THE OXFORD I

LATIN AMERICAN HISTORY

THE OXFORD HANDBOOK OF
LATIN AMERICAN HISTORY

Edited by
JOSE C. MOYA

2011

OXFORD
UNIVERSITY PRESS

Oxford University Press, Inc., publishes works that further
Oxford University's objective of excellence
in research, scholarship, and education.

Oxford   New York
Auckland   Cape Town   Dar es Salaam   Hong Kong   Karachi
Kuala Lumpur   Madrid   Melbourne   Mexico City   Nairobi
New Delhi   Shanghai   Taipei   Toronto

With offices in
Argentina   Austria   Brazil   Chile   Czech Republic   France   Greece
Guatemala   Hungary   Italy   Japan   Poland   Portugal   Singapore
South Korea   Switzerland   Thailand   Turkey   Ukraine   Vietnam

Copyright © 2011 by Oxford University Press, Inc.

Published by Oxford University Press, Inc.
198 Madison Avenue, New York, New York 10016

www.oup.com

Oxford is a registered trademark of Oxford University Press

All rights reserved. No part of this publication may be reproduced,
stored in a retrieval system, or transmitted, in any form or by any means,
electronic, mechanical, photocopying, recording, or otherwise,
without the prior permission of Oxford University Press.

Library of Congress Cataloging-in-Publication Data
The Oxford handbook of Latin American history / edited by Jose C. Moya.
p. cm.
Includes bibliographical references and index.
ISBN 978-0-19-516620-0; 978-0-19-516621-7 (pbk.)
1. Latin America—History.   2. Latin America—Historiography.
I. Moya, Jose C., 1952–
F1410.O95 2010
980—dc22   2009053006

1 3 5 7 9 8 6 4 2

Printed in the United States of America
on acid-free paper

To Paula, Cristina, and Sebastian

Preface

THE most cursory glimpse at a library's catalogue will reveal that the last decades of the twentieth century and first of the twenty-first have witnessed a veritable explosion of publications about Latin American history. A search in WorldCat for books published since 1980 on the history of even the smallest country in the region, the Dominican Republic, returns over 2,300 titles, close to a thousand more than what had been published in the preceding four centuries. A similar query on Mexico generates more than 35,000 volumes, which almost matches the number of books on Mexican history published before 1980.

What could explain this unprecedented boom? At the broadest level, the source for the upsurge in Latin American historiography is the same as for the expansion of academic publications in general: the transformation of higher education from a prerogative of elites to a massively consumed service. The number of students enrolled in institutions of higher education worldwide increased two hundred times during the twentieth century, from half a million in 1900 to ten million in 1960 and one hundred million in 2000.[1] History as a discipline changed from an expensive hobby of gentleman scholars to a profession, one almost completely embedded in academia, which trained the practitioners, employed them, provided their immediate clients (students), and offered outlets for their writings (academic presses and journals).

The tide of historical writings about Latin America has specific sources in various places as well. Some of these preceded the peak of the tide by a decade or two. In the United States, concern about the Cuban Revolution and Cold War politics increased government and other forms of institutional support for Latin American studies during the 1960s and 1970s. Title VI of the National Defense Education Act of 1958 provided, for the first time, a steady flow of public funds for area studies. A majority of the Latin American studies centers in the country appeared during the next two decades. An umbrella organization, the Latin American Studies Association, was founded in 1966. These centers and other expanding programs such as the Social Science Research Council, the Peace Corps, Fulbright fellowships, and the National Endowment for the Humanities greatly increased the level of financial support for travel and research south of the Rio Grande. The expansion of North American academia, the internationalist character of the countercultural movement of the 1960s and '70s, and romantic images of Latin America (including its revolutionary movements) during the period engendered a generation of curious and idealistic North American students eager to take advantage of these increased opportunities. This combination of propitious cultural and institutional trends formed a large cohort of scholars during the 1960s and '70s that would produce much of the Anglophone historiography on Latin America during the next three decades.

Other sources for the historiographical swell are contemporaneous with it. The institutional infrastructure of research universities and centers, foundations, endowments, scholarly presses, journals, associations, and other programs that had developed in the post–World War II decades continued to provide essential support for Latin American studies after the 1970s and even expanded, albeit at a slower pace. The social movements and Sandinista Revolution in Central America during the 1980s had an effect similar to the Cuban Revolution in the 1960s and the Chilean solidarity movement in the 1970s. They attracted a new generation of North American students to Latin American studies. The increased number of Latino students in U.S. colleges and universities had a similar and cumulative effect by enlarging the pool of potential graduate students with an interest in Latin America. Many of them, of course, entered other professions, and others focused their interest on Chicano studies or other forms of U.S. ethnic studies. But many directed their intellectual gaze south of the border. The knowledge of Spanish of first- and second-generation Hispanics and their more recent connections to their natal or ancestral lands made this a more common choice than was the case among black graduate students, who gravitated to African-American studies to a much greater degree than to African history. As the twentieth century ended, about fifty North American research universities were graduating between fifty and sixty PhDs in Latin American history per year, and the Conference on Latin American History, the principal professional association of its type in the United States, had close to a thousand members.[2]

Developments outside the United States added to the historiographical swell. In the United Kingdom, the Parry Report of 1965 had an effect similar to that of Title VI in the United States in increasing public funds for British area studies. The Society for Latin American Studies (the U.K. equivalent of LASA) was founded around the same time, and so were Latin American studies centers at the universities of Oxford, London, Cambridge, and Liverpool. Over the next decades, these institutions expanded, and more modest versions appeared in a dozen other British universities. In Canada, the first Latin American studies center was founded in 1972 at the University of York, in part thanks to an inflow of exiled intellectuals from South America, and six other centers have been founded since. In Germany, the Ibero-Amerikanisches Institut in Berlin (founded in 1930) was one of the oldest institutions of its type anywhere, but its expansion dates from the 1970s. By 2007 it had the largest library in Europe specializing in Latin America, with close to a million volumes, and published eight different journals and series. The Columbian quincentennial in 1992 brought a surge in publications on Latin American history in Italy and particularly in Spain. The contemporaneous economic boom in the latter country, and a wave of immigration that increased the number of Latin Americans in Spain from 100,000 in 1990 to two million in 2008, kept the historiographical surge going. Japan witnessed a similar, though more modest, increase in publications on Latin America that also coincided with the massive immigration of Nisei and Sansei (second- and third-generation Japanese) from Peru and particularly Brazil. A diaspora of Latin American scholars in Europe, Israel, Canada, and Australia have published scores of books and articles on the history of their region of origin.

The other part of the explanation for the sharp increase in publications devoted to Latin American history can be found in the region itself. The almost complete transition to democratic regimes during the last decades of the twentieth century has increased the intellectual freedom for scholarly research. Historical inquiry in particular gained a new vitality as a means to unravel a troubled past. The expansion of intellectual "space" had a literal, physical dimension as institutions of higher learning more than doubled to 8,910 in 2008.[3] Enrollments experienced a similar jump.[4] The expansion and popularization of tertiary education by itself increased the number of students of history at various levels, from undergraduate majors to doctoral candidates.

The diversification of academia intensified the trend. Traditional public universities continued to educate large numbers in the humanities and social sciences. The sharp increase in private universities added new scholarly loci. The growth of provincial universities (or provincial branches of national universities) did the same, and also facilitated a boom in regional history. The increase in institutes has likewise augmented and diversified historical studies with their specialization in different branches of the discipline. Specialized journals have also expanded and popularized branches such as economic, demographic, social, urban, and agricultural history, particularly in the larger Latin American countries. Transnational associations such as the Sociedad Latinoamericana de Estudios sobre América Latina y el Caribe and the Federación Internacional de Estudios sobre América Latina y el Caribe (FIEALC) both founded in Mexico City in 1978, have served to connect scholars from all over Latin America. FIEALC, for example, has organized biannual conferences since its founding. The number of students matriculating and/or graduating with master's or PhD degrees in history from Latin American universities has multiplied in the last generation. Many others receive their degrees from European, and increasingly North American, universities. During the 1990s, the number of Latin American students in U.S. universities increased by 50%. By 2007, the United States had become the main destination for university students from all Latin American countries except Cuba and Paraguay.[5]

Lastly, the upsurge in Latin American historiography was driven by a boom in "new" histories that reflected general tendencies in the discipline. The transformation of the discipline from elite hobby to a profession employing thousands of people came along with a rhetorical need to justify it. Just writing about history did not seem sufficient rationale for the activity when so many were doing it and getting paid for it. Specialization and utilitarian claims—often phrased in the language of national interest and learning from the past to avoid mistakes in the future—served to justify the increase to the public and private decision makers that paid for much of the academic apparatus. Internal justification, however, came mainly from claims of innovation. New practitioners could not simply research the past, at least if they wanted to advance in the profession. They had to challenge, revise, or supersede the work of previous historians.

Such pressure injected historiography with an intrinsic tendency to exaggerate novelty, reminiscent of what had taken place with the jump in the professionalization of the plastic arts half a century before. The tendency fused with the trend toward specialization to create an explosion of self-proclaimed newness: the new economic, new social, new urban, new rural, new labor, new intellectual, new political, and new cultural histories, among others, and "new" historiographies of topics ranging from science to sexuality. As had happened in the plastic arts after the 1890s, "isms," "posts," and "turns" proliferated in academic history after the 1960s: constructionism, postmodernism, poststructuralism, postcolonial theory, and cultural, linguistic, hermeneutic, and postempirical "turns," among others.

The proliferation of new labels may have originated in the changing sociology of a profession, and it clearly surpassed actual innovation. But it also reflected real surges in intellectual effervescence generated by the dramatic increase in the number of historians and in their social diversity and by significant transformations in the discipline. New social historians may have overstated the newness of their enterprise, yet this "history from below" did incorporate groups (peasants, workers, women, migrants, racial and ethnic minorities, children, etc.) who make up the bulk of the population but had mostly been left out of traditional historical narratives. This history of the many offered, by definition, a more complete picture of the human past than the history of the few. The multiplication of "new" specializations moved history beyond its traditional concentration on formal politics, diplomacy, military affairs, and other expressions of manifest power relations. By doing so, it not only made the discipline more socially inclusive, it also expanded its thematic space, illuminating the quotidian universe that encompasses the bulk of our lives and actions: work, family relations, leisure activities, food and drinking habits, sex, and so forth. All those "linguistic" and "hermeneutic" turns may have seemed like navel gazing from a guild whose members make a living by working with language, but they also increased historians' sensitivity to text, semiotics, codes, intertextuality, and omission—the notion that what is not said may be as important as what is said. And trends yet to be named have been redirecting attention to the material foundations of human history.

These trends have affected academic history in general. Indeed, since their source lay in the "massification" of a profession, they first appeared and became more intense in larger fields outside Latin American history, namely European and Anglo-American history. The trends are also discussed more specifically in the chapters of this volume.

The introduction to the volume, therefore, tackles an issue that the specific chapters were not meant to address: the limitations and meaning of Latin America as a historical category. It does so in consecutive sections that explore other categories that could be more meaningful than Latin and North in the conceptual organization of space within the Americas; the commonalities that distinguish the Americas from the rest of the world; the commonalities that distinguish Latin

America from both the rest of the Americas and the rest of the colonized world; and the reasons why a region that is in the Western Hemisphere in many more ways than geographically became excluded from "the West."

The rest of the volume aims to provide a timely state of the field by surveying the swell of publications on Latin American history since the 1980s. Twenty-four of the most renowned historians in the field discuss and assess the principal findings, debates, and trends in this historiography in sixteen chapters that cover the major periods and themes in Latin American history. Originally, we had envisioned a purely thematic organization, but the structure of the field made this an unfeasible option and required the inclusion of time and place as supplemental organizational schema. Colonial historiography, in particular, has long-established traditions and well-defined features that deserve a separate discussion.

The first part of the volume, thus, mixes time, place, and theme with four chapters on the recent historiography of the colonial period. Kevin Terraciano and Lisa Sousa discuss intellectual, legal, urban, environmental, economic, and religious history and studies of Spaniards, blacks, and slavery in New Spain. The largest section of the chapter, however, deals with the Amerindian population, particularly with a corpus of historical studies that, employing indigenous-language sources, have unveiled the long-term survival and adaptation of native culture after the European conquest. Lyman Johnson and Susan Socolow cover Spanish South America, particularly the Andean core of the empire but also a surprisingly rich historical literature on the River Plate, long a marginal corner of the Spanish Empire. The relative lack of surviving documents written in Quechua or other South American indigenous languages has prevented the development of a philological historiography analogous to that of New Spain. But increasingly informed by the work of archeologists, anthropologists, and ethnographers, historians of colonial South America have also revealed the remarkable endurance of native social, cultural, and even political practices during three centuries of Spanish colonial rule. Stuart Schwartz's chapter on Luso-America highlights five themes or trends: the social history of the major groups within the colony (merchants, cane farmers and sugar barons, slaves, and the free population of color); a complementary cultural approach that has added attention to issues such as private life, public rituals, and subaltern agency; Afro-Brazilian life and culture; a surprisingly rich literature on the indigenous population; and studies of colonial governance. Although these three regional chapters also deal with gender and sexuality, the recent literature on this topic is so sizable that it merited a specialized treatment. Asunción Lavrin offers this in a thorough discussion of the scholarship on sexuality (both hetero- and alternative) in pre-Columbian times, during the conquest, and through the centuries of colonial rule that followed. These tales of sex tell us much about power, morality, popular and institutional religion, and cultural encounters.

The fifth chapter, by Jeremy Adelman, bridges the colonial and the national period in a discussion of the independence movements. This topic, part of foundational narratives in the region, once represented the core of Latin American history. The shift to structural and socioeconomic analysis after the 1960s led to a period of neglect of a topic that came to be considered too Whiggish and celebratory or, at best, not particularly consequential. But a renewed interest in political history, and more recently the expectation of several bicentenaries in 2010, have brought a new crop of studies of the emancipation process. By following historians' changing attitudes on the theme, the chapter also tells us much about the intellectual climate in Latin America during the last half century.

The next two chapters are the only ones to deal with a specific country. This was done in part to account for the peculiarities of Brazilian history. This is a country that occupies almost half of South America. It was the only Portuguese colony in the hemisphere, the only nation to gain its independence through the transference of the royal family from the metropole to the colony, the only one to have a long-lasting monarchy, and the last to abolish slavery. In chapter 6, João Reis and Herbert Klein examine African slavery in Brazil, a topic and country that have produced such a rich historiography—much of it regionally based—that we decided to concentrate on it and not include another chapter on the Caribbean, where recent studies of slavery outside of the Anglophone West Indies are surprisingly few. In chapter 7, Barbara Weinstein tackles an even larger body of recent historical studies of postcolonial Brazil that explore the forging of the nation, the abolition of slavery, the fall of the Empire and establishment of the Republic, and urban culture, regional history, and politics in the twentieth century.

The rest of the volume is organized thematically. In chapter 8, a Brazilianist and a historian of Cuba and Colombia, Kim Butler and Aline Helg, team up to discuss race relations in postabolition Afro-Latin America. They find that, contrary to the Lusocentrism of the recent historiography on slavery, much has been written in the past few decades about race and blackness in the Caribbean and in Spanish America. In the next chapter, Florencia Mallon shifts the discussion of race from Afro- to Indo-America, focusing on a corpus of historical studies that underline how Amerindians, anti-Indian racism, and Indigenism have played a central role in the formation of nations and national identities along the mountainous backbone of Spanish America. Originally, we had planned to include a chapter on the third leg of the Latin American racial tripod. But the recent historiography on European immigration, particularly in English, proved to be too scant to merit a separate chapter. The discussion of the topic thus ended up dispersed among the other chapters.

The next two chapters (10 and 11) form a spatial counterpoint. Eric Van Young's essay on rural history treats the environment where most Latin Americans lived until the middle of the twentieth century. Reflecting this basic fact, the region's historiography boasts a long tradition of studies of agrarian movements, haciendas—with a once fiery debate about the putative feudal or capitalist nature of these large landed estates, plantations, estancias, and ejidos (or land-owning Indian villages)—and the peasantry. Van Young surveys both this rich historiographical tradition and newer works on rural life. Latin America has also a long urban tradition. Since the middle of the nineteenth century, it has been more urbanized than any other region on the globe except North America, northwestern Europe, and Australia/New Zealand. This has produced large urban working classes, large labor movements, and an equally large—and by now traditional—labor historiography, particularly in Latin America itself. James Brennan's essay discusses both these classics and newer trends that have shifted the focus from organized labor to workers themselves and their sociocultural world inside and outside the factory. The essay covers working-class formation during the second half of the nineteenth century, the influence of anarchism and socialism on labor and urban life from the 1880s to the Great Depression, the relationship of organized labor and populist regimes from the latter event to the 1960s, and the emergence since then of what has been called "new unionism," a more politically independent and grass-roots form of labor mobilization.

Chapters 12 and 13 form another conceptual pair in so far as they focus on the intersection between domestic and public life. In a temporal counterpart to Lavrin's chapter on the colonial period, Donna Guy discusses gender and sexuality during the national period and the shift from women's history to the study of the social construction of both femininity and masculinity and of various forms of sexuality. This, Guy argues, has problematized "the notion of universalized female oppression," a trend in line with the general historiographical emphasis on individual and collective agency since the 1980s. As in Lavrin's chapter, gender here is both a topic and a category of analysis. The discussion thus sheds much light on other aspects of—in this case, national—society, such as notions of nationality and citizenship, the nature of the modern state and law, populism, and revolutionary and feminist politics. This may be even more pronounced for family history, since unlike women's history it never limited itself to one gender. Nara Milanich argues that the field has been hobbled in recent years—particularly in U.S.-based scholarship—by the political baggage associated with "the family" in contemporary public discourse, by family history's close identification with the empiricism of historical demography and early social history, and by an external perception of narrowness. Yet she discusses a rich literature that both deals directly with the most elemental components of any human society (household, marriage, kinship networks, and social reproduction) and illuminates general "relations of power, patronage, and inequality, as well as of solidarity, affinity, and affect."

The remaining three chapters (14–16) move from the most material to the seemingly ethereal. John Coatsworth and William Summerhill's chapter on economic history explores a scholarly corpus whose robust empiricism stands out from the general antipositivist trends in the historical field and thus contributes—however one may feel about the actual practices—a healthy element of disciplinary pluralism. The field originally rested on two pillars, neoclassical economic theory and cliometrics—that is, the use of quantitative methods, models from applied economics, and counterfactuals to test falsifiable hypotheses. But, inspired by the work of scholars such as the Nobel laureate Douglass North, recent practitioners have added a "new institutionalism" that aims to incorporate an increased sensibility towards cultural norms.

At the outset, the subject of the next chapter, disease and medicine, may seem even more material than the economy. Yet Diego Armus and Adrián López-Denis's essay actually focuses not on the history of physical maladies or the biomedical profession but on three overlapping trends in the historical study of human responses to illness, which they label as "new history of medicine, history of public health, and sociocultural history of disease." The topics range from colonial epidemiology and pharmacopoeia to twentieth-century public health institutions and urban hygiene. But a consistent focus on the social, cultural, and symbolic components of diseases and cures unifies this historiography and distinguishes it from the narrower scope of the long-established field of the history of medicine.

A similar distinction differentiates the recent historiography of religion, discussed by Reinaldo Román and Pamela Voekel in the last chapter, from the traditional field of church history. The emphasis has shifted from the institutional and official to the quotidian and informal. The stress on popular religiosity comes across in the debate over syncretism discussed in the first section of the chapter. Did Catholicism absorb African and indigenous beliefs, in practice if not theologically, to form a sort of Latin American spiritual stew, as the Cuban anthropologist Fernando Ortiz once put it? Did this synthesis become more Christian with time? Did non-European belief systems survive relatively unadulterated, particularly in the understanding of the divine rather than form, as some revisionists proposed? Popular religiosity also occupies a central position in the historical debate about secularism, the nature of millenarianism, and the spread of Protestantism during the national period.

NOTES

1. Evan Schofer and John W. Meyer, "The Worldwide Expansion of Higher Education in the Twentieth Century," *American Sociological Review* 70:6 (2005): 898–920.

2. Marshall C. Eakin, "Latin American History in the United States: From Gentlemen Scholars to Academic Specialists," *The History Teacher* 31:4 (1998): 539.

3. IESALC (Instituto Internacional de la UNESCO para la Educación Superior en América Latina y el Caribe), Conferencia Regional de Educación Superior (Cartagena, 2008). In some countries, as Barbara Weinstein notes in her chapter on Brazil in this volume, the expansion of higher education had actually begun during military dictatorships.

4. Hans de Wit et al., eds., *Higher Education in Latin America: The International Dimension* (Washington, D.C.: The World Bank, 2005), 39.

5. UNESCO, Institute for Statistics, *Global Education Digest, 2007* (Montreal, 2007), 140–41.

Contents

Preface, vii
List of Contributors, xvii

Introduction, 1
Jose C. Moya

1. Historiography of New Spain, 25
   Kevin Terraciano and Lisa Sousa

2. Colonial Spanish South America, 65
   Lyman L. Johnson and Susan M. Socolow

3. The Historiography of Early Modern Brazil, 98
   Stuart B. Schwartz

4. Sexuality in Colonial Spanish America, 132
   Asunción Lavrin

5. Independence in Latin America, 153
   Jeremy Adelman

6. Slavery in Brazil, 181
   João José Reis and Herbert S. Klein

7. Postcolonial Brazil, 212
   Barbara Weinstein

8. Race in Postabolition Afro-Latin America, 257
   Kim D. Butler and Aline Helg

9. Indigenous Peoples and Nation-States in Spanish America, 1780–2000, 281
   Florencia E. Mallon

10. Rural History, 309
    Eric Van Young

11. Latin American Labor History, 342
    James P. Brennan

12. Gender and Sexuality in Latin America, 367
    Donna J. Guy

13. The Historiography of Latin American Families, 382
    Nara Milanich

14. The New Economic History of Latin America: Evolution and Recent Contributions, 407
    John H. Coatsworth and William R. Summerhill

15. Disease, Medicine, and Health, 424
    Diego Armus and Adrián López Denis

16. Popular Religion in Latin American Historiography, 454
    Reinaldo L. Román and Pamela Voekel

    Selected Bibliography, 489
    Index, 509

Contributors

Jeremy Adelman is the Walter Samuel Carpenter III Professor in Spanish Civilization and Culture at Princeton University, where he is also the Director of the Council for International Teaching and Research. The author of several books and articles on nineteenth- and twentieth-century Latin American history, his most recent study is *Sovereignty and Revolution in the Iberian Atlantic* (Princeton University Press, 2006). Also, he has coauthored a textbook in world history, *Worlds Together, Worlds Apart: A History of the World from the Origins of Humankind to the Present* (W.W. Norton, 2008).

Diego Armus teaches at Swarthmore. His most recent book is *La ciudad impura: Salud, tuberculosis y cultura en Buenos Aires, 1870–1950* (2007), English version forthcoming with Duke University Press. Among his other books on the history of medicine and disease are *Avatares de la medicalización en América Latina* (2005); *Cuidar, controlar, curar: Ensaios históricos saúde e doença na América Latina e Caribe* (2004); *Disease in the History of Modern Latin America: From Malaria to AIDS* (2003); and *Entre médicos y curanderos: Cultura, historia y enfermedad en América Latina* (2002). He is currently working on a history of smoking in Buenos Aires.

James P. Brennan received his PhD from Harvard and has taught at the University of California, Riverside since 1996. His most recent publication is a book coauthored with Argentine historian Marcelo Rougier, *The Politics of National Capitalism: Peronism and the Argentine Bourgeoisie, 1946–1976*. He is currently working on an economic, social, and environmental history of mining in the Americas from the seventeenth through the twentieth centuries.

Kim D. Butler is an associate professor of history at Rutgers University in the Department of Africana Studies. Her 1998 book, *Freedoms Given, Freedoms Won: Afro-Brazilians in Post-Abolition São Paulo and Salvador*, received awards from the American Historical Association and the Association of Black Women Historians. Her current work focuses on diaspora theory in addition to her projects on Brazil. She has published numerous book chapters, and her articles have appeared in *Diaspora*, *The African Studies Review*, *The Americas*, and *Slavery and Abolition*. She currently serves on the Executive Board of the Association for the Study of the Worldwide African Diaspora.

John H. Coatsworth is Dean of the School of International and Public Affairs and Professor of History and International and Public Affairs at Columbia University. He is the author or editor of nine books and many scholarly articles on Latin American economic and international history. In 2009–10, he served as president of the Latin American Studies Association. Professor Coatsworth coedited *The Cambridge Economic History of Latin America* (2 vols., Cambridge University Press, 2006) with Victor Bulmer-Thomas and Roberto Cortes Conde. In 2005, he was elected to membership in the American Academy of Arts and Sciences.

Donna J. Guy is a Distinguished Professor of Humanities and History at Ohio State University. She has been the President and Secretary of the Conference on Latin American History. Her publications include *Sex and Danger in Buenos Aires: Prostitution, Family and Nation in Argentina, 1875–1955; Sex and Sexuality in Latin America: An Interdisciplinary Reader; White Slavery and Mothers Alive and Dead: The Troubled Meeting of Sex, Gender, Public Health and Progress in Latin America;* and *Women Build the Welfare State: Performing Charity Creating Rights in Argentina 1880–1955*. She is currently working on an analysis of letters written to Juan and Eva Perón tentatively titled *Write to Me Argentina*.

Aline Helg is a professor of history at the University of Geneva in Switzerland. Her books include *Liberty and Equality in Caribbean Colombia, 1770–1835* (University of North Carolina Press, 2004) and *Our Rightful Share: The Afro-Cuban Struggle for Equality, 1886–1912* (University of North Carolina Press, 1995), both winners of prizes from the American Historical Association, and *La educación en Colombia, 1918–1957: Una historia social, económica y política* (CEREC, 1987, repr. 2001). She also has published several articles and book chapters on Cuba, Colombia, comparative race relations in the Americas, black mobilization, independence, and racial ideas in Latin America.

Lyman L. Johnson is Professor of History at University of North Carolina Charlotte. His current project examines the late colonial laboring class of Buenos Aires and its role in independence. His recent publications include: "Cities and Wealth in the South Atlantic: Buenos Aires and Rio de Janeiro before 1860," *Comparative Studies in Society and History*, 48:3 (2006): 634–68 (with Zephyr Frank); "'A Lack of Legitimate Obedience and Respect': Slaves and Their Masters in the Courts of Late Colonial Buenos Aires," *Hispanic American Historical Review*, 87:4 (2007): 631–57; and the book *Aftershocks: Earthquakes and Popular Politics in Latin America* (University of New Mexico Press, 2009), edited with Jürgen Buchenau.

Herbert S. Klein is Director of the Center for Latin American Studies, Professor of History, and Senior Fellow at the Hoover Institution at Stanford University, as well as Gouverneur Morris Professor Emeritus of History at Columbia University. Klein is the author of some twenty books and 155 articles, the most recent of which are *African Slavery in Latin America and the Caribbean* (coauthor), *Slavery in*

Brazil (coauthor), and a selection of essays on *Escrvismo no Brasil* (coauthor). He has also published on such diverse themes as *The American Finances of the Spanish Empire, 1680–1809* and *A Population History of the United States* and is coauthor of *Brazil Since 1980* and *Mexico Since 1980*.

Asunción Lavrin received a PhD from Harvard University and has published on colonial and twentieth-century women, religion, sexuality, and feminism. Among her best-known books are *Latin American Women: Historical Perspectives* (1978), *Sexuality and Marriage in Colonial Latin America* (1989), *Women, Feminism and Social Change: Argentina, Chile and Uruguay, 1890–1940*, (1995), and *Brides of Christ: Conventual Life in Colonial Mexico* (2008). She is now Emerita from Arizona State University. In 2009 she received the Distinguished Service Award from the Conference on Latin American Hisory.

Adrián López Denis received a BA in biology and an MA in Latin American studies from the University of Havana, an MA in economics from Carleton Univeristy in Canada, and a PhD in history from UCLA. He is now a postdoctoral fellow at Brown University. His primary field of specialization is the cultural and social history of the Spanish Caribbean. He is currently working to expand his dissertation, "Disease and Society in Colonial Cuba, 1790–1840," into a comprehensive history of slave medicine in the island, from the seventeenth to the nineteenth century.

Florencia E. Mallon is the Julieta Kirkwood Professor of History at the University of Wisconsin-Madison. Her book *Peasant and Nation: The Making of Postcolonial Mexico and Peru* (Berkeley, 1995) received LASA's Bryce Wood Award for the Best Book in Latin American Studies, and *Courage Tastes of Blood: The Mapuche Indigenous Community of Nicolás Ailío and the Chilean State, 1906–2000* (Duke University Press, 2005) was awarded the Bolton-Johnson Prize from the Conference on Latin American History. She is one of the founding editors of Duke University Press's book series on "Narrating Native Histories." Her current project is entitled "Travels Inside the Nation-State: Chile in Transnational Perspective."

Nara Milanich is an assistant professor of history at Barnard College, Columbia University. She is the author of *Children of Fate: Childhood, Class, and the State in Chile, 1850–1930* (Duke University Press, 2009) as well as "Whither Family History? A Road Map from Latin America," which appeared in the *American Historical Review* (2007). She is currently working on a book entitled *Latin American Families: A History*, under contract with Cambridge University Press.

Jose C. Moya is Professor Emeritus at UCLA and Professor of History at Barnard College, Columbia University, where he also directs the Forum on Migration. He has been a visiting professor at the universities of San Andrés in Buenos Aires, Santiago de Compostela in Spain, and Paris VII. His book *Cousins and Strangers:*

Spanish Immigrants in Buenos Aires, 1850–1930 (Berkeley, 1998) received the Bolton Prize and four other awards, and the journal *Historical Methods* (Winter 2001) devoted a forum to its theoretical contributions to migration studies. Moya writes extensively on global migrations and anarchism.

João José Reis is Professor of History at the Universidade Federal da Bahia, Brazil. He has been a visiting professor at the universities of Michigan (Ann Arbor), Princeton, Brandeis, and Texas (Austin), and a fellow at the Center for Advanced Studies in the Behavioral Sciences (Stanford) and the National Humanities Center. He is the author, among other books, of *Slave Rebellion in Brazil: The Muslim Uprising of 1835 in Bahia, Death is a Festival: Funeral Rites and Rebellion in Nineteenth-Century Brazil*, and *Domingos Sodré, um sacerdote africano: Escravidão liberdade e candomblé na Bahia no Século XIX*.

Reinaldo L. Román is the author of *Governing Spirits: Religion, Miracles and Spectacles in Cuba and Puerto Rico, 1898–1956* (University of North Carolina Press, 2007). He is currently working on a book about Spiritism in Cuba during the insurgency against Spain and the early republican years. He teaches in the History Department at the University of Georgia.

Stuart B. Schwartz is the George Burton Adams Professor of History at Yale University. Among his books are *Sovereignty and Society in Colonial Brazil* (1973) and *Sugar Plantations in the Formation of Brazilian Society* (1984), and most recently *All Can Be Saved: Religious Tolerance and Salvation in the Iberian Atlantic World* (2008). He is also the coauthor (with James Lockhart) of *Early Latin America* (1983). He served as coeditor of the *Hispanic American Historical Review* (1996–2001). He is presently working on "A Sea of Storms: A History of Caribbean Hurricanes: From Columbus to Katrina."

Susan M. Socolow, Dobbs Professor of Latin American History at Emory University, has done research in colonial social history, women's history, historical demography, and the history of medicine. The author of several articles and books on the history and historiography of colonial Latin America, she is working on a history of the use of public monuments in Buenos Aires and Montevideo. Her books include *The Merchants of Viceregal Buenos Aires* (1978), *The Bureaucrats of Buenos Aires* (1987), *Women in Colonial Latin America* (2000), *Cities and Society in Colonial Latin America* (1986), and *The Countryside in Colonial Latin America*.

Lisa Sousa is an Associate Professor of Latin American History at Occidental College in Los Angeles. She has edited and translated *The Story of Guadalupe* (1998), with James Lockhart and Stafford Poole, and *Mesoamerican Voices* (2005), with Kevin Terraciano and Matthew Restall. She has published numerous articles on indigenous society and culture and is completing a book manuscript on indigenous gender and power in colonial Mexico.

William R. Summerhill is Professor of History at UCLA. He chaired the UCLA Program on Brazil and has held visiting appointments at the École des Hautes Études en Sciences Sociales and the Universidade de São Paulo. He has written on the econometric history of Brazilian railroads, the history of public finance and banking in nineteenth-century Brazil, comparative economic history, and contemporary bank privatization in Brazil. The author of two books and several articles, he is a contributor to the *Cambridge Economic History of Latin America*. His most recent effort is *Inglorious Revolution: Political Institutions, Sovereign Debt, and Financial Underdevelopment in Imperial Brazil* (Yale University Press, forthcoming).

Kevin Terraciano received his PhD from the University of California at Los Angeles in 1994 and joined the faculty as an assistant professor in 1995. He is Professor of History and chair of the Latin American Studies Program at UCLA. He specializes in Colonial Latin American history, especially New Spain and the indigenous cultures and languages of central and southern Mexico. He has received several prizes and awards for his publications, undergraduate teaching, and graduate training.

Eric Van Young (PhD, UC Berkeley 1978) is Distinguished Professor of History at the University of California, San Diego. He has chaired his department and was Interim Dean of Arts and Humanities during 2007 and 2008. His most recent major published work, *The Other Rebellion: Popular Violence, Ideology, and the Struggle for Mexican Independence, 1810–1821* (Stanford University Press, 2001), won the Bolton-Johnson Prize of the Conference on Latin American History in 2003. A specialist on the history of colonial and nineteenth-century Mexico, he is currently writing a biography of the Mexican statesman, entrepreneur, and historian Lucas Alamán.

Pamela Voekel is the cofounder and a member of the organizing collective of the Tepoztlán Institute for Transnational History of the Americas, a weeklong seminar that meets each summer in Mexico. She is the author of *Alone Before God: The Religious Origins of Modernity in Mexico* (Duke University Press, 2002). She is currently at work on a book tentatively titled "Holy Warriors: Religion and Gender in the Age of Revolutions." She teaches at the University of Georgia in Athens, where she is the faculty advisor to the Living Wage Coalition.

Barbara Weinstein is professor of history at New York University and past president of the American Historical Association. Her publications include *The Amazon Rubber Boom, 1850–1920* (Stanford University Press, 1983) and *For Social Peace in Brazil: Industrialists and the Remaking of the Working Class in São Paulo, 1920–1964* (University of North Carolina Press, 1996). She is currently completing a book on race, region, and national identities in twentieth-century Brazil, to be published by Duke University Press, and coediting a volume on the global history of the middle class.

THE OXFORD HANDBOOK OF
LATIN AMERICAN HISTORY

INTRODUCTION: LATIN AMERICA—THE LIMITATIONS AND MEANING OF A HISTORICAL CATEGORY

Does the term Latin America provide an appropriate label for the historiography discussed in this volume? Historians south of the Rio Grande write local and national rather than hemispheric histories. With few exceptions, Brazilians write about Brazil, Mexicans about Mexico, and that is even more true of historians in smaller countries. As a group, historians north of the Rio Grande do not limit their inquiry to a single country. Indeed, it could be said that Latin American studies are an Anglo-American creation. Still, historical studies in the North rarely encompass the entire "South" unless they are textbooks. Most of the works discussed in this volume deal not with Latin America but with specific countries, and more often with specific regions, cities, and towns.

Can the phrase then offer more than an inaccurate but convenient label for books and maps? Is it a meaningful category of historical analysis or, as some have suggested, an artificial and arbitrary invention?[1] From various perspectives, Latin America as a category seems too broad and internally diverse to pack much meaning. What do Hispaniola (a tropical island where 95% of the population traces its roots, at least partially, to Africa), Guatemala (a mountainous region where a similar proportion of the inhabitants are of full or mostly Amerindian descent and close to half speak indigenous languages), and Argentina (a temperate region larger than Western Europe where more than half of the population is of non-Spanish European stock) have in common? In terms of historical development, economy, and social structure, are not São Paulo and Buenos Aires more similar to New York or Toronto than they are to Lima or Salvador do Bahia? Do not the pampas have more in common geographically, historically, socially, and economically with the U.S./Canadian prairies than with the Andean altiplano?

In this respect, a conceptual triad that fuses geographical and ethnohistorical components offers more meaningful criteria for dividing the Western Hemisphere than the traditional categories of Latin and North (or Anglo-) America. The first type in the triad would consist of the western highlands of the hemisphere, which ethnically correspond to Indo- or mestizo America. It includes what anthropologists have called nuclear America: the densest concentrations of Amerindian population, both in pre-Columbian times and today, in Mesoamerica and the central Andean altiplano. Demographically and culturally, these two regions are most indigenous in their core and become more mestizo as one moves either north or south. This historical region developed a colonial economy and social complex based on the exploitation of indigenous labor, silver mines, haciendas, and landowning Indian villages. It contained the wealthiest colonies of the Spanish empire, but also rigid corporatist arrangements and highly unequal social structures that sometimes have persisted, in both obvious and veiled ways, into the present.

The second geographic/ethnohistorical category in the New World would comprise its tropical coastal lowlands, and corresponds to Afro-America. These regions were not densely populated in pre-Columbian times to begin with, and the European conquest and Old World diseases decimated or wiped out the local population. Their historical development was based on the importation of western African and Bantu slaves and the production of tropical cash crops for export to Europe. These plantation complexes developed in tropical lowlands on small islands or close to the coast. Even in places as small as Puerto Rico, the distinction between a coastal complex once based on plantations and slavery and an interior highland ecology once based on independent farming and a Hispanic peasantry is still visible. More so than Indo-America, Afro-America transcends the traditional categories of Anglo-, Spanish-, and Luso-America, because it encompasses the British, French, Hispanic, Dutch, and Danish Antilles; the Northeast and areas of central Brazil; parts of the South of the United States; the Caribbean coasts of Central and South America; and Pacific coastal strips in Peru, Ecuador, Colombia, Panama, and Mexico.

These regions share with Indo-America a wealthy colonial past. Saint-Domingue was probably the richest place in the world in the decades before the 1791 Haitian Revolution, worth to the French much more than the immense expanses of Quebec or Louisiana.[2] Barbados made more money for Britain than all thirteen mainland colonies put together.[3] The South of the United States was wealthier than the North as late as the early nineteenth century, and so was the Northeast in Brazil compared to the South. Yet social inequality probably surpassed that of Indo-America. Saint-Domingue may have been the wealthiest place on earth in relation to its territory, but nine-tenths of its inhabitants were slaves, and the nation constructed on this unbalanced foundation became the poorest one in the Western Hemisphere. The rural population in Afro-America lacked the basic economic and social security that Indian villages and communal land tenure provided in Indo-America. The social consequences are visible even today. For example, divorce or separation rates, out-of-wedlock births, common-law unions, and single-parent households are more common in Afro- than in Indo-America.[4]

The third geographic/ethnohistorical region of the New World encompasses the temperate lands on the northern and southern edges of the hemisphere that correspond to Euro-America. This zone comprises the north of the United States, Canada, and the temperate belt that stretches from São Paulo to southern Argentina and the southern half of Chile. Without precious metals and indigenous labor (the population density here was the lowest in the hemisphere in pre-Columbian times),[5] and with no tropical lands that could grow the cash crops that Old World markets demanded, these regions remained marginal backwaters during colonial times.

This state of affairs was drastically changed by a series of socioeconomic revolutions in Europe during the nineteenth century. The demographic explosion in the Old World created a massive market for New World temperate foodstuffs that had not existed before and provided much of the workforce that would cultivate the crops. The Industrial Revolution created demand for other temperate-zone New World commodities—such as hides, tallow, wool, and flax—that had not existed before; it promoted urbanization in Europe, which in turn further increased the demand for American staples, as fewer people grew their own food; and it provided the transportation innovations (particularly trains and steamships) that made possible the massive movement of goods and people across the Atlantic and across the temperate plains of the New World. The prairies and the pampas, which before the middle of the nineteenth century had been just semi-empty grasslands, became in the next century the biggest producers of agro-pastoral wealth the world had ever seen.

The poorest colonies thus became during the nineteenth century the richest countries of the Americas and the richest regions within those countries. By the early twentieth century, per capita GDP in the United States, Canada, Argentina, Uruguay, and Chile was two to six times higher than the average elsewhere in the hemisphere.[6] The North, the South, and the East of the United States, Brazil, and Argentina respectively—which had been the least developed areas of those countries before 1800—became the wealthiest. The late development of Euro-America proved to be a blessing in the long term. Relatively unencumbered by rigid colonial institutions (from a strong church to commercial monopolies, guilds, latifundia, ejidos, and plantations) and by highly vertical social structures, these regions became not only the richest in the hemisphere but also the most egalitarian in terms of the distribution of material, political, and cultural resources.[7] One can say that they were born "modern" as opposed to "early modern": capitalist and liberal rather than colonial and mercantilist.

This volume takes into account these realities, these categories within the Western Hemisphere that in terms of historical trajectory, ethnoracial composition, economic development, and social structure are more cohesive and meaningful than those of Latin and North America. All four chapters on the colonial period address these divisions. So do many of the thematic chapters, particularly those on rural and religious history. And two chapters deal specifically with postcolonial Afro- and Indo-Latin America.

The works reviewed in this volume's essays, however, also show—although rarely in an explicit way—that despite its diversity and sharp distinctions, Latin America represents more than a convenient label with little inherent meaning. Indeed, a focused interpretation of scattered studies could demonstrate that, as broad categories go, this one has more historical significance and cultural meaning than other continental labels such as Europe, Asia, and Africa.

To begin with, the multiracial history that divides the Western Hemisphere into the three major categories discussed above also distinguishes it from the rest of the globe. Ethno-racial diversity is common in most of the world. But in the case of the Western Hemisphere this is not only the result of ethnolinguistic differences between neighboring groups but also, and most uniquely, of transcontinental migrations. The aboriginal inhabitants were simply the first to come. Sixty million Europeans, eleven million Africans, and five million Asians arrived after 1492. The term "New World," originally a product of Eurocentric arrogance related to the notion of "discovery," does denote a distinctive role and position in the history of humanity. It accurately names a hemisphere where Homo sapiens arrived long after the rest of the planet had been populated, and one that became a receptacle for the people of every other continent.

The newcomers may have concentrated in different regions of the hemisphere, but all New World countries have or had multiracial societies to some extent, and this appears as a unifying motif in the historiography. Mexico and Argentina have no visible African presence today, but Terraciano and Sousa discuss a boom in studies of the African experience in their chapter on New Spain, and Johnson and Socolow as well as Butler and Helg mention numerous studies of blacks in Argentina. Although Amerindians represent less than one-third of 1% of Brazil's population today, histories of the indigenous presence have become so numerous that Schwartz includes a section tellingly titled "The Return of the Natives" in his chapter on colonial Brazil, and Weinstein refers to a recent revival of "Indian" identity in her chapter on postcolonial Brazil. The works discussed in most other chapters remind us that although the proportion of the elements may vary drastically between regions, the Indigenous-African-European demographic and cultural tripod marks the history of the entire hemisphere.[8] Race has thus been a more central theme in the historiography of Latin America and the Western Hemisphere than in that of other parts of the world.

This historiographical feature reflects a historical one: the New World's particular propensity to racialize ethnicity. Phenotypical difference is not a prerequisite for this process. Countless ethnic groups throughout the world that are not physically distinguishable from each other swear that they are and use racial language to define collective identities. But the greater phenotypical dissimilarity that transcontinental migrations produced in the New World facilitated and promoted the tendency to perceive ethnic difference as biological and permanent and to define them in racial terms related to putative pigmentations (white, black, yellow, redskin, *raza cobriza*, pardo, *preto*, etc.).

Racialization, and the resulting racism, is in turn connected to another distinguishing characteristic of the Western Hemisphere: its relatively high levels of social inequality. Those levels have varied historically and geographically. They have been generally lower during periods of labor scarcity and/or redistributive policies and in regions where free immigration played a more significant role than slavery or conquest. But in global comparison all Western Hemisphere countries, with the exception of Canada and Cuba, appear in the top two quintiles in Gini coefficient measures of income inequality in the early twenty-first century.

Transcontinental migration promoted not only a tendency for racialization and exclusion but also, and somewhat contradictorily, an inclusive definition of nationality that eventually found legal expression in the concept of jus soli, which bestows citizenship on the basis of birthplace rather than ancestry and distinguishes the New World from the Old. All thirty-eight countries in the Western Hemisphere except two (Haiti and the Bahamas) confer citizenship to anyone born there (with some exceptions for children of diplomats), compared to only ten of the 156 countries outside of the Americas.

Given all the history and traits that the New World shares, it seems fitting that south of the Rio Grande the Western Hemisphere is thought of as one continent rather than two. The Americas are conceived in the singular: as America, a landmass that stretches from the Bering Strait to Cape Horn rather than from New York to California. Yet Anglo-Americans normally do not include themselves even in the plural "Americas," an ambiguous term that is often associated, including in academic circles, with the countries south of the Rio Grande. The cartographical distinction that makes America a continent rather than a country has important historical, political, and ideological implications. After all, the Rio Grande was until the 1840s just a river rather than a political, socioeconomic, and cultural frontier, and California (and most of the U.S. Southwest and Florida) were once part of "Latin" America. Many of the leaders of the independence wars in Latin America used *americano*, rather than creole or national gentilics, to refer to themselves and establish a separate identity from peninsular Iberians. Many Latin Americans still resent what they view as an imperious appropriation by the United States of a demonym that belongs to all of the inhabitants of America.[9]

The primary element that makes part of America "Latin" is a shared history of Iberian colonialism. Indeed, Ibero-America is a more accurate appellation for the region than Latin America, a controversial term that was first promoted by the French during their imperial adventure in Mexico in the 1860s and became common only in the twentieth century.[10] If speaking a Romance language were really the criterion—the standard explanation for the use of "Latin"—then Quebec too would be considered part of Latin America. The fact that Haiti is sometimes included reflects, then, not the use of a common Latinity as a norm of membership but the tacit application of underdevelopment as a definitional principle for the category—an economicist tendency that surfaced with the post–World War II boom in development studies.

Iberian colonialism distinguishes Latin America not only from the rest of the Western Hemisphere but also from the rest of the developing or postcolonial world. Spanish and Portuguese colonialism in the Americas began much earlier than other

European colonial incursions elsewhere, lasted much longer, ended a century and a half earlier, and left a much deeper impact.

At the most primary level, Iberian colonialism transformed the physical ecology of the Americas to a degree unknown in the history of European colonialism in the Afro-Asiatic world, or for that matter of Arab colonialism in North Africa. This transformation of the hemisphere's biota had momentous demographic, economic, and social consequences. At the most microscopic level, imported pathogens decimated the indigenous population in a demographic catastrophe of a magnitude without parallel anywhere else.[11] Scores of new plants and animals, along with imported technology, transformed elemental aspects of quotidian life that ranged from eating habits, clothing, work, and leisure to land use, specifically the introduction of extensive agriculture, ranching, and equestrian cultures. Whether they were estancias in the pampas, fazendas in Brazil, haciendas in Indo-America, or plantations in Afro-America, the prevalence of latifundia, a land-tenure system dominated by large estates, shaped rural space and social relations in most of Latin America. The precocious development of commercial agriculture—whether export-oriented or domestic—became another distinguishing historical characteristic of the region. Renaissance Mediterranean urban planning—with its central plazas and checkerboard grid—shaped space in towns and cities from Chile to Mexico. Iberian law imposed a unifying legal (and legalistic) culture that affected everything from marriage and domestic relations to inheritance and commercial contracts. Roman Catholicism had a unifying and lasting effect on the entire region, both as a set of beliefs and practices and as a public institution.

The Iberian languages imposed a degree of linguistic unity that sets Latin America apart from any other continent. In colonial Brazil, more than two hundred languages disappeared in the confrontation with Portuguese. In the Spanish possessions, the fact that during the first century of colonization arrivals came basically from Andalusia, Estremadura, and New Castile—rather than Spain in general—shaped and unified American Castilian. Despite the existence of regional accents, Spanish and Portuguese in Ibero-America developed no creole languages similar to the French-based creoles of Haiti, Guiana, or New Caledonia; the English creoles of Belize, Guyana and the West Indies; or the Papiamento of the Netherland Antilles. Indeed, it is revealing that with a single minor exception (Palenquero, a Spanish-Bantu patois spoken by less than two thousand descendants of runaway slaves in a village southeast of Cartagena) the only creoles in Ibero-America are English-based languages introduced by West Indian immigrants in the Atlantic coast of Central America and the Colombian islands of San Andrés and Providencia. The absence does not reflect any intrinsic trait of the Spanish and Portuguese languages or of Iberian imperialism in general. After all, a Spanish-based creole developed in the Philippines (Chabacano), and eighteen Portuguese creoles have emerged in Africa, Asia, and even the Americas (Portuguese accounts for over half of the vocabulary of Papiamento in Aruba, Bonaire, and Curaçao, and for a quarter of Saramaccan in Suriname).

A comparison of the saturation level of colonial languages worldwide highlights the distinctiveness of the Iberian colonial experience in the Americas. English is spoken by only 10% of the population of India and Pakistan, and less than one-quarter of 1% speak it as a first language. The proportion is similar or lower for Tanzania, Uganda, Kenya, Malawi, and Swaziland and higher in other African countries, but the figures include speakers of local pidgins.[12] French-based creoles (generically referred to as African French) are spoken to different degrees in thirty African countries, but only small numbers of urban inhabitants speak French as a first language. The same is true in Haiti. Forty percent of Mozambicans speak Portuguese, but only 6% do so as a first language. The proportion of the population in the ex-Russian colonies that speaks Russian as their main language ranges from less than 15% in Uzbekistan, Turkmenistan, Tajikistan, Kyrgyzstan, Azerbaijan, Armenia, and Georgia to a high of 72% in Belarus.[13] Dutch is spoken as a first language by only 60% of the population in Suriname, the same proportion that speaks Portuguese in Angola and Arabic in Algeria and Morocco, despite the fact that Arab colonialism in Berber North Africa is more than eight centuries older than Iberian colonialism in the Americas. French has practically disappeared from Indochina, and so have Dutch from Indonesia, Portuguese from the Lusitanian ex-colonies in Asia, and Spanish from the Philippines. By comparison, Portuguese is spoken by virtually the entire population of Brazil, as is Spanish in Spanish American countries, with the exception of Paraguay, where it is spoken by 70% of the population, and Guatemala, Bolivia, and Peru, where it is spoken by 86%–88%.[14]

These drastic contrasts in the usage of colonial languages and the absence of Spanish or Portuguese creoles in Ibero-America reflect a broader phenomenon that transcends linguistics: the cultural breadth and depth of Iberian colonialism in the New World. Its impact runs the gamut from the most primary and physical to the most ethereal. It is palpable in the ecology, flora and fauna, agriculture and husbandry, food and cooking, urban space, public and domestic architecture, politics, law, language, literature, music, high and folk art, naming patterns, and just about every aspect of social life. Even some Latin American cultural artifacts that came to be seen as quintessentially indigenous—such as the bowler hats, traditional *polleras* (skirts), and *charangos* (small guitars) of the Andean region—are actually Castilian imports from the sixteenth century. Indeed, the Iberian cultural imprint often became invisible precisely because it was so deep and buried in time that it appeared to most observers as local, natural, and indigenous. And the recent emphasis of the historiography on the Amerindian and African components of Latin America has contributed its share in making such an omnipresent, and presumably obvious, element less visible.[15]

This has obscured two factors crucial in defining Latin America as a meaningful category beyond mere geographical adjacency. One is internal: the Iberian cultural imprint is the principal commonality that warrants including countries and regions that are drastically different in ethnoracial composition, levels of economic development, and social structure in the same category. The other is external.

The Iberian imprint distinguishes Latin America from the rest of the so-called global South. Nowhere in the Afro-Asiatic world did European culture spread so widely and penetrate so deeply. In part this reflects a much thicker inflow of colonial settlers (about one million Spaniards and half a million Portuguese), followed by a bigger wave of seventeen million European immigrants during the national period (43% of them Iberians and 40% Italians).[16] In many regions, the Iberian colonizers and their descendants, and later European settlers, came to represent the majority, making these areas more akin to a southern European version of Australia than to any postcolonial country in Africa or Asia. This is true even in zones outside of Euro-America, such as Antioquia and Caldas in Colombia, the Altos de Jalisco and other areas in northern Mexico, the central highlands of Costa Rica and Puerto Rico, and western and central Cuba. Where this did not happen, populations nonetheless became much more Hispanized or Lusitanized than people in colonies in Africa or Asia became Gallicized or Anglicized. Even in the least Europeanized countries of the region—say, Guatemala or Bolivia—Spanish and Christianity are almost universal, in dramatic contrast to the situation in India, Indonesia, Indochina, Iraq, Iran, or the Ivory Coast—to use just one letter in the postcolonial alphabet.

Latin America's third major unifying and distinguishing trait, besides its shared history of transcontinental multiraciality and deep Iberianization, is its centrality in the twin processes of globalization and modernity. Although vast stretches of Eurasia had been connected since the time of the Mongol empire, it is impossible to speak of globalization (a term that refers to a globe or sphere) before 1492. Eurocentric periodizations used to date the beginning of modern history to the fall of Constantinople in 1453, but the "discovery" of the Indies obviously makes a better candidate for an admittedly arbitrary birthdate.

The aftermath of that event drastically transformed worldviews—literally—and the world itself. Karl Marx described the Columbian exchange as the threshold of the modern world in the first page of the *Communist Manifesto*. Adam Smith, capitalism's philosophical sire, deemed it one of the two "most important events recorded in the history of mankind."[17] The contention may be hyperbolic in regard to the general history of humanity. But it is irrefutable when it comes to the origin of modern capitalism. American silver (which accounted for 85% of the world's output between 1500 and 1800) made possible the development of mercantile capitalism in Europe, as economic historians have long maintained.[18] It spurred the first truly global trade system, according to, among others, the new "California School" of Sinologists, who have shown that for three centuries Europe paid for all of its imports almost exclusively with American silver, and that much of it ended up in China.[19] And, along with other New World resources, it was also the single most important element in explaining the Industrial Revolution, according to bolder—and less convincing—accounts.[20]

Whatever the weight of Latin American silver in ushering Europe's industrialization, it did foster levels of industrialization and urbanization within the region itself that have gone unnoticed in Eurocentric, and more recently Asiacentric, accounts of world economic history. Around 1600, Potosí's population surpassed that of any Western European city with the exception of Paris and Naples, and its silver mines represented the largest industrial complex in the world. Two centuries later, Ibero-America contained forty-five of the fifty largest cities in the New World; the population of Mexico City alone exceeded that of the five largest U.S. cities put together; and in terms of output, technology, the size of the labor force and its organization, and productivity, the mining complex of the Mexican Bajío probably surpassed the presumed cradle of the Industrial Revolution in the English midlands. The effect of that output transcended the silver regions. Western Cuba developed a precocious service economy to supply the silver fleet that turned the island into the most urbanized area in the world around 1800, again, ahead of the putative global vanguard sites of urbanization in England and the Netherlands.[21] A few decades later, steam sugar mills, the seventh railroad in the world, and other technologies made the island a pioneer in the Industrial Revolution—a process that has only been told from the other side of the Atlantic or the northern side of the Mason-Dixon line. And, despite Anglo-Gallic assumptions of Hippocratic supremacy, Cuba had more physicians per capita during the nineteenth century than England or France.[22]

Latin America's central, and at times pioneering, role in the development of globalization and modernity did not cease with the end of colonial rule and the early modern period. Indeed, the region's political independence places it at the forefront of two trends that are regularly considered thresholds of the modern world. The first is the so-called liberal revolution, the shift from the monarchies of the ancien régime, where inheritance legitimated political power, to constitutional republics and the notion of popular sovereignty, where legitimacy originates from the consent of the governed. This presumed shift serves as the basis for the traditional periodization of Western history, with the French Revolution marking the transition from early modern to modern history, or from modern to contemporary in the usage of continental European historians.

Here, Latin America has usually been excluded from a Western current in which it played a pivotal role. The centrality of liberalism since the early nineteenth century makes the region's political history parallel to that of Europe and distinguishes it from that of the rest of the world. Liberalism became a popular ideology, rather than simply an elite creed, earlier in parts of Latin America, particularly in Mexico, than in Eastern and parts of Northern Europe. Latin America's struggles against the Iberian monarchies preceded similar movements in Central and Eastern Europe against the Ottoman, Austro-Hungarian, and Russian empires by fifty to a hundred years. Latin American liberals' crusade against the temporal power of the church during the nineteenth century coincides in content and timing with similar struggles in Catholic Europe but precedes some of them, such as the case of Italy. The fact that Benito Mussolini was named after Benito Juárez may seem just a curious anecdote, but it is indicative of the iconic status that some Latin American liberal leaders attained in the Old World.

The second, and related, trend consistently considered a threshold of modern history that saw Latin America at the forefront is the development of nation-states. No decade since 1800 has failed to witness the birth of at least one of these polities. But the production of these peculiarly modern forms of organizing and delimiting physical space has been concentrated in four temporal booms that coincided with the end of more expansive imperial entities. The first rose from the ashes of the

Iberian dominions in the Americas between 1810 and 1824; the second from the ruins of the Austro-Hungarian, Russian, and Ottoman empires after World War I; the third followed the disintegration of European overseas empires after World War II; and the fourth sprung in the 1990s from the communist carcass of what few now remember used to be the "Second World."

This means that Latin America went through a process that, for better or for worse, is the quintessential expression of political modernity more than a century before all but a dozen or so of the 190-plus countries that control or claim every square inch of the planet today. What is still news in many parts of the world (including parts of Europe) in the twentieth-first century—secessionist movements, regional caudillismo or warlordism, and the struggle to forge cohesive nation-states—forms part of a specific period of nineteenth-century history in Latin America. This gives the region's historiography an element of thematic and temporal unity, since, with the exception of Cuba and Puerto Rico, all its countries went through a similar process (even those, like Brazil and Chile, where the struggle was less pronounced) within roughly the same time period.

Latin America may thus be part of the New World, but it has old countries. Its states are relatively strong and its nations stronger, not only in contrast to newer countries in the Afro-Asiatic world but also in comparison to Western Europe, the reputed cradle and site par excellence of mature and cohesive national polities. Latin America has nothing similar to the Basque, Catalan, Corsican, Flemish, Northern Irish, and Scottish ethnonationalist, and often violent, separatist movements. No Latin American country sends four "national teams" to the World Soccer Cup, like the apparently not-so-united United Kingdom. Only clichés such as "banana republics" or "emerging countries," accumulated prejudice, and unexamined assumptions can sustain the notion of Latin American nations as relatively new and incomplete projects in comparison to Western Europe.

Latin America's connections to the world economy declined during the aftermath of independence. But they revived with such force after the middle of the century that the region came to play as important a role in the second stage of globalization and the parallel spread of global/financial capitalism (circa 1870–1930) as it had played in the first and the accompanying expansion of commercial capitalism after 1492. Transatlantic trade during this period surpassed, in volume and value, that of the colonial era.[23] Hides, wool, and flax from the pampas, rubber from the Amazon, and minerals from Chile and Mexico fueled the Industrial Revolution on the other side of the ocean. Latin America became a major market for this revolution's output, and its most advanced regions became early participants in the process itself. The number of arrivals from Europe dwarfed the number of colonial settlers by a factor of ten to one. So did capital flows, westward in the form of—mostly British—investments, and eastward as immigrant remittances. The transatlantic circulation of goods, money, people, technologies, institutional practices, ideas, and all sorts of material and cultural goods acquired unprecedented intensity and density.

Because the factors in this circulation tended to move in unison and unequally toward different destinations, the process reversed the economic rank of colonial times and opened the regional gaps that came to characterize Latin America and the Western Hemisphere in general during the national period. Europe's exports, capital, technology, and emigrants headed mainly to those New World regions from which it imported the most, namely temperate North and South America and Cuba.

But although the level of integration into the global economy differed significantly, Latin America's geographical situation in what was an Atlantic-dominated system gave it an advantage over other regions of the world. Argentina and Uruguay may have boasted the highest levels of international trade per capita in the world and ranked among the ten richest countries by the outbreak of World War I. But trade and GDP per capita for Latin America in general were higher than for the most of the rest of the world. Mexico's GDP per capita surpassed that of Hungary and Poland, and Peru's doubled that of China.[24] Demographic growth was higher in the countries of immigration. But Latin America in general and Europe increased their share of the world's population during the period, while Asia's and Africa's declined. When it came to those living in cities, Uruguay may have been the most urbanized country in the world after England around 1900, and Cuba, Argentina, and Chile ranked among the top dozen. But Latin America in general has been the most urbanized region in the world outside of Northern Europe and its colonies of settlement since the middle of the nineteenth century. Cuba was the seventh country in the world to have railroads, those quintessential symbols of nineteenth-century modernity. But five other Latin American nations were among the first twenty countries to build them, and all twenty were within the Atlantic world. The advantage of geography could even trump levels of development. The "iron horse" arrived in a dozen Latin American countries (including landlocked and poor Paraguay and Bolivia) before it reached Japan.

A similar pattern of diffusion appears in political and social practices associated with modernity. Mass politics were most advanced in Uruguay—which developed a welfare state in the early 1900s that preceded most of its counterparts in Western Europe—and in Argentina, which established universal, secret, and obligatory male suffrage in 1912, elected the first socialist senator in the Western Hemisphere a year later, and saw the founding of the second communist party in the world in 1918, two months after the October Revolution in Russia itself, and almost a year before Rosa Luxemburg founded the third in Germany. But communist parties appeared in five other Latin American countries (Mexico, Uruguay, Cuba, Chile, and Brazil) before 1922, a timing that coincides with that of the U.S, Canada, Western Europe, and Australia/New Zealand and precedes that of most of Africa and Asia by decades.

The geographical spread of May Day celebrations draws a similar map. This "international" worker's day saw street demonstrations by socialists and anarchists during its debut in 1890 in sixty-three European cities that stretched from Helsinki and Warsaw in the east to London and Lisbon on the west, and in six cities on the other side of the Atlantic: Chicago, New York, Havana, Buenos Aires, Rosario, and Montevideo. From these pioneering loci of working-class activism, the practice spread over the next two decades to Eastern Europe and eight other Latin American countries, but not to any place outside the Atlantic world unless it was a settlement of European immigrants. As James Brennan discusses in his chapter, southern cone countries and Cuba developed some of the earliest and largest organized labor movements in the world.

Whether we consider GDP, demography, urbanization, or the spread of technology, political parties, and workers' collective practices, the pattern is the same. Some Latin American countries occupy the same level and time period as Western Europe and what we would call today the First World, and the others—with the exception of the poorer Central American and Andean countries—occupy a point or time closer to the European periphery than to Asia and Africa.

The pattern persists regarding the major political trends of the twentieth century. In 1910, Mexico had the first social revolution of the twentieth century, seven years ahead of the one that presumably shook the world in ten days. During the 1930s and 1940s, Cuba, Argentina, Uruguay, Brazil, Mexico, and Chile were at the forefront of a global trend in the formation of populist regimes and in the move from liberal/free-trade policies to autarkic plans for import-substitution industrialization. In 1959, Cuba revived the communist dream worldwide, after public awareness of Stalinist purges seemed to have eroded it beyond repair, and led—often with military support—the expansion of communism in the Third World during the next two decades. From the 1970s on, Latin American countries, particularly Chile, were at the vanguard of a reverse curve toward neoliberal, market-oriented reforms. From the 1980s on, the move, or return, to democracy in the region preceded similar trends in Eastern Europe, Asia, and Africa. And in the twenty-first century, countries such as Venezuela, Argentina, Brazil, Bolivia, Ecuador, Uruguay, Paraguay, and Honduras appeared to be leading the way in a global leftist cycle away from neoliberalism and toward more social democratic forms of capitalism. The similar content and timing of these cycles also augment the unity that a shared experience of colonial rule and of liberalism and nation-state formation during the nineteenth century impart to Latin American political history.

Latin America's greater proximity to the West, or to its European semiperiphery, than to the Third World, to which it presumably belongs, transcends political history and runs the gamut from population structures and industrialization to educational levels and gender relations. In the same way that the region followed on Europe's heels during the growth phase of demographic modernization in the long nineteenth century, it has kept close during its downward phase in the last third of the twentieth. Fertility rates, population growth, and infant mortality declined, and life expectancy increased, much earlier and faster than in Africa, the Middle East, and most of Asia.[25] By 2008, Cuba and Uruguay had joined Japan as the only countries outside of Europe with natural population decline, and Puerto Rico will soon join them, since its fertility rate of 1.76 is significantly below the 2.1 replacement level.

The timing of industrialization in the larger Latin American countries also mirrors that of Europe outside its manufacturing core rather than that of even pioneering regions outside the Western world. In a 1989 study of the most industrialized areas of the developing world that stressed Latin America's underperformance, sociologist Gary Gereffi admitted that in contrast to East Asia's so-called Four Tigers

(South Korea, Taiwan, Hong Kong, and Singapore), the conventional phrase "*newly industrializing countries*" was a misnomer when applied to Argentina, Brazil, and Mexico (and he could have added Chile, Uruguay, and Cuba), since rapid industrial growth there dated at least from the 1920s.[26]

Education presents an analogous pattern. Already by the early 1900s, the primary school enrollment rate in Argentina surpassed that of Italy, Chile's and Ecuador's exceeded Finland's, Mexico's and Honduras's were above Russia's, Uruguay's and Costa Rica's doubled that of Yugoslavia, and Brazil's was ten times higher than Korea's.[27] In 1920, Puerto Rico's rate was above that of all seventeen Southern and Eastern European countries, with the exception of Czechoslovakia.[28] During the first decade of the twentieth century, the literacy rates in Chile and Costa Rica were a little higher than in Spain, and that of Mexico was similar to Portugal's.[29] The rates in Uruguay (75%), Cuba (70%), and Argentina (65%) made them some of the most literate societies in the world at the time, ahead—in some cases by a wide margin—of all of Southern and Eastern Europe.[30] India, Pakistan, Morocco and forty-some other countries had not reached those levels a century later. By 1965, enrollment in primary education was universal in nine Latin American countries, and the region's rate in general was similar to that of Europe but 27 percentage points above that of South Asia, 32 points higher than in the Middle East and North Africa, and 50 points higher than in sub-Saharan Africa.[31] The disparities in tertiary education were even more pronounced. In an extreme example, from the 1950s to the 1980s, higher education enrollment in Argentina exceeded the levels in the Western European "core" (France, Germany, and the U.K.).[32]

Gender patterns show similar parallels in various facets. In terms of rural-to-urban migration, demographers have found two distinct global patterns: a female predominant one characteristic of Western Europe, the European areas of settlement, and Latin America, and another where men predominate characteristic of the Middle East, Africa, South Asia, and to a lesser degree East Asia and Eastern Europe.[33] The domestic service became feminized in Latin America, Western Europe, and North America during the eighteenth and nineteenth centuries, while in sub-Saharan Africa and India, men still accounted for 64%–87% of servants in 1970.[34] Latin America shares with Europe and the areas of European settlement early and high ratios of female to male enrollment in primary, secondary, and tertiary education and high levels of female literacy. These are the only regions of the world where women outnumber men among university students.[35] Indeed, Panama was one of the first countries to reach that threshold in the early 1970s, and by the early twenty-first century the female proportion in higher education enrollments in that country and in Argentina, Uruguay, Cuba, Paraguay, Honduras, the Dominican Republic, and at times Brazil surpassed those of the United States and Europe.[36]

Gendered political trends follow a similar direction. In terms of female suffrage, no independent country outside of Europe, the Soviet Union, and the areas of European settlement had granted it in 1929 when Ecuador did; and nine other Latin American countries did so before France extended the right to vote to women in 1945. Since the late twentieth century, Argentina, Cuba, and Costa Rica have ranked, along with Scandinavian countries, among the top ten nations of the world in terms of women's proportional presence in national legislatures. The World Economic Forum's *Global Gender Gap Report* for 2008 shows that thirteen of the nineteen Ibero-American countries ranked higher than the United States and Canada in a composite measure of women's political empowerment. This not only contradicts the persistent North American stereotypes of Latin America as an exceptionally patriarchal region but also makes them particularly ironic.

Why would a region that already by 1800 was the most Europeanized area of the globe outside of Europe itself and its colony of settlement in North America and that continued to have much stronger historical parallels to the West than to the rest of the world during the next two centuries be consistently categorized as non-Western? Part of the answer to this conundrum lies in the early definition of Latin America as the polar opposite of North America. During the nineteenth century and much of the twentieth, the United States defined the hemispheric South in the dichotomous terms it described its own national South. The North was modern, capitalist, industrial, democratic, and rational; the South traditional or backward, feudal, rural, authoritarian, and suffused by premodern codes of honor. Vis-à-vis the hemispheric South, three other dyads were added: Anglo/Latin, Protestant/Catholic, and white/mixed-race. Some of those dualities were still prevalent in modernization theory, and development studies in general, during the 1950s and '60s.

Most scholars in the twenty-first century would either dismiss these dualities as examples of Western orientalism (although "australism" would be a more accurate term, given that they relate to the south rather than the east) or deconstruct them as Derridean binaries.[37] Yet Latin America continues to be categorized as non-Western in various scholarly disciplines. In political science, it is normally studied in the field of comparative politics, which despite the name, focuses, at least de facto, on the non-Western world rather than on comparisons. In economics, it is treated as part of the "developing" world, a supposedly more positive version of the older "underdeveloped," "less-developed," or Third World that still basically coincides with the non-Western world. In most departments of history in North American universities, the Latin American field is grouped with other non-U.S./non-European fields, and Latin American history classes fulfill "multicultural" (a code for non-Western and nonwhite) requirements.

This reflects the fact that the definition of the West continues to be plagued by presuppositions and metanarratives about modernity, development, democracy, and race. The relative economic decline of Spain and Portugal and the weakness of their representative politics during the nineteenth and much of the twentieth century made them ineligible for a label that had become synonymous with modernity and liberal democracy. So, despite the facts that the Iberian Peninsula occupies the western end of Europe and that its inhabitants were the pioneers of western overseas expansion and prime standard-bearers of that process for more than two centuries, Spain and Portugal were relegated from the center to the semiperiphery and from the West to the South.[38] A selective cartography moved them from western to southern or Mediterranean Europe, even though Portugal does not face the

Mediterranean. The linguistic component of this process saw the marginalization of Spanish and Portuguese as French and later English became the dominant global languages of Western culture and power. The West became, at least implicitly, a label for the North, a synonym for Northern Europe and its colonies of settlement. If Iberia moved, at best, to a quasi-Western semiperiphery in Anglo-French conceptual cartography, Ibero-America became stuck in a non-Western periphery. The Spanish "economic miracle" during the last quarter of the twentieth century, the return of democracy, and European Union membership eventually gained that country, and increasingly Portugal, "admission" into the conceptual West. But, despite the almost total consolidation of liberal democracy on the other side of the Atlantic, the Iberian ex-colonies are still assumed to be too poor to join.[39]

The assumption rests on historical myopia and the conceptual homogenization of an economically diverse region. During colonial times, the Indies were associated in Europe with wealth rather than poverty. The phrase "rich as Peru" became a cliché in most western European languages.[40] During the national period, much of Latin America has ranked within the top tenth of the world's population in terms of income. From the middle of the nineteenth century to the 1950s, Argentina's and Uruguay's GDP per capita was regularly higher than those of most European nations, including, at times, France and Germany. Chile, Cuba, Venezuela, and Costa Rica have also had historically higher incomes than most of the world and than most of southern and eastern Europe. In the twenty-first century, many Latin American countries continue to rank in the top third of the world in terms of wealth. The average GDP per capita in this century of Uruguay, Argentina, Chile, and Puerto Rico surpasses those of sixteen European countries.

Broader indicators of social development show similar patterns. In the United Nation's Human Development Index, eight Latin American countries rank in the top third worldwide and none in the bottom third. Infant mortality is significantly lower in even the poorest Latin American countries than in the world as a whole. Life expectancy in ten Latin American countries for 2005–09 surpassed those of fifteen European nations. In the cases of Costa Rica, Puerto Rico, Chile, and Cuba, it exceeded that of the United States. Nine Latin American countries are more urbanized than twenty-five European countries, including Italy, Switzerland, and Austria. And they rank even higher in the HPI, a newer index that combines subjective life satisfaction, life expectancy at birth, and ecological footprint per capita. Latin America accounted for nine of the top ten countries in 2009.[41]

This leaves race as the other criterion that keeps Latin America out of the conceptual West. Although the latter term supposedly corresponds to a geocultural entity, its association with race has been explicit since at least the late nineteenth century. By then whiteness had long surpassed Christianity as an occidental distinguishing marker vis-à-vis the rest of the world.[42] This coincided temporally with the increased identification in the United States of Latin America as racially mixed.[43] The racialization of Latinos in that country strengthened such association and carried it into the twenty-first century. The U.S. government officially defines Hispanics as a nonracial category, but in ordinary usage they are listed as one more group in the conventional racial pentalogy of the country, along with whites, blacks, Native Americans, and Asians. So although Latinos, like Americans in general, represent simply a metacategory made up of the other four, their regular inclusion in this racial classification has helped cement the designation of Latin America as nonwhite in lay, and even scholarly, language. Language, in turn, has naturalized the assumption.

Scholars from various disciplines have contributed their share to cementing the conceptual separation of Latin America from the West by both their choice of topics and their approach to them. Anthropologists, particularly those coming from outside the region, have directed their gaze to the "primitive" and alterity. During the last four decades they have written, for example, more than twenty books in English about the Yanomamo in Brazil but not a single one about Portuguese immigrants, who are forty times more numerous but apparently not "other" enough. Anglo-European literary and cultural studies have tended to stress the exotic and the magical. Literary works in that vein are in turn more likely to be translated, furthering the external association of Latin American literature with the magical rather than the rational. Political scientists have penned hundreds of volumes on dictatorships, repression, and revolutions but few on democracies, institutions, and electoral politics. Economists and economic historians have often underscored underdevelopment and poverty to a point that the history of the region seems one of unmitigated failure.

The lack of a global perspective has compounded the misrepresentations. In terms of economic history, Latin America is rarely placed in a global context but is compared to the United States instead, as if a country that contains less than 5% of the world's population were some sort of universal standard. Political history can be even less comparative. The disproportionate emphasis on tyrannies and repression without any external reference has obscured the fact that compared to most regions of the world, including Western Europe, what stands out about Latin America is the general absence of international wars, genocides, holocausts, and state-organized slaughter.[44]

The point in the last section was not to demonstrate that the West is just a capricious concept. Like many other expansive social categories, including Latin America, it is inconsistent, malleable, and fluctuating but ultimately meaningful. Neither was the intention to decry stereotypes, which are, per se, just cognitive mechanisms. The section aimed to debunk only those clichés that are particularly divorced from empirical evidence and distorting of historical and social realities, and then to explain why and how Northern European and North American economic and political hegemony during the nineteenth and twentieth centuries produced—partly by design and partly through ignorance—a historiography and general discourse that occluded Latin America from "the West" and from narratives of modernity.

This has tended to conceal the critical role the region played in the latter process. Unlike the Old World, Latin America, as a historical category rather than a landmass, has no ancient or medieval history. It both sprang from and spawned modern history. The notion is not original. It has been expressed by thinkers from Marx to post-Marxist literary scholars such as Walter Mignolo, who, in one of the most recent ruminations on the topic, tellingly titled *The Idea of Latin America*, stresses that America was invented rather than discovered and links the invention to the modernity/coloniality dyad.[45]

The argument in this essay, however, has differed in its conceptualization of the dyad. It has treated modernity not only as a Western ideological concoction or metanarrative but also as a factual trend in the history of humanity that encompasses the massification of demographic reproduction, production, exchange, consumption, politics, culture, and long-distance connections, communication, and mobility. It has placed less emphasis on European imperialism, echoing the findings of more than a generation of historians of early Latin America that have shown the limits of Iberian imperial dictates and the primacy of local forces in the development of the region.[46] It has stressed the importance of Iberian colonialism, but as a broad social, economic, and cultural process that gives meaning to Latin America as a historical category and differentiates it from the rest of the Western Hemisphere and the rest of the postcolonial world, rather than as mere political rule. The accent here has been on the American side of the Atlantic and on broad history rather than on the eastern side and ideological/discursive currents. Latin America was indeed invented rather than discovered, but mainly in the first definition of the term (to create something new) rather than the second (to make up something false).

That creation, it is true, seems too internally disparate to make a cohesive category. The contrasts between countries and regions in terms of geography and climate, ethnic composition, social structure, and the distribution of material and cultural resources can be sharp. Vast disparities in levels of development existed in pre-Columbian times, continued with some changes during the colonial period, reversed during the nineteenth century when the most marginal colonies became the most developed countries, and widened during the next century. Around 1900, the richest countries in Latin America were about four times wealthier than the poorest; by 2000, they were six times wealthier (or nineteen times wealthier if one counts Haiti). The income gap between the poorest and richest countries in Ibero-America is twice as wide as that between the latter and the United States.[47]

These gaps, however, are actually wider within most other regions of the world. Tunisia's and Libya's GDP per capita are nine to twenty times higher than those of their neighbors in the Sahel; South Africa's and Botswana's are ten to fifty-two times higher than those of twenty other sub-Saharan countries. In the Middle East, or actually just within the Arabian Peninsula, the "oil kingdoms" are four to thirty-six times wealthier than Jordan and Yemen. In South Asia, Malaysia and Singapore are ten to thirteen times richer than Bangladesh and Indonesia. In East Asia, the per capita GDP of South Korea is sixteen times higher than North Korea's. In Europe, Switzerland, Luxembourg, and the Scandinavian countries are seven to twelve times richer than the poorer countries of the Balkans and Eastern Europe. Only Western Europe has narrower income gaps than Ibero-America, but this is the result of recent convergences. Before the 1960s, the GDP gap between the richest and the poorest countries was similar in both regions (a ratio of about four to one).

If Ibero-America is less internally disparate than most other regions of the world in terms of economic development, it is even less so in most other aspects. The salience of transcontinental immigrations and the resulting particular type of multi-racialism, derived from transoceanic movements rather than ethnolinguistic differences between neighbors, give the region a unifying historical thread that distinguishes it, and the Western Hemisphere in general, from the Old World. The depth of Iberian colonialism imparted a rare level of cultural unity. Ibero-America is the largest contingent area in the world bound by similar legal practices, language, religion, naming patterns, and the arrangement of urban space, among other cultural markers. There are fewer major languages (those with half-million or more speakers) in all of Ibero-America (nine) than in many a single country such as Ghana, Kenya, or Myanmar (ten each), Pakistan and South Africa (eleven), Iran (thirteen), Uganda (fourteen), the Philippines and Mozambique (fifteen), Ethiopia and Nigeria (seventeen), Tanzania (eighteen), the Democratic Republic of Congo (twenty-four), or even part of a country, like the European portion of Russia (eleven) or the island of Sumatra in Indonesia (fourteen), not to mention subcontinental-sized India, where there are more major languages beginning with a single letter (k, sixteen) than in all of Latin America, or in all the Western Hemisphere for that matter.[48]

The depth of Iberian colonialism and its amalgamating capacity makes problematic the application of postcolonial theory to Latin America. "Postcolonial" here is not a neutral temporal term referring to a period after political emancipation in any ex-colony, from Australia to Zimbabwe and from Algeria to the United States. Postcolonial studies emerged from, and responded to, a particular situation: ex-French and particularly ex-English colonies that became independent after World War II or even later, where European cultural penetration was relatively superficial, especially at the level of popular culture, and where, somewhat ironically, the symbolic presence of the ex-colonizer looms large particularly vis-à-vis the Europeanized native intelligentsia. The situation is almost antithetical in Latin America, where Iberian colonialism began centuries earlier, lasted much longer, and left a much deeper cultural impact, not only in contrast to other European overseas colonial ventures but also when compared to Russian colonialism in Eurasia and Arab colonialism in North Africa. Moreover, postcoloniality in Latin America is a two-century-old phenomenon, and the ex-imperial powers declined into semiperipheral status, eliciting more pity than resentment. By the twentieth century, Spaniards and Portuguese in Spanish America and Brazil respectively had become more the butt of popular jokes than the objects of anti-imperialist diatribes or Fanonian meditations by local intellectuals.

Postindependence trends furthered the internal cohesiveness and external distinctiveness that Iberian colonialism had laid down. Despite the continued and indiscriminate application of categories such as "emerging countries" to Ibero-American nations, most countries in the region emerged within the first quarter of the nineteenth century, and even the "young" ones, Cuba and Panama, are over a century old—which is ancient by global standards when it comes to nation-states. During the nineteenth century, most of them shared a sequence of regional struggles and politicoeconomic instability, followed by a period of national consolidation, liberal ascendancy, and reintegration into the Atlantic economy that had no counterpart in the rest of the "postcolonial" world at the time. During the twentieth century, they witnessed the emergence of universal suffrage, of populist, developmentalist states, and of Keynesian economics and the resurgence of liberal democracy and neoliberal economics, followed by a (re)turn to the left in the next century.

Finally, Latin America has been defined and differentiated by the timing of postcolonial modernization—a process that includes the demographic transition, trends toward mass production and market integration, urbanization, the appearance and spread of new technologies, the development of organized labor, mass politics, mass education and literacy, greater global connectivity, and a protracted tendency toward gender parity. The pace has varied internally. In some countries and for some indicators, it kept step with, or even outpaced, that of core Western European countries. More commonly, it resembled that of the European eastern and southern periphery. But Latin America as a whole has outpaced most of the rest of the world with the exception of precisely the countries it has been consistently compared to by economic historians and economists: the Anglo settler societies, Japan, and, since the 1970s, the "four Asian tigers" (South Korea, Taiwan, Hong Kong, and Singapore). Such selective comparisons have fostered myopic and exaggerated notions of laggardness and failure.

This essay's purpose has not been to push forward Latin America's position in a teleological race or claim its admission into the "West," as if this were a membership in an elite club, but to elucidate its meaning as a historical category by placing the region in a global rather than selective perspective.

ACKNOWLEDGMENTS

I would like to thank all the contributors to this volume for their patience, work, and dedication, and Jorge Cañizares-Esguerra, Susan Ferber, Emilio Kourí, Claudio Lomnitz, Nara Milanich, and Paula Soler-Moya for their careful reading and useful comments on this introduction.

NOTES

1. In Mauricio Tenorio Trillo, *Argucias de la historia: Siglo XIX, cultura y "Ameérica Latina"* (Mexico City: Paidoós, 1999), the scare quotes on "Latin America" in the title are repeated throughout the text to stress the arbitrariness of the concept.

2. Alex Dupuy, "French Merchant Capital and Slavery in Saint-Domingue," *Latin American Perspectives* 12:3 (1985): 82, 91–92.

3. David Eltis, "The Total Product of Barbados, 1664–1701," *The Journal of Economic History* 55:2 (1995): 336.

4. Douglas S. Massey, Mary J. Fischer, and Chiara Capoferro, "International Migration and Gender in Latin America: A Comparative Analysis," *International Migration* 44:5 (2006): 63–91 show that the differences in family structure between Afro- and Indo-America also affect the sex ratio of emigration flows. The Dominican Republic, with higher rates of consensual unions, separation, and single-headed households than Mexico, also exhibits a higher level of female participation in emigration.

5. The aboriginal populations of the regions that came to form Euro-America experienced a less severe decline during the colonial period than that of nuclear America precisely because of their low density, spatial dispersal, and limited contact with Europeans, and the fact that those contacts occurred over centuries rather than being temporally concentrated. But they continued to be relatively small. By the middle of the nineteenth century, the entire Amerindian population of the United States (400,000), Canada (100,000), and southern Brazil, Uruguay, and eastern and southern Argentina (80,000) amounted, all together, to less than one-third of the population of the city of London alone. Jose C. Moya, "Immigration, Development, and Assimilation in the United States in a Global Perspective, 1850–1930," *Studia Migracyjne* [Warsaw], 35:3 (2009): 89–104.

6. Data compiled by Angus Maddison in *Monitoring the World Economy, 1820–1992* (Paris: Development Centre of the Organization for Economic Cooperation and Development, 1995) show that by 1900 the United States had the second highest per capita GDP in the world, after New Zealand, and the highest in the Western Hemisphere. An extrapolation of Maddison's data shows that Uruguay ranked second in the Americas, with a per capita GDP that amounted to 81% of the U.S. GDP; Argentina and Canada came next with 68%; and then Chile with 54%. There are no comparable data for Cuba, a country whose per capita GDP was higher than that of the United States as late as the 1820s. But the figures for other Latin American countries are two to five times lower than those for the Southern Cone: Mexico, 24% of the per capita GDP of the United States; Colombia, 24%; Venezuela 20%; and Peru, 17%.

7. Jose C. Moya, "A Continent of Immigrants: Postcolonial Shifts in the Western Hemisphere," *Hispanic American Historical Review* 86:1 (2006): 1–28.

8. The Indigenous-European-African triad in the Americas affects the history of even places where one of the elements disappeared as a cultural group, such as the Caribbean with Amerindians, or arrived relatively late, such as Canada with Afro-descendents.

9. Walter D. Mignolo, "Afterword: Human Understanding and (Latin) American Interests—The Politics and Sensibilities of Geocultural Locations," *Poetics Today* 16:1 (1995): 175.

10. As late as 1918, Aurelio M. Espinosa, a linguist at Stanford University, was dismissing the term Latin America as "an intruder...a new name [that] is not only vague, meaningless, and unjust, but what is much more, unscientific": "The Term Latin America," *Hispania* 1:3 (1918): 135–43. Three years later, the term Latin America was formally repudiated at the Second Spanish-American Congress of History and Geography at its meeting in Seville: *Hispania* 4:4 (1921): 194.

11. The pandemics most similar to the one brought to the New World by the European conquest are the Black Plague in Asia and Europe during the middle of the fourteenth century and the misnamed Spanish influenza of 1918–20. Fatalities were similar in absolute number (estimates range between forty and seventy million in the three cases) but not in

the proportion of the population affected (estimates are 70%–90% for nuclear America, 30%–60% for the Black Death in Europe, and about 3% of the world's population for the 1918–20 global influenza pandemic). There are many other cases in world history, from the Spanish occupation of the Canary Islands to the Austronesian migrations to Polynesia, where mortality rates matched or surpassed those of the Americas, but in these cases the number of people affected was in the tens of thousands rather than the tens of millions.

12. David Crystal, ed., *The Cambridge Encyclopedia of the English Language* (Cambridge University Press, 2004), 100–09; M. Paul Lewis, ed., *Ethnologue: Languages of the World*, 16th ed. (Dallas: SIL International, 2009), also used for the other cases in this paragraph.

13. Jacob M. Landau and Barbara Kellner-Heinkele, *Politics of Language in the Ex-Soviet Muslim States* (Ann Arbor: University of Michigan Press, 2001).

14. Francisco Moreno Fernández and Jaime Otero Roth, *Demografía de la lengua española* (Madrid: Instituto Complutense de Estudios Internacionales, 2006), 19–28.

15. The lack of attention to the Iberian component in recent Latin American historiography is tellingly demonstrated in the chapters on the colonial period. Terraciano and Sousa have only a short section on Spaniards in their essay on New Spain and state that we now know more about indigenous society—and they could have added, the African population—than we know about the colonizer. Johnson and Socolow do not mention a single work on Spaniards in their chapter on Spanish South America. Schwartz has long sections on the African and indigenous population in Brazil but none on the Portuguese. Most of the literature on the Lusitanian side mentioned in the chapter deals with colonial governance and the Portuguese empire, much of it published in Portugal, rather than with the Portuguese in Brazil and their sociocultural impact.

16. Jose C. Moya, "Migration," *Encyclopedia of Latin American History and Culture*, 2nd ed. (New York: Charles Scribner's Sons/Thompson Gale, 2008).

17. *The Wealth of Nations* [1776] (London: Cannan, 1904), Vol. II, 125.

18. See, for example, Earl J. Hamilton, "American Treasure and the Rise of Capitalism, 1500–1700," *Economica* 27 (Nov. 1929): 338–57.

19. Kenneth Pomeranz, *The Great Divergence: Europe, China, and the Making of the Modern World* (Princeton: Princeton University Press, 2000), 159–61 and chap. 6; Richard Von Glahn, *Fountain of Fortune: Money and Monetary Policy in China, 1000–1700* (Berkeley: University of California Press, 1996), chap. 4.

20. See Pomeranz, *The Great Divergence*, chap. 6, which gives the Columbian exchange a prominent role in producing that divergence, and Andre Gunder Frank, *ReOrient: Global Economy in the Asian Age* (Berkeley: University of California Press, 1998), an Asiacentric retort to Eurocentric accounts of the world economy between 1400 and 1800 that diminishes the importance of 1492 outside the Atlantic world (pp. 328–30) but ends up arguing that it was basically American silver, resources, and markets that allowed European economies to keep up with China and India until 1800 and then surpass them, thus having a catalytic effect beyond the Atlantic (pp. 262–63, 277–85, 344).

21. Eric E. Lampard, "Historical Contours of Contemporary Urban Society: A Comparative View," *Journal of Contemporary History* 4:3 (1969): 3–25 claimed that "even as late as 1800 only the Dutch Netherlands and Britain had as many as one person in five regularly domiciled in towns and cities" (p. 3). But calculating the Cuban urban population in 1792 conservatively as those living in cities of over 10,000 inhabitants, from data in Richard Morse, "Trends and Patterns of Latin American Urbanization, 1750–1920," *Comparative Studies in Society and History* 16:4 (1974): 439, produced a figure of 30%. The comparable figures given for 1800 in Jan de Vries, *European Urbanization, 1500–1800* (Cambridge, 1984), 39, are 29% for the Netherlands and 20% for England and Wales.

22. Adrian Lopez-Denis, "Disease and Society in Colonial Cuba, 1790–1840" (PhD diss., University of California, Los Angeles, 2007), 66–67.

23. Kevin H. O'Rourke and Jeffrey G. Williamson, *Globalization and History: The Evolution of a Nineteenth-Century Atlantic Economy* (Cambridge, Mass.: MIT Press, 2001).

24. Data for GDP per capita come from historical sets constructed by the economist Angus Maddison and available at www.ggdc.net/maddison.

25. Wolfgang Lutz and Ren Qiang, "Determinants of Human Population Growth," *Philosophical Transactions: Biological Sciences* 357:1425 (Sept. 29, 2002): 1197–210; *Population and the World Bank: Adapting to Change* (Washington, D.C.: World Bank, 2000), 3, 6, 8; Christopher J. L. Murray et al., "Can We Achieve Millennium Development Goal 4? New Analysis of Country Trends and Forecasts of Under-5 Mortality to 2015," *The Lancet* (London) 370 (Sept. 22–28, 2007): 1040–55.

26. Gary Gereffi, "Rethinking Development Theory: Insights from East Asia and Latin America," *Sociological Forum* 4:4 (1989): 505–33.

27. Richard A. Easterlin, "Why Isn't the Whole World Developed," *The Journal of Economic History* 41:1 (1981): 1–19 (table on pp. 18–19); Iván Molina and Steven Palmer, "Popular Literacy in a Tropical Democracy: Costa Rica, 1850–1950," *Past and Present* 184:1 (2004): 169–207. The educational reforms of the Mexican revolutionary government apparently had an impressive effect. By 1930, the country's rate of primary school enrollment was 50% higher than those of the Soviet Union and Yugoslavia, tripled Turkey's, and surpassed that of Italy. For the impact of the Mexican revolution at a local level, see Stephen A. Kowalewski and Jacqueline J. Saindon, "The Spread of Literacy in a Latin American Peasant Society: Oaxaca, Mexico, 1890 to 1980," *Comparative Studies in Society and History* 34:1 (1992): 110–40.

28. Aaron Benavot and Phyllis Riddle, "The Expansion of Primary Education, 1870–1940: Trends and Issues," *Sociology of Education* 61:3 (1988): 191–210.

29. Literacy around 1900 varied dramatically within Latin America. But even the countries with the lowest rates in the region (Honduras, 18%; Bolivia, 17%; and Guatemala, 13%) did not rank much below Portugal's 25% and Serbia's 21%, surpassed Bosnia's 12%, and doubled or tripled the rates in India (6%), Egypt (5%), and Turkey (5%). The fact that literacy among the black population in Cuba in 1860—that is, eighteen years before the abolition of slavery—was higher than that of the population in general of the last three countries almost half a century later underlines the gap in education levels between Latin America and the non-Western world. From data in UNESCO, *Progress of Literacy in Various Countries* (Paris, 1953), 200–22, and Carlos Newland, "La educación elemental en Hispanoamerica: Desde la independencia hasta la centralización de los sistemas educativos nacionales," *The Hispanic American Historical Review* 71:2 (1991): 378.

30. Literacy rates around 1910 were 35% in Russia and Poland, 42% in Bulgaria, 50% in Spain, and 62% in Italy. The highest rates in the world were found in Great Britain, where it had become universal, among South African whites (97%), and in the United States (92%), Canada (89%), and France (87%): Boris N. Mironov, "The Development of Literacy in Russia and the USSR from the Tenth to the Twentieth Centuries," *History of Education Quarterly* 31:2 (1991): 240; Gabriel Tortella, "Patterns of Economic Retardation and Recovery in South-Western Europe in the Nineteenth and Twentieth Centuries," *The Economic History Review, New Series* 47:1 (1994): 11; UNESCO, *Progress of Literacy in Various Countries*, 144, 200–22.

31. World Bank, *Peril and Promise: Higher Education in Developing Countries* (Washington, D.C.: World Bank, 2000), 104–07. The nine Latin American countries with universal primary school enrollment rates in 1965 were Argentina, Uruguay, Brazil, Chile,

Paraguay, Peru, Cuba, Costa Rica, and Panama. They were followed by Venezuela (94%), Mexico (92%), Ecuador (91%), Dominican Republic (87%), Colombia (84%), El Salvador (82%), Honduras (80%), Bolivia (73%), Nicaragua (65%), and Guatemala (50%).

32. World Bank, *Peril and Promise*, 104–07.

33. Siew-Ean Khoo, Peter C. Smith, and James T. Fawcett, "Migration of Women to Cities: The Asian Situation in Comparative Perspective," *International Migration Review* 18:4 (1984): 1247–63.

34. Jose C. Moya, "Domestic Service in a Global Perspective: Gender, Migration, and Ethnic Niches," *Journal of Ethnic and Migration Studies* 33:4 (2007): 559–79.

35. UNESCO, Global *Education Digest 2007: Comparing Education Statistics across the World* (Montreal: UNESCO Institute for Statistics, 2007), 132.

36. UNESCO, *Global Education Digest 2007*; German W. Rama and Juan Carlos Tedesco, "Education and Development in Latin America, 1950–1975," *International Review of Education* 25:2/3 (1979): 187–211; Karen Bradley and Francisco O. Ramirez, "World Polity and Gender Parity: Women's Share of Higher Education, 1965–1985," *Research in Sociology of Education and Socialization* 11 (1996): 63–91.

37. Román de la Campa, "Latin, Latino, American: Split States and Global Imaginaries," *Comparative Literature* 53:4 (2001): 377, perceives in the term Latin America an Anglo-American effort to establish otherness, a form of North American orientalism.

38. Enrique Dussel, "Eurocentrism and Modernity," *Boundary* 20:2 (1993): 65, briefly mentions the marginalization of Spain and Portugal in the discourse on Western modernity. Jorge Cañizares-Esguerra, *Puritan Conquistadors: Iberianizing the Atlantic, 1550–1700* (Stanford: Stanford University Press, 2006) has recently confronted these assumptions, making a powerful case for the centrality of the Iberian presence in the shaping of not only Latin America but the entire Atlantic world.

39. A good example of Anglo-American assumptions about the backwardness of the Iberian world is unwittingly provided by the English historian Lawrence Stone in "Literacy and Education in England 1640–1900," *Past and Present* 42 (Feb. 1969): 69–139. In a concluding aside that bears little relation to the topic of the article, Stone muses about how "modernizing tyrannies," such as communist and fascist regimes, carry within them the seed of their own undoing because of their emphasis on mass education, and are thus transient, adding: "it is only nonmodernizing tyrannies, such as are found in Iberia and Latin America, which are capable of enduring for centuries" (p. 86). Despite Stone's certainty, these backward and interminable Iberian tyrannies lasted not centuries but five years in Spain and less than two decades in all of Latin America.

40. The phrase "rich as Peru" was still common enough in the late eighteenth and early nineteenth centuries to appear in musical entertainment such as Mozart's opera *Così fan tutte* (1790) and Rossini's *Il viaggio a Reims* (1825).

41. The New Economics Foundation, "The Happy Planet Index, 2009," p. 3. Available at www.happyplanetindex.org/public-data/files/happy-planet-index-2-0.pdf (accessed May 12, 2010).

42. Paul B. Rich, *Race and Empire in British Politics* (New York: Cambridge University Press, 1986).

43. Rubin F. Weston, *Racism in U.S. Imperialism: The Influence of Racial Assumption on American Foreign Policy, 1893–1946* (Columbia: University of South Carolina Press, 1972); and Michael L. Krenn, ed., *Race and U.S. Foreign Policy in the Ages of Territorial and Market Expansion, 1840–1900* (New York: Taylor & Francis, 1998): pp. 43–116 for four chapters on the annexation of Texas and the Mexican-American War, pp. 208–40 for "Imperialism and the Anglo-Saxon," and pp. 254–65 on Cuba and Puerto Rico.

44. Miguel Angel Centeno, *Blood and Debt: War and the Nation-State in Latin America* (University Park: Penn State University Press, 2002), 7–10.

45. Walter D. Mignolo, *The Idea of Latin America* (Oxford: Blackwell, 2005).

46. The shift in emphasis from imperial dictates to local processes in the history of the colonial period was first advanced by social history's concern with quotidian realities and popular culture rather than elite politics and later by the "New Philology," a school of ethnohistory that stressed the importance of using American sources, particularly those written in indigenous languages. See the essay in this volume by Terraciano and Sousa.

47. All data for GDP per capita by country come from Maddison, *Monitoring the World Economy, 1820–1992*, his webpage (see note 24), and United Nation and World Bank reports.

48. Calculated from data on languages and numbers of speakers in Lewis, *Ethnologue*.

CHAPTER 1

HISTORIOGRAPHY OF NEW SPAIN

KEVIN TERRACIANO
LISA SOUSA

Nueva España in the colonial or viceregal period extended from the Isthmus of Tehuantepec in the south to San Luis Potosí and up to Guadalajara in the north.[1] For most of this period, however, the viceroy's reach extended in the north to Nuevo Mexico and in the south to Central America and the Caribbean, not to mention the Philippines in the far west. In this chapter, we strike a compromise between the more restricted and extended boundaries by focusing on central and southern Mexico but not neglecting the far Mexican North and the southernmost boundaries of Mesoamerica, including Yucatan, Chiapas, and Guatemala. This essay will focus especially on publications since the early 1980s.

Trends in the study of New Spain do not diverge very much from the general evolution of the field of early Latin American history, with the one exception that the historiography of the Indians of Mexico is especially rich and robust. Even the study of indigenous peoples reflects a trend in the profession to pay more attention to traditionally underrepresented groups in colonial society. In general, earlier studies of political and economic institutions and the prominent men associated with them gave way in the 1960s and '70s to more social historical concerns with collective mentalities and group behaviors. Whereas earlier social histories treated more elite sectors of the population, from conquerors, judges, and administrators to hacendados, miners, and merchants, many now concern the more populous sectors of society—women, *castas* (mixed race), slaves, peasants, the indigent, and the indigenous. If many historians have emphasized economic and materialist causes and structural relations to explain how groups and individuals acted, now many seek to include cultural reasons for collective behaviors that are more contingent and unpredictable. Cultural studies of a postmodernist nature have had a limited but generally positive impact on our field, as Eric van Young observed.[2] The so-called new history is characterized by the study of mentalities, especially those of subalterns or subordinate groups, and a "thick reading" and problematization of texts that were produced in a colonial context.

This essay is organized into nine unequally weighted parts that represent major areas in the historiography of New Spain. It does not organize the literature into general types of history such as "social" or "cultural," or broad topics such as "race" and "ethnicity," because such overlapping and amorphous categories would include too many works. It does include discussions of "intellectual" and "economic" histories, because there are relatively few works of this nature to consider and most are easy to recognize as such. Most importantly, the nine sections organize bodies of literature that connect in many ways and represent the innovative and interdisciplinary research that characterizes the field.

INDIGENOUS PEOPLES

The remarkable quality and quantity of historical works on the "Indians" of Mexico in the immediate preconquest and colonial periods, which are usually referred to as "ethnohistory," have shifted this area of research from its traditional domain of anthropology toward a central place within the field of early Latin American history. The fact that the *Handbook of Latin American Studies* dedicates an entire section of literature reviews to the topic of Mesoamerican ethnohistory, organized under "History" and comparable in size to other historical sections such as "Colonial Mexico," confirms the importance of this area of study. At the turn of the twenty-first century, in volume 60, for example, the two historians who edited the ethnohistory section included some 240 books and articles that had been published in the previous four years, compared to 189 for the more general section on Colonial Mexico.[3] The quincentennial commemoration of 1492 inspired numerous studies of indigenous society and culture, and histories of indigenous peoples of New Spain have continued to increase since that time. Many excellent research articles on Mesoamerica have been published by scholars from Mexico, the United States and Canada, Central America, and Europe (Denmark, England, France, Germany, Italy, Netherlands, Poland, and Spain) in journals such as *Estudios de Cultura Nahuatl, Tlalocan, Historia Mexicana, Ethnohistory*, and *Mesoamérica*, among others. In Mexico, several national institutions have sponsored publications on indigenous history and culture, including the Instituto Nacional de Antropología e Historia (INAH), the Museo Nacional de Antropología e Historia, the Instituto de Investigaciones Históricas de UNAM (also the Institutos Antropológicas and Filológicas), the Centro de Estudios Superiores en Antropología Social (CIESAS), the Instituto Nacional Indígenista (INI), the Fondo de Cultura Económica, and the Consejo Nacional para la Cultura y las Artes.

This section follows general trends in the historiography of Indians of Mexico in recent decades, proceeding from histories of the immediate preconquest and early postconquest periods based primarily on Spanish-language sources and native pictorial records, and then to more recent scholarship based on the analysis of native-language alphabetic writings from the colonial period. It highlights many studies that stand out for their originality and contributions to the literature, regardless of the types of sources used by their authors. Some areas of research involving Indians are addressed in other sections of this essay, especially "Religion and the Church" and "Women, Gender, and Sexuality."

The "Aztecs," or the Mexica of Mexico Tenochtitlan, have attracted the most attention. Many studies have examined the "triple alliance" empire, its dynastic rulers, their methods of political and economic expansion and control, and the politico-religious ideology that sustained their power and view of the cosmos. Pedro Carrasco's detailed study of the Tenochca empire exemplifies this type of work, as does the study of the *templo mayor* by Johanna Broda, David Carrasco, Leonardo López Luján, and Eduardo Matos Moctezuma.[4] Indeed, scholars have addressed a tremendous range of topics, from Aztec warfare, trade, tribute, and transportation to the economy of central Mexico, from law in Tetzcoco to Mexica dynastic succession, and from "Azteca-Nahuatl" writing to Nahua conceptions of the human body.[5]

Studies of indigenous society and culture spurred the facsimile reproduction and analysis of many preconquest-style pictorial writings from Mesoamerica, often called "codices," especially from highland central and southern Mexico, produced both before and after the Spanish conquest. Luis Reyes García collaborated with Maarten Jansen and Ferdinand Anders to reproduce and analyze several codices from central and southern Mexico. This is only one example of the many collaborative efforts to use pictorial writings for the study of indigenous history before the Spanish conquest. Beyond the Mexica empire, there are many excellent studies of greater Mesoamerica before the arrival of the Spaniards, especially in the south. In the Maya region of southern Mexico and Central America, numerous scholars have worked on writing systems, especially in the more remote Classic period. Likewise, in Oaxaca, many have used pictographic writings from the Postclassic and early colonial period to study Mixtec, Zapotec, and Chocho cultures and societies.[6] One symposium in Mexico, for example, features the study of codices and documents from Mexico, meeting every three years and publishing numerous papers from its lengthy proceedings that attempt to bridge a traditional divide between the preconquest and postconquest periods.[7]

Proceeding from this rich literature on the immediate preconquest period to histories of the postconquest period based mainly on Spanish-language texts from libraries and archives in Mexico, Europe, and the United States, one encounters a type of research for which historians are better equipped than most scholars in other disciplines. Charles Gibson's works on Tlaxcala in 1952 and central Mexico in 1964 brought this type of scholarship to a very high level.[8] In both books, Gibson made extensive use of archival legal records in Mexico to show how indigenous towns actively responded to the conquest and colonial rule before succumbing to demographic decline and colonial deprivation. Gibson demonstrated the extent to which Spaniards utilized indigenous forms of organization and relied on local elites to make the colonial system function to their advantage. By shifting focus from Spaniards to Indians, he pioneered a new area of the field for historians trained to read archival records written in older Spanish. Around the same time, Woodrow Borah and Sherbourne Cook at the University of California, Berkeley published a number of demographic studies that demonstrated the immense size of the indigenous population in the early period and its precipitous decline by the mid-seventeenth century.[9] Many of the findings appeared in the Ibero-Americana series of the University of California Press, a publishing forum for a group of Latin Americanists known as the "Berkeley School." Borah and Cook confirmed the full extent of population loss through the systematic use of quantitative data; even those who disagree with the estimated numbers at contact do not dispute the rate of decline. And yet, despite the massive demographic decline, native peoples continued to make up the majority of the population of New Spain throughout the colonial period, most living in rural communities. This fact alone explains the recent attention given to the indigenous population in this period. Peter Gerhard mapped hundreds of these communities in Mexico, beginning with a dense volume on the center, complemented by separate volumes for the northern and southern "frontiers" of New Spain.[10]

Whereas studies of preconquest central Mexico tend to remain fixed on the Aztec empire, works on the colonial period downplay the importance of imperial structures and instead focus on the autonomous nature of the local state or *altepetl* within the broader Nahua culture area. The independent organization of the *altepetl* helps to explain why the empire, which was really more of a loose and restricted confederation of tribute-paying *altepetl* than a leviathan that lorded over a large territory, unraveled so rapidly at the hands of the Spaniards and their many Indian auxiliaries. The implication of this decentering approach is that native cultures in New Spain did not unravel with the collapse of larger structures, and that thousands of communities could and did function on their own, despite many significant changes.

Earlier studies focused on colonial institutions that regulated the social, political, economic, and religious organization of native communities. More recent works focus on how communities and their leaders responded to these institutions of colonial rule. In general, for much of the colonial period, Spaniards lived in cities surrounded by an indigenous countryside. Communities were "containers" of indigenous culture, represented by hereditary elites who actively sought to defend and promote their local interests. Scholars have studied the survival, adaptation, and decline of the native nobility and lordly establishments in Mesoamerica (defined by Spaniards as *caciques* and *cacicazgos*, respectively), often in relation to broader discussions of the declining population and increasing competition with Spaniards for material resources, especially labor and land. Some portray Indians as victims who were overwhelmed by disease and a colonial system designed to benefit the colonizers; others emphasize indigenous agency and adaptation and relate a complex and uneven process of change and continuity, determined primarily by the degree and timing of indigenous contact with Europeans in a given region. One emphasizes transformation and acculturation, the other adaptation and negotiation. The different emphases are often matters of perspective based on the types of sources consulted, the period, and the place of study. Many works combine aspects of both, assigning agency to both Spanish and indigenous actors but recognizing the colonial context of their interactions.

Several microhistories of communities and regions have illuminated the different dynamics of change in various parts of New Spain to the point that general statements about the status of Indians under Spanish rule should be avoided, because the experiences of the Nahuas of Mexico City, the Itza of Yucatan, and the "Pueblo" of Nuevo México—to name only three groups—differed in so many significant ways. A series sponsored by CIESAS and INI titled *Historia de los pueblos indígenas de México*, edited by Teresa Rojas Rabiela and Mario Humberto Ruz, features dozens of regional studies of indigenous groups, most reaching back into the colonial period. At last count, the series stands at some two dozen volumes on various regions and a few specialized topics. Regional histories abound in Mexico, in part because regionalism is still so important today. There are several hundred regional studies of Indians in New Spain; the notes refer to a few outside of central Mexico, on the Tarascans or Purépecha of Michoacan,[11] the Mixtecs and Zapotecs of Oaxaca,[12] and the Maya of Yucatan.[13] Serge Gruzinski is one of the few scholars to attempt a cross-regional history, ranging broadly across highland Mexico to apply a variety of conceptual approaches from the French school on the history of mentalities, considering the conquest not as an event but as an extended process of westernization.[14]

In the last few decades, the translation and analysis of colonial native-language sources written in the Roman alphabet has had a profound impact on history and ethnohistory. Most of the earliest work involved published texts produced in the sixteenth century under the instruction and auspices of the religious orders and written in the Nahuatl language, which included language instructional materials, catechisms, speeches, songs, and projects of an ethnographic nature, such as the twelve books of the Florentine Codex. Much of the focus was on the texts as literature and as sources for the study of the language and philosophy of the ancients. In Mexico, Ángel María Garibay and Miguel León-Portilla have written numerous books on a variety of translated texts. In addition to participating actively in the production of church-sponsored texts, native writers throughout Mesoamerica generated countless records in their own languages from around the mid-sixteenth century onward. Only a small percentage of this documentation remains, yet it is a massive corpus that seems to expand continuously with each archival search. In the 1970s, a small group of historians, anthropologists, and linguists began to work with archival documentation written in Nahuatl, a major language of central Mexico.[15] The development of a historical approach based on the use of native-language sources proceeds from social historical concerns with the collective behavior and mentalities of groups. Local native-language documents offer an internal or emic perspective on indigenous groups and individuals, their language, and important organizing concepts in their culture and society.

James Lockhart and many of his former students from UCLA have made numerous contributions to this scholarship, as have scholars in Mexico, such as Luis Reyes García. Lockhart was the first to synthesize findings based on these types of documents for the Nahuas of central Mexico, based firmly on his own original research and the work of his students and colleagues, in his monumental book *The Nahuas After the Conquest*.[16] Lockhart used hundreds of Nahuatl-language writings from various *altepetl* in central Mexico to demonstrate the vitality and resilience of Nahua culture and language well into the eighteenth century and beyond, despite the many significant changes. Other works associated with this New Philology, as it has been called, have focused on collections of Nahuatl-language documents from specific communities or areas in central Mexico, including Culhuacan, Cuernavaca, Coyoacan, Tenochtitlan, Cuauhtinchan, Chalco, and Toluca.[17] One prominent historian called research associated with Lockhart and his students "the most innovative and recognizable 'school' of colonial history to yet emerge."[18]

The potential for comparison between Nahuas and other Mesoamerican groups who wrote in their own languages is very promising. Comparative studies for the Maya region began with Ralph Roys and France Scholes, who pioneered the use of colonial Yucatec Maya as early as the 1930s and '40s.[19] Colonial-era texts such as the *Popol Vuh* and the Books of Chilam Balam are comparable in many ways to texts in Nahuatl that record oral traditions. Matthew Restall wrote a history based entirely on a large collection of colonial Maya-language sources, mainly from the late colonial period, following Nancy Farriss's classic work on Yucatan.[20] For Oaxaca, Kevin Terraciano was the first to use colonial Mixtec-language texts, in conjunction with pictorial writings and Spanish-language sources, for a history of the Mixtec or *Ñudzahui* people from the early sixteenth to the eighteenth centuries, making numerous detailed comparisons with the Nahuas. Now Terraciano and Sousa, in collaboration with linguists and historians at UCLA, are also working with Zapotec-language records from the Valley of Oaxaca.[21] Michel Oudijk was the first to complete a comprehensive study of colonial Zapotec pictorial records from the Sierra and the Valley of Oaxaca, including native-language alphabetic texts, and is now also working with Zapotec-language documents.[22] Following José Alcina Franch, David Tavárez is analyzing Zapotec calendars and songs, working with a large, challenging corpus of ritual texts from the later colonial period.[23] Also in Oaxaca, Sebastián van Doesburg is now working with hundreds of Chocho-language (*Ngiwa*) documents from the northwestern Mixteca region.[24]

Studies based on native-language records reveal many of the activities and preoccupations of corporate communities, which were represented by a municipal council of elected male officials who used alphabetic writing as a means to defend and promote their collective and individual interests. Although profiles of certain individuals emerge, especially elites, such studies rarely reach a biographical level;

the Nahua historian, don Domingo de San Antón Chimalpahin Quauhtlehuanitzin, is exceptional, but even he remains an elusive character in many ways, known more for his many writings about the Nahua past than for anything else he did in his life, as Susan Schroeder has shown.[25] "Collective biographies" of indigenous *principales* are more common.[26] Whereas elites tend to stand out in the record, both Spanish- and native-language archival records involve a cross-section of the population, so that social histories of indigenous communities and groups can offer considerable depth and detail, thanks to the Spanish "paper empire," which produced tons of documentation across nearly three centuries. Some scholars who use native-language records have focused not on communities or defined populations but on particular types of texts and genres of writing as forms of cultural expression in a colonial context. Louise Burkhart's study of the Nahua-Christian moral dialogue in the sixteenth century, for example, examines the language of church-sponsored publications for key Christian concepts. Most recently, Burkhart and Barry Sell have studied Nahua theater by translating all extant plays written in Nahuatl.[27] Others have examined particular writings of a historical nature, such as the annals, which were written originally in a pictographic form and then adapted to the alphabet in the sixteenth century.

Research involving native-language writings, especially Nahuatl, has generated numerous translations of these writings into Spanish, English, and other languages. In 1950, Arthur J. O. Anderson and Charles E. Dibble published the first of twelve books of the Florentine Codex, translated from Nahuatl into English, and published the last book thirty-two years later.[28] In Mexico, Ángel María Garibay, Fernando Horcasitas, Miguel León-Portilla, Alfredo López Austin, Luis Reyes García, and Rafael Tena have translated numerous texts into Spanish.[29] Lockhart, Anderson, and Frances Berdan were among the first to compile a collection of fully transcribed and translated mundane documents.[30] Sarah Cline translated a famous collection of testaments from Culhuacan with León-Portilla, and a lengthy census from Morelos.[31] Since Anderson, no scholar has produced more translations of Nahuatl-language texts than Lockhart, who continues to edit a Nahuatl-language series that he founded at UCLA.[32] Many others have contributed to this rich tradition of Nahuatl-language study.[33] One should not view these types of translation projects as endeavors separate from historical scholarship, since many translators also analyze the texts as historical sources. Most recently, several scholars, including Stephanie Wood, Robert Haskett and Paula López Caballero, have worked with *títulos primordiales* and Techialoyan "codices," genres of late colonial indigenous writing that tend to feature discursive native-language documents and pictorials.[34] The location and nature of native-language texts and documents are now more identifiable, thanks to several good guides and indices, and as scholars and archivists become more conscious of their existence and value.[35]

Most studies of indigenous peoples of New Spain, regardless of the types of sources on which they are based, have focused on well-defined pueblos or regions inhabited by predominately indigenous populations, living in relative isolation from Spaniards.[36] At the same time, urban studies tend not to focus on indigenous populations, but rather treat them as part of the ethnically mixed and plebeian population of the city, as Douglas Cope does in his study of Mexico City.[37] John Chance and Norma Angélica Castillo Palma have studied interactions and *mestizaje* in the cities of Oaxaca and Cholula, respectively.[38] Perhaps because the project is so daunting, few have attempted to study the four-part indigenous *altepetl* of Mexico Tenochtitlan after the conquest, which surrounded the Spanish-speaking population of the capital and was absorbed eventually by the city's expansion.[39] Much more work could be done on "urban Indians" and on interethnic interactions involving indigenous peoples and others more generally.

Moreover, most histories of the Indians of New Spain have focused on the dense sedentary native populations in central and southern Mexico, which came into direct contact with Spaniards. North of sedentary central Mexico, beginning as far south as what is now known as the Bajío, lay a vast region inhabited by more dispersed, smaller groups. In general, peoples of the north adapted to the more extreme environments of the arid plains; many of them practiced some agriculture for part of the year, but nearly all moved across an extended territory, and some relied entirely on hunting and gathering. The peoples of the north, including what is now the southwestern United States, were very different from the Mesoamericans.[40] Histories of the northern groups are more challenging in many ways, because sources are more limited and are written entirely in Spanish. Nonetheless, we have some excellent histories of this vast region. Cynthia Radding, for example, analyzed interactions between the Opata, Pima, and Eudeve and the Spanish and mestizo settlers in northwestern Mexico, especially during the Bourbon reforms and the independence period.[41] Seeking to connect their struggles with changes in the environment, Radding demonstrates how the competition for access to resources proved a crucial factor in the survival of indigenous groups, particularly against encroaching frontier institutions such as missions, presidios, and mines. Similarly, Susan Deeds studied how five indigenous groups in Nueva Vizcaya (ranging across the modern states of Sinaloa, Durango, and Chihuahua) responded to two centuries of colonial rule, from the arrival of the Spaniards to the collapse of the Jesuit missions.[42] Deeds explores the issue of cultural ethnogenesis, attempting to explain why only two of five indigenous groups in the region, the Tarahumaras (Rarámuri) and the Tepehuanes, survived into the late colonial period, whereas the other three (Xiximes, Acaxees, and Conchos) were absorbed or depleted by Spanish frontier institutions.

Northern New Spain is known for its mobile populations. Michael Swann followed his work on Durango with a study of mobility in the north.[43] There are a number of works on Tlaxcalans who migrated from central Mexico to the north, such as David Adams's study of the Tlaxcalan communities that formed in Coahuila and Nuevo León.[44] Agueda Jiménez Pelayo has written on the Caxcanes of Zacatecas who collaborated with Spaniards as *indios fronterizos*.[45] Some solid regional histories of the north have been written on Saltillo, Querétaro, and Chihuahua.[46] The mission system continues to attract scholarly attention, but it is now seen in the more expansive context of frontier studies.[47]

BLACKS AND SLAVERY

The study of slavery in New Spain has been limited in comparison to works about other parts of Latin America, especially the Caribbean and Brazil, not only because fewer Africans went to New Spain than the other two areas but because historians have paid so much attention to coerced forms of labor among indigenous peoples, as exemplified by the many works of Silvio Zavala.[48] Also, the relative lack of an apparent or visible Black population and a surge of interest in indigenous cultures deflected historians' attention from Mexico's African population. But now scholars recognize that the African population in New Spain was larger and more important than once thought, thanks to Gonzalo Aguirre Beltrán's *La población negra de México*, first published in 1946.[49] The book revealed that Africans lived not only in Veracruz and along the Pacific coast but also in the interior of New Spain and especially in Mexico City. Aguirre's emphasis on the absorption of the population by indigenous and mestizo groups, resulting in the *afromestizo*, reinforced the ideal of *mestizaje*—the cornerstone of Mexico's nation-building ideology. *La población negra* remains a foundational text, but it was not until the 1970s that others followed Aguirre Beltrán's lead, attending first to the institution of slavery and then to *negros* as a discrete population.

Colin Palmer and Patrick Carroll were among the first historians who followed in Aguirre Beltrán's footsteps. Palmer's *Slaves of the White God* provides a detailed account of the Atlantic and domestic slave trade, and is thus an institutional history of slavery in Mexico. Carroll's *Blacks in Colonial Veracruz*, published a full fifteen years after Palmer's book, departs from a general treatment of Africans in Mexico and moves toward a more focused study of labor conditions, supply and demand, and other features of slavery in Veracruz. Like Palmer, Carroll tells us more about the institution than about peoples of African descent and their cultures. His detailed comparative study of Córdoba and Jalapa, in particular, shows the extent to which the region and the central highlands in general depended on black labor for its sugar *ingenios* and other enterprises. He concludes by considering the active role of Africans, mulattoes, and mestizos in the independence movement against Spain.[50]

Since 2000, studies have focused more on the diversity of African experiences in urban areas and within colonial institutions. Herman Bennett's contribution to the literature focuses on the African population of Mexico City during the peak years of the Mexican slave trade, considering people of African descent as members of a complex, diverse population.[51] Bennett examines marriage petitions among urban blacks, demonstrating a broad endogamous solidarity among Angolans, especially in the early period. Ben Vinson reveals the crucial role that Afro-Mexicans contributed to the formation of New Spain's defense before the implementation of the Bourbon military reforms in the 1760s.[52] Free-colored militiamen were organized into segregated militias called *compañías de pardos y morenos libres* until the creation of racially integrated units in 1792. Whatever legal or monetary benefits these free people of African descent and their families derived from being members of the militia, many sought to join Spanish and mestizo provincial units after 1792, attempting to advance in the colonial ethnic hierarchy. Nicole von Germeten examines motives underlying the foundation of Afro-Mexican *cofradías* and the changes that these societies underwent in the colonial period, sampling confraternities in Mexico City, Valladolid, and Parral.[53] The author considers a number of important issues across time, from the popularity of African saints and the prominence of women as leaders in the early period to distinctions between black and mulatto cofradías. María Elisa Velázquez has written an extensive history of Afro-Mexican women, examining slavery, gender, and racial relations in Mexico City in the seventeenth and eighteenth centuries.[54]

These recent studies are as attentive to the occupations and social status of Afro-Mexicans as to their racial and ethnic designations. The shift from studying Africans on plantations to more urban settings or in communities not oriented toward slave labor has forced scholars to come to terms with the ethnic complexity of colonial spaces, where "blacks" as a group were as diverse as the *casta* society in which they lived and worked. Scholars have paid increasing attention to what "*negro*" means in different times and places of New Spain, and especially to the dynamic population of free blacks and mulattoes. This is particularly the case among historians in the United States, who have focused their research more on analytical categories of race and ethnicity than on culture or class. Interethnic interactions between blacks and native peoples is another promising area of study that is addressed by some urban studies but, in general, is still neglected. Restall edited a compilation of articles which begins to explore African-Indigenous interactions in colonial Latin America, with relevant contributions on New Spain.[55] The essays in this volume tend to downplay the Spanish presence and the idea of cultural dominance and acculturation, including the influence of the church and most other colonial institutions, focusing instead on processes of interculturation and the increasing confluence of indigenous and African populations over the course of the colonial period, as they came into mutual contact in many ways over time.

Finally, a rare contribution by an African historian to the study of colonial Mexico is *L'Afrique Bantu dans la colonization du Mexique, 1596–1640*, by Nicolas Ngou-Mvé, which demonstrates the overwhelmingly Central African provenance of New Spain's slave population, especially from the Loango states, and the importance of Luanda as the continent's main slaving port.[56] Ngou-Mvé is especially strong on the African side of the Atlantic, unlike most historians who treat slavery or Africans in the Americas.

Spaniards

We have reached a point, ironically, where we know as much, if not more, about indigenous society as we know about Spaniards, other Europeans, and criollos in New Spain. One obvious way to examine Spaniards as a group is through the study of migration. Ida Altman has followed Spaniards from Spain to New Spain and other parts of Spanish America.⁵⁷ Robert Himmerich y Valencia examined the *encomenderos* as a social group, compiling biographical sketches of both high-ranking and humble Spaniards.⁵⁸ Not surprisingly, the literature is especially strong for Spanish elites, who played prominent roles in major institutions such as government and the church. Some studies treat ideas, institutions, and individuals on both sides of the Atlantic. Ethelia Ruiz Medrano investigates the government of viceroy don Antonio de Mendoza and the second Audiencia.⁵⁹ María Elena Martínez analyzes the evolution of a Spanish ideology, *limpieza de sangre*, and considers its impact on religion, law, gender, and race relations in Mexico.⁶⁰ Alejandro Cañeque's investigation of the viceregal court is a valuable blend of political and cultural history.⁶¹ Similarly, Cayetana Alvarez de Toledo's book on the life, writings, and reforms of Juan de Palafox provides a biographical and intellectual history of this influential bishop of the seventeenth century that focuses on his association with the viceregal establishment and his writings both in Spain and New Spain.⁶² Surprisingly, there is no comparable, comprehensive study of the life and works of fray Bartolomé de las Casas, although numerous translations and critical editions of his writings continue to be published.⁶³ Stafford Poole's book on don Pedro Moya de Contreras, archbishop and first inquisitor of New Spain, offers a biographical treatment of a high-ranking Spanish official within a broader discussion of Catholic policies and strategies.⁶⁴ Edith Couturier's biography of the Count of Regla documents the rise of a successful Spanish merchant and miner who attained nobility and wealth in New Spain.⁶⁵ Louisa Hoberman profiled merchant elites in the mature colonial period, and John Kicza examined a wide range of entrepreneurs and their social and familial connections in the Bourbon era.⁶⁶ Doris Ladd took up the topic of the Mexican nobility in the latter decades of the period.⁶⁷ Like Kicza's book, Solange Alberro's brief but broad study of Spaniards in Mexico includes both elites and commoners.⁶⁸

Histories of Spaniards in New Spain overlap with urban studies in many ways, because most Spaniards gravitated to cities. A volume of essays on Puebla from the sixteenth to the twentieth centuries, edited by Agustín Grajales and Lilián Illades, contains several pieces on Spaniards in the earlier period.⁶⁹ One study treats non-Spanish Europeans primarily in New Spain, a group which has received little attention, while another examines Spanish and Creole interactions in the late colonial period.⁷⁰ Many histories consider Spanish and indigenous interactions, giving more or less equal attention to both groups.⁷¹ Some include mestizos in the multiethnic mix.⁷²

Women, Gender, and Sexuality

Asunción Lavrin pioneered the study of women in colonial Latin America; her edited volume on women stood alone for years before serious monographs began to appear on the topic.⁷³ One of the first major studies was Sylvia Arrom's book on women in Mexico City, which examined multiple types of data in two districts of the city, representing about 10% of the population.[74] Arrom set out to address some very challenging questions that reflect trends in the study of women: Did men dominate women in law and in practice? What did working women do? How was women's status affected by age, class, and race? Did women's status change across time? This ambitious work set a high standard for the study of women in Mexico. Several more defined studies of women followed, using discrete collections of sources to consider various questions about the status of women; Patricia Seed's study of marriage promise contracts, for example, examines a shift in cultural assumptions that informed parental authority and children's freedom to choose marriage partners, and sheds light on changing notions about individual will, love, and honor in the eyes of church authorities.[75] Speaking of the church, several studies by Lavrin and others have considered the position of nuns in colonial society, as a special group of literate women who produced writings about their lives, albeit in a restricted context.[76]

Very few works addressed indigenous or African women until Susan Kellogg's book on native women in Mexico City.[77] Susan Schroeder, Stephanie Wood, and Robert Haskett organized an excellent anthology entitled *Indian Women of Early Mexico*, which challenged stereotypes about Indian women and illustrated the varied and central roles women played before and after the conquest.[78] The contributors to this anthology provided new approaches for the study of indigenous women's history. Steve Stern's use of sociological theories to describe gender norms and deviance and the reality of domestic violence represents another breakthrough in the field; Stern used criminal records to show how gendered conflict reinforced patriarchal norms, however contested, within households and communities in three different areas of late colonial Mexico.[79] Several other historians have written about male sexual violence and contested relations of power in New Spain.[80] Some studies of Malinche view her fleeting appearance on history's stage through the lens of gender and power.[81]

Proceeding from an interest in women, the field moved to consider gender relations and sexuality. Again, Lavrin edited an influential set of essays on the topic.[82] Various scholars, including Richard Boyer, Martha Few, Ramón Gutiérrez, and Ann Twinam, examined a range of issues such as honor and power that went beyond an exclusive focus on women.[83] Many of these works were consciously influenced by Foucault's *History of Sexuality*, which linked individuals and sexualities with institutions and forms of control and enabled scholars to theorize about sexuality in relation to power. Initially, most studies of sexuality continued to focus on heterosexual relations. Serge Gruzinski was the first to write about homosexuality in colonial Latin America, focusing on Mexico. Others have followed for New Spain, including Federico Garza Carvajal, Alfredo López Austin, Martin Nesvig, Sergio Ortega, Lee Penyak, Pete Sigal, and Zeb Tortorici.[84] In addition to the work edited by Lavrin, three anthologies deserve mention for their inclusion of essays or documents on sexuality.[85] In Mexico, the numerous edited volumes resulting from the Seminario de Historia de las Mentalidades attest to the collaborative efforts of Mexican historians (including Solange Alberro, Alfredo López Austin, Ana María Atondo Rodríguez, María Elena Cortés Jacome, Sergio Ortega Noriega, Dolores

Enciso Rojas, and Jorge René González Marmolejo, among others) to advance the study of moral order, gender, family, and sexuality in colonial Mexico.[86]

Gender and sexuality studies are now accepted and valued by most historians, but some works have been criticized for their use of postmodern/queer/subaltern studies jargon, loosely defined concepts such as "patriarchy," and their attempt to advance a "presentist agenda." There are also questions of interpretation. Some historians such as Irene Silverblatt, Ruth Behar, Noemí Quezada, and Martha Few have examined *curanderas*, sorcery, local healing practices, and sexual witchcraft as evidence of resistance and subversion of colonial domination. Laura Lewis, Richard Boyer, Pilar Gonzalbo Aizpuru, and Ann Twinam argue against this "resistance" reading in history.

Religion and the Church

Many studies of religion and the church in New Spain continue to respond in some way to Robert Ricard's thesis of the "spiritual conquest," first posed in the 1930s.[87] Ricard represents one extreme in the literature in that he immersed himself in the writings of the ecclesiastics to such a degree that he ended up replicating their view of what they had accomplished in the sixteenth century. He was more familiar with the ideologies, aspirations, and achievements of the mendicant orders than with the indigenous sacred beliefs and cosmologies that he supposed had been eradicated. Since Ricard, many scholars have attended to indigenous views of the cosmos and to the limits of the spiritual conquest. Alfredo López Austin, Miguel León-Portilla, and Leonardo López Lujan have written extensively on Nahua worldviews, with implications for how Nahuas imagined and received Christian doctrine.[88] In one of his early works, López Austin explored the "man-god" or charismatic individual who was believed to possess divine energy.[89] Serge Gruzinski followed by identifying the reemergence of the traditional "*hombre-dios*" in colonial times who rallied people against the new order.[90] Christian Duverger returned to Ricard's focus on the activities of the orders but offered a more refined view of Nahua spirituality and the limits of conversion.[91] Guy Stresser-Péan challenged Ricard's notion that paganism was thoroughly eradicated in central Mexico by combining historical and ethnographic research in the Northern Sierra region of Puebla.[92] As Charles Gibson remarked and Stresser-Péan demonstrated, the best evidence for remnants of older, non-Christian practices comes not from the archive but from the contemporary ethnographic record. Thus, a natural response to Ricard's sweeping thesis was to examine evidence of native continuities, attributing more agency to indigenous actors and recognizing the limitations of the spiritual conquest, as many friars did by the end of the sixteenth century. To some scholars, however, resistance did not prevent the fragmentation, acculturation, and eventual "westernization" of the native system envisioned by Ricard.[93]

Christians referred to remnants of native spiritual practices as "idolatries" and "superstitions." The understanding of idolatry by the Inquisition is a subject explored by Carmen Bernand and Gruzinski.[94] Inquisitorial records are among the most commonly used sources on idolatry, although the concerns and obsessions of this policing institution tended to accentuate the most extreme practices. Nonetheless, numerous scholars have pored over these fascinating records with an eye for the same types of information that the inquisitors sought. Richard Greenleaf provided one of the first synoptic studies of the institution of the Mexican Holy Office, followed by Solange Alberro's *Inquisición y sociedad en México, 1571–1700*.[95] The Holy Office of the Inquisition was established in Mexico in 1571, following the commission of a *provisorato de indios* in 1559, which was to deal with Indians under a different set of guidelines.[96] Indebted to Greenleaf's study of Zumárraga and the Inquisition's treatment of Indians, Bernard Grunberg provided a clear review of the main doctrinal and practical issues that preoccupied the Apostolic Inquisition in Mexico (until 1571) and examined several cases against Indians in the early period.[97] Taking as a point of departure the work of France V. Scholes and Eleanor Adams, Inga Clendinnen analyzed the *procesos* of Bishop Diego de Landa's autos-da-fé in 1562 to consider the ritual acts and prophetic literature of the Maya.[98] John Chuchiak has also made several contributions to the study of idolatry and its persecution in Yucatan.[99] Marcelo Carmagnani and Terraciano have used inquisitorial records for the study of Zapotec and Mixtec practices in Oaxaca, respectively.[100]

Many scholars have attended to the incorporation and adaptation of Christian practices by local indigenous populations. These types of studies tend to treat Mesoamerican and Spanish folk beliefs and practices as more congruent than incompatible. One approach to this process of adaptation employs the concept "syncretism" to describe how elements of the two religious systems were mixed or fused, whether consciously or not, to form a stable synthesis that did not fundamentally alter indigenous elements in the mixture. The equation of the Virgin of Guadalupe with Tonantzin, a Nahua female deity, is one example. Some scholars have faulted syncretism for its simplistic, mechanical theory of change. Although most historians agree that conversion involved the adaptation of Christian rites to local practices, the process was much more unpredictable and did not necessarily result in a finished, hybrid product.[101]

In her classic study of the Maya of Yucatan, Nancy Farriss referred to a "creative synthesis," a dynamic and complex convergence of Maya and Christian practices and beliefs that was achieved by native elites and *cofradías* (lay confraternities) in the relative absence of priests in this more remote part of New Spain.[102] It is not that Mesoamericans were opposed to accepting new deities and practices, but that they refused to abandon all older practices and found creative ways to avoid the monotheistic imperative of all or nothing. Like Clendinnen, Farris found that the Maya accommodated certain Christian practices in ways that did not supplant older traditions. Farriss's more refined analysis borrowed from the language of syncretism but expanded the concept to include local, contingent factors in explaining religious change.

Taking a somewhat different tack in his study of the Nahuas, James Lockhart characterized cultural interactions between Spaniards and Nahuas in general as a process of "double mistaken identity" in which "each side takes it that a given form or concept is essentially one already known to it, operating in much the same manner as in its own tradition, and hardly takes cognizance of the other side's interpretation." Working with a tremendous variety of Nahuatl-language sources from especially the sixteenth and seventeenth centuries, Lockhart attributed this process to "the basic similarities between both cultures, each side using its own categories in interpreting the cultural phenomena of the other."[103] Louise Burkhart examined aspects of this process of mutual misrepresentation in Nahuatl-language church-sponsored texts of the sixteenth century, demonstrating how friars carefully selected Nahuatl-language terminology for Christian concepts without resorting to Spanish loanwords, and the theoretical problems inherent in their attempt to bridge the "dialogical gap." Here Burkhart followed Dibble's concept of "Nahuatlization."[104] Georges Baudot also examined the process of "transculturation," in which both Europeans and Indians attempted to understand the "other" within their own discursive categories.[105]

Historians in recent years have paid less attention to the theory and doctrine of Christian conversion and have attended more to ritual and the practice of "local religion." Piety is not to be confused with orthodoxy, as William Christian shows by using those same sixteenth-century questionnaires—the *Relaciones Geográficas*—for towns in Spain that scholars have used for indigenous pueblos in New Spain.[106] And yet, in spite of the limitations of conversion, it is clear that the collective practices of the church appealed to many people. *Cofradías*, as local organizations dedicated to specific saints, sponsored many collective activities.[107] Ritual abounded with possibilities for convergence. Osvaldo Pardo and Sarah Cline examine the sacraments for evidence of interplay and exchange between Christian and Nahua ritual practices. Jaime Lara, Samuel Edgerton, and Richard McAndrew contemplate the sacred spaces of church architecture, following and extending George Kubler's classic study.[108] No Christian introduction was more successful than the cult of saints. The patron saint of the local church became a symbolic head of the community, resembling a patron deity in many ways.[109] And no saint in Mexico is venerated more than the Virgin of Guadalupe, who has inspired a number of excellent studies before and after the canonization of Juan Diego in 2002. Many accomplished scholars, including Solange Alberro, David Brading, Edmundo O'Gorman, Xavier Noguez, Stafford Poole, and William Taylor, have weighed in with books on the origins, evolution, and significance of Guadalupe.[110] Some of these works also treat broader discussions of the formation of local ethnic identities.

William Taylor's magisterial study of local religion in rural parishes of the Archdiocese of Mexico and the Diocese of Guadalajara in the Bourbon period exemplifies the best social and cultural history of religious devotion and the local church in New Spain.[111] The book is really three studies in one: a social history of parish priests; a survey of the religious culture of lay people; and a consideration of the role of priests and parishioners in local politics, looking ahead to the participation of priests in the Mexican Independence movements. By studying priests *and* parishioners together, both Indians and non-Indians, Taylor is able to examine local religion in a more holistic way, without denying agency to subjects on either side of the altar. Whereas most studies of religion in New Spain treat the "spiritual conquest" of the sixteenth century, Taylor considers a complex blend that percolated in Mexico for at least two centuries. In so many ways, this sophisticated study transcends a focus on religion to include broader issues, such as the organization of public life and the consequences of specific Bourbon administrative reforms.

The field continues to benefit from more traditional studies of prominent religious figures and institutions, such as the first ecclesiastical councils, the first archbishop of New Spain and other prominent elites or intellectuals, and regional studies of the church.[112] Many scholars have used ecclesiastical records, especially Inquisition cases, to study cultural concerns and social behavior. These studies are not as interested in religion as they are in the church as an agent of social control and the extent and limitations of the institution's policing practices. Works on penance, confession, and blasphemy, for example, might fall into this category of social control.[113] Madness and magic invited the inquisitorial gaze, and indigenous drinking habits, if we are to believe all the reports, troubled many priests and Spanish officials.[114] Many studies of gender, bigamy, polygyny, perversion, and "unnatural" sexuality involve the Inquisition as well, but these topics are mentioned above in the section on gender and sexuality.

Finally, two excellent anthologies on religion in New Spain, one edited by Martin Nesvig and the other by Susan Schroeder and Stafford Poole, represent the diversity and remarkable quality of works in this area of the field.[115]

Law, Crime, and Rebellion

The study of law, crime, and violent rebellion constitutes another rich vein of research. Studies of law have focused on the Audiencia, the General Indian Court or Juzgado Real, the administration of local justice, and the effect of Spanish law on native societies. Woodrow Borah, for example, shows how the Indian Court was established in the late sixteenth century to ease the introduction of Indians into Spanish law and legal procedures and to protect them from abusive officials. Borah provides overviews of numerous cases which highlight various aspects of the justice system for native individuals and groups.[116] Brian Owensby has extended Borah's work by focusing on the ways in which native pueblos and individuals learned how to use the General Indian Court to pursue their claims.[117] At a more local level, in the Sierra region of Oaxaca, Yanna Yannakakis examines "native intermediaries" who operated within the legal system to negotiate interactions between Spanish officials and native communities.[118]

Studies of law and crime overlap. William Taylor's study of patterns of excessive drinking, homicide, and rebellion in the Mixteca Alta and the Valley of Mexico in the eighteenth century provides a comparative analysis of three crimes that appear frequently in the colonial criminal record.[119] Gabriel Haslip-Viera's book on crime in Mexico City addresses the urban environment of the city, the issue of social disorder, and the mechanics of the criminal justice system.[120] Teresa Lozano Armendares took up the same topic for a more defined period.[121] Lee Penyak explored the archive of the Tribunal Superior de Justicia in his study of criminal law in New Spain.[122] Some have explored the cultural dimensions of crime. Sonya Lipsett-Rivera and Lyman Johnson, for example, edited a volume on honor, shame, and violence in Colonial Latin America, which includes relevant pieces on New Spain. Terraciano examined the same topic in his analysis of a rare Mixtec-language murder note written by a man who killed his wife because he suspected her of committing adultery.[123] One collection of essays focuses on violence in Guatemala and El Salvador in the eighteenth and nineteenth centuries.[124] These many studies show that the criminal justice system, despite its biases and limitations, did not simply police and regulate passive subjects. Criminal records reveal a cross-section of society, including economically marginal people who appear infrequently in notarial or civil records and who used and sometimes manipulated the justice system to their benefit.

Rebellion might be considered the ultimate collective crime in the colonial period, especially if it resulted in violence against individuals and groups. María Teresa Huerta and Patricia Palacios were among the first to consider indigenous rebellions as a category of study, a topic later addressed in a volume edited by Susan Schroeder.[125] Several studies of indigenous rebellions focus on particular regions: William Taylor and Héctor Díaz-Polanco address the topic for Oaxaca.[126] Victoria Bricker, Kevin Gosner, Grant Jones, Severo Martínez Peláez, Juan Pedro Viqueira Albán, and Robert Patch have studied violent conflicts in the Maya area.[127] Michael Ducey and Andrew Kraut address rebellions in the Huasteca region and New Mexico, respectively.[128] Felipe Castro Gutiérrez has written several works on rebellion in Michoacán and in New Spain, in general.[129] Many other works discuss violent rebellions in the context of broader regional histories of Indians.

Another related field of research interprets agrarian violence more in terms of peasant revolts than indigenous uprisings, as Taylor did in his study, placing more emphasis on class divisions than on ethnicity. For example, John Tutino takes a diachronic approach to the study of agrarian violence from 1750 to 1940.[130] The most recent and influential study of popular violence is Eric Van Young's massive study of the Mexican Independence period.[131] Finally, some have studied urban riots or *tumultos*, particularly the infamous Mexico City riot of 1692.[132]

URBAN AND ENVIRONMENTAL STUDIES

Despite the prominence of cities in New Spain, there are relatively few recent urban studies for this period. Three articles defined the state of this research for colonial Latin America in general in the 1980s.[133] For New Spain, Edmundo O'Gorman was among the first in the 1930s to map out the urban spaces of Mexico City, and Alfonso Caso produced a study in the 1950s of the city immediately before and after the conquest.[134] Studies of architecture aside, it was not until 1990 that a team of scholars followed the lead of these two Mexican pioneers.[135] The old viceregal capital continues to attract most of the attention. Douglas Cope used a variety of sources to examine the "plebeian" population in Mexico City between 1660 and 1720, when the *castas* system had reached its full maturity.[136] He questions and qualifies the assumption that the urban poor in Mexico sought to climb the ethnic hierarchy and to "pass" as Spaniards. Cope blends social analysis with statistical methods to address a range of important issues from race relations, patronage networks, and urban spaces to forms of social control, rebellion, and crowd behaviors. Silvia Arrom followed her work on women in Mexico City with a book on the poorhouse of Mexico City from the 1770s to the 1870s.[137] Esteban Sánchez de Tagle has studied popular culture and street life in colonial Mexico City.[138] Outside of Mexico City, John Chance examined ethnicity and identity in Oaxaca City, Eugenia María Azevedo Salomao wrote on urban centers in colonial Michoacan, and María Elena Martínez studied the organization of public space in Puebla de Los Angeles.[139] In fact, there are numerous studies of provincial cities in New Spain, from Zacatecas to Campeche, and one recent volume focuses entirely on the evolution of Querétaro, for example.[140] Outside of Mexico, there are three good studies of Santiago de Guatemala that stretch from the sixteenth to the nineteenth centuries.[141] Some good, more general works treat urban society, urban spaces, and images of the city in Spanish America, including useful material on Mexico City.[142]

A few environmental histories have appeared in the last decade or so. The first studies for New Spain considered the environmental impact of the conquest, particularly the introduction of domestic animals, as exemplified by Elinor Melville's book on the effect of pastoral systems in Hidalgo, and the infamous *desague* project to drain the lake in the Valley of Mexico.[143] Sonya Lipsett-Rivera studied conflicts over the control of water resources in Puebla across the colonial period.[144] Several works have treated the demographic and environmental impact of disease, speaking broadly about the Americas and sometimes focusing on New Spain.[145] One book focuses on the impact of a single epidemic in a specific city.[146]

Intellectual History

Intellectual history is a neglected area of the field, considering its potential, perhaps because the close reading of many texts published in or about New Spain remains more the domain of literary studies. Fortunately, some excellent studies make up in quality for what is lacking in quantity. And several works of an intellectual character, which focus closely on texts and ideas, can be found in other sections in this essay, especially "Religion and the Church," considering how the church dominated intellectual life in this period.

Identity formation is a paramount theme in the intellectual histories of New Spain. Enrique Florescano has written a history of the histories of Mexico, in several volumes, presenting a sweeping view of Mexico's past from its legendary origins to the present, with special attention to the colonial period.[147] His writings on memory and history in the preconquest and colonial periods set him apart, along with David Brading, as one of the foremost intellectual historians of Mexico. Although Brading's *The First America* does not focus exclusively on New Spain, there is enough fascinating material in this massive work to constitute an entire volume on New Spain and early Mexico, and he has published pieces elsewhere that focus on Mexico across the centuries.[148] In *The First America*, Brading traces the evolution of local creole identities from the early sixteenth century to the 1860s. The book is an elegantly written reference work that situates scores of Spanish American texts and writings on Spanish America in their historical and intellectual context. Brading's magnum opus seems to have inspired Jorge Cañizares-Esguerra's enlightening study of eighteenth-century debates about history and identity on both sides of the Atlantic world.[149] In general, many historians have tracked the import and evolution of European ideas in the Americas, creating a perception that intellectual innovation and creativity flowed one way across the Atlantic—a notion that Florescano, Brading, and Cañizares-Esguerra have rejected.

Writings on the Spanish-led conquest of New Spain continue to provoke discussion and debate. This topic is certainly the traditional domain of Spanish literature, as new editions of the writings of *conquistadores* and *cronistas* appear regularly. An entire bibliography could be compiled on just Bernal Díaz del Castillo's *Historia verdadera*, for example. Spanish writings aside, recent works on indigenous accounts of the conquest, done mainly by historians, such as James Lockhart's analysis of Nahua writings on the conquest, add a very different dimension to the conquest literature.[150] Several other histories have revisited Spanish and indigenous writings on the conquest and colonial encounters with a critical eye, especially since 1992.[151] Anthony Pagden's work on European perceptions and imaginations of the New World does not focus on New Spain, but it does represent the best kind of intellectual history.[152] Aside from a flurry of more popular studies that commemorated the quincentennial in both celebratory and disparaging tones, older debates on the black legend, exemplified by the exchanges between Lewis Hanke and Benjamin Keen, have been shelved for the most part.

If we interpret intellectual history in its broadest sense, as Irving Leonard did in his many writings on the Baroque and as Luis Weckmann did in his massive work on the medieval heritage of Mexico, we might also include studies of art, architecture, the book trade, education, public festivals, and other topics that intersect with more traditional cultural histories, namely, studies of "high culture."[153] The production of art in the colonial period is one such area of study. Many art historians have attended to pictorial manuscripts produced in the sixteenth century, focusing first on the aesthetics and artistic production of the texts and then on their content or historical value. Jeannette Petersen's study of the murals in the Franciscan *convento* of Malinalco, Gruzinski's study of Indian fresco paintings in different parts of central

Mexico, and Barbara Mundy's consideration of indigenous maps drawn in the sixteenth century exemplify this type of work.[154] Perhaps no genre of art from New Spain has attracted more attention than the so-called *castas* paintings.[155] Pamela Voekel's book on the religious and political debates about burials in late-eighteenth-century Mexico might be considered more intellectual than religious history, as is Martin Nesvig's study of the inquisitorial censors of New Spain, the jurists and theologians who debated and shaped inquisitorial law and theory.[156] Education and the university are another concern of intellectual history.[157] Studies of public festivals, processions, and rituals of power might also be included here, overlapping with the concerns and methodologies of "new" cultural histories.[158]

Economic History

Whereas social histories have tended to dominate the field in the last few decades, economic histories have remained fairly constant in number. The two types of study are not entirely independent, of course, and both rely increasingly on a variety of sources and interdisciplinary methods. In general, more recent economic histories have moved away from Wallerstein's world systems approach and dependency theory, which focused on inequality and underdevelopment, toward studies that focus on the region as a unique entity with its own regional market imperfections distinct from Europe. Whereas earlier studies tended to focus on the export sector, especially mining, more recent studies have focused on domestic sectors and their role in the economy.[159] Studies of the hacienda and *obraje* in New Spain, for example, show that the systems responded to unique sets of market conditions that defy world systems analysis and dependency theory metanarratives.

Eric Van Young's study of Guadalajara and the agricultural production of its hinterlands is an excellent place to begin a discussion of internal markets in New Spain.[160] He constructed foodstuff prices and production from local archives and crossed these data with population trends and land ownership to determine the nature of the region's urban and hinterland expansion between 1600 and 1800. Internal market constraints and imperfect conditions related to land, labor, and capital allow a better, richer understanding of the conditions that contributed to low returns, low wages, inequalities, and a lack of incentive for innovation. Van Young's study begins after the nadir of the indigenous population and ends after the revolution, demonstrating how the formation and expansion of the hacienda system, the integration of the indigenous population, and the erosion of indigenous systems, resulted in the conflict represented by Hidalgo's *grito*.

Studies of the production of textiles in *obrajes* offer another vista on domestic markets and urban growth. In a major book that covers the three centuries before 1840, Richard Salvucci considers the institution of the *obraje* in Mexico City, Puebla-Tlaxcala, and the Bajío, compiling numerous data that address the supply and demand side of *obraje* production.¹⁶¹ Salvucci sees the *obraje* as a rational local response to an imperfect market. Low wages and coerced labor stifled incentives to innovate or mechanize the industry. Ultimately, the Mexican textile sector was not able to compete with British textiles after the Bourbon Reforms liberalized trade. Another study of *obrajes* by Carmen Viqueira and José Urquiola focuses specifically on the Puebla-Tlaxcala area, a region in which *obrajes* thrived and then declined quite early.¹⁶² These authors conclude that the *obraje* was not transported from Spain but was developed in response to internal market demands and conditions functioning within the world system but not determined by it.

There are several other works in this area of the field that deserve mention for their ambition and originality. Two general but serious works addressed the large issue of the Mexican economy in the Bourbon period.¹⁶³ Jeremy Baskes's study of *repartimiento de mercancías* in Oaxaca examines a good deal of quantitative data in the light of transaction cost theory to argue that the system of cross-cultural trade was more of a benign credit system than a nefarious practice of forced consumption and labor, and that both Spanish *corregidores* and indigenous people made rational choices in advancing and acquiring goods in a cash-starved economy.¹⁶⁴ Baskes' careful analysis of the Oaxacan case contradicts previous studies of this topic in Spanish America and should generate more research. Studies of labor in silver mines, haciendas, and highways deal with this issue of workers' agency without using as much quantitative data.¹⁶⁵ Other economic histories address a range of broad topics, including the expenses and revenues of the Real Hacienda, the copper mining industry, histories of credit and internal markets in Guadalajara, and a comparative study of petty capitalism.¹⁶⁶

By now it is apparent that the study of New Spain represents a major area of Latin American history that continues to attract international scholars. The interdisciplinary nature of many projects has encouraged collaboration at the borders of disciplines, where innovations tend to occur. The intensive study of native pictorial and alphabetic writings, for example, which involves a great deal of specialized training, is an original area of study that has developed independently from trends or models in other influential fields in history.

Some areas of the field offer exciting prospects for future research, especially those in which scholarship has existed for only a matter of years, such as environmental and urban history and the study of women, gender, and sexuality. In some cases, promising areas have not received the systematic, sustained attention that they deserve, leaving much still to be done. The history of women in the early period, for example, is still quite thin. Family history and the study of children are only beginning.¹⁶⁷ Whereas many histories of ethnic groups have focused on Indians, Africans, or Spaniards, mestizos and mulattoes have received much less attention, perhaps because studies of urban populations are still few and far between. Some areas of inquiry that have taken off in other fields, such as the history of science and medicine, have barely touched New Spain, but the potential is rich.

More historians attempt to bridge the colonial and national periods, but most still cling to one period or the other. Regionally, if New Spain extends south to Central America, the vast majority of studies focus on what is now Mexico. And if it includes the very far north, what is now the southwestern United States, few Latin Americanists trained in the study of Mexico have ventured this far, leaving the region more to historians of the United States and to Chicano studies. Comparative studies of New Spain and Peru are still exceptional in number, perhaps because the historiographies of the two areas are so rich and deep that it is challenging to stay abreast of both.

Nevertheless, this essay clearly shows that New Spain is one of the richest and most dynamic areas of Latin American historiography, as it has been for a very long time. And there is no shortage of excellent young scholars to suggest that it will not continue in this tradition.

ACKNOWLEDGMENTS

We are grateful for the suggestions of several advanced graduate students at UCLA, including Molly Ball, León García Garagarza, Veronica Gutiérrez, Pablo Miguel Sierra Silva, Zeb Tortorici, Dana Velasco Murillo, and Peter Villella. We give special thanks also to Susan Schroeder and David Tavárez for their many helpful comments.

NOTES

1. As it is defined in Peter Gerhard's *Historical Geography of New Spain, 1519–1821* (Cambridge University Press, 1972).

2. Eric Van Young, "The New Cultural History Comes to Old Mexico," *The Hispanic American Historical Review* 79:2 (1999): 211–48.

3. Robert Haskett and Stephanie Wood, eds., "Ethnohistory: Mesoamerica," in *Handbook of Latin American Studies* (Austin: University of Texas Press, 2005), no. 60, pp. 73–117.

4. Pedro Carrasco, *Estructura político-territorial del imperio tenochca: La triple alianza de Tenochtitlan, Tetzcoco y Tlacopan* (Mexico City: El Colegio de México/Fondo de Cultura Económica, 1996). Johanna Broda, Davíd Carrasco, and Eduardo Matos Moctezuma, *The Great Temple of Tenochtitlan: Center and Periphery in the Aztec World* (Berkeley: University of California Press, 1987). Leonardo López Luján, *The Offerings of the Templo Mayor of Tenochtitlan* (Albuquerque: University of New Mexico Press, 2005).

5. Ross Hassig, *Aztec Warfare: Imperial Expansion and Political Control* (Norman: University of Oklahoma Press, 1988) and *Trade, Tribute, and Transportation: The Sixteenth-Century Political Economy of the Valley of Mexico* (Norman: University of Oklahoma Press, 1985); Frances Berdan, *The Aztecs of Central Mexico: An Imperial Society* (New York: Holt, Rinehart and Winston, 1982), updated and reprinted in 2005; Jerome Offner, *Law and*

Politics in Aztec Texcoco (Cambridge: Cambridge University Press, 1983); Susan D. Gillespie, *The Aztec Kings: The Construction of Rulership in Mexica History* (Tucson: University of Arizona Press, 1989); Joaquín Galarza, *Estudios de escritura indígena tradicional azteca-náhuatl* (Mexico City: Archivo General de la Nación, 1979); Alfredo López Austin, *Cuerpo humano e ideología: Las concepciones de los antiguos mexicanos*, 2 vols. (Mexico City: UNAM/INAH, 1982).

6. As one of many examples, see Elizabeth H. Boone, *Stories in Red and Black: Pictorial Histories of the Aztecs and Mixtecs* (Austin: University of Texas Press, 2000) for a study that compares Postclassic writing traditions in central Mexico and Oaxaca.

7. The first, edited by Constanza Vega Sosa, is called *Códices y documentos sobre México: Primer simposio* (Mexico City: INAH, 1994). The second and third symposia resulted in publications in 1997 and 2000.

8. Charles Gibson, *Tlaxcala in the Sixteenth Century* (New Haven: Yale University Press, 1952); *The Aztecs under Spanish Rule* (Stanford, Calif.: Stanford University Press, 1964).

9. Woodrow Borah and S. F. Cook, *The Population of Central Mexico, 1548*, Series Ibero-Americana, No. 43 (Berkeley and Los Angeles: University of California Press, 1960); S. F. Cook and Woodrow Borah, *The Population of the Mixteca Alta, 1520–1960*, Series Ibero-Americana, No. 50 (Berkeley and Los Angeles: University of California Press, 1968).

10. Peter Gerhard, *Guide to the Historical Geography of New Spain* (Cambridge: Cambridge University Press, 1972), published in Mexico in 1986.

11. Felipe Castro Gutiérrez, *Los tarascos y el imperio español, 1600–1740* (Mexico City: UNAM, 2004); Hans Roskamp, *La historiografía indígena de Michoacán* (Leiden: Research School CNWS, 1998).

12. For the Mixteca region of Oaxaca: Rudolfo Pastor, *Campesinos y reformas: La mixteca, 1700–1856* (Mexico City: El Colegio de México, 1987); María de los Ángeles Romero Frizzi, *Economía y vida de los españoles en la Mixteca Alta: 1519–1720* (Mexico City: INAH, 1990); Ronald Spores, *The Mixtecs in Ancient and Colonial Times* (Norman: University of Oklahoma Press, 1994); Kevin Terraciano, *The Mixtecs of Colonial Oaxaca* (Stanford, Calif.: Stanford University Press, 2001). For the Valley of Oaxaca: William Taylor, *Landlord and Peasant in Colonial Oaxaca* (Stanford, Calif.: Stanford University Press, 1976). For the Sierra Zapoteca: John Chance, *Conquest of the Sierra: Spaniards and Indians in Colonial Oaxaca* (Norman: University of Oklahoma Press, 1989). For the Isthmus: Judith Frances Zeitlin, *Cultural Politics in Colonial Tehuantepec: Community and State among the Isthmus Zapotec, 1500–1750* (Stanford, Calif.: Stanford University Press, 2005).

13. Nancy Farriss, *Maya Society under Colonial Rule: The Collective Enterprise of Survival* (Princeton: Princeton University Press, 1984). See also Victoria Bricker, *The Indian Christ, The Indian King: The Historical Substrate of Maya Myth and Ritual* (Austin: University of Texas Press, 1981); Grant Jones, *Maya Resistance to Spanish Rule: Time and History on a Colonial Frontier* (Albuquerque: University of New Mexico Press, 1989); Robert Patch, *Maya and Spaniard in Yucatan, 1648–1812* (Stanford, Calif.: Stanford University Press, 1993); Matthew Restall, *The Maya World* (Stanford, Calif.: Stanford University Press, 1997). Sergio Quezada, *Los pies de la república: Los mayas peninsulares, 1550–1750* (Tlalpan: CIESAS/INI, 1997).

14. Serge Gruzinski, *La Colonisation de l'imaginaire: Sociétés indigènes et occidentalisation dans le Mexique espagnol: XVIe–XVIIIe siècle* (Paris: Gallimard, 1988), trans. as *The Conquest of Mexico: The Incorporation of Indian Societies into the Western World, 16th–18th Centuries* (Cambridge: Polity Press, 1993).

15. For example, Arthur Anderson, Frances Berdan, and James Lockhart, *Beyond the Codices: The Nahua View of Colonial Mexico* (Berkeley and Los Angeles: University of

California Press, 1976); Luis Reyes García, *Cuauhtinchan del siglo XII al XVI: Formación y desarrollo histórico de un señorío prehispánico* (Wiesbaden: Steiner, 1977); Johanna Broda and Pedro Carrasco, eds., *Estratificación social en la Mesoamérica prehispánica* (Mexico City: INAH, 1976); James Lockhart and Frances Karttunen, *Nahuatl in the Middle Years: Language Contact Phenomena in Texts of the Colonial Period* (Berkeley and Los Angeles: University of California Press, 1976).

16. James Lockhart, *The Nahuas After the Conquest* (Stanford, Calif.: Stanford University Press, 1992).

17. S. L. Cline, *Colonial Culhuacan, 1580–1600: A Social History of an Aztec Town* (Albuquerque: University of New Mexico Press, 1986); Robert Haskett, *Indigenous Rulers: An Ethnohistory of Town Government in Colonial Cuernavaca* (Albuquerque: University of New Mexico Press, 1991); Rebecca Horn, *Postconquest Coyoacan: Nahua-Spanish Relations in Central Mexico, 1519–1650* (Stanford, Calif.: Stanford University Press, 1997); Susan Kellogg, *Law and the Transformation of Aztec Culture, 1500–1700* (Norman: University of Oklahoma Press, 1995); Luis Reyes García, *Cuauhtinchan del siglo XII al XVI*; Susan Schroeder, *Chimalpahin and the Kingdoms of Chalco* (Tucson: University of Arizona Press, 1991); Stephanie Wood, "Corporate Adjustments in Colonial Mexican Indian Towns: Toluca Region, 1550–1810" (PhD diss., University of California, Los Angeles, 1984); Caterina Pizzigoni, *Testaments of Toluca* (Stanford, Calif.: Stanford University Press, UCLA Latin American Center Publications, 2007). Miriam Melton-Villanueva promises to contribute to this literature with her dissertation at UCLA on a valuable collection of late colonial and early Independence Nahuatl-language wills that she found in Toluca. Another UCLA student, Bradley Benton, is focusing his research on Tetzcoco in the sixteenth century, based in part on a variety of Nahuatl-language documents.

18. Van Young, "The New Cultural History," p. 234.

19. For example, Ralph Roys, *The Titles of Ebtun* (Washington, D.C.: Carnegie Institution, 1939); Ralph Roys, *The Book of Chilam Balam of Chumayel* (Norman: University of Oklahoma Press, 1967); Ralph Roys and France Scholes, *The Maya Chontal Indians of Acalan-Tixchel* (Norman: University of Oklahoma Press, 1968).

20. Matthew Restall, *Maya World*, 1997; Nancy Farriss, *Maya Society*, 1984. For the translation of a collection of last wills and testaments written in Cakchiquel-Maya, see Robert M. Hill, *The Pirir Papers and Other Colonial Period Cakchiquel-Maya Testamentos* (Nashville: Vanderbilt University Publications in Anthropology, 1987).

21. The UCLA Zapotec group currently includes linguists Pamela Munro, Michael Galant, and Aaron Sonnenschein and a doctoral student in history, Xochitl Marina Flores Marcial.

22. Michel Oudijk, *Historiography of the Bènizàa: The Postclassic and Early Colonial Periods (1000–1600 A.D.)* (Leiden: Research School of Asian, African, and Amerindian Studies, 2000).

23. José Alcina Franch, *Calendario y religión entre los zapotecos* (Mexico City: UNAM, 1993); David Tavárez, "La idolatría letrada: Un análisis comparativo de textos clandestinos rituales y devocionales en comunidades nahuas y zapotecas, 1613–1654," *Historia Mexicana* 49:2 (1999): 197–252. See also by Tavárez: "Idolatry as an Ontological Question: Native Consciousness and Juridical Proof in Colonial Mexico," *Journal of Early Modern History* 6:2 (2002): 114–39; "The Passion According to the Wooden Drum: The Christian Appropriation of a Zapotec Ritual Genre in New Spain," *The Americas* 62:3 (2006): 413–44. Tavárez is also completing a book manuscript titled "Invisible Wars: Clandestine Indigenous Devotions, Authorship, and Dissent in Colonial Mexico."

24. Sebastián van Doesburg, *Códices Cuicatecos: Porfirio Díaz y Fernández Leal: Edición facsimilar, contexto histórico e interpretación*, 2 vols. (Mexico City: Editorial Porrúa, 2001). Van Doesburg is collaborating with Michael Swanton on the Chocho-language project, which involves hundreds of colonial-era documents written in this language.

25. *Codex Chimalpahin: Society and Politics in Mexico Tenochtitlan, Tlatelolco, Texcoco, Culhuacan, and Other Nahua Altepetl in Central Mexico: The Nahuatl and Spanish Annals and Accounts Collected and Recorded by Don Domingo de San Antón Muñón Chimalpahin Quauhtlehuanitzin*, ed. and trans. Arthur J. O. Anderson and Susan Schroeder, 2 vols. (Norman: University of Oklahoma Press, 1997); *Annals of His Time: Don Domingo de San Antón Muñón Chimalpahin Quauhtlehuanitzin*, ed. and trans. James Lockhart, Susan Schroeder, and Doris Namala (Stanford, Calif.: Stanford University Press, 2006).

26. Jesús Monjarás-Ruiz, *La nobleza mexica* (Mexico City: Edicol, 1980); Donald Chipman, *Moctezuma's Children: Aztec Royalty under Spanish Rule, 1520–1700* (Austin: University of Texas Press, 2005).

27. Louise Burkhart, *Holy Wednesday: A Nahua Drama from Early Colonial Mexico* (Philadelphia: University of Pennsylvania Press, 1996); Louise Burkhart and Barry Sell, *Nahuatl Theater* (Norman: University of Oklahoma Press, 2004) (one of four volumes on the subject).

28. Arthur J. O. Anderson and Charles E. Dibble, trans., *The Florentine Codex: General History of the Things of New Spain*, 13 parts (Salt Lake City and Santa Fe: University of Utah Press and School of American Research, Santa Fe, 1950–82).

29. Miguel León-Portilla, *Los antiguos mexicanos a través de sus crónicas y cantares* (Mexico City: Fondo de Cultura y Económica, 1983); Miguel León-Portilla, *La filosofía náhuatl estudiada en sus fuentes* (Mexico City: Ediciones Especiales del Instituto Indigenista Interamericano, 1956); Eustaquio Celestino Solís and Luis Reyes García, *Anales de Tecamachalco, 1398–1590* (Mexico City: Fondo de Cultura Económica, 1992); Paul Kirchhoff, Lina Odena Güemes, and Luis Reyes García, *Historia Tolteca Chichimeca* (INAH 1976); Rafael Tena, *Anales de Tlatelolco* (Mexico City: CONACULTA, 2004); Rafael Tena, *Códice Cozcatzin* (Mexico City: INAH, 1994); Rafael Tena, *Diario: Domingo Chimalpáhin* (Mexico City: Consejo Nacional para la Cultura y las Artes, 2001).

30. Anderson, Berdan, and Lockhart, *Beyond the Codices*.

31. S. L. Cline and Miguel León-Portilla, eds., *The Testaments of Culhuacan*, Nahuatl Studies (Los Angeles: UCLA Latin American Center, 1984); S. L. Cline, ed., *The Book of Tributes: Early Sixteenth-Century Nahuatl Censuses from Morelos* (Los Angeles: UCLA Latin American Center Publications, 1993).

32. Nahuatl texts translated into English by Lockhart and his colleagues (excluding those already mentioned above) include: with Berdan and Anderson, *The Tlaxcalan Actas: A Compendium of the Records of the Cabildo of Tlaxcala, 1545–1627* (Salt Lake City: University of Utah Press, 1986); with Frances Karttunen, *The Art of Nahuatl Speech: The Bancroft Dialogues* (Los Angeles: UCLA Latin American Center Publications, 1987); *We People Here: Nahuatl Accounts of the Conquest of Mexico* (Berkeley and Los Angeles: University of California Press, 1993); with Lisa Sousa and Stafford Poole, *The Story of Guadalupe: Luis Laso de la Vega's* Huei tlamahuiçoltica *of 1649* (Stanford and Los Angeles: Stanford University Press and UCLA Latin American Center Publications, 1998); with Susan Schroeder and Doris Namala, *Annals of His Time: Don Domingo de San Antón Muñón Chimalpahin Quauhtlehuanitzin*, Series Chimalpahin (Stanford, Calif.: Stanford University Press, 2006); *Grammar of the Mexican Language*, by Horacio Carochi [1645] (Stanford and Los Angeles: Stanford University Press and UCLA Latin American Center Publications, 2001); *Nahuatl as Written: Lessons in Older Written Nahuatl* (Stanford and Los

Angeles: Stanford University Press and UCLA Latin American Center Publications, 2001); *Nahuas and Spaniards: Postconquest Central Mexican History and Philology* (Stanford and Los Angeles: Stanford University Press and UCLA Latin American Center Publications, 1991). Many of these translations are part of the Nahuatl series established by Lockhart within the UCLA Latin American Center, which now stands at nearly a dozen volumes, the last few published by Stanford University Press.

33. Bernardino de Sahagún, *Primeros Memoriales: Paleography of Nahuatl Text and English Translation*, trans. Thelma Sullivan, rev. H. B. Nicholson et al. (Norman: University of Oklahoma Press, 1997); Hernando Ruiz de Alarcón, *Treatise on the Heathen Superstitions That Today Live Among the Indians Native to This New Spain, 1629*, trans. and ed. J. Richard Andrews and Ross Hassig (Norman: University of Oklahoma Press, 1984); John Bierhorst, *Cantares Mexicanos: Songs of the Aztecs* (Stanford, Calif.: Stanford University Press, 1985); John Bierhorst, *History and Mythology of the Aztecs: The Codex Chimalpopoca* (Tucson: University of Arizona Press, 1992); Matthew Restall, Lisa Sousa, and Kevin Terraciano, eds., *Mesoamerican Voices: Native-Language Writings from Colonial Mexico, Oaxaca, Yucatan, and Guatemala* (Cambridge: Cambridge University Press, 2005); Günter Zimmermann, *Briefe der indianischen Nobilität aus Neuspanien an Karl V und Philipp II um die Mitte des 16. Jahrhunderts*, Beiträge zur mittelamerikanischen Völkerkunde 10 (Hamburg: Hamburgischen Museum für Völkerkunde und Vorgeschichte, 1970); Eike Hinz, Claudine Hartau, and Marie-Luise Heimann-Koenen, eds., *Aztekischer Zensus: Zur Indianischen Wirtschaft und Gesellschaft im Marquesado um 1540*, 2 vols. (Hanover: Verlag für Ethnologie, 1983).

34. Stephanie Wood, *Transcending the Conquest: Nahua Views of Spanish Colonial Mexico* (2003); Robert Haskett, *Visions of Paradise: Primordial Titles and Mesoamerican History in Cuernavaca* (Norman: University of Oklahoma Press, 2005); Paula López Caballero, *Los títulos primordiales del centro de México* (Mexico City: Consejo Nacional para la Cultura y las Artes, 2003); Xavier Noguez, *Códice Techialoyan de San Pedro Tototepec* (Zinacantepec: Colegio Mexiquense, 1999); James Lockhart, *Nahuas and Spaniards* (Los Angeles: UCLA Latin American Center, 1992); Lisa Sousa and Kevin Terraciano, "The 'Original Conquest' of Oaxaca: Late Colonial Nahuatl and Mixtec Accounts of the Spanish Conquest," *Ethnohistory* 50:2 (2003): 349–400. For similar records among the Maya, see Matthew Restall, *Maya Conquistador* (Boston: Beacon Press, 1998).

35. For example, Luis Reyes García, Eustaquio Celestino Solís, Armando Valencia Ríos, Constantino Medina Lima, and Gregorio Guerrero Díaz, *Documentos nahuas de la ciudad de México del siglo XVI* (Mexico City: CIESAS/AGN, 1996); see also John Frederick Schwaller, *Estudios de cultura náhuatl* 18 (1986): 315–83 and *Estudios de cultura náhuatl* 21 (1991): 311–38 for useful catalogs of Nahuatl manuscripts and texts in select libraries in the United States. Most recently, Michel Oudijk and María Castañeda de la Paz have undertaken the ambitious task of organizing catalogs of and editing explanatory essays on all known native-language writings and pictorial writings from Mexico for the *Handbook of Middle American Indians*, intending to update and supersede the older catalogs and descriptions published in volumes 14 and 15 of the HMAI in 1975.

36. One lengthy anthology, for example, contains essays that focus specifically on indigenous issues within given communities: Francisco González-Hermosillo Adams, ed., *Gobierno y economía en los pueblos indios del México colonial* (Mexico City: INAH, 2001). See Margarita Menegus Bornemann, *Del señorío a la república de indios: El caso de Toluca, 1500–1600* (Madrid: Ministerio de Agricultura, Pesca y Alimentación, 1991) and Bernardo García Martínez, *Los pueblos de la Sierra de Puebla* (Mexico City: Colegio de México, 1987) for good regional studies of the transformation of indigenous political institutions.

37. R. Douglas Cope, *The Limits of Racial Domination: Plebeian Society in Colonial Mexico City, 1660–1720* (Madison: University of Wisconsin Press, 1994).

38. John Chance, *Race and Class in Colonial Oaxaca* (Stanford, Calif.: Stanford University Press, 1978); Norma Angélica Castillo Palma, *Cholula, sociedad mestiza en ciudad india: Un análisis de las consecuencias demográficas, económicas y sociales del mestizaje en una ciudad novohispana (1649–1796)* (Mexico City: Universidad Autónoma Metropolitana, Unidad Iztapalapa, Plaza y Valdés, 2001). Verónica Gutiérrez, a doctoral student at UCLA, is focusing on Cholula in the sixteenth century.

39. There are some promising signs of activity in this area, however. William Connell has prepared a manuscript "Indigenous Spaces of Negotiation: Political Culture and Self-Government in Mexico Tenochtitlan, 1524–1730," based on his dissertation at Tulane. And Margarita R. Ochoa, a graduate student at the University of New Mexico, is producing a study on the urban Indian families of late-colonial Mexico City.

40. See Peter Gerhard, *The North Frontier of New Spain* (Princeton: Princeton University Press, 1982) for a mapping of the areas that would have constituted the Spanish north in the colonial period, including Nueva Galicia, Nueva Vizcaya, Sinaloa, Sonora, Baja and Alta California, Nuevo México, Coahuila, Texas, Nuevo León, and Nuevo Santander.

41. Cynthia Radding, *Wandering Peoples: Colonialism, Ethnic Spaces, and Ecological Frontiers in Northwest Mexico, 1700–1850* (Durham: Duke University Press, 1997).

42. Susan Deeds, *Defiance and Deference in Mexico's Colonial North: Indians under Spanish Rule in Nueva Vizcaya* (Austin: University of Texas Press, 2003).

43. Michael M. Swann, *Tierra Adentro: Settlement and Society in Colonial Durango* (Boulder: Westview Press, 1982); *Migrants in the Mexican North: Mobility, Economy and Society in a Colonial World* (Boulder, Westview Press, 1989); see also Irene Vásquez, "The Indigenous Factor in Nueva Vizcaya: the North of Mexico, 1550–1790" (PhD diss., University of California, Los Angeles, 2003).

44. David Adams, *Las colonias tlaxcaltecas de Coahuila y Nuevo León en la Nueva España: Un aspecto de la colonización del norte de México* (Saltillo: Archivo Municipal de Saltillo, 1991). See also Eugene B. Sego, *Aliados y adversarios: Los colonos tlaxcaltecas en la frontera septentrional de Nueva España* (San Luis Potosí: Centro de Investigaciones Históricas de San Luis Potosí, 1998). Two other notable works on Tlaxcalan migrants are Elizabeth Butzer's *Historia social de una comunidad tlaxcalteca: San Miguel de Aguayo, 1686–1820* (Saltillo: Archivo Municipal de Saltillo, 2001) and David Frye's *Indians into Mexicans: History and Identity in a Mexican Town* (Austin: University of Texas Press, 1996), a study of ethnic identity in Mexquitic, a pueblo in San Luis Potosí that was founded as a model Tlaxcalan community.

45. Agueda Jiménez Pelayo, *Haciendas y communidades indígenas en el sur de Zacatecas* (Mexico City: INAH, 1989); Dana Velasco Murillo, "Urban Indians in a Colonial Silver City: Zacatecas, Mexico, 1546–1806" (PhD diss., University of California, Los Angeles, 2009).

46. John C. Super, *La vida en Querétaro durante la Colonia, 1531–1810* (Mexico City: Fondo de Cultura Económica, 1983); Cheryl English Martin, *Governance and Society in Colonial Mexico: Chihuahua in the Eighteenth Century* (Stanford, Calif.: Stanford University Press, 1996).

47. Eric Langer and R. H. Jackson, eds., *The New Latin American Mission History* (Lincoln: University of Nebraska Press, 1995); Evelyn Hu-DeHart, *Missionaries, Miners, and Indians: Spanish Contact with the Yaqui Nation of Northwestern New Spain, 1533–1820* (Tucson: University of Arizona Press, 1981); Steven W. Hackel, *Children of Coyote: Missionaries of Saint Francis: Indian-Spanish Relations in Colonial California, 1769–1850*

(Chapel Hill: University of North Carolina, 2005); Cecilia Sheridan Prieto, *Anónimos y desterrados: La contienda por el "sitio que llaman de Quauyla": Siglos XVI–XVIII* (Mexico City: CIESAS/Miguel Angel Porrúa, 2000); David Weber, *The Spanish Frontier in North America* (New Haven: Yale University Press, 1992); Donna J. Guy and Thomas E. Sheridan, *Contested Ground: Comparative Frontiers on the Northern and Southern Edges of Empire* (Tucson: University of Arizona Press, 1998).

48. Representative works by Silvio Zavala include: *La encomienda indiana* (Madrid: Imprenta Helénica, 1935); *Los esclavos indios en la Nueva España* (Mexico City: Colegio de México, 1968); and *El servicio personal de los indios en la Nueva España*, (Mexico City: Colegio de México, 1984–1989), a four-volume work on the sixteenth century.

49. Gonzalo Aguirre Beltrán, *La población negra de México: Estudio etnohistórico* (Mexico City: Ediciones Fuente Cultural, 1946).

50. Colin Palmer, *Slaves of the White God: Blacks in Mexico, 1570–1650* (Cambridge: Harvard University Press, 1976). Patrick J. Carroll, *Blacks in Colonial Vera Cruz: Race, Ethnicity, and Regional Development* (Austin: University of Texas Press, 1991). Some have focused on active resistance to colonial rule. See, for example, David M. Davidson, "Negro Slave Control and Resistance in Colonial Mexico, 1519–1650," in *Maroon Societies: Rebel Slave Communities in the Americas*, ed. Richard Price (Baltimore: Johns Hopkins University Press, 1979).

51. Herman Bennett, *Africans in Colonial Mexico: Absolutism, Christianity and Afro-Creole Consciousness, 1570–1640* (Bloomington: Indiana University Press, 2003).

52. Ben Vinson, *Bearing Arms for His Majesty: The Free-Colored Militia in Colonial Mexico* (Stanford, Calif.: Stanford University Press, 2001).

53. Nicole von Germeten, *Black Blood Brothers: Confraternities and Social Mobility for Afro-Mexicans* (Gainesville: University Press of Florida, 2005).

54. María Elisa Velázquez Gutiérrez, *Mujeres de origen africáno en la capital novohispana, siglos XVII y XVIII* (Mexico City: UNAM, 2006).

55. Matthew Restall, ed., *Beyond Black and Red: African-Native Relations in Colonial Latin America* (Albuquerque: University of New Mexico Press, 2005). Restall's forthcoming (Stanford University Press) book on Afro-Yucatecans argues that Africans (or peoples of African descent) and Maya (or peoples of Maya descent) became "Afro-Mayas" by the late colonial period, so systemic and complete was integration by this time. Pablo Sierra is writing a dissertation at UCLA on interethnic interactions in Puebla, a major urban center with large indigenous and Afro-Mexican populations.

56. Nicolas Ngou-Mvé, *L'Afrique bantu dans la colonisation du Mexique (1596–1640)* (Libreville, Gabon: CICIBA, 1998).

57. Ida Altman, *Emigrants and Society: Extremadura and Spanish America in the Sixteenth Century* (Berkeley: University of California Press, 1989). For immigrants in the later period, see Charles F. Nunn, *Foreign Immigrants in Early Bourbon Mexico, 1700–1760* (Cambridge: Cambridge University Press, 1979). See also D. J. Robinson, ed., *Migration in Colonial Spanish America* (Cambridge: Cambridge University Press, 1990).

58. Robert Himmerich y Valencia, *The Encomenderos of New Spain, 1521–1555* (Austin: University of Texas Press, 1991).

59. Ethelia Ruiz Medrano, *Gobierno y sociedad en Nueva España: Segunda Audiencia y Antonio de Mendoza* (Zamora: El Colegio de Michoacan, 1991).

60. María Elena Martínez, *Genealogical Fictions: Limpieza de Sangre, Religion, and Gender in Colonial Mexico* (Stanford, Calif.: Stanford University Press, 2008).

61. Alejandro Cañeque, *The King's Living Image: The Culture and Politics of Viceregal Power in Colonial Mexico* (New York: Routledge, 2004).

62. Cayetana Alvarez de Toledo, *Politics and Reform in Spain and Viceregal Mexico: The Life and Thought of Juan de Palafox, 1600–1659* (Oxford: Oxford University Press, 2004).

63. See, for example, Bartolomé de las Casas, *In Defense of the Indians*, tr. and ed. Stafford Poole (DeKalb: Northern Illinois University Press, 1992).

64. Stafford Poole, *Pedro Moya de Contreras: Catholic Reform and Royal Power in New Spain, 1571–1591* (Berkeley and Los Angeles: University of California Press, 1987).

65. Edith Couturier, *The Silver King: The Remarkable Life of the Count of Regla in Colonial Mexico* (Albuquerque: University of New Mexico Press, 2003).

66. Louisa Schell Hoberman, *Mexico's Merchant Elite, 1590–1660: Silver, State and Society* (Durham: Duke University Press, 1991); John Kicza, *Colonial Entrepreneurs: Families and Business in Bourbon Mexico City* (Albuquerque: University of New Mexico Press, 1983).

67. Doris Ladd, *The Mexican Nobility at Independence, 1780–1826* (Austin: University of Texas Press, 1976).

68. Solange Alberro, *Les Espagnols dans le Mexique colonial: Histoire d'une acculturation* (Paris: A. Colin, 1992). Similarly, Maher Memarzadeh's dissertation on medical practitioners in early colonial Mexico focuses on Spanish pharmacists, surgeon/barbers, and physicians as a single social group with pronounced internal distinctions based on status and education: "Medical Practitioners in Early Colonial Mexico" (PhD diss., University of California, Los Angeles, 2005).

69. Agustín Grajales and Lilián Illades, eds., *Presencia española en Puebla, siglos XVI–XX* (Puebla: Instituto de Ciencias Sociales y Humanidades, Benemérita Universidad Autónoma de Puebla/Embajada de España en México, 2002).

70. Tamar Herzog, "'A Stranger in a Strange Land': The Conversion of Foreigners into Members in Colonial Latin America," in *Constructing Collective Identities and Shaping Public Spheres*, ed. Luis Roniger and Mario Sznajder (Brighton: Sussex Academic Press, 1998). Hillel Eyal, "Colonizing the Colonizer: Spanish Immigrants and Creoles in Late Colonial Mexico City" (PhD diss., University of California, Los Angeles, 2006).

71. Murdo J. MacLeod and Robert Wasserstrom, eds., *Spaniards and Indians in Southeastern Mesoamerica: Essays on the History of Ethnic Relations* (Lincoln: University of Nebraska Press, 1983). Romero Frizzi, *Economía y vida de los españoles en la Mixteca Alta*; Jesús F. de la Teja and Ross Frank, eds., *Choice, Persuasion, and Coercion: Social Control on Spain's North American Frontiers* (Albuquerque: University of New Mexico Press, 2005); Chance, *Conquest of the Sierra*; Harry W. Crosby, *Antigua California: Mission and Colony on the Peninsular Frontier, 1697–1768* (Albuquerque: University of New Mexico Press, 1994); John L. Kessell, *Spain in the Southwest: A Narrative History of Colonial New Mexico, Arizona, Texas, and California* (Norman: University of Oklahoma Press, 2002).

72. Danna Levin Rojo and Federico Navarrete, eds., *Indios, mestizos y españoles: Interculturalidad e historiografía en la Nueva España* (Mexico City: Universidad Autonoma Metropolitana, Unidad Azcapotzalco/UNAM, Instituto de Investigaciones Históricas, 2007); Isabel Rodas, *De españoles a ladinos: Cambio social y relaciones de parentesco en el altiplano central colonial guatemalteco* (Guatemala City: Ediciones ICAPI, 2004); Castillo Palma, *Cholula, sociedad mestiza en ciudad india*.

73. Asunción Lavrin, ed. *Latin American Women: Historical Perspectives* (Westport: Greenwood Press, 1978).

74. Silvia Marina Arrom, *The Women of Mexico City, 1790–1857* (Stanford, Calif.: Stanford University Press, 1985).

75. Patricia Seed, *To Love, Honor and Obey in Colonial Mexico* (Stanford, Calif.: Stanford University Press, 1988); Edith Couturier, "Women and the Family in Eighteenth-Century Mexico: Law and Practice." *Journal of Family History*, 10:3 (1985): 305–17.

76. Asunción Lavrin, *Brides of Christ: Conventual Life in Colonial Mexico* (Stanford, Calif.: Stanford University Press, 2008); Elisa Sampson Vera Tudela, *Colonial Angels: Narratives of Gender and Spirituality in Mexico, 1580–1750* (Austin: University of Texas Press, 2000).

77. Susan Kellogg, *Law and Transformation in Aztec Culture, 1500–1700* (Norman: University of Oklahoma Press, 1995).

78. Susan Schroeder, Stephanie Wood, and Robert Haskett, eds., *Indian Women in Early Mexico* (Norman: University of Oklahoma Press, 1997). Lisa Sousa is completing a book manuscript that uses multiple types of sources and methods to examine indigenous women in three parts of Mesoamerica: the Valley of Mexico, the Mixteca Alta, and the Sierra Zapoteca.

79. Steve J. Stern, *The Secret History of Gender: Women, Men, and Power in Late Colonial Mexico* (Chapel Hill: University of North Carolina Press, 1995).

80. Carmen Castañeda, *Violación, estupro y sexualidad: Nueva Galicia, 1790–1821* (Guadalajara: Ed. Hexágono 1989); Stephanie Wood, "Sexual Violation in the Conquest of the Americas," in *Sex and Sexuality in Early America*, ed. Merril D. Smith, 9–34 (New York: New York University Press, 1998); Terraciano, "Crime and Culture in Colonial Mexico: The Case of the Mixtec Murder Note," *Ethnohistory* 45:4 (1998): 709–45. In chap. 6 of *The Mixtecs*, Terraciano analyzed a gender system in which women *cacicas* exercised local political power with men, and examined how Spanish introductions affected this system over time.

81. Camilla Townsend, *Malintzin's Choices: An Indian Woman in the Conquest of Mexico* (Albuquerque: University of New Mexico Press, 2006); Sandra Cypress, *La Malinche in Mexican Literature: From History to Myth* (Austin: University of Texas Press, 1991).

82. Asunción Lavrin, ed., *Sexuality and Marriage in Colonial Latin America* (Lincoln: University of Nebraska Press, 1989).

83. Ramón Gutiérrez, *When Jesus Came, the Corn Mothers Went Away: Marriage, Sexuality and Power in New Mexico, 1500–1846* (Stanford, Calif.: Stanford University Press, 1991); Richard Boyer, *Lives of the Bigamists: Marriage, Family, and Community in Colonial Mexico* (Albuquerque: University of New Mexico Press, 1995); Martha Few, *Women Who Live Evil Lives: Gender, Religion, and the Politics of Power in Colonial Guatemala* (Austin: University of Texas Press, 2002); Ann Twinam, *Public Lives, Private Secrets: Gender, Honor, Sexuality, and Illegitimacy in Colonial Spanish America* (Stanford, Calif.: Stanford University Press, 1999).

84. Federico Garza Carvajal, *Butterflies Will Burn: Prosecuting Sodomites in Early Modern Spain and Mexico* (Austin: University of Texas Press, 2003); Sergio Ortega, ed., *De la santidad a la perversión: O de porque no se cumplía la ley de Dios en la sociedad novohispana* (Mexico City: Grijalbo, 1986); Pete Sigal, *From Moon Goddesses to Virgins: The Colonization of Yucatecan Maya Sexual Desire* (Austin: University of Texas Press, 2000); Richard Boyer and Geoffrey Spurling, *Colonial Lives: Documents on Latin American History, 1550–1850* (New York: Oxford University Press, 2000); Lee Penyak, *El ramo de penales del Archivo Judicial del Tribunal Superior de Justicia* (Mexico City: Instituto Mora, 1993); Zeb Tortorici, "'Heran Todos Putos': Sodomitical Subcultures and Disordered Desire in Early Colonial Mexico," *Ethnohistory* 54:1 (2007): 35–67. Tortorici is writing a dissertation at UCLA on the regulation of "unnatural" sexuality in Colonial Mexico, which uses hundreds of original, unstudied legal cases from the seventeenth and eighteenth centuries, which he found in archives in northern, central, and southern Mexico.

85. Pete Sigal, ed. *Infamous Desire: Male Homosexuality in Colonial Latin America* (Chicago: University of Chicago Press, 2003); Lyman L. Johnson and Sonya Lipsett-Rivera, eds., *The Faces of Honor: Sex, Shame, and Violence in Colonial Latin America* (Albuquerque: University of New Mexico Press, 1998); Pilar Gonzalbo Aizpuru, ed. *História de la vida cotidiana en México* (Mexico City: El Colegio de México, Fondo de Cultura Económica, 2004). Also, a special issue of the journal *Ethnohistory* (vol. 54:1, Winter 2007) contains several relevant articles on Mesoamerica.

86. For example: Seminario de Historia de las Mentalidades, *El placer de pecar y el afán de normar* (Mexico City: INAH, 1988).

87. Robert Ricard, *La "conquéte spirituelle" du Mexique: Essai sur l'apostolat et les méthodes missionaires des ordres mendiants en Nouvelle-Espagne de 1523–24 á 1572* (Paris: Institut d'ethnologie, 1933), tr. Lesley Byrd Simpson as *The Spiritual Conquest of Mexico: An Essay on the Apostolate and the Evangelizing Methods of the Mendicant Orders in New Spain: 1523–72* (Berkeley and Los Angeles: University of California Press, 1966).

88. Miguel León-Portilla, *The Aztec Image of Self and Society: An Introduction to Nahua Culture*, ed. J. Jorge Klor de Alva (Salt Lake City: University of Utah Press, 1992); Miguel León-Portilla, "Los franciscanos vistos por el hombre náhuatl," *Estudios de Cultura Náhuatl* 17 (1984); Alfredo López Austin, *Tamoanchan y Tlalocan* (Mexico City: Fondo de Cultura Económica, 1994); Alfredo López Austin, *Los mitos del tlacuache: Caminos de la mitología mesoamericana* (Mexico City: Alianza Editorial Mexicana, 1990); Alfredo López Austin and Leonardo López Lujan, *El pasado indígena* (Mexico City: COLMEX, 1996), tr. as *Mexico's Indigenous Past* (Norman: University of Oklahoma Press, 2001); Alfredo López Austin and Leonardo López Lujan, *Mito y realidad de Zuyuá: Serpiente emplumada y las transformaciones mesoamericanas del clásico al posclásico* (Mexico City: COLMEX/FCE, 1999). López Austin and Xavier Noguez, eds., *De hombres y dioses* (Michoacán: El Colegio de Michoacán, 1997). Eduardo Matos Moctezuma, David Carrasco, Michel Graulich, and Michael Smith have also made valuable contributions to this literature on Nahua myth and sacred belief.

89. Alfredo López Austin, *Hombre-Dios: Religion y política en el mundo náhuatl* (Mexico City: UNAM, 1973).

90. Serge Gruzinski, *El poder sin límites: Cuatro respuestas indígenas a la dominación española* (Mexico City: Instituto Nacional de Antropología y Historia, Instituto Francés de América Latina, 1988). This work was republished in English as *Man-Gods of the Mexican Highlands* (Stanford, Calif.: Stanford University Press, 1989); the original French title of this classic is *Les Hommes-dieux du Mexique: Pouvoir indien et société coloniale (XVIe–XVIIIe siècles)* (Paris: Éditions des Archives Contemporaines, 1985).

91. Christian Duverger, *La Conversion des Indiens de la Nouvelle Espagne* (Paris: Editions du Seuil, 1987).

92. Guy Stresser-Péan, *Le Soleil-Dieu et le Christ: La christianisation des Indiens du Mexique vue de la Sierra de Puebla* (Paris: L'Harmattan, 2005). León García Garagarza, a doctoral candidate at UCLA, is using early Inquisition records in central Mexico and conducting ethnographic research for his project on the charismatic resistance of native priests to the spiritual conquest.

93. Serge Gruzinski, *La Colonisation de l'imaginaire: Societés indigènes et occidentalisation dans le Mexique espagnol: XVIe et XVIIIe siècle* (Paris: Gallimard, 1988). Jorge Klor de Alva attempted to construct a typology of Nahua responses to the conversion efforts of the church in his article "Spiritual Conflict and Accommodation in New Spain: Toward a Typology of Aztec Responses to Christianity," in *The Inca and Aztec States,*

1400–1800, Anthropology and History, ed. George A. Collier et al., pp. 345–66 (New York: Academic Press, 1982).

94. Carmen Bernand and Serge Gruzinski, *De l'idolâtrie: Une archeólogie des sciences religieuses* (Paris: Edition du Seuil, 1988). On defining idolatry in locally specific terms, see John F. Chuchiak IV, "Toward a Regional Definition of Idolatry: Reexamining Idolatry Trials in the '*Relaciónes de Méritos*' and their Role in Defining the Concept of '*Idolatria*' en Colonial Yucatán, 1570–1780," *Journal of Early Modern History* 6:2 (2002): 140–67.

95. Richard Greenleaf, *The Mexican Inquisition of the Sixteenth Century* (Albuquerque: University of New Mexico Press, 1969); Solange Alberro, *Inquisición y sociedad en México, 1571–1700* (Mexico City: Fondo de Cultura Económica, 1988). See also Joaquín Pérez Villanueva and Bartolomé Escandell Bonet, eds., *Historia de la Inquisición en España y América,* 3 vols. (Madrid: Biblioteca de Autores Cristianos, Centro de Estudios Inquisitoriales, 1984–2000). The historiography of the Mexican inquisition began in earnest with Joaquín García Icazbalceta's *Don Fray Juan de Zumárraga: Primer obispo y arzobispo de México* (Mexico City: Andrade y Morales, 1881) and José Toribio Medina's *Historia del tribunal del Santo oficio de la inquisición en México* (Santiago: Imprenta Elzeviriana, 1905). Two early editions of Zumárraga's indigenous trials by Luis González Obregón made primary sources accessible to many generations of scholars: *Proceso inquisitorial del cacique de Texcoco* (Mexico City: Guerrero Hermanos, 1910), and *Procesos de indios idólatras y hechiceros* (Mexico City: Guerrero Hermanos, 1912).

96. Jorge Traslosheros, *Iglesia, justicia y sociedad en la Nueva España: La audiencia del Arzobispado de México, 1528–1668* (Mexico City: Editorial Porrúa/Universidad Iberoamericana, 2004).

97. Richard Greenleaf, *Zumárraga and the Mexican Inquisition, 1536–1543* (Washington, D.C.: Academy of Franciscan History, 1962) and "The Inquisition and the Indians of New Spain: A Study in Jurisdictional Confusion," *The Americas* 22:2 (1965): 138–66. Bernard Grunberg, *L'Inquisition apostolique au Mexique: Histoire d'une institution et de son impact dans une societé coloniale (1521–1571)* (Paris: L'Harmattan, 1998).

98. France V. Scholes and Eleanor Adams, *Don Diego Quijada, Alcalde Mayor de Yucatán, 1561–1565* (Mexico City: Editorial Porrúa, 1938). Inga Clendinnen, *Ambivalent Conquests: Maya and Spaniard in Yucatan, 1517–1570* (Cambridge: Cambridge University Press, 1987). John Chuchiak has also made insightful contributions to the study of religion in Yucatan; see, for example, his "Pre-Conquest *Ah Kinob* in a Colonial World: The Extirpation of Idolatry and the Survival of the Maya Priesthood in Colonial Yucatán, 1563–1697" in *Maya Survivalism: Acta Mesoamericana,* vol. 12, ed. U. Hostettler and M. Restall (Munich: A. Saurwein, 2001).

99. John Chuchiak, "In Servitio Dei: Fray Diego de Landa, the Franciscan Order, and the Return of the Extirpation of Idolatry in the Colonial Diocese of Yucatán, 1573–1579," *The Americas* 61:4 (2005): 611–46 and "By Faith, Not Arms: Franciscan Reducciones, the Frontier Mission Experience, and the Subjugation of the Maya Hinterland, 1602–1697," in *Francis in the Americas: Essays on the Franciscan Family in North and South America,* ed. John F. Schwaller (Berkeley: Academy of American Franciscan History, 2005), 119–42. Chuchiak is also completing a book manuscript on the topic, titled "Religious Conflicts and Maya Resistance on a Colonial Mexican Frontier, 1563–1721."

100. Marcelo Carmagnani, *El regreso de los dioses: El proceso de la identidad étnica en Oaxaca, siglos XVII y XVIII* (Mexico City: Fondo de Cultura Económica, 1988); Kevin Terraciano, *The Mixtecs of Colonial Oaxaca,* chap. 8, "Sacred Relations" (Stanford, Calif.:

Stanford University Press, 2001). We understand that Nancy Farris is writing a major book on religion in Mexico, involving ethnographic and archival research in the Sierra Zapoteca of Oaxaca and other parts of Mesoamerica.

101. The existence of comparable features between the two belief systems and the way that Christian practices could be put to local uses troubled some priests in the sixteenth century, who feared that native traditions would taint orthodoxy. Fernando Cervantes attributes this fear in part to the church's shifting perception of the Mexican gods from false idols and silly superstitions to devils in disguise. Fernando Cervantes, *The Devil in the New World* (New Haven: Yale University Press, 1994). Similarly, in their insightful introduction to the writings of Hernando Ruiz de Alarcón, a priest who encountered evidence of idolatry in early seventeenth-century Guerrero, J. Richard Andrews and Ross Hassig discuss the ambivalent attitudes of priests toward native beliefs.

102. Nancy Farriss, *Maya Society Under Colonial Rule: The Collective Enterprise of Survival* (Princeton: Princeton University Press, 1984).

103. James Lockhart, *The Nahuas after the Conquest* (Stanford, Calif.: Stanford University Press, 1992), 445.

104. Louise Burkhart, *The Slippery Earth: Nahua-Christian Moral Dialogue in Sixteenth-Century Mexico* (Tucson: University of Arizona Press, 1989); Charles Dibble, "The Nahuatlization of Christianity," in *Sixteenth Century Mexico: The Work of Sahagún*, ed. Munro Edmonson (Albuquerque: University of New Mexico Press, 1974), 225–33. In *The Mixtecs*, Terraciano used similar evidence in native-language texts from the Mixteca Alta region of Oaxaca, demonstrating that this discourse extended beyond Nahuas in central Mexico.

105. Georges Baudot, *México y los albores del discurso colonial* (Mexico City: Nueva Imagen, 1996). Georges Baudot, "Nahuas y españoles: Dioses, demonios y niños," in *De palabra y obra en el Nuevo Mundo*, vol. 1, *Imágenes interétnicas*, ed. Miguel León-Portilla et al. (Madrid: Siglo Ventiuno, 1992).

106. William Christian, *Local Religion in Sixteenth-Century Spain* (Princeton: Princeton University Press, 1981).

107. Alicia Bazarte Martínez, *Las cofradías de españoles en la ciudad de México* (Mexico City: Universidad Autónoma Metropolitana, 1989); Pilar Martínez López-Cano, Gisela von Wobeser, and Juan Guillermo Muñoz, eds., *Cofradías, capellanías, y obras pías en la América colonial* (Mexico City: Universidad Autónoma Metropolitana, 1998); Nicole von Germeten, *Black Blood Brothers: Confraternities and Social Mobility for Afro-Mexicans* (Gainesville: University Press of Florida, 2006); Susan Schroeder, "Jesuits, Nahuas, and the Good Death Society in Mexico City, 1710–1767," *Hispanic American Historical Review* 80:1 (2000): 43–76; John Frederick Schwaller, "Constitution of the Cofradía del Santíssimo Sacramento of Tula, Hidalgo, 1570," *Estudios de Cultura Náhuatl* 19 (1989): 217–44; Barry Sell, "Our Lady of Solitude of San Miguel Coyotlan, 1619: A Rare Set of Cofradía Rules in Nahuatl," *Estudios de Cultura Náhuatl* 31 (2000): 331–58.

108. Osvaldo Pardo, *The Origins of Mexican Catholicism: Nahua Rituals and Christian Sacraments in Sixteenth-Century Mexico* (Ann Arbor: University of Michigan Press, 2004); S. L. Cline, "The Spiritual Conquest Reexamined: Baptism and Christian Marriage in Early Sixteenth-Century Mexico," *Hispanic American Historical Review* 73:3 (1993): 453–80; McAndrew, John, *The Open-Air Churches of Sixteenth-Century Mexico* (Cambridge: Harvard University Press, 1965). Samuel Edgerton, *Theaters of Conversion: Religious Architecture and Indian Artisans in Colonial Mexico* (Albuquerque: University of New Mexico Press, 2001); Jaime Lara, *City, Temple, Stage: Eschatological Architecture and Liturgical Theatrics in New Spain* (Notre Dame: University of Notre Dame Press, 2004).

See also Jaime Lara, *Christian Texts for Aztecs: Art and Liturgy in Colonial Mexico* (Notre Dame, Ind.: University of Notre Dame Press, 2008).

109. Discussions of the saints can be found in numerous works on religion in New Spain. For a few studies of saints not already mentioned elsewhere in this section, see: Félix Baez-Jorge, *Entre los nahuales y los santos* (Jalapa: Universidad Veracruzana, 1998); Gonzalo Aguirre Beltrán, *Zongolica: Encuentro de dioses y santos patronos* (Jalapa: Universidad Veracruzana, 1986); Stephanie Wood, "Adopted Saints: Christian Images in Nahua Testaments of Late Colonial Toluca," *The Americas* 47:3 (1991): 259–93.

110. Solange Alberro, *El águila y la cruz: Orígenes religiosos de la conciencia criolla, México, siglos XVI–XVII* (Mexico City: El Colegio de México, Fondo de Cultura Económica, 1999); Louise Burkhart, "The Cult of the Virgin of Guadalupe in Mexico," in *South and Meso-American Native Spirituality: From the Cult of the Feathered Serpent to the Theology of Liberation*, ed. Gary H. Gossen with Miguel León-Portilla, vol. 4 of *World Spirituality: An Encyclopedic History of the Religious Quest* (New York: Crossroad, 1993), 198–227; Guadalupe Mauro Rodríguez, *Historia o símbolo?* (Mexico City: Editorial Edical, 1980); Joaquín Antonio Peñalosa, *Flor y canto de poesía guadalupana: Siglo XVII* (Mexico City: Editorial Jus, 1987); Xavier Noguez, *Documentos guadalupanos* (Mexico City: Fondo de Cultura Económica, 1993); Stafford Poole, *Our Lady of Guadalupe: The Origins and Sources of a Mexican National Symbol, 1531–1797* (Tucson: University of Arizona Press, 1995); Stafford Poole, *The Guadalupan Controversies* (Stanford, Calif.: Stanford University Press, 2006); Lisa Sousa, Stafford Poole, and James Lockhart, eds. and trans., *The Story of Guadalupe: Luis Laso de la Vega's Huei tlamahuiçoltica of 1649* (Stanford, Calif.: Stanford University Press, 1998); William B. Taylor, "The Virgin of Guadalupe: An Inquiry into the Social History of Marian Devotion," *American Ethnologist* 14:1 (1987): 9–33; Jeanette Favrot Peterson, "The Virgin of Guadalupe: Symbol of Conquest or Liberation?" *Art Journal* 51:4 (1992): 39–47; Edmundo O'Gorman, *Destierro de sombras: Luz en el origen y culto de Nuestra Señora de Guadalupe de Tepeyac* (Mexico City: Universidad Nacional Autónoma de México, 1986); David Brading, *Mexican Phoenix: Our Lady of Guadalupe: Image and Tradition Across Five Centuries* (Cambridge: Cambridge University Press, 2001).

111. William B. Taylor, *Magistrates of the Sacred: Priests and Parishioners in Eighteenth-Century Mexico* (Stanford, Calif.: Stanford University Press, 1996). See also "Two Shrines of the Cristo Renovado: Religion and Peasant Politics in Late Colonial Mexico," *American Historical Review* 110:4 (2005): 945–74.

112. Cristóforo Gutiérrez Vega, *Las primeras juntas eclesiásticas de México (1524–1555)* (Rome: Centro de Estudios Superiores, 1991); Carmen José Alejos-Grau, *Juan de Zumárraga y su "Regla Cristiana Breve"* (Pamplona: Servicio de Publicaciones de la Universidad de Navarra, 1991); John Frederick Schwaller, *The Church and Clergy in Sixteenth-Century Mexico* (Albuquerque: University of New Mexico Press, 1987); Stafford Poole, *Pedro Moya de Contreras: Catholic Reform and Royal Power in New Spain, 1571–1591* (Berkeley and Los Angeles: University of California Press, 1987); Stafford Poole, "The Declining Image of the Indian Among Sixteenth-Century Clergy," in *Indian-Religious Relations in Colonial Spanish America*, ed. Susan Ramírez (Syracuse: Syracuse University Press, 1989); Jesús Bustamante, *Fray Bernardino de Sahagún: Una revisión crítica de los manuscritos y de su proceso de composición* (Mexico City: UNAM, 1990); Luis Nicolau D'Olwer, *Fray Bernardino de Sahagún (1499–1590)*, trans. Mauricio J. Mixco (Santa Fe and Salt Lake City: School of American Research/University of Utah, 1997); Miguel León-Portilla, *Bernardino de Sahagún: Pionero de la antropología* (Mexico City: UNAM/El Colegio Nacional, 1999). John Frederick Schwaller, ed., *Sahagún at 500: Essays on the Quincentenary of the Birth of Fr. Bernardino de Sahagún* (Berkeley: Academy of Franciscan

History, 2003). On the church in Michoacán, for example, see David A. Brading, *Church and State in Bourbon Mexico: The Diocese of Michoacán, 1749–1810* (New York: Cambridge University Press, 1994), and Ricardo León Alanís, *Los orígenes del clero y la iglesia en Michoacán, 1525–1640* (Morelia: Universidad Michoacana de San Nicolás de Hidalgo, Instituto de Investigaciones Históricas, 1997).

113. Luis Martínez Ferrer, *La penitencia en la primera evangelización de México, 1523–1585* (Mexico City: Universidad Pontifica de México, 1998); Antonio Rubial García, *La santidad controvertida* (Mexico City: Fondo de Cultura Económica/Facultud de Filosofía y Artes de UNAM, 1999); Javier Villa-Flores, "To Lose One's Soul: Blasphemy and Slavery in New Spain, 1596–1664," *Hispanic American Historical Review* 82:3 (2002): 435–68.

114. María Cristina Sacristán, *Locura e Inquisición en Nueva España, 1571–1700* (Mexico City: Colegio de Michoacan, Fondo de Cultura Económica, 1992); Laura A. Lewis, *Hall of Mirrors: Power, Witchcraft, and Caste in Colonial Mexico* (Durham, N.C.: Duke University Press, 2003); Sonia Corcuera de Mancera, *El fraile, el indio, y el pulque: Evangelización y embriaguez en la Nueva España (1523–1548)* (Mexico City: Fondo de Cultura Económica, 1991).

115. Martin Nesvig, ed. *Local Religion in Colonial Mexico* (Albuquerque: University of New Mexico Press, 2006); Susan Schroeder and Stafford Poole, eds., *Religion in New Spain: Varieties of Colonial Religious Experience* (Albuquerque: University of New Mexico Press, 2007).

116. Woodrow Borah, *Justice by Insurance: The General Indian Court of Colonial Mexico* (Berkeley: University of California Press, 1983); Ronald Spores and Ross Hassig, *Five Centuries of Law and Politics in Central Mexico* (Nashville: Vanderbilt University Publications in Anthropology, 1984); Ethelia Ruiz Medrano, *Gobierno y sociedad en Nueva España: Segunda Audiencia y Antonio de Mendoza* (Zamora: El Colegio de Michoacan, 1991); Susan Kellogg, *Law and the Transformation of Aztec Culture, 1500–1700* (Norman: University of Oklahoma Press, 1995); Charles R. Cutter, *The Legal Culture of Northern New Spain 1700–1810* (Albuquerque: University of New Mexico Press, 1995).

117. Brian Owensby, *Empire of Law and Indian Justice in Colonial Mexico* (Stanford, Calif.: Stanford University Press, 2008). One work focuses on a how a prominent Nahua community actively shaped Spanish law toward Indians: Jovita Baber, "The Construction of Empire: Politics, Law and Community in Tlaxcala, New Spain, 1521–1640" (PhD diss., University of Chicago, 2005).

118. Yanna Yannakakis, *The Art of Being In-Between: Native Intermediaries, Indian Identity, and Local Rule in Colonial Oaxaca* (Durham, N.C.: Duke University Press, 2008).

119. William B. Taylor, *Drinking, Homicide, and Rebellion in Colonial Mexican Villages*, (Stanford, Calif.: Stanford University Press, 1979).

120. Gabriel Haslip-Viera, *Crime and Punishment in Late Colonial Mexico City, 1692–1810* (Albuquerque: University of New Mexico Press, 1999).

121. Teresa Lozano Armendares, *La criminalidad en la ciudad de México, 1800–1821* (Mexico City: UNAM, 1987).

122. Lee M. Penyak, *El ramo de penales del Archivo Judicial del Tribunal Superior de Justicia* (Mexico City: Instituto Mora, 1993).

123. Lyman L. Johnson and Sonya Lipsett-Rivera, eds., *The Faces of Honor: Sex, Shame, and Violence in Colonial Latin America* (Albuquerque: University of New Mexico Press, 1998); Kevin Terraciano, "Crime and Culture in Colonial Mexico: The Case of the Mixtec Murder Note," *Ethnohistory*, 45:4 (1998): 709–45.

124. Ana Margarita Gómez and Sajid Alfredo Herrera Mena, *Los rostros de la violencia: Guatemala y El Salvador, siglos XVIII y XIX* (San Salvador: UCA Editores, 2007).

125. María Teresa Huerta and Patricia Palacios, *Rebeliones indígenas de la época colonial* (Mexico City: INAH 1976); Susan Schroeder, ed., *Native Resistance and the Pax Colonial in New Spain* (Lincoln: University of Nebraska Press, 1998).

126. Hector Díaz-Polanco, ed., *El fuego de la inobediencia: Autonomía y rebelión india en el obispado de Oaxaca* (Mexico City: CIESAS, 1996).

127. Victoria Bricker, *The Indian Christ, The Indian King: The Historical Substrate of Maya Myth and Ritual* (Austin: University of Texas Press, 1981); Kevin Gosner, *Soldiers of the Virgin: The Moral Economy of a Colonial Maya Rebellion* (Tucson: University of Arizona Press, 1992); Grant Jones, *The Conquest of the Last Maya Kingdom* (Stanford, Calif.: Stanford University Press, 1998); Severo Martínez Peláez, *Motines de indios: La violencia colonial en Centroamérica y Chiapas* (Puebla: Universidad Autónoma de Puebla, 1985); Juan Pedro Viqueira Albán, *Indios rebeldes e idólatras: Dos ensayos históricos sobre la rebelión india de Cancuc, Chiapas, acaecida en el año de 1712* (Mexico City: CIESAS, 1997) and *Encrucijadas chiapanecas: Economía, religión e identidades* (Mexico City: Tusquets Editores, 2002); Robert Patch, *Maya Revolt and Revolution in the Eighteenth Century* (New York: M.E. Sharpe, 2002). Bricker's study crosses over into the nineteenth century; many studies of conflict in the Maya area focus on the caste wars of the nineteenth century. Miguel Alberto Bartolomé, Alicia Barabas, Antonio García de León, and Gilbert Joseph, among others, address these topics.

128. Michael T. Ducey, *A Nation of Villages: Riot and Rebellion in the Mexican Huasteca, 1750–1850* (Tucson: University of Arizona Press, 2004); Andrew L. Knaut, *The Pueblo Revolt of 1680: Conquest and Resistance in Seventeenth-Century New Mexico* (Norman: University of Oklahoma Press, 1995).

129. Felipe Castro Gutiérrez, *Movimientos populares en Nueva España: Michoacán, 1766–1767* (Mexico City: Seminario Rebeliones y Revoluciones en México, UNAM, 1990); *Nueva ley y nuevo rey: Reformas borbónicas y rebelión popular en Nueva España* (Zamora and Mexico City: Colegio de Michoacán/UNAM, Instituto de Investigaciones Históricas, 1996); *La rebelión de los indios y la paz de los españoles* (Tlalpan: CIESAS/INI, 1996).

130. John Tutino, *From Insurrection to Revolution in Mexico: Social Bases of Agrarian Violence, 1750–1940* (Princeton: Princeton University Press, 1986).

131. Eric Van Young, *The Other Rebellion: Popular Violence, Ideology, and the Mexican Struggle for Independence, 1810–1821* (Stanford, Calif.: Stanford University Press, 2001).

132. R. Douglas Cope, *The Limits of Racial Domination: Plebeian Society in Colonial Mexico City, 1660–1720* (Madison: University of Wisconsin Press, 1994).

133. Susan Socolow and Lyman Johnson, "Urbanization in Colonial Latin America," *Journal of Urban History*, 8/1 (1981), 27–59; Woodrow Borah, "Trends in Recent Studies of Colonial Latin American Cities," *Hispanic American Historical Review* 64:3 (1984): 535–54; Frank Bronner, "Urban Society in Colonial Spanish America: Research Trends," *Latin American Research Review* 21:1 (1986): 7–72.

134. Edmundo O'Gorman, *Reflexiones sobre la distribución urbana colonial de la ciudad de México* (Mexico City: Editorial Cultura, 1938); Alfonso Caso, *Los barrios antiguos de Tenochtitlan y Tlatelolco* (Mexico City: Academia Mexicana de la Historia, 1956).

135. Manuel Toussaint, Federico Gómez de Orozco, and Justino Fernández, eds, *Planos de la ciudad de México, siglos XVI y XVII: Estudio histórico, urbanístico y bibliográfico* (Mexico City: XVI Congreso Internacional de Planificación y de la Habitación, 1990). There are also several collections of primary sources for the study of the Mexico City.

136. R. Douglas Cope, *The Limits of Racial Domination*.

137. Silvia Marina Arrom, *Containing the Poor: The Mexico City Poor House, 1774–1871* (Durham: Duke University Press, 2000). See also Silvia Arrom and Servando Ortoll, eds.,

Riots in the Cities: Popular Politics and the Urban Poor in Latin America, 1765–1910 (Wilmington, Del.: Scholarly Resources, 1996).

138. Esteban Sánchez de Tagle, *Los dueños de la calle: una historia de la vía pública en la época colonial* (Mexico City: INAH, 1997).

139. John Chance, *Race and Class in Colonial Oaxaca* (Stanford, Calif.: Stanford University Press, 1978). María Elena Martínez, "Space, Order and Group Identities in a Spanish Colonial Town: Puebla de Los Ángeles," in *The Collective and the Public in Latin America: Cultural Identities and Political Order*, ed. Luis Roniger and Tamar Herzog (Brighton, U.K.: Sussex Academic Press, 2000). Eugenia María Azevedo Salomao, *Espacios urbanos comunitarios durante el período virreinal en Michoacán* (Morelia: Morevallado Editores, 2003).

140. Fernando Núñez, Carlos Arvizu, and Ramón Abonce, *Space and Place in the Mexican Landscape: The Evolution of a Colonial City*, ed. Malcolm Quantrill (College Station: Texas A&M University Press, 2007).

141. Christopher Lutz, *Santiago de Guatemala, 1541–1773: City, Caste, and the Colonial Experience* (Norman: University of Oklahoma Press, 1994); Robinson A. Herrera, *Natives, Europeans, and Africans in Sixteenth-Century Santiago de Guatemala* (Austin: University of Texas Press, 2003); Catherine Komisaruk, "Women and Men in Guatemala, 1765–1835: Gender, Ethnicity, and Social Relations in the Central American Capital" (PhD diss., University of California, Los Angeles, 2000), forthcoming with Stanford University Press.

142. Louisa Hoberman and Susan Socolow, eds., *Cities and Society in Colonial Latin America* (Albuquerque: University of New Mexico Press, 1986); Jay Kinsbruner, *The Colonial Spanish-American City* (Austin: University of Texas Press, 2005); Richard Kagan and Fernando Marias, *Urban Images of the Hispanic World, 1493–1793* (New Haven: Yale University Press, 2000).

143. Elinor G. K. Melville, *A Plague of Sheep: Environmental Consequences of the Conquest of Mexico* (Cambridge: Cambridge University Press, 1994); Emma Pérez-Rocha, *Ciudad en peligro: Probanza sobre el desague general de la ciudad de México, 1556* (Mexico City: INAH, 1996); Charles Gibson, *Aztecs under Spanish Rule* (Stanford: Stanford University Press, 1964).

144. Sonya Lipsett-Rivera, *To Defend Our Water with the Blood of Our Veins: The Struggle for Resources in Colonial Puebla* (Albuquerque: University of New Mexico Press, 1999).

145. Noble David Cook and W. George Lovell, eds., *"Secret Judgments of God": Old World Disease in Colonial Spanish America* (Norman and London: University of Oklahoma Press, 1992); Noble David Cook, *Born to Die: Disease and New World Conquest, 1492–1650* (Cambridge: Cambridge University Press, 1998).

146. Miguel Ángel Cuenya Mateos, *Puebla de los Ángeles en tiempos de una peste colonial: Una mirada en torno al matlazahuatl de 1737* (Puebla: Benemérita Universidad Autónoma de Puebla, 1999).

147. Enrique Florescano, *Memory, Myth, and Time in Mexico* (Austin: University of Texas Press, 1994); *Historia de las historias de la nación Mexicana* (Mexico City: Taurus, 2002); "La reconstrucción histórica elaborada por la nobleza indígena y sus descendientes mestizos," in *La memoria y el olvido: Segundo simposio de historia de las mentalidades* (Mexico City: Instituto Nacional de Antropología e Historia, 1985).

148. David Brading, *The First America: The Spanish Monarchy, Creole Patriots and the Liberal State, 1492–1867* (Cambridge: Cambridge University Press, 1991). See also by Brading: *The Origins of Mexican Nationalism* (Cambridge: Center of Latin American

Studies, 1985); *Prophecy and Myth in Mexican History* (Cambridge: Center of Latin American Studies, 1984).

149. Jorge Cañizares Esguerra, *How to Write the History of the New World: Histories, Epistemologies, and Identities in the Eighteenth-Century Atlantic World* (Stanford, Calif.: Stanford University Press, 2001). Alberro has also made valuable contributions to the discussion of identity formation, among many other topics; see, for example, Solange Alberro, *Del gachupín al criollo: O de cómo los españoles de México dejaron de serlo* (Mexico City: Fondo de Cultura Económica, El Colegio de México, 1999). Salvador Velazco considers the rise of new identities among three prominent mestizo intellectuals; see Velazco, *Visones de Anáhuac: Reconstrucciones historiográficas y etnicidades emergentes en el México colonial: Fernando de Alva Ixtlilxóchitl, Diego Muñoz Camargo y Hernando Alvarado Tezozómoc* (Guadalajara: Universidad de Guadalajara, 2003). Peter Villella, "The True Heirs to Anahuac: Native Nobles, Creole Patriots and the 'Natural Lords' of Colonial Mexico" (PhD diss., University of California, Los Angeles, 2009) inserts indigenous caciques and elites into intellectual history by examining how they constructed legal and philosophical arguments about their rights as natural lords to win titles and privileges in the colonial period.

150. Lockhart, *We People Here*. Miguel León-Portilla, *Broken Spears*. Laura Matthew and Michel Oudijk, *Indian Conquistadors: Indigenous Allies in the Conquest of Mesoamerica* (Norman: University of Oklahoma Press, 2007). Florine Asselbergs, *Conquered Conquistadors: The Lienzo de Quauhquechollan, A Nahua Vision of the Conquest of Guatemala* (Boulder: University of Colorado Press, 2008).

151. José Rabasa, *Writing Violence on the Northern Frontier: The Historiography of Sixteenth-Century New Mexico and Florida and the Legacy of Conquest* (Durham, N.C.: Duke University Press, 2000); James Krippner-Martínez, *Rereading the Conquest: Power, Politics, and the History of Early Colonial Michoacán, Mexico, 1521–1565* (University Park: Penn State University Press, 2001). Rebecca Brienen and Margaret Jackson, *Invasion and Transformation: Interdisciplinary Perspectives on the Conquest of Mexico* (Boulder: University Press of Colorado, 2008).

152. Anthony Pagden, *The Fall of Natural Man: The American Indian and the Origins of Comparative Ethnology* (Cambridge: Cambridge University Press, 1986). Walter Mignolo's *The Darker Side of the Renaissance: Literacy, Territoriality, and Colonization* (Ann Arbor: University of Michigan Press, 1995) does not focus on New Spain, either, but offers a provocative assessment of the intellectual dimensions of the conquest.

153. Irving Leonard, *Baroque Times in Old Mexico* (Ann Arbor: University of Michigan, 1959) and *Books of the Brave: Being an Account of Books and of Men in the Spanish Conquest and Settlement of the Sixteenth-Century New World* (Cambridge: Harvard University Press, 1949); Luis Weckmann, *La herencia medieval de México*, 2 vols. (Mexico City: El Colegio de México, 1984).

154. Jeanette Favrot Peterson, *The Paradise Garden Murals of Malinalco* (Austin: University of Texas Press, 1993); Serge Gruzinski, *El águila y el síbila: Frescos indios de México* (Mexico City: M. Moleiro, 1994); Barbara Mundy, *The Mapping of New Spain: Indigenous Cartography and the Maps of the Relaciones Geográficas* (Chicago: University of Chicago Press, 1996). Several of Cecelia Klein's students in Art History at UCLA (including Dana Leibsohn, Travis Kranz, Eulogio Guzman, Delia Cosentino, and Angelica Afanador) have focused on sixteenth-century pictorial manuscripts from the perspective of art.

155. José Guadalupe Victoria, *Pintura y sociedad en Nueva España* (Mexico City: Universidad Nacional Autonoma de México, 1986). Ilona Katzew, *Casta Painting* (New Haven: Yale University Press, 2004); María Concepción García Sáiz, *Las castas mexicanas: Un género pictórico americano* (Milan: Olivetti, 1989); Jaime Cuadriello, ed., *Juegos de*

ingenio y agudeza: La pintura emblemática de la Nueva España (Mexico City: Museo Nacional de Arte, INBA, Banamex, 1994); Magali Carrera, *Imagining Identity in New Spain: Race, Lineage, and the Colonial Body in Portraiture and Casta Paintings* (Austin: University of Texas Press, 2003).

156. Pamela Voekel, *Alone Before God: The Religious Origins of Modernity in Mexico* (Durham, N.C.: Duke University Press, 2002); Martin Nesvig, *The World of the Censors in Early Mexico* (New Haven: Yale University Press, 2009).

157. Pilar Gonzalbo Aizpuru, *Historia de la educación en la época colonial: La educación de los criollos y la vida urbana* (Mexico City: El Colegio de México, 1999); Magdalena Chocano Mena, *La fortaleza docta: Élite letrada y dominación social en México colonial, siglos XVI–XVII* (Barcelona: Ediciones Bellaterra, 2000).

158. Max Harris, *Aztecs, Moors, and Christians: Festivals of Reconquest in Mexico and Spain* (Austin: University of Texas Press, 2000); Linda A. Curcio-Nagy, *The Great Festivals of Colonial Mexico City: Performing Power and Identity* (Albuquerque: University of New Mexico, 2004); Juan Pedro Viqueira Albán, Sonya Lipsett-Rivera, and Sergio Rivera Ayala, eds. *Propriety and Permissiveness in Bourbon Mexico* (Wilmington, Del.: Scholarly Resources, 1999); Juan Pedro Viqueira Albán, *Relajados o reprimidos? Diversiones públicas y vida social en la ciudad de México durante el siglo de las luces* (Mexico City: Fondo de Cultura Económica, 1987).

159. Actually, the two best studies of mining in New Spain are as much social as economic histories: David Brading, *Miners and Merchants in Bourbon Mexico, 1763–1810* (Cambridge: Cambridge University Press, 1971); Peter Bakewell, *Silver Mining and Society in Colonial Mexico: Zacatecas, 1546–1700* (Cambridge: Cambridge University Press, 1971). A few more recent studies of mining in New Spain can be found in Peter Bakewell, ed., *Mines of Silver and Gold in the Americas* (Aldershot, U.K. and Brookfield, Vt.: Variorum, 1997).

160. Eric Van Young, *Hacienda and Market in Eighteenth-Century Mexico: The Rural Economy of the Guadalajara Region, 1675–1820* (Berkeley and Los Angeles: University of California Press, 1981). Other studies of the hacienda include Herman Konrad, *A Jesuit Hacienda in Colonial Mexico: Santa Lucía, 1576–1767* (Stanford, Calif.: Stanford University Press, 1980) and David A. Brading, *Haciendas and Ranchos in the Mexican Bajío: León 1700–1860* (Cambridge: Cambridge University Press, 1978).

161. Richard J. Salvucci, *Textiles and Capitalism in Mexico: An Economic History of the Obrajes, 1539–1840* (Princeton: Princeton University Press, 1987).

162. Carmen Viqueira and José I. Urquiola, *Los obrajes en la Nueva España* (Mexico City: Consejo Nacional para la Cultura y las Artes, 1990).

163. Arij Ouweneel and Cristina Torales Pacheco, comps., *Empresarios, indios y estado: Perfil de la economía mexicana, siglo XVIII* (Amsterdam: CEDLA, 1988); Nils Jacobsen and Hans-Jürgen Puhle, eds., *The Economies of Mexico and Peru during the Late Colonial Period, 1760–1810* (Berlin: Colloquium Verlag, 1986).

164. Jeremy Baskes, *Indians, Merchants, and Markets: A Reinterpretation of the Repartimiento and Spanish-Indian Economic Relations in Colonial Oaxaca, 1750–1821* (Stanford, Calif.: Stanford University Press, 2000).

165. Doris M. Ladd, *The Making of a Strike: Mexican Silver Workers in Real del Monte, 1766–1775* (Lincoln: University of Nebraska Press, 1988). Lolita Gutiérrez Brockington, *The Leverage of Labor: Managing the Cortés Haciendas in Tehuantepec, 1588–1688* (Durham, N.C.: Duke University Press, 1989). Bruce Castleman, *Building the King's Highway: Labor, Society, and Family on Mexico's Caminos Reales, 1757–1804* (Tucson: University of Arizona Press, 2005).

166. John J. Tepaske and Herbert S. Klein, *Ingresos y egresos de la Real Hacienda de Nueva España*, 2 vols., (Mexico City: Instituto Nacional de la Antropología y Historia,

1986); Elinore M. Barrett, *The Mexican Colonial Copper Industry* (Albuquerque: University of New Mexico Press, 1987); Guy P. C. Thomson, *Puebla de los Angeles: Industry and Society in a Mexican City, 1700–1850* (Boulder: University of Colorado Press, 1989); Linda Greenow, *Credit and Socioeconomic Change in Colonial Mexico: Loans and Mortgages in Guadalajara, 1720–1820* (Boulder: University of Colorado Press, 1983); Antonio Ibarra, *La organización regional del mercado interno novohispano: La economía colonial de Guadalajara, 1770–1804* (Mexico City: UNAM, 2000); Jay Kinsbruner, *Petty Capitalism in Spanish America: The Pulperos of Puebla, Mexico City, Caracas, and Buenos Aires* (Boulder: University of Colorado Press, 1987).

167. Two anthologies on children in Latin America contain essays on New Spain: Tobias Hecht, ed., *Minor Omissions: Children in Latin American History and Society* (Madison: University of Wisconsin Press, 2002) and Ondina González and Bianca Premo, eds. *Raising an Empire: Children in Early Modern Iberia and Colonial Latin America* (Albuquerque: University of New Mexico Press, 2007).

CHAPTER 2

COLONIAL SPANISH SOUTH AMERICA

LYMAN L. JOHNSON
SUSAN M. SOCOLOW

IN the last twenty years, there has been a growing divergence between the literature of Spanish South America written by Spanish Americans concerned with colonial antecedents of their national histories and foreign scholars seeking to apply topics and methods drawn from outside the region. These different emphases are the underlying reasons for important changes in the research agendas that now excite our field. Focusing on a subset of scholarship that we see as suggestive of current trends and interests, our goal is to draw the reader's attention to works of merit across the breadth of this dynamic field.

If the health and vigor of the field of colonial Spanish South America can be demonstrated by the expanding number of researchers and publications, it is also true that communication and debate across increasingly narrow "fields" has been constrained by the growing volume of publications. In the 1960s there was already a separation between the historical literatures devoted to colonial Spanish South America and Mexico. In the early twenty-first century, we can no longer confidently assert that there is an intellectual community that reads broadly across the component fields of colonial Spanish South America itself. Historians of colonial Latin America have effectively developed their careers in smaller subfields defined by both the earlier boundaries of place and time and by newer topical and theoretical markers like identity and gender, among others. As a result, the ability of any book or article to influence the larger community of colonial historians, regardless of intellectual merit, is very limited. Some works of undeniable merit have had little traction outside the confines of the author's small subfield, and as a result have failed to find the audiences they deserve. In other cases, works focused narrowly on the experience of a convent, a village, or a regionally specific political event have proved broadly influential in unexpected ways. This essay seeks to both advertise the merits of neglected work and trace the web of interconnections with subsequent research produced by the most influential studies.

The changes in the field since the early 1990s are manifold.[1] Many fields retain their earlier character but attract smaller audiences. Demographic and economic topics retain a genuine vitality, as do colonial administration and trade. But these fields have resisted the redefinitions and reorientations insisted upon by many historians in the recent past and are now situated on the field's periphery. Newly burgeoning areas include work that emphasizes resistance, riots, and rebellion, as well as a growing interest in the indigenous world stimulated by the recent ascent of ethnohistory. Interest in identity and gender has surged over the last two decades. Finally, some topics have served to transcend or connect the interests of historians located across these fields; slavery in particular continues to draw scholarly attention that illuminates the broad structures of colonial society.

The Conquest Era, Early Settlement, and the Formation of Colonial Society

Some scholarship in the still very dynamic field of precontact cultures directly influences the way in which we understand the collision of civilizations following 1492. One very original and challenging work, *Los últimos Incas del Cuzco* by the late Franklin Pease, can serve as a useful bridge to a discussion of the conquest era. Pease provocatively questioned one of the foundational components of the Andean conquest drama, the "civil war" between Atahualpa and Huascar.[2] He suggests, without resolving the issue in a satisfying way, that this combat may have consisted of, or may have imitated, ritualized struggles tied to the structural expectations of Hanan Cuzco and Urin Cuzco, the moieties that underlay the Inka political order. Although no one can read this work without recognizing the transformative power of his insight, there has been little follow-through by other historians, suggesting to us the confining effects of the limited documentation.

Given the deep interest in the conquest era from the origins of our field and the enduring value still found in the contributions by Lockhart and Hemming in the 1970s, it is encouraging to know that scholars continue to bring new questions and methods to bear on the period, with exciting results.[3] *Transatlantic Encounters*, edited by Kenneth Andrien and Rolena Adorno, provides one of the most useful introductions to new scholarship.[4] Susan Ramirez's important contributions to the literature delve into the indigenous world view and their subsequent reaction to the conquest.[5] Karen Powers's *Women in the Crucible of Conquest* is an example of how susceptible a field with a deep and apparently settled historiography can be to new interpretations.⁶ Powers's innovative synthesis highlights the centrality of the experiences of women to understanding the previously masculine precincts of the conquest and early settlement periods.

The conquest and early colonial consolidation have also benefited from the publication of new work based on more traditional topics, methods, and sources. Rafael Varón Gabai's study of the Pizarro family fills out the Spanish background to the military and political events in Peru and illuminates in very useful ways the role of the Pizarro clan in the immediate postconquest period.⁷ Hermes Tovar Pinzón's work on the Caribbean zone of New Granada⁸ emphasizes the conquest, dislocation, and resistance of indigenous peoples, providing a very useful corrective to older work on this region as well as an argument about the early regional development of the encomienda. The work of Ana María Presta, focused on encomendero families of Alto Peru, offers a particularly rewarding examination of the strategies employed to gain, preserve, and project economic and social power. Powers and Presta offer an exciting reinterpretation of the role of women at the origin of colonial society. José de la Puente Brunke's study of the encomienda in Peru, although more traditional in focus, offers a crucial expansion of our understanding of this foundational colonial institution.⁹

Indigenous reactions to Spanish efforts to impose new institutions, mores, and cultural practices have been among the most controversial topics of recent research. Informed by an increasingly sophisticated understanding of preconquest societies and by the work of anthropologists and archaeologists, ethnohistorians have made great strides in identifying and understanding the strategies used by Andean peoples to survive and respond to conquest.¹⁰ Thomas Abercrombie's work has been particularly helpful in understanding the degree to which some indigenous people adopted Spanish forms while others preserved their own ways of understanding.¹¹ Also of importance is Noble David Cook's *People of the Volcano: Andean Counterpoint in the Colca Valley of Peru*, which provides a complex examination of culture, society, and economy in this important region as it was integrated in the colonial world.¹²

Resistance, Riots, and Rebellions

It may be surprising that historians, a class of people who spend their days talking to students or researching in libraries and archives, are so relentlessly interested in violence in all its settings. Over the past twenty years, historians of colonial South American history have examined disturbances of all kinds, producing a rich harvest of books and articles. Violent crimes as well as riots and more serious uprisings have been interrogated to reveal more fully the structure and functioning of Spanish colonial society. Drawing on seminal works by E. P. Thompson on moral economy, Eric Hobsbawm and George Rudé on preindustrial social rebellions, and James

Scott on everyday resistance, colonial Latin Americanists have excavated disturbances ranging from local riots focused on labor demands and taxes to large-scale risings like the Tupac Amaru rebellion of 1780.[13]

Since Steve Stern's edited volume on uprisings and identity and Rolena Adorno's interpretation of the writing of Guaman Poma as a critique of Spanish colonialism in the 1980s, a veritable tsunami of research has greatly enriched our knowledge of various forms of resistance, centering on, but not limited to, the eighteenth-century Andean world.[14] The net result of this work has transformed the colonial Andes from a region of passive indigenous acceptance of Spanish rule to one of active, ongoing challenge to state and church.

Perhaps the least studied of these three interlocking topics has been the question of resistance, that is, day-to-day personal challenges to the tribute system, patriarchal authority, and church-imposed rules of conduct and religious orthodoxy, events as small as flight from police authorities and the bribing of local officials.[15] Ward Stavig's exploration of the realm of personal conduct, especially his examination of indigenous resistance to changes in their sexual conduct, has been especially enlightening. Try as they would, the Spanish state and the Catholic Church could not repress preconquest practices of trial marriage, an institution deemed essential to a successful marriage by natives. Church and state also encountered resistance to their campaigns to stamp out prostitution, adultery, and socially sanctioned violence against women.[16]

Religious beliefs and practices were other arenas where indigenous resistance undermined efforts by Spanish government officials and Catholic clergymen to enforce conformity. One school of current scholarship indicates clearly that indigenous society, especially those people living away from major centers of Spanish population and institutional power, succeeded in influencing both local practice and belief well into the eighteenth century and beyond. Andean peoples, while accepting those aspects of Christianity that served their purposes, also refused to abandon their preconquest spirituality and practice normative Christianity. In spite of official church pressure to forsake mountain gods (*huacas*), lineage gods (*chancas*), and personal gods of fecundity (*conopas*), Andean and Catholic religious beliefs and practices continually interacted in both religious institutions and the lives of individuals.[17] At least one scholar, Juan Carlos Estenssoro, has taken on the school of Andean "resistance" to Catholicism, arguing that while Indians adopted and subverted European religious practices, they also sought to become accepted as Old Christians.[18]

The Taki Onqoy movement, the earliest rebellion against Spanish government in South America to attract ongoing scholarly interest, illustrates the imperfect, unsettled, and conflicted nature of cultural change in the Andes.[19] The lesser-known seventeenth-century uprising led by Pedro Bohórquez, a Spaniard claiming to be a descendent of the Inca royal line, disturbed the *governación* of Tucumán in the mid-seventeenth century. A study by Argentine anthropologist Ana María Lorandi has demonstrated both the plastic nature of identity (a Spaniard pretending to be the Inca) and the wide audience for neo-Inca representation in this distant periphery of the Inca Empire.[20] However, later uprisings, generally seen as infused with consequential political import, have drawn more attention.

As discontent, population pressures, and taxes rose during the reign of Charles III, urban riots became a common occurrence in the cities of colonial Spanish America. The work of John Leddy Phelan was among the first to bring the accumulating urban problems of the Bourbon period and the resultant social unrest to historians' attention.[21] Leon Campbell's article on an urban uprising of free black militiamen resisting royal tribute collection in Lambayeque, Peru, was another early contribution to this field.[22] Newer work has examined secondary theaters of popular discontent, acknowledging the central role played by urban Indians in the district of Quito. Among these *motines* were riots in Pasto in 1780 and 1800,[23] an uprising in 1780 in Arequipa,[24] and the earlier, better-known Quito insurrection of 1765.[25] In addition, the 1781 Revolt of the Comuneros of Bogotá, although not considered an indigenous uprising, was one of many uprisings in the region.[26] The riots of 1780–81, like the major Indian rebellion of Tupac Amaru II, highlight the social and economic consequences of the ambitious Spanish reform program of the eighteenth century.

Notable recent studies on riots and rebellions concur that the imperial reforms of the late colonial era disrupted long-established understandings between the colonial state and church on the one hand and both colonial elites and masses on the other. With ancient arrangements discarded, efforts to impose new taxes, create new social relationships, and transform commercial connections led to elite conspiracies and remonstrations, regional conflicts, and the disruption of institutional processes, as well as popular protests and acts of violence. As a result, beginning at midcentury, the eighteenth century witnessed a wave of rebellions that shook the colonial order to its core. The mounting protest and social conflict were manifested in both urban and rural settings.[27]

The Spanish crown, intent upon improving the American contribution to the treasury, ignored the early flare-ups and proceeded to introduce a host of new fiscal and administrative reforms after 1770. In response, the indigenous communities of the Andes began to react to more stringent laws such as the forced purchase of goods by indigenous communities (*repartimiento de bienes*), a reconfigured system of governance (intendants and *subdelegados*), and the increasing Hispanization, greed, and general alienation of their community leaders (*curacas*) from the people they were charged with protecting.

Undoubtedly, the complex of related rebellions initiated by Tupac Amaru II was the most important rebellion of the Spanish colonial period. Provoked by the reforms and by accumulated grievances rooted in the distant past, many indigenous communities of the Andean region erupted in rebellion in 1780. New research on the great rebellion that shook the southern Andes in the late eighteenth century, informed by new questions and methods, has broadly revised earlier interpretations. Scarlett O'Phelan argues that by examining a range of Indian uprisings, both large and small, the large forces transforming the Andean region can be illuminated. Although these insurrectionists took aim at different abuses and exploiters, they were all reacting to the same changes in Spanish policy and practice.[28] Underlining the centrality of fiscal concerns in this cycle of rebellions, O'Phelan sees the Tupac Amaru movement as, in effect, a synthesis of all the grievances that had informed earlier risings.²⁹

Leon Campbell, drawn to the rebellion through his earlier work on the Spanish army of Bourbon Peru, published several articles related to individuals and social groups involved in the uprising, suggesting convincingly that Tupac Amaru was able to recruit outside the indigenous world and relied in surprising ways on *castas* and creoles as military lieutenants.³⁰ Ward Stavig, placing his work within an examination of the broad cultural experience of colonial Andeans, investigated the importance of individual indigenous experiences during the rebellion.³¹ Charles F. Walker's *Smoldering Ashes: Cuzco and the Creation of Republican Peru* provides an excellent overview of the rebellion, integrating the best of the recent scholarship and connecting these insights to the formation of regional political identity and the evolution of regional political practice in the decades following Peruvian independence.³²

Historians have also brought new perspectives and sources to bear on the other violent protest movements that along with the Tupac Amaru rising comprised the Great Andean Rebellion.³³ Sometimes ignored in the desire to illuminate the origins and revolutionary trajectory of Tupac Amaru is the earlier Andean leader, the Aymara speaker Tomás Katari. What began as his routine legal protest on behalf of the Macha communities located between Potosí and La Paz in the 1770s served eventually as the platform for what became the Chayanta Rebellion.³⁴ What is sometimes seen as the third stage of the Andean revolution, and has been viewed as the bloodiest episode of this mounting tide of rebellion, was the movement headed by another Aymara speaker, Tupac Catarí, in the highlands of Alto Peru (present-day Bolivia).³⁵

The best of the recent scholarship—that of Sergio Serulnikov for the Tomás Katari movement and that of Sinclair Thomson for Túpaj Katari, among others—has disassembled the earlier heroic narratives in order to provide a richer and more contextualized understanding of the complex interactions between Andean communities with settled understandings of obligation and place and the broadly ambitious Spanish reform project. Such work has illuminated the importance of changes to social and cultural structures and to material conditions within the indigenous communities, the importance of the personalities of the principal leaders, and even the connections of blood and family that served as vectors of political organization by these charismatic leaders. Although some of these studies make mention of indigenous peoples who remained loyal to the Spanish crown, even providing crucial military support, these communities and their leaders are only now beginning to attract attention.³⁶ Although the Spaniards eventually put down the revolts and publicly executed most of the captured insurgent leaders, indigenous dissatisfaction was not entirely suppressed. Movements attempting to impose an Andean utopia or protesting the forced sale of goods and labor obligations continued to spring up years after the end of the Great Rebellion.³⁷ One measure of the continued efficacy of these heroic memories is that as late as 1809 Spanish authorities in Paraguay were forced to confront rumors that the son of Tupac Amaru "has been crowned."³⁸

Outside of the central Andes, historians have recovered other episodes of indigenous resistance in regions as varied as the late-seventeenth-century Colombian Chocó and the Atlantic coast of Panama in the early eighteenth century.[39] In addition, there is growing interest in the long saga of Mapuche resistance to Spanish colonization in Chile, a resistance than lasted for more than three centuries.[40] In all of these incidents, indigenous people along the frontier attempted with varying degrees of success to prevent Spanish incursion into their regions or, once defeated militarily, to retain elements of traditional cultural practice.

In other regions, ethnic groups attempted to organize resistance as the new pressures of the last decades of the eighteenth century began to rearrange long-established relationships. Farmers affected by new monopolies, artisans torn loose from guild protections, and even merchants previously accustomed to the profits of contraband trade saw new laws, new imperial agents, and new taxes as threatening. The most important of these uprisings occurred in the northern Andes, specifically in Bogotá, in the same year that the Tupac Amaru rebellion began. Even though the Comunero Revolt was put down, there was a lasting effect on the political participation of the masses in New Granada.[41]

In other cases, historians have uncovered the shadowy records of prosecuted conspiracies, rather than full-blown rebellions, as markers of these tensions. But the mid-eighteenth-century conspiracy in Lima and the late-eighteenth-century conspiracy in Buenos Aires strongly suggest the breadth of political dissatisfaction in major urban centers.[42] Research on various forms of resistance to colonial rule has transformed our vision of the Spanish colonial world from one of overall tranquility to one of ever-simmering indignation. These were societies more dynamic, fluid, and contentious than previously thought.

The Church, Religious Practices, and Religious Culture

Although the Catholic Church continues to be a field of interest to colonial historians as well as scholars of literature, all regions of colonial Spanish South America still await a work on the order of William Taylor's monumental study of the church in colonial Mexico.[43] Most of the recent work is concentrated on the viceroyalties of Peru and of Río de la Plata, with three areas receiving concerted attention. The first is the church's intellectual and moral influence on the conversion of the Andean peoples during the first hundred years of conquest. The second, and perhaps most productive, is the multiple roles of religious women within the church and greater colonial society. The third is an inquiry into the effects of the Bourbon Reforms on the power and personnel of the church. However, some topics that have been central concerns to students of the Mexican church for decades—the clergy's intellectual resistance to eighteenth-century reforms and the church's role in the intellectual foundations of creole self-awareness—have yet to be fully examined by historians of colonial South America.[44]

One of the most important aspects of the colonial church has been the role of the religious orders in the early life of the colony, centering on their relationship to the indigenous. Sabine MacCormick's examination of the conversion experience of indigenous peoples in the early years following the conquest of Peru and the later turf battle between regular and secular clergy over control of Indian parishes has proved influential.[45] The regular clergy and indigenous peoples also interacted through a mission system used by the state to fix the frontiers of colonial Spanish America. James Saeger and Barbara Ganson have both examined missions and their influence on colonial Paraguay. While Saeger examines the Abipones, Mocobis, and Tobas and Ganson the Guaraní, their works reflect modern scholarly interest in illuminating the agency of indigenous peoples in the creation of the colonial world.[46] Among the most innovative work on religion is Carolyn Dean's *Inka Bodies and the Body of Christ*, which focuses on the Corpus Christi celebrations in colonial Cuzco to explore the role of religious festival, belief, representation, and hierarchy in this culturally diverse environment.[47]

The Jesuits, among all the orders, continue to garner the most attention of scholars of the Río de la Plata. While the classic pathbreaking studies by Nicolas Cushner stressed the local and regional economic roles of the Jesuit order,[48] new work has highlighted the varied interests of the order, both spiritual and financial, in the more marginal regions of the viceroyalty.[49] Celia López's valuable work on the Jesuits in colonial San Juan, Argentina, adds an additional case study focused on the order's integration into both commercial and social networks.[50] The Bethlemites, a far less studied (and far less contentious) order, instrumental in running hospitals throughout colonial Spanish America, have also been the focus of Argentine historian Carlos Mayo, who examined the organization, its social composition, *mentalité*, and finances.[51] While dispensing charity and providing spiritual solace might have central to the day-to-day functions of Bethlemites, Franciscans, and others, with the provision of capital in the form of loans to merchants, landowners, and artisans, the orders acted as rational bankers, centrally interested in the viability of their loans.

The lives, careers, economic roles, and politics of secular priests have not received similar levels of attention. An exception is Scarlett O'Phelan's study of twenty years of ordinations of Indian priests in Lima. While there was a distinctly ambivalent attitude toward Indians entering the priesthood within the church, sons of caciques and descendants of preconquest nobility were admitted and sometimes promoted to positions of influence because of their linguistic talents. O'Phelan contends that high-ranking Indians had much greater access to ordination as secular clergy than to membership in the regular orders, a point worth additional investigation given the role of the orders in the conversion effort.[52] The financing of the secular church, a similarly underserved topic, has been studied in a useful comparative article by John Frederick Schwaller that examines Mexico and Peru.[53]

One of the most interesting areas of recent church scholarship has been the complex place of women, both religious and secular, in the colonial church. Several scholars have contributed significant analyses of the spiritual, political, and economic roles and family ties of female convents, as well as the lives of individual professed nuns.[54] Far more attention has been paid to *beatas*, holy women who chose not to enter the convent but instead to live, alone or in *beaterios*, in the uncloistered world. These "holy women," often poor whites and even mestizas or *indias*, constantly ran the risk of being seen as religious deviants rather than devout and pious.[55] The visibility and persistence of these women in the face of dismissal or repression is arresting. Nancy van Deusen has revealed the world of *recogimientos*, institutions created under the auspices of the church to protect orphans and unmarriageable, widowed, abandoned, and abused women, as well as women who had "fallen" into a life of sin. Her work argues that the colonial Catholic world was not always neatly divided into purely sacred and worldly spaces.[56] She also published the spiritual memoir of Ursula, a *mulata* slave who became a mystic while serving in a Lima convent, and an effective player in convent politics despite the presumed disabilities that attached to her race, status, and poverty. This study contributes to our understanding of how the weak and poor could attain some degree of power within rigidly hierarchical environments like convents.[57]

The Inquisition influenced all of Spanish colonial society, but was especially active in Peru and New Granada.[58] It campaigned for censorship and the punishment of those deemed to be involved in "deviant" behavior. One result of the Inquisition's defense of religious purity was its scrutiny of *judíos conversos*, Jews who had converted to Christianity but were never free of the suspicion of secretly practicing their old religion. Protestants, especially Englishmen who were seen as encroaching on the Spanish dominions, were also subject to the Inquisition's wrath.[59] The maintenance of religious purity also meant preventing contamination by heresy, defined as unacceptable beliefs and practices. Another important component of the Inquisition's work was the ongoing censorship of books.[60]

Within a few years of conquest, the mass of indigenous peoples were exempt from inquisitorial control because they were deemed neophytes, new converts who were still prone to doctrinal errors. Nonetheless, parish priests and friars worked to uncover what they viewed as the continuation of pagan or diabolic practices and destroy these errors of faith. These campaigns of extirpation continued throughout the colonial period, with the church and crown always attempting to enforce orthodoxy but accepting a degree of pre-Columbian religious survivals. Kenneth Mills argues that our polarized concept of the church versus Indian religion should be modified to account for gradual change, adaptation, selection, and unintended consequences. He documents an Andean mixture of Christianity and pre-Colombian beliefs and the survival of Andean religious ideas and practices alongside Catholic ones well into the mid-eighteenth century.[61] A useful edited book by Jean-Jacques Decoster examines the religious and cultural interactions between the Catholic Church and indigenous groups, as well as campaigns against Catholics whose religious purity was under suspicion.[62]

While these functions of the Inquisition have long been studied by historians, more recently attention has turned to the potential of Holy Office sources to provide insights into popular beliefs and practices as well as racial, ethnic, and gender identities.[63] One group deemed "deviant" by the Inquisition were those guilty of the "nefarious sin" of homosexual relations.[64] Women involved in "witchcraft," suspicious *beatas*, and abandoned women were also among the ranks of those liable to be called up before the Holy Tribunal.[65]

Looking at the role the church played in Argentina during the late colonial period, Roberto Di Stefano has explored the internal and external political dealings of the church, including divisions within the clergy over clerical education, power struggles between bishops and the ecclesiastical cabildo, and the church's role in the local economy.[66] In a more postmodern vein, Jaime Peire, using the metaphor of the mirror and the concept of "*lo imaginario*," examines the relationship of secular to regular orders as well as that of the church to an ever more worldly secular society.[67] Still another study of the church in the Río de la Plata concentrates on eleven churchmen who had extraordinary influence on the political and spiritual framework of Independence and early national politics.[68] While these scholars stress the importance of the church in Buenos Aires, Daniel Santamaría reports that, with the exception of the missions, the secular and the regular clergy had scant importance in the political life of the interior.[69]

Administration, Politics, and Reform

The period of the Bourbon Reforms has long been an area of ongoing scholarly inquiry. Even though the examination of colonial administration and political culture has lost momentum since the turn towards cultural topics in the mid-1990s, those historians who remain interested in administrative and political history remain overwhelmingly concentrated in this period. Why?

Although the imperial reformers (an odd collection of individuals pursuing often contradictory ends) are difficult to fit into a single argument about intentions or outcomes, the consequential nature of changes to fiscal policy, administrative practice, military recruitment and training, and commercial structures is undeniable. The string of late colonial rebellions reinforces this point. Since the reform era preceded the even larger transformative events of the American and French revolutions and the independence struggles of Spanish America, it conveniently suggests a direct link to what would follow. Even though the argument that the Bourbon Reforms led to the independence wars has been long dismissed, it has reappeared recently in the deep cover provided by "moral economy" enthusiasts. Finally, because the logic and rhetoric of the reform influenced all of the century's big ideas—secularization, centralization of political authority, an enthusiasm for planning, and a voracious appetite for fiscal resources—the era has successfully been employed to frame (and infuse with implied meaning) the work of cultural historians.

As a result, nearly all of the components of this period have been examined across much of Spanish South America. Among the topics pursued most broadly are the political innovations, the introduction of the intendant system, the creation of new viceroyalties, and fiscal reform.[70] Military reform and modernization were pursued with increasing urgency in the era of Carlos IV when military officers, especially naval officers, were inserted into the highest levels of the colonial bureaucracy. The efforts by the reformers to transform the church, bending it to the purposes of the state and harvesting increased shares of its resources, often led to unforeseen outcomes, especially the expulsion of the Jesuits in 1767. Moreover, eighteenth-century economic reform (mining reforms, *comercio libre*, the tobacco and cacao monopolies, and an altered commercial tax structure) may in the end have had a greater impact on later events than the administrative reforms, which have received much more attention.[71]

The link between the ambitions of the reformers, the local consequences of the reforms, and the eventual appearance of criollo consciousness is broadly assumed but seldom argued convincingly due to the near absence of serious work on colonial politics. Social historians have clearly demonstrated the workings of familial and commercial networks in pursuit of advantage. We know a great deal about the ways that colonial administrators at nearly every level placed clients and dependents in positions of advantage and then worked to thwart efforts by the king and Iberian reformers to limit corruption and impose uniform enforcement of law.[72] What has not been done is to trace these colonial cartels and factions across the chaotic last decade of the colonial period as they assumed ideological characteristics and became integrated in incipient political parties.

Production and Exchange

Economic history, like the history of colonial political and judicial institutions, has lost ground as a colonial research field in the past fifteen years. In general, the participants in this field continue to produce high-quality work, but there has been a clear disengagement with social and cultural historians. Contributors continue to publish in the areas of Atlantic trade, silver production, and the fiscal regime, as well as in the areas of wage and price history.[73] Yet, despite the quality and seriousness of these publications, few young scholars of colonial Latin America in the United States commit themselves to this field, although interest among Latin Americans remains strong.

Given that modern cultural and social historical research often begins with implicit assumptions about class relations, material quality of life, and the working of the market, this disconnection in the United States seems odd, even willful. For example, much of the work on the adaptation of Andean cultures to new colonial realities emphasizes the forced integration of indigenous communities into markets as laborers and producers. What do we actually know about the size and functioning of these markets? What do we know about income and wealth? More central still, what do we know about the intersection of the colonial economy and demographic changes?

How can we explain this field's limited ability to recruit from a growing pool of graduate students in the United States and Canada? From the 1970s into the early 1990s, when social history in the style of James Lockhart's *Spanish Peru* was ascendant among historians of colonial Spanish South America, there was a general interest in economic history, and as a result, studies of Atlantic commerce, wages and prices, silver flows, and markets found a broad readership.[74] The common assumption of the field was that the experience of social groups could best be understood in relationship to the functioning of the colonial economy. By connecting to cycles of economic expansion and contraction, historians presumed that they were discovering the origins of the large dramas of migration, cultural change, riot, rebellion, and, ultimately, the revolutions that led to independence.

As this earlier version of social history gave way to the "New Social History" or, alternatively, to the "New Cultural History," focused on gender, race and ethnicity, and sexuality, the conversation between social historians and economic historians went mute. Historians interested in the idea of human agency were unconvinced by arguments that human action was framed and directed by material conditions and were impatient with the demands that the workings of the economy be elaborated quantitatively. The adoption by economic historians of more complicated and, to most nonspecialists, more opaque quantitative methods also contributed to this rupture. One visible result was a series of intemperate exchanges at academic meetings and in print by partisans of qualitative and quantitative methods.[75]

Despite this loss of traction, the quality of economic research has generally remained excellent. Among the works that deserve attention is the late Enrique Tandeter's *Coercion and Market*, a study of the intersection of mineral production and labor supply at Potosí.[76] Tandeter's study is rooted in his careful estimations of prices and wages, measures of productivity and profitability, as well as in his reading of demographers and students of Atlantic commerce. Dense with original insights, his work convincingly argues that the Potosí mita had evolved by the late eighteenth century from a system of forced labor into a system of forced wealth transfers from indigenous communities to mine owners and colonial officials.

Other Andeanists remain interested in connecting the experience of indigenous communities to the workings of the Spanish colonial economy, especially the impact of the eighteenth-century imperial reforms on the indigenous. Ann Zulawski's *They Eat From Their Labor: Work and Social Change in Colonial Bolivia* is exemplary of this style of inquiry.[77] She links the complex process of cultural adaptation within the region's indigenous agricultural economy to the imposition of markets, forced labor, and elements of European material culture. Kenneth J. Andrien's study of colonial Ecuador serves as another model study that connects the economic role of the colonial state to a series of social historical issues.[78]

The effort to assess the economic impact of the Bourbon Reforms has also promoted research that seeks to interpret late colonial economic performance. More efficient tax collection, new taxes, less constrained commercial links, and new technologies were all intended to promote colonial production and increase the transfer of American wealth to Spain. There has been no effort to measure the global economic effects of the Bourbon Reforms. There have been few studies of Atlantic trade or intracolonial trade in recent years, but María Jesús Arazola Corvera's *Hombres, barcos y comercio de la ruta Cádiz-Buenos Aires (1737–1757)* is an important complement to the earlier work of Pierre Chaunu and others.[79] There has been no comprehensive assessment of *comercio libre*, but a number of essays were collected in *Reform and Insurrection in Bourbon New Granada and Peru*.[80] In addition, Zacarias Moutoukias has explored trade in the Río de la Plata, emphasizing the importance of personal networks, the relationship between merchants and bureaucrats, and the extent to which the late-seventeenth-century Spanish crown financed its administrative and military structure in Buenos Aires from legal, semilegal, and illegal commerce.[81]

The colonial government collected more taxes and fees while at the same it increased expenditure for colonial defense and, in some cases, for infrastructure. Herbert Klein's *The American Finances of the Spanish Empire* offers a synthesis of income and expenditures taken from the colonial accounts.[82] The sources upon which this study was based present significant difficulties, but they do provide a uniform quantitative record over a long period and therefore remain attractive to economic historians. The intersection of the colonial state's fiscal and regulatory functions and economic performance inform a number of other useful studies, including those by Anthony McFarlane, Lance Grahn, and Cristina Ana Mazzeo.[83] In addition, Viviana Grieco has studied the role of the extraordinary contributions (*donativos*) made by American subjects during the wars and fiscal crises of the decades of the 1790s and 1800s.[84]

The Bourbon reforms produced mixed results. Silver production at Potosí and other South American mining centers increased until the indigenous insurrections of the 1780s, but, compared with the steep increases of New Spain, mining did not lead the economic expansion in Spanish South America.[85] A useful article by Juan Carlos Garavaglia traces the flow of gold and silver through Buenos Aires, demonstrating the way in which political reform, including the creation of a new viceroyalty in 1776, led to economic expansion as the interior's mineral production was harvested by the new viceregal capital and by the metropole.[86]

Instead, it was commercial reform, especially the opening of additional colonial ports to direct trade with Spain, and political reform, especially the creation of two new viceroyalties (New Granada and Río de la Plata), that facilitated the expansion of agricultural exports, dramatically increasing public sector spending while taxes flowed from the colonies to Spain in increasing volume. The Río de la Plata was among the regions that benefited most from these alterations. A talented cohort of Argentine historians revolutionized understanding of the rural economy in the late colonial period. They have shown that by that period, a complex mix of livestock grazing and agriculture had appeared in what is now Uruguay and Argentina. Rural enterprise integrated a number of market-driven adaptations to the regions conditions of scarce and expensive labor and erratic markets. That is, essential elements of what would become the region's characteristic estancia economy were present before independence.[87]

SOCIAL HISTORY

Social history continues to be a field of central interest to colonial historians, although the focus and tone of the field have changed. While studies of social groups are still produced, social identity and popular cultural practice, the history of the family, and women's history are now the major foci. Much of the newer work has emphasized social tensions, conflicts, and transgression. Women's history has led to a new interest in the concept of agency, leading to a vision of colonial women that stresses their empowerment rather than their victimization.

Several books fall under the rubric of prosopography or group biography, the study of one social group. This branch of history continues to concentrate on elites—nobles, encomenderos, military officers and merchants—groups that usually left a wealth of archival sources.[88] While expanding its scope to more peripheral regions of the colonial world, almost all of these studies are concentrated on the sixteenth or eighteenth centuries.

The masses of urban dwellers have received some attention, although much remains to be done.[89] People of color—that is, blacks and mulattoes—have lately begun to receive attention in Spanish American colonial history. While the classic study of slaves in Peru was published in the 1970s,[90] for many years interest in urban slavery, the predominant use for African labor in the region, paled by comparison to the plantation slavery studies produced for Brazil and the Caribbean. The situation is finally changing. Carlos Aguirre authored an excellent overview of slavery in Peru, and recent work reflecting a upsurge of interest in the study of slaves and free people of color shows that both groups had an important demographic and economic presence in regions usually not thought of as having an African population, including New Granada, the Misque region of the Eastern Andes, Buenos Aires, Guayaquil, and Cuzco.[91] While urban history is no longer an active field in colonial history, Kris Lane's book provides a convincing and suggestive examination of both urban and rural Quito circa 1599.[92]

Despite a flurry of theoretical interest, promoters of "subaltern" as an umbrella term for the colonial rural and urban masses have gained limited traction among historians of colonial Spanish South America. The belief that a single social category could encompass the lives of African slaves, rural members of *ayllus*, master artisans, unskilled urban laborers, and muleteers represents a comprehensive retreat from the documents. Even limited experience with the words of these often poor and exploited men and women demonstrates their careful efforts to distinguish and define themselves and their contemporaries.[93]

While historians continue to produce high-quality studies focused on diametrically opposite ends of the socioeconomic scale, another body of work has begun to examine day-to-day social practice, especially the effect of traditions and legal institutions on social behavior. Honor, shame, and the effect of illegitimacy on individuals and families in colonial society have been closely examined.[94] Some of this work concentrates on a specific geographical locale, but Ann Twinam's work on the *gracias al sacar* purchased by the elite to remove the stain of illegitimacy takes a wider imperial perspective, as well as examining the wages of conception outside of marriage from the perspective of the woman, the man, and the resultant child.[95] Twinam's book, as well as earlier work on amorous relations between the sexes and marriage, also addresses church and state control of the domestic dimension of colonial social life.[96]

Honor, shame, and illegitimacy are only some of the dimension of "private life," a concept introduced by French social historians Philippe Ariès and Georges Duby, which has produced a veritable windfall of books in Spanish South America, with chapters addressing issues ranging from housing to intimacy, prestige, and sociability.[97] Private life history, like a related field, the history of the family, allows for comparisons across social groups. In addition to analyzing gendered roles within the household, historians of the family have examined family size, romantic love, moral codes, and violence.[98] Sexuality, marriage, and bigamy have also been topics of enduring interest.[99] At least one historian has examined domestic space and its relationship to forms of neighborhood sociability.[100]

Although public life has yet to come under the same scrutiny,[101] historians looking at "everyday life" have produced several books and articles on fiestas, religious processions, games, and diversions, including a new edition of the classic by the late Argentine historian José Torre Revello.[102] Another growing field is that of violence and criminality, including thievery, cattle rustling, and banditry in both highland and lowland Peru.[103] Luxury goods, another aspect of "everyday life" for the elite, and food have also been examined.[104] There is a renewed interest in the history of punishment and colonial penal systems as well as a growing examination of social policy toward groups such as children and the poor.[105]

Women's history is now well established as a fertile field of social history. In addition to Susan Socolow's overview of colonial Latin American women, several important books and articles have appeared on various aspects of the female experience.[106] René Salinas Mesa, a Chilean scholar, has examined changes in women's identity beginning in the late colonial period.[107] Recent studies have continued Elinor Burkett's early work on Andean women, adding greatly to our knowledge of indigenous and mestiza women in early colonial Upper and Lower Peru by examining a host of topics, including identity and transgressive behaviors.[108] Because many of these works focus on one group of women at one time and place, central to much of this research is the question of representation. Unlike other fields of social history, historians of women have produced research concentrating on the seventeenth century, including two recent studies on market women in the Andean region.[109] While Kimberly Gauderman sees women, or at least market women in Quito, as independent and empowered, Jane Mangan presents a more nuanced picture of their role in an urban economy. Emma Mannerelli, focusing on the relations between men and women in seventeenth-century Lima, enlarges her view to include a wide racial and social universe.[110] All three works call attention to the distance between the "ideal" woman and the far more complicated social reality. A host of scholars also call attention to the high degree of violence that women of all social classes were subjected to, usually at the hands of their husbands, lovers, fathers, or brothers.[111]

The assumptions that indigenous women did not participate in the mita, did not pay tribute, and did not often leave their place of birth are also being questioned.[112] Other studies are beginning to examine the position of women in frontier regions of Spanish America.[113] Some work has also analyzed the widespread taking of captives along the frontier and the position of "Spanish" female captives among indigenous societies.[114] The connection of women to witchcraft, a topic first investigated for colonial Mexico,[115] has recently been explored for the Tucumán region; Judith Farberman has extended the more traditional view of female *brujas* engaged in love magic to a consideration of their connection to popular medicine.[116] But witches were not the only women viewed as transgressive. Prostitutes were also clearly among those who rejected the normative female role.[117] Recently the social position of women who repented their years as prostitutes has been examined by one colonial scholar.[118]

Demographic History, Health, and Disease

Demographic history continues to make solid contributions to Latin American social history and, at least in the eyes of some historians, is beginning to be rediscovered by scholars of colonial Spanish America.[119] The more innovative studies concentrate on general population patterns, mortality studies, and the related issues of medicine, curing, and disease. Nevertheless, there have been very few demographic articles published in the most prestigious journals. Moreover, not many "new" social historians feel the need to root their explorations in demographic fundamentals.

Work on the demographic profile of the Buenos Aires region based on close analysis of published censuses continues in Argentina. These studies closely combine demographic description with social analysis, thus providing a quantitative structure to support further investigations on both urban and rural society. José Luis Moreno's coauthored demographic analysis of household size and its relationship to social class and race, based on the 1744 census of Buenos Aires, finds that the number of one-person households was surprisingly large for a traditional society.

In addition, it points out that women had a larger role in the workforce and as heads of household than previously thought.[120] Two other works, based on manuscript censuses, detail the population of Córdoba in 1778 and 1811.[121] Also of note is a study of the population of the rural Magdalena region over approximately 150 years, and pathbreaking and exhaustive work on the population of the province of Córdoba at the end of the eighteenth century.[122]

Mortality, especially among Andean indigenous peoples, continues to be a topic of much interest. Following her study of the postconquest demography of native populations in Honduras, Linda Newson produced a study on early colonial Ecuador that stressed regional and subregional variations.[123] Like Noble David Cook's book on the effects of conquest on the population of Peru,[124] she finds that the greatest depopulation occurred along the Pacific coast. Work has also been done on indigenous populations and disease in the seventeenth and eighteenth centuries.[125] An important edited volume, Cook and W. George Lovell's *Secret Judgments of God*, contains several articles on disease and mortality in Spanish South America, and Cook's book, *Born to Die*, presents a synthesis of the effect of disease on indigenous mortality throughout the early postconquest New World.[126] While all these works have underlined the importance of European disease in the dramatic decline of the indigenous population, Suzanne Austin Alchon has recently argued that disease alone does not explain postconquest mortality and that Spanish mistreatment of indigenous people must be returned to the demographic spotlight.[127] Increasingly, historians are coming to see that over time and space there was great variation in living conditions, diet, the prevalence of epidemic disease, and resultant mortality. Work by the late Aníbal Arcondo confirms that by the second half of the eighteenth century, although there were still outbreaks of disease, at least in Córdoba epidemics did not reach the level of a mortality crisis.[128] Furthermore, there was a general improvement in economic and health conditions, resulting in an increasing number of births throughout the region.

Beyond a purely demographic interest in mortality, social historians have also begun to examine working conditions and the health of workers—especially Andean miners—in the colonial period. While Kendall Brown provides an overview of the environment conditions in the Huancavelica "mine of death" during the entire colonial period, O'Phelan analyzes health conditions in the Hualgayoc mine by examining death records from the late colonial period.[129] Other historians have examined hospital records and Inquisition records to understand mortality as well as institutional and informal health practices.[130]

Finally, historians have begun to examine Andean migration, concentrating both on the numbers of indigenous peoples who left their communities of origin (*forasteros*) and the political, religious, social, and economic reasons and consequences of this movement.[131] While numbers were sometimes manipulated by indigenous and Spanish authorities for their own political purposes or are hard to determine, it is increasingly clear that heavy labor quotas were responsible for much out-migration. This movement of indigenous peoples to both urban and rural settings came to affect wide areas of colonial South America, influencing local markets, race mixture, and wage levels throughout the region.

Conclusion

This essay reviews the major trends in historiography of colonial Spanish America, but as in all such overviews, we have been forced to create arbitrary topical divisions, while giving scant (or no) attention to many valuable subfields in Latin American history.

We clearly believe that there has been a boom in Andean history created by the exciting work of Peruvian, American, and European scholars working closely with colleagues in the allied fields of anthropology and archaeology. Especially noteworthy is the work related to resistance and rebellion, which has produced a more complete vision of eighteenth-century political and economic discontent while elucidating indigenous actions and reactions from an understanding of indigenous culture and values.

We also find that there is an increased interest in several topics of religious history. Historians have made important contributions to the missionizing role of the regular clergy in the years immediately after the Conquest. The Jesuits, a regular order founded in the late sixteenth century, were especially active in Spanish South America. Their multiple activities, in both urban and rural settings, continue to attract historians' attention.

Gender and family history are two subfields of social history that have taken center stage in the work of several Latin American and U.S. scholars. Indeed, it is not unusual for historians to work in both fields. While some of this new work has added new dimensions to our knowledge of elite women, both religious and lay, we applaud the studies that expand our knowledge of urban nonelite women and their family settings. The relative difficulty of finding sources for these "plebeian" women makes the problem of how representative any source is all the more acute, and forces historians to try to place their material within a larger context. We also note the relatively scant work on slave women and free women of color, two groups that were integral to the workforce of every major colonial city. We would also welcome additional studies of rural women, but we recognize the even greater difficulty of locating useful source material.

We note an increase in the use of a new chronology in some recent studies in social history. Instead of using independence as the great dividing line, a growing number of historians now see the latter years of the eighteenth century as the logical beginning in order to understand postindependence developments.[132] To date, this periodization has been most successful in works about women, Afro-Americans, and Indians.

Expanded interest in "agency" and "identity" on the part of some gender and social historians reflects the growing influence of "new" social and cultural history perspectives. While the substantial achievements in this field are clear, problems of method endure. We will mention two here, use of the modern nomenclature of identity without adequate critical scrutiny and failure to situate social action in the context of economic and political structures.

We also note a lessening of interest in colonial economic history, especially among U.S.-based historians. The paradox of scant interest in this field is not lost on those who realize that colonial Latin American sources contain an incredibly rich mix of source materials, ranging from inventories of personal property collected during probate to the little explored records of colonial fiscal authorities. Included here are wage and price series, import/export records, *diezmos*, and *alcabala* records. Where are the young scholars willing to engage these wonderful materials? One of the most important topics to both political and social historians, the colonial consequences of the Bourbon Reforms, begs for economic analysis. What were the sectoral effects of the reforms? Who won, who lost?

As historians we are acutely aware of the pitfalls of predicting future trends in our field. Nonetheless, we believe that the history of children and childhood is one open to exciting research. Political history, a field of study often absent from the field of colonial Latin American history, is another promising field. Studies of local politics—the issues, the alliances, the *intereses creados*, and their change over time—would help to counteract our vision of a rather static polity.

ACKNOWLEDGMENTS

We wish to thank Guiomar Dueñas, Bianca Premo, Ann Twinam, and Charles Walker for their most helpful comments and suggestions.

NOTES

1. Lyman L. Johnson and Susan M. Socolow, "Colonial History," in *Latin American and Caribbean Studies: A Critical Guide to Research Sources*, ed. Paula Covington et al. (Westport, Conn.: Greenwood Press, 1992), 321–32.

2. Franklin Pease, *Los últimos Incas del Cuzco* (Lima: Alianza Editorial, 1991).

3. John Lockhart, *The Men of Cajamarca: A Social and Biographical Study of the First Conquerors of Peru* (Austin: University of Texas Press, 1972), and John Hemming, *The Conquest of the Incas* (New York: Harcourt, Brace, Jovanovich 1970).

4. Kenneth Andrien and Rolena Adorno, eds., *Transatlantic Encounters: Europeans and Andeans in the Sixteenth Century* (Berkeley: University of California Press, 1991).

5. Susan E. Ramírez, *To Feed and Be Fed: The Cosmological Bases of Authority and Identity in the Andes* (Stanford, Calif.: Stanford University Press, 2005); *The World Upside Down: Cross-Cultural Contact and Conflict in Sixteenth-Century Peru* (Stanford, Calif.: Stanford University Press, 1996); Ramírez, ed., *Indian-Religious Relations in Colonial Spanish America* (Syracuse: Maxwell School of Citizenship and Public Affairs, Syracuse University, 1989).

6. Karen Viera Powers, *Women in the Crucible of Conquest* (Albuquerque: University of New Mexico Press, 2005). The classic article by Elinor Burkett also posited the gender-specific role of women as a bridge between the conquered and the conquering:

Burkett, "Indian Women and White Society: The Case of Sixteenth-Century Peru." in *Latin American Women: Historical Perspectives*, ed. Asunción Lavrin (Westport: Greenwood Press, 1978), 101–28.

7. Rafael Varón Gabai, *Francisco Pizarro and His Brothers: The Illusion of Power in Sixteenth-Century Peru*, tr. Javier Flores Espinoza (Norman: University of Oklahoma Press, 1997).

8. Hermes Tovar Pinzón, *La estación del miedo o la desolación dispersa: El Caribe colombiano en el siglo XVI* (Bogotá: Editorial Ariel, 1997).

9. Ana María Presta, *Encomienda, familia y negocios en Charcas Colonial: Los encomenderos de La Plata 1550–1600* (Lima: IEP, 2000); and José de la Puente Brunke, *Encomienda y encomenderos en el Perú* (Seville: Deputación Provincial de Sevilla, 1992).

10. See for example Ramirez, *The World Turned Upside Down*.

11. Thomas Abercrombie, "Tributes to Bad Conscience: Charity, Restitution, and Inheritance in Cacique and Encomendero Testaments of Sixteenth-Century Charcas," in *Dead Giveaways: Indigenous Testaments of Colonial Mesoamerica and the Andes*, ed. Susan Kellogg and Matthew Restall (Salt Lake City: University of Utah Press, 1998), 249–89; Abercrombie, *Pathways of Memory and Power: Ethnography and History among an Andean People* (Madison: University of Wisconsin Press, 1998). In addition, see Frank Salomon, *The Cord Keepers: Khipus and Cultural Life in a Peruvian Village* (Durham, N.C.: Duke University Press, 2004).

12. Noble David Cook (Durham, N.C.: Duke University Press, 2007).

13. E. P. Thompson, "The Moral Economy of the English Crowd in the Eighteenth Century," *Past and Present* 50 (February 1971): 76–136; Eric Hobsbawm, *Primitive Rebels: Studies in Archaic Forms of Social Movement in the 19th and 20th Centuries* (Manchester: Manchester University Press, 1959); James Scott, *Weapons of the Weak: Everyday Forms of Peasant Resistance* (New Haven: Yale University Press, 1985).

14. Steve J. Stern, ed., *Resistance, Rebellion, and Consciousness in the Andean Peasant World: 18th to 20th Centuries* (Madison: University of Wisconsin Press, 1987); Rolana Adorno, *Guaman Poma: Writing and Resistance in Colonial Peru* (Austin: University of Texas Press, 1988).

15. Frank Salomon, "Ancestor Cults and Resistance to the State in Arequipa, ca. 1748–1754," in Stern, *Resistance, Rebellion and Consciousness*, 148–65.

16. Ward Stavig, "'Living in Offense of Our Lord': Indigenous Sexual Values and Marital Life in the Colonial Crucible," *Hispanic American Historical Review* [hereafter *HAHR*] 75:4 (1995): 597–622; Stavig, *Amor y violencia sexual* (Lima: University of South Florida and Instituto de Estudios Peruanos, 1995).

17. Kenneth Mills, *Idolatry and Its Enemies: Colonial Andean Religion and Extirpation, 1640–1750* (Princeton: Princeton University Press, 1997); Mills, *An Evil Lost to View? An Investigation of Post-Evangelisation Andean Religion in Mid-Colonial Peru* (Liverpool: University of Liverpool, Institute of Latin American Studies, 1994).

18. Juan Carlos Estenssoro, *Del paganismo a la santidad: La incorporacion de los Indios del Perú al Catolicisimo 1532–1750* (Lima: La Católica-IFEA, 2003).

19. Steve J. Stern, "El Taki Onqoy y la sociedad andina (Huamanga, siglo XVI)," *Allpanchis* 16:19 (1982): 49–77; Thomas Abercrombie, "La perpetuidad traducida: del 'debate' al Taki Onqoy y una rebelión comunera peruana," in *Incas e indios cristianos: Elites indígenas e identidades cristianas en los Andes coloniales*, ed. Jean-Jacques Decoster (Lima and Cuzco: CBC, IFEA and Asociación Kuraka, 2002), 79–120.

20. Ana María Lorandi, *De quimeras, rebeliones y utopias: La gesta del inca Pedro Bohorques* (Lima, Universidad Católica del Perú, 1997).

21. John Leddy Phelan, *The People and the King: The Comunero Revolution in Colombia, 1781* (Madison: University of Wisconsin Press, 1978).

22. Leon Campbell, "Black Power in Colonial Perú: The 1779 Tax Rebellion of Lambayeque," *Phylon: Review of Race and Culture* 33:2 (1972): 140–52.

23. Rebecca Earle Mond, "Indian Rebellion and Bourbon Reform in New Granada: Riots in Pasto, 1780–1800," *HAHR* 73:1 (1993): 99–124.

24. David P. Cahill, "Taxonomy of a Colonial 'Riot': The Arequipa Disturbances of 1780," in *Reform and Insurrection in Bourbon New Granada and Peru*, ed. John Robert Fisher, Allan J. Kuethe, and Anthony McFarlane (Baton Rouge: Louisiana State University Press, 1990), 255–91.

25. Anthony McFarlane, "The 'Rebellion of the Barrios': Urban Insurrection in Bourbon Quito," in *Reform and Insurrection* ed. Fisher et al., 197–254; Kenneth J. Andrien, "Economic Crisis, Taxes and the Quito Insurrection of 1765," *Past and Present* 129 (November 1990): 104–31.

26. Anthony Macfarlane, "Civil Disorders and Popular Protests in Late Colonial New Granada," *HAHR* 64:1 (1984): 17–54.

27. Oscar Cornbilt, *Power and Violence in the Colonial City: Oruro from the Mining Renaissance to the Rebellion of Tupac Amaru, 1740–1782* (Cambridge University Press, 1995); Brooke Larson, "Insurgent Peasant Politics and Colonial Crisis in the Bolivian Andes during the Late Eighteenth Century," *Colonial Latin American Review* 8:2 (1999): 241–44.

28. Scarlett O'Phelan Godoy, *Rebellions and Revolts in Eighteenth Century Peru and Upper Peru* (Vienna: Bohlau Verlag, 1985); Scarlett O'Phelan Godoy, "La rebelión de Tupac Amaru: Su organización interna, dirigencia y alianzas," *Histórica* 3:2 (1979): 89–122; O'Phelan Godoy, "Elementos étnicos y de poder en el movimiento tupacamarista: 1780–1781," *Nova Americana* 5 (1982): 79–101; O'Phelan Godoy, "Tierras comunales y revuelta social: Perú y Bolivia en el Siglo XVIII," *Allpanchis* 22 (1983): 75–91; O'Phelan Godoy, "Hacia una tipología y un enfoque alternativo de las revueltas y rebeliones del Perú colonial: Siglo XVIII," *Jahrbuch für Geschichte von Staat, Wirtschaft und Gesellschaft Lateinamerikas* 21 (1984): 127–53; O'Phelan Godoy, "Aduanas, mercado interno y élite comercial en el Cusco antes y después de la Gran Rebelión de 1780," *Apuntes* [Lima] 19 (1986): 53–72.

29. O'Phelan's typology of rebellions include anti-fiscal, anti-clerical, anti–ethnic lord, anti–centers of production movements, and conflicts over land.

30. Leon Campbell, "Women and the Great Rebellion in Peru, 1780–1783," *The Americas* 42:2 (1985): 163–96; Campbell, "The Army of Peru and the Túpac Amaru Revolt: 1780–1783," *HAHR* 56:1 (1976): 31–57; Campbell, "Ideology and Factionalism during the Great Rebellion," in Stern, *Resistance, Rebellion, and Consciousness*, 110–39; Campbell, "Rebel or Royalist? Bishop Juan Manuel de Moscoso y Peralta and the Tupac Amaru Revolt in Peru, 1780–1784," *Revista de Historia de América* 86 (1978): 135–68; Campbell, "Banditry and the Túpac Amaru Rebellion in Cuzco, Peru: 1780–1784," *Bibliotheca Americana* 1:2 (1982): 131–62. See also Campbell, "Recent Research on Andean Peasant Revolts, 1750–1810," *Latin American Research Review* 14:1 (1979): 3–49.

31. Ward Stavig, "Face-to-Face with Rebellion: Individual Experience and Indigenous Consciousness in the Thupa Amaro Insurrection," in *Indigenous Revolts in Chiapas and the Andean Highlands*, ed. Kevin Gosner and Arij Ouweneel (Amsterdam: CEDLA, 1996), 132–49; Stavig, *The World of Tupac Amaru: Conflict, Community and Identity in Colonial Peru* (Lincoln: University of Nebraska Press, 1999).

32. Charles F. Walker, *Smoldering Ashes: Cuzco and the Creation of Republican Peru, 1780–1840* (Durham, N.C.: Duke University Press, 1999).

33. Scarlett O'Phelan Godoy, *La gran rebelión en los Andes: De Túpac Amaru a Túpac Catari* (Cuzco, Perú: Centro de Estudios Regionales Andinos Bartolomé de las Casas, 1995).

34. Sergio Serulnikov, *Subverting Colonial Authority: Challenges to Spanish Rule in Eighteenth-Century Southern Andes* (Durham, N.C.: Duke University Press, 2003); Serulnikov, *Tomás Catari y la producción de justicia* (Buenos Aires: CEDES, 1988); Serulniknov, "Disputed Images of Colonialism: Spanish Rule and Indian Subversion in Northern Potosí, 1777–1780," *HAHR* 76:2 (1996): 189–226; Serulnikov, "Customs and Rules: Bourbon Rationalizing Projects and Social Conflicts in Northern Potosí during the 1770s," *Colonial Latin American Review* 8:2 (1999): 245–74.

35. Sinclair Thomson, *We Alone Will Rule: Native Andean Politics in the Age of Insurgency* (Madison: University of Wisconsin Press, 2002); Thomson, "'We Alone Will Rule....': Recovering the Range of Anticolonial Projects among Andean Peasants (La Paz, 1740s to 1781)," *Colonial Latin American Review* 8:2 (1999): 275–99.

36. The exceptions to this statement are a recent article by David T. Garrett, "'His Majesty's Most Loyal Vassals': The Indian Nobility and Túpac Amaru," *HAHR* 84:4 (2004): 575–617, and his book *Shadows of Empire: The Indian Nobility of Cusco, 1750–1825* (New York: Cambridge University Press, 2005).

37. Scarlett O'Phelan Godoy, "Cuzco 1797: El movimiento de Maras, Urubamba," *Histórica* 1:1 (1977): 113–28; Alberto Flores Galindo, "In Search of an Inca," in *Resistance, Rebellion, and Consciousness*, 193–210; David P. Cahill and Scarlett O'Phelan Godoy, "Forging Their Own History: Indian Insurgency in the Southern Peruvian Sierra, 1815," *Bulletin of Latin American Research* 11:2 (May 1992): 125–67.

38. Jerry W. Cooney, "Un rey inca para el Paraguay: Guarambaré en 1809," *Desmemoria: Re-vista de Historia* 5:23–24 (1999): 118–25.

39. Caroline A. Williams, "Resistance and Rebellion on the Spanish Frontier: Native Responses to Colonization in the Colombian Chocó, 1670–1690," *HAHR* 79:3 (1999): 397–414; Ignacio Gallup-Díaz, "'Haven't We Come to Kill the Spaniards?' The Tule Upheaval in Eastern Panama, 1727–1728," *Colonial Latin American Review* 10:2 (2001): 251–71.

40. Guillaume Boccara, "Etnogénesis mapuche: Resistencia y reestructuración entre los indígenas del centro-sur de Chile (siglos XVI–XVIII)," *HAHR* 79:3 (1999): 425–61.

41. Margarita Garrido, *Reclamos y representaciones: Variaciones sobre la política en el Nuevo Reino de Granada, 1770–1815* (Bogotá: Banco de la República, 1993).

42. Scarlett O'Phelan Godoy, "Una rebelión abortada: Lima 1750: La conspiración de los indios olleros de Huarochirí," *Varia História* 24 (2001): 7–32; Lyman L. Johnson, "The Subversive Nature of Private Acts: Juan Barbarín: The 1795 French Conspiracy in Buenos Aires," in *Human Tradition in Colonial Latin America*, ed. Kenneth Andrien (Wilmington, Del.: Scholarly Resources, 2002), 259–77.

43. William B. Taylor, *Magistrates of the Sacred: Priests and Parishoners in Eighteenth-Century Mexico* (Stanford, Calif.: Stanford University Press, 1997).

44. David Brading addresses these issues for eighteenth-century Mexico in *Church and State in Bourbon Mexico: The Diocese of Michoacán, 1749–1810* (New York: Cambridge University Press, 1994).

45. Sabine MacCormack, *Religion in the Andes: Vision and Imagination in Early Colonial Peru* (Princeton: Princeton University Press, 1991); Maria Marsilli, "'I Heard It Through the Grapevine': Analysis of an Anti-Secularization Initiative in the Sixteenth-Century Arequipan Countryside, 1584–1600," *The Americas* 61:4 (2005): 647–72. Karen Vieira Powers, "The Battle for Bodies and Souls in the Colonial North Andes: Intraecclesiastical Struggles and the Politics of Migration," *HAHR* 75:1 (1995): 31–56.

46. James Schofield Saeger, *The Chaco Mission Frontier: The Guaycuruan Experience* (Tucson: University of Arizona Press, 2000); Barbara Ganson, *The Guaraní under Spanish Rule in the Río de la Plata* (Stanford, Calif.: Stanford University Press, 2003).

47. Carolyn Dean, *Inka Bodies and the Body of Christ: Corpus Christi in Colonial Cuzco, Peru* (Durham, N.C.: Duke University Press, 1999). See also Verónica Salles-Reese, *From Viracocha to the Virgin of Copacabana: Representation of the Sacred at Lake Titicaca* (Austin: University of Texas Press, 1997).

48. Nicolas P. Cushner, *Lords of the Land: Sugar, Wine and Jesuit Estates of Coastal Peru, 1600–1767* (Albany: State University of New York, 1980); *Farm and Factory: The Jesuits and the Development of Agrarian Capitalism in Colonial Quito, 1600–1767* (Albany: State University of New York, 1982); *Jesuit Ranches and the Agrarian Development of Colonial Argentina, 1650–1767* (Albany: State University of New York, 1983).

49. See Cushner's overview of the Jesuits, *Soldiers of God: The Jesuits in Colonial America, 1565–1767* (Buffalo, N.Y.: Language Communications, 2002).

50. Celia López, *Con la cruz y con el dinero: Los Jesuitas de San Juan Colonial* (San Juan, Argentina: Editorial Fundación Universidad, 2001).

51. Carlos Mayo, *Los betlemitas en Buenos Aires: Conventos, economia y sociedad* (Sevilla: Excma. Diputación Provincial de Sevilla, 1991); Carlos Mayo and Jaime Peire, "Iglesia y crédito colonial: La política de los conventos de Buenos Aires, 1767–1810," *Revista de Historia America* 112 (1991): 147–57.

52. Scarlett O'Phelan, "'Ascender al estado eclesiástico': La ordenación de indios en Lima a medianos del siglo XVIII," in Decoster, ed., *Incas e indios cristianos*, 311–29.

53. John Frederick Schwaller, "Tithe Collection and Distribution in Mexico and Peru, circa 1600," *Jahrbuch für Geschichte von Staat, Wirtschaft und Gesellschaft Lateinamerikas* 26 (1989): 1–18.

54. For female convents, see Kathryn Burns, *Colonial Habits: Convents and the Spiritual Economy* (Durham, N.C.: Duke University Press, 1999); Burns, "Gender and the Politics of Mestizaje: The Convent of Santa Clara in Cuzco, Peru," *HAHR* 78:1 (1998): 5–44; Burns, "Apuntes sobre la economía conventual: El Monasterio de Santa Clara del Cusco," *Allpanchis* 38 (1991): 67–95; Gabriela Braccio, "Una ventana hacia otro mundo: Santa Catalina de Sena: Primer convento femenino de Buenos Aires," *Colonial Latin American Review* 9:2 (2000): 187–212. The writings of individual nuns are examined by Karen Stolley, "'Llegando a la primera mujer': Catalina de Jesús Herrera y la invención de una genealogía femenina en el Quito del Siglo XVIII," *Colonial Latin American Review* 9:2 (2000): 167–85; Kathleen Ann Myers, *Neither Saints Nor Sinners: Writing the Lives of Women in Spanish America* (New York: Oxford University Press, 2003).

55. Fernando Iwasaki Cauti, "Mujeres al borde de la perfección: Rosa de Santa María y las alumbradas de Lima," *HAHR* 73:4 (1993): 581–613; Nancy E. van Deusen, "Manifestaciones de la religiosidad femenina en el siglo XVII: Las beatas de Lima," *Histórica* 23:1 (1999): 47–78; Kathryn Burns, "Beatas, 'decencia' y poder: La formación de una elite indígena en el Cuzco colonial," in Decoster, ed., *Incas e indios cristianos*, 121–34; Frank Graziano, *Wounds of Love: The Mystical Marriage of Saint Rose of Lima* (New York: Oxford University Press, 2004).

56. Nancy E. van Deusen, *Between the Sacred and the Worldly: The Institutional and Cultural Practice of Recogimiento in Colonial Lima* (Stanford, Calif.: Stanford University Press, 2001); van Deusen, "Determining the Boundaries of Virtue: the Discourse of *Recogimiento* Among Women in Seventeenth-Century Lima," *Journal of Family History* 22:4, (1997): 373–89; Nancy E. van Deusen, "Defining the Sacred and the Worldly: *Beatas* and *Recogidas* in Late-Seventeenth-Century Lima," *Colonial Latin American Historical*

Review 6:4 (1997): 441–77; van Deusen, *Dentro del cerco de los muros: El recogimiento en la época colonial* (Lima: Centro de Documentación sobre la Mujer, 1987).

57. Van Deusen, *The Souls of Purgatory: The Spiritual Diary of a Seventeenth-Century Afro-Peruvian Mystic, Ursula de Jesus* (Albuquerque: University of New Mexico Press, 2004). This typically feminine form of writing is closely examined by Myers, *Neither Saints Nor Sinners*.

58. For an interesting interpretation of the Inquisition that links it to the emergence of the modern state, see Irene Silverblatt, *Modern Inquisitions: Peru and the Colonial Origins of the Civilized World* (Durham, N.C.: Duke University Press, 2004).

59. Anna Maria Splendiani, "Los protestantes y la Inquisición," *Anuario Colombiano de Historia Social y de la Cultura* 23 (1996): 1–14.

60. Teodoro Hampe Martínez, *Santo Oficio e historia colonial: Aproximaciones al Tribunal de la Inquisición de Lima, 1570–1820* (Lima: Ediciones del Congreso del Perú, 1998).

61. Kenneth Mills, *Idolatry and Its Enemies: Colonial Andean Religion and Extirpation, 1640–1750* (Princeton: Princeton University Press, 1997); Mills, "The Limits of Religious Coercion in Midcolonial Peru," *Past and Present* 145 (1994): 84–121.

62. Decoster, ed., *Incas e indios cristianos*.

63. See for example Anna Maria Splendiani, J. E. Sanchez, and E. Luque de Salazar, *Cincuenta anos de la Inquisición en el Tribunal de Cartagena de Indias 1610–1660* (Bogota: Centro de Educación Javeriana, 1997); Anna Maria Splendiani, *Documentos para la historia del Santo Tribunal de la Inquisición en Cartagena de Indias, siglo XVII, años 1610–1636*, vols. 1–4 (Bogota, 1994).

64. Ward Stavig, "Political 'Abomination' and Private Reservation: The Nefarious Sin, Homosexuality and Cultural Values in Colonial Peru," in *Infamous Desire: Male Homosexuality in Colonial Latin America*, ed. Pete Sigal (Chicago: University of Chicago Press, 2003), 134–51; Geoffrey Spurling, "Honor, Sexuality, and the Colonial Church: The Sins of Dr. González, Cathedral Canon," in *The Faces of Honor: Sex, Shame and Violence in Colonial Latin America*, ed. Lyman Johnson and Sonya Lipsett-Rivera (Albuquerque: University of New Mexico Press, 1998), 45–67; Spurling, "Under Investigation for the Abominable Sin: Damián de Morales Stands Accused of Attempting to Seduce Antón de Tierra de Congo," in *Colonial Lives: Documents on Latin American History, 1550–1850*, ed. Richard Boyer and Geoffrey Spurling (Oxford: Oxford University Press, 2000), 112–29.

65. María Emma Mannarelli, *Hechiceras, beatas y expósitas: Mujeres y poder inquisitorial en Lima* (Lima: Ediciones del Congreso del Perú, 1999).

66. Roberto Di Stefano, *El púlpito y la plaza: Clero, sociedad y política de la Monarquía Católica a la República Rosista* (Buenos Aires: Siglo Veintiuno, 2004); Di Stefano, "Magistri clericorum: Estudios eclesiásticos e identidades sacerdotales en Buenos Aires a fines de la época colonial," *Anuario IEHS* 12 (1997): 177–95; Di Stefano, "Poder episcopal y poder capitular en lucha: El conflicto entre el Obispo Malvar y Pinto y el Cabildo Eclesiástico de Buenos Aires por la cuestión de la liturgia," *Memoria Americana* 8 (1999): 67–82.

67. Jaime Peire, *El taller de los espejos: Iglesia e imaginario, 1767–1815* (Buenos Aires: Editorial Claridad, 2000).

68. Nancy Calvo, Roberto Di Stefano, and Klaus Gallo, eds., *Los curas de la Revolución: Vidas de eclesiásticos en los orígenes de la Nación* (Buenos Aires: Emecé, 2002).

69. Daniel J. Santamaría, "La Iglesia en el Jujuy colonial, siglos XVII y XVIII," in *Jujuy en la historia: Avances de investigación* (Jujuy, Argentina: Facultad de Humanidades y Ciencias Sociales, Universidad Nacional de Jujuy, 1995), 2: 27–42.

70. Anthony McFarlane, *Colombia before Independence: Economy, Society, and Politics under Bourbon Rule* (Cambridge: Cambridge University Press, 2002) presents a good

overview of the reforms and their results in Nueva Granada. For the effects of the reforms in Quito, see Christiana Borchart de Moreno and Segundo E. Moreno Yánez, "Las reformas borbónicas en la Audiencia de Quito," *Anuario Colombiano de Historia Social y de la Cultura* (Bogotá) 22 (1995): 35–57, and their "La historia socioeconómica ecuatoriana del siglo XVIII: Análisis y tendencias," *Revista de las Indias* 49:186 (1989): 379–409. For the impact of the intendent system in the Río de la Plata, see Enrique Orduña Rebollo, *Intendentes e intendencias* (Buenos Aires: Ediciones Ciudad Argentina, 1997); and Edberto Oscar Acevedo, *Las intendencias altoperuanas en el Virreinato del Río de la Plata* (Buenos Aires: Academia Nacional de la Historia, 1992). For Venezuela, see Juan Andreo García, *La intendencia en Venezuela: Don Esteban Fernández de León, intendente de Caracas, 1791–1803* (Murcia, Spain: Universidad de Murcia, 1991).

71. For mining reforms in Alto Perú, see María Concepción Gavira Márquez, "Caja Real, reforma y minería en Oruro, 1776–1810," *Anuario del Archivo y Biblioteca Nacionales de Bolivia* (Sucre) (1996): 199–227, and her "Producción de plata y comercio en Oruro a fines del período colonial: Análisis a través de las fuentes fiscales," *Revista de las Indias* 61:222 (2001): 377–405. Also of significant value are Serena Fernández Alonso, "Minería peruana y reformismo estatal: Las Ordenanzas del Real Banco de San Carlos de la Villa de Potosí," *Anuario de Estudios Americanos* 47 (1990): 259–77, and Adrian J. Pearce, "Huancavelica 1700–1759: Administrative Reform of the Mercury Industry in Early Bourbon Peru," *HAHR* 79:4 (1999): 669–702. For the tobacco monopoly, see Jerry W. Cooney, "La Dirección General de la Real Renta de Tabacos and the Decline of the Royal Tobacco Monopoly in Paraguay, 1779–1800," *Colonial Latin American Historical Review* 1:1 (1992): 101–15. See also Ana Inés Punta, *Córdoba borbónica: Persistencias coloniales en tiempo de reformas, 1750–1800* (Córdoba, Argentina: Universidad Nacional de Córdoba, 1997). For an example of work on the slave trade, see Cristina Ana Mazzeo de Vivó, "Esclavitud y acumulación mercantil: El tráfico negrero en el contexto de las reformas borbónicas," *Histórica* (Lima) 17:2 (1993): 149–78, which provides some original data on the slave trade between Buenos Aires and Lima in the late eighteenth and early nineteenth centuries.

72. For Paraguay during the Bourbon Reform era, see Jerry W. Cooney, "Fraude y burócratas: Tabaco y Paraguay, 1789–1790," *Revista Paraguaya de Sociologia* 29:85 (1992): 29–40. Scarlett O'Phelan Godoy, "Tiempo inmemorial, tiempo colonial: Un estudio de casos," *Procesos* (Corporación Editora Nacional Quito) 4 (1993): 3–20 is a particularly useful reminder of how colonial subjects resisted the reforms using the argument of prior practice.

73. See Lyman L. Johnson and Enrique Tandeter, eds., *Essays on the Price History of Eighteenth-Century Latin America* (Albuquerque: University of New Mexico Press, 1990). A slightly different version is published in Spanish as *Economías coloniales* (Buenos Aires: Fondo de Cultura Económica, 1992).

74. James Lockhart, *Spanish Peru 1532–1560: A Colonial Society* (Madison: University of Wisconsin Press, 1968).

75. Although there is little direct discussion of the colonial period, see the essays in *HAHR*, 79:2 (May 1999) for an example of the ways in which historians have taken to talking past each other on these issues. The actual exchange among the participants was more heated in the AHA session that led to this special issue of the journal.

76. Enrique Tandeter, *Coercion and Market: Silver Mining in Colonial Potosí, 1692–1826* (Albuquerque: University of New Mexico Press, 1993).

77. Ann Zulawski, *They Eat from Their Labor: Work and Social Change in Colonial Bolivia* (Pittsburgh: University of Pittsburgh Press, 1995).

78. Kenneth J. Andrien, *The Kingdom of Quito, 1690–1830: The State and Regional Development* (New York: Cambridge University Press, 1995). See also Michael Hamerly,

Historia social y económica de la Antigua provincial de Guayaquil, 1763–1842 (Guayaquil, 1973), and María Laviana Cuetos, *Guayaquil en el siglo XVIII: Recursos naturales y desarrollo económico* (Sevilla, 1987).

79. María Jesús Arazola Corvera's *Hombres, barcos y comercio de la ruta Cádiz-Buenos Aires, 1737–1757* (Sevilla: Diputación de Sevilla, 1998). The foundation for current work remains Pierre and Huguette Chaunu, *Séville et l'Atlantique, 1504–1650*, 8 vols. (Paris: Colin, 1955–59).

80. Fisher et al., eds., *Reform and Insurrection*, 123–96.

81. See his "Réseaux personnels et autorité coloniale: Les négociants de Buenos Aires au XVIIIe siècle," *Annals* 47:4/5 (1992): 889–915, and "Power, Corruption, and Commerce: The Making of the Local Administrative Structure in Seventeenth-Century Buenos Aires," *HAHR*, 68:4 (1988): 771–801.

82. Herbert S. Klein, *The American Finances of the Spanish Empire* (Albuquerque: University of New Mexico Press, 1998). A good place to begin examining the reliability for this accounts is Samuel Amaral, "Public Expenditure Financing in the Colonial Treasury: An Analysis of the Real Caja de Buenos Aires Accounts, 1789–1791," *HAHR*, 64:2 (1984): 287–95.

83. Anthony McFarlane, "The State and the Economy in Late Colonial and Early Republican Colombia," *Ibero-Amerikanisches Archiv* (Berlin) 23:1/2 (1997): 61–89; Lance Grahn, *The Political Economy of Smuggling* (Boulder, Colo.: Westview Press, 1997); and Cristina Ana Mazzeo, "Repercusiones y consecuencias de la aplicación del comercio libre en la elite mercantil limeña a fines del siglo XVIII," *Revista de Indias* 55:203 (1995): 101–26.

84. Viviana L. Grieco, "Socializing the King's Debt: Local and Financial Transactions of the Merchants of Buenos Aires, 1793–1808," *The Americas* 65:3 (2009): 321–50.

85. An introduction to this topic is provided by Kendall W. Brown, "The Spanish Imperial Mercury Trade and the American Mining Expansion Under the Bourbon Monarchy," in *The Political Economy of Spanish America in the Age of Revolution, 1750–1850*, ed. Kenneth J. Andrien and Lyman L. Johnson (Albuquerque: University of New Mexico Press, 1994), 137–68.

86. Juan Carlos Garavaglia, "El ritmo de la extracción de metálico desde el Río de la Plata a la Península, 1779–1783" in *Revista de Indias* 36:143/144 (1976): 247–68.

87. See Samuel Amaral, *The Rise of Capitalism on the Pampas: The Estancias of Buenos Aires, 1785–1870* (New York: Cambridge University Press, 1998), 290. Among the many fine studies included in this literature are Juan Carlos Garavaglia and Jorge D. Gelman, *El mundo rural rioplatense a fines de la época colonial: Estudios sobre producción y mano de obra* (Buenos Aires: Biblos, 1989); Raul O. Fradkin, ed., *La historia agraria del Río de la Plata colonial: Los establecimientos productivos*, 2 vols. (Buenos Aires: Centro Editor de América Latina, 1993); and María Mónica Bjerg and Andrea Reguera, eds., *Problemas de historia agraria* (Tandil, Argentina: IEHS, 1995). See also Juan Carlos Garavaglia and Jorge D. Gelman, "Rural History of the Río de la Plata, 1600–1850," *Latin American Research Review* 30:3 (1995): 75–105, for an informative overview of the literature.

88. Recent work on encomenderos includes Paul Rizo-Patrón, *Linaje, dote y poder: La nobleza de Lima de 1700 a 1850* (Lima: Pontificia Universidad Católica del Perú, 2000); Miguel León Gómez, *Paños e hidalguía: Encomenderos y sociedad colonial en Huánuco* (Lima: Instituto de Estudios Peruanos, 2002); Ana María Presta, *Los encomenderos de La Plata, 1550–1600* (Lima, Instituto de Estudios Peruanos, 2000); Javier Ortiz de la Tabla Duchase, *Los encomenderos de Quito (1534–1660): Origen y evolución de una elite colonial* (Seville: Escuela de Estudios Hispano-Americanos, 1993); Gabriel Guarda, *Los encomenderos de Chiloé* (Santiago: Ediciones Universidad Católica de Chile, 2002).

Merchants and other members of the elite are examined in Enriqueta Vila Vilar, *Los Corzo y los Mañana: Tipos y arquetipos del mercader con Indias* (Seville: Escuela de Estudios Hispanoamericanos, 1991); Cristina Ana Mazzeo de Vivó, ed., *Los comerciantes limeños a fines del siglo XVIII: Capacidad y cohesión de una elite, 1750–1825* (Lima: Pontificia Universidad Católica del Perú, 1999); Clara López Beltrán, *Alianzas familiares: Elite, género y negocios en La Paz, siglo XVII* (Lima: Instituto de Estudios Peruanos, 1998); Juan Marchena Fernández, "The Social World of the Military in Peru and New Granada: The Colonial Oligarchies in Conflict, 1750–1810," in Fisher et al., *Reform and Insurrection*, 54–95; Robert J. Ferry, *The Colonial Elite of Early Caracas: Formation and Crisis, 1567–1767* (Berkeley: University of California Press, 1989).

89. Martin Minchom, *The People of Quito, 1690–1810: Change and Unrest in the Underclass* (Boulder, Colo.: Westview Press, 1994); Minchom, "La economía subterránea y el mercado urbano: Pulperos, 'indias gateras' y 'regatonas' del Quito colonial, siglos XVI–XVII," *Revista Ecuatoriana de Historia Económica* 3:5 (1989): 93–104; Tamar Herzog, *La administración como un fenómeno social: La justicia penal de la ciudad de Quito, 1650–1750* (Madrid: Centro de Estudios Constitucionales, 1995).

90. Frederick P. Bowser, *The African Slave in Colonial Peru, 1524–1650* (Stanford, Calif.: Stanford University Press, 1974).

91. Aguirre, *Breve historia de la esclavitud en el Perú: Una herida que no deja de sangrar* (Lima: Congreso del Perú, 2005); Renée Soulodre-La France, "Socially Not So Dead! Slave Identities in Bourbon Nueva Granada," *Colonial Latin American Review* 10:1 (2001): 87–103; Rafael Antonio Díaz Díaz, *Esclavitud negra urbana en el Nuevo Reino de Granada: Ensayo sobre la necesidad de una investigación global de la población negra durante el periodo colonial* (Bogota: Universidad Javeriana, 1992); Diaz, "Esclavos, amos y escribanos: Perspectivas metodológicas y de investigación para el estudio de la población esclava en la sección de notarías del Archivo General de la Nación," *Revista del Archivo General de la Nación* (Bogota), (1997): 32–55; Diaz, "La manumisión de los esclavos o la parodia de la libertad: Santafé de Bogotá," *Anuario Colombiano de historia social y de la cultura* 23 (1996): 49–72; Lolita Gutiérrez Brockington, "The African Diaspora in the Eastern Andes: Adaptation, Agency, and Fugitive Action, 1573–1677," *Americas* 57:2 (2000): 207–24; Brockington, "Trabajo, etnicidad y raza: El afro-boliviano en el corregimiento de Mizque, 1573–1787," *Anuario* (Sucre) (1996): 107–22; Marta Goldberg, "Los negros de Buenos Aires," in *Presencia africana en Sudamérica*, ed. Luz María Martínez Montiel (Mexico City: Consejo Nacional para la Cultura y las Artes, 1995), 529–607; Marta B. Goldberg and Silvia C. Mallo, "La población africana en Buenos Aires y su campaña: Formas de vida y subsistencia, 1750–1850," *Temas de África y Asia* 2 (1993): 15–69; María Eugenia Chaves, *Honor y libertad: Discursos y recursos en la estrategia de libertad de una mujer esclava (Guayaquil a fines del período colonial)* (Gotenburg, Sweden: Universidad de Gotemburgo, 2001); Chaves, "Slave Women's Strategies for Freedom and the Late Spanish Colonial State," in *Hidden Histories of Gender and the State in Latin America*, Elizabeth Dore and Maxine Molyneux, eds. (Durham, N.C.: Duke University Press, 2002), 108–26; *María Chiquinquirá Díaz: Una esclava del siglo XVIII (Acerca de las identidades de amo y esclavo en el puerto colonial de Guayaquil)* (Guayaquil: Archivo Hitórico de Guayas, 1998); Jean-Pierre Tardieu, *El negro en Cusco: Los caminos de la alienación en la segunda mitad del siglo XVII* (Lima: Banco Central de Reserva del Perú, 1998). Bernard Lavallé, *Amor y opresión en los Andes coloniales* (Lima: Instituto francés de estudios andinos y Instituto de Estudios Peruanos, 1999), chaps. 7 and 8: Camile Townsend, "'Half My Body Free, the Other Half Enslaved': The Politics of the Slaves of Guayaquil at the End of the Colonial Era," *Colonial Latin American Review* 7:1 (June 1998): 105–28; Sherman Bryant, "Enslaved Rebels, Fugitives, and

Litigants: The Resistance Continuum in Colonial Quito," *Colonial Latin American Review* 13:1 (June 2004): 7–46.

92. Kris Lane, *Quito, 1599* (Albuquerque: University of New Mexico Press, 2002).

93. A strong argument for the utility of the term and a good introduction to the literature that sustains it is found in Florencia Mallon, "The Promise and Dilemma of Subaltern Studies: Perspectives from Latin American History," *American Historical Review* 99:5 (December 1994): 1491–515.

94. Lyman L. Johnson, "Dangerous Words, Provocative Gestures, and Violent Acts: The Disputed Hierarchies of Plebeian Life in Colonial Buenos Aires," in Johnson and Lipsett-Rivera, eds., *The Faces of Honor*, 127–51; María Emma Mannarelli, *Pecados públicos: La ilegitimidad en Lima, siglo XVII* (Lima: Ediciones Flora Tristán, 1993); José Luis Moreno, "Sexo, matrimonio y familia: La ilegitimidad en la frontera pampeana del Río de la Plata, 1780–1850," *Boletín del Instituto de Historia Argentina y Americana Dr. E. Ravignani* 16/17, 3rd series (1998): 61–84.

95. Ann Twinam, *Public Lives, Private Secrets: Gender, Honor, Sexuality, and Illegitimacy in Colonial Spanish America* (Stanford, Calif.: Stanford University Press, 1999); Twinam, "The Negotiation of Honor," in Johnson and Lipsett-Rivera, eds., *The Faces of Honor*, 68–102.

96. Susan M. Socolow, "Acceptable Partners: Marriage Choice in Colonial Argentina, 1778–1810," in Asunción Lavrin, ed., *Sexuality and Marriage in Colonial Latin America* (Lincoln: University of Nebraska Press, 1989), 209–51; Della M. Flusche and Eugene H. Korth, *Forgotten Females: Women of African and Indian Descent in Colonial Chile 1535–1800* (Detroit: Blame Ethridge, 1983); Flusche and Korth, "Dowry and Inheritance in Colonial Spanish America: Peninsular Law and Chilean Practice," *The Americas* 43:4 (April 1987): 395–410; José Angel Rodríguez, "Voluntad contra calidad: De los matrimonios desiguales en el siglo XVIII venezolano," in Scarlet O'Phelan et al., eds., *Familia y vida cotidiana en América Latina, Siglos XVIII–XX* (Lima: Instituto Riva-Agüero, 2003), 253–72; Bernard Lavallé, "El argumento de la 'notoria desigualdad' en la relación de pareja (Lima y Quito, siglo XVII y XVIII)," in O'Phelan et al., eds., *Familia y vida cotidiana*, 231–52.

97. Ricardo Cicherchia, *Historia de la vida privada en la Argentina* (Buenos Aires: Editorial Troquel, 1998); Fernando Devoto y Marta Madero, eds., *Historia de la vida privada en la Argentina*, Vol I: *País antiguo, de la colonia a 1870* (Buenos Aires: Taurus, 1999); José Pedro Barrán et al., eds., *Historias de la vida privada en el Uruguay: Entre la honra y el desorden, 1780–1870* (Montevideo: Taurus, 1996).

98. José Luis Moreno, *Historia de la familia en el Río de la Plata* (Buenos Aires: Editorial Sudamericana, 2004); Ricardo Cicerchia, ed., *Formas familiares, procesos históricos y cambio social en América Latina* (Quito: Ediciones Abya-Yala, 1998); Scarlet O'Phelan et al., eds., *Familia y vida cotidiana en América Latina, siglos XVIII–XX* (Lima: Instituto Riva-Agüero, 2003). One historian has found that in five major cities of late colonial Nueva Granada, households headed by single and widowed women and those who took in borders were as common as the more "traditional" consanguineous family households: Pablo Rodríguez Jiménez, "Una manera difícil de vivir: Las familias urbanas neogranadinas del siglo XVIII," in Pilar Gonzalbo Aizpuru and Cecilia Rabell Romero, *Familia y vida privada en la historia de Iberoamérica* (Mexico City: El Colegio de México and Universidad Nacional Autónoma de México, 1996), 309–23.

99. For work on sexuality and sin, see Susan Migden Socolow, "Dos mujeres: Límites a la sexualidad femenina de Buenos Aires colonial," in O'Phelan Godoy et al., eds., *Familia y vida cotidiana*, 299–314; Ann Twinam, "Oficiales reales en el papel de 'casamenteros': Sexualidad, ilegitimidad y familia en Hispanoamérica borbónica," O'Phelan et al., eds.,

Familia y vida cotiadiana, 273–98; José Angel Rodríguez, *Babilonia de pecados: Norma y transgresión en Venezuela, siglo XVIII* (Caracas: Alfadil Ediciones, 1998). For marriage, see M. Mónica Ghirardi, *Matrimonios y familias en Córdoba, 1700–1850: Prácticas y representaciones* (Córdoba: Universidad Nacional de Córdoba, 2004); Pablo Rodríguez, *Sentimientos y vida familiar en el Nuevo Reino de Granada* (Bogotá: Ariel, 1977). An interesting bigamy case is the subject of Noble David Cook and Alexandra Parma Cook, *Good Faith and Truthful Ignorance: A Case of Transatlantic Bigamy* (Durham, N.C.: Duke University Press, 1991). For colonial family history, see Ana Inés Punta, *Córdoba borbónica* (Córdoba: Universidad Nacional de Córdoba, 1997); Ana María Bascary, *Familia y vida cotidiana: Tucumán a fines de la colonia* (Tucumán: Universidad Nacional de Tucumán, 1999); Pablo Rodriquez, ed., *La familia en Iberoamérica 1550–1980* (Bogotá: Universidad Externado de Colombia 2004); Guiomar Duenas Vargas, *Los hijos del pecado: Ilegitimidad y vida familiar en la Santa fe de Bogotá colonial* (Bogota: Editorial Universidad Nacional, 1997).

100. René Salinas Meza, "Espacio doméstico, solidaridades y redes de sociabilidad aldeana en Chile tradicional, 1750–1880," *Contribuciones Científicas y Tecnológicas: Area Ciencias Sociales y Humanidades* (Universidad de Santiago de Chile), 26:118 (1998): 1–19.

101. One exception to this statement is the article by Ann Twinam, "Estrategias de resistencia: Manipulación de los espacios privado y públicos por mujeres latinoamericanas de la época colonial," in Pilar Gonzalbo Aizpuru and Berta Ares Queija, eds., *Las mujeres en la construcción de las sociedades iberoamericanas* (Mexico and Seville: El Colegio de Mexico and Escuela de Estudios Hispanoamericanos, 2004), 251–69.

102. Pablo Rodríguez, *En busca de lo cotidiano: Honor, sexo, fiesta y sociedad, siglos XVII–XIX* (Bogotá: Universidad Nacional de Colombia, 2002); José Torre Revello, *Crónicas del Buenos Aires colonial*, 2nd ed. (Buenos Aires: Taurus, 2004); Carlos Mayo, ed., *Juego, sociedad y Estado en Buenos Aires, 1730–1830* (La Plata: Universidad Nacional, 1998); Rosa María Acosta de Arias Schreiber, *Fiestas Coloniales Urbanas: Lima, Cuzco, Potosí* (Lima: Editorial Logos, 1997).

103. Ward A. Stavig, "Violencia cotidiana de los naturales de Quispicanchis, Cañas, y Canchis en el siglo XVIII," *Revista Andina* 3:2 (1985): 451–68; Stavig, "Ladrones, cuatreros y salteadores: Indios criminales en el Cuzco rural a fines de la colonia," in Carlos Aguirre and Charles Walker, eds., *Bandoleros, abigeos y montoneros: Criminalidad y violencia en el Perú, siglos XVIII–XX* (Lima: Instituto de Apoyo Agrario, 1990), 69–103; Stavig, *The World of Túpac Amaru: Conflict, Community, and Identity in Colonial Peru* (Lincoln: University of Nebraska Press, 1999); Carmen Vivanco Lara, "Bandolerismo colonial peruano, 1760–1810: Caracterización de una respuesta popular," in Aguirre and Walker, *Bandoleros, abigeos y montoneros*, 25–56; Alberto Flores Galindo, "Bandidos de la costa," in Aguirre and Walker, *Bandoleros, abigeos y montoneros*, 57–68. See also Flores Galindo, *La ciudad sumergida: Aristocracia y plebe en Lima, 1760–1830*, 2nd ed. (Lima: Editorial Horizonte, 1991) for pioneering work on an urban lower sector.

104. Nelly Raquel Porro Girardi and Estela Rosa Barbero, *Lo suntuario en la vida cotidiana del Buenos Aires virreinal: De lo material a lo espiritual* (Buenos Aires, PRHISCO-CONICET, 1994); Aníbal Arcondo, *Historia de la alimentación en Argentina: Desde los orígenes hasta 1920* (Córdoba: Ferreyra, 2002). Perhaps because Arcondo was a colonial historian, more than half of the book deals with the colonial period.

105. Tamar Herzog, *Upholding Justice: Society, State, and the Penal System in Quito (1650–1750)* (Ann Arbor: University of Michigan Press, 2004); Osvaldo Barreneche, *Crime and the Administration of Justice in Buenos Aires, 1785–1853* (Lincoln: University of Nebraska Press, 2006); René Salinas Meza, "Orphans and Family Disintegration in Chile:

The Mortality of Abandoned Children, 1750–1930," *Journal of Family History* 16:3 (1991): 315–29; José Luis Moreno, "El delgado hilo de la vida: Los niños expósitos de Buenos Aires, 1779–1823," *Revista de Indias* 60:220 (2000): 663–85; Cynthia E. Milton, *The Many Meanings of Poverty: Colonialism, Social Compacts, and Assistance in Eighteenth-Century Ecuador* (Stanford, Calif.: Stanford University Press, 2007); Cynthia E. Milton, "Wandering Waifs and Abandoned Babes: The Limits and Use of Juvenile Welfare in Eighteenth-Century Audiencia of Quito," *Colonial Latin American Review* 13:1 (2004): 103–28; Bianca Premo, *Children of the Father King: Youth, Authority and Legal Minority in Colonial Lima* (Chapel Hill: University of North Carolina Press, 2005); Ondina E. González and Bianca Premo, ed., *Raising and Empire: Children in Early Modern Iberia and Colonial Latin America* (Albuquerque: University of New Mexico Press, 2007).

106. Susan M. Socolow, *Women of Colonial Latin America* (New York: Cambridge University Press, 2000); María Himelda Ramírez, *Las mujeres en la sociedad colonial de Santafé, 1750–1810* (Bogotá: Instituto Colombiano de Antropología, 2000); Jorge Augusto Gamboa, *El precio de un marido: El significado de la dote matrimonial en el Nuevo Reino de Granada: Pamplona, 1570–1650* (Bogota, 2003); Fernanda Gil Lozano et al., *Historia de las mujeres en la Argentina*, Vol. I: *Colonia y siglo XIX* (Buenos Aires: Taurus, 2000).

107. René Salinas Meza, "El ideario femenino chileno, entre la tradición y la modernidad: Siglos XVIII al XX," *Estudos CEDHAL* (Centro de Estudos de Demografia Histórica da América Latina, Universidade de São Paulo) 8 (1993).

108. Burkett, "Indian Women and White Society: The Case of Sixteenth-Century Peru." For Lower Peru, see Karen B. Graubart, *With Our Labor and Sweat: Indigenous Women and the Formation of Colonial Societyy in Peru, 1550–1700* (Stanford, Calif.: Stanford University Press, 2007); Karen B. Graubart, "Indecent Living: Indigenous Women and the Politics of Representation in Early Colonial Peru," *Colonial Latin American Review* 9:2 (2000): 213–35; Berta Ares Queija, "Mancebas de españoles, madres de mestizos: Imágenes de la mujer indígena en el Perú colonial temprano," in Gonzalbo and Queija, eds., *Las mujeres*, 15–39. The classic biography of the daughter of Francisco Pizarro and Quispe Sisa and granddaughter of the Inca Huayna Capac has been republished: María Rostworowski Tovar de Diez Canseco, *Doña Francisca Pizarro: Una ilustre mestiza, 1534–1598* (Lima: IEP, second edition, 2003). For Upper Peru, see Ana María Presta, "Portraits of Four Women: Traditional Female Roles and Transgressions in Colonial Elite Families in Charcas, 1550–1600," *Colonial Latin American Review* 9:2 (2000): 237–62; Presta, "Acerca de las primeras doñas mestizas de Charcas colonial, 1540–1590," in Gonzalbo and Queija, eds., *Las mujeres*, 41–62.

109. Kimberly Gauderman, *Women's Lives in Colonial Quito: Gender, Law, and Economy in Spanish America* (Austin: University of Texas Press, 2003); Jane Mangan, *Trading Roles: Gender, Ethnicity and the Urban Economy in Colonial Potosí* (Durham, N.C.: Duke University Press, 2005).

110. María Emma Mannarelli, *Private Passions and Public Sins: Men and Women in Seventeenth-Century Lima*, tr. Sidney Evans and Meredith D. Dodge (Albuquerque: University of New Mexico Press, 2007).

111. Lavallé, *Amor y opresión*; René Salinas Meza, "La violencia conyugal y el rol de la mujer en la sociedad chilena tradicional: Siglos XVIII y XIX," *Demografía, familia e inmigración en España y América* (Santiago: Universidad de Chile, Universidad de Santiago de Chile, Universidad Católica de Valparaíso, Universidad Metropolitana de Ciencias de la Educación y la Embajada de España, 1992), 117–33; René Salinas Meza and Igor Goicovic Donoso, "Amor, violencia y pasión en el Chile tradicional, 1700–1850," *Anuario Colombiano de Historia Social y de la Cultura* 24, (1997): 237–68; José Luis Moreno, "Conflicto y

violencia familiar en el Río de la Plata, 1770–1810," *Revista de Historia Social y de las Mentalidades* (Santiago) 6 (2002): 13–38; Viviana Kluger, *Escenas de la vida conyugal: Los conflictos matrimoniales en la sociedad virreinal rioplatense* (Buenos Aires: Editorial Quórum, 2003).

112. Bianca Premo, "From the Pockets of Women: The Gendering of the Mita, Migration and Tribute in Colonial Chucuito, Peru," *Americas* 57:1 (2000): 63–94; Guillermo Lohmann Villena and Enriqueta Vila Vilar, "Juana de Rojas: Una mujer emigrante, empresaria y matriarca del siglo XVII," in Gonzalbo and Queija, eds., *Las mujeres*, 87–101; Judith Farberman, "Los que se van y los que se quedan: Familia y migraciones en Santiago del Estero a fines del período colonial," *Quinto Sol* (Santa Rosa) 1:1 (1997): 7–40; Socolow, "Women and Migration in Colonial Latin America," in M. Anore Horton, ed., *New Perspective on Women and Migration in Colonial Latin America* (Princeton University, Program in Latin American Studies, Cuaderno 4, 2001), 1–20.

113. Socolow, "Women of the Frontier: Buenos Aires, 1740–1810 (or The Gaucho Turned Upside Down)," in Donna Guy, ed., *Contested Ground: Comparative Frontiers in the Greater South West and the Río de la Plata* (Tucson: University of Arizona Press, 1998), 67–82; Gregorio Saldarriaga, "Redes y estrategias femeninas de inserción social en tierra de frontera: Tres mujeres desarraigadas en Antioquia (siglo XVII)," in Gonzalbo and Queija, eds., *Las mujeres*, 141–61.

114. Gabriel Guarda, "Los cautivos en la guerra de Arauco," *Boletín de la Academia Chilena de. Historia* 54:98 (1987): 93–157; Susan M. Socolow, "Spanish Captives in Indian Societies: Cultural Contact along the Argentine Frontier, 1600–1835," *HAHR* 72:1 (1992): 73–99.

115. Ruth Behar, "Sexual Witchcraft, Colonialism, and Women's Powers: Views from the Mexican Inquisition," in Lavrin, ed., *Sexuality and Marriage*, 178–206.

116. Judith Farberman, "Sobre brujos, hechiceros y médicos: Prácticas mágicas, cultura popular y sociedad colonial en el Tucumán del siglo XVIII," *Cuadernos de Historia* (Córdoba) 4 (2001): 67–104; Farberman, "La hechicera y la médica: Prácticas mágicas, etnicidad y género en el Tucumán del siglo XVIII," in Gonzalbo and Queija, eds., *Las mujeres*, 163–92; Carlos Garcés, *Brujas y adivinos en Tucumán: Siglos XVII y XVIII* (Jujuy, Argentina: Universidad Nacional de Jujuy, 1997).

117. Pablo Rodríguez, "Servidumbre sexual: La prostitución en los siglos XV–XVIII," in Aída Martínez and Pablo Rodríguez, eds., *Placer, dinero y pecado: Historia de la prostitución en Colombia* (Bogotá: Aguilar, 2002), 67–89. In the same volume Rodríguez also considers Spanish mistresses (*mancebas*) as a forerunner of prostitution: Pablo Rodríguez, "Las mancebías españolas," 39–65.

118. Pilar Jaramillo de Zuleta, "Las 'arrepentidas,'" in Martínez and Rodríguez, eds., *Placer, dinero y pecado*, 91–128.

119. José Luis Moreno and José Antonio Mateo, "El 'redescubrimiento' de la demografía histórica en la historia económica y social," *Anuario IEHS* 12 (1997): 35–55.

120. For *porteño* urban society, see José Luis Moreno and Marisa M. Díaz, "Unidades domésticas, familias, mujeres y trabajo en Buenos Aires a mediados del siglo XVIII," *Entrepasados* (Buenos Aires) 8:16 (1999): 25–42. For rural society, see José Luis Moreno, "Población y sociedad en el Buenos Aires rural a mediados del siglo XVIII," *Desarrollo Económico* 29:114 (1989): 265–83. Both articles use the 1744 censuses of the region. Similar findings for eighteenth-century Bogotá are seen in Duenas Vargas, *Los hijos del pecado*.

121. Aníbal Arcondo, *La población de Córdoba según el empadronamiento de 1778* (Córdoba: Universidad Nacional de Córdoba, 1998); *La población de Córdoba en 1813* (Córdoba: Facultad de Ciencias Económicas, 1995).

122. César A. Garcia-Belsunce, *El pago de la Magdalena: Su población (1600–1765)* (Buenos Aires: Academia Nacional de la Historia, 2003); Dora Celton, *La población de la provincia de Córdoba a fines del siglo XVIII* (Buenos Aires: Academia Nacional de la Historia, 1993).

123. Linda Newson, *Life and Death in Early Colonial Ecuador* (Norman: University of Oklahoma Press, 1995), and Newson, *The Cost of Conquest: Indian Decline in Honduras under Spanish Rule* (Boulder: Westview Press, 1986).

124. Noble David Cook, *Demographic Collapse: Indian Peru, 1520–1620* (New York: Cambridge University Press, 1981).

125. Suzanne Austin Alchon, *Native Society and Disease in Colonial Ecuador* (New York: Cambridge University Press, 1991).

126. Noble David Cook and W. George Lovell, eds., *"Secret Judgments of God"; Old World Disease in Colonial Spanish America* (Norman: University of Oklahoma Press, 1991); Noble David Cook, *Born to Die: Disease and New World Conquest, 1492–1650* (New York: Cambridge University Press, 1998). See the articles by Linda A. Newson, "Old World Epidemics in Early Colonial Ecuador," 84–112; Juan A. Villamarín and Judith E. Villamarín, "Epidemic Disease in the Sabana de Bogotá, 1536–1810," 113–41; Brian M. Evans, "Death in Aymaya of Upper Peru, 1580–1623," 142–58; Suzanne Austin Alchon, "Disease, Population, and Public Health in Eighteenth-Century Quito," 159–82; and Fernando Casanueva, "Smallpox and War in Southern Chile in the Late Eighteenth Century," 183–212.

127. Suzanne Austin Alchon, *A Pest in the Land: New World Epidemics in a Global Perspective* (Albuquerque: University of New Mexico Press, 2003).

128. Aníbal Arcondo, "Mortalidad general, mortalidad epidémica y comportamiento de la población de Córdoba durante el siglo XVIII," *Desarrollo Económico* 33:129 (1993): 67–85.

129. Kendall Brown, "Workers' Health and Colonial Mercury Mining at Huancavelica, Peru," *The Americas* 57:4 (2001): 467–96; Scarlett O'Phelan Godoy, "Vivir y morir en el mineral de Hualgayoc a fines de la colonia," *Jahrbuch für Geschichte von Staat, Wirtschaft und Gesellschaft Lateinamerikas* 30 (1993): 75–127.

130. Nancy E. van Deusen, "The 'Alienated' Body: Slaves and *Castas* in the Hospital de San Bartolomé in Lima, 1680–1700," *The Americas* 56:1 (1999): 1–30; Susan Socolow, "Women and Health: Córdoba, 1815–1829," *Revista de la Junta Provincial de Historia de Córdoba* 21 (2004): 191–227; Kathryn Joy McKnight, "'En su tierra lo aprendió': An African *Curandero*'s Defense before the Cartagena Inquisition," *Colonial Latin American Review* 12:1 (2003): 63–84.

131. For both Upper and Lower Peru, see Noble David Cook, "Patrones de migración indígena en el Virreinato del Perú: Mitayos, mingas y forasteros," *Histórica* (Lima) 13:2 (1989): 125–52. For Cuzco, see Wightman, *Indigenous Migration and Social Change: The Forasteros of Cuzco, 1570–1720* (Durham, N.C.: Duke University Press, 1990). For the Audiencia of Quito, see Karen Vieira Powers, "The Battle for Bodies and Souls in the Colonial North Andes: Intraecclesiastical Struggles and the Politics of Migration," *HAHR* 75:1 (1995): 31–56; Powers, *Andean Journeys: Migration, Ethnogenesis, and the State in Colonial Quito* (Albuquerque: University of New Mexico Press, 1995); Gerardo Fuentealba, "Forasteros, comunidades indígenas, Estado y grupos de poder en la Audiencia de Quito, siglo XVIII," *Revista Ecuatoriana de Historia Económica* 4:8 (1990): 59–98. See also David J. Robinson, ed., *Migration in Colonial Spanish America* (Cambridge: Cambridge University Press, 1990), which includes Powers, "Indian Migration in the Audiencia of Quito: Crown Manipulation and Local Co-optation," 313–23; Ann Zulawski, "Frontier Workers and Social Change: Pilaya y Paspaya, Bolivia in the Early Eighteenth Century," 112–27; Ann M. Wightman, "' … Residente en esa ciudad … ': Urban Migrants in Colonial Cuzco," 86–111;

Brian M. Evans, "Migration Processes in Upper Peru in the Seventeenth Century," 62–85; Edda O. Samudio A., "Seventeenth-Century Indian Migration in the Venezuelan Andes," 295–312. At least one scholar has examined the effect of Indian immigration on Buenos Aires: Eduardo R. Saguier, "Economic Impact of Indian Inmigration and Commercial Capital on the Formation of a Colonial Labor Force: The Case of Buenos Aires in the Early Seventeenth Century," *Revista de Historia de América* (México) 101 (1986): 65–104.

132. Sarah Chambers, *From Subjects to Citizens: Honor, Gender and Politics in Arequipa, Peru 1780–1854* (University Park: Pennsylvania State Press, 1999); Arlene Diaz, *Female Citizens, Patriarch, and the Law in Venezuela, 1786–1904* (Lincoln: University of Nebraska Press, 2004); Christine Hunefeldt, *Paving the Price of Freedom: Family and Labor among Lima's Slaves 1800–1854* (Berkeley: University of California Press, 1994); Aline Helg, *Liberty and Equality in Caribbean Colombia: 1770–1835* (Chapel Hill: University of North Carolina Press, 2004); Walker, *Smoldering Ashes*.

CHAPTER 3

THE HISTORIOGRAPHY OF EARLY MODERN BRAZIL

STUART B. SCHWARTZ

While most scholars would agree that early modern Brazil stood in a classic colonial relationship to its metropole, Portugal, the peoples who lived in Brazil during its first 322 years believed for the most part that they resided in either the "State of Brazil" or the "State of Maranhão," parts of "*América portuguesa*," and only slowly did they perceive or think of their status as dependent or colonial. This point, emphasized recently by historian Laura de Mello e Souza, among others, places a renewed emphasis on perception and on the beliefs and understandings of the people in the past rather than on modern analytical labels and interpretations. In some ways it represents a shift in the writing and conceptualization of Brazil's early history.[1] While certainly not all scholars have abandoned the analytical category of "colonial Brazil," the new emphasis on contemporaneous ideas and patterns of thought is a change symbolic of a number of transformations in historical methods and approaches that have characterized the recent past of historical writing on Brazil prior to independence.

In the past two decades, the study of early modern Brazil in the United States has remained far behind that of Spanish America in popularity and publication for linguistic and geographical reasons as well, because there are far fewer Americans of Brazilian origin than there are persons of Hispanic descent. Globally, however, scholarship on the early modern era in Brazil has been booming since the 1980s. This trend has been influenced theoretically by developments in the social sciences and by the cultural turn in history, by new information technologies of digitalization and the internet, and by a series of centenaries that have generated institutional support for publications, conferences, and research.[2] This essay will identify a number of major themes and questions that have organized much of this historical production, note the major writings that have moved the field in new directions, and discuss the shifts in emphasis in historical inquiry by concentrating on some of the works that have been seminal in the study of colonial Brazil.

During the period from 1985 to 2010, Brazil commemorated both the quincentenary of 1492 and that of Cabral's voyage of 1500, which was part of the cycle of voyages initiated by Vasco da Gama in 1498 and extensively celebrated by Portugal's National Commission on the Discoveries, as well as the transfer of the Portuguese court to Brazil in 1808. These commemorations, as well as the centennial in 1988 of the abolition of slavery in Brazil, were not merely causes for national celebration, they were hotly debated and criticized and often served as outlets for frustration and condemnation by groups who felt betrayed by the subsequent history. Thus in Brazil, the general public turned toward Brazil's early history with renewed curiosity, as did a variety of groups and movements, from those seeking to advance indigenous peoples' rights to Afro-Brazilian political movements and those seeking political and economic change in a country with among the world's worst distributions of income.[3] But whatever the political motives of such questioning, the commemorations and anticommemorations focused attention on the course of Brazil's history, and in Brazil, Portugal, and elsewhere there was renewed interest in the first centuries of Brazilian history.[4] Probably the most important institutional results of this celebratory impulse for the study of early Brazil were the monographs, conferences, journals, and editions of classic texts and documents sponsored by various governmental and nongovernmental institutions in Brazil, as well as the extensive and valuable scholarly program supported by the Portuguese Commission on Discoveries.[5]

Also developing from the availability of resources and institutional support made possible by the quincentennial was the extensive project to microfilm and make available the documentary sources on colonial Brazil in foreign archives. This Projecto Resgate initiated its program by placing on CD-ROMs all of the materials related to Brazil in the Arquivo Histórico Ultramarino, Portugal's principal colonial archive, which has greatly facilitated research in one of the principal sources of early Brazilian history.[6] Along with this has been the development of a number of new online journals such as *Journal of Portuguese History* and *Almanack braziliense*, which have joined such first-rate historical journals as *Tempo* and *Topoi* (Rio de Janeiro), *Revista Brasileira de História*, *Vária História* (Minas Gerais), *Afro-Ásia* (Salvador), *Revista de História* (São Paulo), and *Anais de História de Além-mar* and *Penelope* (Lisbon), among others that consistently publish important work on colonial Brazil. There are now scholars who work on early Brazil in virtually every state of that country, and there are strong centers of colonial history based at the Cátedra Jaime Cortesão and the Laboratório de Estudos de Intolerância at the University of São Paulo, the Federal University of Rio de Janeiro, the Fluminense Federal University (Niterói), the Federal University of Minas Gerais, and the University of Campinas.

From Social to Cultural History

A Marxist or structuralist vision of Brazil prior to 1808 as a slave-based export economy tied to the developing merchant capitalism of an expanding Europe has been the paradigm dominating historical thinking about Brazil since the 1930s. Authors like Gilberto Freyre, Roberto Simonson, Caio Prado Jr., and Florestan Fernandes, not all of them Marxists, contributed in various ways to a vision of early Brazil that emphasized its patriarchal and semifeudal social relations, the "inescapable economic imperative" of slavery, and the negative aspects of its export orientation and dependence on world markets. This vision, closely related to dependency theory, had advantages. It provided a coherent interpretation of the Brazilian past that elided the vagaries of political chronologies, and it placed the continuing problems of economic dependency, class, and race at the heart of Brazilian history. This interpretation, emphasizing Brazil's colonial situation, oriented much of the work done from the 1960s to the 1980s and continues to influence scholarship today, but its emphasis on economic structures and on the commercial nature of the colony seemed to represent a certain kind of teleology that made Europe or the metropole the protagonist of colonial history. It also left out or downplayed large segments of the population, and it barely touched on issues such as sexuality, gender, belief systems, ritual, identity, and forms of representation, the themes and topics that preoccupied the new cultural history.

The reaction to this structuralist interpretation came in two stages. By the 1970s, there were a series of studies emphasizing the social contexts and activities of institutions and the composition and actions of various social groups such as merchants, cane farmers (*lavradores de cana*), sugar planters, New Christians, and free people of color. As part of the social history movement of the time, these studies were often characterized by a methodological focus on collective behaviors and uniformities that made the use of quantitative methods appealing, although Brazilian scholars often sought (with greater or lesser success) to avoid the worst deficiencies of North American positivism, which often seemed unaware of its ideological and methodological bias by turning to theories, usually of a Marxist origin. In many ways the social history movement in Brazil was not a rejection of the structuralist paradigm but a development within it that shifted focus to the colony itself and agency to local groups and individuals. By the 1980s, the move toward social history and economic history had generated a series of important studies of institutions and social groups that sought to examine the way in which collective historical actors responded to the structural constraints of the colonial regime. Nowhere was this more apparent than in the study of slavery, where a series of fundamental analyses of the slave system in the 1960s was followed in the 1970s and 1980s by an increasing production of studies of resistance, rebellion, family, demography, and manumission that emphasized slave action, resilience, and volition, what was called the "agency" of slaves, in the face of the structural limitations and asymmetries of power. These studies shifted focus to local conditions and individual or collective efforts in Brazil and away from the colonial system as a whole.[7] Methodologically, much work during this period continued to make use of quantitative analysis, and some of the best work was done in economic and demographic studies that lent themselves to that approach. Overall, the historiographical accomplishments of social history were impressive, and it had the advantage of demonstrating the complexity and contingency of history in which the dynamic interplay of social and political forces often challenged the predominant structuralist interpretation.

The social history movement in colonial Brazilian history was by the 1990s overtaken by a second wave of studies that demonstrated discontent with overarching interpretations that seemed to stress conformities, state power, and structural constraints on human action. Influenced by newer approaches in Europe and by gender studies, the history of *mentalités*, ethnohistory, and literary and cultural criticism, scholars in Brazil, as everywhere, began to turn to subjects such as childhood, the body, sexualities, language, representations, and identities. In this change of focus, Brazilians had their own endogenous precursors, especially in the work of the polyfaceted social anthropologist Gilberto Freyre, whose fascination with a range of topics from family to sexuality and table manners had been a kind of cultural history *avant la lettre* and whose legacy within Brazilian cultural life is still greatly debated.[8] The cultural history movement in Brazil, however, has not replaced the social history of the previous decade but has rather expanded it, and has offered a variety of opportunities for combinations and methodological hybridities of various types.

Two large collaborative projects announced and ratified the cultural turn that Brazilian historiography had been taking since the mid-1980s. The *História da vida privada* (4 vols., 1997) under the general direction of Fernando A. Novais was based on an earlier French collection on the same theme. The volume dedicated to the colonial era included many of the major Brazilian historians who had been moving from social to cultural history. The essays in this volume emphasized aspects of family life, sexuality, material culture, and religiosity. Subsequently, the two-volume collection *Festa* published in 2002 marked another aspect of the cultural turn by emphasizing festivals, processions, public displays, and other ludic activities that cultural historians have emphasized as revelatory of deeper cultural understandings.[9] Together these volumes served as benchmarks for the cultural turn in colonial Brazilian historiography. Cultural history in the study of early Brazil has not taken much of a "linguistic turn" and has remained closely allied with social history, and both have remained under the shadow of, or at least have been influenced by, the structuralist visions of the Brazilian past. Thus, even when seeking to overturn aspects of those interpretations, the terms and agendas of the debates continue to be those developed in the mid-twentieth century: the place of the colony in a global mercantile system, the role of the state and its relationship to local power, the asymmetry of social relations, and the form and function of slavery as an economic system and a determinant of human relationships and attitudes. Concern with the private sphere and intimate life, however, has developed alongside the more traditional concern with the public sphere, and the two have tended to become analytically joined. Finally, it is important to note here that colonial Brazilian historiography, like that of Spanish America, has been strongly influenced by Anglo-American social history, by Italian microhistory, and by French social and cultural historiography, but it has also been considerably impacted in the past two decades by the rebirth of early modern history in post-Salazar Portugal, a singular development that has greatly enriched and deepened analysis of Portugal and its empire, including Brazil. This essay examines the historiographical trends in this period by examining four important themes around which much of the historical writing of the last two decades has centered.

The Return of the Natives

The quincentenaries of Columbus' first voyage (1992) and Cabral's landing in Brazil (2000) provided a stimulus to new interest in the histories of the native peoples of Brazil. At a time when tribal indigenous people and languages have been increasingly marginalized but during which the self-identification of rural people as Indians has grown due to legal advantages in land acquisition and to their search for improved ethnic or economic status, the historiography related to the indigenous peoples of Brazil in the colonial era entered into a period of increasing sophistication. Their increasingly prominent place in the scholarly literature now more adequately reflects their importance in the early stages of the colony's formation. A turning point was surely the publication of *História dos índios do Brasil* (1992), edited by the anthropologist Manuela Carneiro da Cunha. Concentrating on Amazonia but with articles on other regions as well, it was an intentional effort to bring historians and anthropologists together in a common project, but without a unifying method or approach. That volume was followed in 1999 by the *Cambridge History of the Native Peoples of the Americas, Vol. III: South America*, which included broad overviews of Brazilian indigenous history by Brazilian and foreign scholars such as Robin Wright, John Monteiro, and Manuela Carneiro da Cunha. Both of these works reflected a movement away from, but not a rejection of, structuralist approaches, or at least their integration into methods that might be broadly termed ethnohistorical.[10] Nevertheless, the *Cambridge History* was attacked by those who insisted on seeing Indians only as victims or as subjects of colonial policy.[11]

John Hemming's *Red Gold: The Destruction of the Brazilian Indians* (1978) set out in broad detail that sad story, and his subsequent volume has taken the story from the mid-eighteenth to the twentieth century.[12] John Monteiro's *Negros da terra* (1998) was a major contribution on Indian societies and their contact with the Portuguese in southern Brazil.[13] Bringing together historical and ethnological materials, Monteiro emphasized the integration of indigenous peoples into the colonial economy and the importance of Indian labor as a stage in southern Brazil's development, just as earlier work had done for the Northeast.[14] The study of early contact has been enhanced by new editions of classic texts such as those of Fernão Cardim and Simão de Vasconcellos. Notable among them is Whitehead and Harbsmeier's study and edition of Hans Staden's classic account, which emphasizes its ethnographic value in both text and illustrations.[15] There has also been a resurgent interest in *La France antarctique*, the French outpost in Guanabara Bay, and by extension in the French attempts to explore and exploit the Brazilian coast.[16] Leyla Perrone Moisés presents an interesting literary and historical analysis of the early voyage of Paulmier de Gonneville in 1503–05. The work of Frank Lestringant has been particularly important in stimulating a renewed interest in France Antarctique and in the question of perception and representation of the Tupi and especially their practice of cannibalism.[17] On the later French colony in Maranhão that failed, Andrea Daher has written a close analysis of the Capuchin missionaries and their encounter with the indigenous inhabitants that reflects recent cultural and religious approaches used in Early Modern European studies.[18]

To some extent the reinvigoration of studies of indigenous history in Brazil was stimulated by important modern ethnographic studies by anthropologists who were aware of the historical sources and chronicles of the early contacts but whose own work also gave new direction and impulse to historians to return to classic texts with a new focus. Important in this regard were the studies of Eduardo Viveiros de Castro on violence and cannibalism and Hélène Clastres on Tupi-Guarani messianism.[19] Whereas the Tupinamba and Tupinikin and other related groups and their contacts with the Europeans in the sixteenth century had dominated the historiography of the previous generation of scholars, serious and innovative work has been emerging in the last twenty years on non-Tupi speakers and on the later periods of conquest and contact. There has been interesting work on the Taiririu Tapuya in Dutch Brazil.[20] Pedro Puntoni's *A guerra dos bárbaros: Povos indígenas e a colonização do sertão nordeste do Brasil, 1650–1720* (2000) examined the opening of the *sertão* of Pernambuco, Paraíba, and Rio Grande do Norte. Its detailed account of the expeditions in the conquest of the *sertão* and the destruction of its peoples is a chronicle of the last half of the seventeenth century. Marcos Galindo has examined the opening of the cattle frontier on the São Francisco in the *sertão* of Rodelas and the efforts of Capuchins and Jesuits to carry out missionary efforts there.[21] Two important studies by Langfur and Espindola have examined the penetration of the Rio Doce into Minas Gerais and the resistance of the Grens or Botocudos in the eighteenth and nineteenth centuries.[22] These studies demonstrate that the penetration of the *sertão* was discontinuous, the colonial territory not contiguous, and that large patches of territory remained outside of colonial control well into the nineteenth century. The extension of that control and the process of contact were taken up in new studies of *bandeirismo* in a special issue of *The Americas* published in 2005.[23] Langfur and Schwartz have examined the still mostly understudied relations between indigenous peoples and Afro-Brazilians, a theme also taken up by Santos Gomes, and Alida Metcalf has suggested that indigenous millenarian ideas were eventually shared by fugitive African slaves as well.[24] Mary Karasch in a number of detailed studies on the opening of the Brazilian Far West has given great attention to the dynamic relationships and creation of identities among whites, Indians, and Africans on the frontier.[25]

The definition of religion in the process of missionary contact has become a major focus in many studies. Christina Pompa's *Religião como tradução: Missionários, Tupi e Tapuia no Brasil colonial* emphasizes the "translation" of symbolic meanings in the effort to transform the universe of indigenous peoples. The study of the missionary effort itself has been transformed from an exercise of filial piety to a study of interaction, failures, adjustments, and compromises. Dauril Alden's *The Making of an Enterprise* (1996) has provided a baseline study of the Jesuits in the Portuguese empire that places Brazil in a global context. New work like that of Charlotte de Castelnau-L'Estoile's *Les Ouvriers d'une vigne sterile: Les Jésuites et la conversion des Indiens du Brésil 1580–1620* (Lisbon: Fondation Gulbenkian, 2000) has taken on the question of conversion in the period after the great successes of the initial contact when spiritual victories were more fleeting and when the ardor of the missionaries and their personal qualities no longer matched their task. Focus has also been narrowed from the vision and objectives of the missionary enterprise to the everyday realities of life in the *aldeias*.[26] An excellent example is Celestino de Almeida's study of the functioning of the indigenous villages in Rio de Janeiro. Her attention to their integration into the local labor market, as well as the creation of new identities as a result of the mixing and fusion of groups under missionary control, underlines the thrust of the recent studies toward cultural as well as material aspects of indigenous life in the colonial setting. Forced adaptation to European models, however, is only part of the story of contact. João Azevedo Fernandes has emphasized the active role of Tupinamba women and institutions of marriage and kinship in creating cultural spaces of interaction during the first generations of contact.[27]

Studies on Indians and Indian-Portuguese relations in the eighteenth century have had a strongly regional concentration on the Amazonian region. Perhaps the most ambitious study is that of Rita Heloísa de Almeida on the Directory system and the secularization of the missions, which uses Pará and Maranhão as its geographical focus.[28] That period is also the focus of Angela Domingues, Patricia Melo Sampaio, and Barbara A. Sommer, who have all produced studies of the Pombaline reforms and their sweeping effects on the indigenous populations of the region.[29] Indian resistance to Portuguese pressures and policy shifts has been studied by Santos, while Nadia Farage in an excellent study has examined the situation of indigenous peoples in the frontiers of the Rio Branco caught between the competing aims and demands of the Portuguese, Dutch, and Spanish colonial regimes.[30]

The shift toward cultural studies and toward cultural interactions has found in the exchanges and conflicts between Europeans and native peoples an ideal arena for study. Rolando Vainfas's *A heresia dos índios* (1995) on the syncretic *santidade* movement among the Indians of Bahia emphasized its fusion of religious elements in a movement of resistance against the colonial regime. This same theme in regards to *santidade* was taken up by Alida Metcalf in her study of cultural go-betweens in the first century of contact.[31] The Inquisition trials on which their studies are based provide fascinating evidence of syncretism and cultural "passing," but need to be contextualized within the peculiar genre of "renegade" confessions in which those returning to the church always tell a tale of separation because of necessity or adversity and then return because of conviction.

The cultural turn has allowed for a refocusing on various themes. The concern with language and its manipulation has found resonance in the work of João Adolfo Hansen on the early perception of indigenous languages and in Bessa Freire's work on linguistic strategies in Amazonia, but it also underlies the interpretative structure of Claudia Pompa's study of interaction and catechism in the first century of contact.[32] Representation, another concern of cultural historians, has also generated a series of new studies on the way in which America and its native inhabitants were described, portrayed, and analyzed by European observers.[33]

Indigenous peoples were often treated along with the flora and fauna as part of the natural history of Brazil and, like them, an obstacle to progress. Environmental history is still in its infancy in Brazil, but the pioneering work of Warren Dean on the Atlantic forest, which included much on its indigenous inhabitants, is now beginning to attract followers. José Augusto Pádua has examined environmental thought from the late eighteenth century to the period of the Republic, and Shawn Miller has examined both the forests and the mangroves of Bahia from an environmental and economic perspective.[34] This field is poised to grow in importance in the next decade.

Afro-Brazilian Life and Culture

The centenary of abolition in 1988 seemed to represent a culmination of interest in the topic of slavery and Afro-Brazilian culture, but the field has continued to flourish and has taken a number of new directions, although students of the nineteenth century have been more active than colonial historians.[35] The important quantitative studies of the 1970s and 1980s by scholars like Robert Slenes, Manolo Florentino, Mary Karasch, and Katia Queirós de Mattoso and her students have resulted in a continuing series of studies, usually with a strong regional focus. Excellent books of the 1980s, like Leila Algranti's study of urban slavery in Rio de Janeiro or Silvia Lara's on the violence of slavery in Campos de Goitacases, demonstrated the continuity of this tradition.[36] Minas Gerais has been particularly favored in the number and quality of studies on slavery. Take, for example, Kathleen Higgins's *Licentious Liberty*, a study of slavery in Sabará (Minas Gerais) that includes analyses of manumission, godparentage, and other subthemes, all developed during the expansion of slavery studies and the turn toward slave actions and agency, or Eduardo Paiva França's analysis of slave strategies to gain and enjoy freedom based on wills and testaments, or the work of Douglas Libby on manumission and demography, and Donald Ramos on the slave family.[37] The

1990s witnessed a continuation of important studies in this mode. José Roberto Góes' study of slavery in the captaincy of Rio de Janeiro was an imaginative exploration of the operation of godparentage and family organization among slaves, which was expanded in his later book coauthored with Manolo Florentino.[38] Robert Slenes did similar work on imperial era São Paulo, but with implications for the colonial period as his own work turned increasingly from social-demographic to cultural history.[39] Excellent studies, like Elizabeth Kuznesof and José Flávio Mota on São Paulo and Sheila Faria de Castro on Campos de Goitacases, have demonstrated the pervasive influence of slavery on all social groups and on the dynamic of colonial life.[40]

Not all recent work has focused on the slaves themselves. The meanings and implications of slavery have been the subject of two important studies of Rafael Marquese on the question of slave management, and a number of studies have examined the meanings of color and race in colonial society.[41] Some of the most innovative quantitative work has been done on Minas Gerais and on southern Brazil, both on slavery and on free persons of color. Laird Bergad has done an impressive study on Minas Gerais that has undercut the vision of slavery there as a contracting institution in the decline of the mining economy, while Herbert Klein has by himself and in a number of studies with Clothilde Paiva explored both slavery and the *libertos* (freed persons) in Minas Gerais and São Paulo. Klein and Francisco Vidal Luna have demonstrated the importance of slavery in the economy of São Paulo, but also the fact that slave marriages were far more frequent in this region than elsewhere in Brazil, pointing out that this situation had an impact on the legal status and role of freed persons in the region.[42]

Along with the continuing and strong tradition of social and economic studies of slavery as an institution and of slaves as human actors, the historiography of slavery has continued to broaden, and an Atlantic dimension has become increasingly important in the way in which historians of Brazil approach the history of slavery in its economic and social as well as its political dimensions. This framework, of course, was inherent in the topic and was clearly marked out in Charles Boxer's excellent study of *Salvador de Sá and the Struggle for Brazil and Angola* (1952) and in Pierre Verger's classic on the flow of people and culture between Bahia and the Bight of Benin (1968), but with the publication of John Thornton's *Africa and Africans*, Joseph Miller's *Way of Death*, and Luiz Felipe Alencastro's *Trato dos viventes*, a renewed recognition was given to the integrated nature of the Portuguese South Atlantic, where slaves moved continually from Africa to Brazil, administrators often circulated from Brazil to Africa, and imperial policies were usually conceived with an attention to the interdependency of the two colonial spheres.[43] Of course, the South Atlantic dimension naturally carries over into the newer studies of the slave trade, like Jaime Rodrigues's *De costa a costa* (2005) which deals with the crews, slave and free, on the ships in the Angola-to-Brazil slave route in a book that parallels in some ways the work on the North Atlantic of Marcus Rediker and Peter Linebaugh.[44]

This Atlantic dimension is also a fundamental aspect of the new cultural histories linked to diaspora studies of African and Afro-American themes. Much of this work has centered on the task of demonstrating the transference and persistence of specific African ethnicities, religions, or cultural practices, and a rejection of creolization as the most useful way of conceptualizing the formation of Afro-Brazilian culture.[45] Daniela Calainho and to a lesser extent James Sweet have used Inquisition cases involving witchcraft and heresy to reveal African practices, although, in fact, because of Portuguese folk practices it is very difficult at times to distinguish whether the origins of certain amulets and rites of divination are African or European.[46] Joao José Reis's study of the Bahian Malê revolt of 1835 and subsequent work continued a Bahian tradition of concern with aspects of African culture in Brazil but has also served as a point of departure and an example for the recent wave of interest.[47] Among the best of these studies have been Mariza de Carvalho's *Devotos de cor* on the black sodalities of *minas* (Gbe and Yoruba speakers) in Rio de Janeiro and her exploration of other ethnic and religious groups.[48] While these studies have deepened our understanding of the African aspect of Afro-Brazilian culture, they have sometimes enthusiastically pushed beyond the evidence substantiating continuities and have been unwilling to recognize that other "colonial" identities based on color, status, or place of birth sometimes trumped African ethnic associations.

The Africanist and creole viewpoints sometimes provide the basis for quite different interpretative strategies. Take, for example, Marina de Mello e Souza's study of the tradition among various black brotherhoods of the crowning of kings and queens of the Congo. Her study of the practice concentrates on the history of the Kongo kingdom and its contact with Portuguese Catholicism in her search for the roots of the tradition in Brazil, but Elizabeth Kiddy in her study of the brotherhoods of the Rosary in Minas Gerais, while not dismissing African influences, presents considerable evidence that the origins of the practice lie in Catholic traditions associated with the cult of Our Lady of the Rosary itself rather than in Africa, and that in Minas Gerais these brotherhoods were not organized by African ethnicity but by color. Silvia Lara's study shows how the religiosity and ritual of Afro-Brazilians in their brotherhoods and in the crowning of kings and queens can be woven into the fabric of a larger discussion of Brazilian cultural history.[49]

One very positive result of the renewed interest in slaves and their descendants as historical agents and of the concerns of cultural history with identity and representation has been a number of works that reconstruct the lives of individual Afro-Brazilians and through them the social relations and beliefs of their times. Luiz Mott's biography of a previously unknown black street prophet and popular "saint" in eighteenth-century Rio de Janeiro, discussed below, and Junia Furtado's study of the mythically famous Chica da Silva, "queen" of the diamond district of Minas Gerais, are fine examples of the intersection of biography, microhistory, and cultural approaches to social history.[50]

Social and Cultural History

The growing interest in cultural history has not been limited to studies of Indians or Africans, and since the 1980s it has in various forms been used first as an adjunct to the history of Brazilian society and then increasingly as a method or approach in itself. Seeking to break with structuralist interpretations and hoping to reveal human agency, especially of those with little access to power, like slaves, women, and free persons of color, the new historiography has been able to move inquiry in new directions, but at the same time it has also allowed historians to reconsider important traditional questions from a new perspective. Take, for example, the issue of local power and the formation of regional elites within the imperial system. In a septet of stunning monographs, former diplomat Evaldo Cabral de Mello has traced the history of Pernambuco, concentrating on the major events (the Dutch occupation, 1630–54; the War of the Mascates, 1711–13; the movements for independence, 1817–1824), but he has really been preoccupied with the self-consciousness and self-representation of the dominant planter class of the region. It is the mentality and self-projected image of this class, rather than government or institutions, that serve as his focus, but a close appreciation of the regional economy and the structures of government is never far from the center of his analysis. Taken as a corpus, the works of Cabral de Mello must be seen as one of the major historiographical accomplishments of the last two decades and an effective demonstration of the relationship between cultural, social, and political history.[51]

Important work has been produced in the last two decades within the traditional contexts of twentieth-century scholarship. Study of the political configuration of Brazil and its place within the imperial rivalries of the seventeenth century has been advanced by a resurgence of interest in the union of Spain and Portugal (1580–1640) and its imperial implications.[52] Studies of the Brazilian economy continue to flourish. For the seventeenth century, Christopher Ebert's study of the sugar trade and Leonor Freire Costa's fundamental study of the Brazil Company's fleets and organization make the role of mercantile trade and the importance of merchants in defining Brazil's role in the empire clear, and Daviken Studnicki-Gizbert demonstrates the impact of Portuguese merchants in the broader Atlantic world.[53] For the eighteenth century, a fine collection edited by Júnia Furtado contains a number of articles linking Minas Gerais to the broader Atlantic system of commerce and politics, and her own earlier monograph examined the life and activities of a merchant of the period.[54] The works of Novais, Arruda, Valentim, and Pedreira on the Atlantic economy are essential in the interpretative debate on the end of the colonial regime in Brazil.

Law and legal institutions have also merited renewed interest. My own social history of the High Court (*Relação*) of Bahia and its judges has now been joined by Arno and Maria José Wehling's parallel study of the *Relação* of Rio de Janeiro, which delves far more deeply into the questions and origins of Portuguese law. Guilherme Pereira das Neves discusses the operation of the *Mesa da Consciência*, Portugal's council on religious matters, in the context of the dislocation of the Portuguese court to Brazil.[55] Questions of legal practice and legal culture are also primary in Linda Lewin's two-volume study of inheritance law and its changes.[56] The relationship of slaves and freed persons to the law and legal institutions has been explored by Russell-Wood but still awaits further study.[57] No one has yet tackled the great collection of court proccedings in the *arquivo dos feitos findos* in Lisbon, which contains much material on Brazil.

Urban history has merited continuing interest from a number of approaches. It is well represented by Nireu Cavalcanti's study of the construction, form, and social organization of eighteenth-century Rio de Janeiro, as well as by a detailed study of the development and construction of Recife under the Dutch by Nederveen Merkerk. The late Ilana Blaj's study of the networks of power and trade in the transformation of São Paulo into an important regional center shows that access to indigenous laborers and the internal market were crucial factors in that process.[58] Rio de Janeiro and its governance has been the focus of the work of Fernanda Bicalho and Maria da Fátima Gouvêa, who have used it as a vantage point from which to examine the question of municipal power and imperial governance in general.[59] Small towns also have their historians. Laurant Vidal's model study of the town and inhabitants of Mazagão, a Portuguese outpost in Morocco transplanted to the Amazon, is a true Atlantic odyssey. Nestor Goulart Reis has continued his contributions in this area with a volume of town plans and views of the colonial cities.[60] Cláudia Damasceno Fonseca has provided a detailed study of the formation of the urban network of Minas Gerais and the use of space within the towns that unites geographical and social analyses.[61] Urban institutions have also received new attention. C.R. Boxer used Salvador in his comparative study of the *câmaras* (town councils) in various parts of the Portuguese empire, and Isabel dos Guimarães Sá did the same in her book on the charitable brotherhoods of the *Misiericórdia* found throughout the Portuguese empire.[62]

The history of the great estates has continued, although it has only slowly emerged from the long shadow of Gilberto Freyre's cultural interpretation from the *varanda* of the plantation house. Sugar has been a major focus, and a number of studies have centered on Bahia. Vera Ferlini's study of the cane farmers (*lavradores de cana*) broke new ground, and my own book on Bahian sugar society was an attempt to break away from a planter-dominated view of that history by examining other rural classes as well. B. J. Barickman has pushed the Bahian story into the nineteenth century and expanded its focus to include social relations in other agricultures. Pernambuco, except for the Dutch period, has not had similar attention. An important and somewhat overlooked study by Jean Baptiste Nardi on tobacco cultivation and commerce demonstrates that there is still much to be done on economic activities other than sugar. For example, tanneries (*curtumes*), colonial Brazil's first industry, have never been studied. Still, the great latifundia and their generations of owners continue to fascinate some historians, as Moniz Bandeira's volume on the lands of Garcia D'Avila shows.[63]

Perhaps one of the most important developments in social history has been the concern with the poor nonslave sectors of the population. The breakthrough book in this regard was Laura de Mello e Souza's *Os desclasificados do ouro* (1982), which examined the poor of Minas Gerais in its age of opulence, but other scholars like Iraci del Nero da Costa and Maria Luiza Marcilio were also working on the mass of the free and freed population, often using census materials and other quantitative sources to examine the Brazilian peasantry. In the context of Brazil, however, such studies always raised the issue of the relationship between slave and free labor and between peasants and slaves. The complexity of those relationships, the commonality of slaveholding by relatively poor people or by ex-slaves, and the long-term impact of the export economy on all social relations have raised provocative questions about the concept of "subalternity" in the context of a racially divided slave society.[64]

The private sphere and topics such as family, gender, and sexuality have been a principal venue for the close relationship of social and cultural history. The work of Muriel Nazzari on the changing importance of the dowry in colonial São Paulo as a way of gauging the changing status of women remains a model of imaginative research, as does Alida Metcalf's community study of family structure and change in the Paulista frontier community of Santana de Parnaíba. The works on family history by Mesquita, Marcilio, and Nizza da Silva all grew out of the social science tradition.[65] But the related themes of gender and sexuality have opened questions about attitudes and representations to be considered along with law, norms, and practices. Ronaldo Vainfas has written a key work on sexuality and intimate life, and Luiz Mott has written a series of works on lesbianism, homosexuality, pederasty, and other aspects of what was considered deviant sexuality that has been especially sensitive to its interplay with asymmetries of class and race.[66] In 1993, Luciano Figueiredo published a fine study of lower-class women in Minas Gerais that provided great detail on their role in the economy as well as on their sexuality in the social science tradition, and in that same year Leila Algranti published a book on the ideology and interior life of cloistered women and Mary del Priore in her *Ao sul do corpo* attempted to deal with social and theological attitudes about women's bodies as well as with women's own perceptions.[67] Since then, women's history has become a field of growing complexity, as the studies that serve as the basis for Nizza da Silva's able overview demonstrate.[68]

Religiosity has been an area in which cultural approaches have had a particularly strong impact. The history of religion is no longer exclusively a history of the institutional church or of missionary activities. The concept of "popular" religion, as an aspect of a putative "popular culture," has become a major focus of theoretical concern. It is increasingly clear that the first formulation of a "popular religion" as distinct from an official cult was too crude or simple a conceptualization, and that there were often variations between religion as prescribed and religion as practiced that were expressed sometimes in terms of region, sometimes in terms of class, and sometimes as simply changing over time.[69] Influenced by the thinking of Roger Chartier, Peter Burke, Adriano Prosperi, and Carlo Ginzburg, scholars of the Brazilian past are now writing a far fuller and more integrated kind of history of religion. We can start with some essential overviews.[70] Caio Boschi's chapters

"O enquadramento religioso," on ecclesiastical administration, missionary activity, religious orders, the Inquisition, and lay religiosity, in the *Historia da expansão portuguesa*, vols. 2 and 3 (1998), now provide an excellent entry point into the religious history of empire, especially from the Catholic side. Added to this is the now fundamental *Historia religiosa de Portugal*, with excellent articles not only on the formal institutions of the church and its relationship to the state but also on the spaces, sociability, and practices of popular religion, or what it calls "O Deus de todos os dias." These general surveys serve as a starting point to which can be added Luiz Mott's "Cotidiano e vivencia religiosa: Entre a capela e o calundu" in the *História da vida privada* (vol. 1, 1997), as well as the chapters in the same collection by Mary del Priore and Ronaldo Vainfas, which deal with syncreticism and with practices and customs specific to Brazil.[71] Together, these essays now provide an excellent introduction to the various dimensions of colonial religious life.

The old division between a normative European Catholicism and its deformation in colonial areas by the attempts of missionaries to inculcate it among "savage" peoples has undergone considerable rethinking. We now know that bringing post-Trentine Catholicism to the European laity in places like Beira Baixa, Galicia, and Apulia was often as frustrating and difficult as the attempts to inculcate orthodox practice in the overseas missions, and in some respects not much different than converting the heathen of Mexico or Maranhão.[72] The history of the missions in Brazil, above all those of the Jesuits, has been considerably advanced in recent years. Dauril Alden's monumental *The Making of an Enterprise* gives us an empirewide vision of the Society of Jesus in the Portuguese world exhaustive in detail and broad in scope. There have also been fine studies of particular areas and periods like that of Castelnau-L'Estoile, or José Eisenberg's study of the political ideology of the Brazilian Jesuit missions.[73] The other Brazilian orders—Carmelites, Benedictines, Franciscans, and others—have not, as a whole, fared as well.

The important subject of religious fusion, overlapping, and syncreticism has witnessed a virtual explosion in Brazil. Two fundamental books of Laura de Mello e Souza on popular religion, witchcraft, and the devil demonstrate how a European vision (*olhar*) of the Inquisitors was imposed on the multicultural American reality.[74] Her work has been made even more intelligible by the excellent studies of J. Paiva and F. Bethencourt on the concept of witchcraft in metropolitan Portugal itself. Paiva's work is especially important because it points out that many practices condemned by the church were prosecuted by the episcopal courts rather than the Inquisition, so that sorcery and magic were, in fact, a far more widespread problem than the statistics of the Inquisition alone might lead us to believe.[75]

We now have studies in depth of syncretic religious practice in Brazil like Vainfas's *A heresia dos indios* (1995) on *santidade*, an anticolonial messianic movement among the Tupinamba and some *mamelucos* in late-sixteenth- and early-seventeenth-century Bahia. While, John Thornton's *The Kongolese Saint Anthony*, on a syncretic movement to restore the Kingdom of Kongo, led by a Kongolese woman, Dona Beatriz Kimpa Vita, at the end of the seventeenth century.

reminds us that an imperial or European transatlantic perspective is not the only requirement for understanding the dimensions of hybridity and religiosity. Such influences could, like people, move from one imperial region to another.[76]

The cultural history of popular religion draws on Emile Durkheim and on Clifford Geertz's emphases on ceremony, ritual, and spectacle as demonstrations of projects of social reality and social possibilities. Here an attention to social and economic considerations might be especially useful. Increased urbanization and the wealth in cities like Salvador, Ouro Preto, and Rio de Janeiro allowed for traditional religious and secular forms such as saint's-day processions or viceregal entries to be aesthetically and culturally elaborated. In that sense, popular religion and politico-administrative history were intimately tied together in the historical process.[77] Mary Del Priore has produced a short introduction to these public festivals, and the two substantial volumes of *Festa* (2001) organized by István Jancsó and Iris Kantor contain outstanding examples of the religious and social themes that can be developed from such materials.[78] The critical edition of the 1676 panegyric biography and funeral description of the Visconde de Barbacena provides an example of the kind of texts that can be used for this purpose, but the study of the Corpus Christi processions by Beatriz Cruz Santos is the most complete study of these activities in colonial Brazil to date.[79]

One area in the history of religion in Brazil that has seen great expansion in recent decades has been studies of the Inquisition. This scholarship was based on a firmer quantitative understanding of the Inquisition's operation in Portugal and on a better understanding of its operations in comparison with civil courts or with the judicial process in other countries.[80] The measure of the Inquisition's rigor is always dependent on what numbers and what groups are placed in the denominator in any measure of the tribunal's operations. But the new interest in the Inquisition as institution and its exploitation by historians as a vast documentary resource has produced positive results. A work like Francisco Bethencourt's comparison of the Spanish, Portuguese, and Italian Inquisitions facilitates sounder cross-national comparisons.[81]

In Brazil, Inquisition studies have taken a number of new directions. The earlier and fundamental work of Sonia Siqueira and Anita Novinsky and the publication of the various inquisitorial visits to Brazil had already established an excellent foundation for understanding both the institution and its effects. More recently, Anita Novinsky and her students like Tucci Carnero and Lina Gorenstein Ferreira da Silva have shown that the Holy Office continued operations primarily against New Christians well into the eighteenth century, especially in Minas Gerais and Rio de Janeiro, and they have argued that its operations had important social and economic effects.[82] But it also must be acknowledged that the predominant interest of the Portuguese Inquisition in "New Christians," and the question of whether they were really Jews or not, has also at times had a curious impact on Brazilian scholarship. Other studies demonstrate that the Holy Office also remained active in northeastern Brazil, as the work of Bruno Feitler on Paraíba and Luiz Mott on Maranhão and Sergipe makes clear.[83] How the tribunal of the Holy Office operated in the eighteenth century has been clarified by a careful quantitative study of its operations and its agents in Pernambuco by J. Wadsworth.[84] How the tribunal sought to suppress political as well as religious dissent at the close of the colonial era has been the object of a series of studies by the Canadian historian David Higgs.[85]

Parallel to this line of investigation on the political and social dimensions of the Inquisition has been the exploitation of Inquisition records to reveal much about popular practices and attitudes as well as religiosity, and a range of heterodox and heretical ideas. Two scholars, Gerardo Pieroni and Timothy Coates, both independently and in collaboration, have taken on the long-neglected topic of penal exile or *degredo* within the Portuguese empire, using the records of both civil and ecclesiastical courts.[86] Inquisition records reveal a great deal about orthodoxy and heterodoxy in the colony, where the opportunities for sexual license and exploitation paralleled and intersected with the power and status disparities according to gender, color, or ethnicity or were based on the civil status of slave and free. Such records allow a close understanding of the discrepancy between theology and practice.[87] My own study on attitudes of religious relativism or tolerance in the Luso-Hispanic Atlantic world defined by the Inquisition as heretical falls into this category.[88]

Inquisition records with their attention to situation and personal detail have also brought some remarkable individual cases to light that have served as the basis for a growing number of biographical studies. While not exactly achieving the fame or methodological subtlety of Ginzburg's *The Cheese and the Worms*, studies of these Brazilian cases offer fascinating views of the mental, social, and political contexts of their protagonists. We have, for example, two studies of Pedro Rates Henequim, a long-time resident in Minas Gerais, executed by the Inquisition in 1744; that of Freire Gomes emphasizes Henequim's heretical religious hybridity, while that of Adriana Romeiro concentrates on his millenarian ideas and political plotting.[89] There is also the remarkable "life and times" biography of an ex-slave street prophetess in eighteenth-century Rio de Janeiro done by Luiz Mott, who in other studies has explored the many varieties of popular dissidence and deviation from church norms.[90]

The growth of interest in the forms of Baroque expression, not only the spectacles, festas, and processions but also the arts and literature, and in the various dimensions of the Catholicism of the Counter-Reformation has enriched the field and added new dimensions to cultural and social history. Diogo Ramada Curto has provided a broad overview of intellectual production on an imperial scale.[91] The remarkable missionary, preacher, diplomat, and writer Padre Antônio Vieira has been the center of a whole new cultural, literary, and textual historiography that has analyzed and commented on his prophetic, political, and theological positions as well as his missionary activities.[92] The works of Vieira Nascimento, van den Besselaar, Muhama, Cohen, and Pécora, as well as the controversial essays by Alfredo Bosi on both Vieira and the Italian Jesuit Antonil, have refocused interest on the interplay of literature and history. Perhaps the outstanding examples of the beneficial union of literary analysis and history have been the works of João Adolfo Hansen, particularly his study of the seventeenth-century Bahian satiric poet and social critic

Gregório de Matos, and those of Alcir Pécora on Vieira and Baroque culture.[93] These works form part of the intellectual history of Brazil, a field that has been resuscitated and reinvigorated by the cultural turn. Iris Kantor's study *Esquecidos e renascidos* on the ephemeral Bahian literary societies of the eighteenth century has revealed a colonial elite searching in the study of history for its own place in the intellectual and social life of the colony.[94] Lilia Moritz Schwarcz's sumptuously produced volume on the transfer of the Portuguese court and the royal library from Lisbon to Rio de Janeiro provides a cultural history of both social and intellectual life when local elites and Portuguese courtiers were thrown together by the vissisitudes of the Atlantic revolutions.[95]

GOVERNING COLONIES

Given the turn toward cultural history, few people would have predicted two decades ago that administrative history would become a central focal point of new interpretations and controversy, but the dominant role that the state has always played in Brazilian history perhaps assured its principal role in the modern historiography as well. In Brazil as elsewhere, the past twenty years have witnessed a questioning of a narrative that makes the nation-state the invariable protagonist, especially in works dealing with the period of independence, but on the whole, scholars concerned with Brazil have not had to put the "state back in," since the social history approaches never dislocated it from consideration. Since Raimundo Faoro published *Os donos do poder* (1958), debate has centered on his interpretation of the state and its bureaucracy developing in opposition to society, as well as on various alternative interpretations in which the state is seen as representative or captive of particular interest groups in society. There were classic Anglo-American studies in the 1970s, such as those of Alden, Boxer, Maxwell, Russell-Wood, and Schwartz, that examined how local and regional powers sought to subvert or control state power or how institutions like charitable brotherhoods might reflect the struggle between public and private power. Despite the fact that the 1980s witnessed a move toward privatization and a withdrawal of the state from aspects of social and economic planning in contemporary Brazil, a concern with the state and its intersection with society has been at the heart of recent debates among historians of colonial Brazil. The predominant concept that has reigned in Brazil has been that of the "old colonial regime" developed by Fernando Novais in an often reprinted essay and in his monograph on the development of imperial thought in eighteenth-century Portugal.[96] Growing from the earlier Marxist interpretations of Caio Prado Jr., Novais's interpretation stressed the mercantilist nature of the colonial relationship, its dependence on coerced labor, and the inherent economic and thus social disadvantages in it for Brazil. It posited an inherently conflictive relationship between the colony and the metropolis while recognizing their changing interdependence, and it argued that the Portuguese mercantilist system had inherent contradictions that created an economic crisis resulting in the independence of Brazil. His thesis was sustained in a more quantitative and formal way in a series of studies by José Jobson de Andrade Arruda, and in works by other scholars who adopted the paradigm advocated by Novais and who bolstered his argument with a firm database drawn from trade statistics.[97]

This paradigm, however, has come under increasing scrutiny from a number of angles in the last two decades. First of all, a series of studies by Portuguese economic historians like Valentim Alexandre and Jorge Pedreira raised serious questions about the "inherent structural anomalies" of the Portuguese colonial system and have argued that whatever crisis characterized the relationship between metropole and colony at the beginning of the nineteenth century was due to the political events of 1807–08 and their economic effects and not to a systemic breakdown of colonialism.[98] Novais, Arruda, and others have not been willing to yield the field to this critique, and both sides have sought to reinforce their interpretation, integrating new studies such as Ernst Pijning's important work on contraband.[99] Another line of reinterpretation has come from João Fragoso and some of his colleagues in Rio de Janeiro. In a series of innovative and challenging studies, he has emphasized the autonomous growth of capital accumulation and political power within the colony, especially among the merchants of Rio de Janeiro, and has stressed the growth of local production and trade rather than international commerce as the driving force of that growth. This emphasis parallels the work of others on the internal economy and the importance of "peasant" farming in Brazil, although it strives more than others to break away from slavery's long shadow over the nature of colonial history. The interpretative problem is that the slave trade, slavery, latifundia, and the export economy were so intertwined with small-scale farming and the provisioning of cities and plantations that it is difficult to analytically separate the two aspects of the economy at any point.

Fragoso and his colleagues have also emphasized the origin, persistence, and importance of colonial groups in the institutions of government. To some extent, their emphasis has been made possible by the coming of age of a new generation of historians in post-Salazar Portugal whose reinterpretation of early modern Portugal has had direct implications for the study of Brazil. The Portuguese legal historian António Manuel Hespanha and a group of scholars associated with the Universidade Nova de Lisboa have set about reexamining basic institutions, structures and social groups of early modern Portugal. Hespanha's major study, *As vésperas do Leviathan*, while it did not address the overseas colonies at all, suggested that royal power and state resources remained limited well into the seventeenth century. Hespanha also penned a suggestive study using Marcel Mauss's concept of the gift to explain the essentially patrimonial nature of the royal dispensation of office and honor and the methods of rule in Early Modern Portugal.[100] These ideas provided a stimulus to Brazilian scholars who wished to emphasize the parallel situation in the colony, where local elites continued to exercise social and economic control and where the manipulative use of an economy of reward allowed an imperial system to integrate local elites. These scholars have also found particularly important a seminal essay by the Coimbra historian Joaquim Romero Magalhães emphasizing that membership in the Portuguese municipal councils (*conselhos, senados da câmaras*) created a kind of provincial nobility, with important social and political consequences.[101]

Drawing on these interpretative models and on work stressing the dynamic relation between the imperial center and its peripheries, a group of scholars mostly working on (and living in) Rio de Janeiro have challenged the Novais paradigm. Instead, they have suggested that a better way to understand Brazil is summarized in the term "the ancien régime in the tropics," emphasizing the adjustments and cooperation of certain groups in the colony with the imperial apparatus of government and thus breaking with a "dualist" and competitive structural model of colony versus empire. Among the major authors of this new school, João Fragoso has concentrated on the early manipulation of bureaucratic positions as a springboard to personal power and elite status among the first settlers of Rio de Janeiro, and then on the development of a local merchant class in the eighteenth century whose control of an ever more important local economy provided the basis of their wealth and authority. He has argued, however, that the continued investment of these elites in land and slaves, which were less profitable than commerce, indicates that their thinking was still precapitalist.[102] Fernanda Bicalho has examined the growth of local power as expressed by the *câmara* of Rio de Janeiro through the course of the eighteenth century, while the late Maria de Fátima Gouvêa studied the circulation of officials within the empire and the changing administrative forms used to incorporate Brazil into the imperial system.[103] The focus has been on local powers with aristocratic pretensions acting like a colonial nobility, but whether their proclamation of that status really qualified them as a nobility remains in question.

In any case, we are now fortunate to have a better baseline to evaluate such claims because our understanding of the role of the nobility in Portuguese and Brazilian society has been transformed by works like Mafalda Soares da Cunha's examination of the house of Bragança, and especially by the works of Nuno Freitas Monteiro. His carefully constructed and monumental analysis of the great Portuguese noble houses in the eighteenth century, their strategies, and their holdings, demonstrate the reasons why this social class remained politically powerful for so long. His work is suggestive in many ways of how the presence or absence of a nobility might be understood in the colonial context. That, in fact, is the subject of Nizza da Silva's book on the Brazilian aristocracy, which always sought to enjoy noble status.[104] The impulse to see the nobility as one among a number of potential elites—social, bureaucratic, and economic, both metropolitan and colonial—underlies a number of studies contained in the collection *Optima pars*, and this concept lies at the heart of a major tendency in the recent historiography of the social and political organization of the Portuguese empire and its component parts.[105] The studies of Gonçalves Monteiro on the nobility, Subtil on the Desembargo do Paço and the legal bureaucracy, Cardim on the Cortes and the court, Freire Costa on the fleets of the Brazil Company, and Fernanda Olival on the military orders have all opened new perspectives on the functioning of the Brazilian colony within the parameters and models of the metropolis, although the first generation of their works were about Portugal, not its colonies.[106] That too is now changing. A major research effort has been mounted on elites in the Ibero-American world that now integrates Brazilian, Portuguese, and Spanish historians. That project has also produced an excellent proposographical study of all of the governors and captains-major of the Portuguese Atlantic empire in the seventeenth and eighteenth centuries.[107] But in a similar fashion, Brazilian scholarship is repaying its debt to Portugal with fine books of cultural history on early modern Portugal produced by Brazilian historians.[108]

The interpretative dispute about administration and the nature of authority in which some authors focus on the conflictive nature of the relation between colony and metropolis and others on the collaborative relation between local elites and imperial government has generated a great deal of renewed interest in the nature of government and rule. A number of conference volumes have been published centered on these themes, and various historical journals have dedicated issues to the theme of colonial administration.[109] Laura de Mello e Souza has addressed the question directly in a series of essays drawing on her work in Minas Gerais, and has suggested that the slave-based nature of Brazilian society marked it so profoundly that labels such as "ancien régime" are not particularly helpful in understanding its dynamic and an overemphasis on the legal arrangements of power results in a misleading image of colonial reality, but hers is surely not the last volley in this exchange.[110] These exchanges have demonstrated how the historians of early modern Brazil have been drawn into increasingly transnational, global, and imperial contexts, whether the particular focus is a south Atlantic system that links Brazil to Angola and West Africa or the intertwined histories of the empires of Portugal and Spain during the first age of globalization.[111] The history of early modern Brazil can no longer be written in isolation from these other perspectives, nor can those broader histories ignore Brazil and its historiographies.

The period from the fall of Pombal to Brazilian independence and the formation of a nation-state has now become a focus of intense interest. The debates focus on the nature of the economic crisis of the colonial regime and whether its "crisis" was structural or depended on the peculiar political conjuncture of the Napoleanic invasions. It has also centered on the relationship of imperial government to local powers in the colony.[112] That has led in turn to a renewed interest in the creators and executors of imperial policy in the eighteenth century. The studies of Diniz Silva on dom Luís da Cunha at the beginning of the period, of Maxwell on Pombal in mid-century, and of Mansuy-Diniz Silva on dom Rodrigo de Souza Coutinho at the century's end have all sought to use the lives and thought of these men as a pathway to understand imperial policy.[113] To those issues, recent scholarship has added other dimensions, exploring like Lily Schwarcz and Maria Beatriz Nizza da Silva the cultural context of the period as a whole, like Iris Kantor the intellectual ferment in learned academies or Ronald Raminelli the interest in cartography and natural history, like J. Pinto Furtado the uses and representation of the 1788 Minas Gerais conspiracy, or like Kirsten Schulz the political and cultural aspects of the transfer of the court to Lisbon.[114] István Jancsó published two excellent collections that represent the work of a growing number of imaginative studies of the period of nation building in the 1820s and 1830.[115] The commemorations in 2008 for the bicentennial of the arrival of the Portuguese court in Rio de Janeiro have occasioned a boom of new works on the period of transition to independence and national definition, both in terms of the intellectual origins of that transition and in regard to political struggles over the form of the new nation.[116] It is fair to say that they have demonstrated that the former periodization based on political chronology is no longer very useful in the face of the new social and cultural studies. These have revealed the continuities between a slave-based Portuguese America that had come to see itself as a colony of empire and a newly independent Brazil in which those in control viewed coerced labor and monarchy as their own and their nation's destiny. At the same time, many people, slave, freed, and free, increasingly sought to liberate themselves and their country from the burdens of both slavery and empire.

ACKNOWLEDGMENTS

The author wishes to thank Hal Langfur and Mariza de Carvalho Soares for their help and suggestions.

NOTES

1. See the interview with Laura de Mello e Souza in "Entrevistas," *Póshistória* 6 (1998). She edited *Cotidiano e vida privada na América portuguesa*, vol. I of *História da vida privada no Brasil*, Fernando A. Novais, ed., 4 vols. (Sao Paulo: Companhia das Letras, 1997–98) and chose the title because the term "colonial Brazil" was an invention of the nineteenth century.

2. Other historiographical assessments that discuss recent developments in the study of colonial Brazil are José Jobson Arruda and José Manuel Tengarrinha, eds., *Historiografia Luso-Brasileira contemporânea* (Bauru: EDUSC, 1999); José Jobson Arruda and Luís Adão da Fonseca, *Brasil-Portugal: História, agenda para o milênio* (Bauru: EDUSC, 2001); A. J. R. Russell-Wood, "Archives and the Recent Historiography on Colonial Brazil," *Latin American Research Review* 36:1 (2001): 75–103; "United States Scholarly Contributions to the Historiography of Colonial Brazil," *Hispanic American Historical Review* 65:4 (1985): 683–723; Júnia Furtado, "Novas tendências da historiografia sobre Minas Gerais no período colonial," in *Historiografia mineira nos últimos 20 anos*, ed. Roberto Martins and Amilcar Vianna Martins (Belo Horizonte: ICAM, 2007). I have discussed some of these historiographical issues previously in Stuart B. Schwartz, "Somebodies and Nobodies in the Body Politic: Mentalities and Social Structures in Colonial Brazil," *Latin American Research Review* 31:1 (1996): 113–34; "The Colonial Past: Conceptualizing Post-*Dependentista* Brazil," in *Colonial legacies*, ed. Jeremy Adelman (New York: Routledge, 1999), 175–93; and "Brazil: Ironies of the Colonial Past," *HAHR* 80:4 (2000): 681–94.

3. There were general essays on the colonial era like Jorge Caldeira, *A nação mercantilista* (Rio de Janeiro: Editora 34, 1999), and handbooks like Ronaldo Vainfas, ed., *Dicionário do Brasil colonial* (Rio de Janeiro: Editora Objectiva, 2000), as well as much coverage in the media.

4. These years witnessed the great popularity of books on the early history of Brazil, like the series written by journalist Eduardo Bueno, a popular TV *novela* entitled *A muralha* on the settlement of early São Paulo, the publication of two useful dictionaries of colonial Brazilian history, and a number of syntheses of the colonial era. See Vainfas, *Dicionário*; Maria Beatriz Nizza da Silva, ed., *Dicionaário da história da colonização portuguesa no Brasil* (Lisbon: Verbo, 1994); Arno Wehling and Maria José C. de Wehling, *Formação do Brasil colonial* (Rio de Janeiro: Nova Fronteira, 1994).

5. See António Manuel Hespanha, *Há 500 anos: Balanço de três anos de comemorações dos descobrimentos portugueses 1996–98* (Lisbon, 1999) for a summary of many of the Commission's activities in those years. It published a notable journal, *Oceanos*, in an oversize format that included excellent articles and stunning visual images, with many issues dedicated wholly or in part to early Brazil. See, for example, "Vieira, 1697," *Oceanos*, 30–31 (1997); "Azulejos: Portugal e Brasil," *Oceanos*, 36–37 (1998–99); "A formação territorial do Brasil," *Oceanos* 40 (1999); "A Construção do Brasil," *Oceanos*, 41 (2000); "Viver no Brasil colónia," *Oceanos*, 42 (2000). Two of the most important documentary collections published in the period were the seventeenth-century gubernatorial and other correspondence of Luís and Gaspar de Sousa and the letters of the Conde da Torre published by the Portuguese Commission on Discoveries [hereafter abbreviated as CNCDP] and the important Códice Costa Matoso, a collection of materials related to Minas Gerais. See João Paulo Salvado and Susana Münch Miranda, eds., *Livro 1º do Governo do Brasil (1607–1633)* (Lisbon: CNCDP, 2001); *Livro 2º do Governo do Brasil (1615–1634)* (Lisbon: CNCDP, 2001); *Cartas para Álvaro de Sousa e Gaspar de Sousa* (Lisbon: CNCDP, 2001); *Cartas do 1º Code da Torre*, 4 vols. (Lisbon: CNCDP, 2001); Luciano Raposo de Almeida Figueiredo and Maria Verônica Campos, eds., *Códice Costa Matoso: Coleção das noticias dos primeiros descobrimentos das minas na Ameérica que fez o doutor Caetano da Costa Matoso sendo ouvidor-geral das do Ouro Preto...*, 2 vols. (Belo Horizonte: Sistema Estadual de Planejamento, Fundação Joaão Pinheiro, Centro de Estudos Histoóricos e Culturais, 1999). Another important collection has been the series of translations and beautifully produced facimile editions from the Dutch period in Northeastern Brazil (1630–54) funded by Petrobras and published by Editora Index. See, for example, *The "Thierbuch" and "Autobiography" of Zacharias Wagener*, 2 vols. (Rio de Janeiro: Editora Index, 1997); B. N. Teensma, ed., *Vincent Joachim Soler's Seventeen Letters, 1636–43* (Rio de Janeiro: Editora Index, 1999); Nelson Papavero and Dante Martins Teixeira, eds., *Cudburt Pudsey: Journal of a Residence in Brazil* (Petrópolis: Editora Index, 2000). Important monographs were also produced in this period. For example, Jorge Couto, *A construção do Brasil* (Lisbon: Cosmos, 1998).

6. Over 250,000 documents were microfilmed at the Arquivo Histórico Ultramarino. The Projecto Resgate de Documentação Histórica Barão Rio Branco was decentralized to some extent, and thus the distribution of the CD-ROMs and the publication of the catalogues and guides for the documents from each captaincy was administered by the Brazilian state cultural offices or universities for each region. This caused considerable problems in the distribution of the discs and in the completion of the guides. For examples of some of the guides, see Caio Boschi, ed., *Inventário dos manuscritos avulsos relativos a Minas Gerais existentes no Arquivo Histórico Ultramarino (Lisboa)*, 3 vols. (Belo Horizonte: Fundação João Pinheiro, Centro de Estudos Históricos e Culturais, 1998); *Catálogo de*

verbetes dos documentos manuscritos avulsos da capitania de Matto Grosso (1720–1827) (Campo Grande: Casa da Memória Arnaldo Estevão de Figueiredo/Universidade Federal de Mato Grosso, 1999); Gisafran Nazareno Mota Jucá, ed., *Catálogo dos documentos manuscritos avulsos da capitania de Ceará (1618–1832)* (Brasília and Fortaleza: Ministério da Cultura/Universidade Federal de Ceará, 1999).

7. Jacob Gorender, *A escravidão reabilitada* (São Paulo: Atica, 1990) suggested that emphasis on slave agency exculpated slavery from its sins and presented a rosy picture of the institution, but his critique did not have a profound influence on later studies.

8. Gilberto Freyre, *Casa grande e senzala*, critical ed., Guillermo Giucci, Enrique Rodríguez Larreta, Edson Nery da Fonseca, eds. (Madrid: ALLCA XX, 2002). See also, Maria Lúcia Pallares Burke, *Gilberto Freyre: Um vitoriano nos trópicos* (São Paulo: UNESP, 2005); Ricardo Benzaquen de Araujo, *Guerra e paz: Casa grande e senzala e a obra de Gilberto Freyre nos anos 30* (São Paulo: Editora 34, 2004).

9. Fernando A. Novais, *História da vida privada*, 4 vols. (São Paulo: Companhia das Letras, 1997); István Jancsó and Iris Kantor, *Festa: Cultura e sociabilidade na América portuguesa* (São Paulo: Hucitec, 2001).

10. Manuela Carneiro da Cunha, ed. *História dos índios do Brasil* (São Paulo: Companhia das Letras, 1992); Frank Salomon and Stuart B. Schwartz, eds., *Cambridge History of the Native Peoples of the Americas*, Vol. III: *South America*, parts 1 and 2 (Cambridge: Cambridge University Press, 1999–2000).

11. See Claude Lévi-Strauss, review of the *Cambridge History of the Native Peoples of the Americas*, Vol. III: *South America*, in *L'Homme* 158–159 (2001): 439–42; Carmen Bernand, "L'américanisme à l'heure du multiculturalisme: Projets, limites, perspectives," *Annales* 5 (2002): 1293–310, and the rejoinders in Stuart Schwartz, "Denounced by Lévi-Strauss," *The Americas* 59:1 (2002): 1–8; Stuart Schwartz and Frank Salomon, "Réponse à Claude Lévi-Stauss," *L'Homme* 158–159 (2001): 439–42; and Stuart B. Schwartz and Frank Salomon, "'Un américain (imaginaire) à Paris,' Réponse à Carmen Bernand," *Annales* n. 2 (2003): 499–512.

12. John Hemming, *Amazon Frontier: The Defeat of the Brazilian Indians* (London: MacMillan, 1987).

13. John Monteiro, *Negros da terra: Índios e bandeirantes nas origens de São Paulo* (São Paulo: Companhia das Letras, 1994). See also his overview essay, "The Crises and Transformations of Invaded Societies: Costal Brazil in the Sixteenth Century," *Cambridge History of the Native Peoples of the Americas*, Vol. III, pt. 1, pp. 973–1023.

14. For example, Stuart B. Schwartz, "Indian Labor and New World Plantations," *American Historical Review* 83:1 (1978): 43–79; *Sugar Plantations in the Formation of Brazilian Society* (Cambridge: Cambridge University Press, 1985), 51–72.

15. Neil L. Whitehead and Michael Harbsmeier, *Hans Staden's True History: An Account of Cannibal Captivity in Brazil* (Durham, N.C.: Duke University Press, 2008). See also Neil L. Whitehead, "Hans Staden and the Cultural Politics of Cannibalism," *HAHR* 80:4 (2000): 721–51.

16. Jean de Léry, *History of a Voyage to the Land of Brazil*, Janet Whatley, trans. and ed. (Berkeley: University of California Press, 1990). See also Tom Conley, "Thevet Revisits Guanabara," *HAHR* 80:4 (2000): 753–81.

17. Leyla Perrone-Moisés, *Vinte luas: Viagem de Paulmier de Gonneville ao Brasil: 1503–1505* (São Paulo: Companhia das Letras, 1992); Frank Lestringant, *Le Huguenot et l'sauvage*, 3rd ed. (Geneva: Droz, 2004; the original edition is Paris: Amateur des Livres, 1990). See also Lestringant, *Cannibals: The Discovery and Representation of the Cannibal from Columbus to Jules Verne*, trans. Rosemary Morris (Cambridge: Polity Press, 1997).

18. Andrea Daher, *Les singularités de la France Équinoxiale* (Paris: Honoré Champion, 2002). See also the more general study of Maurice Pianzola, *Des Français à la conquête du Brésil (XVII siècle): Les perroquets jaunes* (Paris: L'Harmattan, 1991).

19. Hélène Clastres, *The Land-without-Evil: Tupí-Guaraní Prophetism*, trans. Jacqueline Grenez Brovender (Urbana: University of Illinois Press, 1995); Eduardo Viveiros de Castro, *From the Enemy's Point of View: Humanity and Divinity in an Amazonian Society*, trans. Catherine V. Howard (Chicago: University of Chicago Press, 1992).

20. See, for example, Ernst van den Boogart, "Infernal Allies: The Dutch West India Company and the Tararirú," in *Johan Maurits van Nassau-Siegen, 1604–1679*, ed. E. van den Boogart (The Hague: Johan Maurits van Nassau Stichting, 1979), 518–38; Ronald Raminelli, "Habitus caníbal: Os índios de Albert Eckhout," in *O Brasil e os holandeses*, ed. Paulo Herkenhoff (Rio de Janeiro: Sextante, 1999), 104–21.

21. Marcos Galindo, *O governo das almas: A expansão colonial no país dos tapuia, 1651–1798* (PhD diss., Leiden Universiteit, 2004).

22. Hal Langfur, *The Forbidden Lands: Colonial Identity, Frontier Violence, and the Persistence of Brazil's Eastern Indians, 1750–1830* (Stanford: Stanford University Press, 2006); Haruf Salmen Espindola, *Sertão do Rio Doce* (Bauru: EDUSC, 2005).

23. A. J. R. Russell-Wood, "Introduction: New Directions in *Bandeirismo* Studies in Colonial Brazil," *The Americas* 61: 3 (2005): 353–71. The issue included studies by H. Langfur, A. Metcalf, A. J. R. Ruseell-Wood, and M. Karasch.

24. Stuart B. Schwartz and Hal Langfur, "Tapanhuns, Negros da Terra, and Curibocas: Common Cause and Confrontation between Blacks and Natives in Colonial Brazil," in Matthew Restall, ed., *Beyond Black and Red: African-Native Relations in Colonial Latin America* (Albuquerque: University of New Mexico Press, 2006), 81–115; Alida Metcalf, "Millenarian Slaves? The Santidade de Jaguaripe and Slave Resistance in the Americas," *AHR* 104:5 (1999): 1531–59. The theme is also touched upon in Flávio dos Santos Gomes, *A hydra e os pântanos: Mocambos, quilombos e comunidades de fugitives no Brasil (séculos XVII–XIX)* (São Paulo: UNESP, 2005).

25. Mary Karasch, "Catequese e cativeiro: Política indigenísta em Goiás, 1780–1889," *História dos Índios no Brasil*, 397–412; "Interethnic Conflict and Resistance on the Brazilian Frontier of Goiás, 1750–1890," *Contested Ground: Comparative Frontiers on the Northern and Southern Edges of the Spanish Empire*, ed. Donna Guy and Thomas E. Sheridan (Tucson: University of Arizona Press, 1998), 115–34.

26. Geographer Pasquale Petrone's *Aldeamentos paulistas* (São Paulo: EDUSP, 1995), written in 1965 but not published at the time, provides an excellent analysis of the origins of Santos and São Paulo as missionary villages.

27. João Azevedo Fernandes, *De cunhã a mameluca* (João Pessoa: Editora Universitária, 2003).

28. Rita Heloísa de Almeida, *O direitório dos Índios* (Brasília: Editora Universidade de Brasília, 1997).

29. Angela Domingues, *Quando os índios eram vassalos* (Lisbon: CNCDP, 2002), trans. as *When the Indians Were Vassals: Power Equations in Northern Brazil* (New Delhi: Transbooks, 2007); Patrícia Maria Melo Sampaio, "Espelhos partidos: Etnia, legislação e desigualdade na colônia sertões do Grão-Pará" (PhD diss., Universidade Federal Fluminense, 2001); Barbara A. Sommer, "Negotiated Settlements: Native Amazonians and Portuguese Policy in Pará, Brazil, 1758–1798" (PhD diss., University of New Mexico, 2000).

30. Francisco José dos Santos, *Além da conquista: Guerras e rebeliões indígenas na Amazônia pombalina* (Manaus: Editora da Universidade de Amazonas, 1999); Nádia Farage,

As muralhas dos sertões: Os povos indígenas no Rio Branco e a colonização (Rio de Janeiro: Paz e Terra/ANPOCS, 1991).

31. Ronaldo Vainfas, *A heresia dos índios: Catolicismo e rebeldia no Brasil colonial* (São Paulo: Companhia das Letras, 1996); Alida Metcalf, *Go-Betweens and the Colonization of Brazil, 1500–1600* (Austin: University of Texas Press, 2005).

32. João Adolfo Hansen, "Sem F, sem L, sem R: Cronistas, jesuítas e índios no século XVI," in *A conquista de América*, ed. Elisa A. Kossovitch (Campinas: Cedes, 1993 [Cadernos Cedes 30]); José Ribamar Bessa Freire, *Rio Babel: A história das línguas na Amazônia* (Rio de Janeiro: Atlântica, 2004); José Ribamar Bessa Freire and Maria Carlota Rosa, *Línguas gerais: Política lingüística e catequese na América do Sul no período colonial* (Rio de Janeiro: EDUERJ, 2003).

33. Paulo de Assunção, *A terra dos brasis: A natureza da América portuguesa vista pelos primeiros jesuítas (1549–1596)* (São Paulo: Annablume, 2000); Ronald Romaneli, *Imagens da colonização* (São Paulo: Jorge Zahar/EDUSP, 1996); Zinka Ziebell, *Terra de canibais* (Porto Alegre: Universidade Federal de Rio Grande do Sul, 2002).

34. Warren Dean, *Wih Broadax and Firebrand: The Destruction of the Brazilian Atlantic Forest* (Berkeley: University of California Press, 1995); José Augusto Pádua, *Um sopro de destruição: Pensamento político e crítica ambiental no Brasil escravista (1786–1888)* (Rio de Janeiro: Jorge Zahar, 2002); Shawn Miller, *Fruitless Trees: Portuguese Conservation and Brazil's Colonial Timber* (Stanford: Stanford University Press, 2000); "Stilt-Root Subsistence: Colonial Mangroves and Brazil's Landless Poor," *HAHR* 83:2 (2003): 223–54.

35. I have included an extensive bibliography on Brazilian slavery in Stuart B. Schwartz, *Escravos, roceiros, e rebeldes*, trans. Jussara Simões (Bauru: EDUSC, 2001), 21–88, which updates the earlier review published in the English-language edition of this book published in 1988. (I have limited my comments here because the topic is covered in this volume by the essay of João José Reis and Herbert Klein.)

36. Leila Mezan Algranti, *O feitor ausente: Estudo sobre a escravidão urbana no Rio de Janeiro* (Petropolis: Vozes, 1988); Silvia Hunold Lara, *Campos de vioência: Escravos e senhores na capitania do Rio de Janeiro* (Rio de Janeiro: Paz e Terra, 1988).

37. Kathleen Higgins, *Licentious Liberty in a Brazilian Gold-Mining Region* (University Park: Penn State University Press, 1999); Eduardo França Paiva, *Escravos e libertos nas Minas Gerais do século XVIII* (São Paulo: Annablume, 1996); Douglas Cole Libby and Afonso de Alencastro Graça Filho, "Reconstruindo a liberdade-alforrias e forros na freguesia de São José do Rio das Mortes, 1750–1850," *Varia História* 30 (2003): 112–51; and Tarcíso R. Filos de Deus, "Batismos de crianças legítimas e naturais na paróquia de Nossa Senhora do Pilar de Ouro Preto, 1712–1810," *Varia História*, 31 (2004): 69–97; Donald Ramos, "Single and Married Women in Vila Rica, Brazil, 1754–1838," *Journal of Family History* 16:3 (1991): 261–81.

38. José Roberto Góes, *O cativeiro imperfeito: Um estudo sobre a escravidão no Rio de Janeiro da primeira metade do século XIX* (Vitória: Governo do Estado de Espírito Santo, 1993); Manolo Florentino and José Roberto Góes, *A paz das senzalas: Famílias escravas e tráfico atlântico, c. 1790–1850* (Rio de Janeiro: Civilização Brasileira, 1997). Some of their results can be read in English in "Slavery, Marriage and Kinship in Rural Rio de Janeiro, 1790–1830," in *Identity in the Shadow of Slavery*, ed. Paul E. Lovejoy (London and New York: Continuum, 2000), 137–62.

39. Robert W. Slenes, *Na senzala, uma flor: Esperanças e recordações na formação da família escrava* (Rio de Janeiro: Editora Nova Fronteira, 1999).

40. Elizabeth Kuznesof, *Household Economy and Urban Development: São Paulo, 1765–1836* (Boulder, Colo.: Westview Press, 1986); José Flávio Motta, *Corpos escravos,*

vontades livres: Posse de cativos e família escrava em Bananal, 1801–1829 (São Paulo: Annablume, 1999); Sheila de Castro Faria, *A colônia em movimento: Fortuna e família no cotidiano colonial* (Rio de Janeiro: Nova Fronteira, 1998).

41. Rafael de Bivar Marquese, *Administração e escravidão: Idéias sobre a gestão da agricultura escravista brasileira* (São Paulo: Hucitec, 1999); *Feitores do corpo, missionários da mente: Senhores, letrados e o controle dos escravos nas Américas, 1660–1860* (São Paulo: Companhia das Letras, 2004).

42. Laird Bergad, *Slavery and the Demographic and Economic History of Minas Gerais, Brazil, 1720–1888* (Cambridge: Cambridge University Press, 1999); Herbert Klein, "A demografia do tráfico atlântico de escravos para o Brasil," *Estudos Econômicos* 17:2 (1987): 129–50; Clotilde Paiva, "Slave And Free in Nineteenth-Century Minas Gerais, Campanha, 1831," *Slavery and Abolition* 15:1 (1994): 1–21; Francisco Vidal Luna and Herbert Klein, *Slavery and the Economy of São Paulo, 1750–1850* (Stanford: Stanford University Press, 2003).

43. Charles R. Boxer, *Salvador de Sá and the Struggle for Brazil and Angola* (London: University of London/Athlone Press, 1952); Pierre Verger, *Flux et reflux de la traite des nègres entre le golfe de Bénin et Bahia de Todos os Santos du XVIIe au XIXe siécle* (Paris: Mouton, 1968), Brazilian ed. 1987; John Thornton, *Africa and Africans in the Making of the Atlantic World*, 2nd ed. (Cambridge: Cambridge University Press, 1998); Joseph Miller, *Way of Death: Merchant Capitalism and the Angolan Slave Trade, 1730–1830* (Madison: University of Wisconsin Press, 1988); Luiz Felipe de Alencastro, *O trato dos viventes: Formação do Brasil no Atlântico sul, séculos XVI e XVII* (São Paulo: Companhia das Letras, 2000). His ideas are also summarized in "Le versant brésilien de l'Atlantique-sud: 1550–1850," *Annales. Histoire, Sciences Sociales* 61:2 (2006): 339–82. See also Alberto da Costa e Silva, *Um rio chamado Atlântico: A África no Brasil e o Brasil na África* (Rio de Janeiro: Nova Fronteira, 2003).

44. Jaime Rodrigues, *Da costa a costa: Escravos, marinheiros e intermediários do tráfico negreiro de Angola ao Rio de Janeiro (1780–1860)* (São Paulo: Companhia das Letras, 2005); *O infame comércio: Propostas e experências no final do tráfico de africanos para o Brasil* (Campinas: Unicamp, 2000). Cf. Marcus Rediker, *Between the Devil and the Deep Blue Sea* (Cambridge: Cambridge University Press, 1989); Peter Linebaugh and Marcus Rediker, *The Many-Headed Hydra: Sailors, Slaves, Commoners, and the Hidden History of the Revolutionary Atlantic* (Boston: Beacon Press, 2000).

45. There are excellent articles on Central African cultural influences in Brazil in Linda M. Heywood, ed., *Central Africans and Cultural Transformations in the American Diaspora* (Cambridge: Cambridge University Press, 2002). See, for example, Mary Karasch, "Central Africans in Central Brazil," pp. 117–52; Elizabeth W. Kiddy, "Who Is the King of the Congo? A New Look at African and Afro-Brazilian Kings in Brazil," pp. 153–82; Robert Slenes, "The Great Porpoise-Skull Strike: Central African Water Spirits and Slave Identity in Early Nineteenth-Century Rio de Janeiro," pp. 183–210. For, a statement of the Africanist approach, see Paul E. Lovejoy, "The African Diaspora: Revisionist Interpretations of Ethnicity, Culture and Religion under Slavery," *Studies in the World History of Slavery, Abolition, and Emancipation* 2 (1997): 1–23. Richard Price has characterized and criticized this new "Africanist" emphasis as a "cultural nationalist" perspective; see Richard Price, "The Miracle of Creolization: A Retrospective," *New West Indies Guide* 75:1–2 (2001): 35–64.

46. Daniela Calainho, "Metrópole das mandingas: Religiosidade negra e Inquisição portuguesa no antigo regime" (PhD diss., Federal University Fluminense, 2000); James Sweet, *Recreating Africa: Culture, Kinship, and Religion in the African Portuguese World, 1441–1770* (Chapel Hill: University of North Carolina Press, 2003). See also Gwendolyn Midlo Hall, *Slavery and African Ethnicities in the Americas* (Chapel Hill: University of North Carolina Press, 2005); Michael A. Gomez, *Reversing Sail: A History of the African*

Diaspora (Cambridge: Cambridge University Press, 2005); and as editor, *Diasporic Africa: A Reader* (New York: New York University Press, 2006).

47. João José Reis, *Rebelião esclava no Brasil: A história do levante dos Malês* (São Paulo: Brasiliense, 1986; 2nd ed., São Paulo: Compañía das Letras, 2004); "Magia jeje na Bahia: A invasão do calundu do Pasto de Cachoeira, 1785," *Revista Brasileira de História* 8:16 (1988): 57–82; "African Drumming and Dance between Repression and Concession: Bahia, 1808–1855," in M. Gomez, ed., *Diasporic Africa*, 45–63.

48. Mariza de Carvalho Soares, *Devotos de cor: Identidade étnica, religiosidade e escravidão no Rio de Janeiro, século XVIII* (Rio de Janeiro: Civilização Brasileira, 2000); "From Gbe to Yoruba: Ethnic Changes within the Mina Nation in Rio de Janeiro," in *The Yoruba Diaspora in the Atlantic World*, ed. Toyn Falola and Matt Childs (Bloomington: Indiana University Press, 2005). These studies build upon the solid foundation of work on lay brotherhoods in Minas Gerais such as Caio César Boschi, *Os leigos e o poder: Irmandades leigas e politica colonizadora em Minas Gerais* (São Paulo: Ática, 1986); Julieta Scarano, *Devoção e escravidão: A Irmandade de Nossa Senhora do Rosário dos Pretos no Distrito Diamantino no século XVIII* (São Paulo: Nacional, 1976).

49. Elizabeth W. Kiddy, *Blacks of the Rosary: Memory and History in Minas Gerais, Brazil* (University Park: Penn State University Press, 2005); Silvia Hunold Lara, *Fragmentos setecentistas: Escravidão, cultura e poder na América portuguesa* (São Paulo: Companhia das Letras, 2007).

50. Luiz Mott, *Rosa Egipcíaca: Uma santa africana no Brasil* (Rio de Janeiro: Bertrand, 1993); Júnia Ferreira Furtado, *Chica da Silva e o contratador dos diamantes* (São Paulo: Companhia das Letras, 2003).

51. Evaldo Cabral de Mello, *Olina restaurada: Guerra e açúcar no Nordeste, 1630–1654* (Rio de Janeiro: Forense, 1975); *Rubro veio: O imaginário da Restauração pernambucana* (Rio de Janeiro: Nova Fronteira, 1986), *A fronda dos mazombos: Nobres contra mascates, Pernambuco, 1666–1715* (São Paulo: Companhia das Letras, 1995); *O Negócio do Brasil: Portugal, os Países Baixos e o Nordeste, 1641–1669* (Rio de Janeiro: Topbooks, 1998); *A outra independencia: O federalismo pernambucano de 1817 a 1824* (São Paulo: Editora 34, 2004); *Nassau* (São Paulo: Companhia das Letras, 2006).

52. See, for example, Jean Frédéric Schaub, *Le Portugal au temps du comte-duc de Olivares (1621–1640)* (Madrid: Casa de Velázquez, 2001); *Portugal na monarquia hispânica, 1580–1640* (Lisbon: Livros Horizonte, 2001); Rafael Valladares, *La rebelión de Portugal, 1640–1680* (Madrid: Junta de Castilla y León, 1998); Fernando Bouza Alvarez, *Portugal en la monarquía hispánica, 1580–1640* (Madrid: Universidad Complutense, 1987); Joaquim Veríssimo Serrão, *O tempo dos Filipes em Portugal e no Brasil, 1580–1668* (Lisbon: Edições Colibrí, 1994); Maria da Graça M. Ventura, ed., *A união ibérica e o mundo Atlântico* (Lisbon: Edições Colibrí, 1997); Stuart B. Schwartz, "The Voyage of the Vassals: Royal Power, Noble Obligations, and Merchant Capital before the Portuguese Restoration of Independence, 1624–1640," *American Historical Review* 96:3 (1991): 735–62.

53. Christopher Ebert, "The Trade in Brazilian Sugar: Brazil, Portugal, and Northwestern Europe, 1550–1630" (PhD diss., Columbia University, 2004); Leonor Freire Costa, *O transporte no Atlântico e a Companhia Peral do Comércio do Brasil, 1580–1663*, 2 vols. (Lisbon: CNCDP, 2002); *Império e grupos mercantis: Entre o Oriente e o Atlântico, século XVII* (Lisbon: Livros Horizonte, 2002); Daviken Studnicki-Gizbert, *A Nation upon the Ocean Sea: Portugal's Atlantic Diaspora and the Crisis of the Spanish Empire, 1492–1640* (New York: Oxford University Press, 2006).

54. Júnia Furtado, ed., *Diálogos oceânicos: Minas Gerais e as novas abordagens para uma história do Imperio Ultramarino Português* (Belo Horizonte: UFMG, 2001); Maria

Odila Silva Dias, *Homens de negócio: A interiorização da metrópole e do comércio nas Minas setecentistas* (São Paulo: Hucitec, 1990).

55. Stuart B. Schwartz, *Sovereignty and Society in Colonial Brazil* (Berkeley: University of California Press, 1978); Arno Wehling and Maria José Wehling, *Direito e justice no Brasil colonial: O tribunal da Relação do Rio de Janeiro, 1751–1808* (Rio de Janeiro: Renovar, 2004); Guilherme Pereira das Neves, *E receberá mercê: A Mesa da Consciência e Ordens e o clero secular no Brasil, 1808–1828* (Rio de Janeiro: Ministério da Justiça/Arquivo nacional, 1997).

56. Scholars now have at their disposal a website that makes available the collections of Portuguese legislation for the early modern period; see *Ius Lusitaniae. Fontes Históricas do Direito Português* at www.iuslusitaniae.fcsh.unl.pt.

57. A. J. R. Russell-Wood, "Vassalo e soberano: Apelos extrajudiciais de africanos e de indivíduos de origen africana na América portuguesa," in *Cultura portuguesa na terra de Santa Cruz*, ed. Maria Beatriz Niza da Silva (Lisbon: Editorial Estampa, 1995), 215–33.

58. Ilana Blaj, *A trama das tenções: O processo de mercantilização de São Paulo colonial, 1681–1720* (São Paulo: Universidade de São Paulo, 2002).

59. See below n. 103. See also Maria Fernanda B. Bicalho, "As câmaras municipais no império português: O exemplo do Rio de Janeiro," *Revista Brasileira de História* 18:36 (1998): 251–80; Maria de Fátima Gouvêa, "Redes de poder na América portuguesa: O caso dos homens bons do Rio de Janeiro, ca. 1790–1822," *Revista Brasileira de História* 18:36 (1998): 297–330.

60. Hannedea van Nederveen Meerkerk, *Recife: The Rise of a 17th-Century Trade City from a Cultural-Historical Perspective* (Assen, The Netherlands: Van Gorcum, 1989); Nireu Calvalcanti, *O Rio de Janeiro setecentista: A vida e a construção da cidade da invasão francesa até a chegada da Corte* (Rio de Janeiro: Jorge Zahar, 2004); Laurent Vidal, *Mazagão: La ville qui traversa l'Atlantique* (Paris: Aubier, 2005).

There are good studies of Pernambuco that raise these issues. See, for example, Kalina Vanderlei Silva, *O miserável soldo e a boa ordem da sociedade colonial: Militarização e marginalidade na Capitania de Pernambuco dos sécalos XVII e XVIII* (Recife: Fundação de Cultura Cidade do Recife, 2001).

61. Cláudia Damasceno Fonseca, *Des terres aux villes de l'or: Pouvoirs et territories urbains au Minas Gerais (Brésil, XVIII siècle)* (Paris: Centre Culturel Calouste Gulbenkian, 2003).

62. Isabel dos Guimarães Sá, *Quando o rico se faz pobre: Misericordias, caridade e poder no imperio português, 1500–1800* (Lisbon: CNCDP, 1997). Cf. A. J. R. Russell-Wood, *Fidalgos and Philanthropist: The Santa Casa da Misericórdia of Bahia, 1550–1755* (Berkeley: University of California Press, 1968). See also *Colectânea de estudos: Universo urbanístico português, 1415–1822* (Lisbon: CNCDP, 1998), which contains articles by Nelson Goulart Reis and Roberta Delson on Brazilian urban topics.

63. Vera Lúcia Amaral Ferlini, *Terra, trabalho e poder: O mundo dos engenhos no Nordeste colonial* (São Paulo: Brasiliense, 1988); Stuart B. Schwartz, *Sugar Plantations in the Formation of Brazilian Society, Bahia, 1550–1835* (Cambridge: Cambridge University Press, 1985); B. J. Barickman, *A Bahian Counterpoint: Sugar, Tobacco, Cassava, and Slavery in the Recôncavo, 1780–1860* (Stanford: Stanford University Press, 1998); Luiz Alberto Moniz Bandeira, *O feudo: A casa da Torre de Garcia d'Avila* (Rio de Janeiro: Civilização Brasileira, 2000).

64. See Iraci del Nero da Costa, *Arraia-miuda: Um estudo sobre os não proprietários de escravos* (São Paulo: MGSP, 1992); Maria Luiza Marcilio, *Crescimento demográfico e evolução agrária paulista, 1700–1836* (São Paulo: Hucitec, 2000); Bert Barickman, "'A Bit of Land, Which They Call *Roça*': Slave Provision Grounds in the Bahian Recôncavo, 1780–1860,"

HAHR 74:4 (1994): 469–87; Schwartz, *Peasants, Slaves, and Rebels*, pp. 65–101. There are good studies of Pernambuco that raise these issues; see, for example, Guillermo Palacios, *Cultivadores libres, Estado y crisis de la esclavitud en Brasil en la época de la Revolución Industrial* (Mexico City: Colegio de México and Fondo de Cultura Económica, 1998); Kalina Vanderlei Silva, *O miserável soldo e a boa ordem da sociedade colonial: Militarização e marginalidade na Capitania de Pernambuco dos séculos XVII e XVIII* (Recife: Fundação de Cultura Cidade do Recife, 2001).

    65. Eni de Mesquita, *Familia e grupos de convívio* (São Paulo: Marco Zero, 1989); *As mulheres, o poder e a familia* (São Paulo: Marco Zero, 1989); Maria Luiza Marcílio, *Crescimento demográfico e evolução agrária paulista, 1700–1836* (São Paulo: EDUSP, 2000); Maria Beatriz Nizza da Silva, *História da família no Brasil colonial* (Rio de Janeiro: Nova Fronteira, 1998).

    66. Luiz Mott, *Escravidão, homossexualidade e demonologia* (São Paulo: Icone, 1988); *O lesbianismo no Brasil* (Porto Alegre: Mercado Aberto, 1987). This line of research continues. See the articles by Mott and other scholars in the volume dedicated to him, Harold Johnson and Fracis A. Dutra, eds., *Pelo Vaso Traseiro: Sodomy and Sodomite in Luso-Brazilian History* (Tucson: Fenestra Books, 2007).

    67. Luciano Figuereido, *O avesso da memória: Cotidiano e trabalho da mulher em Minas Gerais no século XVIII* (Rio de Janeiro: José Olympio, 1993); Leila Mean Algranti, *Honradas e devotas: Mulheres da Colônia* (Rio de Janeiro: José Olympio, 1993); Mary del Priore, *Ao sul do corpo: Condição feminina, maternidades e mentalidades no Brasil colônia* (Rio de Janeiro: José Olympio, 1993).

    68. Maria Beatriz Nizza da Silva, *Donas e plebeias na sociedade colonial* (Lisbon: Editorial Estampa, 2002). See also her edited volume, *Sexualidade, família e religião na colonização do Brasil* (Lisbon: Livros Horizonte, 2001).

    69. For an interesting discussion of the elements of popular religion, see Ellen Badone, ed., "Introduction," *Religious Orthodoxy and Popular Faith in European Society* (Princeton: Princeton University Press, 1990), 3–23. See also Luis E. Rodriguez-San Pedro Bezares and José Luis Sánchez Lora, eds., *Historia de España Tercer milenio*, Vol. 13: *Los siglos XVI–XVII: Cultura y vida cotidiana* (Madrid: Editorial Síntesis, 2000), 207–55.

    70. Two fine overviews of the recent historiography of religion in Portugal and Brazil can be found in Isabel dos Guimarães Sá, "História religiosa em Portugal e no Brasil: Algumas perspectivas (séculos XVI–XVII)," in *Brasil-Portugal: História, agenda para o milênio*, José Jobson Arruda and Luís Adão da Fonseca, eds. (Bauru: EDUSC, 2001), 29–54; and in the same volume, Ronaldo Vainfas, "História da cultura e das religiosidades no império colonial português (séculos XV–XVIII)," 97–106. See also Lara Mancuso and Fernando Torres-Lodoño, "Los estudios sobre lo religioso en Brasil: Un balance historiográfico," *Istor* 9 (2002): 55–81.

    71. Ronaldo Vainfas, "Moralidades brasílicas: Deleites sexuais e linguagem erótica na sociedade escravista," *Historia da vida privadano Brasil*, I, 221–274; Mary Del Priore, "Ritos da vida privada," *ibid.*, 275–330.

    72. Jean Delumeau, *Catholicism betweeen Luther and Voltaire: A New View of the Counter-Reformation* (London: Burns and Oates, 1977); Adriano Prosperi, *Tribunali della coscienzia: Inquisitori, confessori, tribunali* (Turin: Einaudi, 1996).

    73. Dauril Alden, *The Making of an Enterprise: The Society of Jesus in Portugal, Its Empire, and Beyond, 1540–1750* (Stanford: Stanford University Press, 1996); Charlotte de Castelnau-L'Estoile, *Les ouvriers d'une vigne sterile: Les jésuites et la conversion des Indien au Brésil* (Lisbon/Paris: Centre Culturel Calouste Gulbenkian, 2000); José Eisenberg, *As*

missões jesuíticas e o pensamento político moderno (Belo Horizonte: Universidade Federal de Minas Gerais, 2000).

74. Laura de Mello e Souza, *The Devil in the Land of the Holy Cross* (Austin: University of Texas Press, 2003), originally published as *O diabo e a terra da Santa Cruz* (São Paulo: Compañía das Letras, 1986); *Inferno atlântico: Demonologia e colonização, séculos XVI–XVIII* (São Paulo: Companhia das Letras, 1993).

75. Francisco Bethencourt, *O imaginário da magia: Feiticeiras, adivinhos e curandeiros em Portugal no século XVI* (Lisbon: Universidade Aberta, 1987); José Pedro Paiva, *Práticas e crenças mágicas: O medo e a necesidade dos mágicos na diocese de Coimbra (1650–1740)* (Coimbra: Livraria Minerva, 1992), and his *Bruxaria e superstição num país sem caça às bruxas, 1600–1774*, 2nd ed. (Lisboa: Notícias, 2002). Also useful is Maria Benedita Araújo, *Mágia, demónio e força mágica na tradição portuguesa, séculos XVII e XVIII* (Lisbon: Edições Cosmos, 1994).

76. See note 44 above. Cf. Marina de Mello e Souza, *Reis negros no Brasil escravista: História da festa de coroação de rei Congo* (Belo Horizonte, 2002); João José Reis, *Slave Rebellion in Brazil* (Baltimore: Johns Hopkins University Press, 1993).

77. See the discussion in Chandra Mukerji and Michael Schudson, *Rethinking Popular Culture: Contemporary Perspectives in Cultural Studies* (Berkeley: University of California Press, 1991).

78. István Jancsó and Iris Kantor, eds., *Festa: Cultura e sociabilidade na América portuguesa*, 2 vols. (São Paulo: Hucitec, 2001). Cf. José Pedro Paiva, *Religious Ceremonials and Images: Power and Social Meaning (1400–1750)* (Coimbra: Palimage Editores, 2002). The fullest analysis of the place of religious festivals in popular culture is found in Marta de Abreu Esteves, *O império do divino: Festas religiosas e cultura popular no Rio de Janeiro (1830–1900)* (Rio de Janeiro: Nova Fronteira 1999), which deals with the nineteenth century.

79. Stuart B. Schwartz and Alcir Pécora, eds., *As excelências do governador: O panegírico fúnebre a d. Afonso Furtado, de Juan Lopes Sierra* (São Paulo: Companhia das Letras, 2002); Beatriz Catão Cruz Santos, *O corpo de Deus na América: A festa de Corpus Christi nas cidades da América portuguesa, século XVIII* (São Paulo: Anna Blume, 2005).

80. See, for example, Joaquín Pérez Villanueva and Bartolomé Escandell Bonet, *Historia de la Inquisición en España y América*, 3 vols. (Madrid: Biblioteca de Autores Cristianos, 2000); Henry Kamen, *The Spanish Inquisition: An Historical Revision* (New Haven: Yale University Press, 1997).

81. Francisco Bethencourt, *História das Inquisições: Portugal, Espanha e Itália* (Lisbon: Circulos dos Leitores 1994). Recent work on Portugal, like J. Coelho's study of the Inquisition of Evora or M. Tailland's study of that tribunal from 1660 to 1821, E. Mea's book on the Inquisition of Coimbra, José Pedro Paiva's studies of Portuguese witchcraft and its prosecution in Coimbra, and the thoroughly researched examinations of particular groups (foreigners, *mouriscos*, renegades) or particular categories of offense (bigamy, sodomy), now make it easier to place evidence from Brazil in a larger context. See António Borges Coelho, *Inquisição de Évora*, 2 vols. (Lisbon: Caminho, 1987); Michèle Janin-Thivos Tailland, *Inquisition et société au Portugal: Le cas du tribunal de Évora* (Paris: Centre Cultural Calouste Gulbenkian, 2002); Elvira Cunha de Azevedo Mea, *A Inquisição de Coimbra no século XVI* (Oporto: Fundaçao Eng. António de Almeida, 1997). Unfortunately, the Lisbon tribunal where all cases from the overseas colonies were tried still remains without a major study.

82. Anita Novinsky, *Cristãos novos na Bahia* (São Paulo: Perspectiva, 1972); Sonia Siqueira, *A inquisição portuguesa e a sociedade colonial* (São Paulo: Atica, 1978); Anita Novinsky, *Inquisição: Prisioneiros do Brasil (Séculos XVI a XIX)* (Rio de Janeiro: Perspectiva,

2002); Maria Luiza Tucci Carneiro, *Preconceito racial no Brasil-colônia* (São Paulo: Brasiliense, 1983); Lina Gorenstein Ferreira da Silva, *Heréticos e impuros: A Inquisição e os cristãos-novos no Rio de Janeiro, século XVIII* (Rio de Janeiro: Secretaria de Cultura do Municipio do Rio de Janeiro, 1995).

83. Bruno Feitler, *Inquisition, juifs et nouveaux-chrétiens au Brésil: Le Nordeste, XVIIe et XVIIIe siècles* (Louvain, 2003). French historian Nathan Wachtel, whose *La foi du souvenir* (Paris: Seuil, 2002) dealt with Portuguese New Christians in Spanish America, has been conducting research on the Paraíba New Christians as well. See Luiz Mott, *A Inquisição em Sergipe* (Aracajú: Fundação Estadual de Cultura, 1989); *A Inquisição no Maranhão* (São Luis: EDUFMA, 1995).

84. James E. Wadsworth, "In the Name of the Inquisition: The Portuguese Inquisition and Delegated Authority in Colonial Pernambuco," *The Americas* 61:1 (2004):19–52. See also his "Joaquim Marques de Araújo: O poder da Inquisição em Pernambuco no fim do periodo colonial" in *De Cabral a Pedro I: Aspectos da colonização portuguesa no Brasil*, ed. Maria Beatriz Nizza da Silva (Oporto: Universidade Portucalense Infante d. Henrique, 2001), 309–28.

85. See, for example, David Higgs, "O Santo Ofício da Inquisição de Lisboa e a 'Luceferina Assembléia' do Rio de Janeiro na década de 1790," *Revista do Instituto Histórico e Geográfico Brasileiro* 412 (2001): 239–384.

86. Timothy Coates, *Convicts and Orphans: Forced and State-Sponsored Colonizers in the Portuguese Empire* (Stanford: Stanford University Press, 2001); Gerardo Pieroni, *Os excluídos do Reino: A Inquisição portuguesa e o degredo para o Brasil colônia* (Brasília: Universidade de Brasília, 2000).

87. Ronaldo Vainfas, *Trópico dos pecados: Moral, sexualidade e Inquisição no Brasil*, 2nd ed. (Rio de Janeiro: Campus, 1997); Eliana Maria Rea Goldschmidt, *Convivendo com o pecado na sociedade colonial paulista* (São Paulo: Annablume, 1998); Luiz Mott, *Escravidão, homosexualidade e demonologia* (São Paulo: Icone, 1988).

88. Stuart B. Schwartz, *All Can Be Saved: Salvation and the Origins of Tolerance in the Iberian Atlantic World* (New Haven: Yale University Press, 2008).

89. Plínio Freire Gomes, *Um herege vai ao paraíso* (São Paulo 1997); Adriana Romeiro, *Um visionário na corte de D. João V* (Belo Horizonte: Universidade Federal de Minas Gerais, 2001).

90. Luiz Mott, *Rosa Egipcíaca: Uma santa africana no Brasil* (Rio de Janeiro: Bertrand Brasil, 1993). See, for example, Luiz Mott, *Escravidão, homosexualidade, e demonologia* (São Paulo: Companhia das Letras, 1988).

91. Diogo Ramada Curto, "A literatura e o império," *História da expansão portuguesa*, F. Bethencourt and K. Chauduri, eds., 5 vols. (Lisbon: Círculo dos Leitores, 1998–2000), I, 413–33; "As practicas de escrita," III, 421–62.

92. The third centenary of Padre Vieira's death in 1997 stimulated a renewed interest in his work. See, for example, the outstanding collection of essays in the special number of *Oceanos* 30/31 (1997) dedicated to Vieira. Among the important new contributions to scholarship on Vieira are José van den Besselaar, *Antônio Vieira: Profecia e polêmica* (Rio de Janeiro: Editora da Universidade do Estado do Rio de Janeiro, 2002), and his critical edition of *Livro anteprimeiro da História do futuro* (Lisbon, 1985); Thomas Cohen, *The Fire of Tongues: António Vieira and the Missionary Church in Brazil and Portugal* (Stanford: Stanford University Press, 1998); Margarida Vieira Mendes, *A oratória barroca de Vieira* (Lisbon: Caminho, 1989); Paulo Alexandre Esteves Borges, *A plenificação da história em Padre António Vieira* (Lisboa: Imprensa Nacional-Casa da Moeda, 1995); and Alcir Pécora, *Teatro do sacramento: A unidade teológico-retórico-política dos sermões de Antônio Vieira*

(São Paulo: UNICAMP/EDUSP, 1994). Pécora has also done a critical edition of a selection of Vieira's sermons. *Sermões: Padre Antônio Vieira*, 2 vols. (São Paulo: Hedra, 2000–2001). Alfredo Bosi, *Dialética da colonização* (São Paulo: Companhia das Letras, 1992).

93. João Adolfo Hansen, *A sátira e o engenho: Gregório de Matos e a Bahia do século XVII*, 2nd ed. (Campinas: Ateliê Editorial, 2004); Alcir Pécora, *Máquina dos gêneros* (São Paulo: EDUSP, 2001).

94. Iris Kantor, *Esquecidos e renascidos: Historiografia acadêmica luso-americana 1724–59* (São Paulo: Hucitec/Centro de Estudos Bahianos, 2004).

95. Lilia Moritz Schwarcz, *A longa viagem da biblioteca dos reis* (São Paulo: Companhia das Letras, 2002).

96. See "O Brasil nos quadros do antigo sistema colonial," in Carlos Guilherme Mota, ed., *Brasil em Perspectiva* (São Paulo: Difusão Européia do Livro, 1968), 47–62 It has most recently been republished along with Novais' principal articles in Fernando A. Novais, *Aproximações: Estudos de história e historiografia* (São Paulo: Cosac e Naify, 2006), 45–60. See also Fernando A. Novais, *Portugal e Brasil na crise do antigo sistema colonial, 1777–1808*, 4th ed. (São Paulo: Hucitec, 1986).

97. José Jobson de Andrade Arruda, *O Brasil no comércio colonial* (São Paulo: Ática, 1980); "Colonies as Mercantile Investments," in *The Political Economy of Merchant Empires*, ed. James Tracy (Cambridge: Cambridge University Press, 1991), 360–420.

98. Valentim Alexandre, *Os sentidos do imperio: Questão nacional e questão colonial na crise do antigo regime portugués* (Porto: Afrontamento, 1993); Jorge M. Pedreira, *Estrutura industrial e mercado colonial: Portugal e Brasil* (Lisbon: Difel, 1994).

99. Ernst Pijning, "Controlling Contraband: Mentality, Economy, and Society in Eighteenth-Century Rio de Janeiro" (PhD diss., Johns Hopkins University, 1997). There was direct exchange between Jobson Arruda and Pedreira: see Jorge M. Pedreira, "From Growth to Collapse: Portugal, Brazil, and the Breakdown of the Old Colonial System (1760–1830)," *HAHR* 80:4 (2000): 839–64; José Jobson de Andrade Arruda, "Decadence or Crisis in the Luso-Brazilian Empire: A New Model of Colonization in the Eighteenth Century," *HAHR* 80:4 (2000): 865–78, followed by an exchange between Pijning and Pedreira in *HAHR* 81:3–4 (2001): 733–44. See the summary evaluation of the debate in Guilherme Pereira das Neves, "Del imperio Luso-Brasileiro al imperio del Brasil (1789–1822)," in *De los imperios a las naciones: Iberoamérica*, ed. A. Annino, L. Castro Leiva, and F. X. Guerra (Zaragoza: Ibercaja-Obra Cultural, 1994), 169–93. Further contributions to the debate can be seen in José Luís Cardoso, *A economia política e os dilemas do imperio luso-brasileiro, 1790–1822* (Lisbon: CNCDP, 2001). On the routes and practices of contraband, see Paulo Cavalcante, *Negócios de trapaça: Caminhos e descaminhos na América portuguesa* (Sao Paulo: Hucitec, 2006).

100. António Manuel Hespanha, *As vésperas do Leviathán: Instituições e poder político, Portugal, séc. XVII*, 2nd ed. (Coimbra: Livraria Almedina, 1994); *La gracia del derecho: Economía de la cultura en la Edad Moderna* (Madrid: Centro de Estudios Constitucionales, 1994).

101. Joaquim Romero Magalhães, "As estruturas sociais de enquadramento da economia portuguesa de Antigo regime: Os concelhos," *Notas Econômicas* 4 (1994): 23–34. The work of A.J.R. Russell-Wood has also been influential in this new direction; see especially his "Centro e periferia no mundo luso-brasileiro," *Revista Brasileira de História* 18:36 (1998): 187–250.

102. I have summarized Fragoso's argument more extensively in "Somebodies and Nobodies in the Body Politic: Mentalities and Social Structures in Colonial Brazil," *Latin American Research Review* 31:1 (1996): 113–34.

103. João Fragoso, "A nobreza da república: Notas sobre a formação da primeira elite senhorial do Rio de Janeiro (séculos XVI e XVII)," *Topoi. Revista de História* 1 (2000): 45–122; *Homens da grossa aventura: Acumulação e hierarquia na praça mercantile do Rio de Janeiro, 1790–1830*, 2nd ed. (Rio de Janeiro: Civilização Brasileira, 1998); Maria Fernanda Bicalho, *A cidade e o império: O Rio de Janeiro no século XVIII* (Rio de Janeiro: Civilização Brasileira, 2003); Maria de Fátima Gouvêa, "Redes de poder na América portuguesa: O caso dos homens bons do Rio de Janeiro, 1790–1822," *Revista Brasileira de História* 18:36 (1998): 297–330; "Poder, justiça e soberania no Império colonial português, século XVIII," *Leituras: Revista da Biblioteca Nacional* (Lisbon), 6 (2000). A major statement of the position of the Carioca school and examples of some of its best work is found in João Fragoso, M. Fernanda Bicalho, and Maria de Fátima Gouvêa, eds., *O antigo regime nos trópicos: A dinâmica imperial portuguesa, séculos XVI–XVIII* (Rio de Janeiro: Civilização Brasileira, 2001). See also João Fragoso, Maria de Fátima Gouvêa, and Maria Fernanda Baptista Bicalho, "Uma leitura do Brasil colonial: Bases de materialidade e da governabilidade no Império," *Penelope* 23 (2000): 67–88João Fragoso, Maria de Fátima Gouvêa, and Maria Fernanda Baptista Bicalho, "Uma leitura do Brasil colonial: Bases de materialidade e da governabilidade no Império," *Penelope* 23 (2000): 67–88.

104. Mafalda Soares da Cunha, *A Casa da Bragança, 1560–1640* (Lisbon: Editora Estampa, 2000); Nuno Gonçalo Freitas Monteiro, *O crepúsculo dos grandes, 1750–1832* (Lisbon: Imprensa Nacional, 1996); *Elites e poder: Entre o antigo regime e o liberalismo* (Lisbon: Imprenta de Ciencias Sociais, 2003); Maria Beatriz Nizza da Silva, *Ser Nobre na Colônia* (São Paulo: UNESP, 2005).

105. Nuno G. F. Monteiro, Pedro Cardim, and Mafalda Soares da Cunha, eds., *Optima pars: Elites Ibero-Americanas do Antigo Regime* (Lisbon: Imprensa de Ciências Sociais, 2005).

106. José M. Subtil, *O Desembargo do Paço, 1750–1833* (Lisbon: Universidade Autónoma de Lisboa, 1996); Pedro Cardim, *Cortes e cultura política no Portugal do Antigo Regime* (Lisbon: Edições Cosmos, 1998); Fernanda Olival, *As ordens militares e o estado moderno: Honra, mercê, e venalidade em Portugal, 1641–1789* (Lisbon: Estar, 2001).

107. Mafalda Soares da Cunha and Nuno Gonçalo F. Monteiro, "Governadores e capitães-mores do império Atlântico português nos séculos XVII e XVIII" in Maria Fernanda Bicalho, Vera Lúcia Amaral Ferlini, *Modos de governor* (São Paulo: Alameda, 2005).

108. Notable in this regard are Jacqueline Hermann, *No reino do desejado: A construção do sebastianismo em Portugal séculos XVI e XVII* (São Paulo: Companhia das Letras, 1998); Ana Paula Torres Megiani, *O rei ausente: Festa e cultura política nas visitas dos Felipes a Portugal, 1581–1619* (São Paulo: Alameda, 2004); Mary Del Priore, *O mal sobre a terra: Uma história do terremoto de Lisboa* (Rio de Janeiro: Topbooks, 2003); Rodrigo Bentes Monteiro, *O rei no espelho: A monarquia portuguesa e a colonização da América, 1640–1720* (São Paulo: Hucitec, 2005). Deserving mention as well as a predecesor is Eduardo D'Oliveira França, *Portugal na época da Restauração* (São Paulo: Hucitec, 1997), which had circulated as an underground "classic" since it was completed as a thesis in 1951.

109. Maria Fernanda Bicalho and Vera Lúcia Amaral Ferlini, *Modos de governor* (São Paulo: Alameda, 2005). Some historical journals that have dedicated considerable space to the topic of colonial administration are *Revista Brasileira de História* 18:36 (1998), "Do Império português ao Império do Brasil"; *Penelope* (Lisbon), 27 (2002), "Política e administração no Atlântico"; *Tempo*, 7:13 (2002), "Política e administração no mundo Luso-brasileiro."

110. Laura de Mello e Souza, *O sol e a sombra: Política e administração na América portuguesa do século XVIII* (São Paulo: Compañía das Letras, 2006), especially pp. 44–69.

António Manuel Hespanha has responded in "Depois do Leviathán," *Almanack Brasiliense* 5 (2007), available at http://www.almanack.usp.br.

111. For example, Joseph Miller, *Way of Death: Merchant Capitalism and the Angolan Slave Trade* (Madison: University of Wisconsin Press, 1988); Alencastro, *Trato dos viventes*; Sanjay Subrahmanyam, "Holding the World in Balance: The Connected Histories of the Iberian Overseas Empires, 1500–1640," *American Historical Review* 112:5 (2007): 1359–85; Serge Gruzinski, *Les quatre parties du monde: Histoire d'une mondalisation* (Paris: Editions de La Martinière, 2004).

112. José Luís Cardoso, *A economia política e os dilemas do imperio luso-brasileiro, 1790–1822* (Lisbon: CNCDP, 2001).

113. Luís da Cunha, *Instruções políticas*, Abílio Diniz Silva, ed. (Lisbon: CNCDP, 2001); Kenneth Maxwell, *Pombal: Paradox of the Enlightenment* (Cambridge: Cambridge University Press, 2001); Andrée Mansuy-Diniz Silva, *Portrait d'un homme d'État: D. Rodrigo de Souza Coutinho, Comte de Linhares, 1755–1812*, 2 vols. (Paris: Centre Culturel Calouste Gulbenkian, 2006).

114. Schwarcz, *A longa viagem*; Maria Beatriz Nizza da Silva, *A cultura luso-brasileira: Da reforma da Universidade à independencia do Brasil* (Lisbon: Editorial Estampa, 1999); Ronald Raminelli, *Viagens ultramarinas* (Sao Paulo: Alameda, 2008); Iris Kantor, *Esquecidos e renacidos* (Sao Paulo: Hucitec, 2004); Kristin Schultz, *Tropical Versailles: Empire, Monarchy, and the Portuguese Royal Court in Rio de Janeiro* (New York: Routledge, 2001).

115. István Jancsó, ed., *Independência: História e historiografia* (São Paulo: Hucitec, 2005); *Brasil: Formação do estado e da nação* (São Paulo: Hucitec, 2003).

116. Ana Rosa Cloclet da Silva, *Inventando a nação: Intelectuais ilustrados e estadistas Luso-Brasileiros na crise do Antigo regime portugués* (São Paulo: Hucitec, 2006); Andréa Slemian, *Vida política em tempo de crise: Rio de Janeiro, 1808–1824* (São Paulo: Hucitec, 2006); Denis Antônio de Mendonça Bernardes, *O patriotismo constitucional: Pernambuco, 1820–22* (São Paulo: Hucitec/Editora Universidade Federal de Pernambuco, 2006).

CHAPTER 4

SEXUALITY IN COLONIAL SPANISH AMERICA

ASUNCIÓN LAVRIN

WITH the arrival of the conquistadors and settlers in Spanish America, a peculiar and constant pattern of sexual behavior began to unfold. The curiosity and sometimes amazement shown by the earliest discoverers and travelers about the naked bodies of men and women in the tropics and their uninhibited (to European eyes) sexual behavior led to natural consequences. As soon as the mostly young males, arriving after several months of sea travel, stepped onto the shores of the New World, they began to sexually intermingle with the indigenous women. Whether these liaisons were forced or natural remains under debate, but the massive miscegenation that ensued for several centuries—known as *mestizaje*—was to become one of the key demographic features of the Spanish colonies.

There was more than mere sex to this process. The personal and social behavior of the several ethnic and racial groups involved was deeply colored by religious and social rules. Prescriptions and proscriptions developed throughout three centuries, creating a complex mixture of ethic, religious, and legal guidelines which the population either accepted or challenged. The intersection of civil legislation, religious condemnation, and real personal behavior form a corpus of evidence that is the basis of contemporary research.

As the process of colonization took place, these various patterns had to accommodate to each other, which they did, we know, rather imperfectly. The moral values attached to sexuality by Roman Catholicism were not necessarily similar to those upheld by indigenous societies, although sometimes they coincided on some issues. Throughout the colonial period, the theological views of Christianity reinforced by the stern reinterpretation of the Counter-Reformation authorities became the "correct" vision of sexual behavior for all peoples. As such, they were officially applied to all subjects by the church and the lay authorities. Local indigenous practices struggled to survive alongside the official views, and they did so to various degrees. Their success depended on the lack of official supervision or the geographical isolation of the group.¹ Despite the assumption that Catholic morality ruled sexual behavior, "popular" interpretations of what was sexually correct or acceptable thrived among the non-Spanish populace. Even those of Spanish descent were not immune to nonorthodox practices. The appeal of research on sexuality is that a good deal of information stems from common people, whose conduct attests to their desire to escape the straitjacket of confessional morality. The upper layers of society have also left their track, as some of their members searched for legal means to cover their slips. There is something satisfyingly "democratic" about the history of sin and sex.

This essay will follow some of the works that have tackled the sometimes thorny issue of how to recover and interpret the historical memory of sexual behavior. Sexuality will be defined as the set of activities and forms of behavior directly related to contact between the sexes, as well as the ideas and ideology developed to understand the nature of sexual relations and the mechanisms devised to control it. That ideology was mostly formulated by religious authorities and enforced by the state through institutions such as the Inquisition and the ecclesiastical and civil courts. What seems to be lacking in the current historiography is the extension of some concepts based on human sexuality to larger arenas of human relations and governance, such as the analysis of medical views on sex and its effects on the development of health policies, the influence of the religious discourse on sex and on legislation affecting the social order, the sexual content of the religious discourse, the erotic content of religious writings, and the hidden sexual meanings of political discourse.

Pre-Columbian Sexuality

Information on this topic is of interest in order to reach a balanced understanding of the meeting of the sexes in the sixteenth century and the biological and cultural changes it elicited. At present, most of our knowledge is culled from postconquest Spanish sources or archaeological findings. The latter field seems to be opening up much relevant and fascinating information. Figurines, paintings in pottery, wall paintings, and reliefs inform us about gender roles and sexual practices in the preconquest world, while mythological accounts provide important cultural elements that may be broadly applied to social and political life. Both are especially useful for the Andean area, which lacked any form of writing. Pottery described as "erotic," often rather blatant representations of sexual acts, are abundant among the Moche culture of northern Peru, whose rich palette of sexual symbols include phallic and vaginal sex as well as uninhibited depictions of anal and homosexual sex, pictures of shamed male prisoners in the nude, and even sexual acts among skeletal figures.

Whether these objects suggest a view of sex as a natural part of life, as catering to the fantasies of some individuals, or as having deeper underlying religious and political meanings remains under study. Clearly, Andean peoples have a long tradition of sexual representation addressing behavior as well as symbolic ideology. Information on sexual behavior as reflected in archaeological data and in the earliest chroniclers indicates a deep concern with sexual behavior and reproduction, but not all of it was related to sex per se. Some recent interpretations point to symbolic meanings of power and fertility in sexual acts. The mythology of the region provides other clues. The myths of Huarochirí as well as Inca foundational myths have plenty of explicit and implicit information on sexual taboos as well as sexual behavior. Inca moral rules, as translated by postconquest narratives, seemed to condemn adultery and same-sex practices even though other sexual practices offensive to Catholic Spaniards, such as premarital sex, were normal and acceptable to them. Doubts have been raised about the ability of postconquest inquiries to fully comprehend the meaning of indigenous sexuality in this region and elsewhere. Mary Weismantel reminds us that meanings ascribed to such sources may not be accurate as long as we filter them through Western value systems, a warning that applies to all information on pre-Columbian sexuality.[2] In fact, the analysis of all myths, Andean or Mesoamerican, is subject to contradictory interpretations.

For Mesoamerica, the sources are richer and have the advantage of a written language to support explanations and interpretations. Maya and Aztec artifacts and mythology, as well as cultural materials collected by early chroniclers, indicate a complex incorporation of sexual meaning into political and religious behavior. Archaeology has provided additional evidence, although the Mesoamerican civilizations lack the abundant explicitness of Moche sexual imagery. Recent writings on the pre-Columbian Maya note the fluid nature of sexual roles in their mythology. Recent ethnographic studies point to the translation of gendered notions of sexual roles to different visual and plastic media. The representation of bodies, costumes, and gender-related activities helped define gender roles, whether in monumental construction, representations of the ruling class, or small artifacts used in everyday devotional practices. Male genital bloodletting among the Maya and other phallic displays have raised questions about male bonding, the symbolism of maleness and power yielding, the transmission of power, and the meaning of sexual acts themselves.[3] Studies of gender systems and social values ascribed to the male and female sex among the Aztecs are based largely on data gathered after the conquest by friars or male chroniclers from the leading men of the Nahua communities. As such, they favor a male viewpoint of social and sexual mores, possibly in need of correction by analysis more sensitive to the female input in society. In sum, postconquest sources coupled with archaeological data form the base of current studies exploring sexually charged gender roles through a variety of cultural expressions. Architecture, pottery, murals and sculpture, spindles, and clothing are among the vast array of products of material culture that are under scrutiny as conveyors of information of gender roles. While there is a considerable element of clever interpretation in this field, this trend is also an exciting turn for archaeology as a tool to understand ancient cultures.⁴ The relevance of all pre-Columbian data in the understanding of colonial sexual practices is now understood as being paramount.

THE CONQUEST PERIOD

The conquest period, as the crucial moment of mutual discovery, was carried out as much through sexual encounters as it was in the fields of war. Few historians in the past discussed the sexual nature of the Spanish conquest. When Robert Padden characterized the conquest of Mexico as the conquest of the penis, he raised a few eyebrows, but once the veil was lifted, others followed suit in seeing a strong dosage of heterosexual behavior in the formation of the new society and the core of changes in the population's profile.⁵ The assumption that heterosexual sexuality had its heyday in the process of conquest and the first decades of the settlement underlies these general surveys of the topic. However, the inclusion of other forms of sexuality has changed the tone of the discussion and expanded the frontiers of sexuality, as discussed below.⁶

The conquest period, as recorded in most narratives, highlights the male experience of the Spanish men receiving Indian women as gifts or taking them for their own personal sexual use, and sometimes marrying them if they were socially desirable.⁷ Accounts such as those of Huamán Poma de Ayala and Gonzalo Fernández de Oviedo are among the many that have served as bases for recent inquiries into the sexual behavior of conquerors and early settlers, as well as into their own perception of Indian women and men. Coming from antagonistic viewpoints, these and similar sources describe and moralize using their own standards and require careful analysis. The discussions of the role of Marina-Malinche in the conquest of Mexico by Frances Karttunen and Camilla Townsend shed much light on the controversial nature of the role of this and other women in the conquest saga.⁸ The sexual violence implicit in the conquest and how it affected women—mostly indigenous, but also early settlers—deserves further research and reinterpretation. To date, there are few studies that stretch into the colonial period, other than a few concerned with rape and domestic abuse. Research in criminal courts would help delineate not only a better profile of sexual violence against women of all races but delve deeper into the nature of violence itself and its symbolic meaning as an exercise in gender power.⁹

The cultural understanding of the meeting of peoples with their own perceptions of sexual values and practices posed new questions on how to read the body as a text for conquest. The nudity of tropical peoples was the first step in the development of new concepts of "perversion" if not lack of civilization for the Spaniards, who, at the same time, discovered and enacted sexual activities that contradicted their own moral mandates. In general, the view of the body that prevailed in the colonial period was inherited from late medieval and early sixteenth-century Christianity. The opposition of flesh and spirit was generalized through religious indoctrination, but it certainly was not a view that had any great purchase among the masses, even if they declared much contrition after transgressions. The manipulation of the body for sexual purposes through witchcraft was but one manifestation of the gap between the theological culture and the popular culture.

The first generation of evangelizers was obsessed with indigenous polygamy, usually reserved for the nobility, and encountered numerous "aberrations" in indigenous practices that prompted the construction of an elaborate discourse on sexuality for the "neophytes."[10] The indigenous population took time to assimilate and accept Roman Catholicism in its entirety. Shamanism and "idolatry" persisted and, along with them, unorthodox practices such as "tying" and potions for sexual purposes.[11] On the other hand, the way in which Catholic and indigenous notions of gender and sexual behavior melded with or confused each other is also an important aspect of postconquest analysis. Louise Burkhart has studied the conceptual change from Nahua morals to Christian morals as an intense "dialogue" on sin, purity, and pollution, virginity, incest, and other forms of behavior. Some of these concepts were more easily adaptable to Nahua (and by extension other indigenous) thought than others. Burkhart suggests that in the end, Christianity was "Nahuatlized." Because the friars appropriated the moral authority of the elders and took the upper hand in the definition of proper sexual behavior, the colonial indigenous moral world remained a slippery one.[12] On the other hand, the persistence of pagan practices and their implicit moral meaning tainted the adoption of Christianity. In fact, through these underground practices some members of the group maintained positions of power in their communities.[13] However, by adopting Christian practices they could also gain power while transforming their understanding of gender, albeit not always in tandem with normative Christianity.

POSTCONQUEST: COLONIAL PERIOD

While the indigenous population is paramount in the study of the conquest, the African population is a harder subject to cope with as long as the various African roots remain unexplored. The friars' lack of interest in the African background stood in contrast with their avid collection of materials on the Indians. Conjugal arrangements and master-slave sex are often culled from sources such as the Inquisition. The sexual use of female slaves added a gendered dimension that has been easy to document, while a similar use of male slaves remained difficult to document, although it was by no means unknown.[14] Conjugal love was difficult among slaves, despite official royal and ecclesiastical encouragement, with masters often becoming an obstacle to regular marital sex. Illicit relationships were formed out of necessity. In general, the population of African ancestry was tightly hemmed in by Christian moral teachings, whether as *bozales* or criollos, and their transgressions and challenges closely resemble those of other racial groups.[15] Unlike other members of society, Africans were associated with the devil and sexuality. The most common personal representation of the devil in the mind of many colonial people was that of a black man. The demonization of blackness explains the connection of sexuality with Inquisitorial materials on witchcraft.[16]

Demographic studies in the 1970s delved into the phenomenon of *mestizaje* as the factor that, by the middle of the seventeenth century, had counterbalanced the loss of indigenous populations. *Mestizaje* has been treated as a demographic phenomenon rather than as a sexuality issue, which was not always the case during the colonial period, when sex and race were more tightly knitted. *Mestizaje* has also been the base for many studies in race relations and racial policies. A different slant is now offered by studies that openly acknowledge the sexual base of *mestizaje* and probe into the human aspect of the liaisons that produced such racial mixing. In pursuing this line of research, historians have expanded the boundaries of demography into social and cultural history.[17] However, demographic analysis remains indispensable to validate the sexuality underlying the process of miscegenation. Among other facts, it helps to assess the breadth of unions outside wedlock by testing the number of illegitimate children and single mothers that helped to create and define an alternative form of family formation. Although those unions were outside the legal and religious frame, they were the "pattern" followed by in many areas of Spanish America, truly "public sins" regarded with unusual complacency in a society presumably upholding rigid prescriptions of personal behavior.[18]

The theological debates over the nature of marriage and how to apply it to the Indians engaged many minds, while the unfettered sexual behavior of Spaniards received relatively little attention. Given the widespread practice of unbridled sex by men of all classes and colors, the Inquisition eventually began to investigate seriously the sexuality of the non-Indian population by the end of the sixteenth century and accelerated this process in the ensuing years. The promiscuity of the population at large was acknowledged and addressed. Crown and church devised new forms of surveying personal behavior in an attempt to regulate how their subjects followed the canons of proper sexual behavior.[19] Ecclesiastical courts took the reins of control over the sexual life of the population in general by supervising personal mores and establishing the canons of propriety that would support the edifice of official Counter-Reformation sexuality. Marriage was prescribed as the sole conduit for sexual relations; any other form of contact among the sexes was deemed punishable in various degrees. The church increasingly used the confessional as a means to probe into the sexual behavior of the faithful of all races. However, neither the official posture nor the punishments meted out for sin and its "illegitimate" fruits proved to be strong deterrents to the populace. People continued to misbehave and even poke surreptitious fun at the judges. As Águeda Méndez has amply corroborated, erotically charged popular writings, songs, and dances circulated in the urban area, reaffirming the tradition of challenging prescribed sexual behavior.[20]

The exploration of the broad spectrum of sexual behavior and the lack of observance of ecclesiastical norms is at the core of studies of colonial sexuality. One of the earliest collections of essays on sexual behavior, published in Mexico in the mid-1980s, carried the subtitle "why the law of God was not obeyed in novo-Hispanic society," a question that seems to have guided the historical curiosity of works on Spanish America published since then.[21] Throughout the colonial period, heterosexual sexuality expressed itself in behavior that had its roots in the sixteenth century. While demographic data indicate that mestizos of different racial mixtures perpetuated irregular forms of sexual couplings through many generations, the source of *mestizaje* lies at the feet of the white males who first exercised their sexual privilege with women of all races, setting a trend throughout the end of the colonial period. The failure in the enforcement of policies of sexual regulation was well recorded in the many civil and ecclesiastical courts, where transgressions were duly recorded while being judged.[22] Among the spectrum of challenges to official canon are witchcraft, bigamy, adultery, rape, incest, illicit cohabitation, marital abuse, solicitation by religious males, and sodomy.

As this brief and incomplete "catalog" of transgressions suggests, one of the liabilities of research on sexuality is that the behavior officially recorded has been labeled as "sinful" and aberrant a priori, and is treated as such in most sources. Historians must sift through evidence that is tainted by prejudgment and separate the grain from the chaff. While the viewpoints of church and civil authorities are a key element in the construction of sexuality, so too are the personal voices of the transgressors, a much sought after and scarce historical commodity. Judicial processes are the best sources in which to detect the viewpoints of the purveyors of moral law as well as those who transgressed it.[23] Prescriptive sources, even if disconnected from reality, are also crucial to understanding the moral constructions that influenced the law and attempted to shape the mind of the people. As such, they gain real validity on their own as expressions of cultural canons. Ecclesiastical and civil records open windows into the interplay of personal attitudes and the laws. They allow us to witness the assimilation of social mores, the social pressures to conform as well as the desire to challenge them and escape. When the balance between the willingness to conform and the desire to challenge was broken, one had "sinful" and punishable behavior. Recidivists were punished as criminals, and sexual criminality was a serious concern for the authorities at the end of the colonial period.[24]

Given the intimate nature of sexual behavior and the tight privacy that most people wished to maintain around it in compliance with traditional prescriptions received from ecclesiastical authorities, what we know today about it was what became out of control, spilling from private chambers or hideouts to the public arena. Intimacy, betrayed by the actors themselves or by eager witnesses, opened itself up to the curious gaze of historians in the cases of bigamy, incest, deflowering, rape, and same-sex sexual activity.[25] When it became public, sexual intimacy became a "scandal" and put the machinery of justice into action. Behavior that became "de pública voz y fama" was subjected to the curiosity and judgment of the entire community—whether it was proper or improper. "Public sins" were offensive because they eroded the accepted codes of morality. Knowledge of the intimate was gained through the grapevine and gossip that detected the transgression. Indictment and sometimes eventual conviction resulted from denunciation (sometimes self-denunciation) of domestic witnesses.[26]

All private life had a public nature. Female virginity, legitimate marriage, legitimate birth, and female modesty or immodesty were all public matters that allowed the community to establish accountability and pass judgment.

The impact of the public eye on the private realm of sexual behavior can be observed and analyzed in several ways. The most common venue is the Inquisition and its records, which cover all offenses against the sacraments. The Inquisition was an astute institution that worked on the assumption that peer pressure and public interest in other people's lives helped to maintain control over the population. People were the best keepers of their neighbors. Richard Boyer's study of bigamy through Inquisitorial records illustrates the peculiar origins of bigamy as well as its successful detection. His findings corroborate and expand previous studies.[27] Irrational as it may appear, those who transgressed the law wished nothing more than to pretend to obey it. Bigamists were caught because of their desire to maintain "propriety" by marrying and appearing to be following the law of God and the land. They were concerned about the public image of a relationship and therefore counterfeited legality. Their behavior was also a mirror of forms of sexual seduction and persuasion that sheds much light on other forms of colonial sexuality.[28]

The flow of information helped the Inquisition and the ecclesiastic tribunals maintain their hold on society not just in cases of bigamy but with other forms of sexual "misconduct" such as rape, incest, and sexual violence. The Provisorato de Indios fulfilled the same function for the indigenous population.[29] The majority of cases begin with the denunciation of self-appointed keepers of propriety and afflicted parties, but self-denunciation was also a factor pointing to the weight of internalized religious indoctrination. Not surprisingly, one learns about marital intimacies in suits for personal separation—the so-called "divorce" that allowed married couples to abandon marital duties and live separate lives. Domestic violence rather than adultery was the most common reason for separation, and these suits expose the vagaries of sadistic punishment of women and the misunderstandings of sexually incompatible couples.[30]

Since the preservation of women's virginity before marriage remained a paramount concern for colonial subjects, the forceful violation of physical virginity was, officially, a heinous crime. However, despite the strong letter of the law, punishment for rape was influenced by race and class: the lower the status of the woman, the weaker the effectiveness of the law. The flexible sexual behavior of some women also suggests that sometimes it was difficult to establish the boundaries between forced sex and consensuality.[31] Indeed, this was one of the most contentious aspects of sexual contact when submitted to the close scrutiny of the law.

If the physical aspects of sexuality will continue to elicit interest among historians, the more subtle and abstract element of personal and public behavior, honor, was its compulsory companion. Honor is a concept that embraces nuances of public and private behavior that have nothing to do with sex. However, honor also had the closest association with sexuality insofar as it implied an obligation to be responsible for one's own sexual behavior. The overarching topic of "honor," the base of all forms of proper and improper behavior, affected both genders and all racial and ethnic variations. It is now embedded in studies of sexual behavior. Historians of honor agree that women bore the greater weight of maintaining their own honor and that of the family, although there are disagreements as to whether or not the concept of honor changed throughout time and as to the precise nature and variations of the interplay of men and women in negotiating honor in different communities. In fact, the injections of time, locality, and race have problematized the discussion of honor.[32]

Female honor was heavily predicated on sexual behavior and largely, although not solely, applied to single women who lost their virginity as a result of willing or forced sex. However, if force was an issue, married women could argue they would lose social honor if a man forced sex on them. Ecclesiastical and civil law recognized and endorsed the responsibility of men as patresfamilias and husbands for the sexual honor of women, but stressed the moral burden women incurred if they abandoned their commitment to virtue and chastity. Therefore, both sexes were rewarded with personal and social "legitimation" and full protection of personal legal rights when they obeyed the prescriptions on sexual behavior. In her thorough study of honor and legitimacy, Ann Twinam redefines the meaning of honor as a mixture of personal values and public opinion, but one that had important nuances and situational variations. Her analysis of class, gender, and legitimation uses the sexual behavior of both genders as an analytical tool to understand the boundaries of honor and the parameters between rigidity and flexibility it offered to colonial subjects. She has introduced the theme of male honor and single fathers, stretching the meaning of the concept of honor beyond the more traditional assumption that it was a "female" issue.[33] Lipsett-Rivera argues that men were not the sole "protectors" (as well as debunkers) of women's sexual honor; women themselves stood up in their own defense, aware of the social repercussions dishonor could have for themselves and their close relatives.[34]

Prostitution was a sexual transgression of moral norms, and yet also an acceptable practice within well-defined circumstances. While this statement applies to the practice as known among Europeans, there are some uncertainties about how it functioned in pre-Columbian societies. Information on indigenous "prostitutes" culled from postconquest sources is mediated by the vision of the friars who first collected it. However, there is no doubt that some forms of prostitution existed among the Aztecs.[35] After the conquest, there was a very fine line of distinction between a woman of "loose" morals, who would have sexual affairs with several men, and women who engaged in paid sex as a way of life. There were no authorized brothels similar to those in the peninsula, and sometimes "prostitution" was more a perception in the mind of the witness than a reality comparable to that in Europe. Huamán Poma de Ayala called the Indian women who slept with Spaniards "whores" and continually castigated all forms of sexual misbehavior among the different ethnic groups.[36] As Pablo Rodríguez has suggested, the availability of Indian women throughout the conquest period, and of *casta* women throughout the colonial period, conspired against the establishment of a booming prostitution business.[37] Yet all urban centers contained women of ill repute, whose trade was broadcast by the public grapevine. "Public sinning" irked ecclesiastical authorities, but a clear line of demarcation did not exist between a woman available for sex with men and another of loose morals who would have sequential multiple partners.

Although José Toribio Medina heatedly denounced the sexual misconduct of the colonial clergy, few historians ventured deeply into the topic until recently. There is more than circumstantial evidence that priests and friars abused the confidence of their female advisees and that sodomy and pederasty were not beyond the experience of some. Paulino Castañeda and René Millar have analyzed the Inquisition's handling of sexual transgressions among the religious in Peru. Castañeda notes that in the sixteenth century the Inquisition ignored the situation, apprehensive of the clergy's reputation in its protracted struggle with Protestantism. A drive for the reform of the clergy in the eighteenth century changed this, and the Inquisition adopted a more aggressive policy in the punishment of all forms of transgressions by members of the church.[38]

For Mexico, Jorge René González Marmolejo has thoroughly investigated male ecclesiastical sexuality, using the Inquisition records of New Spain as his main source. He has surveyed cases in Puebla and has completed a study of all the cases of solicitation in the archbishopric of Mexico in the eighteenth century. Other inquiries into clerical sexuality have defined the circumstances surrounding such behavior as well as the targets of their sexual desire.[39] The investigation of what constituted "misbehavior" rested in the church's hands, and because of the carefully framed definition of solicitation and the cautious and discreet procedures of the investigation, it is evident that the church tried to protect its members as much as to punish those who were obviously guilty. However, that "punishment" rarely led to defrocking or expulsion from the orders. Solicitation tells us more about the problems of controlling sexuality among men of the cloth than about the disciplinarian practices of the church. Since Inquisitors were far from squeamish, the records also often reveal intimate details that might have shocked the prudish ears of the time, but they are fertile ground for modern researchers in search of popular understanding of the most forbidden and tempting of all sexual conduct.

Anthropologists began to raise interest in sexual witchcraft as they explored the practical uses of indigenous, African, and Spanish cosmic conceptions of the relatedness of a "magic," or demonic, and a natural world. The powers of the spirits of animals, or the devil among Christians, could be managed to serve the interest of the flesh; natural substances could be used to "bind" and subdue the will of lovers and obtain control over the sexual behavior. The pre-Hispanic past linked this type of beliefs to the colonial period, as shown by Noemí Quezada's investigation of the world of Aztec and postconquest New Spain. In her search she looked for the characterization of the practices, the personality of the practitioners, and the use of supernatural powers as a mean of sexual control.[40] However, the use of witchcraft did not create a polarity between Indian and Spaniards, or even the *castas*, because all groups resorted to it. Afro-criollos often learned practices from the Indians. Ruth Behar has reminded us of the Spanish origins of witchcraft and has argued that it was an expression of female subversion of male power in general. Witchcraft, in her view, could be a tool of the colonized (who could be women as well as men) against the colonizers and an expression of racial distrust and rejection of the white masters by indigenous and mixed-bloods.[41] "Unsanctioned power" is what Laura A. Lewis calls the use of witchcraft to subvert Spanish power.[42] Perhaps the colonial subjects were not thinking such sophisticated thoughts when they exercised themselves in the arts of the "occult." The simple desire to affect the conduct of others and the profit made by the sale of products seem to have guided those individuals caught by the authorities. Witchcraft was also linked to forms of prostitution, according to Ana Sánchez, who underlines their connection with pseudo-medicine and the clerical campaign against idolatry.[43] A large-scale campaign against unorthodoxy had an obvious connection with witchcraft and the threat it seemed to pose to Catholic canon. It also targeted the human element in the lower rungs of society to find evidence for its social fears and sexual insecurities, and to search for evidence of criminal behavior, a common accompaniment of sexual transgressions.[44]

Another facet of the connection between sexuality and religion revealed by research on diabolism points to the complex meanings of the devil in the theological imagination as well as in folk beliefs. The devil was associated with lust, among other things, and lured men and women into lewdness, a symbol of all that was undesirable about the flesh. As such, he was a ubiquitous figure in many texts associated with religious pedagogy or indoctrination, such as sermons, religious chronicles, and hagiography, and remained deeply embedded in the colonial imagination as a source of sexual misconduct.[45] The devil pursued everybody, transcending gender, class, and race, and remained the deus ex machina of all sinful behavior.[46] Witchcraft and diabolism are signs of cracks in the system of belief, which remain tantalizing possibilities for further cultural explorations.

Conquerors, first settlers, and evangelizers detecting homosexual activities in the indigenous population reacted with vigorous denunciation. The "nefarious" sin would become first the object of curiosity and revulsion, and later a crime of the highest order for colonials as the Counter-Reformation church fixed its gaze on this behavior in the seventeenth century and held the first public burnings of proven homosexuals. Serge Gruzinski led in the study of this still developing aspect of colonial sexuality.[47] Pierre Ragon explored the theme of the discovery of the sexual "otherness" of the indigenous in New Spain, as revealed in the many observations and comments recorded by the conquerors and settlers.[48] Since then, several other authors have explored this topic in search of one of the most secret and reviled sexual practices of the period. They seek to reinterpret the "encounter" of sexualities, the meaning of sexual behavior during the conquest, and the "unorthodox" sexuality of those who did not fit the narrow definitions of Catholic morality.

Since the sixteenth century, two visions have dominated the sexual practices of indigenous males by those who observed and studied them. The first was that of the Indian as an "effeminate" sodomite, an interpretation reaffirmed by theologians and historians with transparent imperial undertones. The second was that of the lusty Indian, in opposition to the deviant practitioner of sodomitic sex or the "transvestites" that came to be known as "berdaches." In the 1520s, he lust of Indian chiefs surrounded by harems of women, as well as the sexual desire of some indigenous women, mesmerized Gonzalo Fernández de Oviedo, who was also appalled by parallel examples of sodomy. Such abrasive sensuality was interpreted as lessening intellectual faculties, a theme clearly intended to cast doubts on indigenous rationality. However, this view was increasingly undermined by a discourse more suitable to the colonized in which the indigenous, rather than an active agent of sexuality, became phlegmatic and feminized by the conquest.

Richard Trexler in his *Sex and Conquest: Gendered Violence, Political Order, and the European Conquest of the Americas* (London: Polity Press, 1995) took the issues of masculinity, power, and empire to formulate a "gendered" interpretation of the conquest along homoerotic lines, based on native homosexual practices and the conquerors' view of such behavior. The study of these "practices" itself served a greater cause: that of seeing the conquest as a stupendous act of penetration—physical and intellectual. This, he claims, was not a new way of understanding conquest to men who carried it out, such as the natives, who were themselves conquerors of others, and the Europeans who eventually conquered them. Another grand interpretation of sex and power is that of Federico Garza Carvajal, who pursues the meaning of sodomy to those men in charge of defining and punishing it as a base for a political imperialistic scheme.[49] He posits that the definition of sodomy rested on the definition of the model "total" man ("Vir") and his counterpart, the model total woman. In his view, the physical and political expansion of Spain in the sixteenth century used the concept of masculinity in solidifying its imperial designs at home and abroad. Seeing the need to accept a theory of culturally variable notions of homosexuality, he studies the perception and punishment of sodomites in Spain. There, he claims, sodomy had entailed a more "virile" notion of man on man, but by the end of the seventeenth century the notion had changed and sodomy was seen as a sign of moral perversion and eventually a sign of moral decay. The concept of "feminizing" the conquered is one that has been picked up by Laura Lewis in her work, which deals with identities as well as transgressions. Political and cultural interpretation of the conquest through the lens of same-sex notions and practices remains intriguing, although still not corroborated or accepted by all historians.[50]

Beyond the grand interpretation of the conquest, the perception, practice, and control of same-sex sexual activity in the colonies is under close examination. Pete Sigal took a first step towards engaging a debate on homoeroticism by setting a theoretical framework in his introduction to *Infamous Desire: Male Homosexuality in Colonial Latin America* (Chicago: University of Chicago Press, 2003).[51] Michel Foucault argued that homosexuality, as understood today, did not exist as a form of self-identity in the early modern period. As an exception to the rule, the Brazilian Louis Mott contends that in seventeenth-century Brazil, a gay identity was already taking shape, a thesis that some historians of Spain support. Indeed, the bottom line of Segal's arguments is to deny the complete applicability of Foucault's argument. Segal's own analysis addresses the question of the interplay of sexual desire and sexual power among eighteenth-century Yucatecan Mayas as well as among early colonial Nahua-speaking peoples in central Mexico. Segal seeks, in particular, to understand the discourse of power, desire, and fear about sodomy in both the pre-Columbian and the Spanish colonial period and how the respective cultures understood alternative sexualities and understood or misunderstood their respective sexual values and canons. In general, theories of third-gender subjectivity mediating between the two opposing biological genders seem to preoccupy some contemporary researchers, while others argue for a flexible categorization that would accommodate individuals who shifted from one to the other following cultural idiosyncrasies that did not fit neatly into each other. That is the position of Ana Mariella Bacigalupo, who introduces the term "co-gender" to identify shamans whose sexual identity fluctuated between the masculine and the feminine. The field has moved forward from testimonial history into interpretive history.[52] Works published in the last five years indicate that the pre-Columbian past has gained legitimacy and weight in the interpretation of colonial forms of behavior, and the debate over definitions of masculinity and third-sex identities suggests the need to recast the concept of gendered sexuality.

While the literature challenges the credibility of colonial sources, the fact is that the new research depends heavily on their information. A tighter reading of the archival materials is the path followed by those seeking to find new clues to explain behavior regarded as deviant or transgressing Christian European norms.[53] A theme yet to be fully explored is that of sexuality and erotics within the church and in conjunction with religion.[54] The question also remains whether sixteenth-century perceptions and behavior changed throughout time. By the end of the colonial period, much water had passed under the bridge, and Catholic indoctrination had left deep tracks among all sectors of the population. Did popular understanding of same-sex, as well as heterosexual, sex undergo significant changes? Stavig assumes a considerable overlapping of values by that period and argues that offense at homosexuality was taken more seriously when it was public rather than private.[55] Popular understanding of gender models and gender behavior was not necessarily similar to that of the elite or the ecclesiastic and civil authorities, but so far, works on colonial sexuality suggest that there was not a radical change or "liberalization" in the understanding or judgment of sexual practices at the end of the eighteenth century.[56]

Most of the studies carried out on colonial sexuality have had the double task of unearthing the facts and interpreting the information on raw sexual behavior that abounds in the sources. Inescapably, our own current interest in sexuality and our own understanding of theories to explain sexual behavior are essential elements in these studies. The effort to understand the past on its own terms and to understand the mental universe of the historical actors is a challenging task demanding ample contextualization and the utmost caution in interpreting with sensitivity to the period. There is a need to escape linearity and overinterpretation in the choice of themes and sources. Doubtless, in the colonial period the complexity of sexual behavior was only matched by the complexity of the desire to regulate it. The tension between these two sources of "power" was constant, but it did not express itself in the same manner throughout time. Shifts in the attention of secular and ecclesiastic authorities result in the highlighting of some forms of "transgression" and the neglect of others. Factors such as race, class, and gender are obvious elements of analysis for reported behavior; the nuances and interplay of what is visible as behavior is intimately tied to the intellectual constructions that those who teach, rule, and punish use to exercise their power. In response, those at the receiving end also had a complex universe of ideas and sentiments that created their own rules while transforming those they received. It is desirable to extend the study of sexuality to a broader cultural field that would include art, literature, fashion, spirituality, and politics, among others. Researching behavior and thought through the lens of sexuality has changed the understanding of important aspects of colonial history and enriched its meaning, a trend likely to continue.

NOTES

1. Ward Staving, "'Living in Offense of Our Lord': Indigenous Sexual Values and Marital Life in the Colonial Crucible," *Hispanic American Historical Review* 75:4 (1995): 597–622.

2. Fernando Cabieses, *Dioses y enfermedades: La medicina en el antiguo Perú* (Lima: Artegraf, 1974); Federico Kauffman Doig, *Comportamiento sexual en el antiguo Perú* (Lima: Kompaktos, 1978) and *Sexo y magia sexual en el antiguo Peru* (Lima, n.p., 2001); Frank Salomon and George L. Urioste, eds., *The Huarochirí Manuscript: A Testament of Ancient and Colonial Andean Religion* (Austin: University of Texas Press, 1991); José Alcina Franch, "*Erotismo y procreación en el arte mochica: Del amor en los tiempos antiguos,*" *Precolombart* 2 (1999): 5–17; Justo Cáceres Macedo, *La sexualidad en la antigua sociedad moche del Peru* (Lima, n.p., 2000); Steve Bourget, *Sex, Death, and Sacrifice in Moche Religion and Visual Culture* (Austin: University of Texas Press, 2006); Juan José Vega, "La prostitución en el incario," in *Historia de las mujeres en América Latina*, ed. Juan Andreo and Sara Beatriz Guardia (Murcia: Universidad de Murcia, 2002), 45–53; Mary Weismantel, "Moche Sex Pots: Reproduction and Temporality in Ancient South America," *American Anthropologist* 106:3 (2004): 495–505. For the historical roots of contemporary eroticized music and dance, see Raphael Parejo-Coudert, "La flûte *pinkuyllu* des Provincias Altas du Cuzco (Pérou): Organologie et symbolique érotique d'un aérophone andin," *Journal de la Société des Américanistes* 87 (2001): 211–64, and *Eros en el Arte Ecuatoriano* (Quito: Banco Central del Ecuador, 1998).

3. See comments on homosexuality and alternative sexualities below.

4. Alfredo López Austin, "La sexualidad entre los antiguos Nahuas," in *Familia y sexualidad en Nueva España* (Mexico City: Fondo de Cultura Económica, 1980), 177–206; Jan G. R. Elferink, "Aphrodisiac Use in Pre-Columbian Aztec and Inca Cultures," *Journal of the History of Sexuality* 9:1–2 (2000): 25–36; Serge Gruzinski, "Matrimonio y sexualidad en México y Texcoco en los albores de la conquista o la pluralidad de los discursos," in *La actividad del Santo Oficio de la Inquisición en Nueva España, 1571–1990*, ed. Solange Alberro (Mexico City: Instituto Nacional de Antropología e Historia, 1981), 19–74; Pete Sigal, "The Politicization of Pederasty Among the Colonial Yucatecan Maya," *Journal of the History of Sexuality* 8:1 (1997): 1–24; Cecelia F. Klein, ed., *Gender in Pre-Hispanic America* (Washington, D.C.: Dumbarton Oaks Research Library and Collection, 2001). See Klein's

essay "None of the Above: Gender Ambiguity in Nahua Ideology" in *Gender in Pre-Hispanic America*, and her "Fighting with Femininity: Gender and War in Aztec Mexico" in *Gender Rhetorics: Postures of Dominance and Submission in History*, ed. Richard C. Trexler (Binghamton, N.Y.: Medieval and Renaissance Texts and Studies, 1994), 107–46. Rosemary A. Joyce has carried out extensive work on the interpretation of gender among the Classic Maya; her bibliography is cited in "Negotiating Sex and Gender in Classic Maya Society," in *Gender in Pre-Hispanic America*, 109–41. Inga Clendinnen correlated gender roles to sexuality in her *Aztecs: An Interpretation* (Cambridge: Cambridge University Press, 1991); Geoffrey Kimball, "Aztec Homosexuality: Textual Evidence," *Journal of Homosexuality* 26:1 (1993): 7–24; John Bierhorst (trans.), *History and Mythology of the Aztecs: The Codex Chimalpopoca* (Tucson: University of Arizona Press, 1992); Guilhem Olivier, "Homosexualidad y prostitución entre los nahuas y otros pueblos del posclásico," in *Historia de la vida cotidiana en Mexico*, Vol. 1: *Mesoamérica y los ámbitos indígenas de la Nueva España*, ed. Pablo Escalante Gonzalbo (Mexico City: El Colegio de Mexico/Fondo de Cultura Económica, 2004), 301–38, and "Conquistadores y misioneros frente al pecado nefando," *Historias* 28 (1992): 47–63; Camilla Townsend, "'What in the World Have You Done to Me, My Lover?': Sex, Servitude and Politics among the Pre-Conquest Nahuas as Seen in the Cantares Mexicanos," *The Americas* 62:2 (2005): 349–89; Kay A. Read and Jane Rosenthal, "The Chalcan Woman's Song: Sex as a Political Metaphor in Fifteenth-Century Mexico," *The Americas* 62:3 (2006): 313–48.

5. Robert Padden, *The Hummingbird and the Hawk: Conquest and Sovereignty in the Valley of Mexico, 1503–1541* (Columbus: Ohio State University Press, 1967); Magnus Morner, *Race Mixture in the History of Latin America* (Boston: Little Brown, 1967).

6. Richard C. Trexler, *Sex and Conquest: Gendered Violence, Political Power, and the European Conquest of the Americas* (Ithaca, N.Y.: Cornell University Press, 1995); Araceli Barbosa Sánchez, *Sexo y conquista* (Mexico City: Universidad Nacional Autónoma de México, 1994); Ricardo Herren, *La conquista erótica de las Indias* (Barcelona: Planeta, 1991).

7. Karen Vieira Powers, "Conquering Discourses of 'Sexual Conquest': Of Women, Language and Mestizaje," *Colonial Latin American Review* 11:1 (2002): 7–32.

8. Frances Karttunen, "Rethinking Malinche," in *Indian Women of Early Mexico*, ed. Susan Schroeder, Stephanie Wood, and Robert Haskett (Norman: University of Oklahoma Press, 1997), 291–312; Camilla Townsend, *Malitzin's Choices: An Indian Woman in the Conquest of Mexico* (Albuquerque: University of New Mexico Press, 2006).

9. Felipe Guamán Poma de Ayala, *Nueva corónica y buen gobierno*, ed. John V. Murra and Rolena Adorno (Mexico City: Siglo Veintiuno, 1980); Gonzalo Fernández de Oviedo y Valdés, *Historia general y natural de las Indias, islas y Tierrafirme del mar océano* (Madrid: Real Academia de la Historia, 1851–55); Mathew Restall, "'He Wished it in Vain': Subordination and Resistance Among Maya Women in Post-Conquest Yucatan," *Ethnohistory* 42:4 (1995): 577–94; Ward Stavig, *Amor y violencia sexual: Valores indígenas en la sociedad colonial* (Lima: Instituto de Estudios Peruanos/University of Southern Florida, 1996); Brian T. McCormack, "Conjugal Violence, Sex, Sin and Murder in the Mission Communities of Alta California," *Journal of the History of Sexuality* 16:3 (2007): 391–415.

10. Pierre Ragon, *Les Indiens de la découverte: Evangélisation, mariage et sexualité* (Paris: L'Harmattan, 1992).

11. See section on witchcraft below.

12. Louise M. Burkhart, *The Slippery Earth: Nahua-Christian Moral Dialogue in Sixteenth-Century Mexico* (Tucson: University of Arizona Press, 1989).

13. Ana Mariella Bacigalupo, "The Struggle for Mapuche Shamans' Masculinity: Colonial Politics of Gender, Sexuality, and Power in Southern Chile," *Ethnohistory* 51:3 (2004): 489–533. See also Ramón A. Gutiérrez, "A Gendered History of the Conquest of America: A View from New Mexico," in Trexler (ed.), *Gender Rhetorics*, 47–63.

14. Geoffrey Spurling, "Under Investigation for the Abominable Sin: Damián de Morales Stands Accused of Attempting to Seduce Antón de Tierra de Congo," in *Colonial Lives: Documents on Latin American History, 1550–1850*, ed. Richard Boyer and Geoffrey Spurling (New York: Oxford University Press, 2000), 112–29.

15. Solange Alberro, "Las representaciones y realidades familiares de los negros bozales en la predicación de Alonso de Sandoval (Cartagena de Indias, 1627) y Nicolás Duque de Estrada (La Habana, 1769)," in *La familia en el mundo iberoamericano*, ed. Pilar Gonzalbo Aizpuru and Cecilia Rabell (Mexico City: UNAM, 1994), 73–89; Adriana Maya Restrepo, "Las brujas de Zaragoza: Resistencia y cimarronaje en las minas de Antioquia, Colombia, 1619–1622," *América Negra* 4 (Diciembre 1992): 85–99.

16. Rosa Soto Lira, "Matrimonio y sexualidad de las mujeres negras en la Colonia," *Nomadías* 1 (1999): 61–70; Paloma Fernández-Resines, "Matrimonio restrictivo y política sexual bajo el régimen esclavista," *Memoria* (Ecuador), 8 (2000): 129–43; Heather Rachelle White, "Between the Devil and the Inquisition: African Slaves and the Witchcraft Trials in Cartagena de Indies," *The North Star: A Journal of African American Religious History* 8:2 (2005): 1–15; Joan Cameron Bristol, *Christians, Blasphemers, and Witches: Afro-Mexican Ritual Practice in the Seventeenth Century* (Albuquerque: University of New Mexico Press, 2007); Juan Carlos Garza Reyes, "Del mal de amores y de otros males: Curanderismo y hechicería en la villa de Colima del siglo XVIII," *Estudios de Historia Novohispana* 16 (1996): 83–98, and *Familia y sexualidad en Nueva España* (Mexico City: SEP/Fondo de Cultura Económica, 1982); Alejandra Cárdenas, *Hechicería, saber y transgresión: Afromestizas frente a la Inquisición, Acapulco, 1621–1622* (Mexico City: n.p., 1997); Colin A. Palmer, "Religion and Magic in Mexican Slave Society," in *Race and Slavery in the Western Hemisphere: Quantitative Studies*, ed. Stanley L. Engerman and Eugene D. Genovese (Princeton: Princeton University Press, 1975), 311–28; María Eugenia Chaves, "Honor y libertad: Discursos y recursos en la estrategia de libertad de una mujer esclava (Guayaquil a fines del periodo colonial)" (PhD diss., University of Göteborg, 2001).

17. María Cristina Navarrete, "De amores y seducciones: El mestizaje en la Audiencia del Nuevo Reino de Granada en el siglo XVII," in *La escritura de la historia de las mujeres en América Latina: El retorno de las diosas*, ed. Sara Beatriz Guardia (Lima: CEHMAL, 2005), 201–13.

18. Robert McCaa, "Tratos nupciales: La constitución de uniones formales e informales en México y España, 1500–1900," in *Familia y vida privada en la historia de Iberoamérica*, ed. Pilar Gonzalbo Aizpuru and Cecilia Rabell Romero (Mexico City: El Colegio de Mexico/UNAM, 1996), 21–57; Thomas Calvo, "Concubinage et métissage en milieu urbain: Le cas de Guadalajara au XVIIe siècle," in *La ville en Amérique espagnole coloniale* (Paris: University de la Sorbonne Nouvelle-Paris III, 1984), 147–58, and "The Warmth of the Hearth: Seventeenth-Century Guadalajara Families," in *Sexuality and Marriage in Colonial Latin America*, ed. Asunción Lavrin (Lincoln: University of Nebraska Press, 1989), 287–312; Claudio Esteva-Fabregat, *Mestizaje in Ibero-America* (Tucson: The University of Arizona Press, 1994); Guiomar Dueñas Vargas, *Los hijos del pecado: Ilegitimidad y vida familiar en la Santafé de Bogotá Colonial* (Bogotá: Editorial Universidad Nacional, 1997); Agustín Grajales Porras and José Luis Aranda y Romero, "Hijos naturales del sagrario angelopolitano a mediados del siglo XVIII," *Coloquio sobre Puebla* (Puebla: Comisión Puebla Centenario, 1991), 21–32; Martha Few, *Women Who Live Evil Lives:*

Gender, Religion, and the Politics of Power in Colonial Guatemala (Austin: University of Texas Press, 2002).

19. See essays in *Familia y sexualidad en Nueva España* (Mexico City: Sep/Fondo de Cultura Económica, 1982); Solange Alberro, "El discurso inquisitorial sobre los delitos de bigamia poligamia y solicitación," in *Seis ensayos sobre el discurso colonial relativo a la comunidad doméstica* (Mexico City: Dirección de estudios históricos, 1980); Regina Harrison, "Confesando el pecado en los Andes: Del siglo XVI hacia nuestros días," *Revista Crítica de Literatura Latinoamericana* 19:37 (1993): 169–85, and "The Theology of Concupiscence: Spanish-Quechua Confessional Manuals in the Andes," in *Coded Encounters: Writing, Gender, and Ethnicity in Colonial Latin America*, ed. Francisco Javier Cevallos-Candau, Jeffrey A. Cole, Nina M. Scott, and Nicomedes Suárez-Araúz (Amherst: University of Massachusetts Press, 1994), 135–50.

20. María Águeda Méndez, ed., *Catálogo de textos marginados novohispanos: Inquisición, siglos XVIII y XIX* (Mexico City: Archivo General de la Nación/El Colegio de México/UNAM, 1992) and *Catálogo de textos marginados novohispanos: Inquisición, siglo XVII* (Mexico City: El Colegio de México/Archivo General de la Nación/Fondo Nacional para la Cultura y las Artes, 1997); Georges Baudot and María Águeda Méndez, *Amores prohibidos: La palabra condenada en el México de los virreyes* (Mexico City: Siglo XXI, 1997); Sergio Rivera Ayala, "Lewd Songs and Dances from the Streets of Eighteenth-Century New Spain," in *Rituals of Rule, Rituals of Resistance: Public Celebrations and Popular Culture in Mexico*, ed. William Beezley, Cheryl Martin, and William French (Wilmington, Del.: Scholarly Resources, 1994).

21. Sergio Ortega et al., *De la santidad a la perversión: O por que no se cumplía la ley de Dios en la sociedad mexicana* (Mexico City: Editorial Grijalbo, 1985); Aída Martínez and Pablo Rodríguez, eds., *Placer, dinero y pecado: Historia de la prostitución en Colombia* (Bogotá: Aguilar, 2002); Solange Alberro et al., *El placer de pecar y el afán de normar: Ideologías y comportamientos familiares y sexuales en el México colonial* (Mexico City: Planeta, 1988); Asunción Lavrin, ed., *Sexuality and Marriage in Colonial Latin America* (Lincoln: University of Nebraska Press, 1989), and "La sexualidad y las normas de la moral sexual," in *La ciudad barroca*, Vol. II of *Historia de la vida cotidiana en Mexico*, ed. Antonio Rubial and Pilar Gonzalbo Aizpuru (Mexico City: El Colegio de Mexico/Fondo de Cultura Económica, 2005), 489–518; Luis Martín, *Daughters of the Conquistadors: Women of the Viceroyalty of Peru* (Albuquerque: University of New Mexico Press, 1983), 141–70.

22. Pilar Gonzalbo Aizpuru, *Familia y orden colonial* (Mexico City: El Colegio de Mexico, 1998), chaps. 1–3; Eduardo Cavieres and René Salinas, *Amor, sexo y matrimonio en Chile tradicional* (Valparaíso: Universidad Católica de Valparaíso, 1991); Ana María Presta, "Portraits of Four Women: Traditional Female Roles and Transgressions in Colonial Elite Families in Charcas, 1550–1600," *Colonial Latin American Review* 9:2 (2000): 237–62.

23. Asunción Lavrin, "Sexuality in Colonial Mexico: A Church Dilemma," in *Sexuality and Marriage in Colonial Latin America*, 47–92; Serge Gruzinski, "Individualization and Acculturation: Confession Among the Nahuas of Mexico from the Sixteenth to the Eighteenth Century," in Lavrin, *Sexuality*, 96–115; Kathy Waldron, "The Sinners and the Bishop in Colonial Venezuela: The *Visita* of Bishop Mariano Martí, 1771–1784," in Lavrin, *Sexuality*, 156–77; Sylvia Marcos, "Indigenous Eroticism and Colonial Morality in Mexico: The Confession Manuals of New Spain," *Numen* 39:2 (1992): 157–74; Solange Alberro, "La sexualidad manipulada en Nueva España: Modalidades de recuperación y de adaptación frente a los tribunales eclesiásticos," in *Familia y sexualidad en Nueva España*, 238–57.

24. Lee Michael Penyak, "Criminal Sexuality in Central Mexico 1750–1850" (PhD diss, University of Connecticut, 1993); Pilar Jaramillo de Zuleta, "Las Arrepentidas," in *Placer, dinero y pecado: Historia de la prostitución en Colombia*, ed. Aída Martínez and Pablo Rodríguez (Bogotá: Aguilar, 2002), 91–128; María Emma Mannarelli, *Hechiceras, beatas y expósitas: Mujeres y poder inquisitorial en Lima* (Lima: Ediciones del Congreso de la República, 1998), and *Private Passions and Public Sins: Men and Women in Seventeenth-Century Lima* (Albuquerque: University of New Mexico Press, 2007).

25. Asunción Lavrin, "Intimidades," in *Des Indes occidentales a l'Amérique latine*, ed. Alain Musset and Thomas Calvo (Paris: CEMCA/ENS/IHEAL, 1997), Vol. 1, 195–218.

26. Roxana Boixadós, "Una viuda de 'mala vida' en la colonia riojana," in *Historia de las mujeres en la Argentina: Colonia y siglo XIX*, ed. Fernanda Gil Lozano, Valeria Silvina Pita, and María Gabriela Ini (Buenos Aires: Taurus, 2000), Vol. 1, 135–52; René Salinas Meza, "Uniones ilegítimas y desuniones legítimas: El matrimonio y la formación de la pareja en Chile colonial," in *La familia en el mundo iberoamericano*, ed. Pilar Gonzalbo Aizpuru and Cecilia Rabell (Mexico City: UNAM/Instituto de Investigaciones Sociales, 1994), 145–92; Ana María Atondo Rodríguez, "El amor venal y el amor conyugal," in *Amor y desamor: Vivencias de parejas en la sociedad novohispana* (Mexico City: CONACULTA/INAH, 1999), 83–102; Jorge Pinto Rodríguez, "La familia en una sociedad del Chile colonial: Las modalidades alternativas al vínculo matrimonial en el Norte Chico, 1700–1800," in *Demografía, familia e inmigración en España y América* (Santiago: Univ. de Santiago de Chile, 1992), 91–116; Lee M. Penyak and Verónica Vallejo, "Expectations of Love in Troubled Mexican Marriages During the Late Colonial and Early National Periods," *The Historian* 65:3 (2003): 563–86.

27. Richard Boyer, *Lives of the Bigamists: Marriage, Family, and Community in Colonial Mexico* (Albuquerque: University of New Mexico Press, 1995), and "Women, *La Mala Vida*, and the Politics of Marriage," in *Sexuality and Marriage in Colonial Latin America*, ed. Asunción Lavrin (Lincoln: University of Nebraska Press, 1989), 252–86; Dolores Enciso Rojas, "Matrimonio y bigamia en la capital del virreinato: Dos alternativas que favorecían la integración del individuo a la vida familiar social," in *Familias Novohispanas: Siglos XVI al XIX*, ed. Pilar Gonzalbo Aizpuru (Mexico City: El Colegio de Mexico, 1991), 12–133; Enciso Rojas, "Amores y desamores en las alianzas matrimoniales de los bígamos del siglo XVIII," in *Amor y desamor*, 103–28; and Pete Sigal and Neil L. Whitehead, eds., *Ethnopornography: Sexuality, Colonialism, and Anthropological Knowing* (unpublished manuscript).

28. Patricia Seed, "La narrativa de Don Juan: El lenguaje de la seducción en la literatura y la sociedad hispánica del siglo XVI," in Pilar Gonzalbo Aizpuru and Cecilia Rabell, ed., *La familia*, 91–125; Pablo Rodríguez, *Seducción, amancebamiento y abandono en la colonia* (Bogotá: Fundación Simón y Lola Guberek, 1991).

29. John Chuchiak, "Secrets behind the Screen: *Solicitantes* in the Colonial Diocese of Yucatan and the Yucatec Maya, 1570–1785," in *Religion in New Spain*, ed. Susan Schroeder and Stafford Poole (Albuquerque: University of New Mexico Press, 2007), 83–109.

30. Bernard Lavallé, *Amor y opresión en los Andes coloniales* (Lima: Instituto Francés de Estudios Andinos, 1999), and "Amor y desamor en el Sur Peruano a finales del Siglo XVIII," in *Mujer y Familia en América Latina: Siglos XVIII–XIX* (Málaga: Asociación de Historiadores Latinoamericanistas Europeos, 1996), 27–56. On domestic violence, see Sonya Lipsett-Rivera, "La violencia dentro de las familias formal e informal," in *Familia y vida privada en la historia de Iberoamérica*, ed. Pilar Gonzalbo Aizpuru and Cecilia Rabell Romero (Mexico City: El Colegio de Mexico/UNAM 1996), 325–40; Christiana Borchart de Moreno, "Violencia cotidiana y de género en Quito a fines del siglo XVIII," *Memoria* 7 (1999): 1–31; Juan Javier Pescador, "Entre la espada y el olivo: Pleitos matrimoniales en el

Provisorato Eclesiástico de México, siglo XVIII," in Gonzalbo Aizpuru and Rabell, *La familia*, 193–226; Susan M. Deeds, "Double Jeopardy: Indian Women in Jesuit Missions of Nueva Vizcaya," in *Indian Women of Early Mexico*, ed. Susan Schroeder, Stephanie Wood, and Robert Haskett (Norman: University of Oklahoma Press, 1997), 255–89; Richard Boyer, *Lives of the Bigamists*, passim.

31. Carmen Castañeda, *Violación, estupro y sexualidad: Nueva Galicia 1790–1821* (Guadalajara: Editorial Hexágono, 1989); Gerardo González Reyes, "Familia y violencia sexual: Aproximaciones al estudio del rapto, la violación y el estupro en la primera mitad del siglo XVIII," in *Familias iberoamericanas: Historia, identidad y conflictos*, ed. Pilar Gonzalbo Aizpuru (Mexico City: El Colegio de México 2001), 93–115; Sonya Lipsett-Rivera, "The Intersection of Rape and Marriage in Late-Colonial and Early-National Mexico," *Colonial Latin American Historical Review* 6:4 (1997): 559–90.

32. Lyman L. Johnson and Sonya Lipsett-Rivera, "Honor and Honors in Colonial Spanish America," in *The Faces of Honor: Sex, Shame, and Violence in Colonial Latin America*, ed. Lyman L. Johnson and Sonya Lipsett-Rivera (Albuquerque: University of New Mexico Press, 1998), 1–17; Lyman Johnson, "Dangerous Words, Provocative Gestures, and Violent Acts: The Disputed Hierarchies of Plebeian Life in Colonial Buenos Aires," in *The Faces of Honor*, 127–51; Patricia Seed, *To Love, Honor, and Obey in Colonial Mexico: Conflicts over Marriage Choice, 1574–1821* (Stanford: Stanford University Press, 1988); Richard Boyer, "Honor Among Plebeians: *Mala Sangre* and Social Reputation," in *The Faces of Honor*, 152–78; Ramón A. Gutiérrez, *When Jesus Came, the Corn Mothers Went Away: Marriage, Sexuality, and Power in New Mexico, 1500–1846* (Stanford: Stanford University Press, 1991); Steve J. Stern, *The Secret History of Gender* (Chapel Hill: University of North Carolina Press, 1995); Carlos Herrera, "Infidelity and the Presidio Captain: Adultery and Honor in the Lives of María Rosa Tato y Anza and José Antonio Vidósola, Sonora, New Spain, 1769–1783," *Journal of the History of Sexuality* 15:2 (2006): 204–27.

33. Ann Twinam, *Public Lives, Private Secrets: Gender, Honor, Sexuality, and Illegitimacy in Colonial Spanish America* (Stanford: Stanford University Press, 1999). See also Frederic Langue, *Aristócratas, honor y subversión en la Venezuela del siglo XVIII* (Caracas: Biblioteca de la Academia Nacional de la Historia, 2005).

34. Sonia Lipsett-Rivera, "A Slap in the Face of Honor," in Johnson and Lipsett-Rivera (eds.), *The Faces of Honor*, 179–200.

35. Guilhem Olivier, "Entre diosas y prostitutas: Las alegres del mundo mesoamericano," in Martínez and Rodríguez (eds.), *Placer, dinero y pecado*, 17–37; María J. Rodríguez, *La mujer azteca* (Toluca: Universidad Autónoma del Estado de Mexico, 1991), 185–233.

36. Huaman Poma, *Nueva Corónica*, 668, 807, 812–16.

37. Pablo Rodríguez, "Servidumbre sexual: La prostitución en los siglos XV–XVIII," in Martínez and Rodríguez (eds.), *Placer, dinero y pecado*, 67–89.

38. Paulino Castañeda and Pilar Hernández Aparicio, *La Inquisición de Lima*, 2 vols. (Madrid: Editorial Deimos, 1989), I: 385–416, gives information on the "marriage" of clergymen. René Millar Carvacho, *La Inquisición de Lima*, Vol. 3 (1697–1820) (Madrid: Editorial Deimos, 1998), 385–400.

39. Jorge René González Marmolejo, "Correspondencia amorosa de clérigos del siglo XVIII: El caso de Fray José Ignacio Troncoso," in *Amor y Desamor: Vivencia de parejas en la sociedad novohispana* (Mexico Instituto Nacional de Antropología e Historia, 1999), 155–80, "Clérigos solicitantes, perversos de la confesión," in *De la santidad a la perversión*, ed. Sergio Ortega, 239–52, "Pecados virtuosos: El delito de solicitación en la Nueva España (siglo XVIII), *Historias* 11 (1985): 73–84, and *Sexo y confesión: La iglesia y la penitencia en los siglos XVIII y XIX en la Nueva España* (Mexico City: Conaculta/INAH/Plaza y Valdés,

2002). González Marmolejo has published several other articles on this subject. Asunción Lavrin, "Los hombres de Dios: Aproximación a un estudio de la masculinidad en Nueva España," *Anuario Colombiano de Historia Social y de la Cultura* 31 (2004): 283–309. Asunción Lavrin has a chapter on solicitation in the convents of nuns in *The Brides of Christ: Conventual Life in Colonial Mexico* (Stanford: University Press, 2008), 209–43.

40. Noemí Quezada, *Amor y magia amorosa entre los Aztecas: Supervivencia en el México colonial* (Mexico City: UNAM/Instituto de Investigaciones Antropológicas, 1989); *Sexualidad, amor y erotismo: México prehispánico y México colonial* (Mexico City: UNAM/ Plaza y Valdés, 1996).

41. Ruth Behar, "Sexual Witchcraft, Colonialism, and Women's Powers: Views from the Mexican Inquisition," in *Sexuality*, ed. Asunción Lavrin, 178–206, and "Sex and Sin: Witchcraft and the Devil in Late-Colonial Mexico," *American Ethnologist* 14:1 (1987): 34–54; María Emma Mannareli, "Inquisición y mujeres: Las hechiceras en el Perú durante el siglo XVII," *Revista Andina* 3:1 (1985): 141–54; Ramón A. Gutiérrez, "Women on Top: The Love Magic of Indian Witches of New Mexico," *Journal of the History of Sexuality* 16:3 (2007): 373–90. See also his *When Jesus Came, the Corn Mothers Went Away*.

42. Laura A. Lewis, *Hall of Mirrors: Power, Witchcraft, and Caste in Colonial Mexico* (Durham, N.C.: Duke University Press, 2003). See also "From Sodomy to Superstition: The Active Pathic and Bodily Transgressions in New Spain," *Ethnohistory* 54:1 (2007): 129–56, an exploration of the connection of gender values and the religious values of commoners and elites.

43. Ana Sánchez, *Amancebados, hechiceros y rebeldes, Chancay, siglo XVII* (Cuzco: Centro de Estudios Regionales Andinos Bartolomé de Las Casas, 1991).

44. Pierre Duviols, *Cultura andina y represión: Procesos y visitas de idolatría y hechicería, Cajatambo, siglo XVII* (Cuzco: Centro de Estudios Andinos Bartolomé de Las Casas, 1988); Diana Luz Ceballos Gómez, *Hechicería, brujería e Inquisición en el Nuevo Reino de Granada: Un duelo de imaginarios* (Medellín: Editorial Universidad Nacional, 1994); Judith Farberman, "Las hechiceras de Tuama: Mujeres y delito en un pueblo de indios colonial, Santiago del Estero (actual noroeste Argentino) 1761," in *Familias iberoamericanas: Historia, identidad y conflictos*, ed. Pilar Gonzalbo Aizpuru (Mexico City: El Colegio de México, 2001), 117–39. See also Farberman, "La fama de la hechicera: La buena reputación femenina en un proceso criminal del siglo XVIII," in *Historia de las mujeres en la Argentina: Colonia y siglo XIX*, ed. Fernanda Gil Lozano, Valeria Silvina Pita, and María Gabriela Ini, Vol. 1, 27–43.

45. Rosalva Loreto López, "The Devil, Women and the Body in Seventeenth-Century Puebla Convents," *The Americas* 5:2 (2002): 183–99. For a general study, see Fernando Cervantes, *The Devil in the New World: The Impact of Diabolism in New Spain* (New Haven: Yale University Press, 1994).

46. Sonya Lipsett-Rivera, "Mira Lo Que Hace El Diablo: The Devil in Mexican Popular Culture, 1750–1856," *The Americas* 59:2 (2002): 201–19; Lisa Sousa, "The Devil and Deviance in Native Criminal Narratives from Early Mexico," *The Americas* 59:2 (2002): 161–79.

47. Serge Gruzinski, "The Ashes of Desire: Homosexuality in Mid-Seventeenth-Century New Spain," in *Infamous Desire: Male Homosexuality in Colonial Latin America*, ed. Pete Sigal (Chicago: University of Chicago Press, 2003), 197–214. This article was first published in 1985 in *De la santidad a la perversión*, ed. Sergio Ortega.

48. Pierre Ragon, *Les Amours indiennes, ou, l'imaginaire du conquistador* (Paris: Armand Colin, 1992).

49. Federico Garza Carvajal, *Butterflies Will Burn: Prosecuting Sodomites in Early Modern Spain and Mexico* (Austin: University of Texas Press, 2003).

50. Lewis, *Hall of Mirrors*, passim.

51. Other works by Peter Sigal include "Gendered Power, the Hybrid Self, and Homosexual Desire in Late Colonial Yucatan," in *Infamous Desire*, 102–32; *From Moon Goddesses to Virgins: The Colonization of Yucatecan Maya Sexual Desire* (Austin: University of Texas Press, 2000); "The *Cuiloni*, the *Patlache*, and the Abominable Sin: Homosexualities in Early Colonial Nahua Society," *Hispanic American Historical Review* 85:4 (2005): 555–93; "Queer Nahuatl: Sahagún's Faggots and Sodomites, Lesbians and Hermaphrodites," *Ethnohistory* 54:1 (2007): 9–34.

52. Martin Nesvig, "The Complicated Terrain of Latin American Homosexuality," *Hispanic American Historical Review* 81:3–4 (2001): 689–729; Ana Mariella Bacigalupo, "The Struggle for Mapuche Shamans' Masculinity: Colonial Politics of Gender, Sexuality and Power in Southern Chile," *Ethnohistory* 51:3 (2004): 489–533.

53. Zeb Tortorici, "'Heran Todos Putos': Sodomitical Subcultures and Disordered Desire in Early Colonial Mexico," *Ethnohistory* 54:6 (2007): 35–67; Martha Few, "Chocolate, Sex, and Disorderly Women in Late-Seventeenth- and Early-Eighteenth-Century Guatemala," *Ethnohistory* 52:4 (2005): 637–87; Kimberly Gauderman, "It Happened on the Way to the *Temascal* and Other Stories: Desiring the Illicit in Colonial Spanish America," *Ethnohistory* 54:1 (2007): 177–86; Caterina Pizzigoni, "Alternative Sex and Gender in Early Latin America," *Ethnohistory* 54:1 (2007): 187–94.

54. Laura Lewis, "From Sodomy to Superstition"; Geoffrey Spurling, "Honor, Sexuality and the Colonial Church"; Asunción Lavrin, "Los hombres de Dios"; John Chuchiak, "The Secrets Behind the Screen" and "The Sins of the Fathers: Franciscan Friars, Parish Priests, and the Sexual Conquest of the Yucatec Maya," *Ethnohistory* 54:1 (2007): 69–127; and Zeb Tortorici, "Masturbation, Salvation, and Desire: Connecting Sexuality and Religiosity in Colonial Mexico," *Journal of the History of Sexuality* 16:3 (2007): 355–72.

55. Ward Stavig, "Political 'Abomination' and Private Reservation: The Nefarious Sin, Homosexuality, and Cultural Values in Colonial Peru," in *Infamous Desire*, ed. Pete Sigal, 134–51; Carolina Giraldo Botero, "Homoerotismo femenino en la Nueva Granada, 1745–1822," *En Otras Palabras* 9 (2001): 23–43; Michael J. Horswell, "Toward an Andean Theory of Ritual Same-Sex Sexuality and Third-Gender Subjectivity," in *Infamous Desire*, 25–69. See also his *Decolonizing the Sodomite: Queer Tropes of Sexuality in Colonial Andean Culture* (Austin: University of Texas Press, 2005).

56. Martha Few, "'That Monster of Nature': Gender, Sexuality and the Medicalization of a 'Hermaphrodite' in Late Colonial Guatemala," *Ethnohistory* 54:1 (2007): 159–76.

CHAPTER 5

INDEPENDENCE IN LATIN AMERICA

JEREMY ADELMAN

LATIN America's secession from Spain and Portugal occupies an important yet enigmatic place in the region's historiography. Like many epochal struggles, it has been the source of endless romanticizing and heroic storytelling. But it has also been singled out as a period in which things that might have happened, often presuming that these would have been for the good, did not. The result is a distinctive blend of worshiping and bashing of the principal figures of the age, and conclusions that the struggles for sovereignty were redeeming, lamentable, or simply inconsequential. Simón Bolívar, who more than any other founder shouldered this polarized view of the independence period, pronounced to the Colombian assemblymen in 1830: "Fellow citizens! I blush to say this: Independence is the only benefit we have acquired, to the detriment of all the rest." As if to ensure that his handiwork could cut both ways, he also added: "But independence opens the door to us to win back the others under your sovereign authority, in all the splendor of glory and freedom."[1] It is easy to let the stirring invocations of glory dominate the final sentence of what was one of Bolívar's adieus to Colombians. But from the historian's vantage point, the notion of recovering what was lost evokes what has been so thorny about this period. After all, wasn't independence about realizing something new, not retrieving what was gone?

The writing of modern history has been tied up with the fortunes and visions of the nation-state. For colonial societies especially, decolonization or independence is the epochal moment in which nations come into being; at the hands of historians, it is the quintessential subject for epic nationalist tales. What has been distinctive about Latin America, however, is that the rather unsettled (some might say dismal) view of the "national question" has translated into an unresolved debate over how to write the history of the moment that gave birth to Latin American nations. While other countries and regions created triumphal narratives of the struggle for sovereignty, such a formulation was never easily accepted or universalized in Latin America. National creation myths, even the best ones, condense potential narratives into one or a few privileged stories with an eye to assimilating a national people with and into their history. The task of integrating histories, like integrating peoples, has not fared as well as Latin American nationalists of all shapes and sizes would have liked. Instead of a historical consensus, there has been a contest—at times more explicit than others—over the significance of independence to Latin America. Indeed, Latin America's historiography of the making of its sovereignty is the history of a debate over the region's somewhat complicated experience of modern life.

What this means is that the founding epics of national history in Latin America were less constrained but more confused than narratives of national purpose and realization in other corners of the Atlantic world. Thomas Bender has recently noted of the United States that the bounded unity of the nation inspired, while limiting, history writing in the "other" America. Quite the opposite has been true, as this essay will illustrate, of Latin American historiography. The disunity of nationhood was more often the departure point for narratives of Latin American independence. Even recent historians' efforts to transcend nation-centric stories are less discontinuous with a heritage of almost two centuries of Latin American history writing premised on—and often vexed by—the unbounded sovereignty of the Latin American nation-states.[2]

NATION BUILDING AND NATIONAL HISTORIES

By definition, there was no history of independence until it happened. Accordingly, the writing of Latin America's secession from Spain and Portugal emerged just as a particular brand of history was coming into vogue in the 1820s and 1830s: grand narratives written in the idiom of the nation. Thomas Macaulay, Jules Michelet, and George Bancroft were more than great epic writers—with the revolutions in England, France, and the United States being the charmed *sujets du jour*—they were great national synthesizers; revolutions were epochal moments of nations coming into being. Nations had a collective past, shared a cathartic and bonding experience in toppling an old order, and were thus poised for a common future.

Much the same spirit inspired the first generation of Latin American historians, but they had quite different views of their subject. On the heels of the declarations of independence, *letrados* rushed to pen their epics of "Colombian," "Mexican," or "Brazilian" histories. The stories they told were never divorced from the ideological or partisan struggles that endured after independence. Indeed many of these *letrados* were combatants in these brawls, and their histories were scarcely disguised tomes to lend legitimacy to one side or the other. But they did conform to some common models of what "history" was supposed to look like. First and foremost, the language of the nation was hard to disentangle from the language of history—few details were spared for stories that did not fit the nation-building enterprise. Secondly, the history of independence was associated with models of constitutionalism, so that narratives of independence dwelled on the fortunes of centralism, federalism, and democracy as the legal principles needed in order to attach civil society to its nation-state.

Epic-writing about Latin American nationhood lent itself to a plurality of narratives because so many of the first great accounts began from the premise that the nations were themselves still works in progress. This was as true for liberal pessimists like José Manuel Restrepo and liberal optimists like Bartolomé Mitre as it was for conservative authors like Lucás Alamán. While fixating on the great men of the era of Colombian, Argentine, or Mexican independence, they also had to contend with the flawed characters of the liberators and the liberated in order to point to the unfinished business of the struggles they unleashed.[3] The nineteenth century was the classic age for writing about independence as a national saga through the martyred efforts of great men: Bolívar, San Martín, Hidalgo, and even Iturbide. This vision has echoed to the present in the cultish views of many of these leaders, as Germán Carrera Damas has shown provocatively in the case of Bolívar.[4] It may well be that images of sacrifice, and the notion that the revolutions remained unfulfilled, gave these leaders a significance that could be easily adapted to contemporary valences (so Peronists could trace a genealogy from San Martín to Perón; and of course Hugo Chávez is distinctly unabashed in his self-portraits as a reincarnation of Bolívar). Brazilian independence was more difficult to fit into this personalized mold of national history, but there were nonetheless efforts to portray Pedro I, for instance, as a national hero, guided by the pragmatic visionary, José Bonifacio, in making the decisive break with Lisbon. And if the continued popularity of Oliveira Lima's 1922 study, published on the centenary of Brazilian independence, is any gauge, the preeminent role of sagacious men who personified a national spirit resonated in Brazil too.[5]

The cult of the founding fathers—which was always accepting of their flaws, and got a great deal of narrative mileage from their tragic traits—has been an enduring strain of Latin American historiography about independence. It reached its acme around the time of the first centenary of independence in 1910 in Spanish America and 1922 in Brazil. Documentary collections, official histories, and hagiographies rolled off the printing presses across the region. The burgeoning cities were decorated with statutes and iconography to the great leaders. The sesquicentennials of independence revitalized nationalistic accounts and the importance of creole leaders and liberators. The *Colección documental de la independencia del Perú* was one such impressive effect, gathering a staggering number of basic documents—but, by reaching back into earlier decades of unrest and revolt, implying that Peruvian nationalism was maturing and outgrowing the Spanish cast.[6] Another was the massive collection of documents published by the Argentine Senate, *Biblioteca de Mayo: Colección de obras y documentos para la historia argentina*, issued in 1960.

While flawed leaders dominated the foreground, there had to be something to personify. The nation that was born with independence took the stage along with its heroic "fathers." While there was not much examination of the history of this "nation," it was assumed that a popular consensus and spirit were coherent enough to reject colonialism and follow a prophet to a new land. For the uplifting national historians, this was the formulation. But it was never wholly accepted; it never yielded to a bounded unity to the region's historiography, one which mapped itself onto the visions of the nation it was supposed to serve. Thus, while there was a celebratory streak in the classical historiography, there was also much more discord and disunity regarding the properties of the nation that came into being with independence. Not even the pomp and ceremony of the centenaries of independence could drown out the uneasy feelings that writing the history of independence was not the same thing as celebrating it. It did not help that 1910 was a climactic year in Latin America as social revolution, anarchism, and millenarianism swept the region.

The centrality of the unbounded nation-state in the history of independence remains current to this day. This combination of a personified but fractured history of Latin American independence found its most famous rendition in John Lynch's classic synthesis, *The Spanish American Revolutions, 1808–1826*.[7] This has been, for over a quarter century, possibly the single most popular book on the period. What is important to note, aside from its ability to condense a complex set of stories into a single volume, is its resonance with a deeper historiographical tradition, one that follows the trails of military and constitutional leaders but presumes, in an important opening chapter, the prominence of an "incipient nationalism" among creoles. What stirred their political passions was as much the waning of an old order as the ability of charismatic men to bring nations into the world. Lynch did not simply echo the by now ragged centennial epics but resonated with the more skeptical pioneering works of Restrepo and Alamán, which figure in the citations in the Colombian and Mexican chapters. Indeed, the independence revolutions not only created nations but also fostered political styles and habits, personified in regional caudillos, that would plague modern Spanish America in part because nations were incipient, not mature. The legacies were distinctly ambiguous, therefore; independence shattered old structures but did not quite recompose the fractions into national wholes, a theme which Lynch proceeded to explore in subsequent books. John Chasteen's recent synthesis updates Lynch's classic by adding some forgotten figures, women and common folk, but he shares much of Lynch's framework.[8]

Personalizing history did not mean simplifying it; whereas American history continues to be bogged down in the celebration of the "character" of the founding fathers, historians of Latin America have not been given to the euphoric (or distempered) style. If Karen Racine's wonderful biography of Francisco de Miranda, David Bushnell's of Bolívar, Iván Jaksic's on Andrés Bello, Timothy Anna's of Iturbide, and Neill Macaulay's on Dom Pedro I are any gauge, this genre enabled historians to take a close look at the internal contradictions and agonies of movements that did anything but move in a straight, cohesive line. Perhaps this also explains why the saga of Latin American revolutions has also provided material for novelistic renditions by

Gabriel García Márquez, Carlos Fuentes, and others. For Jorge Luis Borges, the political upheaval was the setting for a drama of the mind. In Borges's "A Page to Commemorate Colonel Suárez, Victor at Junín," his subject reflects thus:

> What does my battle at Junín matter if it is only
> a glorious memory, or a date learned by rote
> for an examination, or a place in the atlas?
> The battle is everlasting and can do without
> the pomp of actual armies and of trumpets.
> Junín is two civilians cursing a tyrant
> on a street corner,
> or an unknown man somewhere, dying in prison.[9]

THE STRUCTURALIST MOMENT

If the epics of the classic age stressed the agency of great—and not so great—men as flawed prophets of imperfect nations, it was not very clear why Portuguese and Spanish colonies should give way to nations without recourse to explanations that relied on a natural, almost preordained logic. It was, ironically, the turn in Latin American nationalism during the 1930s that compelled historians to query some of the precepts of the classic age without dislodging the centrality of the national question. What emerged was a much more structuralist style of history that distanced itself from many of the earlier narratives that had emphasized the voluntarism of its great actors. The revisionist work took place against the backdrop of a world economic crisis, rising anticolonial sentiment around the world, and increasing awareness across the political spectrum that the liberal ideas, intellectual styles, and accompanying political and social regimes of the previous century were more than simply exhausted. Liberalism was, in a sense, the ideology that perpetuated fragmentation of national communities rather than transcending it.

The 1930s was the heyday of revisionism and a self-conscious effort to reject much of the official, "centenary"-style history. In Argentina, *revisionistas* went to work to debunk the illusory world that Mitre, as President and as historian, had concocted. Not only did the revolutions fail, their progeny, and especially the landowning classes and merchants of Buenos Aires, delivered the vital interests of the *patria* to foreign, imperialist interlopers waving the Union Jack. "Independence" was thus a formal sham covering up an underlying informal process of reconquest by industrial powers. Peruvian historians echoed José Carlos Mariátegui and Víctor Raúl Haya de la Torre and denounced the oligarchic republics for having betrayed the national and popular interests. In Mexico, after the Revolution of 1910, nationalists decried liberals and conservatives alike; as elsewhere, they began to examine the "nation" in a distinctly indigenous and autochthonous idiom.

Of the historical reworkings of this era, few were more influential than the coincidence of three Brazilian landmarks: Sérgio Buarque de Holanda's *Raízes do Brasil* (1936), Gilberto Freyre's *Casa grande e senzala* (1933), and Caio Prado Júnior's *Formação do Brasil contemporâneo* (1942). Echoing the recent turns to economic, social, and cultural history associated with the Annales school in France, but with personalities all their own, each of these works had altered the significance of independence—indeed, all three in their own ways pricked the bubble that assumed that independence was the cathartic experience of nation building. The caesura of 1822 and the declaration of national sovereignty were contextualized within much deeper, structural shifts. Within colonial societies emerged social formations and identities that made the nation what it was—patrimonial, corporatist, rural, and feudal—so that independence, far from being the culmination of a heroic struggle, appears as an afterthought. For some, like Sérgio Buarque de Holanda, "our" revolution was less the triumph of a national cause than a process of removing formal colonial institutions that ruled over two clashing propensities that were part and parcel of Iberian efforts to implant European cultures in American settings: the egalitarian and integrative forces associated with republicanism (like the provincial secessionist movements of 1817) and the forces of aristocracy and social hierarchy. As he and other authors of the 1930s were aware, these same drives were rekindling revolutionary and reactionary tendencies which, while they sat on opposite ends of the ideological spectrum, shared an aversion to the middle ground of liberalism.[10]

By the 1940s and 1950s, independence began to look less like a national climacteric than one, albeit dramatic, point in a series of clashing tendencies nested within colonial and postcolonial societies. Indeed, many were beginning to wonder whether "independence" had a seismic logic at all. For Marxists like Mariátegui and many of his readers, capitalism was still locking horns with persistent feudalism; for writers influenced by Max Weber and what later became called "modernization theory," the basic contradiction was between traditional, ascriptive, personalizing forces and the forces of modernity—rational, impersonal, and prescriptive. Both views found themselves combined into, or adapted to, the third-worldist vocabulary of "underdevelopment."

Marxist debates had a profound effect on post–World War II historical writing in Latin America, especially as the intellectual climate of the region grew increasingly radical. One such pioneering work was the short interpretive volume by the Chilean Marxist, Hernán Ramírez Necochea, whose 1959 study, *Antecedentes económicos de la independencia de Chile*, maintained that the old Spanish regime collapsed because it thwarted a capitalist transformation of its empire. Pressures by industrial societies for access to colonial markets, combined with colonial elites with more "bourgeois" inclinations than their rulers, gave the breakdown an economic motivation that had little to do with national teleologies. Sergio Bagú, an Argentine historian who labored to apply sociological methods to social and economic history, composed one of the masterworks of Marxist history in Latin America, *El plan económico del grupo rivadaviano, 1811–1827: Su sentido y sus contradicciones, sus proyecciones sociales, sus enemigos*. These works argued that independence was less a political struggle for national sovereignty than a social upheaval on the part of a proto-bourgeoisie clamoring to break loose from the patrimonial and feudal strictures of imperial control without achieving it. The "proto" prefaces the class nature of the upheaval because these were not mature bourgeoisies aiming to topple the ancien régime and supplant it with a fully capitalist order (which is how many French Marxist historians saw the events of 1789); accordingly, the weaknesses of local elites—their incomplete transformation into agents of capitalism—prevented them from installing a new capitalist or developmental order. The penetration of British interests—that is, more robust capitalists—truncated whatever possible mutation creole elites might have made into agents of capitalist development. The result was a highly uneven but nonetheless integrated model of modernity. This became a powerful framework for many social and economic historians, invigorated even more in the 1970s with the spread of a "dependency" approach to the region's history. But, it is worth reminding ourselves, it merely supplanted a national teleology (and its failures) with another one about capitalism; where the nation was only partially realized with independence, now it was the bourgeoisie that suffered the same fate.[11]

The social and economic aspects of independence, and their incomplete transformations, also became popular abroad. North American historians wrote in a less Marxisant strain, but nonetheless shifted the emphasis to the structural dynamics of independence. One was Richard Graham's 1972 *Independence in Latin America*.[12] For Graham, "national" leaders may have moved about the stage, but the motivating forces of history were less the volitions of heroes than the interests of elites, the struggles of working peoples, and the shifts in the world economy as a result of the industrial revolution—whose compound effects sidelined the Iberian powers and pushed Latin America, its elites and subaltern folk, into the market orbits of rising commercial powers. The same tone was struck in another fine synthesis, Jay Kinsbruner's 1973 study *Independence in Spanish America*, which explicitly shifted the emphasis from nation building to strivings among creole elites for economic development that did not sit well with either peninsular magnates or ordinary people. The result was—and it took some time for people to pick up on this insight—not just a "revolution" but a civil war within it over rival visions of the future.[13] In the shadow of the Cuban revolution, which did so much to transform the language of sovereignty and give it a Marxisant tone, it was hard to deny that formal independence had scarcely resolved the colonial tensions that had contributed to its eruption, and that the issues of development, poverty, and social cohesion lingered from the era of Iberian rule.

Elite Crisis of the Ancien Régime

With the maturing of a more structuralist view of history and the shift away from nation-centric approaches to independence, a generation of historians began to look closely at the crisis of the late eighteenth and early nineteenth centuries as the breakdown of long-lasting colonial pacts—an elite crisis that induced some creoles to devise national frameworks to supplant old imperial ones once the ancien régime was on its last legs. The corrosion of elite fealty and integration set the stage for the implosion of the state. Yet even here there was a basic enigma. Doris Ladd's important study of the Mexican high elite illustrated the degree of elite integration through extended fictive and real kin networks, as well as the sharp creolization of the aristocracy (in contrast to the view that creoles were marginalized by the Bourbon reforms) in the late eighteenth and early nineteenth centuries. Other works on late colonial elites in Rio de Janeiro and Buenos Aires, for example, concurred. Indeed, as the political scientist Jorge Domínguez noted in his study of the crisis of a "patrimonial" Spanish empire, elite competition was accommodated within ancien régime rules—except where emergent elites displayed "incipiently modernizing" orientations. But this was, he concluded, rare.[14] So, given the integration of elites and unprecedented incorporation of American fractions, how did the elite crisis transpire?

For some, ideology and the effects of the Enlightenment fractured an elite whose cohesion could not rest only on common interests or fears. Simon Collier, for instance, wrote a peerless study of the breakdown of consensus among Chilean elites (who ranked among the most tightly knit and stable of the colonial outposts) and the struggle to forge a new alliance, emboldened perhaps more by political conviction than by economic interests—a book which would inaugurate an important series of monographs published by Cambridge University Press (and which Collier himself edited). At the same time, Carlos Guilherme Mota looked at the *mentalités* of Brazilian plutocrats to show the uneven and partial local consumption and adaptation of European ideas, which confirmed Brazilians' sense of prospective modernization while fueling an anxiety that they were falling short of some universal (read: Europeanized) norm. The result was a simultaneous fascination with and revulsion against the idea of revolution. On the whole, however, the intellectual history of the period was surprisingly scant, in contrast to the current of idealism that so decisively shaped North American historiography.[15] There is one important exception: Renán Silva's recent study of education, libraries, books, and reading in the half century before 1808 follows the recent turn in the history of learned cultures to take a fresh look at figures of the New Granadan Enlightenment without assuming that an interpretive community synthesized into a nationalist elite bursting to topple the ancien régime.[16]

Closer examinations of colonial elites did suggest that the story of independence required a prior account of the breakdown of colonialism and elite fealty to the Iberian systems. Conflict over ideas paled beside a more "realist" conflict over power, accentuated once its central bastion, the monarchy, collapsed. Timothy Anna, Brian Hamnett, and John Fisher contributed important accounts of the administrative, social, and economic decomposition of elite unity in Mexico and Lima—but while they looked closely at the capitals of the two major viceroyalties, the struggles they charted operated within the imperial frameworks that held local elites together. Writing in the wake of the sesquicentennials of Mexican and

Peruvian independence, and in response to what was then becoming a more open debate about whether revolutions were national or not, the issue was not the rise of a new elite to challenge the old order but rather the collapse of the old order, which drove wedges into colonial alliances and thus yielded new elites. For Hamnett and Anna, independence could not be separated from the larger effects of the French Revolution and the hammer blows to the Spanish monarchy. These were crises caused by Napoleon's invasion, which occasioned elite defection and then provoked a failure of governmental structures. Both historians also opened up peninsular archives for systematic reference (something earlier nationalists had not done, because they were looking for the autochthonous aspects of independence). Fisher examined the ways in which regional forces, while still loyal to the crown, fought for autonomy within Peru. Later, Anna, joined by Michael Costeloe, argued that "independence" put the historical cart before the horse—for far from bringing new nations into being, Spain's crisis or mismanagement (depending on how you look at it) "lost" American possessions; nations were the aftereffects of an imperial crisis. This was a perspective shared by Kenneth Maxwell in what has become a classic study of Brazil, with the rather obvious point that the "loss" of Brazil was much more anticipated, as Maxwell noted in the failure of the Braganza monarchy to hang on to the metropolis. More recently, Roderick Barman synthesized a much broader period, going back to the 1790s and reaching forward to the 1850s, to chart the more extended breakdown of elite pacts, whose ultimate effects were to yield something new, the nation. What all these historians argued was that the birth of the "nation" per se did not anticipate or cause a change in ruling systems, but the other way around.[17]

It is tempting to see this counter-national history of independence as a vision that could be most easily grasped by non-Latin Americans, especially in the high tide of revolutionary nationalism among intellectual circles in the 1960s and 1970s. But this would be too simple. For the Brazilian economic historian Fernando Novais, independence was not a story about decolonization; it was the effect of a crisis of the ancien régime and its elites, social regimes that could no longer sustain mercantilist colonialism and absolutism and whose colonial elites had already began making the transition to something more than just primitive accumulation, so that independence was a de jure conclusion to de facto developments. Indeed, the edited volume in which Novais's influential essay appeared, edited by Carlos Guilherme Mota, was an important touchstone among Brazilian historians who wanted to advance accounts of independence that marginalized or at least contextualized the national question.[18] Peruvians began to argue that independence was less a conquest than a concession, something motivated from without by industrial powers dueling with a moribund Spain or by San Martín's and Bolívar's "foreign" armies. Peruvian elites, driven more by fear, simply switched allegiance. Heraclio Bonilla and Karen Spalding, in part reacting to the hoopla of the sesquicentennial, published a polemical and influential 1972 essay, "La Independencia en el Perú: Las palabras y los hechos," which argued that the large structures of the world economy, and not national aspirations, caused independence. Notable was the rising sense among historians that the classical framework confused a postdictive rhetoric of nation builders with the causes and course of the breakdown of Iberian empires.[19]

Perhaps the most influential study of the elite crisis that led to independence came from the pen of the Argentine historian Tulio Halperín Donghi. In a series of important articles, and subsequently in his majestic monograph *Revolución y guerra: Formación de una élite dirigente en la Argentina criolla*, he detailed the complex unwinding of systems of rulership, the opening of the centrifugal forces contained by elite unity, and the cascade into revolutionary militarization and civil war. In the dense political narrative, it is sometimes easy to forget that Halperín Donghi was attentive to the underlying social and economic shifts in trade and production that made it harder and harder to keep old mercantilists and new commercial interests within the same bloc. Halperín Donghi later expanded to a general level the notion of elite crisis in response to the schisms unleashed by empires struggling to cope with war and commercial competition; in *Reforma y disolución de los imperios ibéricos, 1750–1850* he argued, along with Anna and others, that independence was intricately linked with, if not caused by, imperial dissolution.[20] Fernando Novais and other Brazilian historians were even more insistent that independence was driven by underlying structural forces and had little to do with national aspirations, and using an approach like Halperín Donghi's they argued that Brazil's secession was a response to a broader crisis of the Portuguese empire, a crisis that had sundered the consensus among ruling elites and propelled them to secede, albeit with far less friction and discord than in Spanish America.

Structural models of history transcended personalized narratives and national teleologies; they did not dismiss them, but contextualized people and movements within more sociological frames. The focus tended to be on political and economic elites, and how their collaboration extracted revenues and rents from colonial societies. It was when the institutional conditions that supported these alliances broke down, either under the weight of the fiscal and commercial pressures of Atlantic warfare or faced with changing ideological precepts of rulership and rights, that revolutions erupted. And when colonial agents could no longer see their interests upheld within a framework of empire, they broke loose. Thus it was that the idyll of a coherent "nation" pursuing liberation stepped aside in favor of a more instrumental approach to history, one which conformed to a more general turn in history and the social sciences towards "realist" approaches that accentuated the struggle for political power in the absence of a dominant legitimating system, or Marxian approaches that dwelled on the conflict of material interests between old mercantilist peninsular concerns and a rising, possibly even "bourgeois," class in the colonies. As one suggestive synthesis recently argued, independence was simply one dimension of a more general crisis of the Spanish state which broke the institutional fetters on capitalist development. As such, Peter Guardino and Charles Walker argued, the period qualifies as a bourgeois revolution (albeit without a thoroughbred bourgeoisie to lead it).[21]

THE FAILED REVOLUTION?

As Weberian and Marxist concepts of class elbowed aside national frames for understanding the struggles of the early nineteenth century, many historians began to question whether there was a "revolution" at all. For Octavio Paz, whose 1959 *El laberinto de la soledad* made explicit what was implicit about the classical approach to Latin American history, the region's past was caught in a set of countervailing trajectories that altered the world while reinforcing the power of its heritages. Flux and reflux. Conquistadors had created something anew while prolonging the past, and now "liberators" cleared the stage to become "the Spanish American dictator." Thus, observed Paz, "the newness of the new Spanish American nations is deceptive: in reality they were decadent or static societies, fragments and survivals of a shattered whole." John J. Johnson, in writing a history of the military of the region, pointed to the revolutionary caudillos who had trumpeted the cause of national liberty as the perpetuators of an authoritarian tradition. This more skeptical view of what if anything had changed acquired greater valence in the 1970s as Latin American societies plunged from the heady decades of democratic populism into serial dictatorship.[22]

The view of a revolution that failed, or that never was, found the most currency in a series of important monographs about popular insurrections for a different, more inclusive new order that were crushed by peninsular reactionaries and scared creole elites whose visions of a new order stopped short of spreading the social dividends of change more broadly. For Marxists looking for a bourgeoisie to topple a feudal system, as well as for liberals looking for enlightened *penseurs* determined to bring reason to a backward regime of estates, there may have been a break with independence, but not a social revolution. For Bonilla and Spalding, the rupture of independence was decisive because it enabled a fundamentally colonial society to subsist precisely because it declared independence. What *limeño* elites did was to cash in the formal rule of Spain for the informal domain of Great Britain. For Indians, rural folk, and the great majority, "independence" was a word, little more—Túpac Amaru's rebellion, far from being one of the protonational precursors, represented a terminal defeat (that is, until the specter of a socialist revolution came along) for aspirants of a new order, whose spectral presence frightened elites into clinging onto old systems.[23]

It may be argued that Peruvians were especially inclined to view independence as less than a triumphal moment because of the lateness of secession and the prevalence of outside armies. But they were not. The shift can best be seen in the emergence of important studies of rural folk who seized upon the political rupture to effect a different social order. In 1966, Hugh Hamill published a pioneering study of Father Hidalgo, recasting him less as a national (or protonational) hero or misguided lunatic than as a prophetic leader of a people who were fed up with the violations of their moral economy—and who carried an anti-Spanish flag not because they were "Mexicans" but because they objected to their colonial status and its burdens. Hidalgo therefore helped inaugurate the regime's legitimacy crisis and thus usher in independence, even though the social order that eventuated bore little resemblance to the one he and his followers would have wanted.[24] Another example of a failed, or foiled, movement that articulated something different was Carlos Guilherme Mota's study of the 1817 uprising in Pernambuco. While Mota put greater stress on the interethnic and cross-class alliances that challenged the old order than did Hamill, what was important was the opposition to rulers in Rio de Janeiro and not Lisbon. Mota argued that the movement was less successful at realizing its own affirmative goals than at crippling an already wobbly Braganza dynasty. Yet what the federalist spirit of 1817 expressed was a localized, and not national, concept of sovereignty. Indeed, one of the running concerns for the rebels was a struggle against "monopoly" of all sorts.[25] Like Hamill's study, Mota's explored a failed revolution, but one that ensured that there was no return to the status quo ante.

One of the most celebrated of the "failed" alternative movements was that of José Gervasio Artigas and the federalists of the Banda Oriental. In 1959, John Street published a little-known but very important study of the rural insurrection in the borderlands between Brazil and Buenos Aires, where country folk were as suspicious of the urban potentates of Rio de Janeiro, Buenos Aires, and Montevideo as they were of distant powers. His book lacked some of the structural flavor of most subsequent works and did not examine in depth the social structure of the region, sticking mainly to a political narrative of a people who took the language of freedom to mean not just home rule but a radical alternative to who got to rule at home.[26] Artigas and his army of Indians, ex-slaves, and mixed-blood peons nonetheless exemplified the idea of a different social order nestled within a political project. Lucía Sala de Touron, Nelson de la Torre, and Julio Rodríguez published *Artigas y su revolución agraria, 1811–1820* in Mexico in 1978, while they were in exile from Uruguay. The book became a touchstone for historians who felt that the obsession with the nation had occluded a more fundamental struggle to create a social, egalitarian order in the countryside once dominated by landed estates. Artigas's 1815 proclamation, not of independence but of the defense of a new rural order, was what was at stake—especially Article Six, which gave rights to land and cattle to the region's "*infelices.*"[27] Theirs was a history of the development not of a national consciousness but of a social one—which was doomed by the conspiracies and treasons of Spanish, Portuguese, *and* creole magnates who, whatever their political differences, agreed that the River Plate should be dominated by great estancias and coerced labor systems.

It should be stressed that failure did not mean permanent defeat. What these case studies showed was that there was a latent meaning to independence that had been crushed, but whose legacies survived. For Mota, the Pernambucan rebels, especially the more populist elements, lived on to rally behind the 1824 creation of the Confederation of the Equator; for Hamill, there endured an Indian and mestizo resistance to any restoration, which informed liberals across the nineteenth-century Mexican political landscape; and for Sala de Touron and her coauthors, Artigas lived on in the spirit of federalist insurgents, which could be read, not unreasonably, as a genealogical founding of the Tupamaro guerrillas fighting for a cause that had not been won in 1810.

After the Revolution

By the early 1980s there existed a plenitude of narratives about the significance and meaning of independence in Latin American history. In a sense, this was already implicit in the classical formulation, which had never managed to stabilize a bounded unity to national histories. What changed was how historians were choosing to see the disunity within the national framework, or giving bounded structures to struggles that decentered national aspirations. But as the 1980s unfolded, in a context in which the region emerged from years of dictatorship and civil war, historians returned to the political content of independence. They were now less dismissive of some of the formal changes that accompanied it. After all the traumas of the repression, the formalities of citizenship acquired new, and vital, significance. What is more, as intellectual life became less radical, the urge to find hidden transformative possibilities within the upheavals of the early nineteenth century lost its charm. Indeed, a historiographical preference once so resolutely dismissed, military history, showed signs of some recovery. Clément Thibaud, for instance, shows—at some length—how the military played a central role in nation making, not as a result of its triumphant feats but out of the sociability within colonial militias that evolved into standing armies.[28]

And yet, despite the historiographical turns of the 1980s, the "national question" remained as fractured and unresolved as ever. This change within continuity is expressed in two major directions in which historians pursued their research on independence. The first was a return to the study of the formal political arena cast across a broad "Atlantic" framework. The second involved a closer examination of some of the social and cultural developments that were associated with independence but had very little to do with any process of nation building.

It could be argued that the restorations (or, in some cases, the first instantiations) of democracy in the 1980s motivated historians to look at formal politics in the early nineteenth century. But this, as with so many other historiographical shifts, had its pioneering anticipators. To begin with, the classical histories, anthologies of documents, and constitutional collections had explored state formation, albeit from a somewhat rigid perspective. But there were many historians who defied the simplifying nationalist mold. Among them was the Texas-based scholar Nettie Lee Benson, who authored several important articles and compiled a formative group of essays written by a group of graduate students that centered on the effects that the convocation of deputies to the Spanish Cortes, with the Junta reeling from the pressures of Napoleon's armies. *Mexico and the Spanish Cortes, 1810–1822* was published in 1966, and in a sense looked back to an earlier constitutional history. However, it also anticipated by several decades a fascination with the sudden intervention of electoral and representative activity in Spain and the empire. To be sure, as Benson argued, the Cortes for the first time claimed to represent the parts of the empire (provinces, colonies, estates) as a single "Spanish" nation, thereby forcing the national question into the political arena, but it also charted a new course for resolving the regime's legitimacy, elections. For all the studies of political leadership, Benson struck a nerve when she wrote that "few developments in the history of the Spanish colonial system have been more carelessly treated or more misinterpreted than the attempt to establish constitutional government under the Spanish monarchy..." What emerged from the essays, and in her later monograph *The Provincial Deputation in Mexico* (originally published in Mexico in 1955), was how the rupture in the fundaments of political rule sent riptides across the Spanish dominions that altered the practice of politics and gave rise to understandings of political identity that could not be reduced to social class, economic interest, or location in the world economy.[29] And if the efforts to create new foundations for political legitimacy within the Spanish empire had been overlooked, the situation was even more obscure in the Portuguese empire.

There was a reason why constitutionalism under the Spanish monarchy had been so ill treated: in the rush to establish a narrative of a colony becoming a nation and repudiating its overlords, there was little room for examining how the empires broke up, since the result was so foreordained. The structural emphasis on inevitable decay was no more illuminating than the classical approach it sought to replace. With relatively few exceptions, most historians were willing to accept at face value the language of rebels who believed that nothing Spanish or Portuguese could ever accommodate itself to a more reasoned and representative system. It did not help that this often dovetailed with an Anglo-American propensity to think of constitutionalism as a uniquely Anglo-Saxon art. What Benson called for, and what historians began to pick up in the 1980s, was thus the long history of imperial crisis which presaged independence. Accordingly, there proliferated a great many case studies of elections.

One important collection of essays, edited by Antonio Annino, explored the effects of electoral life in a wide array of settings, from Buenos Aires and Rio de Janeiro to the Yucatán peninsula. One of the goals of this work is to dispense with the bacilli of the Black Legend which presumed that the experience of modern political representation in Latin America had (and has) been a failure, a view reinforced by the overwhelming echo of nineteenth-century elite voices that decried the disorder and anarchy of voting. Greater attention to suffrage dislodged the more familiar story about caudillos and caciques as the political inheritors of the Liberators' efforts. This direction of research, it is worth saying, paid less attention to "parties" and electoral outcomes (whose polls were, in any event, very uneven predictors of who actually won these contests) and more on electoral practices as "inputs" contributing to political cultures in formation, and this being a conditioning force for state formation. The result is that political citizenship conditioned states as much as the other way around. What this meant for how historians understand independence is clear enough: it was one of a series of larger unresolved questions about sovereignty, and making sense of independence requires a prior analysis of some of the ways in which political life changed in the wake of an imperial crisis in the metropolis. In the case of Mexico, for instance, Virginia Guedea has charted the manifold ways in which insurgents and loyalists alike turned to elections to rally support and popular practices of suffrage coexisted with military activity to sort out allegiances and alignments across New Spain between 1810 and 1821. And as Karen Caplan has observed, it was not just Spaniards and creoles who turned to elections; Indians in Oaxaca and Yucatán also embraced voting as a means to resolve disputes over municipal leadership. If Mexicans developed a national consciousness, they did so during, or perhaps because of, a fundamental rupture in the practice of politics.[30]

There have also been a series of very important studies of the deliberative work of the Cortes itself, showing how the parliament wrestled with reintegrating the components of an empire or monarchy into a single, multicontinental, and multiethnic "nation." Márcia Regina Berbel, for instance, has published an account of how the elected deputies to the Cortes in Lisbon went to the metropolis to defend the unity of the Portuguese nation and the consequential equality of subjects within it. Almost two years of deliberation yielded to divergent notions of what it meant to belong to a single nation. As Berbel's book shows, the justifications for "Brazilian" secession did not mean that "Brazilians" subscribed to a common framework of national membership; some of the very same fissures that opened in Lisbon remained open when sovereignty was repatriated to Rio de Janeiro.[31] Other historians have taken seriously the political theory, or theories, that informed what became an increasingly polarized set of positions over the statehood that was supposed to sustain nationhood within empire or monarchy. To José Carlos Chiaramonte, for instance, rebellious and reactionary proponents of sovereignty operated within a doctrinal framework of natural rights and a cult of civic virtue, not national rights, equally defensible at subnational (municipal or provincial) levels and at supranational ones (like a "monarchy"). In this way, ancient norms could give way to new political forms. Brazil's constitutional break was therefore with Lisbon, not with monarchy, and was not a mere outlier, simply one expression of a new combination of political sentiments, which relocated the spatial boundaries of the political community with independence without repudiating empire or monarchy as the means to bond a political regime to its social composition. Nationhood was therefore but one of the progeny of a shift in models of citizenship; Chiaramonte made explicit what was becoming an implicit recognition: it was the state that created the conditions for the nation, and not a maturing national *esprit* that created new states.[32]

In the 1980s, therefore, historians were turning full circle to the analysis of the institutional structures of rulership, restoring the autonomy of the political field but sidelining the heroes of the nations they were supposed to personify. There was also another important departure from the classical legacies: greater attention was paid to the contingencies of political decomposition and recomposition of empire before the independence of its colonies, thus sparing the analysis of its predestined, nationalizing outcome. Independence was becoming a political effect, not a cause of political change. For María de Lourdes Viana Lyra, Brazilian secession came after several decades of imperial tinkering and efforts on the part of colonists and metropolitans alike to reimagine the empire before ditching it in favor of something else, like the nation-state—or, to be more accurate, to reinvent the empire as a nation-state. Roberto Breña's important recent study of Mexico goes a step further: it argues that the crisis within the Spanish empire evolved within the understandings of liberalism in all corners of Madrid's dominion, which had itself evolved from Bourbon Enlightenment trends; the crisis was internal to the ideological makeup of the system itself.[33]

Indeed, there has been a full reevaluation of loyalism and the stresses and strains of the ancien régime before its final collapse as conditions of rebellion. John Fisher for Peru and Christon Archer for Mexico, for instance, have shown how much loyalists feuded and wrangled over what to do after 1808—a dimension of the conflict which had been completely occluded by the nationalist accounts, which preferred to leave loyalists as an undifferentiated mass of reactionaries. Scarlett O'Phelan Godoy has compiled an important collection of essays specifically dealing with life in Peru from 1808 to the 1820s, that is, the years between the monarchy's collapse and the final defeat of peninsular armies. What becomes clear is that Peru did not conform to the image of unflinching loyalty and stasis. Indeed, as O'Phelan Godoy remarked in a critique of Bonilla and Spalding's view that independence was simply "conceded" rather than achieved, there was a great deal more unrest and discontinuity even within the most "loyal" of Iberian viceroyalties than historians have admitted—in large part because they have been so obsessed with locating the origins of a national quest for sovereign redemption rather than conflict and violence over what it meant to persist in empire and monarchy. In a nuanced study by Víctor Peralta of José Fernández de Abascal, the formidable viceroy in Lima from 1806 to 1816, it is clear that for all the Spaniard's cunning, he was running a tough gauntlet between subjects itching to try on new liberties and loyalists who despised the change but were reluctant to fund the suppression of its more radical proponents. Gustavo Montoya, in a fine-grained essay, explored the waverings of *limeño* dominant classes during San Martín's occupation of the city, with royalist armies camped just outside. In these circumstances, it was not at all clear what to do—and to slap simplified causal models onto complex contingencies seems increasingly ahistorical (though perhaps no less tempting just because the scenarios of collapsing systems are so complex).[34]

There is now a welter of very good studies of what it meant to be on the "other," loyalist, side of the political line to complement the increasingly complex view of the divisions and changes within the patriot cause. In a sense, Germán Carrera Damas's study of the Venezuelan loyalist Boves, while still a blood-curdling read, no longer stands alone in urging readers to take the defenders of empire seriously as historical subjects. Valentim Alexandre charted the step-by-step ways in which the "colonial question" was magnified into the powder keg of the Portuguese regime. Maria de Lourdes Viana Lyra has shown how conservative reformers struggled from the 1790s to shore up the Portuguese empire by recasting it as a grand trans-Atlantic utopia whose inheritors were José Bonfacio and the Brazilian Empire born in 1822. Kirsten Schultz's close study of urban political culture in Rio de Janeiro between 1808 and 1821 shows just how much potentates of all inclinations labored to recombine traditional notions of monarchy and empire with newer principles of representation and newer realities of the Americanization of power.[35]

The most important and provocative intervention has come from Jaime E. Rodríguez O., who in a series of essays and edited books, and finally in *The Independence of Spanish America*, has recast the breakup of the Spanish empire as a civil war among Spaniards, many of whom happened to live in the Americas. The 1998 edition of *The Independence of Spanish America* winnows out references to colony and empire to make way for an image of a "heterogeneous confederation" of more or less equal parts bound by a "Spanish Monarchy." There was friction but no colonial identity brewing in the peripheries, waiting, as the classical historians had argued, for the apposite moment for their birth into a national form. The problem came when Spanish subjects were forced to deal with the absence of their monarch. Spanish Americans and Spaniards could not agree on what kind of structure to put in his stead. As a result, independence was not only the end of a long political process, nation-states were the "fragments and survivals of a shattered whole" (in Octavio Paz's words) of a multicontinental cosmopolitan kingdom.

What is important to underscore about Rodríguez's argument is that colonies did not secede from an empire; it was the protracted metropolitan crisis of the ancien régime that eventuated in nations. Rodriguez crystallized a growing historical view of independence as anything but inevitable, the old regime as anything but a brittle framework incapable of adapting old practices to new ways, the nation being "Hispanic" before labels like "Colombian" or "Argentine" were assigned to the post-Hispanic shards. If the national teleology is gone, Rodríguez fills the narrative vacuum with the idea of an enduring "Spanish" and "monarchical" imagined community of preference. Here, the revisionism runs into some problems. It downplays the multiple legal principles and practices involved in being a Spanish subject on the peripheries that membership in the Monarchy did not resolve, or at least explains conflict as a contingent clash and not a structural dilemma. Sidelining the words "empire" and "colony" certainly creates more room to think about the ancien régime without presuming its demise. But dispensing with structured notions of asymmetry and inequity makes it hard to explain the violence and discord that followed the crisis of 1808. While Rodríguez challenges both the view that creoles were bound to defy imperial authority and the structuralist assumption that the old regime could not adapt to modern mores, he is forced to restore the Liberators back to the center of the political stage, albeit shorn of their heroic vestments, as the saboteurs of the system.[36]

Rodríguez's works comprise a landmark in the making of modern Latin American history, having crystallized a growing view that there was a political logic to imperial change that was not reducible to underlying structural drives and their inevitability. He, and others, located the emergence of nationhood as a more truly revolutionary outcome precisely because it was so unforeseen, and not the result of a preexisting propensity.

The Unbounded Unity of Independence

Is there a position between viewing independence as a contingent event with structural consequences and treating it as a structural manifestation that unleashed contingent disorders? This last section will explore several ways in which historians have sought to locate the struggle for sovereignty within several sets of conflicts, only one of which has to do with abrasive concepts of nationhood. They fall within quite a different model of politics than the one described above. If some historians in the 1980s began to take seriously the domain of an autonomous political sphere, others reframed politics not so much as the space in which political subjects grappled with the challenge of choosing and acknowledging state authority but as an activity which defines the boundaries and limits of citizenship. This shift owed its inspiration to the works of Alexis de Tocqueville and Jürgen Habermas, who observed a more general structural disjuncture between eighteenth-century efforts to centralize state authority in absolutist and interventionist hands and ideas of the Enlightenment and the republic of letters, according to which political subjects possessed abilities to reason and consequential rights. What was vital was not just shifting formal *political* rules but, as Habermas put it, a "structural transformation" of the public sphere that constituted the citizenry. As social scientists were arguing during the 1980s "transitions" to democracy, what was at stake for the system was not just elections and formal rules of the game, but also the freedom and energy of an autonomous civil society to buttress them.

This sphere, comprised of public spaces, parks, cafés, newspapers, and salons, was no less important to the shaping of politics than its coeval political sphere. One of the presumptions, however, about the emergence of a public "sphere" lies in its singular rather than plural origins and development. Indeed, what is so important about *Latin American* historical scholarship is that is demonstrates how the fracturing of political systems can be traced to the fragmentation and polarization of publics themselves, driven above all by transformations in the principles and practices of representation within empires. Isabel Lustosa's in-depth study of how Luso-Brazilian journalists exchanged a war of printed words—printed insults, in her words—set the stage for Brazilian secession in spite of elite and royalist efforts to keep the two sides of the Luso-Atlantic worlds together. In this sense, the emergent public activity associated with new patterns of sociability and exchange did more than alter political rules and norms; it could fragment and reaggregate them in novel ways.[37]

The most important work in this vein has come from the Paris-based historian François-Xavier Guerra and his many students. For Guerra, the revolutions were not disruptive moments in an otherwise integrated system but an acceleration of processes that had begun under the ancien régime and were carried forward, vertiginously, with secession. There was therefore a deeply discontinuous aspect to independence, but its novelty can be ascribed to a more global transformation in a system of references, ideas, social imaginations, and values that amounts to nothing less than the eruption of modernity within old regime monarchies. What is important about the transformation within the old political vessel is that what was novel did not necessarily imply or require a new order to realize it. In this sense, the "filiation" or likening of the Latin American revolutions to the French Revolution needs some serious qualification (since in any event French revisionists were busy dismantling old verities about their revolution as well). Rather than a sharp new order, what emerged were much more hybrid systems and experiments in empires (like Brazil and Mexico), monarchies (like Belgrano's Incan restoration), or even triumvirates, protectorates, and directorates that amalgamated new principles with old absolutist ones.

What is more, revolutionary syncretisms tried to resolve the problems of state legitimacy against the backdrop of new practices of sociability, symbolic activity, and media for determining what did quickly acquire an undeniable force: public opinion. In a study of Mexico around independence, Rafael Rojas has shown how reading, writing, and the circulation of books and other media kindled an incipient public opinion as old imperial structures waned—though the causal ties between the two developments remain, perhaps necessarily so, unclear. Guerra and Annick Lempérière edited an important volume that tackled these ambiguities head-on and explored the fascinating variations with which increasingly localized combinations of new and old practices tried to resolve what historians had traditionally treated in binary ways: tradition and modernity. And yet, Latin America's independence process still acquired an important determining power. Unlike other societies of the Latinate world (including Portugal and Spain) after the revolutions, there was no restorationist undertow that swept countries back into monarchical or neoabsolutist regimes. Latin Americans had constitutions that checked the powers of rulers; legitimacy was predicated on popular sovereignty. Such principles, honored perhaps only in the breach, nonetheless altered the fundamental course of state formation in Latin America.[38]

We are, therefore, some distance from the idealized images of heroes delivering their societies to the promised land of the nation's bounded unity and the state's universalized identification with the rule of law. Free of the view that tarred Latin American revolutions as somehow manqué, historians have turned away from postdictive narratives in which the "failure" or "success" of the outcome guided the story of social and political change in favor of accounts of how old and new forces combined, clashed, and compromised. Of late, historians have been looking more closely at the many manifestations of the shifting hybrid systems in which declarations of independence were embedded. New formal rules may have been inscribed in charters, public opinion may have begun to enjoy an influence over state affairs that no one imagined before 1810, but the values, norms, and behavior of societies and households did not necessarily calibrate themselves to the same rhythm of change. Indeed, in many ways, they continued to be "traditional" precisely because state sovereignty was so shaky.

To get at how public norms and institutions intersected, historians have looked closely at how the vocabulary of "honor" persisted in distinguishing permissible and legitimate activity from that which was impermissible and stigmatized by public norms. Margarita Garrido's study of appeals and petitions to colonial and revolutionary authorities describes the enduring appeal—and effectiveness—of a particular supplicative style of collective representation before authorities. She shows that the diminishing returns on this traditional convention of the ancien régime taxed its legitimacy, as well as its successor's. Victor Uribe's study of the legal *letrado* elite of Nueva Granada explores the ways in which attorneys and magistrates—and their families—shared a familiar world, replete with strong behavioral customs that gave ballast to a highly litigious society, and an increasingly polarized one as the revolution unfolded. Within a profession and its reproductive networks devoted to upholding legality and honorable conduct, there was hatched a series of subversive ideas and proposals which ensured that lawyers would be at the center, and on both sides of the line, of the revolution. Throughout, however, "honor" was a way to gauge private citizens' compliance with law, as well as a public language with which to vilify opponents. The world had changed, while redoubling the force of its heritages. Flux and reflux.

Living an honorable life, indeed elevating "honor" as a means to distinguish between active rights-bearing citizens and passive subjects, is the theme of Sarah Chambers' study of Arequipa. "Honorable citizens" were those endowed with the ability to contribute to public affairs. In courts, the streets, and newspapers, public authorities from colonial officials to rival caudillos were celebrated or decried for their compliance with accepted notions of honor (though, it is worth noting, this was hardly a transparent ideal and was itself the source of much feuding). What independence did was to democratize honor; the republic had to accept that all citizens could in theory be honorable, and thus active members of the political community. The ultimate custodian of honor shifted from the king to the constitution without dispensing with traditional understandings of labor discipline, Indian subservience, and patriarchal mores that reproduced social inequalities through the nineteenth century. Flux and reflux.

José Murilo de Carvalho's study of the Braganza court shows how Brazil's dominant classes handled the disruptions of secession and constitutional change without letting the former colony splinter by hanging on to Portuguese colonial habits, which had been the source of a great deal of ideological homogeneity. This was only in part a doctrinal matter; it also depended on forms of elite socialization, training, and courtly rituals that distinguished civil rulers from the rest while blurring the lines that had been so divisive within Spanish American elites. At the same time, Brazilian elites acknowledged that their hold on power depended on their ability to accommodate new groups (especially from the provinces) and aspirants into the charmed circle of potentates lest they be accused (and they often were) of being as despotic as Portuguese rulers. Flux and reflux.[39]

To say that older concepts survived the break of independence while acquiring new meaning or significance need not diminish the violence that accompanied the friction between flux and reflux. Indeed, the flux-reflux that Octavio Paz invoked need not imply lack of motion. If political historians have looked at how citizenship changed, and thus challenged the view that independence achieved little, social historians have been even more probing of the stubborn view that change stopped at the doorstep of formality and did not enter the private world of domesticity or social power. For instance, historians have examined how the wars shaped the lives of slaves—and how, in turn, slaves seized upon mass violence to expand the boundaries of their freedom. In Lima, as Alberto Flores Galindo and Christine Hunefeldt have shown in their works, the public tumult of Spain's invasion, and eventually San Martín's occupation of the viceregal capital, shook up without militarizing the most dichotomous relations between wealthy potentates and slaves. Disturbances may have spiked, but elites nonetheless (or in response to the social instability) remained unified and able to preserve social hierarchies—but barely. Gustavo Montoya, for instance, shows how the popular *cuerpos cívicos* mobilized during the Protectorate years in Lima (1821–22), rearranging fundamental social relations.[40]

If social upheavals convulsed even the most stable of colonial outposts, they had the capability of transforming plantation belts into battlefields. Centuries of slaveholding practices went up in flames, even though, on the books, slavery was only annulled in most societies in the 1850s. Peter Blanchard has followed the trails of slaves who became foot soldiers in patriot armies and who forced their claims upon the Liberators, so that the new states soon passed laws ending the slave trade before cutting their ties with Spain. Some legislators freed all the children born thereafter; meanwhile, slaves, as Camilla Townsend has shown for the area around Guayaquil, did not sit around waiting to be freed but took the language of liberty to heart, fleeing, litigating, and manumitting themselves in unprecedented numbers. Marixa Lasso has shown how the image of Haiti functioned as a double-edged sword, simultaneously as a potent threat from slaves who wanted freedom from republicans and royalists alike and as a menace to be avoided. Haiti inspired a radical republican tradition among free people of color, and thus added to polarized social relations that cut across rebellious and royal armies. This compelled both sides to free slaves as recruits to armies while struggling to keep black troops from radicalizing their commanders' cause. And in some cases, racial lines were drawn across the commanders themselves. Aline Helg has argued that Black and mulatto commanders ran headlong into white leaders like Bolívar and Francisco de Paula Santander's fears that Colombian republicanism would cascade into a anarchic *pardocracia*. Not a few found themselves executed in the panic to avoid radicalization of independent countries. Helg's analysis suggests that the revolution for independence was a lost opportunity for creating a different, more egalitarian racial order. But the effect of the struggles on slavery's role in basic productive relations cannot be ignored: from the sugar estates in New Spain to the cacao plantations of Venezuela and the *estancias* of the Banda Oriental, property owners had to look beyond slaves as the cornerstones for capital accumulation. Even in Brazil, where social stasis has been a running theme, an anthology of excellent essays about runaways and their fugitive communities, edited by João José Reis, illustrates how the political convulsions and provincial uprisings shook the ability of planters to enforce labor discipline and led to spasms of slave flight.[41]

Where the dynamic between flux and reflux, accelerated by independence, is most evident is in recent scholarship on the shifting social geography of ethnicity. Not surprisingly, the historiographical activity is concentrated on the Andes and, especially, Mexico. In the Andes, of course, there was a longstanding view that the lingering fears of Túpac Amaru ensured that elites recoiled at the thought of opening the political domain to new, subaltern actors. Flores Galindo's elegant *Aristocracia y plebe* certainly evokes this sense, albeit in the neurological core of the Peruvian viceroyalty. At best, historians invoke the unrest in Huánuco and Cuzco (1811–12 and 1814) as spasmodic echoes of the past rather than part of a syncopated, and still incomplete, process of integrating Indian villagers into a new order. Jorge Cornejo Bouroncle's classic study of Mateo García Pumacahua's insurgency was an important exception to this rule—though he cast his narrative as a heroic nationalist alliance against Spanish despots.[42] In Mexico, Hidalgo's and Father Morelos's insurrections got a similar treatment. They helped spark the beginnings of independence and struck fear in the hearts of magnates (and thus stifled whatever enthusiasm they might have for the "Mexican" cause), but once the old regime began to forfeit the loyalty of elites, the political action shifted to the capital and subaltern actors faded into the background.

It would be hard to exaggerate how much historians have toppled this view of spasmodic popular insurgency. Charles Walker, for instance, carries his story of *cuzqueño* politics from Túpac Amaru to Pumacahua and on into the postcolonial decades. What is clear is that there were certainly waves of insurgency. Yet conflict, and not the passivity of a "*grand peur*," marked the highlands throughout the revolutionary era. This was why Cuzco's colonial intendant referred to "smoldering ashes" that threatened to flare up at any time. While it is true that liberals had a tough time dealing with the "Indian question" and in many ways preferred to let the status quo ante endure rather than shower the highlands with the liberties they advocated in urban salons, Cuzco's Indians remained a force to be reckoned with—an insight that the caudillo Agustín Gamarra took to heart, much to the chagrin of his liberal detractors.[43]

The effect of popular insurgency on the course and outcome of independence and on the remapping of the social landscape is most developed in the work on Mexico. Brian Hamnett, whose studies of infraelite struggles in the capital were so important in putting "independence" into a larger imperial setting, shifted his attention to the provinces, arguing that the insurgency had vital popular taproots and thus succeeded in compromising the legitimacy of royalist power in Mexico City. Insurgent bands, led by chieftains and their clans, hammered away at viceregal power until, in many regions, it was they and not Spanish officers who governed, well before Iturbide carried the military over to the Mexican side. Peter Guardino looked at one region in particular, Guerrero, where peasants fought for a new model of state sovereignty and citizenship. Mulatto sharecroppers and Indian villagers who grew cotton on the Costa Grande kept up a fight against Spanish power and eventually proved to be critical popular constituents in Vicente Guerrero's guerrilla war from 1815 to 1821—and eventually a bastion of his brand of popular liberalism, which continued to echo through the nineteenth century. Finally, Eric Van Young's in-depth and sprawling epic makes it all but impossible to envision "independence" as a process of national liberation involving elite bargaining and feuding over principles of state sovereignty without accounting for subaltern agency. As much as Hidalgo sparked Mexican nationalism, his insurgency also unleashed an internal war between classes and ethnic formations that sapped the colonial administration of its dominion over the viceroyalty while transforming the ways of life of villagers. These were the conditions that set the stage for secession, not its products. And with this sequence in mind, what Van Young insists is that the complex alliances of Indians, slaves, mixed folk, and creole ideologues should not let the image of a national synthesis against Spain overshadow very important and unresolved struggles for local resources, power, and communal identities. The anticolonial struggle therefore often blurred into an internecine one. It may be that Van Young has captured why it has been so hard for historians to settle the issue of which revolution was more important and how to bring some closure to either. Seeing the revolution as a convergence of cultural, social, and political struggles occasioned by the crisis of a regime that had legitimated centuries of a colonial social order has become a way to unbind the unrealized unity that been so elusive for the classical raconteurs of independence.[44]

Conclusion

In spite of the shifting views of Latin American independence there is a persistent undertow, and it is the way in which independence was simultaneously a moment of promise and frustration for historians who were trying to tell stories about political subjects struggling to fix new models of sovereignty out of colonial parts—and thus trying to answer the entwined questions of independence of what, and for whom. Such a tension ensured that independence never achieved the status of a culminating or redemptive moment in Latin American nation building. This does not mean that many historians in the nineteenth and twentieth centuries did not try to give a bounded unity to this moment as one of national birth; they did. But even in the classic narratives of independence, heroic national founders were as famous for their flaws as for their achievements; for all their daring selfless acts, they imprinted their imperfections on the fissiparous communities they "liberated."

Paradoxically, the unbounded unity of independence has had some liberating effects for Latin American historians, who have not had to labor under the burdens of quite such a triumphalist and exceptionalist mold as have Americans when it comes to their revolution. Historians have been able to be much more open about its ambiguities, incompletions, and imperfections. There has been, to be sure, a strong sense among many that independence was a failed moment in which nations struggled but failed to cohere, and more recently in which political liberties never had the leveling social effects that many, especially more radical, historians inscribed into the very meaning of the term "revolution." But increasingly, especially since the 1980s, seeing that the revolution was not an announcement of a new order but rather a structured transition between orders which remains unresolved, historians have been able to recapture some of the very discontinuous dimensions of the period precisely because creating nations was simply one of many potential stories and significances of the period. In such a fashion, the organized violence that accompanied the breakup of empires could reflect the diversity of colonial societies and the pluralism of their causes. The combination of improvising a new public stage while polarizing and militarizing the discord between its actors has reinforced the indefinite or unbounded view of the independence era, where so much could happen while remaining so unresolved.

NOTES

1. "Address to the 'Congreso Admirable': Message to the Constituent Congress of the Republic of Colombia," in *El Libertador: Writings of Simón Bolívar*, ed. David Bushnell (New York: Oxford University Press, 2003), 108.

2. Thomas Bender, "Introduction: Historians, the Nation, and the Plenitude of Narratives," in *Rethinking American History in the Global Age*, ed. Bender (Berkeley: University of California Press, 2002), 2.

3. José Manuel Restrepo, *Historia de la revolución de Colombia* (Medellín: Bedout, 1969), 6 vols.; Bartolomé Mitre, *Historia de Belgrano y de la independencia argentina* (Buenos Aires: Angel Estrada, 1947), 4 vols.; Lucas Alamán, *Historia de Méjico*, 5 vols. (Mexico City: Editorial Jus, 1942). For background reviews of these historiographical founders, see Germán Colmenares, *Las convenciones contra la cultura: Ensayos sobre la historiografía hispanoamericana del siglo XIX* (Bogotá: TM Editores, 1986), 87–90.

4. Germán Carrera Damas, *El culto a Bolívar: Esbozo para un studio de la historia de las ideas en Venezuela* (Caracas: Instituto de Antropología e Historia, 1969).

5. Oliveira Lima, *O Movimento da Independência, 1821–1822* (5th ed., Rio de Janeiro: Topbooks, 1997).

6. Issued by the Comisión Nacional del Sesquicentenario de la Independencia del Perú between 1971 and 1974.

7. John Lynch, *The Spanish American Revolutions, 1808–1826* (New York: W.W. Norton, 1973, 2nd ed. 1986).

8. John Lynch, *Caudillos in Spanish America, 1800–1850* (Oxford: Oxford University Press, 1992); John Charles Chasteen, *Americanos: Latin America's Struggle for Independence* (Oxford: Oxford University Press, 2008).

9. From Jorge Luis Borges, *Selected Poems* (New York: Penguin, 2000), p. 171; Karen Racine, *Francisco de Miranda: A Transatlantic Life in the Age of Revolution* (Wilmington, Del.: Scholarly Resources, 2003); David Bushnell, *Simón Bolívar: Liberation and Disappointment* (New York: Longman, 2004); Timothy E. Anna, *The Mexican Empire of Iturbide* (Lincoln: University of Nebraska Press, 1990); Iván Jaksic, *Andrés Bello: Scholarship and Nation-Building in Nineteenth-Century Latin America* (Cambridge: Cambridge

University Press, 2001); Neill Macaulay, *Dom Pedro: The Struggle for Liberty in Brazil and Portugal, 1798–1834* (Durham, N.C.: Duke University Press, 1986); see also Robert Harvey, *The Liberators: Latin America's Struggle for Independence* (London: Overlook Press, 2000).

10. See Sérgio Buarque de Holanda, *Raízes do Brasil* [1936] (São Paulo: Companhia das Letras, 1998), with fascinating reflections by Antonio Candido in an introduction and postscript on the reception of this work among writers and historians in Brazil.

11. Hernán Ramírez Necochea, *Antecedentes económicos de la independencia de Chile* (Santiago: Editorial Universitaria, 1959); Sergio Bagú, *El plan económico del grupo rivadaviano, 1811–1827: Su sentido y sus contradicciones, sus proyecciones socials, sus enemigos* (Rosario: Instituto de Investigaciones Historicas, 1966).

12. Richard Graham, *Independence in Latin America: A Comparative Approach* (New York: McGraw-Hill, 1972, updated in 1994).

13. Jay Kinsbruner, *Independence in Spanish America: Civil Wars, Revolutions, and Underdevelopment*, 2nd ed. (Albuquerque: University of New Mexico Press, 1994).

14. Doris M. Ladd, *The Mexican Nobility at Independence, 1780–1826* (Austin: University of Texas Press, 1976); Susan M. Socolow, *The Merchants of Buenos Aires, 1778–1810: Family and Commerce* (Cambridge: Cambridge University Press, 1978); João Luis Ribeiro Fragoso, *Homens de grossa aventura: Acumulação e hierarquia na praça mercantil do Rio de Janeiro (1790–1830)* (Rio de Janeiro: Arquivo Nacional, 1992); Jorge I. Domínguez, *Insurrection or Loyalty: The Breakdown of the Spanish American Empire* (Cambridge, Mass.: Harvard University Press, 1980). For Domínguez, the cause of independence lay more at the feet of international great power competition rather than inframperial elite competition.

15. Simon Collier, *Ideas and Politics of Chilean Independence, 1808–1833* (Cambridge: Cambridge University Press, 1967); Carlos Guilherme Mota, *Idéia de revolução no Brasil (1789–1801)*, 4th ed. (São Paulo: Atica, 1996).

16. Renán Silva, *Los ilustrados de Nueva Granada, 1760–1808: Genealogía de una comunidad de interpretación* (Medellin: Banco de la República, 2002).

17. Brian Hamnett, *Revolución y contrarrevolución en México y el Perú* (Mexico City: Fondo de Cultura Económica, 1978); Timothy Anna, *The Fall of Royal Government in Mexico City* (Lincoln: University of Nebraska Press, 1978), *The Fall of Royal Government in Peru* (Lincoln: University of Nebraska Press, 1979), and *Spain and the Loss of America* (Lincoln: University of Nebraska Press, 1983); John Fisher, "Royalism, Regionalism and Rebellion in Colonial Peru, 1808–1815," *Hispanic American Historical Review* 59:1 (1979): 232–57; Michael P. Costeloe, *Response to Revolution: Imperial Spain and Spanish American Revolutions, 1810–1840* (Cambridge: Cambridge University Press, 1986); Rebecca A. Earle, *Spain and the Independence of Colombia, 1810–1825* (Exeter: Exeter University Press, 2000); Kenneth R. Maxwell, *Conflicts and Conspiracies: Brazil and Portugal, 1750–1808* (Cambridge: Cambridge University Press, 1973); Roderick J. Barman, *Brazil: The Forging of a Nation, 1798–1852* (Stanford: Stanford University Press, 1988).

18. Fernando A. Novais, "As Dimensões da Independencia," in *1822: Dimensões*, ed. Carlos Guilherme Mota (São Paulo: Perspective, 1972), 15–26, and his later *Portugal e Brasil na crise do antigo sistema colonial* (São Paulo: Hucitec, 1979).

19. Heraclio Bonilla and Karen Spalding, "La Independencia en el Perú: Las palabras y los hechos," in Bonilla et al., *La Independencia en el Perú* (Lima: Instituto de Estudios Peruanos, 1972), 15–64.

20. Tulio Halperín Donghi, "La Revolución y la crisis de la estructura mercantil colonial en el Río de la Plata," *Estudios de Historia Social* 2:2 (1966): 78–125, "Revolutionary Militarization in Buenos Aires, 1806–1815," *Past and Present* 40 (1968): 84–107, *Politics,*

Economics and Society in Argentina in the Revolutionary Period (Cambridge: Cambridge University Press, 1975), and *Reforma y disolución de los imperios ibéricos, 1750–1850* (Madrid: Alianza Editorial, 1985).

21. Peter Guardino and Charles Walker, "The States, Society and Politics in Peru and Mexico in the Late Colonial and Early Republican Periods," *Latin American Perspectives* 19:2 (1992): 10–43. For a more Weberian approach, see George Reid Andrews, "Spanish American Independence: A Structural Analysis," *Latin American Perspectives* 12:1 (1985): 105–32.

22. Octavio Paz, *The Labyrinth of Solitude: Life and Thought in Mexico* (New York: Grove Press, 1961), 121; John J. Johnson, *The Military and Society in Latin America* (Stanford: Stanford University Press, 1964), 13–34.

23. Bonilla and Spalding, "La Independencia en el Perú: Las palabras y los hechos," 44–48.

24. Hugh Hamill, *The Hidalgo Revolt: Prelude to Mexican Independence* (Gainesville: University of Florida Press, 1966).

25. Carlos Guilherme Mota, *Nordeste 1817* (São Paulo: Editora da Universidade de São Paulo, 1972).

26. John Street, *Artigas and the Emancipation of Uruguay* (Cambridge: Cambridge University Press, 1959).

27. Lucía Sala de Touron, Nelson de la Torre, and Julio C. Rodríguez, *Artigas y su revolución agraria, 1811–1820* (Mexico City: Siglo XXI, 1978).

28. Clément Thibaud, *Repúblicas en armas: Los ejércitos bolivarianos en la Guerra de Independencia en Colombia y Venezuela* (Bogotá: Planeta, 2003).

29. Nettie Lee Benson, ed., *Mexico and the Spanish Cortes, 1810–1822: Eight Essays* (Austin: University of Texas Press, 1966), 5, and Benson, *The Provincial Deputation in Mexico: Harbinger of Provincial Autonomy, Independence, and Federalism* (Austin: University of Texas Press, 1992). See her own harbinger, "The Contested Mexican Election of 1812," *Hispanic American Historical Review* 26:3 (1946): 336–50.

30. Antonio Annino (coord.), *Historia de las elecciones en Iberoamérica, siglo XIX* (Mexico City: Fondo de Cultura Económica, 1995); Virginia Guedea, "La primeras elecciones populares en la ciudad de México, 1812–1813," *Mexican Studies/Estudios Mexicanos* 7:1 (1991): 1–28, "Los procesos electorales insurgentes," *Estudios de Historia Novohispana* 11 (1991): 201–49, and "The Process of Mexican Independence," *American Historical Review* 105:1 (2000): 116–30; Karen Caplan, "The Legal Revolution in Town Politics: Oaxaca and Yucatán, 1812–1825," *Hispanic American Historical Review* 83:2 (2003): 255–93; Guillermo Sosa Abella, *Representación e independencia, 1810–1816* (Bogotá: Instituto Colombiano de Antropología e Historia, 2006).

31. For an important early view, see James F. King, "The Colored Castes and American Representation in the Cotres of Cádiz," *Hispanic American Historical Review* 33:1 (1953): 33–64, and more recently Joaquín Varela Suances-Carpegna, *La teoría del estado en los orígenes del constitucionalismo hispanico (Las Cortes de Cádiz)* (Madrid: Centro de Estudios Constitucionales, 1983); Marie Laure Rieu-Millan, *Los diputados americanos en las Cortes de Cádiz* (Madrid: Consejo Superior de Investigaciones Científicas, 1990); Manuel Chust, *La cuestión nacional Americana en las Cortes de Cádiz (1810–1814)* (Valencia: Centro Francisco Tomás y Valiente/UNED, 1999). See Márcia Regina Berbel, *A nação como artefato: Deputados do Brasil nas Cortes Portugesas, 1821–1822* (São Paulo: Hucitec, 1999).

32. Two good examples are Brian Hamnett, "Constitutional Theory and Political Reality: Liberalism, Traditionalism and the Spanish Cortes, 1810–1814," *Journal of Modern History* 49:1 (1977): 1071–109, and José Carlos Chiaramonte's suggestive "Fundamentos iusnaturalistas de los movimientos de independencia," *Boletín del Instituto de Historia*

Argentina y Americana Dr. Emilio Ravignani 22:2 (2000): 33–71. For an exploration of how political cultures and theories changed in Argentina, see his more developed essays in *Ciudades, provincias, estados: Orígenes de la nación Argentina, 1800–1846* (Buenos Aires: Ariel, 1997).

33. María de Lourdes Viana Lyra, *A utopia do poderoso império: Portugal e Brasil, bastidores da política, 1798–1822* (Rio de Janeiro: Sette Letras, 1994); Roberto Breña, *El primer liberalismo español y los procesos de emancipación de América, 1808–1824* (Mexico City: Colegio de México, 2006).

34. See the essays in Christon Archer, ed., *The Wars of Independence in Spanish America* (Wilmington, Del.: Scholarly Resources, 2000) and his important studies of the Spanish military in "The Army of New Spain and the Wars of Independence, 1790–1821," *Hispanic American Historical Review* 64:4 (1981): 705–14 and "Insurrection–Reaction–Revolution–Fragmentation: Reconstructing the Choreography of Meltdown in New Spain During the Independence Era," *Mexican Studies/Estudios Mexicanos* 10:1 (1994): 63–98; John R. Fisher, "The Royalist Regime in the Viceroyalty of Peru, 1820–1824," *Journal of Latin American Studies* 32:1 (2000): 55–84. It should be noted that Anna and Hamnett have also added to our understanding of the loyalist cause and its internal conflicts. For good military histories of the loyalist side, see Stephen K. Stoan, *Pablo Morillo and Venezuela, 1815–1820* (Columbus: Ohio State University Press, 1974). Scarlett O'Phelan Godoy (comp.), *La independencia del Perú: De los Borbones a Bolívar* (Lima: Instituto Riva-Agüero, 2001) and "El mito del la 'independencia concedida": Los programas politicos del siglo XVIII y del temprano XIX en el Perú y Alto Perú, 1730–1814," *Historica*, 9:2 (1985): 155–91; Gustavo Montoya, *La independencia del Peru y el fantasma de la revolución* (Lima: Instituto de Estudios Peruanos, 2002).

35. Víctor Peralta Ruíz, *En defense de la autoridad: Política y cultura bajo el gobierno del Virrey Abascal, Peru, 1806–1816* (Madrid: Consejo Superior de Investigaciones Científicas, 2002); Valentim Alexandre, *Os sentidos do império: Questão nacional e questão colonial na crise do antigo regime português* (Lisboa: Biblioteca das Ciências do Homem, 1993); Maria de Lourdes Viana Lyra, *A utopia do poderoso império: Portugal e Brasil, bastidores da política, 1798–1822* (Rio de Janeiro: Sette Letras, 1994); Kirsten Schultz, *Tropical Versailles: Empire, Monarchy and the Portuguese Royal Court in Rio de Janeiro, 1808–1821* (New York: Routledge, 2001).

36. Jaime E. Rodríguez O., "The Emancipation of America," *American Historical Review* 105:1 (2000): 147; "From Royal Subject to Republican Citizen: The Role of the Autonomists in the Independence of Mexico," in his *The Independence of Mexico and the Creation of the New Nation* (Los Angeles: UCLA Latin American Center Publications, 1989), 19–44; and *The Independence of Spanish America* (Cambridge: Cambridge University Press, 1998), 131–52.

37. Isabel Lustosa, *Insultos impressos: A guerra dos jornalistas na independência, 1821–1822* (São Paulo: Companhia das Letras, 2000).

38. Rafael Rojas, *La escritura de la independencia: El surgimiento de la opinion pública en México* (Mexico City: Taurus, 2003); François-Xavier Guerra, *Modernidad e independencias: Ensayos sobre las revoluciones hispánicas* (Mexico City: Fondo de Cultura Económica, 1993); Guerra and Annick Lempérière et al., *Los espacios públicos en Iberoamérica: Ambigüedades y problemas, Siglos XVIII–XIX* (Mexico City: Fondo de Cultura Económica, 1998); Véronique Hebrard, *Le Venezuela indépendant: Une nation par le discours, 1808–1830* (Paris: L'Harmattan, 1996). A very good survey of the evidence on the public sphere is Victor M. Uribe-Uran, "The Birth of a Public Sphere in Latin America During the Age of Revolution," *Comparative Studies in Society and History* 42:2 (2000):

425–57. A useful anthology on the press on the heels of independence is Paula Alonso, *Construcciones impresas: Panfletos, diarios y revistas en la formación de los estados nacionales en América Latina, 1820–1920* (Mexico City: Fondo de Cultura Económica, 2004).

39. Margarita Garrido, *Reclamos y representaciones: Variaciones sobre la política en el Nuevo Reino de Granada, 1770–1815* (Bogotá: Banco de la República, 1993); Victor M. Uribe-Uran, *Honorable Lives: Lawyers, Family, and Politics in Colombia, 1780–1850* (Pittsburgh: University of Pittsburgh Press, 2000); Sarah C. Chambers, *From Subjects to Citizens: Honor, Gender, and Politics in Arequipa, Peru, 1780–1854* (University Park: Penn State University Press, 1999); José Murilo de Carvalho, *A Construção da Ordem: A Elite Política Imperial* (Rio de Janeiro: UFRJ, 1996). In my own work I have sought to connect longer-term changes in understandings of possession to political development. Independence mattered because it sealed the fate of restrictive mercantilist policies that were already crumbling before 1807, thus shaking the commercial orders that upheld imperial regimes. See *Republic of Capital: Buenos Aires and the Legal Transformation of the Atlantic World* (Stanford: Stanford University Press, 1999). This is a subtheme of a much broader study, *Sovereignty and Revolution in the Iberian Atlantic* (Princeton: Princeton University Press, 2006).

40. Alberto Flores Galindo, *Aristocracia y plebe: Lima, 1760–1830* (Lima: Mosca Azul, 1984); Christine Hunefeldt, *Paying the Price of Freedom: Family and Labor among Lima's Slaves, 1800–1854* (Berkeley: University of California Press, 1994); Montoya, *La independencia del Perú*, chap. 3.

41. Peter Blanchard, "The Language of Liberation: Slave Voices in the Wars of Independence," *Hispanic American Historical Review* 82:3 (2002): 499–523 and "Black Soldiers Between Independence and Abolition in Spanish South America," in *The Arming of Slaves in World History*, ed. Christopher Brown and Philip Morgan (New Haven: Yale University Press, 2004); Camilla Townsend, "'Half My Body Free, the Other Half Enslaved': The Politics of the Slaves of Guayaquil at the End of the Colonial Era," *Colonial Latin American Review* 7:1 (1998): 105–28; Marixa Lasso, "Haiti as an Image of Popular Republicanism in Caribbean Colombia: Cartagena Province (1811–1828)," in *The Impact of the Haitian Revolution in the Atlantic World*, ed. David P. Geggus (Columbia: University of South Carolina Press, 2001), 176–92, and "A Republican Myth of Racial Harmony: Race and Patriotism in Colombia, 1810–1812," *Historical Reflections* 29:1 (2003); Aline Helg, *Liberty and Equality in Caribbean Colombia, 1770–1835* (Chapel Hill: University of North Carolina Press, 2004). We still know rather more about slavery and its demise after than during independence. See, for instance, James Ferguson King, "The Latin American Republics and the Suppression of the Slave Trade," *Hispanic American Historical Review* 24:3 (1944): 387–411; John V. Lombardi, *The Decline and Abolition of Negro Slavery in Venezuela, 1820–1854* (Westport, Conn.: Greenwood, 1971); Peter Blanchard, *Slavery and Abolition in Early Republican Peru* (Wilmington, Del.: Scholarly Resources, 1992).

42. Jorge Cornejo Bouroncle, *Pumacahua: La Revolución del Cuzco en 1814* (Cuzco: Editorial Rozas, 1956).

43. Charles Walker, *Smoldering Ashes: Cuzco and the Creation of Republican Peru, 1780–1840* (Durham, N.C.: Duke University Press, 1999).

44. Brian R. Hamnett, *Roots of Insurgency: Mexican Regions, 1750–1824* (Cambridge: Cambridge University Press, 1986); Peter F. Guardino, *Peasants, Politics, and the Formation of Mexico's National State: Guerrero, 1800–1857* (Stanford: Stanford University Press, 1996); Eric Van Young, *The Other Rebellion: Popular Violence, Ideology, and the Mexican Struggle for Independence, 1810–1821* (Stanford: Stanford University Press, 2001).

CHAPTER 6

SLAVERY IN BRAZIL

JOÃO JOSÉ REIS
HERBERT S. KLEIN

STUDIES about slavery in Brazil have increased enormously, both within and outside of Brazil, particularly in the past two decades. The celebration of the 100th anniversary of abolition in 1988 heightened interest and promoted funding for research on slavery, but it does not alone explain this phenomenon. More enduring factors can be invoked, such as the increase in the number of history graduate programs and of historical journals put out by these programs, which multiplied venues for publications, as well as a renewed interest in racial relations since the last years of the military regime (1964–85). Of course, Brazil was the largest importer of Africans in the era of the slave trade, slavery was a fundamental aspect of the history of the country up until its abolition, today Brazil has the largest African-descent population in the Americas, and all these factors combined make the region an exception in Latin America. Brazil is surrounded by countries where African slavery was generally unimportant compared to other forms of coerced labor and where descendents of European or indigenous peoples predominate in the population. These factors, plus the sheer volume of the scholarship on the topic, justify considering the historiography of slavery in Brazil on its own terms.

The renewal of the Brazilian scholarship of slavery in the 1970s and 1980s was largely influenced by the vibrant historiography produced in the United States, but more recently, while this dialogue continues and has even intensified, much of the research agenda, methods, narrative strategies, and interpretive tools have come to differ, sometimes substantially. In terms of quantitative studies, the most dynamic and important research on slavery in any American country today is probably being done in Brazil. Not only have traditional themes been explored by using new and nontraditional sources, but new methods have been developed for the study of slavery which can be applied to other former slave societies.

Until recently, the historiography of slavery tended to be divided into two moments: the first centered on the work of Gilberto Freyre, who viewed slavery basically as an integrative system in which conflict, though not absent, tended to give way to cooperation between masters and slaves; the second would be represented by what is known as the Paulista School (Florestan Fernandes, Fernando Henrique Cardoso, Octavio Ianni, Emilia Viotti da Costa), a group of scholars who viewed slavery as a closed social and economic structure in which the slave appears almost always in the position of a passive victim.[1] This division has the defects of all generalizations. Freyre, for example, who emphasized the impact of so many facets of the African and Indian cultures on "Brazilian civilization," wrote that Indian and African slaves were the victims of a "social and economic system in which they functioned passively and mechanically."[2] Such a description compares closely with the perspective of Fernando Henrique Cardoso, who wrote that in the formation of Brazil as a nation, the slaves—as well as other subaltern classes in Latin America in general—were "mute testimonies of a history to which they do not count except as a sort of passive instrument over whom acted the changing forces of history."[3] Or, more to the point, in his classic *Capitalismo e escravidão*, Cardoso wrote: "The slave consciousness only registered and mirrored, passively, the social meanings imposed on him."[4] On the other hand, historian Emilia Viotti da Costa showed slaves to be historical subjects with greater nuance and complexity than did sociologist Cardoso and others in the Paulista School. In the same vein, a decade earlier Stanley Stein had published his classical *Vassouras*.[5]

The Paulistas, nevertheless, were interested in structural questions, namely the transition from slavery to capitalism, or, as Florestan Fernandes puts it in a Weberian mode, the transition from a society of estates (*estamental*) or orders to one more fully based on class stratification. This "systemic" preoccupation continued into the following generation of historians, in particular those inspired by the new developments of Marxism in the 1970s, when the concept of mode of production became a main tool of historical interpretation. The studies about the "colonial slave mode of production," begun in Brazil by Ciro Cardoso and continued by Jacob Gorender (in spite of considerable theoretical differences between the two), characterized the debates in the 1970s and early 1980s, and formed a third moment in the historiography of slavery since Freyre.[6] Finally, there is what historian Maria Helena P. T. Machado has called "the social history of slavery," which developed in the last two and a half decades. It is this last current of thought that the first part of this essay primarily addresses. In the second part, we cover the remarkable advance in quantitative slavery studies in Brazil, to which we add those dedicated to economic and demographic history.[7]

It is important to point out at the start that such an "evolution" in the historiography of slavery is arbitrary in many ways. Distinct developments in the historiography of slavery can be traced if we focus on subthemes or on regional scholarship, very important in a vast area such as Brazil. Studies about slave resistance, family, and abolition would have, most likely, their own individual trajectory or chronology; the historiography of slavery in Bahia does not follow the same paths seen in the historiography of slavery in Rio Grande do Sul, which in turn is different from that of slavery in São Paulo, and so on.

It is possible to trace the principal characteristics of the recent historiography of slavery, which include: 1) a diverse methodological-theoretical focus, which is multidisciplinary and involves greater dialogue with the historiography of slavery in other parts of the Americas without necessarily being comparative; 2) far greater research, employing very diversified primary, mainly manuscript, sources; 3) sophisticated quantitative methods, using the creation of complex databanks and advanced computer programs; 4) a diversification of themes; 5) an emphasis on the lives of slaves and freed persons and on their views of slavery and freedom; and 6) an emphasis on local studies, sometimes drawing close to or fully following a microhistorical perspective, including biographical studies.

Heavy theoretical models and essays written with little or no empirical research gave way to studies centered on regional history, often local history, along with monographs and thematic works, almost always based on archival primary sources, without abandoning interpretation. Unlike those of older generations of slavery scholars, studies have been developed almost exclusively at the university and have been directly associated with the above-mentioned proliferation of history graduate programs created in the last thirty years or so. In this way, the recent historiography of slavery—like the recent production of Brazilian historiography in general—marks the emergence of the professional historian, superseding independent scholars or those working isolated in research institutions and universities.

One of the perspectives of greatest importance in the recent development of the historiography of slavery relates to efforts to reconstruct the lives of slaves, including their day-to-day sociability and their worldviews. Such an approach does not conform to preestablished theoretical models; it does not respond either to the old view that overemphasized shared slave/master values—the usually paternalistic master and the accommodating slave—nor to that (not so old) view that considers the relations of masters and slaves only through the logic of the whip—the brutal owner and the victimized slave. This is not to say that the recent historiography has been uniform or monolithic or that the scholars involved agree about everything. It is also simplistic to say that most of these scholars seek only to choose a placid third way between the logic of paternalism/accommodation, on one hand, and the logic of the whip/victimized slave, on the other. Actually, both paternalism and violence are seen as complementary forms of slave control.

It seems that among the majority of historians there is a greater resistance to simple answers to complex questions. Historians tend to agree that slavery constituted one of several systems of social relations. We might even say that the notion of "system" has disappeared altogether in recent studies to give way to the notion of process, and principally to that of daily life experience; or, better yet, daily life is seen as a privileged window through which the slave experience can be rescued. There is agreement that slavery was a social regime based on physical coercion. No scholar ever questioned this premise, Gilberto Freyre included. To say this is not enough, however. Many other social regimes past and present have been based on the use of force. Despite accusations that recent historiography conceptualizes slavery as a contractual system,[8] violence is still considered the founding act and it remains central to the interpretation of slavery, but it represents only the beginning of a discussion, not its epilogue. In fact, violence demonstrates the incapacity of masters to control slaves; it can be seen as a sign of weakness and not of strength, of an absence of hegemonic domination, to use a Gramscian concept employed in studies of slavery since the late 1960s.[9]

As Silvia Lara warns, there is a need to distinguish the type of force used to maintain slavery, which was exemplary and didactic, not erratic.[10] In spite of many cases of extreme brutality, such as that perpetrated by the master of the Casa da Torre (House of Torre) clan in Bahia studied by Luiz Mott, exemplary beatings prevailed, a type of violence that was punitive but most importantly didactic and discriminative.[11] Violence occurred alongside compensations by and compromise on the part of masters. Such gestures included permission for slave families to exist and remain together; slave access to provision gardens; quotas of sugar, cotton, coffee, cattle, and gold on plantations, farms and mines; an extra bit of clothing; and a degree of cultural autonomy. Studies about such "breaches" in slavery have already been done for Bahia, Rio de Janeiro, Minas Gerais, and São Paulo from different and at times controversial perspectives.[12] In Brazil, the concession of manumission was facilitated by the law and represented a favorite expedient of control at the micro level, a form of reward usually obtained, as written in the documents, "for good services rendered." This expression of subalternity and reciprocity, which also appears in paid manumission documents, almost hides the fact that the money used for the transaction was mainly the fruit of work done by the slave, although with the acquiescence of the owner. From this point of view, the hope of attaining freedom by means of a letter of manumission represented a powerful mechanism of control, but one that was not imposed with a whip. Studies on this subject have grown substantially since the mid-1970s, when Stuart Schwartz and Katia Mattoso published their pathbreaking essays on Bahia.[13]

Seigniorial concession, however, is but one angle from which to grasp the relations between masters and slaves, given that they represented an outcome of disputed interests. Acts of compromise were not the result of a master's moral duty alone, but also a response to a slave's attempt to overcome complete subjugation. Scholars in Brazil disagree on the relative weight of seigniorial concession on one hand and slave initiative on the other, but in general they agree on the active role of slaves in conquering manumission and other gains. Negotiation is a key concept in this respect. Achievements that appear—and actually needed to appear in the eyes of society, above all the master class—as concessions were in truth the result of acts by slaves that redesigned the limits of slavery. Such gains ended up becoming informal rights that in turn were defended zealously by slaves, while masters naturally sought to reduce them. Thus negotiation usually implied some measure of resistance; in other words, masters would not negotiate terms of subalternity without the potential threat of rebellion. When slave rights were not respected, or masters refused to negotiate over them, slaves carried out acts of revenge, fled, or reacted with violence, either individually or collectively. A few committed suicide. In this sense, there existed a sort of "moral economy" of slaves, similar to the moral economy of the crowd suggested by British historian E. P. Thompson for the eighteenth-century English food rioters. Thompson, not surprisingly, has inspired several studies of slavery in Brazil.[14]

There were moral rights, but there were legal rights as well, and here again a Thompsonian reading of law as contested arena has been influential. To obtain rights consecrated by the law, slaves took a wide range of initiatives. Following Sidney Chalhoub's pioneering work on the city of Rio de Janeiro, a growing number of historians have investigated the *ações de liberdade* (acts of liberty), which were legal cases brought to courts by slaves who considered themselves to be illegally enslaved, or who for some reason believed they deserved freedom.[15] Often they had obtained the legal right to freedom or the promise of freedom, either through purchase or in bequests after their owners died, but descendents of the deceased refused to abide by the terms of the will. Legal actions of this sort, more common in the last decades of slavery (1870s to 1880s), also existed in an earlier period. Keila Grinberg, for example, uncovered in Rio de Janeiro the story of the slave woman known as Liberata, who at the beginning of the nineteenth century demanded her freedom, arguing that her master/lover had promised it in return for carrying out sexual favors that resulted in several children being born.[16]

Legal cases associated with the end of the international slave trade and reforms of the slave regime increased dramatically in the courts from the middle of the nineteenth century. Many Africans transported to Brazil after the prohibition of the transatlantic slave trade in 1831 understood the illegality of their enslavement and appealed their condition in court. Many others appealed in the hope of benefiting from the Law of September 28, 1871 ("Law of the Free Womb"), for example demanding manumission for a price determined by an arbitration judge, or contesting their enslavement against masters who failed to register them as the law required. Eduardo Spiller Pena focused his study on such legal cases in Curitiba, and Ricardo Tadeu Caires Silva studied the province of Bahia as a whole. Like Chalhoub and Hebe Mattos for Rio de Janeiro, Pena and Silva demonstrated that the law, instead of pacifying slaves, politicized them in their day-to-day relations with owners.[17]

The judicial arena, an important new field in Brazilian slavery studies, was clearly a place often frequented by slaves whose interests conflicted with those of masters, and magistrates increasingly became a key figure in deciding disputed rights.[18] One could claim that often slaves followed the lead of—or, as masters complained, were "seduced by"—free whites or blacks personally involved with the victim, enemies of masters involved, or abolitionists. Black abolitionist Luiz Gama, for example, was one of these persons, whose courageous and militant performance in the courts of São Paulo has recently been studied by Elciene Azevedo.[19] More common in this regard were networks established by slaves that involved companions, friends, relatives, and particularly mothers, who, once having gained their freedom, struggled to free their children and sometimes their grandchildren. Slaves were defended by free *curadores* in these legal battles, but it was the slaves who risked confronting their masters in court.

The 1871 Law inspired resistance up until abolition, particularly among slaves who used their savings to purchase their freedom. But the practice of buying manumission letters had already been a fact of common law long before 1871.[20] Freed slaves came to constitute an important sector of slave society, especially in the cities. Slaves who attained their freedom, on the other hand, in time were often able to purchase captives to serve them. Slaves made history move in different, sometimes disconcerting, directions. African freedmen and women enslaved other Africans, often of the same ethnic group or "nation," as shown in several studies for Bahia, Rio Grande do Sul, Minas Gerais, and Rio de Janeiro, among other places. Ethnic identity, so important for the recruitment and mobilization of anti-slavery rebels, did not inhibit intraethnic enslavement. Oliveira even argues that communication based on a common language facilitated control and labor productivity. Candomblé specialists were slave owners, and there is evidence that some high priests and priestesses enslaved initiates of their own nations.[21]

Slaves who had revolted against their own enslavement, once defeated, and hardened by their experiences, could become themselves slave masters and mistresses. However, research for Bahia in this regard suggests that during a revolt, ethnic solidarity could prevail over the ideology of slavery. Unlike other Africans who owned slaves of their own ethnic group, the Malê or Islamic rebels who shook Bahia in 1835, all of them Africans and the vast majority Yoruba, may have sought to make free mulattos into slaves, but they declared they had no intention of enslaving other Africans.[22]

Slaves entered the logic of slavery in Brazil deploying other, sometimes amazing, deeds. They often sought and obtained freedom by means of their own capacity to enslave others. Although not widespread, the phenomenon of a slave owning another slave occurred. Slaves could, for instance, save up money, purchase a "new negro" (meaning an African captive recently imported from Africa), train him or her in a skill, and then offer him or her in exchange for freedom.[23] There are even several cases of slaves who owned slaves, not necessarily to exchange for their freedom, and such ownership was recognized by their masters as legitimate, notwithstanding the lack of legal basis. Enslaved slaveowners challenged the tenets of slavery at the same time that they affirmed it. Agency, it should be emphasized, is above all the ability to choose, and therefore compromise with slavery, like resistance against it, can be judged as part of slave agency.[24]

Slaves and freedmen moved between accommodation or integration and rebellion more often than they fixed themselves in one of the two extremes. More common was the daily tension, and sometimes conflicts, in the day-to-day relations between masters and slaves. This is not to say that slavery was not functional as a form of exploitation, but that it functioned poorly—to perform the role of a slave did not necessarily mean to be a good slave. Slaves performed a role, their public as opposed to their hidden transcripts, which does not mean they pretended all the time to be someone they were not.[25] They simply tried to learn how to exploit the chances to attain liberties within the limits of slavery by choosing the best moment to comply and the best moment to react. There cannot be any mistake about this: the supposedly loyal and peaceful slave one day could become a fierce rebel the next. Furthermore, a rebel one day could turn conscientious worker the next.[26]

Slavery involved a mix of profoundly contradictory social relations. It meant social death only in the abstract, as a model, or philosophically, so to speak.[27] Slavery actually functioned all the time with the seeds of its own destruction, which were the slaves themselves. As has been suggested by Antonio Barros de Castro, slavery cannot be understood by means of explanatory models that are strictly economic, much less by "economic laws," as Jacob Gorender attempted to do in a rather rigid Marxist format.[28] Masters were actually never able to make slaves into the sort of ideal property that submitted and only worked, a mere soulless, inert commodity. The slave was a "troublesome property," in the words of U.S. historian Kenneth Stampp, although not in the sense of seeking all the time to subvert the social relations of production.[29] More often, slaves would try to fool masters and take advantage of the latter's most consecrated rules. For example, they pretended to be naïve and even stupid to justify stealing from the master's chicken coop, arguing that a theft had not been committed because both slave and chicken were property. "To steal from master is not to steal," Henry Koster heard from a slave in Pernambuco in the early nineteenth century.[30] The notion that domestic theft, particularly in a time of need, did not constitute a crime or a sin was shared by enslaved men and women throughout the Americas. A subtle culture of resistance, with artful ways, means, and rules, evolved within the slave community.

Before slaves considered the idea of total abolition, and even when this hope changed from a distant horizon to a more realistic and likely possibility, they struggled for small freedoms within the institution of slavery; they negotiated—and this is a key concept—breathing space. Historians of slavery tend to see resistance only in terms of flight, the formation of *quilombos*, or runaway communities, and especially rebellion. We side with Michel-Rolph Trouillot when he writes about "the infinite spectrum of human reactions to forms of domination."[31] Slaves possessed quite particular visions of freedom, as has been suggested by Chalhoub in his penetrating study about the last decades of slavery in the city of Rio de Janeiro.[32] "[F]reedom," wrote Barbara Fields about a comparable context, "was no fixed condition but a constantly moving target."[33]

Slavery, like freedom, was a moving target. In other words, bondsmen and bondswomen had their own ideas concerning the acceptable limits of subordination to their masters. There are numerous studies from the four corners of Brazil that depict slaves who refused to be sold or, on the contrary, fought to be sold to another master. Slave flight and even the theft of slaves were often linked to such decisions. In a pioneering study, Marcus Carvalho shows how slaves in Pernambuco in the first half of the nineteenth century allowed themselves to be stolen so they could be sold by the thief to another master.[34] Others chose to flee from their owners while looking for someone willing to buy them. Sometimes masters themselves allowed their slaves to seek buyers. A note in Bahia's newspaper *Correio Mercantil* (Aug. 8, 1839) tells the story of a domestic servant who refused to continue serving his owner, who in turn let him negotiate his sale to another owner. The slave complained that his master's family had grown too large, thereby increasing his daily responsibilities. Having chosen another master, the transaction was made. However, when the slave arrived at the house of his new owner, he realized that the latter's family was even larger than the one he had just left behind, and he decided to go back on his decision, which was accepted by all the parts involved. It is tempting to consider such attitudes legacies of slavery in Africa, where the practice of changing owners has been documented.[35]

On the other hand, there were slaves who refused to allow themselves or their relatives to be sold to another master. Isabel Reis has unearthed cases from nineteenth-century Bahia in which whole families fled together for this reason. Some of these episodes ended in tragedy, with mothers killing their children and committing suicide when slave hunters attempted to arrest them.[36] There are a number of examples of slaves who committed suicide only because they were threatened with being sold away. After the end of the transatlantic slave trade in 1850 and the intensification of the internal, southbound trade, this kind of disruption of slave life became a daily threat. Slaves threatened to rebel, or became rebels at their destination, as studies on slave criminality in the Southeast of Brazil have shown repeatedly. Whatever the angle, the sale of slaves represented a moment of great tension. The reasons were many. The slave had become accustomed to the manners and style of control of his or her present owner. Everything could be different and perhaps worse with the new master, a change that meant jumping into the unknown. More importantly, being sold away meant severing social ties forged over the years. It meant leaving behind friends, lovers, relatives, and well-known environments, familiar human and geographic territory. Sales were particularly traumatic when slaves had to move to another city or province, or even another country. Export sales often represented a form of punishment, so much so that newspapers often published advertisements specifying that buyers must take their human merchandise out of the province. Recurrent flights often resulted in owners selling their slaves out of town as punishment.[37]

The most common form of active slave resistance, flight and the formation of maroon communities, happened for a number of reasons, as noted in several recent and not so recent studies.[38] Slaves did not flee from their masters only to escape bad treatment. Often the important thing was not from what, where, or whom they fled, but instead, to what, where, and whom. As Flávio Gomes has shown for Rio de Janeiro, José Maia for Pará, and Silmei Petiz for Rio Grande do Sul, there were many purposes in escaping, flight routes, and destinations. Hendrik Kraay has written about slaves who left the service of masters to serve in the army. One extreme type of flight was the act of suicide, which could be described as flight to the beyond, often to a sacred land of ancestors usually located back in Africa. Slaves could also escape to a large city where they could pass as free persons of color. Finally, there were temporary flights, which could last from a few hours to a few days, with the goal of participating in parties or street festivals, fulfilling religious obligations, or visiting lovers or parents. Eduardo Silva has suggested a typology of flights: "bargaining flights" to demand concessions from masters, and "permanent flights" to break away completely from their authority. The latter could be of two kinds: "flight to outside the system," which ended up in the formation of maroon settlements, and "flight to within the system," to the anonymity of the large urban centers that were formed over the course of the nineteenth century with the growth in free and freed populations of Africans and their descendents. In the outskirts of large cities, abolitionist *quilombos* were formed in the last years of slavery. Ademir Gebara described flights to cities in general as flight toward the free labor market, an interpretation that has been questioned by several slave flight and *quilombo* historians who suggest that, from the slave's point of view, the perspective of freedom was not restricted to the mere passage from slavery to wage labor. It might have been more enticing for a slave to become an independent worker, a small farmer, or a street vendor, for instance. However, an abolitionist *quilombo* in Santos served as a pool from which to recruit strikebreakers.[39]

Whatever the kind of flight, it usually proved to be a difficult choice. One should not doubt the capacity of a slave to discern and judge between the certain dangers of continued enslavement and the uncertainty of life astray, or even life when freedom had been legally obtained. Slaves who purchased their manumission no longer had owners, but they subsequently had to regard their former masters or other free persons as patrons. Until 1871, even freedom that had been purchased by slaves could be revoked if ex-masters considered themselves or their interests to be threatened or in some way offended by former slaves. Such ties of dependence became more important each step of the way over the course of the nineteenth century as a mechanism to control the increasing population of free and freed blacks.[40] In a slave society, freedom demanded protection of the privileged free person, and this had a price. For a black person, it was dangerous to be alone, without a patron, in a society where there was always someone superior. Free blacks and *mestiços* were often kidnapped and enslaved, particularly children, sometimes whole families. Or they were arrested as fugitive slaves, and sometimes rotted in prison before proving their cases. At the time of their abduction, such persons had no one to protect them, or found themselves away from those who could.[41]

Under certain circumstances, it was better to be a slave, meaning that affirmation of such a status would ensure more protection. Archival research often reveals examples of individuals who used—and at times abused—their condition as slaves in their daily disputes with police officers. Confronted or detained by the latter, they reacted in a very Brazilian manner with words such as "Do you know with whom you are speaking? My master is the influential Baron so-and-so" or "My master is not a pauper." Silvia Lara has discussed this form of impudence in her book on late eighteenth-century Campos dos Goitacazes, Rio de Janeiro. There were complaints over slave boldness by both small and great authorities, from local judges and militia captains to colonial governors and presidents of provinces. Such persons protested against slaves who used the influence of their masters for their own purposes in the routine struggles with the police, with poor whites, and even with other slaveowners. Such complaints were invoked against both slaves and their masters, because the latter, in the opinion of authorities, allowed and at times encouraged arrogant behavior as a means to propagate their prestige in society. Here is a case in which slave and master interests converged.[42]

When describing such situations, it is important not to generalize. A slave could conquer greater autonomy in an urban setting, in spite of the fact that the police tried to control cities in the same way overseers controlled plantations. As has been suggested in several studies—abundant for the city of Rio de Janeiro, but also available for Salvador, Recife, São Paulo, Porto Alegre, Pelotas, Teresina, Juiz de Fora and so on—urban slavery necessarily meant greater independence for the so-called slaves for hire, or *negros de ganho*. These workers went out into the streets on their own to sell goods, carry crates and sedan chairs, wash clothes, and contract out all kinds of services. Masters often allowed urban slaves to rent and even own rooms and houses, and only return home to pay the daily, or more often weekly, sum previously contracted between the two. Such autonomy gained other social and cultural dimensions, expressed in the formation of a complex network in which family, friends, work partners, ethnic cohorts, and coreligionists met in private and public celebrations to give meaning to life in spite of slavery.[43]

Recent research has also demonstrated that on landed estates, in the mines, and on sugar plantations and small farms, as much as in towns and larger cities, slaves managed to win some degree of autonomy. One can no longer imagine that rural properties functioned like completely closed institutions, where slaves resided in a condition of complete despair. In such institutions, for example, there could exist no form of family life. In spite of enormous restrictions, however, slaves carried on amorous relationships, married at times, formed extended family ties, and struggled to abide by their own kinship rules.[44] Slaves residing on different properties did not live completely isolated from each other. Despite police prohibition, on Sundays and holidays slaves from different plantations in Bahia, for example, gathered to dance, beat drums, and at times to conspire. Studies on the *Jongo* suggest precisely that.[45] Slaves residing in the interior of the province of Rio de Janeiro studied by Flávio Gomes circulated through slave quarters, taverns, markets, and maroon fields, shaping what the author has called a *campo negro* ("black territory"), meaning a geographic and social ambience where slaves moved around with some degree of protection from other slaves, freed, and free people interested in dealing with them for different reasons, economic, religious, affective, and so on.[46]

Slavery was deeply based on personal relations, and the roles of the individual and of individual creativity, resilience, negotiation, and resistance emerge as an important aspect in the recent historical narrative, which is so dependent on primary sources rich in these personal stories. Microhistoric, detailed accounts of individual lives and thoughts allow for a greater degree of understanding of slave life. In the absence of the slave narratives so common in the United States, some sources—such as parish, probate, criminal, and trial records—allow for a greater degree of understanding of slave life. The bits and pieces of life histories of individual slaves and more often freed persons, though extremely difficult to retrieve, can be extended significantly when the lucky historian is able to successfully link different sources around one or a group of characters.[47] The result is an analytical method akin to Clifford Geertz's "thick description" combined with the Italian "microhistory" perspective.[48]

The new social history of slavery has revealed individual slaves and freed people who made personal decisions, men and women who thought, evaluated, decided, and acted in their own behalf, at times forging amazing careers. Some studies can be defined as biographies, such as Luiz Mott's book about the "black saint" Rosa Egipcíaca, an extraordinary African visionary whose sect for a while included, alongside slaves and common folk, members of the aristocracy, colonial bureaucrats, and representatives of the low and high clergy in both Minas Gerais and Rio de Janeiro. Also from Minas comes the revisionist study of the famous *liberta* Chica da Silva, whom Junia Furtado uses as a guide to understand the world of the free black women of the mining region, a subject that had already been explored by Luciano Figueredo and Eduardo Paiva. A similar perspective, although adopting a heavily quantitative approach absent in other studies, is Zephyr Frank's book on Antonio Dutra, a freed African, slave-owning barber-surgeon representative of what the author calls the "middling sector" of property-owners in mid-nineteenth-century carioca society. Rio is also the backdrop for Eduardo Silva's biography of Dom Obá II of Africa, a Bahian free black who traced his ancestry to Yoruba kings, fought in the Paraguayan war, and afterwards established residence in Rio de Janeiro, where he became an influential figure in the local black community, which he promoted in newspaper articles in favor of abolition and other good causes. The list of case studies such as these is growing in the literature on slavery in Brazil. Rosa, Chica, Dutra, and Dom Obá were exceptional individuals, but there are others whose lives have been dug from the archives, while still others await rescue from anonymity. Of course, these biographical studies are in most cases based on fragmented data on each specific individual, the context assuming a major part of the story being told.[49]

The emphasis on the individual also crops up in studies on slave resistance. In slavery, individual acts of rebellion played a considerable role. Sabotage, violence against masters, and flight did not destroy slavery as a mode of production and a way of life, but they did undermine it in a fundamental way by revealing that slaves did not accept the absolute personal subalternity implicit in slavocratic ideology and mentality. In order to be challenged, the institution of slavery did not need to be entirely threatened in an economic, ideological, or political sense, although this sort of minor resistance could profit from larger crises faced by the slave society. The subtle resistance of slaves in Brazil gave rise to the image of a cancer so frequently used by nineteenth-century Brazilian abolitionists to describe slavery. As James Scott has observed, day-to-day resistance did not make headlines as collective rebellions did, but it slowly wore away the slave regime and other oppressive social systems. To represent day-to-day resistance, Scott has suggested the metaphor of coral rocks that one day, transformed into reefs, prevent the passage of the ocean water to the beach. In other words, in the long run history cannot but be affected by these microscopic pressures. Slavery would have been an even greater hell were it not for these small acts of individual resistance by slaves.[50]

Though preoccupied with their daily individual struggles, enslaved persons could develop wide-ranging worldviews and thereby become more able to judge the social and political environment around them and act accordingly as a group. Historians have come to appreciate their capacity to move from small acts of resistance to much larger actions, from micro to macro rebelliousness. Slaves frequently understood when the world of the slaveholders confronted a crisis. At such moments, their opportunities to bargain could increase because the master class and the political elite were involved with other problems—and their guns were pointed in other directions. At such moments, individual confrontations were often accompanied by collective resistance. Slave flights, the formation of maroon communities, and the enactment of revolts increased in frequency and size when rulers were divided. Thus, the famous Palmares *quilombo* benefited from the Dutch occupation of Pernambuco and the conflict between colonial powers—involving Portugal, Spain, and Holland—that followed.[51] Everywhere in nineteenth-century Brazil, slave resistance flourished whenever political crisis and social conflicts emerged among the free classes, namely during the independence turmoil in 1821–23, the several military, federalist, liberal, and republican rebellions between 1824 and the early 1840s, the war against Paraguay in the late 1860s, and the abolitionist campaigns in the following years. The rhetoric of political dissent and liberal and abolitionist ideologies were heard by slaves in the master's house, markets, and taverns and were disseminated in the slave quarters. In various parts of Brazil, slaves translated in their own way the patriotic, anticolonial discourse that depicted Brazil as a slave of Portugal. Just as Brazil sought freedom, so too did the slaves. The same phenomenon was replicated during the movements that followed independence in the 1820s and 1830s, except that now regional rebels associated the image of the Imperial Court in Rio de Janeiro with that of a master the enslaved provinces needed to separate from or develop new, less dependent terms of relationship with. Slaves observed closely such discourses, as well as the measures implemented by the government in 1831, 1850, and 1871, which abolished the slave trade and reformed slavery. Many slaves conspired at these moments, motivated by the belief that the government, and specifically the emperor, had conceded freedom to them but their owners had refused to obey. It should be added with great emphasis that, contrary to traditional historiography, slaves and free blacks were a decisive factor in the abolition of slavery, being active both in the direct resistance and in the social movements that sealed the end of slavery in the 1880s. These findings are all part of the repertoire of recent historical research.[52]

A couple of examples can be mentioned of how slaves seized moments of crisis to rebel collectively. Maria Januária Vilela Santos has studied how slaves in Maranhão, led by a freedman from Ceará named Cosme Bento das Chagas, took advantage of the Balaiada liberal rebellion to rise up, in the words of Chagas, "so as not to have slavery." The leader even adopted the somewhat messianic title of "Tutor and Emperor of Liberty" in letters that he wrote in 1840. The Balaiada rebels, on the other hand, were not abolitionists, and many joined the government forces precisely when the black insurrection became part of the movement. In Bahia, slave revolts also intensified in the period following Independence, when anti-Portuguese riots and military and federalist rebellions abounded. What distinguishes the two regions is that liberal ideology, incorporated into the slave movement in Maranhão, did not surface in Bahia, where bondsmen and freedmen invoked an African ideology, namely Islam, in their struggle against slavery.[53]

Besides revolts, religion and religious leadership played a key role in several aspects of slave life. Historians have recently shown renewed interest in Calundu, Candomblé, Afro-Catholicism—the religion of the popular black brotherhoods—and Islam. In the past, few scholars have touched on the subject, Roger Bastide's classic *Les religions africaines au Brésil* being an exception. It should be noted, however, that Bastide used mainly travelers' accounts and other published sources. New data have now emerged from manuscripts deposited in Brazilian and Portuguese archives which allow a much richer picture of the slaves' religious practices. For the colonial period, Luiz Mott and Laura de Mello e Souza pioneered in the investigation of spirit possession religions and magical beliefs persecuted by the Inquisition, presenting the reader of their works with detailed ethnographic accounts. More recently, James Sweet used basically the same sources to emphasize African continuity in the religious practices of slaves in Brazil. With regard to the nineteenth century, several recent studies focus on Candomblé and other religious practices Africans brought with them from Africa or (re)invented in Brazil. Islam, usually portrayed in its militant dimension, is now being investigated as a day-to-day, problem-solving religion akin to Candomblé and Calundu, in which divination, ritual healing, witchcraft, and amulet making prevailed.[54]

Afro-Christianity continues to be a subject of intense research. Perhaps the most surprising findings come from mid-nineteenth-century Recife, where Marcus Carvalho uncovered the preaching of a protestant free black, Agostinho José Pereira, who taught other blacks to write using popular verses that threatened whites with a Haitian-style destruction of slavery. In the meantime, the study of black brotherhoods continues to receive attention, mainly because sources on the subject have always been more copious. One of the most controversial aspect of the black confraternity, the question of affiliation along ethnic lines, is covered by several of the recent studies. Mariza Soares's study of the Mahi is probably the most original in terms of unveiling new sources and establishing the connection of brotherhood leadership with a particular African origin.[55]

The formation of new, complex, often fluid and negotiated African ethnic identities in Brazil is a theme of rising interest in the recent historiography of slavery, as is creolization. The different meanings of Mina identity for slaves imported from the Bight of Benin ports are being investigated in different regions of Brazil, as well as the development of more specific ethnic groups such as Nagô (Yoruba-speakers), Jeje (Gbe-speakers), Hausa, Angola, Moçambique, and Benguela. The Mina have been studied especially in Rio de Janeiro and Rio Grande do Sul. The formation of a Bantu-speaking identity in the Southeast has for some time been explored with great insight by Robert Slenes. These studies relate ethnicity with market control, social mobility, family life, religion, and resistance. One consistent result for different regions—particularly Rio de Janeiro, São Paulo, and Rio Grande do Sul—is the relative success of West African slaves in winning their freedom, usually through purchase, often as a result of their control of profitable urban professions, in particular that of market women. Ethnic identity has also been related to the formation of Candomblé and slave revolts, particularly in Bahia. The formation of a "Brazilian" identity by African returnees to West Africa is an old theme that has been the subject of recent investigation. Many of these studies are now being conducted by historians trained in African history, which has thrown a new light on a complex question, namely what is a New World creation and what is African continuity in slave cultures and identities in Brazil.[56]

New Sources and the Quantitative Study of Slavery in Brazil

Cultural practices and meanings, and many other aspects of the slave experience, including life histories, family life, daily work, manumission, resistance, and crime, have all benefited from diverse research strategies that have been present in the recent historiography. Truly outstanding has been an outpouring of quantitative studies on all aspects of slavery and slave life in the past quarter century that has brought Brazilian historiography to the forefront in this area of research in the Americas. In no other country has so much new material been analyzed to date from this perspective. New quantitative sources have been unearthed, and much innovative use has been made of them. Many of these notarial records,[57] parish records,[58] and unpublished eighteenth- and nineteenth-century censuses (*mapas*) were underutilized before the development of this new group of studies.[59] Traditional judicial records have been systematically studied to produce quantitative assessments of crime and slavery.[60] Even newspapers have been mined for quantitative data.[61] These sources have been used to analyze topics as diverse as the Atlantic and internal slave trades, slave demography and slave production, and slave prices and their change over time, as well as manumission and the size of slaveholdings and their structure. Family life and friendship patterns, occupations, and even heights and weights of criminals have been measured. All of this research has been surprisingly coherent because of systematic attempts to be comparative and to relate local findings to general trends even when dealing with microhistorical studies of individual parishes, so the accumulation of knowledge has been impressive.

The area which has been most rapidly resolved in the past quarter century has been the volume, origin, and direction of the Atlantic slave trade to Brazil. Mostly the work of an international group of scholars who have mined the European, American, and even African archives, there now exists a rather extensive set of slave voyages to Brazil that have been made available for research.[62] The internal slave trade within Brazil itself was originally less studied and more difficult to analyze because of the lack of systematic records, but even here recent original studies based on new sources have appeared.[63]

But without question the single most dramatic increase in knowledge has been in the study of slave demography and of slavery itself within Brazil in the eighteenth and nineteenth centuries, largely developed on the basis of new and previously unexplored census data. Starting with eighteenth-century unpublished census data for Minas Gerais, a group of Paulista scholars led by Francisco Vidal Luna and Iraci Costa del Nero da Costa laid out a basic set of models to examine the distribution among slaveholders and their basic demographic characteristics as revealed in local census data.[64] These initial studies from the colonial records were followed by a major demographic exploration of the unpublished and unanalyzed censuses of the 1830s for Minas Gerais finally made available by Clotilde Paiva and her colleagues.[65] Along with these studies, the Martins brothers proposed a major revision of nineteenth-century historiography by arguing that Minas remained Brazil's largest slave state despite the eclipse of gold mining and the lack of a major international export trade, a situation unique to slavery in the Americas.[66] One part of their model suggested that Minas remained a net importer of Africans throughout the nineteenth century, a position which has been challenged by Bergad, Paiva, and others, who have argued for positive natural population growth for the region by the early nineteenth century.[67] But their basic query has led to a reevaluation of the nineteenth-century Minas economy and the role of African slaves not only in Minas but in all parts of Brazil.[68]

On the basis of his earlier Minas Gerais studies, Francisco Vidal Luna and his University of São Paulo students launched a major analysis of the *mapas* for the state of São Paulo for the period from the 1750s to the 1850s, the most complete encountered up to this date for any province in the empire. There have now been detailed studies in a number of books and essays that have produced probably the most sophisticated analysis we have of the distribution of slaves by occupation and slave ownership, as well as their demographic characteristics.[69]

The question of the size of slave holdings and the nature of the slave-owning class, and the relation between holdings and slave demography, issues that Luna and his collaborators explored, have been major themes analyzed in studies from Pernambuco to Paraná.[70] Another area of research that has used these *mapas* along with relevant parish registers is the quantitative analysis of marriage, kinship, godparenthood, and legitimacy of births. This has been one of the more dramatically expanding areas in slave studies, and aside from the work by Luna and Costa on eighteenth-century Minas Gerais[71] has also been much influenced by the work of Herbert Gutman on slave families in the United States. There have been a large number of studies that suggest a significant rate of legal slave marriages almost everywhere in Brazil, with these marriages often correlated with the size of the slaveholdings from which they come. In turn, size of holdings often influences legitimacy rates, and even godparenthood patterns of slaves using other slaves or free persons as fictive kin. Surprisingly, the few very detailed studies of kinship and naming patterns find that Brazilian slaves differed significantly from the norms found for the U.S. slave population.[72]

Probably one of the oldest and most quantitatively analyzed subjects in Brazilian slavery is the question of manumission. Detailed studies are still being produced on patterns of manumission in all the regions of Brazil. Almost all find the same bias toward younger ages and women and a correspondingly higher ratio of Africans among the self-purchased slaves.[73] There has also been a major reevaluation of the important role of the dominant free colored in the nineteenth-century economy and society.[74]

The extraordinary distribution of slaves throughout the economy and their occupations is now coming under more precise evaluation, often on the basis of *mapas* as well as notarial records.[75] Finally, an area of continued concern is that of the changing prices of slaves over time and region, with the recent work of Bergad being one of the few which covers an entire province over a long period of time.[76]

Slavery in Brazil is a vast, varied, and fertile research field.[77] The main perspective in historiography in the last decades, a shift that has enabled a far greater understanding of the social history of slavery, has been an awareness of slaves as active agents of their own history—of course, a history they made together with masters and other sectors of society. It has also involved a major growth of sophisticated quantitative archival research, which has reconstructed the basic structure of Brazilian slave society and economy as never before and demonstrated both the common features Brazil shared with all slave societies and the unique patterns which developed in this crucial Afro-American society.

Moreover, by insisting on the centrality of the slave experience, the recent historiography has also gained a role outside of the academic world. When its findings migrate to textbooks and classrooms, Brazilian children and youth will get to know a vision of slavery far different from the one their parents and grandparents learned in school and the media. Future generations will meet great heroes and defenseless victims, but above all millions of men and women who fought small and constant daily battles, often managed to negotiate peace with their masters, and did not give up hope while enduring the pain of living as the property of other men and women, including black slaveowners.

The role of historians should not be overestimated, however. History as an academic discipline plays only a small though important part in constructing a political consciousness that will help to bring about necessary social change, racial justice in particular. Social movements play a much bigger role, even in the study of history. The emergence of black movements in the 1970s and 1980s may be counted as one of the key influences behind much of what is being written about slavery in Brazil today. Black movements not only showed that racial democracy was an unfulfilled ideal but also dethroned the idea that Afro-Brazilians were not able to organize and mobilize themselves, not able to be agents of history. After the rise of the new black movement, Afro-Brazilians would never be the same; nor would the historiography of slavery, even though that connection has yet to become apparent to many historians.

ACKNOWLEDGMENTS

We would like to thank Professor Dale Graden for his assistance with the translation of parts of the section of this paper written by João Reis. Reis would also like to thank the Conselho Nacional de Desenvolvimento Científico e Tecnológico (CNPq) for its support, as well as the National Humanities Center, where this chapter was revised and updated in the fall of 2008.

NOTES

1. On the Paulista group, see Richard Graham, *Escravidão, reforma e imperialismo* (São Paulo: Perspectiva, 1979), chap. 1.
2. Gilberto Freyre, *Casa Grande & Senzala: A formação da família brasileira sob o regime de economia patriarcal*, 14th ed. (Recife: Companhia Editora de Pernambuco, 1970), vol. 2: 341.
3. Fernando Henrique Cardoso, *Autoritarismo e democratização* (São Paulo: Paz e Terra, 1975), 112.
4. Fernando Henrique Cardoso, *Capitalismo e escravidão: o negro na sociedade escravocrata do Rio Grande do Sul* (São Paulo: Civilização Brasileira, 2003), 76.
5. Emilia Viotti da Costa, *Da senzala à colônia* (São Paulo: DIFEL, 1966); Stanley J. Stein, *Vassouras, a Brazilian Coffee County, 1850–1890: The Roles of Planter and Slave in a Changing Plantation Society* (New York: Atheneum, [1957] 1974). On the importance of Stein for the historiography of slavery in Brazil, see Silvia Hunold Lara, "*Vassouras* e os sons do cativeiro no Brasil," in *Memórias do jongo: As gravações históricas de Stanley Stein, Vassouras, 1949*, ed. Silvia Hunold Lara and Gustavo Pacheco (Rio de Janeiro: Folha Seca; São Paulo: CECULT, 2007), 45–67. Built on the same model was the excellent study by Warren Dean, *Rio Claro: A Brazilian Plantation System, 1820–1920* (Stanford, Stanford University Press, 1976).
6. The "colonial slave mode of production" thesis argued that the internal dynamics of the colonial society was defined by production based on slavery, not by mercantilist colonial relations. The "colonial" nature of the mode of production pointed to an external expropriation of a good deal of the wealth produced through taxes, metropolitan comercial privileges, and unequal exchange. See Ciro Flamarion Cardoso, "El modo de producción esclavista colonial en America," in Cardoso et al., *Modos de producción en America Latina*, Cuadernos Pasado y Presente 40 (Córdoba, 1973): 193–242; Jacob Gorender, *O escravismo colonial* (São Paulo: Ática, 1978).
7. Maria Helena P. T. Machado, "Em torno da autonomia escrava: Uma nova direção para a história social da escravidão," *Revista Brasileira de História* 16 (1988): 143–60. Reviews of the literature on slavery in Brazil have also been made by Silvia H. Lara, "Escravidão no Brasil: Um balanço historiográfico," *LPH: Revista de História* 3:1 (1992): 215–44, and Stuart B. Schwartz, *Slaves, Peasants, and Rebels: Reconsidering Brazilian Slavery* (Urbana and Chicago: University of Illinois Press, 1992), chap. 1. An updated version of this chapter was published in the Brazilian edition of this book, *Escravos, roceiros e rebeldes* (Bauru: Edusc, 2001). Another good review of the literature, though concentrated on freed persons, is A. J. L. Russell-Wood, "Preface to the New Edition: Free and Freed Persons of

African Descent in Colonial Brazil: Trends and Historiography," in *Slavery and Freedom in Colonial Brazil* (Oxford: Oneworld, 2002), xiii–liii.

8. Jacob Gorender, *A escravidão reabilitada* (São Paulo: Ática, 1990).

9. For an influential Gramscian interpretation of U.S. slavery, see Eugene D. Genovese, *Roll Jordan Roll: The World the Slaves Made* (New York: Pantheon Books, 1972), in which the author develops the concept of paternalism as a form of the master class's political and cultural hegemony.

10. Silvia H. Lara, *Campos da violência: Escravos e senhores na capitania do Rio de Janeiro, 1750–1808* (São Paulo: Paz e Terra, 1988).

11. Luiz Mott, "Terror na Casa da Torre: Tortura de escravos na Bahia colonial," in *Escravidão e invenção da liberdade*, ed. João José Reis (São Paulo: Brasiliense, 1988), 17–32. On the ideology of didactic slave punishment in colonial Brazil, see Ronaldo Vainfas, *Ideologia e escravidão: Os letrados e a sociedade escravista no Brasil colonial* (Rio de Janeiro: Vozes, 1986), 115ff.

12. The list is long. See for instance: Schwartz, *Slaves, Peasants, and Rebels*, esp. chaps. 2, 3, and 5; Russell-Wood, *Slavery and Freedom*; B. J. Barickman, "'A Bit of Land they Call *Roça*': Slave Provision Grounds on Sugar Plantations and Cane farms in the Bahian Recôncavo, 1780–1860," *Hispanic American Historical Review* 74: 4 (1994): 649–87; João José Reis and Eduardo Silva, *Negociação e conflito: A resistência negra no Brasil escravista* (São Paulo: Companhia das Letras, 1988); Manolo Florentino and José Roberto Góes, *A paz das senzalas: Famílias escravas e tráfico atlântico, Rio de Janeiro, c. 1790– c. 1850* (Rio de Janeiro: Civilização Brasileira, 1997); Robert Slenes, *Na senzala uma flor: Esperanças e recordações na formação da família escrava—Brasil sudeste, século XIX* (Rio de Janeiro: Nova Fronteira, 1999); Flávio dos Santos Gomes, *História de quilombolas: Mocambos e comunidades de senzalas no Rio de Janeiro, século XX* (São Paulo: Companhia das Letras, 2006), esp. chap. 3.

13. Stuart B. Schwartz, "The Manummission of Slaves in Colonial Brazil: Bahia, 1684–1750," *Hispanic American Historical Review* 54:4 (1974): 603–35; Katia Mattoso, "A propósito de cartas de alforria," *Anais de História* 4 (1972): 23–52; Peter Eisenberg, *Homens esquecidos* (Campinas: UNICAMP, 1989), chaps. 10 and 11; Eduardo França Paiva, *Escravos e libertos nas Minas Gerais do século XVIII* (São Paulo: Anablume, 1995), chap. 2; Kathleen Higgins, *Licencious Liberty in a Brazilian Gold-Mining Region: Slavery, Gender, and Social Control in Eighteenth-Century Sabará, Minas Gerais* (University Park: University of Pennsylvania Press, 1999), chap. 5; Russell-Wood, *Slavery and Freedom*, esp. chap. 2; Enidelce Bertin, *Alforrias na São Paulo do século XIX: Liberdade e dominação* (São Paulo: Humanitas/FFCH/USP, 2004). A catalogue of 10,055 manumissions in Porto Alegre (with name of slave, age, color/origin, price, reasons and conditions when appropriate, and name of master, among other information) was published by Paulo Roberto S. Moreira (who also wrote a long introductory essay) and Tatiani de Souza Tassoni, *Que com seu trabalho nos sustenta: As cartas de alforria de Porto Alegre, 1748–1888* (Porto Alegre: EST, 2007), 9–96 for the introductory essay. For a discussion of the long-run seigniorial politics of manumission, see Rafael de Bivar Marquese, "A dinâmica da escravidão no Brasil: Resistência, tráfico negreiro e alforrias," *Novos Estudos* 74 (2006): 107–23. Other titles on manumission are listed in note 73 below.

14. On Thompson's influence on Brazilian historiography of slavery, see Silvia H. Lara, "'Blowing in the Wind': E. P. Thompson e a experiência negra no Brasil," *Projeto História* 12 (1995): 43–56.

15. Sidney Chalhoub, *Visões da liberdade: Uma história das últimas décadas da escravidão na Corte* (São Paulo: Companhia das Letras, 1990), esp. chap. 2.

16. Keila Grinberg, *Liberata: A lei da ambigüidade* (Rio de Janeiro: Relume Dumará, 1994).

17. Beatriz Mamigonian, "'Do que o preto mina é capaz': Etnia e resistência entre africanos livres," *Afro-Asia* 24 (2000): 71–95; Eduardo Spiller Pena, *O jogo da face: A astúcia escrava frente aos senhores e à lei na Curitiba provincial* (Curitiba: Aos Quatro Ventos, 1999); Ricardo Tadeu Caires Silva, "Os escravos vão à justiça: A resistência escrava através das ações de liberdade" (master's thesis, Universidade Federal da Bahia, 2000); idem, "Caminhos e descaminhos da abolição: Escravos, senhores e direitos nas últimas décadas da escravidão, Bahia, 1850–1888," (PhD diss., Universidade Federal do Paraná, 2007), chap. 4. More on the background of the 1871 law in Sidney Chalhoub, *Machado de Assis historiador* (São Paulo: Companhía das Letras, 2003), esp. chap. 4. On the juridical debate, see also Eduardo Spiller Pena, *Pajens da Casa Imperial: Jurisonsultos, escravidão e a lei de 1871* (Campinas: UNICAMP/CECULT, 2001). On the making of another important law towards gradual slave emancipation, the sexagenarian law of 1885, see Joseli Maria Nunes Mendonça, *Entre a mão e os anéis: A lei dos sexagenários e os caminhos as abolição no Brasil* (Campinas: UNICAMP/CECULT, 1999).

18. See Lenine Naquete, *Escravos e magistrados no segundo reinado* (Brasília: Fundação Petrônio Portela, 1988).

19. Elciene Azevedo, *Orfeu de carapinha: A trajetória de Luiz Gama na Imperial Cidade de São Paulo* (Campinas: UNICAMP/CECULT, 1999). See also her "Para além dos tribunais: Advogados e escravos no movimento abolicionista em São Paulo," in *Direitos e justiças no Brasil: Ensaios de história social*, ed. Silvia H. Lara and Joselice Maria N. Mendonça (São Paulo: UNICAMP, 2006), 199–238.

20. Manuela Carneiro da Cunha, *Antropologia do Brasil: Mito, história, etnicidade* (São Paulo: Brasiliense, 1986), 123–44.

21. Maria Inês Côrtes de Oliveira, "Viver e morrer no meio dos seus," *Revista USP* 28 (1996–96): 187–91; Lisa Earl Castillo and Luis Nicolau Parés, "Marcelina da Silva e seu mundo: Novos dados para uma historiografia do candomblé ketu," *Afro-Ásia* 36 (2007): 111–50; João José José Reis, *Domingos Sodré, um sacerdote africano: Escravidão, liberdade e candomblé na Bahia no século XIX* (São Paulo: Companhia das Letras, 2008), chaps. 6 and 7; B. J. Barickman, "As cores do escravismo: Escravistas 'pretos,' 'pardos' e 'cabras' no Recôncavo Baiano, 1835," *População e Família* 2:2 (1999), 7–59; Moreira, *Que com seu trabalho nos sustenta*; Francisco Vital Luna, "Estrutura de posse de escravos," in Francisco Vital Luna e Iracy del Nero Costa, *Minas colonial: Economia e sociedade* (São Paulo: FIPE/Pioneira, 1982), 43–47; Zephyr L. Frank, *Dutra's World, Wealth and Family in Nineteenth-Century Rio de Janeiro* (Albuquerque: University of New Mexico Press, 2004); Manolo Florentino, "Alforria e etnicidade no Rio de Janeiro oitocentista: Notas de pesquisa," *Topoi* 5 (2002): 25–40.

22. João José Reis, *Slave Rebellion in Brazil: The Muslim Uprising of 1835 in Bahia* (Baltimore: Johns Hopkins University Press, 1993), 121–22.

23. Schwartz, "The Manumission of Slaves in Colonial Brazil"; Mattoso, "A propósito de cartas de alforria," Mieko Nishida, "Manumission and Ethnicity in Urban Slavery: Salvador, Brazil, 1808–1888," *Hispanic American Historical Review*, 73:3 (1993): 361–91.

24. Reis, *Domingos Sodré*, 228–29.

25. On hidden and public transcripts of subalterns, see James Scott, *Domination and the Arts of Resistance: Hidden Transcripts* (New Haven and London: Yale University Press, 1990).

26. See Eugene Genovese, *In Red and Black: Marxian Explorations in Southern and Afro-American History* (New York: Vintage, 1968), chap. 4.

27. We are refering to Orlando Patterson's seminal *Slavery and Social Death: A Comparative Study* (Cambridge, Mass.: Harvard University Press, 1982).

28. Antonio Barros de Castro, "A economia política, o capitalismo e a escravidão," in *Modos de produção e realidade brasileira*, ed. José Roberto do Amaral Lapa (Rio de Janeiro: Vozes, 1980), 67–107; Gorender, *O escravismo colonial*.

29. Kenneth M. Stampp, *The Peculiar Institution: Slavery in the Ante-Bellum South* (New York: Vintage: 1956), chap. 3.

30. Henry Koster, *Travels in Brazil, 1809–1815* (London: Longman, Hurst, Rees, Orme, and Brown, 1817), 443.

31. Michel-Rolph Trouillot, *Silencing the Past: Power and the Production of History* (Boston: Beacon Press, 1995), 84.

32. ªChalhoub, *Visões da liberdade*.

33. Barbara J. Fields, *Slavery and Freedom on the Middle Ground: Maryland during the Nineteenth Century* (New Haven: Yale University Press, 1985), 193.

34. Marcus J. M. Carvalho, "Quem furta mais e esconde: O roubo de escravos em Pernambuco," *Estudos Econômicos*, 17 (1987): 89–110. Republished as chap. 13 of Carvalho, *Liberdade: Rotinas e rupturas do escravismo: Recife, 1822–1850* (Recife: UFPE, 2002).

35. See, for instance, Martin Klein, "Servitude among the Wolof and Serer of Senegambia," in *Slavery in Africa*, ed. Suzanne Miers and Igor Kopytoff (Madison: University of Wisconsin Press, 1977), 347–48.

36. Isabel Cristina F. Reis, *A vida familiar e afetiva dos escravos na Bahia do século XIX* (Salvador: Centro de Estudos Baianos da UFBA, 2001).

37. Chalhoub, *Visões da liberdade*, chap. 1; João Reis, "Escravos e coiteiros no quilombo do Oitizeiro," in *Liberdade por um fio: História dos quilombos no Brasil*, ed. Reis and Flávio Gomes (São Paulo: Companhia das Letras, 1997), 332–72; Hebe Mattos, *Das cores do silêncio: Os significados da liberdade no sudeste escravista*, 2nd ed. (Rio de Janeiro: Nova Fronteira, 1998); Elione Silva Guimarães, *Violência entre parceiros de cativeiro: Juiz de Fora, segunda metade do século XIX* (São Paulo: Annablume/Fapesp, 2006); Maria de Fátima Novaes Pires, *O crime na cor: Escravos e forros no sertão da Bahia (1830–1888)* (São Paulo: Annablume/Fapesp, 2006), 182–90; Jackson Ferreira, "'Por hoje acaba a lida': Suicídio escravo na Bahia, 1850–1888," *Afro-Ásia* 31 (2004): 197–234.

38. On recent research about maroon communities in Brazil, see essays in Reis and Gomes, eds., *Liberdade por um fio: A história dos quilombos no Brasil*.

39. Flávio dos Santos Gomes, "Jogando a rede e revendo as malhas: Fugas e fugitivos no Brasil escravista," *Tempo* 1 (1996): 67–93; ídem, *Histórias de quilombolas*; idem, *A hidra e os pântanos: Mocambos, quilombos e comunidades de fugitivos no Brasil (séculos XVII–XIX)* (São Paulo: UNESP, 2005); José Maia B. Neto, "Histórias urbanas de liberdade: Escravos em fuga na cidade de Belém, 1860–1888," *Afro-Ásia* 28 (2002): 221–50; Silmei Petiz, *Buscando a liberdade: As fugas de escravos da província de São pedro para o além-fronteira (1815–1851)* (Passo Fundo: EPF, 2006); Hendrik Kraay, "O abrigo da farda: O Exército brasileiro e os escravos fugidos, 1800–1888," *Afro-Ásia* 17 (1996): 29–56; João José Reis and Eduardo Silva, *Negociação e conflito: A resistência negra no Brasil escravista* (São Paulo: Companhia das Letras, 1989), chap. 4; Carvalho, *Liberdade*, chap. 12; Ademir Gebara, *O mercado de trabalho livre no Brasil* (São Paulo: Brasiliense, 1986), chap. 3; Chalhoub, *Visões da liberdade*, 58–59; Mattos, *Das cores do silêncio*, esp. chap. 10; Maria Helena P. T. Machado, "From Slave Rebels to Strikebreakers: The Quilombo of Jabaquara and the Problem of Citizenship in Late-Nineteenth-Century Brazil," *Hispanic American Historical Review* 86:2 (2006): 246–74. On the abolitionist *quilombo* seen from the perspective of its free organizers, see Eduardo Silva, *As camélias do Leblon: Uma investigação em história cultural* (São Paulo: Companhia das

Letras, 2003). On slave suicide, see, for instance, Renato Pinto Venâncio, "A última fuga: Suicídio de escravos no Rio de Janeiro (1870–1888)," *LPM: Revista de História* 1 (1990): 80–89; and Ferreira, "'Por hoje acaba a lida.'"

40. Manuela Carneiro da Cunha, *Negros, estrangeiros: Os escravos libertos e sua volta à África* (São Paulo: Brasiliense, 1985), esp. 17–61.

41. See, for example, Luiza Volpato, *Cativos do Sertão: Vida cotidiana e escravidão em Cuiabá em 1850–1888* (Rio de Janeiro: Marco Zero, 1993), 213–14; Sidney Chalhoub "The Politics of Silence: Race and Citizenship in Nineteenth-Century Brazil," *Slavery and Abolition* 27:1 (2006): 73–87.

42. See, for instance, Lara, *Campos da violência*, 204; Reis and Silva, *Negociação e conflito*, chap. 3; João Reis, "A greve negra de 1857 na Bahia," *Revista USP* 18 (1993): 29.

43. What follows is just a sample of available studies on different aspects of urban slavery. For Rio de Janeiro: Mary C. Karasch, *Slave Life in Rio de Janeiro, 1808–1850* (Princeton: Princeton University Press, 1987); Leila Algranti, *O feitor ausente: Estudo sobre a escravidão urbana no Rio de Janeiro* (Petrópolis: Vozes, 1988); Chalhoub, *Visões da liberdade*; Sandra Lauderdale Graham, *House and Street: The Domestic World of Servants and Masters in Nineteenth-Century Rio de Janeiro* (Cambridge: Cambridge University Press, 1988); Marilene R. N. Silva, *Negro na rua: A nova face da escravidão* (São Paulo: Hucitec, 1988); Luiz Carlos Soares, *O "povo de cam" na capital do Brasil: A escravidão urbana no Rio de Janeiro do século XIX* (Rio de Janeiro: Faperj/7 Letras, 2007); Carlos Eugênio Líbano Soares, *A negregada instituição: Os capoeiras no Rio de Janeiro* (Rio de Janeiro: Secretaria Municipal de Cultura, 1994); idem, *Capoeira escrava e outras tradições rebeldes no Rio de Janeiro (1808–1850)* (Campinas: UNICAMP, 2001); idem, *Zungú: Rumor de muitas vozes* (Rio de Janeiro: Arquivo Público do Estado, 1998); Martha Abreu, *O Império do Divino: Festas religiosas e cultura popular no Rio de Janeiro, 1830–1900* (Rio de Janeiro: Nova Fronteira, 1999); Juliana B. Farias, Carlos Eugênio L. Soares, and Flávio dos Santos Gomes, *No labirinto das nações: Africanos e identidades no Rio de Janeiro, século XIX* (Rio de Janeiro: Arquivo Nacional, 2005); Luiz Alberto Couceiro, *Bumerangue encapsulado: Um estudo sobre a construção social da subjetividade numa cidade escravista, Rio de Janeiro, c. 1860–c. 1888* (Rio de Janeiro: 7 Letras, 2003). For Salvador: Katia M. de Queirós Mattoso, *To Be a Slave in Brazil, 1550–1888* (New Brunswick: Rutgers University Press, 1986), where passages on urban slavery are often based on this author's extensive research on Salvador; idem, *Da Revolução dos Alfaiates à riqueza dos baianos no século XIX* (Salvador: Corrupio, 2004); Oliveira, *O liberto*; Maria José Andrade, *A mão-de-obra escrava em Salvador, 1811–1888* (Salvador: Corrupio, 1988); Cecília Moreira Soares, *Mulher negra na Bahia no século XIX* (Salvador: Eduneb, 2006); Mieko Nishida, *Slavery and Identity: Ethnicity, Gender, and Race in Salvador, Brazil, 1808–1888* (Bloomington and Indianápolis: Indiana University Press, 2003). For Recife: Carvalho, *Liberdade*, as an example of many studies by him; see also Luiz Geraldo Silva, "Da festa à sedição: Sociabilidades, etnia e controle social na América portuguesa, 1776–1814," in *Festa: Cultura e sociabilidade na América portuguesa*, ed. István Jancsó and Iris Kantor (São Paulo: Hucitec/EDSUP/FAPESP, 2001), vol. 1: 313–35. For São Paulo: Maria Odila S. Dias, *Quotidiano e poder em São Paulo no século XIX* (São Paulo: Brasiliense, 1984); Maria Cristina Wissenbach, *Sonhos africanos, vivências ladinas: Escravos e forros em São Paulo (1850–1888)* (São Paulo: Hucitec, 1998). For Rio Grande do Sul: Paulo Roberto S. Moreira, *Faces da liberdade, máscaras do cativeiro: Experiências de liberdade e cativeiro percebidas através das cartas de alforria—Porto Alegre (1858–1888)* (Porto Alegre: EDPUCRS, 1996); idem, *Os cativos e os homens de bem: Experiências negras no espaço urbano* (Porto Alegre: EST, 2003); Marco Antonio L. de Mello, *Reviras, batuques e carnavais: A cultura de resistência dos escravos em Pelotas* (Pelotas: UFPel, 1994); and Valéria Zanetti,

Calabouço urbano: Escravos e libertos em Porto Alegre (1840–1860) (Passo Fundo: UPF, 2002); Mário Maestri, *O sobrado e o cativo: A arquitetura erudita no Brasil escravista: O caso gaúcho* (Passo Fundo: UPF, 2001). See also Elione Silva Guimarães, *Múltiplos viveres de afrodescendentes na escravidão e no pós-abolição: Família, trabalho, terra e conflito (Juiz de Fora-MG, 1828–1928)* (São Paulo: Annablume/Juiz de Fora: Funalfa, 2006), esp. chap. 1.

44. See for example Higgins, *Licencious Liberty*; Luciano Figueiredo, *O avesso da memória: Cotidiano e trabalho da mulher em Minas Gerais no século XVIII* (Rio de Janeiro: José Olympio/Brasília: Ednub, 1993); Slenes, *Na senzala uma flor*; Góes, *Cativeiro imperfeito*; Florentino e Góes, *A paz na senzala*; Hebe M. Castro, "Laços de família e direitos no final da escravidão," in *História da vida privada no Brasil*, ed. Luiz Felipe de Alencastro (São Paulo: Companhia das Letras, 1999), vol. 2: 337–83; Sandra Graham, *Caetana Says No: Women's Stories from a Brazilian Slave Society* (Cambridge: Cambridge University Press, 2002). See also several articles on slave family and *compadrio* in the pages of *Afro-Ásia*, available at www.afroasia.ufba.

45. See, for example, chapters in Lara and Pacheco, eds., *Memórias do jongo*.

46. Gomes, *Histórias de quilombolas*.

47. See, for example, Robert Slenes, "Senhores e subalternos no Oeste paulista," in Alencastro, ed., *História da vida privada no Brasil*, 2: 233–90; Regina Xavier, *A conquista da liberdade: Libertos em Campinas na segunda metade do século XIX* (Campinas: Centro de Memória da UNICAMP, 1996).

48. Giovanni Levi, "Sobre a micro-história," in *A escrita da história: Novas perspectivas*, ed. Peter Burke (São Paulo: Unesp, 1992), 133–63; Carlo Ginzburg, *Mitos, emblemas, sinais: Morfologia e história* (São Paulo: Companhia das Letras, São Paulo, 1991), 243–79; Clifford Geertz, *The Interpretation of Cultures* (New York: Basic Books, 1973) chap. 1; A. Biersack, "Local Knowledge, Local History: Geertz and Beyond," in *The New Cultural History*, ed. Lynn Hunt (Berkeley: University of California Press, 1989), 72–96.

49. Luiz Mott, *Rosa Egipcíaca: Uma santa africana no Brasil* (Rio de Janeiro: Bertrand Brasil, 1993); Júnia F. Furtado, *Chica da Silva e o contratador de diamantes: O outro lado do mito* (São Paulo: Companhia das Letras, 2003); Frank, *Dutra's World*; Eduardo Silva, *Prince of the People: The Life and Times of a Brazilian Free Man of Colour* (London: Verso, 1993). See also Graham, *Caetana Says No*; Grinberg, *Liberata*; Gabriela dos Reis Sampaio, *Juca-Rosa, um pai-de-santo na corte imperial* (Rio de Janeiro: Arquivo Nacional, 2009); Regina Xavier, *Religiosidade e escravidão no século XIX: Mestre Tito* (Porto Alegre: UFRGS, 2008); Reis, *Domingos Sodré*; João Reis, Flávio Gomes and Marcus "África e Brasil entre margens: aventuras e desventuras do africano Rufino José Maria, c. 1822–1853," *Estudos Afro-Asiáticos* 26:2 (2004): 257–302; Farias, Eugênio Soares and Gomes, *No labirinto das nações*, chap. 6; Roberto Guedes, "De ex-escravo a elite escravista: A trajetória de ascensão social do pardo alferes Joaquim Barbosa Neves (Porto Feliz, São Paulo, século XIX)," in *Conquistadores e negociantes: Histórias de elites no Antigo Regime nos trópicos*, ed. João Luís R. Fragoso, Carla Maria C. de Almeida, and Antonio Carlos J. de Sampaio (Rio de Janeiro: Civilização Brasileira, 2007), 337–76; and chapters by Hebe Mattos, Mariza de Carvalho Soares, Daniela Buono Calainho, and Sheila de Castro Faria in Ronaldo Vainfas, Georgina S. dos Santos, and Guilherme P. Neves, eds., *Retratos do império: Trajetórias individuais no mundo português nos séculos XVI a XIX* (Rio de Janeiro, EDUFF, 2006), among many other titles.

50. James C. Scott, "Everyday Forms of Peasant Resistance," *The Journal of Peasant Studies* 13:3 (1986): 5–35; idem, *Domination and the Arts of Resistance*. For a critique and Scott's reply, see Mathews C. Gutman, "Rituals of Resistance: A Critique of the Theory of Everyday Forms of Resistance," *Latin American Perspectives* 20:2 (1993): 54–96. In slavery

studies, the concept of day-to-day resistance has been available since Raymond and Alice Bauer's pathbreaking 1942 article in the *Journal of Negro History*, reprinted as "Day to Day Resistance to Slavery" in *American Slavery: The Question of Resistance*, ed. J. H. Bracey Jr, A. Meier, and E. Rudwick (Belmont: Wadsworth, 1971), 37–60.

51. Recent studies on Palmares include Schwartz, *Slaves, Peasants, and Rebels*, chap. 4; Flávio dos Santos Gomes, *Palmares* (São Paulo: Contexto, 2005); and Silvia H. Lara, "Marronage et pouvoir colonial: Palmares, Cucaú et la frontière de la liberté au Pernambuco à la fin du XVIIe siècle," *Annales: Histoire, Sciences Sociales* 67 (2007), 639–62.

52. See among many others, Carvalho, *Liberdade*, chaps. 8 and 9; Glacyra Leite, *Pernambuco 1824: A Confederação do Equador* (Recife: Massangana, 1989); Mundinha Araujo, *Insurreição de escravos em Viana, 1867* (São Luís: Sioge, 1994); Reis and Silva, *Negociação e conflito*, chap. 5; Marcos Andrade, "Rebelião escrava na comarca do Rio das Mortes, Minas Gerais: O caso Carrancas," *Afro-Ásia* 21/22 (1998–99): 45–82; Vilma P. F. Almada, *Escravismo e transição: O Espírito Santo (1850–1888)* (Rio de Janeiro: Graal, 1984), 154–74; Volpato, *Cativos do sertão*, 182–97; Suely R. R. Queiroz, *Escravidão negra em São Paulo* (Rio de Janeiro: José Olympio, 1977), chap. 4 and pp. 207–15; Ricardo F. Pirola, "A conspiração escrava de Campinas, 1832: Rebelião, etnicidade e família," (master's thesis, Universidade de Campinas, 2005); Célia Marinho Azevedo, *Onda negra, medo branco: O negro no imaginário das elites—século XIX* (Rio de Janeiro: Paz e Terra, 1987); Maria Helena P. T. Machado, *O plano e o pânico: Os movimentos sociais na década da abolição* (São Paulo: EDUSP/Rio de Janeiro: EDUFRJ, 1994); João Reis, "Quilombos e revoltas escravas no Brasil," *Revista USP* 28 (1995–96): 27–31; Gomes, *A hidra e os pântanos*.

53. Maria Januária V. Santos, *A Balaiada e a insurreição dos escravos no Maranhão* (São Paulo: Ática, 1983); Reis, *Slave Rebellion*.

54. Mott, *Rosa Egipcíaca*; idem, *Escravidão, homossexualidade e demonologia* (São Paulo: Ícone, 1988); Laura de Mello e Souza, *O Diabo e a Terra de Santa Cruz* (São Paulo: Companhia das Letras, 1986), of which there is a recent English edition from the University of Texas Press; James Sweet, *Recreating Africa: Culture, Kinship and Religion in the African-Portuguese World, 1441–1770* (Chapel Hill: University of North Carolina Press, 2003); Reis, *Slave Rebellion*; idem, "Magia jeje na Bahia: A invasão do calundú do Pasto de Cachoeira, 1785," *Revista Brasileira de História* 16 (1988): 57–82; idem, "Candomblé in Nineteenth-Century Bahia: Leaders, Followers, Clients," *Slavery and Abolition* 22:1 (2001): 116–34; idem, *Domingos Sodré*; Reis and Silva, *Negociação e conflito*, chap. 3; Dale T. Graden, "'So Much Superstition among These People!': Candomblé and the Dilemmas of Afro-Bahian Intellectuals, 1864–1871," and Fayette Wimberly, "The Expansion of Afro-Bahian Religious Practices in Nineteenth-Century Cachoeira," both in *Afro-Brazilian Culture and Politics: Bahia, 1790s to 1990s*, ed. Hendrik Kraay (Armonk, N.Y.: M. E. Sharpe, 1998), 57–73 and 74–89 respectively; Rachael E. Harding, *A Refuge in Thunder: Candomblé and Alternative Spaces of Blackness* (Bloomington: Indiana University Press, 2000); Renato da Silveira, *O candomblé da Barroquinha: Processo de constituição do primeiro terreiro baiano de Keto* (Salvador: Maianga, 2006); Luís Nicolau Parés, *A formação do candomblé: História e ritual da nação jeje na Bahia* (Campinas: UNICAMP, 2006); Sampaio, *Juca-Rosa*; Robert Slenes, "The Great Porpoise-Skull Strike: Central África Water Spirit and Slave Identity in Early-Nineteenth-Century Rio de Janeiro," in *Central Africans and Cultural Transformations in the American Diaspora*, ed. Linda M. Heywood (Cambridge: Cambridge University Press, 2002), 183–208, among others.

55. Marcus J. M. Carvalho, "'Que crime é ser cismático?': As transgressões de um pastor negro no Recife patriarcal," *Estudos Afro-Asiáticos* 36 (1999): 97–121; idem, "'É fácil serem sujeitos de quem já foram senhores': O ABC do Divino Mestre," *Afro-Ásia* 31 (2004):

327–334. Studies on black brotherhoods and devotion are many. Just a few titles: A. J. R. Russell-Wood, "Black and Mulatto Brotherhoods in Colonial Brazil: A Study in Collective Behavior," *Hispanic American Historical Review*, 54:4 (1974): 567–602; Patricia Mulvey, "The Black Lay Brotherhoods of Colonial Brazil: A History" (PhD diss., CUNY, 1976); Karasch, *Slave Life*, chap. 9; Julita Scarano, *Devoção e escravidão* (São Paulo: Companhia Editora Nacional, 1975); João Reis, "Identidade e diversidade étnicas nas irmandades negras no tempo da escravidão," *Tempo* 3 (1997): 7–33; Anderson José M. de Oliveira, *Devoção negra: Santos e catequese no Brasil colonial* (Rio de Janeiro: Quartet/FAPERJ, 2008); Elizabeth Kiddy, *Blacks of the Rosary: Memory and History in Minas Gerais, Brazil* (Philadelphia: Penn State University Press, 2005); Carlos A. M. Lima, "Escravos da Senhora do Rosário," in Ana Maria da S. Moura and Carlos A. M. Lima, *Devoção e incorporação: Igreja, escravos e índios na América Portuguesa* (Curitiba: Peregrina, 2002), 9–267; and Mariza Soares, *Devotos da cor: Identidade étnica, religiosidade e escravidão no Rio de Janeiro, século XVIII* (Rio de Janeiro: Civilização Brasileira, 2000).

56. See, for example, pertinent essays in several collective works such as Kristin Mann and Edna Bay, eds., *Rethinking the African Diaspora: The Making of a Black Atlantic World in the Bight of Benin and Brazil* (London: Frank Cass, 2001); Paul Lovejoy and David Trotman, eds., *Trans-Atlantic Dimension of Ethnicity in the African Diaspora* (London and New York: Continuum, 2003); Toyin Falola and Matt D. Childs, eds., *The Yoruba Diaspora in the Atlantic World* (Bloomington and Indianapolis: Indiana University Press, 2004); José C. Curto and Paul E. Lovejoy, eds., *Enslaving Connections: Changing Cultures of Africa and Brazil During the Era of the Slave Trade* (Amherst, Humanity Books, 2004); José C. Curto and Renèe Soulodre-France, eds., *Africa and the Americas: Interconnections During the Slave Trade* (Trenton, N.J.: Africa World Press, 2005); Barreto, Soares, and Gomes, *No labirinto das nações*; Mariza de Carvalho Soares, ed., *Rotas atlânticas da diáspora africana: Da Baía do Benim ao Rio de Janeiro* (Niterói: EDUFF, 2007); Florentino, "Alforria e etnicidade no Rio de Janeiro"; Zanetti, *Calabouço urbano*; Moreira, *Faces da liberdade*; Robert Slenes, "'Malungo Ngoma vem': África encoberta e descoberta no Brasil," *Revista USP* 12 (1991–92): 48–67; idem, *Na senzala uma flor*; Pirola, "A conspiração escrava de Campinas"; Oliveira, "Viver e morrer no meio dos seus"; idem, "Quem eram os 'negros da Guiné'? A origem dos africanos na Bahia," *Afro-Ásia* 19/20 (1997): 37–73; idem, "Retrouver une identité: Jeux sociaux des africains de Bahia (vers 1750–vers 1890)" (PhD diss., Université de Paris IV [Sorbonne], 1992); Nishida, *Slavery and Identity*; Reis, *Slave Rebellion*; Nicolau Parés, *A formação do Candomblé*; idem, "O processo de 'crioulização' no Recôncavo da Bahia," *Afro-Ásia* 33 (2005): 87–132.

57. Though not dealing primarily with slaves, the classic model study for using these notarial and inventory records for social analysis is Katia M. de Queirós Mattoso, *Bahia, uma provincial no Império* (Rio de Janeiro: Nova Fronteira, 1992). Recent studies that systematically use inventories to study slavery regionally are Laird W. Bergad, *Slavery and the Demographic and Economic History of Minas Gerais, Brazil, 1720–1888* (Cambridge: Cambridge University Press, 1999) and Sheila de Castro Faria, *A colônia em movimento: Fortuna e família no cotidiano colonial* (Rio de Janeiro: Nova Fronteira, 1988). They have also been used in a host of local studies, see for example, Mônica Ribeiro de Oliveira, "Cafeicultura mineira: Formação e consolidação, 1809–1870," *Anais do IX Seminário sobre a Economia Mineira* (2000), and Dora Isabel Paiva da Costa, "Mecanismos de redistribuição de riqueza e formação de famílias proprietárias em área de fronteira: Campinas, 1795–1850," *Anais do III Congresso Brasileiro de História Econômica, ABPHE* (1999), which has an interesting comparative discussion of the sampling problems related to using these inventories. The detailed study of Flávio Rabelo Versiani and José Raimundo Oliveira

Vergolino, "Posse de escravos e estrutura da riqueza no agreste e sertão de Pernambuco: 1777–1887" (Universidade de Brasília, Departamento de Economia, Textos para discusão, Texto no. 231 Brasília, Agosto de 2002) is based on these inventories, as are the dissertations of Heloísa Maria Teixeira, "Reprodução e famílias escravas em Mariana (1880–1888)" (PhD diss., Universidade de São Paulo-FFCH, 2001) and Marcia Cristina Roma de Vasconcellos, "Famílias escravas em Angra dos Reis, 1801–1888" (PhD diss., Universidade de São Paulo-FFCH, 2006); and Juliana Garavazo, "Relações familiares e estabilidade da família escrava: Batatais (1850–88)," XIV Encontro Nacional de Estudos Populacionais, ABEP (2004); Paiva, *Escravos e libertos*, and his *Escravidão e universo cultural na colônia, Minas Gerais, 1716–1789* (Belo Horizonte: UFMG, 2001).

58. These traditional sources have been used to study manumission at the baptismal font and legitimacy of births, as well as fictive kinship—or godparenthood—among slaves. On manumission, see James Patrick Kiernan, "Baptism and Manumission in Brazil: Paraty, 1789–1822," *Social Science History* 3:1 (1978): 56–71; Cristiano Lima da Silva, "Senhores e pais: Reconhecimento de paternidade dos alforriados na pia batismal na Freguesia de Nossa Senhora do Pilar de São João del-Rei (1770–1850)," *Anais do I Colóquio do Lahes* (2005) (no page numbers); and Roberto Guedes, "Na pia batismal: Família e compadrio entre escravos na freguesia de São José, Rio de Janeiro (primeira metade do século XIX)" (master's thesis, Universidade Federal Fluminense, 2000). On the question of legitimacy of slave births, see, for example, Maísa Faleiros da Cunha, "A legitimidade entre os cativos da Paróquia Nossa Senhora da Conceição de Franca—Século XIX," *XIV Encontro Nacional de Estudos Populacionais, ABEP* (2004), 1–14; Rafael Ribas Galvão, "Bastardia e legitimidade na Curitiba dos Séculos XVIII e XIX," *XIII Encontro da Associação Brasileira de Estudos Populacionais ABEP* (2002), 1–23; Silvia Maria Jardim Brügger, "Legitimidade, casamento e relações ditas ilícitas em São João del Rei (1730–1850)," *Anais do IX Seminário sobre a Economia Mineira* (2000): 37–64; Vanda Lúcia Praxedes, "A teia e a trama da 'fragilidade humana': Os filhos ilegítimos em Minas Gerais (1770–1840)," *Anais do XI Seminário sobre a Economia Mineira* (2004): 1–23. Worth looking at is the attempt to measure multiple illegitimate births for the same mothers in Maria Adenir Peraro, "Mulheres de Jesus no universo dos ilegítimos," *Diálogos: Revista do Departamento de História da UEM* 4:4 (2000): 1–15; also see her essay "O princípio da fronteira e a fronteira de princípios: Filhos ilegítimos em Cuiabá no séc. XIX," *Revista Brasileira de História* 19:38 (1999): 55–80. For studies of godparenthood (*compadrio*) among slaves, see José Luis R. Fragoso and Manolo Florentino, "Marcelino, filho de Inocência Crioula, neto de Joana Cabinda: Estudo sobre famílias escravas em Paraíba do Sul, 1835–1872," *Estudos Econômicos* 17:2 (1987), 151–74; Ana Maria Lugão Rios, "Família e compadrio entre escravos nas fazendas de cafe: Paraiba do Sul, 1871–1920," *Cadernos do ICHF, Universidade Federal Fluminense* 23 (1999), 103–28, and her recent essay, "The Politics of Kinship: Compadrio Among Slaves in Nineteenth-Century Brazil," *The History of the Family An International Quarterly* 5:3 (2000): 287–98; Maria de Fatima Rodrigues das Neves, "Infância de faces negras: A cria escrava brasileira no século XIX" (PhD diss., Universidade de São Paulo, 1993); Jonis Freire, "Compadrio em uma freguesia escravista: Senhor Bom Jesus do Rio Pardo (MG) (1838–1888)," *XIV Encontro Nacional de Estudos Populacionais, ABEP* (2004); Cacilda Machado, "Casamento & Compadrio: Estudo sobre relações sociais entre livres, libertos e escravos na passagem do século XVIII para o XIX (São José dos Pinhais—PR)," *XIV Encontro Nacional de Estudos Populacionais, ABEP* (2004); Marcia Cristina de Vasconcellos, "O compadrio entre escravos numa comunidade em transformação (Mambucaba, Angra dos Reis, século XIX)," *Afro-Ásia* 28 (2002), 147–78; Stuart B. Schwartz and Stephen Guderman, "Cleaning the Original Sin: Godparenthood and Baptisms of Slaves in Eighteenth-Century Bahia," in

Kinship Ideology and Practice in Latin America, ed. Raymond Thomas Smith (Chapel Hill: University of North Carolina Press, 1984), 35–58. A more extended version of this essay is found in Schwartz, *Slaves, Peasants, and Rebels*, 137–60.

59. The previously unpublished *mapas* have been studied by Francisco Vidal Luna and Herbert S. Klein, *Slavery and the Economy of São Paulo, 1750–1850* (Stanford, Calif.: Stanford University Press, 2003; Portuguese edition, São Paulo, 2006); José Flávio Motta, *Corpos escravos, vontades livres: Estrutura da posse de cativos e família escrava em um núcleo Cafeeiro (Bananal, 1801–1829)* (São Paulo: Ananablume, 1999); Ramón García Fernández, "Concentração da riqueza e crescimento econômico no Litoral Norte paulista (1778–1836)," *Estudos Sociedade e Agricultura* 10 (1998): 165–89; Horacio Gutiérrez, "Demografia escrava numa economia não-exportadora: Paraná, 1800–1830," *Estudos Econômicos* 17:2 (1987): 297–314; and Armênio de Souza Rangel, "A economia do município de Taubaté: 1798 a 1835," *Estudos Econômicos* 23:1 (1993): 149–79. For Minas Gerais, see the works cited in note 64 below.

60. Among the numerous studies on slaves and crime, see Ilton César Martins, "Veredicto culpado: A pena de morte enquanto instrumento de regulação social em Castro—PR (1853–1888)" (master's thesis, Universidade Federal de Paraná, 2005); Maria Helena P. T. Machado, *Crime e escravidão: Trabalho, luta e resistência nas lavouras paulistas, 1830–1888* (São Paulo: Editora Brasiliense, 1987); Solimar Oliveira Lima, *Triste Pampa: Resistência e punição de escravos em fontes judiciárias no Rio Grande do Sul, 1818–1833* (Porto Alegre: EDIPURCS, 1997); Maria de Fátima Novaes Pires, *O crime na cor: Escravos e forros no alto sertão da Bahia (1830–1888)* (São Paulo: Annablume, 2003); Elione Silva Guimarães, *Violência entre parceiros de cativeiro: Juiz de Fora, segunda metade do seculo XIX* (São Paulo: Annablume, 2006); idem, "Rixas e brigas entre companheiros de cativeiro (Juiz de Fora 1850–88)," *Revista Universidade Rural, Serie Ciencias Humanas* 24:1–2 (2002): 89–100; Alysson Luiz Freitas de Jesus, *No sertão das Minas: Escravidão, violência e liberdade (1830–1888)* (São Paulo: Annablume, 2007); Alan Nardi de Souza, "Crime e castigo: A criminalidade em Mariana na primeira metade do século XIX" (master's thesis, Universidade Federal de Juiz de Fora, 2007); and Cesar Mucio Silva, *Processos-crime: Escravidão e violência em Botucatu* (São Paulo: Alameda, 2004). Among the earlier models cited by many of the recent works are Algranti, *O feitor austente*, and the discussion of this theme in Karasch, *Slave Life*.

61. One of the earliest studies using newspapers to study slavery was done by Gilberto Freyre, *O escravo nos anúncios de jornais brasileiros do século XIX* (São Paulo: CBBA Propeg, 1984). The shipping sections of such newspapers have been used to study the Atlantic slave trade to Brazil. See Herbert S. Klein, "O tráfico de escravos africanos para o porto de Rio de Janeiro, 1825–1830," *Anais de História* 5 (1973): 85–101; and Manolo Garcia Florentino, *Em costas negras: Uma história do tráfico atlântico de escravos entre a Africa e o Rio de Janeiro [séculos XVIII e XIX]* (Rio de Janeiro: Arquivo Nacional, 1995).

62. For older studies of the Atlantic slave trade to Brazil, see Pierre Verger, *Flux et reflux de la traite de nègres entre le golfe de Benin et Bahia de Todos os Santos* (Paris: Mouton 1968); Antonio Carreira, *As companhias pombalinas de navegação, comércio e tráfico de escravos* (Porto: Centro de Estudos da Guiné Portuguesa, 1969); David Eltis, *Economic Growth and the Ending of the Transatlantic Slave Trade* (New York: Cambridge University Press, 1987); Herbert S. Klein, *The Middle Passage, Comparative Studies in the Atlantic Slave Trade* (Princeton: Princeton University Press, 1978); and Joseph Miller, *The Way of Death: Merchant Capitalism and the Angolan Slave Trade, 1730–1830* (Madison: University of Wisconsin Press, 1988). A summary of much of this older research is found in Herbert S. Klein, "Demografia do tráfico atlântico de escravos para o Brasil," *Estudos*

Econômicos 17:2 (1987): 129–50. Recent new research has begun on traders as well as on the international trade; see also Florentino, *Em costas negras*; Jaime Rodrigues, *De costa a costa: Escravos, marinheiros e intermediários do tráfico negreiro de Angola ao Rio de Janeiro (1780–1860)* (São Paulo: Companhia das Letras, 2005); and his *O infame comércio, propostas e experiências no final do tráfico de africanos para o Brasil (1800–1850)* (Campinas: Unicamp, 2000). There have also appeared several new collections of essays on African-Brazilian relations; see Soares, ed., *Rotas atlânticas*; Heywood, ed., *Central Africans and Cultural Transformations*; Selma Pantoja and José Flávio Sombra Saraiva, eds., *Angola e Brasil nas rotas do Atlântico Sul* (Rio de Janeiro, 1999). Moreover, David Eltis has led an ongoing compilation of slave voyages which has involved Florentino and many other Brazilian scholars. A first approximation appeared as David Eltis, Stephan D. Behrendt, David Richardson, and Herbert S. Klein, *The Transatlantic Slave Trade, 1562–1867: A Database CD-Rom* (Cambridge: Cambridge University Press, 1998), with an updating in 2008 and now available online at http://www.slavevoyages.org/tast/index.faces. A recent survey of the entire trade is found in Herbert S. Klein, *The Atlantic Slave Trade* (Cambridge: Cambridge University Press, 2000). An important reconceptualization of the role of the slave trade in the formation of Brazil is Luiz Felipe de Alencastro, *O trato dos viventes: formação do Brasil no Atlântico Sul* (São Paulo: Companhia das Letras, 2000).

    63. An early study on the internal slave trade was Herbert S. Klein, "The Internal Slave Trade in Nineteenth-Century Brazil: A Study of Slave Importations into Rio de Janeiro in 1852," *Hispanic American Historical Review* 51:4 (1971): 567–68. A major new approach using local census materials has been developed in a series of studies by José Flávio Motta, "Tráfico interno de cativos: O preço das mães escravas e sua prole," *Anais do XI Encontro Nacional de Estudos Populacionais, ABEP* (1999): 1397–416; idem, "O tráfico de escravos na Província de São Paulo: Areias, Silveiras, Guaratinguetá e Casa Branca, 1861–1887" (Texto para discussão, São Paulo: IPE/USP, 2001); and most recently "Escravos daqui, dali e de mais além: O tráfico interno de cativos em constituição (Piracicaba), 1861–1880," *Revista Brasileira de História* 26:52 (2006), 15–47; and José Flávio Motta and Renato L Marcondes, "O comércio de escravos no Vale do Paraíba paulista: Guaratinguetá e Silveiras na década de 1870," *Estudos Econômicos* 30:2 (2000): 267–99, Also see Cláudio Heleno Machado, "Tráfico interno de escravos na região de Juiz de Fora na segunda metade do século XIX," *Anais do III Congresso Brasileiro de História Econômica ABPHE* (1999) (no page numbers); and Richard Graham, "Nos tumbeiros mais uma vez?: O comércio interprovincial de escravos no Brasil," *Afro-Ásia* 27 (2002): 121–60. Alternative sources have been examined by Carolina Perpétuo Corrêa, "Comércio de escravos em Minas Gerais no século XIX: O que podem nos ensinar os assentos de batismo de escravos adultos," *Anais do XII Seminário sobre a Economia Mineira* (2006), 1–21; and in the latest of a series of articles using special tax records for studying the trade, see Cristiano Corte Restitutti, "A circulação entre o Rio de Janeiro e o Sul de Minas Gerais, c. 1800–1830," *XVI Encontro Nacional de Estudos Populacionais* (2008), 1–20; and Gabriel Santos Berute, "A concentração do comércio de escravos na capitania do Rio Grande de São Pedro do Sul, c. 1790–c. 1825," *II Encontro "Escravidão e Liberdade no Brasil Meridional* (2005), and Fábio W. A. Pinheiro, "O tráfico atlântico de escravos na formação dos plantéis mineiros, Zona da Mata (c.1809–c.1830)" (master's thesis, Rio de Janeiro: UFRJ, 2007).

    64. See the books by Francisco Vidal Luna and Iraci del Nero da Costa. For see also Luna, *Minas Gerais: Escravos e senhores* (São Paulo: IPE/USP, 1981); and Costa, *Vila Rica: População (1719–1826)* (São Paulo: IPE/USP, 1979); idem, *Populações mineiras: Sobre a estrutura populacional de alguns núcleos mineiros no alvorecer do século XIX* (São Paulo:

IPE-USP, 1981), and his *Minas Gerais: Estruturas populacionais típica* (São Paulo: EDEC, 1982). There is also a series of works done jointly by Francisco Vidal Luna and Iraci del Nero da Costa, *Minas colonial: Economia e sociedade* (São Paulo: FIPE/Pioneira, 1982); "Contribuição ao estudo de um núcleo urbano colonial (Vila Rica—1804)," *Estudos Econômicos* 8:3 (1978): 41–68; "A presença do elemento forro no conjunto de proprietários de escravos," *Ciência e Cultura* 32:7 (1980): 836–41; "Demografia histórica de Minas Gerais no período colonial," *Revista Brasileira de Estudos Políticos* 58 (1984): 15–61. Some of this material was also used by Demétrio Ramos, "Vila Rica: Profile of a Colonial Brazilian Urban Center," *The Americas* 35:4 (1979): 495–525.

65. Clotilde Andrade Paiva, "População e economia nas Minas Gerais do século XIX" (PhD diss., Universidade de São Paulo, 1996); idem, "A natalidade de Minas Gerais no século XIX: Algumas hipóteses," paper presented at the Conference on the Population History of Latin America (Ouro Preto, 2–6 July, 1989); idem, "Minas Gerais no século XIX: Aspectos demográficos de alguns núcleos populacionais," in *Brasil: História econômica e demográfica*, ed. Iraci del Nero da Costa (São Paulo: IPE-USP, 1986), 173–88. Clotilde Andrade Paiva et al., "Estrutura e dinâmica da população de Minas Gerias no século XIX" (unpublished CNPQ Research Report of 1990); and a series of joint articles she has written with others based on her archival data: Clotilde Paiva and Herbert S. Klein, "Slave and Free in Nineteenth-Century Minas Gerais: Campanha in 1831," *Slavery & Abolition* 15:1 (1994): 1–21; Clotilde Paiva and Douglas Cole Libby, "The Middle Path: Alternative Patterns of Slave Demographics in Nineteenth-Century Minas Gerais" (paper presented at the World Demographic History Conference, Vera Cruz, Mexico, 1992). Also see Douglas Cole Libby and Márcia Grimaldi, "Equilíbrio e estabilidade: Economia e comportamento demográfico num regime escravista, Minas Gerais no século XIX," *Anais: VI Encontro Nacional de Estudos Populacionais, ABEP* (1988): 413–95; and Carolina Perpétuo Corrêa, "Aspectos da demografia e vida familiar dos escravos de Santa Luzia, Minas Gerais, 1818–1833," *Anais XIV Encontro Nacional de Estudos Populacionais, ABEP* (2004): 1–24. All the data generated by Paiva and her associates are compared to the findings from São Paulo in Herbert S. Klein and Francisco Vidal Luna, "Slave Economy and Society in Minas Gerais and São Paulo: Brazil in 1830," *Journal of Latin American Studies* 36:1 (2004): 1–28, and is also used extensively in the book by Bergad, *Slavery and the Demographic and Economic History of Minas Gerais*.

66. See Roberto Borges Martins, "Growing in Silence: The Slave Economy of Nineteenth Century Minas Gerais, Brazil" (PhD diss., Vanderbilt University, 1980); and Amilcar Martins Filho and Roberto B. Martins, "Slavery in a Non-Export Economy: Nineteenth-Century Minas Gerais Revisited," *Hispanic American Historical Review* 63:3 (1983): 537–68, and "Reply," *Hispanic American Historical Review* 64:1 (1984): 135–46.

67. Aside from the works of Bergad and Paiva previously cited, see Alexandre Mendes Cunha, "Paisagem e população: Algumas vistas de dinâmicas espaciais e movimentos da população nas Minas do começo do Dezenove," XIII Encontro da Associação Brasileira de Estudos Populacionais, Ouro Preto, MG (2002). A finding for a positive rate of slave population growth also has been seen for the southern region of Paraná in the same period. See Horacio Gutierrez, "Demografia escrava numa economia não-exportadora Paraná, 1800–1830," *Estudos Econômicos* 17:2 (1987): 297–314.

68. Much of the recent work of Bergad and Douglas Libby has dealt with the economy of nineteenth-century Minas. See Douglas C. Libby, *Transformações e trabalho em uma economia escravista: Minas Gerais no século XIX* (São Paulo: Editora Brasiliense, 1988), and his article "Proto-industrialization in a Slave Society: The Case of Minas Gerais," *Journal of Latin American Studies* 23:1 (1991): 1–35.

69. Aside from the work on São Paulo *mapas* cited in note 59, and that of the censuses of the 1830s in Minas Gerais developed by Clotilde Paiva and her associates cited in note 65, see the recent analysis of an 1830s *mapa* for Bahia in B. J. Barickman, "Reading the 1835 Parish Censuses from Bahia: Citizenship, Kinship, Slavery, and Household in Early Nineteenth-Century Brazil," *The Americas* 59:3. (2003): 287–323.

70. For a sample of these many local studies, see Versiani and Vergolino, "Posse de escravos e estrutura da riqueza"; Renato Leite Marcondes and Juliana Garavazo, "A propriedade escrava e a hipótese de crescimento vegetativo em Batatais: a classificação dos escravos (1875)," *XIII Encontro da Associação Brasileira de Estudos Populacionais*, ABEP (2002); Márcia Cristina de Vasconcellos, "Estrutura de posse de escravos em angra dos reis, século XIX," *Anais do V Congresso Brasileiro de História Econômica*, ABPHE (2003) (no page numbers); Jonas Rafael dos Santos, "Senhores e escravos: a estrutura da posse de escravos em Mogi das Cruzes no início do Século XIX," *XIV Encontro Nacional de Estudos Populacionais, ABEP* (2004); Carlos A. M. Lima, "Sobre as posses de cativos e o mercado de escravos em Castro (1824–1835): Perspectivas a partir da análise de listas nominativas," *Anais do V Congresso Brasileiro de História Econômica*, ABPHE (2003): 1–25; Luciana Suarez Lopes, "A estrutura da posse de cativos nos momentos iniciais da cultura cafeeira no novo oeste paulista: Ribeirão Preto: 1849–1888," *XIV Encontro Nacional de Estudos Populacionais, ABEP* (2004); and Renato Leite Marcondes, "Small and Medium Slaveholdings in the Coffee Economy of the Vale do Paraíba, Province of São Paulo," *Hispanic American Historical Review* 85:2 (2005): 259–81. Also see B. J. Barickman, *A Bahian Counterpoint: Sugar, Tobacco, Cassava, and Slavery in the Recôncavo, 1780–1860* (Stanford: Stanford University Press, 1998); and his essay, "As cores do escravismo," both passed partially on local *mapas*. One of the earliest attempts to show how these slaveholding patterns fit into the general American slave system was the classic study of Stuart B. Schwartz, "Patterns of Slaveholding in the Americas: New Evidence from Brazil," *American Historical Review*, 87:1 (1982): 55–86, which is more fully elaborated in his study *Sugar Plantations in the Formation of a Brazilian Society (Bahia, 1550–1835)* (Cambridge: Cambridge University Press, 1985).

71. The classic study which opened up this theme of slave marriage was Francisco Vidal Luna and Iraci del Nero da Costa. "Vila Rica: Nota sobre casamento de escravos (1727–1826)," *África—Revista do Centro de Estudos Africanos* 4 (1981): 3–7. Also see Francisco Vidal Luna, "Casamento de Escravos em São Paulo: 1776, 1804, 1829," in *História e População: Estudos sobre a América Latina*, ed. Sérgio Nadalin et al. (São Paulo: SEADE, 1990), 226–36.

72. A good summary of much of the earlier literature is found in Slenes, *Na senzala, uma flor*. The Rio de Janeiro "school" has been particularly active in this area. See Góes, *O cativeiro imperfeito*; Florentino and Góes "Parentesco e família entre os escravos no século XIX: O caso do meio rural fluminense entre 1790 e 1830," *Revista Brasileira de Estudos de População* 13:2 (1995): 183–98; and Florentino and Góes, *A paz das senzalas*; plus a series of important studies which were published in the *Anais* of the Encontro da Associação Brasileira de Estudos Populacionais in various years (and are available at http://www.abep.org.br/usuario/GerenciaNavegacao.php). These include Marcia Cristina Roma de Vasconcellos, "Casamento e maternidade entre escravas de Angra dos Reis, século XIX," *Anais do XIV Encontro Nacional de Estudos Populacionais, ABEP* (2004): 1–13; Jonis Freire, "Compadrio em uma freguesia escravista: Senhor Bom Jesus do Rio Pardo (MG) (1838–1888)," *Anais do XIV Encontro Nacional de Estudos Populacionais, ABEP* (2004): 1–24; Renato Leite Marcondes and José Flávio Motta, "A família escrava em Lorena e Cruzeiro (1874)," *Anais XIII Encontro Nacional de Estudos Populacionais, ABEP*, 2000; Juliana Garavazo, "Relações familiares e estabilidade da família escrava: Batatais (1850–88)," *Anais*

do XIV Encontro Nacional de Estudos Populacionais, ABEP (2004); and Carolina Perpétuo Corrêa, "Aspectos da demografia e vida familiar dos escravos de Santa Luzia, Minas Gerais, 1818–1833," *Anais do XIV Encontro Nacional de Estudos Populacionais, ABEP* (2004): 1–24. Also see Linda Wimmer, "Ethnicity and Family Formation among Slaves on Tobacco Farms in the Bahian Recôncavo, 1698–1829," in Curto and Lovejoy, eds., *Enslaving Connections: Changing Cultures of Africa and Brazil during the era of slavery* (Amherst, N.Y.: Humanity Books, 2004), 149–62, as well as Rômulo Andrade, "Ampliando estudos sobre famílias escravas no século XIX," *Revista Universitaria Rural, Serie Ciencias Humanas* 24:1–2 (2002): 101–13; and Hebe Maria Mattos de Castro and Eduardo Schnoor, eds., *Resgate: Uma janela para o Oitocentos* (Rio de Janeiro: Topbooks, 1995); as well as Heloísa Maria Teixeira, "Meninos-dos-olhos do senhor: Crianças escravas nas propriedades de Mariana (1850–1888)," *Anais do XIV Encontro Nacional de Estudos Populacionais, ABEP* (2004): 1–18; Rômulo Andrade, "Casamentos entre escravos na região cafeeira de Minas Gerais," *Revista da Universidadade Rural, Serie Ciencias Humanas* 22:2 (2000): 177–97.

73. Mattoso, "A propósito de cartas de alforria"; idem, "A carta de alforria como fonte complementar para o estudo de rentabilidade de mão de obra escrava urbana, 1819–1888," in Carlos Manuel Pelaez and Mircea Buescu, eds, *A moderna história econômica* (Rio de Janeiro: APEC, 1976); and those by Schwartz, "The Manumission of Slaves"; Peter L. Eisenberg, "Ficando livre: As alforrias em Campinas no século XIX," *Estudos Econômicos* 17:2 (1987): 176–216; James P. Kiernan, "The Manumission of Slaves in Colonial Brazil: Paraty, 1789–1822" (PhD diss., New York University, 1976); and Robert W. Slenes, "The Demography and Economics of Brazilian Slavery: 1850–1888" (PhD diss., Stanford University, 1976), for his estimates of rural patterns of manumission. An excellent discussion of slave prices and the impact of the laws of emancipation is found in the classic work of Pedro Carvalho de Mello, "The Economics of Labor in Brazilian Coffee Plantations, 1850–1888" (PhD diss., University of Chicago, 1977). Recent additions to this literature have included the two books by Paiva, *Escravos e libertos* and *Escravidão e universo cultural*; Nishida, "Manumission and Ethnicity"; Bertin, *Alforrias em São Paulo do século XIX*; Douglas Cole Libby and Clotilde Andrade Paiva, "Alforrias e forros em uma freguesia mineira: São José d'El Rey em 1795," *Revista Brasileira de Estudos de População* 17:1/2 (2000): 17–46; Higgins, *'Licentious Liberty'*; and Manolo Florentino, "Sobre minas, crioulos e a liberdade costumeira no Rio de Janeiro, 1789–1871," in *Tráfico, cativeiro e liberdade Rio de Janeiro, séculos XVII–XIX*, ed. Manolo Florentino (Rio de Janeiro: Civilização Brasileira, 2005), 331–66, and his essay with José Roberto Góes, "Do que Nabuco já sabia: Mobilidade e miscigenação racial no Brasil escravista" (unpublished manuscript presented at the Congresso Internacional Brasil-Portugal Ano 2000—Sessão de História). Also see the essays presented at the *Anais do X Seminário sobre a Economia Mineira* (2002) by Cristiano Lima da Silva, "Senhores e pais: Reconhecimento de paternidade dos alforriados na pia batismal na Freguesia de Nossa Senhora do Pilar de São João del-Rei (1770–1850)"; Antônio Henrique Duarte Lacerda, "Economia cafeeira, crescimento populacional e manumissões onerosas e gratuitas condicionais em Juiz de Fora na segunda metade do século XIX."

74. Aside from Luna and Klein, *Slavery and the Economy of São Paulo*, chap. 7, see Herbert S. Klein and Clotilde Paiva, "Freedmen in a Slave Economy: Minas Gerais in 1831," *Journal of Social History* 29:4 (1996): 933–62; Frank, *Dutra's World*; João José Reis,"'The Revolution of the Ganhadores': Urban Labour, Ethnicity and the African Strike of 1857 in Bahia, Brazil," *Journal of Latin American Studies* 29:2 (1997): 355–93; Reis, *Domingos Sodré*, among other titles. A good summary of the recent literature is Russell-Wood, "Preface." See also, for the colonial era, Russell-Wood, *Slavery and Freedom*, esp. chaps. 3 and 4.

75. Along with the work of Libby cited above, see the essays by Marcelo Magalhães Godoy, "Uma província artesã: O universo social, econômico e demográfico dos artífices da Minas do oitocentos," *Anais do XII Encontro Nacional de Estudos Populacionais, ABEP* (2000): 1–34, and "Fazendas diversificadas, escravos polivalentes—caracterização sóciodemográfica e ocupacional dos trabalhadores cativos em unidades produtivas com atividades agroaçucareiras de Minas Gerais no século XIX," *Anais do XIV Encontro Nacional de Estudos Populacionais, ABEP* (2004): 1–23; Luiz Carlos Soares, "A escravidão industrial no Rio de Janeiro do século XIX," *Anais do VII Congresso Brasileiro de História Econômica, ABPHE* (2003): 1–27.

76. Aside from Bergad, *Slavery and the Demographic*, see Flávio Rabelo Versiani and José Raimundo Oliveira Vergolino, "Preços de escravos em Pernambuco no século XIX" (Brasilia: Universidade de Brasília, Departamento de Economia, Textos para discussão, Texto no. 252, October 2002); Kátia M. de Queirós Mattoso, Herbert S. Klein, and S. L. Engerman, "Trends and Patterns in the Prices of Manumitted Slaves: Bahia, 1819–1888," *Slavery & Abolition* 7:1 (1986): 59–67; Afonso de Alencastro Graça Filho, "As flutuações dos preços e as fazendas escravistas de São João del Rei no século XIX," *Anais do IX Seminário sobre a Economia Mineira* (2000): 147–78; the two essays by Luiz Paulo Ferreira Nogueról, "Preços de bois, de cavalos e de escravos em porto alegre e em Sabará no século XIX: Mercadorias de um mercado nacional em formação," *Anais do XI Seminário Sobre a Economia Mineira* (2004): 1–23; idem, "Mercado Regional de Escravos: Padrões de preços em Porto Alegre e em Sabará, no século XIX—elementos de nossa formação econômica e social," *Ensaios FEE*, Porto Alegre, 23, Número especial, 2002: 539–64; Carlos A. M. Lima, " Sobre preços de escravos com ofícios artesanais na cidade do Rio de Janeiro (1789–1839)," *Anais do III Congresso Brasileiro de História Econômica* (1999) (no page numbers); and the classic work by Carvalho de Mello, "The Economics of Labor in Brazilian Coffee Plantations, 1850–1888."

77. We should add that collections of essays and special issues of journals have been published, some of which we have already mentioned as sources for specific works. A few examples not mentioned before include: João José Reis, ed., *Escravidão e invenção da liberdade: Estudos sobre o negro no Brasil* (São Paulo: Brasiliense, 1988), with essays on slave treatment, baptism, manumission, and revolts in Bahia; François Crouzet and Denis Rolland, eds., *Pour l'histoire du Brésil: Mélanges oferts à Katia de Queirós Mattos* (Paris: L'Harmattan, 2000), Part iii on slave resistance, religion, ethnicity, slave trade, demography, freed people of color, abolition, and slave memory; Maria Beatriz Nizza da Silva, ed., *Brasil: Colonização e escravidão* (Rio de Janeiro: Nova Fronteira, 1999), with chapters on Indian slavery, slave family, daily life, resistance, religion, ethnicity, dress, work, manumission, and abolitionism; Manolo Florentino and Cacilda Machado, eds., *Ensaios sobre a escravidão I* (Belo Horizonte: UFMG, 2003), with essays on the slave trade, African religion in Portugal (16th–17th century), state and private violence also in Portugal, "management" of slaves, slave demography and hierarchies, slave rebellion and criminality, among others; special issues of *Estudos Econômicos* 13:1 (1983), on economics, labor, demography, trade, slave property, etc; *Estudos Econômicos* 17 (1987), on resistance; *Revista Brasileira de História* 8:16 (1988), on historiography, demography, family, religion, law; of *Estudos de História* 9:2 (2002), with articles on Atlantic and internal slave trade, size of slaveholding property, freed people, black militia, slave family, religion and crime. Journals such as *Estudos Afro-Asiáticos, Afro-Ásia, Topoi*, and *Tempo*, among others, regularly publish articles on slavery in Brazil.

CHAPTER 7

POSTCOLONIAL BRAZIL

BARBARA WEINSTEIN

The challenges of summarizing recent trends in the historiography of postcolonial (modern) Brazil are much greater today than they were a few decades ago. Interest in Brazil among North America- and Europe-based historians has grown steadily during the last twenty years, but far more impressive is the virtual explosion in the production of historical scholarship in Brazil itself. The fruit of the opening that accelerated the dissolution of the military regime and initiated Brazil's newest republic, as well as the dramatic expansion of university education that began, ironically, under military rule, this vastly larger historical profession, with its attendant PhD programs and armies of graduate students, has transformed the historiography of Brazil, both quantitatively and qualitatively. Meanwhile, increased attention to theory among North American historians and increased emphasis on archival research among Brazilian historians have erased many of the differences that once distinguished the North American historical corpus from the Brazilian scholarly production; intensified collaboration among historians regardless of geographic location has meant that to discuss Brazilian historiography today without due recognition of the research and publications of Brazilian historians of Brazil is simply impossible. Furthermore, within Brazil the historical profession has become increasingly decentralized, so that the metonymic relationship between Rio/São Paulo and the nation, sustained by the earlier concentration of research and scholarship in those academic locales, has been disrupted, and it would be a disservice to these important new trends to revert to using Rio/São Paulo as a shorthand for Brazil as a whole.

This essay should be treated as a portal into the rapidly expanding historiography of modern Brazil. It highlights the major nodes of discussion and debate among historians of Brazil over the last two decades, and describes how these debates have been shaped by broader shifts in the historical profession. Two themes frame this survey of the new historiographical trends for postcolonial Brazil. One is the impact of the linguistic or cultural turn on that historiography. As in the United States and Europe, the shift from social to cultural history as the ascendant mode of historical interpretation has had a profound effect on research and writing about Brazil. Moreover, many of the key (often French) theorists and historians associated with this turn—Michel Foucault, Pierre Bourdieu, Roger Chartier, Michel de Certeau—were being eagerly consumed by Brazilian scholars long before they became fashionable in the United States.[1] Slower to have an impact in the Brazilian historiography were the writings of the Subaltern Studies scholars and postcolonial theorists. This I would explain in two ways. First of all, the postcolonial anxiety about "provincializing Europe" has been of relatively little concern to Brazilian historians. On the contrary, an identification with European historical theory has allowed Brazilian scholars to deflect the imposition of North American modes of historical interpretation and research, to maintain autonomy from the North American academy, and to be more selective in their adoption of ideas and approaches from the Anglophone milieu. Whereas Dipesh Chakrabarty and other postcolonial theorists collapse North America and Western Europe into a single "hyperreal" Europe that is the dominant subject of history,[2] Brazilian historians have constructed their intellectual identities primarily in dialogue with continental European (as opposed to Anglophone) historical approaches.

Secondly, the notions of "popular liberalism" or "everyday forms of state formation" that have informed much of the recent Spanish American historiography (especially of Mexico, but also of Colombia, Argentina, and Cuba) have been slow to find a purchase in Brazilian historiography.[3] Given the deeply rooted and often quite accurate assumptions about Brazil's exclusionary and authoritarian politics, its heritage of slavery and violence, and the weight of patron-client relations on the one hand, and the presumed distance between the lives of elites and popular classes on the other, it has been unusually difficult for historians of Brazil to imagine liberalism as "popular" or to think of the popular classes as participating, directly or indirectly, in state formation. Even historical sociologist Sérgio Adorno, who acknowledges the "demands asserted by the popular classes during the decolonizing revolution and even in the course of the construction of the National State," nonetheless goes on to conclude that there was not the slightest echo of these demands in the academic milieu that produced the majority of Brazil's professional politicians and public actors.[4] Adorno does go further than most of the scholars of his generation by acknowledging the political manifestations of the poorer segments of Brazilian society, but he still situates them within a continuous narrative of defeat and/or marginalization.

These deeply ingrained assumptions have begun to shift as scholars have become increasingly attentive to evidence that Brazilian society in the nineteenth, and even into the twentieth, century was not simply a nation composed of a tiny, ever-powerful, and privileged white elite and a huge disenfranchised multicolored popular collectivity, with the two factions divided by a yawning chasm. Whether it be statistical evidence showing widespread slave ownership (including among some people of color), or documented instances of freepersons refusing to allow the public use of racist language (or even racial categories), or a fascinating anecdote about a slave-owning "spinster" from an aristocratic family having to ask one of her slaves to draw up a document because she was illiterate and he was not, or unexpectedly large turnouts for electoral contests, scholars have begun to rethink the trope of the "Two Brazils," an organizing concept that has proved remarkably durable, but hopefully not indestructible.

INVENTING THE NATION

The peculiar trajectory of Brazil in the immediate postindependence decades—the relatively peaceful transition from colony to nation, the installation of a constitutional monarchy rather than a republic, and the new nation's geographic cohesion (as opposed to the fragmentation of Spanish America)—continues to define the contours of the historiographical debates on this period. However, there has been considerable rethinking of the decades from the 1820s to the 1840s, and questioning of certain earlier suppositions about the political and social order that emerged with the break from Portugal. At least one major issue appears to be "settled" for the time being: the idea that "independence" was not a significant event or process has vanished as a serious scholarly proposition. Whereas historians writing in the 1960s and '70s emphasized the (economic) shift from colonialism to neocolonialism and the failure of independence to shake up the social order, recent research—influenced by the cultural turn and the historiography of the nation, political authority, and the public sphere—examines closely and seriously the various challenges posed by the transition from colony to nation.[5] This has meant a firm dismissal of Roberto Schwarz's claim, with reference to liberal ideologies in Brazil, that these "ideas were out of place." Rejecting this normative approach to nineteenth-century liberalism, historians have sought instead to understand how both elites and popular groups drew on traditional forms of honor, authority, and power, and new ideas about rights and citizenship, and adapted them to the particular circumstances of Brazil's transition to nationhood. Thus, for example, Kirsten Schultz has argued that the transfer of the court from Lisbon to Rio de Janeiro destabilized the symbols and hierarchies of Portuguese colonial rule; this did not destroy the legitimacy of the monarchy per se, but made its absolutist form increasingly untenable. In a similar vein, Iara Lis Carvalho Souza traces the way in which postcolonial rituals of rule during the reign of Dom Pedro I (1822–31) drew on premodern notions of the king's persona as the embodiment of empire. This representation of the empire, however, could not survive the increasing tensions and popular unrest of the postindependence decade, and gave way to a set of symbols and commemorations that disembodied the empire/nation. Here we can see a clear shift from the social history paradigm, with its attention to the causes of the emperor's abdication, to a cultural history paradigm more attentive to the shifts in the political culture that made it possible to imagine imperial politics without Dom Pedro I or the absolutist tendencies he represented.[6]

Whether from a social or cultural history perspective, a major trend in recent studies, and one that constitutes a break with the dominant views of an earlier historiography, is an emphasis on the subaltern as a *political* actor. Whereas most earlier works depicted a rigidly elitist political system that left no room for popular *political* action, thereby relegating collective protest to the realm of inchoate, prepolitical resistance, several recent historical works insist not only that popular groups (slaves, free laborers, foot soldiers, etc.) participated, even if informally, in public life, but that they were aware of the political events and ideological trends of that era, and were alert to the radical potential of certain liberal ideas. The rethinking of liberalism in nineteenth-century Brazil dates back to works such as Emilia Viotti da Costa's *The Brazilian Empire* and Alfredo Bosi's *A Dialética da Colonização*, but recent research has expanded the concept of politics and uncovered debates about rights and citizenship in previously unexamined spaces.[7] João José Reis, in his study of slave rebellion in Bahia, details the many acts of protest by underpaid soldiers or dissatisfied plebeians that paralleled various forms of slave protest. Hendrik Kraay, also writing about Bahia, includes a rich account of the social turbulence of the period from independence to the mid-1830s; Kraay's study explores the role of the military—both officers and lower ranks—in politics during the transition from colony to nation, and the importance of the army in creating a space for political activity by people of color. Gladys Ribeiro maps the conflicts between Portuguese and people of color in nineteenth-century Rio, and shows how these conflicts both reflected and induced tensions at other levels of Brazilian society. Ivana Stolze Lima traces the idea of Brazil as a "mixed" nation—in contrast to the Portuguese—back to the very earliest years following independence. Other works, such as those by Hebe Mattos and Keila Grinberg, highlight the presence of people of color, both "respectable" and plebeian, in public life and the important implications this had for the role of race in political discourse, especially with regard to slavery.[8]

This rethinking of the subaltern presence in the (informal) political arena has also provoked a reexamination of the regional uprisings that exploded throughout Brazil during the period of the Regency (1831–41). Revolts such as the Farroupilha, Balaiada, and Cabanagem had been seen either as failed attempts by elite liberals (in their more radical version, known as *exaltados*) to solidify greater provincial power, or as genuine acts of insurrection by popular groups quickly suppressed by fearful elites. Aspects of these interpretations endure, but now the emphasis is on the efforts by popular groups to incorporate their demands into the political discourses of the time rather than to smash the existing order. Even rebellious slaves sometimes adopted the language of liberalism, though the most famous slave rebels of this era—the so-called Malês of Bahia—articulated their protest within an "African" framework. Attention has also been paid to the way the writings of conservatives opposed to the changes (and the presumed disorder) these movements promoted created a delegitimizing memory of these insurrections as irrational outbreaks of violence. As for the rebel leadership, it is portrayed as wavering between accommodation with those in power and attempting to construct a genuinely different liberal/republican politics.[9]

To be sure, not all of the recent works on early nation building and imperial politics have adopted this perspective. Several studies emphasize the relative cohesion of imperial elites and the extremely weak popular presence in the imperial political system. Roderick Barman, in *Brazil: The Making of a Nation*, sees most of these uprisings as caused by a retrogressive preference for the local over the national, and he ultimately stresses the strength of the conservative impulse.[10] Perhaps most influential along these lines has been the work of José Murilo de Carvalho, whose *A construção da ordem* claims that the shared socialization of the first generation of elite politicians in the Portugal's University of Coimbra allowed for a degree of cooperation across regions that kept the nation intact and made stable forms of political rule more likely in Brazil than in the other newly independent nations. In this and subsequent work on imperial politics (e.g., *Teatro de sombras*), Murilo de Carvalho also contends that the capacity of the imperial administration to create a network of officials loyal in the first instance to the emperor rather than to the planter or merchant elites accounts for the relative stability of Brazilian politics in the nineteenth century.[11]

Contesting this view are two major studies of imperial politics that offer other explanations for the "stability" of imperial politics, especially after the brief experiment with partial decentralization of power under the regency ended with the precipitous crowning of Emperor Dom Pedro II in 1841. Richard Graham, in *Patronage and Politics in Nineteenth-Century Brazil*, disputes Murilo de Carvalho's claims about state autonomy under the emperor, arguing instead that regional economic elites were connected to politicians through elaborate webs of patronage. Graham argues as well that electoral participation in the early empire was more widespread than previously assumed, but that its democratizing potential was limited by the power of patronage networks to discipline voters. Indeed, Graham goes further than most students of patronage to argue that ideology was of little consequence in the empire because politicians typically decided whom to support based on personal ties, not ideological positions.[12] Ilmar Rohloff de Mattos, in *O tempo saquarema*, also disputes the elite socialization/imperial autonomy argument offered by Murilo de Carvalho, but from a very different perspective. Mattos claims that there were real disagreements among the various groups involved in imperial politics, and that the conservative turn in Brazilian politics after 1840 should be attributed to the successful machinations of a particular political faction, with considerable power in the court, from the province of Rio de Janeiro. Hence, the dominance of Conservatives in the Second Reign was due to the triumph of a particular regional oligarchy, which succeeded in imposing its political project and expunging the potentially democratic aspects of liberalism (especially the variety advocated by the *exaltados*), rather than the formation of a political system autonomous from the interests of elite factions.[13] With its critical emphasis on the role of a particular sociopolitical class in promoting antidemocratic hierarchies of wealth and authority, *O tempo saquarema* also differs sharply from subsequent work on Brazil's nineteenth-century Conservatives by Jeffrey Needell. In *The Party of Order*, Needell portrays that same political cohort as principled defenders of stability and parliamentary rule under the Empire, as against the supposedly anarchic and violent impulses of the Liberal Party and the patronage-based politics of the emperor's advisors. Needell goes so far as to contend that the coffee-planter Conservatives' opposition to the proposed Free Womb Law reflected their concern with constitutionalism rather than their stubborn commitment to slaveholding.[14]

Finally, the fashion for cultural history has moved historians to return to the question of the monarchy as a source of national unity and political order, but now with attention to the various symbols, rituals, spectacles, and texts produced by Brazil's "tropical monarchy." The massive study by historical anthropologist Lilia Moritz Schwarcz, *The Emperor's Beard*, has been a major contribution to the historiography of the culture of the Empire. Schwarcz traces the very deliberate efforts of the monarchy, during the reign of Dom Pedro II (1841–89), to craft a national identity that drew on European royal traditions while foregrounding certain symbols and motifs peculiar to Brazil, particularly those associated with a romanticized image of indigenous culture. Dom Pedro was a devoted patron of the Instituto Histórico e Geográfico Brasileiro, an institution whose principal mission was to construct a foundational historical narrative for the Brazilian nation. It quickly became a bastion of romantic-nationalist historical writing and "Indianist" literature.[15]

Slave Emancipation

No topic has seen more dramatic shifts in historical interpretation over the last two decades than slave emancipation. Whereas an earlier historiography emphasized either the activism of abolitionist leaders or a shift in structural economic conditions, most of the recent work sees slave emancipation as a result of popular mobilization and resistance to slavery by the slaves themselves. In addition, works by Murilo de Carvalho and George Reid Andrews cite the role of foreign pressure as well as the abolitionist inclinations of the emperor and his advisors (who supposedly were able to adopt this dissident position because of their "autonomy" from the planter class). Structural determinants have disappeared from the interpretive landscape, with most historians accepting the idea that slavery was not necessarily incompatible with various forms of agrarian modernization, and that abolition was primarily a political and social process.[16] At the same time, the erstwhile heroes of the narrative of slavery's decline and fall, the abolitionist leaders, have been charged with opposing slavery chiefly on racist grounds, proposing overly gradualist strategies, having excessively cozy relations with the planter class, or effacing the role of the enslaved in their own liberation.[17] Rejecting earlier assumptions about the slaves' incapacity to develop a political consciousness, historians such as Warren Dean,

Hebe M. Mattos, Maria Helena Machado, and Eduardo Silva have emphasized various ways in which slaves accelerated the process of abolition through massive desertions of the plantations and other "immediatist" strategies,[18] while others such as Keila Grinberg, Sidney Chalhoub, and Joseli de Mendonça have emphasized slaves' use of the courts, especially after the passage of the Free Womb Law (1871) and the Sexagenarian Law (1885), to contest their bondage and secure their freedom.[19] In the process historians have also considered the different meanings attributed to "liberty" in the tortuous course of slave emancipation.

The economics of slaveholding continues to influence interpretations of slave emancipation, though differently from an earlier literature. It is now generally agreed that slave ownership, until the mid-nineteenth century, was more widely distributed than previously recognized, both in the urban and rural economies. We also know, from the work of Roberto and Amílcar Martins, that fazendas in Minas Gerais outside the export sector depended upon large numbers of slave laborers throughout the nineteenth century. Moreover, even in the booming plantation regions, smallholders with a few slaves had a larger presence than previously assumed. A corollary of this—though resting largely on speculation—is that the shortage of slaves generated by the simultaneous boom in coffee production and the closing of the transatlantic slave trade in the 1850s redistributed slaveownership upward to the wealthiest landowners, thereby concentrating slaveholding for the first time among the plantation elite, who then found themselves increasingly isolated in their defense of slavery (or more accurately, their critique of abolition).[20]

Whereas "the impact of abolition" once meant its effect on different regional plantation economies, in recent work attention has shifted to the impact of emancipation on the former slaves themselves.[21] The opportunities and struggles that freedpersons confronted after 1888 varied considerably from region to region—though government indifference to their plight seems to have been quite uniform throughout Brazil. In urban centers such as Salvador and Rio, where slaves had long worked alongside free people of color, the transition to freedom often did not have a dramatic impact on the work processes or webs of sociability among *afrodescendentes*. Research by João Reis, Maria Cecília Velasco e Cruz, and Marcelo Badaró Mattos indicates some important continuities between forms of work organization that preceded abolition and forms of labor organizing and protest that followed it, disputing the view that labor militancy in Brazil sprung exclusively from European immigrant roots.[22] Kim Butler argues that the Afro-Bahian community, though excluded from regional political power, maintained African consciousness through cultural activities, especially the *candomblé* houses that would become so crucial to Afro-Brazilian cultural identity in general. She contrasts this with the black political consciousness expressed by former slaves in São Paulo, where the marginalizing effects of European immigration meant that blackness became a meaningful basis for political unity and activism.[23]

George Reid Andrews, in his study of Blacks in São Paulo, also emphasizes the marginalization of ex-slaves by the influx of European immigrants from the late 1880s on. At the same time, he effectively refutes Florestan Fernandes's thesis that slavery's damaging effects on the ex-slaves put them at a disadvantage vis-à-vis immigrants in the job market, arguing instead that racist preferences among employers for white workers, immigrant hiring networks, and the choices of the ex-slaves themselves were more crucial in excluding freedpersons from both established and new employment opportunities in the decades following abolition. Andrews's work and research by Maria Helena Machado (also on São Paulo) and Joan Bak (on Porto Alegre) indicate efforts by immigrant workers to exclude *afro-descendentes* from the workplace or newly formed worker associations.[24]

Abolition and the Fall of the Empire

One of the most durable issues in the historiography of postcolonial Brazil is the possible relationship (or lack thereof) between the abolition of slavery in May of 1888 and the overthrow of Dom Pedro II and installation of the First Republic in November of 1889. Given the proximity of these two major events, it is difficult to resist the temptation to see some cause-and-effect relationship, or some shared discursive tendency that explains the origins of both episodes. Perhaps most influential in reviving the notion that abolition helped provoke the collapse of the empire has been the work of Murilo de Carvalho, with its claim that the emperor and his advisors pressured the planter class to abolish slavery more rapidly than might have otherwise been the case (thereby earning the coffee planters' enmity). Richard Graham, in contrast, emphasizes the increasing tensions between the military (immediately responsible for the overthrow of the Empire) and Dom Pedro II. The republican movement, meanwhile, has been portrayed in much recent work not as a bulwark of progressive change but as hostage to the slavocratic coffee planters of São Paulo.[25] From this perspective, the overthrow of the empire is seen not so much as the close of an era of slavery and rigid hierarchies of wealth and prestige, but as the onset of a regime of intensified elite dominance (absent the supposedly restraining influence of the emperor's moderating power) and conservative modernization led by the burgeoning province of São Paulo.

The emergence of São Paulo and the decentralization of politics under the First Republic are typically seen as signs of a resurgent regionalism. The final decades of the empire witnessed not only the founding of a Republican Party (with federalism a major plank of its platform) but also mounting expressions of regional identity, in print and in politics, as Brazil's political and economic center of gravity shifted to the southeast. The pioneering studies of Love, Levine, and Wirth on regional politics in the Old Republic focused on the construction of regional networks of political influence among elites. Their research illuminated the workings of the First Republic, with its "politics of the governors" and political bossism (*coronelismo*), but devoted little space to regional identity beyond the sphere of elite politics.[26] Subsequent discussions of regionalism have placed more emphasis on the relationship between socioeconomic structures, regional economic trajectories, and the assertion of political power at the national level. My own study of the Amazon rubber boom traces the rise of support among liberals in the province of Pará for a more decentralized political system that would allow their home region greater autonomy and control over fiscal resources.[27] The latest studies of regionalism—predictably influenced by the cultural turn—have looked at the process of regional identity construction, the circulation of elite and popular notions of regional culture, and the tension involved in forming an identity that is regionally distinctive yet compatible with some (unstable and contested) notion of *brasilidade*. Most significantly, rather than seeing region and nation as counterposed, they have emphasized the relationship between regionalism and the process of nation building. Judy Bieber's study of Minas Gerais, for example, reveals the "ethnographic" work that produced a notion of *mineiro* identity under the Empire. Also notable is Durval Muniz de Albuquerque's *A invenção do Nordeste e outras artes*, where he traces the construction, through literary and print materials, of a region—the Northeast—that is portrayed as uniform in its misery and backwardness despite the enormous variations in regional social structure, economy, ethnicity, and topography.[28]

Not the Republic of Their Dreams

Recent works on the early decades of republican rule highlight the violent and repressive responses of the new republican power elites to the scattered instances of popular insurgency and political dissidence.[29] Most infamous is the case of Canudos, the millenarian community in the interior of Bahia that resisted repeated incursions by federal troops, only to be crushed and most of its residents massacred in 1897. Though criticism of the republican government's overreaction to the threat represented by Canudos dates back to Euclides da Cunha's classic chronicle of this clash between a modernizing state and a backlands community, *Os sertões*, more recent interpretations have been even harsher in their judgments of the newly installed republican regime. Robert Levine, in *Vale of Tears*, constructs a very different image of Canudos from the Euclidean view, portraying the community as a rational response to hardships posed by conditions in the Northeast and insisting that the preachings of Antonio Conselheiro, Canudos's charismatic leader (depicted by Euclides as a madman), were well within the strictures of Catholic doctrine. From Levine's perspective, the "threat" posed by Canudos was entirely invented by a republican regime irrationally fearful of political dissent. In contrast, Marco Antonio Villa portrays Canudos as a genuine social movement with revolutionary potential, crushed by a regime eager to protect its conservative/authoritarian vision of Brazil's future.[30]

The less famous War of the Maragatos, set in the far south of Brazil, has received innovative treatment from John Chasteen in his *Heroes on Horseback*. This insurgency, led by remnants of the regional elite displaced by the new urban-based republicans in Rio Grande do Sul, drew widespread support from the popular classes, mobilized by the charismatic caudillo Gumercindo Saraiva. Using the methods of the new cultural history, Chasteen demonstrates how caudillo and followers constructed a politically meaningful relationship that, despite its personalistic tendencies, reflected common values and cultural norms that could be translated into political allegiances. Chasteen's analysis is also distinguished by its attention to the border region and the role it played in constructions of the nation on both the Brazilian and the Uruguayan sides, thereby challenging a view that national identification tends to weaken as one moves away from the alleged "center" of the nation.[31]

Though much briefer and less bloody than either of the above-mentioned revolts, the 1904 Revolt against the Vaccine in Rio has attracted a remarkable amount of attention from historians, probably because it provides a perfect context in which to explore tensions produced by the modernizing republican regime. Indeed, the literature on this episode forms a microcosm of the new developments in the field of history over the last twenty years. Teresa Meade, working within a Thompsonian social history framework, portrays the revolt as part of a larger series of struggles against urban renewal (which ejected the poorer residents of Rio from the city center) and emphasizes the role of labor leaders and an incipient working class in the protests. Murilo de Carvalho highlights the leadership of positivist republicans who opposed obligatory vaccination and successfully employed gendered and moralizing images of honor and the sanctity of the home to rally popular support. Like Meade, he highlights an "urban renewal" program insensitive to the needs of the poor as a cause of the protest, though he emphasizes the new sanitary regime's incompatibility with daily social and cultural practices rather than the challenge of socioeconomic change. Nicolau Sevcenko, in a lyrical but overheated account of the revolt (which left twenty-three dead—not an insignificant body count, but not one of the twentieth century's major tragedies), attempts to reinject an element of the irrational, portraying the carioca poor as driven to revolt "against history" by the misery and oppressiveness of their circumstances. Jeffrey Needell's work introduces the element of race, citing the repression of Afro-Brazilian culture as a major cause of popular unrest. Most recently, Sidney Chalhoub has insightfully noted that all these explanations start from the premise that the problem was not actually the vaccine, but that the issue of mandatory vaccination condensed other resentments and became the lightning rod for more general forms of discontent. Chalhoub argues that the vaccine was not just a metaphor for other controversies percolating within the popular classes but was an issue in and of itself. In his revisionist interpretation, he recuperates a long history of alternative medical forms of immunization, possibly derived from African practices, and a popular tradition of questioning the newer forms of smallpox vaccination.[32]

Urban Culture and Society through the Early Twentieth Century

Although the coffee economy of the *fluminense* (Rio de Janeiro province) hinterland—plagued by overcultivation and soil erosion—would be in decline for much of the second half of the nineteenth century, its port city and commercial center, Rio de Janeiro, the imperial court and then republican capital, would remain Brazil's premier city and cultural hub for this entire period. One consequence of the shift away from social and economic history toward an emphasis on culture, both elite and popular, has been an intensified interest in the culture and politics of the city at the turn of the nineteenth century—even though it would be many decades before Brazil would cease to be a predominantly agrarian nation.

Unlike Argentina, where a strong conservative/nationalist tradition persistently portrayed the countryside as the heartland of the nation and Buenos Aires as a fragment of foreignness lodged in that nation's heart, Brazilian intellectuals, past and present, have tended to distinguish between the city of the elite and the city of the popular classes, rather than constructing a dichotomy of urban versus rural. To be sure, there is a tradition of critiquing the elites for their often superficial imitation of European styles and trends—thus the famous phrase "for the English to see." But it has been more common (as in the Revolt against the Vaccine) to cite the tensions and conflicts between privileged groups yearning for modernity and security in the urban milieu and the struggles of popular groups, especially people of color, for physical and cultural space, for resources, and for freedom from the repressive arm of the municipal government.[33] At the same time, the most recent studies of the city have emphasized not just the conflicts but also the connections between elite and popular urban culture. They have eschewed both the "social control" approach, which portrayed festivities such as carnival as a version of "bread and circuses," and an overly essentialized notion of what constitutes resistance or subversion. Studies of popular festivals (including carnival) and religious practices, such as Martha de Abreu Esteves's *O império do divino*, presume interaction between plebeian groups and church authorities, and see popular forms of religious expression as crucial markers of identity and community, but not necessarily as instruments of resistance, whether conscious or unconscious.[34]

Several recent books—such as those by Nicolau Sevcenko and Jeffrey Needell—refer to Rio's "Belle Époque." The references to this period, which Needell fixes as 1898 to 1914, and the use of this phrase typically have a slightly ironic quality. Sevcenko titles a chapter "Brazil's compulsory insertion into the Belle Époque," and Needell dates the beginning of this era from the consolidation of *paulista* domination of the new republic and the subsequent marginalization of more popular and inclusive political and cultural projects.[35] The 1890s were, for the most part, a period of continuous unrest, with political and social challenges ranging from Canudos and the War of the Maragatos to struggles between the military/positivist republicans and the so-called oligarchies of São Paulo and Minas for power in the new republican regime. It was also a period of economic instability, with the Encilhamento—an 1891 episode of unrestrained financial speculation caused by new government policies—being the most dramatic example of this.[36] In contrast, the period following the *paulistas*' accession to power is seen as an era of elite political and economic consolidation, accompanied (in Rio, and on a lesser scale, in other cities such as Belém and Porto Alegre) by concerted efforts at civic beautification and cultural "elevation"—in other words, the Europeanization of urban life.[37] Sevcenko contrasts this era (unfavorably) with the 1820s, when elites concerned with constructing a specifically Brazilian identity embraced indigenous cultural and linguistic influences (or at least their notion of them), whereas he portrays carioca elites and middling groups in the early 1900s as distancing themselves as much as possible from the rural, the indigenous, and, above all, the African in Brazilian society. At the same time, he emphasizes the turn to realism in the work of two major writers of the era, Euclides da Cunha and Lima Barreto, who sought to use their literary production as an instrument of social reform.[38]

Behind the veneer of modernity and European manners lurked another urban milieu, this one marked by substandard housing (whether it be the *cortiços* of Rio and São Paulo or the *mocambos*, swollen with drought victims, of Recife), unstable employment patterns (including forms of petty criminality and prostitution), and vibrant religious and cultural practices that vigorously defied elite attempts at Europeanization.[39] Indeed, recent studies have begun to note a degree of elite ambivalence, even desire, with regard to this resilient popular culture, and increasingly emphasize the circulation of cultural images between elite and popular contexts. Meanwhile, though the poor may have struggled to maintain their own cultural traditions, they were by no means immune to the appeal of the new styles and tastes being disseminated by popular magazines or the mushrooming movie theaters. And many journalists and writers expressed *saudades* for an older, often idealized, Rio that was less modern and disciplined than the early-twentieth-century version. Sueann Caulfield, in her fascinating discussion of Rio's cosmetic preparations for the visit of King Albert and Queen Elizabeth of Belgium, notes the controversy that emerged over the music that would accompany the festivities, with some influential figures pressing for a more "Brazilian" musical program.[40] To be sure, moving into the 1920s, a period of renewed nationalist sentiment and organizing, this reassertion of *brasilidade* among elites becomes more apparent, with Hermano Vianna's *The Mystery of Samba* citing a 1926 encounter between intellectuals (among them Gilberto Freyre) and samba musicians in Rio as the originating point for Brazil's discourse of "racial democracy." Bryan McCann and Carlos Sandroni similarly explore the mainstreaming of samba as a crucial element of Brazilian national identity in the 1930s.[41]

Race, Gender, and Nation

Race and racism are issues that have been central to the historiography of Brazil in virtually every time period and sociopolitical context. As recent works have noted, Brazil's status as a country with a racially diverse or "mixed" population served, early on, as a source of concern for political elites regarding the viability of the new Brazilian nation and as a resource for constructing a national identity distinctive from that of the European colonizers. While evidence of racial discrimination based on skin color or descent is everywhere in Brazilian society throughout its history, so is the affirmation, by members of both the popular and dominant classes, that such discrimination is somehow un-Brazilian. Historians struggle with the slipperiness of race as a category of identity in Brazil and the persistent distance between discourses of racial tolerance and everyday practices of racial discrimination.

One ongoing theme in the historical literature that has been a focal point of considerable discussion is the "myth" or discourse of racial democracy—its origins and its impact. Several historians have traced elements of this discourse to the immediate postindependence period, not only as a component of a new national identity but as part of the struggle to produce a color-blind approach to citizenship and political rights by free men of color who had a presence in the public sphere. Keila Grinberg and Hebe Mattos examine efforts by political actors of color to insist on a nonracialized justification for slavery (indicating that opposition to racism did not automatically imply opposition to African slavery). João Reis's research in Bahia demonstrates that the most meaningful dividing line in Bahian society in the decades following independence was Brazilian/African, not white/nonwhite or even free/slave.[42] In other words, race (meaning variously skin color, descent, or appearance) rarely operated alone as an indicator of ascribed status or self-perception. Even the classic addition of class to race does not exhaust the range of possible affinities and differences.

From the mid-nineteenth century on, the struggle for emancipation also generated new claims and concerns about racial identity. Focusing on the popular roots of the discourse of racial democracy, Hebe Mattos notes that in the course of the process of emancipation, newly freed slaves avoided calling themselves "*preto*"— black—not because of a desire to whiten themselves, but because they regarded the term "black" as applying only to those still enslaved, whereas these *libertos* were joining the now numerically preponderant population that was neither white (i.e., European) or "black" (i.e., African/enslaved). Thus, one of the foundational ideas of racial democracy—that citizens of any color were "Brazilians" first and foremost— was a positive source of identity in an era of emancipation.[43]

Other authors, focused on the racial discourses of elites (including both abolitionists and slavery's shrinking pool of defenders), have revealed the anxieties expressed by these segments of Brazilian society at the prospect of a nation without slavery, and without the "constraints" on the poor and the people of color that elites in a slave society enjoyed.[44] These fears and concerns were magnified by the timing of abolition—Brazil was gradually dismantling the institution of slavery precisely at a time when, among scientists and intellectuals in Europe and North America (and Latin America), the term "race" was taking on what some would describe as its modern meaning, and intellectuals and authorities of various sorts were using and abusing new forms of scientific knowledge and expertise to construct theories of racial determinism. All of this was made even more ominous by the enthusiasm with which Europeans in the second half of the nineteenth century went about carving up the world into colonies inhabited by those presumed to be "racially inferior." Thomas Skidmore, in his book *Black into White*, recounts the various strategies being debated and proposed in the final decades of the nineteenth century for the "whitening" of Brazilian society, and Jeffrey Lesser details the continuing opposition to Chinese immigration.[45] In a somewhat different vein, Lilia M. Schwarcz chronicles the rise of "scientific racial" thinking in Brazil during the same time period, looking at how incipient scientific institutions and museums adopted the ideas emanating from Europe about race and racial "types." Schwarcz does note, however, that Brazilian adepts of scientific-racialist thinking from the outset adapted these "European" ideas to the circumstances of a nation with a large population of color, generally expressing a more "optimistic" view of race and acculturation.[46] This argument is foreshadowed in Julyan Peard's *Race, Place, and Medicine*, about Bahia's "*tropicalista*" school of medical research. It is further elaborated in Nancy Stepan's important study "*The Hour of Eugenics*," in which she argues that eugenic discourse in Brazil, as elsewhere in Latin America, was based on a Lamarckian view of evolution that allowed for environmental change rather than genetic determinism, and therefore could advocate "positive" eugenic policies that called for better hygiene and sanitation.[47]

Other studies have sought to understand (or demonstrate) how racism operated in a society that disavowed racial discrimination, at least in the strictly legal sense, and in which publicized instances of explicit racial prejudice often provoked cries of outrage from all quarters. Andrews focuses on the exclusion of Blacks from the more stable forms of employment in São Paulo (city and state), though he does conclude that the industrial workforce gradually became more racially diverse from the 1930s on. Still, he goes perhaps the farthest in arguing that racial discrimination in Brazil is a matter of black and white, with the supposedly "intermediate" mulattos or *pardos* being excluded from most of the privileges of whiteness. In using statistics to advocate a unified racial identity for people of color, Andrews's study takes its cues from the field of social history—it is about social actors whom he defines as Black, rather than about race as a shifting historical and analytical category.[48]

In contrast, much of the recent scholarship is about *race* rather than about fixed categories of racially defined historical actors. A number of historians and anthropologists—most influential here would be the work of Olívia Gomes da Cunha—have emphasized the way in which new scientific categories, languages, and methods created policies on hygiene, criminality, juvenile reform, among others, that were profoundly engaged with assumptions about the relationship between race and behavior—without necessarily making that engagement overt.

Often reflecting the influence of Michel Foucault, these scholars assert that the modernizing state, far from eroding scientific-racialist discourses, institutionalized race as a category of scientific analysis. Looking at the other side of the question—how the valorization of whiteness leads to the devaluation of blackness—Jerry Dávila examines the way in which educators in the first half of the twentieth century constructed an educational policy with the intent of culturally whitening Brazil through education.[49]

Just as the last twenty years have seen a shift from an emphasis on the social history of Black Brazilians (or to use the more contemporary term, *afro-descendentes*) to a discussion of how race itself operates as a historical category, producing difference, hierarchy, and conflict, a similar process has occurred with the shift from the history of women to the study of gender. Pioneering works of women's history, such as Maria Odila Leite da Silva Dias's study of poor women in nineteenth-century São Paulo, June Hahner's chronicle of the struggle for female suffrage, or Miriam Moreira Leite's biographical account of the radical feminist Maria Lacerda de Moura, took the category of woman, its meaning, and the disadvantages it entailed as givens.[50] In contrast, Susan Besse's influential study, *Restructuring Patriarchy*, begins to consider gender and gender roles as historically unstable and shifting; she argues for an enduring patriarchal order in Brazilian society, but one that shifts away from the family-based power of the father to the modernized patriarchy of the state. Similarly, Margareth Rago's *Do cabaré ao lar* shifts the discussion of working-class women in São Paulo away from quantitative studies of their employment patterns and working conditions to the question of sexuality and women's increasing presence in public spaces.[51]

The most innovative recent research on gender has been particularly interested in issues of sexuality, proper femininity/masculinity, honor, and social control. Cristiana Schettini Pereira's study of prostitution in early republican Rio explores the ways in which these "public women" asserted their right to control their own bodies and struggled to maintain access to the increasingly policed spaces of urban geography.[52] In works that examine court cases and other discussions of "fallen women" in consecutive eras of the First Republic, Martha Abreu and Sueann Caulfield use the legal and juridical literature on "deflowering" to investigate the changing images of plebeian or working-class women, the claims of these women to be treated as honorable citizens, and the changing legal definitions of honor and sexuality. Caulfield is particularly bold in delving into the ramifications of her research, which examines poor families' attempts to legally coerce a seducer into treating a "ruined" daughter honorably. She uses this documentation to explore leading jurists' evolving legal arguments and how these reflect the tensions created by the emergence of modern gender roles. Going even further, she links the efforts to define the woman deserving of honorable treatment to concerns over constructing an identity for Brazil as an honorable nation. In a similar vein, Peter Beattie uses the concept of honorable masculinity to trace shifting attitudes and discourses about military recruitment and service, and the circumstances under which such service might be regarded as a source of honor or dishonor. His study provides a particularly interesting window on the changing meanings of national identity and citizenship from the mid-nineteenth century to the end of World War II.[53]

Beattie's discussion of same-sex intercourse in the barracks, and its role in creating an image of military service as unsavory or dishonorable, contributes to a small but growing historical literature on gay and lesbian (or nonheteronormative) sexuality. Luiz Mott has produced a number of pioneering topics on this theme, but by far the most influential study is James N. Green's *Beyond Carnival*. In the same vein as Beattie's discussion of nonnormative intercourse in the military, Green discusses the process by which the notion of a "homosexual" was constructed in the press, in the medical journals, and in the very practices of gay men, who gradually constructed self-images that defied traditional notions of dominant and passive partners (with only the latter being considered, at the time, the true "deviants"). Green then traces the formation of a gay subculture, especially in Rio de Janeiro, and the spaces that gay men managed to carve out for themselves, not only on the margins of carioca society but also in the very heart of carnival celebrations, even under the military regime.[54]

São Paulo: Region and Nation

The beginning of Rio's "Belle Époque," ironically, coincided with the consolidation of the *paulista* elite's dominance in the political and economic spheres, and the spectacular expansion of the city of São Paulo, which would in short order emerge as Brazil's largest and most dynamic urban center. Not surprisingly, the foundational texts for the history of São Paulo (city and state) sought to understand how this colonial backwater could be so rapidly transformed into the most dynamic agro-exporting region of Brazil and then, defying the archetypal Brazilian boom-bust cycle, go on to become South America's leading industrial center. These books—Emilia V. da Costa's *Da senzala à colonia*, Warren Dean's *The Industrialization of São Paulo* and *Rio Claro*, Wilson Cano's *Raízes da concentração industrial em São Paulo*, Boris Fausto's *Trabalho urbano e conflito social*, Joseph Love's *São Paulo in the Brazilian Federation*—simultaneously examined the process by which São Paulo emerged as Brazil's dominant economic and political center and illuminated the uneven distribution of power and resources that resulted from this unrestrained "progress."[55]

The large and diverse historiography that has appeared over the last two decades has shifted away from explaining São Paulo's exceptionalism (itself increasingly regarded as a problematic construct), and has either focused instead on social history topics such as immigration, labor movements, and criminality or has taken up the question of how politicians, journalists, artists, and intellectuals in this burgeoning urban center constructed an identity that explained and endorsed what contemporaries saw as São Paulo's special position within the Brazilian union. With regard to immigration, the dominant image continues to be that of the Europeans as "*brava gente*"—a courageous and combative community that organized strikes, formed unions, and actively resisted exploitation by *fazendeiros* and factory owners (many of the latter being immigrants as well).⁵⁶ But as early as 1980, Thomas Holloway was arguing that many Italian immigrants experienced considerable social mobility and succeeded in becoming small-scale coffee planters.⁵⁷ Mauricio Font even went so far as to claim that these small immigrant planters became the backbone of the Paulista Republican Party by the late 1920s, though there is considerable disagreement on that matter.⁵⁸ Jeffrey Lesser has provided us with vivid accounts of the experiences of non-European immigrants to São Paulo (especially Japanese and Syro-Lebanese), who could not easily assimilate into a "white" *paulista* middle class and who faced continuous pressures for cultural assimilation from political elites who feared the formation of "ethnic cysts" in the Brazilian body politic.⁵⁹ Still other research—including work by George Reid Andrews and Maria Helena Machado—raises the issue of the tense relationship between the European immigrant communities and the "native" Brazilian workers (with the latter often being portrayed by the immigrant press as either abusive cops or strikebreakers, rather than comrades in struggle).⁶⁰

Despite the many new studies that have appeared on the *paulista* labor movement, the themes and interpretations that have defined the historiography of early working-class life and activism have remained relatively stable over the last twenty years. But some new questions and assumptions have been introduced. The first wave of historiography, which only slowly absorbed the influence of Thompsonian social history, portrayed the labor movement in one of two ways: either as split between highly ideological and class-conscious anarchist leadership and a largely apolitical but intermittently galvanized rank and file, or as a largely undifferentiated militant/class-conscious collectivity often pushed in inappropriate directions by a leadership somewhat divorced from the day-to-day interests of the working class.⁶¹ The more complex, less a priori approaches to consciousness (now more often called "identity") that emerged first under the influence of E. P. Thompson and the centrality of "experience," and then as a result of the linguistic turn, have moved historians to go beyond these dichotomous views of the leadership and rank and file, and to go outside the workplace to understand working-class politics and culture. This has meant more attention to issues such as forms of recreation and religious devotion and the search for housing and sexual respectability. Within the factory, it has meant more attention to hierarchies of skill, gender, and race/ethnicity that make it increasingly difficult to talk about a homogeneous working-class identity.⁶² It has also meant going beyond the familiar locales of industrializing Rio and São Paulo to, for example, a massive textile plant in the Northeast.⁶³ Finally, it has meant taking more seriously elite and middle-class initiatives to promote solutions to the "social question" other than police repression, and workers' involvement in political organizations and movements previously regarded as entirely foreign to the working-class experience.⁶⁴ This has also placed in question the long-standing assumption that the pre-1930s labor movement was highly autonomous and ideological and faced unrelenting repression from the authorities, whereas the post-1930s labor movement was coopted into the state's corporatist/populist project and hence was short on ideology and militancy. John French's study of working-class militancy and populist politics in the industrial suburbs of São Paulo has been a particularly influential contribution in this regard.[65]

The other major trend in the historiography of São Paulo during these decades addresses a set of questions related to the political, cultural, and intellectual history of the region more germane to the attitudes and activities of the political and cultural elites. First, there has been a series of challenges to the very idea of a unitary *paulista* oligarchy with its core in the coffee-planting elite. As far back as Warren Dean's *Industrialization of São Paulo*, historians have been arguing against a sharp distinction between planter class and emerging industrial bourgeoisie, and over recent decades there has been a general agreement that the Paulista Republican Party, far from remaining the redoubt of the rural oligarchy, became increasingly urban-based, with a growing middle-class constituency, and with urban merchants and industrialists playing an ever more prominent role in the direction of the party. Some have gone so far as to argue that the declining coffee planters, resentful of their marginalization within the PRP, migrated to the only "mainstream" opposition party of the Old Republic, the Partido Democrático, but this view has been widely disputed. Conversely, Edgar de Decca has contended that the *paulista* elites, regardless of specific political affiliation, shared a commitment to a bourgeois project of industrialization by the 1920s.[66]

Closely related to this is a rethinking of the political ideologies of the era, and the particular forms that liberal discourse took in early twentieth-century São Paulo. For the most part, the emphasis is on the limits of *paulista* liberalism, with its strongly elitist bent and its tendency to advocate decentralization only to the extent that São Paulo maintained its hegemonic position within the union. Historians have certainly discerned variations in liberal thinking, with the Partido Democrático being the most explicit alternative to the politically dominant PRP. Maria Lígia Prado sharply revised our image of the PD by moving the discussion away from previous attempts to draw a direct connection between the socioeconomic composition of the party and its political platform toward an emphasis on the party's reformist orientation as an alternative elite project (though one limited in its impact and appeal by the reluctance of even reformist elites in São Paulo to mobilize the popular classes).[67] Prado and others have used the many newspapers published in São Paulo as crucial primary sources, while some historians have made the press their specific object of inquiry. Despite the robust state of newspaper journalism in this era, with at least a dozen mainstream dailies being published along with more ephemeral popular and working-class publications, these are rarely portrayed as forming the basis for a bourgeois public sphere.[68] This perspective may begin to change with the publication of James Woodard's *A Place in Politics*, which makes the case for a much more robust political sector, and more extensive grass-roots engagement with Republican Party politics than previously recognized.[69]

Again, in most existing studies, the emphasis continues to be on the limits of liberal discourse, with the mainstream press expressing anxiety and fear about changing gender roles, the growing urban working class, and the menace of radical foreign ideologies. Nationalism becomes a more common political idiom in the 1920s, but serious political reform is never imagined as involving a radical break with the past, and journalists were more likely to bemoan the unfitness of the average Brazilian for the exercise of full citizenship rights than to see the "masses" as a source of political renovation. Indeed, the only two serious challenges to the existing republican order in the 1920s came from military revolts—led by young reformist/nationalist officers (*tenentes*)—that elicited considerable support among São Paulo's new middle class and more reform-minded elites, but stopped short of explicitly rallying the masses to their cause.[70] And the one homegrown "revolutionary" movement with a mass following, the Constitutionalist Revolution of 1932, had neither radical nor democratic goals.[71]

This historiography, with its appreciation of the fluidity of the relationship between economic interests and political projects, represents a major shift away from the more rigidly structuralist approach to history that defined much of the earlier scholarship. It continues to rely, however, on a set of assumptions about the defects of Brazilian/*paulista* liberalism to explain the glacial pace of real social change. Whether due to a faulty liberal tradition or the lingering influence of an authoritarian slavocratic society, elites, and even middle-class groups, are portrayed as ultimately failing to adopt a genuinely enlightened approach to a range of issues, whether popular participation in politics, improved standards of living, or economic development. Yet this moves me to ask two questions: first, defective compared to whom? Implicit in the critique of the *paulista* "liberals" is an assumption that elsewhere more enlightened elites were constructing hegemonic positions around a project genuinely concerned with popular standards of living and broad-based political participation. But to the extent that this might be the case (though I think the instances are few in number), it is a result of specific political struggles (often aided by catastrophic international conflicts), not of elite disposition. The other is whether we can explain the political discourse of the *paulista* elites in terms of the residues of the past, as remnants of a traditional Brazilian society, or as emerging from a new identity associated with a particular view of modernity. In this vein, there have been a series of important studies that illuminate the construction of *paulista* identity during the First Republic and demonstrate the way in which intellectuals and politicians during those years reconfigured the history and trajectory of São Paulo to explain their region's apparent aptitude for modernity. These include Antonio Celso Ferreira's insightful discussion of the construction of the *bandeirante* myth and Tania de Luca's excellent analysis of the *Revista do Brasil*, a journal published in São Paulo in the early 1920s. De Luca's study is especially interesting for its attention to the way *paulistas* in that era married regionalism with an emergent nationalism.[72]

In a similar vein, there has been increasing attention from historians and historically minded social scientists to the artistic and intellectual milieu of São Paulo in this era, and specifically the role of the modernists (artists, poets, polemicists) in the construction of *paulista* identity and the reinvention of São Paulo city. Until the famed Modern Art Week of 1922, São Paulo had languished far behind Rio with regard to cultural capital; thereafter, regional spokesmen would claim that *paulistas* were in the front ranks of artistic innovation as well as economic and social progress. Though the modernists themselves liked to emphasize the outraged response to their work, meant to skewer the self-satisfied bourgeoisie of urban São Paulo, they were for the most part well patronized and well connected to the regional elite, and many of the writers were also journalists for mainstream publications. Indeed, far from puncturing São Paulo's inflated image of itself, the modernists typically fed regional chauvinism with their paeans to modernity and a *"verde-amarelismo"* (named for the colors of the Brazilian flag) that asserted patriotism while, as Tania de Luca notes, conflating São Paulo with the nation.[73]

The "Crisis" of the 1920s and the "Revolution" of 1930

The repeated use of the hedging quotation marks in the section heading above indicates the extent to which recent historiography has challenged long-standing assumptions and periodizations of twentieth-century Brazilian history. Until recently, historians wrote (with few dissenting opinions) as if there were an evident and growing crisis of liberalism in Brazilian society and politics from the proclamation of the republic on, and that the pace of this crisis accelerated sharply in the 1920s, making the Revolution of 1930, and its supposed rupture with the liberal-oligarchic past, virtually inevitable. Whether or not the 1930 seizure of power by Getúlio Vargas and his *tenente* allies constituted a "bourgeois revolution" in the Marxist sense was a matter for debate, but its status as a moment of rupture with the past went largely unquestioned.[74]

Over the last twenty-five years, however, historians writing from a wide range of perspectives have challenged various components of this dominant scenario, including the teleological notion of an unfolding crisis of oligarchic liberalism that reached its apogee in the late 1920s. To be sure, the 1920s could be characterized as a turbulent decade, considering the *tenente* revolts, intermittent urban unrest, agitation for women's suffrage, the increasing interregional tensions, the instability of the economy, and the impact of the onset of the Great Depression. But our tendency to see these events, collectively, as amounting to a crisis of a certain variant of liberalism is the result of ideological work, not some inevitable and transparent historical process. In effect, historians had largely accepted a metahistorical narrative—and one that I still think can be, in certain respects, quite useful—within which shifts in economic and social structure produce pressures for "real" political change, and if such changes do not occur, a crisis of legitimacy results and a revolution occurs. The primary and most obvious strategy for questioning this historical logic is to argue that the Revolution of 1930, in fact, produced little "real" political and social change, or, following Edgar de Decca, was not a revolution at all. The other is to highlight the extent to which some significant and substantial changes had already occurred prior to 1930 (with some historians combining both arguments).[75]

Much of the scholarship published in the 1980s and early 1990s—when the most recent military dictatorship (also dubbed a "revolution" by its leadership) was still fresh in historians' minds—sought to challenge the *getulista* discourse of rupture with the past. Susan Besse acknowledged that the Vargas regime did seek to modernize gender relations, but noted that many of the key concepts related to such a modernizing project had already been articulated and advocated prior to the revolution. Furthermore, her ultimate point was that this "modernization" resulted in the restructuring, rather than undermining, of patriarchy.[76] A new school of labor historians, many of them connected to the University of Campinas, vigorously criticized the claim that Vargas's policies had benefited and empowered workers, arguing instead that the state-controlled union system, and the attendant labor legislation, merely strengthened the hand of the industrial bourgeoisie.[77] As for the agrarian oligarchy that Vargas had supposedly displaced from power, historians asserted that industrialization was already widely embraced by elite and middle-class Brazilians prior to 1930; some historians even went so far as to claim that Vargas, at least initially, had been anti-industrialization.[78] In effect, these studies (with widely varying degrees of subtlety and sophistication) denied that there had been significant social and political change, and argued instead for continuity. To the extent that change had occurred, it involved strengthening of the role of the state, but for the purpose of reproducing the existing social order and "modernizing" the forms of worker discipline and social control. By extension, the military regime that had just finished its twenty-one-year rule in 1985, with its exaltation of the "strong state" and its disdainful attitude toward civil liberties, was the heir apparent of the 1930 Revolution.[79]

This wave of critical scholarship, however, rapidly exhausted its capacity to illuminate the impact of the political events of the early 1930s. First of all, its very critique of the use of the word "revolution" came into question in the wake of the linguistic turn. Not that new cultural historians would unproblematically accept the term "revolution," but they would argue that the meaning or referents of the term were neither fixed nor stable, and its "legitimate" use would always be an effect of power. In other words, there was no single historically sound definition of "revolution." In a sense, this provides a way out of the change-versus-continuity impasse, as historians begin to consider how the early Vargas regime altered the political landscape in terms of the meanings, expectations, and possibilities for political discourse and demands among those with access to the political arena (itself an unstable entity whose parameters expanded and contracted at different points in his regime). Departing from the earlier emphasis on cooptation versus repression, works by John French, Angela de Castro Gomes, Jorge Ferreira, Fernando Teixeira da Silva, Seth Garfield, and Cliff Welch indicate how workers and other subaltern groups appropriated the populist language and the legal innovations of the Vargas era to press their claims for material benefits and to rethink their roles and rights as Brazilian citizens.[80] Having been largely excluded from even symbolic participation in the formal political sphere of the Old Republic, large segments of the popular classes welcomed Vargas's efforts at mass mobilization, even if contained and controlled (Vargas himself portrayed their new circumstances as the result of an "*outorga*"—rights benevolently granted to workers by his regime, and not the fruit of their own struggles). Sueann Caulfield closes her important study of gender and honor in early twentieth-century Rio with a discussion of a letter written to Getúlio Vargas by a woman of very modest means. In the letter, she called upon Vargas to force a man who had promised to marry her to honor his pledge. She felt entitled to make this request because, as a worker, she was an honorable citizen and deserved to be treated honorably—a leap of logic she was unlikely to have made before the Revolution of 1930.[81] To be sure, the connection between changing discursive practices and general material conditions continues to be a vexing question for historians. For example, very few of the new labor laws issued during the early 1930s were actually implemented, and the absence of formal democratic processes meant that popular groups could not call Vargas to account for failures to make good on his promises.[82] Several recent studies also remind us that the construction of citizenship rights around the figure of the worker entailed the exclusion of those Brazilians who, by virtue of race, gender, or unemployment, could not claim that status.[83] At the same time, it seems impossible any longer to argue that nothing significant had changed about the relationship between previously excluded groups and the State.

The Estado Novo: What's New?

One of the difficulties historians have faced in analyzing and categorizing the Vargas regime (1930–45) is that the regime itself (leaving aside, for now, Vargas's later abbreviated term in office as elected president) can be broken down politically into three distinct phases, including a "constitutional" interregnum (1934–37) when Vargas ruled as provisional president. Nonetheless, fully half of the regime took place within the parameters of the Estado Novo (1937–45), a "New State" inaugurated when Vargas suspended elections and issued a new, more authoritarian constitution. Inevitably, when historians have been moved to consider what kind of regime it was—totalitarian/fascist? a regime of emergency? social democratic (without the democracy)? authoritarian-corporatist? Bonapartist? populist?—they have had to reckon with the Estado Novo era and its legacy.[84]

Through the 1970s, much of the literature on the Estado Novo highlighted its fascist features, including the centralization of power, the adoption of a corporatist government structure, the absence of civil liberties, the routine (if uneven) censorship of the press, the production of propaganda, and the imprisonment and torture of the regime's opponents. These were likely points of concern for scholars in a nation where the existing military dictatorship had revived and extended many of these practices. But by the early 1980s, historians were beginning to question or dispute the characterization of the Estado Novo as fascist. These doubts arose from both empirical and epistemological inspirations. As Maria Helena Capelato observes, the Estado Novo was more about demobilization than mobilization of the masses; with the declaration of the "New State," Vargas dissolved all political associations and made no attempt to create a mass organization on the order of the European fascist parties.[85] Similarly, there was no concerted attempt to disseminate a rigid political doctrine, and Vargas retained among his closest political and cultural advisors men of diverse ideological orientations. And while Vargas had entertained Nazi overtures earlier in his regime, once the European war began in earnest, he moved with dispatch to negotiate a deal with the United States and to ally Brazil with the "United Nations" against Nazi Germany and fascist Italy. Whatever fascist tendencies Vargas exhibited, they were certainly not of an orthodox strain.

Perhaps more important, historians have become increasingly critical of attempts to fit the historical specificities of the Estado Novo into categories constructed a priori, based on European political models. It has become less important—even pointless—to decide whether the Estado Novo was "really" fascist, and more pressing to examine what correlation of social and political forces had allowed Vargas, under the explicitly authoritarian regime of the Estado Novo, to dispense with the rituals of (limited) democratic rule, and to what ends. Two studies of state-labor relations in this period—Angela Castro Gomes's *A invenção do trabalhismo* and John French's *The Brazilian Workers' ABC*—dramatically revised our view of the workers' attitudes toward Vargas and his policies. Until the appearance of these two studies, scholars assumed either that Brazilian workers were vulnerable to Vargas's entreaties because of their rural roots and their lack of class consciousness, or that those same workers militantly resisted the state's policies for industrialization and work discipline but a combination of repression and an opportunistic union leadership insensitive to the needs of the rank and file allowed Vargas to implement his strategy for social control. Gomes and French, by contrast, emphasized the extent to which Vargas's policies built on previous struggles by urban workers, and responded to already existing labor demands. And like recent revisionist works on Peronism in Argentina, these authors argued that the Vargas regime allowed workers a claim to citizenship and a legitimate voice in public life that had been denied them under previous political administrations. Gomes also emphasizes the extent to which Vargas's nationalist/modernizing economic policies appealed to labor leaders, while French cites the obduracy of the industrial bourgeoisie as a major inducement for union officials to throw in their lot with a state that at least intermittently supported their demands. Jorge Ferreira, in his *Trabalhadores do Brasil*, similarly draws on new theoretical insights into populism and working-class identity to construct a more fluid and reciprocal relationship between Brazilian workers and the Vargas regime.[86]

Related conclusions have been drawn about Vargas's relationship with other social and corporate groups. Whereas an earlier historiography either cited a vacuum in power caused by the weakness of the "national" bourgeoisie (the corollary of the weak working class) or claimed a virtual congruity between Vargas and industrial interests, more recent studies have challenged both arguments. In my own monograph on industrialists and workers in São Paulo, I explore the way Vargas built on industrialist discourse about productivity and national greatness, yet also pressured employers in general to modify their narrow vision of social peace, while making concessions to industrialists that allowed him to count on the support of the very *paulistas* who, a few years earlier, actively supported a regional uprising against his dictatorship.[87] Looking at a very different segment of Brazilian society, the Xavante Indians, Seth Garfield acknowledges that the nationalist rhetoric of the Estado Novo imparted "social and cultural prestige to Indian groups through their consecration as primordial Brazilians." At the same time, the continuing use of racial distinctions among Estado Novo policy makers, and Vargas's energetic support for westward expansion, encouraged land invasion and cultural loss among indigenous peoples.[88]

To be sure, historians writing in the aftermath of a two-decade-long military dictatorship were unlikely to ignore the fascistic features of the Estado Novo, even if they no longer argued in terms of an "ideal-type" fascism. In a highly influential essay, the philosopher Marilena Chauí located the origins of the exaltation of the "strong state" by both the right and the left in the Vargas era. In this vein, historians have analyzed the political imaginary of the Vargas regime. Alcir Lenharo's pathbreaking *Sacralização da política* explores the rhetoric of the "March to the West" and the use of bodily and religious imagery in the construction of the political imaginary of the era, though it still relies on a conception of the state as unitary, and thus allows little agency for its political subjects. More recent studies by Eliana Dutra and Jorge Ferreira acknowledge the use of symbols clearly derived from totalitarian regimes (both Nazism and Stalinism), but also recognize that their meanings were unstable and their effectiveness relied less on systematic repression than resonance with the popular classes.[89] Examining more concrete manifestations of the Vargas regime, Silvana Goulart detailed press censorship and government propaganda orchestrated by Vargas's Departamento de Imprensa e Propaganda (DIP), and Elizabeth Cancelli explored the grim world of state-sponsored violence and repression during the regime.[90] Reid Andrews and Kim Butler chronicled the short life and sudden death of the Frente Negra Brasileira—banned as a political party by the Estado Novo, which then eagerly promoted Gilberto Freyre's vision of Brazil as a racial democracy.[91] Maria Luiza Tucci Carneiro's research exposed the widespread anti-Semitism of the Vargas regime, though the more recent and nuanced study by Jeffrey Lesser indicates that here, too, the Estado Novo eschewed rigid adherence to ideological orthodoxy and allowed Jewish refugees from Nazi aggression to enter the country in relatively large numbers, especially if they could be of some service to Vargas's plans for national development.[92]

A topic of enduring fascination for historians is the role of artists, writers, and intellectuals in the cultural and political apparatus of the Estado Novo. The expansion of state capacity and Vargas's eclectic approach to (intellectual) labor recruitment meant that a startling variety of distinguished intellectuals and artists participated in the cultural productions of the Vargas era. Earlier work focused almost exclusively on the repression or cooptation of intellectuals by the regime, but more recent studies have treated such formulations as too simplistic, and more specifically as incapable of accounting for the diversity of intellectual and artistic participation in the regime. Monica Velloso, in her study of the "cultural politics" of the Vargas regime, observes that the cultural discourse of the Estado Novo rejected the liberal separation of political and cultural spheres, situating intellectuals as crucial mediators of "public opinion" and national identity. To be sure, this implied a potential for state restrictions on artistic expression, but it also implied greater prestige and influence for those artists and intellectuals—many of them overtly opposed to the politics of the regime—who gained access to the state apparatus.[93]

Particularly influential in reorienting the discussion on this theme has been Sérgio Miceli's *Intelectuais e classe dirigente no Brasil (1920–1945)*, in which he contends that, rather than the state coopting intellectuals, it was the latter that coopted the state—that is, used the semiautonomous spaces created by the state to advance specific cultural/political projects, especially in a nation where the "private" market for cultural products was continually cramped. This contention, itself derived from Pierre Bourdieu's sociological insights into "habitus" and "fields of force," denotes a more general rethinking of the state. Neither an instrument of a particular social class nor a monolithic structure operating according to its own logic, the state becomes a process rather than a thing, and a process through which diverse groups contend for power, even under an authoritarian regime, and both create and compete for access to the means of implementation.[94] Taking this analytical approach a step further, Daryle Williams, in his *Culture Wars in Brazil*, demonstrates the notable cultural and artistic eclecticism of the Vargas regime, but also discerns certain patterns that favored the more conservative neocolonial faction for matters of historic preservation, even as the regime anointed left-leaning figures like the architect Oscar Niemeyer to convey an image of "tropical modernism" abroad.[95]

The End of the Estado Novo and the Beginning of the Populist Republic

The weight of scholarly opinion still favors a view of the Estado Novo as planting the seeds of the subsequent military-authoritarian regime and as consolidating an ideology of a strong, centralized state that has repeatedly hampered the formation of a robust civil society in Brazil. There is, however, an alternative view of the Estado Novo that emphasizes the democratic-populist implications of its dismantling of the regional political machines and state military forces that were the domain of the most reactionary party bosses. Vargas also helped shift the center of political gravity from the boss-ruled rural areas to the growing metropolises, where, presumably, voters were less susceptible to *coronelismo* or other traditional patronage or coercive relationships (and were more likely to be literate, and hence able to vote in the first place). In addition, Gomes, French, Maranhão, and others note the crucial opening for greater union autonomy that began during the final years of the Estado Novo and that produced a major mobilization of industrial workers following the end of World War II.[96]

While certain basic political histories remain essential for sketching out and contesting political narratives of the post-1945 era, most accounts of the Vargas and Kubitschek presidencies or studies of the political parties of the Populist Republic or of developmental nationalism have been the work of political scientists and sociologists, not historians.[97] The new historiography of this era is, for the most part, not as tightly engaged with these political narratives, and seeks instead to flesh out the emerging intellectual, social, and cultural world of Brazil in the decades between the end of the Estado Novo and the onset of the military dictatorship, especially in the mushrooming urban centers. As Leandro Konder observes in a recent historiographical essay on Brazilian intellectuals in the 1950s, scholars writing at that time—despite the apparent loosening of restraints with the conclusion of the Estado Novo—did not perceive that decade as a moment that was propitious for significant political or social change.[98] In part, the Cold War and its repercussions in Brazil (including the banning of the Communist Party within a year of its relegalization) cast a pall on movements to revitalize the political and social spheres.[99] Yet it was a period of considerable intellectual effervescence, which witnessed the emergence of the São Paulo school of sociology and the publication of now classic works by Sergio Buarque de Holanda and Antonio Candido. Meanwhile, social scientists such as Hélio Jaguaribe became directly involved in constructing the ideological edifice that supported both the discourse and the policies of developmental nationalism so central to the Kubitschek presidency (1956–60).

With the decline of the relentless post-1960s emphasis on "history from the bottom up," historians and other historically minded scholars have begun to pay closer attention to these developments in the artistic and scholarly community, as well as to groups that are neither of the elite, conventionally defined, nor of the popular classes. Networks of sociability among journalists, artists, intellectuals, and political activists in the years from 1945 to 1964 have become a major focus of attention, with Lúcia Helena Gama's *Nos bares da vida* serving as an exceptionally intriguing example. Gama's book locates the formation of a new artistic/intellectual/political sensibility in the bohemian milieu of the bars in São Paulo's "new downtown" around the Praça da República.[100] Brian Owensby, in his *Intimate Ironies*, takes up the question of middle-class identity and culture in Brazil during these decades, and rescues this theme from the reductionism of earlier structuralist interpretations. Owensby's most innovative contribution is to emphasize not the socioeconomic characteristics of a specific middle-class population but the cultural processes that produced a middle-class identity, and the way an emerging Brazilian middle class drew on class images from other industrializing/urbanizing societies while forming an identity that incorporated features peculiar to the historical circumstances of its construction. Thus discourses of merit—common to emerging middle-class cultures—combined with "traditional" notions of patronage and personal influence, rather than simply replacing them. Owensby also argues that there was no specific middle-class party or politics in post-1930s Brazil, but rather a more generalized sense of disenchantment among middling groups with regard to the political sphere.[101]

Although labor history is no longer the hot topic it was in the wake of the social history boom, several studies of organized labor and working-class culture continue to influence the interpretation of this era. The most important innovation has been a shift away from structuralist assumptions about populism and the state and labor histories based on preconceptions of different ideological factions within organized labor, and toward more carefully researched studies demonstrating that union leaders often had closer connections to workers on the shop floor than previously assumed, and that affiliations with the Communist Party or Catholic movements did not necessarily mean that a union official had an agenda that was sharply different from that of the rank and file. Historians have shown that state policies and populist rhetoric, far from demobilizing workers, opened up new opportunities to press "legitimate" demands and organize effective strikes without fear of violent repression. To be sure, the opening of the archives of the political police (DOPS) is already revealing extensive infiltration of unions and left-wing political groups by police agents, even during the supposedly democratic interregnum of the Populist Republic. But no longer could employers simply assume that the government apparatus would automatically act in its favor. The Kubitschek presidency—long seen as only vaguely populist and very friendly to industrialist interests—turns out to be a period of intense strike activity and real gains for organized labor.[102]

While most post-'45 labor history continues to be confined to the urban centers of Rio and São Paulo, some regional studies have expanded the scope of research. Yonne de Souza Grossi's *Mina de Morro Velho*, on mineworkers in Minas Gerais, carefully traces the rise of a particular union local, the relationship between the union and the community, and the complicated interactions between leaders with specific ideological affiliations and a rank and file increasingly disposed to militant action but with more protean ideological positions. Alexandre Fortes's *Nós do quarto distrito* examines immigrants and migrants who gradually create a working-class community in the far southern city of Porto Alegre, while Paulo Fontes demonstrates the role of *nordestino* identity in the construction of class consciousness and solidarity in an industrial suburb of São Paulo. On the agrarian front, a pioneering work is Cliff Welch's *The Seed Was Planted*, which challenges the longstanding assumption that rural workers had been unaffected by the populist politics and the corporatist legislation of the post-1930 era. Typically, rural workers and small cultivators are seen as only making their voices heard politically in the 1960s, and then mainly in the Nordeste. Instead, Welch argues that the interior of São Paulo saw considerable rural activism starting in the 1950s, and that rural workers shared many of the same aspirations, concerns, and ideological tendencies as urban workers.[103]

Historians have paid surprisingly little attention to the Vargas presidency and the dramatic suicide that ended it prematurely, but the subsequent presidency of Juscelino Kubitschek has been the focus of research by several historians and numerous political scientists.[104] Indeed, it would be startling if scholars weren't interested in the Kubitschek era, a period of remarkable industrial growth, rising standards of living for industrial workers, and the creation of the new national capital, Brasília. Yet the literature on this era is anything but celebratory. Much of the research published in the 1970s and early '80s emphasized the massive influx of multinational capital (with primarily negative implications), the corruption and patronage involved in the building of Brasília, and the spiraling inflation that would set the stage for the crises of the early 1960s. Kubitschek was also portrayed as entirely identified with the interests of big business and making only feeble efforts to incorporate workers and their concerns into his developmentalist project. Finally, several important studies, such as Caio Navarro de Toledo's *ISEB: Fábrica de ideologias*, critically explored the way in which a certain Marxist-influenced construction of national development led scholars, including many on the left, to participate in and endorse the policies of the Kubitschek presidency, with the effect of colluding with the expansion of foreign capital and the cooptation of workers.[105]

Historians writing today, from the perspective of a neoliberal world economy, tend to see the Kubitschek era, with its valorization of economic planning and state participation in the economy, in a somewhat more positive and nostalgic light. To be sure, the undiluted enthusiasm for modernity and unchecked economic progress—exemplified by the slogan "fifty years in five"—grates on contemporary sensibilities. But increasingly, the historical evidence points to some substantial gains for industrial workers under Kubitschek, both in terms of living standards and union autonomy, and a not entirely harmonious relationship between his government and private economic interests. Salvador Sandoval's study of strike waves in twentieth-century Brazil, for example, provides evidence of heavy strike activity during the Kubitschek government, a trend that owed more to the loosening of corporatist controls than to mounting worker discontent.[106] Various labor histories also indicate that union leaders could be enthusiastic about nationalist/developmentalist projects, and even support the strengthening of the "national bourgeoisie," but that did not mean that they suspended or muffled their criticism of industrial employers or actively restrained workers from striking. Instead, they took advantage of the increasingly central role of labor unions in the developmentalist project to press long-standing demands.[107] Meanwhile, my own work on the *paulista* industrialists, as well as Maria José Trevisan's *50 anos em 5*, observe that while Kubitschek adopted much of the language of rationalization and productivity central to industrialist discourse, employers were increasingly concerned that work stoppages and inflation would undermine "social peace" and that unions were using the political sphere to advance a "subversive" workers' agenda.[108] Indeed, many of the comments about the JK era would foreshadow the similar, if more vociferous, attacks on the ill-fated Goulart presidency of the early 1960s.

Urban Space and Postwar Popular Culture

One of the repercussions of the cultural turn in history has been a shift away from older political narratives and chronologies to privilege topics such as music, consumption, public celebrations, and national identity. Brazil is an especially likely locale for such a shift in historians' attention, since it provides a particularly rich array of popular cultural traditions and innovations. Furthermore, the dramatic expansion of the urban centers in the period from the 1930s on has meant that popular culture is, in effect, equivalent to urban culture.

Any discussion of popular music in this period still begins with samba. In the late 1920s, according to historian Bryan McCann, *paulista* modernist Mário de Andrade "lamented that samba was an urban genre," since in his eyes (or ears) urban music—unlike authentic rural traditions—would be corrupted by commercialization and international influences. In other words, its Brazilianness would always be in danger of dilution by market and foreign forces. Until recently, historians and cultural critics writing about popular music and urban culture have generally echoed Mário's concerns, now couched in the "mass culture" language of the Frankfurt School or the neo-Marxist concept of cultural imperialism.[109] However, over the last decade both Brazilian and North American scholars of urban and popular culture, influenced by the work of Walter Benjamin, have sought to draw a less rigid distinction between "mass" and "popular" culture, and have adopted a more sympathetic view of samba and its musical progeny. Deconstructing notions of "authenticity" and "purity," not only have works such as Bryan McCann's *Hello, Hello Brazil* rejected the notion that concern for commercial appeal inevitably degrades or dilutes "national" cultural expressions, they see the expansion of the urban market (both in Brazil and abroad) for cultural products as sparking creativity and generating strategies to advance Brazilian popular music while allowing the strategic absorption of foreign trends. And these trends are, in turn, modified by their contact with Brazilian innovations.[110]

A similar perspective can be found in Christopher Dunn's study of Brazilian popular music at the height of the military dictatorship. In *Brutality Garden*, Dunn traces the rise of *tropicália*—a musical trend that emerged in the late 1960s, at the height of military repression—and notes that traditional leftists denounced this trend as too friendly to foreign influence and not sufficiently engaged with political struggle. Dunn, however, insists that *tropicália* was a way to discard stifling nationalist preoccupations with authenticity, on the one hand, and to express searing critiques of the military regimes without alarming the censors on the other. And in his provocative book *The Mystery of Samba*, anthropologist Hermano Vianna laments the historical trajectory by which samba—which he regards as the *mestiço* musical genre par excellence—became an instrument of orthodoxy and homogenization in the hands of the state.[111]

Although postwar urbanization is still largely the terrain of anthropologists and urban planners, historians are beginning to explore the dramatic transformations of urban space during this era. The single most spectacular change was, of course, the transfer of the federal capital from Rio de Janeiro to the invented interior city of Brasília, a monument to the modernist architecture and planning of Oscar Niemeyer and Lúcio Costa and the relentless pursuit of *"Brasil Grande."*[112] But perhaps just as intriguing as this macrotransformation are the microchanges in the urban landscape wrought by rural migrants from the Northeast and the expanding urban population of limited means, who began to invade unoccupied urban terrain and construct makeshift neighborhoods commonly known as "favelas." Reversing a trend common to cities in the twentieth century, whereby neighborhoods of the poor and the wealthy become ever more spatially separated, these urban squatter settlements often appeared in the interstices of middle- or upper-class neighborhoods, on lands that had not been developed because they were tied up in some juridical dispute, were rights-of-way for highway construction, or simply were inappropriate for large-scale construction—for example, the marsh communities on the bay in Salvador and, most famous of all, the favelas on the granite hills (*morros*) ringing Rio's fashionable Southern Zone.

Not surprisingly, the initial wave of publications about favelas portrayed them as a den of anomie and social pathology. Particularly influential was the celebrated firsthand chronicle of favela life by Carolina Maria de Jesús, *Child of the Dark*, an account that undoubtedly owed much of its initial success to its tendency to confirm all the worst prejudices of middle-class readers about the *favelados* (as residents of favelas were pejoratively termed).[113] A second wave of studies, which combined historical and social-scientific methods, presented a dramatically different image of the favela-dweller; in works such as Janice Perlman's 1976 study *The Myth of Marginality* or Julio Pino's *Family and Favela*, published twenty years later, the inhabitants of these new urban residential formations emerge as socially and racially diverse, as having values and aspirations similar to those of middle-class Brazilians (Perlman), and as placing even more importance on family ties than other Brazilians (Pino).[114] Numerous studies have also showcased the capacity of favela residents to organize community associations and to pressure local governments for schools and other services. In this scenario, it is not the impoverished *favelados* who are a problem but rather the developmentalist state and a middle class terrified of crime and disorder.[115] However, the intensified urban violence of recent decades, the alarming expansion of the drug trade, and the desperate recourse to strategies such as "popular lynchings" to punish criminals has made this optimistic construction of life in the favelas more difficult to sustain. Most recently, Brodwyn Fischer has argued, in *A Poverty of Rights*, that the precarious legal status of "shacktowns," rather than being a deviation from the norm, became an entrenched feature of urban political culture, and a key factor in reproducing material disadvantages.[116]

Scholars have also explored the considerable contribution of the "*morro*" to carioca popular culture, particularly through the "samba schools" that have dominated carnival celebrations in Rio de Janeiro since the 1930s. Though much of this work has focused on Rio de Janeiro, that city has not been the exclusive site of popular cultural studies for this period. The other major locale for such studies has been Salvador da Bahia, with its rich African cultural and religious traditions and its highly influential *candomblé* houses. Of particular interest here is the way in which prominent religious figures—most of them *afro-descendente* women—have become powerful political brokers in Salvador even as the political apparatus and economic power largely remain in the hands of the "white" elite. Anthropologists have also explored the use of Yoruba cultural practices (or practices designated as Yoruba) to claim cultural authenticity and religious authority, at the same time that *candomblé* has gained acceptance, official and informal, as a constitutive element of Brazilian national identity.[117]

From Populist Republic to Military Dictatorship

If knowledge of the impending collapse of civilian/democratic rule cast a pessimistic pall over histories of the Kubitschek era, this has been doubly the case for studies of the early 1960s and the short-lived Goulart presidency, widely seen as setting the stage for twenty-one long years of military rule. The narrative of intensifying crisis in the three years spanning 1961 to 1964 is very well known, beginning with President Jânio Quadros's stunning resignation in late 1961, which was followed by Vice President João Goulart's contested ascendancy to the presidency, increasing peasant mobilization in the Northeast, growing labor militancy in the center-south, right-wing demonstrations in the major cities, and a series of "revolts" within the lower ranks of the military, all taking place within the context of the post–Cuban Revolution Cold War.[118] Not surprisingly, the first wave of scholarly studies designed to explain the military seizure of power on April 1, 1964, portrayed the "collapse of populism" and the rise of the "bureaucratic-authoritarian regime" as virtually inevitable. One line of argument—most widely associated with the work of Guillermo O'Donnell—sees the rise of military regimes (with Brazil being only the earliest instance of this process) as being due to the shift from import-substitution industrialization, typically accompanied by nationalist-populist political projects, to a phase of heavy industrialization and massive foreign investment, with its negative implications for the popular classes as both workers and consumers, thereby requiring an authoritarian/repressive regime forged through an alliance of military officials and technocrats.[119] Then there were the sociological studies of Octávio Ianni and Francisco Weffort, which explained the military coup as a result of the (also inevitable) contradictions of populist politics—that is, each successive populist administration has to deal with an ever more militant and mobilized working class, and it becomes more and more difficult to sustain a reformist position in the face of rising popular demands and growing elite disaffection. Thus, the populist political project eventually leads either to revolution or, as happened in Brazil, counterrevolution.[120]

For several decades, historians (as opposed to social scientists) proved reluctant to tackle the military rise to power and the subsequent military dictatorship, partly because the topic seemed too "contemporary" to be history, and partly because, understandably, discussions of the military regime in its immediate aftermath tended to focus almost exclusively on such issues as human rights violations, worsening income distribution, and near-universal resistance to the regime. The era of military rule provides a classic example of a topic that required a certain temporal distance before a critical mass of historians could think about it in intellectually innovative ways. Thus, it is somewhat predictable that the first major history of the regime, *The Politics of Military Rule in Brazil, 1964–1985*, was written by a North American historian of Brazil, Thomas Skidmore, who maintained the largely narrative approach that had defined his earlier work on the period from Vargas to Goulart.[121] The narrative style, however, does not imply a lack of interpretation. Rather, Skidmore's account emphasized the role of particular figures within the military in both the rise and decline of the regime. Unlike the handful of other studies that appeared during the military dictatorship, which had typically emphasized the role of civilian elites in prodding the military to seize power or had insisted that popular resistance was forcing the military, against its will, to accept a gradual return to civilian rule,[122] Skidmore saw the entire process as traceable, in the first instance, to conflicts, alliances, and changes internal to the armed forces. This approach is even more evident in the highly narrative (and widely read) four-volume history of the rise and fall of the regime by journalist Elio Gaspari; indeed, at times Gaspari almost seems to be arguing that two figures within the military, Ernesto Geisel and Golbery do Couto e Silva, were responsible for all the political twists and turns of that era.[123]

Thus, when historians steeped in social and cultural history methods finally began to take on the military regime as a subject for historical interpretation, they entered an intellectual field where production had oscillated between two extremes: structuralist explanations that tended to be deterministic in their approach and allow for very little human agency, and narrative accounts that tended to overstate the agency of a handful of military officials. And it was a field where virtually all the studies had been organized around two questions: why did the military seize power, and why did the military leave power? In contrast, much of the recent work—which began as a trickle in the mid-1990s and has turned into a flood of new studies with the fortieth anniversary of the military seizure of power—deals with such questions only indirectly.[124] As is generally the case in the aftermath of the cultural turn, these new studies are more likely to be microhistories, or to be informed more by the question of "how?" than "why?" In other words, how did the military regime manage to normalize its rule and to create a certain degree of consent despite its myriad violations of individual and political rights? How did its repressive-modernizing policies intersect with national and transnational movements for personal liberation and cultural change (particularly in the realms of race, gender, and sexual preference)? How did various movements and institutions adapt to the challenges of an explicitly authoritarian regime?

Many impressive works have reoriented the historiography of the military regime. Some of these works have made a particularly important contribution by uncovering entirely new source material; this is the case with Kenneth Serbin's *Secret Dialogues*, which reveals the extensive meetings and negotiations between the Catholic Church and the military-controlled state through the "Bipartite Commission" at the height of the repression (1970–74). Serbin's study has required a considerable revision in the image of the church as an oppositional institution that avoided any sort of complicity with the military regime, arguing instead for a more pragmatic church that sought both social justice and institutional protection.[125] Focusing on a similar period, Carlos Fico's *Reinventando o otimismo* explores not the more infamous aspects of the Médici regime (1969–74) but the massive media and publicity campaign to gain popular support for its nationalist project of creating *Brasil Grande* during the period of the so-called economic miracle—a campaign that had considerable success despite the cruel repression of those years.[126] Studies such as this one have made it increasingly untenable to assume that the military ruled through force alone, or enjoyed support only from a narrow segment of Brazilian society. They have also urged us to contemplate to what extent this "regime of exception" was truly exceptional. In the 1980s, when Brazil was still in the precarious process of transition to civilian rule, those writing about the regime were likely to draw a sharp contrast between military rule and democratic/civilian government. And for the many who were victims of military repression, those contrasts continue to be real and profoundly significant. But at this "safer" chronological distance, it also becomes possible to think about aspects of the military regime as not so extraordinary or anomalous, and as sharing many of the goals and assumptions that informed, for example, the Kubitschek era. Increasingly, historians and cultural theorists recognize that, ironically, the authoritarian regime, by intensifying a series of trends such as urbanization, university education, women's employment, transnational cultural influences, and middle-class identity formation, actually opened the way (though often unintentionally) for many cultural and political innovations—some of which certainly contributed to the military's retreat from power and fall from grace.[127]

Yet another emerging area of historical scholarship on the military regime, and one that inevitably requires a degree of distance from the events under study, is the question of historical memory. Here the issue of resistance, and especially of the armed left, looms large (indeed, a great deal larger than it ever loomed during the dictatorship). Marcelo Ridenti, in several works on this subject, warns of the tendency toward mystification of the armed struggle, and a retrospective rereading of the guerrilla movement as part of the "democratic" resistance (given the current consensus that the only good politics are democratic politics). At the same time, he reminds his readers that the left was certainly no less democratic than the right or center at that time, and arguably more so.[128] There are also a number of historians who, drawing heavily on oral histories, are exploring more specific aspects of the dictatorship, and especially the "*anos de chumbo*"—the most repressive period, lasting from approximately 1968 to 1976.[129] Themes include forms of censorship and repression, the experiences of imprisonment and exile, and changing attitudes toward democracy, feminism, and homosexuality on the left. Most of these historians actively avoid the temptation to romanticize or exaggerate the resistance to the military regime, but there is a danger that this inevitably more appealing theme will end up skewing historical memory and obscuring the extensive civilian support, or complacency, that the military enjoyed. In this regard, Daniel Aarão Reis rightly notes the difficulties experienced by Brazilians in remembering a regime that so few of them actively resisted. According to Reis, "there is no denying, no matter how painful it may be, that the military dictatorship was a process of social/historical construction, not an accident along the way. It was a process that was not imposed, or invented by aliens, but one in which Brazilians participated."[130]

Past and Present

For the moment, the contemporary history of Brazil seems to stop with the fall of the military dictatorship, though we now have at least one survey of the politics and economics of the decades following the transition to civilian rule by two distinguished economic historians.[131] And certainly there are some scholars who are already casting a historical eye on recent decades, especially on the ways new social initiatives prompt us to rethink the past. These include movements organized around environmental issues and indigenous and African identities.[132] The latter are particularly fascinating for the historian, since, in the past decade, indigenous groups and *afro-descendentes* have actively and deliberately used historical arguments and documentation to make claims for land or for social programs to address past inequities. This has meant the revival of "Indian" identities by communities that had gone for generations without such identification, and the search for roots in runaway slave communities (*quilombos*) by rural villages. It is still too early to say what impact this will have on Brazilian historiography, but it certainly promises to make historical knowledge a major resource, and probably a major source of contention, for some time to come.

Notes

1. Sergio Miceli (a historical sociologist) was using Pierre Bourdieu as a major theoretical reference in his work in the late 1970s. See his *Intelectuais e classe dirigente no Brasil, 1920–45* (São Paulo: DIFEL, 1979).

2. Dipesh Chakrabarty, *Provincializing Europe: Postcolonial Thought and Historical Difference* (Princeton: Princeton University Press, 2000).

3. Concerning the limited impact of this literature on Brazilian historiography, see Barbara Weinstein, "As novas tendências historiográficas nos Estados Unidos e a pesquisa sobre a América Latina," *CEDHAL: Série Seminários de Pesquisa*, Texto 4 (São Paulo, 1997).

4. Sérgio França Adorno de Abreu, *Os aprendizes do poder: O bacharelismo liberal na política brasileira* (Rio de Janeiro: Paz e Terra, 1988), 237.

5. On independence as a shift from colonialism to neocolonialism, see Emilia Viotti da Costa, "Independence: The Building of a Nation," in *The Brazilian Empire: Myths and Histories* (Chicago: University of Chicago Press, 1985), 23. Recently, Stephen Haber and Herbert S. Klein have maintained that there were no major economic transformations as a result of independence; however, they dismiss the "neocolonial" explanation for the persistence of colonial period economic patterns: "The Economic Consequences of Brazilian Independence," in Haber, ed., *How Latin America Fell Behind* (Stanford: Stanford University Press, 1997), 243–59.

6. Kirsten Schultz, *Tropical Versailles: Empire, Monarchy, and the Portuguese Royal Court in Rio de Janeiro, 1808–1821* (New York: Routledge, 2001); Iara Lis de Carvalho Souza, *A pátria coroada: O Brasil como corpo politico autônomo, 1780–1831* (São Paulo: UNESP, 1998). See also Jurandir Malerba, *A corte no exílio: Civilização e poder no Brasil às vésperas da independência, 1808–1821* (São Paulo: Companhia das Letras, 2000).

7. Viotti da Costa, "Liberalism: Theory and Practice," in *The Brazilian Empire*, 53–77; and Alfredo Bosi, *Dialética da colonização* (São Paulo: Companhia das Letras, 1992).

8. João José Reis, *Slave Rebellion in Brazil: The Muslim Uprising of 1835 in Bahia* (Baltimore: Johns Hopkins University Press, 1993); Hendrik Kraay, *Race, State, and Armed Forces in Independence-Era Brazil: Bahia, 1790s–1840s* (Stanford: Stanford University Press, 2001); Gladys Sabina Ribeiro, *A liberdade em construção: Identidade nacional e conflitos antilusitanos no primeiro reinado* (Rio de Janeiro: Relume Dumará, 2002); Ivana Stolze Lima, *Cores, marcas e falas: Sentidos da mestiçagem no Império do Brasil* (Rio de Janeiro: Arquivo Nacional, 2003); Hebe Maria Mattos (de Castro), *Escravidão e cidadania no Brasil monárquico* (Rio de Janeiro: Jorge Zahar, 2000); Keila Grinberg, *O fiador dos brasileiros: Cidadania, escravidão e direito civil no tempo de Antonio Pereira Rebouças* (Rio de Janeiro: Civilização Brasileira, 2002). See also Linda Lewin, *Surprise Heirs: Illegitimacy, Inheritance Rights, and Public Power in the Formation of Imperial Brazil, 1822–1889* (Stanford: Stanford University Press, 2003), chap. 1.

9. Reis, *Slave Rebellion*, chap. 2; Matthias Röhrig Assunção, "Elite Politics and Popular Rebellion in the Construction of Post-colonial Order: The Case of Maranhão, Brazil, 1820–1841," *Journal of Latin American Studies* 31:3 (1999): 1–38; Kraay, *Race, State, and Armed Forces*.

10. Roderick J. Barman, *Brazil: The Forging of a Nation, 1798–1852* (Stanford: Stanford University Press, 1988).

11. José Murilo de Carvalho, *A construção da ordem: A elite política imperial* (Rio de Janeiro: Campus, 1980); *Teatro de sombras: A política imperial* (São Paulo: Vértice, 1988). This argument about the autonomy of the imperial bureaucracy was first elaborated in Eul-Soo Pang and Ron L. Seckinger, "The Mandarins of Imperial Brazil," *Comparative Studies in Society and History* 14:2 (1972): 215–44.

12. Richard Graham, *Patronage and Politics in Nineteenth-Century Brazil* (Stanford: Stanford University Press, 1990).

13. Ilmar Rohloff de Mattos, *O tempo saquarema: A formação do estado imperial* (Rio de Janeiro: ACCESS, 1994).

14. Jeffrey Needell, *The Party of Order: The Conservatives, the State, and Slavery in the Brazilian Monarchy, 1831–1871* (Stanford: Stanford University Press, 2006). Two studies of imperial politics beyond Rio and São Paulo that offer a very different image of the Conservatives are Judith Bieber, *Power, Patronage, and Political Violence: State Building on a Brazilian Frontier, 1822–1889* (Lincoln: University of Nebraska Press, 1999), and Roger

A. Kittleson, *The Practice of Politics in Postcolonial Brazil: Porto Alegre, 1845–1895* (Pittsburgh: University of Pittsburgh Press, 2005).

15. Lilia Moritz Schwarcz, *The Emperor's Beard: Dom Pedro II and the Tropical Monarchy of Brazil* (New York: Hill and Wang, 2004 [1998]), especially chap. 7. See also the chapter on Indianist novelist José de Alencar in Doris Sommer, *Foundational Fictions: The National Romances of Latin America* (Berkeley: University of California Press, 1991).

16. Warren Dean's *Rio Claro: A Brazilian Plantation System, 1820–1920* (Stanford: Stanford University Press, 1976) was a crucial contribution to this trend.

17. Célia M. Marinho de Azevedo, *Abolitionism in the United States and Brazil: A Comparative Perspective* (New York: Garland, 1995). On new trends in the narrative of abolition, see Barbara Weinstein, "The Decline of the Progressive Planter and the Rise of Subaltern Agency: Shifting Narratives of Slave Emancipation in Brazil," in *Reclaiming the Political in Latin American History: Essays from the North*, ed. Gilbert Joseph (Durham, N.C.: Duke University Press, 2001), 81–101.

18. Dean, *Rio Claro*; Sidney Chalhoub, *Visões da liberdade* (São Paulo: Companhia das Letras, 1990); Hebe M. Mattos de Castro, *Das cores do silêncio: Os significados da liberdade no sudeste escravista* (Rio de Janeiro: Arquivo Nacional, 1995); Maria Helena Machado, *O plano e o pânico: Os movimentos sociais na década da abolição* (Rio/São Paulo: UFRJ/Edusp, 1994); Eduardo Silva, *As camélias de Leblon e a abolição da escravatura: Uma investigação da história cultural* (São Paulo: Schwarcz, 2003). Contrary to an earlier historiography that situated the immediatist strategy for abolition in the radical wing of the organized abolitionist movement, Silva claims that immediatism arose within a *quilombo* on what was then the outskirts of Rio.

19. Chalhoub, *Visões da liberdade*; Keila Grinberg, *Liberata: A lei da ambiguidade* (Rio de Janeiro: Relume-Dumará, 1994); Joseli Maria Nunes Mendonça, *Entre a mão e os anéis: A lei dos sexagenários e os caminhos da abolição no Brasil* (Campinas: Unicamp, 1999).

20. Hebe M. Mattos (de Castro), *Ao sul da história* (São Paulo: Brasiliense, 1987); Stuart B. Schwartz, "Patterns of Slaveholding in the Americas: New Evidence from Brazil," *American Historical Review* 87:1 (1982): 55–86; Bert Barickman, "As cores do escravismo: Escravistas 'pretos,' 'pardos' e 'cabras' no Recôncavo baiano em 1835," *População e Família* 2:2 (1999): 7–62; Renato Leite Marcondes, "Small and Medium Slaveholdings in the Coffee Economy of the Vale do Paraíba, Province of São Paulo," *Hispanic American Historical Review* 85:2 (2005): 259–81; Zephyr L. Frank, *Dutra's World: Wealth and Family in Nineteenth-Century Rio de Janeiro* (Albuquerque: University of New Mexico Press, 2004).

21. An excellent entry point into this new literature would be Olívia Maria Gomes da Cunha and Flávio dos Santos Gomes, eds., *Quase-cidadão: Histórias e antropologias da pós-emancipação no Brasil* (Rio de Janeiro: FGV, 2007).

22. João José Reis, "'The Revolution of the Ganhadores': Urban Labour, Ethnicity and the African Strike of 1857 in Bahia, Brazil," *Journal of Latin American Studies* 29:2 (1997): 355–93; Maria Cecília Velasco e Cruz, "Puzzling out Slave Origins in Rio de Janeiro Port Unionism: The 1906 Strike and the Sociedade de Resistência dos Trabalhadores em Trapiche e Café," *Hispanic American Historical Review* 86:2 (2006), 205–45; Marcelo Badaró Mattos, *Escravizados e livres: Experiências comuns na formação da classe trabalhadora carioca* (Rio de Janeiro: Bom Texto, 2008).

23. Kim D. Butler, *Freedoms Given, Freedoms Won: Afro-Brazilians in Post-Abolition São Paulo and Salvador* (New Brunswick: Rutgers University Press, 1998). For a historical-anthropological approach to Bahia's place in the "Afro-Atlantic dialogue," see J. Lorand Matory, *Black Atlantic Religion: Tradition, Transnationalism, and Matriarchy in the Afro-Brazilian Candomblé* (Princeton: Princeton University Press, 2005).

24. George Reid Andrews, *Blacks and Whites in São Paulo, Brazil, 1888–1988* (Madison: University of Wisconsin Press, 1991); Maria Helena P. T. Machado, "From Slave Rebels to Strikebreakers: The Quilombo of Jabaquara and the Problem of Citizenship in Late-Nineteenth-Century Brazil," *Hispanic American Historical Review* 86:2 (2006): 247–74; Joan L. Bak, "Race, Respectability and Reformist Workers in Porto Alegre, 1908–1913," *História: Debates e tendências*, VI Encontro Estadual de História—ANPUH/RS, 4:1 (2003), 65–72.

25. Carvalho, *Teatro de sombras*; Graham, *Patronage and Politics*; Andrews, *Blacks and Whites*.

26. Joseph L. Love, *Rio Grande do Sul and Brazilian Regionalism, 1882–1930* (Stanford: Stanford University Press, 1971), and *São Paulo in the Brazilian Federation, 1889–1937* (Stanford: Stanford University Press, 1980). The latter was part of a series that included John D. Wirth, *Minas Gerais and the Brazilian Federation, 1889–1937* (Stanford: Stanford University Press, 1977) and Robert Levine, *Pernambuco in the Brazilian Federation, 1889–1937* (Stanford: Stanford University Press, 1978). See also Eul-Soo Pang, *Bahia in the First Brazilian Republic: Coronelismo and Oligarchies, 1889–1934* (Gainesville: University of Florida Press, 1979).

27. Barbara Weinstein, *The Amazon Rubber Boom, 1850–1920* (Stanford: Stanford University Press, 1983). See also Evaldo Cabral de Mello, *O Norte agrário e o Império* (Rio de Janeiro: Nova Fronteira, 1984); Linda Lewin, *The Politics of Parentela in Paraíba: A Case Study of Family-Based Oligarchy in Brazil* (Princeton: Princeton University Press, 1987); Marcos A. Silva, ed., *República em migalhas: História regional e local* (São Paulo: Marco Zero, 1990); Angela M. de Castro Gomes, ed., *Regionalismo e centralização política: Partidos e Constituinte nos anos 30* (Rio de Janeiro: Nova Fronteira, 1980).

28. Bieber, *Power, Patronage, and Political Violence*; Durval Muniz de Albuquerque Jr., *A invenção do Nordeste e outras artes* (Recife: Ed. Massangana, 2001); Nísia Trindade Lima, *Um sertão chamado Brasil: Intelectuais e representação geográfica da identidade nacional* (Rio de Janeiro: IUPERJ/Revan, 1999); Tania Regina de Luca, *A Revista do Brasil: Um diagnóstico para a n(ação)* (São Paulo: UNESP, 1999); Barbara Weinstein, "Racializing Regional Difference: São Paulo vs. Brazil, 1932," in *Race and Nation in Modern Latin America*, ed. Nancy Appelbaum, Anne Macpherson, and Karin Rosemblatt (Chapel Hill: University of North Carolina Press, 2003), 237–62.

29. The classic studies of dissenting movements in the Old Republic—royalism on the one hand, and jacobin nationalism on the other—are Maria de Lourdes M. Janotti, *Os subsversivos da república* (São Paulo: Brasiliense, 1986), and Suely Robles Reis de Queiróz, *Os radicais da república: Jacobinismo—ideologia e ação* (São Paulo: Brasiliense, 1986).

30. Robert M. Levine, *Vale of Tears: Revisiting the Canudos Massacre in Northeastern Brazil, 1893–1897* (Berkeley: University of California Press, 1992); Marco Antonio Villa, *Canudos: O povo da terra* (São Paulo: Atica, 1995). For a classic structuralist explanation, see Maria Isaura Pereira de Queiróz, *O messianismo no Brasil e no mundo* (São Paulo: Dominus, 1965). For an account of a millenarian movement that emerged soon after Canudos that had a very different trajectory, see Ralph della Cava, *Miracle at Joaseiro* (New York: Columbia University Press, 1970). For an excellent discussion of the culture of millenarianism in Brazil, see Patricia Pessar, *From Fanatics to Folk: Brazilian Millenarianism and Popular Culture* (Durham, N.C.: Duke University Press, 2004). Not all millenarian movements were based in the Northeast; see Todd A. Diacon, *Millenarian Vision, Capitalist Reality: Brazil's Contestado Rebellion, 1912–1916* (Durham, N.C.: Duke University Press, 1991), and Duglas Teixeira Monteiro, *Os errantes do novo século: Um estudo sobre o surto milenarista do Contestado* (São Paulo: Livraria Duas Cidades, 1974).

31. John C. Chasteen, *Heroes on Horseback: The Life and Times of the Last Gaucho Caudillos* (Albuquerque: University of New Mexico Press, 1995).

32. Teresa A. Meade, *"Civilizing" Rio: Reform and Resistance in a Brazilian City, 1889–1930* (University Park: Penn State University Press, 1997); José Murilo de Carvalho, *Os bestializados: O Rio de Janeiro e a República que não foi* (São Paulo: Companhia das Letras, 1987); Nicolau Sevcenko, *A Revolta da Vacina: Mentes insanas em corpos rebeldes* (São Paulo, Scipione, 1993); Jeffrey Needell, "The *Revolta contra Vacina* of 1904: The Revolt against 'Modernization' in Belle-Époque Rio de Janeiro," *Hispanic American Historical Review* 67:2 (1987): 233–69; Sidney Chalhoub, *Cidade febril: Cortiços e epidemias na Corte Imperial* (São Paulo: Companhia das Letras, 1996); Marco A. Pamplona, *Riots, Republicanism, and Citizenship: New York City and Rio de Janeiro during the Consolidation of the Republican Order* (New York: Garland, 1996).

33. For the imperial period, see Thomas H. Holloway, *Policing Rio de Janeiro: Repression and Resistance in a Nineteenth-Century City* (Stanford: Stanford University Press, 1993).

34. Martha de Abreu Esteves, *O império do Divino: Festas religiosas e cultura popular no Rio de Janeiro, 1830–1900* (Rio de Janeiro: Nova Fronteira, 1999); see also Schwarcz, *The Emperor's Beard*, chap. 10. For studies of carioca carnaval that put more emphasis on its "subversive" portential, see Maria Clementina Pereira Cunha, *Ecos da folia: Uma história social do carnaval carioca entre 1880 e 1920* (São Paulo: Companhia das Letras, 2001); Cunha, ed., *Carnavais e outras f(r)estas: Ensaios de história social de cultura* (Campinas: Unicamp, 2002); Rachel Soihet, *A subversão pelo riso: Estudos sobre o carnaval carioca da Belle époque ao tempo de Vargas* (Rio de Janeiro: FGV, 1998).

35. Jeffrey D. Needell, *A Tropical Belle-Époque: Elite Culture and Society in Turn-of-the-Century Rio de Janeiro* (Cambridge: Cambridge University Press, 1987); José Murilo de Carvalho, *A formação das almas: O imaginário da república no Brasil* (São Paulo: Companhia das Letras, 1990).

36. On the Encilhamento and the fiscal policies of the Old Republic, see Steven Topik, *The Political Economy of the Brazilian State, 1889–1930* (Austin: University of Texas Press, 1987).

37. On the campaign to make Belém a modern city with a civic life, see Geraldo Mártires Coelho, *O brilho da supernova: A morte bela de Carlos Gomes* (Rio de Janeiro: Agir, 1995); *No coração do povo: O monumento à República em Belém, 1891–1897* (Belém: Paka-Tatu, 2002).

38. Nicolau Sevcenko, *Literatura como missão: Tensões sociais e criação cultural na Primeira República* (São Paulo: Brasiliense, 1983).

39. Sidney Chalhoub, *Trabalho, lar e botequim: O cotidiano dos trabalhadores no Rio de Janeiro da Belle Époque* (São Paulo: Brasiliense, 1986); Marcos Luiz Bretas, *Guerra das ruas: Povo e polícia na Cidade do Rio de Janeiro* (Rio de Janeiro: Arquivo Nacional, 1997).

40. Sueann Caulfield, *In Defense of Honor: Sexual Morality, Modernity, and Nation in Early Twentieth-Century Brazil* (Durham, N.C.: Duke University Press, 2000). Even Sidney Chalhoub, whose pioneering study of working-class culture in Rio had constructed a cultural world very much separate from and in conflict with that of the elite, recently added a preface to a new edition of the book that modified this "clash of cultures" scenario. See *Trabalho, lar e botequim*, 2nd ed. (Campinas: Unicamp, 2001).

41. Hermano Vianna, *The Mystery of Samba: Popular Music and National Identity in Brazil* (Chapel Hill: UNC Press, 1999); Bryan McCann, *Hello, Hello Brazil: Popular Music in the Making of Modern Brazil* (Durham, N.C.: Duke University Press, 2004); Carlos Sandroni, *Feitiço decente: Transformações do samba no Rio de Janeiro, 1917–1933* (Rio de Janeiro: Jorge Zahar/UFRJ, 2001).

42. Mattos, *Das cores do silêncio*; Grinberg, *O fiador dos brasileiros*; Reis, *Slave Rebellion in Brazil*.

43. Mattos, *Das cores do silêncio*.

44. Célia M. Marinho de Azevedo, *Onda negra, medo branco: O negro no imaginário das elites—século XIX* (Rio de Janeiro: Paz e Terra, 1987).

45. Thomas Skidmore, *Black into White: Race and Nationality in Brazilian Thought* (New York: Oxford University Press, 1974); Jeffrey Lesser, *Negotiating National Identity: Immigrants, Minorities, and the Struggle for Ethnicity in Brazil* (Durham, N.C.: Duke University Press, 1999).

46. Lilia M. Schwarcz, *The Spectacle of the Races: Scientists, Institutions, and the Race Question in Brazil, 1870–1930* (New York: Hill and Wang, 1999); Dain Borges, "'Puffy, Ugly, Slothful and Inert': Degeneration in Brazilian Social Thought, 1880–1940," *Journal of Latin American Studies* 23 (1993): 235–56.

47. Julyan G. Peard, *Race, Place, and Medicine: The Idea of the Tropics in Nineteenth-Century Brazilian Medicine* (Durham, N.C.: Duke University Press, 1999); Nancy L. Stepan, *"The Hour of Eugenics": Race, Gender, and Nation in Latin America* (Ithaca: Cornell University Press, 1991). See also Marcos Chor Maio and Ricardo Ventura Santos, eds., *Raça, ciência, e sociedade* (Rio: Fiocruz, 1996); Gilberto Hochman, *A era do saneamento: As bases da política de saúde pública no Brasil* (São Paulo: Hucitec, 1998), and Sidney Chalhoub, "The Politics of Disease Control: Yellow Fever and Race in Nineteenth-Century Rio de Janeiro," *Journal of Latin American Studies* 25 (1993): 441–63.

48. Andrews, *Blacks and Whites*.

49. Olívia Gomes da Cunha, *Intenção e gesto: Pessoa, cor e a produção cotidiana da (in) diferença no Rio de Janeiro, 1927–1942* (Rio de Janeiro, Arquivo Nacional, 2002); "Sua alma em sua palma: Identificando a 'raça' e inventando a nação," in Dulce Pandolfi, ed., *Repensando o Estado Novo* (Rio de Janeiro: FGV, 1999), 257–88; Jerry Dávila, *Diploma of Whiteness: Race and Social Policy in Brazil, 1917–1945* (Durham, N.C.: Duke University Press, 2003).

50. Maria Odila Leite da Silva Dias, *Power and Everyday Life: The Lives of Working Women in Nineteenth-Century Brazil* (New Brunswick: Rutgers University Press, 1995); June Hahner, *Emancipating the Female Sex: The Struggle for Women's Rights in Brazil, 1850–1940* (Durham, N.C.: Duke University Press, 1990); Miriam Moreira Leite, *Outra face do feminismo: Maria Lacerda de Moura* (São Paulo: Atica, 1984).

51. Susan K. Besse, *Restructuring Patriarchy: The Modernization of Gender Inequality in Brazil, 1914–1940* (Chapel Hill: University of North Carolina Press, 1996); Margareth Rago, *Do cabaré ao lar: A utopia da cidade disciplinar—Brasil, 1890–1930* (Rio de Janeiro: Paz e Terra, 1985).

52. Cristiana Schettini Pereira, *'Que tenhas teu corpo': Uma história social da prostituição no Rio de Janeiro das primeiras décadas republicanas* (Rio de Janeiro: Arquivo Nacional, 2006).

53. Martha de Abreu Esteves, *Meninas perdidas: Os populares e o cotidiano do amor no Rio de Janeiro da Belle Époque* (Rio de Janeiro: Paz e Terra, 1989); Caulfield, *In Defense of Honor*; Peter M. Beattie, *The Tribute of Blood: Army, Honor, Race, and Nation in Brazil, 1864–1945* (Durham, N.C.: Duke University Press, 2001).

54. James N. Green, *Beyond Carnival: Male Homosexuality in Twentieth-Century Brazil* (Chicago: University of Chicago Press, 1999). See also the pioneering studis of Luiz R. B. Mott, including *O lesbianismo no Brasil* (Porto Alegre: Mercado Aberto, 1987); *Escravidão, homossexualidade e demonologia* (São Paulo: Icone Editora, 1988); *Sexo proibido: Virgens, gays e escravos nas garras da Inquisição* (Campinas: Papirus, 1989).

55. Emilia Viotti da Costa, *Da senzala à colônia* (São Paulo: DIFEL, 1966); Warren Dean, *The Industrialization of São Paulo, 1880–1945* (Austin: University of Texas Press, 1969); Wilson Cano, *Raízes da concentração industrial em São Paulo* (Rio de Janeiro: DIFEL, 1977); Boris Fausto, *Trabalho urbano e conflito social, 1890–1920* (São Paulo: DIFEL, 1976); Love, *São Paulo and the Brazilian Federation.*

56. A good example of this approach to immigration is Zuleika Alvim, *Brava gente! Os italianos em São Paulo, 1870–1920* (São Paulo: Brasiliense, 1986).

57. Thomas H. Holloway, *Immigrants on the Land: Coffee and Society in São Paulo, 1886–1934* (Chapel Hill: University of North Carolina Press, 1980).

58. Mauricio A. Font, *Coffee, Contention, and Change in the Making of Modern Brazil* (Cambridge, Mass.: Basil Blackwell, 1990). For a critique of this argument, see James P. Woodard, "History, Sociology and the Political Conflicts of the 1920s in São Paulo, Brazil," *Journal of Latin American Studies* 37 (2005): 333–49.

59. Lesser, *Negotiating National Identity*; see also his study of Jewish immigrants, *Welcoming the Undesirables: Brazil and the Jewish Question* (Berkeley: University of California Press, 1995).

60. Andrews, *Blacks and Whites*; Maria Helena P. T. Machado, "From Slave Rebels to Strikebreakers: The Quilombo of Jabaquara and the Problem of Citizenship in Late Nineteenth-Century Brazil," *Hispanic American Historical Review* 86:2 (2006): 247–74.

61. One of the first major historical studies of the Brazilian working class from a social-historical perspective was Francisco Foot and Victor Leonardi, *História da indústria e do trabalho no Brasil* (São Paulo: Global, 1982).

62. Eva Alterman Blay, *A mulher na indústria paulista* (São Paulo: Atica, 1978); *Eu não tenho onde morar: Vilas operárias na cidade de São Paulo* (São Paulo: Nobel, 1985); Rago, *Do cabaré ao lar*; Maria Auxiliadora Guzzo, *A vida fora das fábricas: O cotidiano operário em São Paulo, 1920–1934* (Rio de Janeiro: Paz e Terra, 1987); Boris Fausto, *Crime e cotidiano: A criminalidade em São Paulo, 1880–1924* (São Paulo: Brasiliense, 1984); Joel Wolfe, *Working Women, Working Men: São Paulo and the Rise of Brazil's Industrial Working Class, 1900–1955* (Durham, N.C.: Duke University Press, 1993); Maria Izilda Santos de Matos, *Trama e poder: Um estudo das indústrias de sacaria para o café, São Paulo, 1888–1934* (Brasília: SESI/DN, 1994).

63. Particularly important in this regard is the work of José Sérgio Leite Lopes, including *A tecelagem dos conflitos de classe na "Cidade das Chaminés"* (São Paulo: Marco Zero, 1988).

64. A pioneering work in this regard is Angela M. de Castro Gomes, *Burguesia e trabalho: Política e legislação social no Brasil, 1917–1937* (Rio de Janeiro: Campus, 1979); see also Barbara Weinstein, *For Social Peace in Brazil: Industrialists and the Remaking of the Working Class in São Paulo, 1920–1964* (Chapel Hill: University of North Carolina Press, 1996).

65. John D. French, *The Brazilian Workers' ABC: Class Conflict and Alliances in Modern São Paulo* (Chapel Hill: University of North Carolina Press, 1992).

66. Dean, *Industrialization of São Paulo*; Décio Saes, *Classe media e política na Primeira República brasileira, 1889–1930* (Petrópolis: Vozes, 1975); *A formação do estado burguês no Brasil, 1888–1891* (Rio de Janeiro: Paz e Terra, 1985); Edgar Salvadori de Decca, *O silêncio dos vencidos* (São Paulo: Brasiliense, 1981).

67. Maria Lígia Coelho Prado, *A democracia ilustrada: O Partido Democrático de São Paulo, 1926–1934* (São Paulo: Atica, 1986).

68. Maria Helena Capelato and Maria Lígia Coelho Prado, *O bravo matutino: Imprensa e ideologia no jornal "O Estado de São Paulo"* (São Paulo: Alfa-Omega, 1980); Maria Helena Capelato, *Os arautos do liberalismo* (São Paulo: Brasiliense, 1988).

69. James Woodard, *A Place in Politics: São Paulo, Brazil, From Seigneurial Republicanism to Regionalist Revolt* (Durham, N.C.: Duke University Press, 2009).

70. Vavy Pacheco Borges, *Tenentismo e revolução brasileira* (São Paulo: Brasiliense, 1992); Anna Maria Martinez Corrêa, *Rebelião de 1924 em São Paulo* (São Paulo: Hucitec, 1976).

71. Vavy Pacheco Borges, *Getúlio Vargas e a oligarquia paulista* (São Paulo: Brasiliense, 1979); Maria Helena Capelato, *O Movimento de 1932: A causa paulista* (São Paulo: Brasiliense, 1982); Weinstein, "Racializing Regional Difference."

72. Antonio Celso Ferreira, *A epopéia bandeirante: Letrados, instituições, invenção histórica, 1870–1940* (São Paulo: UNESP, 2001); de Luca, *A Revista do Brasil*.

73. Nicolau Sevcenko, *Orfeu estático no metrópole: São Paulo, sociedade e cultura nos frementes anos 20* (São Paulo: Companhia das Letras, 1992); Sérgio Miceli, *Nacional estrangeiro: História social e cultural do modernismo artístico em São Paulo* (São Paulo: Companhia das Letras, 2003).

74. Key texts for studying the Revolution of 1930 include Florestan Fernandes, *A revolução burguesa no Brasil: Ensaio de interpretação sociológica* (São Paulo: Zahar, 1975); Boris Fausto, *A revolução de 1930: Historiografia e história* (São Paulo: Brasiliense, 1970).

75. Paulo Sérgio Pinheiro, *Política e trabalho no Brasil: Dos anos vinte a 1930* (Rio de Janeiro: Paz e Terra, 1975); Capelato and Prado, *O bravo matutino*; Weinstein, "Impressões da elite sôbre os movimentos da classe operária: A cobertura da greve em 'O Estado de São Paulo,' 1902–1917," in Capelato and Prado, *O bravo matutino*; de Decca, *O silêncio dos vencidos*.

76. Besse, *Restructuring Patriarchy*.

77. For views of the Vargas regime as creating a new disciplinary state apparatus that would produce more compliant workers for an emerging industrial bourgeoisie, see Kazumi Munakata, *A legislação trabalhista no Brasil* (São Paulo: Brasiliense, 1981); "Compromisso do Estado," *Revista Brasileira de História* 7 (1984), 58–71; Zélia Lopes da Silva, *A domesticação dos trabalhadores nos anos 30* (São Paulo: Marco Zero, 1990); Alcir Lenharo, *A sacralização da política* (Campinas: Papirus, 1986).

78. Robert M. Levine, *The Vargas Regime: The Critical Years, 1934–1938* (New York: Columbia University Press, 1970); Fausto, *A revolução de 1930*.

79. See, for example, Marilena Chauí, "Apontamentos para uma crítica da ação integralista brasileira," in Chauí and Maria Sylvia Carvalho Franco, *Ideologia e mobilização popular* (Rio de Janeiro: Paz e Terra, 1978), 17–149.

80. French, *Brazilian Workers' ABC*, Angela M. de Castro Gomes, *A invenção do trabalhismo* (Rio de Janeiro: IUPERL/Vértice, 1988); Jorge L. Ferreira, *Trabalhadores do Brasil: O imaginário popular, 1930–1945* (Rio de Janeiro: FGV, 1997); Fernando Teixeira da Silva, *Operários sem patrões: Os trabalhadores de Santos no entreguerras* (Campinas: Unicamp, 2003); Seth Garfield, *Indigenous Struggle at the Heart of Brazil: State Policy, Frontier Expansion, and the Xavante Indians, 1937–1988* (Durham, N.C.: Duke University Press, 2001); Cliff Welch, *The Seed was Planted: The São Paulo Roots of Brazil's Rural Labor Movement, 1924–1964* (University Park: Penn State University Press, 1999).

81. Caulfield, *In Defense of Honor*.

82. John D. French, *Drowning in Laws: Labor Law and Brazilian Political Culture* (Chapel Hill: University of North Carolina Press, 2004).

83. Brodwyn Fischer, *A Poverty of Rights: Citizenship and Inequality in Twentieth-Century Rio de Janeiro* (Stanford: Stanford University Press, 2008); Adriano Duarte, *Cidadania e exclusão: Brasil, 1937–1945* (Florianópolis: EdUFSC, 2007).

84. I owe many of the insights in this section of the article to Maria Helena Capelato's splendid essay, "Estado Novo: Novas histórias," in *Historiografia brasileira em perspectiva*, ed. Marcos Cezar de Freitas (São Paulo: EdUSF/Context, 1998). See also Dulce Pandolfi, ed., *Repensando o Estado Novo* (Rio de Janeiro: FGV, 1999).

85. Capelato, "Estado Novo"; *Multidões em cena: Propaganda política no varguismo e no peronismo* (São Paulo: FAPESP, 1998).

86. French, *Brazilian Workers' ABC*; Gomes, *Invenção do trabalhismo*; Ferreira, *Trabalhadores do Brasil*. A similar study located outside Rio and São Paulo is Alexandre Fortes, *Nós do Quarto Distrito: A classe trabalhadora porto-alegrense e a Era Vargas* (Rio de Janeiro: Garamond, 2004).

87. Weinstein, *For Social Peace in Brazil*; Borges, *Getúlio Vargas e a oligarquia paulista*.

88. Garfield, *Indigenous Struggle*.

89. Chauí, "Apontamentos"; Lenharo, *Sacralização da política*; Eliana de Freitas Dutra, *Ardil totalitário: Imaginário politico no Brasil dos anos 30* (Rio de Janeiro: UFRJ, 1997); Ferreira, *Trabalhadores do Brasil*.

90. Silvana Goulart, *Sob a verdade oficial: Ideologia, propaganda e censura no Estado Novo* (São Paulo: Marco Zero, 1990); Elizabeth Cancelli, *O mundo da violência: A polícia na era Vargas* (Brasília: UnB, 1993).

91. Andrews, *Blacks and Whites*; Butler, *Freedoms Given, Freedoms Won*; Darién J. Davis, *Avoiding the Dark: Race and the Forging of National Culture in Modern Brazil* (Brookfield: Ashgate, 1999). On the work of Gilberto Freyre in this period, see Ricardo Benzaquen de Araújo, *Guerra e paz: Casa Grande e Senzala e a obra de Gilberto Freyre nos anos 30* (Rio de Janeiro, Editora 34, 1994).

92. Maria Luiza Tucci Carneiro, *O anti-semitismo na era Vargas: Fantasmas de uma geração, 1930–1945* (São Paulo: Brasiliense, 1988); Lesser, *Welcoming the Undesirables*.

93. Monica Pimenta Velloso, *Os intelectuais e a política cultural do Estado Novo* (Rio de Janeiro: FGV/CPDOC, 1987); also Lúcia Lippi Oliveira, Monica Pimenta Veloso, and Angela M. de Castro Gomes, eds., *Estado Novo: Ideologia e poder* (Rio de Janeiro: Zahar, 1982).

94. Miceli, *Intelectuais e classe dirigente*. See also Maria Stella M. Bresciani, *O charme da ciência e a sedução da objetividade: Oliveira Vianna entre intérpretes do Brasil* (São Paulo: UNESP, 2005).

95. Daryle Williams, *Culture Wars in Brazil: The First Vargas Regime, 1930–1945* (Durham, N.C.: Duke University Press, 2001).

96. Gomes, *Invenção do trabalhismo*; John D. French, "The Populist Gamble of Getúlio Vargas in 1945: Political and Ideological Transitions in Brazil," in *Latin America in the 1940s: War and Postwar Adjustments*, ed. David Rock (Berkeley: University of California Press, 1994), 141–65; Ricardo Maranhão, *Sindicatos e democratização: Brasil, 1945–50* (São Paulo: Brasiliense, 1979).

97. For example, Maria Celina Soares d'Araújo, *O segundo governo Vargas* (Rio de Janeiro: Zahar, 1982); Maria Vitória de Mesquita Benevides, *O governo Kubitschek: Desenvolvimento econômico e estabilidade política, 1956–1961* (Rio de Janeiro: Paz e Terra, 1976). Both authors are political scientists.

98. Leandro Konder, "História dos intelectuais nos anos 50," in Freitas, ed., *Historiografia brasileira em perspectiva*, 355–74.

99. On anticommunism in Brazil, see Rodrigo Patto Sá Motta, *Em guarda contra o "perigo vermelho," 1917–1964* (São Paulo: Perspectiva, 2002); Carla Simone Rodeghero, *O anticommunismo brasileiro sob o olhar norte-americano* (Rio de Janeiro: FGV, 2006).

100. Lúcia Helena Gama, *Nos bares da vida: Produção cultural e sociabilidade em São Paulo, 1940–1950* (São Paulo: SENAC, 1998).

101. Brian P. Owensby, *Intimate Ironies: Modernity and the Making of Middle-Class Lives in Brazil* (Stanford: Stanford University Press, 1999). For a different view of middle-class politics in the postwar era, see Bryan McCann, "Carlos Lacerda: The Rise and Fall of a

Middle-Class Populist in 1950s Brazil," *Hispanic American Historical Review* 83:4 (2003): 661–96.

102. Wolfe, *Working Women, Working Men*; Salvador A. M. Sandoval, *Social Change and Labor Unrest in Brazil since 1945* (Boulder, Colo.: Westview, 1993); Paulo Fontes, *Trabalhadores e cidadãos: Nitro Química, a fábrica e as lutas operárias nos anos 50* (São Paulo: Annablume, 1997).

103. Yonne de Souza Grossi, *Mina de Morro Velho: A extração do homem* (Rio de Janeiro: Paz e Terra, 1981); Fortes, *Nós do Quarto Distrito*; Paulo Fontes, *Um Nordeste em São Paulo: Trabalhadores migrantes em São Miguel paulista, 1945–66* (Rio de Janeiro: FGV, 2008); Welch, *The Seed Was Planted*.

104. On Vargas's presidency (1951–54), see D'Araújo, *O segundo governo Vargas*; on Vargas's suicide, see Daryle Williams and Barbara Weinstein, "*Vargas Morto:* The Death and Life of a Brazilian Statesman," in *Death, Dismemberment and Memory: Body Politics in Latin America*, ed. Lyman Johnson (Albuquerque: University of New Mexico Press, 2004), 273–315. On Kubitschek, see Benevides, *O governo Kubitschek*.

105. Caio Navarro de Toledo, *ISEB: Fábrica de ideologias* (São Paulo: Atica, 1977); Maria Sylvia Carvalho Franco, "O tempo das ilusões," *Ideologia e mobilização popular*, 151–209; Carlos Guilherme Mota, *Ideologia da cultura brasileira, 1933–1974* (São Paulo: Atica, 1980).

106. Sandoval, *Social Change and Labor Unrest*.

107. Weinstein, *For Social Peace in Brazil*; Amélia Cohn, *Previdência social e processo politico no Brasil* (São Paulo: Moderna, 1981).

108. Weinstein, *For Social Peace in Brazil*; Maria José Trevisan, *50 anos em 5: A FIESP e o desenvolvimentismo* (Petrópolis: Vozes, 1986).

109. See, for instance, Antonio Pedro Tota, *O imperialismo sedutor: A americanização do Brasil na época da Segunda Guerra* (São Paulo: Companhia das Letras, 2000); for a nationalist view of musical "authenticity," see José Ramos Tinhorão, *História social da música popular brasileiro* (Lisboa: Caminho, 1990).

110. Bryan McCann, *Hello, Hello Brazil: Popular Music in the Making of Modern Brazil* (Durham, N.C.: Duke University Press, 2004). See also Tânia da Costa Garcia, *O "it verde e amarelo" de Carmen Miranda, 1930–1946* (São Paulo: Annablume, 2004).

111. Christopher Dunn, *Brutality Garden: Tropicália and the Emergence of a Brazilian Counterculture* (Chapel Hill: University of North Carolina Press); Vianna, *Mystery of Samba*.

112. James Holston, *The Modernist City: An Anthropological Critique of Brasília* (Chicago: University of Chicago Press, 1989).

113. Carolina Maria de Jesús, *Child of the Dark: The Diary of Carolina Maria de Jesus* (New York: Dutton, 1962). It was published two years earlier in Brazil as *Quarto de despejo: Diário de uma favelada* (São Paulo: Liv. F. Alves, 1960). See also Robert M. Levine and José Carlos Sebe Bom Meihy, *The Life and Death of Carolina Maria de Jesus* (Albuquerque: University of New Mexico Press, 1995).

114. Janice E. Perlman, *The Myth of Marginality: Urban Poverty and Politics in Rio de Janeiro* (Berkeley: University of California Press, 1976); Julio C. Pino, *Family and Favela: The Reproduction of Poverty in Rio de Janeiro* (Westport, Conn.: Greenwood Press, 1997).

115. Alba Zaluar and Marcos Alvito, *Um século de favela* (Rio de Janeiro: FGV, 1998); Teresa Pires do Rio Caldeira, *City of Walls: Crime, Segregation, and Citizenship in São Paulo* (Berkeley: University of California Press, 2000).

116. Fischer, *A Poverty of Rights*. For a study that also uses citizenship rights as its point of departure but places greater emphasis on favelas as a base for social mobilization,

see James Holston, *Insurgent Citizenship: Disjunctions of Democracy and Modernity in Brazil* (Princeton: Princeton University Press, 2008).

117. Hendrik Kraay, ed., *Afro-Brazilian Culture and Politics: Bahia, 1790s to 1990s* (Armonk, N.Y.: M. E. Sharpe, 1998); Matory, *Black Atlantic Religion*.

118. There is a large literature on the peasant leagues and rural mobilization in the Brazilian Northeast during the early 1960s. These studies include José de Souza Martins, *Os camponeses e a política no Brasil* (Petrópolis: Vozes, 1981); Luciana de Barros Jaccoud, *Movimentos sociais e crise política em Pernambuco, 1955–1968* (Recife: Massangana, 1990); Clodomir Santos de Morais, *História das Ligas Camponesas do Brasil* (Brasília: Iattermund, 1997); Anthony Pereira, *The End of the Peasantry: The Rural Labor Movement in Northeast Brazil, 1961–1988* (Pittsburgh: University of Pittsburgh Press, 1997). On U.S.-Brazilian relations in this period, see W. Michael Weis, *Cold Warriors and Coups d'Etat: Brazilian-American Relations, 1945–1964* (Albuquerque: University of New Mexico Press, 1993).

119. Guillermo A. O'Donnell, *Modernization and Bureaucratic Authoritarianism: Studies in South American Politics* (Berkeley: University of California Press, 1973). For a major study of the military seizure of power that emphasizes the role of industrial interests and multinational capital, see René Armand Dreifuss, *1964, conquista do estado: Ação política, poder e golpe de classe* (Petrópolis: Vozes, 1981).

120. Octávio Ianni, *Crisis in Brazil* (New York: Columbia University Press, 1970); Francisco C. Weffort, *O populismo na política brasileira* (Rio de Janeiro: Paz e Terra, 1978).

121. Thomas E. Skidmore, *The Politics of Military Rule in Brazil, 1964–85* (New York: Oxford University Press, 1988); his previous political history was *Politics in Brazil: An Experiment in Democracy, 1930–1964* (New York: Oxford University Press, 1967).

122. Dreifuss, *1964, conquista do estado*; Maria Helena Moreira Alves, *State and Opposition in Military Brazil* (Austin: University of Texas Press, 1985); Heloisa M. Murgel Starling, *Os senhores das Gerais: Os novos inconfidentes e o golpe military de 1964* (Petrópolis: Vozes, 1986).

123. The four volumes are *A ditadura envergonhada* (São Paulo: Companhia das Letras, 2002); *A ditadura escancarada* (2002); *A ditadura derrotada* (2003) and *A ditadura encurralada* (2004). Gaspari refers to Geisel as "*o sacerdote*" (the priest) and Golbery as "*o feiticeiro*" (the wizard).

124. A good introduction to this new literature would be the following collections of essays: Daniel Aarão Reis, Marcelo Ridenti, and Rodrigo Patto Sá Motta, eds., *O golpe e a ditadura militar 40 anos depois, 1964–2004* (Bauru: Edusc, 2004), and Carlos Fico et al., *1964–2004, 40 anos do golpe: ditadura militar e resistência no Brasil* (Rio de Janeiro: 7 Letras, 2004).

125. Kenneth P. Serbin, *Secret Dialogues: Church-State Relations, Torture, and Social Justice in Authoritarian Brazil* (Pittsburgh: University of Pittsburgh Press, 2000).

126. Carlos Fico, *Reinventando o otimismo: Ditadura, propaganda e imaginário social no Brasil* (Rio de Janeiro: FGV, 1997).

127. Eder Sader, *Quando novos personagens entraram em cena* (Rio de Janeiro: Paz e Terra, 1988); Sônia Alvarez, *Engendering Democracy in Brazil: Women's Movements in Transition Politics* (Princeton: Princeton University Press, 1990); Andrews, *Blacks and Whites*; Dunn, *Brutality Garden*; Green, *Beyond Carnival*; João Pinto Furtado, "Engajamento politico e resistência cultural em múltiplos registros," in Reis et al., *O golpe e a ditadura militar*, 229–45.

128. Marcelo Ridenti, *O fantasma da revolução brasileira* (São Paulo: UNESP, 1993); "Resistência e mistificação da resistência armada contra a ditadura: Armadilhas para pesquisadores," in Reis et al., *O golpe e a ditadura militar*, 53–65.

129. Beatriz Kushnir, "Cães de guarda: Entre jornalistas e censores," in Reis et al., *O golpe e a ditadura militar*, 249–64; Marieta de Moraes Ferreira, "Vozes da oposição: Ditadura e transição política no Brasil," in *1964–2004, 40 anos do golpe*, 183–91; Samantha Viz Quadrat, "Os porões internacionais da repressão," in *1964–2004, 40 anos do golpe*, 153–62; Denise Rollemberg, "Vidas no exílio," in *1964–2004, 40 anos do golpe*, 192–206; Maria Paula Araújo, *A utopia fragmentada: novas esquerdas no Brasil e no mundo na década de 1970* (Rio de Janeiro: FGV, 2000).

130. "A ditadura militar, não há como negá-lo, por mais que seja doloroso, foi um processo de construção histórico-social, não um acidente de percurso. Foi processada pelos brasileiros, não imposta, ou inventada, por marcianos." Daniel Aarão Reis, "Ditadura e sociedade: As reconstruções da memória," in Reis et al., *O golpe e a ditadura militar*, 50; see also Daniel Aarão Reis Filho, *A revolução faltou ao encontro* (São Paulo: Brasiliense, 1991).

131. Francisco Vidal Luna and Herbert S. Klein, *Brazil since 1980* (Cambridge: Cambridge University Press, 2006). On the economic crisis of 1981–94 and its impact on the urban middle class, see Maureen O'Dougherty, *Consumption Intensified: The Politics of Middle-Class Daily Life in Brazil* (Durham, N.C.: Duke University Press, 2002).

132. The foundational text for rethinking Brazilian history from the perspective of the environment is Warren Dean, *With Broadax and Firebrand: The Destruction of the Brazilian Atlantic Forest* (Berkeley: University of California Press, 1997). On movements around indigenous and Afro-Brazilian identities, see Jonathan W. Warren, *Racial Revolutions: Antiracism and Indian Resurgence in Brazil* (Durham, N.C.: Duke University Press, 2001); Eliane Cantarino O'Dwyer, ed., *Quilombos: Identidade étnica e territorialidade* (Rio de Janeiro: FGV, 2002); Jan Hoffman French, "*Mestizaje* and Law Making in Indigenous Identity Formation in Northeastern Brazil: 'After the Conflict Came the History,'" *American Anthropologist* 106:4 (2004): 663–74; "Dancing for Land: Law-Making and Cultural Performance in Northeastern Brazil," *Political and Legal Anthropology Review* 25:1 (2002): 19–36.

CHAPTER 8

RACE IN POSTABOLITION AFRO-LATIN AMERICA

KIM D. BUTLER
ALINE HELG

IN considering the articulation of racial issues and ideology in postabolition Latin America, it is helpful to begin with the themes that define the region as a historical and cultural whole. Despite the many differences that make each country and community unique, the Americas are linked by a shared history that brings together the stories of the Atlantic slave trade; European colonization; the cultural fusion of indigenous, African, European, and Asian peoples; the region's distinct role in a global network of trade that led to industrialization and capitalism; and the movement to political independence. There are resonances of each of these stories in the critical and formative discourse of race in the postabolition era.

Race has many meanings in Latin America: the Día de La Raza in some countries recalls indigenous heritage on the anniversary of Christopher Columbus's arrival; the "*raça côsmica*" was theorized in Brazil to envision a new multiethnic humanity; "race" is even used to identify fans of soccer teams. In the years surrounding abolition, however, race was the vehicle by which Latin America was to transition from slavery and colonial racial castes, resituating its overwhelmingly black and brown populations in ostensibly democratic republics. It did so in an era of biological determinism, social Darwinism, and eugenics, and its experience bore implications for former colonies hoping to rise to parity with quintessentially "modern" Europe.

Yet race as a social ideology could not be mandated by elites; it was discursively produced by all members of society. In this regard, emancipation both created new social spaces for nonenslaved people of color and provided them locations from which to articulate and manifest their own politics of identity. It is precisely at this juncture that the black presence, once closely monitored because most persons of African ancestry were considered transferable property, begins to slip away in the historical record.

The present essay focuses on race scholarship primarily in regard to African descendants and the sociopolitical discourses of the postabolition era. Yet it should be remembered that Afro-Latin America developed in contexts that also involved the negotiations of indigenous, Asian, Middle Eastern, and European peoples as, together, they shaped the modern Americas.

The end of slavery in Latin America, whether by abolition or decree, extended from 1791, with the start of the Haitian Revolution, through May 1888, when Brazil became the last country to abolish slavery—that is, over almost one hundred years. It was, therefore, one of several major historical trends that defined the nineteenth century, which also marked the start of American independence movements following the U.S. declaration of independence in 1776 and the beginnings of "free" market economies. Formal abolition occurred in societies where free populations of color had already come to occupy significant social space through manumission. These economic, political, and social shifts are deeply intertwined and cannot be considered in isolation. In continental Latin America, abolition typically was negotiated in the debates surrounding founding constitutions, but national independence involved numerous regional insurrections that predate the present contours of political states. Thus, the origins of much postabolition racial discourse lie in discarded debates over failed constitutions. The involvement of people of color in independence movements (presidents Bernardino Rivadavia of Argentina and Vicente Guerrero of Mexico, for example, were partially of African ancestry), the discourses over property rights and human rights, and the forging of new national identities all took place at a time when scientific thought was deeply imbued with racialized constructs.[1] The weight of this legacy in discussing race in the postabolition era is a fundamental consideration for Latin Americanists, and, as will be discussed below, recent scholarship is increasingly contextualizing the nineteenth-century debates as a panhemispheric conversation.[2]

Because of slavery's long and defining history, it dominates the scholarship on the African Americas. However, increasing interest has focused on the transition to postabolition society, and how decisions made during that period were to affect the modern Americas and their cultural ideologies of race and ethnicity. With major demographic relocations, new arrivals, and the shaping of new nations and national identities, "race" in Latin America is more widely understood now as a dynamic construct that moves through shifting political contexts.

Despite these recent trends, one of the historiographical conventions shaping the literature has been an adherence to the geographic boundaries defining Latin American scholarship, separating the Spanish Americas, Anglophone North America, the circum-Caribbean regions of continental America, and the various colonial spheres within the Caribbean. This practice has hindered a more holistic view of the issues surrounding the constructions and politics of race in the hemisphere, which resulted from intensive cross-influences between its nations. Because much of the scholarship is nationally defined, we have traced it along those lines in this essay, but we also attempt to consider some scholarship outside the formal confines of Latin American studies that helps contextualize the debates of the postabolition era.[3]

Haiti's huge slave uprising in 1791 and declaration of national independence in 1804 represented a watershed whose importance was long overlooked in Latin American historiography. While Haiti lies outside the scope of this volume's focus on Latin America, it bears mention here because of its revolution's impact on slave societies elsewhere in the region.[4] Several collected essays examine how the ideals of the Haitian Revolution, as well as the fear of "another Haiti" and transnational conspiracies among people of color, permeated the Americas, affecting the ways in which the transition to independence and free labor economies would be negotiated.[5] In like manner, the Haitian Revolution deepened concerns about maintaining socioeconomic hegemonies—fears ultimately inscribed in American interpretations and practice of democracy during the nationalist period. Haiti's invasion of the Dominican Republic in 1822, which ended slavery by decree, seemed to confirm the anxieties of American slaveholders endeavoring to forestall similar developments in their territories. Although such episodes as Simón Bolívar's successful appeal to Haiti for assistance in the independence wars have been documented in regional histories, the Haitian Revolution and its aftermath remain to be fully appreciated as a major element in the evolution of race in postabolition Latin America.[6]

As was often the case with slave insurrections, the alarm generated by the Haitian Revolution was disproportionate to the likelihood of its replication elsewhere. Slave societies in continental Spanish America differed in significant ways from the Caribbean, and those differences would affect patterns of postabolition transitions. First, the indigenous population remained a significant demographic presence in such areas as Mexico, Central America, Peru, and Bolivia, thus creating distinct regions where indigenous peoples rather than African descendants comprised the backbone of the working class. Second, in Brazil and Argentina, where immigration programs could be adequately financed, Europeans came in large numbers to constitute the incipient industrial working class in the late nineteenth century. Third, the beginning of the process of abolition of slavery in Spanish continental America coincided with the end of colonial rule, thus situating postabolition transitions as defining experiments in national identity and politics.

The involvement of African descendants in the wars of independence gave people of color a further claim for citizenship as the political economies of new nations were worked out. African American involvement in the military had a long history, but was particularly important in the negotiations of nineteenth-century freedom—for slaves as well as for emerging nations. Peter Voelz offers a good hemispheric overview of black military history, and recent studies have focused on specific cases.[7] Yet few of them examine the contribution of former colonial militias of free mulattoes and blacks (*milicias de pardos y morenos*) to the independence process.[8] Also underrepresented in the literature is the decisive role played by slaves in the patriot and royalist armies during the wars of independence of the 1810s and

1820s—slaves who joined the troops under the promise of freedom.[9] According to Robin Blackburn's comparative study of abolition in the Americas, the independence movements were more vigorous in regions with slaveholding ranchers and planters, such as the River Plate, Venezuela, and New Granada.[10] However, despite slaves' participation in the wars, few nations abolished slavery at the onset of independence. Only Chile, Central America, and Mexico, where slaves were few, fully ended slavery in the 1820s as a logical consequence of the principles of freedom and equality (and, in the case of Mexico, also to deter further colonization of Texas by Anglo-American slaveholders). The other former Spanish colonies abolished the slave trade (under British pressure) and issued laws of manumission that merely freed the newborn (nonetheless submitting them to free service to their mothers' masters until adulthood). In fact, slavery in continental Spanish-speaking America was abolished only three decades after independence, in the 1850s (in Bolivia and Paraguay, in the 1860s), whereas the British had done so in their colonies in 1838 and the French in 1848. The historiography on this long and complex process remains scarce: no comprehensive study focuses on the nations that freed their slaves in the 1820s, notably Chile, where half of the troops that came from Argentina to liberate the territory were made up of men of African ancestry. Among the bulk of continental Spanish American nations, where slaveholders managed to maintain slavery until the midcentury without being challenged by a popular abolitionist movement, only Venezuela and Peru have received substantial scholarly attention, notably from John Lombardi, Peter Blanchard, and Christine Hunefeldt.[11]

Despite their conformity with slavery, Latin American nations opted not to inscribe colonial caste systems in the constitutions and laws adopted in the aftermath of independence, which typically made no mention of the race of the free. Race was inscribed, however, in immigration policies that explicitly excluded people of African and Asian descent in such countries as Brazil and Costa Rica. "Race-neutral" conventions prevailed domestically. Such practices extended to eliminating racial identifications on official statistical reports, including the national censuses of several nations, such as Colombia, Argentina, and Brazil. Advocates of these policies argued that they helped erase the Iberian notion of the "stain of slavery" and integrate free people of full and mixed African ancestry in the citizenry. Because this racial inclusion generally was neutralized by economic or cultural exclusion, it has been marginally taken into account in the recent and rich literature on citizenship and suffrage in Latin America.[12]

The protracted abolition process in Brazil, Cuba, and to a lesser extent Puerto Rico, and the transition of their African-descended population to socioeconomic liberalism have been the topic of more extended scholarship.[13] Brazil took seven decades to fully end slavery nationally, beginning with its de jure prohibition of the transatlantic trade in 1815, which failed to prevent the mass importation of Africans up to 1850 and a brisk domestic slave trade. Final abolition came in 1888 after a series of intermediate measures. As in other Latin American nations, the transition toward abolition was closely bound up with the transition toward national independence. However, Brazil was unique in that its break with the Portuguese monarchy came when the prince regent, Pedro I, declared himself emperor of a newly independent nation in 1822. The quest for abolition and social change continued under the empire; there were armed uprisings and conspiracies challenging not only the political order, but slavery and racial inequality as well. Works by Hendrik Kraay and Peter Beattie explore the implications of Afro-Brazilian participation in the regional conflicts predating abolition in 1888 and the establishment of a republic in 1889.[14]

Most scholarship on race in postabolition Brazil has focused on the period beginning in the mid-twentieth century, in part because of its strong social science orientation, but also because a lack of recorded data on race has presented a challenge for historians. In the decades immediately following abolition, racial identifications appeared inconsistently in census statistics and such records as police, labor, medical, and ecclesiastical documents. Nonetheless, scholars have begun to find ways to investigate this important transitional era. George Reid Andrews utilized company records in his São Paulo study, testing the theories of Brazilian scholars such as Florestan Fernandes that slavery had handicapped Afro-Brazilians' ability to adapt to a capitalist economy.[15] São Paulo was also the site of Brazil's only black political party, the Frente Negra Brasileira (1933–37), and a flourishing black press, the subject of research by scholars who also incorporated oral history.[16] Similarly, Olívia Maria Gomes da Cunha and Flávio dos Santos Gomes utilize oral sources to profile the many facets of postabolition activism in Brazil.[17] Walter Fraga Filho uses notarial records to trace community and personal histories in the state of Bahia around the time of abolition, also the focus of work by Dale Graden.[18] Scholars have also looked at the broader implications of the era's activism. Kim D. Butler compares the political history of Afro-Brazilians in São Paulo with that of Salvador da Bahia, highlighting fundamental principles of postabolition black politics that link the cities with each other and with the rest of the Afro-Atlantic. Elisa Larkin Nascimento examines the interrelationships of the social and cultural movements that have attempted, since the early twentieth century, to challenge and eradicate racial and gender inequalities in Brazil.[19]

Seminal texts from the early and mid-twentieth century, most notably the works of Gilberto Freyre and Florestan Fernandes, largely established the parameters of the scholarly discussion on race in Brazil, and continue to have resonance even today. Contesting the outright vilification of all things African by some Brazilian intellectuals, Freyre recast Afro-Brazilians, their culture, and their relationships with the rest of Brazilian society with a determined optimism; his writings became the foundation of what would be called the myth of racial democracy. Several decades later, Fernandes acknowledged the persistence of racism, and opened a new line of debate by social scientists on the intersections of race and class.[20] Because of the cycles of political instability and repressive regimes in Brazil, the extent of what was considered leftist class analysis (and who could produce it with relative impunity) was limited.[21] Nonetheless, research on the postabolition obstacles facing Afro-Brazilians continued at a steady pace, with contributions from such scholars as Octavio Ianni, Clovis Moura, and the Afro-Brazilian artist, activist, and intellectual Abdias do Nascimento.[22]

Alongside the social science literature, anthropologists were particularly involved in studies of race and culture. Donald Pierson's *Negroes in Brazil* set the stage for much investigation into Afro-Brazilian cultures.[23] One of the hallmarks of recent works on race in Brazil is a shift away from the insularity of ethnography and toward explorations of Brazil's role in a global discourse on race in the modern era. Comparisons with the racial orders of the United States and apartheid South Africa are the focus of works by George Fredrickson and Anthony Marx, who explore how the absence of legally inscribed racialism nonetheless can result in a discriminatory racial order.[24] Collaborative works have enabled exploration of race from Brazilian and foreign perspectives, as reflected in several anthologies focusing on the twentieth century.[25] Both come from long-term projects between scholars in the United States and Brazil and, through their publications, are encouraging the scholarly development of Afro-Brazilian researchers. Livio Sansone, an Italian scholar working in Brazil, has challenged the explicitly race-conscious perspectives of some foreign scholars as well as the countervailing tendency of Brazilian scholars to subordinate race to class analyses. He proposes an approach that lies in between those extremes as a more accurate rendering of the complexities of race in Brazil.[26] In that regard, scholarship exploring the shaping of identities beyond the strictures of race has greatly expanded our understanding of multiple Afro-Brazilian realities.[27]

Regardless of how it is characterized or explained, the persistence of racial inequality and the social constructions and usages of race have been dominant themes blurring the boundaries between history and social science. The other predominant area of scholarship—cultural studies on Afro-Brazilian sacred traditions, *capoeira* and other martial art forms, and popular culture generally—has also informed work in the humanities, so that there has been rich cross-influencing contributing to Afro-Brazilian studies. Micol Seigel looks at the construction of Afro-Brazilian and national culture in the postabolition years as a transnational project linking the politics and the creativity of the jazz age. Darién Davis documents the linkages between the political and the racial project, a theme taken up in several case studies on the specific ways of inscribing racial hierarchies in the modern era.[28] The degree to which culture is a tool of social liberation and political expression is explored in works ranging from general studies to specific artistic moments, and has recently come to include studies of the new hip-hop cultures emerging in the urban south.[29]

Tracing midcentury Afro-Brazilian culture and politics, Michael Hanchard argues against a disproportionate emphasis on culture as the sine qua non of sociopolitical mobilization.[30] His work facilitates greater discourse between cultural analysts and the political scientists whose statistically based work has documented some of the real-life implications of racism in Brazil. Work by such scholars as Edward Telles, Carlos Hasenbalg, and Nelson do Valle Silva, as well as a major study from the *Folha de São Paulo*, have not only provided hard evidence of the illusory nature of Brazil's fabled "racial democracy," but have also interrogated the different implications of being "black" or "brown."[31]

Regardless of their specific disciplinary focus, new studies on race in postabolition Brazil appear regularly due to increasing interest, and also to such research centers as the Centro de Estudos Afro-Asiáticos in Rio de Janeiro, the Centro de Estudos Afro-Orientais in Salvador, and the Federal University campuses in Campinas and Rio de Janeiro, along with the ongoing work at major universities such as the University of São Paulo. All these institutions frequently publish master's theses, occasional papers, and reports. Despite the voluminous literature on race in Brazil, the evolution of racial dynamics in the postabolition era remains a lesser-studied aspect of Afro-Brazilian history, but it is an area increasingly enriched by ongoing research on both ethnic history and its relation to this era.

The historiography on these topics in the Spanish-speaking Caribbean has been principally on Cuba, the most important and longest-lasting slave society in the area. Christopher Schmidt-Nowara focuses on the role of the Spanish Abolitionist Society in the destruction of Puerto Rican and Cuban slavery in 1873 and 1886, respectively. For Cuba, Rebecca Scott looks at the interplay between the Ten Years' War for Independence (1868–78) and Cuban abolition, as well as the various ways planters substituted for slave labor and slaves struggled to gain freedom. Philip Howard and Fannie Rushing examine black societies and *cabildos de nación* (religious and mutual aid societies allowing descendants of distinct African ethnic identity to perpetuate their heritage) as prominent spaces for African and Afro-Cuban solidarities and political activism. Focusing on Cuba's three wars for independence, from 1868 to 1898, Ada Ferrer investigates the tensions between racism and antiracism contained within Cuban nationalism. Challenging Cuba's myth of racial democracy, Aline Helg analyzes Afro-Cubans' postslavery mobilization, notably the Independent Party of Color, up to the massacre of thousands of them by the Cuban army in 1912. Alejandro de la Fuente examines race and racial equality in the labor market, education, and political representation in Cuba's twentieth-century process of national formation and socialist revolution. A central question in these works is whether in a racially stratified society such as Cuba, the empowerment and racial pride of the historically oppressed Afro-Cuban minority are key to the decline of racism and racial discrimination. If Helg tends to conclude so, Ferrer and de la Fuente believe that the existence of a national rhetoric of racial inclusiveness creates significant opportunities for Afro-Cubans to influence the nation-state project.[32] Linked to this debate is the scholarship on the intellectual and military role of mulatto general Antonio Maceo in Cuba's independence process.[33]

Race in nineteenth-century Puerto Rico is the topic of a work by Jay Kinsbruner demonstrating that racial prejudice, both legal and social, has produced cumulative disadvantage for free Afro-Puerto Ricans, especially women. Free working-class women of color and their strategies against inequality are also at the core of a study by Félix V. Matos Rodríguez. Teresita Martínez-Vergne examines how San Juan's bourgeoisie attempted to impose its power over the capital's popular classes, above all poor and "deviant" people of African descent and women, through the control of the public space. Eileen Suárez Findlay examines the island's antiprostitution campaigns and marriage reforms and the responses they generated, especially among Afro-Puerto Rican women during the shift from Spanish to U.S. colonialism. The project of "Americanization" of the island by U.S. colonial authorities and its impact on race and gender up to 1932 is analyzed by Pedro A. Cabán.[34]

Since Haiti's occupation from 1822 to 1844, issues of race in the Dominican Republic have been shaped by the nation's relationship with its "black" neighbor. Dominicans, a people with significant African ancestry, have tended to ascribe blackness, Africanness, and other forms of otherness to Haitians, defining themselves, in contrast, as *indios*. Harry Hoetink argues that Dominican racial studies are inseparable from the study of Haitians in the Spanish-speaking portion of Hispaniola. The presence of Haitian migrant workers on sugar plantations during the long U.S. occupation of Hispaniola in the 1910s and 1920s further exacerbated racial tensions, which exploded in the now well-researched massacre of thousands of Haitian settlers on the border engineered by Dominican dictator Rafael Trujillo in 1937. In particular, Ernesto Sagás looks closely at the pervasive doctrine of *antihaitianismo*, which has enabled Dominican elites to reject blackness, silence the darker and poorer Dominicans, and unite Dominicans around the myth of a racially harmonious society. Focusing in part on the border with Haiti, Lauren Derby and Richard Turits explore the role played by the 1937 massacre in the ambivalent support of the Dominican peasantry to Trujillo.[35] Less researched has been the influence of U.S. occupations (1916–24) on Dominican racial construct and tensions.

Despite having a population comprising a majority of *pardos* (people of mixed African ancestry), Venezuela has been the focus of few historical studies. For more than three decades, anthropologist Angelina Pollak-Eltz has examined Venezuela's "black culture" in its many spheres of influence, such as religion, folklore, music, and family structure. In 1990, Winthrop R. Wright's *Café con leche* (coffee with milk) analyzed the antiblack prejudice and discrimination prevalent in Venezuelan society as well as the government's whitening policies concomitant with a public discourse celebrating *mestizaje*. But in Venezuela as elsewhere, racism has also permeated part of the Afro-American middle class, which has stereotyped African-derived cultures and lower-class lifestyles as inferior, a phenomenon known as endoracism and studied by María Marta Mijares.[36]

For Colombia as well, until recently the history of its populations of African descent has been the work of anthropologists or limited to the field of colonial slavery.[37] Starting in the 1990s, however, the adoption of a new constitution recognizing Colombia's diversity and of a law legalizing the traditional communal landholdings of the "black communities" in the Pacific lowlands has given impetus to Afro-Colombian historical studies. Building on anthropologist Peter Wade's analysis of the regionalization of race in Colombia, several works show that Colombia's national pursuit of *mestizaje* and whitening has masked racial conflicts and the continuing marginalization of the indigenous and Afro-Colombian population. Francisco U. Zuluaga examines how during the independence wars and their aftermath, some free Afro-Colombian communities in Southern Cauca negotiated their support first for the patriot or royalist armies and later for the Liberal or Conservative parties in order to defend their own interests. Aline Helg analyzes the historical roots of Colombia's neglect of its Afro-Caribbean identity by exploring the role of free and enslaved blacks, elite whites, and indigenous peoples in the processes of independence and early nation building in the Caribbean region. Marixa Lasso examines the aspirations of Afro-Colombian participants in patriot struggles during the same period, when an ideology of racial equality conflicted with entrenched racism. Nancy Appelbaum reveals the hidden history of usurpation and displacement of indigenous and African-descended communities that led to the establishment of the legendary white pioneer families of the western coffee region of Riosucio from the mid-nineteenth to the mid-twentieth century. Focusing on Antioquia during Colombia's civil war of the Violencia (1948–53), Mary Roldán shows how race, ethnicity, and class marked the partisan conflict and allowed for the seizure of lands and natural resources in a predominantly Afro-Colombian area.[38]

In contrast, for Ecuador and Peru the historiography on people of African descent has remained modest in comparison with anthropological studies. Still, looking at the Pacific coast of Ecuador and Colombia, Norman Whitten's pioneer examination of the culture of this predominantly black region includes a strong historical perspective, as do two more recent case studies, on lowland Esmeraldas and on Concepción in the highlands, respectively.[39] Denys Cuche's 1981 study of Afro-Peruvians in postslavery plantations remains isolated, but Ramón Aranda de los Rios has since contributed the first inquiry into an uprising by black hacienda workers during the War of the Pacific (1879–83).[40]

Until recently, relatively little has been published on the postabolition era in Uruguay, although, like Brazil, it had a flourishing black press and active black organizations in the early twentieth century. The treatment of blacks in Uruguay's nineteenth-century regional wars and their subsequent marginalization in Uruguayan society, in particular, informed Afro-Uruguayan political expressions. Romero J. Rodríguez provides a much-needed contribution to the historiographical lacuna with his 2006 overview of Afro-Uruguayan history. Although it opens with African antecedents and slavery, the book emphasizes the eras from postabolition through the present. Romero includes a detailed discussion of early-twentieth-century Afro-Uruguayan organizations and initiatives, including youth groups, black women's social and political organizations, and the black press.[41] An earlier work by Romero is part of a wider body of literature focusing on the mid- to late twentieth century and contemporary Afro-Uruguayan politics.[42]

Argentina's historiography on race is dominated by the conundrum of the virtual disappearance of the once numerous African-descended population concentrated in the viceregal capital of Buenos Aires. George Reid Andrews's exploration of this question in 1980 combined conventional demographic explanations with a serious consideration of social attitudes privileging whiteness and promoting assimilation.[43] Recent scholarship has sought to probe this phenomenon further, utilizing insights from research elsewhere in Latin America. Oscar Chamosa's analysis of Afro-Argentinian organizations during the transition to postabolition and Andrews's study of Uruguayan black societies from 1865 to 1930 echo themes explored recently in Brazil and Cuba, particularly the move away from African nation-based identity toward color identity and the shift in the primary functions of these organizations as other structures came to address the needs of the black community.[44] Similarly, Carmen Bernand, Lucía Dominga Molina, and Mario Luis López address this period, citing extensive evidence of Argentina's rich African-descended past.[45] The processes by which that past was negated, and attempts to now reclaim it, have repercussions for understanding race politics throughout Latin America.[46] With few full-length historical treatments available, Constance García-Barrio has pointed to alternative sources, such as literature, to document the complex relationships between Afro-Latins and early nationalist politics.[47]

Argentina is but one apparent anomaly that helps reveal some of the nuances in ethnic identity in the Americas. Along the Atlantic coast of Central America, Africans intermingled with indigenous peoples to create what are known today as Black Carib and Garifuna communities in Honduras, Belize, and Nicaragua. Edmund Gordon looks at the creation of these multiethnic communities and the evolution of their history with the dominant Spanish-speaking culture in Nicaragua in a treatment that also layers in an analysis of present-day cultural interactions.[48] Closely focused studies such as this have helped unravel the many ways in which ethnicities have been created, defended, and reimagined in the Americas. With the changing conditions attendant on abolition, ethnicity among African descendants took distinct trajectories, related less to African origins and increasingly to issues of class and political organization in each community. Thus, rather than a commonly shared identity across Afro-Latin America, multiple variations arose, each with its own political implications. These issues have been explored in several postabolition works. Helg and Butler suggest that "blackness" as an identity emerged only under specific conditions, leading to the larger question of who chooses race as a primary political identity, and why. One factor that seems clearly related is the degree to which the state and society racialized its black citizens. If the decrees and practices of states and elites were racially determined, it is likely that the response would have been, too. It is also important to consider the new internationalized consciousness of the early twentieth century, which led to pan-Africanism, the Garvey movement, and Negritude.

Garveyism came to Latin America through the multiple migrations stemming from the Caribbean as its labor market adapted to postabolition opportunities in a global economy increasingly dominated by U.S. entrepreneurship. The various efforts to build transcontinental shipping avenues, such as the railroad projects in Brazil and Costa Rica and, most successfully, the Panama Canal, along with plantation agriculture in Central America and Cuba, attracted frustrated Caribbean workers, mostly from Jamaica.[49] The less lucrative projects tend to be overshadowed by the history of the Canal, but they are nonetheless significant episodes in Afro-Latin history. Construction of the failed Madeira-Mamoré Railroad (1878–1912), for example, brought to Brazil over 20,000 workers from more than fifty countries, the majority from the Caribbean. Of these, most were Barbadian, but their numbers included immigrant workers from Grenada, St. Vincent, St. Lucia, Jamaica, Martinique, and Trinidad as well.[50]

In general, these seasonal or permanent migrations were closely related to the expansion of U.S. imperialism in the Caribbean and continental America through military occupations, Washington's support for exploitative Spanish-American dictators, and the acquisition of immense agricultural properties by U.S. companies. Although no existing study focuses globally on these U.S.-engineered migrations of non-Spanish-speaking Afro-Caribbean workers, several works look at the experience mostly of Jamaicans and Barbadians in Panama and Costa Rica. Jeffrey Casey Gaspar, Philippe Bourgois, Elisavinda Echeverri-Gent, Trevor Purcell, and Aviva Chomsky focus on the United Fruit Company in their research, whereas Lancelot Lewis, Velma Newton, and Michael Conniff highlight the Panama Canal. Elizabeth Petras examines the relationships between Jamaica and Panama and Cuba. In addition, sugar plantations in Cuba and the Dominican Republic also received high numbers of Haitian workers. Generally, the push and pull factors, labor conditions, and workers' resistance are well-researched topics in the literature on Central America, as are the relationships between these migrants and their host societies, from rejection to gradual acceptance with continuing racial discrimination. In addition, West Indian strikes and the role played by Garveyism in them are analyzed by Ronald Harpelle. Less examined for Central America are the experiences of Afro-Caribbean women migrants, the culture of the immigrant communities, and ethnic differences between immigrants.[51] In contrast, historians of Cuba, such as Marc McLeod, Barry Carr, and Aviva Chomsky, have explored the cultural and religious differences between British West Indian and Haitian immigrants, their insertion in the labor movement, Cuban reactions to their coming, and the diffusion of Garveyism among them.[52]

As they traveled and resettled, these workers, largely from Jamaica and Barbados, but including a broad cross section of the Caribbean in its total, experienced disillusionment with the promises of postabolition labor opportunities, which too often situated them in slavery-like conditions and race hierarchies in the workforce. Their frustrations and political interpretations linking proletarianism and race were inscribed in the pages of *The Negro World* and circulated throughout the Caribbean enclaves in the Americas, which also became host to branches of the United Negro Improvement Association (UNIA). Along with concern with, and response to, the partitioning of Africa among European colonial powers, and eventually World War I, black migrations and cosmopolitan centers gave rise to a transnational conversation that resulted in the Harlem Renaissance, Négritude, and Pan-Africanism. While scholars such as Irma Watkins-Owens, Winston James, Brent Edwards, and Michelle Stephens look to New York or Paris, few center Afro-Latin perspectives on these ideological trends.[53] Négritude, although a Francophone expression, nevertheless engaged with literary and artistic works in Brazil and the Spanish-speaking Caribbean.[54]

Just as the politics of the early twentieth century inspired transnationalism, so too did developments such as African independence struggles, the antiapartheid movement in South Africa, and broader geopolitical debates on racism, slavery, economic inequality, and other concerns of social justice that increasingly transcended race.[55] The movement of Black Power and revolutionary black nationalism of the 1960s and '70s had a profound impact on Cuba, where at the beginning activists from the United States were welcome. Later on, however, the government of Fidel Castro feared their influence on Afro-Cuban youth.[56] Simultaneously, some

African-American visitors became critical of the regime's paternalist solution to racial discrimination. This chapter of the history of Afro-American internationalism is still to be completely investigated. Similarly, Cuba was a key figure in Cold War politics, particularly in its role as supporter of armed anticolonial forces in Africa, some of them hosted for training on the island.[57]

Historical treatments of the role of Afro-Latin peoples in the philosophical movements of the early twentieth century have yet to fully realize the dream of Arturo Alonzo Schomburg, the Puerto Rican scholar-activist who collected one of the most extensive archives of literature on the black world (now the Schomburg Center for Research in Black Culture, part of the New York Public Library). Much of the literature dealing with internationalism addresses Afro-Latin contributions abroad to some extent, but the depth and extent of their interactions with other African descendants both in and outside Latin America is most indelibly inscribed in the art born of those relationships. The larger body of arts scholarship is too extensive to survey in the present essay, but it is useful to address several points connecting cultural analyses to questions of race.

In the early twentieth century, cultural studies were an important vehicle for understanding race in Latin America. Fueled by a desire to interrogate biological determinism and later by the new discipline of anthropology, scholars generated a body of literature focused on African descendants that became the foundation for future research on race. This first generation of cultural studies was primarily ethnographic in nature, characterized either as recording primitive traditions challenged by the confrontation with modernity or as inscriptions of race differences. In the context of the time, the European ideal versus the African opposite informed a hierarchical consideration of culture. Contemporaries tended to negate or condemn the African roots of national cultures. This resulted in poor peoples' cultural expressions being more deeply tied to African traditions and thus considered lowbrow due to their dual roots in poverty and Africanity. Yet it is precisely in these forms that scholars have begun to mine a rich archive of embedded historical memory. Scholars of the latter twentieth century often had first to identify and claim African-based cultures before moving on to more recent work which goes beyond ethnographic recording of traditions to a reading of culture for its historical, sociological, and political implications.

The profound African imprint on American cultures was historically denied due to racism; as a result, a significant focus of scholarship on culture has been to situate and identify the components of national cultures stemming from their African descendants. Writing against historical invisibility, scholars have revealed the African roots of such quintessentially national expressions as the Argentinian tango and are increasingly able to disentangle the intertwined creolized elements to locate specific antecedents on the continent.[58] Robin Moore analyzes the implications of the appropriation of segments of Afro-Cuban culture in the forging of national identity, a process repeated throughout the hemisphere and treated in most of the postabolition studies mentioned elsewhere in this essay. Elements of African-based culture considered acceptable to national identity were valorized by erasing the mark of race, thereby maintaining the association of "black" culture as undesirable, lowbrow, and even antipatriotic.[59]

Music has been a particularly rich avenue for the investigation of race, ethnicity, and their attendant history and politics. Even where historical literature is scarce, such as Argentina, Peru and Uruguay, scholarship on music has greatly enhanced race studies. Recent works have been especially important for disentangling the complexities of national identity formation and the national project in general as it impacted, and was influenced by, racialized peoples.[60] Because music has often reflected transnational connections, it has also revealed how racial construction takes place beyond the national level. Some of these questions are explored in recent works on Brazil by Christopher Dunn and Micael Herschmann.[61]

Many other forms of culture help interpret race in Latin America. In her work on Cuban rumba, Yvonne Daniel argues that social change is inscribed in dance.[62] Robert Stam engaged cinema as a vehicle for exploring race in Brazil.[63] Literature, mentioned above, has been important in its own right, but some novelists such as Quince Duncan (Costa Rica) and Manuel Zapata Olivella (Colombia) have also published analytical works of importance.[64] The literature on religion is too extensive to be discussed in this essay, but it is an essential component of research on race. In addition, the religious cultures of the Americas reflect their diversity beyond the black/white binary.[65]

The ongoing racial disparities documented by research on Latin America have also affected the latter's nature; scholars of African descent are sorely underrepresented in universities and in the historical literature. In addition, despite historians' broad use of national, regional, and local archives, the voices of the subaltern have remained elusive and, when they exist, are often transcribed and transformed by others in the hostile context of police investigations, trials, or journalistic accounts. As stressed by Stephan Palmié in his critique of historians' use of hegemonic Western "rational" categories (notably modernity versus tradition) to account for Afro-Cubans' actions and ideas, closer attention should be given to the discourse of subaltern men and women—a complex and problematic task.[66]

Afro-Latin culture has more commonly been recorded in cultural expressions and oral traditions. Just as scholars have mined culture for its social, political, and historical content, several oral histories have appeared in recent years that serve as rich complements to other sources. Perhaps the most widely read and critiqued Cuban slave narrative is Miguel Barnet's *Biografía de un cimarrón*, originally published in 1966. Daisy Rubiera Castillo edited an autobiographical narrative by her mother, *Reyita, sencillamente*, which provides a black woman's reflections on nine decades of Cuban history.[67] While oral history has informed much of the scholarship on twentieth-century Afro-Brazilian history, the interviews themselves are often not readily available. Shortly after the death of activist José Correia Leite, São Paulo scholar Cuti published an extensive series of interviews compiled over years which recovers the voice of one of the most important activists of the era. Though not formally interviews, several other texts capture the voices of Afro-Brazilian women, ranging from the diary of a homeless woman surviving on scraps of refuse to the memoir of Benedita da Silva, the first Afro-Brazilian woman to sit in Congress and former governor of Rio de Janeiro.[68] Ben Vinson III offers a fresh take on both the techniques of oral history and the parameters of Afro-Latin history in his memoir of the life of Virgil Richardson, a former Tuskegee Airman who, like many African Americans under various conditions since the nineteenth century, ultimately settled in Mexico.[69]

The general studies of race and African culture in the Americas tend to be historical overviews, and very few focus specifically on the postabolition era. One exception is the comparative study of emancipation and its aftermath by Frederic Cooper, Thomas Holt, and Rebecca Scott.[70] A 1995 anthology by the Minority Rights Group includes contributions by scholars of individual nations with historical overviews as context for contemporary social, economic, and political issues.[71] More typical of comparative studies or overviews of Afro-Latin America is a focus on slavery and African cultural heritage. Written with a polemical tone uncharacteristic today, but in easily accessible language, Leslie Rout's study of Spanish-speaking America chronicles a comprehensive history of the region through the 1970s.[72] Michael Conniff and Thomas J. Davis have coauthored one of the very few overviews of slavery and its aftermath focusing on all the Americas. Written specifically as a textbook, it takes a primarily regional approach distinguishing the United States, Brazil, and Spanish America.[73] Since the early 1990s, several overviews, anthologies, and edited volumes have increasingly explored the postemancipation era and taken a more nuanced approach to race, ethnicity, and class.[74] An important addition to this literature is Reid Andrews's *Afro-Latin America*, a comparative study focusing on the evolution of African descendants' roles in Latin American societies after 1800. Andrews draws on a wealth of recent scholarship detailing black agency, organizations, and struggles as they worked through defining issues such as immigration, labor market adjustments, black consciousness movements, and contemporary politics.[75]

While the literature on race in the Americas has focused primarily on African descendants, the interplay of ethnic dynamics is now being explored more widely to include indigenous peoples, Asians, and other ethnic groups represented in Latin American societies. Notably, Jeffrey Lesser studies the experiences of immigrants from Japan, China, the Middle East, and North Africa to Brazil in the context of the debates over national identity in the twentieth century.[76]

A clear direction for new research has been scholarly conversation across disciplines and regional boundaries.[77] In addition, communications technology has facilitated dialogue between local and foreign scholars of specific countries, although the distribution of resources continues to privilege scholars able to access them. Further, while graduate schools in the United States have trained increasing numbers of students of color and students from Latin America, higher education in Latin America has not yet benefited fully from the diversity of voices of its population.

However, in increasingly diverse ways, a multitude of voices are speaking out about racial constructions and their meanings in the Americas.[78] Despite the wide range of the literature considered here, historians concur that slavery and colonialism continue to impact the nations of the Americas, and that racial inequality has clearly persisted. In a recent publication, Quince Duncan articulates some new takes on the debate about race, particularly as it is studied in Latin America.[79] Under the construct of "unity in diversity," Duncan defends the study of, and connection with, ancestral ethnicity not as segregationist, but as empowerment and enrichment of the nation as a whole. He raises the political issue of reparations, which can be extended to land claims by indigenous and black peoples, both as explosive as the African independence struggle and both connected to the ways we write and interpret the history of race in Latin America. Finally, Duncan looks to collaboration with other African descendants (a term borrowed from Latin Americans' use of *afrodescendientes*) in Latin America and beyond, transcending the boundaries of language and colonial borders that have impeded a more holistic understanding of ethnicity and race for the many diasporas of the region. To the extent that we can expand our understanding of this complex topic, we will better understand the infinitely intriguing world of the Americas.

NOTES

1. Ted Vinent, *The Legacy of Vicente Guerrero: Mexico's First Black Indian President* (Gainesville: University Press of Florida, 2001).

2. Anthologies providing a regional overview of these issues include Nancy Naro, ed., *Blacks, Coloureds and National Identity in Nineteenth Century Latin America* (London: London Institute of Latin American Studies, 2003); and Nancy P. Applebaum, Anne S. Macherson, and Karin Alejandra Rosemblatt, eds., *Race and Nation in Modern Latin America* (Chapel Hill: University of North Carolina Press, 2001).

3. Notably, Michael Gomez examines the African diaspora and its links with Africa across time and continents in *Reversing Sail: A History of the African Diaspora* (Cambridge, U.K.: Cambridge University Press, 2005). New frameworks for graduate programs are facilitating comparative contexts for Latin American studies (Jack P. Greene, "Beyond Power: Paradigm Subversion and Reformulation and the Re-Creation of the Early Modern Atlantic World," in *Crossing Boundaries: Comparative History of Black People in Diaspora*, ed. Darlene Clark Hine and Jacqueline McLeod (Bloomington: Indiana University Press, 1999), 319–42. The African diaspora as a framework for Latin American studies is addressed by Ben Vinson in his introduction to a special issue of *The Americas*: Ben Vinson III, "African (Black) Diaspora History, Latin American History," *The Americas* 63:1 (2006): 1–18.

4. On the Haitian Revolution, see Thomas O. Ott, *The Haitian Revolution, 1789–1804* (Knoxville: University of Tennessee Press, 1973); Jean Fouchard, *The Haitian Maroons: Liberty or Death*, translated by A. Faulkner Watts (New York: Edward W. Blyden Press, 1981); David Patrick Geggus, *Slavery, War, and Revolution: The British Occupation of Saint Domingue, 1793–1798* (Oxford and New York: Clarendon Press and Oxford University Press, 1982); Carolyn Fick, *The Making of Haiti: The Saint Domingue Revolution from Below* (Knoxville: University of Tennessee Press, 1990); Franklin W. Knight, "The Haitian Revolution," *American Historical Review* 105:1 (2000): 103–15; David Patrick Geggus, *Haitian Revolutionary Studies* (Bloomington: Indiana University Press, 2002); Laurent Dubois, *Avengers of the New World: The Story of the Haitian Revolution* (Cambridge, Mass.: The Belknap Press, 2004). On Haiti

after independence in 1804, see David Nicholls, *From Dessalines to Duvalier: Race, Colour and National Independence in Haiti* ([1979] New Brunswick: Rutgers University Press, 1996); Michel-Rolph Trouillot, *Haiti: State against Nation: The Origins and Legacy of Duvalierism* (New York: Monthly Review Press, 1990); Anne Greene, *The Catholic Church in Haiti: Political and Social Change* (East Lansing: Michigan State University Press, 1993); Mary A. Renda, *Taking Haiti: Military Occupation and the Culture of U.S. Imperialism, 1915–1940* (Chapel Hill: University of North Carolina Press, 2001).

5. On the impact of the Haitian Revolution in Latin America, see Julius Scott, "The Common Wind: Currents of Afro-American Communication in the Era of the Haitian Revolution" (PhD diss., Duke University, 1986); Anthony P. Maingot, "Haiti and the Terrified Consciousness of the Caribbean," in *Ethnicity in the Caribbean: Essays in Honor of Harry Hoetink*, ed. Gert Oostindies (London: MacMillan Caribbean, 1996), 53–80; David Barry Gaspar and David Patrick Geggus, eds., *A Turbulent Time: The French Revolution and the Greater Caribbean* (Bloomington: Indiana University Press, 1997); David P. Geggus, ed., *The Impact of the Haitian Revolution in the Atlantic World* (Charleston: University of South Carolina Press, 2001).

6. For example, Leslie Manigat, "Haiti dans les luttes d'indépendance vénézuélienne (Pétion et Bolivar: Naissance du Panaméricanisme)," in *Bolívar et les peoples de Nuestra América: Des sans-culotte noirs au libertador*, ed. Alain Yacou (Bordeaux: Presses Universitaires de Bordeaux, 1990), 29–42; Ada Ferrer, "Noticias de Haiti en Cuba," *Revista de Indias* 63:229 (2003): 675–94; Michel-Rolf Trouillot, *Silencing the Past: Power and the Production of History* (Boston: Beacon Press, 1995).

7. Peter Voelz, *Slave and Soldier: The Military Impact of Blacks in the Colonial Americas* (New York: Garland, 1993). See also Ben Vinson III, *Bearing Arms for His Majesty: The Free-Colored Militia in Colonial Mexico* (Stanford: Stanford University Press, 2001); Matt D. Childs, *The 1812 Aponte Rebellion in Cuba and the Struggle against Atlantic Slavery* (Chapel Hill: University of North Carolina Press, 2006); Zachary Morgan, "Legislating the Lash: Race and the Conflicting Modernities of Enlistment and Corporal Punishment in the Brazilian Military during the Empire," *Journal of Colonialism and Colonial History* 5:2 (2004).

8. Peter Beattie, *The Tribute of Blood: Army, Honor, Race and Nation in Brazil* (Durham, N.C.: Duke University Press, 2001); George Reid Andrews, "The Afro-Argentine Officers of Buenos Aires Province, 1800–1860," *Journal of Negro History* 64 (Spring 1979): 85–100; Clément Thibaud, *Repúblicas en armas: Los ejércitos bolivarianos en la guerra de Independencia en Colombia y Venezuela* (Bogotá: Planeta, 2003); Aline Helg, *Liberty and Equality in Caribbean Colombia, 1770–1835* (Chapel Hill: University of North Carolina Press, 2004).

9. Peter Blanchard, *Under the Flags of Freedom: Slave Soldiers and the Wars of Independence in Spanish South America* (Pittsburgh: University of Pittsburgh Press, 2008); Helg, *Liberty and Equality*.

10. Robin Blackburn, *The Overthrow of Colonial Slavery, 1776–1848* (London: Verso, 1988), 337.

11. John V. Lombardi, *The Decline and Abolition of Negro Slavery in Venezuela, 1820–1854* (Westport, Conn.: Greenwood Press, 1971); Peter Blanchard, *Slavery and Abolition in Early Republican Peru* (Wilmington, Del.: Scholarly Resources, 1992); Christine Hunefeldt, *Paying the Price of Freedom: Family and Labor among Lima's Slaves, 1800–1854* (Berkeley: University of California Press, 1994); Carlos Aguirre, *Agentes de su propia libertad: Los esclavos de Lima y la desintegración de la esclavitud, 1821–1854* (Lima: Pontificia Universidad Católica del Perú, 1993). For an institutional approach, Margarita González, "El proceso de manumisión en Colombia," *Cuadernos Colombianos* 2 (1974): 145–240.

12. For en excellent review of this literature, see Hilda Sabato, "On Political Citizenship in Nineteenth-Century Latin America," *American Historical Review* 106 (October 2001): 1290–315. For a discussion of the Colombian case, see Helg, *Liberty and Equality*.

13. On gender and abolitionism and emancipation in Brazil and Cuba, see the chapters by Roger Kittleson and Michael Zeuske, respectively, in *Gender and Slave Emancipation in the Atlantic World*, ed. Pamela Scully and Diana Paton (Durham, N.C.: Duke University Press, 2005).

14. Hendrik Kraay, *Race, State and Armed Forces in Independence-Era Brazil: Bahia, 1790s–1840s* (Stanford: Stanford University Press, 2001); Beattie, *The Tribute of Blood*.

15. George Reid Andrews, *Blacks and Whites in São Paulo, Brazil, 1888–1988* (Madison: University of Wisconsin Press, 1991); Florestan Fernandes, *The Negro in Brazilian Society* (New York: Columbia University Press, 1969).

16. Miriam Nicolau Ferrara, *A Imprensa Negra Paulista, 1915–1963* (São Paulo: FFLECH-USP, 1986); Cuti (Luiz Silva), *E disse o velho militante José Correia Leite* (São Paulo: Secretaria Municipal de Cultura, 1992); Michael Mitchell, "Racial Conscious and the Political Attitudes and Behavior of Blacks in São Paulo, Brazil" (PhD diss., Indiana University, 1977).

17. Olívia Maria Gomes da Cunha and Flávio dos Santos Gomes, eds. *Quase-cidadão: Histórias e antropologias da pós-emancipacão no Brasil* (Rio de Janeiro: FGV, 2007).

18. Walter Fraga Filho, *Encruzilhadas da liberdade: Histórias de escravos e libertos na Bahia, 1870–1910* (Campinas: Unicamp, 2006); Dale Torston Graden, *From Slavery to Freedom in Brazil: Bahia, 1835–1900* (Albuquerque: University of New Mexico Press, 2006).

19. Kim D. Butler, *Freedoms Given, Freedoms Won: Afro-Brazilians in Post-Abolition São Paulo and Salvador* (New Brunswick: Rutgers University Press, 1998); Elisa Larkin Nascimento, *The Sorcery of Color: Identity, Race, and Gender in Brazil* (Philadelphia: Temple University Press, 2007).

20. Gilberto Freyre, *The Masters and the Slaves* (New York: Alfred Knopf, 1946); Fernandes, *The Negro in Brazilian Society*.

21. Some of the leading scholars of race were victims of the purge of the faculty of the prestigious University of São Paulo in 1969, including Fernandes, Octavio Ianni, and future Brazilian president Fernando Henrique Cardoso.

22. Octavio Ianni, *Raças e classes sociais no Brasil* ([1966] São Paulo: Brasiliense, 1987); Clóvis Moura, *O Negro, de bom escravo a mau cidadão?* (Rio de Janeiro: Conquista, 1977); Abdias do Nascimento, *Brazil: Mixture or Massacre? Essays in the Genocide of a Black People*, 2nd ed., rev. (Dover, Mass.: Majority Press, 1989).

23. Donald Pierson. *Negroes in Brazil: A Study of Race Contact at Bahia* (Chicago: University of Chicago Press, 1944).

24. Anthony W. Marx, *Making Race and Nation: A Comparison of the United States, South Africa, and Brazil* (New York: Cambridge University Press, 1998); George M. Frederickson, *The Comparative Imagination: On the History of Racism, Nationalism, and Social Movements* (Berkeley: University of California Press, 1997); Charles V. Hamilton, ed., *Beyond Racism: Race and Inequality in Brazil, South Africa and the U.S.* (Boulder, Colo.: Lynne Rienner, 2001). An earlier significant comparative study was Carl N. Degler, *Neither Black nor White: Slavery and Race Relations in Brazil and the United States* (New York: Macmillan, 1971).

25. Michael G. Hanchard, ed., *Racial Politics in Contemporary Brazil* (Durham, N.C.: Duke University Press, 1999); Georgia A. Persons, ed., *Race and Democracy in the Americas* (New Brunswick: Transaction, 2003); Pierre-Michel Fontaine, ed., *Race, Class and Power in Brazil* (Los Angeles: UCLA Center for Afro-American Studies, 1985).

26. Livio Sansone, *Blackness without Ethnicity: Constructing Race in Brazil* (New York: Palgrave, 2003).

27. J. Lorand Matory, "The English Professors of Brazil: On the Diasporic Roots of the Yoruba Nation," *Comparative Studies in Society and History* 41:1 (1999): 72–103.

28. Micol Seigel, *Uneven Encounters: Making Black and White in Brazil and the United States, 1918–1933* (Durham, N.C.: Duke University Press, 2009); Darién Davis, *Avoiding the Dark: Race and the Forging of National Culture in Modern Brazil* (Brookfield, Vt.: Ashgate, 1999); France Winddance Twine, *Racism in a Racial Democracy: The Maintenance of White Supremacy in Brazil* (New Brunswick: Rutgers University Press, 1998); Jeferson Bacelar, *A hierarquia das raças: Negros e brancos em Salvador* (Rio de Janeiro: Pallas, 2001).

29. Larry Crook and Randal Johnson, eds., *Black Brazil: Culture, Identity and Social Mobilization* (Los Angeles: UCLA Latin American Center Publications, 2000); Christopher Dunn, *Brutality Garden: Tropicalia and the Emergence of a Brazilian Counterculture* (Chapel Hill: University of North Carolina Press, 2001); Micael Herschmann, *O Funk e o Hip Hop invadem a cena* (Rio de Janeiro: UFRJ, 2000); Micael Herschmann, *Abalando os anos noventa: Funk e Hip Hop* (Rio de Janeiro: Rocco, 1997).

30. Michael George Hanchard, *Orpheus and Power: The* Movimento Negro *of Rio de Janeiro and São Paulo, Brazil, 1945–1988* (Princeton: Princeton University Press, 1994).

31. Edward Telles, *Race in Another America: The Significance of Skin Color in Brazil* (Princeton: Princeton University Press, 2004); Cleusa Turra and Gustavo Venturi, eds., *Racismo Cordial* (São Paulo: Atica, 1995); Carlos Hasenbalg, *Disriminação e desigualdades raciais no Brasil* (Rio de Janeiro: Graal, 1979); Nelson do Valle Silva and Carlos Hasenbalg, *Relações raciais no Brasil contemporâneo* (Rio de Janeiro: Rio Fundo, 1992); Hanchard, ed., *Racial Politics in Contemporary Brazil*; Rebecca Reichman, ed., *Race in Contemporary Brazil: From Indifference to Inequality* (University Park: Pennsylvania State University Press, 1999); Lilia Moritz Schwarcz, *Racismo no Brasil* (São Paulo: Publifolha, 2001).

32. Christopher Schmidt-Nowara, *Empire and Antislavery: Spain, Cuba, and Puerto Rico, 1833–1874* (Pittsburgh: University of Pittsburgh Press, 1997); Rebecca J. Scott, *Slave Emancipation in Cuba: The Transition to Free Labor, 1860–1899* (Princeton, N.J.: Princeton University Press, 1985); Philip A. Howard, *Changing History: Afro-Cuban Cabildos and Societies of Color in the Nineteenth Century* (Baton Rouge: Louisiana State University Press, 1998); Fannie Theresa Rushing, "Afro-Cuban Social Organization and Identity in a Colonial Slave Society, 1800–1888," *Colonial Latin American Historical Review* 11:2 (2002): 177–202; Ada Ferrer, *Insurgent Cuba: Race, Nation, and Revolution, 1868–1898* (Chapel Hill: University of North Carolina Press, 1999); Aline Helg, *Our Rightful Share: The Afro-Cuban Struggle for Equality, 1886–1912* (Chapel Hill: University of North Carolina Press, 1995); Alejandro de la Fuente, *A Nation for All. Race, Inequality, and Politics in Twentieth-Century Cuba* (Chapel Hill: University of North Carolina Press, 2001). See also Serafín Portuondo Linares, *Los Independientes de Color. Historia del Partido Independiente de Color* ([1950] Havana: Editorial Caminos, 2002); Pedro Serviat, *El problema negro en Cuba y su solución definitiva* (Havana: Editora Política, 1986); Tomás Fernández Robaina, *El negro en Cuba, 1902–1958: Apuntes para la historia de la lucha contra la discriminación racial* (Havana: Editorial de Ciencias Sociales, 1990); Silvio Castro Fernández, *La masacre de los independientes de color en 1912* (Havana: Editorial de Ciencias Sociales, 2002); Olga Portuondo Zúñiga and Michael Max P. Zeuske, eds., *Ciudadanos en la nación* (Santiago de Cuba: Oficina del Conservador de la Ciudad-Fritz Thyssen Stiftung, 2002); Carlos Moore, *Castro, the Blacks, and Africa* (Los Angeles: UCLA Center for Afro-American Studies, 1989).

33. See José L. Franco, *Antonio Maceo: Apuntes para una historia de su vida*, 3 vols. ([1951] Havana: Editorial de Ciencias Sociales, 1975); Philip S. Foner, *Antonio Maceo: The*

"Bronze Titan" of Cuba's Struggle for Independence (New York: Monthly Review Press, 1977); Eduardo Torres-Cuevas, *Antonio Maceo: Las ideas que sostienen el arma* (Havana: Editorial de Ciencias Sociales, 1995); Aline Helg, "La Mejorana Revisited: The Unresolved Debate between Antonio Maceo and José Martí," *Colonial Latin American Historical Review* 10:1 (2001): 61–89.

    34. Jay Kinsbruner, *Not of Pure Blood: The Free People of Color and Racial Prejudice in Nineteenth-Century Puerto Rico* (Durham, N.C.: Duke University Press, 1996); Félix V. Matos Rodríguez, *Women in San Juan, 1820–1868* (Princeton, N.J.: Markus Wiener Publishers, 2001); Teresita Martínez-Vergne, *Shaping the Discourse on Space: Charity and Its Wards in Nineteenth-Century San Juan, Puerto Rico* (Austin: University of Texas Press, 1999); Eileen A. Suárez Findlay, *Imposing Decency: The Politics of Sexuality and Race in Puerto Rico, 1870–1920* (Durham, N.C.: Duke University Press, 1999); Pedro A. Cabán, *Constructing a Colonial People: Puerto Rico and the United States, 1898–1932* (Boulder, Colo.: Westview, 1999). On women and race in the Caribbean in general, see Verena Shepherd, Bridget Brereton, and Barbara Bailey, eds., *Engendering History: Caribbean Women in Historical Perspective* (Kingston: Ian Randle, 1995).

    35. H[arry] Hoetink, *The Dominican People, 1850–1900: Notes for a Historical Sociology*, trans. Stephen K. Ault (Baltimore: Johns Hopkins University Press, 1982), and *"Race" and Color in the Caribbean* (Washington, D.C.: Woodrow Wilson International Center for Scholars, 1985); Lauren Derby, "Haitians, Magic and Money: Raza and Society in the Haitian-Dominican Borderlands, 1900 to 1937," *Comparative Studies in Society and History* 36:3 (1994): 488–526; Eric Roorda, "Genocide Next Door: The Good Neighbor Policy, the Trujillo Regime and the Haitian Massacre of 1937," *Diplomatic History* 20:3 (1996): 301–19; Ernesto Sagás, *Race and Politics in the Dominican Republic* (Gainesville: University Press of Florida, 2000); Richard Lee Turits, *Foundations of Despotism: Peasants, the Trujillo Regime, and Modernity in Dominican History* (Stanford: Stanford University Press, 2003). See also David J. Howard, *Coloring the Nation: Race and Ethnicity in the Dominican Republic* (Oxford and Boulder, Colo.: Signal Books-L. Rienner, 2001).

    36. Angelina Pollak-Eltz, *La negritud en Venezuela* (Caracas: Lagoven, 1991), also in English translation; Winthrop R. Wright, *Café con Leche: Race, Class, and National Image in Venezuela* (Austin: University of Texas Press, 1990); María Marta Mijares, *Racismo y endoracismo en Barlovento: Presencia y ausencia en Rio Chico: Autoimagen de una población barloventeña* (Venezuela, s.n.: Fundación Afroamérica, 1996?). See also Jesús Chucho García, *Afrovenezolanidad: Esclavitud, cimarronaje y luchas contemporáneas* (Caracas: Ministerio de Educación, Cultura y Deportes, 2001).

    37. For anthropological studies, see Aquiles Escalante, "Notas sobre el Palenque de San Basilio, una comunidad negra de Colombia," *Divulgaciones Etnológicas* 3:5 (1954): 207–358; Michael Taussig, *The Devil and Commodity Fetishism in South America* (Chapel Hill: University of North Carolina Press, 1980); Nina S. de Friedemann and Jaime Arocha, *De sol a sol: Génesis, transformación y presencia de los negros en Colombia* (Bogotá: Planeta Colombiana Editorial, 1986). For historical works, see William F. Sharp, *Slavery on the Spanish Frontier: The Colombian Chocó, 1680–1810* (Norman: University of Oklahoma Press, 1976); Anthony McFarlane, "*Cimarrones* and *Palenques*: Runaways and Resistance in Colonial Colombia," *Slavery and Abolition* 6 (1985): 131–51; Hermes Tovar Pinzón, *De una chispa se forma una hoguera: Esclavitud, insubordinación y liberación* (Tunja: Universidad Pedagógica y Tecnológica de Colombia, 1992).

    38. Peter Wade, *Blackness and Race Mixture: The Dynamics of Racial Identity in Colombia* (Baltimore: Johns Hopkins University Press, 1993); Francisco U. Zuluaga R., *Guerrilla y sociedad en el Patía: Una relación entre clientelismo político y la insurgencia social*

(Cali: Universidad del Valle, Facultad de Humanidades, 1993); Helg, *Liberty and Equality*; Marixa Lasso, *Myths of Harmony: Race and Republicanism during the Age of Revolution, Colombia, 1795–1831* (Pittsburgh: University of Pittsburgh Press, 2007); Nancy P. Appelbaum, *Muddied Waters: Race, Region, and Local History in Colombia, 1846–1948* (Durham, N.C.: Duke University Press, 2003); Mary Roldán, *Blood and Fire: La Violencia in Antioquia, Colombia, 1946–1953* (Durham, N.C.: Duke University Press, 2002). On more contemporary issues, see Patricia Vásquez de Urrutia, ed., *La democracia en blanco y negro: Colombia en los años ochenta* (Bogotá: Ediciones Uniandes, Departamento de Ciencia Política-CEREC, 1989); Claudia Mosquera, Mauricio Pardo, and Odile Hoffman, eds., *Afrodescendientes en las Américas: Trayectorias sociales e identitarias. 150 años de la abolición de la esclavitud en Colombia* (Bogotá: Universidad Nacional de Colombia, 2002); Juana Camacho and Eduardo Restrepo, eds., *De montes, ríos y ciudades: Territorios de la gente negra en Colombia* (Bogotá: Fundación Natura/Ecofondo/Instituto Colombiano de Antropología, 1999).

39. Norman E. Whitten, Jr., *Black Frontiermen: A South American Case* (Cambridge, Mass.: Schenkman, 1974); Sabine Speiser, *Leben ist mehr als Uberleben: Afroamerikanische Totenriten in Esmeraldas (Ekuador) und ihr Beitrag zur kulturellen Kontinuitat* (Saarbrucken and Fort Lauderdale: Breitenbach, 1989); Henry Medina Vallejo, *Comunidad negra y cambio cultural: El caso de Concepción en la sierra ecuatoriana* (Quito: Ediciones Afroamérica, Centro Cultural Afroecuatoriano, 1996).

40. Denys Cuche, *Pérou nègre: Les descendants d'esclaves africains du Pérou: Des grands domaines esclavagistes aux plantations modernes* (Paris: L'Harmattan, 1981); Ramón Aranda de los Ríos, *Sublevación de campesinos negros en Chincha, 1879* (Lima: Herrera Editores, 1990). See also José Carlos Luciano Huapaya, *Los afroperuanos: Trayectoria y destino del pueblo negro en el Perú* (Lima: Centro de Desarrollo Etnico, 2002).

41. Romero J. Rodríguez, *Mbundo malungo a mundele: Historia del movimiento afrouruguayo y sus alternativas de desarrollo* (Montevideo: Rosebud Ediciones, 2006).

42. Romero J. Rodríguez, *Racismo y derechos humanos en Uruguay* (Montevideo: Organizaciones Mundo Afro, 2003); Luis Ferreira, *El movimiento negro en Uruguay, 1988–1998* (Montevideo: Ediciones Etnicas/Mundo Afro, 2003). The 1994 *Historias de Vida: Negros en el Uruguay*, a collection of ten short autobiographical essays on Afro-Uruguayan life, was republished as Teresa Porzecanski, ed., *Historias de exclusión: Afrodescendientes en el Uruguay* (Montevideo: Linardi y Risso, 2006).

43. George Reid Andrews, *The Afro-Argentines of Buenos Aires, 1800–1900* (Madison: University of Wisconsin Press, 1980).

44. Oscar Chamosa, "To Honor the Ashes of their Forebears: The Rise and Crisis of African Nations in the Post-Independence State of Buenos Aires, 1820–1860," *Americas* 59:3 (2003): 347–78; George Reid Andrews, "Remembering Africa, Inventing Uruguay: *Sociedades de Negros* in the Montevideo Carnival, 1865–1930," *Hispanic American Historical Review* 87:4 (2007): 693–726.

45. Carmen Bernand, "Entre pueblo y plebe: Patriotas, pardos, africanos en Argentina, 1790–1852," in *Blacks, Coloureds and National Identity in Nineteenth-Century Latin America*, ed. Nancy Priscilla Naro (London: Institute of Latin American Studies, 2003), 60–80; Lucía Dominga Molina and Mario Luis López, "Afro-Argentinians: 'Forgotten' and 'Disappeared'—Yet Still Present," in *African Roots/American Cultures: Africa in the Creation of the Americas*, ed. Sheila S. Walker (Lanham, Md.: Rowman & Littlefield, 2001), 332–347.

46. Dina V. Picotti, *La Presencia africana en nuestra identidad* (Buenos Aires: Ediciones del Sol, 1998); Alejandro Solmianski, *Identidades secretas: La negritude argentina*

(Rosario: Beatriz Viterbo, 2003); Marvin Lewis, *The Afro-Argentine Discourse: Another Dimension of the Black Diaspora* (Columbia: University of Missouri Press, 1996).

47. Constance García-Barrio, "The Black in Literature about the Rosas Era," *Revista/Review Interamericana* 10:4 (1980–81): 476–87.

48. Edmund T. Gordon, *Disparate Diasporas: Identity and Politics in an African Nicaraguan Community* (Austin: University of Texas Press, 1998).

49. Judith Stein, *The World of Marcus Garvey. Race and Class in Modern Society* (Baton Rouge: Louisiana State University Press, 1986); Ronald N. Harpelle, *The West Indians of Costa Rica: Race, Class and the Integration of an Ethnic Minority* (Kingston: Ian Randle, 2001). See also below the works on migrant British West Indian workers.

50. Francisco Foot Hardman, *Trem fantasma: A modernidade na selva* (São Paulo: Companhia das Letras, 1988).

51. Jeffrey Casey Gaspar, *Limón, 1880–1940: Un estudio de la industria bananera en Costa Rica* (San José: Editorial Costa Rica, 1979); Philippe I. Bourgois, *Ethnicity at Work: Divided Labor on a Central American Banana Plantation* (Baltimore: Johns Hopkins University Press, 1989); Elisavinda Echeverri-Gent, "Forgotten Workers: British West Indians and the Early Days of the Banana Industry in Costa Rica and Honduras," *Journal of Latin American Studies* 24:2 (1992): 275–308; Trevor Purcell, *Banana Fallout: Class, Color, and Culture among West Indians in Costa Rica* (Los Angeles: UCLA Center for Afro-American Studies, 1993); Aviva Chomsky, *West Indian Workers and the United Fruit Company in Costa Rica, 1870–1940* (Baton Rouge: Louisiana State University Press, 1996); Lancelot S. Lewis, *The West Indian in Panama: Black Labor in Panama, 1850–1914* (Washington, D.C.: University Press of America, 1980); Velma Newton, *The Silver Men: West Indian Labour Migration to Panama, 1850–1914* (Kingston, Jamaica: Institute of Social and Economic Research, 1984); Michael L. Conniff, *Black Labor on a White Canal: Panama, 1904–1981* (Pittsburgh, Pa.: University of Pittsburgh Press, 1985); Elizabeth McLean Petras, *Jamaican Labor Migration: White Capital and Black Labor, 1850–1930* (Boulder, Colo.: Westview Press, 1988); Harpelle, *The West Indians of Costa Rica*; Rhonda Denise Frederick, *"Colón Man a Come": Mythographies of Panama Canal Migration* (Lanham, Md.: Lexington Books, 2005). See also Carlos Meléndez Chaverri and Quince Duncan, *El negro en Costa Rica: Antología* (San José: Editorial Costa Rica, 1972). A useful and readily accessible overview of migration from the Caribbean is Bonham C. Richardson, "Caribbean Migrations, 1838–1985," in *The Modern Caribbean*, ed. Franklin W. Knight and Colin A. Palmer (Chapel Hill: University of North Carolina Press, 1989), 203–28.

52. Marc McLeod, "Garveyism in Cuba, 1920–1940," *Journal of Caribbean History* 30:1–2 (1996), 132–68, and "Undesirable Aliens: Race, Ethnicity, and Nationalism in the Comparison of Haitian and British West Indian Immigrant Workers in Cuba, 1912–1939," *Journal of Social History* 31:3 (1998): 599–623; Barry Carr, "Identity, Class, and Nation: Black Immigrant Workers, Cuban Communism, and the Sugar Insurgency, 1925–1934," *Hispanic American Historical Review* 78:1 (1998): 83–116; Aviva Chomsky, "'Barbados or Canada?': Race, Immigration, and Nation in Early-Twentieth-Century Cuba," *Hispanic American Historical Review* 80:3 (2000): 415–62. On Haitian workers in the Dominican Republic, see above and Orlando Inoa, *Azúcar: Arabes, cocolos y haitianos* (Santo Domingo: FLACSO, 1999).

53. Frank Andre Guridy, *Forging Diaspora: Afro-Cubans and Afro-Americans in a World of Empire and Jim Crow* (Chapel Hill: University of North Carolina Press, 2010); Irma Watkins-Owens, *Blood Relations: Caribbean Immigrants and the Harlem Community, 1900–1930* (Bloomington: Indiana University Press, 1996); Winston James, *Holding Aloft the Banner of Ethiopia: Caribbean Radicalism in Early Twentieth Century America* (London: Verso, 1998); Brent Hayes Edwards, *The Practice of Diaspora: Literature, Translation, and the*

Rise of Black Internationalism (Cambridge, Mass.: Harvard University Press, 2003); Michelle Ann Stephens, *Black Empire: The Masculine Global Imaginary of Caribbean Intellectuals in the United States, 1914–1962* (Durham, N.C.: Duke University Press, 2006).

54. Richard Preto-Rodas, *Negritude as a Theme in the Poetry of the Portuguese-Speaking World* (Gainesville: University of Florida Press, 1970); Nancy Morejón, *Nación y mestizaje en Nicolas Guillén* (Habana: Unión de Escritores y Artistas de Cuba, 1982); Keith Ellis, *Cuba's Nicolas Guillén: Poetry and Ideology* (Toronto: University of Toronto Press, 1983); Zila Bernd, *Negritude e literatura na America Latina* (Porto Alegre: Mercado Aberto, 1987); Robert Linsley, "Wilfredo Lam: Painter of Negritude," *Art History* 7:4 (1988): 527–44; and René Dépestre, "Hello and Goodbye to Negritude," in *Africa in Latin America: Essays on History, Culture, and Socialization*, ed. Manuel Moreno Fraginals (New York: Holmes & Meier, 1984), 251–72.

55. A broad analysis of the interaction of geopolitics on the local working class, with its implications for racial constructions, is Walter Rodney, *A History of the Guyanese Working People, 1881–1905* (Baltimore: Johns Hopkins University Press, 1981).

56. See Carlos Moore, *Pichón, A Memoir: Race and Revolution in Castro's Cuba* (Chicago: Lawrence Hill, 2008).

57. John Clytus, *Black Man in Red Cuba* (Miami: University of Miami Press, 1970). See also Piero Gleijeses, *Conflicting Missions: Havana, Washington, and Africa, 1959–1976* (Chapel Hill: University of North Carolina Press, 2002); Moore, *Castro, the Blacks, and Africa*; de la Fuente, *A Nation for All*.

58. Donald S. Castro, *The Afro-Argentine in Argentine Culture: El negro del acordeón* (Lewiston, N.Y.: E. Mellen Press, 2001).

59. Robin Dale Moore, *Nationalizing Blackness:* Afrocubanismo *and Artistic Revolution in Havana, 1920–1940* (Pittsburgh: University of Pittsburgh Press, 1997).

60. Gerard H. Béhague, ed., *Music and Black Ethnicity: The Caribbean and South America* (New Brunswick: Transaction Publishers, 1994); Isabelle Leymarie, *Du tango au reggae: Musiques noires d'Amérique latine et des Caraïbes* (Paris: Flammarion, 1996); Peter Wade, *Music, Race, and Nation: Música Tropical in Colombia* (Chicago: University of Chicago Press, 2000); Alejandro Frigerio, *Cultura negra en el Cono Sur: Representaciones en conflicto* (Buenos Aires: Ediciones de la Universidad Católica Argentina, 2000); Carlos Aguirre et al., *Lo africano en la cultura criolla* (Lima: Fondo Editorial del Congreso del Perú, 2000); Heidi Carolyn Feldman, *Black Rhythms of Peru: Reviving African Musical Heritage in the Black Pacific* (Middletown, Conn.: Wesleyan University Press, 2006).

61. See note 24; also Charles A. Perrone and Christopher Dunn, eds., *Brazilian Popular Music and Globalization* (Gainesville: University Press of Florida, 2001).

62. Yvonne Daniel, *Rumba: Dance and Social Change in Contemporary Cuba* (Bloomington: Indiana University Press, 1995).

63. Robert Stam, *Tropical Multiculturalism: A Comparative History of Race in Brazilian Cinema and Culture* (Durham, N.C.: Duke University Press, 1997).

64. For example, Quince Duncan, *The Best Short Stories of Quince Duncan—Mejores historias de Quince Duncan*, ed. Dellita Martin-Ogunsola (San José: Editorial Costa Rica, 1995), and *Contra el silencio: Afrodescendientes y racismo en el Caribe continental hispánico* (San José: Editorial Universidad Estatal a Distancia, 2001); Manuel Zapata Olivella, *Chambacú: Corral de negros* (Medellín: Editorial Bedout, 1967), *Changó el gran putas* (Bogotá: Editorial La Oveja Negra, 1983), and *La rebelión de los genes: El mestizaje americano en la sociedad futura* (Bogotá: Altamir Ediciones, 1997).

65. For basic introductions, see Roger Bastide, *African Civilizations in the New World*, transl. Peter Green (New York, Harper & Row, 1971); George Eaton Simpson, *Black*

Religions in the New World (New York: Columbia University Press, 1978); Sandra T. Barnes, ed., *Africa's Ogun: Old World and New* (Bloomington: Indiana University Press, 1989); George Brandon, *Santería from Africa to the New World: The Dead Sell Memories* (Bloomington: Indiana University Press, 1993).

66. Stephan Palmié, *Wizards and Scientists: Explorations in Afro-Cuban Modernity and Tradition* (Durham, N.C.: Duke University Press, 2002).

67. Miguel Barnet, *Biografía de un cimarrón* ([1966] Havana: Editorial de Ciencias Sociales, 1986), also in English translation as Esteban Montejo, *Biography of a Runaway Slave*, ed. Miguel Barnet (Willimantic, Conn.: Curbstone Press, 1994); María de los Reyes Castillo Bueno, *Reyita, sencillamente: Testimonio de una negra cubana nonagenaria*, ed. Daisy Rubiera Castillo (Havana: Instituto Cubano del Libro/Prolibros, 1997), also in English translation as Maria de los Reyes Castillo Bueno, *Reyita: The Life of a Black Cuban Women in the Twentieth Century* (Durham, N.C.: Duke University Press, 2000); William Luis, *Literary Bondage: Slavery in Cuban Narrative* (Austin: University of Texas Press, 1990).

68. Cuti, *E disse o velho militante Jose Correia Leite*; Medea Benjamin and Maisa Mendoça, *Benedita da Silva: An Afro-Brazilian Woman's Story of Politics and Love* (Oakland, Calif.: The Institute for Food and Development Policy, 1997); Robert M. Levine, ed., *Bitita's Diary: The Childhood Memoirs of Carolina Maria de Jesus*, trans. Emanuelle Oliveira and Beth Joan Vinkler (Armonk, N.Y.: M.E. Sharpe, 1998); Daphne Patai, *Brazilian Women Speak: Contemporary Life Stories* (New Brunswick: Rutgers University Press, 1988). Although it is not by definition a testimonial, Ruth Landes's strikingly personal ethnography of her fieldwork in Brazil in 1938 and 1939 with the *candomblé* community, which includes her conversations with the most remarkable figures in Afro-Bahian cultural history, was rereleased in 1994 (Ruth Landes, *The City of Women*, [1947] Albuquerque: University of New Mexico Press, 1994). See also Gomes da Cunha and dos Santos Gomes, eds. *Quase-cidadão*.

69. Ben Vinson III, *Flight: The Story of Virgil Richardson, a Tuskegee Airman in Mexico* (New York: Palgrave Macmillan, 2004).

70. Frederick Cooper, Thomas C. Holt, and Rebecca J. Scott, *Beyond Slavery: Explorations of Race, Labor, and Citizenship in Postemancipation Societies* (Chapel Hill: University of North Carolina Press, 2000). See also their useful bibliographic guide: Rebecca J. Scott, Thomas Holt and Aims McGuiness, eds., *Societies after Slavery: A Select Annotated Bibliography of Printed Sources on Cuba, Brazil, British Colonial Africa, South Africa, and the British West Indies* (Pittsburgh: University of Pittsburgh Press, 2002), as well as Rebecca J. Scott, *Degrees of Freedom: Louisiana and Cuba after Slavery* (Cambridge, Mass.: The Belknap Press, 2005). On the transition to free labor, see also Manuel Moreno Fraginals, Frank Moya Pons, and Stanley L. Engerman, eds., *Between Slavery and Free Labor: The Spanish-Speaking Caribbean in the Nineteenth Century* (Baltimore: Johns Hopkins University Press, 1985).

71. Minority Rights Group, ed., *No Longer Invisible: Afro-Latin Americans Today* (London: Minority Rights Group, 1995).

72. Leslie B. Rout, *The African Experience in Spanish America, 1502 to the Present Day* ([1976] Princeton: Markus Weiner, 2003). Other early comparative studies and edited volumes include Franklin Knight, *The African Dimension in Latin American Societies* (New York: MacMillan, 1974); Robert Brent Toplin, ed., *Slavery and Race Relations in Latin America* (Westport, Conn.: Greenwood Press, 1974); Ann M. Pescatello, ed. *The African in Latin America* (New York: Knopf, 1975); Ann M. Pescatello, ed., *Old Roots in New Lands: Historical and Anthropological Perspectives on Black Experiences in the Americas* (Westport, Conn.: Greenwood Press, 1977); Margaret E. Crahan and Franklin W. Knight, eds., *Africa*

and the Caribbean: The Legacies of a Link (Baltimore: Johns Hopkins University Press, 1979); Manuel Moreno Fraginals, ed., *Africa in Latin America: Essays on History, Culture, and Socialization* (New York: Holmes & Meier, 1984).

73. Michael L. Conniff and Thomas J. Davis, *Africans in the Americas: A History of the Black Diaspora* ([1994] Caldwell, N.J.: Blackburn, 2002).

74. Richard Graham, ed., *The Idea of Race in Latin America, 1870–1940* (Austin: University of Texas Press, 1990); Peter Wade, *Race and Ethnicity in Latin America* (London: Pluto Press, 1997); Norman E. Whitten and Arlene Torres, eds., *Blackness in Latin America and the Caribbean. Social Dynamics and Cultural Transformation*, 2 vols. (Bloomington: Indiana University Press, 1998); Martín Sagrera, *Los Racismos en las Américas: Una interpretación histórica* (Madrid: IEPALA, 1998); Nancy Priscilla Naro, ed., *Blacks, Coloureds and National Identity in Nineteenth-Century Latin America* (London: Institute of Latin American Studies, 2003). See also Darién J. Davis, ed., *Slavery and Beyond: The African Impact on Latin America and the Caribbean* (Wilmington, Del.: Scholarly Resources Inc., 1995); Carlos Moore et al., eds., *African Presence in the Americas* (Trenton, N.J.: Africa World Press, 1995); Luz María Martínez Montiel, *Negros en América* (Madrid: Editorial MAPFRE, 1992), and the various volumes edited by Luz María Martínez Montiel in the collection "Claves de América Latina, Nuestra Tercera Raíz": *Presencia africana en el Caribe*; *Presencia africana en Centroamérica (Belice, Honduras, Nicaragua, Costa Rica y Panamá)*; *Presencia africana en México*; *Presencia africana en Sudamérica (Colombia, Venezuela, Perú, Brazil, Uruguay, Paraguay y Argentina)* (México: Consejo Nacional para la Cultura y las Artes, 1995); Juan Angola Maconde, *Raíces de un pueblo: Cultura afroboliviana* (La Paz: Producciones CIMA/Embajada de España/Cooperación Española, 2000); Darlene Clark Hine and Jacqueline McLeod, eds., *Crossing Boundaries: Comparative History of Black People in Diaspora* (Bloomington: Indiana University Press, 1999); Sheila S. Walker, ed., *African Roots/American Cultures: Africa in the Creation of the Americas* (Lanham, Md.: Rowman & Littlefield, 2001); Darién J. Davis, ed., *Beyond Slavery. The Multilayered Legacy of Africans in Latin America and the Caribbean* (Lanham, Md.: Rowman & Littlefield, 2007).

75. George Reid Andrews, *Afro-Latin America, 1800–2000* (New York: Oxford University Press, 2004).

76. Jeffrey Lesser, *Negotiating National Identity: Immigrants, Minorities and the Struggle for Ethnicity in Brazil* (Durham, N.C.: Duke University Press, 1999). For other books in this line of inquiry, see the series Latin America Otherwise published by Duke University Press. See also Luz María Martínez Montiel, *Asiatic Migrations in Latin America* (Mexico City: Colegio de México, 1981).

77. George Reid Andrews, "Diaspora Crossings: Recent Research on Afro-Latin America," *Latin American Research Review* 48:3 (2008): 209–24.

78. See in particular two special issues of the *Journal of Latin American and Caribbean Anthropology* 12:1 and 12:2 (2007).

79. Duncan, *Contra el silencio*.

CHAPTER 9

INDIGENOUS PEOPLES AND NATION-STATES IN SPANISH AMERICA, 1780–2000

FLORENCIA E. MALLON

SINCE the 1970s, much of Spanish America has witnessed the rise of indigenous revitalization movements that, drawing on discourses of international human rights and on the increasing importance of cultural and identity politics, have demanded from nation-states the recognition of their rights to territory, cultural difference, and political autonomy as "First Peoples." At a time when more historically established and familiar social movements based on class have been on the decline throughout the hemisphere, indigenous movements have acquired a great deal of visibility and have contributed to a rethinking of the role of Native peoples in the formation of postcolonial societies. With these developments in mind, this essay traces the evolution of Native-state relations in Spanish America in the postcolonial period, using them as a window into the role of race in societies marked predominantly by the interaction between indigenous groups and Europeans. Its main message is that, in order to understand the conflictual underpinnings of nation and citizenship in these regions of Latin America, we need to get beyond a history of *mestizaje* to a deeper understanding of how the silencing of indigenous histories of expropriation and exclusion, as well as of ongoing struggles for restitution and recognition, everywhere left colonial tracings in even the most progressive forms of the national-popular state.[1]

Given the vastness of the topic and the region to be covered, the approach will of necessity be synthetic and geographically selective. The main focus will be on providing a broad overview and periodization. With the crisis of the Spanish colonial system and the rise of independence movements, emerging elites interested in projects of nation-state formation entered into new forms of negotiation and confrontation with indigenous peoples and their visions for both inclusion and autonomy. While these negotiations differed markedly from those that had earlier taken place between Natives and the colonial state, they were conditioned by the forms of conquest and colonization that had gone before, as well as by emerging political, geographic, military, and economic distinctions among the newly independent societies. Notwithstanding these important variations, however, significant similarities also emerged. Given the common project of national unification, for example, despite distinct political systems the notion of indigenous autonomy as part of a decentralized, more horizontal politics was everywhere rejected. The goal became instead a unitary nation, based on an abstract, generic, "one-size-fits all" concept of citizenship rooted in European liberalism. People who did not immediately fit this concept were to be educated or sanitized until they did, or else there was no place for them as participants in the national community. By the turn of the twentieth century, such notions underwrote a variety of exclusionary political systems based on limited citizen participation, often legitimated through concepts borrowed from positivism or eugenic social engineering.[2]

Between the Mexican Revolution of 1910 and the national-popular governments of the 1960s and 1970s, a new, and to some extent more tempting, version of the unitary nation emerged. No longer an exclusively positivist or eugenic project, the socialist- and Marxist-inspired models of "one-size-fits-all" citizenship were based on more inclusionary and empowering visions of class liberation. Any person, no matter what his or her gender, race, or ethnic identity, could claim participation and social rights based on membership in the productive classes of society. This dream, which I will call the "national romance," would come apart under the combined assault of authoritarianism and neoliberalism in the 1970s and beyond. It was at that point, with the failure of the national-popular project and in the context of the rising tide of international human rights activism and indigenous revitalization, that indigenous demands for cultural recognition and political autonomy reemerged as a potential alternative strategy for democratization.

The tension between unity and inclusion on the one hand, and autonomy and respect for difference on the other, was at the center of nation-state formation in indigenous and mestizo parts of Spanish America, but the sides did not line up in easy, neat, or predictable ways. Given contemporary indigenous political and cultural claims, one might expect that movements for autonomy and respect for difference would also line up historically with the more "progressive" or "democratic" political factions or forces, but this was often not the case. Indeed, depending on the case and the historical moment, autonomy could mean segregation and lack of citizenship, just as unity or inclusion might mean both forced assimilation along with certain kinds of empowerment. Puzzling out the ways in which these various tendencies worked themselves out for indigenous populations across Spanish America in the nineteenth and twentieth centuries helps us understand from a different vantage point some of the particular contradictions involved in any attempt to make nations in this piece of the postcolonial world. It also adds much-needed historical depth to our attempts at puzzling through the implications of today's indigenous demands for autonomy and participation.³

From Colony to Nation? Indigenous Peoples and the Transition to Independence

Starting with the so-called Andean Civil War in Peru and Bolivia (1780–81) and ending with the "pacification" of indigenous groups on the frontiers of northern Mexico, southern Chile, and the Argentine pampas (1880s), Native peoples throughout the Americas responded with creativity and dynamism to the political and economic crisis of the colonial regime that had ruled, partially incorporated, and partially exterminated them across the better part of three centuries. When faced with the possibility of creating a new postcolonial order, distinct groups imagined a variety of potential alternatives, from integration, citizenship, and shared national identity on one side to diverse forms of negotiated autonomy on the other. The results differed from place to place, largely due to previous differences in patterns of colonization, political, and military confrontation, and varied projects for consolidation of the state. But everywhere across the region, the nineteenth century ended with processes of exclusion and repression. In this section I use the cases of the southern cone (Chile and Argentina), Mexico, and Peru in order to explore how different colonial strategies vis-à-vis indigenous populations created distinct postcolonial options.

Throughout the colonial period, relations between Spaniards and Natives on the southern cone frontiers oscillated back and forth between a certain economic interdependence and latent, often open, warfare. Despite some variations between the two sides of the Andes Mountains, what the southern cone colonial societies had in common was the achievement of a certain balance of forces on the frontier in which Native groups remained unconquered and neither politically nor economically dominated. When they were still a part of the Spanish empire's periphery, the creole inhabitants of Buenos Aires or central Chile did not feel an overwhelming need to subjugate these populations, with whom they maintained interdependent, if conflictual, relations. Mapuche military power, which as of the eighteenth century existed on both sides of the Andes, was also a notable impediment to creole victory. This combination of factors resulted, throughout the eighteenth and first half of the nineteenth centuries, in a dynamic and prosperous exchange economy based on cattle smuggling that led to rising prosperity and prestige for some Mapuche lineages on both sides of the Andes, as well as increasing socioeconomic differentiation within indigenous society.

The presence of unconquered indigenous groups within the territory now claimed by nations in formation became a problem only with the potential emergence of autonomous nation-states. Indeed, as the nineteenth century advanced, the integration of the region into a new international market and technological advances in weaponry and ammunition would combine with projects for national and territorial unification to increase the importance—as well as the viability—of frontier conquest. Beginning in 1860 and culminating in the 1880s, centralizing liberal states on both sides of the mountains launched parallel projects that would ultimately lead to the violent subjugation of these rebel groups who had continued to exist at the very core of the nation. The Chilean and Argentine states would seek a solution to this problem between 1880 and 1882, when the so-called pacification of Native groups on the pampas and along the Araucanian frontier was accomplished through mutual military collaboration on both sides of the international boundary.[4]

The story was a different one in the Andes and in central Mexico, centers of pre-Columbian indigenous civilization where the colonial project was based precisely on the conquest and domination of significant Native populations, who then labored for Spanish entrepreneurs in mines, haciendas, and textile workshops. The mature colonial system rested, broadly speaking, on a sort of agreement between indigenous communities and the Spanish colonial state: indigenous labor and tribute, in exchange for the legal protection of communal institutions. On this agreement rested the famous division between the *república de indios* and the *república de españoles*, conceptualized as two distinct worlds or "republics." And the Spanish crown's indigenous subjects learned early on how to use the politico-legal discourses and practices of the colonial system to their advantage.[5]

Indeed, across the colonial period Native communities were reorganized and reconstructed in the interaction between their preexisting cultural, social, and political characteristics and the colonial state's strategies for Christianization and the extraction of tribute and labor power. While there were endless variations across region and culture, the ongoing interactions with colonial power created, over time, distinct opportunities for different groups within indigenous society. At moments of particularly dramatic change or crisis, fissures tended to emerge within Native society along lines of generation, gender, lineage, or wealth. Again and again, indigenous authorities faced the challenge of legitimacy, as their difficult balancing act as mediators between their communities and the colonial system was called into question.

Such a moment occurred in the eighteenth century, when a common colonial crisis worked itself out differently in Mexico and in the Andes. In the highlands of what is today Peru and Bolivia, the mediation of ethnic and communal authorities became progressively less effective, especially with the attempt to enforce the Bourbon Reforms (1760–80). In central Mexico, on the other hand, an expanding population and the rise of regional commercial economies based in communities and haciendas pressed in on communal resources and generated confrontations among peasants, merchants, and *hacendados*, in effect uniting indigenous and mestizo peasants against outside exploiters. To this was added the crisis of commercial agriculture, mining and textile sectors, and commercial routes in the Bajío that set the backdrop for social unrest during the wars of independence.[6]

As a result of these variations, in the Andes between 1780 and 1782 Tupaq Amaru and Tupaq Katari claimed their authority as legitimate descendants of Andean lineages and opposed to the existing political system a vision of social reorganization that would begin from Andean principles. The quick and violent repression of this movement took an ethnic form, and the final result of the Andean Civil War (1780–82) was the reaffirmation of royalist and conservative sentiments among the creoles of the Peruvian viceroyalty.[7] In Mexico, by contrast, the crisis of 1810 was manifested in a popular movement led by two radical priests, Miguel Hidalgo and José María Morelos. The greatest strength of this social movement, according to the dominant historiographical interpretation, was in the indigenous and mestizo communities in the central part of the country, from Guadalajara and Michoacán to Morelos and Guerrero, and in the mining region of the Bajío. This multiethnic and multiclass revolution rapidly became a guerrilla war that established a social agenda of legal equality, the abolition of slavery, and political federalism. Despite repression and a conservative declaration of independence in 1821, this social agenda continued to inspire a series of popular movements in favor of radical liberalism in central Mexico throughout the nineteenth century.[8]

In the regions that had been at the center of both pre-Columbian and colonial systems of power, therefore, the challenge for newly independent states was not how to establish control over a previously unconquered indigenous population, but how to reconstruct and rethink an already existing colonial relationship in a postcolonial context. How would the indigenous community, which had stood at the center of negotiations with the colonial state, be reconceptualized? What would happen to the ethnic and racial separation between the "republic of Indians" and the "republic of Spaniards" in a postcolonial setting, when a nation was supposed to evolve based, at least theoretically, on the legal equality of all citizens? In regions with such demographically large and diverse indigenous populations, these questions would be at the heart of all attempts at consolidation by modernizing liberal states. And at least in Mexico's more indigenous municipalities, as Antonio Annino has shown, many people took seriously the promise of legal equality as contained in the notion of the *municipio libre*.[9]

LIBERALISM, NATION-STATE CONSOLIDATION, AND INDIGENOUS PEOPLES DURING THE "LONG NINETEENTH CENTURY"

In nineteenth-century debates on liberalism in Latin America, the case of Mexico stands out dramatically, precisely because of the comparative success of its liberal project. In the middle of the nineteenth century, Mexican liberalism managed to break the economic power of the Catholic Church and install, by the 1870s, a hegemonic liberal regime that, despite internal conflicts and disagreements, generated the highest level of economic growth and political stability of the republican era.

When examining this period of liberal ascendancy, some historians have emphasized that liberal anticorporativism targeted indigenous communities, not only for their collectivist approach to property but also for their religiosity, thus prompting the rise of popular conservatism. Others, however, have highlighted the popular liberalism of irregular military forces that served as key allies in the 1850s and 1860s and helped defeat Mexican conservatives and French interventionists.[10]

The best way to explain this apparent contradiction is by examining the diverse regional and historical articulations of liberalism to questions of political autonomy. The 1855 Liberal revolution had at its base a federalist popular political culture rooted in rural communities in the central part of the country through an alliance between peasants and populist caciques. Some indigenous groups—especially in the northern sierra of the state of Puebla; parts of Oaxaca, Morelos, and Cuernavaca districts in the state of Mexico; and important parts of the state of Guerrero— accepted this alliance because they thought federalism would provide them with political autonomy, while the privatization of communal lands could be carried out in favor of the community inhabitants themselves. In these regions, liberalism took on the character of a popular movement, and indigenous and peasant guerrillas made important contributions to the defeat of conservative and imperialist forces between 1858 and 1867.[11]

But the opposite tendency also existed, sometimes in the same central regions of Mexico but especially among the Native groups inhabiting the "periphery" of the country—the north, the extreme south, the Huasteca. Among many of these groups, resistance against a centralizing liberal state and the agrarian policies of a militant liberalism facilitated an alliance between Natives and conservatives, or between indigenous peoples and Maximilian's imperial policies. Here the desire for political autonomy did not pass through a popular federalism or liberalism but instead was articulated directly to a conservative and monarchist project. And indeed, as Antonio Annino has recently suggested, it may even be possible that, in indigenous Mexico, the division between popular federalism and monarchism may not have been so clear once we explore historically the notions of inherent rights to autonomy as developed in the Spanish monarchical tradition and taken up in the post-Cádiz practices of the autonomous indigenous municipalities.[12]

At a general level, therefore, the relationship between the Mexican liberal state, modernizing and expansionist, and indigenous groups and communities revolved around two main questions: communal agrarian property, and the organization and decentralization of political power. As had been the case during the crisis of the Independence period, preexisting divisions within communities according to generation and lineage could influence community decisions in a variety of ways. When liberalism was able to establish alliances with indigenous peasant communities, these were usually mediated by the younger generation of male leaders and soldiers around notions of municipal autonomy that promised local control over land and political institutions. When it was impossible to establish such an alliance, the more cautious strategies around local autonomy came to the fore, increasing the influence of the older generation and concentrating power around more conservative ethnic leaders. There were also cases in which specific communities or regions negotiated partially with each side, accepting the alliances or relationships that were most convenient at any given moment.[13]

By the last decades of the nineteenth century, during the stability of the Porfiriato, the majority of national territory had been pacified, even though there were still some pockets of rebellion and resistance. In the central part of the country, local populist caciques mediated between communities and the state, often relying on their legitimacy as veterans of the resistance movement against the French Intervention. In the northeastern part of the country, the war against the Yaqui continued in Sonora, and the indigenous prisoners from this war were shipped to Yucatán as forced labor for the henequen plantations. The war against the Apache had ended in the state of Chihuahua, thanks in large part to an agreement with some of the communities in Guerrero district, through which in exchange for defending the frontier against the Indians colonists had received land and municipal autonomy. This stability would not last for long once the twentieth century began, however, for the development of commercial agriculture and the colonization of northern lands would begin to break the agreements the liberal state had established with northern and southern indigenous peasant groups. Indeed, the largest concentrations of popular rebellion during the 1910 revolution would occur precisely in the regions where these old agreements with the state were most dramatically ruptured.[14]

In nineteenth-century Peru, on the other hand, agreements between an emerging state and indigenous groups remained elusive, something that emerged with particular clarity after the War of the Pacific (1879–84). When General Andrés Cáceres, hero of the resistance against the Chilean occupation, became president in 1886, one of his first priorities was to pacify the country's central region, where peasant and indigenous *montoneras* remained armed and mobilized. These irregular forces had been part of Cáceres's own resistance movement against the Chilean occupation, but now they remained in control of lands claimed by the large landowners of the area. Cáceres therefore sent Emiliano Carvallo to the central sierra departments of Junín and Huancavelica as his own special envoy, in order to hammer out an agreement about land tenure and the distribution of property.[15] In July 1887, Carvallo sent a proposal back to Lima in which he suggested putting an end to the system of indigenous communal property in the country as a whole. His justification for such a radical proposal was that, despite various attempts at privatization in the first decades after Independence, "we have returned, almost unconsciously, to the same colonial agrarian regime." The time had come, Carvallo emphasized, for indigenous people to respond to the incentive of private property that would be theirs through a well planned and executed land distribution program, becoming educated and participating in the national economy and society. If land were distributed as private property to all indigenous peasants, the state could auction off the surplus and use the income generated to build schools in the villages.[16]

It is fascinating to note not only the many similarities between Carvallo's proposal and the 1856 Mexican Lerdo Law privatizing corporate lands but also the fact that Carvallo was suggesting this measure in 1887, three decades later. In addition, while in Mexico the Lerdo law in effect transformed the system of land tenure in many parts of the country, in Peru this much later proposal remained essentially on the drawing board. The difference between the Mexican and Peruvian cases is, therefore, dramatic. When faced with a similar need for dialogue between a modernizing state and indigenous communities, why did the Mexican state take an activist route, while the Peruvian state was still unable or unwilling to transform rural property relations?

To begin to answer this question requires examining the differential construction of liberalism in each case. If in Mexico the radical and revolutionary liberalism that emerged with the 1855 revolution was supported by popular federalist movements in the central region of the country, nothing analogous had taken place in Peru before the War of the Pacific. During that war, the Cacerista alliance that sustained the La Breña resistance against the Chilean army (1882–84) could arguably be seen as containing the seeds of precisely such a more radical alternative, but Cáceres was not able to take advantage of this opportunity to construct a new political coalition. The political and economic autonomy of the communities, especially at the end of the war with Chile, was frightening to political elites, and represented the reconstruction of a more egalitarian political order in the areas mobilized during the war. Would it have been possible to break the autonomy of the communities by privatizing communal lands, but without unleashing a revolutionary movement that demanded authentic citizenship and real political participation? With the opposition of the landowning class hanging in the balance, not even the Cacerista government was willing to risk it. The result, especially after the beginning of Nicolás de Piérola's presidency in 1895, was a "recolonization" of relations between the state and indigenous communities.[17]

The state that emerged in Peru at the end of the nineteenth century, therefore, reproduced the "republic of Indians," no longer as a protectionist policy in a corporate colonial order but instead as fragmentation, isolation, and exclusion in a supposedly national society. After bloodily repressing the remaining pockets of indigenous and peasant mobilization between 1895 and 1902, Nicolás de Piérola claimed the title of "protector of the indigenous race." But he and his successor in fact presided over the aptly named Aristocratic Republic, where for the first time in the independent history of Peru literacy became a requirement in order to exercise the right to vote.[18] Thus at the beginning of the twentieth century, the political dialogue between the state and indigenous communities, begun in Mexico with the 1855 revolution, was at best a distant possibility in Peru.[19]

Although space limitations prevent an equal consideration of other Spanish American cases with indigenous majorities where creole elites faced similar challenges to their projects of rule, additional cases where analogous issues emerged across the "long nineteenth century" would have to include Bolivia and Guatemala. In the former, the 1899 Civil War involved highland Aymara communities in an effort to expand definitions of the nation, and the postwar repression took a path of refragmentation and marginalization in some ways similar to the Peruvian case, though, as we shall see below, the paths of Peru and Bolivia would begin to diverge dramatically during the first half of the twentieth century.[20] In Guatemala, on the other hand, after an earlier civil war had installed a conservative regime with the support of indigenous communities, by the end of the nineteenth century an authoritarian liberal state consolidated itself on the foundations of export production and forced labor put into place by conservative governments, effectively segregating and marginalizing the Maya population. As Greg Grandin has shown, Q'ich'e Maya elites in the highland city of Quetzaltenango were relatively successful at claiming for themselves the power of civilization and mediation vis-à-vis the Maya peasantry of their region, but at the cost of giving up any possibility for a broader, more horizontal project of social justice for Guatemala's multiethnic rural poor.[21]

What these various cases of indigenous Latin America have in common, then, is that by the end of the nineteenth century, emerging states established control over their Native populations by engaging in a complex and contradictory dialogue between autonomy and inclusion. If in most cases the former meant segregation, isolation, and poverty, the latter meant integration through "civilization." What both models had in common was that they elided any recognition of indigenous territorial or cultural rights, and made ongoing access to resources—even if in a reduced and impoverished form—contingent on accepting the new postcolonial rules of the game. For indigenous peoples, this meant a difficult choice between equally unacceptable alternatives, a choice that would continue to haunt them well into the twentieth century.

Chile: A Centralist State and a War to the Death

In 1851 and 1859, two bloody civil wars presented the last viable challenge to the centralization of the Chilean state. General José María Cruz, maximum leader of the 1851 uprising, and Bernardino Pradel, a liberal merchant with quite a bit of influence among Mapuche caciques, had convinced an alliance of Mapuche lineages to participate in the two conflicts with the goal of stopping the infiltration of Chilean colonists into indigenous territory, a process that had been going on for nearly a decade through the illegal purchase of lands and ensuing pressures on Mapuche resources. By 1862, when a new president was elected, the guerrilla resistance had come to an end, but there were no longer any Chilean settlements within Mapuche territory. Former colonists, after having fled in the face of the threats of war, now began to pressure the government to provide them with protection.[22] To this was added, between 1857 and 1861, the first crisis in the economic export model that had connected the haciendas of Chile's central valley with the California market. Among the country's economic and political elites, there was a generalized perception that it was time for a change. Where could capital most profitably be invested? The idea of opening the frontier began to gain popularity. And this idea presupposed, finally, the "pacification" and "civilization" of the Mapuche.[23]

Newly elected president Joaquín Pérez, eager to gather opinions about the conquest of the Araucanía region, convened a meeting in Santiago with the most important Mapuche caciques. Thanks to the efforts of mediator Bernardino Pradel, according to historian Arturo Leiva, thirteen caciques, accompanied by "nothing less than the entire general staff of the 1859 rebels," traveled to Santiago in April 1862. Representing three distinct territorial units and, according to surviving documentation, fifty-six different lineages, they met with President Pérez. In a separate and private meeting with Pérez, Pradel also presented his proposal for a solution to the Mapuche problem. He suggested the creation of a separate indigenous province in the territory known as Araucanía, which would then be divided into departments administered by Mapuche caciques who would receive a salary from the government. Each cacique would then organize a public security force composed of the young warriors under his protection, and these would also receive a salary from the state. Land sales and commercial relations would be subject to special laws in order to prevent fraud or other abuses.[24]

According to Leiva, Pradel's proposals contained an original, "almost revolutionary" perspective on the indigenous problem in southern Chile. They envisioned "a political alliance with the Araucanos in the short run, with a view toward acquiescence in the long run, but without destroying the structure of Araucanian society, and even less breaking its pattern of settlement, but rather taking advantage of it."[25] Indeed, what Pradel was proposing was a sort of negotiated autonomy, in which the forms of indigenous organization and political culture could form part of a national space organized according to notions of coalition rather than integration. Such a project, however, did not turn out to be viable. In part, this was because it was presented by the losing faction in the recent civil war, but another important reason was that the interests of the colonists could not be ignored in the context of a frontier society.[26] If the government created a province administered by Mapuche caciques, lands previously colonized through illegal infiltration would need to be returned legally to indigenous hands. This, however, would run counter to the interests of the colonists on the front lines, so to speak, who were serving the interests of the government by occupying new territory and attaching it to what was considered national space.[27]

But President Pérez also had national security concerns. In what was at the time a secret correspondence with federalist General José María Cruz, he took seriously Cruz's suggestion that, in the territories of the south where the Chilean state still had no direct control and authority, conspiracies between Argentine federalists and Mapuche leaders might result in the claiming of territory by European powers. And this was, of course, not entirely a fantasy, since around the same time the French Interventionist army was advancing into Mexico and French adventurer Orélie-Antoine de Tounens had just been captured after his failed attempt to create an independent kingdom in Patagonia and Araucanía.[28]

Rather than provide the Mapuche with any advantages, therefore, Pérez ordered a military expedition, led by southern landowner and avid centralist Cornelio Saavedra, to refound the colonial fort at Angol, south of the Bío-Bío River. This they did by December 1862. As the first official postcolonial incursion into Mapuche territory, to the region known as "Ultra Bío-Bío," the expedition brought to an end any possibility of political coalition, of serious consideration of autonomy for indigenous groups in southern Chile.[29] As of 1862, therefore, the decision had already been made to use force as a last resort in solving the Mapuche "problem"; but another twenty years would pass before the military defeat of the Mapuche people, known euphemistically as the "Pacification," was completed.

Similarly, in Argentina, it would not be until 1880, after several failed attempts, that General Julio A. Roca finally blazed a path to Patagonia, closing the mountain passes between Chile and Argentina and, in a campaign known as "the Conquest of the Desert," exterminating and subduing the Araucanos and Tehuelches who still lived on the pampas north of the Negro river. The governments of Chile and Argentina coordinated their final campaigns against the indigenous peoples of the south, thus preventing the easy escape of defeated groups from one side of the international border to the other. On the Argentine side, the few survivors were placed in special territories or reservations. On the Chilean side, the government initiated the settlement of militarily defeated populations through a policy called *reducción*, a word with deep colonial roots whose meaning, reduction or shrinkage, was also doubly relevant. On the one hand, the amount of land allocated to the Mapuche was reduced to a fraction of what they had earlier occupied or claimed; on the other hand, the definition of Mapuche lineage was also reduced to include only the direct descendants of a particular cacique, thus subdividing broader territorial alliances in order to divide and conquer. In both cases, indigenous defeat in the context of a war to the death made the survivors into savage "others" without rights to citizenship.[30]

And yet the very name of General Roca's campaign suggests an important difference between the Chilean and Argentine cases. The conquest of a desert presupposes, discursively and implicitly, the occupation of unoccupied space. Despite the effects of epidemic and war, however, we know that the pampas were still occupied by a mixed population composed of indigenous groups, semi-independent gauchos, and colonists.[31] How and when did this frontier become a desert?

After independence, the relatively stable network of labor and product exchanges that had characterized pampas society was disrupted. As both creoles and Indians became interested in claiming specific territorial rights as a more secure form of access to resources, in 1825 Juan Manuel de Rosas, then governor of the province of Buenos Aires, negotiated the first treaty with a group of pampas caciques that established a system of annual rents. Those caciques who accepted the payment of such an annual quota were forced to develop a relationship with a specific livestock rancher, or *estanciero*, who then received a special permit from the government. In this way Rosas was able to tie certain indigenous groups to the system of *caudillismo* and use the Native warriors from these groups as allies in his wars against others who remained in a state of rebellion.[32]

Between 1830 and 1852, Juan Manuel de Rosas used the territorial and military alliances underlying the system of *caudillismo* in order to control, from Buenos Aires, a substantial portion of the Argentine coast and interior. A good number of the approximately 35,000 indigenous people who still inhabited the pampas during these years established alliances with Rosas through the system of annual rents. But after Rosas's defeat in 1852 and the short respite under the alliance between Federalist General Justo José Urquiza and Mapuche leader Kalfukurá, the unitarian forces that took power under the command of General Bartolomé Mitre in 1861 saw federalism's Native allies as one of the principal causes of the "barbarism" that had characterized the previous system. This image of barbarism received further support in the 1860s and 1870s when the system of exchange based on the *pulperías* entered crisis. Without access to their accustomed resources, Native groups attempted to make up the difference through war and raids known as *malones*, in which a particular settlement was targeted in an effort to procure livestock and captives. The cattle acquired in this way were sent as contraband to Chile along a network of clandestine markets. The *malones* that occurred during these two decades were especially destructive, as a single raid could destroy the annual production of an entire region. And particularly during the War of the Triple Alliance (1865–71), when the national army was otherwise occupied in fighting against Paraguay, indigenous groups once again were able to raid with relative impunity within Buenos Aires province.[33]

Against this background, war to the death against indigenous groups was constructed, in the 1870s, as the "conquest of the desert." Intellectuals and politicians who consolidated power in the post-Rosas era were men dedicated to the civilization, education, and settlement of their country, and to the destruction of the last vestiges of the previous system of *caudillismo*. The principal victims of this effort were Native peoples, whose very existence had already been denied even before they were defeated, eradicated, or exterminated.[34]

The military conquest of the pampas was immediately followed by the construction of railroads and the expansion of the agrarian and livestock economies on the plains. Together with British investment and European immigration, the agricultural and livestock "boom" of the last decades of the nineteenth century brought Argentina unprecedented prosperity and economic growth. Indeed, by 1910, with the centennial of Independence, the dreams of prosperity, political unification, and "civilization" nurtured by the anti-Rosas generation of 1880 seemed to have become reality.[35]

In Chile, as in Argentina, the final defeat of the Mapuche in 1882 opened a rich region of forest and agricultural lands to colonization and investment. Taking advantage of the government's policy of demarcating and auctioning off "surplus" indigenous lands, as well as of the process of urbanization, both Chilean and immigrant entrepreneurs were able to accumulate dramatic amounts of land between 1880 and 1920. Wheat haciendas and lumber companies grew rapidly in the area between the Bío-Bío and Toltén rivers, and by 1907 the entire territory between Santiago and Valdivia was connected by railroad.[36]

THE RISE AND FALL OF THE NATIONAL-POPULAR: INDIGENOUS PEOPLES CONFRONT THE TWENTIETH CENTURY

Despite some differences between the two southern cone frontier societies that won "wars to the death" against their indigenous peoples, most notably the much more substantial demographic presence of the Mapuche in Chile after their military defeat, the similarities between the two southern cone societies are more notable when we compare them with Mexico and Peru. In Argentina and Chile, states in the process of consolidation used armies seasoned in international conflict (the War of the Triple Alliance for Argentina, the War of the Pacific for Chile) in the final push against an internal enemy. Indigenous autonomy was, in both cases, terminated through military defeat, and the result was "rule by exception," in the sense that the surviving indigenous populations, whether in reservations or settlement communities, were defined as populations of noncitizens. The very success of this process of marginalization made possible the survival of a mythical view of these defeated peoples into the twentieth century. In Chile, the "Araucano" was constructed as the original seed of national identity, and as the first force resisting Spanish colonialism.[37] In Argentina, the "barbarous" populations of the interior are idealized in the ever more nostalgic image of the gaucho, more easily romanticized precisely because he no longer existed in reality.[38]

As Rebecca Earle has recently shown, by the beginning of the twentieth century this kind of mythmaking about indigenous peoples had come to an end in most other countries, especially in those where they had not been successfully marginalized, whether demographically or politically. Such cases would include Guatemala, Bolivia, Mexico, and Peru.[39] In Mexico, however, the 1910 Revolution generated a discourse of *mestizaje* within which the postrevolutionary state would supervise the long-term incorporation of indigenous peasants into the process of national development, thus leading to the eventual disappearance of the "problem." As recent work has shown for the revolutionary decades between 1920 and 1940, Mexican *indigenismo* oscillated back and forth between a certain respect for the positive aspects of indigenous cultures and an implicitly racist assumption that a people not wishing integration into the revolutionary project must of necessity be considered "primitive." And yet at the heart of this oscillation stood a dialogue between indigenous and mestizo traditions that can be seen as building on the practices of multi-ethnic movements that since 1810 had envisioned a popular agenda of agrarian justice and political participation in the indigenous and mestizo communities of central Mexico. Indeed, it is not an exaggeration to suggest that the 1910 Revolution managed to articulate this nineteenth-century tradition of radical liberalism—and of political dialogue between the state and indigenous communities—to an emerging postrevolutionary political project.[40]

The situation was quite different in Peru, where *indigenista* legislation began to take shape as of 1920, under the regime of Augusto B. Leguía. In contrast to Mexico, where multiethnic struggles had yielded a politics and discourse of dialogue and *mestizaje*, in Peru the various neocolonial reconstructions of the separation between European and Native continued to have a strong impact. Thus, while Article 58 of the new 1920 Peruvian Constitution recognized the legal right of indigenous communities to their communal lands, this was done in the context of a new protectionist and paternalistic policy toward indigenous peoples in general. The 1920 Constitution also created an Indian Affairs section within the Ministry of Development (*Fomento*) through which communities could request from the state official recognition, thus establishing a direct and "special" relationship between indigenous peoples and the state.[41] Within indigenous communities, interestingly enough, new opportunities for the claiming of communal land tenure offered by national-level legislation sometimes allowed local factions interested in maintaining egalitarianism to struggle against emerging economic elites who wanted to privatize communal holdings.[42]

Beyond these important differences, however, what all these societies in Spanish America had in common was the extent to which the new projects for civilization and national unification that took hold between 1880 and 1930 created a political and discursive field within which the very survival of an autonomous indigenous population was seen as contradictory to the existence of a modern nation. Recent work has explored how indigenous intellectuals themselves sometimes attempted to work within the confines of a civilizing discourse. When a more educated and economically privileged indigenous elite accepted the terms of an integrationist discourse and took it upon themselves to serve as designated mediators between indigenous peasants and the larger society, by definition they excluded the underprivileged members of their own racial or ethnic group from autonomous participation. But there are also examples of indigenous leaders and intellectuals who attempted to use existing discourses of citizenship to wring concessions on land, labor, and suffrage from national states.[43]

From the perspective of indigenous peasantries, however, the problem of land could not be easily resolved simply through education and integration. As part of a broader social problem with roots in the colonial period, and one that affected non-indigenous peasants as well, the question of land tenure throughout Spanish America was linked to issues of social welfare that, increasingly, leftist and reformist parties would make theirs. And herein lay the attraction of the national-popular project for the indigenous peasantry: its promises of redistribution and support for the lower classes taken as a whole. But as we shall see, the notion of national inclusion for all the productive classes, which lay at the very center of national-popular movements and promises, remained problematic for indigenous people.

While the contradictions of an inclusive social reform project that claimed to represent all as culturally homogeneous citizens were everywhere felt by Spanish America's "first peoples," here I will explore this larger question by comparing the experience of two prominent indigenous leaders in the three decades between 1910 and 1940: Manuel Aburto Panguilef in Chile and Manuel Quintín Lame in Colombia. Though the contexts of their struggles were very different, what unified the experience of these two leaders was the centrality of the struggle for indigenous lands and the difficulty of finding a consistent and successful political strategy that would lead to state recognition of indigenous demands and the restitution of their historic territory.

Between 1910 and 1939, Páez leader Manuel Quintín Lame led two major campaigns for the restitution of indigenous lands (*resguardos*) in highland Colombia. The first of these occurred in the Gran Cauca between 1910 and 1921, when Quintín Lame was elected by several indigenous cabildos to defend their *resguardos* against a recent wave of colonization. After several years of increasingly militant resistance, around 6,000 Native soldiers confronted the army in what became known as the Tierradentro uprising. Lame was captured in 1917 after a number of battles and massacres, and remained in jail until 1921. He subsequently led another restitution campaign between 1922 and 1939 in Tolima state, where he was once again captured, tortured, and jailed. Although throughout these years Lame was courted by a variety of political parties, the most tempting alliance seems to have been with the labor movement and the left. In 1925, Lame accepted the vice presidency of the Second Workers' Congress, a group already clearly aligned with the Communist left; yet in the end he chose to abandon such an alliance in favor of a more purely indigenous strategy of rebuilding the *resguardos* and reconstituting indigenous governments. By 1930, Lame was considered a sellout by leftist leaders earlier allied with him, and he would fade into obscurity until a revitalized indigenous movement discovered him as "precursor" in the 1970s.[44]

In many ways, Manuel Aburto Panguilef followed a strikingly parallel path in Chile between 1927 and 1940. As the only Mapuche leader consistently to oppose the breakup and privatization of indigenous lands, Aburto suffered imprisonment and internal exile twice between 1927 and 1930, as well as being the focus of criticism from more integrationist Mapuche organizations. As an alternative, Aburto began to explore an alliance with the Chilean working-class movement and its allied leftist political parties, envisioning a common front on the issue of land redistribution. This policy of coalition with the Chilean left culminated in the participation of Aburto's organization the Federación Araucana in the 1938 Popular Front coalition that brought Pedro Aguirre Cerda to the presidency with the support of Radical, Communist, and Socialist parties. But Aburto's participation in the leftist coalition would be short-lived, since the new president quickly made concessions to the landowners in his own Radical party by shelving the issue of agrarian reform. Shortly thereafter Aburto began to emphasize the more traditional cultural forms and practices of Mapuche community leaders, and earned the contempt of those self-defined progressive Mapuche who joined the Communist and Socialist parties. As in the case of Lame, Aburto would once again come to the attention of analysts with the Mapuche revitalization movement of the 1980s and 1990s.[45]

The experiences of Lame and Aburto highlight the kinds of pressures felt by indigenous leaders to integrate themselves into a national-popular project that marginalized ethnic and cultural demands in exchange for promises of participation in and protection by a welfare state. Whether such a project was actually supported by sitting governments, such as the postrevolutionary state in Mexico or the Popular Front governments in Chile, or whether it was the counterhegemonic project of a left out of power, the result for indigenous peoples was to some extent similar. With the exception of the Mexican postrevolutionary state, which by the 1930s had made agrarian reform a central part of its process of consolidation, no other welfare-state or populist government would take seriously the issue of land redistribution until the 1960s. If indigenous leaders sidelined a crucial part of their political and cultural agenda, therefore, they did so in exchange for very little, since land restitution was simply not in the cards during the first half of the twentieth century. And even in Mexico, the exception to this rule, indigenous communities would learn that access to land—and thus the material survival of their communities and local cultural and religious practices—came at a heavy price: integration into a centralized and increasingly authoritarian political system which helped transform local leaders into caciques who delivered votes to the Institutionalized Revolutionary Party.[46]

It is a strong testament to the power of the national-popular dream that the emergence of indigenous revitalization movements did not become a general phenomenon until the national-development states entered crisis. And indeed, this would not happen until the national-popular projects organized from the left—which included a popular coalition hegemonized by progressive and leftist forces, social and political mobilization, agrarian reform, and redistribution of political and economic power—everywhere failed to deliver on their promises. This, in conjunction with the decline of the socialist model across the world, inspired indigenous intellectuals and activists to rethink their strategies and programs and refocus on issues of identity, culture, and autonomy. The conditions under which national-popular projects envisioned citizenship, whether from a socialist or a liberal-populist perspective, had forced Native peoples to pay a high price: cultural and ethnic clandestinity in exchange for a coalition with other peasants and workers. Once these supposedly broader projects were shown to be impractical, why continue to sacrifice other rights and demands?

At the same time, beginning in the 1970s the changing balance of forces at the international level had generated in the United Nations a series of debates and resolutions concerning oppressed populations within existing nation-states. These included discussions on the status of national and ethnic minorities, women, and Native peoples. As part of an ever more international discourse on human rights, and with the participation of indigenous activists from many different countries who had worked in Geneva for more than twenty years, the resolutions and discussions began to focus international attention on the subject of Native rights. Indigenous leaders and movements in Spanish America have used the documents created at the United Nations to pressure the governments of their countries to formulate new policies that can put into practice multiethnic and multicultural notions of the state. Rethinking citizenship as a coalition of hybrid practices and identities where "Native" and "citizen" are no longer contradictory terms, the new generation of indigenous activists has used international declarations such as the Convention for the Elimination of All Racial Discrimination and ILO Convention 169 on Indigenous and Tribal Peoples to reclaim the right to difference within constitutional law.[47] Even in Mexico, where the 1990s brought about the final crisis of the postrevolutionary model of national development, the Zapatista Army of National Liberation (EZLN) has participated with other indigenous organizations in transforming the rules of the game and putting back on the table the question of cultural autonomy within notions of citizenship and nation.[48]

Beyond these broad commonalities of context, however, the narrative of indigenous revitalization had distinct contours and complexities in each case. If in Mexico indigenous organizations emerged in the mobilizations responding to the erosion of a postrevolutionary authoritarian order, in Guatemala and Chile they emerged (in very different ways) as responses to authoritarian violence and to assaults on Native groups as such.[49] In Bolivia and Colombia, indigenous organizations arose out the dissatisfactions Native peasants and workers have with the nature of class-based organizations.[50] Native peoples of the Brazilian Amazon, in responding to ecological and commercial attacks on their very survival, made common cause with other anti-dictatorship forces and became a symbolic cause célèbre for the democratic movement as a whole.[51] In Nicaragua, even though the movement for autonomy along the Atlantic coast began in contradiction with the Sandinista government, it wrung political and cultural concessions from that very government that for a while looked quite impressive in comparison to other parts of the hemisphere.[52] And finally, in Ecuador, the impressive grassroots capabilities of indigenous organizations at the regional level, especially in the Amazonian region, ended up coalescing into a broad, national-level political force in that country's deepening crisis.[53]

Countries where large revitalization movements did not emerge also exhibited diverse histories.[54] While in some cases, such as Argentina, Costa Rica, and El Salvador, one might conclude that an extremely small demographic presence was the deciding factor, this would be disproved by the fact that in Colombia and Brazil, where Native populations are under 1% of the population, visible indigenous movements scored important political victories, such as recognition in the Colombian constitution and the granting of autonomous territories. In Peru, despite the much larger demographic presence of Native groups, both in the Amazonian and highland regions, in the 1920s the fierce repression of an indigenous movement in favor of citizenship and participation convinced an entire generation of Quechua leaders that their best survival strategy was through a certain kind of cultural *mestizaje*. Thus Andean cultures in Peru would increasingly find a "mestizo" expression inside expanding urban centers and in class-based political movements in the highlands and on the coast.[55]

This extreme complexity of historical narratives and political outcomes does, however, yield a common conceptual thread. Everywhere in Spanish America, indigenous peoples lived a painful contradiction between a desire for cultural autonomy and recognition—which if fulfilled often led to a new postcolonial version of the segregationist *república de indios*—and the dream of full and equal citizenship, which usually resulted in a culturally destructive form of integration without full equality. Discourses of *mestizaje* and the "cosmic race" could seem liberating when the alternative was isolation and marginalization in small and impoverished "autonomous" communities. But so, too, could autonomy seem liberating when integration meant giving up so much, in exchange for at most half a loaf of citizenship.

Today's indigenous revitalization movements, while calling attention to this contradiction, can sometimes still remain mired within it. In the process of denouncing the trap of integrationism and *mestizaje*, some indigenous leaders can lose sight of the fact that autonomy does not, by itself, assure equality or full participation. Whether demographically or territorially speaking, moreover, few Native peoples can realistically aspire to building an independent nation. Even those who might, such as the Maya in Guatemala and the Aymara in Bolivia, are historically so poor in resources that their economic viability—even if we assume an amicable solution to partition—would be hard to envision. So ultimately, the contradiction faced by postcolonial Latin Americans, both Native and non-Native, between cultural difference that reproduced inequality and a version of unitary citizenship that erased cultural difference, remains entirely relevant today.

The difference now, at the start of the new millennium, is that the resurgence of indigenous movements and organizations throughout Latin America has once again placed on the political agenda the possibility of full citizenship alongside cultural diversity and autonomy. Despite the impressive variety of indigenous experiences in different Latin American countries, which took shape thanks to the distinct demographic presence of Native groups and diverse forms of postcolonial state consolidation, it is only at the end of the twentieth century and the beginning of the twenty-first, when the national-popular development model has lost its capacity to unify and inspire a multiethnic people-nation, that a different vision of the nation and the citizen can perhaps be taken seriously.[56] This intercultural vision, based on regional autonomy and cultural diversity, has emerged out of conflict and imperfectly, from within the postcolonial struggles of indigenous peoples. In an ever more globalized world, such a vision, with its respect for difference within coalition, becomes ever more current. It also makes possible new historical reflections on the nature of nation-state formation in Latin America, and on the failure of this process truly to deal with the postcolonial legacies of the dispossession, usurpation, and marginalization endured by the region's "first peoples."

NOTES

1. *Mestizaje*, defined as racial mixture between people of indigenous and of European descent, emerged as a discourse of equality and of Latin American specificity in the early twentieth century, especially in the context of the Mexican revolution of 1910. For an

introduction to the evolution of indigenous revitalization movements in different parts of Latin America, see Rachel Sieder, ed., *Multiculturalism in Latin America: Indigenous Rights, Diversity and Democracy* (New York: Palgrave Macmillan, 2002); Kay B. Warren and Jean E. Jackson, eds., *Indigenous Movements, Self-Representation, and the State in Latin America* (Austin: University of Texas Press, 2002). Although in many parts of Spanish America, such as Argentina, Colombia, Ecuador, Mexico, Nicaragua, and Peru, there has been more recent—and very salutary—attention paid to the role of peoples of African origin, this essay will not address the role of Afro-Latin Americans.

2. The foundational discussion of eugenics in Latin America can be found in Nancy Leys Stepan, *"The Hour of Eugenics": Race, Gender and Nation in Latin America* (Ithaca, N.Y.: Cornell University Press, 1991).

3. A burgeoning literature has developed, over the past ten years or so, on the contemporary indigenous autonomy movements throughout Spanish America. It is much too large to cite in its entirety. For some important examples, see, for the region as a whole, Xochitl Leyva, Aracelio Burguete, and Shannon Speed, eds., *Gobernar en la diversidad: Experiencias indígenas desde América Latina: Hacia la investigación de co-labor* (Mexico City: CIESAS, 2008); José Antonio Lucero, *Beyond the Lost Decade: Indigenous Movements, Development, and Democracy in Latin America* (Princeton, N.J.: Princeton University Press, 2003); Nancy Grey Postero and Leon Zamosc, *The Struggle for Indigenous Rights in Latin America* (Brighton, U.K.: Sussec Academic Press, 2004); Kay B. Warren, *Indigenous Movements, Self-Representation, and the State in Latin America* (Austin: University of Texas Press, 2002). For Bolivia: Nancy Grey Postero, *Now We Are Citizens: Indigenous Politics in Multicultural Bolivia* (Stanford, Calif.: Stanford University Press, 2007); Esteban Ticona Alejo, *Organización y liderazgo aymara: La experiencia indígena de la política boliviana, 1979–1996* (La Paz: Universidad de la Cordillera/Cochabamba: Agroecología Universidad Cochabamba, 2000). For Chile: Diane Haughney, *Neoliberal Economics, Democratic Transition, and Mapuche Demands for Rights in Chile* (Gainesville: University Press of Florida, 2006). For Colombia: Joanne Rappaport, *Intercultural Utopias: Public Intellectuals, Cultural Experimentation, and Ethnic Pluralism in Colombia* (Durham, N.C.: Duke University Press, 2005). For Guatemala: Edward F. Fischer and R. McKenna Brown eds., *Maya Cultural Activism in Guatemala* (Austin: University of Texas Press, 1996); Víctor D. Montejo, *Maya Intellectual Renaissance: Identity, Representation, and Leadership* (Austin: University of Texas Press, 2005); Kay B. Warren, *Indigenous Movements and Their Critics: Pan-Maya Activism in Guatemala* (Princeton, N.J.: Princeton University Press, 1998). For Mexico: Natividad Gutiérrez, *Nationalist Myths and Ethnic Identities: Indigenous Intellectuals and the Mexican State* (Lincoln: University of Nebraska Press, 1999); Maya Lorena Pérez Ruiz, *¡Todos somos zapatistas! Alianzas y rupturas entre el EZLN y las organizaciones indígenas de México* (Mexico City: INAH, 2005); Jan Rus, Rosalva Aída Hernández Castillo, and Shannan L. Mattiace, eds., *Mayan Lives, Mayan Utopias: The Indigenous Peoples of Chiapas and the Zapatista Rebellion* (Lanham, Md.: Rowman & Littlefield, 2003); Lynn Stephen, *Zapata Lives! Histories and Cultural Politics in Southern Mexico* (Berkeley: University of California Press, 2002). For Peru: María Elena García, *Making Indigenous Citizens: Identities, Education, and Multicultural Development in Peru* (Stanford, Calif.: Stanford University Press, 2005). On globalization from below, see Arturo Escobar, *Más allá del Tercer Mundo: Globalización y diferencia* (Bogotá: Instituto Colombiano de Antropología e Historia, 2005).

4. A useful overview of Native-Spanish relations on the southern cone frontiers can be found in Kristine L. Jones, "Warfare, Reorganization, and Readaptation at the Margins of Spanish Rule: The Southern Margin (1573–1882)," *The Cambridge History of the Native*

Peoples of the Americas, Vol. III: *South America*, ed. Frank Salomon and Stuart B. Schwartz, Part 2 (Cambridge, U.K.: Cambridge University Press, 1999), 138–87. For the case of Chile, see Mario Góngora, *Origen de los "inquilinos" de Chile Central* (Santiago: Editorial Universitaria, 1960); Sergio Villalobos R., "Tres siglos y medio de vida fronteriza," in Villalobos et al., *Relaciones fronterizas en la Araucanía* (Santiago: Ediciones Universidad Católica de Chile, 1982), 11–86; Jorge Pinto Rodríguez et al., *Misioneros en la Araucanía, 1600–1900: Un capítulo de historia fronteriza en Chile* (Temuco: Ediciones Universidad de la Frontera, 1988). The indigenous perspective emphasizes the violence and confrontation of this period, and the importance of constant frontier war in the process of social change and politico-cultural realignment within Native groups. See Pablo Marimán, Sergio Caniuqueo, José Millalén and Rodrigo Levil, *¡…Escucha, winka…!: Cuatro ensayos de Historia Nacional Mapuche y un epílogo sobre el futuro* (Santiago: LOM Editores, 2006), especially 53–218; José Bengoa, *Historia del pueblo mapuche (siglos XIX y XX)* (Santiago: Ediciones Sur, 1985); Guillaume Boccara, "Análisis de un proceso de etnogénesis: El caso de los Reche-Mapuche de Chile en la época colonial," *Memoria Americana 7: Cuadernos de etnohistoria* (Facultad de Filosofía y Letras, Universidad de Buenos Aires, 1998), 11–27. Boccara suggests that the word *Mapuche* was not used until the end of the eighteenth century, when the indigenous groups in south central Chile, who had previously referred to themselves as *Reche*, had undergone a major social, political, and military reorganization in response to war and the development of a prosperous livestock economy on both sides of the Andes mountains. For the Argentine case, see Kristine Jones, "Conflict and Adaptation in the Argentine Pampas, 1750–1880" (PhD diss., University of Chicago, 1984); Axel César Lazzari, "'¡Que vivan los indios argentinos!' Análisis de las estrategias discursivas de etnización/nacionalización de los ranqueles en una situación de frontera" (master's thesis, Universidad Federal de Rio de Janeiro, 1996). On the nature of the frontier, see Jorge Pinto Rodríguez, ed., *Araucanía y pampas: Un mundo fronterizo en América del Sur* (Temuco: Ediciones Universidad de la Frontera, 1996); Patricia Cerda-Hegert, *Fronteras del Sur: La región del Bío Bío y la Araucanía chilena, 1604–1883* (Temuco: Instituto Latinoamericano de la Universidad Libre de Berlin/Ediciones Universidad de la Frontera, n.d.); Leonardo León Solís, *Maloqueros y conchavadores en Araucanía y las Pampas, 1700–1800* (Temuco: Universidad de La Frontera, Serie Quinto Centenario, 1991); Jorge Pinto Rodríguez, *De la inclusión a la exclusión: La formación del estado, la nación y el pueblo mapuche* (Santiago: Instituto de Estudios Avanzados/ Universidad de Santiago de Chile, 2000).

5. Steve J. Stern, *Peru's Indian Peoples and the Challenge of Spanish Conquest: Huamanga to 1640* (Madison: University of Wisconsin Press, 1982); Karen Spalding, *Huarochirí: An Andean Society Under Inca and Spanish Rule* (Stanford, Calif.: Stanford University Press, 1984) and *De indio a campesino: Cambios en la estructura social del Perú colonial* (Lima: Instituto de Estudios Peruanos, 1974); Friedrich Katz, "Rural Uprising in Preconquest and Colonial Mexico," in *Riot, Rebellion, and Revolution: Rural Social Conflict in Mexico*, ed. Katz (Princeton, N.J.: Princeton University Press, 1988), 65–94; Mark Thurner, *From Two Republics to One Divided: Contradictions of Postcolonial Nationmaking in Andean Peru* (Durham, N.C.: Duke University Press, 1997). The idea of a "colonial pact" was first suggested, for the case of Bolivia, by Tristan Platt, *Estado boliviano y ayllu andino: Tierra y tributo en el norte de Potosí* (Lima: Instituto de Estudios Peruanos, 1982).

6. Florencia E. Mallon, "Indigenous Communities, Political Cultures, and the State in Latin America, 1780–1990," *Journal of Latin American Studies*, Suppl. (1992): 35–53; Sinclair Thomson, *We Alone Shall Rule: Native Andean Politics in the Age of Insurgency* (Madison: University of Wisconsin Press, 2003). Brian R. Hamnett, *Roots of Insurgency: Mexican Regions, 1750–1824* (Cambridge: Cambridge University Press, 1985); Eric Van Young,

"Moving Toward Revolt: Agrarian Origins of the Hidalgo Rebellion in the Guadalajara Region," in Katz, *Riot, Rebellion, and Revolution*, 176–204; William B. Taylor, "Banditry and Insurrection: Rural Unrest in Central Jalisco, 1790–1816," in Katz, *Riot, Rebellion, and Revolution*, 65–94.

7. The literature on the Andean Civil War is extremely rich. In addition to Thomson, *We Alone Shall Rule*, some of the more helpful sources are: Steve J. Stern, "The Age of Andean Insurrection, 1742–1782: A Reappraisal," in *Resistance, Rebellion, and Consciousness in the Andean Peasant World, 18th to 20th Centuries*, ed. Stern (Madison: University of Wisconsin Press, 1987), 29–93; Stern, *Resistance, Rebellion and Consciousness*, 94–210; René Zavaleta Mercado, *Lo nacional-popular en Bolivia* (Mexico City: Siglo XXI, 1986); and Charles F. Walker, *Smoldering Ashes: Cuzco and the Creation of Republican Peru, 1780–1840* (Durham, N.C.: Duke University Press, 1999).

8. The classic explanation of Mexican independence can be found in John Lynch, *The Spanish American Revolutions, 1808–1826* (New York: Norton, 1973); Hugh M. Hamill Jr., *The Hidalgo Revolt: Prelude to Mexican Independence* (Gainesville: University of Florida Press, 1966); Wilbert H. Timmons, *Morelos: Priest, Soldier, Statesman of Mexico* (El Paso: Texas Western College Press, 1963); Brian R. Hamnett, "Royalist Counterinsurgency and the Continuity of Rebellion: Guanajuato and Michoacán, 1813–1820," *Hispanic American Historical Review* 62:1 (1982): 19–48; and summarized in Mallon, "Indigenous Communities," 42–44. The continuity of social movements in this central region across the nineteenth century is explored in Leticia Reina, *Las rebeliones campesinas en México (1819–1906)* (Mexico City: Siglo XXI, 1980); John M. Hart, "The 1840s Southwestern Mexico Peasants' War: Conflict in a Transitional Society," in Katz, *Riot, Rebellion, and Revolution*, 249–68; Peter F. Guardino, *Peasants, Politics, and the Formation of Mexico's National State: Guerrero, 1800–1857* (Stanford: Stanford University Press, 1996); Florencia E. Mallon, *Peasant and Nation: The Making of Postcolonial Mexico and Peru* (Berkeley: University of California Press, 1995). Most recently, Eric Van Young has advanced a revisionist perspective on Mexican Independence by arguing that there was no unified multiclass and multiethnic movement, but instead two separate rebellions, a popular village-bounded one and a broader movement led by mediators and powerbrokers. See *The Other Rebellion: Popular Violence and Ideology in Mexico, 1810–1821* (Stanford: Stanford University Press, 2001).

9. For his most recent and most ambitious statement of these issues, see Antonio Annino, "The Two-Faced Janus: The Pueblos and the Origins of Mexican Liberalism," in Elisa Servín, Leticia Reina, and John Tutino, eds., *Cycles of Conflict, Centuries of Change: Crisis, Reform, and Revolution in Mexico* (Durham, N.C.: Duke University Press, 2007), 60–90. For another example of how Independence opened up new possibilities in the indigenous communities of southern Mexico, see Peter Guardino, *The Time of Liberty: Popular Political Culture in Oaxaca, 1750–1850* (Durham, N.C.: Duke University Press, 2005), esp. chap. 6.

10. Jean Meyer, *Problemas campesinos y revueltas agrarias (1821–1910)* (Mexico City: Secretaría de Educación Pública, 1973); T. G. Powell, "Priests and Peasants in Central Mexico: Social Conflict During 'La Reforma,'" *Hispanic American Historical Review* 57:2 (1977): 296–313; Alan Knight, "El liberalismo mexicano desde la Reforma hasta la Revolución (una interpretación)," *Historia Mexicana* 35:1 (1985): 59–91; Guy P. C. Thomson, "Popular Aspects of Liberalism in Mexico, 1848–1888," *Bulletin of Latin American Research* 10:2 (1991): 265–92; Mallon, *Peasant and Nation*; Alicia Hernández Chávez, *La tradición republicana del buen gobierno* (Mexico City: Fideicomiso Historia de las Américas/El Colegio de México/Fondo de Cultura Económica, 1993), and *Anenecuilco: Memoria y vida de un pueblo* (Mexico City: El Colegio de México, 1991).

11. Reina, *Las rebeliones campesinas*; Guardino, *Peasants, Politics, and State Formation*; Mallon, *Peasant and Nation*; Patrick J. McNamara, *Sons of the Sierra: Juárez, Díaz, and the People of Ixtlán, Oaxaca, 1855–1920* (Chapel Hill: University of North Carolina Press, 2007).

12. Jean Meyer, *Revueltas campesinas* and *Esperando a Lozada* (Zamora: El Colegio de Michoacán, 1984); John Tutino, "Peasants and Politics in Nineteenth-Century Mexico," *Latin American Research Review* 22:3 (1987): 237–44; Evelyn Hu-DeHart, *Yaqui Resistance and Survival: The Struggle for Land and Autonomy* (Madison: University of Wisconsin Press, 1984); Andrés Lira, *Comunidades indígenas frente a la ciudad de México: Tenochtitlán y Tlatelolco, sus pueblos y sus barrios, 1812–1919* (Zamora: El Colegio de Michoacán, 1983); Rodolfo Pastor, *Campesinos y reformas: La mixteca, 1700–1856* (Mexico City: El Colegio de México, 1987); Antonio Escobar O., *Indio, Nación y Comunidad en el México del Siglo XIX* (Mexico City: Centro de Estudios Mexicanos y Centroamericanos/Centro de Investigaciones y Estudios Superiores en Antropología Social, 1993); Guy P. C. Thomson, "Agrarian Conflict in the Municipality of Cuetzalán (Sierra de Puebla): The Rise and Fall of 'Pala' Agustín Dieguillo, 1861–1894," *Hispanic American Historical Review* 71:2 (1991): 205–58. For my last comment, see Annino, "The Two-Faced Janus," op. cit.

13. Antonio Escobar O., "Los ayuntamientos y los pueblos indios de la Sierra Huasteca: Conflictos entre nuevos y viejos actores, 1812–1840," in *La reindianización de América, siglo XIX*, ed. Leticia Reina (Mexico City: Siglo XXI, 1997), 294–316; "Los condueñazgos indígenas en las Huastecas hidalguense y veracruzana: ¿Defensa del espacio comunal?," in Escobar O., *Indio, nación y comunidad en el México del siglo XIX*, 171–88; "Movimientos socio-rurales en las actuales Huastecas hidalguense y veracruzana (México), en la primera mitad del siglo XIX," in *Jahrbuch für Geschichte Latinamerikas* 38 (2001): 157–81; and "Del gobierno indígena al ayuntamiento constitucional en las Huastecas hidalguense y veracruzana, 1780–1853," in *Mexican Studies/ Estudios Mexicanos* 12:1 (1996): 1–26; Michael Ducey, "Hijos del pueblo y ciudadanos: Identidades políticas entre los rebeldes indios del siglo XIX," in *Construcción de la legitimidad política en México en el siglo XIX*, ed. Brian Connaughton, Carlos Illades, and Sonia Pérez Toledo (Zamora and Mexico City: El Colegio de Michoacán/UAM-Iztapalaba/UNAM/El Colegio de México, 1999), 127–51.

14. Mallon, *Peasant and Nation*; Ana María Alonso, *Thread of Blood: Colonialism, Revolution and Gender on Mexico's Northern Frontier* (Tucson: University of Arizona Press, 1995); María Teresa Koreck, "Space and Revolution in Northeastern Chihuahua," in *Rural Revolt in Mexico and U.S. Intervention*, ed. Daniel Nugent (La Jolla, Calif.: Center for U.S. Mexican Studies, 1988), 127–48; Nugent, *Spent Cartridges of Revolution: An Anthropological History of Namiquipa, Chihuahua* (Chicago: University of Chicago Press, 1993); Nugent and Alonso, "Multiple Selective Traditions in Agrarian Reform and Agrarian Struggle: Popular Culture and State Formation in the Ejido of Namiquipa, Chihuahua," in Gilbert Joseph and Daniel Nugent, eds., *Everyday Forms of State Formation: Revolution and the Negotiation of Rule in Modern Mexico* (Durham, N.C.: Duke University Press, 1994), 209–46. A recent work that examines the limits of the Porfirian order, as well as the forms of resistance that were possible, is Romana Falcón, "Límites, resistencias y rompimiento del órden," in *Don Porfirio Presidente... nunca omnipotente: Hallazgos, reflexiones y debates, 1876–1911*, ed. Romana Falcón and Raymond Buve (Mexico City: Universidad Iberoamericana, 1998), 385–406.

15. Florencia E. Mallon, *The Defense of Community in Peru's Central Highlands: Peasant Struggle and Capitalist Transition, 1860–1940* (Princeton, N.J.: Princeton University Press, 1983) and *Peasant and Nation*, 207–19; Nelson Manrique, *Campesinado y nación: Las guerrillas indígenas en la guerra con Chile* (Lima: Ital-Perú-C.I.C., 1981) and *Yawar mayu: Sociedades terratenientes serranas, 1879–1910* (Lima: Instituto Francés de Estudios Andinos/DESCO, 1988).

16. "Proyecto de ley sobre la repartición de las tierras de comunidad, enviado por Emiliano Carvallo al Sr. Director General de Gobierno," Biblioteca Nacional de Perú, Sala de Investigaciones, #D12842, f. 11. I thank Mark Thurner for giving me access to a copy of this document.

17. Manrique, *Yawar mayu*; Mallon, *Peasant and Nation*.

18. Mallon, *Peasant and Nation*, 274–75; Thurner, *From Two Nations to One Divided*.

19. In a recent dissertation, Ponciano del Pino Huamán has explored the long-lasting consequences for Peruvian Andean communities, especially in the highland regions of Huanta, Ayacucho, of this closing down of Peruvian politics at the end of the nineteenth century. See del Pino Huamán, "'Looking to the Government': Community, Politics, and the Production of Memory and Silences in Twentieth-Century Peru, Ayacucho" (PhD diss., University of Wisconsin-Madison, 2008).

20. For the case of Bolivia across the nineteenth century, as well as a most instructive comparison with other Andean cases, see Brooke Larson, *The Trials of Nation Making: Liberalism, Race, and Ethnicity in the Andes, 1810–1910* (Cambridge, U.K.: Cambridge University Press, 2004).

21. Greg Grandin, *The Blood of Guatemala: A History of Race and Nation* (Durham, N.C.: Duke University Press, 2000). For an updated analysis of the continuities between Conservative and Liberal regimes in nineteenth-century Guatemala on issues of labor and export production, see René Reeves, *Ladinos with Ladinos, Indians with Indians: Land, Labor, and Regional Ethnic Conflict in the Making of Guatemala* (Stanford, Calif.: Stanford University Press, 2006).

22. Arturo Leiva, *El primer avance a la Araucanía: Angol, 1862* (Temuco: Ediciones Universidad de la Frontera, 1984), 54–79; José Bengoa, *Historia del pueblo mapuche (siglo XIX y XX)* (Santiago: Ediciones Sur, 1985), 164–70; Ricardo Ferrando Keun, *Y así nació la frontera: Conquista, guerra, ocupación, pacificación, 1550–1900* (Santiago: Editorial Antártica, 1986), 321–22; and Rolando Arturo Leiva, "Araucanía—Etnía y Política" (PhD diss., Free University of Berlin, 2006).

23. Jorge Pinto Rodríguez, "Crisis económica y expansion territorial: La ocupacion de la Araucanía en la segunda mitad del siglo XIX," *Revista Estudios Sociales* (Santiago) 72 (1992): 85–126; and *La formación del Estado y la nación, y el pueblo mapuche: De la inclusión a la exclusión* (Santiago: DIBAM, 2003).

24. Leiva, *El primer avance*, 91–133; direct quotation on p. 115.

25. Ibid., 125–26.

26. Maurice Zeitlin, *The Civil Wars in Chile (Or, the Bourgeois Revolutions That Never Were)* (Princeton, N.J.: Princeton University Press, 1984); Andrew Daitsman, "Popular Mobilization and Liberal Rebellion in Chile: The Civil Wars of the 1850s" (PhD diss., University of Wisconsin-Madison, 1995); Esteban Valenzuela, *Alegato histórico regionalista* (Santiago: LOM, 1999).

27. Leiva, *El primer avance*, 28–41, 131–33; direct quotation on p. 132.

28. For the correspondence between Pérez and Cruz, see "Cartas del Presidente Pérez y del General Cruz," in *Revista Chilena de Historia y Geografía* 123 (1954–55): 73–120.

29. Pinto, "Crisis económica," *De la inclusión a la exclusión*; Leiva, *El primer avance*; Bengoa, *Historia*.

30. Jones, "Conflict and Adaptation," 158, 170–76; Ferrando Keun, *Y así nació la frontera*, 468, 470, 481; Bengoa, *Historia*, 149, 259–63, 285–336.

31. Jones, "Conflict and Adaptation," 92, 117, 140; Lazzari, "¡Que vivan los indios argentinos!"; Richard W. Slatta, *Gauchos and the Vanishing Frontier* (Lincoln: University of Nebraska Press, 1992); Isabel Hernández et al., *La identidad enmascarada: Los Mapuche de*

Los Toldos (Buenos Aires: Editorial Universitaria de Buenos Aires, 1993); Curruhuinca-Roux, *Las matanzas del Neuquén: Crónicas mapuches* (Buenos Aires: Editorial Plus Ultra, 1984).

32. Jones, "Conflict and Adaptation," 16–20, 41–46, 60, 67, 78.

33. Nicolas Shumway, *The Invention of Argentina* (Berkeley: University of California Press, 1991), esp. 214–96; George Reid Andrews, *The Afro-Argentines of Buenos Aires, 1800–1900* (Madison: University of Wisconsin Press, 1980), esp. 93–112; Slatta, *Gauchos*; Jones, "Conflict and Adaptation," 92–93, 100–103, 110–23, 147–48, 159–70, 189, 196–97; Curruhuinca-Roux, *Matanzas del Neuquén*, 111–14; Jorge Pinto Rodríguez, "Integración y desintegración de un espacio fronterizo: La Araucanía y las pampas, 1550–1900," in Pinto Rodríguez, ed., *Araucanía y pampas*, 11–46.

34. Jones, "Conflict and Adaptation;" Gladys Varela and Luz María Font, "La erradicación indígena y el nuevo poblamiento en el noroeste neuquino," in Pinto Rodríguez, ed., *Araucanía y pampas*, 201–11; Hernández et al., *La identidad enmascarada*; Curruhuinca-Roux, *Matanzas del Neuquén*; Domingo Faustino Sarmiento, *Civilización y barbarie: La vida de Juan Facundo Quiroga* ([1845] Mexico: Editorial Porrúa, 1977); Shumway, *Invention of Argentina*. The similarities with the process of "disappearance" of the Afro-Argentines of Buenos Aires, so painstakingly narrated by Andrews, *Afro-Argentines*, is a subject that warrants further discussion and research.

35. David Rock, *Argentina 1516–1987: From Spanish Colonization to Alfonsín* (Berkeley: University of California Press, 1987), 118–61; Mark D. Szuchman, *Order, Family and Community in Buenos Aires, 1810–1860* (Stanford, Calif.: Stanford University Press, 1988); James Scobie, *Revolution on the Pampas: A Social History of Argentine Wheat, 1860–1910* (Austin: University of Texas Press, 1964).

36. Ferrando Keun, *Y así nació la frontera*, 488–543; Bengoa, *Historia*, 345–46, 353–55.

37. Bengoa, *Historia*; Quezada, *La frontera*; Hernán San Martín, *Los Araucanos* (Santiago: Editora Nacional Quimantú, 1972); Stephen E. Lewis, "Myth and the History of Chile's Araucanians," *Radical History Review* 58 (1994): 112–41; Ziley Mora Penroz, *Verdades mapuches de alta magia para reencantar la Tierra de Chile* (Temuco: Editorial Kushe, 1989); Museo Chileno de Arte Precolombino, *Mapuche!* (Santiago: Compañía General de Electricidad Industrial, 1985); *Mapuche: Seeds of the Chilean Soul* (Philadelphia: Port of History Museum, 1992); Yosuke Kuramochi, *Me contó la gente de la tierra: Relatos orales de los mapuches del centro sur de Chile* (Santiago: Ediciones Universidad Católica de Chile, 1992); Miguel Laborde, *La selva fría y sagrada* (Santiago: Editorial Contrapunto, 1990); Tulio Mora, *El libro de Paloma: Ensayos mapuches* (Santiago: Editorial La Noria, 1987).

38. Slatta, *Gauchos*; Shumway, *Invention of Argentina*.

39. Rebecca Earle, *The Return of the Native: Indians and Myth-Making in Spanish America, 1810–1930* (Durham, N.C.: Duke University Press, 2007).

40. Alan Knight, "Racism, Revolution, and *Indigenismo*: Mexico, 1910–1940," in *The Idea of Race in Latin America, 1870–1940*, ed. Richard Graham (Austin: University of Texas Press, 1990), 71–113; Marjorie Becker, "Black and White and Color: Cardenismo and the Search for a Campesino Ideology," *Comparative Studies in Society and History* 29 (1987): 453–65; Mallon, "Indigenous Communities." An alternative vision is presented in Guillermo Bonfil Batalla, *México profundo: Una civilización negada* (Mexico City: Secretaría de Educación Pública/ CIESAS, 1987). The most recent work that has tempered our views of *indigenismo* during the early revolutionary decades has been done by Alexander S. Dawson, "From Models for the Nation to Model Citizens: *Indigenismo* and the 'Revindication' of the Mexican Indian, 1920–40," *Journal of Latin American Studies* 30 (1998): 279–308, and *Indian and Nation in Revolutionary Mexico* (Tucson: University of Arizona Press, 2004). For a different look at the role of indigenous intellectuals in twentieth century Mexico, and their

relationship with nationalism, see Natividad Gutiérrez, *Nationalist Myths and Ethnic Identities: Indigenous Intellectuals and the Mexican State* (Lincoln: University of Nebraska Press, 1999).

41. Thomas M. Davies, *Indian Integration in Peru: A Half-Century of Experience, 1900–1948* (Lincoln: University of Nebraska Press, 1974).

42. Florencia E. Mallon, *The Defense of Community in Peru's Central Highlands: Peasant Struggle and Capitalist Transition, 1860–1940* (Princeton, N.J.: Princeton University Press, 1983), 268–333. See also del Pino Huaman, "'Looking to the Government': Community, Politics, and the Production of Memory and Silences in Twentieth-Century Peru, Ayacucho" (PhD diss., University of Wisconsin-Madison, 2008).

43. Examples of more educated and economically privileged indigenous elites using civilizing discourses can be found in Grandin, *The Blood of Guatemala*, esp. 110–97, and Florencia E. Mallon, "La doble columna y la doble conciencia en la obra de Manuel Manquilef," *Revista Chilena de Antropología* (April 2010). For a more transgressive use of civilizing discourses, see Laura Gotkowitz, *A Revolution for Our Rights: Indigenous Struggles for Land and Justice in Bolivia, 1880–1952* (Durham, N.C.: Duke University Press, 2007).

44. Gonzalo Castillo Cárdenas, *Liberation Theology From Below: The Life and Thought of Manuel Quintín Lame* (New York: Orbis Books, 1987); Diego Castrillón Arboleda, *El indio Quintín Lame* (Bogotá: Ediciones Tercer Mundo, 1973); Quintín Lame, *Los pensamientos del indio que se educó dentro de las selvas colombianas* (Organización Nacional Indígena de Colombia, 1987), and *En defensa de mi raza* (Bogotá: Rosca de Investigación y Acción Social, 1973); Joanne Rappaport, *The Politics of Memory: Native Historical Interpretation in the Colombian Andes* (New York: Cambridge University Press, 1990); and Ricardo Sánchez, "Las ideas socialistas en Colombia," Universidad Nacional de Colombia, *El Marxismo en Colombia* (Bogotá: Facultad de Ciencias Sociales, 1983), 117–43.

45. On Aburto's commitment to the restitution of Mapuche lands and his subsequent repression, see Bengoa, *Historia del pueblo mapuche*; Foerster and Montecino; Archivo Nacional Histórico-Miraflores, Santiago, Intendencia de Cautín, Vol. 242: "Oficio del gobernador de Mariluan al Intendente de Cautín, sobre cumplimiento de providencia que recayó sobre un telegrama del Ministerio del Interior acerca de Manuel Menque, Aburto Panguilef y Arturo Huenchullan," Victoria, 7 April 1927; Vol. 279: "Solicitud de varios caciques al Gobernador de Imperial para que recomiende una comisión frente al Supermo Gobierno," Nueva Imperial, 11 Oct. 1929; Vol. 283: "Oficio de Manuel Aburto Panguilef, presidente del Comité Ejecutivo de la Araucanía, al Intendente de Cautín," Loncoche, 10 Sept. 1929; "Oficio del Comité Ejecutivo de la Araucanía de Chile al Intendente de Cautín, transcribiendo comunicaciones de su sesión del 10 de Septiembre," Loncoche, 16 Sept. 1929; Vol. 305: "Oficio de Manuel Aburto Panguilef, presidente del Comité Ejecutivo de la Araucanía al Intendente de Cautín," Loncoche, 22 April 1930; "Oficio de Manuel Aburto Panguilef al Intendente de Cautín," Loncoche, 30 April 1930; "Oficio de Manuel Aburto Panguilef, Presidente del Comité Ejecutivo de la Araucanía de Chile, al Intendente de Cautín," Loncoche, 17 Dec. 1930. See also Archivo Siglo XX (Santiago), Ministerio del Interior, Oficios Confidenciales, N° 7401: "Guillermo Edwards Matte, Ministro del Interior, al Intendente de Cautín, sobre necesidad de mantener reservadas informaciones sobre Manuel Aburto Panguilef," Santiago, 18 Feb. 1929; N° 7669: "Oficio del Ministerio del Interior al Intendente de Cautín, sobre la relegación de Aburto Panguilef a Caldera," Santiago, 2 June 1930; N° 7670: "Criptograma Nr 0 47 al Intendente de Temuco [sic], sobre autorización que Aburto Panguilef vuelva a Loncoche," 13 Sept. 1930, y N° 7670: "Solicitud de Manuel Aburto Panguilef al Ministro del Interior, pidiendo se resuelva la situación de su relegación," Santiago, 3 Sept. 1930. On his alliance with the left see Bengoa, Foerster and

Montecino, and Intendencia de Cautín, Vol. 432: "Oficio de Manuel Aburto Panguilef, Presidente de la Federación Araucana al Intendente de Cautín, informándole de los acuerdos de la reunión de la Federación," Temuco, 22 July 1935; Vol. 283: "Oficio del Comité Ejecutivo de la Araucanía de Chile al Intendente de Cautín, transcribiendo comunicaciones de su sesión del 10 de Sept. de 1929," Loncoche, 16 Sept. 1929. The renewed attention being given to Aburto in the contemporary period can be seen in André Menard and Jorge Pávez, "El Congreso Araucano: Ley, raza y escritura en la política mapuche," *Política* (Universidad de Chile) 44 (2005): 211–32; André Menard, "Manuel Aburto Panguilef: De la República Indígena al sionismo mapuche," Working Paper Series 12, Ñuke Mapuförlaget, 2003, 63 pp; and Florencia E. Mallon, "El Siglo XX Mapuche: Esferas públicas, sueños de autodeterminación y articulaciones internacionales," in *Las disputas por la etnicidad en América Latina: Movilizaciones indígenas en Chiapas y Araucanía*, ed. Christian Martínez Neira and Marco Estrada Saavedra (Santiago: Catalonia, 2009), 155–90.

46. Perhaps the most dramatic case of this in Mexico that has received additional attention in the wake of the Neo-Zapatista uprising is Chiapas. On these issues historically in the highland region of that state, see Jan Rus, "The 'Comunidad Revolucionaria Institucional': The Subversion of Native Government in Highland Chiapas, 1936–1968," in *Everyday Forms of State Formation: Revolution and the Negotiation of Rule in Modern Mexico*, ed. Gilbert Joseph and Daniel Nugent (Durham, N.C.: Duke University Press, 1994), 265–300; and June C. Nash, *Mayan Visions: The Quest for Autonomy in an Age of Globalization* (New York: Routledge, 2001), especially 31–117.

47. Beyond the collections cited in footnote 2, sources dealing with indigenous rights and international human rights include: Guillermo Bonfil Batalla, ed., *Utopía y revolución: El pensamiento político contemporáneo de los indios en América Latina* (Mexico City: Editorial Nueva Imagen, 1981); Héctor Díaz Polanco, *Indigenous Peoples in Latin America: The Quest for Self-Determination*, Lucía Rayas, trans. (Boulder, Colo.: Westview Press, 1997); Documentos de la Segunda Reunión de Barbados, *Indianidad y descolonización en América Latina* (Mexico City: Editorial Nueva Imagen, 1979); Alexander Ewen, ed., *Voice of Indigenous Peoples: Native People Address the United Nations* (Santa Fe, N.M.: Clear Light Publishers, 1994); Rigoberta Menchú, with Dante Liano and Gianni Mina, *Rigoberta: La nieta de los mayas* (Mexico City: Aguilar, Altea, Taurus, Alfaguara, S.A. de C.V., 1998); Rodolfo Stavenhagen, *Ethnic Conflicts and the Nation-State* (New York: St. Martin's Press, 1996), "Indian Ethnic Movements and State Policies in Latin America," *IFDA Dossier* 36 (July/August 1983): 3–16; *Derecho Indígena y derechos humanos en América Latina* (Mexico City: El Colegio de México, 1988); Stavenhagen and Diego Iturralde, eds., *Entre la ley y la costumbre: El derecho consuetudinario indígena en América Latina* (Mexico City: Instituto Indigenista Interamericano/Instituto Interamericano de Derechos Humanos de San José, Costa Rica, 1990). A particularly creative example of the use of international human rights discourse in relation to the situation of the Maya people in Guatemala can be found in the work of Demetrio Cojtí Cuxil. See, for example, Demetrio Cojtí Cuxil, "The Politics of Maya Revindication," in *Maya Cultural Activism in Guatemala*, ed. Edward F. Fischer and R. McKenna Brown (Austin: University of Texas Press, 1996), 19–50. For an overview of the discourse of the Guatemalan Maya revitalization movement, see Kay B. Warren, *Indigenous Movements and their Critics: Pan-Maya Activism in Guatemala* (Princeton, N.J.: Princeton University Press, 1998).

48. On the 1980s indigenous movement in Juchitán, Oaxaca, known as COCEI, see Jeffrey W. Rubin, *Decentering the Regime: Ethnicity, Radicalism, and Democracy in Juchitán, Mexico* (Durham, N.C.: Duke University Press, 1997); and Howard Campbell, *Zapotec Renaissance: Ethnic Politics and Cultural Revivalism in Southern Mexico* (Albuquerque:

University of New Mexico Press, 1994). On the EZLN, see George A. Collier and Elizabeth L. Quaratiello, *Basta! Land and the Zapatista Rebellion in Chiapas* (Oakland, Calif.: Food First, 1994); Neil Harvey, *The Chiapas Rebellion: The Struggle for Land and Democracy* (Durham, N.C.: Duke University Press, 1998); Lynn Stephen and George Collier, eds., *Reconfiguring Ethnicity, Identity and Citizenship in the Wake of the Zapatista Rebellion*, Special Issue of the *Journal of Latin American Anthropology* 3:1 (1997); and Lynn Stephen, *Zapata Lives! Histories and Cultural Politics in Southern Mexico* (Berkeley: University of California Press, 2002). An interesting example of the impact indigenous revitalization had on the historiography of the twentieth century is Reina, ed., *La reindianización de América*.

49. For the case of Guatemala, see Fischer and Brown, *Maya Cultural Activism* and Warren, *Indigenous Movements and their critics*. For Chile, see Rosa Isolde Reuque Paillalef, *When a Flower Is Reborn: The Life and Times of a Mapuche Feminist*, ed., trans. Florencia E. Mallon (Durham, N.C.: Duke University Press, 2002); Kyle Steenland, *Agrarian Reform Under Allende: Peasant Revolt in the South* (Albuquerque: University of New Mexico Press, 1977); José A. Mariman, "Transición democrática en Chile: Nuevo ciclo reivindicativo mapuche?" 1994, available at http://www.xs4all.nl/~rehue/art/jmar5a/html; Christián Martínez Neira, *Comunidades y Territorios Lafkenche, los mapuche de Rucacura al Moncul* (Temuco: Instituto de Estudios Indígenas/Universidad de la Frontera, Serie de Investigación, 1995); Florencia E. Mallon, "Cuando la amnesia se impone con sangre, el abuso se hace costumbre: El pueblo mapuche y el Estado chileno, 1881–1998," in *El modelo chileno: Democracia y desarrollo en los noventa*, ed. Paul W. Drake and Iván Jaksic (Santiago: LOM Ediciones, 1999), 435–64; and Mallon, *Courage Tastes of Blood: The Mapuche Community of Nicolás Ailío and the Chilean State, 1906–2001* (Durham, N.C.: Duke University Press, 2005).

50. On the case of Colombia, see Rappaport, *The Politics of Memory*, 134–36; Leon Zamosc, *The Agrarian Question and the Peasant Movement in Colombia: Struggles of the National Peasant Association, 1967–1981* (New York: Cambridge University Press, 1986); and Myriam Jimeno, "Juan Gregorio Palechor: Tierra, identidad y recreación étnica," in Joanne Rappaport, ed., *Ethnicity Reconfigured: Indigenous Legislators and the Colombian Constitution of 1991*, Special Issue of *Journal of Latin American Anthropology* 1:2 (1996): 46–77. On Bolivia, see, in addition to sources already cited and as an introduction to an extremely rich and diverse literature, Xavier Albó, "From MNRistas to Kataristas to Katari," in Stern, *Rebellion, Resistance, and Consciousness*, 379–419; Albó, *Pueblos indios en la política* (La Paz: CIPCA, 2002); and Esteban Ticona Alejo, *Organización y liderazgo aymara: La experiencia indígena en la política boliviana, 1979–1996* (La Paz: Universidad de la Cordillera, 2000).

51. Alcida Rita Ramos, *Indigenism: Ethnic Politics in Brazil* (Madison: University of Wisconsin Press, 1998).

52. Charles R. Hale, *Resistance and Contradiction: Miskitu Indians and the Nicaraguan State, 1894–1987* (Stanford, Calif.: Stanford University Press, 1994).

53. For an introduction to the Ecuadorian case, in addition to the collections already cited, see Melina Selverston-Scher, *Ethnopolitics in Ecuador: Indigenous Rights and and the Strengthening of Democracy* (Coral Gables, Fla.: North-South Center Press, 2001). For an overview of recent work on the general subject of indigenous struggles that includes additional bibliography, see Donna Lee Van Cott, "Indigenous Struggle," *Latin American Research Review* 38:2 (2003): 220–33.

54. In Argentina, for example, a Mapuche revitalization does exist, despite the small size of the population. See Claudia Briones and José Luis Lanata, eds., *Contemporary Perspectives on the Native Peoples of Pampa, Patagonia, and Tierra del Fuego: Living on the*

Edge (Westport, Conn.: Bergin and Garvey, 2002), especially 91–120. And in El Salvador, Jeffrey Gould's recent work on the 1932 massacre has also shown the emergence of a small but dedicated indigenous movement in the western region of the country. See especially *1932: Scars of Memory (Cicatriz de la Memoria)*, a film by Jeffrey Gould and Carlos Henriquez Consalvi (First Run/Icarus Films, 2002).

55. Marisol de la Cadena, *Indigenous Mestizos: The Politics of Race and Culture in Cuzco, 1919–1991* (Durham, N.C.: Duke University Press, 2000); Frank Salomon, "Unethnic Ethnohistory: On Peruvian Peasant Historiography and Ideas of Autochthony," *Ethnohistory* 49:3 (2002): 475–506. At the same time, as recent work has shown, notions of indigeneity and politicized identity in the Peruvian Andes are complex and shifting. See, in addition to the relevant sources cited in footnote 3, María Elena García, ed., *Latin American and Caribbean Ethnic Studies: Special Issue: Indigenous Encounters in Contemporary Peru*, 3:3 (November 2008).

56. The case that comes to mind here is, of course, the government of Evo Morales in Bolivia. For an especially stimulating reflection about Evo Morales and his Movimiento al Socialismo that places him in broad Bolivian historical perspective, see Forrest Hylton and Sinclair Thomson, *Revolutionary Horizons: Past and Present in Bolivian Politics* (New York: Verso, 2007).

CHAPTER 10

RURAL HISTORY

ERIC VAN YOUNG

THE history of Latin America has been written on and by the land. This is not an invocation of Physiocratic dogma, and still less a piece of folkloric nostalgia—it is simply a fact. While the silver pouring from Mexico and Peru, and later the gold and diamonds of Brazil, tied the colonized areas of the New World irrevocably into the economy of the Old through the Iberian Peninsula, precious metals also integrated huge regions of Ibero-America internally (although hard cash was often scarce), oiling the wheels of commerce, greasing the palms of state officials, and stimulating all sorts of local economic activities from shoe making to sugar refining. Until relatively recent times, certainly well into the twentieth century, most Latin Americans got their living directly or indirectly from farming.[1] In late colonial Mexico, for example, estimates of the percentage of the labor force engaged in agriculture, including both people linked to the market and those producing for subsistence, would stand at approximately 85%–90%. This direct dependence on the land persisted during the great export booms of the late nineteenth and early twentieth centuries, while the demand for labor thus generated induced millions of Europeans to migrate westward across the Atlantic Basin, as it had earlier driven the involuntary migration of millions of enslaved Africans.

These processes profoundly transformed the human face, economies, and cultures of societies such as Brazil, Argentina, and Uruguay, and to a lesser extent Chile and other areas of South America. But by the end of the twentieth century the situation had changed radically under the impact of industrialization, urbanization, and the expansion of service sectors in the national economies of the region. The percentage of the labor force still engaged in agriculture provides a gross indicator of the change, falling in Argentina from about 14% in 1980 to 1% in 2000, and during the same period in Brazil from 41% to 24%, and in Mexico from 55% to 24%. Furthermore, ownership of the land in one form or another configured colonial and postcolonial space, and long molded the social and political identity of indigenous and peasant communities, the overall social structure, the power of elite groups, and the aristocratic (and racialist) values reflected in literature, art, and social practice. Great political struggles—among them the Mexican and Cuban revolutions and the 1994 Zapatista uprising in Chiapas—were in large measure carried forward to redress social and economic inequalities arising from the skewed distribution of land, the oppressive power of landowning groups, and the influence of foreign governments and markets mediated through the export sector. It should hardly be surprising, therefore, that scholarly writing about Latin American rural history has a long and deep tradition itself, stretching back into the nineteenth century.

A major problem with writing a historiographical survey of this literature while simultaneously conveying along very general lines some of its substantive findings lies in the way that "rural history" sprawls in so many different directions. If one were to follow the *histoire totale* approach, for instance, there would be virtually no principle of exclusion in writing about what were still until recently, after all, overwhelmingly agrarian societies. To take but one example, the Catholic Church was and is intimately entwined with the lives of rural people. Until some time around the middle of the nineteenth century, in most places, rural curates bought, inherited, and owned land as private farmers employing other people, typically among their parishioners, and until liberal reforms abolished the mandatory tithe, such men had derived much of their income from it. If churchmen were regular clergy, their orders often owned vast tracts of productive land. The Jesuits were especially notable for this, but many of the other orders supported their activities in part from landed income as well, occupying large shares of the market and struggling judicially and extrajudicially against peasant farmers for the control of resources. Furthermore, when fertility rituals and prayers were performed at the edge of peasant fields dedicated to raising crops, Christian and indigenous belief and ceremonial systems jostled each other in the process. So while this range of activities may not have been dedicated exclusively to getting a living from the land, some of it was, and the activities certainly involved rural people and the disposition of surpluses and wealth produced by farming, thus bringing into significant overlap two spheres of life—the economic and the spiritual—often thought removed from each other, and traditionally treated that way by historians.

"Rural life" can therefore embrace almost anything that takes place outside urban areas. The solution that I have adopted to avoid this sprawl—which could also embrace spatial systems, gender relations, material culture,[2] forms of popular political mobilization, and so forth—will be to focus principally on historical writings about economic activities involving farming and the land (whether subsistence or commercial, large-scale or small, mechanized or "traditional," indigenous or European), and to work outward from there, where appropriate touching upon social, political, and cultural life. Writing in economic history has been the core of rural historiography across national traditions, and while interest in economic matters has waned among historians of Latin America (at least among Anglophone scholars) in the face of the rise of cultural history over the last two decades or so, writing on the cultural history of rural areas per se, as opposed to that of village Indians, say, or women who happened to live outside cities, has yet to wax in compensation.[3] Furthermore, to avoid lapsing into a cataloguish recitation of rural historiographies on a country-by-country basis, on the one hand, or into a strictly analytical discussion by theme that strips regional systems and localities of their historical particularities, on the other, this essay tacks back and forth between countries and themes, paying the most attention to Mexico, Argentina, Brazil, and the Andean region, and bringing in other literatures where relevant. There is ample justification for this approach, since the agrarian, rural, and regional historiography of these four areas has developed quite noticeably around distinct narratives whose breadth and overlap covers much of Latin American history: that on Mexico related to the feudal/capitalist dichotomy in the rural economy, Argentina's on the pampas export sector beginning in the eighteenth century, and Brazil's around the problematics of initially slave-based sugar production, and later export booms (especially coffee, still in its early stages dependent upon the labor of African slaves) cognate to Argentina's.[4]

Historical studies of Latin American rural life have a significant prehistory going well back into the nineteenth and early twentieth centuries, much of it, not surprisingly, spurred either by a critique of plantation slavery and its social sequelae or by agrarian problems, with their attendant political upheavals. To cite but one example, the Cuban writer José Antonio Saco published an important early study of slavery in the 1870s,[5] in an era when abolitionism was tightly intertwined with the island colony's belated movement for independence from Spain. In a related fashion, the run-up to the Mexican Revolution, with its building agrarian pressures and political ferment, triggered the reformist critique of the Porfirio Díaz regime by the Mexican Andrés Molina Enríquez, *Los grandes problemas nacionales* (1909), in which he made the gnomic but oft-quoted remark, "La hacienda no es negocio [the hacienda is not a business]."[6] It is worth noting that Saco was a philosopher and Molina Enríquez a lawyer, that both men were involved in journalism and politics, and that their work was quite characteristic of a late-nineteenth-century liberal reformist tradition with a strongly meliorist bent reflected in their views of rural society and how to transform it.

By the interwar period, when Euro-Atlantic social science had already gained a strong foothold among Latin American intellectuals, a refashioned concern with slavery and race relations gave impulse to a new generation of studies with an explicitly anthropological, culturalist approach, in part inspired by the desire to suss out the origins of African cultural survivals within Latin American nations. Published within a year of each other, for example, the Brazilian Gilberto Freyre's *The Masters and the Slaves* (1946) and the Cuban Fernando Ortiz's *Cuban Counterpoint: Tobacco and Sugar* (1947) sought the origins of their societies' modern social problems in an analysis of the colonial and nineteenth-century plantation complex, African slavery, and race relations.[7] Although these now classic works and others of their ilk certainly discussed the plantation complex and its economic context, they were not studies of rural history per se, since they were more centrally concerned with viewing contemporary social problems in a historical light, and their authors were therefore prompted to formulate national metanarratives as much out of political concerns as the logic of historical inquiry.[8]

National "traditions" in rural historiography have thus developed along somewhat different trajectories during the last half century or so, although the outlines of these literatures in some cases announced themselves quite obviously long before the 1950s. These trends were mostly nourished by some of the factors already alluded to: liberal-reformist political critiques, the need to explain revolutions with notable agrarian components, the problems presented by postemancipation race relations, local antiquarian traditions, the maturing of social science in the region, and so forth. The Brazilian scholarly literature developed principally around the northeastern sugar and central-southern coffee plantation complexes, coalescing quite understandably around issues of slavery, and the Argentine historiography around the successive waves of pampas export economy in the nineteenth and twentieth centuries. Andean writing on colonial rural history tilted somewhat toward labor systems, chiefly because of the difficulties of mobilizing indigenous people for the Spanish estate and mining sectors, and followed the wide documentary trail these conflicts left in the historical record; it also focused on certain postindependence export activities (sugar on the coast, wool in the highlands). The Mexican literature, in the absence of a dominant agro-export activity, developed a fixation on the mixed-production hacienda, which serviced primarily domestic markets. In addition to these endogenous considerations, many historians in Latin America, Europe, and the United States who later focused on rural history were influenced by the works of Saco, Molina Enríquez, Freyre, Ortiz, and others of the proto-rural historians, but also by those of European scholars such as Marc Bloch, Pierre Goubert, Emmanuel Le Roy Ladurie, Bernhard Slicher Van Bath, R. H. Tawney, and Joan Thirsk, among others.

The Feudalism/Capitalism Debate: Mexico

If one were to single out an avatar of more modern approaches to rural history, it would be a work very closely related to the European historiography of Marc Bloch's generation: François Chevalier's *La formation des grands domaines au Mexique* (1952).[9] Chevalier's work raised the question of whether the great colonial landed estate was feudal or capitalist in spirit and practice (we have seen Molina Enríquez's verdict from the early twentieth century), but he worked out his response through attacking a mass of primary documentation rather than arguing from theoretical abstraction or upstreaming from later political events. Chevalier presented a *tableau vivant* of the feudal-looking north Mexican seigneur and the patriarchal frontier society over which he ruled, suggesting that the origin of the colonial hacienda's feudalization lay in an economic contraction led by a seventeenth-century decline in silver mining production. This contraction of market demand, he reasoned, had turned the rural estate in upon itself, reinforcing what had already been an ecologically adaptive tendency in such estates toward extensive (livestock-raising) rather than intensive (grain-producing) practices, but also allowing scope for the mentality of the "grand seigneur" imported in the cultural baggage of the Spanish conquerors.[10]

In one guise or another, the argument over whether landed estates in the Iberian New World were primarily feudal or capitalist in form or some sort of hybrid—and if capitalist, when they became so—has been the grand theme of much of the writing on rural history ever since Chevalier. The issue spilled over into much writing about Latin America not even centrally focused on rural history, since a broader characterization of the region's entire history with reference to whether its major economic formations were feudal or capitalist could provide the foundation of large interpretive schemes.[11] From this point of view, the discussion also had important political implications. For if the transition to capitalism had come early, a socialist revolution might be expected sooner rather than later; whereas if feudalism had prevailed until recent times, the phase of capitalism must still be passed through, and political expectations and social revolutionary aspirations adjusted accordingly. Particularly where the colonial period—the foundational moment of Latin American agro-social forms—was concerned, the historiographic seed planted by Chevalier's great study flowered most exuberantly during a relatively brief period, between about 1965 and 1985.[12] Latin American, European, and North American scholars have debated endlessly and robustly whether commercialized rural estates can be called capitalist, protocapitalist, precapitalist, or cryptocapitalist, whether forms of coerced labor disqualified them or could be accommodated theoretically to what remained basically a Marxian framework of understanding, whether apparently rational economic behaviors were driven by aristocratic values, and so forth.

Although it played itself out most clearly in the Mexican historiography of the colonial era and the prerailroad age, this discussion produced loud echoes in the rich Argentine literature as well, especially for the period between about 1750 and the onset of the great export booms in the mid-nineteenth century.[13] And what seemed at first a parochial debate played a significant role from the 1960s in the rise of dependency perspectives (and some theoretical oddities, such as ideas about the articulation of modes of production). Dependency theory—perhaps "perspective" is a better word than theory, since at this remove in time it is difficult to see what was very theoretical about it—took the form in the Mexicanist literature of works such as André Gunder Frank's extended essay (published in 1979, but written many years earlier) on the transformation of the mode of production from feudalism to an early dependent capitalism in the sixteenth century,[14] although this approach was later to find its most florid application in studies of the nineteenth and twentieth centuries.[15] In regions removed from the core silver-mining centers of Mexico and Peru, economic dynamism and social change within a dependent colonial framework were portrayed by some scholars as substantial but still amounting only to a nascent form of capitalism manqué, as in Marcello Carmagnani's detailed study of Chile between 1680 and 1830. Carmagnani found that during the eighteenth century, Peruvian demand for Chilean wheat transformed the agrarian economy of the sleepy colony's central valleys, in the process reinforcing landlord hegemony over a resident service tenantry (*inquilinos*) and establishing an urban hierarchy in which other cities were subordinate to Santiago, and Santiago to commercial interests in Lima and Cádiz.[16]

The view that the colonial landed estate was a messily capitalist institution—commercialized, profit-oriented, economically rational, and so forth, but organized internally along paternalistic lines and capable of contracting in on itself when labor and/or market conditions warranted a turn toward autarchy—had hardened into orthodoxy as studies of rural economic history reached their high-water mark in the 1970s and early 1980s. In Mexico, the economic historians Jan Bazant and Enrique Semo, among others, refined this model in research on multiple haciendas in the central parts of the country, and studies by Anglophone historians (e.g., David Brading, Eric Van Young) demonstrated roughly the same thing.[17] For the Andean area, Robert G. Keith's book on colonial estates along the Peruvian coast and Keith A. Davies's more focused study of the Arequipa region, on the south coast of Peru, supported and expanded these findings for a different environment that nonetheless shared much with Mesoamerica, especially the presence of dense, sedentary indigenous populations in relatively close proximity to urban markets. A more theoretically sophisticated treatment was that on Peru of the French scholar Jean Piel, whose study embraced the entire country from the Spanish conquest up to the mid-nineteenth century, passing majestically through the wars of independence from Spain, which he characterized in Braudelian fashion as "only a political and juridical phenomenon" subordinate to changes in the land and productive arrangements. Piel remarked that there was at the time he published his book no Peruvian equivalent of Chevalier's great work, although he himself apparently aspired to create one. In tracing the development of "agrarian capitalism" in Peru, Piel saw the incipient rationalized commercial agriculture of the colonial era blossom into a more truly capitalist agricultural regime between about 1840 (with the advent of the guano export industry and the capital it made available) and 1920, which he dubbed the period of "neolatifundism" in the central Andean region.[18] A pair of fine studies by Nicholas Cushner—who, like Piel, called large-scale commercial farming production "agrarian capitalism"—were devoted to sugar and wine production on the north coast of Peru and the still more northerly region of Quito, in what is today Ecuador, during the period 1600–1767, and a third to the colonial Río de la Plata region, today's Argentina. Cushner's studies shared both the strength and the weakness that they were based on the activities of the Jesuit order, expelled from the Spanish realms in 1767. The Jesuits' punctilious accounting practices, substantial networked capital resources, and access to the highest levels of colonial power made their records unusually continuous and therefore invaluable sources, but raised questions of how representative their enterprises were.[19] The same was true of the historical anthropologist Herman

W. Konrad's dense study of a Jesuit hacienda complex in central Mexico during the same period as Cushner's work on the order's Andean estates. Konrad strongly emphasized the social ecology of the Jesuit latifundia, especially their destructive effects on nearby indigenous peasant villages, thereby painting a much less sanguine picture than Cushner of rural capitalist enterprise in the colonial heartlands, and assimilating Jesuit haciendas to what other scholars had found for secular landholdings.[20]

Theoretical leverage for drawing these distinctions had long since been provided by an important but now curiously little-cited article by the distinguished anthropologists Eric Wolf and Sidney Mintz.[21] They analyzed the differences between lowland plantations (staple-producing and characterized by wage-labor systems in the twentieth century, but in many areas slave-based well into the nineteenth century) and highland haciendas (nominally free-labor, farming and/or livestock) in terms of six variables—capital, labor, land, markets, technology, and modes of social control—rather than phenomenologically, as static ideal types, thus creating a typological matrix into which New World agro-social forms might be fitted. Of these variables, it has been the nature of markets (i.e., the degree of commercialization in the countryside) and forms of labor that have proven to pack the greatest diagnostic punch. Most studies of non-export-oriented rural economy for the colonial period and the earlier nineteenth century will devote some attention to the way farming and livestock surpluses were moved around domestic market spaces and disposed of, and it is hardly surprising that many works on rural Mexico turn their attention to such relationships, given the centrality of agricultural commercialization in the historiography of haciendas. My own study of rural estates in the Guadalajara region of western-central Mexico in the later colonial period is one of the few to do this in detail, however, describing in terms of central-place theory a regional rural economy increasingly integrated and reconfigured by the growth of urban demand over the course of a century.[22] One of the most penetrating studies on the Mexican countryside, that of Simon Miller, tackles the issue of economic modernization during the longer nineteenth century, concluding that in response to improving means of transport (the railroads) and the consolidation of domestic security, great Mexican landlords were able to produce grain profitably for distant urban markets, thus following a "Junker path" toward an economic modernization whose flowering was blocked by the eruption of the Mexican Revolution of 1910. Macroeconomic studies, primarily of the late colonial period (although for the immediate postconquest era see the excellent work of Ross Hassig), have demonstrated how large urban concentrations, burgeoning smaller cities, and mining complexes constituted markets that could organize rural production systems economically, like magnets orienting iron filings, and over the course of time reconfigured large regions in Mexico, the Andean area, and Argentina. Such works demonstrate on the whole a marked theoretical concern with the power of central places and with regionality. The studies on the Andean area are also strongly oriented toward the analysis of spatiality, but vertically rather than horizontally. They have stressed the uneven distribution of poles of economic growth there and the importance of the famous "Andean verticality," the distribution of native subsistence activity in an archipelago of complementary population concentrations and ecological niches corresponding to the imposing Andean geography of mountain tiers interrupted by intermontane valleys.[23]

The use of unfree or semifree forms of labor has drawn most attention in the debate over the hacienda, since the more coercive end of the labor continuum was anchored in African slavery.[24] This has proven a theoretical quagmire for most students of highly commercialized, staple-producing estates, no less in Anglo-America than in the Iberian colonies, since the presence of a wage-labor market with relatively free factor mobility has long been considered the single most important desideratum for defining capitalism, especially (although not exclusively) in the Marxian tradition. Theoretical problems show up in this regard from the very first labor institutions (coexistent with African slavery) established by the Spanish in the New World to control native labor, although it must be admitted that these problems arise primarily if the observer is committed beforehand to model building rather than a more eclectic, empiricist approach.

In general, early coercive labor arrangements involving colonists and indigenous people—slavery, labor tribute, corvée service—can be conceived of as mechanisms of primitive accumulation, since they created the infrastructure (urban and rural buildings, agricultural enterprises, roads, some mining facilities, etc.) of many of the colonies. The enslavement of Indians under doubtful royal authorization, or absent such license altogether, was the motive for great controversy from Columbus's time, lasted surprisingly long in some areas (especially in peripheral regions of the Spanish New World empire, often under the nominal justification of warfare), and has received some attention from modern authors, particularly the Mexican Silvio Zavala, who pioneered the study of indigenous labor history.[25] More important than indigenous slavery for the Spanish settlers was the institution of the encomienda, which enjoyed its heyday during the sixteenth century, although as in the case of slavery it survived in peripheral areas until quite late, even after it was officially abolished at midcentury. The encomienda was imported to Spain's American realms from Old Spain, where it had served late medieval Christian monarchs and their aristocratic allies in controlling newly conquered Muslim Iberians and extracting labor from them. The institution was adapted to dominate New World Indian populations through granting the right to conqueror-settlers to collect tribute from them in the form of labor (within strict limits often observed more in the breach than the observance) and commodities in return for some wages, indoctrination in Christian belief, and protection by their Spanish overlords (*encomenderos*). Because of the delegated sovereignty, the language of vassalage in which the grants were couched, and the elements of coercion in it, the encomienda has often been painted as a feudal institution. Much of the pioneering historiography, again, was done for colonial Mexico, but scholars have looked at its history in colonial Chile, Paraguay, Colombia, Guatemala, and even Argentina.[26]

Encomienda studies have flourished most, however, for the Andean area, probably because the native population there declined more slowly than in Mesoamerica under the impact of epidemic disease, the labor market was stickier, the impact of the silver mining economy focused on Potosí (in modern-day Bolivia) was more disruptive, and so forth. In the colonial-era historiography, in fact, there is an inverse relationship between Mexico and the Andean zone, the former having produced many fewer studies of the encomienda and related forms of labor mobilization but developed an obsession with the hacienda, while the latter has been much less preoccupied with the hacienda than with the encomienda and the form of corvée labor known as mita. One of the best of these Andean-area studies is that of Efraín Trelles, who traces the career of the Peruvian conquistador-*encomendero* Lucas Martínez Vegazo (1512–67) during the middle third of the sixteenth century. Trelles demonstrates very clearly that the encomienda was not only a form of military parasitism but also a fundamental mode of accumulating capital and building an early colonial economy, albeit against the backdrop of implicit state coercion and with the collaboration of members of the native ruling class who intervened as mediators in the process.[27]

Although there were technical and legal differences between them, the encomienda was in some ways similar to the widely known labor practice called *repartimiento*, a form of village-based, rotating, paid corvée labor established in some places in the sixteenth century, and which lasted in a somewhat attenuated form nearly until the end of the colonial period. The harshest form of this (known as the mita, a term taken over from the Incas)—a practice deeply disruptive of the complex kinship, spatial, and political forms of Andean native society, since many Indians fled their villages permanently to escape it—was employed at the great silver mining complex at Potosí, although it also provided labor for grain cultivation, sugar production, and livestock operations elsewhere.[28] A very different institution of a similar name, variously known as the *reparto* or *repartimiento de mercancías*, was also established during the early colonial period and officially outlawed by the Bourbon administrative reforms of the late eighteenth century, although it continued to exist de facto even after that. Particularly notorious for its abusiveness in Mexico and the Andes, this was a form of extractive arrangement whereby royal officials in the countryside compelled Indian villagers to buy goods from them on credit at inflated prices, thus forcing them into the labor market for money wages (as the payment of royal tribute also did) and in the process making tidy profits for themselves and their merchant backers. Jürgen Golte's study of the commercial *repartimiento* in the Andean area in the late eighteenth century suggested a direct relationship between its degree of exploitiveness and the propensity of indigenous communities to join the great wave of antiwhite and antigovernment rebellion that lashed the area in the early 1780s, and the view of most historians of the practice has at best been a very dark one. Turning this view on its head, however, the American scholar Jeremy Baskes has argued plausibly that during the late eighteenth century in the heavily Indian region of Oaxaca, in southeastern Mexico, a variant of the practice fueled small-scale production for export of the valuable dye-stuff cochineal (Spanish *cochinilla*) very much to the benefit of the Indian producers, for whom credit for living costs and production inputs was essential. He finds that force was minimal or nonexistent, and that the high prices of goods given on credit represented a reasonable risk premium for merchant backers and the provincial officials who fronted for them.[29]

Despite the long endurance of formally coerced labor in the Latin American countryside, at least nominally free labor existed alongside it from the beginning and grew steadily in importance. Free labor as such has received surprisingly limited scholarly attention, not because historians are not interested in it but because sources are lacking, or at best fragmented, and at least for the modern period depend heavily upon finding account books for agricultural estates or labor recruiters, which survive only sporadically. Most studies of estate complexes, regions, or export sectors touch heavily on labor, however. One of the most powerful formulations of the rise of free wage labor for areas of heavily indigenous population (Mesoamerica, the Andes) is still that of Charles Gibson. He suggested that for the colonial Mexican heartland the sequence encomienda labor→ repartimiento (corvée labor)→debt peonage occurred in response to the notorious declining demographic curve for native peoples, concomitantly increasing the difficulties for estate owners in recruiting, retaining, and controlling laborers. Gibson and other scholars (e.g., Lolita Gutiérrez Brockington) have even proposed that debt peonage in colonial times depended upon the ability of workers in relatively labor-scarce environments to maximize their position by extracting credit from their employers as a wage premium. But we are still left with the puzzle of why the practice should have persisted even in areas where the population curve trended upward from the mid-colonial period and the pressure to recruit labor in this fashion would presumably have abated.[30]

The extent and even the function of debt peonage, of course, would have varied with local population trends, peasant access to subsistence lands, and other conditions.[31] In modern times, forms of debt peonage overlapping with slavery have existed in rubber-producing areas, including the Putumayo region of Colombia and Peru, and in Chiapas, Tabasco, and Campeche in Mexico, as well as in Yucatán's henequen plantations. A pair of elegant studies, by Peter Klarén and Michael Gonzales, have delved into labor recruiting practices (the system of *enganche*, a sort of indenture contract) on Peru's sugar-producing north coast, and another, by Roger Plant, into the experience of Haitians recruited to work in the sugar industry in the Dominican Republic.[32] Still sparser than the historiography of rural labor, and a direct outgrowth of it, are works on the history of rural wages themselves, so well developed for Europe and the United States. A lamentable result of this lacuna is that while we have some fine works on the history of prices and on agricultural fluctuations and crises, especially for the colonial era, we still have very little writing on the standard-of-living debate for the mass of the Latin American rural population over time, which has proved so suggestive for the rest of the Atlantic world.[33]

Export Economies in Full Flower: Argentina

After Spanish America and Brazil achieved their independence from the metropolitan powers in the early 1820s, the successor states faced the necessity of reintegrating themselves into the world economy along relatively free-market lines rather than within the often stultifying mercantilist framework only just being overhauled in the last half-century or so of colonial rule.[34] Some of the new nations were so disrupted by the very process of sundering the colonial bond that they never regained their footing; Haiti is notoriously the Western Hemisphere's most extreme case of this. Others, such as Gran Colombia (which broke up into three nations) or Central America (which ended up as five), took time to recover their balance, collectively investing their energies in the consolidation of their boundaries and the establishment of their new state structures, an effort that cost all the new states dearly in greater or lesser degree, the notable exception being Brazil. Moreover, nearly everywhere (again, Brazil excepted) the costs of independence included ruined countrysides, widespread mortality, impaired or nonexistent state fiscal capacity, disrupted trade, and so forth.[35] As they struggled to consolidate themselves, almost all the new states of Latin America reentered the international market through mining (silver in Mexico and Peru, and somewhat later, copper in Chile and Mexico and guano in Peru from the 1840s) and/or agro-pastoral production for foreign markets. Indeed, livestock and agricultural exports tell much (though by no means all) of the history of rural Latin America for the nearly two centuries since independence was consummated. Many of the products are familiar, even mundane, but they formed the basis for enormous landed and commercial wealth in the region up to the Great Depression and beyond—coffee, sugar, bananas, beef and mutton, wool, and wheat are among the best known such commodities, along with some less familiar products such as henequen (also called sisal, a hard fiber produced in Mexico's Yucatan Peninsula)—leaving a permanent imprint on export-oriented economies.

Much of the narrative of Latin America's history in the later nineteenth and twentieth centuries can also be organized in terms of the economic distortions, opportunity costs, concentration of wealth, demographic changes, and social and political stresses the export economies brought in their wake, as well as the social solutions invented or adapted to deal with these problems.[36] The most common of these nostrums has been the market solution, which involves expanding export industries already in place, encouraging new ones, or engaging in import substitution industrialization, all strategies more or less covered by the discursive fig leaf that a rising tide lifts even the smallest boats. A second solution is political intervention to redress imbalances in the social distribution of wealth, either in the shape of land reform (e.g., Peru in the 1960s) or outright revolution (Mexico, Cuba, Nicaragua, etc.), which theoretically runs counter to the market solution, although in the end one of its goals may be to situate smaller commercial producers and peasants more advantageously in relation to markets. A third solution can be wrapped up in efforts to increase agricultural productivity through technological interventions (i.e., the Green Revolution). In practice none of these measures has been completely effective in the long term, and they may create as unintended consequences even worse social problems than they solve. Argentina constitutes a classic case of the market solution in the form of overlapping waves of export commodities dating from the late colonial period. It serves to introduce a range of historical issues touching on export economies, but also to illustrate the ways in which the picture of the socially reductive power of exports has been significantly complicated by recent research.[37]

As with other historiographies, that on Argentine rural life had its prehistory, as exemplified by now classic works such as Ricardo Levene's investigation into the colonial economy, Jacinto Oddone's study of landholding families in Buenos Aires province, Alfredo Montoya's on the salt-beef industry, and Horacio Giberti's on the Argentine livestock industry, the locus classicus of conventional wisdoms about economic development in the Río de la Plata.[38] The much-studied sequence of overlapping pampean export booms that began in the eighteenth century—cattle hides, salt beef, mutton and wool, wheat, and a turn back to beef again—has been portrayed as sweeping all before it, producing an enduring and highly skewed distribution of landed wealth (the top rung of which was occupied by large estancias and the landowning clans which held them), extensive proletarianization (of which both the hero and tragic victim was the gaucho), a radically dependent economic structure, and a political sphere long dominated by the export oligarchy. This has been a long accepted vision absorbed into some influential general works on the Argentine economy, such as those of Aldo Ferrer and (to a lesser degree) Jonathan Brown. Superimposed upon this picture was the need to explain the late unification of Argentina as a nation-state in even the most restricted technical sense, and beyond that to account for the peculiarly unmediated relationship, generally not so overt in others of the new successor states, between large-scale landownership and political power, most impressively exemplified by the figure of Juan Manuel de Rosas, dictator of Buenos Aires province for almost the entire period 1829–52.[39]

As late as the end of the 1990s, some excellent, now classic works added much substance and nuance to this general picture, looking at a single economic sector here, a different subregion there. Among the many such works are James Scobie's somewhat earlier but still canonical economic and social history of wheat production on the pampas between 1860 and 1910, Ian Rutledge's investigation of the development of agrarian capitalism (a favorite theme of the literature) in the interior province of Jujuy, Jeremy Adelman's books on property rights, capital formation, and the pampas economy in comparative (Argentina-Canada) and Atlantic contexts (along with the older, complementary work of Carl Solberg, which concentrates heavily on government policy toward the wheat industry), Samuel Amaral's study of Buenos Aires estancias from the late eighteenth century to 1870, the two-volume work of Osvaldo Barsky and his collaborators on pampas livestock development up to 1900, and Hilda Sabato's book on the sheep industry in the last half of the nineteenth century.⁴⁰ Sabato's empirically rich study echoes in its central thematic emphasis the feudalism/capitalism debate played out not only in the Mexican historiography but also for other areas of the former colonies (such as the works of Cushner and Piel on the Andean region). In theoretical terms, she places her investigation of sheep culture between what she calls, on the one hand, the "pragmatic" perspective, which traces the nineteenth-century concentration of landed property in the form of large estancias to international market forces that funneled to large landowners "Ricardian rents" from the availability of fertile soils, and, on the other hand, the "critical" perspective (what we might now call the institutional, or Northian view), in which large estates are seen to be created through public land giveaways during the early nineteenth century and consolidated through the associated political practices.⁴¹ While her synthetic approach leans toward a somewhat simplified picture of labor (it was furnished either by foreign immigrants or natives driven off the land, she writes), it does allow Sabato to devote her attention not only to large estancias, but also to what she calls small, family-worked sheep farms whose existence was long thought incompatible with market forces and concentrated property in land. A comparison of productive types with Mexico might yield the following suggestive analogy: sheep farms/estancias = ranchos/haciendas.

The historical writing on Argentine rural life has shifted during the last fifteen or twenty years—not to abandon the era of the classic export economy beginning around 1850, which the writers mentioned above and many others have served so well in their writings, but certainly to emphasize more strongly internal market logics, and to concentrate on an earlier period, a nineteenth century embracing the years 1750–1850. The historiography began to undergo a renaissance about the mid-1980s, when the wave of Mexican hacienda studies (from which the Argentine scholarship in part took inspiration) had already begun to recede from its high-water mark.⁴² This renaissance shared some of the same origins as the changes that had brought about the reorientation of the Mexican rural historiography a generation earlier: first, a revisionist reaction against an earlier orthodoxy (in the Mexican case the "feudal" model of the traditional hacienda, in the Argentine the Atlantic export market); and second, a turn toward ever more granular, localized sorts of documentation—notary records, estate account books, parish records, accounts of criminal trials of rural people, and so forth. It is hard to overestimate the importance of the writings of Carlos Sempat Assadourian in this shift of focus.⁴³ His work drew attention to the organizing power of an internal "economic space" in Spanish South America during the colonial era, centered on the great Andean silver mining complexes, primarily Potosí, in what is today Bolivia. While one might feel inclined to debate whether this relationship was any less of an export economy than the Atlantocentric one that developed starting with the production of cattle hides in the late eighteenth century, it nonetheless pushed much further back in time the history of the commercial agriculture and livestock sectors and laid the groundwork for more detailed studies of the pre–export boom period, which has been the major terrain of the historiographical renaissance. The work that came along after Assadourian, of which one of the major architects has been Juan Carlos Garavaglia, is typified by Garavaglia's own essays on topics ranging from regional differentiation within the Río de la Plata area to the economics of Jesuit missions in Paraguay, Carlos Mayo's study of late colonial pampean estancias, Jorge Gelman's very detailed reconstruction of a single merchant fortune, and the interesting anthology of Raúl Fradkin and Garavaglia on the rural and commercial economy of Buenos Aires province in the 1750–1850 period, as well as a number of studies on the interior provinces of Salta and Tucumán.[44]

In general, these and other works in the impressive wave of the new pampas historiography have emphasized the diversity of the rural production structure and of the labor force, the importance of African slaves as workers until quite late, the little-researched presence of Indians, the region's social fluidity, and so forth.[45] Three of the best exemplars of the new approaches are Jorge Gelman's study of agrarian structure at the end of the colonial period in the Banda Oriental, the area that would later make up much of Uruguay; Garavaglia's companion study on the Buenos Aires countryside, to the southwest of the Río de la Plata, over a somewhat longer extension of time; and Ricardo Salvatore's investigation of rural working people in the Rosas period. The books share a heavily quantitative methodology, Gelman and Garavaglia deploying numbers to trace the shape of property holding, production, and population in the countryside, Salvatore to profile rural working people—gauchos, it is fair to say—to help delineate their social and political consciousness, and to define from a subalternist perspective the parameters of their freedom as social actors. Salvatore concludes that subaltern actors enjoyed a more complex political worldview and a much greater degree of agency vis-à-vis the actions of the *rosista* state than historians had heretofore suspected, while Gelman and Garavaglia arrive at analogous conclusions about the diversity of rural society before the great export boom age, the importance of intraregional markets for agricultural products, the capacity of smaller production units to survive next to large estancias, and the complexity of rural labor arrangements. Garavaglia, in particular, provides an encyclopedic description of everything from natural resource endowment (his description of the *pampa ondulada* reminds one of Braudel describing an inland, pampean sea), to demography and household economic cycles, to agricultural and livestock technology and the movement of prices for agricultural commodities.[46]

While Argentina has come to be seen as the poster child for the power of commodities to mediate relations among human beings (what has been called "the social life of things"),[47] and thereby to shape political, social, and economic practices in exporting societies, the forces in play there have not been unique to the country; Latin American rural history is replete with other examples, especially since the late eighteenth century or so. Robert Ferry has written a social and economic history of colonial Caracas and its hinterland, for example, by interweaving the genealogy of elite clan social reproduction over several generations (a theme common in the rural history literature) with the transition from a cereal-based hacienda economy to the slave-based production of cacao for export. Other tropical exports, such as Mexican henequen, have generated their own separate, in some cases quite substantial, literatures, often concentrating on the role of coerced labor in the process of production for international markets, as in the work of Allen Wells. The wool export sector in the Peruvian altiplano has been investigated over the span of a long nineteenth century by Nils Jacobsen. To take another case, there has been some very interesting historical writing on the Amazon export boom in natural rubber between 1850 and 1920, Barbara Weinstein stressing the coercion exerted upon rubber tappers and the resistance they offered and Warren Dean the environmental aspects, while Michael Taussig examines the social conditions and belief systems of native laborers in another rubber-producing region, the Colombian Putumayo. More recently, Bradford Barham and Oliver Coomes have completely recast the discussion of the Amazon rubber era through the application of initiating questions and explanatory schema drawn from the fields of industrial organization economics and environmental anthropology, demonstrating among other findings that the structure of production was much more varied than had once been thought, primarily within an upriver/downriver geography.[48] Moreover, their explicit starting point is to learn from a historical case something of the relationship between an export boom and distorted economic development in light of a recent return by a number of Latin American countries under neoliberal doctrines to commodity exports, a policy long eschewed in favor of import substitution industrialization.[49]

Other export booms have stimulated studies, some of them within international frameworks and some embracing a model of intense commodity commercialization within one region but at least nominally within a single polity, which somewhat complicates the notion of "export economy." Among the former may be counted the "McDonaldization" of the international trade in beef cattle in the late twentieth century, for example from Costa Rica to the United States.[50] Among the latter were the colonial tobacco industry in Spanish America and the less well known but regionally significant yerba maté industry in Paraguay, both important commercialized intracolonial products of long spatial reach serving large numbers of consumers, and in the case of tobacco, since its processing and distribution comprised a royal monopoly from the late eighteenth century, a major source of revenue for the colonial government.[51] One such export product whose development occasioned a huge historical literature is coffee, produced for both domestic consumption and international markets, which dominated the economies of large parts of Central America, Brazil, and Colombia from some time in the nineteenth century onward and has been a major player in Mexico, Venezuela, Puerto Rico, and elsewhere. General economic histories of Colombia have emphasized the role of coffee production in resource allocation, the dynamics of the export sector, capital accumulation, and peasant agriculture, while more specialized investigations, regional monographs, and works in historical geography and anthropology have delved into local development, land usage patterns, the politics of export-boom successions, and forms of peasant protest.[52] Two penetrating studies take an even longer view, Lowell Gudmundson for Costa Rica and David McCreery for Guatemala.[53] Gudmundson demonstrates convincingly that before the decade of the 1840s, on the cusp of the coffee export boom, Costa Rica was hardly the idealized, egalitarian, smallholder paradise that came to comprise the mythified post-coffee national image. Rather, it was a stratified society with already obvious indices of social inequality and spatial concentration of population, an image that significantly modifies our understanding of the effects of large-scale commercial agriculture on a peasant society. For highland Guatemala, on the other hand, McCreery shows clearly that during a (very) long nineteenth century Indian peasants were shifted by national labor recruitment laws into the coffee plantation sector, effectively subsidizing it through their low wages and creating just the sort of break with traditional rural structures that Gudmundson minimizes for Costa Rica.

TROPICAL COMMODITIES AND SLAVERY: BRAZIL

As Sidney Mintz eloquently pointed out two decades ago (and other authors before him, such as Noël Deerr), and as daily practice in the West confirms, coffee and tea came to be associated with sugar, a tropical export commodity whose worldwide consumption (save for periods of international warfare, when supplies were disrupted but demand remained very strong) has risen uninterruptedly since the age of Columbus, and which for centuries after 1492 was overwhelmingly produced in the Americas.[54] Until the mid-seventeenth century or so, the Old World sated its sweet tooth with Brazilian production, and thereafter increasingly from the British, French, and Spanish Caribbean islands.[55] Moreover, sugar production also supported domestic consumption in the coastal Andean region (e.g., northern Peru), in northern South America, and in Mesoamerica (e.g., parts of Central America and Mexico), and does to this day. Although production on a small scale was possible, sometimes within the framework of a sharecropping arrangement or by sale of cane from small independent producers to mill owners, the economic logic of economies of scale in growing sugarcane, and even more that of the substantial capital investment needed to refine sugar from raw cane—the buildings, equipment, credit chains, and so on—pushed in the direction of large-scale production units. And almost everywhere in the Americas, up until the abolition of slavery (Mexico 1829, Peru 1854, the Spanish Caribbean 1886, Brazil 1888), sugar production was strongly associated with African slavery and the trans-Atlantic slave trade.[56] So strong was this linkage, in fact, that the burgeoning field of Atlantic history becomes much more problematic as an analytical framework after the disappearance of the trade in enslaved Africans in the nineteenth century.

In terms of the scale of African slavery there, Brazil was by a large margin the most important slavocratic society in mainland Ibero-America, although the institution left no corner of the Spanish or Portuguese empires untouched. Over the nearly four centuries between 1494 and the late 1860s, Latin America and the Caribbean received about 85% of the ten million or so Africans shipped in bondage to the New World. Of the ten million, Brazil got about 35%, the Caribbean islands a bit more, and mainland Spanish America perhaps 10%. The first African slaves arrived in the Portuguese colony in the late 1530s, a scant three decades after the chance "discovery" of the region in 1500, and the sugar industry was established about the same time, coming to thrive particularly in the northeastern zone, although it eventually spread further south. Over time Brazil's economic and political center of gravity shifted southward, too, responding to overlapping waves of export economies—gold mining, then coffee production—that shared some of the same characteristics of similar economies elsewhere; and until abolition in 1888, the labor was primarily supplied by slaves of African origin. The colonial phase of this story has been dealt with by a number of Brazilian scholars after Freyre, among the most theoretically informed and empirically dense works being that of Jacob Gorender, who was much concerned with exploring the slave mode of production in the Marxist mold. Clearly agnostic from a theoretical point of view, but basically materialist, was Stuart B. Schwartz's admirable economic and social history of the colonial Brazilian sugar economy. Based in large measure on the intensive study over a long period of records from a single large sugar estate and refining operation (*engenho*, Spanish *ingenio*) in the Bahia area, Schwartz's book eclipsed at the time of its publication almost all previous studies of sugar and slavery in Brazil and established the baseline for subsequent work. In great detail he reconstructed the labor relations, cane-growing practices and milling technology, credit linkages, slave demography, and other aspects of the industry over more than three centuries. Among his most important interpretive findings was that slavery was so tightly woven into the fabric of Bahian society that its presence tended over time to degrade all forms of labor, free and unfree.[57]

Other studies of Brazilian rural slavery showed the variability of the institution across regions, periods, and economic sectors, but on the whole produced findings cognate to those for Bahia. Also working on Bahia, for example, Bert Barickman produced a fine study of the tensions and complementarities between the export economy and a local commercial sector supplying bread made from cassava flour. Where Stuart Schwartz left off his study chronologically around 1835, the earlier study of Peter Eisenberg took up the fate of sugar in Pernambuco, a neighboring area in the Brazilian northeast, from 1840 to the eve of World War I, tracing the declining arc of the sugar economy under the impact on the international market of sugar-beet production, and on labor accessibility of the abolition of slavery in 1888. Alida Metcalf's study of a sparsely settled area to the west of São Paulo, corresponding roughly to the period of Schwartz's investigation, demonstrated the enduring social inequalities that slavery and large landholdings could give rise to even in frontier situations. By the time the coffee industry kicked into high gear in about the third decade of the nineteenth century, the basic pattern of large production units, slave labor, and external markets had been established. Stanley Stein's classic study of a coffee-producing area to the northwest of Rio de Janeiro (1850–90), while it demonstrated the nonaristocratic background of the planter elite and the role that racialist ideology played in undergirding the slave labor system, also showed the ruthlessness of capitalist exploitation of both the slaves and the natural environment to optimize production within a paternalistic and patriarchal social framework. Later studies on the São Paulo region have tended to confirm these conclusions while adding rich empirical detail.[58]

The findings of these and other historians have contributed to a highly polemical debate about the "cruelty continuum" that had raged among Latin Americanist scholars at least since the days of Gilberto Freyre, and which saw an even more developed, indeed hypertrophied, counterpart in the historical literature on slavery in the United States. Much of the discussion revolved around the nature of postemancipation race relations in the formerly slavocratic societies of the Americas, and what might account for the putatively more tolerant and inclusive attitudes in Ibero-America as opposed to Anglo-America.[59] Schwartz, for example, argued convincingly that contrary to the views of Freyre and some other earlier students of Brazilian race relations, Brazilian slavery could be just as cruel and dehumanizing as Anglo-American or Spanish versions *when such treatment was profitable*, that slave mortality was high and natality low, and that the long Iberian experience of black Africans and the supposed mellowness of Portuguese tropical Catholicism did little if anything to alleviate the condition of slaves.

With the economic issues largely resolved in favor of the slaveowners' cruelty and opportunism, the interest of many historians turned toward the culture of Brazilian slave society, the slave community and family, slave demography, forms of resistance, and so forth, all within what would later come to be called a subalternist perspective. As in the North American historiography, greater emphasis came to be placed upon the slaves' subjective experience of their condition. An example of such work is Kátia M. de Queirós Mattoso's attempt to reconstruct the slaves' experience over the entire history of the institution in Brazil, a sensitive and innovative (if not entirely convincing) study of how slaves asserted their personhood within what she calls a "contractualist" legal and customary framework vis-à-vis their masters, and of the forms of "voice" and "exit" that facilitated such an assertion. In this approach, forms of slave accommodation and resistance received a good deal of attention. But as in the Mexicanist rural historiography, a turn toward social history, subalternist approaches, and cultural history seems to have implied a significant ratcheting down of effort on the economic history of slave systems, so that the excellent study of Francisco Vidal and Herbert Klein even looks a bit anachronistic, while Nancy Naro's slightly earlier book devotes relatively little space to the economics of nineteenth-century slave-worked coffee *fazendas* and a great deal to social structure and demographic trends.[60] In some ways, this is the structural equivalent of the strong current among Mexicanists toward ethnohistory, which, although it deals with native peoples who were mostly peasants, is not devoted to rural history in the traditional sense of the term.

The other great receiving area for African slaves, apart from the northern Anglo-American colonies, was of course the Caribbean area, which has an enormous historical literature on sugar and slavery. This is particularly well developed for the English islands, with a tradition stretching from Lowell Ragatz's, Eric Williams's (a kind of urtext in the field), and Richard Pares's works on capitalism, the planter class, and sugar, to the later works of Orlando Patterson and Richard Dunn on the same theme and the more strictly slave- and production-centered studies of scholars such as Elsa Goveia, and Jerome Handler and Frederick Lange.[61] The Spanish islands are well represented in this sugar-and-slavery literature as well, going back to the nineteenth century, even well before José Antonio Saco. Among the major modern works here are Manuel Moreno Fraginals's monumental study of the sugar industry in Cuba, primarily from the production point of view, and Leví Marrero's even grander and more inclusive economic history of the island from the colonial period through the second third of the nineteenth century, much of which (especially the latter volumes) is necessarily devoted to sugar and slavery. Focused more on the side of the social history of the Cuban slave community is Franklin Knight's book, while Laird Bergad's emphasizes economic aspects. For Puerto Rico, Francisco Scarano's compact revisionist study of sugar and slavery in the first half of the nineteenth century demonstrates convincingly that sugar production on the island received a major fillip with the collapse of the industry on the French sugar colony of Saint Domingue in 1791, also benefiting from the sagging productive capacity of the British islands, Spain's more open commercial policies, and the possibilities of continuing slave labor imports through an illicit trade that lasted until midcentury. Although smaller in scale than Cuban sugar plantations, those of Puerto Rico also relied for their core labor force on enslaved Africans and continued to do so in the main until abolition in 1873.[62]

Finally, the sugar-slavery nexus in mainland Spanish America has received its share of attention.[63] One of the best studied cases, interestingly enough, although after the mid-sixteenth century or so it was not a major player in the international sugar market, is Mexico, probably in large measure because the major sugar-producing region of the country was in the State of Morelos, around Cuernavaca, to the south of Mexico City, which proved to be the locus of the peasant wing of the Revolution of 1910 led by Emiliano Zapata. Despite its lurid title, Colin Palmer's study provides a good survey of the African slave trade and slavery in Mexico during the early colonial period, complementing Gonzalo Aguirre Beltrán in this respect, and there are two good studies of slavery and commercial agriculture along the Gulf coast, in the Veracruz area—Patrick Carroll's on tobacco, and Adriana Naveda Chávez-Hita's on sugar. For the Morelos area proper, there are a number of fine studies dealing with the period between about 1750 and 1880. Gisela Von Wobeser nominally provides an excellent overview of the colonial sugar industry, but in fact limits her study to the Cuautla-Cuernavaca area, even though sugar was produced in respectable quantities (if on a smaller scale) elsewhere in Mexico (the Guadalajara area, Michoacan, Veracruz). Beatriz Scharrer Tamm focuses on sugar technology in the later colonial period, Ernest Sánchez Santiró on social structure and mercantile activity in the sugar zone, and Gisela Landázuri Benítez and Verónica Vázquez Mantecón on the domestic political economy of the industry from 1750 to 1880. Cheryl Martin's excellent book looks primarily at the tensions between sugar haciendas and the Indian villages from which they drew much of their labor, and upon whose lands they continually encroached.

It is worth noting that all these fine agrarian histories pay relatively little attention to African slavery, mostly because for much of the history of sugar production in the region slaves constituted a relatively small, if extremely valuable, core labor force, and free Indian peasants were the majority of laborers in an industry highly seasonal in its labor requirements. One of the first students of the colonial Mexican sugar industry to make this important point, and to look more deeply into the social ecology of the Morelos haciendas, was Ward Barrett, a historical geographer whose minute examination of agricultural techniques, production processes and costs, capital requirements, prices for the finished product, labor needs, and profit levels constitutes not only a brilliant X-ray of a highly industrialized commercial agricultural sector but one of the outstanding works in Latin American economic history more generally. The sugar industry did survive the colonial period, of course, albeit with a reconstituted labor force after the abolition of African slavery in the newly independent Mexico in 1829. One of the newest books mentioned in this historiographical survey, that of Paul Hart, deals insightfully with the industry up to the eve of the Revolution of 1910, showing how an increasing dependence on wage labor by peasant villagers, overproduction of sugar in the last decades before the fall of the Porfirian regime, and the failure of sugar hacendados to find external markets for their products all converged to sow widespread impoverishment and political discontent in the land of Zapata. Hart's work reflects current theoretical trends in the study of Latin American historical peasantries and politics that see rural people much more as the agents of their own histories than as passive objects and production factors; but that is the theme for another essay.[64]

In conclusion, it is difficult to predict how the study of Latin American rural history will evolve in the coming decades. A look at the bibliography accompanying this essay conveys the impression that over the last fifteen years or so, scholarly energies devoted to traditional themes in the field—labor systems; the traditional hacienda, estancia, and rancho; and economic history more broadly—have flagged somewhat. Within this overall scenario, however, certain areas of research interest have waned while others have waxed. The study of colonial and nineteenth-century Mexican rural history, although not exactly moribund, took a nosedive from about the mid-1980s, particularly in its economic aspects, as archival investigation reached a point of diminishing returns and historians grew to know more and more about less and less. Investigation into the same period and themes in Argentina, however, began to flourish and continues to do so. Slavery, slave societies, and the social and economic effects of the "peculiar institution" have remained areas of fascination because so much of the Western Hemisphere is still dealing with their legacies.

Apart from the interest in filling in the rural history of certain regions (e.g., Central America) and periods (the seventeenth century), some questions in the field clearly warrant further work. Among these is the social history of life on the land up to the middle of the nineteenth century or so. This is relatively easier to do for slave-dominated areas, and much harder for free and nominally free labor areas. Since slaves were a valuable form of property, legal records of all sorts are likely to have documented slave life, while the social relations of free but humble, generally uninscribed rural people are the soft tissue of an agrarian society that vanishes over time. Another promising theme well worth pursuing is the environmental history of the countryside under various forms of economic exploitation—traditional peasant agriculture, undercommercialized large estates, forestry and the expansion of livestock production, and export agriculture. Life on the land in Latin America has been so very important for so many centuries (and remains so in large areas today) that it is difficult to believe that, whatever the fashions of scholarly investigation, it will not remain a theme of perennial fascination for historians and other social scientists.

NOTES

1. Louisa Schell Hoberman and Susan Migden Socolow, eds., *The Countryside in Colonial Latin America* (Albuquerque: University of New Mexico Press, 1996).

2. See, for example, Arnold J. Bauer, *Goods, Power, History: Latin America's Material Culture* (Cambridge: Cambridge University Press, 2001).

3. There are, of course, problems of sources (mostly their absence or thinness) to be reckoned with in writing the cultural history of rural life. For the relationship of cultural to economic history, and some thoughts on the decline of the latter within the context of Mexicanist historiography, see Eric Van Young, "The 'New Cultural History' Comes to Old Mexico," *Hispanic American Historical Review* 79 (1999): 211–48; Van Young, "La pareja dispareja: Algunos comentarios sobre la relación entre la historia cultural e historia económica," *Historia Mexicana* 52 (2003): 831–70; Van Young, "Two Decades of Anglophone Writing on Colonial Mexico: Continuity and Change since 1980," *Mexican Studies/Estudios Mexicanos* 20 (2004): 275–326; Van Young, "El lugar de encuentro entre la historia económica y la historia cultural," Segundo Congreso de Historia Económica, Asociación Mexicana de Historia Económica, Universidad Nacional Autónoma de México, 27–29 October, 2004.

4. There is also admittedly a strong (to be honest, almost exclusive) temporal emphasis on the colonial period and an extended nineteenth century—say, up to 1930 or so. In part this is because of the early modernist bias in the European agrarian history literature, which was so influential in molding the agrarian historiography of Latin America; in part because work on agrarian structures in the latter part of the twentieth century tended to shade over into policy and economic studies, and to that degree became less historical; and in part due to my own expertise. There is also a case to be made that the colonial agrarian historiography is richer, deeper, and more accomplished. The essay's emphasis on the economic history of production processes, in the face of the enormous literature on that and related themes, has also meant leaving aside, except in passing, discussions of peasantries and forms of political and social resistance by subaltern groups.

5. José Antonio Saco, *Historia de la esclavitud desde los tiempos mas remotos hasta nuestros días* (Paris: Tipografía Lahure, 1875–77).

6. Andrés Molina Enríquez, *Los grandes problemas nacionales* (Mexico City: A. Carranza e Hijos, 1909).

7. Gilberto Freyre, *The Masters and the Slaves: A Study in the Development of Brazilian Civilization*, translated by Samuel Putnam ([1933] New York: A.A. Knopf, 1946); Fernando Ortiz, *Cuban Counterpoint: Tobacco and Sugar*, translated by Harriet de Onís ([1940] New York: A.A. Knopf, 1947); and see also Philip D. Curtin, *The Rise and Fall of the Plantation*

Complex: Essays in Atlantic History (Cambridge: Cambridge University Press, 1998). A related work, published just a few years after Freyre and Ortiz, is that of the Mexican anthropologist Gonzalo Aguirre Beltrán, *La población negra de México, 1519–1810: Estudio etnohistórico* (Mexico City: Ediciones Fuente Cultural, 1946), on the African-origin population of Mexico.

8. It is interesting to note that of the more than twenty published papers from a recent academic conference devoted to Fernando Ortiz's scholarship and intellectual legacy, only a couple touch on his work as a rural historian, and those only lightly; Mauricio A. Font and Alfonso W. Quiroz, eds., *Cuban Counterpoints: The Legacy of Fernando Ortiz* (Lanham, Md.: Lexington Books, 2005). It should be added that an important local historiographical tradition of a more antiquarian nature within Latin America itself added its rivulet to the headwaters of what would later become a much more cosmopolitan approach to rural history. From the late nineteenth century, in particular, every city or region of any importance was likely to count (as they still do) vocational genealogists and historians among its lawyers, physicians, engineers, school teachers, priests, and other educated professionals, often with interests in the history of local dynastic families and their landholdings. These men often produced works of real value based upon careful archival research and the painstaking reconstruction of local landholdings and political life, even if they worked within relatively restricted limits and in a style strongly narrative rather than analytic. An example of this genre of work from the area of Latin America I happen to know best is Jesús Amaya Topete, *Ameca, protofundación mexicana* (Mexico City: Lumen, 1951), a detailed reconstruction of colonial landholding patterns and the genealogy of landed magnate families in the Ameca Valley, at the western end of Lake Chapala in central western Mexico. For Chile, a similarly detailed, foundational study in agrarian history was the work on one of the country's central valleys, the Valle del Puangue, by Jean Borde and Mario Góngora, both academics: *Evolución de la propiedad rural en el Valle del Puangue*, 2 vols. (Santiago: Editorial Universitaria, 1956).

9. François Chevalier, *La formation des grands domains au Mexique: Terre et société aux XVIe–XVIIe siècles* (Paris: Université de Paris, Institut d'Ethnologie, 1952). The book appeared in Mexico as *La formación de los grandes latifundios en México (Tierra y sociedad en los siglos XVI y XVII)*, trans. Antonio Alatorre (Mexico City: n.p., 1956), and in English as *Land and Society in Colonial Mexico: The Great Hacienda*, ed. Leslie B. Simpson, trans. Alvin Eustis (Berkeley: University of California Press, 1966). The third Mexican edition, *La formación de los latifundios en México: Haciendas y sociedad en los siglos XVI, XVII y XVIII*, 3rd rev. ed. (Mexico City: Fondo de Cultura Económica, 1999), includes a new introductory essay by Chevalier reviewing the writings on the Mexican hacienda after the initial appearance of his book, along with an updated bibliography. Chevalier's great study adopts a derived medievalist framework for the development of the great landed estate in colonial Mexico, emphasizing the politico-institutional dimension highlighted by his own teacher, Marc Bloch, in his masterwork *Feudal Society*, trans. L. A. Manyon, 2 vols. ([1939–40] Chicago: University of Chicago Press, 1961). It is only in the new bibliography of the 1999 edition of his book that Chevalier includes Bloch's other great work on the French countryside, *French Rural History: An Essay on its Basic Characteristics*, trans. Janet Sondheimer (Berkeley: University of California Press, 1966), originally published in 1931 (before the treatise on feudalism), which deals with rural society from a more strictly economic angle, and for a time period corresponding exactly to Chevalier's own, the sixteenth through eighteenth centuries.

10. Chevalier's treatment of regional and temporal variations in the economic and social morphology—the term is that of Herbert Nickel, *Morfología social de la hacienda*

mexicana (Mexico City: Fondo de Cultura Económica, 1988)—was in fact more nuanced than either his critics or his admirers acknowledged, although his model for the Mexican north was applied rather promiscuously by other scholars to the rest of the country and beyond. In the 1999 edition of his book, he was prepared to concede that his general model of the colonial hacienda might accommodate the notion (from Eric Van Young, "Mexican Rural History Since Chevalier: The Historiography of the Colonial Hacienda," *Latin American Research Review* 18 (1983): 5–62) that these agro-social units were capitalist (or at least highly commercialized) economically and feudal (or at least patriarchal) socially. In his masterful study of agrarian capitalism in Peru, *Capitalisme agraire au Pérou*, Vol. 1: *Originalité de la société agraire péruvienne au XIXe siécle* (Paris: Éditions Anthropos, 1975), Jean Piel makes much the same suggestion, characterizing the functioning of the colonial hacienda as capitalist externally (allowing for the accumulation of capital resources), and precapitalist internally (insofar as its relations of production were concerned).

11. Cristóbal Kay, *El sistema señorial europeo y la hacienda latinoamericana* (Mexico City: Ediciones Era, 1980); William Schell, Jr., *Medieval Iberian Tradition and the Development of the Mexican Hacienda* (Syracuse: Maxwell School of Citizenship and Public Affairs, Syracuse University, 1986); Alan Knight, *Mexico: The Colonial Era* (Cambridge: Cambridge University Press, 2002); Marcello Carmagnani, *Formación y crisis de un sistema feudal: América Latina del siglo XVI a nuestros días* (Mexico City: Siglo Veintiuno).

12. Eric Van Young, *Hacienda and Market in Eighteenth-Century Mexico: The Rural Economy of the Guadalajara Region, 1675–1820*, 2nd rev. ed. (Lanham, Md.: Rowman & Littlefield, 2006). There have been some notable *desfases* in this general periodization. The impressive outpouring of scholarly work on the pampean rural economy and society of Argentina in the late colonial and early national periods, for example, picked up momentum only as the literature on Mexico began to wane.

13. In what follows I only scratch the surface of the rich historiography on haciendas and rural life in colonial and nineteenth-century Mexico. Among a multitude of other studies, readers may wish to consult the following: for more northerly parts of Mexico, María Vargas-Lobsinger, *La hacienda de "La Concha": Una empresa algodonera de la Laguna, 1883–1917* (Mexico City: Universidad Nacional Autónoma de México, 1984); Agueda Jiménez Pelayo, *Haciendas y comunidades indígenas en el sur de Zacatecas* (Mexico City: Instituto Nacional de Antropología e Historia, 1989); and Frédérique Langue, *Mines, terres et société à Zacatecas (Mexique) de la fin du XVIIe siècle à l'indépendance* (Paris: Publications de la Sorbonne, 1992); for the more central and southerly parts of the country, Willliam B. Taylor, *Landlord and Peasant in Colonial Oaxaca* (Stanford: Stanford University Press, 1972); Edith B. Couturier, *La Hacienda de Hueyapan, 1550–1936* (Mexico City: Secretaría de Educación Pública, 1976); Heriberto Moreno García, *Guaracha: Tiempos viejos, tiempos nuevos* (Mexico City: El Colegio de Michoacán, 1980) and the same author's *Haciendas de tierra y agua en la Antigua Ciénega de Chapala* (Guadalajara: El Colegio de Michoacán, 1989); Juan Felipe Leal and Mario Huacuja Rountree, *Economía y sistema de haciendas en México: La hacienda pulquera en el cambio, siglos XVIII, XIX y XX* (Mexico City: Ediciones Era, 1982); Richard B. Lindley, *Haciendas and Econonomic Development: Guadalajara, Mexico, at Independence* (Austin: University of Texas Press, 1983); Arístides Medina Rubio, *La iglesia y la producción agrícola en Puebla, 1540–1795* (Mexico City: El Colegio de México, 1983); María Guadalupe Rodríguez Gómez, *Jalpa y San Juan de los Otates, dos haciendas en el Bajío colonial* (León: El Colegio del Bajío, 1984); Michael E. Murphy, *Irrigation in the Bajío Region of Colonial Mexico* (Boulder, Colo.: Westview Press, 1986); Ricardo Rendón Garcini, *Dos haciendas pulqueras en Tlaxcala, 1857–1884* (Tlaxcala: Gobierno del Estado de Tlaxcala/Universidad Iberoamericana, 1990); Marta Eugenia García

Ugarte, *Hacendados y rancheros queretanos, 1780–1920* (Mexico City: Consejo Nacional para la Cultura y las Artes, 1992); a trio of works by Rodolfo Fernández: *Latifundios y grupos dominantes en la historia de la Provincia de Ávalos* (Guadalajara: Instituto Nacional de Antropología e Historia, 1994), *Mucha tierra y pocos dueños: Estancias, haciendas y latifundios avaleños* (Mexico City: Instituto Nacional de Antropología e Historia, 1999), and *La gran propiedad en Cocula de Ávalos, 1539–1700* (Mexico City: Instituto Nacional de Antropología e Historia, 2003); Sonya Lipsett-Rivera, *To Defend Our Water with the Blood of Our Veins: The Struggle for Resources in Colonial Puebla* (Albuquerque: University of New Mexico Press, 1999); and for Yucatán, Robert W. Patch, *Maya and Spaniard in Yucatan, 1648–1812* (Stanford: Stanford University Press, 1993).

14. Andre Gunder Frank, *Mexican Agriculture, 1521–1630: Transformation of the Mode of Production* (Cambridge: Cambridge University Press, 1979).

15. Gabriel Palma, "Dependency: A Formal Theory of Underdevelopment or a Methodology for the Analysis of Concrete Situations of Underdevelopment?," *World Development* 6 (1978): 881–924; Enrique Semo, *The History of Capitalism in Mexico: Its Origins, 1521–1763*, trans. Lidia Lozano (Austin: University of Texas Press, 1993); Ciro F. S. Cardoso and Héctor Pérez Brignoli, *Historia económica de América Latina*, 2 vols. (Barcelona: Crítica, 1984); Andre Gunder Frank, *Capitalism and Underdevelopment in Latin America: Historical Studies of Chile and Brazil* (New York: Monthly Review Press, 1967).

16. Marcello Carmagnani, *Los mecanismos de la vida económica en una sociedad colonial: Chile, 1680–1830* ([1973] Santiago: Ediciones de la Dirección de Bibliotecas, Archivos y Museos, Centro de Investigaciones Diego Barros Arana); and for a later period in Chile, Arnold J. Bauer, *Chilean Rural Society from the Spanish Conquest to 1930* (Cambridge: Cambridge University Press, 1975).

17. Jan Bazant, *Cinco haciendas mexicanas: Tres siglos de vida rural en San Luis Potosí (1600–1910)* (Mexico City: El Colegio de México, 1975); Enrique Semo, ed., *Siete ensayos sobre la hacienda mexicana, 1780–1880* (Mexico City: Instituto Nacional de Antropología e Historia, 1977); David A. Brading, *Haciendas and Ranchos in the Mexican Bajío: León, 1700–1860* (Cambridge: Cambridge University Press, 1978); Van Young, *Hacienda and Market in Eighteenth-Century Mexico*.

18. For an interesting and sometimes sharp polemic over the development of large-scale commercial agriculture from the colonial period to the twentieth century in Bolivia, see Brooke Larson, *Cochabamba, 1550–1900: Colonialism and Agrarian Transformation in Bolivia* ([1988] Durham, N.C.: Duke University Press, 1998); and Robert H. Jackson, *Regional Markets and Agrarian Transformation in Bolivia: Cochabamba, 1539–1960* (Albuquerque: University of New Mexico Press, 1994).

19. A useful collection of original documentary sources that deals with the entrepreneurial activities of the Jesuits and other regular orders is Hermes Tovar Pinzón, *Fuentes para el estudio de las actividades socio-económicos de la Compañía de Jesús y otras misiones religiosas* (Bogotá: Universidad Nacional de Colombia, Facultad de Ciencias Humanas, 1971–); and on haciendas more generally for colonial New Granada, which would later become Colombia, see also Tovar Pinzón, *Grandes empresas agrícolas y ganaderas: Su desarrollo en el siglo XVIII* (Bogotá: Universidad Nacional de Colombia, Ediciones CIEC, 1980), and the same author's *Hacienda colonial y formación social* (Barcelona: Sendai Ediciones, 1988).

20. Robert G. Keith, *Conquest and Agrarian Change: The Emergence of the Hacienda System on the Peruvian Coast* (Cambridge, Mass.: Harvard University Press, 1976); Keith A. Davies, *Landowners in Colonial Peru* (Austin: University of Texas Press, 1984); Jean Piel, *Capitalisme agraire au Pérou*, Vol. 1: *Originalité de la société agraire péruvienne au XIXe*

siécle (Paris: Éditions Anthropos, 1975); Nicholas P. Cushner, *Lords of the Land: Sugar, Wine and Jesuit Estates of Coastal Peru, 1600–1767* (Albany: State University of New York Press, 1980); Cushner, *Farm and Factory: The Jesuits and the Development of Agrarian Capitalism in Colonial Quito, 1600–1767* (Albany: State University of New York Press, 1982); Cushner, *Jesuit Ranches and the Agrarian Development of Colonial Argentina, 1650–1767* (Albany: State University of NewYork Press, 1983); Herman W. Konrad, *A Jesuit Hacienda in Colonial Mexico: Santa Lucia, 1576–1767* (Stanford: Stanford University Press, 1980).

    21. Eric R. Wolf and Sidney W. Mintz, "Haciendas and Plantations in Middle America and the Antilles," *Social and Economic Studies* 6 (1957): 380–412; Magnus Mörner, "The Spanish American Hacienda: A Survey of Recent Research and Debate," *Hispanic American Historical Review* 53 (1973): 183–216.

    22. In a closely reasoned study of the same urban area, Antonio Ibarra Romero, *La organización regional del mercado interno novohispano: La economía colonial de Guadalajara, 1770–1804* (Mexico City: Universidad Nacional Autónoma de México, 2000), has argued that at the close of the colonial period, the Guadalajara region was much more deeply linked to outside markets than my model of regional semi-autarchy would admit. Ramón María Serrera Contreras, *Guadalajara ganadera: Estudio regional novohispano, 1760–1805* (Seville: Consejo Superior de Investigaciones Científicas, 1977), argues much the same thing for a long-range livestock trade between this area and Mexico City for the last half century of the colonial era. Under this discussion lurks the more theoretical issue of what exactly regions are, and how they change over time, a discussion with relevance well beyond the bounds of colonial Mexico; on this issue see Eric Van Young, ed., *Mexican Regions: Comparative History and Development* (La Jolla: Center for U.S.-Mexican Studies, University of California, San Diego, 1992), and Pedro Pérez Herrero, *Región e historia en México (1750–1850): Métodos de análisis regional* (Mexico City: Instituto de Investigaciones Doctor José María Luis Mora and Universidad Autónoma Metropolitana, 1992).

    23. Simon Miller, *Landlords and Haciendas in Modernizing Mexico: Essays in Radical Reappraisal* (Amsterdam: CEDLA, 1995); Ross Hassig, *Trade, Tribute, and Transportation: The Sixteenth-Century Political Economy of the Valley of Mexico* (Norman: University of Oklahoma Press, 1985); Carlos Sempat Assadourian et al., *Minería y espacio económico en los Andes, siglos XVI–XX* (Lima: Instituto de Estudios Peruanos, 1980); Assadourian, *El sistema de la economía colonial: Mercado interno, regiones y espacio económico* (Lima: Instituto de Estudios Peruanos, 1982); Juan Carlos Garavaglia, *Mercado interno y economía colonial* (Mexico City: Editorial Grijalbo, 1983); Richard L. Garner and Spiro E. Stefanou, *Economic Growth and Change in Bourbon Mexico* (Gainesville: University Press of Florida, 1993); Arij Ouweneel, *Shadows Over Anahuac: An Ecological Interpretation of Crisis and Development in Central Mexico, 1730–1800* (Albuquerque: University of New Mexico Press, 1996); Manuel Miño Grijalva, *El mundo novohispano: Población, ciudades y economía, siglos XVII y XVIII* (Mexico City: El Colegio de México, 2001); Jonathan D. Amith, *The Möbius Strip: A Spatial History of Colonial Society in Guerrero, Mexico* (Stanford: Stanford University Press, 2005); Herbert S. Klein, *Haciendas and 'Ayllus': Rural Society in the Bolivian Andes in the Eighteenth and Nineteenth Centuries* (Stanford: Stanford University Press, 1993); John V. Murra, *The Economic Organization of the Inca State* ([1956] Greenwich, Conn.: JAI Press, 1980).

    24. Arnold J. Bauer, "Rural Workers in Spanish America: Problems of Peonage and Oppression," *Hispanic American Historical Review* 59 (1979): 34–63; Steve J. Stern,

"Feudalism, Capitalism, and the World-System in the Perspective of Latin America and the Caribbean," *American Historical Review* 93 (1988): 829–72.

25. Silvio Zavala, *Los esclavos indios en Nueva España*, 3rd rev. ed. (Mexico City: El Colegio de México, 1994); for Central America, William L. Sherman, *Forced Native Labor in Sixteenth-Century Central America* (Lincoln: University of Nebraska Press, 1979); and for Chile, Jorge Randolph, *Las guerras de Arauco y la esclavitud* (Santiago: Sociedad Impresora "Horizonte," 1966); Eugene H. Korth, *Spanish Policy in Colonial Chile: The Struggle for Social Justice, 1535–1700* (Stanford: Stanford University Press, 1968); Mario Góngora, *Encomenderos y estancieros: Estudios acerca de la constitución social aristocrática de Chile después de la conquista, 1580–1660* (Santiago: Editorial Universitaria, 1971); and Alvaro Jara, *Guerra y sociedad en Chile: La transformación de la guerra de Arauco y la esclavitud de los indios* (Santiago: Editorial Universitaria, 1981).

26. Silvio Zavala, *La encomienda indiana*, 3rd rev. ed. ([1935] Mexico City: Editorial Porrúa, 1992); Zavala, *El servicio personal de los indios en la Nueva España, 1521–1550* (Mexico City: El Colegio de México, 1984); Lesley B. Simpson, *The Encomienda in New Spain: The Beginning of Spanish Mexico*, rev. ed. ([1950] Berkeley: University of California Press, 1982); José Miranda, *La función económica del encomendero en los origines del régimen colonial (Nueva España, 1525–1531)* (Mexico City: Instituto de Investigaciones Históricas, Universidad Nacional Autónoma de México, 1965); Robert Himmerich y Valencia, *The Encomenderos of New Spain, 1521–1555* (Austin: University of Texas Press, 1991); Gonzalo Aguirre Beltrán, *Pobladores del Papaloapan: Biografía de una hoya* (Mexico City: CIESAS, 1992); Elman R. Service, *Spanish-Guarani Relations in Early Colonial Paraguay* ([1954] Westport, Conn.: Greenwood Press, 1971); Luis Enrique Rodríguez Baquero, *Encomienda y vida diaria entre los indios de Muzo, 1550–1620* (Bogotá: Instituto Colombiano de Cultura Hispánica, 1995); Luis Fernando Calero, *Chiefdoms Under Siege: Spain's Rule and Native Adaptation in the Southern Colombian Andes, 1535–1700* (Albuquerque: University of New Mexico Press, 1997); Silvio A. Zavala, *Contribución a la historia de las instituciones coloniales en Guatemala* (Guatemala City: Universidad de San Carlos en Guatemala, 1967); Wendy Kramer, *Encomienda Politics in Early Colonial Guatemala, 1524–1544: Dividing the Spoils* (Boulder, Colo.: Westview Press, 1994); Robinson Herrera, *Natives, Europeans, and Africans in Sixteenth-Century Santiago de Guatemala* (Austin: University of Texas Press, 2003); Otto Vargas, *Sobre el modo de producción dominante en el Virreinato del Río de la Plata* (Buenos Aires: Editorial Agora, 1983).

27. Manuel Belaúnde Guinassi, *La encomienda en el Perú* (Lima: Ediciones Mercurio Peruano, 1945); Silvio Zavala, *El servicio personal de los indios en el Perú: Extractos del Siglo XVI* (Mexico City: El Colegio de México, 1978); Andrés Guerrero, *De la economía a las mentalidades* (Quito: El Conejo, 1991); José de la Puente Brunke, *Encomienda y encomenderos en el Perú: Estudio social y político de una institución colonial* (Sevilla: Excma. Diputación de Sevilla, 1992); Javier Ortiz de la Tabla Ducasse, *Los encomenderos de Quito, 1534–1660: Orígen y evolución de una élite colonial* (Sevilla: Escuela de Estudios Hispano-Americanos, 1993); Efraín Trelles Arestegui, *Lucas Martínez Vegazo: Funcionamiento de una encomienda peruana inicial* (Lima: Fondo Editorial, Pontificia Universidad Católica del Perú, 1982). For further studies that look at Indian slavery and encomienda within the context of other labor forms and the colonial economy in general, see Juan A. Villamarin and Judith E. Villamarin, *Indian Labor in Mainland Colonial Spanish America* (Newark: Latin American Studies Program, University of Delaware, 1975); Javier Tord Nicolini, *Hacienda, comercio y luchas sociales (Perú colonial)* (Lima: Biblioteca Peruana de Historia,

Economía y Sociedad, 1981); Silvio Zavala et al., *Peones, conciertos y arrendamientos en América Latina* (Bogotá: Centro Editorial, Universidad Nacional de Colombia, 1987); and Silvio Zavala, *Estudios acerca de la historia del trabajo en México: homenaje del Centro de Estudios Históricos a Silvio Zavala* (Mexico City: El Colegio de México, 1988).

28. Peter J. Bakewell, *Miners of the Red Mountain: Indian Labor in Potosí, 1545–1650* (Albuquerque: University of New Mexico Press, 1984); Lesley Byrd Simpson, *Studies in the Administration of the Indians in New Spain: III. The Repartimiento System of Native Labor in New Spain and Guatemala*, Ibero-Americana 13 (Berkeley: University of California Press, 1938); Andrés Guerrero, *La semántica de la dominación: El concertaje de indios* (Quito: Ediciones Libri Mundi/Enrique Grosse-Luemern, 1991).

29. Jürgen Golte, *Repartos y rebeliones: Túpac Amaru y las contradicciones de la economía colonial* (Lima: Instituto de Estudios Peruanos, 1980); and also on the Andes, see Alfredo Moreno Cebrián, *El corregidor de indios y la economía peruana del siglo XVIII: Los repartos forzosos de mercancías* (Madrid: Consejo Superior de Investigaciones Científicas, Instituto G. Fernández de Oviedo, 1977). On Mexico, see Jeremy Baskes, *Indians, Merchants, and Markets: A Reinterpretation of the Repartimiento and Spanish-Indian Economic Relations in Colonial Oaxaca, 1750–1821* (Stanford: Stanford University Press, 2000); but for somewhat different findings, see Brian R. Hamnett, *Politics and Trade in Southern Mexico, 1750–1821* (Cambridge: Cambridge University Press, 1971) and Carlos Sánchez Silva, *Indios, comerciantes y burocracia en la Oaxaca poscolonial, 1786–1860* (Oaxaca: Instituto Oaxaqueño de las Culturas/Fondo Estatal para la Cultura y las Artes/Universidad Autónoma Benito Juárez de Oaxaca, 1998).

30. Charles Gibson, *The Aztecs under Spanish Rule: A History of the Indians of the Valley of Mexico, 1519–1810* (Stanford: Stanford University Press, 1964); Lolita Gutiérrez Brockington, *The Leverage of Labor: Managing the Cortés Haciendas in Tehuantepec, 1588–1688* (Durham, N.C.: Duke University Press, 1989); Van Young, *Hacienda and Market*, 2nd ed.; Van Young, "Mexican Rural History Since Chevalier."

31. For the Mexican north in the late eighteenth and early nineteenth centuries, when labor was quite scarce, see Charles H. Harris, III, *A Mexican Family Empire: The Latifundio of the Sánchez Navarros, 1765–1867* (Austin: University of Texas Press, 1975); and more generally, Friedrich Katz, ed., *La servidumbre agraria en México en la época porfiriana* (Mexico City: Ediciones Era, 1984); Herbert J. Nickel, *Relaciones de trabajo en las haciendas de Puebla y Tlaxcala (1740–1914): Cuatro análisis sobre reclutamiento, peonaje y remuneración* (Mexico City: Universidad Iberoamericana, 1987); Nickel, *Morfología social de la hacienda mexicana* (Mexico City: Fondo de Cultura Económica 1988); Nickel, *El peonaje en las haciendas mexicanas: Interpretaciones, fuentes, hallazgos* (Mexico City: Universidad Iberoamericana, 1997); Nickel, ed., *Paternalismo y economía moral en las haciendas mexicanas del porfiriato* (Mexico City: Universidad Iberoamericana, 1989). On Latin America more generally, consult Kenneth Duncan and Ian Rutledge, eds., *Land and Labour in Latin America: Essays on the Development of Agrarian Capitalism in the Nineteenth and Twentieth Centuries* (Cambridge: Cambridge University Press, 1977).

32. Peter F. Klarén, *Modernization, Dislocation, and Aprismo: Origins of the Peruvian Aprista Party, 1870–1932* (Austin: University of Texas Press, 1973); Michael J. Gonzales, *Plantation Agriculture and Social Control in Northern Peru, 1875–1933* (Austin: University of Texas Press, 1985); Roger Plant, *Sugar and Modern Slavery: A Tale of Two Countries* (London: Zed Books, 1987).

33. Enrique Florescano, *Precios del maíz y crisis agrícolas en México (1708–1810)* (Mexico City: El Colegio de México, 1969); Elías Trabulse, ed., *Fluctuaciones económicas en*

Oaxaca durante el siglo XVIII (Mexico City: El Colegio de México, 1979); Lyman L. Johnson and Enrique Tandeter, eds., *Essays on the Price History of Eighteenth-Century Latin America* (Albuquerque: University of New Mexico Press, 1990); Ruggiero Romano, *Coyunturas opuestas: La crisis del siglo XVII en Europa e Hispanoamérica* (Mexico City: El Colegio de México, 1993); for some exceptions, see Eric Van Young, *La crisis del orden colonial: Estructura agraria y rebeliones populares de la Nueva España, 1750–1821* (Mexico City: Alianza, 1992), and indirectly Arnold J. Bauer, *Goods, Power, History: Latin America's Material Culture* (Cambridge: Cambridge University Press, 2001).

34. Stanley J. Stein and Barbara H. Stein, *The Colonial Heritage of Latin America: Essays on Economic Dependence in Historical Perspective* (New York: Oxford University Press, 1970); Victor Bulmer-Thomas, John H. Coatsworth, and Roberto Cortés Conde, eds., *The Cambridge Economic History of Latin America*: I. *The Colonial Era and the Short Nineteenth Century* (Cambridge: Cambridge University Press, 2006).

35. Tulio Halperín Donghi, *The Aftermath of Revolution in Latin America*, trans. Josephine de Bunsen (New York: Harper and Row, 1973); Leadro Prados de la Escosura and Samuel Amaral, eds., *La Independencia americana: Consecuencias económicas* (Madrid: Alianza, 1993); Roberto Schmit, *Ruina y resurrección en tiempos de Guerra: Sociedad, economía y poder en el Oriente entrerriano posrevolucionario, 1810–1852* (Buenos Aires: Prometeo, 2004).

36. For three case studies, see Steven C. Topik and Allen Wells, eds., *The Second Conquest of Latin America: Coffee, Henequen, and Oil during the Export Boom, 1850–1930* (Austin: University of Texas Press, 1998).

37. My treatment in this section of the chapter owes much to the thematic and organizational guidance afforded by several fine historiographical essays by Argentine scholars, primarily Raúl Fradkin, "La historia agraria y los estudios de establecimientos productivos en Hispanoamérica colonial: Una mirada desde el Río de la Plata," in Raúl Fradkin, ed., *La historia agraria del Río de la Plata colonial: Los establecimientos productivos*, 2 vols. (Buenos Aires: Centro Editor de América Latina, 1993), 1: 7–44; Juan Carlos Garavaglia and Jorge D. Gelman, "Rural History of the Río de la Plata, 1600–1850: Results of a Historiographical Renaissance," *Latin American Research Review* 30 (1995): 75–105; and Raúl Fradkin and Jorge Gelman, "Recorridos y dasafíos de una historiografía: Escalas de observación y fuentes en la historia rural rioplatense," in Beatriz Bragoni, ed., *Microanálisis: Ensayos de historiografía argentina* (Buenos Aires: Prometeo, 2004), 31–54. Sugar as an export staple has been left aside for the moment, since its intimate association with African slavery makes it more logical to deal with it in the section of the essay on Brazil.

38. Ricardo Levene, *Investigaciones acerca de la historia económica del Virreinato del Plata* (Buenos Aires: Universidad Nacional de la Plata, 1927–28); Jacinto Oddone, *La burguesía terrateniente argentina: Buenos Aires colonial, Capital Federal, Provincia de Buenos Aires, Provincia de Entre Ríos, Territorios Nacionales*, 2nd ed. ([1936] Buenos Aires: Libera, 1975); Alfredo Montoya, *Historia de los saladeros argentinos* (Buenos Aires: Raigal, 1956); Horacio Giberti, *Historia económica de la ganadería argentina* (Buenos Aires: Raigal, 1954; rev. edd. Buenos Aires: Solar, 1961, 1970, 1981).

39. Aldo Ferrer, *The Argentine Economy* (Berkeley: University of California Press, 1967); Jonathan C. Brown, *A Socioeconomic History of Argentina, 1776–1860* (Cambridge: Cambridge University Press, 1979); Jorge Gelman, *Rosas, estanciero: Gobierno y expansión ganadera* (Buenos Aires: Capital Intelectual, 2005); John Lynch, *Argentine Dictator: Juan Manuel de Rosas, 1829–1852* (Oxford: Oxford University Press, 1981).

40. James R. Scobie, *Revolution on the Pampas: A Social History of Argentine Wheat, 1860–1910* (Austin: University of Texas Press, 1964); Ian Rutledge, *Cambio agrario e*

integración: El desarrollo del capitalismo en Jujuy, 1550–1960 (Buenos Aires: Centro de Investigaciones en Ciencias Sociales, 1987); Jeremy Adelman, *Frontier Development: Land, Labour, and Capital on the Wheatlands of Argentina and Canada, 1890–1914* (Oxford: The Clarendon Press, 1994); Adelman, *Republic of Capital: Buenos Aires and the Legal Transformation of the Atlantic World* (Stanford: Stanford University Press, 1999); Carl E. Solberg, *The Prairies and the Pampas: Agrarian Policy in Canada and Argentina, 1880–1930* (Stanford: Stanford University Press, 1987); Samuel Amaral, *The Rise of Capitalism on the Pampas: The Estancias of Buenos Aires, 1785–1870* (Cambridge: Cambridge University Press, 1998); Osvaldo Barsky, et. al., *Historia del capitalismo agrario pampeano*, 2 vols. (Buenos Aires: Universidad de Belgrano/Siglo Veintiuno, 2003–05); Hilda Sabato, *Agrarian Capitalism and the World Market: Buenos Aires in the Pastoral Age, 1840–1890* (Albuquerque: University of New Mexico Press, 1990).

41. The concentrated wealth stored up in the rich soils of the River Plate area raises the issue of how natural environments are perceived and used, and how they mediate human relationships. To date, the field of environmental history has not developed as one might have hoped, given the relatively early success in this vein of Warren Dean, *Brazil and the Struggle for Rubber: A Study in Environmental History* (Cambridge: Cambridge University Press, 1987), a study of the environmental effects of the Amazon rubber boom, and his later work on the destruction of Brazil's Atlantic-litoral forests, Dean, *With Broadax and Firebrand: The Destruction of the Brazilian Atlantic Forest* (Berkeley: University of California Press, 1995). For early colonial Mexico, we have the elegant study of Elinor G. K. Melville, *A Plague of Sheep: Environmental Consequences of the Conquest of Mexico* (Cambridge: Cambridge University Press, 1994), in which she shows that the environmental degradation of the Mezquital Valley even in modern times was due not to the weight of human habitation in the preconquest era, but rather to the overgrazing of sheep introduced by Spanish stockmen in the sixteenth century and the "ungulate irruption" unleashed by it.

42. The term "renaissance" is that of Garavaglia and Gelman, "Rural History of the Río de la Plata, 1600–1850."

43. Carlos Sempat Assadourian, *El sistema de la economía colonial: Mercado interno, regiones y espacio económico* (Lima: Instituto de Estudios Peruanos, 1982).

44. Juan Carlos Garavaglia, *Economía, sociedad y regiones* (Buenos Aires: Ediciones de la Flor, 1987); Sara Mata de López, *Tierra y poder en Salta: El noroeste argentino en vísperas de la independencia* (Sevilla: Diputación de Sevilla, 2000); Jorge D. Gelman, *De mercachifle a gran comerciante: Los caminos del ascenso en el Río de la Plata colonial* (Huelva: Universidad Internacional de Andalucía, 1996); Raúl Fradkin and Juan Carlos Garavaglia, eds., *En busca de un tiempo perdido: La economía de Buenos Aires en le país de la abundancia 1750–1865* (Buenos Aires: Prometeo, 2004); Carlos Mayo, *Estancia y sociedad en la pampa (1740–1820)* (Buenos Aires: Biblos, 1995); Cristina López de Albornoz, *Los dueños de la tierra: Economía, sociedad y poder: Tucumán, 1770–1820* (Tucumán: Universidad Nacional de Tucumán, 2003).

45. Raúl Mandrini and Andrea Reguera, *Huellas en la tierra: Indios, agricultores y hacendados en la pampa bonaerense* (Tandil: Instituto de Estudios Histórico-Sociales, 1993).

46. Jorge D. Gelman, *Campesinos y estancieros: Una región del Río de la Plata a fines de la época colonial* (Buenos Aires: Libros del Riel, 1998); Juan Carlos Garavaglia, *Pastores y labradores de Buenos Aires: Una historia agraria de la campaña bonaerense 1700–1830* (Buenos Aires: Ediciones de la Flor, 1999); Ricardo D. Salvatore, *Wandering Paysanos: State Order and Subaltern Experience in Buenos Aires during the Rosas Era* (Durham, N.C.: Duke

University Press, 2003); and for a somewhat different view of gauchos, see Richard W. Slatta, *Gauchos and the Vanishing Frontier* (Lincoln: University of Nebraska Press, 1983).

47. Arjun Appadurai, ed., *The Social Life of Things: Commodities in Cultural Perspective* (Cambridge: Cambridge University Press, 1986).

48. On cacao, see Robert J. Ferry, *The Colonial Elite of Early Caracas: Formation and Crisis, 1567–1767* (Berkeley: University of California Press, 1989); Andrés Guerrero, *Los oligarcas del cacao: Ensayo sobre la acumulación originaria en el Ecuador: Hacendados cacaoteros, banqueros, exportadores y comerciantes en Guayaquil (1890)* (Quito: Editorial El Conejo, 1980); Jaime Torres Sánchez, *Haciendas y posesiones de la Compañía de Jesús en Venezuela: El Colegio de Caracas en el siglo XVIII* (Sevilla: Universidad de Sevilla, 2002); on the hard fiber henequen, Allen Wells, *Yucatán's Gilded Age: Haciendas, Henequen, and International Harvester, 1860–1915* (Albuquerque: University of New Mexico Press, 1985); on wool, Nils Jacobsen, *Mirages of Transition: The Peruvian Altiplano, 1780–1930* (Berkeley: University of California Press, 1993); and on rubber, Barbara Weinstein, *The Amazon Rubber Boom, 1850–1920* (Stanford: Stanford University Press, 1983); Dean, *Brazil and the Struggle for Rubber*; Michael T. Taussig, *Shamanism, Colonialism, and the Wild Man: A Study in Terror and Healing* (Chicago: University of Chicago Press, 1991); and Bradford L. Barham and Oliver T. Coomes, *Prosperity's Promise: The Amazon Rubber Boom and Distorted Economic Development* (Boulder, Colo.: Westview Press, 1996).

49. This instrumentalist view of what such studies can accomplish clearly points up the fact—perhaps too obvious to bear much comment—that historical literatures respond to more than just an internalist logic of investigation. Garavaglia and Gelman, "Rural History of the Rio de la Plata," point out, for example, that the end of the military regime in Argentina in the mid-1980s, by allowing the return of exiled scholars, paved the way for the renaissance in River Plate rural history they review. Similarly, the political and intellectual effects of the Vietnam War in the United States in part stimulated among my own generation the interest in peasant resistance movements and wars of national liberation that later came to fuller fruition under the subaltern studies banner.

50. Marc Edelman, *The Logic of the Latifundio: The Large Estates of Northwestern Costa Rica Since the Late Nineteenth Century* (Stanford: Stanford University Press, 1992); and for an earlier era in Costa Rica, Lowell Gudmundson, *Hacendados, políticos y precaristas: La ganadería y el latifundo guanacasteco* (San José: Editorial Costa Rica, 1983).

51. Juan Carlos Garavaglia, *Mercado interno y economía colonial* (Mexico City: Grijalbo, 1983); Susan Deans-Smith, *Bureaucrats, Planters, and Workers: The Making of the Tobacco Monopoly in Bourbon Mexico* (Austin: University of Texas Press, 1992).

52. Laird W. Bergad, *Coffee and the Growth of Agrarian Capitalism in Nineteenth-Century Puerto Rico* (Princeton: Princeton University Press, 1983); Héctor Pérez Brignoli and Mario Samper Kutschbach, eds., *Tierra, café y sociedad: Ensayos sobre la historia agrarian centroamericana* (San José: Programa Costa Rica, FLACSO, 1994); William Roseberry, Lowell Gudmundson, and Mario Samper Kutschbach, *Coffee, Society, and Power in Latin America* (Baltimore: Johns Hopkins University Press, 1995); William Gervase Clarence-Smith and Steven C. Topik, eds., *The Global Coffee Economy in Africa, Asia and Latin America, 1500–1989* (Cambridge: Cambridge University Press, 2003 [electronic book]); William P. McGreevey, *An Economic History of Colombia, 1845–1930* (Cambridge: Cambridge University Press, 1971); José Antonio Ocampo, *Colombia y la economía mundial, 1830–1910* (Mexico City: Siglo Veintiuno, 1984); Marco Palacios, *El café en Colombia, 1850–1970: Una historia económica, social y política*, 3rd rev. ed. (Bogotá: Planeta, 2002); Darío Fajardo, *Haciendas, campesinos y políticas agrarias en Colombia, 1920–1980* (Bogotá: Editorial Oveja Negra, 1983); Fajardo, *Espacio y sociedad: Formación de las regiones agrarias*

en Colombia (Bogotá: Corporación Colombiana para la Amazonia-Araracuara, 1993); José Chalarca, *Vida y hechos del café en Colombia* (Bogotá: Común Presencia, 1998); Renzo Ramírez Bacca, *Colonización del Líbano: De la distribución de baldíos a la consolidación de una región cafetera, Tolima, Colombia 1849–1907* (Bogotá: Universidad Nacional de Colombia, 2001); Ramírez Bacca, *Formación y transformación de la cultura laboral cafetera en el siglo XX* (Medellín: Carreta, 2004); Jaime Vallecilla Gordillo, *Café y crecimiento económico regional: El Antiguo Caldas, 1870–1970* (Manizales, Colombia: Universidad de Caldas, 2001); Renée Souldre-La France, *Región e imperio: El Tolima Grande y las reformas borbónicas en el siglo XVIII* (Bogotá: Instituto Colombiano de Antropología e Historia, 2004); Catherine LeGrand, *Frontier Expansion and Peasant Protest in Colombia, 1850–1936* (Albuquerque: University of New Mexico Press, 1986); William Roseberry, *Coffee and Capitalism in the Venezuelan Andes* (Austin: University of Texas Press, 1983).

53. Lowell Gudmundson, *Costa Rica before Coffee: Society and Economy on the Eve of the Export Boom* (Baton Rouge: Louisiana State University Press, 1986); David McCreery, *Rural Guatemala, 1760–1940* (Stanford: Stanford University Press, 1994).

54. Sidney Mintz, *Sweetness and Power: The Place of Sugar in Modern History* (New York: Penguin Books, 1986); Noël Deerr, *The History of Sugar*, 2 vols. (London: Chapman and Hall, 1949–50).

55. For reasons of space, the Caribbean region, in which peasant, plantation, and export agriculture had just as complex a history as in mainland Ibero-America and left marks just as deep on contemporary societies, is alluded to here only in passing. Nor, for the same reason, have I delved into the social and cultural aspects of Africans in the New World, although as with the ethnohistory of Native American peoples, rural history should by all rights include them. In terms of its historiographical and bibliographical orientation, this section of my essay owes much to João José Reis and Herbert S. Klein, "The New Historiography of Slavery in Brazil," in this volume, and to Herbert S. Klein and Ben Vinson III, *African Slavery in Latin America and the Caribbean*, 2nd rev. ed. (New York: Oxford University Press, 2007).

56. Herbert S. Klein, *The Middle Passage: Comparative Studies in the Atlantic Slave Trade* (Princeton: Princeton University Press, 1978); Klein, *African Slavery in Latin America and the Caribbean* (New York: Oxford University Press, 1986); Klein, *The Atlantic Slave Trade* (Cambridge: Cambridge University Press, 1999); Hugh Thomas, *The Slave Trade: The Story of the Atlantic Slave Trade, 1440–1870* (New York: Simon and Schuster, 1997); Philip D. Curtin, *The Rise and Fall of the Plantation Complex: Essays in Atlantic History* (Cambridge: Cambridge University Press, 1998).

57. Laird Bergad, *Slavery and the Demographic and Economic History of Minas Gerais, Brazil, 1720–1888* (Cambridge: Cambridge University Press, 1999); Jacob Gorender, *O escravismo colonial*, 5th rev. ed. (São Paulo: Atica, 1988); Stuart B. Schwartz, *Sugar Plantations in the Formation of Brazilian Society: Bahia, 1550–1835* (Cambridge: Cambridge University Press, 1985); Schwartz, *Slaves, Peasants, and Rebels: Reconsidering Brazilian Slavery* (Urbana: University of Illinois Press, 1992).

58. Bert J. Barickman, *A Bahian Counterpoint: Sugar, Tobacco, Cassava, and Slavery in the Recôncavo, 1780–1860* (Stanford: Stanford University Press, 1998); Peter L. Eisenberg, *The Sugar Industry in Pernambuco: Modernization Without Change, 1840–1910* (Berkeley: University of California Press, 1974); Alida C. Metcalf, *Family and Frontier in Colonial Brazil: Santana de Parnaíba, 1580–1822* (Berkeley: University of California Press, 1992); Stanley J. Stein, *Vassouras: A Brazilian Coffee County, 1850–1900* ([1957] New York: Atheneum, 1976); Warren Dean, *Rio Claro: A Brazilian Plantation System, 1820–1920* (Stanford: Stanford University Press, 1976); Francisco Vidal Luna and Herbert S. Klein,

Slavery and the Economy of São Paulo, 1750–1850 (Stanford: Stanford University Press, 2003); and on the sugar-beet industry in Peru, see Peter F. Klarén, *Modernization, Dislocation, and Aprismo: Origins of the Peruvian Aprista Party, 1870–1932* (Austin: University of Texas Press, 1973).

59. Marvin Harris, *Patterns of Race in the Americas* (New York: Norton, 1964); Carl N. Degler, *Neither Black nor White: Slavery and Race Relations in Brazil and the United States* ([1971] Madison: University of Wisconsin Press, 1986).

60. Kátia M. de Queirós Mattoso, *To Be a Slave in Brazil, 1550–1888* ([1979] New Brunswick, N.J.: Rutgers University Press, 1986); Silvia H. Lara, *Campos da violencia: Esclavos e senhores na Capitania do Rio de Janeiro, 1750–1808* (Rio de Janeiro: Paz e Terra, 1988); João José Reis and Eduardo Silva, *Negociação e conflito: A resistencia negra no Brasil esclavista* (São Paulo: Companhia das Letras, 1989); Vidal Luna and Klein, *Slavery and the Economy of São Paulo*; Nancy P. Naro, *A Slave's Place, a Master's World: Fashioning Dependency in Rural Brazil* (London: Continuum, 2000).

61. Lowell J. Ragatz, *The Fall of the Planter Class in the British Caribbean, 1763–1833: A Study in Social and Economic History* ([1928] New York: Octagon Books, 1971); Eric Williams, *Capitalism and Slavery* ([1944] New York: Capricorn Books, 1966); Richard Pares, *A West-India Fortune* ([1950] Hamden, Conn.: Archon Books, 1968); Orlando Patterson, *The Sociology of Slavery: An Analysis of the Origins, Development and Structure of Negro Slave Society in Jamaica* (London: MacGibbon and Kee, 1967); Richard S. Dunn, *Sugar and Slaves: The Rise of the Planter Class in the English West Indies, 1624–1713* (New York: W.W. Norton, 1973); Elsa Goveia, *Slave Society in the British Leeward Islands at the End of the Eighteenth Century* (New Haven: Yale University Press, 1965); Jerome S. Handler and Frederick W. Lange, *Plantation Slavery in Barbados: An Archaeological and Historical Investigation* (Cambridge, Mass.: Harvard University Press, 1978).

62. José Antonio Saco, *Historia de la esclavitud desde los tiempos mas remotos hasta nuestros días* (Paris: Tipografía Lahure, 1875–77); Manuel Moreno Fraginals, *El ingenio* ([1964] Barcelona: Crítica, 2001); José A. Piqueiras, *Azúcar y esclavitud en el final del trabajo forzado: Homenaje a M. Moreno Fraginals* (Madrid: Fondo de Cultura Económica, 2002); Leví Marrero, *Cuba, economía y sociedad*, 15 vols. (Rio Piedras, P.R.: Editorial San Juan, 1972–); Franklin W. Knight, *Slave Society in Cuba During the Nineteenth Century* (Madison: University of Wisconsin Press, 1970); Laird Bergad, *Cuban Rural Society in the Nineteenth Century: The Social and Economic History of Monoculture in Matanzas* (Princeton: Princeton University Press, 1990); Francisco A. Scarano, *Sugar and Slavery in Puerto Rico: The Plantation Economy of Ponce, 1800–1850* (Madison: University of Wisconsin Press, 1984).

63. On Peru, see Frederick P. Bowser, *The African Slave in Colonial Peru, 1524–1650* (Stanford: Stanford University Press, 1974), which is admittedly mostly urban history; Peter Blanchard, *Slavery and Abolition in Early Republican Peru* (Wilmington, Del.: Scholarly Resources, 1992); and Carlos Aguirre, *Breve historia de la esclavitud en el Perú: Una herida que no deja de sangrar* (Lima: Fondo Editorial del Congreso del Perú, 2005); and on Colombia, Germán Colmenares, *Cali, terratenientes, mineros y comerciantes, siglo XVIII* (Bogotá: Carlos Valencia, 1980).

64. Colin A. Palmer, *Slaves of the White God: Blacks in Mexico, 1570–1650* (Cambridge, Mass.: Harvard University Press, 1975); Gonzalo Aguirre Beltrán, *La población negra de México, 1519–1810: Estudio etnohistórico* (Mexico City: Fuente Cultural, 1946); Patrick J. Carroll, *Blacks in Colonial Veracruz: Race, Ethnicity, and Regional Development*, 2nd ed. (Austin: University of Texas Press, 2001); Adriana Naveda Chávez-Hita, *Esclavos negros en las haciendas azucareras de Córdoba, Veracruz, 1690–1830* (Xalapa: Universidad Veracruzana,

Centro de Investigaciones Históricas, 1987); Gisela von Wobeser, *La hacienda azucarera en le época colonial* (Mexico City: Secretaría de Educación Pública, 1988); Beatriz Scharrer Tamm, *Azúcar y trabajo: Tecnología de los siglos XVII y XVIII en el actual Estado de Morelos* (Mexico City: Centro de Investigaciones y Estudios Superiores en Antropología Social, 1997); Ernest Sánchez Santiró, *Azúcar y poder: Estructura socioeconómica de las alcaldías mayores de Cuernavaca y Cuautla de Amilpas, 1730–1821* (Mexico City: Praxis, 2001); Gisela Landázuri Benítez and Verónica Vázquez Mantecón, *Azúcar y Estado (1750–1880)* (Mexico City: Fondo de Cultura Económica, 1988); Cheryl E. Martin, *Rural Society in Colonial Morelos* (Albuquerque: University of New Mexico Press, 1985); Horacio Crespo et al., *Historia del azúcar en México*, 2 vols. (Mexico City: Fondo de Cultura Económica, 1988–90); Ward Barrett, *The Sugar Hacienda of the Marqueses del Valle* (Minneapolis: University of Minnesota Press, 1970); Paul Hart, *Bitter Harvest: The Social Transformation of Morelos, Mexico, and the Origins of the Zapatista Revolution, 1840–1910* (Albuquerque: University of New Mexico Press, 2005).

CHAPTER 11

LATIN AMERICAN LABOR HISTORY

JAMES P. BRENNAN

The history of Latin American labor in the sense of human toil, the history of work, is as old as the region itself. The labor systems established by the Spanish and Portuguese colonists extracted a surplus from indigenous and African peoples in complex, exhausting, rapacious ways. Such work was the foundation of the Iberian empires' wealth and the source of immeasurable suffering for those who performed it. Though a vital area of research for any historian of Latin America, when we speak of "labor history" proper we generally and more accurately are referring to the history of labor in modern capitalism. Nowhere, save perhaps in the mining sector, can bona fide capitalist labor systems be said to have appeared in Latin America before the early to mid-nineteenth century. Indeed, the extractive, coerced labor of the colonial period lingered on into the nineteenth century, and in some places, such as Guatemala, with astonishing resilience into the twentieth century. Yet everywhere in Latin America, by the mid-nineteenth century a modern capitalist labor market of some size had appeared. With the dominance of capitalism as a mode of production, the working class became increasingly important, and labor history as a subfield in Latin American historiography had its object of study defined: to record and explain "the labor movement."

A review of Latin American labor historiography is a much simpler task than it is for many subfields. Barely a quarter century old, labor history is certainly a newcomer compared to the deep scholarship on colonialism, the Independence movements, slavery, rural history, and many other topics.[1] The study of Latin America labor until the 1970s remained largely the preserve of economists, political scientists, and some sociologists, but even among them attention was slight compared to issues of economic development, political systems, and rural society. The few studies concerned with labor, such as Victor Alba's *Historia del movimiento obrero en América Latina* (1964), quite understandably focused on the most public and visible manifestations of labor: labor politics. The study of labor was thus the study of the trade union movement as represented by the role of the large labor confederations and most powerful unions in civil society, especially their relationship with the state, political parties, and regimes. A notable exception to the emphasis on the politics of labor was Robert Alexander's pioneering and still very useful study of the industrial relations systems in Argentina, Brazil, and Chile.[2] Nonetheless, studies of labor and the working class beyond its most public activities and institutions were very few. Through the 1960s and early 1970s, historical scholarship on the subject amounted to a handful of scattered monographs, also essentially institutional and political.[3] The underdeveloped state of historical scholarship for Latin American labor contrasted with the welter of studies being published at the time on the working class in Europe and North America, increasingly of a social and cultural nature.

The foundational study for Latin American labor history was in many ways was Hobart Spalding's *Organized Labor in Latin America: Historical Case Studies of Urban Workers in Dependent Societies* (1977). As its title indicates, Spalding's book was heavily influenced by dependency theory and found in the international economy the keys to unraveling the trajectories of the Latin American labor movements. It would take several years for dissertations and books on labor topics to appear, but Spalding's monograph established labor as a serious object of study for Latin Americanists. The book dispelled prejudices that the agrarian nature of the region for most of its history, and the comparatively small size of its industrial base and industrial working class, perforce made workers a subject of secondary interest. Spalding demonstrated that workers, unions, and labor movements had unquestionably become influential players in Latin American society and politics in its modern history. Almost a decade later, a second study, Charles Bergquist's *Labor in Latin America: Comparative Studies on Chile, Argentina, Venezuela and Colombia* (1986), sought to allay any reservations that lingered about labor's importance. Bergquist argued for Latin America's specificity and the primacy of the workers in the export sector as the main influences in the Latin American labor movements. Though rather strangely disavowing any affinity with Spalding's dependency perspective, it did in fact offer a similar explanation, albeit providing a more historically detailed and optimistic account of the Latin American labor movements.

Written at a time when historical scholarship was still seeking a dialogue with the social sciences, both Spalding and Bergquist's studies sought to come up with a single, unifying explanation for what were in reality greatly diverse national labor movements whose histories were not easily reduced to exogenous influences, not even one so important as the international economy. The "boom," as it has frequently described in Latin American labor studies in the two decades since Bergquist's monograph, has followed a different path than that chartered by the historian of Colombia. Rather than broad interpretive studies, the "new Latin American labor history," both by anglophone historians and by Latin Americans themselves, has celebrated the diversity of the national experiences and found the explanations for the distinct trajectories of the labor movements in history and culture.[4] This essay will review the recent literature, organized according to my own periodization of the history of labor and the working class in the region, highlighting the main schools of interpretations, themes, and analytical perspectives. I conclude with an assessment and some suggestions about a possible future course for Latin American labor studies.

Working Class Formation (1850–80)

The early years of working class formation and the origins of the labor movement, one of the best and most intensely studied periods in U.S. labor history, has been relatively neglected, especially by anglophone historians. Of the some two dozen most important monographs published over the past two decades by English-speaking historians and listed in the bibliography, only one, David Sowell's study of artisans and the origins of the Colombian labor movement in nineteenth-century Bogotá, deals with this formative period, and even that study is not about the working class per se. Sowell's findings on the mobilization of artisans in post-Independence Bogotá, echoes the studies of Sean Wilentz and other historians of the U.S. working class for these same decades, but differs substantially from them. Bogotá's artisans mobilized in response more to foreign imports and increased competition than to an industrialization process that threatened artisans' crafts with proletarianization and deskilling.[5] The neglect of this period generally can be explained by the retrenchment in capitalism's growth in the post-Independence decades, a weak industrialization process, and the comparatively small size of the Latin American working class. No identifiable working-class culture had yet emerged, and workers' organizations were by and large confined to mutual aid societies. Nonetheless, in several countries, Argentina and Chile certainly, Mexico to a certain extent after midcentury, capitalist enterprise and capitalist labor markets grew significantly, enough to be able to speak of at least a proto–working class and labor movements.

Three pioneering studies by Latin American historians have demonstrated the importance of these neglected years, and also the period's intrinsic interest. For Argentina, Luis Alberto Romero and Hilda Sabato analyzed the conformation of Latin America's first unadulterated capitalist labor market, that of Buenos Aires, in a magisterial study, *Los trabajadores de Buenos Aires: La experiencia del mercado, 1850–1880*. Latin America's most flourishing export economy created in its great port and capital city during the middle decades of the nineteenth century an economy characterized by occupational mobility, wild fluctuations in employment according to the business cycle, and penny capitalism in the form of self-employment and seasonal, largely unskilled work. Though there were some well-paid jobs for more highly skilled labor in a flourishing export economy evolving towards specialization in the international division of labor, the experience of work in the city tended more toward the impermanent, the part-time, all the loading, carting, and digging of a robust but still rudimentary economy. Romero and Sabato's exhaustive use of census materials from the period paints a portrait of a city of immigrants and native-born criollos in which work was abundant and social and spatial mobility more feasible than in the estates, farms, and small towns that both immigrant and criollo had left behind. The availability of work and the possibility of material progress would leave its mark on a working class in which class identities would always compete with a larger urban environment that attenuated them.[6]

A second study, by Chilean historian Gabriel Salazar, rather than revealing the opportunities for social mobility made possible by the expansion of capitalism, demonstrated the transition to capitalism in all its brutal, disruptive dimensions. Chile's mining sector, the battering ram in breaking down precapitalist social relations, experienced a profound transformation in these decades. The consolidation of the mining sector in a few diversified firms and, to a lesser extent, increased capitalization altered the ad hoc labor contracting arrangements and desultory production in the mines that characterized the late colonial and early national periods. The mineworkers and peripatetic prospectors who migrated with considerable freedom of movement gave way to the indebted worker in the new mining camps controlled by merchant capital. Thus, despite the stunted development of industry, some Latin American countries did experience a process similar to Europe and North America in the transition to capitalism, albeit with characteristics of their own. Salazar's study is also important because it analyzes how "proletarianization" was a process that affected not only men but also women, with the breakdown of the household economy and the end of the rudimentary textile industry dominated by women and ancillary to agriculture.[7]

A third study, Mario Trujillo Bolio's *Operarios fabriles en el valle de México, 1864–1884*, examined that sector of the working class, textile workers, who along with mineworkers had long constituted and would for some time continue to be the largest part of the Latin American proletariat. Though largely a social history, Trujillo Bolio's study does at least raise the issue of ideology and political culture among textile workers in Mexico's central valley. With so much attention of late being given by historians to the impact of a popular liberalism on the Mexican peasantry, it would seem a pressing task for labor historians to assess whether something similar occurred among the nineteenth-century Mexican working class. Trujillo Bolio does not offer any clear answers here. Though the Liberals drew more support from the capital city's artisans than from local textile workers, one faction of the latter did support the candidacies of Juárez and Lerdo de Tejada in the presidential elections of 1867 and 1872. Still another faction adhered to socialist positions. The content of this liberalism and socialism is not analyzed, and Trujillo Bolio's treatment is only suggestive. Liberalism might appeal to workers' sense of nationalism and opposition to aristocratic privilege, but its anticlericalism and much of its economic program did not. The textile workers' "socialism" appears to have more affinities with Proudhon, Bakunin, and Kropotkin than with Marx. Still, something of a working-class political consciousness appears to have been germinating in

Mexico among the textile workers in the central valley, albeit one that adumbrated the tensions in working-class political culture between liberalism and socialism that would be apparent during the Porfiriato and the Revolution.[8]

This first, formative period in Latin American history lacked the great defining issue that for British and U.S. historians was the Industrial Revolution and the transition to industrial capitalism. Such monumental, historically transcendent changes provided the grist for E. P. Thompson's *The Making of the English Working Class* and for Thompson's many imitators in the United States who worked on this period and wrote some of the best American labor history. A small working class in what were overwhelmingly rural societies meant that historians of Latin American chose other, more important subjects to study, while labor historians devoted their research to later periods. Nonetheless, these three studies by Latin American historians do suggest three areas for future research during the genesis of the Latin American working class: the conformation of capitalist labor markets, the process of proletarianization in a commercial capitalism with some ancillary industrialization and a burgeoning mining sector, and the political culture of workers in the heyday of liberalism but also in the decades of the birth of the international socialist movement.

Anarchism, Socialism, and the Patterns of Everyday Life (1880–1930)

Capitalism's rapid expansion, globally and within Latin America itself, in the final decades of the nineteenth century allowed the working class for the first time to emerge as a significant sector of Latin American society. Among the effects of capitalism's expansion were the lowering of passage rates and great international movements of population, including to Latin America. The largest concentration of workers were found in those countries where capitalism was growing most rapidly, where economic opportunities were increasing exponentially, and which were attracting the greatest numbers of foreign immigrants. In the port cities especially, in Rio de Janeiro, Montevideo, Buenos Aires, Rosario, Valparaíso, and Santos and its upland sister São Paulo, large contingents of immigrant workers, overwhelmingly young and male, clustered in working class neighborhoods and immigrant tenements, the Brazilian *cortiço* and Argentinian *conventillo*, while expanding into other parts of the city as well. The new arrivals forged sodalities and even a class identity in such neighborhoods, evidenced in the self-appellation they increasingly employed: *el proletariado*. Spatial concentration facilitated a sense of common identity and was reinforced by shared confrontations with the employers and the state as well as similar work experiences. Identifiable working-class cultures emerged, most famously in Buenos Aires with its *tango* and *lunfardo*, but everywhere workers gained a sense of distinctiveness in their societies. Such a sense of collective identity allowed them to create or expand organizations: mutual aid societies, unions, and even the first labor confederations.

Adding to that sense of distinctiveness were ideologies—anarchism, socialism, and, to a much lesser extent in these years, communism—that were all preaching a special role, even a mission, for the workers in building a better society, a new order free from the exploitation and hardships they were suffering. There was thus a contradiction in the process of acculturation and naturalization of the immigrant working class in the various Latin American nations, and that was their intense internationalism. They saw themselves as part of a worldwide movement, the local representatives of the international proletarian struggle, hence the names they gave their new labor confederations, such as Mexico's Casa del Obrero Mundial or Argentina's Federación Obrera Regional Argentina (FORA). As the names of these organizations indicate, they were regarded as merely the local branches, indeed the *casa*, their very home away from home, for fellow workers linked across the superstition and atavism that were national borders in a common cause of international proletarian struggle to topple the old order and build a new one.

Much of the labor historiography for these years, produced by both anglophone and Latin American historians, deals with the ideological disputes stemming from the First International and their reverberations in individual Latin American countries. Of the three ideologies competing for working-class loyalties, anarchism was until World War I the most successful and hence the most studied. Anarchism had a strong, though difficult to gauge, impact beyond the leadership even in those countries that did not experience large-scale European immigration. Studies of the Mexican working class and labor movement have asserted a similar influence even in a country in which European immigration was insignificant. Most recently, John Lear's study of the working class in Mexico City during the Mexican Revolution emphasized the anarchists' leadership of Mexican labor during these years. Lear's monograph nonetheless strips away much of the mythology surrounding the Casa del Obrero Mundial, and while acknowledging the influence of anarchist ideas on the leadership, questions their impact on the great mass of workers. What emerges is an anarchism that flourished because of its greater ability to articulate the lived experiences of workers, "to provide a vocabulary for articulating class differences and an imperative for independent organization," but was constrained by the nationalism and religious sensibilities of the Mexican working class.[9]

For Chile, Peter De Shazo's monograph, the first in the wave of detailed anglophone studies of the national dynamics of Latin American labor, also demonstrated the strength of the anarchists. At least in Santiago and Valparaíso, the anarchists were the dominant force in the Chilean labor movement through the first three decades of the twentieth century, even in the country that would have the strongest socialist and communist parties in the region, and ones with large working-class constituencies. As in Mexico, the anarchists had more success than others because their insistence on direct economic action and their disdain for politics best expressed the needs of a working class that had little faith in the willingness of the ruling classes or the ability of the state to redress their demands.[10] Likewise for

Brazil, Boris Fausto's classic study of the labor movement, *Trabalho urbano e conflito social*, emphasized the anarchists' dominance in these years but also Brazilian anarchism's affinities with a Spencerian liberalism and the labor movement's innate weakness. The anarchists contributed to such weakness through their hyperindividualism, their preoccupation with issues like anticlericalism, and their distaste for organization, not to mention politics.[11]

Not surprisingly, historical scholarship on the anarchist question has been richest in that country which at the time had the largest working class in the region and the most vibrant anarchist movement in the world outside of Spain, Argentina. Some of the best testimonial literature by working-class militants of the period dealt with anarchism and the anarchists, such as Diego Abad de Santillán's history of the FORA. There were also classic narrative accounts such as Osvaldo Bayer's of the 1919 Patagonia uprising, as well as a sizable body of more specialized, scholarly studies. Juan Suriano's recent book, deeply researched and elegantly written, adds yet another contribution to the bibliography on anarchism. Suriano's rich tapestry of Buenos Aires's variegated anarchist subculture, with its boisterous press, popular theater, libertarian schools, secret rituals, and emotive symbols, conveys the dynamism of this underground, working-class culture in the heyday of liberalism and belle époque Argentina. Yet Suriano also cogently analyzes and trenchantly criticizes the contradictions, and even the anachronistic character, of the anarchists' intransigent, at times chiliastic project. In the midst of the anarchists' denigration of the state and vitriolic harangues about the innately wicked and corrupt nature of politics, the Argentine elite passed the first prolabor legislation, citizenship was given real meaning through electoral reform, public education expanded, and acculturation and genuine possibilities for social advancement took place. State policies and legislation, the discovery of the "social question," and some state initiatives to palliate the hardships collectively undermined the anarchists' intransigent positions and the attractiveness of international proletarian revolution.[12]

The post–World War I advance of socialist parties and unions among the working class has been less studied than the anarchist question. The explanation advanced by Bergquist, using Chile as the paradigmatic case, that countries characterized by foreign-owned enclave economies tended to evolve towards socialist labor movements does not seem borne out by the experience of other Latin American countries. William French's study of mineworkers in the foreign-owned copper mines of northern Mexico reveals a working class that aspired to respectability and status as the *gente decente*.[13] Indeed, in the case of Chile itself, Chilean historian Julio Pinto Vallejos's study of Chilean mineworkers, *Trabajos y rebeldías en la pampa salitrera*, presents an open-ended process in which the mineworkers' socialist politics developed out of the specific contingencies of history and was by no means inevitable because of the structural position they occupied in the national economy.[14] This question of anarchism's decline and socialism's rise is one calling for further research. Some classic studies assess the impact of the Russian Revolution and the Second International on the labor movements, but they are largely confined to the labor leadership as revealed in the latter's public statements and the political positions adopted by the trade unions.[15] The development of Marxist ideologies or worldviews on the workers goes almost unnoticed. Similarly, a working-class ideology on the rise in a number of countries after the war and through the 1920s, syndicalism, with its stress on an apolitical but pragmatic trade unionism, remains neglected save as manifested in the syndicalist unions' public history.[16]

The most notable change in the historiography of labor for this period, one made largely by anglophone historians, has been including the role of women and developing gender as a category of analysis in the study of Latin American workers. Joel Wolfe's *Working Women, Working Men*, though following an older model of women's history as opposed to gender analysis, does at least restore agency to women in Brazil's largely feminine workforce in the textile industry, including their role in the great 1917 strike. Wolfe's controversial interpretation posits that women's concerns animated the strike, indeed that São Paulo's women workers initiated it.[17] Elizabeth Hutchison's work on the Chilean working class similarly makes a persuasive case for the importance of women and specific women's concerns in the early Chilean labor movement.[18] Also for Chile, the country whose recent historical scholarship has been most "engendered," Thomas Klubock's study of the mineworkers at the great El Teniente copper mine during the early decades of the century and through the popular front years stressed gender relations and the miners' particular definition of masculinity as the decisive components in the development of a militant union tradition and political radicalism among the copper miners.[19]

Whether one agrees or not with Klubock's argument, his study does have the merit of adding a new dimension to the scholarship on the Chilean working class. Ann Farnsworth-Alvear's study of textile workers in Colombia, however, marks the most sophisticated use of gender on a Latin American labor history topic to date. Farnsworth-Alvear chose a single geographic area and industrial sector, Medellín's textile workers, to explore relations between employers and workers and the crucial role that gender played in them. Gender here, as in Klubock's study but with greater analytical power and theoretical sophistication, is understood not simply as restoring women's agency but as a series of social negotiations over sexual identity. Farnsworth-Alvear unravels a heretofore hidden component in the industrialization process and capital-labor relations. She also more effectively combines cultural and social history than many of the recent engendered labor histories. Much of this new scholarship, as labor history, tends too often to be very near-sighted, working almost entirely with a concern for "gender," as if only that mattered. Farnsworth-Alvear is also guilty of some of this deficiency (where is the murderously violent world of Colombian local politics in her study of Medellín?), though her book is theoretically sharper than the other gender studies on Latin American labor. She does make a compelling case for the influence if not the primacy of gender issues among the textile workers she studies.[20]

Much of the working-class history of the period, particularly that dealing with workers' everyday lives as opposed to their unions and politics, belongs more to urban and immigration literature than to labor history strictly speaking. The intensity of the urbanization process and the profound impact of mass European immigration altered in manifold ways the residential patterns, families, and consumption habits of the urban working class. A study such as José Moya's *Cousins and Strangers* perhaps reveals more about what it meant to be an Argentine worker at the turn of the century than the many studies on the organized labor movement and labor politics for this period. Only a small number of workers belonged to unions or were militants in anarchist or socialist organizations, but all were coworkers, neighbors, and family members. Other studies that belong more to the urbanization literature than labor historiography offer similar insights on working-class life in these decades. To take just one example, the edited volume *Cities of Hope* demonstrates the clash between modernizing elites and the urban working class. Urban social protest, including but not confined to the working class, was more widespread and intense in this period than perhaps in any other in modern Latin American history. The historians of urbanization analyze the geography of urban protest and its roots in the trials and tribulations—housing, public health, and others—that workers experienced in their neighborhoods and communities separate from their status as producers and union members.[21]

Popular Fronts and Populism (1930–60)

If there has been a "boom" in Latin American labor history over the last decades, especially among anglophone historians, it has been on the populist era. Taken together, these studies have led to a deep revision in the understanding of the working class's relationship to populism. Rejecting the highly schematic interpretations and working-class heteronomy posited by the classic studies on the populist phenomenon, such as those of Gino Germani, this new historical scholarship stresses the agency and identity of the workers themselves, especially as revealed through oral history, discourse analysis, and working-class biography. These studies have argued that rather than being manipulated masses, the workers who followed Perón, Cárdenas, Vargas, and lesser populist leaders gained from these movements an identity and a sense of empowerment, and therefore a real ability to advance their interests. This new scholarship has not emphasized the instrumentalist factors and concrete benefits awarded to the working class by these leaders, things they take as a given. Instead, they have focused on the cultural configurations and working-class consciousness that developed in conjunction with but were not solely constituted by improvements in wages, working conditions, and collective bargaining rights.

The new Latin American labor history has been less concerned with other aspects of the period. In addition to populism, the other outstanding development in the history of the Latin American working class in these years, indeed in many ways a crucial precipitant of the populist phenomenon, was the emergence of the communists as the dominant force in the labor movements in most of Latin America in the 1930s. Following the Third International and the Comintern's support for popular front strategies to defeat fascism, communist trade unionists followed pragmatic tactics of building strong union structures and winning tangible gains for their members. Their growth was phenomenal, particularly in manufacturing, construction, and mining. The greatest change in the Latin American labor movements in the 1930s was the drive to organize unskilled workers and create industrial unions. In this, the communists played the decisive role. The anticommunist thrust to Latin American populism has not been stressed enough by the new scholarship, yet it is the essential background to understanding people like Cárdenas, Perón, and Vargas. The idea that the populists spoke "truthfully" to the workers in a language that they could understand while communists engaged in wooly abstractions about class struggle and proletarian revolution—a favorite trope of the New Left–inflected Latin American labor history of the last two decades—certainly does not appear to have been the case in the 1930s and early 1940s. Indeed, populism was in part a deliberate attempt to stanch a deepening identity of at least sectors of the working class with the communist leadership of the unions whose influence was in ascendance.

This process was first played out in Mexico, where Cárdenas built a popular front of his own in the form of a revamped revolutionary party and sought to cooperate with the communists who had created Mexico's first industrial unions and the new labor confederation, the Confederación de Trabajadores Mexicanos (CTM). There still is no deeply researched, thorough study of the Mexican labor movement for the Cárdenas years. Some older books, by Joel Ashby and Marjorie Clark, are still useful, but are dated in a number of ways.[22] Mexican contributions have been only slightly better. Labor history has not until very recently been a favorite area of scholarship by Mexican historians, and the Spanish-language literature therefore is also thin. Arturo Anguiano's study of the Cárdenas years, and especially Alicia Hernández's contribution to the multivolume series *Historia de la revolución mexicana*, serve well as political histories of labor but have nothing on political economy, shop floor politics, labor law, gender, or cultural issues.[23] Among the unexplored questions given the dearth of historical scholarship on labor was the history of the communists in Mexico. Only Barry Carr's general history of Mexican communism broaches the subject in any depth.[24]

Cárdenas, a figure of the 1930s, the popular fronts, the Spanish Civil War, and the antifascist struggle, though often included as part of the Latin American populist trinity, was actually in many ways quite a different figure. The situation in Mexico in the 1930s was radically unlike that of Argentina or Brazil in the immediate postwar period. To strengthen his government, Cárdenas at first accepted the support of the PCM, offered as part of the communists' popular front strategies. Such support saved Cárdenas from a military coup in 1936, whereupon he built his agrarian reform, which allowed him to create an independent peasant base through the creation of the Confederación Nacional de Campesinos (CNC). Cárdenas then divided labor and the peasantry in the new Partido Revolucionario Mexicano (PRM) in 1938. Perón and the reinvented Vargas, products more of the Cold War, undertook more direct frontal assaults against the communists and against labor's independence generally. In Vargas's case, such policies obviously revealed continuities with the labor policies of the Estado Nôvo. The revisionist literature has regrettably missed, or at least underestimated or downplayed, the coercive side of the populist story. The role of the communists in the labor movements in the 1930s and the war years especially awaits further research.

Despite this omission, the historical scholarship of the so-called "new Latin American labor history" has marked a great advance in our understanding of the relationship between Latin American workers and populism. Certainly no one will ever think the same way again about the populist phenomenon as a result of these studies. The magnum opus in this scholarship was unquestionably Daniel James's study of Peronism and the working class, *Resistance and Integration*.[25] Some of the book's arguments are certainly open to debate. Though a useful device for his own thesis about the working-class predisposition for Peronism's discourse, James probably overstates (replicating the official Peronist discourse) the degree of working-class defeats, disarray, and demoralization in the 1930s and early 1940s as the prelude to Peronism. As Joel Horowitz's meticulous study of five unions in this period demonstrates, unions had learned to bargain fairly effectively, according to their strategic weight and political influence, with both private authorities and the state.[26] Not all was disarray and despair in the unions in the years preceding Perón's rise to power. Nonetheless, James shifted the focus of Peronism and the working class away from instrumentalist interpretations and on to the questions of the workers' Peronist identity in all its complexity and contradictions in a way no scholar, including Argentine scholars, had ever done. The book brilliantly analyzed the working class's conversion to a *peronista* political culture that proved protean, resilient, and formidable in its dealings with the state and employers.

James's study, for all its insightful and pathbreaking qualities, was nonetheless the culmination of a reassessment of Peronism and the working class that Argentine scholars had been engaged in for some time. In the late 1960s, Celia Durruty had first broken with the "Peronism as a pathology" interpretations and argued for Peronism's authenticity as a working-class movement and as a product of a history, not a mere instrument of demagoguery.[27] At around the same time, Miguel Murmis and Juan Carlos Portantiero had questioned the idea of an old versus new working class in the rise of Perón. In *Estudios sobre los orígenes del peronismo*, Murmis and Portantiero had argued that Perón's appeal had been across the board among the workers and not been confined to the new migrants, who supposedly lacked class identity and were prone to populist manipulation.[28] Juan Carlos Torre had similarly demonstrated with solid empirical evidence that in the origins of the Peronist movement, and specifically the October 17, 1945, protests that propelled Perón to power, the older, established unions had played the pivotal role in the mobilizations.[29] Finally, Hugo del Campo had analyzed the links and continuities with a previous union tradition that had influenced Perón's success in courting union support during his rise to power.[30]

Some of this revisionist literature had come from outside Argentina. For example, a foreign scholar, Walter Little, had shown that while in power, Perón was not able to absorb and subordinate completely the unions, despite the many institutions that the regime established (labor courts, collective bargaining practices, union certification). The Peronist unions retained a greater degree of autonomy than is generally thought, including the ability to strike. A deepening Peronist identity and the ability to represent rank-and-file interests were not necessarily incompatible with a genuine and effective representation of working-class interests.[31] Yet James's contribution was unique in its melding of oral testimony and working-class discourse as it appeared in such diverse sources as the labor press, union broadsides, and artifacts of popular culture such as tango lyrics. His study was unique in richness of detail and profound insights into Peronism as a political culture.

James's influence on Argentine historians who work on Peronism and the working class has been enormous. *Resistance and Integration* is an obligatory reference for any Argentine historian who studies the period, and oral history and working-class culture have become respectively the methodology of preference and dominant paradigm among them. In lesser hands, this has led sometimes to repetitive invocations of E. P. Thompson, Raymond Williams's "structure of feelings," and the tendency to always see culture and identity as the driving force in working class politics at the expense of issues of political economy, class interests, and power politics. The best historical scholarship, however, has fused James's cultural insights with the Latin Americans' continued preoccupation with material realities. Perhaps the signal example of an Argentine historian building on James's influence yet retaining her own distinctly Latin American sensibility is Mirta Lobato's recent book on the working-class community of Berisso. Lobato's analysis of the immigrant community and meatpacking center is among the most successful attempts to integrate social, political, and cultural history on a Latin American labor topic. Her intimate knowledge of the world of work in the meatpacking plants, the impact of the broader political conjunctures on the working-class community, and the changing perceptions and reconfigured identities of the workers make her book a major contribution to Argentine labor historiography for the period.[32]

Though not with the same sweep and analytical power as James's book, John French's study had a similar impact on the study of Brazilian populism. Like James's study, French's monograph, *The Brazilian Workers' ABC*, took issue with the classic interpretations that stressed populism's corporatist aspirations, its tendency towards social control, working-class demobilization, and union bureaucratization, represented in Brazilian political folklore in the symbol of the *pelego*.[33] Leônicio Martins Rodrigues, Francisco Weffort, and the sundry anglophone scholars who upheld the image of populism as working-class betrayal were reproached for a "flawed vision" of Brazilian labor history but also offered a compelling alternative interpretation. As in James's book, there are some questionable assertions in French's reappraisal of populism. In his effort to rescue the populist labor tradition, he dismisses too facilely the extent to which the post-1964 so-called new unionism that repudiated the populist legacy really was something entirely new and a more militant and authentic labor movement. Changes in the very structure of Brazilian industry, global economic forces, new collective bargaining practices, and political circumstances all helped to shape a unionism that was in some important ways a rupture with a discredited populist tradition. That tradition had become discredited not only with intellectuals but with the workers themselves, in a process that was not unique to Brazil.

Nonetheless, French convincingly argued that the workers effectively exploited the political alliances that populism made possible as well as the institutions, such as the labor courts, established by Vargas. French's interpretation was in some ways an even more heretical one than James's study for the Argentines, coming as it did in the midst of the enthusiasm over Lula, the new unionism, and the establishment of the Partido dos Trabalhadores, all of which based their claims to legitimacy on a repudiation of the populist labor tradition. Moreover, unlike James's study, it could not build its arguments as much on a rich revisionist literature written by Brazilians themselves, and confronted a more hostile intellectual environment in Brazil. Like James's study, it recast the debate on Brazilian populism and the working class, influencing interpretations not only of anglophone historians of Brazil but also Brazilian historians. A recent example of French's influence can be seen in the collection of essays *Na luta por direitos: Estudios em historia social do trabalho*, which picks up on *The Brazilian Workers' ABC*'s conclusions and demonstrates how, through their strikes, their identities, and union practices, populism opened a space for greater working-class activism and influence.[34] Rather than a betrayal, populism now appears as a vehicle, albeit one with certain contradictions and liabilities, for organized workers to advance their interests in both the public and private spheres. Historians have not studied populism in other countries characterized by populist movements such as Peru and Cuba with the same sophistication and critical acumen as Brazil and Argentina. Nonetheless, both James and French employed new social theories and methodologies and established a new paradigm, not to mention standards for studying the phenomenon, that will surely influence the subsequent studies of populism there and elsewhere in the region,

The populist era was a watershed in Latin American labor history in manifold ways. The period witnessed the decline of strictly class-based ideologies such as anarchism, socialism, syndicalism, and communism. Nationalism was in ascendance everywhere among the working class, and even the communists were forced to frame their trade union struggles in national terms. Indeed, it was the inability to do that as global events grew in their consequences and caused the communists to subordinate union tactics to the antifascist struggle and Moscow's directives that caused them to lose much of their hard-earned support among the workers. Populist leaders such as Cárdenas, Perón, and Vargas both articulated and were constituted by this working-class nationalism. Changes in the international and Latin American economies similarly were a catalyst and an outcome of this new working-class nationalism. State-supported industrialization and talk of a "national bourgeoisie" promised to uplift the nation and better distribute its wealth in a new emancipating project. At their May Day celebrations, workers might well now listen to government functionaries drably recount the latest accomplishments in building steel plants or industrial production rather than incendiary speeches on the evils of capitalism and calls for class war and international proletarian solidarity. The state had also implemented policies to incorporate them into the national mainstream, an incorporation that, as the new Latin American labor history has compellingly demonstrated, worked on multiple levels: political, institutional, and emotional.

Revolution, the New Unionism, and Transnationalism (1960–2000)

The most dramatic decades in Latin America's twentieth-century history, its age of revolution and counterrevolution in the postwar years, have received considerably less attention by the new anglophone Latin American labor history than did the populist era. Even when chronologically touching on these years, as the James and French monographs both do, its greatest insights have been on the populism and the working class. The vastly changed world that emerges with the onset of the Cold War, the triumph of the Cuban Revolution, and the consolidation of a new international economic order, commonly referred to as transnationalism, in some ways belied the revisionist interpretations offered by them on populism and the workers. New, grassroots currents within organized labor in the region, often openly repudiating the populist past, appeared. Their demands for union democracy, extending to calls for broader social and political reform, introduced a novel current within the labor movements of several countries. This "new unionism" has been extensively studied by political scientists, but less by the new labor history. Nonetheless, a number of important monographs on the period were written, though not necessarily adhering to the agenda set by the new Latin American labor history.

The most important changes affecting the Latin American working class in this period involved the increasing difficulties experienced by the state-supported industrialization policies and the weakening in economic nationalism generally, reflected in the growing presence of multinational enterprises, especially in manufacturing. With their global strategies for capital accumulation, modern technologies, and managerial practices, the multinationals represented the most advanced sectors of the industrial economy. The labor forces of these enterprises, once thought to constitute a privileged labor aristocracy, turned out to be some of the most militant and politically radicalized sectors of the organized working class. They were not the only ones. Increasingly, public sector workers, many of them employed in the tertiary sector as teachers, civil servants, and the like, assumed an important role in their labor movements and were key participants in the labor insurgencies of the 1960s and 1970s. Yet it was the workers in the most advanced sectors of industrial capitalism who held the strategic power and who led the great working protests of these years, establishing the first trade union and political alternatives to the populist politics that had characterized the middle decades of the twentieth century.

This process was played out with its greatest consequences in Brazil, which in these years emerged decisively as Latin America's most industrial nation. There the workers employed in São Paulo's industrial belt, especially in the large automotive complexes, led the first successful general strike against the military dictatorship in 1978, serving as the cynosure for sundry social movements that called for the end of military rule. These shop floor rebellions shook both the political and social foundations of the military government, coming as they did from the very place and very people who had most benefited from the so-called Brazilian miracle. This new labor movement and its leader, Lula da Silva, were also instrumental in the founding of a new political party, the Partido dos Trabalhadores (PT). The PT figured as the most important left-of-center party in the final two decades of the twentieth century in Latin America, and one that would, after many failed attempts, finally succeed in coming to power at the national level in the 2002 presidential elections. Brazilian labor history of this period is the most intensely studied of any in Latin American labor history, though curiously not by anglophone historians, who have yet to produce a single monograph on the topic. Brazilian historians, in contrast, have published a wide array of factory studies, oral histories, and sociocultural analyses of increasing sophistication and detail, both as published monographs and as PhD dissertations.[35]

If the new working class had its most transcendent expression in Brazil, its most dramatic one was in Argentina, and specifically in the wave of social movements and working-class protests there between 1969 and 1975. The epicenter of this social ferment and political agitation was the country's second urban center, Córdoba, which experienced a rapid industrialization process in the decade and a half following Perón's fall from power in 1955. In Córdoba's automotive plants and ancillary industries, a new working class formed in the space of a few years and quickly assumed a leadership role in the local labor movement while spearheading political opposition to military rule. These same workers also provided the shock troops for the 1969 *Cordobazo*, the greatest protest by the organized working class in postwar Latin America. This working-class and labor movement has been studied in depth, both in my sociopolitical history and in Córdoban historian Mónica Gordillo's more sociocultural study.[36] Both books have served as starting points for an explosion in research by a younger generation of Argentine historians. These historians are deepening the scholarship on the many issues, making Córdoba, after Brazil, the best and most intensely researched of any locale in postwar Latin America.[37] The question that has driven their research, as it did Brennan and Gordillo's, is why such militancy and political radicalism failed to generate a viable independent working-class movement and political party such as Brazil's. This interrogative leads them back to the perennial question of Peronism's complex and contradictory relationship with the working class, but also to the praxis and practices of the Argentine left in these years and to the effects of the country's murderous state terrorism.

For Latin America's other large industrial economy, Mexico, the so-called new unionism class has not received the same attention. Twentieth-century Mexican historiography generally continues to be dominated by agrarian history and peasant studies, with comparatively much less work having been done on industry and labor than for Brazil or Argentina. The postwar period is the most neglected of all.[38]

Some research on the labor insurgencies of the 1970s has produced worthy contributions to the historiography, and there have been a handful of studies on the great 1958 general strike. Otherwise, the Mexican working class of these years remains all but invisible. The most important contribution to labor history for this period is actually not a conventional labor history per se but Jeffrey Bortz's very good study of industrial wages for Mexico City. Bortz demonstrates the deterioration of Mexican workers' wages relative to the increase in workers productivity and inflation rate and in the process provides a corpus of invaluable information for future political and social histories of the Mexico City working class.[39] Otherwise, the shining exception to historians' deafness to the Mexican working class as a social and political actor in the postwar period is Rosalina Estrada Urroz's study of the "condición obrera" in Puebla, *Del telar a la cadena de montaje*. Puebla, already a major textile center, experienced rapid industrialization and investment by foreign multinationals, mainly automotive and ancillary plants. In a process reminiscent of Córdoba's, the former ecclesiastical center's industrial base was transformed, the size of the industrial working class greatly augmented, and a militant labor movement created. Though not sufficiently analytical, Estrada Urroz's work is unique for Mexico and has few competitors elsewhere in the region for the richness of its data, detail, and scope. Her study covers virtually every aspect of working-class life in these years—work, wages and living standards, strikes—though it is silent on the favorite paradigm of the new anglophone labor history, identity and working-class culture, which perhaps explains why it has been ignored.[40]

The starting point for interest in a new political history for Latin American workers and for the vogue in oral history as a methodology was undoubtedly Peter Winn's *Weavers of Revolution*. Almost thirty years after its original publication, Winn's book still remains the most complete labor history for Latin America. Winn engages no social theory, uses oral sources in a more traditional way than do the current practitioners of "popular memory," yet presents an impeccably integrated history that analyzes both capital and labor, masterfully weaving together broader political events with a microhistory of the factory, all in a compelling if slightly romanticized account of workers and revolution.[41] Winn's book also reminds us that, all the justified attention to the "new unionism" in this period notwithstanding, the vast majority of Latin American workers continue to labor in the traditional industries such as textiles and are immersed in industrial relations systems inherited from the populist period. Such continuities justify the new anglophone scholarship's concentration on the populist era as the crucible of twentieth-century labor history. For workers and revolution, there is no comparable study for revolutionary Cuba, though Linda Fuller's *Work and Democracy in Socialist Cuba* offers a sober analysis and useful counterpoint to Winn's epic account of a socialist transformation of the workplace.[42]

For the vast majority of Latin American workers, these years were not so public or dramatic as they were for the new working class or workers in Allende's Chile or revolutionary Cuba. For workers living through the apogee and then collapse of the national capitalist model, their history was first one of greater access to state-supported education, health, and social security programs, rising living standards, and new consumption habits. The first postwar government did not dismantle the reforms of the populist period in that regard, and in fact extended and deepened the activities of the *estado bienestar*. The dramatic effects of such monumental changes for the Latin American working class have yet to be studied, either in their populist origins or during the *desarrollista* governments of the 1950s and 1960s. The history of consumption, a well-established field in European and U.S. labor history, is a particularly surprising lacuna, given the current fashion for working-class identity and culture outside of production.[43] More understandable has been the scant attention paid to the collapse of the national capitalist model, the neoliberal ascendancy, and survival in the harsh realities of a hostile social environment. The very identity as a worker, an identity gaining in intensity over the course of a century, crumbled or was profoundly altered in the final decades of the century. Neither the assault on working-class identity nor the global economic processes underlying these changes have been studied yet by historians, though a rich sociological and economic literature has appeared on these issues, one that historians in the future will be able to tap. A final lacuna is the precise impact of the Cold War on the Latin American movements and what might be more generally described as "Americanization," particularly, again, on the issue of consumption and its effects on consciousness and world views.

An Alternative Agenda?

Perhaps the best way to assess the current state of Latin American labor history is to consider recent studies by the two anglophone historians who have done the most to promote the field over the last twenty years. Daniel James's *Doña María's Story* and John French's *Drowning in Laws* highlight the achievements, but also expose some of the limitations, of the recent Latin American labor history.[44] As in their previous books, both historians are primarily concerned in their new monographs with the relationship between populism and the working class. Neither has recanted his revisionist vision of populism's ability, even against its own intentions, to provide a vehicle for working-class identity and interests. Both books have a number of virtues. James deftly and with a sharp critical eye deconstructs Doña María's testimony as he explores the most unknown element of Peronism's history, indeed one absent from his own *Resistance and Integration*: the gendered dimension of the Peronist working-class identity. French rightly stresses the importance of the law as a locus of labor politics and Brazil's industrial relations system, entering into an area of historical research rich with possibilities but virtually ignored by historians of Latin American labor.

Yet the approach of both in these monographs also has some shortcomings, ones that I would extend to the new Latin American labor history's minimalist agenda generally. James's foray into testimony and working-class biography in *Doña María's*

Story probably should not be imitated by other historians, particularly younger ones. In attempting to understand groups such as a particular social class (as opposed to conventional biography on dominant personalities), historical scholarship generally does not rely on individual character studies or psychological portraits (or its academic equivalent, discourse analysis), something we leave to novelists and others, but to collective human experience. As I read James's book, I thought of my own Doña María, my landlady during the years that I was living and doing research in Córdoba. Mine was not so admirable or even likable a personality as James's, truculently nationalist, fiercely anticommunist, faintly anti-Semitic, and "a lifelong *peronista,*" just like the former Berisso meatpacking worker. Who is to say whose individual testimony tells us more about what it means to be a Peronist working-class woman?

I see nothing wrong with a talented historian like James, with such an intimate understanding of Peronism and so many cogent insights on Argentine working-class culture, writing a book like this. Indeed, the book should probably be read as much as James's ruminations on the methodology of oral history as a statement on gender and identity. Yet the results in less expert hands would surely be more pedestrian; and even in his, the explanatory power of an approach such as that employed in *Doña María's Story* is limited. All this is not to say that oral history cannot be a valuable methodology in reconstructing working-class biography. It clearly can, but the emphasis needs to be on the collective rather than individual experience, prosopography rather than a cappella autobiography. Similarly, French's treatment of the law as a cultural artifact, as both the expression of a highly legalistic and litigious industrial relations system and the shaper of a peculiar working-class consciousness barely exploits the possibilities of studying the law. A thorough, painstaking, and meticulous study of case law (important in civil law systems like Brazil's, not just in common law ones) would probably do much more to explain the conundrum that French admirably elucidates but never really resolves: why did workers remain loyal to, or at least ambivalent about, the *getulista* labor code that apparently did so little for them? His response is strictly ideational: the creation of a "juridical consciousness of class." Perhaps, but to have acquired such a consciousness surely is a more complicated story than simply the propagation of a powerful discursive myth. Some of the explanation is probably to be found in the intricacies of the law itself and the role of the law in Brazilian society beyond its duplicities and apparent formalism.[45]

In a recent interview, James and French noted a certain loss of momentum, even interest, in labor history among the upcoming generation of Latin Americanists.[46] Multiple factors explain this, among them professional pressures and the lack of interest in labor history in the dominant U.S. and European fields and the implications of that for hiring practices. So some loss of interest is probably inevitable and beyond our ability to do much of anything about. Yet a degree of gravitas, if not vitality, can be injected by reconceptualizing the field. At least one of them has proposed as a solution greatly widening the parameters of what constitutes labor history, to the point that it becomes conterminous with virtually everything in the Latin American past, from the history of slavery to agrarian history to that of the middle class, apparently wherever subalterns and identity appear.[47] That does not strike me as a happy resolution to a genuine dilemma that both James and French have correctly pointed out. Restoring some momentum to Latin American labor history does not seem to me best served by going poaching in distant or even nearby fields. Widening the parameters too broadly undermines the very rationale of having any specialized field: to establish common sets of interests, a common vocabulary, and common standards with which to evaluate one another's work. The histories of slavery, of rural society, even of the middle class raise their own complicated issues. Moreover, there is still so much yet to learn about Latin American labor and the working class that it is unnecessary; we have more than enough to keep ourselves busy.[48]

Labor history needs to be more broadly defined, but also with clear limits. My own preference is to widen labor history beyond the issues of identity and political culture that now dominate the scholarship. The object of study should be nothing more and nothing less than the many industrial worlds of modern Latin America. In part, this would mean a return to political economy and undertaking new studies of work. Studies of technology, work practices, and labor politics by industrial sector have virtually disappeared from labor history, where they were never very prominent in the first place. They need to be encouraged and the research published. But the broader political economy also needs to be addressed. One of the hallmarks of labor in modern capitalism, a characteristic that merely intensified in the postwar period, is its physical mobility. "Transnationalism" refers not only to the spread of multinational corporations and the internationalization of production, it also implies the creation of a kind of global capitalist labor market. The movements of Latin American workers internationally and within countries, the development of segmented labor markets—these and other questions should find a place among labor historians. Demography should also be revived. A field with a long and distinguished tradition for colonialists, historical demography is needed to provide some sociological precision about the region's working populations, and it can contribute to debates, for example, on the formal versus informal economy and standards of living.

Good labor history will also be good business history. The two fields, the first already well established and the second only now developing, will evolve, or stagnate, in unison. This Latin American business history will include but go beyond Chandlerian study of the firm, and with a more critical perspective that addresses larger issues of capitalist development and those appropriate to peripheral capitalist economies. Just as labor history is more than simply a study of unions and deals with the working class on multiple levels, so business history of the sort I am proposing will move beyond the study of the firm to become a history of the Latin American industrial bourgeoisie. This bourgeoisie's relationship with the state, with their workers, and with one another will form the critical counterpoint to the history of labor, and indeed, I would argue that one cannot be understood without the other.[49] Such a business history should consider not only the national bourgeoisie but also the international one and the pressures and constraints exercised by the global economy, an issue that Bergquist bravely raised but one that became too restrictive and monocausal in his analysis. The capital accumulation strategies of global corporations and their connections to national economies and local business groups certainly matter a great deal to the workers affected by them, and they are vitally important issues for labor historians to grapple with.

Among the implications for what I am proposing is that labor historians will gain greater knowledge of other disciplines of direct bearing on labor history. For those interested in the enormously important area of labor law, a formal training in the law and legal theory will raise the level of scholarship. Some background in labor economics and familiarity with the industrial relations literature also seem to me obligatory for anyone who seriously seeks to study working people. Workers do have identities, but those identities are contingent on larger forces, ones that their identities can perhaps resist but cannot avoid. Therefore, no one can seriously hope to study those who have toiled in Latin America's factories, mines, and workshops without some understanding of how labor markets work. There should also be some space again in our ranks for the econometricians, since their quantification adds enormously to our understanding of the larger forces at play for Latin American workers. More studies such as Jeffrey Bortz's study of wages in postwar Mexico City are absolutely vital.[50] In addition to formal training in such things as the law, labor economics, and econometrics, I would urge more eclectic, wide-ranging interests than we currently find among labor historians. Some interest in the history of technology, for example, not just the ability to invoke Foucault, Derrida, or Bourdieu, seems essential to me, as does research in the kinds of sources labor historians rarely, if ever, utilize: engineering manuals, miners' handbooks, and business archives, among others.[51]

The same can be said for cultural studies of labor and the working class. The world of perceptions, identities, and representations, relying heavily on oral history as a methodology, will and should continue to be written. My opinion is that this area of historical research needs to be done in close collaboration with Latin American scholars. In an area of research in which the nuances, inflections, and elliptical meanings of language are everything, it is more than a little presumptuous to think a foreign scholar can plumb the depths of language and working-class argot with anything approaching the understanding of a native speaker. Indeed, reading (and hearing) some of the more strident advocates of oral history and popular memory, one has to seriously question the rigor of some of the recent forays into oral history. When they reproduce textually parts of their interviews, a regrettably infrequent procedure, debatable and even mistaken translations are all too common. I personally have deep reservations about the ability of anyone to conduct serious oral history without the ability to speak fluent, idiomatic Spanish or Portuguese. I am afraid far too few practitioners of oral history and popular memory actually do. Anglophone (read North American) historians should swallow some of their hubris, recognize the limitations that inevitably exist when studying a foreign culture, and undertake oral histories in tandem with Latin American scholars. Those who do so should not only show some natural talent for language but also probably have some formal training in linguistics. Empathy and a tape recorder are fine, but identity and culture as they are discernible through language require a more rigorous training in the intricacies of language itself. If historians want to work as ethnographers, they have will have to use the tools of a real ethnography.

As a general proposition, the cultural approaches that have steadily become more prevalent in the Latin American labor history of the last two decades need to establish a dialogue with the theories and methods of social history if they are to avoid a fixation on the merely anecdotal, even trivial.[52] In some ways, this would mean simply finding common ground between the continuing preoccupations of Latin American historians with issues of the economy, social class, and power politics and the recent contributions of anglophone historians on political culture and gender. Ideally, a good labor historian will have the ability to integrate all these things. So I am proposing an open-minded and less parochial stance from all sides. Labor history has produced a solid corpus of monographs and has come a long way from rather humble beginnings just over two decades ago. The studies discussed above have all advanced our knowledge, which is the purpose of scholarship. A few have even fundamentally reshaped our understanding of the history of the Latin American working class. But labor history has the ability to do much more than celebrate workers' identity and chronicle their resistance.[53] A more ambitious labor history will also permit the field to overcome its current doldrums and even a certain ghettoization, making its own unique and important contributions to explaining the Latin American dilemma.

Labor history does have the ability to engage bigger questions about the Latin American past, and those possibilities should be exploited. The region's defining issues, the ones that Latin Americans most discuss in public discourse and that have animated the preoccupations of its historians and social scientists, indeed its very art and literature, are the resilience of poverty and inequality in the region and how they have buttressed dictatorship. Why should not labor historians add their voice to the debates on Latin American industrialization, for example, and contribute their unique insights to the social, political, and technological factors that influenced industrialization beyond the state policies and comparative cost and benefits that figure so prominently in the neoclassical perspectives of many economic historians? Is not labor, and the greater power of Argentine unions politically and of workers on the shop floor compared to Brazil, an important part of the explanation for the more successful postwar capital accumulation strategies of the Brazilian bourgeoisie and the greater stability of military rule there compared to Argentina? To help answer these and other great, historically momentous questions, Latin American labor history will have to build on the recent achievements reviewed in this essay, but also set a more ambitious agenda for the future.

NOTES

1. I am speaking here of academic scholarship. There is, of course, a long, distinguished tradition of labor history written by union militants and party activists. This literature is particularly rich for Argentina; see, for example, Diego Abad de Santillán,

La F.O.R.A.: Ideología y trayectoria del movimiento obrero revolucionario en la Argentina (Buenos Aires: Nervio, 1933); Sebastián Marotta, *El movimiento sindical argentino: Su génesis y desarrollo*, 3 vols. (Buenos Aires: Lacio, 1960); Jacinto Oddone, *Gremialismo proletario argentino* (Buenos Aires: La Vanguardia, 1949). An example for Mexico is Alfonso López Aparicio, *El movimiento obrero en Mexico, antecedentes, desarrollo y tendencias* (Mexico City: Editorial Jus, 1952).

2. Robert J. Alexander, *Labor Relations in Argentina, Brazil, and Chile* (New York: McGraw–Hill, 1962).

3. There exist various attempts by anglophone scholars to provide an overview of Latin American labor historiography, beginning with some that took stock of the existing scholarship just as the field was entering a period of relative dynamism. Within the last few years, more recent assessments of the scholarship of the previous quarter century have appeared. All provide a useful perspective of the field at given moments in its development: Kenneth Paul Erickson, Patrick V. Peppe, and Hobart A. Spalding, "Research on the Urban Working Class and Organized Labor in Argentina, Brazil, and Chile: What is Left to be Done?" *Latin American Research Review* 9:2 (1974): 15–42; Judith Evans, "Results and Prospects: Some Observations on Latin American Labor Studies," *International Labor and Working-Class History* 16 (Fall 1979): 15–42; Eugene Sofer, "Recent Trends in Latin American Labor Historiography," *Latin American Research Review* 15:1 (1980): 165–76; Ian Roxborough, "The Analysis of Labour Movements in Latin America: Typologies and Theories," *Bulletin of Latin American Research* 1:1 (1981): 81–95; Emilia Viotti da Costa, "Experience versus Structures: New Tendencies in the History of Labour and the Working Class in Latin America: What Do We Gain? What Do We Lose?" *International Labor and Working Class History* 36 (Fall 1989): 3–24; John D. French, "The Latin American Labor Studies Boom," *International Review of Social History* 45:2 (August 2000): 279–308; Joel Wolfe, "The Social Subject versus the Political: Latin American Labor Studies at a Crossroads," *Latin American Research Review* 37:2 (2002): 244–62.

4. Viotti da Costa's above-cited review essay was the first to speak of a "new labor history" for Latin America. In reality, given the recent emergence and underdeveloped nature of labor history for Latin America at the time, it was "new" only in the sense of joining, belatedly, already established currents in the dominant European and U.S. fields. That new labor history for Europe and the United States had rebelled decades before against the old institutional labor history, still being practiced at the time and appearing in venerable if somewhat stodgy journals such as *Labor History*.

5. David Sowell, *The Early Colombian Labor Movement: Artisans and Politics in Bogotá, 1832–1919* (Philadelphia: Temple University Press, 1992).

6. Luis Alberto Romero and Hilda Sabato, *Los trabajadores de Buenos Aires: La experiencia del mercado, 1850–1880* (Buenos Aires: Sudamericana, 1992).

7. Gabriel Salazar, *Labradores, peones y proletarios: Formación y crisis de la sociedad popular chilena del siglo XIX* (Santiago: LOM Ediciones, 2000), 263–69.

8. Mario Trujillo Bolio, *Operarios fabriles en el valle de México, 1864–1884* (Mexico City: El Colegio de México, 1997), 168–72.

9. John Lear, *Workers, Neighbors, and Citizens: The Revolution in Mexico City* (Lincoln: University of Nebraska Press, 2001), 173–74. Though neither centrally concerned with the anarchist question nor a labor history strictly speaking, another notable contribution to the history of labor during the Mexican Revolution is Jonathan Brown's study of the oil industry, *Oil and Revolution in Mexico* (Berkeley: University of California Press, 1993).

10. Peter DeShazo, *Urban Workers and Labor Unions in Chile, 1902–1927* (Madison: University of Wisconsin Press, 1983), 245–46.

11. Boris Fausto, *Trabalho urbano e conflito social* (São Paulo: DIFEL, 1977), 62–79.

12. Santillán, *La F.O.R.A.*; Osvaldo Bayer, *Los vengadores de la Patagonia trágica* (Buenos Aires: Galerna, 1973); Juan Suriano, *Anarquistas: Cultura y política libertaria en Buenos Aires, 1890–1910* (Buenos Aires: Manantial, 2001).

13. William E. French, *A Peaceful and Working People: Manners, Morals, and Class Formation in Northern Mexico* (Albuquerque: University of New Mexico Press, 1996).

14. Julio Pinto Vallejos, *Trabajos y rebeldías en la pampa salitrera: El ciclo del salitre y la reconfiguración de las identidades populares (1850–1900)* (Santiago: Editorial Universidad de Santiago, 1998).

15. Julio César Jobet, *El partido socialista de Chile*, 2 vols.(Santiago: Ediciones Prensa Latinoamericana, 1971), and Jacinto Oddone, *Gremialismo proletario argentino* (Buenos Aires: La Vanguardia, 1949) are just two of many examples.

16. The best study on the 1920s, especially strong on labor's ideological disputes and political conflicts, is Leticia Gamboa, *La urdimbre y la trama: Historia social de los obreros textiles de Atlixco, 1899–1924* (Mexico City: Fondo de Cultura Económica, 2001).

17. Joel Wolfe, *Working Women, Working Men: São Paulo and the Rise of Brazil's Industrial Working Class, 1900–1955* (Durham, N.C.: Duke University Press, 1993), 16–25.

18. Elizabeth Quay Hutchison, *Labors Appropriate to Their Sex: Gender, Labor, and Politics in Urban Chile, 1900–1930* (Durham, N.C.: Duke University Press, 2001).

19. Thomas M. Klubock, *Contested Communities: Class, Gender, and Politics in Chile's El Teniente Copper Mine, 1904–1951* (Durham, N.C.: Duke University Press, 1998). One can speculate that the engendering of Chilean history was the result of the conjugation of the end of the long Pinochet dictatorship, and the greater possibilities for research the restoration of democracy provided, with the North American boom in gender studies. This engendering is not confined to labor history and covers everything from the popular front to the *Unidad Popular* agrarian reform.

20. Ann Farnsworth-Alvear, *Dulcinea in the Factory: Myths, Morals, Men, and Women in Colombia's Industrial Experiment, 1905–1960* (Durham, N.C.: Duke University Press, 2000).

21. Ronn Pineo and James A. Baer, eds., *Cities of Hope: People, Protests, and Progress in Urbanizing Latin America, 1870–1930* (Boulder, Colo.: Westview Press, 1998).

22. Joel C. Ashby, *Organized Labor and the Mexican Revolution under Lázaro Cárdenas* (Chapel Hill: University of North Carolina Press, 1963) and Marjorie Clark, *Organized Labor in Mexico* (Chapel Hill: University of North Carolina Press, 1934).

23. Arturo Anguiano, *El estado y la política obrera del cardenismo* (Mexico City: Ediciones Era, 1975); Alicia Hernández Chávez, *La mecánica cardenista*, vol. 16 of *La historia de la revolución mexicana*, ed. Luis González (Mexico City: El Colegio de México, 1979).

24. Barry Carr, *Marxism and Communism in Twentieth-Century Mexico* (Lincoln: University of Nebraska Press, 1992). There are also good pages on Cárdenas and the communists in Michael Snodgrass, *Deference and Defiance in Monterrey: Workers, Paternalism, and Revolution in Mexico, 1890–1950* (Cambridge: Cambridge University Press, 2003), and Myrna Santiago makes interesting connections between labor and environmental history in *The Ecology of Oil: Environment, Labor and the Mexican Revolution, 1900–1938* (Cambridge: Cambridge University Press, 2006).

25. Daniel James, *Resistance and Integration: Peronism and the Argentine Working Class, 1946–1976* (Cambridge: Cambridge University Press, 1988).

26. Joel Horowitz, *Argentine Unions, the State, and the Rise of Perón, 1930–1945* (Berkeley: Institute of International Studies, 1990).

27. Celia Durruty, *Clase obrera y peronismo* (Córdoba: Pasado y Presente, 1969).

28. Miguel Murmis and Juan Carlos Portantiero, *Estudios sobre los orígenes del peronismo* (Buenos Aires: Siglo XXI, 1972).

29. Juan Carlos Torre, "La CGT y el 17 de octubre de 1945," *Todo es historia* 103 (March 1976).

30. Hugo del Campo, *Sindicalismo y peronismo: Los comienzos de un vínculo perdurable* (Buenos Aires: CLACSO, 1983).

31. Walter Little, "La organización obrera y el estado peronista, 1945–1955," *Desarrollo Económico* 19:75 (1979).

32. Mirta Z. Lobato, *La vida en las fábricas: Trabajo, protesta y política en una comunidad obrera, Berisso (1904–1970)* (Buenos Aires: Prometeo/Entrepasados, 2001).

33. John D. French, *The Brazilian Workers' ABC: Class Conflict and Alliances in Modern São Paulo* (Chapel Hill: University of North Carolina Press, 1992).

34. Alexandre Fortes et al., *Na luta por direitos: Estudos recentes em história social do trabalho* (Campinas: Unicamp, 1999).

35. See the extensive historiography on this period in John D. French and Alexander Fortes, *Urban Labor History in Twentieth-Century Brazil: An Annotated Introduction to the Bibliography* (Albuquerque: Latin American Institute, University of New Mexico, 1998).

36. James P. Brennan, *The Labor Wars in Córdoba: Ideology, Work, and Labor Politics in an Argentine Industrial City, 1955–1976* (Cambridge: Harvard University Press, 1994); Mónica Gordillo, *Córdoba en los '60: La experiencia del sindicalismo combativo* (Córdoba: Universidad Nacional de Córdoba, 1996). Brennan and Gordillo have recently coauthored a book that combines their findings along with some new research and conclusions in *Córdoba rebelde: El Cordobazo, el clasismo, y la movilización social, 1969–1976* (Buenos Aires: De la Campana, 2008).

37. A sampling of some of this work can be read in Mónica Gordillo, ed., *Actores, prácticas, discursos en la Córdoba combativa: Una aproximación a la cultura política de los '70* (Córdoba: Ferreyra, 2001).

38. Two fine doctoral dissertations, however, have helped to remedy the situation: Kenneth Maffett, "Alternating Currents in Mexican Labor: Electrical Manufacturing Workers in Mexico City, 1968–1986" (PhD diss., University of California at San Diego, 2000) and Steven Bachelor, "The Edge of Miracles: Postrevolutionary Mexico City and the Remaking of the Industrial Working Class, 1925–1982" (PhD diss., Yale University, 2003).

39. Jeffrey Bortz, *El salario en México* (Mexicto City: El Caballito, 1986), 40–52.

40. Rosalina Estrada Urroz, *Del telar a la cadena de montaje: La condición obrera en Puebla, 1940–1976* (Puebla: Universidad Autónoma de Puebla, 1997).

41. Peter Winn, *Weavers of Revolution: The Yarur Workers and Chile's Road to Socialism* (Oxford: Oxford University Press, 1986).

42. Linda Fuller, *Work and Democracy in Socialist Cuba* (Philadelphia: Temple University Press, 1992).

43. Some work has been done on consumption for the populist period. For the Argentine case, see the pathbreaking essay by Juan Carlos Torre and Elisa Pastoriza, "La democratización del bienestar," *Nueva historia argentina*, vol. 8 (Buenos Aires: Sudamericana, 2002), 257–312, and also the doctoral dissertation by Eduardo Elena, "Justice and Comfort: Peronist Political Culture and the Search for a New Argentina, 1930–1955" (PhD diss., Princeton University, 2002).

44. Daniel James, *Doña María's Story: Life History, Memory, and Political Identity* (Durham, N.C.: Duke Universtity, 2000) and John D. French, *Drowning in Laws: Labor Law and Brazilian Political Culture* (Chapel Hill: University of North Carolina Press, 2004).

45. On the emerging field of Latin American labor law, see Line Schjolden, "Suing for Justice: Labor and the Courts in Argentina, 1900–1943" (PhD diss., University of California,

Berkeley, 2002) and William Suárez-Potts, "The Making of Labor Law in Mexico, 1875–1934" (PhD diss., Harvard University, 2004).

46. "Pensar a America Latina: Entrevista de Daniel James e John French," in *Na luta por direitos*, p. 207.

47. John D. French, "The Laboring and Middle-Class Peoples of Latin America and the Caribbean: Historical Trajectories and New Research Directions," in *Global Labour History: A State of the Art*, ed. Jan Lucassen (Bern: Peter Lang, 2006), 289–333.

48. I am, of course, not suggesting that labor historians fail to read widely and shut themselves off from the findings in other fields. As I have stated in this essay, I believe the immigration-urbanization literature, to mention just one example, is of direct relevance to labor history. I am suggesting, however, that to say labor history is everything is ultimately to say it is nothing, to deny that it has its own unique concerns and should develop its own methods to address them.

49. An exception to the general neglect of the industrial bourgeoisie's history is Barbara Weinstein, *For Social Peace in Brazil: Industrialists and the Making of the Working Class in São Paulo, 1920–1964* (Chapel Hill: University of North Carolina Press, 1996). Though she examines only one aspect of the *paulista* bourgeoisie's history, its welfare and worker-training programs, Weinstein at least recognized the importance of capital's history to labor history. For the Argentine case, see James P. Brennan and Marcelo Rougier, *The Politics of National Capitalism: Peronism and the Argentine Bourgeoisie, 1946–1976* (University Park: Penn State University Press 2009).

50. For a brilliant example of how econometrics can contribute to labor history, see Aurora Gómez-Galvarriato, "Measuring the Impact of Institutional Change in Capital-Labor Relations in the Mexican Textile Industry, 1900–1930," in *The Mexican Economy, 1870–1930: Essays on the Economic History of Institutions, Revolution, and Growth*, ed. Jeffrey L. Bortz and Stephen Haber (Stanford: Stanford University Press, 2002). Gómez Galvarriato has developed the first modern index of real wages in Mexico for the period 1900–30.

51. This point is forcefully made in John Womack's new book, *Posición estratégica obrera: Hacia una nueva historia de los movimientos obreros* (Mexico City: Fondo de Cultura Económica, 2008). Though I do not think labor history should be limited to issues of work, strategy, and strategic position, Womack does certainly make a compelling case for their neglect by labor historians, of Latin America and elsewhere.

52. This is not something I would confine only to labor history but would extend to other areas of historical scholarship; indeed, it is hardly a position original with me and is becoming a widespread sentiment among professional historians. For a recent terse but eloquent statement in support of a reevaluation of social history's importance to cultural history, see Paula S. Fass, "Cultural History/Social History: Reflections on a Continuing Dialogue," *Journal of Social History* 37:1 (2003): 39–45.

53. Perhaps it is time for labor historians who are interested in resistance to address a related issue: the absence of it. Workers devise all kinds of strategies to escape their class status, and "resistance" of the kind favored by the new Latin American labor history is usually a last resort. Latin American scholars, confronted by the region's harsh realities on a daily basis, are far more aware of this than their North American counterparts. See for example, Jorge Parodi, *To Be a Worker: Identity and Politics in Peru*, trans. James Alstrum and Catherine Conaghan (Chapel Hill: University of North Carolina Press, 2000).

CHAPTER 12

GENDER AND SEXUALITY IN LATIN AMERICA

DONNA J. GUY

Now is an ideal moment to reflect upon the accomplishments and future challenges of Latin American gender and sexuality history since 1810. Although it has been more noticeable since the late 1970s, there has always been an ethnographic and historical tradition of gender and sexuality studies within the region. One only has to glance at the voluminous bibliography of pre-1977 works on Latin American women compiled by Meri Knaster and Lynn Stoner's subsequent 1988 bibliography to demonstrate the long-standing interest.[1]

Theories regarding gender and sexuality have developed principally in Europe and the United States, but Latin America has always been at the forefront of challenging and/or reaffirming notions that have been formulated by researchers working on other parts of the world. That does not mean that gender and sexuality have had a different historical evolution in Latin America, or that they necessarily have different meanings. Culture plays an important role in the development of gender and sex roles, and so do other factors such as religion, capitalism, the nature of the state, race and ethnic relations, colonialism, and law. Latin America has been more willing than other postcolonial regions to recognize the intersections of European, Indigenous, and African cultures in ways that were not initially considered central to early European and U.S. gender studies. Latin American gender and sexuality studies also have not always been affected by the demands of U.S. and Western European sexual politics. Equally important, even when similar patterns have been observed in Latin America, Europe, and the United States, the timing and meanings have often been different. The result has been fresh insights that, in the twenty-first century, should position the history of Latin American gender and sexuality at the center of theoretical and case studies rather than at the margins. This has been shown clearly in the edited volume of William French and Katherine Bliss, where the editors and contributors show the tremendous impact that both gender and sexuality theories have had on Latin American history.[2] This essay focuses on a series of questions that have been addressed in modern Latin American history and interdisciplinary studies and points out the universality, rather than the particularity, of their contributions. It will also raise some questions for future research.

One of the thorniest questions posed by the rise of women's history and gender studies has been the centrality of male oppression in proposing definitions of gender and sexuality and how they can be examined historically. After all, if the sexual and social relations between men and women have no patterns of change as well as continuity over time, then historians would have great difficulty historicizing this experience. At the same time, however, we need to understand the implications of historicizing the history of sexuality and gender studies generally, particularly their implications and relationship to women's studies.

Early proponents of women's studies focused almost exclusively on the power battles between men and women. While forcing us to confront inequality as the central endeavor of the field, gendered subordination sometimes obscured the complex patterns of gender relations among people of the same sex as well as between men and women. In 1974 Sherry Ortner published a pathbreaking essay, one that has become part of the canonical literature of anthropological and women's studies. It was titled "Is Female to Male as Nature Is to Culture?" and in it Ortner argued that the "secondary status of women in society is one of the true universals, a pan-cultural fact."[3] The ubiquitousness of female subordination, argued Ortner, meant that the differences separating the experiences of women across time and space were shaped less by cultural practices and more by differences essentialized by concepts of nature. She argued carefully that this was not simply the result of biological determinism. Instead women had become "a symbol of something that every culture devalues, something that every culture defines as being of a lower order of existence than itself... and that is 'nature' in the most generalized sense." Men, in contrast, were closer to culture, which she defined as "human consciousness and its products."[4]

The resulting gender differences were internalized and accepted by both women and men. She then gave examples of many cultures where this observation was apparent to her, and concluded that no societies had been either egalitarian or matrifocal, and that concepts of ritual pollution had aided the development of women's inferior status.

In this essay, Ortner contributed to the idea of pancultural female subordination by emphasizing that women socialized themselves to accept their inferiority, an argument expressed in class terms by Brazilian pedagogue Paulo Freire in his 1970 classic *Pedagogy of the Oppressed*. Freire argued that education could lead to the liberation of the poor from their oppression, both male and female, whereas Ortner argued that for women this could not be accomplished without structural change, an argument that was particularly Latin American, as education had always been seen as the road to civilizing the indigenous population.[5]

At the same time, however, Latin American gender specialists have made us painfully aware of how, even during revolutionary movements that present structural changes, gender oppression has impeded not only the advancement of women but also that of the larger society. This inquiry began with feminist analysis of the 1959 Cuban Revolution, which espoused liberation for all, and even promoted an antipatriarchal 1975 family law, but never really shared power with women. More recent works on political and land reform have shown systemic resistance to power sharing with women, no matter what the law or political ideology of the government in power. Among the few successful gender-focused strategies utilized by women to gain access to power have been the emphasis on women's rights through motherhood and the use of community-based political movements to advance women's rights. These are not typical of Western European countries, and Latin American patterns relate to factors such as an often unsympathetic left, the influence of Catholic ideology, and the role of conservative women in these societies. Furthermore, recent works on Mexico during and after the 1910 Revolution, particularly those of Jocelyn Olcott and the edited collection by Olcott, Mary Kay Vaughn, and Gabriela Cano, show contradictory records of gendered and sexual success for revolutionary women and men.[6]

In the long run, I think that Freire and the early advocates of education had the more accurate perception of how people could free themselves in both sexual and class terms, and this has been borne out by early as well as recent studies. These have shown, among other things, that declining reproductive rates throughout the world are linked to female education and employment. Furthermore, state politics, rather than religious values, masculine opposition, or feminist efforts, can be catalysts promoting greater gender equity. Other studies show how women have broken the boundaries of labor segmentation by gender, but not always by following the course chosen by male laborers working through labor unions. The absence of early urban industrialization in many countries, the impact of female-headed households, and local customs emphasizing female morality have all had their impact, impacts that have changed significantly over time.[7]

Many decades have passed since Ortner published her essay, and historians have uncovered a wealth of information about women, gender relations, and sexuality, much of which shows the spirit and agency of some women who learned how to defeat or adapt to the Latin American ideological and political system, while others focused on changing them. Recent works reaffirm that there have indeed been patterns of female inequality in Latin America, but they also suggest that men have their own hierarchies of inequality, which should help us question whether there is real distance between nature and culture as Ortner defined it. This has meant that women's studies specialists have been confronted with the need to incorporate men and masculinity into Joan Scott's dictum that gender, like class, should be a category of analysis. The study of social movements since the end of dictatorship in many Latin American countries after 1980 reveals a growing interdependency between female activists and their male relatives and community leaders.[8]

The desire to historicize gender and sexuality studies in Latin America has pushed the field in a number of directions, all of which further complicate the notion of universalized female oppression. It has also brought a new focus of masculinity studies to Latin America, with fresh insights on the military, the working classes, and the state's relationship to private patriarchy.

Before the advent of cultural and women's studies, Latin American historians viewed the nineteenth-century state as relatively weak due to the frequency of coups and political instability, while Latin American men loomed larger than life through the portrayal of dictators and military men. The new focus on the social aspects of state formation, however, paints another picture, this one of states that had relatively consistent attitudes towards race, class, and sexuality with strong roots in colonial attitudes and of progressive men and women who had to modernize notions of gender and sexual relationships in order to construct the new state. In this way, some male politicians recognized the need to modernize social relations through legal reform, and often they enacted legislation without feminist influence, and their actions, while improving the status of women, maintained male privileges related to sexuality and *patria potestad*, the legal control and custody of children. Jeffrey Shumway's book on Argentina just after independence focuses on the cleavages between parents and children, not just men and women, as a way to debate the modernization of the family and the state. Similarly, Katherine Sloane examined abduction cases among indigenous couples throughout nineteenth-century Oaxaca, Mexico, to explain how a nonindigenous custom became a common practice to empower children, particularly girls, and help them force parents to accept their sexual freedom.[9] The pace and timing of these reforms varied considerably from one country to another, and moments of reformist fervor usually resulted in a series of changes including the granting of divorce, civil marriage, and the limitation of male patriarchy over wives who worked outside the home. Interestingly, this could often be accomplished more easily during authoritarian regimes. Examples of this include the passage of female suffrage under several Latin American dictators and the promulgation of divorce during the Peronist years in Argentina. In this way, Latin America, once seen as the bastion of absolute patriarchy, now appears to have been inhabited by men who had to resolve conflicting notions of both masculinity and state practices.

The theory of a more coherent nation-state emerging in the nineteenth century contradicted other traditional historiographical emphases on the enduring political power of the Catholic Church over women in Latin America. How could the state challenge church power at such an early moment? Instead of looking at formal accords between church and state, gender scholars have looked at how marriage served as an index of liberal change. Studies of marital conflict as well as marital choice after independence have uncovered a relatively greater role of secular authority in the lives of married couples, including a relatively greater autonomy for young couples than before independence. The state exerted itself in other ways, ranging from civil marriage and separation to the use of police powers to punish men and women for sexual behaviors that the church had heretofore regulated. Furthermore, some sexual behaviors such as homosexuality, bestiality, and incest were excluded from the list of sexual crimes in postindependence penal legislation. The church continued to have a moral authority in Latin American communities, but it was the state that increasingly attempted to regulate or ignore sexual behavior.[10]

From the late nineteenth century onward, the evolving nation state utilized technologies such as public health and direct challenges to church authority, and through civil marriage, divorce, and revised penal codes replaced the church as the official arbiter of sexual practices. The results were new codes for appropriate masculinity and femininity, with decriminalization of sodomy except with minors and greater protection of male sexual freedom. Whereas civil laws could quickly deny married women custody of their children for an act of adultery, men had to be proven to have long-standing and notorious affairs or to be financially irresponsible, and even then it was difficult to remove their custody rights. Females remained within the domain of moral standards, especially married women, but their wombs became targets of anti–infant mortality campaigns. Whereas initial reforms designed to shape new sexual norms for women were slow to develop, nation-states had to incorporate the female and her reproductive potential into the body politic as well as delineate the powers of men. It soon became clear that governments were not willing to moderate male sexual privilege, while they might be willing to attenuate male gender rights. Traditional discrimination against married women who had sex outside of marriage remained, while men could not be forced to declare that they were fathers of out-of-wedlock children. The rape of a prostitute was less of a crime than the rape of a respectable woman, and most rape crimes were difficult to prosecute except, in some countries with high proportions of mestizo and multiracial inhabitants, for deflowering virgins. Arlene Díaz shows this for Venezuela.[11]

Male gender rights, on the other hand, were open to reform, but only when men wanted to limit their personal and familial power for the sake of the nation. The rise of universal state education and mandatory military service, as well as reforms of the civil code that allowed married women to work and keep their own wages, directly challenged patriarchal rights to select occupations for their family and decide whether wives should work or not. Public health campaigns against infant mortality did not include provisions to allow male heads of households to contradict medical advice. And violence toward female members of the household came under scrutiny in the modern nation-state, but, until recently, with great difficulty.[12]

What about women who thwarted private and public patriarchal plans for women? The loosening of patriarchal control with the growth of the medicalized state provides an opportunity to explore this topic. Recent works on the history of female prostitution in Latin America, for example, argue that the presence of sex workers in nineteenth- and twentieth-century Latin American cities is not simply evidence of the "world's oldest profession," but also the product of changes in the world economy, colonialism, racism, public health, the emerging state, and familial pressures. Whether looking at Rio; Ponce and San Juan, Puerto Rico; Guatemala City; Mexico City; or Buenos Aires, male oppression has been an insufficient explanation for legal and clandestine prostitution, because other local and international factors influenced the regulation of prostitution, as did the resistant behavior of female sex workers and the willingness of male family members to insist on female sexual commerce as a female familial obligation. At the same time, many of the women studied did not always appear to be particularly willing to accept long-term stigmatization as sex workers, and instead used commercial sex as a part-time survival strategy to help support family members as well as themselves. Some actually expressed pleasure and a kind of independence that horrified moral reformers. The works have also shown the complexity of state-driven campaigns to promote public health, and demonstrate that ideas about contagion and genetic traits could not escape the prejudices of medical and religious reformers, who often believed that prostitutes were beyond rehabilitation and needed to suffer other stigmas such as menial jobs to redeem themselves within the community.[13]

Gender and sexuality studies have also influenced mid-twentieth-century Latin American historiography. The strong Latin American emphasis on the state has perhaps been its most fruitful contribution to debates on the nature of gender and sexual oppression. Historians of feminism have been quick to see how Latin American feminists relied on the liberal and revolutionary states, despite all of their problems, to restructure patriarchy through civil code reforms. Unlike in the United States, where there was a maze of individual state laws and common legal practices related to the division of power and responsibility within the family combined with feminist reluctance to view the state as an ally, reformers in code law countries viewed national civil codes and family law reforms as the ideal way to renegotiate patriarchy. Indeed, many civil code reforms were enacted without a strong feminist influence, often in response to changing economic and political realities. Some of the most effective changes have resulted from antifeminist regimes such as the Peronist government in Argentina in the 1940s and the Vargas government in Brazil. Both leaders pushed through female suffrage, although all voting was suppressed in Brazil soon after the legislation was passed.[14]

The history of feminism paralleled the history of the Latin American welfare states that began as charitable efforts that expanded in the 1930s, often in surprising ways. Whereas the study of the welfare state in Europe and the United States has engaged many women's history scholars in the last few years, social historians of Latin America have always felt far more comfortable thinking about the role of the state, although we recognized the significance of the welfare state much later than U.S. and European historians. Initially, studies of welfare programs ignored gender as a central category, but soon the discussion of women and children redirected the debate. And soon it became clear that women, both conservative and progressive, were deeply involved in the regulation of welfare. This was clearly seen in a special issue of *The Americas*, published in 2001 and devoted to the Latin American welfare state, in which all of the contributions discussed the gendered nature of reform movements, and in Christine Ehrick's 2005 work on Uruguay.[15]

What are the relationships between this public patriarchy and the private form that was supposed to be the basis of female oppression? An early comparison of Catholic Latin America with the Muslim Middle East by Nadia Haggag Youssef suggested strong conflicts between the desire of the Latin American state to educate women and have them participate in the public world of work, and the desire of husbands and fathers to determine the fate of the women and children in the family. This observation has been reaffirmed in many studies. Motherist public health campaigns, forced labor laws that affected women, campaigns to create bourgeois family norms as part of the modernizing state, all have limited the authority of the lower-class male within the family while empowering as well as controlling women.[16]

In this new view of the state, male sexual privileges were preserved, but in exchange poor men lost many patriarchal rights and privileges compared to their rich counterparts. From the more public question of whether a woman received her citizenship through her husband, father, or place of birth (in this case, prior to World War I more Latin American countries granted women social citizenship rights based on place of birth than their European or U.S. counterparts) to the more private question of whether a husband could control the education of his children, the profession of his wife, and children whose age of majority was lower than ever before, public authorities attacked, shaped, but ultimately never controlled private gender relations.[17]

Gradually we are learning how these debates evolved, and in what context. We know, for example, that laws protected men from being forced to declare paternity, but there has been little research on the phenomenon of women refusing to acknowledge maternity, something that I have found throughout Argentina in the late nineteenth and early twentieth century. Illegitimacy statistics need to be studied from the perspective of the parents as well as the children. We know that incest laws, in some cases, were never enacted, and yet there is clear evidence of social disapproval of incest when a man was taken to court. How did social disapproval mediate family relations? The accumulation of this information should lead to new insights regarding nation building in Latin America, one that will reshape our interest in code laws, and perhaps place political events such as gradualist slave emancipation laws, almost always phrased as "Law of the Free Womb," in new contexts.

How have men reacted to the changing status of women in society? Traditional Latin American stereotypes of the *machista* man incapable of change have fallen by the wayside. Anthropologists Roger Lancaster, Joseph Carrier, Stephen O. Murray, and others have attacked the canonical literature by studying the many diverse patterns of hetero- and homosexuality in Latin America and linked them specifically to a more multidimensional definition of masculinity. This work has important consequences for the study of female sexual oppression, since it argues that men have a more contingent masculine identity, part of which needs to be reaffirmed by other men, and takes on sexual meanings unrelated to heterosexuality. Whereas traditional gender studies often posited that women were central to the definition of male sexuality, this hypothesis needs reexamination. Similarly, the relationship of men to lesbian women is very unclear and understudied, partly because of the absence of a tradition of women keeping diaries and partly due to legal frameworks that defined masculine sexual freedom without commenting on female sexual privilege.

Other anthropologists have reexamined heterosexual masculine values. Eduardo Archetti has explored the melding of European and Latin American masculinities in Argentina and linked it to a notion of hybridity, one that implicitly has transformative aspects, while Matthew Guttman reaffirmed this by studying the impact of economic crises in a lower-class Mexico City suburb and found that fathering has taken on new nuances as men are more willing to share the burden of household responsibilities.[18]

Gender and sexuality historians have made important contributions to this question as well. Susan Besse's essay on wife killing and her book on the modernization of patriarchy in Brazil both analyze state campaigns in early-twentieth-century Brazil to limit male rights associated with patriarchy and reproductive sex and place the power of the state above the rights of men.[19] Asunción Lavrin's work on the feminists of the Southern Cone clearly delineates the efforts to limit male patriarchs as a goal not only of feminists but also of male reformers cognizant of the need to reform patriarchy as part of the modernization process, something that Lynn Stoner also pointed out in her work on Cuban feminism.[20] My own work on child custody cases in late-nineteenth-century Argentina, however, reveals a judicial reluctance to take rights of custody, or *patria potestad*, away from men unless absolutely necessary. Although they argued against a popular interpretation that *patria potestad* was a biological right of fatherhood and championed the view that it was a legal privilege, judges almost always favored fathers over mothers in these battles.[21] This observation reinforces Besse's view that modernization of patriarchy did not always result in clear benefits for women, a view that has been expressed in recent work on women, patriarchy, and the Mexican Revolution.

Nevertheless, the work on state and private patriarchy has fundamentally changed our perception of how patriarchy operates and what its relationship with the state entails. It posits that even though men were supposed to be the kings of the household, just as they had been in the colonial period, new forces were at work reshaping appropriate notions of fathering, being a husband and a provider. Men often protested these changes, but in many countries with a clear vision of the function of the modern nation-state, the patriarchal prerogatives of poor men were consistently eroded.

Another way that male privileges were contested within the family was through the workplace. At the same time that protective labor legislation increasingly limited female access to the workplace for the sake of ensuring the reproductive capacity of women, men were encouraged to marry, live more stable lives, and adopt bourgeois norms of sobriety and responsibility. Thomas Klubock's study of workers in the El Teniente copper mine in the first half of the twentieth century is premised on the belief that "the process of class formation in the copper mines must be understood as a 'gendered' process in which formal gender ideologies and informal norms, values, and practices surrounding sexuality shaped working-class structures of feeling and political consciousness." In so doing, he supports the contentions of Donna Haraway and Judith Butler that the social construction of sexuality is at the root of the history of gender.[22]

In the U.S.-run Chilean copper mines, management sought to stabilize the transient and often unmarried male labor force and eliminate the impact of independent single women who often worked near the mines in bars and bordellos. This resulted in a higher rate of marriage, and women dependent upon the male salary and access to the company store. While that was useful to the company during moments of boom, this strategy led to women becoming ardent strike supporters during lean times. Karin Rosemblatt has extended this analysis of the sex and gender components of Chilean politics to argue that in the 1930s and 1940s they shaped state practices and relations between popular classes and political and economic elites during the popular-front era.[23] Based upon a reproductive vision of a healthy and united working-class family, many political groups of the time supported temperance movements to control male drinking, make men more responsible breadwinners, and thereby enhance national productivity as well.

I could go on and list many other worthy books and articles that contemplate these questions, but rather than enumerate them all, I would like to go back to the original issue. If we can no longer say that "female is to male as nature is to culture," how do we describe the nature of gender relations and its relationship to sexuality? Originally we perceived gender as those attributes or qualities assigned to males and females by a particular culture and always in the context of female oppression, whereas sex attributes were genetically coded and immutable. Whether it was gender- or sex-related, men controlled female destiny. Historically, this view has been challenged both by historicizing sexuality and by introducing other factors that have helped shape the destinies of women and men. Now we know that patterns of sexuality can be as easily affected by political, social, and economic currents as gender relations. Furthermore, male sexuality is defined in part by relations with other men, just as women's sexuality is defined in part by same-sex relations. Relations between men and women are linked by a series of factors, often mutating and changing over time, and the interactions between men and women delineate the consequences of both sex and gender relations. Thus, if I had to choose a metaphor, I would define male-female relations to be like the double helix of DNA. Interrelated, connected, and sometimes appearing farther apart rather than close together, nevertheless their fates are inexorably intertwined. Oppression may be a common characteristic of male-female relations, but there are other spaces that men and women inhabit, and these must be included in the process. The bridges between male and females appears to be the most distant between patriarchal males and lesbian females, but cross-dressers, transvestites, and men who view themselves as heterosexual but who have sex with other men appear to be able to cross the bridges from time to time. By learning the various codes, hopefully we will gradually uncover the diverse patterns that have affected the lives of women and men in Latin America.

NOTES

1. Meri Knaster, *Women in Spanish America: An Annotated Bibliography from Pre-Conquest to Contemporary Times* (Boston: G. K. Hall, 1977); K. Lynn Stoner, *Latinas of the Americas: A Source Book* (New York: Garland, 1989). It is hoped that there will be similar

publications for men and masculinity studies. Currently there is, however, an online bibliography of studies on sex and sexuality in Latin America at http://library.stanford.edu/depts/hasrg/latinam/balder.html (accessed May 22, 2010) as well as a fine bibliography of literary works related to gay literature compiled by David Foster: David William Foster, *Latin American Writers on Gay and Lesbian Themes; A Bio-Critical Sourcebook* (Westport, Conn.: Greenwood Press, 1994).

2. William E. French and Katherine Elaine Bliss, eds., *Gender, Sexuality, and Power in Latin America since Independence* (Lanham, Md.: Rowan & Littlefield, 2007).

3. Sherry B. Ortner, "Is Female to Male as Nature is to Culture?" in *Woman, Culture, and Society*, ed. Michelle Zimbalist Rosaldo and Louise Lamphere (Stanford: Stanford University Press, 1974), 67.

4. *Ibid.*, 73.

5. Paulo Freire, trans. Myra Bergman Ramos, *Pedagogy of the Oppressed* (New York: Seabury Press, 1970). I would like to thank Rebecca Haidt for help with this point.

6. Lynn Stoner provided the history of the feminist movement before the revolution in K. Lynn Stoner, *From the House to the Streets: The Cuban Woman's Movement for Legal Reform, 1898–1940* (Durham, N.C.: Duke University Press, 1991). Since the revolution, see Lois M. Smith, *Sex and Revolution: Women in Socialist Cuba* (New York: Oxford University Press, 1996); Margaret Randall, *Cuban Women Now: Interviews with Cuban Women* (Toronto: Women's Press, 1974); and her study of Nicaragua, "Gathering Rage: The Failure of Twentieth-Century Revolutions to Develop a Feminist Agenda, the Case of Nicaragua," in Kate Conway-Turner, Suzanne Cherrin, Jessica Schiffman, and Kathleen Doherty Turkel, eds., *Women's Studies in Transition: The Pursuit of Interdisciplinarity* (Cranbury, N.J.: Associated Univ. Presses, 1998); and Muriel Nazzari, "The 'Woman Question' in Cuba: Analysis of Material Constraints on its Solution," *Signs* 9:2 (1983): 246–63. More recent studies of change include Karin Alejandra Rosemblatt, *Political Cultures and the State in Chile, 1920–1950* (Chapel Hill: University of North Carolina Press, 2000); Carmen Diana Deere and Magdalena León de Leal, *Empowering Women: Land and Property Rights in Latin America* (Pittsburgh: Pittsburgh University Press, 2001); Elisabeth J. Friedman, *Unfinished Transitions: Women and the Gendered Development of Democracy in Venezuela, 1936–1996* (University Park: University of Pennsylvania Press, 2001); Karen Kampwirth, *Women & Guerrilla Movements: Nicaragua, El Salvador, Chiapas, Cuba* (University Park: Pennsylvania State University Press, 2002). For recent studies of women and the right, see Victoria González and Karen Kampwirth, *Radical Women in Latin America: Left and Right* (University Park: Penn State University Press, 2001); Margaret Power, *Right-Wing Women in Chile; Feminine Power and the Struggle Against Allende 1964–1973* (University Park, Penn State University Press, 2002); Donna J. Guy, *Women Build the Welfare State: Performing Charity, Creating Rights in Argentina, 1880–1955* (Durham, N.C.: Duke University Press, 2009). The works on Mexico that dispute the revolutionary successes of women include Jocelyn Olcott, *Revolutionary Women in Postrevolutionary Mexico* (Durham, N.C.: Duke University Press, 2005); Jocelyn Olcott, Mary Kay Vaughn, and Gabriela Cano, eds., *Sex in Revolution: Gender, Politics, and Power in Modern Mexico* (Durham, N.C.: Duke University Press, 2006); Stephanie Mitchell and Patience Schell, eds., *The Women's Revolution in Mexico, 1910–1953* (Albuquerque: University of New Mexico Press, 2006); and Stephanie Smith, *Gender and the Mexican Revolution: Yucatecan Women and the Realities of Patriarchy* (Raleigh: University of North Carolina Press, 2009). See also the massive study of women's history in Latin America and Spain published in four volumes: Isabel Morant, ed., with various coordinators for each volume, *Historia de las mujeres en España y América Latina*, 4 vols. (Madrid: Cátedra, 2004–06).

7. On fertility rates, see Nora Scott Kinzer, "Priests, Machos, and Babies: Or, Latin American Women and the Manichaean Heresy," *Journal of Marriage and the Family* 35:2 (1973): 300–12. For a more recent quantitative study, see Edith A. Pantelides and Sarah Bott, eds., *Reproducción, salud y sexualidad en América Latina* (Buenos Aires: Biblos, 2000). Recent works on women and labor in Latin America include María del Carmen Arnaiz and Patricia Chomnalez, *Mujeres que trabajan, 1930–1940* (Buenos Aires: Centro Editor Latinoamericana, 1992); Hector Recalde, *Mujer, condiciones de vida, de trabajo y salud*, 2 vols. (Buenos Aires: Biblioteca Política Argentina, 1989); Heather Fowler Salamini and Mary Kay Vaughan, *Women of the Mexican Countryside, 1850–1990: Creating Spaces, Shaping Transition* (Tucson: University of Arizona Press, 1994); Helen Safa, *The Myth of the Male Breadwinner: Women and Industrialization in the Caribbean* (Boulder, Colo.: Westview Press, 1995); Smith, *Sex and Revolution, Women in Socialist Cuba*; Asunción Lavrin, *Women, Feminism and Social Change*; Elizabeth Quay Hutchison, *Labors Appropriate to their Sex: Gender, Labor, and Politics in Urban Chile, 1900–1930* (Durham, N.C.: Duke University Press, 2001); Susie S. Porter, *Working Women in Mexico City; Public Discourses and Material Conditions, 1879–1931* (Tucson: University of Arizona Press, 2003).

8. Joan Scott, "Gender: A Useful Category of Historical Analysis," in *Gender and the Politics of History*, rev. ed. (New York: Columbia University Press, 1999). For studies of social movements in Latin America, see Arturo Escobar and Sonial E. Alvarez, *The Making of Social Movements in Latin America: Identity, Strategy, and Democracy* (Boulder, Colo.: Westview Press, 1992); Magdalena León de Leal and Sonia Alvarez, eds., *Mujeres y participación política: Avances y desafíos en América Latina* (Bogotá: Académica, 1994); Lynn Stephen, *Women and Social Movements in Latin America: Power from Below* (Austin: University of Texas Press, 1997); Sonia E. Alvarez, Evelina Dagnino, and Arturo Escobar, eds., *Cultures of Politics/Politics of Cultures: Re-Visioning Latin American Social Movements* (Boulder, Colo.: Westview Press, 1998); Maxine Molyneux, *Women's Movements in International Perspective: Latin America and Beyond* (New York: Palgrave, 2001).

9. Jeffrey Merrill Shumway, *The Case of the Ugly Suitor and Other Histories of Love, Gender and Nation in Buenos Aires* (Lincoln: University of Nebraska Press, 2005); Kathryn A. Sloan, *Runaway Daughters: Seduction, Elopement, and Honor in Nineteenth-Century Mexico* (Albuquerque: University of New Mexico Press, 2008).

10. See Silvia Lamadrid Alvarez and Soledad Muñoz, *La investigación social en sexualidad en Chile, 1984–1994* (Santiago: Universidad de Chile, 1996); Eugenia Rodríguez Sáenz, "Civilizando la vida doméstica en el Valle Central de Costa Rica (1750–1850)," in Eugenia Rodríguez Sáenz, ed., *Entre silencios y voces: Género e Historia en América Central (1750–1990)* (San José: Centro Nacional para el Desarrollo de la Mujer y la Familia, 1997), 41–78; Susana Menéndez, *En búsqueda de las mujeres: Percepciones sobre género, trabajo y sexualidad, Buenos Aires, 1900–1930* (Amsterdam: CEDLA, 1997); Manuel Angel Urrego Arila, *Sexualidad, matrimonio y familia en Bogotá, 1880–1930* (Santa Fé de Bogotá: Ariel/Fundación Universidad Central-DIUC, 1997); María del Rosario Romero Contreras, *Amor y sexualidad en Santander: Siglo XIX* (Bucaramanga: Universidad Industrial de Santander, 1999); Christine Hunefeldt, *Liberalism in the Bedroom: Quarreling Spouses in Nineteenth-Century Lima* (University Park: Penn State University Press, 2000); José M. Gordillo, *Campesinos revolucionarios en Bolivia: Identidad, territorio y sexualidad en el Valle Alto de Cochabamba, 1952–1964* (La Paz: PROMEC/Universidad de la Cordillera, 2000); Sonya Lipsett-Rivera, "Marriage and Family Relations In Mexico during the Transition from Colony to Nation," and Elizabeth Anne Kuznesof, "Gender Ideology, Race, and Female-Headed Households in Urban Mexico, 1750–1850," in Victor M. Uribe, ed., *State and Society in Spanish America during the Age of Revolution* (Wilmington, Del.: Scholarly Resources,

2001); Cristián Berco, "Silencing the Unmentionable: Non-Reproductive Sex and the Creation of a Civilized Argentina," *The Americas* 53:3 (2002): 419–41; Gabriela Castellanos and Simone Accorsi, *Género y sexualidad en Colombia y en Brasil* (Cali: La Manzana de la Discordia/Centro de Estudios de Género, Mujer y Sociedad, 2002).

11. Maxine Molyneaux and Elizabeth Dore, *The Hidden Histories of Gender and the State in Latin America* (Chapel Hill: Duke University Press, 2000); Arlene J. Díaz, *Female Citizens, Patriarchs, and the Law in Venezuela, 1786–1904* (Lincoln: University of Nebraska Press, 2004).

12. Steve Stern, *The Secret History of Gender: Women, Men, and Power in Late Colonial Mexico* (Chapel Hill: University of North Carolina Press, 1995) suggested that colonial understandings of domestic violence helped explain domestic violence in modern Mexico. His thesis directly implies a weakness of the modern nation-state in Mexico.

13. Donna J. Guy, "Stigma, Pleasures, and Dutiful Daughters," *Journal of Women's History* 10:3 (1998): 180–91 places recent publications on Latin American prostitution in a global context. Recent works specifically on Latin America include Katherine Bliss, "The Science of Redemption: Syphilis, Sexual Promiscuity, and Reformism in Revolutionary Mexico City," *Hispanic American Historical Review* 79:1 (1999): 1–40; José Flores Ramos, "Virgins, Whores and Martyrs: Prostitution in the Colony, 1898–1919," in Félix V. Matos Rodríguez and Linda C. Delgado, eds., *Puerto Rican Women's History: New Perspectives* (Armonk, N.Y. and London: M.E. Sharpe, 1998), 83–104; Sueann Caulfield, "The Birth of Mangue: Race, Nation, and the Politics of Prostitution in Rio de Janeiro, 1850–1942," in Daniel Balderston and Donna J. Guy, eds., *Sex and Sexuality in Latin America* (New York: New York University Press, 1997), 86–100; William E. French, "Prostitutes and Guardian Angels: Women, Work and Family in Porfirian Mexico," *Hispanic American Historical Review* 72:4 (1992): 529–53; Robert M. Buffington and Pablo Piccato, "Tales of Two Women: The Narrative Construct of Porfirian Reality," *The Americas* 55:3 (1999): 391–424; Eileen J. Findlay, "Decency and Democracy: The Politics of Prostitution in Ponce, Puerto Rico, 1890–1900," *Feminist Studies* 23:3 (1997): 471–99; Eileen Findlay, *Imposing Decency: The Politics of Sexuality and Race in Puerto Rico, 1870–1920* (Durham, N.C.: Duke University Press, 2000); Katherine Elaine Bliss, *Compromised Positions: Prostitution, Public Health, and Gender Politics in Revolutionary Mexico City* (University Park: Penn State University Press, 2002); Beatriz Kushnir, *Baile de máscaras: Mulheres judias e prostituição; As polacas e suas associaçáoes de ajuda mútua* (Rio de Janeiro: Imago, 1996); Yvette Trochón Ghislieri, *Mercenarias del amor: Prostitución y modernidad en el Uruguay (1880–1932)* (Buenos Aires: Taurus, 2003); Alvaro Góngora Escobedo, *La prostitución en Santiago, 1813–1931: Visión de las elites* (Santiago: Editorial Universitaria, 1994); Marlene Sánchez Moncada, "La prostitución en Bogotá, 1880–1920," *Anuario Colombiano de Historia Social y de la Cultura* 25 (1998): 146–87; Jorge Salessi, "Medics, Crooks, and Tango Queens: The National Appropriation of a Gay Tango," in Celeste Fraser Delgado and José Esteban Muñoz, eds., *Everynight Life; Culture and Dancing in Latin/o America* (Durham, N.C.: Duke University Press, 1997), 141–74.

14. Benedict Anderson, *Imagined Communities: Reflections on the Origin and Spread of Nationalism* (London: Verso, 1983). Among the first responses to Anderson by Latin Americanists are those to be found in Andrew Parker, Doris Sommer, et al., eds., *Nationalism and Sexualities* (New York: Routledge, 1992); Emilie Bergmann, Janet Greenberg, and Gwen Kirkpatrick, eds., *Women, Culture, and Politics in Latin America: Seminar on Feminism and Culture in Latin America* (Berkeley: University of California Press, 1992). See also Anna Macias, *Against All Odds: The Feminist Movement in Mexico to 1940* (Westport, Conn.: Greenwood Press, 1982); Donna J. Guy, "Lower-Class Families,

Women and the Law in Nineteenth-Century Argentina," *Journal of Family History* 10:3 (1985): 318–31; June Edith Hahner, *Emancipating the Female Sex: The Struggle for Women's Rights in Brazil, 1850–1940* (Durham, N.C.: Duke University Press, 1990); Sonia Alvarez, *Engendering Democracy in Brazil: Women's Movements in Transition Politics* (Princeton, N.J.: Princeton University Press, 1990); K. Lynn Stoner, *From the House to the Streets: The Cuban Woman's Movement for Legal Reform, 1898–1940* (Durham, N.C.: Duke University Press, 1991); Francesca Miller, *Latin American Women and the Search for Social Justice* (Hanover, N.H.: University Press of New England, 1991); Asunción Lavrin, *Women, Feminism, and Social Change in Argentina, Chile, and Uruguay, 1890–1940* (Lincoln: University of Nebraska Press, 1995); Donna J. Guy, *Sex and Danger in Buenos Aires: Prostitution, Family and Nation in Argentina* (Lincoln: University of Nebraska Press, 1991); Sarah C. Chambers, *From Subjects to Citizens: Honor, Gender, and Politics in Arequipa Peru, 1780–1854* (University Park: Penn State University Press, 1999); Hunefeldt, *Liberalism in the Bedroom*; Elizabeth Dore, *Gender Politics in Latin America: Debates in Theory and Practice* (New York: Monthly Review Press, 1997); Elizabeth Dore and Maxine Molyneux, eds., *Hidden Histories of Gender and the State in Latin America* (Durham, N.C.: Duke University Press, 2000); Díaz, *Female Citizens, Patriarchy and the Law in Venezuela, 1786–1904*.

15. Pioneering work on the welfare state came initially from studies of social security. See Carmelo Mesa Lago, *Social Security in Latin America: Pressure Groups, Stratification, and Inequality* (Pittsburgh: Pittsburgh University Press, 1978). Guillermo V. Alonso, *Política y seguridad social en la Argentina de los '90* (Buenos Aires: FLACSO, 2000). See also Ann S. Blum, "Public Welfare and Child Circulation in Mexico City, 1877–1925," *Journal of Family History* 23:3 (1998), 240–72, and *The Americas* 58:1 (July 2001), the special issue on the rise of the welfare state in Latin America, as well as, more recently, Anne-Emanuelle Birn, Raquel Pollero, and Wanda Cabella, "No se debe llorar sobre leche derramada: El pensamiento epidemiológico y la mortalidad infantil en Uruguay, 1900–1940," *Estudios Interdisciplinarios de América Latina y el Caribe* 14:1 (2003), available at www.tau.ac.il/eial/XIV_1/birn.html (accessed May 21, 2010). A 2004 special issue of the *Journal of Jewish History* on the history of Jews in Latin America has also revealed the role of immigrant women in welfare: see http://www.kluweronline.com/issn/0334-701X/contents; Christine Ehrick, *The Shield of the Weak: Feminism and the State in Uruguay, 1903–1933* (Albuquerque: University of New Mexico Press, 2005). For a review article on the state of female welfare-state history, see Donna J. Guy, "Feminists, Philanthropists, the Rise of the Welfare State, and Child Welfare Policies," *Brújula* 4:1 (December 2005), 45–59, and *Women Build the Welfare State: Performing Charity, Creating Rights in Argentina, 1880–1955* (Durham, N.C.: Duke University Press, 2009).

16. Nadia Haggag Youssef, *Women and Work in Developing Societies* (Westport, Conn.: Greenwood Press, 1976); Donna J. Guy, "Women, Peonage and Industrialization Argentina, 1810–1914," *Latin American Research Review* 16:3 (1981): 65–89; Donna J. Guy, "Emilio and Gabriela Coni: Reformers, Public Health, and Working Women," in *The Human Tradition in Latin America: The Nineteenth Century*, Judith Ewell and William H. Beezley, eds. (Wilmington, Del.: Scholarly Resources, 1989); Héctor Recalde, *La higiene y el trabajo: 1870–1930*, 2 vols. (Buenos Aires: Centro Editor de América Latina, 1988); Eugenia Rodríguez Sáenz, ed., *Entre silencios y voces: Género e historia en América Central 1750–1990* (San José: Centro Nacional para el Desarrollo de la Mujer y la Familia, 1997); Susan K. Besse, *Restructuring Patriarchy: The Modernization of Gender Inequality in Brazil, 1914–1940* (Chapel Hill: University of North Carolina, 1996). Sarah Buck, "El control de la natalidad y el día de la madre: Política feminista y reaccionaria en México, 1922–1923," *Signos históricos* 5 (2001), 9–53; many of the essays in Fernanda Gil Lozano, Valeria Silvina

Pita, and María Gabriela Ini, eds., *Historia de las mujeres en la Argentina*, 2 vols. (Buenos Aires: Taurus, 2000); Sandra McGee Deutsch, "Christians, Homemakers, and Transgressors: Extreme Right-Wing Women in Twentieth-Century Brazil," *Journal of Women's History* 16:3 (2004), 124–37; María Fernanda Lorenzo, Ana Lia Rey, and Cecilia Tossounian, "Images of Virtuous Women: Morality, Gender and Power in Argentina between the World Wars," *Gender & History* 17:3 (2005), 567–92; Barbara Weinstein, "They Don't Even Look Like Women Workers: Femininity and Class in Twentieth-Century Latin America," *International Labor and Working-Class History* 69:1 (2006), 161–76; Kelly Hayes, "Wicked Women and Femmes Fatales: Gender, Power and *Pomba Gira* in Brazil," *History of Religions* 48:1 (2008): 1–21.

17. Donna J. Guy, "'White Slavery,' Citizenship, and Nationalism in Argentina," in *Nationalisms and Sexualities*, ed. Andrew Parker, Mary Russo, Doris Sommer and Patricia Yeager (New York: Routledge, 1992): 201–17. The history of women hiding pregnancy and refusing to acknowledge maternity dates from colonial traditions of honor. Scholars of Argentina have been at the forefront in linking the arrival of both positivism and psychoanalysis as tools for governmental reform of gender and sexuality. Mariano Ben Plotkin, ed., *Argentina on the Couch: Psychiatry, State and Society, 1880 to the Present* (Albuquerque: University of New Mexico Press, 2003); Kristen Ruggiero, *Modernity in the Flesh: Medicine, Law, and Society in Turn of the Century Argentina* (Stanford: Stanford University Press, 2003).

18. Carlos Luis Jáuregui, *La homosexualidad en la Argentina* (Buenos Aires: Colección Cultura y Sociedad, 1987); Eduardo Archetti, *Masculinities: Football, Polo and the Tango in Argentina* (New York: Berg, 1999); Roger N. Lancaster, "Subject Honor and Object Shame: The Construction of Male Homosexuality and Stigma in Nicaragua," *Ethnology* 27:2 (1988): 111–25; "Sexual Positions: Caveats and Second Thoughts on 'Categories.'" *The Americas*, 54:1 (July 1997): 1–16; Stephen O. Murray et al., *Latin American Male Homosexualities* (Albuquerque: University of New Mexico Press, 1995); Ian Lumsden, *Machos, Maricones and Gays: Cuba and Homosexuality* (Pennsylvania: Temple University Press, 1996); Richard Parker, *Bodies, Pleasures and Passions: Sexual Culture in Contemporary* Brazil (Boston: Beacon Press, 1991) and *Beneath the Equator: Cultures of Desire, Male Homosexuality, and Emerging Gay Communities in Brazil* (New York: Routledge, 1999); Matthew Gutmann, *The Meanings of Macho: Being a Man in Mexico City* (Berkeley: University of California Press, 1996). Historians have also made major contributions to this field. See Jorge Salessi, *Médicos maleantes y maricas: Higiene, criminología y homosexualidad en la construcción de la nación argentina* (Buenos Aires, 1871–1914) (Rosario: B. Viterbo, 1995); James Naylor Green, *Beyond Carnaval: Male Homosexuality in Twentieth-Century Brazil* (Chicago: University of Chicago Press, 1999) and "Challenging National Heroes and Myths: Male Homosexuality and Brazilian History," *Estudios Interdisciplinarios de América Latina y el Caribe* 12:1 (2001). There are several historical articles in Peter McKee Irwin, Edward J. McCaughan, and Michelle Rossio Nasser, eds., *The Famous 41: Sexuality and Social Control in Mexico, 1901* (New York: Palgrave, 2003).

19. Susan K. Besse, "Crimes of Passion: The Campaign Against Wife-Killing in Brazil, 1910–1940," *Journal of Social History* 22:4 (1989): 653–66; *Restructuring Patriarchy: The Modernization of Gender Inequality in Brazil, 1914–1940* (Chapel Hill: University of North Carolina, 1996).

20. Asunción Lavrin, *Women, Feminism, and Social Change in Argentina, Chile, and Uruguay, 1890–1940* (Lincoln: University of Nebraska Press, 1995). K. Lynn Stoner, *From the House to the Streets: The Cuban Woman's Movement for Legal Reform, 1898–1940* (Durham, N.C.: Duke University Press, 1991).

21. Donna J. Guy, "Parents Before the Tribunals: The Legal Construction of Patriarchy in Argentina," in Maxine Molyneux and Elizabeth Dore, eds., *The Hidden Histories of Gender and the State in Latin America* (Durham, N.C. and London: Duke University Press, 2000).

22. Thomas Miller Klubock, *Contested Communities: Class, Gender, and Politics in Chile's El Teniente Copper Mine, 1904–1951* (Durham, N.C. and London: Duke University Press, 1998): 7, fn 11.

23. Arlene J. Díaz, *Female Citizens, Patriarchs, and the Law in Venezuela, 1786–1904* (Lincoln: University of Nebraska Press, 2004); Karin Alejandra Rosemblatt, "Domesticating Men: State-Building and Class Compromise in Popular-Front Chile," in Dore and Molyneux, *Hidden Histories of Gender and the State*, 262–90.

CHAPTER 13

THE HISTORIOGRAPHY OF LATIN AMERICAN FAMILIES

NARA MILANICH

"Few topics of fundamental importance have generated so much numbing literature as the family," mused sociologist Perry Anderson in a 2005 essay in *The Nation*.[1] Anderson and others have described the decline of family studies within disciplines where they once thrived. For most of the twentieth century, kinship was the bread and butter of the anthropological métier, but by the 1980s it had largely receded from view.[2] Family never occupied the central place in history that kinship did in anthropology, but at one time the history of family appeared destined to become one of social history's favored progeny. In 1981, the field figured alongside intellectual history, the history of science, and economic history in an appraisal of history's future. As it turned out, such historiographical stature would prove fleeting. Ten years later, a review essay asked, "Whatever Happened to Family History?" Twenty years later, one practitioner groused, "Where is the next [Philippe] Ariès or [Lawrence] Stone who will write a personal, idiosyncratic synthesis of the field" and breath new interpretive life into it?[3]

Such assessments refer to the history of family in Europe and the United States. In Latin America, the field has exhibited its own trajectory and a different chronology, yet it is hard to avoid characterizing it too as a narrative of decline. Today there are individual works that may be categorized, by their authors or audience, as family history, and in some national historiographies in Latin America, family history endures as a vigorous field. But among U.S.-based scholars in particular, it is difficult to discern a body of historical scholarship on family that has retained an analytic character discrete from other, related fields such as women's history. There is arguably no critical mass of work that engages in a collective conversation using shared methods and frameworks in order to answer questions about family patterns historically. The very category "family" appears much less frequently in Latin American historiography than it once did.[4] Thus, where review essays often begin with the caveat that they cannot possibly achieve exhaustive coverage of their field, this essay faces a different challenge: it cannot be taken as given that the field of Latin American family history exists in the first place.

The waning of family as a category of historical analysis is a noteworthy development in U.S. and European historiography, but it is even more striking in the case of Latin America. In the 1860s, Chilean historian and statesman Benjamín Vicuña Mackenna characterized Santiago as "not a city of men but of relatives."[5] A century later, social scientists had a term for such a condition: Latin America was "familistic," an affliction associated with underdevelopment. Meanwhile, household and family have figured at the center of some of the most influential twentieth-century interpretations of Latin American society and culture, from Gilberto Freyre's *The Masters and the Slaves* to Oscar Lewis's *Five Families* to Gabriel Gárcia Márquez's *One Hundred Years of Solitude*. The waning of family history thus reflects the tacit renunciation of a long intellectual tradition.

The first part of this essay describes the methods and frameworks that historians have used to examine Latin American families, sketches some of their findings, and speculates about the reasons why family has become marginalized as a category of historical inquiry. The essay tacks back and forth between scholarship written in the vein of family history and work that addresses such issues as domesticity and patriarchy but does not necessarily take family as its central analytic concern. If one query running through the discussion concerns the extent to which family history endures as a recognizable historiographical enterprise, a second and perhaps more trenchant question is whether it should exist as such. I argue that family history has much to contribute to our understanding of Latin America's past and present, and I conclude by identifying several areas for future inquiry.

Throughout, I refer to *families*, *households*, and *kinship*. The terms are obviously not synonymous. The *household* is often defined as a coresident domestic unit whose members often, but not always, share kin or marriage ties. *Kinship* can be defined as "relatedness," whether biological or social, with recent anthropological literature mindful of any a priori distinction between the two.[6] In historical scholarship, *family* often stands in for *kinship* or *household* and refers to the broadly defined gamut of relationships deemed private or domestic. I use the term *family* in this way, and use the more analytically specific *kinship* and *household* where relevant.

From Social Science Perspectives to the Emergence of Family History

The most famous piece of social science scholarship in twentieth-century Latin America—Gilberto Freyre's classic *The Masters and the Slaves*—is usually regarded as a meditation on race, but it may also be the region's first social history of family. Freyre introduced the notion that family was central to understanding social, political, and economic structures beyond the household: "[A]ll that political and military history has to offer in the way of striking events holds little meaning in comparison with a mode of life that is almost routine; but it is in that routine that the character of a people is most readily to be discerned."[7] Freyre's anecdotal methods did not meet later standards of historical analysis, and his claims about the centrality of the patriarchal plantation household to Brazil's historical development did not ultimately survive sustained scrutiny. But in identifying the domestic sphere as a locus of race and class relations and the site of the social reproduction of Brazilian "civilization," his work foreshadowed future generations of scholarship on family.

By the 1950s and 1960s, very different analytic problems animated social science scholarship, but family was still accorded a central place. Research on urbanization, economic modernization, and the massification of politics manifested a keen interest in the role family relations played in these processes. Scholars asked about the functional role of family in maintaining social stability, generating tolerance for adversity, and mediating disruptive social change. They disagreed about whether modernization would lead to a weakening of "traditional" extended kinship bonds and the extent to which those bonds could thwart the alienation and political unrest attendant to modern capitalism. They also assigned different normative valences to family: while many saw "familism" as an obstacle to the development of modern political and economic institutions and civil society, others considered kin networks and household strategies to be "resources of poverty" in the context of material deprivation and economic uncertainty. But regardless of whether family was "good" or "bad" for development, there existed a widespread consensus that it was "the primary group in society," shaping everything from the (non)emergence of political parties and stock markets to the survival of the urban poor.[8] Indeed, in modernization theory, part of what distinguished "modern" societies from "traditional" ones was the nature of family structure (egalitarian nuclear versus patriarchal extended) as well as family's relative preponderance in economy and society.[9]

By the 1980s, historical studies of Latin American families had come into their own among both U.S.- and Latin America–based historians. Their emergence in part reflected Latin Americanists' embrace of historiographical trends developing elsewhere: the expansion of historical demography and its discovery of household and family as subjects of study, the explosion of social history generally, the influential sensibilities of the French Annales school. But the field also bore the mark of specifically Latin American problematics. Questions about the interaction between kinship structures and capitalism, urbanization, and modernization first posed in the social science literature were at the forefront of historical scholarship as well.[10] The field was also markedly interdisciplinary, with particularly strong ties to anthropology and ethnohistory.[11]

In retrospect, what emerged in the 1980s might more appropriately be characterized as two Latin American family histories, each drawing on different sources and methods and evolving largely independently of one another. One family history intersected with economic and political history and explored elite kinship networks and their significance for organizing economic and political power in Latin American societies. Another family history, drawing its methods, concepts, and questions from demographic and social history, focused on plebeian family patterns. On the surface, this division of labor made sense: elite and plebeian families not only appear to have served different functions, but they exhibited basic morphological dissimilarities in terms of marriage (or nonmarriage) patterns, filiation, child rearing, sexuality, and gender roles.

A spate of works in the 1980s explored elite kinship, with an emphasis on Mexico and Brazil.[12] This scholarship tended to focus on the late eighteenth and nineteenth centuries and examined how family practices both mediated and were transformed by the transition from colonies to republics and by ensuing processes of economic and political modernization. One abiding concern was the relationship of elite families to state formation, as scholars argued either that such kin networks filled a power vacuum left by weak states or that they developed in a symbiotic relationship to them. Several works identified families as key linkages between politics and patronage at the local and national levels. While their primary focus was on the relationship of these "notable family networks" to political economy, a subset of works drew on cultural history and historical ethnographic approaches to excavate the symbolic dynamics of family. For example, Larissa A. Lomnitz and Marisol Pérez-Lizaur explored how the Gómez clan, the bourgeois Mexican family they traced over a century and a half, constructed and maintained a collective identity through public and private rituals, from sending birth announcements to throwing grand weddings. "A big Gómez party is more than an occasion for merriment," they noted. "It is an arena of ostentation and power, aspirations to leadership, loyalty and spite, solidarity and discrimination."[13]

To the extent it argued that strong family networks hindered the development of modern political and economic structures, the historical scholarship on elite families echoed the earlier social science literature. But as historian Elizabeth Kuznesof points out, these studies hardly attributed omnipotence to their subjects. Flexible and resilient, elite families responded as best they could to economic and political circumstances that were often adverse and largely beyond their control.[14] Ultimately, kinship in these studies is portrayed as a resource and survival strategy for power holders, not unlike its function in many ethnographic and historical portrayals of plebeian families.

Concurrently with the scholarship on elite kin networks, but surprisingly disengaged from it, a very different family history began to explore plebeian, slave, peasant, and other nonelite families and household structures.[15] Perhaps the single most salient finding of these studies has been the extraordinarily widespread and enduring existence of nonnormative practices surrounding family, gender, and sexuality in diverse Latin American societies. Where dominant religious and cultural scripts have prescribed patriarchy, marriage, conjugal sexuality, and endogamy, popular and subordinate groups in particular exhibited low rates of formal marriage and rampant consensual unions, illegitimate births, and female-headed households.[16] Pablo Rodríguez's characterization of family in Colombia as "regulated more by community beliefs, traditions, and values than by abundant and strict juridical codes" probably holds true for many communities across the hemisphere.[17]

In 1992, Silvia Arrom observed that among Latin America–based scholars, the study of family history was considerably more developed than women's history.[18] Indeed, family history found fertile terrain in Latin American historiographies, particularly in Brazil and Mexico, where it evinced particular national inflections. In Brazil, historical studies of family grew directly out of demographic history. The field has been distinguished by a special concern with slave families and by a conceptual preoccupation with the structure of households and *parentela* (kinship).[19] Such issues derive from an ongoing debate with Gilberto Freyre's claim about the centrality of the plantation "big house" in Brazilian history.[20] In Mexico, family history took its cues not only from historical demography but also from the history of mentalities. This scholarship has emphasized sexuality, religion, and the interplay of Catholic norms and popular transgression in the colonial context. It has often drawn on Inquisition records and given particular attention to indigenous subjects.[21] In both Brazil and Mexico, family history developed in the context of collaborative centers or seminars working with labor-intensive sources. These collective projects in turn served as bases for the development and diffusion of family history on other areas of Latin America. Outside of Brazil and Mexico, the field tends to be identified less with institutional hubs than with prominent individual scholars.

Probably in part as a result of available sources, family history has tended to focus disproportionately on the late colonial period and the nineteenth century. As such, the scholarship has given particular attention to the transition from colonies to republics.[22] A number of studies have explored the articulation of household structures and early capitalist development.[23] Reflecting a burgeoning interest in state formation, recent scholarship has also examined family, conjugality, and property in the context of secularization and liberalism in postcolonial Latin America.[24]

An enduring theme running through this work concerns the historical evolution of patriarchy, understood to encompass power relations involving both gender and generation. *Longue durée* studies of colonial and imperial Brazil have emphasized the waning of patriarchy and extended kinship as new commercial opportunities arose and marriage and kin relations no longer constituted the sole means by which to establish one's economic and status position.[25] While patriarchy is not her analytic focus, Elizabeth Kuznesof's classic study of household structure in early-nineteenth-century São Paulo may be read as further evidence for the decline of patriarchy. Kuznesof found that protoindustrialization was associated with a rise in female headship, a finding replicated in other Latin American communities. Her broad point is not only that households were shaped by commercialization, urbanization, and early industrialization but that they mediated the specific forms these processes took in Latin America.[26]

In Spanish America, studies of late colonial patriarchy have drawn heavily on *disensos*, the disputes between parents and offspring over marriage choice. A centerpiece of these discussions is the Royal Pragmatic on Marriage of 1776, which expanded the prerogatives of fathers to control their children's choice of marriage partners.

Generally, the Pragmatic is seen as a last-ditch (and not very successful) effort to shore up beleaguered paternal prerogatives rather than the opening salvo in a new escalation of patriarchal power.[27] More generally, the Pragmatic reflected how attempts to manage social and racial took the form of regulations governing marriage, suggesting dynamics that sociopolitical order and family order were intertwined.[28] In her exploration of intergenerational authority and the changing textures of patriarchy in colonial Lima, Bianca Premo also seeks to link household politics to broader political change. Moving beyond *disensos*, her wide-ranging exploration of children and childrearing in all facets of *limeño* society also finds evidence of an embattled late-eighteenth-century patriarchy. She contends that an enlightened "new politics of the child" emphasized affective bonds, good treatment, and education aimed at creating economically useful subjects. Drawing on these ideas, unlikely patriarchs— mothers, wet nurses, slave parents—successfully challenged fathers and even the masters of slave children for custody of young people.[29]

If the emphasis of late colonial studies has been on the tempering of patriarchy, it is striking that the story seems to reverse in the nineteenth century. Scholars generally agree that the secularization of family law undermined the emphasis on free will and the thread of gender (as well as class and racial) egalitarianism that had historically characterized canon marriage law.[30] The codification of criminal and civil law introduced new discriminatory measures, such as a double standard in the treatment of male and female adultery.[31] In Chile, Andrés Bello's Civil Code applied liberal notions of free will, private property, and contract to illegitimate kin relations, empowering men at the expense of women and children. The liberal logic of kinship law has endured until the present day.[32]

Yet the impact of liberalism on family relations was decidedly contradictory. Elizabeth Dore, for example, has argued that in Nicaragua the privatization of property during the liberal coffee revolution devastated indigenous communities but gave women unprecedented access to land and spurred an increase in female headship. Focusing on liberalism as a set of philosophical tenets, Christine Hunefeldt contends that in nineteenth-century Peru, women drew on liberal notions of "personal rights and freedom, equal opportunities, and civil rights" to challenge patriarchal authority in conjugal disputes. Carmen Deere and Magdalena León find that liberal reforms of marriage law enhanced the "bargaining power and economic autonomy of married women," especially in Mexico and Central America.[33] These apparently contradictory findings about the effects of liberal law, doctrine, and policy on patriarchy likely reflect the heterogeneity both of liberalism as a political and economic ideology and of patriarchy, which denotes a range of gender and generational relationships within and beyond kin networks. These studies suggest that patriarchy needs to be disaggregated by class, by family type, and by specific social relations (because, for example, patriarchs' control over an extended kin group may decline even as husbands gain power over wives, as Muriel Nazzari shows in her study of the dowry's disappearance in Brazil). It is precisely the multifarious nature of patriarchal relations that family history is especially well suited to illuminate.

Sources and Methods

In its diverse guises, family history has been distinguished by an exceptionally rich source base. Demographic scholarship has utilized sources such as parish records and census manuscripts, often relying on methods first developed by Europeanists. But some of these methods proved inapplicable, spurring methodological innovation and giving the historical demography of Latin American families a distinct cast. For example, English family reconstitution techniques, in which parish registries are used to painstakingly reconstruct genealogical webs, proved unfeasible in most Latin American communities due to the instability of names, the mobility of populations, and the fact that family ties were frequently informal and unrecorded in such sources.[34] On the other hand, a number of Latin American societies boast high-quality household-based sources, ranging from Nahuatl-language registries for Central Mexico in the 1530s and 1540s, which Robert McCaa has characterized as "some of the richest household listings... in the early modern world," to the house-to-house enumerations carried out by military, clerical, and medical authorities in the late eighteenth and early nineteenth centuries. In the latter vein, Guiomar Dueñas Vargas made innovative use of an 1801 smallpox census to reconstruct household size and structure in Santa Fe de Bogotá.[35] Latin American census manuscripts tend to include much more extensive information than the European equivalents, providing opportunities for such techniques as life course analysis, which reconstructs how individuals' roles within households, and by extension in broader social structures, change over their lifetimes. The technique can identify such patterns as widespread servitude among Indian and *casta* adolescents, to give just one example from eighteenth-century Oaxacan registries studied by Cecilia Rabell and Robert McCaa.[36]

Qualitative approaches to family history have made use of wills and other notarial documentation, bureaucratic procedures such as legitimation petitions, and of course Inquisition records and judicial sources.[37] These last materials in particular have shaped the field's contours. The "dossier-oriented rather than adversarial" nature of law generated voluminous records of judicial proceedings with no functional equivalent in Anglo-American legal culture.[38] Such sources narrate everyday domestic life with a richness unparalleled in perhaps any other source, particularly for popular and plebeian sectors. Materials from ecclesiastical and secular courts, both civil and criminal, have been used to reconstruct relationships between spouses, between parents and children, within broader kin networks, and across kinship and community. Court proceedings reflect the striking frequency with which relationships and practices deemed private breached public space and were discussed, debated, and litigated.

On the other hand, a heavy reliance on such sources may overemphasize intrafamilial violence and gender conflict. As Susan Socolow has suggested, reconstructing colonial Mexican patriarchy through criminal records may be "akin to analyzing modern wife batterers and murderers to understand gender relations in the late twentieth century United States."[39] Even seemingly more innocuous evidence, such as marriage rates drawn from censuses, can create a mirage of "deviance." In many countries, marriage rates plummeted and illegitimacy rates rose with the nineteenth-century secularization of marriage. The vertiginous spike in illegitimacy rates in Guatemala in the 1870s, especially in indigenous communities, reflects the enduring cultural validity of marriage rites that newly established civil law no longer recognized. Likewise, in Chile a decade later, marriage rates fell and illegitimacy increased as poor couples ignored civil marriage and continued to contract now civilly invalid Catholic unions.[40] In such cases, low nuptiality and high illegitimacy reflected not subaltern deviance but an adherence to traditional definitions of marriage in the face of the state's attempt to impose new ones. Yet even if the ensuing statistical blips reflect changes in law rather than in social practice, such legal developments affected which families enjoyed legal recognition and who enjoyed the rights to mutual support or inheritance accorded kin. As such, these "fictitious" changes had very real social and material consequences.

Even taking into account the fact that certain sources may magnify nonnormativity, it is difficult to ignore the persistent and ubiquitous divergence of family practices from dominant prescription, especially among popular sectors, in Latin American societies historically. Historians disagree, however, about how to interpret that divergence. Invoking the preponderance of extramarital sexuality, concubinage, and consensual unions in Latin American societies, Swedish sociologist Göran Therborn has colorfully suggested that "Iberian colonial America and the West Indies were the stage of the largest-scale assault on marriage in history."[41] But did creole nonmarriage reflect an "assault" in the sense of a deliberate rejection of dominant norms by (mostly plebeian) subcultures? In some places it may have, but in nineteenth-century Brazil, for example, Sandra Lauderdale Graham has argued that poor people desired to marry but were stymied by economic and bureaucratic hurdles. Whether nonnormative practices reflected a repudiation of normative structures or discriminatory exclusion from them in turn feeds into broad debates over the relative autonomy of popular versus elite cultures.[42]

Familial nonnormativity has generated questions about the consequences of such practices for the relative status and power of those embedded in them. For example, did women become household heads because of their relative economic and social empowerment? Or did the absence of men in such households reflect women's relative lack of bargaining power and their economic marginalization? In other words, did this nonnormative household form reflect an attenuation of patriarchy or an expression of it?

Meanwhile, family history's reliance on such sources as parish registries, census manuscripts, and notarial records has lent a distinctly local cast to the scholarship. Scholars working with demographic data have uncovered striking variations in family patterns across relatively small geographic areas, reflecting variations in land tenure, modes of economic production, and ethnic and class composition.[43] Pablo Rodríguez has suggested that the regional diversity of Colombia "makes it impossible to discern the existence of a specific type of Colombian family."[44] In Brazil, challenging Gilberto Freyre's unitary "Brazilian family" has involved the laborious construction of a portrait of regional variation through work in local archives far from Freyre's native Pernambuco. Such local and regional perspectives have conferred a fine-grained empirical richness to the study of family.

Yet even as local studies abound, the nation-state commands a central place in conceptual frameworks, particularly in scholarship produced in Latin America. Multivolume series explore the histories of "private life" in Argentina, Brazil, Chile, and Uruguay.[45] Such efforts raise obvious questions. Is there such a thing as an Argentine family, and if so when did it come into existence? Is it distinct from the Brazilian family or the Uruguayan family, and if so, how? Clara López Beltrán's observation about the difficulties of generalizing about families in Bolivia due to the cultural heterogeneity of populations spanning the Andean sierra, the Amazon basin, and the Chaco raises the fundamental question of whether constructing a Bolivian family history is even possible, or useful, in the first place.[46]

The centrality of the nation-state in family history reflects its continuing primacy in Latin American historiography generally, global and transnational currents notwithstanding. But studies of family are probably especially predisposed to such a framework because of the strong discursive identification of "family" and "nation," which emerged soon after independence.[47] It may also reflect the notion—articulated most famously by Gilberto Freyre for the Brazilian context—that the family harbors some essential collective identity. As Freyre argued, the Brazilian family refracts nothing less than the essence of Brazilian civilization: "It is in the Big Houses that, down to this day, the Brazilian character has found its best expression...In studying the domestic life of our ancestors we feel that we are completing ourselves: it is...another means of finding ourselves in others, in those who lived before us and whose life anticipates our own."[48] More recently, Pablo Rodríguez has echoed a parallel sentiment in asserting, "in the family Colombians have learned regional ways of being [*maneras de ser*], tastes, speech, and temperament. In a definitive sense, the family has contrived the destiny of every individual but also of our social structure."[49] Such perspectives help explain why family history's privileging of the nation-state is not necessarily incongruous with the preponderance of colonial-era scholarship. "Nation" here is conceived of less as a political unit than as the collective character of a people.

The Decline of Family History

In retrospect, the 1980s and 1990s represented a high-water mark for Latin American family history. Those decades witnessed a surge of scholarship on marriage, gender relations in the household, patriarchy, conjugality, domesticity, sexuality, and honor. Interest in such themes continues unabated in the new millennium. Yet it has occurred concomitantly with a quiet decline in family history as a field. For increasingly, these themes have been explored in the context not of family history but of the history of women, gender, and sexuality, fields that have experienced an extraordinary boom in Latin

American historiography. As Louise Tilly noted in an influential essay, women's history and family history intersect but are animated by different analytic questions, conceptual categories, and political agendas.[50] Indeed, women's history was in part born of the conviction that women had histories outside of the domestic sphere. Family history engages with certain social relationships (kinship, generation), categories (age, household), and historical subjects (children) that are relevant to women's and gender history only as they intersect with other, primary concerns. Today, many of family history's time-honored themes—marriage, domesticity, and the like—continue to attract widespread interest, but their analysis has become reoriented around the frameworks and categories of gender history, particularly in U.S.-based scholarship. It is thus increasingly difficult to discern family history as a discrete subfield with a distinct agenda.[51]

The decline of family as a category in Latin American historiography reflects the fate of family history generally. There are several reasons for that decline. In the context of "cultural wars" in U.S. political culture, "the family" is freighted with normative connotations and political associations (think Focus on the Family, Dr. James Dobson's right-wing evangelical organization). The field's trajectory also reflects trends in the academy. With its strong empiricist roots, family history as traditionally conceived is not especially compatible with poststructural approaches. Finally, the field has suffered from its association with discredited models of social change. As discussed above, "family" first emerged as a subject of Latin Americanist scholarship in analyses of modernization and underdevelopment, in which it served as a key signifier of "tradition." As modernization frameworks were discarded, the family apparently went with them.

These observations about family history's decline are claims less about individual works of scholarship than about the historiography collectively. Undoubtedly, some works pointedly engage with the concepts and frameworks of family history, and some individual scholars embrace the category of family and the field of family history, sometimes quite deliberately.[52] But the very need for such a self-consciously unapologetic stand only reinforces the perception of a field on the wane. Meanwhile, in Latin America–based scholarship, "the family" enjoys a greater currency than in U.S. circles. This may stem from the lesser influence of poststructural approaches or simply the greater stature the field has traditionally enjoyed in Latin American historiographies. Scholars also seem less concerned with drawing a distinction between women's history and family history, a hallmark of feminist history elsewhere. The coexistence of the two fields may reflect the distinct tenor of Latin American feminism.[53]

Looking Forward

Many of the foregoing observations about family history contain implicit suggestions as to where the field might go next. One of the strengths of Latin American family history is its attentiveness to regional and local variation, ethnic heterogeneity, and class difference. At the same time, the field's local sources and its abiding attachment to the nation mean that it has not systematically engaged in the sort of comparative analysis that would generate higher-order generalizations about family patterns historically.[54] It is not surprising that one of the boldest efforts on this score is the work not of a historian but of a sociologist. Göran Therborn's *Between Sex and Power: Family in the World, 1900–2000* posits the existence of five global family systems, of which one is the "creole" family of Latin America, the Caribbean, and the U.S. south: extending "from the Mason-Dixon Line to the Rio de la Plata," this family pattern, he suggests, exhibited a logic that was "dualistic, hierarchical and violent."[55] The notion of "a" hemispheric family culture, quite aside from Therborn's characterization of it, will surely give some historians pause, and yet no one has conducted a systematic search for the commonalities (or differences) that would confirm (or refute) his hypothesis. Meanwhile, where Therborn emphasizes commonality, other evidence suggests variation. In a recent study examining gendered patterns of transnational migration, several sociologists discern a link between family forms in sending societies and the propensity of men and women to migrate. Comparing several Latin American centers of out-migration, they find low rates of informal unions, illegitimacy, and marital disruption in Mexico and Costa Rica, but high rates of marital separation, informal unions, illegitimacy, and female headship in the Dominican Republic and Nicaragua. They conclude that "patriarchal" societies like Mexico give rise to different patterns of male and female migration than do "matrifocal" ones like the Dominican Republic.[56]

Historians will no doubt recoil at such reifications. But it is striking that we must rely on sociologists with no specific expertise in the region and with other research agendas to ask critical questions concerning patterns of convergence and divergence in family forms across Latin America. For historians, such studies raise as many questions as they answer. Are the differential patterns they discern of recent or long-standing historical vintage? Do they reflect the deep legacies of landowning peasant communities versus plantation slavery, for example? Or might they reflect the varying success with which different twentieth-century states have shaped family forms through family wages, pensions, and other incentives? And does this emphasis on variation obscure fundamental hemispheric commonalities, of the kind Therborn emphasizes? Such unresolved questions should inspire Latin Americanist historians to engage in more far-reaching comparative analysis.

One obvious axis of comparison involves the Caribbean and the rest of the hemisphere. This overview of family history has not treated kinship and family studies in the Caribbean, a discrete subfield that has focused on Anglophone societies and is primarily associated with anthropologists. Caribbean family studies emerged out of analytic debates about the origins of Afro-descended cultures in the West Indies and the Americas. This scholarship asked whether the family forms that characterized West Indian kinship and household structures (matrifocality, female headship, child circulation, etc.) reflected African cultural survivals or adaptations to slavery and (post)colonial circumstance. But many of the family forms this literature identified as West Indian have parallels across the hemisphere. Nor are they limited to plantation societies or to Afro-descended populations. Mid-twentieth-century rates of illegitimacy in Guatemala and Honduras were roughly equivalent to or exceeded those in the anglophone Caribbean and the Dominican Republic.[57] Child circulation or "shifting"—the rearing of children by adults other than their parents—is historically ubiquitous in the West Indies but also in urban Mexico, the Andes, and Chile.[58] The division between Caribbean and Latin American family studies consequently appears an artificial creation of originary debates. Scholarship that takes a wide-angle view of family structures across the hemisphere will help to clarify the causes, meanings, and consequences of its diverse family practices.[59]

Comparison also invites engagement with theories based on the historical experience of other world regions. Since the 1960s, a central claim of European family historiography has been that the family regime that emerged in Western Europe by 1500 differed from all other agrarian societies globally. European families were distinguished by at least two key features: women and men married relatively late, and significant numbers of women never married.[60] In a recent book, Mary Hartman argues that in fomenting particular patterns of property ownership, capital formation, investment strategies, and labor markets, Europe's unique family pattern catalyzed nothing less than the transition to capitalism and the rise of the nation-state—that is, the emergence of the modern West.[61] How do we read this theory against the evidence from Latin America, and how might it in turn inform our understanding of hemispheric family patterns? While existing demographic data is scattered, evidence from diverse communities, from early-nineteenth-century Mexico City to nineteenth- and early-twentieth-century rural Chile, suggests that low and late marriage was also common in Latin America.[62] Does such evidence challenge the claim of European exceptionalism? Or does it indicate the fundamentally European character of marriage patterns in the hemisphere? If the latter, it is surely crucial that in Latin America low marriage rates were historically associated with extreme class and racial hierarchies. And they cannot be said to have catalyzed the modern economic and political forms to which, in Hartman's interpretation, they gave rise in Europe. That is, nuptial patterns that look similar across regions may be imbued with starkly different meanings and outcomes. Demographic particularities, in short, do not exist outside of a broader social and cultural matrix—an obvious point, but one that comparative dialogue helps bring into focus.[63]

A second area for further research is the twentieth century. Family history has focused primarily on the colonial period and the nineteenth and early twentieth centuries, leaving the peculiar impression that "family" is a category that belongs to the past. To the extent that historians of the twentieth century have engaged with the family, it is primarily as an object of social engineering on the part of developmentalist, revolutionary, or authoritarian political projects. We know a considerable amount about the policies and discursive postures of twentieth-century states, political parties and movements, parastatal professionals, and law vis-à-vis family and gender.[64] We know very little about household structures, kin relations, and familial practices outside these moments of pointed political interest and orchestration.

What we do know derives primarily from the work of anthropologists and other social scientists. Recent social science scholarship has explored the impact of changing labor markets, shrinking social provision, and burgeoning poverty—trends associated with neoliberal reform—on household structures, gender politics, and kin networks.[65] We need additional research that explores the historical antecedents of these developments. For example, many observers have remarked on the increase in female household headship in the past two decades. Does this development represent yet another iteration of a household pattern ubiquitous since at least the eighteenth century? Or is there something new and unprecedented about contemporary female headship?[66] Such questions seem particularly important given the fact that political rhetoric and legal reforms often have less impact on families than do prevailing economic circumstances. As Heidi Tinsman has shown, Augusto Pinochet espoused a rhetoric of traditional family roles even as his policies increased women's labor force participation and catalyzed "the erosion of male dominance, an increase in women's political agency, and the emergence of gender equality as an ideal."[67] Focusing on family as political discourse may tell us relatively little about what is happening to actual families.

Beyond the expansion of its geographic or temporal scope, another task for family history involves a more self-conscious evaluation of its working categories. The earliest scholarship on Latin American family history cautioned that "since the local context and culture are...crucial in conceptualizing what is meant by 'family' or 'household,' kinship units must be defined with reference to local patterns of communication and exchange."[68] The field has not yet fully realized such broad and culturally grounded concepts. For example, we have little systematic historical work on cultural practices such as spiritual kinship (*compadrazgo/compadrio*) or the rearing of children by nonprogenitors (*crianza/criação*), both important aspects of Latin American kin relations.[69] Yet such "para-kinship" networks may have far-reaching significance, not least because they blur the distinction between "family" and community. As David Lehmann has suggested, relationships of *compadrazgo* "represent a nuancing or greying of the boundaries of the family nucleus, an extension of kin-like obligations through an expanding network." Through such networks, "people can arrange fostering of children, labour exchange, sharecropping contracts, or, where the status of the compadres is unequal, patronage in economic relationships and access to benefits from the state machine."[70] This may be particularly true in plebeian communities. Lara Putnam has suggested that among poor migrants in Caribbean Costa Rica, kinship and community formed a seamless continuum.[71] However we define them (and their definition should be part of family history's intellectual project), family and kinship constitute a central dimension of, and a window onto, the cultural texture and logic of social relations of power, patronage, and inequality, as well as of solidarity, affinity, and affect.

Another challenge is to integrate the two class-specific literatures on Latin American families. This organization of knowledge reflects differences in the methods and frameworks that originally characterized these subfields, but ultimately it does little to advance our understanding of Latin American families. For one, it obscures the fact that even in the face of starkly different family cultures, commonalities characterized kin relations across class, ethnic, and rural-urban boundaries. For example, Larissa A. Lomnitz and Marisol Pérez-Lizaur identified the three-generation "grand family" as a common form of kinship organization within the Mexican upper and lower classes alike.[72] *Compadrazgo/compadrio* is another shared characteristic.

Second, the bifurcated historiography implies that families of different social groups inhabited different social universes and obscures the extent to which households and kin networks themselves served as sites where social groups came together. Through spiritual kinship, patronage, servitude, or slavery, families of subordinate and superordinate status shared multigenerational ties to each other. As Sandra Lauderdale Graham observes of Brazil, "the conduct of family life reached to include servants, labourers, and other dependent clients, sometimes kin. Family thus becomes an appropriate metaphor for the larger society."[73] Of course, individuals of different social backgrounds also formed relationships (often proscribed by social norms) and had children together.

Finally, and perhaps most importantly, we need to understand how class-specific concepts of "family" were constituted in the first place. Families of different social statuses were always defined in relation to one another, with the contrasts (sometimes supposed contrasts) between them accorded great normative significance. Socially and legally recognized family was an entitlement that conferred invaluable material and symbolic resources—status, respectability, support, solidarity, social networks, affect, inheritance. Not all individuals had access to this entitlement, because law and social norms did not recognize all families. Yet the distinction between "formal" and "informal" families, to use Lauderdale Graham's terms, was a socially and legally constructed one. And if *las familias decentes* differed in fundamental ways from their plebeian counterparts, this divergence was a historically produced outcome rather than an a priori fact. This process is precisely what family history's traditional division of labor obscures.

Paying attention to the historically constructed boundaries between formal and informal families in turn directs out attention to how family patterns emerged in, and were sustained by, a social order riven by class and ethnic hierarchies. Patterns of elite prescription and popular practice, indeed the very definitions of norm and transgression, have often mapped on to the fissures of class, race, and ethnicity. Not surprisingly, marital and sexual "nonconformity" has been concentrated in (though not limited to) particular socially and racially marginalized populations. Meanwhile, the hierarchical social order itself generated "nonconformity." Social and legal norms of endogamy have been a major factor in encouraging consensual unions and illegitimacy, and marriage could be inaccessible to the poor. In other words, family opens up a lens onto the social reproduction of class and racial inequality in colonial and postcolonial Latin America—questions first posed, albeit in a different analytic guise, by Freyre in 1933 and explored in a number of influential works since.[74] If modernization long served as the traditional interpretive framework for histories of family and children, perhaps colonialism provides a more appropriate and productive paradigm for Latin America, as Bianca Premo has argued.[75]

By invoking colonialism, I do not mean to return family history to a distant past. The field has substantial work to do in the present, not least in contemporary public discussions of family issues. The "family disintegration" narratives so voluble in U.S. political discourse also resonate in Latin America. Historians have an obligation to challenge the deeply ahistorical premises of these narratives and to debunk myths of an imagined past.[76] These narratives are at times unwittingly abetted by contemporary social science. In the recent scholarship on contemporary households and gender roles, as in public discourse, the foil of the "traditional" family lives on. Scholars invoke such novelties as "the weakening of a model of family based on the stable exercise of authority…by the adult male head" and the "new concept of paternity-maternity that does not necessarily involve a stable relationship among the progenitors."[77] Severed from history, contemporary patterns invite misinterpretation.

Family appears in a very different guise in cultural determinist explanations of underdevelopment. In one recent assessment, Frances Fukuyama repeats the old refrain that Latin America "suffers from familism." Revamping (somewhat) the terms of the original modernization literature, he and others have identified the supposed hypercentrality of family relations with a lack of trust, a dearth of social capital, and corruption.[78] Samuel Huntington has repeated the well-worn contention that familistic values represent an obstacle to economic advancement among Mexican Americans.[79]

But family history's role is not limited to debunking imagined households and spurious claims about deleterious family cultures. Diverse contemporary social and political phenomena implicate kinship, household, and family relations, though not necessarily in the ways the cultural determinists would suggest. The significance of kin ties in structuring migration is of course well known, and transnational motherhoods, fatherhoods, childhoods, and households have moved to the center of migration studies.[80] Meanwhile, neoliberalism's impact on public safety nets appears to have accentuated the significance of private ones. The economic strategies of the urban poor indicate the enduring importance of household and kinship strategies, "not only for survival, but also for accumulation and gain."[81] And if Maria Rosaria Stabili's oral history of elite Chilean women is any indication, family lineage continues to constitute an important source of group identity and solidarity among the upper classes.[82]

Less obvious is the role households may play in contemporary social movements. Alejandro Portes and Kelly Hoffman have argued that political mobilization in Latin America is increasingly community- rather than workplace-based and revolves around protests over prices and basic public services rather than wages and working conditions.[83] Given that households are the primary units of consumption of increasingly elusive goods and services, it may well be that they constitute a logical focus for analyzing these mobilizations. What contributions might family historians make to understanding households as loci of political mobilization?[84]

The significance of family is found well beyond the household. Carlos Vilas has shown that in Nicaragua, dense kin ties linked the Sandinista leadership to traditional elite families, perhaps attenuating the most acute tensions between the two groups.[85] Meanwhile, the experience of, and ensuing forms of resistance to, political violence in Cold War and post–Cold War Latin America have been structured not only by gender, as many scholars have pointed out, but also by family roles and relationships. The Madres de la Plaza de Mayo were joined by the Abuelas, and more recently, by the H.I.J.O.S., a group representing the children of victims of state violence.[86] The members of all these organizations have claimed family relationships as the basis for political identities. Most participants invoke their status as relatives of victims of political violence. Some claim a kinship that is figurative.[87] Yet even if they "only" represent expedient labels, they suggest familial claims enjoy legitimacy in the political sphere and that kinship's power can be metaphorical. These political manifestations of kinship deserve historical analysis.[88]

Ultimately, it is possible to appraise the significance of family relationships and kin identities to social organization, economic survival, political power, class and status distinctions, and sociopolitical identities in Latin America's past and present without falling into facile stereotypes of Latin "familism." Indeed, through systematic and wide-ranging investigation of families in Latin American societies, family history is particularly well poised to challenge such stereotypes in the first place.

NOTES

1. Perry Anderson, "The Family World System," *The Nation*, May 30, 2005.

2. Jack Goody, "The Labyrinth of Kinship," *New Left Review* 36, November-December 2005.

3. See the two-volume special issue "The New History: The 1980s and Beyond," *Journal of Interdisciplinary History* 12:1 (1981), in which Lawrence Stone authored the contribution on family history, "Family History in the 1980s: Past Achievements and Future Trends," *ibid.* 51–87; Jane Turner Censer, "What Ever Happened to Family History? A Review Article," *Comparative Studies in Society and History* 33:3 (1991): 528–38; Cissie Fairchilds, "Review of *Family Life in Early Modern Times, 1500–1789*," *Journal of Social History* 37:2 (2003): 523–25, 525.

4. Ann Blum offers a similar assessment of the historiography in "Bringing It Back Home: Perspectives on Gender and Family History in Modern Mexico," *History Compass* 4:5 (2006): 906–26.

5. Benjamín Vicuña Mackenna, *Historia crítica y social de la Ciudad de Santiago, desde su fundacion hasta nuestros dias (1541–1868)*, vol. 2 (Santiago: Imprenta del Mercurio, 1869), 74.

6. Marianne Schmink, "Household Economic Strategies: Review and Research Agenda," *Latin American Research Review* 19:3 (1984): 87–101, 89; Janet Carsten, "Introduction: Cultures of Relatedness," in *Cultures of Relatedness: New Approaches to the Study of Kinship*, ed. Janet Carsten (New York: Cambridge University Press, 2000), 1–36.

7. Gilberto Freyre, *The Masters and the Slaves: A Study in the Development of Brazilian Civilization*, 2nd ed. (New York: Alfred A. Knopf, 1956), xliii.

8. The concept of "resources of poverty" derives from Mercedes González de la Rocha's book of the same name, *Los recursos de la pobreza: Familias de bajos ingresos de Guadalajara* (Guadalajara: El Colegio de Jalisco/CIESAS/SPP, 1986), subsequently published as *The Resources of Poverty: Women and Survival in a Mexican City* (Cambridge: Blackwell, 1994). "Primary group": Edelmann, 1965, cited in Manuel L. Carlos and Lois Sellers, "Family, Kinship Structure, and Modernization in Latin America" *Latin American Research Review* 7:2 (1972): 95–124, 95. For a review of work on household-based survival strategies among the urban poor, see Schmink, "Household Economic Strategies."

9. Carlos and Sellers, "Family, Kinship Structure, and Modernization"; Raymond T. Smith, *Kinship Ideology and Practice in Latin America* (Chapel Hill: University of North Carolina, 1984), 3–4; Francesca M. Cancian, Louis Wolf Goodman, and Peter H. Smith, "Introduction to special issue on The Family in Latin America," *Journal of Family History* 3:4 (1978): 314–17; Charles Wagley, "Luso-Brazilian Kinship Patterns: The Persistence of a Cultural Tradition," in *Politics of Change in Latin America*, ed. Joseph Maier and Richard W. Weatherhead (New York: Praeger, 1964), 174–89; Oscar Lewis, *Five Families: Mexican Case Studies in the Culture of Poverty* (1959); *The Children of Sánchez, Autobiography of a Mexican Family* (1961); *La Vida: A Puerto Rican Family in the Culture of Poverty—San Juan and New York* (1966).

10. European family history was also concerned with the relationship of kinship to modernization, but in Latin America the issue had particular salience because of the abiding preoccupation with development. See for example Cancian et al., "Introduction," and Elizabeth Anne Kuznesof and Robert Oppenheimer, "The Family and Society in Nineteenth-Century Latin America: An Historiographical Introduction," *Journal of Family History* 10:3 (1985): 215–34.

11. A special issue of the *Journal of Family History* on Latin America—the first ever of its kind—included seven empirical essays, only two of which were authored by historians The 1978 issue was the product of an interdisciplinary working group sponsored by the ACLS and the SSRC.

12. Mary Lowenthal Felstiner, "Family Metaphors: The Language of an Independence Revolution," *Comparative Studies in Society and History* 25:1 (1983): 154–80; Doris M. Ladd, *The Mexican Nobility at Independence, 1780–1826* (Austin: University of Texas Press, 1976); Susan Migden Socolow, *The Merchants of Buenos Aires, 1778–1810: Family and Commerce* (Cambridge: Cambridge University Press, 1978); Susan Migden Socolow, *The Bureaucrats of Buenos Aires, 1769–1810: Amor al real servicio* (Durham, N.C.: Duke University Press, 1987); John E. Kicza, *Colonial Entrepreneurs, Families and Business in Bourbon Mexico City* (Albuquerque: University of New Mexico Press, 1983); Diana A. Balmori, Stuart F. Voss, and Miles Wortman, *Notable Family Networks in Latin America* (Chicago: University of Chicago Press, 1984); David W. Walker, *Kinship, Business, and Politics: The Martínez del Río Family in Mexico, 1824–1867* (Austin: University of Texas Press, 1986); María Collado, *La burguesia mexicana: El emporio Braniff y su participación política, 1865–1920* (Mexico City: Siglo XXI, 1987); Darrell Levi, *The Prados of São Paulo, Brazil: An Elite Family and Social Change, 1840–1930* (Athens: University of Georgia Press, 1987); Linda Lewin, *Politics and Parentela in Paraíba: A Case Study of Family-Based Oligarchy in Brazil* (Princeton: Princeton University Press, 1987); Larissa Adler Lomnitz and Marisol Pérez-Lizaur, *A Mexican Elite Family, 1820–1980: Kinship, Class, and Culture* (Princeton: Princeton University Press, 1987); Robert J. Ferry, *The Colonial Elite of Early Caracas: Formation and Crisis, 1567–1767* (Berkeley: University of California Press, 1989); John Tutino, "Power, Class and Family: Men and

Women in the Mexican Elite, 1750–1810," *The Americas* 39:3 (1983): 359–81; Dain Borges, *The Family in Bahia, Brazil, 1870–1945* (Stanford: Stanford University Press, 1994); Beatriz Bragoni, *Los hijos de la revolución: Familia, negocios y poder en Mendoza en el siglo XIX* (Buenos Aires: Taurus, 1999); and from a sociological perspective, Maurice Zeitlin and Richard Earl Ratcliff, *Landlords and Capitalists: The Dominant Class of Chile* (Princeton: Princeton University Press, 1988). An excellent overview of several of these works is Elizabeth Anne Kuznesof, "The History of the Family in Latin America: A Critique of Recent Work," *Latin American Research Review* 24:2 (1989): 168–86.

13. Lomnitz and Pérez-Lizaur, *A Mexican Elite Family*, 5–6; 157–91; quote is from p. 157. See also Kuznesof, "History of Family," 178.

14. Kuznesof, "History of Family," 184.

15. A much smaller body of works applied social history sensibilities to elite families, for example, Muriel Nazzari, *Disappearance of the Dowry: Women, Families, and Social Change in São Paulo, Brazil, 1600–1900* (Stanford: Stanford University Press, 1991), and more recently Ann Twinam, *Public Lives, Private Secrets: Gender, Honor, Sexuality, and Illegitimacy in Colonial Spanish America* (Stanford: Stanford University Press, 1999). A few scholars have looked at families across the social spectrum, for example, Alida Metcalf, *Family and Frontier in Colonial Brazil: Santana de Parnaíba, 1580–1822* (Berkeley: University of California Press, 1992; repr. University of Texas Press, 2005).

16. The literature on these issues is voluminous. Some influential studies of marriage and concubinage include Pablo Rodríguez, *Seducción, amancebamiento y abandono en la colonia* (Bogotá: Fundación Simón y Lola Guberek, 1991); Verena Martínez-Alier [Stolke], *Marriage, Class and Colour in Nineteenth-Century Cuba: A Study of Racial Attitudes and Sexual Values in a Slave Society* (Ann Arbor: University of Michigan Press, 1974); on illegitimacy, Guiomar Dueñas Vargas, *Los hijos del pecado: Ilegitimidad y vida familiar en la Santafé de Bogotá colonial* (Bogotá: Editorial Universidad Nacional, 1997); María Emma Mannarelli, *Pecados públicos: La ilegitimidad en Lima, siglo XVII* (Lima: Flora Tristán, 1993); Twinam, *Public Lives, Private Secrets*. See also the contributions to the special issue "Female and Family in Nineteenth-Century Latin America" of the *Journal of Family History* 16:3 (1991).

17. Pablo Rodríguez, "La familia en Colombia," in *La familia en Iberoamérica, 1550–1980*, ed. Pablo Rodríguez (Bogotá: Universidad Externado de Colombia, 2004), 277.

18. Silvia Arrom, "Historia de la mujer y de la familia," *Historia Mexicana* XLII:2 (1992): 379–418.

19. In Brazil, some of the major figures in family history, such as Maria Luiza Marcilio, were trained as demographic historians. The University of São Paulo's Centro de Estudos de Demografia Histórica da América Latina (CEDHAL) has been an important center for the development of family history as well as the history of children and childhood. On the historiography of slave families in Brazil, which also grew out of historical demography, see Stuart Schwartz, "Recent Trends in the Study of Brazilian Slavery," in *Slaves, Peasants, and Rebels: Reconsidering Brazilian Slavery* (Urbana: University of Illinois Press, 1996), 10–11. Of course, the importance of demographic approaches has not precluded an interest in cultural values, perceptions, and meanings, evident in such works as Maria Odila Silva Dias, *Power and Everyday Life: Working Women in Nineteenth-Century Brazil* (New Brunswick, N.J.: Rutgers University Press, 1995); Angela Mendes de Almeida, *O gosto do pecado: Casamento e sexualidade nos manuais de confessores dos séculos XVI e XVII* (Lisbon: Rocco, 1994); Laura de Melo e Souza, *The Devil and the Land of the Holy Cross: Witchcraft, Slavery, and Popular Religion in Colonial Brazil* (Austin: University of Texas, 2004).

20. Eni de Mesquita Samara has offered particularly influential refutations of the Freyrean model in such works as *As mulheres, o poder e a família: São Paulo, século XIX*

(São Paulo: Marco Zero, 1989) and *A família brasileira* (São Paulo: Brasiliense, 1983). See also Elizabeth Kuznesof, "Sexuality, Gender and the Family in Colonial Brazil," *Luso-Brazilian Review* 30:1 (1993): 119–32; Eni de Mesquita Samara and Dora Isabel Paiva da Costa, "Family, Patriarchalism, and Social Change in Brazil," *Latin American Research Review* 32:1 (1997): 212–25; B. J. Barickman, "Revisiting the *Casa-grande*: Plantation and Cane-Farming Households in Early Nineteenth-Century Bahia," *Hispanic American Historical Review* 84:4 (2004): 619–59.

21. The Seminario de Historia de las Mentalidades of the Instituto Nacional de Antropologia e Historia has been a particularly productive center for the history of colonial family and sexuality, generating a multitude of works on these topics, especially in the 1980s and early 1990s: *Familia y sexualidad en Nueva España* (Mexico City: Fondo de Cultura Económica, 1982); *La memoria y el olvido*, Segundo Simposio de Historia de las Mentalidades (Mexico City: INAH-SEP, 1985); Sergio Ortega, ed., *De la santidad a la perversión o de porqué no se cumplía la ley de Dios en la sociedad novohispana* (México, Grijalbo, 1986); *Del dicho al hecho: Transgresiones y pautas culturales en Nueva España* (Mexico City: INAH, 1989); *El placer de pecar y el afán de normar: Ideologías y comportamientos familiares y sexuales en el México colonial* (Mexico City: Joaquin Moritz, 1986); *Familia y poder en Nueva España: Memoria del Tercer Simposio de Historia de las Mentalidades* (Mexico City: INAH, 1991); *Amor y desamor: Vivencias de parejas en la sociedad novohispanas* (Mexico City: INAH, 1992); *Comunidades domésticas en la sociedad novohispana: Formas de unión y transmisión cultural* (Mexico City: INAH, 1994); *Vida cotidiana y cultura en el México virreinal: Antología* (Mexico City: INAH, 2000).

22. Sarah C. Chambers, *From Subjects to Citizens: Honor, Gender, and Politics in Arequipa, Peru, 1780–1854* (University Park: Penn State University Press, 1999); Arlene J. Díaz, *Female Citizens, Patriarchs, and the Law in Venezuela, 1786–1904* (Lincoln: University of Nebraska Press, 2004); Eugenia Rodríguez Sáenz, *Hijas, novias y esposas: Familia, matrimonio y violencia doméstica en el Valle Central de Costa Rica (1750–1850)* (Heredia, Costa Rica: Editorial Universidad Nacional, 2000); Jeffrey Shumway, *The Case of the Ugly Suitor and Other Histories of Love, Gender, and Nation in Buenos Aires, 1776–1870* (Lincoln: University of Nebraska Press, 2005); as well as a number of the elite family studies cited above.

23. Elizabeth Anne Kuznesof, *Household Economy and Urban Development, São Paulo, 1765–1836* (Boulder, Colo.: Westview Press, 1986); Ann Hagerman Johnson, "The Impact of Market Agriculture on Family and Household Structure in Nineteenth-Century Chile," *Hispanic American Historical Review* 58:4 (1978): 625–48; Donald Ramos, "Single and Married Women in Vila Rica, Brazil, 1754–1838," *Journal of Family History* 16:3 (1991): 261–82; Dore, "Property, Households and Public Regulation."

24. See footnote 33.

25. Alida Metcalf, *Family and Frontier*; Nazzari, *Disappearance of the Dowry*. At the same time, Nazzari argues that the disappearance of the dowry increased wives' dependence on husbands since they could no longer fall back on this independent source of economic support.

26. Elizabeth Anne Kuznesof, "The Role of the Female-Headed Household in Brazilian Modernization," *Journal of Social History* 13:4 (1980): 589–613. See also Dias, *Power and Everyday Life*.

27. There is, however, some disagreement on this point. Patricia Seed argues that late-eighteenth-century Mexican parents enjoyed expanded power over their children's marriage choices, a contention disputed by Arrom and Socolow in their reviews of her book, Patricia Seed, *To Love, Honor, and Obey in Colonial Mexico* (Stanford: Stanford University Press, 1988). The Royal Pragmatic also secularized these disputes, shifting

jurisdiction over them from the church to the state. See also Socolow, "Acceptable Partners," in Asunción Lavrin, ed., *Sexuality and Marriage in Colonial Latin America* (Lincoln: University of Nebraska Press, 1989); Shumway, *Case of the Ugly Suitor*; Mark D. Szuchman, "A Challenge to the Patriarchs: Love Among the Youth in Nineteenth-Century Argentina," in *The Middle Period in Latin America: Values and Attitudes in the 17th–19th Centuries*, ed. Szuchman (Boulder, Colo.: Lynne Rienner, 1989), 141–65.

28. Martínez-Alier, *Marriage, Class and Colour*.

29. Bianca Premo, *Children of the Father King: Youth, Authority, and Legal Minority in Colonial Lima* (Chapel Hill: University of North Carolina Press, 2005).

30. Socolow, "Acceptable Partners."

31. Elizabeth Dore, "One Step Forward, Two Steps Back: Gender and the State in the Long Nineteenth Century," in *Hidden Histories of Gender and the State in Latin America*, ed. Elizabeth Dore and Maxine Molyneux, (Durham, N.C.: Duke University Press, 2000), 3–32.

32. Nara Milanich, *Children of Fate: Childhood, Class, and the State in Chile, 1850–1930* (Durham, N.C.: Duke University Press, 2009).

33. Elizabeth Dore, "Property, Households and Public Regulation of Domestic Life: Diriomo, Nicaragua, 1840–1900," in Dore and Molyneux, ed., *Hidden Histories of Gender*, 147–71; Elizabeth Dore, *Myths of Modernity: Peonage and Patriarchy in Nicaragua* (Durham, N.C.: Duke University Press, 2006); Christine Hunefeldt, *Liberalism in the Bedroom: Quarreling Spouses in Nineteenth-Century Lima* (University Park: Penn State University Press, 2000), 178; Carmen Diana Deere and Magdalena León, "Liberalism and Married Women's Property Rights in Nineteenth-Century Latin America," *Hispanic American Historical Review* 85:4 (2005): 627–78, 630. See also Sueann Caulfield, Sarah Chambers, and Lara Putnam, eds. *Honor, Status, and Law in Modern Latin America* (Durham, N.C.: Duke University Press, 2005).

34. Robert McCaa, "Families and Gender in Mexico: A Methodological Critique and Research Challenge for the End of the Millennium," in *IV Conferencia Iberoamericana Sobre Familia: Historia de Familia* (Cartagena: Universidad Externado de Colombia, 1997), 1–2.

35. McCaa, "Families and Gender," 2; Dueñas Vargas, *Hijos del pecado*. In contrast to most household registers, the smallpox census recorded with particular care the presence of children and youth. On household-based sources, see also Kuznesof and Oppenheimer, "Family and Society," 223.

36. Cecilia Rabell Romero, "Trayectoria de vida familiar, raza y género en Oaxaca colonial," in *Familia y vida privada en la historia de Iberoamérica*, ed. Pilar Gonzalbo Aizpuru and Cecilia Rabell Romero (Mexico City: El Colegio de México/Universidad Nacional Autónoma de México, 1996), 75–118. McCaa offers a spirited critique of the sometimes misguided application of European demographic methods to Latin American contexts and urges scholars to capitalize on the tremendous potential of the available sources and to use methods specifically suited to them, "Families and Gender," 10.

37. A sample of the numerous works relying on judicial and police records includes many of the essays in Dore and Molyneux, eds., *Hidden Histories of Gender*; Shumway, *Ugly Suitor*; Díaz, *Female Citizens*; Hunefeldt, *Liberalism in the Bedroom*; Steve Stern, *The Secret History of Gender: Women, Men, and Power in Late Colonial Mexico* (Chapel Hill: University of North Carolina Press, 1995); Eduardo Cavieres F. and René Salinas Meza, *Amor, sexo, y matrimonio en Chile tradicional* (Valparaíso: Universidad Católica de Valparaíso, 1991); Lara Putnam, *The Company They Kept: Migrants and the Politics of Gender in Caribbean Costa Rica, 1870–1960* (Chapel Hill: University of North Carolina Press, 2002); Sueann Caulfield, *In Defense of Honor: Sexual Morality, Modernity, and Nation in Early-Twentieth-Century Brazil* (Durham, N.C.: Duke University Press, 2000). Inquisition records: many of

the contributions in Lavrin, *Sexuality and Marriage*; Ronaldo Vainfas, *Trópico dos pecados: Moral, sexualidade e inquisição no Brasil* (Rio de Janeiro: Campus, 1989); and the many works of the Seminario de Historia de las Mentalidades in Mexico, cited in footnote 21. Twinam, *Public Lives, Private Secrets* draws on legitimation petitions.

38. Amy Chazkel, *Laws of Chance: Brazil's Clandestine Lottery and the Making of Urban Public Life* (Durham, N.C.: Duke University Press, forthcoming, 2011), Appendix A. I would like to thank Herb Sloan for clarifying this issue.

39. Susan Socolow, "Review of *The Secret History of Gender: Women, Men, and Power in Latin Colonial Mexico* by Steve Stern," *The Americas* 53:1 (1996): 163–65.

40. Norbert Ortmayr, "Modelos de ilegitimidad en Guatemala (1860–1950)," *Cuadernos de Historia Latinoamericana* 4 [Asociacion de Historiadores Latinoamericanistas Europeos] (1996): 89–123; Robert McCaa, *Marriage and Fertility in Chile: Demographic Turning Points in the Petorca Valley, 1840–1976* (Boulder, Colo.: Westview Press, 1983).

41. Therborn, *Between Sex and Power*, p. 157.

42. Sandra Lauderdale Graham, *House and Street: The Domestic World of Servants and Masters in Nineteenth-Century Rio de Janeiro* (Austin: University of Texas Press, 1992): 73–74, 77. Kuznesof discusses debates over the meaning of nonmarriage in nineteenth-century Brazil in "Sexuality, Gender, and the Family," especially pp. 124–27. On debates about the relative autonomy of popular gender cultures, see Sueann Caulfield, "The History of Gender in the Historiography of Latin America," *Hispanic American Historical Review* 81:3/4 (2001): 449–90.

43. Hector Pérez Brignoli, "Deux siècles d'illégitimité au Costa Rica," in *Marriage and Remarriage in Populations of the Past*, ed. J. Dupâquier et al. (London: Academic Press, 1981), 481–93; Ortmayr, "Modelos de ilegitimidad;" Johnson, "Impact of Market Agriculture."

44. Rodríguez, "La familia en Colombia," in Rodríguez, ed., *La familia en Iberoamérica*, 247.

45. Ricardo Cicerchia, *Historia de la vida privada en la Argentina*, 2 vols. (Buenos Aires: Troquel, 1998–2001); Fernando Devoto y Marta Madero, eds., *Historia de la vida privada en la Argentina*, 3 vols. (Buenos Aires: Taurus, 1999–2002); Fernando A. Novais, ed., *História da vida privada no Brasil*, 4 vols. (São Paulo: Companhia das Letras, 1997–98); Rafael Sagredo and Cristián Gazmuri, eds., *Historia de la vida privada en Chile*, 3 vols. (Santiago: Aguilar Chilena Taurus, 2005–07); José P. Barrán, Gerardo Caetano, and Teresa Porzecanski, eds., *Historias de la vida privada en Uruguay*, 3 vols. (Montevideo: Taurus, 1996–98). See also Rodríguez, ed., *Familia en Iberoamérica*, in which each chapter explores the family history of a different country.

46. Clara López Beltrán, "Familia y sociedad en Bolivia," in Rodríguez, ed., *Familia en Iberoamérica*, 387.

47. Dore, "One Step Forward."

48. Freyre, "Preface to the Second English-Language Edition," *Masters and Slaves*, xxxiii; xliii–xliv.

49. Rodríguez, "La Familia en Colombia," 247.

50. Louise A. Tilly, "Women's History and Family History: Fruitful Collaboration or Missed Connection?" *Journal of Family History* 12:1/3 (1987): 303–15.

51. The relationship between family history and women's/gender history in Latin American historiography is also explored in Blum, "Bringing It Back Home" and in Milanich, "Whither Family History?"

52. For example, Ann Blum argues for the value of family history in "Bringing It Back Home." Recent works that incorporate approaches or concepts associated with family history include Twinam, *Public Lives, Private Secrets*; Putnam, *Company They Kept*;

Hunefeldt, *Liberalism in the Bedroom*; Ann S. Blum, *Domestic Economies: Family, Work, and Welfare in Mexico City, 1884–1943* (Lincoln: University of Nebraska Press, 2010), and Shumway, *Ugly Suitor*. These works also draw on aspects of women's and gender history. Of course, pigeonholing any given work in a historiographical field is a matter of subjective and potentially simplifying interpretation.

53. Take for example the edited volume *Mujeres, familia y sociedad*, published in Peru in 2006. The volume is organized into thematic units, some of which (at least from the point of view of North American and European scholarship) reflect classic themes of family history ("Hijos naturales y paternidad responsible"), while others fall squarely into women's or gender history ("Educación femenina"). Scarlett O'Phelan Godoy and Margarita Zegarra Florez, eds. *Mujeres, familia y sociedad en la historia de América Latina, siglos XVIII–XXI* (Lima: CENDOC, 2006).

54. A rare comparative analysis is Deere and León's "Married Women's Property Rights." Stern's *Secret History of Gender* develops a comparative perspective on regional gender cultures in Mexico.

55. Göran Therborn, *Between Sex and Power: Family in the World, 1900–2000* (New York: Routledge, 2004), 158.

56. Douglas S. Massey, Mary J. Fischer, and Chiara Capoferro, "International Migration and Gender in Latin America: A Comparative Analysis," *International Migration* 44:5 (2006): 63–91.

57. Pérez Brignoli, "Deux siècles," 482; Norbert Ortmayr, "Church, Marriage, and Legitimacy in the British West Indies (Nineteenth and Twentieth Centuries)," *The History of the Family* 2:2 (1997): 141–70, 156.

58. Ann Blum, "Public Welfare and Child Circulation, Mexico City, 1877–1925," *Journal of Family History* 23:3 (1998): 240–71; Jessaca Leinaweaver, *The Circulation of Children: Adoption, Kinship, and Morality in Andean Peru* (Durham, N.C.: Duke University Press, 2008); Nara Milanich, "The Casa de Huérfanos and Child Circulation in Late-Nineteenth-Century Chile," *Journal of Social History* 38:3 (2004): 311–40.

59. As David Lehmann notes, "(urban) Latin American and Caribbean patterns of kinship are less divergent than their separate literatures might suggest." "Female-Headed Households in Latin America and the Caribbean: Problems of Analysis and Conceptualization," in *Pour l'histoire du Brésil: Hommage à Katia de Queirós Mattoso*, ed. François Crouzet and Denis Rolland (Paris: L'Harmattan, 2000), 21.

60. This finding is associated with John Hajnal, especially his essay "European Marriage Patterns in Perspective," in *Population in History: Essays in Historical Demography*, ed. David V. Glass and David E.C. Eversley (London: Edward E. Arnold, 1965), 101–43. Hajnal identified additional features of the Western European family pattern, such as life-cycle service among children, that have figured less prominently in theories about the historical significance of household regimes.

61. Mary S. Hartman, *The Household and the Making of History: A Subversive View of the Western Past* (New York: Cambridge University Press, 2004). See also Wally Seccombe, *A Millenium of Family Change: Feudalism to Capitalism in Northwestern Europe* (New York: Verso, 1992), conclusion.

62. Silvia Arrom, *The Women of Mexico City, 1790–1857* (Stanford: Stanford University Press, 1985), chap. 3; McCaa, *Marriage and Fertility in Chile*. Arrom explores the similarities in nuptial patterns between Latin America and Europe in "Historia de la mujer."

63. This is all the more true given Hartman's claim that the Western European nuptial regime was associated with attenuated social class demarcations, *Household and the Making of History*, 247–48.

64. This is particularly true of the U.S.-based scholarship: Sandra McGee Deutsch, "Gender and Sociopolitical Change in Twentieth-Century Latin America," *Hispanic American Historical Review* 71:2 (1991): 259–71; Thomas Miller Klubock, *Contested Communities: Class, Gender, and Politics in Chile's El Teniente Copper Mine, 1904–1951* (Durham, N.C.: Duke University Press, 1998); Maxine Molyneux, "Mobilization without Emancipation? Women's Interests, the State, and Revolution in Nicaragua," *Feminist Studies* 11:2 (1985): 227–54; Alfred Padula and Lois M. Smith, *Sex and Revolution: Women in Socialist Cuba* (New York: Oxford, 1996); Karin Alejandra Rosemblatt, *Gendered Compromises: Political Cultures and the State in Chile, 1920–1950* (Chapel Hill: University of North Carolina Press, 2000); Heidi Tinsman, *Partners in Conflict: The Politics of Gender, Sexuality, and Labor in the Chilean Agrarian Reform, 1950–1973* (Durham, N.C.: Duke University Press, 2002); Mary Kay Vaughan, *Cultural Politics in Revolution: Teachers, Peasants, and Schools in Mexico, 1930–40* (Tucson: University of Arizona Press, 1997); Barbara Weinstein, *For Social Peace in Brazil: Industrialists and the Remaking of the Working Class in São Paulo, 1920–1964* (Chapel Hill: University of North Carolina Press, 1996).

65. Sylvia Chant, "Researching Gender, Families and Households in Latin America: From the 20th into the 21st Century," *Bulletin of Latin American Research* 21:4 (2002): 545–75.

66. Chant, "Researching Gender" explores the recent literature on female headship. Elizabeth Dore discusses the linkages of historical and contemporary household forms and the political discourses that obfuscate these linkages in "The Holy Family: Imagined Households in Latin American History," in *Gender Politics in Latin America: Debates in Theory and Practice*, ed. Elizabeth Dore (New York: Monthly Review Press, 1997), 101–17.

67. Heidi Tinsman, "Reviving Feminist Materialism: Gender and Neoliberalism in Pinochet's Chile," *Signs: Journal of Women in Culture and Society* 26:1 (2000): 143–85, 147.

68. Cancian et al., "Introduction," 314.

69. Historical perspectives on child circulation include Blum, "Public Welfare" and Milanich, "Casa de Huérfanos." On *compadrazgo*, a classic anthropological study is Sidney Mintz and Eric Wolf, "An Analysis of Ritual Co-parenthood (Compadrazgo)," *Southwestern Journal of Anthropology* 6 (1950): 341–68. We have relatively few historical studies, which tend to focus on slave communities. See Stephen Gudeman and Stuart Schwartz, "Cleansing Original Sin: Godparenthood and the Baptism of Slaves in Eighteenth-Century Bahia," in Smith, ed. *Kinship Ideology and Practice*, 35–58; Stuart Schwartz, "Opening the Family Circle: Godparentage in Brazilian Slavery," in *Slaves, Peasants and Rebels*, 137–60; Ana Maria Lugão Rios, "The Politics of Kinship: *Compadrio* Among Slaves in Nineteenth-Century Brazil," *The History of the Family* 5:3 (2000): 287–98; Paul Charney, "The Implications of Godparental Ties between Indians and Spaniards in Colonial Lima," *The Americas* 47:3 (1991): 295–313.

70. Lehmann, "Female-Headed Households," 5.

71. Putnam, *Company They Kept*, 137–38; Milanich, *Children of Fate*, chap. 5.

72. "Dynastic Growth and Survival Strategies: The Solidarity of Mexican Grand-Families," in Smith, *Kinship Ideology and Practice*. Lomnitz is one of the few scholars to have conducted systematic research into families of different social classes.

73. Sandra Lauderdale Graham, "Review of Dain Borges, *The Family in Bahia*," *Journal of Latin American Studies* 25:2 (1993): 399–401, 401. Her study of households in nineteenth-century Rio de Janeiro illustrates this point: Lauderdale Graham, *House and Street*.

74. Martínez-Alier, *Marriage, Class and Colour*; Ramón A. Gutiérrez, *When Jesus Came, the Corn Mothers Went Away: Marriage, Sexuality, and Power in New Mexico, 1500–1846* (Stanford: Stanford University Press, 1991); Muriel Nazzari, "Concubinage in Colonial

Brazil: The Inequalities of Race, Class and Gender," *Journal of Family History* 21:2 (1996): 107–24. The relationship of family to social hierarchies is the subject of Milanich, "Whither Family History?"

75. Premo, *Raising an Empire*, conclusion.

76. Works that provide historical perspectives on contemporary family issues include Ricardo Cicerchia, "The Charm of Family Patterns: Historical and Contemporary Change in Latin America," in Elizabeth Dore, ed., *Gender Politics in Latin America*, 118–33, and the historical contributions in Sergio Marras, ed., *A partir de Beijing: La familia chilena del 2000* (Santiago: Ediciones de Chile, 1998). See also Dore, "Holy Family."

77. Invocations of "traditional" models or norms include: Tiano cited in Chant, "Researching Gender," 551; Cerruti and Zenteno cited in Chant, "Researching Gender," 550; "weakening model": Castells cited in Chant, "Researching Gender," 546; "new concept of paternity/maternity": Ignacio Irarrázaval and Juan Pablo Valenzuela, "La ilegitimidad en Chile: ¿Hacia un cambio en la conformación de la familia?" *Estudios Públicos* 52 (Santiago), 1992: 145–90, 185.

78. The quote is Fukuyama's, "Social Capital and Development: The Coming Agenda," *SAIS Review* 22:1 (2002): 23–37; Lawrence E. Harrison and Samuel P. Huntington, eds. *Culture Matters: How Values Shape Human Progress* (New York: Basic Books, 2000). See also Lawrence E. Harrison, *Who Prospers? How Cultural Values Shape Economic And Political Success* (New York: Basic Books, 1992), especially 39–41; Anu Realo et al., "Radius of Trust: Social Capital in Relation to Familism and Institutional Collectivism," *Journal of Cross-Cultural Psychology* 39:4 (2008): 447–62.

79. Samuel P Huntington, "The Hispanic Challenge," *Foreign Policy* 141 (2004): 30–45, 44.

80. See, among many others, Pierrette Hondagneu-Sotelo and Ernestine Avila, "'I'm Here but I'm There': The Meanings of Latina Transnational Motherhood," *Gender & Society* 11:5 (1997): 548–71, and Rhacel Salazar Parreñas, *Children of Global Migration: Transnational Families and Gendered Woes* (Stanford: Stanford University Press, 2005).

81. Frances Abrahamer Rothstein, "Declining Odds: Kinship, Women's Employment, and Political Economy in Rural Mexico," *American Anthropologist* 101:3 (1999): 579–93, 579.

82. Maria Rosaria Stabili, *Il sentimento aristocratico: Elites cilene allo specchio (1860–1960)* (Lecce: Congedo, 1996).

83. Alejandro Portes and Kelly Hoffman, "Latin American Class Structures: Their Composition and Change during the Neoliberal Era," *Latin American Research Review* 38:1 (2003): 41–82.

84. The gendered nature of these "practical interests" has been explored by scholars of contemporary women's movements; see for example Molyneux, "Mobilization without Emancipation."

85. Carlos M. Vilas, "Family Affairs: Class, Lineage and Politics in Contemporary Nicaragua," *Journal of Latin American Studies* 24:2 (1992): 309–41.

86. H.I.J.O.S. is the acronym for Hijos por la Identidad y la Justicia contra el Olvido y el Silencio, a human rights group active in Argentina as well as Guatemala.

87. In Argentina, H.I.J.O.S.'s Comisión de Hermanos works to uncover the identities of the hundreds of infants born to political prisoners and reared by military families: "We say that they are our siblings [*hermanos*] because some members of the organization are searching for their biological brothers and sisters but also because generationally (although

they are not part of our biological family) we consider them siblings [, b]ecause they are children of our parents' generation and are their friends [compañeros]." Available at http://www.hijos-capital.org.ar/index.php?option=com_content&task=view&id=144&Itemid=67- (accessed May 22, 2010).

88. Another very different example of kin metaphors in contemporary political language is Daniel M. Goldstein, "Orphans of the State: Conceptualizing Citizenship, Space, and Kinship in Bolivian Municipal Politics," *Cultural Dynamics* 17:5 (2005): 5–31.

CHAPTER 14

THE NEW ECONOMIC HISTORY OF LATIN AMERICA: EVOLUTION AND RECENT CONTRIBUTIONS

JOHN H. COATSWORTH

WILLIAM R. SUMMERHILL

RESEARCH on the economic history of Latin America has grown considerably in scope, depth, and sophistication over the last thirty years. While much of this work has come from scholars within the disciplines of history and economics, investigators in political science and sociology have made major contributions as well. The principal motivation for most of these investigations involves a search for the conditions that made Latin American economies relatively poor in comparison with nations where commerce and industrialization created high standards of living early on, such as the Netherlands, Britain, and the United States. While such an approach ruffles the feathers of adherents to the view that Latin America must be considered "on its own terms," to reject it is to accept a history of poverty as predestination. The region's "social indicators," which are nothing less than measures of economic outcomes, remain well behind those of OECD nations. For much of Latin America, the pace of economic progress since the colonial period can be defined as successful only through comparison with sub-Saharan Africa.[1] The puzzle of the origins of Latin American underdevelopment has inspired most of the work on the region's economic history.

The expansion of research and publication in Latin American economic history in the last decades, while appreciable, has not been as rapid as that of some other subfields of history, though economic history tends to be cumulative in ways that are less likely to occur in more humanistically oriented subfields. Nonetheless, the state of the field is in no way comparable to a "recession."[2] Economic history exhibits strong relevance to practical and policy concerns.[3] Most recently, the new historicization of research in political economy and development has engendered an appreciation for historical work on Latin America that runs across several social science disciplines, and that has not been seen to this extent since the 1960s.

This steady growth of the literature is not limited to monographs and articles; the increase in the number of historiographical and interpretive essays on economic history is yet another indicator. Many assessments focus on specific countries, with essays on Mexico surely figuring most prominently.[4] Countries that have traditionally been the subject of relatively less research have also seen their economic historiographies expand appreciably.[5] In addition to subject essays on particular time periods, the literature on particular economic sectors has developed to the point where it justifies focused assessments.[6] Broader interpretive essays, regionwide in scope, give historians much to think about (especially since they fail to see eye to eye), and precisely because of their disagreements provide a rich array of testable implications of their own.[7]

At the risk of redundancy, the present chapter tackles the task once again. Historiographical essays serve varied purposes, from cataloging works and identifying research trends to making the case for the precedence of particular interpretations. The present essay eschews any effort at comprehensive cataloguing. Its goal, more modest, is to trace out some basic tendencies and trajectories in recent work and extrapolate from them to identify opportunities and needs for the near future.

A simple but insightful measure of the advance of research on the economic history of Latin America can be gleaned by comparison of key compendia over the last few decades. Two efforts stand out as milestones in the evolution of the field. The first is the project sponsored by the (regrettably now defunct) Joint Committee on Latin American Studies of the American Council of Learned Societies and the Social Science Research Council. This project produced two core volumes. The first, Roberto Cortés Conde and Stanley J. Stein's *Latin America: A Guide to the Economic History, 1830–1930* (1977), melded interpretive and historiographical essays with a guide to printed source materials. It was, and remains, an extraordinarily valuable reference for research scholars. A related set of case studies, *The Latin American Economies: Growth and the Export Sector, 1880–1930*, edited by Cortés Conde and Shane Hunt, appeared in 1985, providing some country-specific chapters. With hindsight, three features of the research component of the overall project stand out. First, and most obviously, the literature was, overall, thin. The problem was not that there were not fewer monographs and articles than in later decades. Rather, much of the work, circa 1977, while strongly interpretive, lacked the depth and sophistication of analysis that characterized later studies, contributing to a severe disconnect within the historiography. Work on the ostensible social and political *consequences* of economic conditions, however, far outstripped research on economic history per se, ultimately leaving many of the era's "big" characterizations in doubt (in the ensuing decades, a number of historians exploited this relative backwardness, and the economic historiography began to catch up). Second, partly due to the "behavioralist" impulse in the social sciences, reference to quantitative indicators of economic processes was by the 1970s already considered an important way of establishing facts and documenting changes. Third, overtly cliometric inquiry—explicit hypothesis testing and the drawing of inferences from statistical manipulation—was still uncommon. The tension between the "new" economic history and the old, which pervaded the historiography on the United States in the 1970s, was simply not very strong, not because it was suppressed but because there had been so little work of a cliometric variety done on Latin America.

The appearance of the *Cambridge Economic History of Latin America* (edited by Victor Bulmer-Thomas, John Coatsworth, and Roberto Cortés Conde) nearly three decades after the publication of the Cortés Conde and Stein volume underscores just how far things have progressed and how much richer the research agenda now is. The chapters and bibliographic essays contributed to the work confirm casual impressions drawn from journals and monographs: there has been a tremendous expansion of research. The growth has been most rapid in the cliometric and new institutional tracks, but there have also been important noncliometric advances. The use of quantitative evidence continues to be a centerpiece of the literature (though equally important arguments are made by means of qualitative evidence as well). And hypothesis testing—of more or less formal varieties—has become more prominent than ever before. The field has expanded along multiple fronts, especially interpretively and methodologically. Three dimensions of this evolution stand out as particularly salient: the exploitation of formal theory and models to generate testable hypotheses, the use of a greater volume of primary evidence, and the increasing sophistication of statistical inference. They are evident in varying degrees, in works on a variety of countries and periods.

Economic historians trained mainly in history departments now also deploy formal models, long the domain of economics, and increasingly of political science as well. Formalized deductive approaches are largely choice-theoretic in nature, focusing on strategic interactions that strive to yield as predictions the actual outcomes observed in polities and economies. Such models are invaluable because they discipline thinking, requiring that logical implications conform to the original assumptions. Importantly, they supply hypotheses that can be tested for congruence with fact, and thus serve as important device for improving on the quality of analysis in history. There are losses to eschewing such models, because intuition alone—like empiricism—can be a poor guide to understanding the outcomes of interest. The use of explicit models and formal theory has informed the bulk of recent work in the field, and the quality of findings is the better for it. Assessments by economic historians of profitability, efficiency, productivity change, social savings, the extent of tariff protection, the impact of immigration, and the like are characteristically neoclassical in their underpinnings. Researchers have also exploited models of transactions costs and institutions to fill gaps where neoclassical frameworks are not satisfying. It is worth noting that choice-theoretic approaches are not the exclusive domain of neoclassical models; investigators working in a Marxist tradition have found it useful to employ such approaches as well.[8] To the extent that formal models encompass political processes and not just markets, it is not only price theory that is a valuable tool, but game theory as well.

As important as hypotheses derived from rigorous modeling (as opposed to those derived from what the previous generation of historians asserted) have become for practitioners of the new economic history of Latin America, models are only useful in a practical way when there is evidence available to test their implications. The greater reliance on (and creation of) new bodies of primary evidence has been an important advance as well as a persistent need. The existence of more and better evidence from primary sources is endogenous to the greater specificity of the questions that historians pose. Nothing about the actual archives available to historians over the last thirty years changed very much; however, the use of primary sources has become more systematic and more targeted. The distinction between "diggers," who mainly produce new evidence, and "synthesizers," who exploit existing data to make inferences about development, is imperfect. Both play an important role, but the value-added has been greatest from the corner of synthesizers who did their own digging. Squeezing new insights from the existing published compilations of evidence (the *Estadisticas historicas* types of volumes that exist for many countries) depended heavily on innovations in statistical technique. These were increasingly exhausted by the 1990s, and new answers to old questions have thus required new evidence. The sources long used by traditional historians—newspapers, legal archives, correspondence, under-utilized or unnoticed contemporary publications—have been fruitfully tapped (or even uncovered) by practitioners of the new economic history. While this step seems obvious now, in the past the collection and systematic use of evidence was weaker and spottier. The most striking examples are the classic interpretive treatments of Latin American economies that appeared around midcentury.[9] These works had a persistently strong impact, yet relied more on expert divination than they did on quantitative indicators or new evidence culled from either archival collections or earlier published sources. For the last thirty years, nearly every major characterization about Latin American economies has been vulnerable to revision (or even rejection) by historians not only equipped with hypotheses drawn from deductive reasoning but also armed with better evidence.

The third tendency in the economic historiography has been one of increasing statistical sophistication. Quantification long predates the emergence of the new economic history. The possibility of easily generating inferences from quantitative facts by means of statistical manipulation is one of the major breakthroughs, and it provides a large array of tools to the investigator. Analysis of this sort runs well beyond tables that summarize quantitative facts in fairly obvious ways. Basic techniques like sampling make large bodies of original evidence manageable. Explicit hypothesis testing drawing on a host of statistical regression techniques, including those designed for large panels of data across cases and over time, along with techniques that address the peculiar properties of high-frequency time series data, is now reasonably common. It is well known that the growth in the use of powerful statistical applications is attributable in large measure to the rapid decline in the cost of computation, a trend that has obviously accelerated since the early 1980s. The potential this has created for more—and more reliable—inferences is difficult to exaggerate. Deriving a simple regression coefficient involves inverting a matrix of numbers. Inverting even a small matrix by hand was a daunting and unenviable task. Today inverting a huge matrix is trivially easy and quick. The affordability of computation has put relatively advanced statistical procedures within reach of anyone with access to a desktop machine. The result is that more economic historians than ever before can directly and systematically test hypotheses regarding economic relationships, limited only by the availability of evidence suited to the task.

In addition to these three trends, other patterns in the historiography stand out. The bread and butter of economic historians of Latin America has been the case study (in either article or book form). This type of study is completely unremarkable for scholars within the discipline of history, but less satisfying to economists, where the larger the number of cases (countries, regions, markets, firms, and measurement over time to increase further the number of observations), the more satisfying the findings. Some of the emphasis on cases studies has to do with the area studies, soak-and-poke tradition of research on Latin America. Some of it has to do with the view that working more superficially across a large number of cases yields less robust findings than can be obtained by working deeply on a single case. Within history, large comparative studies across countries have been less commonly pursued. Even for historians willing to follow this course, the lack of standing data sets that make it possible to address many different cases over long spans of time complicate the investigation. This lack also no doubt helps explain the persistence of the country-study approach within history. Country-specific studies nonetheless enjoy a symbiotic relationship with "large N" investigations. The findings of case studies make it possible to qualify broader generalizations, while the generalizations help to inform the design and implementation of the case studies themselves.

A second persistent pattern involves an imbalance in geographic coverage. While the frontier of knowledge in the economic history of Latin America has moved out dramatically, it has done so unevenly. There is a bias in favor of research on what today are the largest countries in Latin America. Indisputably most of the research on economic history focuses on Mexico, Argentina, and Brazil. To a lesser degree, there is a strong body of work on Cuba. Despite the size of its population (which is larger than that of Argentina), there is not much more published on Colombian economic history than there is on, say, Chile, a much smaller country. This unevenness makes it difficult to grapple with big questions on a broader scale. For example, did the terms of trade get better or worse in the era of export-led growth? For Mexico, Brazil, Cuba, or Argentina, there exist data (and even results) that provide an answer. For Guatemala or Bolivia, the question has not yet even been posed. For other areas, such as Venezuela, Ecuador, or Paraguay, the new economic history is nearly nonexistent.

These patterns and tendencies can be best illustrated by reference to some of the more recent work in specific areas of inquiry. The history of prices, long a staple of U.S. and European economic historiography, has developed more slowly in Latin America. Gaps in price history, in turn, have made it more difficult for economic historians of Latin America to assess the mountains of data on colonial tax revenues, mineral production, and agricultural output published during the past two decades, hampered efforts to assess interregional and international economic integration, and increased error margins in estimates of GDP and other economic variables well into the twentieth century.

Among the pioneers in this field, Earl Hamilton's work on the impact of colonial silver on prices in Spain stands out.[10] Hamilton looked for data all over Spain, finding much of his information in the account books of monasteries and other religious institutions. Historians of Mexico were among the first to recognize the importance of price history. Charles Gibson, for example, published a famous scattergram of maize prices in the Valley of Mexico that showed a marked upward trend between 1520 and 1810.[11] Despite these contributions, the price history of the first two postconquest centuries remains to be written. Consumer and producer price indices would make it possible to revisit the masses of published data on Spanish colonial tax revenues compiled by TePaske, Klein, and their collaborators,[12] reexamine tithe data that reflect agricultural production in many regions,[13] better assess both the impact of colonial silver production within the colonies and the health of the mining industry itself,[14] and rewrite the history of wages and living standards.

In contrast to earlier centuries, the price history of the eighteenth century has benefited from a series of important works since Ruggiero Romano's influential essay on Chile and Argentina appeared in 1963. Florescano dedicated his 1969 book *Precios del maíz y crisis agrícolas en México (1708–1810)* to Romano. It adapted the methods of the Annales School to rethink the economic and social history of central Mexico by analyzing trends and cycles in Mexico City maize prices. Later work has added considerable depth and breadth to Florescano's pioneering work.[15] Data on Mexican maize prices at diverse locations throughout the colony raised the issue of market integration first addressed by Lindo[16] and subsequently by others.

For Latin America as a whole, the most influential work on eighteenth-century prices to date is undoubtedly the volume edited by Johnson and Tandeter.[17] The essays in this volume contributed significantly to knowledge of trends in commodity prices and wages in diverse locations throughout Latin America, from Buenos Aires and Santiago in the south through Potosi and Arequipa in the Andes to Brazil, Venezuela, and Mexico. Just as price movements in Mexico's grain markets appear to have been linked across regions within the colony, the studies in this volume suggested fragmentation rather than integration in the markets for export commodities. For example, while sugar prices in Santiago, Arequipa, and Lima tended to move together, they did not correlate at all with the price of sugar in more distant markets, such as Salvador in Brazil, Potosi in the high Andes, or Buenos Aires.

The history of prices in the first half of the nineteenth century is less abundant because record keeping deteriorated due to civil and political conflict. Lyman

Johnson's work on Buenos Aires wages early in the century is a notable exception.[18] Indices for consumer goods and wages for the second half of the century are now available for a growing list of countries. The pioneering efforts organized at the Colegio de México for the Porfirian era (1877–1910), for example, have recently been updated and corrected by Gómez-Galvarriato and Musacchio, while Williamson has used his own index of urban unskilled wages in an important essay on inequality.[19] Price histories for individual commodities as well as indices for consumer prices in the second half of the nineteenth century now exist for a growing number of countries, along with wholesale price indices and indices used as GDP deflators for many. Luis Catão's work on wholesale prices in Brazil between 1870 and 1913 is a good example of this trend, as is the work of Roberto Cortés Conde for Argentina for the same period.[20]

In the twentieth century, especially after World War II, official statistical agencies of the Latin American governments have assumed responsibility for assembling and publishing price data. Nonetheless, as Jeffrey Bortz's work on Mexican wages suggests, economic historians can still have much work to do examining, testing, and even revising official figures.[21]

Much of the social science research on Latin America in the last decades of the twentieth century intersected in some way with the question of industrialization. Industry—whether because of its importance to unionization and the labor movements, its role in technology transfer and foreign investment, its contribution to rapid urbanization, or its presumed importance in explaining large political shifts—became an important topic of study. Industry's income-raising potential—the shift of resources out of agriculture and into manufacturing disproportionately increases average income, because of the latter's higher productivity—led economic historians to focus on two features: the implicit costs of Latin America's failure to industrialize earlier, and the character of the industrialization that did occur beginning in the nineteenth century. The primitive manufacturing capacity that Latin America did possess was hammered by the opening to relatively unrestricted foreign trade in the early nineteenth century. A growing body of empirical work uses new evidence to flesh out long-standing interest in the possibilities that trade protection could have offered industry. The degree and impact of tariff protection for manufacturing has been an especially active area of research on Mexico.[22] The timing of tariff changes and the extent of protection have also been recently reassessed for nineteenth-century Brazil.[23] Strikingly, despite the tardiness of industrialization, independent Latin America as a whole was characterized by high tariff protection from early on.[24]

When Latin American countries did make the transition from artisanal shops to modern manufactories, a hallmark feature of the emerging sector was its high degree of concentration. Relatively few firms accounted for the lion's share of manufacturing output. Oligopoly resulted from the confluence of at least three factors. Technological change during the nineteenth century had shifted costs curves down for many branches of manufacturing. By the time Latin American nations industrialized, the minimum-efficient scale of factories was large. Second, Latin American manufacturing firms operated not in the high-income settings of northwestern Europe and the United States but in relatively poor societies where the typical consumer had low purchasing power. These two features promoted concentration, since only a few firms were required to satisfy demand. A third factor was the institutional arrangements governing the efficiency of financial markets. In Mexico, by way of example, limited access to capital meant that sectors of manufacturing that should have featured many small, competitive firms, such as textiles, were nonetheless concentrated, while institutional changes that increased access to the stock and bond markets in Brazil led to a rapid decline in concentration.[25] Overall, Mexico had a high degree of concentration across nearly all sectors of manufacturing.[26] Chile had sectors of industry dominated by only a few firms, as did Brazil before 1890 (Kirsch, 1977; Haber, 1991). Though oligopoly was apparent in some sectors of Argentine industry, with powerful *grupos* in some instances, concentration was comparatively less prevalent than in Mexico or Brazil, a feature consistent with the country's higher incomes and rapidly growing class of consumers in the late nineteenth century (Pineda, 2010).

One especially illuminating line of work has involved the construction of new estimates of annual flows of industrial investment. Such efforts have been particularly valuable because consistent measures of manufacturing output are not available for most Latin American countries until well into the twentieth century. The investment figures rely on innovative manipulations of equipment import data drawn from official trade statistics. Since Latin American countries lacked appreciable capital-goods industries before the 1930s, changes in the value of machinery imports serve as a reasonable proxy for the rate and timing of investment in manufacturing. Work on Brazilian imports of British machinery from the 1860s through the early twentieth century was the first contribution in this vein.[27] We now have manufacturing investment figures derived using this approach for Mexico in the decades before and after the Revolution.[28] Estimates have also been made for Argentina in the late nineteenth and twentieth centuries.[29] Detailed estimates for every Latin American nation from 1890 to 1930, based on all of the major trading partners for each country, will doubtless lead to entirely new insights into patterns of industrialization in the region.[30]

Somewhat surprisingly, cliometric studies on the agricultural sector are relatively less abundant, despite the sector's importance both to overall levels of economic activity and as a point of origin for mobilizing savings for industrial investment. Argentina's transformation from a pastoral economy to a high-productivity grain exporter has been well documented, but the microeconomics of farming has only recently begun to be explored.[31] Where enslaved Africans and their descendents formed a large share of the agricultural labor force, there have been considerable advances in research. The markets for slaves in Cuba have been examined in enviable detail.[32] Unsurprisingly, nineteenth-century Brazil, with the largest slave population outside of the United States, has seen explosive growth in the demographic and economic historiography of slavery. Work on Bahia, by way of example, reveals a slave-based economy that was less monocultural than many scholars previously imagined.³³ There has been an outpouring of research on São Paulo and Minas Gerais drawing less from new techniques than from archival discoveries.³⁴

One of most active areas of research in quantitative economic history over the last decade has been finance. This emphasis on finance is consistent with the long-standing concern with industrialization. The ability to form real physical capital was central to economic growth, and finance was a key ingredient for capital formation. Capital markets in Latin America, however, were quite weak at independence. Several centuries of colonial rule had done little to support, and likely worked against, financial development. The creation of banks and securities markets continued to be stymied after independence by violence, instability, and politicized market interventions. Various facets of this experience have increasingly fallen under the scrutiny of new economic historians. Work on Brazilian monetary history (influenced by Friedman and Schwartz's classic work on U.S. monetary history) was at the forefront of the cliometric revolution in Latin America.³⁵ Argentine monetary history has also been the subject of careful quantitative and institutional research.³⁶ The roles of banking and securities markets in finance have been subjected to probing and detailed research informed by the state of the art in theory and methods, as well as a keen sensitivity to the crucial relationships between banking and politics. Brazilian banking in the early twentieth century was a crucible of efforts to manage the exchange rate, disputes over regional economic interests, and the country's position in the international market.³⁷ The transformation of São Paulo from an up-country farming town to South America's main industrial center had much to do with the way local capital markets intermediated between savers and entrepreneurs.³⁸ Maurer's work on the Banco Nacional de México examines the intersection of the revitalization of public debt service, the profit motives of merchant financiers, and the emergence of a strongly concentrated banking system.³⁹ Musacchio's work on Brazil provides a valuable case study demonstrating the possibilities and limitations facing civil code nations seeking to create vibrant stock and bond markets.⁴⁰

Transportation improvements, in the form of investments in railroads, figured prominently in the transition to improved economic performance in the late nineteenth and early twentieth centuries. The strength of this impact varied no doubt by country (with the weakest effects likely found in the Andean nations, on average). Pioneering cliometric work on Mexico demonstrated the extraordinary importance of railroads, which dramatically reduced transport costs and forged ties from the country's interior to external markets.⁴¹ The critical importance of government regulatory approaches and subsidy policies in attracting and controlling foreign investments in railroads has been made especially clear for Argentina.⁴² That railroads could have a large direct economic impact without disproportionately favoring the export sector is now clear from the case of Brazil.⁴³ Mexican railroads, too, contributed to conditions in which the internal sector benefited.⁴⁴ State-of-the-art statistical techniques have illustrated in rich detail the market-integrating consequences of railroad development in twentieth-century Colombia.⁴⁵ Clearly, as in the areas of industry and finance, much has been done and much remains to do.

If historians have sometimes viewed these sectoral and country studies as excessively impersonal or even "unpeopled," there is in fact no shortage of work on the distributive components of economic change in Latin American. In the past decade, new work on the history of living standards and the distribution of wealth and income has created what amounts to a new field of historical research on the Latin American economies, replete with new sources of data, sophisticated quantitative methods, and a growing literature on the significance of these topics for Latin America's economic development over the past five centuries. This new field took inspiration in part from the rapid development of anthropometric history pioneered by Robert William Fogel and others in the United States and Western Europe.[46] In addition, the use of data from census, tax, and notarial records and from assets documented in estate inventories, have also contributed to this field.

In Latin America, the world's most unequal region for as long as data have been systematically collected (roughly from the 1960s or 1970s), economic historians have worried about inequality for at least a century. In the new work, however, attention has shifted somewhat from the social and cultural dimensions of inequality (e.g., slavery, caste and class divisions, gender) to economic inequality indexed by inequality in income or wealth or by differences in biological welfare. Especially noteworthy has been the use of historical data on heights (from military and census records as well as skeletal remains) to measure trends in net nutrition over time.

Meanwhile, a lively debate has emerged on the significance of inequality for the development of economic institutions and the performance of the Latin American economies since the colonial era. A seminal essay by U.S. economic historians Stanley Engerman and the late Kenneth Sokoloff argued that factor endowments (mainly land and climate) predisposed the region to economic activities where large enterprises predominated (slave plantations and large haciendas), and small elites came to dominate institutions and policies to the detriment of majorities, whose property and civic rights suffered.[47] The authors contrasted this situation to that of the United States, where family farms and more egalitarian institutions encouraged broad participation in markets and thus faster economic growth. Daron Acemoglu, Simon Johnson, and James Robinson made a similar argument about the negative effect of elite-dominated economic institutions in an influential essay, but suggested exploitative colonial regimes (as opposed to majority-European settlement colonies) rather than factor endowments as the main cause.[48]

More recent work on inequality has called into question the empirical basis for these arguments. Studies of late colonial and nineteenth-century wealth distribution by Frank, Gelman and Santilli, Johnson and Frank, and others, summarized in Coatsworth, suggested that wealth distribution was unequal, but probably not more unequal than in the United States or England.[49] Moreover, highly unequal slave colonies in the late colonial era had the highest per capita GDP in the Americas.[50] Williamson, Coatsworth, and others have argued that Latin America's unusually high inequality was not a colonial phenomenon, but originated in the late nineteenth century with the onset of export-oriented economic growth.[51]

The anthropometric contribution to this debate has been growing steadily in recent years. In the premodern era, data on average heights are often the only measure, albeit indirect, of overall economic performance. Work on Mexico has advanced furthest, starting with data on the stature of the pre-Colombian and early postconquest populations based on skeletons.[52] Larsen's work on the Guale indigenous people of Santa Catalina Island off the Florida coast is especially interesting because it compares the preconquest foragers with their descendants in Jesuit missions, who were shorter and less healthy.[53] Work on the eighteenth and nineteenth centuries by Salvatore on Argentina and Challu on Mexico based on military records showed that class and regional differences in adult height at the end of the colonial era were significant, but smaller than in most European studies.[54]

This work has also contributed new perspectives on economic trends. In Challu's work, for example, the eighteenth century, once thought to be a golden age of prosperity in Mexico, has emerged as an era of long-term deterioration in stature and rising inequality. And the independence era, long thought to be economically disastrous, was not accompanied by a fall in living standards. Inequality in net nutrition may have peaked in the mid to late nineteenth century, during the era of export-led growth.[55] Twentieth-century studies have also produced some unexpected results, including periods of stagnation and even decline in heights,[56] though Colombia may have been an exception.[57] Recent work on Brazil has shown persistent regional as well as social inequalities in stature,[58] while Guatemalan data show a similar persistence of stagnation in stature and even severe stunting of children among the indigenous majority of the population.[59]

The contribution of germ theory and the massive investments in public health it inspired (better sanitation, drinking water, medical care) in Latin America along with rising incomes due to economic growth appear to explain the overall upward trend in stature in most countries in the twentieth century, though inequality and persistent poverty tended to dampen the trend. Thus, trends in welfare and inequality measured by stature have reinforced the conclusions reached by more conventional measures of welfare and productivity that show improvement, but at long-term rates well below most other world regions.

Beyond the case studies of countries, regions, sectors, and firms, there is also a new generation of comparative studies for which Latin American economic history has been indispensable. Arguably, this "rediscovery" of Latin America by social scientists with little to no specialization in the region has had a much greater scholarly impact of late than have the sorts of case studies that are typical of traditional cliometric inquiry. The most prominent clusters of papers in this growing body of work are those of Engerman and Sokoloff and of Acemoglu, Johnson, and Robinson.[60] As important as the role of history is in these arguments, they do not involve (nor did they require) a large, archival-based research project or immersion in the historiography of any particular country. They enjoy outsized success because they seized two existing opportunities in new and highly creative ways. The first was the potential of Latin American economies to serve as important body of cases in the latest investigations of the general problem of economic growth. The second is the reliance on the past to identify the initial, exogenous conditions that shaped the trajectory of a time-bound process of change. This potential of past events aids greatly in resolving problems of causal inference. The resulting papers have garnered tremendous (and warranted) attention, while thrusting particular details of Latin American history front and center for economists and political scientists working on big problems of development.

One might be tempted to think that there is not much that is actually new in the newfound importance of Latin American history for the study of development. Latin American experiences figured importantly in debates about development in the 1960s and 1970s. There are, however, at least a couple of key differences this time around. Latin America mattered for the earlier generation of economics because it inspired critiques of the mainstream thinking on the determinants of economic growth. In simplest terms, "modernization" gave way to "dependency" as the predominant interpretive framework, because of the examples provided by Latin American (and African) cases. Although Rostovian modernizationist thinking had already been badly damaged in the attack mounted by Gerschenkron (without any particular reference to Latin America), the reinforcements from the south finished it off. There is one important difference between that first cycle of revision and what has occurred more recently. Debates on the Washington consensus aside, the ideological and methodological gulf between the mainstream thinking on development within economics and the details of the record of Latin America is much reduced. Latin America is used less frequently now to generate a critique of thinking about development and viewed more as typifying precisely the kinds of problems that development economics tackles directly. Because of this sensibility, the empirical fit between current models and Latin American facts is stronger than what came before.

For all the merits of the approaches of Acemoglu, Johnson, and Robinson and of Engerman and Sokoloff, they also present a discomfiting puzzle to historians. History, as an initial set of conditions, is of critical importance to the arguments they make, and methodologically indispensable (in the case of Acemoglu et al.). At the same time, much of Latin American history does *not* matter to the outcomes they seek to explain, including, ironically, much of its economic history. Any events that transpired, or processes that unfolded, between the time of the initial conditions (original factor endowments in the case of Engerman and Sokoloff, early settler mortality for Acemoglu et al.) and the recent past have no independent impact on the course of Latin American economic history. For Engerman and Sokoloff, almost any proximate cause of underdevelopment or inequality (low outlays on education, restricted political franchise, labor-repressive systems of production) can be traced to initial factor endowments. Similarly for Acemoglu et al., where variables that other scholars have highlighted—say, the quality of property rights—are themselves taken as a function of early settler mortality. A powerful determinism is thus embedded in their arguments, one similar to that use by Barrington Moore, for whom causes and effects were separated by centuries.

Conclusions

We conclude not with a general assessment, but rather with some specific concerns. With the exceptions perhaps of Colombia and Chile, cliometric inquiry remains in short supply for Andean countries, and for smaller, poorer countries in general. Though lack of previous research is not necessarily the strongest rationale to allocate attention to some of these cases, there can be no doubt that there are important findings that await discovery, and important lessons to be learned, by broadening the emphasis from large countries to smaller ones. Inequality, for which Latin America is infamous, now seems to be less rooted in the eighteenth and nineteenth centuries than previously believed, especially when compared to advanced, industrializing economies. If true, this implies that most of the action in the area of inequality is to be found in the twentieth century, which most certainly warrants detailed research. Beyond places and processes of long-term change, particular sectors remain woefully underresearched. Other than for a few large entities, business history of the type that digs deep inside firms to look at problems of incentives and contracting is scarce. The most glaring omission involves the lack of systematic studies of education (beyond tallying up numbers of students), skill acquisition, and human capital formation, which were so critical for growth and social mobility in the twentieth-century United States. These studies continue to be nearly nonexistent for Latin America. The investments required—in terms of time, creativity, and human energy—to expand the intensive and extensive margins of research on these areas will be high. There is little doubt in the end that the payoff will be worth it.

Notes

1. Leandro Prados de la Escosura, "Lost Decades? Economic Performance in Post-Independence Latin America," *Journal of Latin American Studies* 41 (2009): 279–307.

2. Paul Gootenberg, "Between a Rock and a Softer Place: Reflections on Some Recent Economic History of Latin America," *Latin American Research Review* 39:2 (2004): 239–57.

3. A few examples: two economic historians, Gustavo Franco and Winston Fritsch, were part of the team that forged the inflation-defeating Plano Real in Brazil. The economic historian Miguel Urrutia served as governor of Colombia's central bank. That the chairman of the U.S. Federal Reserve is a specialist on the economic history of the Great Depression suggests that the policy relevance of economic historians is not limited to Latin America.

4. John H. Coatsworth, "Cliometrics and Mexican History," *Historical Methods* 18:1 (Winter 1985): 31–37; Coatsworth, "La historiografía económica de México," *Revista de Historia Económica* 6:2 (1988): 277–91; Noel Maurer, "Progress without Order: Mexican Economic History in the 1990s," *Revista de Historia Económica—Journal of Iberian and Latin American Economic History*, special issue, 17 (1999): 13–36.

5. Adolfo Meisel, "La cliometria en Colombia: una revolucion interrumpida, 1971–1999," *Revista de Historia Económica—Journal of Iberian and Latin American Economic History*, special issue, 17 (1999): 37–52; Luis Bértola, "La historia económica en Uruguay: desarrollo y perspectivas," *ibid.*, 77–100.

6. Stephen H. Haber, "La industrialización de México: historiografía y análisis," *Historia Mexicana* 167 (1993): 649–88; Gail Triner, "The Delayed Development of Early Brazilian Financial Historiography, 1890–1930," *Revista de Historia Económica—Journal of Iberian and Latin American Economic History*, special issue, 17 (1999): 53–76.

7. Haber, *How Latin America Fell Behind: Essays on the Economic Histories of Brazil and Mexico, 1800–1914* (Stanford: Stanford University Press, 1997); Gootenberg, "Between a Rock"; Coatsworth, "Structures, Endowments, and Institutions in the Economic History of Latin America," *Latin American Research Review* 40:3 (2005): 126–44.

8. John E. Roemer, ed., *Analytical Marxism, Studies in Marxism and Social Theory* (Cambridge, U.K.: Cambridge University Press/Paris: Maison des sciences de l'homme, 1986); Adam Pzreworski, *Democracy and the Market: Political and Economic Reforms in Eastern Europe and Latin America, Studies in Rationality and Social Change* (Cambridge, U.K.: Cambridge University Press, 1991).

9. Aldo Ferrer, *La economía argentina: Las etapas de su desarrollo y problemas actuales* (Mexico City: Fondo de Cultura Económica, 1963); Celso Furtado, *Formação econômica do Brasil* (Rio de Janeiro: Fundo de Cultura, 1959).

10. Earl Hamilton, *American Treasure and the Price Revolution in Spain* (Cambridge, Mass.: Harvard University Press, 1934).

11. Charles Gibson, *The Aztecs Under Spanish Rule: A History of the Indians of the Valley of Mexico, 1519–1810* (Stanford: Stanford University Press, 1964), 314.

12. Herbert Klein and John TePaske, *The Royal Treasuries of the Spanish Empire in America*, 3 vols. (Durham, N.C.: Duke University Press, 1982); Klein and TePaske, *Ingresos y egresos de la Real Hacienda de Nueva España*, 2 vols. (Mexico City: Instituto Nacional de Antropología e Historia: Colección Fuentes, 1986).

13. Cecilia Rabell Romero, *Los diezmos de San Luis de la Paz: Economía de una región del Bajío en el siglo XVIII* (Mexico City: Universidad Nacional Autónoma de México, 1986); Claude Morin, *Michoacán en la Nueva España del siglo XVIII: Crecimiento y desigualdad en una economía colonial* (Mexico City: Fondo de Cultura Económico, 1979).

14. Coatsworth, "The Mexican Mining Industry in the Eighteenth Century," in *The Economies of Mexico and Peru During the Late Colonial Period, 1760–1810*, ed. Nils Jacobsen and Hans Jürgen Puhle (Berlin: Colloquium, 1986), 26–45; Enrique Tandeter, *Coercion and Market: Silver Mining in Colonial Potosí, 1692–1826* (Albuquerque: University of New Mexico Press, 1993).

15. Virginia García Acosta, *Los precios del trigo en la historia colonial de México* (Mexico City: Casa Chata, 1988); Amilcar Challu, "Grain Markets, Food Supply Policies and Living Standards in Late Colonial Mexico" (PhD diss., Harvard University, 2007).

16. Hector Lindo Fuentes, "La utilidad de los diezmos como fuente para la historia económica," *Historia mexicana* 30:2 (1980): 273–89.

17. Lyman L. Johnson and Enrique Tandeter, eds., *Essays on the Price History of Eighteenth-Century Latin America* (Albuquerque: University of New Mexico Press, 1990).

18. Johnson and Zephyr Frank, "Cities and Wealth in the South Atlantic: Buenos Aires and Rio de Janeiro before 1860," *Comparative Studies in Society and History* 48:3 (2006): 634–68.

19. Colegio de México, *Estadísticas económicas del porfiriato: Fuerza de trabajo y actividad económica por sectores* (Mexico: El Colegio de México, n.d.); Aurora

Gómez-Galvarriato and Aldo Musacchio, "Un nuevo índice de precios para México, 1886–1929," *El Trimestre Económico* 67 (2000): 47–91; Jeffrey G. Williamson, "Real wages inequality and globalization in Latin America before 1940," *Revista de Historia Económica* 17 (1999): 101–42.

20. Luis A. V. Catão, "A new wholesale price index for Brazil during the period 1870–1913," *Revista Brasileira de Economia* 46 (1992): 519–33; Roberto Cortés Conde and Marcela Harriague, *Estimaciones del producto bruto interno de Argentina, 1875–1935* (Buenos Aires: Universidad de San Andres, 1994).

21. Jeffrey Bortz, *Industrial Wages in Mexico City, 1939–1975* (New York: Garland, 1987).

22. Richard J. Salvucci, "The Origins and Progress of U.S.-Mexican Trade, 1825–1884: 'Hoc Opus, Hic Labor Est,'" *The Hispanic American Historical Review* 71:4 (1991): 697–735; Graciela Márquez, "Tariff Protection in Mexico, 1892–1909: Ad Valorem Tariff Rates and Sources of Variation," in *Latin America and the World Economy since 1800*, ed. Coatsworth and Alan M. Taylor (Cambridge, Mass.: Harvard University/David Rockefeller Center for Latin American Studies, 1998); Edward Beatty, "The Impact of Foreign Trade on the Mexican Economy: Terms of Trade and the Rise of Industry 1880–1923," *Journal of Latin American Studies* 32:2 (2000): 399–433; Gómez-Galvarriato, "The Political Economy of Protectionism: The Mexican Textile Industry, 1900–1950," in *The Decline of Latin American Economies: Growth, Institutions, and Crises*, ed. Sebastian Edwards, Gerardo Esquivel, and Graciela Marquez (Chicago: University of Chicago Press, 2007), 363–406.

23. André Vilella, "Política tarifária no II Reinado: Evolução e impactos, 1850–1889," *Nova Economia* 15:1 (2005): 35–68.

24. Coatsworth and Williamson, "Always Protectionist? Latin American Tariffs from Independence to Great Depression," *Journal of Latin American Studies* 36:2 (2004): 205–32.

25. Haber, "Industrial Concentration and the Capital Markets: A Comparative Study of Brazil, Mexico, and the United States, 1830–1930," *The Journal of Economic History* 51:3 (1991): 559–80.

26. Haber, *Industry and Underdevelopment: The Industrialization of Mexico, 1890–1940* (Stanford: Stanford University Press, 1989).

27. Wilson Suzigan, *Indústria brasileira: Origem e desenvolvimento* (São Paulo: Brasiliense, 1986).

28. Haber, Maurer, and Armando Razo, *The Politics of Property Rights: Political Instability, Credible Commitments, and Economic Growth in Mexico, 1876–1929* (Cambridge, U.K.: Cambridge University Press, 2003).

29. Yovanna Pineda, *Industrial Development in a Frontier Economy: The Industrialization of Argentina, 1890–1930* (Stanford: Stanford University Press, 2010).

30. Xavier Tafunell, "Capital Formation in Machinery in Latin America, 1890–1930," Working Paper 1905, Department d'Economia i Empresa, Universitat Pompeu Fabra, June 2008.

31. Samuel Amaral, *The Rise of Capitalism on the Pampas: The Estancias of Buenos Aires, 1785–1870* (Cambridge, U.K.: Cambridge University Press, 1998).

32. Laird W. Bergad, Fe Iglesias García, and María del Carmen Barcia, *The Cuban Slave Market, 1790–1880* (Cambridge, U.K.: Cambridge University Press, 1995).

33. B. J. Barickman, *A Bahian Counterpoint: Sugar, Tobacco, Cassava, and Slavery in the Recôncavo, 1780–1860* (Stanford: Stanford University Press, 1998).

34. Laird W. Bergad, *Slavery and the Demographic and Economic History of Minas Gerais, Brazil, 1720–1888* (New York: Cambridge University Press, 1999); Francisco Vidal Luna and Klein, *Slavery and the Economy of São Paulo, 1750–1850* (Stanford: Stanford University Press, 2003).

35. Carlos M. Peláez and Wilson Suzigan, *História monetaria do Brasil: Análise da política, comportamento e instituições monetárias* (Rio de Janeiro: Instituto de Planejamento Econômico e Social/Instituto de Pesquisas, 1976).

36. Cortés Conde, *Dinero, deuda y crisis: Evolucion fiscal y monetaria en la Argentina, 1862–1890* (Buenos Aires: Editorial Sudamericana/Instituto Torcuato di Tella, 1989); Gerardo Della Paolera and Alan M. Taylor, *Straining at the Anchor: The Argentine Currency Board and the Search for Macroeconomic Stability, 1880–1935* (Chicago: University of Chicago Press, 2001).

37. Gail D. Triner, *Banking and Economic Development: Brazil, 1889–1930* (New York: Palgrave, 2000).

38. Anne G. Hanley, *Native Capital: Financial Institutions and Economic Development in São Paulo, Brazil, 1850–1920* (Stanford: Stanford University Press, 2005).

39. Maurer, *The Power and the Money: The Mexican Financial System, 1876–1932* (Stanford: Stanford University Press, 2002).

40. Aldo Musacchio, "Can Civil Law Countries Get Good Institutions?" *Journal of Economic History* 68:1 (2008): 80–108.

41. Coatsworth, *Growth against Development: The Economic Impact of Railroads in Porfirian Mexico* (DeKalb: Northern Illinois University Press, 1981).

42. Colin M. Lewis, *British Railways in Argentina, 1857–1914: A Case Study of Foreign Investment* (London: Athlone, 1983).

43. Flávio Azevedo Marques de Saes, *As ferrovias de São Paulo, 1870–1940* (São Paulo: Hucitec, 1981); William Roderick Summerhill, *Order against Progress: Government, Foreign Investment, and Railroads in Brazil, 1854–1913* (Stanford: Stanford University Press, 2003).

44. Sandra Kuntz Ficker, *Empresa extranjera y mercado interno: El Ferrocarril Central Mexicano, 1880–1907* (Mexico City: El Colegio de México, 1995).

45. Maria Teresa Ramirez, "Los ferrocarriles y su impacto sobre la economía colombiana," *Revista de Historia Economica* 19:1 (2001): 81–119.

46. Robert William Fogel, "Economic Growth, Population Theory, and Physiology: The Bearing of Long-Term Processes in the Making of Economic Policy," *American Economic Review* 84:3 (1994): 369–95; John Komlos, ed., *The Biological Standard of Living in Europe and America, 1700–1900* (Aldershot, U.K.: Variorum, 1995); Richard Steckel, ed., *The Backbone of History: Health and Nutrition in the Western Hemisphere* (Cambridge, U.K.: Cambridge University Press, 2002).

47. Stanley L. Engerman and Kenneth L. Sokoloff, "Factor Endowments, Institutions, and Differential Paths of Growth Among New World Economies: A View from Economic Historians of the United States," in *How Latin America Fell Behind: Essays on the Economic History of Brazil and Mexico, 1800–1914*, ed. Haber (Stanford: Stanford University Press, 1997), 260–304.

48. Daron Acemoglu, Simon Johnson, and James A. Robinson, "The Colonial Origins of Comparative Development: An Empirical Investigation," *American Economic Review* 91:5 (2001): 1369–401.

49. Frank, "Wealth Holding in Southeastern Brazil, 1815–60," *Hispanic American Historical Review* 85:2 (2005): 223–58; Jorge Gelman and Daniel Santilli, *Historia del capitalismo agrario pampeano*, vol. 3: *De Rivadavia a Rosas: Desigualdad y crecimiento económico* (Buenos Aires: Siglo XXI, 2006); Johnson and Frank, "Cities and Wealth in the South Atlantic: Buenos Aires and Rio de Janeiro before 1860," *Comparative Studies in Society and History* 48:3 (2006): 634–68; Coatsworth, "Inequality, Institutions, and Economic Growth in Latin America," *Journal of Latin American Studies* 40 (2008): 545–69.

50. David Eltis, "The Total Product of Barbados, 1664–1701," *Journal of Economic History* 55:2 (1995): 321–38; Coatsworth, "Economic and Institutional Trajectories in Nineteenth-Century Latin America," in *Latin America and the World Economy Since 1800*, ed. Coatsworth and Taylor (Cambridge, Mass.: Harvard University Press, 1998).

51. Williamson, "Real Wages Inequality"; Coatsworth, "Inequality, Institutions, and Economic Growth."

52. Rebecca Storey, *Life and Death in the Ancient City of Teotihuacan: A Modern Paleodemographic Synthesis* (Tuscaloosa: University of Alabama Press, 1992).

53. Clark S. Larsen, ed., *Bioarchaeology of Spanish Florida: The Impact of Colonialism* (Gainesville: University Press of Florida, 2001).

54. Challu, "Grain Markets"; Ricardo Salvatore, "Heights and Welfare in Late-Colonial and Post-Independence Argentina," in *The Biological Standard of Living in Comparative Perspective*, ed. John Komlos and J. Baten (Stuttgart: Steiner, 1998).

55. Moramay López Alonso, "Growth with Inequality: Living Standards in Mexico, 1850–1950," *Journal of Latin American Studies* 39:1 (2007): 81–105; Meisel and Margarita Vega, "La estatura de la élite colombiana antes de la industrialización, 1870–1919," *Cuadernos de historia económica y empresarial—economía regional*, Paper 002998 (Banco de la República, Colombia, 2005).

56. Ricardo Salvatore, "Stature Decline and Recovery in a Food-Rich Export Economy: Argentina 1900–1934," *Explorations in Economic History* 41:3 (2004): 233–55; López Alonso, "Growth with Inequality."

57. Meisel and Vega, "The Biological Standard of Living (and Its Convergence) in Colombia, 1870–2003: A Tropical Success Story," *Economics and Human Biology* 5:1 (2007): 100–22.

58. Leonardo Monasterio, "Stature and Immigration in Southern Brazil, 1889–1919," working paper, 2009.

59. Luis Ríos Frutos and Barry Bogin, "An Anthropometric Perspective on Guatemalan History," in *Living Standards in Latin American History*, ed. Challu, Coatsworth, and Salvatore (Cambridge, Mass.: Harvard University Press and the David Rockefeller Center for Latin America Studies, 2010).

60. See principally Stanley L. Engerman and Kenneth L. Sokoloff, "Factor Endowments, Institutions, and Differential Paths of Growth Among New World Economies: A View from Economic Historians of the United States," in *How Latin America Fell Behind*, 260–304; "Factor Endowments, Inequality, and Paths of Development among New World Economies," *Economía* 3:1 (2002): 41–88; Acemoglu, Johnson, and Robinson, "Colonial Origins of Comparative Development."

CHAPTER 15

DISEASE, MEDICINE, AND HEALTH

DIEGO ARMUS
ADRIÁN LÓPEZ DENIS

SINCE the 1970s, the historical study of human responses to disease has produced a significant amount of highly influential literature worldwide. Developments in the field have been shaped by (and have contributed to) some of the most radical transformations at the core of the humanities and social sciences. Established disciplines like population studies, history of medicine, and the sociology of public health are evolving to accommodate more aspects of the complex interaction between the sick, health care practitioners, and the society at large. The history of medicine has been enriched by the incorporation of fresh anthropological perspectives on the cultural determinants of health and healing. Scholars working at the intersection of literary theory and cultural studies are acquiring a taste for the historical analysis of biomedical narratives, while social scientists interested in central categories like gender, race, and class are intrigued by multiple connections between medical knowledge, health policy, and identity politics. The role of disease and healing practices in the articulation of geopolitical units at global and local levels attracts the attention of specialists in the history of imperial expansion, colonialism, neocolonialism, modernities and the environment. As a whole, and in no more than four decades, the social and cultural history of disease, medicine, and health became a dynamic source of intellectual renovation in contemporary academic circles.[1]

Like medicine itself, scholarly knowledge about the history of human responses to disease has been circulating along asymmetric channels and passing through multiple colonial and neocolonial filters. The heterogeneous body of historical literature generated through this complex process has been and continues to be shaped by cultural transmissions, appropriations, and innovations. This essay attempts to present an overview of this fast-developing subfield of historical inquiry, based on thematic units organized along a roughly chronological sequence. Although extremely hard to characterize in general terms, some major patterns emerge from a systematic evaluation of the existent bibliography. First of all, when dealing with the history of health, medicine, and disease in the region, a conventional distinction between "colonial" and "national" periods seems less relevant than a division based on the diffusion of bacteriology—slow and with unequal intensity and success, not only in the rural and urban worlds but also among countries—during the last quarter of the nineteenth century.

Studies on the dynamics of disease and healing in Latin America before the introduction of modern bacteriology are unevenly integrated within global academic trends. Environmental and epidemiological considerations provide a framework for a rich historiography dealing with the impact of disease in the early stages of European colonization and conquest.[2] While this literature discusses the consequences of transoceanic biological integration, a parallel line of inquiry explores other dimensions of early globalization. Developed in relative isolation up to the sixteenth century, multiple healing practices and ideas about disease came together for the first time when peoples from Europe, sub-Saharan Africa, and the Americas collided in the New World. This complex interaction was framed by an array of colonial approaches to sanitary policy and medical practice throughout the hemisphere. Formal institutions for professional supervision, medical training, and hospital care were transplanted from France, Portugal, and Spain to their overseas territories. Guilds, universities, the Catholic Church, and the crown had jurisdiction over most aspects of legal medical practice in these colonies. In the British territories, however, the administration of health matters was relatively decentralized, medical knowledge was typically acquired outside the classroom, and healers operated under less hierarchical arrangements.[3] Although more important in theory than in practice, and keeping in mind the very limited dimensions of the medicalization process during the colonial times, this contrast between formal approaches to health issues in Protestant and Catholic colonies had a great influence on the development of their medical historiography.

Framed by global rather than regional chronologies, most studies on the post-bacteriological or "modern" period are particularly well integrated into worldwide developments in the historiography of the field.[4] However, these features do not translate themselves into globalized or comparative narratives of the history of a certain disease or a certain biomedical process. Instead, the emphasis has been on the local, regional, and national dimensions; only on a few occasions does Latin America emerge as a category of analysis. In any case, and independently of their geographical scope, this historiography results from a research agenda that could be read as the product of two paths of inquiry. The first encompasses approaches that started out with the history of medicine and the biosciences and ended up weaving rich social, political, and cultural narratives and analyses. The second took the opposite path, and departing from broader problems initially defined in terms of society, politics, and culture, these studies not only discovered illness as an intriguing and contentious historical issue but came to make disease the organizing theme of their historical accounts. It evolved following three historiographical styles that somewhat try to address the powerful interplay among culture, history, medicine, and society. These styles could be labeled as new history of medicine, history of public health, and sociocultural history of disease. Although all these approaches overlap in many respects and see diseases, health, and medicine as settings marked by consensus, tensions, and conflicts, their research agendas are not necessarily similar.

Traditionally, the subject of disease has been a kind of boundary controlled by historians of medicine. They wrote histories of changes in treatments and biographies of famous doctors. Beyond their specific contributions, these histories appear to have attempted to reconstruct the "inevitable progress" generated by university-certified medicine, to unify the past of an increasingly specialized profession, and to emphasize a certain ethos and moral philosophy presented as distinctive, unaltered, and emblematic of medical practice throughout time. The new history of medicine, by contrast, tends to see the development of medicine as a more irregular and faltering process. Engaging in dialogue with the history of science, it discusses the social, cultural, and political contexts in which certain doctors, institutions, and treatments "triumphed," making a place for themselves in history. And it also examines others less successful, which have been forgotten. It strives to understand the natural history of the disease and some aspects of its social dimensions.[5]

The history of public health looks at power, the state, the medical profession, the politics of health, and the impact of public health interventions on mortality and morbidity trends. In general, and to a large extent, this is a history focused on the relations between health institutions and economic, social, and political structures. For some of its practitioners, the goal is to know better certain health-related problems in the past and perhaps inform somewhat the understanding of public health issues of the present.[6] For others, practicing the history of public health is also practicing history in public health, in the sense that they search the past in order to find certain evidence that, they think, can legitimate public health actions and interventions that should shape the immediate and future public health agendas. It is, no doubt, a history that regards itself as useful and instrumental, seeking in the past lessons for the present and future because it assumes that health is an open-ended process.[7]

Thus, the history of public health aims at researching the past in order to reduce the inevitable uncertainties that mark every decision-making process in public health, thereby facilitating in general rather than specific ways interventions in the contemporary scene. To be sure, this approach continues two overlapping legacies, from late-nineteenth- and early-twentieth-century hygiene practice and research and also from certain national histories of public health written since the 1950s. Both efforts, which recognized and underlined the social dimensions of disease, are important antecedents when evaluating scholarship on public health issues from a historical perspective. These, then, are the points of departure for studies which in some cases do nothing more than celebrate the first public health physicians and practitioners and their actions, much like the traditional history of medicine.[8] In others, writing the biographies of key public health practitioners and policymakers aims more at a critical contextualization than a celebration.[9] Aside from these biographical accounts, other studies attempt to analyze the issue of health and medicine in structuralist code as epiphenomena of the relations of production.[10] Either way, the emphasis of these accounts is on the study of state interventions—or lack of them—to encourage preventive policies and preserve or restore collective health. It focuses on the moments in which the state—based on considerations that go beyond the strictly medical and are shaped by political, economic, cultural, scientific, and technological factors—has promoted actions intended to combat a particular disease.

Most of the time in the history of public health, public medicine appears in a positive and progressive light, as the fortunate outcome of the association of biomedical sciences with a rational organization of society in which certain professionals—public health doctors, above all—offer solutions for the diseases of the modern world. While this association was seen as potentially beneficial, its concrete achievements were found wanting. This unhappy result was presented as a reflection of the dependent condition of the region, without regard for any temporal or national distinctions. According to this approach, this dependency determined the existence of a ruling elite and a structure of economic power that were unable or unwilling to create and distribute public health resources and services in an equitable and efficient manner.[11] Other studies reacted against the schematic use of the dependency model. They summarized the achievements and failures of national or municipal projects aimed at creating or modernizing the basic sanitary infrastructure and reducing mortality. This underlined that, despite the peripheral condition of Latin America and at least in certain countries or cities, the balance was not that negative.[12]

The sociocultural history of disease is more recent than the history of public health. While the latter emphasizes an interventionist agenda aimed at lacking, getting, or preserving health, the former articulates its narrative on the disease as such. It is a history written by historians, sociologists, anthropologists, and cultural critics who have discovered the complexity and possibilities of disease and health, either as problems in themselves or as excuses for discussing other topics. In the first case, and when it is done in its more convincing and sophisticated way, these histories seem to assume—as was stated by one of the most influential historians in this field, who does not study Latin America—that diseases do not exist until we have agreed that they do, by perceiving, naming, and responding to them.[13] In the second, diseases serve broader agendas to understand social and cultural dimensions of the past. This approach barely skims the history of a given etiology; rarely is there any attempt to set up a dialogue between sociocultural history and the history of biomedical science. Instead, it spreads out over topics such as the sociopolitical or sociodemographic dimensions of a particular disease, medical professionalization processes, welfare and social control instruments and institutions, or the state's role in building health infrastructure.[14]

Some of these histories do not go beyond gathering relevant data and basic information. But others, in a deliberate effort to discuss health and disease problems from a critical perspective, argue for a small set of overriding explanatory factors.[15] At times, these studies tend toward top-down and somewhat conspiratorial explanations: the poor have always been wretched because of a lack of political will on the part of elites and middle classes; every public health initiative resulted from an effort to increase the productivity or guarantee the reproduction of labor; elites got involved in sanitary reforms for their own security; pioneering initiatives were the product of the workings of a new professional state bureaucracy interested in imposing public health measures; or dependent capitalism needed those changes. There have also been Foucauldian interpretations of medicalization, an undoubtedly inspiring line of thinking that has consistently found in medicine and state public health interventions an arsenal of normalizing resources aimed at the consolidation of a modernity that most of the time is vaguely defined and lacking in substantial specific historical references to the place under study. Thus medicine was understood as one of the rationalization enterprises that, having developed particular disciplinary languages and practices, tried to control bodies, individuals, and society.[16] In this context, diseases and medical actions attempting to address them have been seen—quite often overlooking mediations and particularities—as instruments for regulating society, labeling difference, and legitimizing ideological and cultural systems. Finally, there have been ambitious studies in which a certain disease is used as an excuse to discuss broader problems, from metaphors of nation building to literary narratives of the malady, the formulation of public health policies and their consequences, and people's experiences with the disease.[17]

These three lines of inquiry—the new history of medicine, the history of public health, and the sociocultural history of disease—undoubtedly reflect an effort to both build on the empirical information offered by the traditional history of medicine and escape from its limitations. All of them take medicine to be an unstable field where the biomedical is shaped as much by human subjectivity as by objective facts and the medical initiatives are discussed taking into account, not always with similar emphasis, its disciplining and/or progressive dimensions. In a more or less convincing way, all of them try to discuss disease and illness as problems that have a biological dimension but are also loaded with social, cultural, political, and economic connotations. Also, and again with more or less success, these works want to be attentive to the rich mediations between the state, medical knowledge, public health policies, the requirements of the economic system, perceptions and representations of illnesses, and the responses of ordinary people.

In general, the literature on the demographic and social consequences of European conquest has been produced by Anglo-American authors operating on a hemispheric scale to satisfy the needs of a comparative agenda. Studies on the consolidation of healing practices and the socioeconomic impact of disease during the colonial period have flourished in Mexico, a country with a long tradition of scholarly research in fields like medical history, urban demography, and colonial studies. As a result, reconstructions of medico-sanitary developments in New Spain constitute a disproportionately large fraction of the existent literature.

The period between the Spanish American wars of independence and the rise of bacteriology has received only minimal attention. This is not the case for the decades between the 1870s and the 1930s, for which the historiography has been and continues to be particularly prolific. As with other topics, studies on the interplay of disease, health, and medicine for this period reveal many of the similarities and differences that qualify the ways Latin American nations entered modern times. Although most of them shared a neocolonial condition, the processes of urbanization and industrialization did not take place at the same time everywhere, a heterogeneity that is also apparent in the nation- and state-building processes, in the relative position of each nation vis-à-vis multiple and shifting metropolitan references, in the ethnic and racial makeup of national populations, and in the relevance of international migration influences. This diversity of national historical experiences and the many modernities that have been in the making in these decades are clearly present in the historiography of disease and health. Thus, for some countries historians have been focusing their attention on tropical diseases such as malaria, yellow fever, hookworm, and Chagas disease as a consequence of the relevant roles played in the incorporation of the countryside into their national histories—even, at times, as a sort of national pathology. But in other cases, that focus was on diseases and health-related problems such as tuberculosis, syphilis, and urban hygiene, associated not as much with the rural world as with modern city life and industrial growth. Studies focused on the 1940s and 1950s dealing with the expansion of the public health agenda under the populist experiences that marked many Latin American countries are not abundant but are already showing very promising results. Finally, the return of old epidemic diseases such as cholera and the arrival of new ones such as HIV-AIDS during the last decades of the twentieth century are receiving consistent scholarly attention, more by medical anthropologists and public health specialists than by historians interested in the recent past.

The historiographical production for the period from the 1870s onwards has grown in an uneven way. In Brazil, the field has been showing a vibrant and perdurable expansion, with research institutions such as the Casa Oswaldo Cruz–Fiocruz with well-articulated agendas focused on the relations among history, science, technology, health, and biomedicine, excellent academic journals such as *História, Ciências, Saúde—Manguinhos*, ongoing debates, and a steady production of original work resulting from well-established graduate programs and well-organized archives. In the rest of Latin America, even in the large and medium-sized countries, the balance is much more modest, and the resulting picture only highlights emerging networks of researchers, academic journals in process of consolidation, and topics and issues for which there are no more than a handful of works.

In the mid-1960s, a handful of world historians began investigating the complex interactions between biogeography, epidemiology, and sociocultural development. According to these scholars, the European expansion of the sixteenth century could be better understood as a transoceanic exchange of people, crops, animals, and germs, with dramatic consequences at the ecological, socioeconomic, and cultural levels.[18] Opening a new line of historical reasoning, they argued that before 1492 the aboriginal population of the Americas was free of some of the most common infectious diseases that had ravaged the Old World for centuries. The hardships of early migratory movements through the cold land bridge connecting Asia to North America kept out of the New World many of the vectors and intermediary hosts essential to the spread of mite-, tick-, and mosquito-borne diseases like relapsing fever, schistosomiasis, malaria, and yellow fever. The lack of large herds of domestic animals limited the development of infections such as smallpox, which presumably evolved from centuries of continuous interaction between humans and their cattle. A relatively small population density explained the absence of crowd-related diseases like measles, chickenpox, influenza, and rubella. The Americas were not a disease-free paradise, but having been isolated from Eurasian and African pools of infection, their population had developed a particular set of immunities that made it susceptible to the ravages of many Old World pathogens. Under such circumstances, the first contact with overseas invaders was bound to be deadly for those aborigines lacking most forms of acquired or inherited protection against common European and African diseases.[19]

The notion that differential immunities played an important role in the early colonization of the tropics has been elevated to the category of historical paradigm. Woven together with other evolutionary and technological notions into the so-called guns and germs theories, it appeals to general readers in their search for comprehensive interpretations of the past.[20] Many scholars have been seduced by the explanatory power of this argument and the apparent simplicity of its biomedical foundations. It proved to be particularly useful in redirecting a long-standing debate on the size of the hemispheric aboriginal population before 1492. Wildly ranging from ten to a hundred million, the very existence of these figures represented a challenge for historical demography as a discipline.[21] By accepting estimates on the high end of the spectrum, scholars were automatically compelled to provide an explanation for the implicit demographic catastrophe of the sixteenth century. A series of deadly epidemics was the most obvious candidate to complete the picture, and this in turn encouraged the development of a fertile crossover between the efforts of demographers and historical epidemiologists.[22]

Like many other historical generalizations, this paradigm has been severely criticized. After retracing the genealogy of both lines of research, some specialists claimed that many demographic estimates based upon high mortality rates were the result of epidemiological assumptions regarding the size of the aboriginal populations. From this point of view, the entire model seemed to be based on a circular argument. According to other critics, the basic methodology applied to most estimates of aboriginal population size was mathematically and historically questionable. Most operations were based on a series of progressively distorting multipliers that rendered any result almost meaningless, while the original sources were simply mistranslated, poorly chosen, or misread.[23] Beyond its original generalizations, however, the notion of differential immunities provided a very flexible foundation for more sophisticated evaluations of population dynamics. The very idea of immunity as something that individuals and groups could acquire after a prolonged exposure to disease allowed this revised version of the model to explain both short-term ecological failure and long-term success. Survival and demographic recovery became legitimate topics alongside more traditional stories of disaster and breakdown, while peripheral regions within the continent received more attention.[24] The inclusion of socioeconomic variables, spatial considerations, and nutritional trends opened the doors of the field to other scholars. Geographers, paleopathologists, paleodemographers, and archeologists contributed a great deal of ecological, dietary, and epidemiological evidence to the reconstruction of early epidemiological dynamics and population patterns in the hemisphere.[25]

In a parallel line of inquiry, other scholars have attempted to clarify the role of differential immunities, nutritional trends, and ecological changes in the development of African slavery in the Americas. Behind these studies is the notion that some African populations enjoyed specific forms of resistance to many Old World pathogens while remaining particularly susceptible to the ravages of other diseases related to their dual condition as slaves and newcomers in the Americas. Some specialists argue that the transatlantic circulation of malaria and yellow fever was a determining factor in the development of the plantation system. According to them, by bringing these and other exotic maladies to the New World, along with their relatively immune human carriers, the first slave traders were in fact replicating the West African disease environment in the Caribbean, Brazil, and the American South.[26] In these particular settings, the relative biological success of people of African descent was so notorious that a combination of natural selection, racial prejudice, and biomedical perceptions fueled new waves of forced transatlantic migration, shaping the final demographic configuration of entire New World regions.[27]

As a complex ecosystem, the plantation depended on a continuous input of labor, food staples, capital, and technology. Under such circumstances, the health of the slaves was severely affected by changes in the composition of their traditional diet, workload, psychological makeup, and reproductive strategies. There is a substantial amount of literature on the living conditions of the slaves and its demographic consequences, with emphasis on the combined effects of malnutrition, exploitation, and infection.[28] Although some scholars overplay the role of ecological and epidemiological factors in the configuration of the plantation system, models based on the interaction of local environments and differential immunities have been useful to explain many significant historical developments in the region, from the outcome of imperial wars in the eighteenth century to the dynamics of smallpox epidemics in colonial Brazil or the cyclical character of Afro-Caribbean religious festivals.[29]

While the biological exchanges triggered by colonization in Latin America can be understood using relatively simple ecological models, studying the complex integration of healing practices that resulted from successive waves of transatlantic migration presents more challenging problems. Peoples from sub-Saharan Africa, the Americas, and Eurasia developed their own responses to disease in a context of relative isolation up until the sixteenth century. Along with its dramatic epidemiological and demographic consequences, the colonization of the New World forced the creation of hybrid healing cultures. Given the nature of the available written sources, most of the research on indigenous "pre-Columbian" medicine consists in fact of studies dealing, more or less openly, with the early stages of this integration.[30] However, some scholars have produced valuable contributions to the understanding of medical knowledge in the region in their effort to distill some "pure" indigenous or European ingredients from the complex healing practices documented by Iberian chroniclers.[31]

In recent decades, historical, anthropological, and ethnographic research carried out not only among indigenous communities but also on rural or urban communities with a well-defined sense of belonging to what can be called a peripheral and Western world has provided an enormous amount of new evidence regarding the use of natural resources, the cosmological dimensions of healing practices, and the extent to which current beliefs are the result of creative exchanges between traditional and modern forms of medical knowledge.[32] Rather than celebrating folk medicine, these studies explore the transactions that take place between hegemonic and popular knowledge. They emphasize the varied and multifaceted meanings that illness acquires among disparate social, ethnic, or racial groups as well as the importance and complexity of the mutual influences, exchanges, and competition between officially certified, alternative, hybrid, and popular medicines well into the twentieth century. In many cases, particularly from the end of the nineteenth century onwards, this pluralistic scenario has been seen as evidence of the limitations of the process of medicalization or of the broader repertoire of resources available to the sick who used them, in a complementary manner or not, even for goals that go beyond any attempt to get basic care or assistance. That is why the presence of healing practices not controlled by biomedicine is apparent in poorly medicalized societies as well as in others where there were successful medicalization efforts based on universal medical coverage or segmented systems of health care. Of course, and as with many other historical issues, any generalization is problematic. In fact, there are plenty of periods and areas where medical pluralism underlines more pragmatic tolerance than bitter rivalries as well as the other way around, marked by violent encounters between competing medical ideologies.[33]

With the arrival of African slave healers, plantation medicine became another important vehicle for the reformulation of colonial therapeutics. This new wave of practitioners was equipped with a completely different set of healing strategies, embedded in a highly complex cosmology. Their contributions have been explored by historians and anthropologists, but integrating the diachronic and synchronic dimensions of all this research remains a major challenge for the historiography of the field.[34] A promising line of research has been opened by scholars interested in the production of more flexible models for the understanding of medico-religious practices in a context of power asymmetries, renegotiation, and conflict. Mainly for Mexico, but also for other areas of Latin America, there are systematic studies on the sociopolitical and cultural significance of alternative healing in colonial times.[35] These efforts have been based on an imaginative use of inquisitorial records and biomedical literature. Such an approach would be particularly relevant for researchers interested in a reconstruction of the complex channels through which medical knowledge circulated across the Atlantic. Original sources documenting Iberian colonial contributions to the pharmacopoeia of the Old World have been carefully edited and studied in the last two decades. This material has provided the referential and methodological foundations for a more balanced assessment of early transatlantic exchanges in other biomedical fields.[36]

A long tradition of institutional history based on the rich archives of professional organizations, universities, and hospitals could easily be transplanted from Europe to Latin America. As a result, studies on professional training, medical regulation, and hospital administration were among the first areas cultivated by the pioneers of medical history in Latin America. Today, this type of approach continues to flourish, and some of the most informative literature on the region for the period before the arrival of bacteriology is produced under the aegis of institutional history.[37] Official reactions to disease in colonial times required a high degree of coordination between bureaucratic agents, thus generating huge amounts of paperwork that in turn became valuable sources for the reconstruction of the biomedical past. In recent years, issues like urban sanitation, vaccination, and general prophylaxis have received some scholarly attention.[38]

When dealing with the postbacteriological period, this institutional history acquires not only a quite different tone but also much more density, mainly resulting from the steady (although unequal among and within countries) process of medicalization that took place throughout the twentieth century. On the one hand, there are studies which basically offer raw and very basic information on hospitals, sanatoriums, medical schools, public health government agencies, or philanthropic organizations, but without much effort at contextualization. On the other hand, more ambitious analysis written by social historians, political scientists and sociologists aims not only at reconstructing the emergence of segmented health care networks based on state and civil society institutions, public health state agencies, and international health organizations but also at studying the making and increasing specialization of the medical and paramedical professions, the role played by key public health doctors, the origins of the national social security systems, and the political conflicts and alliances that accompanied the formulation of certain public health policies, sometimes even going beyond the discursive level in order to explore their real impact.[39]

The study of particular epidemic outbreaks and long-term public responses to endemic maladies constitute another important area of historical inquiry in the region. The existing literature on social responses to epidemic disease before and after the advent of modern bacteriology illustrates multiple instances of continuity and change. For the period before the arrival of bacteriology, approaches range from the discussion of specific medical doctrines and public health procedures to the use of epidemics as tools for socioeconomic, ecological, demographic, political, and racial analysis.[40] Although the pandemic and recurrent nature of many outbreaks could provide an excellent opportunity for transnational contrasts and diachronic interpretations, these comparative dimensions of the topic are still uncharted.

For the postbacteriological period, these histories emphasize the social conditions of emergence of epidemics, the reactions of elites and common people, and the role played by state policies and external—colonial or neocolonial—forces combating the outbreaks. Others use epidemics as a way to explore the state of collective health and the infrastructure of sanitation and health care, its role facilitating initiatives in public health and accelerating the presence of state authority, both in social policy and in private life. Less common is a careful examination of the biological and ecological factors present in an epidemic, opening in that way a dialogue between social history and the history of the biomedical sciences.[41] To be sure, the history of epidemics in Latin America adds to a kind of dramaturgy common to all epidemics, interweaving themes of contagion, fear, stigma, blame, salvation, and individual and social responsibility, suggesting on the one hand that continuities seem to be more apparent than changes and on the other that the local dimension should be approached as a chapter of disease history that at least in some cases is global. But this dramaturgy, it is worth stressing, merely defines the framework for an epidemic event, not its specific cultural, religious, or political features. It also does not speak to the ways societies and certain social groups give meanings to the experience of the epidemic, the availability and use of certain strategies and resources for combating it, and the effective implementation of certain general discourses into policies.

In any case, epidemics lay bare the state of collective health and the infrastructure of sanitation and health care and offer a promising entry to the examination of broader problems. They can facilitate initiatives in public health, and in this way play an accelerating role in expanding state authority, both in social policy and in private life. Nevertheless, society's familiarity with an illness might well lead to ignoring it. This may be either because its persistent presence makes it less extraordinary and surprising, transforming epidemics into endemics, or because the political, social, or geographic contexts in which these epidemics or endemics take place do not allow them to become public, political issues, even though, by definition, they are collective matters.

Before and after the takeoff of modern bacteriology, epidemics were closely associated with urban life, particularly that of great cities. From the end of the nineteenth century until well into the twentieth, this association was also linked to the so-called social question. Thus, with the growing acceptance of monocausal explanations for every illness, references to the larger context were inescapable: the precariousness of garbage disposal, sewer and drinking water systems, housing, biological or racial inheritance, daily habits of hygiene, the work environment, diet and poverty, massive immigration, and the "dangerous" teeming multitudes in the cities. At the beginning of the twentieth century, statistics became a common staple of social analysis, and in some countries state agencies specifically concerned with public health issues were created. First hygienists, and later public health physicians, would play a decisive role in modernizing collective urban facilities and the institutional networks of public assistance, reform, and social control, acting almost as a specialized bureaucracy along with other professionals and political, religious, or governmental agents. At times, the struggle against epidemics took on the character of quasi-military campaigns in rhetoric, by defining microorganisms as enemies, and, in practice, by encouraging intrusive and violent interventions. Perhaps for that reason, these interventions were resisted on certain occasions, even when their methods were not entirely new to the population. At other times, the larger struggle also included persuasion, aiming to educate the population and disseminate so-called hygienic ways of living.

In certain contexts, diseases like syphilis or leprosy were classified as epidemic even though they did not massively affect the population. They were turned into national problems for social, cultural, or political reasons, legitimated by medical expertise, attracting public attention and spurring campaigns designed specifically to eradicate them. Illnesses, such as cholera, that did not break out suddenly but were well established in everyday life, and sometimes killed and afflicted more people than epidemic diseases, did not always manage to mobilize sufficient material, professional, or symbolic resources to be perceived as national problems. These might be chronic maladies, such as tuberculosis and gastrointestinal diseases, or endemic, such as malaria and hookworm. While less spectacular, these diseases had an impact in cities, the countryside, or both. But because they were more widespread, more difficult to treat, more closely associated with poverty, more socially or geographically distant from centers of power, and more easily overlooked, these diseases could be made visible to public opinion and elite consciousness only with enormous effort, and therefore particular policies to combat them were rare or nonexistent. In the urban world, some of these diseases did manage to become public issues because they came to be seen as part of the "social question" or to be strongly associated with broader national problems.[42] In the countryside, endemic illnesses expanded the area of action of public health interventions, fostering initiatives of rural sanitation that ignited efforts to launch social policies, state expansion agendas, the centralization of power, and, more generally, nation-building processes.[43]

Another relevant topic discussed in some historiographical detail has been the ways in which the state and society confronted disease and health problems. At the core of this topic is the development of public health policies resulting from the interplay between external powers and the emerging of more or less consolidated national states. Here two approaches are apparent. On the one hand, a diffusionist interpretation assumes a clear division between centers and peripheral areas in the production of biomedical knowledge, portraying the latter as passive receptors of knowledge and practices constructed outside the region. On the other hand, a more critical reading of that diffusionism emphasizes not the importing and transplanting of ideas about certain pathologies—yellow fever, malaria, hookworm, Chagas disease—but either the infrequent production of local scientific knowledge or the certainly more relevant and widespread processes of creative selection, assembly, reelaboration, and modification of knowledge produced in the metropolitan centers vis-à-vis the specific, local, and peripheral cultural, political, and institutional contexts. In this interpretive frame, the practices of medical doctors, hygienists, and scientists from the Latin American peripheries are sometimes allied with, sometimes competing against, and sometimes challenging what comes from scientific and culturally hegemonic Europe or North America. Thus, these studies reveal the existence of a group of Latin American medical professionals actively producing knowledge, debating—before and after the triumph of modern bacteriology—the possible etiologies of certain diseases, creating institutions of scientific excellence, and devoting themselves to more or less original efforts to make a difference in local and regional mortality and morbidity trends.[44]

The politicization of health and the reception and transfer of expertise and practices associated with the fight against malaria, yellow fever, and hookworm have been and continue to be a relevant topic in the historiography. At its core is the role played by some international agencies, in particular the Rockefeller Foundation. Its missions were decisive in the organization of single-disease services and the promotion of technical approaches and specific cures to the detriment of more comprehensive, educational, and preventive strategies. They were also, especially from the 1910s onwards, a proof of the growing presence and influence of the United States as a new metropolitan world player with an increasing hegemonic role in the region. But along with these novelties, what some studies are underlining is that in many countries, small and large, health- and disease-related problems had already become a public issue before these missions arrived. In fact, during the first two-thirds of the nineteenth century, miasmatic and environmentalist approaches dominated medical perceptions of health and disease without producing major changes in the sanitary infrastructure or overall mortality. But toward the end of the century, modern bacteriology took center stage and profoundly shaped the dynamics of many undertakings in public health. It was in this context that some national scientific communities gave greater priority to the study of certain tropical diseases. These doctors, often trained in Western Europe, developed novel and quite specific approaches to research and intervention, sometimes even before their North American peers.[45]

However, the arrival of the Rockefeller missions was crucial in the orientation of sanitary reforms, particularly for rural areas and for diseases which, it was believed, could be eradicated with little cost and in a short time. Despite varied and uneven results in different countries and with different diseases, there is no doubt that the Rockefeller Foundation projects mobilized public opinion, especially with regard to the living and health conditions of the rural poor, contributed enormously to centralizing sanitary efforts, reinforced the power of the central government vis-à-vis the traditional local and regional ones, and consolidated the position of the United States as the dominant external reference in matters of public health. The missions' technical-elitist approaches had to confront the challenge of adapting to the local population's idiosyncrasies and perceptions of specific diseases, particularly in the countryside. This was something that the Rockefeller representatives found as difficult, and did as badly, as most of the native, mainly urban doctors. At the end, what this historiography is trying to underline is that the relations between national and foreign medical groups were complex, at times involving subordination, cooptation, alliance, pragmatism, conflict, or mutual adaptation. In the rural and urban areas, dealing with various diseases, they faced the unavoidable problems of when to interfere in people's everyday routines and customs and when to leave them alone, and when to use persuasion and when to resort to coercion in order to achieve public health goals. In their original design, missions may have been conceived as purely technical or instrumental endeavors in keeping with a neocolonial philanthropic or economics-based agenda. But when these interventions materialized, they contributed, whether intentionally or not, to establishing precedents and laying the institutional foundations for future preventive medicine projects and, in general, a culture of health that local professional actors would lead and try to disseminate.[46] This scholarship has been the starting point of a new trend of studies focused on global health, international organizations, philanthropic and cooperation initiatives, and colonial and neocolonial encounters rather than global histories of diseases, strongly influenced by and also aiming to influence the relatively new but vibrant field of international and global health.[47]

Studies focused on the sociocultural uses of disease have been in full expansion. Many of them offer historical narratives particularly focused on examining medical discourses on the one hand and the metaphorical uses of disease on the other. Here we see the influence of the Foucauldian interpretative framework shaping studies of madness in general as well as the specific institutions, theoretical systems, and processes of professionalization associated with both the psychiatric order and criminology. Thus, madness has been discussed as a subject that is born and transformed in a field of intersections that range beyond psychiatry itself, and include public hygiene, the spaces of insane asylums, utopian enterprises for collective moral improvement, and the history of nation building and state formation.[48] Some of these pioneering studies have focused on the emergence of a medical power dedicated to disciplining bodies, normalizing general sanitary status, and shaping the political practices of society on an immanent, rather than exterior, level.[49] But quite soon, and as a result of this almost ahistorical tone, they received some criticism. The dominant approaches now tend to be more cautious and more anchored in empirical information, emphasizing both the instrumental and controlling aspects of psychiatry and its humanitarian and liberating possibilities with regard to mental health, and exploring its relations with culture and society at large.[50]

As for the cultural and metaphorical uses of illnesses, an increasing number of studies have explored the connection between literature and disease. The slippery meanings that lie between physical and spiritual disorders and the different written and visual discourses that spiraled around them are at the very core of these interpretative efforts. Many times these interpretations are based on a limited number of texts or sources, read with as much imagination as audacity. Others are the result of more careful exercises of testing these narratives with other sources, exploring and contextualizing the diverse tones as well as the limitations and risks of using the literary register as the only or the most relevant dimension and source at the moment of writing the history of a certain disease.[51]

The struggle against sexually transmitted diseases, particularly syphilis, has also attracted the attention of scholars, who discuss it as part of the effort to construct a population more susceptible to the interests of a certain biopolitics. Implicitly or explicitly, studies of those campaigns seem to have proposed to deal with the sex drive by self-control and by the rational and conscious assumption of biological responsibilities. Focused in this way, these histories are framed as chapters in the Western civilizing process, which, in the worst cases, end up dissolving or ignoring regional or national specificities. When they do take into account these specificities, historical narratives seek to connect the disease to broader issues such as degeneration, race, immigration, and national identity or to more focused ones such as prostitution and state efforts to control, regulate, or prohibit commercial sex.[52]

In studying the process of concentration of power that doctors acquired as a result of society's increasing medicalization, some scholars have analyzed the emergence of medical models of exclusion based on stereotyping, stigmatizing, and pathologizing behaviors supposedly characteristic of women, homosexuals, and certain immigrant and racial groups.[53] These studies have paid some attention to the complex, porous border between "private" and "public" in public health issues—an especially important question in current studies of AIDS, but obviously also relevant at other times and with other diseases. This porous and ever-changing border is at the very heart of the historical construction not only of health rights as individual and social entitlements but also of more or less ambitious public health state interventions. In line with these concerns, the study of Latin American eugenics has directly touched on the interplay among race, science, medicine, nationalism, and the future of Latin American nations. These issues structured the anxieties of many Latin American intellectuals and physicians between the last third of the nineteenth and first third of the twentieth century. They speculated about the potential contributions as well as limitations of blacks, Indians, mixed-race peoples, and immigrants, and they did so following what they thought were very distinctive national features. The majority of these studies discussed eugenics as a bet not only on social improvement associated with sanitation, education, school hygiene, or matrimonial control but also on racial, ethnic, and immigration selection aimed at building healthy national races.[54] Sophisticated mainly on the discursive level, these histories of eugenics did not explore consistently the making of these social and public health policies, still less their results. Only a very few studies are in dissonance with this dominant historiographical interpretation. Particularly invested in highlighting the violent and racist dimensions of Latin American eugenic discourses, among them sterilization, these studies are not only neglectful of their effective materialization in social policies but also unable to put in perspective what seem to have been no more than marginal voices in the general climate of ideas of those decades. Although more ambitious in scope, some social control studies—focusing partly on medicine but mainly on criminology—should be included in this group as a result of addressing discourses as the only historical dimension, as well as giving (without much evidence) quite weak national states an enormous capability of shaping social life.[55]

The topics of women and children's health, state policies, and public welfare have been receiving increasing attention as well.[56] The way in which these topics have been discussed shares common ground with studies focused on the ideology of hygiene as a means of articulating political concerns in technical terms and the ideology of public health as an instrument in the nation-building process.[57] Looking at the cultural dimensions of hygiene, some studies have shown how it achieved great social acceptance as a set of values over the medium and long term. Like education, the modern hygienic code seems to have been incorporated into the everyday life of elites and poor alike, regardless of their political or ideological differences. Certainly these social groups, whether in terms of age, wealth, or gender, may not all have had equal access to hygienic practices or have given to hygiene exactly the same meanings. But what these studies tend to underline is the relevance of individual and collective hygiene as a "civilizing" practice not only encouraged and at times imposed from above—from the state to the professional and enlightened elites to the labor leadership to advertising—but also strongly embraced from below, by the common people.[58]

Some studies have explored responses to intrusive and at times compulsory public health efforts. The history of smallpox vaccination reveals layers of social issues that went well beyond this preventive health measure. In fact, while in certain periods and places studies reconstruct a long and ultimately successful process of acceptance of this preventive health practice, at certain junctures this history is marked by individual resistances or even collective and highly politicized revolts. The available literature on this issue offers an array of interpretative approaches, ranging from making sense of these revolts as ways of articulating a sort of moral opposition against the government, to evidences of elite manipulation of popular discomfort, to examples of popular resistance to urban sanitary and health policies, to the behaviors and perceptions of certain racial groups with regard to smallpox control measures.[59] In the case of tuberculosis, some studies explored the ability of the sick to negotiate or even defy medical power. Whether individually, by ignoring its recommendations, or collectively, by organizing strikes, pressuring the political class and using (and being used by) the mass printed media, patients asserted their right to try a treatment and a vaccine that were not approved by the medical establishment.[60] Cancer also motivated the emergence of a social movement aimed at gaining access to drugs patients believed were effective in spite of the negative evaluation of the scientific community.[61] And malaria, yellow fever, and cholera ignited some resistance as a result of public health measures some popular sectors perceived as ineffective or contrary to a mix of indigenous and traditional Hippocratic perceptions about their illnesses.[62] In line with these approaches, other studies tried to introduce voices of the sick using oral history and in so doing are able to begin exploring a very personalized account of the illness experience.[63]

In the end, these studies of the experiences of the sick and their reactions to resources aimed at dealing with diseases seem to point to at least three issues. First, public health interventions and medical practices could be resisted, accepted, or demanded according to local, cultural, social, political, and disease-specific contexts. Second, its impact needs to be discussed in the short and long run, paying attention not only to particular moments of contention but also to the very successful incorporation of these new practices in people's lives, probably less studied and taken for granted because of their success. Finally, it is important to realize the existence of a degree of historical agency by the sick that reveals that people dealing with diseases are not merely passive objects of medical practices and knowledges. However, the relevance of that agency, especially in the complex process of broadening the meanings of social citizenship and the development of public health policies, should be a subject for careful reflection. In fact, health and disease seem not to have been central to the agenda of the labor movement, nor were they central issues for social movements during the first half of the twentieth century. This relationship can only be made pertinent when health and disease are defined in very general terms, diluted into other labor problems such as the long struggle for shortening the working day, the efforts aimed at improving labor conditions at the workplace, or the development of workers' mutual-aid societies. But it was not until the 1940s that occupational health became a substantial component of the social agendas of the state and organized labor. Still in its early stages, studies on the world of work and disease for that period were perhaps announcing the emergence of what could become a new occupational health history subfield.[64]

The historical agency of the sick and the individual experiences of the illness are also present in studies of HIV-AIDS. In general, the examination of this disease has not been done by historians but by social scientists and medical anthropologists. Since its irruption, the epidemic was initially associated with the homosexual and drug-using communities. Quite soon, this emphasis incorporated poverty as a relevant dimension, and lately a number of international factors that marked Latin American politics during the last third of the twentieth century, such as war, the drug trade, migrations and other global issues, which not only shaped local and national responses from Mexico to Argentina but also unveiled the very diverse—and in comparison with other regions of the world relatively mild—current state of the epidemic.[65]

If for decades after the commercial launch of penicillin in 1945, pathogenic microorganisms seemed finally under control and the great epidemics conquered, only in 1979—a year after the World Health Organization proclaimed victory over smallpox—HIV-AIDS came to the fore as a new deadly infectious disease. Since then, infectious diseases once thought under control, such as tuberculosis, have made a global comeback, and old and never eradicated endemic illnesses such as malaria continue to kill people in the thousands. The scenario is to a certain extent similar to that at the beginning of the bacteriological era, from the 1870s onwards, in which the Pasteurian revolution was speaking of pathogenic microorganisms as invisible enemies to be conquered in the body, just as defensive military battles are a matter of life or death for the social organism. No doubt, then as now, diseases followed not only epidemiological, but also cultural patterns; they were fought using measures of defense and protection, which particularly in epidemic cases always combined both military and hygienic-medical dispositives. In order to understand their history, the historiography of disease, health, and medicine of the bacteriological period has paid attention to the political and cultural logic of these diseases, their mode of action, and social attitudes toward them. Thus, diseases, particularly infectious diseases, were associated with a myriad of phantasms and fears, and quite often even their medical descriptions were and are structured by metaphors rooted not only in the laboratory but also, and sometimes primarily, in political and cultural traditions.

Discourses about infection feature tiny, invisible, contagious, and uncontrollable organisms as well as transgressions of boundaries through intimate or fleeting contact. Infection supplies a host of metaphors for describing social processes in the language of epidemics. In this current age of increasingly global networking and circulation of people and goods, infection has become the master metaphor. It shapes the emergent political and social discourse of order and its associated technologies of surveillance for controlling borders and immigration. These very contemporary discussions might find in the historiography of disease, health, and medicine not so much a specific blueprint for anti-epidemic political agendas as a sense of how complex the relations among power, society, cultures and medicine were in the past.

This complexity has been the subject of the historiography of the postbacteriological period. The tone of the discussion has been quite plural, with some interpretations strongly articulated around Foucauldian, economistic, institutional, or social-control models of analysis but many more particularly invested in avoiding any rigidity. This effort to move away from determinism is quite apparent in the articles included in a half a dozen anthologies and special issues of academic journals dealing with the region at large or with some of its countries.[66] It is also the case of many studies not only focused on a certain country, city, or disease but also focused on certain health- or disease-specific issues. Worth mentioning as illustrations of these historiographical trends is, for instance, an exhaustive examination of the conditions in which yellow fever was studied and confronted in Brazil when bacteriology was still trying to dominate biomedical thinking.[67] Or books centered on the institutional and political interplay acted out by medical and professional groups, local and national governments, and civil society in the making of the health care systems of Chile, Brazil, and Argentina.[68] Or an ambitious history of medicine in Uruguay that discusses the consolidation of what is characterized as medical monopoly of health care in the context of an emerging new and modern sensibility, all of them topics that for Costa Rica were analyzed highlighting not only the consolidation of the process of medicalization but also the existence of a vibrant and diverse world of popular, alternative, and hybrid healers.[69] For the multicultural Caribbean region and for Revolutionary Mexico, two studies have explored the interaction among international health organizations, local and national public health agencies, and official and nonofficial medicine in the achievements and limitations of the heath care systems.[70] Some books on Brazil, Mexico, Peru, and Bolivia discuss diseases and public health campaigns in very specific settings and for relatively short time periods.[71] In other cases, the emphasis aims at the examination of specific public health campaigns on malaria in Mexico and leprosy in Colombia, but over longer periods of time.[72] And in few instances, such as a study of tuberculosis in Buenos Aires between 1870 and 1950, the goal was to write a total history of the disease (inevitably elusive) in which culture, society, power, and official and nonofficial medicines are discussed not only as metaphors, politics, and individual and collective experiences but also as problems that exceed the disease itself, ending up metamorphosed into broader historical processes.[73]

The symbolic meanings and social impact of certain illnesses and public health efforts can be properly understood in historical terms only when a broad range of factors are taken into consideration. These include demographic structures and specific epidemiological histories; colonial and neocolonial contexts; levels of urbanization and industrialization; public health and social policies; the agendas and priorities of international agencies and professional experts involved in disease control; and the state of scientific, medical, and technological knowledge and practices. They also can include specific moments of social demands; the politics of nationalism and national self-image; the greater or lesser presence and influence of the mass media in people's lives; broader debates and negotiations between state policies and medical, social, and individual responsibilities; and the political and cultural uses of illnesses. These are some of the most decisive factors explaining how, when, and why diseases and public health interventions are perceived and lived in specific ways. No wonder different diseases have played, over time, different roles at the national, regional, and local levels. No wonder what became relevant in epidemiological terms in one country has no significance in another. And no wonder that even taking into account all these variables, making historical sense of a disease is in and of itself a risky enterprise, given the fact that human well-being and ill-being can hardly be fully captured through the lens of a single illness.

These challenges, perplexities, and possibilities have marked the historiography of this subfield of studies in Latin America. If half a century ago the field was the territory of physicians writing more or less celebratory histories of official medicine, since the 1970s it has become clear that diseases, health, and medicines are not only sites where society, culture, and politics interact in a certain period or time, but also analytical tools to understand the always elusive complexity of the historical experience.

NOTES

1. In *Locating Medical History: The Stories and Their Meanings*, ed. Frank Huisman and John Harley Warner (Baltimore and London: John Hopkins University Press, 2004), which discusses historiographical developments but deals only with the Anglo-American and Western European worlds.

2. Suzanne Austin Alchon, *A Pest in the Land: New World Epidemics in a Global Perspective* (Albuquerque: University of New Mexico Press, 2003).

3. Ronald L. Numbers, ed., *Medicine in the New World: New Spain, New France, and New England* (Knoxville: University of Tennessee Press, 1987).

4. The discussion on the modern, postbacteriological period updates some issues already analyzed in Diego Armus, "Disease in the Historiography of Modern Latin

America," in *Disease in the History of Modern Latin America: From Malaria to AIDS*, ed. Diego Armus (Durham, N.C.: Duke University Press, 2003).

5. Nancy Stepan, *Beginnings of Brazilian Science: Oswaldo Cruz, Medical Research and Policy, 1890–1920* (New York: Science History Publications, 1976); Marcos Cueto, *Excelencia científica en la periferia: Actividades científicas e investigación biomédica en el Perú, 1890–1950* (Lima: Tarea, 1989); Jaime Benchimol and Luiz Antonio Texeira, *Cobras, lagartos e outros bichos: Uma história comparada dos Institutos Oswaldo Cruz e Butantan* (Rio de Janeiro: UFRJ/Casa Oswaldo Cruz, 1993); Emilio Quevedo Vélez et al., "Ciencias médicas, estado y salud en Colombia," in *Historia social de la ciencia en Colombia*, vol. 8 (Bogotá: Tercer Mundo, 1993); François Delaporte, *La maladie de Chagas: Histoire d'un fléau continental* (Paris: Payot, 1999); Jaime Benchimol, *Dos micróbios aos mosquitos: Febre amarela e a revolução pasteuriana no Brasil* (Rio de Janeiro: Fiocruz/UFRJ, 1999); Simone Petraglia Kropf, Nara Azevedo, and Luiz Octavio Ferreira, "Biomedical Research and Public Health in Brazil: The Case of Chagas Disease," *Social History of Medicine* 16 (2003): 11–129; Jorge Márquez Valderrama, *Ciudad, miasmas y microbios: La irrupción de la ciencia pasteuriana en Antioquia* (Medellín: Editorial Universitaria de Antioquia, 2005).

6. Susana Belmartino, Carlos Bloch, María Isabel Carnino, and Ana Virginia Persello, *Fundamentos históricos de la construcción de relaciones de poder en el sector salud: Argentina, 1940–1960* (Buenos Aires: OPS/OMS, 1991); Gilberto Hochman, *A era do saneamento: As bases da política de saúde pública no Brasil* (São Paulo: Hucitec/ANPOCS, 1998); and the special issue of *Dynamis: Acta Hispanica ad Medicinae Scientiarumque Historiam Illustrandam* 25 (2005), with articles on Central America, Brazil, Mexico, Cuba, and Argentina.

7. Aldo Neri, *Salud y política social* (Buenos Aires: Hachette, 1982); Mario Hernández, "Proceso político y salud en Colombia: 1958–1993," *Tierra Firme* 18 (2000): 663–82; Anne-Emanuelle Birn, "Federalist Flirtations: the Politics and Execution of Health Services Descentralization for the Uninsured Population in Mexico, 1985–1995," *Journal of Public Health Policy* 20:1 (1999): 81–108.

8. Jonathan Leonard, "Carlos Finlay's Life and the Death of Yellow Jack," *Bulletin of the Pan American Health Organization* 23 (1989): 438–52; "Oswaldo Cruz y el florecimiento de la salud pública en el Brasil," *Boletín de la Oficina Sanitaria Panamericana* 115:3 (1993): 222–34.

9. Gilberto Hochman, "A saúde pública em tempos de Capanema: Continuidades e innovações," in H. Bomeny, ed., *Constelação Capanema: Intelectuais e políticas* (Rio de Janeiro: FGV, 2001); Carlos Huneeus and María Paz Lanas, "Eduardo Cruz Coke y el estado de bienestar en Chile, 1937–1938," *Historia* 35 (2001): 151–86.

10. Juan César García, "La medicina estatal en América latina (1880–1930)," *Revista Latinoamericana de Salud* 1 (1981): 70–110; *Pensamiento social en salud en América latina* (Mexico City: Interamericana McGraw Hill/OPS, 1994).

11. Vicente Navarro, "The Underdevelopment of Health or the Health of Underdevelopment: An Analysis of the Distribution of Human Resources in Latin America," *International Journal of Health Sciences* 4:1 (1974): 5–27.

12. Carlos Escudé, "Health in Buenos Aires in the Second Half of the Nineteenth Century," in D. C. Platt, ed., *Social Welfare, 1850–1950: Australia, Argentina and Canada Compared* (London: Macmillan, 1989); Christopher Abel, *Health, Hygiene, and Sanitation in Latin America, 1870–1950* (London: Institute of Latin American Studies, University of London, 1996).

13. Charles E. Rosenberg, "Framing Disease: Illness, Society, and History," in *Framing Disease: Studies in Cultural History*, ed. Charles E. Rosenberg and Janet Golden (New Brunswick, N.J.: Rutgers University Press, 1992).

14. Jaime Benchimol, *Pereira Passos: Um Haussmann tropical* (Rio de Janeiro: Secretaria de Turismo, 1990); Teresa Meade, *"Civilizing" Rio: Reform and Resistance in a Brazilian City, 1889–1930* (University Park: Penn State University Press, 1997); Adrián Carbonetti, *Enfermedad y sociedad: La tuberculosis en la ciudad de Córdoba, 1906–1947* (Córdoba: Emecor, 1998); Ricardo González Leandri, *Curar, persuadir, gobernar: La construcción histórica de la profesión médica en Buenos Aires, 1852–1886* (Madrid: CSIC, 1999); Claudia Agostoni, *Monuments of Progress: Modernization and Public Health in Mexico City, 1876–1910* (Calgary: University of Calgary Press, 2003); Ana María Carrillo, "Profissões da saúde e lutas de poder no México, 1821–1917," in *Cuidar, controlar, curar: Ensaios históricos sobre saúde e doença na América Latina e Caribe*, ed. Gilberto Hochman and Diego Armus (Rio de Janeiro: Fiocruz, 2004).

15. Carl J. Murdock, "Physicians, the State and Public Health in Chile, 1881–1891," *Journal of Latin American Studies* 27 (1995): 551–67; Ronn Pineo, "Public Health Care in Valparaiso, Chile," in *Cities of Hope: People, Protests, and Progress in Urbanizing Latin America, 1870–1930*, ed. Ronn Pineo and James A. Baer (Boulder, Colo.: Westview Press, 1998); Héctor Recalde, *La salud de los trabajadores en Buenos Aires (1870–1910) a través de las fuentes médicas* (Buenos Aires: Grupo Editor Universitario, 1997); Nilson do Rosario Costa, *Lutas urbanas e controle sanitário: Origens das políticas de saúde no Brasil* (Petropolis: Vozes, 1985); Vera Blin Reber, "Misery, Pain and Death: Tuberculosis in Nineteenth Century Buenos Aires," *The Americas* 56:4 (2000): 497–528.

16. Jurandir Freire Costa, *Ordem médica e norma familiar* (Rio de Janeiro: Graal, 1979); Oliva López Sánchez, *Enfermas, mentirosas y temperamentales: La concepción médica del cuerpo femenino durante la segunda mitad del siglo XIX* (Mexico City: Plaza y Valdés, 1998); Nicolau Sevcenko, *A revolta da vacina: Mentes insanas em corps rebeldes* (São Paulo: Brasiliense, 1984); Hugo Vezzetti, "El discurso psiquiátrico," in Hugo Biagini, ed., *El movimiento positivista argentino* (Buenos Aires: Editorial de Belgrano, 1985); Teresita Martínez-Vergne, *Shaping the Discourse on Space: Charity and its Wards in Nineteenth-Century San Juan, Puerto Rico* (Austin: University of Texas Press, 1999).

17. Sérgio Carrara, *Tributo a Vênus: A luta contra a sífilis no Brasil, da passagem do século aos anos 40* (Rio de Janeiro: Fiocruz, 1996); Diego Armus, *La ciudad impura: Salud, tuberculosis y cultura en Buenos Aires, 1870–1950* (Buenos Aires: Edhasa, 2007).

18. Alfred W. Crosby, *The Columbian Exchange: Biological and Cultural Consequences of 1492* (Westport, Conn.: Greenwood, 1973); William H. McNeill, *Plagues and Peoples* (Garden City, N.Y.: Anchor Press, 1976).

19. Alfred W. Crosby, *Germs, Seeds and Animals: Studies in Ecological History* (Armonk, N.Y.: M.E. Sharpe, 1994); Philip D. Curtin *Migration and Mortality in Africa and the Atlantic World, 1700–1900* (Aldershot, U.K.; Burlington, Vt.: Ashgate-Variorum, 2001).

20. Alfred W. Crosby, *Ecological Imperialism: The Biological Expansion of Europe, 900–1900* (Cambridge; New York: Cambridge University Press, 1986); Jared Diamond, *Guns, Germs, and Steel* (New York: W.W. Norton, 1997); George Raudzens ed., *Technology, Disease, and Colonial Conquests, Sixteenth to Eighteenth Centuries: Essays Reappraising the Guns and Germs Theories* (Leiden; Boston: Brill, 2001); Philip Pomper and David Gary Shaw, eds., *The Return of Science: Evolution, History, and Theory* (Lanham, Md.: Roman & Littlefield, 2002).

21. Ángel Rosenblat, *La población de América en 1492: Viejos y nuevos cálculos* (Mexico City: El Colegio de México, 1967); Sherburne F. Cook and Woodrow Borah, *Essays in Population History: Mexico and the Caribbean* (Berkeley: University of California Press, 1971–79); William M. Denevan, ed., *The Native Population of the Americas in 1492* (Madison: University of Wisconsin Press, 1976).

22. Henry F. Dobyns, "Estimating Aboriginal American Population: An Appraisal of Techniques with a New Hemispheric Estimate," *Current Anthropology* 7:4 (1966): 395–416; "Brief Perspective on a Scholarly Transformation: Widowing the 'Virgin' Land" *Ethnohistory* 23:2 (1976): 95–104, and "Disease Transfer at Contact," *Annual Review of Anthropology* 22 (1993): 273–91.

23. Rudolph A. Zambardino, "Mexico's Population in the Sixteenth Century: Demographic Anomaly or Mathematical Illusion?" *Journal of Interdisciplinary History* 11:1 (1980): 1–27; David P. Henige, *Numbers from Nowhere: The American Indian Contact Population Debate* (Norman: University of Oklahoma Press, 1998); Francis J. Brooks, "The Impact of Disease," in Raudzens ed., *Technology, Disease, and Colonial Conquests.*

24. Noble David Cook, *Demographic Collapse, Indian Peru, 1520–1620* (Cambridge; New York: Cambridge University Press, 1981); Noble David Cook and W. George Lovell eds., *Secret Judgments of God: Old World Disease in Colonial Spanish America* (Norman: University of Oklahoma Press, 1991); John W. Verano and Douglas H. Ubelaker, eds., *Disease and Demography in the Americas* (Washington, D.C.: Smithsonian Institution Press, 1992); Suzanne Austin Alchon, *Native Society and Disease in Colonial Ecuador* (Cambridge: Cambridge University Press, 1991); Daniel T. Reff, *Disease, Depopulation, and Culture Change in Northwestern New Spain, 1518–1764* (Salt Lake City: University of Utah Press, 1991); Linda A. Newson, *The Cost of Conquest: Indian Decline in Honduras under Spanish Rule* (Boulder, Colo.: Westview Press, 1986), *Indian Survival in Colonial Nicaragua* (Norman: University of Oklahoma Press, 1987), and *Life and Death in Early Colonial Ecuador* (Norman: University of Oklahoma Press, 1995).

25. Thomas M. Whitmore, *Disease and Death in Early Colonial Mexico: Simulating Amerindian Depopulation* (Boulder, Colo.: Westview Press, 1992); Brenda J. Baker and George J. Armelagos, "Origin and Antiquity of Syphilis: Paleopathological Diagnosis and Interpretation," in *Biological Consequences of the European Expansion, 1450–1800*, ed. Kenneth F. Kiple and Stephen V. Beck (Aldershot, U.K.; Burlington, Vt.: Ashgate-Variorum, 1997), 1–35; Richard H. Steckel and Jerome C. Rose, eds., *The Backbone of History: Health and Nutrition in the Western Hemisphere* (Cambridge: Cambridge University Press, 2002).

26. Reinhard Hoeppli, *Parasitic Diseases in Africa and the Western Hemisphere: Early Documentation and Transmission by the Slave Trade* (Basel: Verlag für Recht und Gesellschaft, 1969); Philip D. Curtin, "Epidemiology and the Slave Trade," *Political Science Quarterly* 83:2 (1968): 190–216; Kenneth F. Kiple, *The Caribbean Slave: A Biological History* (Cambridge: Cambridge University Press, 1984); "A Survey of Recent Literature on the Biological Past of the Black," in *The African Exchange: Toward a Biological History of Black People*, ed. Kenneth F. Kiple (Durham, N.C.: Duke University Press, 1987).

27. Kenneth F. Kiple and Brian T. Higgins, "Yellow Fever and the Africanization of the Caribbean," in Verano and Ubelaker, *Disease and Demography in the Americas*; Philip D. Curtin, "Malarial Immunities in Nineteenth-Century West Africa and the Caribbean," *Parassitologia* 36:1–2 (1994): 69–82; Philip R. P. Coelho and Robert A. McGuire, "African and European Bound Labor in the British New World: The Biological Consequences of Economic Choices," *The Journal of Economic History* 57:1 (1997): 83–115.

28. Kenneth F. Kiple and Virginia H. King, *Another Dimension to the Black Diaspora: Diet, Disease, and Racism* (Cambridge: Cambridge University Press, 1981); Richard B. Sheridan, *Doctors and Slaves: A Medical and Demographic History of Slavery in the British West Indies, 1680–1834* (Cambridge: Cambridge University Press, 1985); Frantz Tardo-Dino, *Le collier de servitude: La condition sanitaire des esclaves aux Antilles Françaises du XVIIe au XIXe siècle* (Paris: Editions Caribéennes, 1985); Michael Tadman, "The Demographic Cost of Sugar: Debates on Slave Societies and Natural Increase in the Americas," *The American Historical Review* 105:5 (2000): 1534–75.

29. Francisco Guerra, "The Influence of Disease on Race, Logistics and Colonization in the Antilles," in Kiple and Beck, eds., *Biological Consequences of the European Expansion*; John R. McNeill, *Mosquito Empires: Ecology and War in the Greater Caribbean, 1620–1914* (New York: University Press, 2010); Dauril Alden and Joseph C. Miller, "Unwanted Cargoes: The Origins and Dissemination of Smallpox via the Slave Trade from Africa to Brazil, c. 1560–1830," in Kiple, ed., *African Exchange*; Robert Dirks, *The Black Saturnalia: Conflict and its Ritual Expression on British West Indies Slave Plantations* (Gainesville: University Presses of Florida, 1987); Linda A. Newson and Susie Minchin, *From Capture to Sale: The Portuguese Slave Trade to Spanish South America in the Early Seventeenth Century* (Leiden: Brill, 2007); Vincent Brown, *The Reaper's Garden: Death and Power in the World of Atlantic Slavery* (Cambridge: Harvard University Press, 2008).

30. María Teresa Sepúlveda y Herrera, *La medicina entre los Purépecha prehispánicos* (Mexico City: Universidad Nacional Autónoma de México, Instituto de Investigaciones Antropológicas, 1988); Bernard Ortiz de Montellano, *Aztec Medicine, Health, and Nutrition* (New Brunswick, N.J.: Rutgers University Press, 1990); Carlos Viesca Treviño, *Medicina prehispánica de México: El conocimiento médico de los Nahuas* (Mexico City: Panorama, 1992); Rafael Valdez Aguilar, *Medicina prehispánica en Sinaloa y en el noroeste de México* (Sinaloa: Universidad Autónoma de Sinaloa, 1997); José Rozo Gauta, *Alimentación y medicina entre los Muiscas* (Bogotá: Naidí, 1998); José Alcina Franch, *Temazcalli: Higiene, terapéutica, obstetricia y ritual en el nuevo mundo* (Sevilla: Escuela de Estudios Hispano-Americanos, Consejo Superior de Investigaciones Científicas, 2000).

31. George M. Foster, *Hippocrates' Latin American Legacy: Humoral Medicine in the New World* (Langhorne: Gordon and Breach, 1994); Alfredo Lopez Austin et al., *The Human Body and Ideology: Concepts of the Ancient Nahuas* (Salt Lake City: University of Utah Press, 1988); Bernard Ortiz de Montellano, "Caida de Mollera: Aztec Sources for a Mesoamerican Disease of Alleged Spanish Origin," *Ethnohistory* 34:4 (1987): 381–99.

32. Arturo Leiva and Emanuele Amodio, eds., *Los espíritus aliados: Chamanismo y curación en los pueblos indios de Sudamérica* (Quito: Ediciones ABYA-YALA, Movimiento Laicos para América Latina, 1991); Silvia Ortiz Echániz, *La medicina tradicional en el norte de México* (Mexico City: Instituto Nacional de Antropología e Historia, 1999); Roberto Campos Navarro, ed., *El empacho en la medicina mexicana: Antología (siglos XVI–XX)* (Mexico City: Instituto Nacional Indigenista, 2000); Angelina Pollak-Eltz, *La medicina tradicional venezolana* (Caracas: Universidad Católica Andrés Bello, 2001); Brad R. Huber and Alan R. Sandstrom, eds., *Mesoamerican Healers* (Austin: University of Texas Press, 2001).

33. María Andréa Loyola, *Médicos e curandeiros: Conflito social e saúde* (São Paulo: DIFEL, 1984); Libbet Crandon-Malamud, *From the Fat of Our Souls: Social Change, Political Process, and Medical Pluralism in Bolivia* (Berkeley: University of California Press, 1991); Joseph Bastien, *Drums and Stethoscope: Integrating Ethnomedicine and Biomedicine in Bolivia* (Salt Lake City: University of Utah Press, 1992); Nancy Scheper-Hughes, *Death Without Weeping: The Violence of Everyday Life in Brazil* (Berkeley: University of California Press, 1992); María Eugenia Módena, *Madres, médicos y curanderos: Diferencia cultural e identidad ideológica* (Mexico City: Ciesas, 1990); Beatriz Texeira Weber, *Medicina, religião, magia e positivismo na República Rio-Grandense, 1889–1928* (Bauru: Educs, 1999); Jane Felipe Beltrão, "A arte de curar dos profissionais de saúde popular em tempo de cólera: Grão-Pará do século XIX," *História, Ciências, Saúde. Manguinhos* VI (2000): 833–66; Ann Zulawski, "Hygiene and 'the Indian Problem.' Ethnicity and Medicine in Bolivia, 1910–1920," *Latin American Research Review* 35:2 (2000): 107–29; David Sowell, *The Tale of Healer Miguel Perdomo Neira: Medicine, Ideologies and Power in the Nineteenth-Century Andes* (Wilmington, Del.: Scholarly Resources, 2001); Steven Palmer, *From Popular Medicine: Doctors, Healers, and Public Power in Costa Rica, 1800–1940* (Durham, N.C.: Duke University Press, 2003); María Silvia Di Liscia,

"Viruela, vacunación e indígenas en la pampa argentina del siglo XIX," in *Entre médicos y curanderos: Cultura, historia y enfermedad en la América latina moderna*, ed. Diego Armus (Buenos Aires: Norma, 2002); Gabriela dos Reis Sampaio, *Nas trincheras da cura: As diferentes medicinas no Río de Janeiro Imperial* (São Pablo: Unicamp, 2005).

34. Paula Montero, *Da doença à desordem: A magia na umbanda* (Rio de Janeiro: Graal, 1985); Michel S. Laguerre, *Afro-Caribbean Folk Medicine* (South Hadley, Mass.: Bergin & Garvey, 1987); Gonzalo Aguirre Beltrán, *El negro esclavo en Nueva España: La formación colonial, la medicina popular y otros ensayos* (Mexico City: Fondo de Cultura Económica, 1994); Robert A. Voeks, *Sacred Leaves of Candomblé: African Magic, Medicine, and Religion in Brazil* (Austin: University of Texas Press, 1997); Johan Wedel, *Santería Healing: A Journey into the Afro-Cuban World of Divinities, Spirits, and Sorcery* (Gainesville: University Press of Florida, 2004); Karol K. Weaver, *Medical Revolutionaries: The Enslaved Healers of Eighteenth-Century Saint Domingue* (Urbana and Chicago: University of Illinois Press, 2006).

35. Gonzalo Aguirre Beltrán, *Medicina y magia: El proceso de aculturación en la estructura colonial* (Mexico City: Instituto Nacional Indigenista, 1963); María del Carmen Anzures y Bolaños, *La medicina tradicional en México: Proceso histórico, sincretismos y conflictos* (Mexico City: Universidad Nacional Autónoma de México, 1983); Noemí Quezada, *Enfermedad y maleficio: El curandero en el México colonial* (Mexico City: Universidad Nacional Autónoma de México, 1989); Jose Luis Fresquet Febrer and José M. López Piñero, eds., *El mestizaje cultural y la medicina novohispana del siglo XVI* (Valencia: Instituto de Estudios Documentales e Históricos sobre la Ciencia, 1995); Manuel Neira Barragán, *La medicina popular y la brujería en Nuevo León y Coahuila durante los siglos XVIII y XIX* (Monterrey: Centro de Información de Historia Regional de la Universidad Autónoma de Nuevo León, 1995); Suzanne Austin Alchón, "Tradiciones médicas nativas y resistencia en el Ecuador colonial," in Marcos Cueto, ed., *Saberes andinos: Ciencia y tecnología en Bolivia, Ecuador y Perú* (Lima: Instituto de Estudios Peruanos, 1995); Diana Luz Ceballos Gómez, *"Quyen tal haze que tal pague": Sociedad y prácticas mágicas en en el Nuevo Reino de Granada* (Bogotá: Ministerio de Cultura, 2002); Sherry Fields, *Pestilence and Headcolds: Encountering Illness in Colonial Mexico* (New York: Columbia University Press, 2009).

36. Martín de la Cruz and Juan Bandiano, *Libellus de medicinalibus Indorum herbis: Manuscrito azteca de 1552* (Mexico City: Fondo de Cultura Económica, 1991); José Luis Fresquet Febrer, *La experiencia americana y la terapéutica en los "Secretos de Chirurgia" (1567), de Pedro Arias de Benavides* (Valencia: Instituto de Estudios Documentales e Históricos sobre la Ciencia, 1993); Carmen Martín Martín et al., *La farmacia en la América colonial: El arte de preparar medicamentos* (Granada: Universidad de Granada, 1995); José M. López Piñero and José Pardo Tomás, *La influencia de Francisco Hernández (1515–1587) en la constitución de la botánica y la materia médica modernas* (Valencia: Instituto de Estudios Documentales e Históricos sobre la Ciencia, 1996); José Enrique Campillo Álvarez, *Francisco Hernández: El descubrimiento científico del Nuevo Mundo* (Toledo: Diputación Provincial de Toledo, 2000); Simon Varey, Rafael Chabrán, and Dora B Weiner, eds., *Searching for the Secrets of Nature: The Life and Works of Dr Francisco Hernández* (Stanford: Stanford University Press, 2000); Simon Varey, ed., *The Mexican Treasury: The Writings of Dr. Francisco Hernández* (Stanford: Stanford University Press, 2000) *Remedios para el imperio: Historia natural y la apropiación del nuevo mundo*; Mauricio Nieto Olarte, (Bogotá: Instituto Colombiano de Antropología e Historia, 2000); Londa L. Schiebinger, *Plants and Empire: Colonial Bioprospecting in the Atlantic World* (Cambridge, Mass.: Harvard University Press, 2004); Antonio Barrera-Osorio, *Experiencing Nature: The Spanish American Empire and the Early Scientific Revolution*(Austin: University of Texas Press, 2006); Daniela Bleichmar, Paula De Vos, and Kristin Huffine, eds., *Science in the Spanish and Portuguese Empires, 1500–1800* (Stanford: Stanford University Press, 2008).

37. John Tate Lanning and John Jay TePaske, *The Royal Protomedicato: The Regulation of the Medical Profession in the Spanish Empire* (Durham, N.C.: Duke University Press, 1985); Gregorio Delgado García, *Historia de la enseñanza superior de la medicina en Cuba, 1726–1900* (Havana: Ministerio de Salud Pública, 1990); Líder Mendieta, *Hospitales de Lima colonial, siglos XVII–XIX* (Lima: UNMSM, 1990); Lilia V. Oliver Sánchez, *El hospital real de San Miguel de Belán, 1581–1802* (Guadalajara: Universidad de Guadalajara, 1992); Francisco Guerra: *El hospital en Hispanoamérica y Filipinas, 1492–1898* (Madrid: Ministerio de Sanidad y Consumo, 1994); *La educación médica en Hispanoamérica y Filipinas durante el dominio español* (Madrid: Universidad de Alcalá, 1998).

38. Marcela Dávalos, *Basura e ilustración: La limpieza de la ciudad de México a fines del siglo XVIII* (Mexico City: Instituto Nacional de Antropología e Historia, 1997); Martha Eugenia Rodríguez, *Contaminación e insalubridad en la ciudad de México en el siglo XVIII* (Mexico City: Departamento de Historia Filosofía de la Medicina, UNAM, 2000); Miguel Angel Cuenya Mateos, ed., *Cabildo, sociedad y política sanitaria en la ciudad de Puebla, 1750–1910* (Puebla: Benemérita Universidad Autónoma de Puebla, 2003).

39. Juan Carlos Veronelli, *Medicina, gobierno y sociedad: Evolución de las instituciones de atención de la salud en Argentina* (Buenos Aires: El Coloquio, 1975); Carmelo Mesa-Lago, *Social Security in Latin America: Pressure Groups, Stratification, and Inequality* (Pittsburgh: Pittsburgh University Press, 1978); Patricio V. Márquez and Daniel J. Joly, "A Historical Overview of the Ministries of Public Health and the Medical Programs of the Social Security Systems in Latin America," *Journal of Public Heath Policy* 7 (1986): 378–94; García, *Pensamiento social en salud en América latina*; Susana Belmartino, *La atención médica argentina en el siglo XX: Instituciones y procesos* (Buenos Aires: Siglo XXI, 2005); Palmer, *From Popular Medicine*; Ana María Carrillo, "Profissoes da saúde e lutas de poder no México, 1821–1917," in Hochman and Armus, *Cuidar, controlar*; Marcos Cueto, *El valor de la salud: Historia de la Organización Panamericana de la Salud* (Washington, D.C.: OPS, 2004); André Pereira Neto, Emilio Quevedo, and Martha Rodriguez, "Vital Brazil, García Media y Liceaga, constructores de la salud en América latina: El rescate del sujeto en el proceso histórico," in Cecilia Minayo, ed., *Criticas e atuantes: Ciências sociais e humanas em saude na America latina* (Rio de Janeiro: Fiocruz, 2005); Adriana Alvarez and Adrián Carbonetti, eds., *Saberes y prácticas médicas en la Argentina: Un recorrido por historias de vida* (Mar del Plata: EUDEM, 2008).

40. Donald B. Cooper, *Epidemic Disease in Mexico City, 1716–1813: An Administrative, Social, and Medical Study* (Austin: University of Texas Press, 1965); Enrique Florescano and Elsa Malvido, eds., *Ensayos sobre la historia de las epidemias en México* (Mexico City: Instituto Mexicano del Seguro Social, 1982); Lilia V. Oliver Sánchez, *Un verano mortal: Análisis demográfico y social de una epidemia de cólera: Guadalajara, 1833* (Guadalajara: Gobierno de Jalisco, Secretaría General, Unidad Editorial, 1986); Lourdes Márquez Morfín, *La desigualdad ante la muerte en la ciudad de México: El tifo y el cólera (1813 y 1833)* (Mexico City: Siglo XXI, 1994); Marcelo Frías Núñez, *Enfermedad y sociedad en la crisis colonial del antiguo régimen: Nueva Granada en el transito del siglo XVIII al XIX: Las epidemias de viruelas* (Madrid: Consejo Superior de Investigaciones Científicas, 1992); Renán Silva, *Las epidemias de viruela de 1782 y 1802 en la Nueva Granada: Contribución a un análisis histórico de los procesos de apropiación de modelos culturales* (Cali: Centro Editorial Universidad del Valle, 1992); Miguel Ángel Cuenya Mateos, *Puebla de los Ángeles en tiempos de una peste colonial: Una mirada en torno al Matlazahuatl de 1737* (Zamora: El Colegio de Michoacán, Universidad de Puebla, 1999); Greg Grandin, *The Blood of Guatemala: A History of Race and Nation* (Durham, N.C.: Duke University Press, 2000); Alvaro León Casas Orrego, "Epidemias y salud pública en Cartagena en el siglo XIX," in *Cartagena de Indias en el siglo XIX*, ed. Haroldo Stevenson and Adolfo Mieisel Roca (Bogotá: Universidad de Bogotá,

2002); Adrián López Denis, "Higiene pública contra higiene privada: Cólera, limpieza y poder en La Habana colonial," *EIALC* 14 (2003): 2–23.

41. Miguel Angel Scenna, *Cuando murió Buenos Aires* (Buenos Aires: La Bastilla, 1974); Rodolpho Telarolli Jr., *Poder e saúde: As epidemias e a formação dos serviços de saúde em São Paulo* (São Paulo: UNESP, 1996); Beatriz Cano, "La influenza española en Tlaxcala (1918)," in *Historia de la salud en México*, ed. Elsa Malvido and María Elena Morales (Mexico City: INAH, 1996); Agustina Prieto, "Rosario: Epidemias, higiene e higienistas en la segunda mitad del siglo XIX," in Mirta Lobato, ed., *Política, médicos y enfermedades: Lecturas de historia de la salud en la Argentina* (Buenos Aires: Biblos/Universidad Nacional de Mar del Plata, 1996); Marcos Cueto, *El regreso de las epidemias: Salud y sociedad en el Perú del siglo XX* (Lima: Instituto de Estudios Peruanos, 1997); Diego Armus, "El descubrimiento de la enfermedad como problema social," in Mirta Lobato, ed., *El progreso, la modernización y sus límites: Nueva Historia Argentina*, vol. 5 (Buenos Aires: Sudamericana, 2000); Ronn Pineo, "Misery and Death in the Pearl of the Pacific: Health Care in Guayaquil, Ecuador, 1870–1925," *Hispanic American Historical Review* 70 (1990): 609–38; Sam Adamo, "The Sick and the Dead: Epidemic and Contagious Disease in Rio de Janeiro, Brazil," in Pineo and Baer, *Cities of Hope*; Nara Azevedo de Brito, "La dansarina: A gripe espanhola e o cotidiano na cidade do Rio de Janeiro," *História, Ciências, Saúde–Manguinhos* 4:1 (1997): 11–30; Charles L. Briggs and Clara Mantini-Briggs, *Stories in the Time of Cholera: Racial Profiling During a Medical Nightmare* (Berkeley: University of California Press, 2003); Liane María Bertucci, *Influenza, a medicina enferma: Ciência e práticas de cura na época da gripe espanhola em São Paulo* (São Paulo: Unicamp, 2004); Jorge Márquez Valderrama, "Políticas, tráficos y epidemias en Colombia a comienzos del siglo XX," in Jorge Márquez, Alvaro Casas, and Victoria Estrada, eds., *Higienizar, medicar, gobernar: Historia, medicina y sociedad en Colombia* (Medellín: Universidad Nacional de Colombia, 2004); Mariola Espinosa, *Epidemic Invasions: Yellow Fever and the Limits of Cuban Independence, 1878–1930* (Chicago: University of Chicago Press, 2009).

42. Diego Armus, "Consenso, conflicto y liderazgo en la lucha contra la tuberculosis: Buenos Aires, 1870–1950," in Juan Suriano ed., *La cuestión social en la Argentina, 1870–1943* (Buenos Aires: La Colmena, 2000); Diana Obregón Torres, *Batallas contra la lepra: Estado, medicina y ciencia en Colombia* (Medellín: EAFIT, 2002) and "The State, Physicians and Leprosy in Modern Colombia," in Armus, *Disease in the History of Modern Latin America*.

43. Luiz Castro Santos, "Estado e saúde pública no Brasil (1889–1930)," *Dados: Revista de Ciências Sociais* 23:2 (1980): 237–50, and "A reforma sanitária 'pelo alto': O pionerismo paulista no início de século XX," *Dados: Revista de Ciências Sociais* 36:3 (1993): 361–92; Saúl Franco Agudelo, *El paludismo en América latina* (Guadalajara: Editorial de la Universidad de Guadalajara, 1990); Nisia Trinidade Lima and Nadia Britto, "Salud y nación: Una propuesta para el saneamiento rural. Un estudio de de la revista Saúde (1918–1919)," in Marcos Cueto, ed., *Salud, cultura y sociedad en América latina: Nuevas perspectivas históricas*.

44. Flavio Coelho Edler, "O debate en torno da medicina experimental no segundo reinado," *Historia, Ciência, Saúde–Manguinhos* 3:2 (1996): 284–99; Julyan G. Peard, *Race, Place and Medicine: The Idea of the Tropics in Nineteenth-Century Brazilian Medicine* (Durham, N.C., and London, Duke University Press, 1999); Benchimol, *Dos micróbios aos mosquitos*; Marcos Cueto, "Tropical Medicine and Bacteriology in Boston and Peru: Studies of Carrion's Disease in the Early Twentieth Century," *Medical History* 40 (1996): 344–64; Simone Petraglia Kropf, Nara Azevedo, and Luiz Otávio Ferreira, "Doença de Chagas: A construção de um fato científico e de um problema de saúde pública no Brasil," *Ciência & Saúde Coletiva* 5:2 (2000): 347–65; Nancy Stepan, "'The Only Serious Terror in these Regions': Malaria Control in the Brazilian Amazon," in Armus, *Disease in the History of*

Modern Latin America; Marilia Coutinho, "Tropical Medicine in Brazil: The Case of Chagas's Disease," in Armus, *Disease in the History of Modern Latin America*.

45. Steve Palmer, *From Popular Medicine to Medical Populism*; Benchimol, *Dos microbios aos mosquitos*.

46. Castro Santos, "Estado e saúde pública no Brasil (1889–1930)"; Marcos Cueto, ed., *Missionaries of Science: The Rockefeller Foundation in Latin America* (Bloomington: Indiana University Press, 1994); Steven Palmer, "Central American Encounters with Rockefeller Public Health, 1914–1921," in *Close Encounters of Empire: Writing the Cultural History of U.S.-Latin American Relations*, ed. Gilbert Joseph, Catherine Legrand, and Ricardo Salvatore (Durham, N.C., and London: Duke University Press, 1998); Luiz Antonio de Castro Santos, "Poder, ideologias e saúde no Brasil da Primeira República: Ensaio de sociología histórica," in Hochman and Armus, *Cuidar, controlar*; Anne-Emanuelle Birn, *Marriage of Convenience: Rockefeller International Health and Revolutionary Mexico* (Rochester, N.Y.: University of Rochester Press, 2006); Marcos Cueto, *Cold War, Deadly Fevers: Malaria Eradication in Mexico, 1955–1975* (Baltimore: Johns Hopkins University Press, 2007).

47. Cueto, *El valor de la salud*; special issue on "History of International Health: Latin American Perpectives," in *História, Ciências, Saúde–Manguinhos* 13:3 (2006); Anne-Emanuelle Birn, "Going Global in Uruguay. Child Well-being and the Evolution of International Health," *American Journal of Public Health* 95:9 (2005): 2–13; Steven Palmer, *Launching Global Health: The Caribbean Odyssey of the Rockefeller Foundation* (Ann Arbor, Mich.: University of Michigan Press, 2010).

48. Hugo Vezzetti, *La locura en la Argentina* (Buenos Aires: Folios, 1983); Rafael García-Huertas, *El delincuente y su patología: Medicina, crimen y sociedad en el positivismo argentino* (Madrid: Cuadernos Galileo, CSIC, 1991); Sérgio Carrara, *Crime e loucura: O aparecimento do manicômio judiciário na passagem do século* (Rio de Janeiro/São Paulo: Eduerj/Edusp, 1998); Kristin Ruggiero, *Modernity in the Flesh: Medicine, Law and Society in Turn-of-the-Century Argentina* (Stanford: Stanford University Press, 2004).

49. Roberto Machado, Angela Loureiro, Rogerio Luz, and Katia Muricy, *Danação da norma: Medicina social e constituição da psiquiatria no Brasil* (Rio de Janeiro: Graal, 1978).

50. Joel Birman, ed., *Precursos na história da psicoanálise* (Rio de Janeiro: Taurus, 1988); Augusto Ruiz Zevallos, *Psiquiatras y locos: Entre la modernización contra los Andes y el nuevo proyecto de modernidad* (Lima: Instituto Pasado y Presente, 1994); Cristina Rivera Garza, "La vida en reclusión: Cotidianidad y estado en el Manicomio General La Castañeda (México, 1910–1930)," in Armus, *Entre médicos y curanderos*, and "Dangerous Minds: Changing Psychiatric Views of the Mentally Ill in Porfirian Mexico, 1876–1911," in *Journal of the History of Medicine and Allied Sciences* 56:1 (2001): 36–67; Hugo Vezzetti, *Aventuras de Freud en el país de los argentinos: De José Ingenieros a Enrique Pichón Rivière* (Buenos Aires: Paidós, 1996); Jorge Balán, *Cuéntame tu vida: Una biografía colectiva del psicoanálisis argentino* (Buenos Aires: Planeta, 1991); Mariano Plotkin, *Freud in the Pampas: The Emergence and Development of a Psychoanalytic Culture in Argentina* (Stanford: Stanford University Press, 2001); Ann Zulawski, "Mental Illness and Democracy in Bolivia: The Manicomio Pacheco, 1935–1950," in Armus, *Disease in the History of Modern Latin America*; Jonathan Ablard, *Madness in Buenos Aires: Patients, Psychiatrists, and the Argentine State, 1880–1983* (Calgary: University of Calgary Press, 2008).

51. Michael Aronna, *"Pueblos Enfermos": The Discourse of Illness in the Turn-of-the-Century Spanish and Latin American Essay* (Chapel Hill: North Carolina Studies in the Romance Languages and Literatures, 1999); Gabriela Nouzeilles, *Ficciones somáticas: Naturalismo, nacionalismo y políticas del cuerpo (Argentina, 1880–1910)* (Rosario: Beatriz Viterbo, 2000) and "An Imaginary Plague in Turn-of-the-Century Buenos Aires:

Hysteria, Discipline, and Languages of the Body," in Armus, *Disease in the History of Modern Latin America*; Nancy Stepan, *Picturing Tropical Nature* (Ithaca, N.Y.: Cornell University Press, 2001); Benigno Trigo, *Subjects of Crisis: Race and Gender as Disease in Latin America* (Hanover, N.H., and London: Wesleyan University Press, 2000); Zandra Pedraza Gómez, *En cuerpo y alma: Visiones del progreso y de la felicidad* (Bogotá: Universidad de los Andes, 1999); Angela Porto, "A vida inteira que podia ter sido e que não foi: Trajetória do um poeta tísico," *História, Ciências, Saúde–Manguinhos* 6 (1999–2000): 523–50; Diego Armus, "Tango, Gender and Tuberculosis in Buenos Aires, 1900–1940," in Armus, *Disease in the History of Modern Latin America* and "Curas de reposo y destierros voluntarios: Narraciones de tuberculosos en los enclaves serranos de Córdoba," in *Literatura, cultura, enfermedad*, ed. Wolfgang Bongers and Tanja Olbrich (Buenos Aires: Paidós, 2006).

52. Sérgio Carrara, "Estrategias anticoloniales: Sífilis, raza e identidad nacional en el Brasil de entreguerras," in *Avatares de la medicalización en América latina, 1870–1970*, ed. Diego Armus (Buenos Aires: Lugar, 2005); David McCreery, "'This Life of Misery and Shame': Female Prostitution in Guatemala City, 1880–1920," *Journal of Latin American Studies* 18:2 (1986): 333–53; Magali Engel, *Meretrizes e doctores: O saber médico e a prostituição na cidade do Rio de Janeiro, 1840–1890* (Rio de Janeiro: Brasiliense, 1989); Martha de Abreu Esteves, *Meninas perdidas: Os populares e o cotidiano do amor no Rio de Janeiro da "Belle Epoque"* (Rio de Janeiro: Paz e Terra, 1989); Donna Guy, *Sex and Danger in Buenos Aires: Prostitution, Family and Nation in Argentina* (Lincoln: University of Nebraska Press, 1991); Eileen J. Suárez Findlay, *Imposing Decency: The Politics of Sexuality in Puerto Rico, 1870–1920* (Durham, N.C., and London: Duke University Press, 1999); Katherine Bliss, *Compromised Positions: Prostitution, Public Health and Gender Politics in Revolutionary Mexico* (University Park: Penn State University Press, 2001).

53. Marvin Leiner, *Sexual Politics in Cuba: Machismo, Homosexuality and AIDS* (Boulder, Colo.: Westview Press, 1993); López Sánchez, *Enfermas, mentirosas y temperamentales*; Jorge Salessi, *Médicos, maleantes y maricas: Higiene, criminología y homosexualidad en la construcción de la nación Argentina: Buenos Aires: 1871–1914* (Rosario: Beatriz Viterbo, 1995); Lilia Moritz Schwarcz, *Espetáculo das raças: Cientistas, instituições e questão racial no Brasil, 1870–1930* (São Paulo: Companhia das Letras, 1993); Sérgio Carrara, "Estratégias anticoloniais: Sífilis, raça e identidade nacional no Brasil do entre-guerras," in Hochman and Armus, *Cuidar, controlar*; María Silvia Di Liscia and Ernesto Bohoslavsky, *Instituciones y formas de control social en América latina, 1840–1940* (Buenos Aires: UNLP/UNGS/Prometeo, 2005).

54. Nancy Stepan, *"The Hour of Eugenics": Race, Gender, and Nation in Latin America* (Ithaca, N.Y.: Cornell University Press, 1991); Consuelo Naranjo Osorio and Armando García González, *Medicina y racismo en Cuba: La ciencia ante la inmigración canaria en el siglo XX* (La Laguna, Tenerife: Taller de Historia, 1996); Armando García González y Raquel Alvarez Peláez, *En busca de la raza perfecta: Eugenesia e higiene en Cuba (1898–1958)* (Madrid: CSIC, 1999); Alexandra M. Stern, "Responsible Mothers and Normal Children: Eugenics and Nationalism in Post-Revolutionary Mexico, 1920–1940," *Journal of Historical Sociology* 12:4 (1999): 369–96; Eduardo Zimmermann, "Racial Ideas and Social Reform: Argentina 1890–1916," *Hispanic American Historical Review* 72:1 (1992): 23–46; Vera Regina Beltrão Marques, *A medicalização da raça: Médicos educadores e discurso eugênico* (São Paulo: Unicamp, 1994); Gilberto Hochman, Nísia Trindade Lima, and Marcos Chor Maio, "The Paths of Eugenics in Brazil: Dilemmas of Miscegenation," in *The Oxford Handbook of the History of Eugenics*, ed. Alison Bashford and Philippa Levine (New York: Oxford University Press, 2010).

55. Marisa Miranda and Gustavo Vallejo, *Darwinismo social y eugenesia en el mundo latino* (Buenos Aires: Siglo XXI, 2005); Yolanda Eraso, "Biotypology, Endrocrinology and Sterlization: The Practice of Eugenics in theTreatment of Argentinian Women during the 1930s," *Bulletin of the History of Medicine* 81 (2007): 793–822; Julia Rodríguez, *Civilizing Argentina: Science, Medicine and the Modern State* (Chapel Hill: University of North Carolina Press, 2006).

56. Annette B. Ramírez de Arellano and Conrad Seipp, *Colonialism, Catholicism, and Contraception: A History of Birth Control in Puerto Rico* (Chapel Hill: University of North Carolina Press, 1983); Ann Blum, "Public Welfare and Child Circulation, Mexico City, 1877–1925," *Journal of Family History* 23:3 (1998): 240–71; Marcela Nari, "Las prácticas anticonceptivas, la disminución de la natalidad y el debate médico en Argentina, 1890–1940," in Lobato, ed., *Política, médicos y enfermedades*; Donna J. Guy, "The Pan American Child Congresses, 1916–1942: Pan Americanism, Child Reform, and the Welfare State in Latin America," *Journal of Family History* 23:3 (1998): 272–91: Anne-Emanuele Birn, "Doctors on Record: Uruguay's Infant Mortality Stagnation and its Remedies, 1895–1945," *Bulletin of History of Medicine* 82:2 (2008): 311–54; Armus, *La ciudad impura*.

57. Sidney Chalhoub, *Cidade febril: Cortiços e epidemias na Corte Imperial* (São Paulo: Companhia das Letras, 1996); Nísia Trindade Lima and Gilberto Hochman, "'Pouca saúde e muita saúva': Sanitarismo, interpretações do país e ciências sociais," in Hochman and Armus, *Cuidar, controlar*; Carlos Ernesto Noguera, *Medicina y política: Discurso médico y prácticas higiénicas durante la primer mitad del siglo XX en Colombia* (Medellín: EAFIT, 2003).

58. Diego Armus, "Salud y anarquía: la tuberculosis en el discurso libertario argentino, 1870–1940," in Lobato, ed., *Política, médicos y enfermedades*; Diego Armus, "O discurso da regeneração: Espaço urbano, utopías e tuberculose em Buenos Aires, 1870–1930," *Estudos Históricos* 8:16 (1995): 235–50; Diego Armus, "La idea del verde en la ciudad moderna: Buenos Aires, 1870–1940," *Entrepasados: Revista de Historia* 10 (1995): 9–22; Dora Barrancos, *La escena iluminada: Ciencias para trabajadores, 1890–1930* (Buenos Aires: Plus Ultra, 1996); María Emma Mannarelli, *Limpias y modernas: Género, higiene y cultura en la Lima del novecientos* (Lima: Flora Tristán, 1999); David Palmer, "Civilizing the City of Kings: Hygiene and Housing in Lima, Peru," in Pineo and Baer, eds., *Cities of Hope*; Heloísa Helena Pimenta Rocha, *A higienização dos costumes: Educação escolar e saúde no projeto do Instituto de Hygiene de São Paulo, 1918–1925* (Campinas: Fapesp, 2003); María Silvia Di Liscia and Graciela Nélida Salto, *Higienismo, educación y discurso en la Argentina 1870–1940* (Santa Rosa: Edunlp/Reun, 2004); Víctor M. García G. and Jorge Márquez V., "Estrategias publicitarias del medicamento en Colombia, 1850–1930," in Márquez, Casas, and Estrada, eds., *Higienizar, medicar, gobernar*.

59. Gilberto Hochman, "Priority, Invisibility, and Erradication: The History of Smallpox and the Brazilian Public Health Agenda," *Medical History* 53:2 (2009): 229–52; José Murilo de Carvalho, *Os bestializados: O Rio de Janeiro e a República que não foi* (São Paulo: Companhia das Letras, 1987); Jeffrey D. Needell, "The *Revolta contra a Vacina* of 1904: The Revolt against 'Modernization' in Belle Epoque Rio de Janeiro," *Hispanic American Historical Review* 67:2 (1987): 233–69; Teresa Meade, "Civilizing Rio de Janeiro: the Public Health Campaign and the Riot of 1904," *Journal of Social History* 20:2 (1986): 301–32; José Carlos Sebe Meihy and Cláudio Bertolli Filho, "Historia social da saúde: Opinião pública versus poder: A campanha da vacina, 1904," *Estudos CEDHAL* 5 (1990); Chalhoub, *Cidade febril*; Luiz Antonio Teixeira, "A rebelião popular contra a vacina obrigatória," *Estudos em Saúde Coletiva* 103 (Rio de Janeiro, IMS/UERJ, 1994).

60. Diego Armus, "Historias de enfermos tuberculosos que protestan: Argentina 1920–1940," in Armus, *Avatares*; José Pedro Barrán, *Medicina y sociedad en el Uruguay del*

novecientos (Montevideo: Ediciones de la Banda Oriental, 1994); Claudio Bertolli Filho, "Antropologia da doença e do doente: Percepções e estratégias da vida dos tuberculosos," *História Ciências Saúde–Manguinhos* 6:3 (1999): 493–522.

61. Emilio de Ipola, "Estrategias de la creencia en situaciones críticas: El cáncer y la crotoxina en Buenos Aires a mediados de los años ochenta," in Armus, *Entre médicos y curanderos*.

62. Noemí Goldman, "El levantamiento de montoneras contra 'gringos' y 'masones' en Tucumán, 1887: Tradición oral y cultura popular," *Boletín del Instituto de Historia Argentina y Americana Dr. Emilio Ravignani* 2 (1990): 47–74; Cueto, *El regreso de las epidemias*; Mirta Fleitas, "Queremos a Mano Santa!: Actores y significados de una revuelta popular acontecida en 1912 en San Salvador de Jujuy (Argentina)," *Salud Colectiva* 3:3 (2007): 301–13.

63. Fernando Sergio Dumas dos Santos and Mariana de Aguiar Ferreira Muaze, *Uma etnohistória da saúde a da doença nos vales dos rios Acre e Purus* (Brasilia: Paralelo 15, 2002); Dilene Raimundo de Nascimento and Diana Maul de Carvalho, eds., *Uma história brasileira das doenças* (Brasilia: Paralelo 15, 2004).

64. Libia J. Restrepo, *La práctica médica en el Ferrocarril de Antioquia, 1875–1930* (Medellin: La Carreta, 2005); Angela Vergara, "The Recognition of Silicosis: Labor Unions and Physicians in the Chilean Copper Industry, 1930–1960," *Bulletin of the History of Medicine* 79 (2005): 723–48.

65. Paul Farmer, "Sending Sickness: Sorcery, Politics and Changing Concepts of AIDS in Rural Haiti," *Medical Anthropology Quarterly* 4:1 (1990): 6–27; Shawn Smallman, *The AIDS Pandemic in Latin America* (Chapel Hill: University of North Carolina Press, 2007); Joao Biehl, *Will to Live: AIDS Therapies and the Politics of Suvival* (Princeton: Princeton University Press, 2007).

66. Cueto, ed., *Salud, cultura y sociedad en América latina*; Armus, *Entre médicos y curanderos*; Armus, *Disease in the History of Modern Latin America*; Hochman and Armus, *Cuidar, Controlar*; Armus, *Avatares*; *História, Ciências, Saúde–Manguinhos* 13:3 (2006); *Dynamis*, 25 (2005).

67. Benchimol, *Dos micróbios aos mosquitos*.

68. María Angélica Illanes, *'En nombre del pueblo, del estado y de la Ciencia…': historia social de la salud pública. Chile 1880–1973* (Santiago: Colectivo de Atención Primaria, 1993); Hochman, *A era do saneamento*; Belmartino, *La atención médica argentina en el siglo XX*.

69. Barrán, *Medicina y sociedad en el Uruguay del novecientos*; Palmer, *From Popular Medicine*.

70. Palmer, *Launching Global Health*; Birn, *Marriage of Convenience*.

71. Cueto, *El regreso de las epidemias*; Chalhoub, *Cidade febril*; Nascimento and Carvalho, eds., *Uma história brasileira das doenças*; Claudia Agostoni, ed., *Curar, sanar, educar: Enfermedad y sociedad en México, siglos XIX y XX* (Mexico City: UNAM/BUAP, 2008); Ann Zulawski, *Unequal Cures: Public Health and Political Change in Bolivia, 1900–1950* (Durham, N.C., and London: Duke University Press, 2007).

72. Obregón Torres, *Batallas contra la lepra*; Cueto, *Cold War, Deadly Fevers*.

73. Armus, *La ciudad impura*.

CHAPTER 16

POPULAR RELIGION IN LATIN AMERICAN HISTORIOGRAPHY

REINALDO L. ROMÁN

PAMELA VOEKEL

THERE was a time when the narrative arcs were clear. It was said that the violent encounter between Africans, Iberians, and the indigenous people of the Americas initiated a steady march to religious disenchantment. Imperfect as the European evangelical and civilizing enterprises may have been, the direction was apparent and the momentum inexorable. Sooner or later, modernization would reach Latin America and the Caribbean, even if secularization tarried.

For several decades, the keepers of the Weberian faith have been in the minority. Since the 1970s and even before, scholars have probed the social, cultural, and epistemological transformations colonial encounters engendered. Faced with distinctly Indian and African understandings of the divine, historians and anthropologists have pondered whether syncretism, often limned as the "blending" of religious cultures, should be counted as evidence of modernization's triumph, or as an indication of the resilience of tradition—a concept that has also come under considerable scrutiny. Historically minded scholars have carefully documented shifts in pious sensibilities and practices, while insisting on the centrality of popular religiosity to our own understanding of the modern (and postmodern) order, politics, the state, gender and racial configurations, and even the economy.

Our own times, charged as they are with high-energy Pentecostal services and the currents of religious pluralism, have made it plain that secularization did not materialize as expected. The signs of reenchantment are now seen everywhere. Even as specialists insist on the relative autonomy of religion, there are few areas of inquiry that have not been subject to reconsideration in light of abiding religious faith. Labor radicals and economic historians, chroniclers of high politics and lowly subalterns, gender and race theorists—all now ignore religion at their peril. It is not surprising then, that several generations of Latin American and Caribbean scholars have busied themselves disassembling foundational dichotomies that opposed Western rationality to local magic, and true religion to superstition.

Faith and Masks: Debating Syncretism

Syncretism has had a storied career among students of the African diaspora. Roger Bastide credited Raimundo Nina Rodrigues, Brazil's pioneering forensic physician and ethnographer, with the first systematic use of the term, which has come to mean the amalgamation, combination, or synthesis of formerly separate religious forms. In 1900, Nina Rodrigues interpreted Afro-Brazilians' apparent conflation of Catholic saints and African deities as a subtle slave strategy for deceiving their masters. Glosses, revisions, and critiques of Nina Rodrigues's theory were to the fore, with the pace quickening perceptibly during the last century's middle decades. Why such intellectual ardor? To speak of syncretism was to take a position in the foundational debate between Melville J. Herskovits and E. Franklin Frazier—to champion either African survivals in the Americas or the notion that enslavement had decimated African cultures, forcing blacks to acculturate to European religious and cultural norms.[1]

Many scholars who favored the term understood the hybrid religious practices syncretism described as markers of progress, as halfway points on the route to Westernization. But even these scholarly proponents of Westernization remained leery of the concept. Acknowledging his debt to Nina Rodrigues, in 1940 Fernando Ortiz proposed an alternative functionalist model of cultural change. He introduced the neologism "transculturation" to describe the historical processes of deculturation and acculturation that indigenous, African, and European cultures underwent in the Americas.[2] Ortiz insisted that European ways had undergone their own syncretism, and formed part of the proverbial *ajiaco*, or Cuban stew. But he never jettisoned his older evolutionary schemes entirely; deculturation, he intimated, transformed Indians and Africans more than Europeans. Cuba's native people had been unable to "adjust" to the Spanish cultures introduced into the island.

Translated into English in 1978, nearly two decades after its French debut, Bastide's *The African Religions of Brazil* proposed another reappraisal of the concept. Although concerned with the interpenetration of civilizations, Bastide nevertheless tagged syncretism a "pseudo problem." Western scholars had misunderstood the Africans' capacity to draw analogies between Catholic saints and African deities; observers like Nina Rodrigues had read assertions of equivalence as confounded identity. In fact, African deities and civilization had persisted in the Americas in both syncretized and relatively pure forms. Syncretism, often a symptom of a civilization's degeneration, was limited to specific locales under identifiable circumstances.

In short, African cultures had defied the odds. This civilization, Bastide explained, had reasserted itself in the Americas after slavery had disarticulated the infrastructure that bound Africans into societies, leaving religious and cultural superstructures adrift. The complex workings of collective memory explained this resurgence. Africans had created new social structures such as the Afro-Brazilian "nations" following the templates—the values, symbols, and collective representations—of African civilization. Critics charged Bastide with an essentialist understanding of things African and an imprecise use of the term "civilization." Bastide's interpretation was certainly at odds with the early synthesis model, whose proponents underscored the American origins of new social institutions such as "nations."

But while stressing African civilization's uncanny resilience, Bastide also embraced historical change. Afro-Brazilian religions were not mere facsimiles of the originals; they prevailed precisely because they adapted. In Brazil, collective representations irrelevant to the altered social realities faded, while more functional ones remained. Bastide conceded that the absence of appropriate personnel, mutual influences between Africans themselves, and the reordering of social categories in a slaveholding society created lapses. Myths, for example, were less durable than ritual because of the "utilitarian" orientation of most Africans. These gaps created the niches in which syncretism prospered.

The loss of African culture that syncretism implied was a function of measurable factors. Urban institutions proved most resilient to change, and thus cities fostered African civilizations in their purest form, Bahia's *candomblés* being a case in point. In the countryside, African religions deteriorated toward the magical, and magic, Bastide affirmed, was by its very logic prone to incorporating foreign elements. But syncretism also responded to social crises. In circumstances of rapid urbanization and industrialization, participants in autonomous African spheres were forced to assimilate into a social order in which class superseded the racial and ethnic affiliations that the pure African religions symbolized. In that sense, modernization and syncretism reinforced one another.[3]

After its publication in 1976, Sidney Mintz's and Richard Price's programmatic essay *The Birth of African-American Cultures* quickly became a touchstone for syncretism's naysayers and champions alike.[4] The concept most often associated with the book is the much-bandied-about "creolization," although, as Stephan Palmié has pointed out, Mintz and Price rejected that term, believing it to be too encumbered with a century's worth of interpretive baggage.[5] Instead, the two deans of historical anthropology referred to the process in question as "early synthesis." African-American institutions responsible for generating distinctive African-American cultures emerged with surprising swiftness, and indeed the middle passage itself generated social germs in the form of dyadic bonds. Relationships such as the shipmates' bonds allowed Africans in the Americas to build new kinship systems and social identities. Rather than crediting direct retentions of specific African cultural traits to explain the process's pace, Mintz and Price described the synthesis as a creative undertaking. For this reason, critics refer to this model as "creationist."

One-to-one correspondences between African and African-American cultural practices rarely emerged, Mintz and Price argued; instead, deeper "grammatical" principles connected cultures across the Atlantic. Even African-Americans' capacity for reinvention suggested vital continuities: the West African cultures ravaged by the slave trade had long dealt with cultural differences through accretion. While acknowledging instances of direct African survivals, particularly in the religious sphere, they nevertheless insisted that individual priests, not entire priesthoods, traveled. African-Americans had forged viable communities by creating new American institutions that transformed crowds into peoples.

Although a critique of the retention model, the early synthesis proposal implied criticism of Bastide's model and of syncretism as well. Popularizations of the latter concept generally described African-American culture as the product of admixtures of European and African elements. Like Bastide, Mintz and Price underscored the heterogeneity of the African cultural inputs and the disarticulating effects of enslavement. No single African or even West African culture could be brought into a blend, nor did ethnic communities survive the middle passage to present a united front. Hence, like Bastide, they believed that African heterogeneity contributed to African-derived hybrid forms. They saw African-Americans and Euro-Americans embroiled in a dynamic of mutual conditioning and influence. The historical results of this dynamic could hardly be called African. Africans and Europeans both had failed to transplant their cultures. Variegated and populated with heterogeneous hybrids rather than single creole forms, American societies were indeed American in every meaningful historical sense.

For over two decades, critics of the early synthesis model have reasserted the African character of the diaspora with evidence drawn from multiple locales in Africa and Europe's far-flung empires. The most influential scholarship in this vein, which Paul Lovejoy calls "revisionist," has sought to offer empirical substantiation of continuities in ethnic affiliation, religion, language, kinship systems, and social institutions. Rather than focusing on syncretism or creolization as such, scholars like Lovejoy, Philip D. Curtin, Michael A. Gomez, Colin Palmer, and John Thornton have aimed to place African history at the center of the narrative of diaspora and to emphasize the agency of Africans and their descendants.[6]

James H. Sweet's 2003 *Recreating Africa* offers a snapshot of the current state of the debate from a revisionist vantage point. Relying on a seldom-used archive of Inquisition records and a command of colonial African historiography, Sweet found that Central African slaves and their descendants maintained a common cultural repertoire that reproduced their core values in Brazil late into the eighteenth century. Instead of early synthesis, Sweet makes a case for a creolization process that was both uneven and painfully slow.[7] Prior to the emergence of syncretic Afro-Brazilian forms, Sweet finds a steady "Africanization" of the black population. A dominant

Central African cultural complex offered slaves from various regions and ethnicities an axis for the nucleation of an African identity in the Americas.

Sweet's evidence for a shared cultural repertoire is derived from inquisitorial accounts of divination, healing, and witchcraft practices that had precise counterparts in Central Africa. These core practices survived because Africans deployed them to resist slavery's dehumanizing effects on individuals and communities. Central Africans understood chattel slavery itself as a form of witchcraft, and thus resorted to divination and other self-defense measures that the Portuguese cast as demonic. In Sweet's view, Catholicism had a limited claim on the loyalties of Brazil's Africanized peoples. Though Africans and their descendants adopted some Catholic trappings, things Catholic and things African remained distinct. For Africans in colonial Brazil, he concludes, Catholicism was no more than a "superficial mask."

Since the 1990s, there have been a number of efforts to reconcile the retention and early synthesis approaches. Although none of these proposals has succeeded in ending the dispute, they have contributed to the revitalization of a debate that showed some signs of stagnation. In 1992, Leslie Desmangles argued in *The Faces of the Gods* that the Haitian religious complex known as Vodou was a "by-product" of Catholicism and religious traditions from various regions of Africa. But rather than invoke syncretism as such, Desmangles proposed that Vodou and Catholicism developed side by side without fusing, a dynamic he dubbed "symbiosis." "Just as tiny parts of a stained-glass window are juxtaposed to form a whole," Desmangles argued, "so too parts of the Vodou and Catholic traditions are juxtaposed in space and in time to constitute the whole of Vodou."[8] Within this framework, Desmangles accommodated distinctly American innovations such as the emergence of a *nanchon* of fierce Petro deities during the days of the Haitian Revolution and many instances of African continuity. Desmangles noted, however, that African traditions had not precisely persisted unchanged; they had been recreated in Haiti, often in the context of prophetic movements that emerged in response to enslavement and colonial oppression.

The syncretism debate has proved every bit as contentious among scholars of the Spanish encounter with native Americans. Although today Mayan missionaries knock on doors in Texas neighborhoods and Europe stands alone as a secular island amidst an international religious revival, scholars still hotly debate just what kind of Christians the natives became. The debate has pivoted around the classic question of continuity or change. Maya specialist Nancy Farriss has a rather startling answer: the Yucatec Maya actually became less monotheistic after the Spanish conquest. If modern Christianity is defined as the belief in the articles of the Nicene Creed, then the Maya mocked the missionary venture. As the *conquistadores* displaced native elites from trade, warfare, and diplomacy and then retreated back into the cities, formerly cosmopolitan indigenous rulers became the masters of small worlds, their influence shrinking to control of the individual villages dotting the countryside.

Farriss drew a structuralist conclusion from the Mayas' forced provincialization: their religious imagination followed suit, as transcendent, all-encompassing divinities like Itzamma or Hunabku lost adherents to the local patron deities who reflected the Mayas' new social ken. Weber's typology of universal versus traditional religions falls flat in this world-shattering encounter; elite Spaniards and Mayans shared a notion of an all-powerful God and, a few odd Erasmians notwithstanding, both cultures had a crowded cosmos of lesser deities or mediators. Mayan and Spanish religions, then, interacted on three levels; there was never a clear shift from one to another, and certainly no teleological march from polytheism to monotheism. The all-encompassing divinity at the top level died off among the newly provincialized Maya, not to be replaced. The lowest level, that of discrete and highly localized supernatural forces, remained essentially Mayan and intact throughout the colonial period, if not beyond. The real syncretic action occurred in the middle level among the village cults with their patron deities, the Catholic saints.[9]

Initially, public ritual at the local level involved "idols behind the altars," saints whom the Maya associated with their own local deities. But by the end of the colonial period, Farriss asserts, the Catholic saints had won out. Had alien images and rituals seized hold of the sacred? Not exactly. What made these patron saint cults syncretic was not their form but their meaning, which remained entirely Mayan. Through their patron saints, Mayans maintained a corporate bond with the sacred; no evidence suggests that individuals approached the saints or God on their own. Moreover, gentle Mary and the blessed saints were morally neutral beings and thus decidedly Mayan, capricious and demanding infants whose benevolence came at the price of their physical comfort. The towns fed these demigods at elaborate festivals so they would in turn feed the citizens.[10] Farriss indeed argues for syncretism, but hardly the clunky sorting of traits into Mayan or Spanish origins that critics of the concept love to hate.

In an important 1990 article that pushed the syncretism debate in new directions, Inga Clendinnen, like Farriss, found inspiration in Clifford Geertz's emphasis on shared cultural understandings and the importance of social meaning over form; she too believed that native religiosity's essence lay beyond its choice of deities. But she parted company with her fellow ethnohistorian on what constituted that essence, asserting that the enduring path to the sacred, not conscious belief, best indicated the outcome of Catholicism's epic encounter with native religion. Precontact Indian culture had distinctive kinetic experiences of the sacred, and these sensory and emotional experiences endured well into the colonial period, despite the outward focus on Christian saints or invocations of Mary.

Priests, friars, and scholars have often turned a blind eye to the dance and fasting that led to the trance state that opened one to the sacred. These activities, however, were not incidental to union with God but rather constitutive of it. Serge Gruzinski's 1989 *Man-Gods in the Mexican Highlands* provides a succinct case study of Clendinnen's insights: although their beliefs become increasingly Catholic over the course of the colonial period, his "man-gods"—Indian spiritual and political leaders—justify their political authority by an enduring Mesoamerican relationship to the divine. By Gruzinski and Clendinnen's lights, Robert Ricard, whose 1933 work asserted a rapid and near-complete Christianization of the natives, was beguiled into this error not only by a desire to eulogize the earliest religious evangelizers but because he ignored the continuity of the Indians' sacred path.[11] Those who look to idols behind altars or to consent to formal theological principles to gauge Indian Christianity search in vain.

Both Clendinnen and Farriss stress the continuities in native religiosity after the Conquest, although Farriss insists that Mayan religion persisted more at the bottom and middle levels of her triune model. But it is Guillermo Bonfil Batalla's 1987 work that deserves pride of place in the continuity camp. His portrayal of enduring structures of native thought traverses six centuries of Mexican history. Mesoamerica's cultural and religious core has survived waves of both secular and religious missionaries, including Franciscan friars, Bourbon bureaucrats, Liberal statesmen, Porfirian *científicos, indigenista* scholars, and the PRI's cultural cadres—this is the gist of Bonfil Batalla's intriguing thesis. The national museum treats tourists to Mexico's *past* Indian glories, but this denial of the Indian present is the ideological ploy of the Mexico *imaginario*, those deracinated elites who have always tried to recreate Mexico in the West's image. The real, deep Mexico, the majority, the *profundo*, lives on not in frozen dioramas but in the countryside and urban tenements. And what characterizes the *profundo*, what makes it Mesoamerican in Bonfil Battalla's reckoning? A belief in the circular notion of time; alternative healers; an economy oriented toward subsistence, not individual profit; land as history rather than commodity; political authority based on community service to the saints and wealth redistribution rather than individual accumulation; the unity of the sacred and the profane—in short, much of the popular and distinctly Indian religiosity described by Clendinnen and Farriss. Focused on the cities, Spanish colonialism allowed for considerable Indian autonomy and thus cultural continuity.[12]

Continuity theorists like Bonfil Batalla reveal resilience in the face of cultural onslaught but often downplay creative adaptation. Andeanist Alberto Flores Galindo was continuity's stalking alter ego. Many colonial-era Andean rebels inspired their followers with promises of a restored Incan utopia. Rather than read this animating myth as a pre-Hispanic religious notion of eternal return, Flores Galindo tagged it a decidedly postconquest invention—an invention that owed as much to Christianity as to native religiosity. Where continuity theorists run the risk of underplaying the intellectual work inherent in the continuous reinvention of religious myths and cultural essences, Flores Galindo found the Andean utopia myth to be "not only a force to understand the past or to offer an alternative to the present. It is also an attempt to envision [*vislumbrar*] the future."[13]

Although he has no use for the hybrid cultures described by Flores Galindo, James Lockhart also offers an implicit critique of continuity models of native religiosity. His understanding of Nahua popular religion stands in stark contrast to that of scholars like Clendinnen and Farriss, who stress meaning over form, who find Mayan understandings of how men connect to God even in the midst of a Catholic saint's festival. For Lockhart, as for Sweet, Christianity and native religions remained two separate systems. Preconquest modes of dealing with the divine persisted in those spaces where Christianity left a niche unfilled, primarily in thinly populated areas remote from the centers of Hispanic population. Indian and Spanish cultures are separate and locked in a zero-sum game; with increasing Spanish incursions, preconquest relations to the divine retreat, although not without leaving traces. Although unconcerned with the national period as such, Lockhart is at loggerheads with Bonfil Batalla, asserting that in spite of the continuities, preconquest traditions are rural-based remnants rather than the core of the nation.[14]

Juan Pedro Viqueira Albán shares Lockhart's implicit critique of Bonfil Batalla's monolithic and enduring Mesoamerican religious culture while also challenging Farriss and Clendinnen's Geertzian assumption of native consensus on matters religious and cultural. In 1712, the Virgin appeared to a pubescent Indian girl, instructing her to build a hermitage in her hometown of Canuk, Chiapas. Viqueira underscores that two religious systems vied for supremacy in the towns surrounding the popular shrine. One group challenged the Church's monopoly but not all of its dogmas; the other, captained by the *maestros nagualistas*, wizards who transformed themselves into animals and natural forces, tapped a more traditionally Indian supernatural. Although the two worked together against the Spanish, they frequently competed for, and occasionally shared, followers.

In stressing spiritual conflict within the towns, Viqueira has no doubt been influenced by the religious polarization currently dividing Chiapas's Indian communities as well as the proliferation of groups vying to lead native resistance to Mexico's current neoliberal government. But if his work reflects Chiapas's fractious religious climate, it also bears the imprint of larger trends in the academy, particularly the rejection of shared meaning in favor of cultural contestation and increased attention to the often violent suppression of alternative views that lurks behind the facade of social or interpretive consensus. Viqueira's narrative technique even mirrors these poststructuralist insights. He wraps his 1993 analysis of the shrine around an enigma at its center: the footsore pilgrims came to the holy spot to pour out their adoration upon—what, exactly? A curtain divided the small chapel, and no direct account can tell us precisely what lay behind it. Viqueira entertains three possibilities: an image of the Virgen del Rosario, a woman-god akin to the native man-gods famously described by Alfredo López Austin and Serge Gruzinski, or an indigenous idol.[15] The author provides solid evidence for all three interpretations and no definitive conclusion—a superbly inventive challenge to traditional narrative techniques.

Viqueira's well-researched analysis and innovative narrative technique place him at the center of a new trend in approaches to popular religiosity. While the 1980s work of Farriss, Clendinnen, and Bonfil Batalla was characterized by underlying structures that influenced religious behavior (Farriss), a Geertzian penchant for shared meaning, and deep continuities in preconquest religious mentalities even up to the present, a newer generation of scholars influenced by poststructuralism have stressed contested meanings and the socially productive nature of Spanish colonial discourses. This trend has produced several exemplars.

Where Farriss cites Indians' knowledge of the local terrain as key to their magical powers, Laura Lewis' 2003 work found a decidedly colonial devil at play in sixteenth- and seventeenth-century New Spain. Spaniards justified their rule by casting the Indians as weak, as a feminized underclass who, like women, needed Spanish men's tutelage. European women and natives of both sexes were beset by frequent lapses of self-control, which necessitated their confinement to spaces—the Indian village, the home—under Spanish male supervision. But this same feminine weakness opened a gateway to significant powers: the Indians wielded authority in the unsanctioned colonial underworld through demonic pacts that both terrified and attracted their overlords. Allied with Satan, Indian magicians could both harm and heal, Lewis argues, just as natives occasionally found succor from Spanish abuse through the colonial courts' healing magic. While Farriss allows for a substratum of Mayan magic in her religious typology, Lewis's decidedly Foucauldian theoretical sorcery makes the autonomous realm of popular religion disappear: when Spaniards persecuted witchcraft, they merely exorcised demons of their own discursive making.

This leads Lewis to a rather shocking conclusion: far from indicating revolutionary resistance, witchcraft instead merely reinforced Spanish hegemony. She proposes that Indian witches embraced a diabolical power dependent upon their weakness, femininity, and closeness to nature rather than challenging those depictions themselves; Spanish discourses created diabolical Indian subjects.[16] But although perhaps not colonial *superbarrios*, surely the Indian dogs who flew through walls to afflict their elite Spanish tormenters with swollen legs, feet, and faces made many think twice before crossing them; resistance can limit abuse without toppling an entire system.

Or so says Irene Silverblatt, who shares Lewis's Foucauldian penchant for productive discursive power but nonetheless maintains that colonial Andean women parlayed Spaniards' devil fears and their own handmaiden status into considerable social power. By the seventeenth century, she explains, self-proclaimed indigenous witches regularly confessed to diabolic pacts and to sex with the Fallen Angel. Although their clients ran the social gamut all the way up to elite Spaniards, Andean witches often acted on behalf of their fellow Indians: turning away tribute collectors in one case, killing an abusive mayor in another, devising potions to remove a negligent parish priest in yet another. As men fled their communities to avoid tribute or the dreaded mita, women armed with diabolical powers became the guardians of ever-changing native traditions—traditions that now included a new dichotomy of good and evil forces where formerly morally ambiguous gods had reigned.[17]

Foucault's explanation of the productive power of knowledge has focused attention not only on social categories but on the historically specific construction of reason and the concomitant production of irrationality. Western scientific rationality's pretense of universality depended on relegating other histories and epistemologies to the realm of the fantastic, the implausible, the traditional, and the stagnant. Far from supplanting the category of religious magic, scientific progress creates it.

Historians now document the knowledge—and the bodies—sacrificed on provincial Western magic's violent journey to universal scientific rationality. Keen to recast the heroic black soldiers of Cuba's independence as the new nation's moral saboteurs and return them to the fields, Cuban men of science fell under the spell of Lombroso's physiological theories of criminality. They concocted the child-sacrificing black brujo, whose skull revealed his criminal bent to the initiated. The brujos were accused of trafficking in human remains, that classic slur of colonialism. As Stephan Palmié explains, however, it was the brujos' own skulls that found their way into the Anthropology Museum. There scientists spun their authority out of these prize possessions, just as some present-day Afro-Cuban religious leaders claim competence based on the possession of the dead.[18]

But where Lewis's *curanderos* are doomed to reiterate their oppressors' categories rather than challenge them, Afro-Cuban wizards provide up-to-the-minute critiques of the ills of a modern order in the making. Scholars need, Palmié insists, to think of the "rationality of others who lived through Western rationalities as a form of social diagnosis."[19] Not capitalist magic but poor wage earners make money, for surplus value comes from exploitation; therefore, the local magic that works against wealth accumulation or speaks of *zonbis* lucidly dissects and rejects a system that puts production ahead of man, exchange value in front of use value. Certainly Michael Taussig has made this claim before, and historians like Paul Vanderwood provide vivid illustrations of peasants who deploy religious ethics that correspond to a former mode of production to critique capitalism and modernity.[20] But under the influence of Jacques Derrida's call to gut all false binaries like modern and traditional, we have witnessed an upsurge in the disassembly of dichotomies. Palmié is an exemplar of this trend. He has no patience for the moral economy model of traditional-societies-assaulted-by-modernity in his analysis: Cuban brujos were born of the encounter between Africa and the West—they did not exist prior to it, and thus there is no primordial place of innocence; if they critique capitalism they also participate in it.

But although poststructuralism has influenced scholars of popular religion since at least the 1980s, it does not dominate the field; deep, enduring religious sensibilities and determining economic and political structures have also found their scholarly champions in our new century. Less interested in the Spaniards' creation of the demons that haunted them, Martha Few's 2002 work found that colonial Santiago de Guatemala's female sorcerers, witches, and midwives based their authority on their knowledge of the human body and the natural world. The Inquisition confronted shape-changers whose powers originated from ancient Indian beliefs described in the Mayan *Popul Vuh*, although certainly the tribunal created social norms and thus deviants. Few's work emerges out of the tradition of Noemí Quezada's and Gonzalo Aguirre Beltrán's erudite studies of popular healers' and magicians' own, somewhat autonomous cultural logics—logics that often have little to do with Spanish devils.[21]

Like Few, Quezada, and Beltrán, Laura de Mello e Souza gives the devil his due but also explicates other influences on popular religiosity. The late Middle Ages witnessed a growing rift between elite and popular culture, resulting in the demonization of popular magic. The end of the Dark Ages was also the dawn of empire, and while early modern intellectuals cast New World nature as Edenic, they also demonized its inhabitants, as Sabine MacCormack's study of the Andes revealed. Brazilian elites believed in and thus feared the sorcerers, diviners, and witches who trafficked with Lucifer; Montaigne's befuddlement that people could be burned for impossible crimes had yet to be born. That would happen with the Enlightenment, or, as Fernando Cervantes points out for the case of New Spain, with the rise of rational Catholic currents like Jansenism, which called for a stricter separation between the sacred and the profane world.[22] But it is what de Mello e Souza reveals along the way to this grand theorizing that makes her work such a tour de force. She moves with brio through the scholarly literature on witchcraft, early traveler's accounts, and Inquisition cases from three centuries to craft a glimpse of Brazil's syncretic popular religion, the *bolsas de mandinga* that contained altar stones and pilfered hosts, the powerful spells cast against slave masters.

FAITHS UNMASKED: DEBATING SECULARIZATION

While the colonial period, with its dramatic encounter of religious worlds, has exerted a magnetic attraction upon interpreters, the nineteenth and early twentieth centuries have exercised a weaker force, with studies of millenarianism emerging as the exception that proves the rule. A rock-ribbed belief in secularization partially explains this trend. Scholars have long held that the rise of science, capitalism, and modernity sounded a death knell for other rationalities, particularly religious ones; Palmié's insight that science invented religious magic had few adherents until recently. Influential British historian of religion Keith Thomas stated the traditional wisdom succinctly: the rise of capitalism and scientific rationality "killed the concept of miracles, weakened the belief in the physical efficacy of prayer, and diminished faith in the possibility of direct divine intervention."[23]

The secularization thesis held sway in the Latin American context in part because it attracted some eloquent historians. Published in the late 1980s and early 1990s respectively, Patricia Seed's and Ramón Gutiérrez's award-winning books differed on the etiology of individualism but nonetheless concurred on the secularization question, on the waning of the union with God as a justification for social mores and political action. Seed's work on central Mexico charted the waning of romantic love between couples as an indication of God's will and the promotion of economic self-aggrandizement from a base passion to the definition of rationality itself. Gutiérrez hewed to a more classical narrative of the rise of romantic love and individual marriage choice, but ultimately concurred with Seed on the waning of religious ethics across the eighteenth century. In line with Seed and Gutiérrez, María Cristina Sacristán found scientific discourse eclipsing religious paradigms of mental illness by century's end.[24]

Critics of this classic narrative of creeping secularization have become more vocal in our new century, resulting in heightened attention to religious sensibilities and increased suspicion of religion and modernity as a zero-sum game. This renewed historical interest can be attributed in part to scholars' concern about an increasingly theocratic U.S. government with its messianic market faith and its indulgence of Manichean world visions.[25] Secularization's champions have evaporated as fundamentalist megachurches have boomed—and become politically active.[26] For some, untangling religion's historical relationship to politics and economics may seem particularly urgent at our current juncture. Other scholars have come to religion through a different route: membership in the same denominations that strike fear into the hearts of the religious and secular left. Conservative evangelical Christians constitute the largest student groups on the very Ivy League campuses that have traditionally sent students on for history graduate training, even while evangelical colleges have moved steadily up the educational scale. A Harvard minister noted that his campus probably now housed "more evangelicals than at any time since the 17th century."[27] At LASA religion panels, Mormons and evangelicals in ties or long skirts now rub elbows with the disheveled children of altar boys, hippies, and Popular Front warriors. As well, the explosion of Protestantism in Latin America has sent historians scrambling to explain its historical origins; the recent efflorescence of cultural history and women's and gender history has also fueled the boom.

The current religious revival has forced a new look at the past, and the secularization thesis has taken some hard hits. Mexico's Independence-era rural rebels certainly had economic grievances, Eric Van Young argues in his 2001 *The Other Rebellion*, but they also fought a culturally defensive movement with local religion at its core; increasing nonchalance about connection with the divine might be an elite or urban phenomenon, but it did not prevail in rural Mexico. One of cultural history's most outspoken devotees, Van Young recognizes that while social groups' existences are rooted in the material world, they are also shaped by language—groups are born of the stories they tell of themselves, and Mexico's peasant rebels spun decidedly religious narratives. Pamela Voekel found an animating religious ethos propelling Mexico's nineteenth-century Liberals—the group cast by most historians as the century's secularizing force par excellence. Patricia Londoño Vega's 2002 work warns against the blithe assumption of fading religious fervor in the nineteenth century as well as the uncritical deployment of a two-tiered model of popular and elite religion. She uncovered a lush and steadily growing world of Catholic voluntary associations in Antioquia, Colombia, during the late nineteenth and early twentieth centuries. Drawn from across the social spectrum, members of these thriving groups displayed a uniform religious sensibility centered on the palpable presence of the divine in the world; at the same time, the Church promoted the latest scientific farming techniques and a redoubled work ethic. In a polemical work, Michael P. Carroll reached a similar conclusion for nineteenth-century New Mexico: the religious zeal of the area's famous flagellant brotherhoods was a recent invention, not a remnant of traditional religion; settler religiosity in earlier centuries had been tepid at best.[28]

Silvia Arrom, Margaret Chowning, and Sol Serrano suggest that the former historiographical enthusiasm for secularization may be attributable to the timeworn—and tiresome—assumption that men are history's main actors. They make a strong case for gender as key to understanding nineteenth-century Christianity; as men's adherence to the traditional church and to religion waned over the century, women's devotion waxed. Working on the early twentieth century, Kristin Boylan, Laura O'Dogherty Madrazo, and Patience Schell all prove the utility of this insight: they reject the image of pious women as frustrated, moralizing hysterics mired in superstition to inquire what women gained by supporting the church and religion against Mexico's revolutionary Jacobins. Boyland in particular insists that the outcome of the era's conflict between church and state cannot be understood without examining women's activism.[29] The turning of analytical attention to popular religion's actual adherents bespeaks an increased respect.[30]

Historical work on popular religion has also gotten a shot in the arm from new avenues of inquiry and newly discovered primary sources, as well as redoubled attention to local religiosity. Jennifer Hughes's graceful consideration of popular devotion to a miraculous Mexican crucifix over five centuries demonstrates that local religiosity has much to offer the analyst of large-scale historical processes like state building. Processions, carnivals, shrines, and devotional practices in particular have also come under scrutiny.[31] Locating evidence of popular religious beliefs has long vexed historians. Elite-generated sources, especially those created by religious proselytizers, often reveal more about the authors than about their targeted converts.[32] Theological tracts and the writings of religious dignitaries have given way to the use of wills, inquisition and trial records, career-pattern approaches, and oral histories in the last several decades. William B. Taylor's 1996 *Magistrates of the Sacred* is a case in point, though ambition, scale, and authority mark this work as exceptional rather than representative. In his 1991 study of attitudes toward death in Bahia, Brazil, around the turn of the nineteenth century, João José Reis put on a veritable clinic on how to research ever-elusive popular religious sensibilities. He examined the pious proclivities contained in 200 Bahian wills, as well as a large corpus of documentation generated by an 1836 popular riot against a new suburban cemetery that threatened church burials in particular and the city's magnificent African-inflected baroque religious culture in general. Reis's pathbreaking book has inspired a spate of intriguing studies that use sepulchral dramas as an entryway into religious mentalities and the relationship between religion and modernity; works by Douglass Sullivan-González, Pamela Voekel, Greg Grandin, Martina Will de Chaparro, Adam Warren, and Heather McCrea, although each posing unique questions to the sources, all owe a debt to Reis.[33]

New sources and the obvious failure of the secularization paradigm are revitalizing the study of national-era religiosity, but the literature on Brazilian millenarianism has long been a hot spot in the historiography. It too reveals a similar sidling away from structuralism toward a profound unwillingness to reduce religion to epiphenomena of some deeper economic or political reality. The debate also reveals increasing unease with the false binary of secular modernity versus religious tradition. Provoked by a jealous church, a secular state wielding maps and measures at odds with local knowledge, droughts, intraclan fighting, and economic turmoil, messiahs wandered Brazil's backlands at century's turn. Euclydes da Cunha's 1906 account of an army massacre of religious pilgrims occupies pride of place in the musings on these religious rebels, in no small part because of its lyrical rendering.[34] Da Cunha's is a tale of two Brazils, a civilization divided between its religious and atavistic backlands and a modernizing and secular coastal elite who nervously espy their countrymen through the scrim of racist science. Millenarian revolts led by miraculous curers who demanded moral rectitude of their followers flared across the backlands after the 1889 military coup that replaced the monarchy with a republic. The interpretive battle has proven almost as tumultuous.

Maria Isaura Pereira de Queiroz, grande dame of millenarianism, finds an unusual application for the classically urban concept of anomie when she proposes it as the root cause of Brazil's rural eschatological fervor. The fundamental building block of northeast and mountain south society was the vertically integrated clan comprised of close and distant kin, bastard sons, godchildren, clients, and assorted hangers-on, all under the patronage and protection of a chieftain or colonel. Individuals barely existed; to know someone was to identify his kin group. Clans tended to splinter, of course, in part due to a testy masculinity that required blood vengeance for the slightest insult, but it was only at times of great intraclan conflict that millenarian visions arose. Antonio the Counselor gained his Canudos following, she explains, while Bahia's governor squared off against a host of formidable fellow chieftains. Holy redoubts like Canudos provided moral order amidst chaos, even reproducing local social hierarchies—no class-conscious rebels here. Rather than signifying a battle between Brazil's coast and its interior or a showdown between secular modernity and rural religious traditions, millenarian movements regrouped refugees from within the conflictive hinterlands themselves.[35]

Todd Diacon takes a more classically moral economy approach in his explanation of a millenarian uprising in the Brazilian state of Santa Catarina. Heavily influenced by James Scott, he emphasizes that in the short span of just fifteen years, exterior modernizing forces—a new railroad, government-sponsored immigration, avaricious lumber companies—rent asunder the area's traditional social relations. Land values soared, and former patrons with godparentage ties to their tenant clients sold lands out from under them and further opted for Mammon over man by delivering their now landless and not-so-sacred charges to the railroad as wage laborers. Promising moral regeneration, the millenarian rebels called the elites out of the impending moral chaos into holy redoubts with venerable if idealized norms of religiously mandated reciprocity. Diacon provides a vivid illustration of rural denizens who deploy religious ethics that correspond to a former mode of production to critique encroaching capitalism.[36]

Diacon's—and Scott's—moral economy approach has drawn heavy fire in recent years. Influenced by subaltern studies and by secularization theorists like Talal Asad, a new wave of scholars reject the paradigm of secular capitalist societies encroaching on static religious ones in favor of "alternative modernities." No premodern religious past waits to be transformed into the modern secular future. Patricia Pessar, for example, demonstrated that the leaders of Bahia's Santa Brigida millenarian community from the 1930s to the present prescribed drafts of their own miraculous bathwater to the infirm and encouraged penitent flagellation. Meanwhile, however, they ran a thriving capitalist agricultural cooperative with highly disciplined workers and a truck fleet that frustrated rival merchants. The church's attempt to monopolize God, rather than the state, rival clans, or the modern economy, plagued these millenarianists. Pessar implicitly endorses Michael Hardt and Antonio Negri's notion of capitalist relations encircling the globe: there can be no more talk of capitalist penetration anywhere, for it is indeed always already everywhere. But she also voices a resounding no to capitalist culture's millenarian prophets, those who proclaim that the end of history is nigh, that modernity has but one secular telos. To the contrary: many thoroughly contemporary Bahian millenarians consider connecting with the divine a higher purpose than shopping till they drop.[37]

At our current economic juncture, we may need this wisdom more than ever. Early capitalism wrought a moral holocaust, promoting vices like acquisitiveness to innate virtues, as Seed demonstrates for the Mexican case; from the 1970s to at least 2009, millennial capitalism, Jean and John Comaroff argue, moved gambling from the moral margins to the center; an "electronic herd" of venture capitalists roamed the planet and the world became a huge casino, as Fidel Castro lamented.[38] The workers were no longer outside the gates in Flint, and thus it appeared to many that consumption ran the economy, unseating noble production. Neoliberalism's apologists cited downright ethereal means to wealth, like market speculation, as the road to riches. Space and time seemed to magically collapse with new information technologies. Never before had capitalism's magic been so powerful, its ability to seemingly create something from nothing more pronounced, and its mystification of the labor theory of value so total.

But hope springs eternal: where the economic quickening of the late nineteenth century helped birth millenarian rebels, the post-Fordist capitalist era, the Comaroffs propose, witnessed an outbreak of "occult economies," often coupled with the hunt for witches and monstrous creatures. Religious mobilizations of this kind followed the times in employing magical means for material ends, but they also criticized those who accumulated wealth by such foul means. The *chupacabras*, the notoriously elusive bloodsucking predator that stalked animals in Puerto Rico and Mexico during the 1990s, generated films, an *X-Files* episode, countless talk shows, a video game, dozens of Web pages, a comedy festival, and Mexico's official declaration of 1996 as the Year of the *Chupacabras*. The creature also provides a perfect case in point, at least according to one interpretation.

Robin Derby's and Reinaldo Román's divergent analyses of the *chupacabras* outbreak demonstrate the continuing purchase of structuralist readings that present popular beliefs as metaphors for concrete material economies, as well as the rise of phenomenological understandings.[39] In her 2003 work, Derby presented the monstrous creature in the spirit of the Comaroffs: the discursive explosion surrounding a diabolical half-man, half-beast provides a barely coded metaphorical language that reveals fin de siècle U.S. imperialism hiding behind free market fundamentalism. With its vampiric overtones, the chupacabras provided a way for small farmers buffeted by baffling global economic forces to discuss "the extraction of vital fluids, such as water, money, and life force (read blood) from Latin America under NAFTA."[40]

In subsequent work, both Derby and Román have interrogated the connections between the chupacabras and neoliberalism, underscoring local dynamics and polysemy. In a 2008 essay, Derby contended that Puerto Rico's neocolonial relationship with the United States sheltered the island from the most recent globalizing trends. Under the commonwealth system that links the island to the United States, "the very concealment of Federal authorities and their motivations produces a particular kind of 'state effect' as people wonder and talk about what transpires behind the mask of power[.]" For that reason, Derby argued, Puerto Ricans undertake spectacular "rites of exposure," unmasking federal officials for their role in numerous depredations.[41]

Román has also questioned the connection between the *chupacabras* and capitalism's newest iteration. He proposes instead that the attacks may be understood as occasions for a public dialogue regarding citizenship and state power in Puerto Rico. Self-proclaimed *chupacabras* experts lured the government's officious bureaucrats to a "discursive pit"; they lampooned experts for failing to end the attacks while simultaneously poking fun at them for conceding the *chupacabras*'s existence. Irony more than a folksy critique of capitalism characterized the beast's pursuers, who forced unresponsive officials to talk to them in their own terms.[42]

The *chupacabras* represents the tip of the iceberg of the proliferation of beliefs in turn-of-the-century Latin America. As Derby notes, many of the early witnesses to the *chupacabras*'s depredations were evangelical Christians who ascribed a demonic character to the creature. This was no accident. A sizeable proportion of the Latin American population now identifies themselves as *evangélicos*: 2005 figures indicate that Protestants accounted for 6% of the population in Mexico, 11% in Chile, 15.4% in Brazil, and 40% in Guatemala. Incredibly, this Protestant growth dates back to the 1970s—a mere thirty years ago.[43]

Faith and Marketplace: Debating the Rise of Protestantism

Studies of the diffusion of Protestantism and especially Pentecostalism, the fastest growing non-Catholic faith in twentieth-century Latin America, constitute a distinct and distinctly polemical field. Although seminal works date to the late 1960s, when Emilio Willems and Christian Lalive d'Epinay limned the popularization of Protestantism in Chile and Brazil, Sidney W. Mintz's 1960 *Worker in the Cane* constitutes a vital if often unheralded precursor.[44]

Mintz analyzed the conversion of Taso Zayas, a nominally Catholic Puerto Rican sugar worker who became a leader in the Socialist movement and joined the nascent Popular Democratic Party in response to the hacienda system's dissolution and the subsequent rise of industrial agriculture. He later abandoned labor and party politics in favor of Pentecostalism. Like many subsequent scholars, Mintz read Taso's conversion as an adaptive response to the social tumult that accompanied industrialization and proletarianization, with their tendencies to destabilize rural communities, especially their gender and domestic orders, and to disarticulate the patronage networks that provided a precarious sense of security. Prefiguring arguments that remain widely current, Mintz concluded that Pentecostalism appealed to the "detribalized" poor, especially landless workers residing in areas where recurrent waves of evangelizing activity had occurred. While Pentecostalism originated in the United States, it had quickly gone native; its rapid spread in the island reflected Puerto Rican initiatives. Most subsequent scholarship concurs with this early assessment and describes contemporary Protestantism and Pentecostalism as "Latin Americanized."

Mintz also examined the conversion process. Conversions followed kinship lines, and women typically came into the Pentecostal fold before their male relatives, a tendency that Elizabeth Brusco and others since have explored systematically. Taso experienced conversion as a means to cure social, economic, and physical maladies that he suffered as personal, even psychological afflictions.[45] The new faith assuaged Taso's feelings of guilt, restored his sense of community, and delivered tranquility and modest economic stability to his household. Taso's conversion engendered adaptive behaviors rather than precipitating a retreat into apathy or false consciousness.

While Mintz's concerns with uprooted populations, curing, and gender have proven long-lasting, it would be misleading to imply an interpretive consensus. In his pioneering *Followers of the New Faith* (1967), Emilio Willems argued that beginning in the tumultuous 1930s, Brazil and Chile's social upheavals steadily alienated the lower classes from their communities, the local elite, and the larger society, afflicting them with anomie that Protestant churches redressed effectively. Dramatic economic changes caused conversions, he explained, because they frayed the moral tenets underlying social control mechanisms. Certainly some Protestants retained folk Catholicism's experiential content, but rapid industrialization, urbanization, internal migration, and the opening of agricultural frontiers had rendered Catholic practice obsolete. With its seasonal ritual calendar and its local saints, folk Catholicism fit the specific needs of "primitive peasantries," one of many phrases that revealed that Willems did not see peasants and proletariats, haciendas and industries as coeval. Converts to Protestantism and Pentecostalism experienced the strain between social structures and folk Catholicism as loss of community and even as loss of self. And it was precisely here that the new faiths intervened; they protested the failing order and its religion, and generated new identities within communities better adapted to the modern milieu.

Lalive d'Epinay's 1969 *Haven of the Masses* shared Willem's stress on anomie but reached a different conclusion about Protestantism's relationship to modernity and politics. In an emerging industrializing order, Willems believed, the Protestant ethic could prove rewarding economically and socially. Moreover, their new religion enabled converts to contend with emerging electoral politics. Although democratic and authoritarian tendencies coexisted within schism-prone Pentecostalism, Chilean and Brazilian Protestants were nevertheless true protagonists of democracy. Protestantism existed in a paradoxical relationship to modernity: it emerged because of modernization and stimulated further social transformations. Lalive d'Epinay, on the other hand, highlighted the continuities between Chilean Pentecostalism and the old rural order, particularly the resilience of authoritarian patronage. In their pastors, anomie-ridden rural transplants found "the *patrón* of their dreams," an "incarnation of the father-figure who has been lost—or rejected, because he has been found to be unjust."[46]

The causal role of anomie in the growth of Latin American Protestantism is by no means discredited, but it has been demoted, and its scholarly proponents tend to see it as merely the starting point for journeys leading elsewhere. David Stoll, David Martin, and Andrew Chestnut all find a place for both anomie and other causes of conversion in their 1990s works. For Martin, "local adaptors" explain Pentecostalism's success. The individualist, participatory tradition of Pentecostalism, an organizational tendency to fragment, and an emphasis on the somatic experience of the divine facilitated the indigenization of the religion. Stoll found that the Left led tractable Guatemalan peasants in the war-torn western highlands into danger: liberation theologians encouraged rebellion even when death was the likely outcome. When evangelical dictator Efraín Ríos Montt unleashed his brutal campaign, the Ixil abandoned Catholicism and embraced evangelical leaders to protect themselves from army massacres. Chestnut found relief from health problems stemming from desperate poverty at the heart of Pentecostal conversion in Brazil, although his expansive definition of illness—domestic problems, alcoholism, unemployment—resembled anomie in the end. Faith healing, he observed, appealed especially to people left out of the modernization process. In Chestnut's most recent book, as well as in Anthony Gill's work, rational, individual economic actors choose Pentecostalism's superior healing powers out of the abundant choices provided by the region's free market in religious products.[47]

John Burdick found little use for anomie, emphasizing instead that the poor in São Jorge, a town of eight thousand in Rio's urban periphery, turned to what Victor Turner famously called "cults of affliction," namely Pentecostalism and Umbanda. These religions freed converts from earthly afflictions and created new secular identities. Liberation theology and CBCs (Christian Base Communities) proved less attractive than these rivals because in spite of all the progressive reforms, Catholicism remained a "cult of continuity." The CBCs, Burdick observed, emphasized the engagement of the church with an unjust world. These communities raised their members' consciousness to inspire them to change the deep political and economic structures underlying their worldly afflictions. Burdick, Daniel Levine, and others have shown that ordinarily this call failed to galvanize the poor.[48] A growing number of factors—from affliction to local adaptors to political maelstroms to free markets—now compete with anomie as causes of Protestant conversion.

The debate on this Protestant Reformation's political consequences has also heated up, although scholars tend to agree that Evangelical and Pentecostal religions flow more naturally toward conservative politics or political apathy. Rowan Ireland shows that within a single town in Recife's periphery distinct political dispositions jostled for prominence within any one religious tradition. Pentecostal *crentes* demonstrated a sectarian orientation that resisted political engagements; total devotion to God was simply incompatible with loyalty to corruptible political causes. But other church-oriented *crentes* accepted the bureaucratic-authoritarian state's overtures when recognized church leaders acted as mediators. The notion that the church triumphant offered protection from a sinful world disposed the congregation of the Assembly of God, for instance, to strike electoral bargains with conservative politicians. Others share Ireland's conclusions: Stoll highlighted the risks associated with the growing influence of the U.S. religious right; Jean Pierre Bastian detected in Latin America's Pentecostal organizations a worrisome retrenchment of home-grown forms of authoritarianism; Chestnut argued that once the Catholic Church expressed its opposition to Brazil's 1960s military regime, Pentecostal congregation leaders managed to secure a comfortable position in a refurbished clientelistic network. This brought concrete gains, including government funds for a new seminary.[49]

Bethany Moreton takes the evangelical religion and politics literature out for a decidedly more transnational spin. She found that Central Americans educated by the Wal-Mart fortune at Arkansas Christian colleges in the 1980s helped spread the gospel of free market fundamentalism in their war-torn countries; the famed "Washington Consensus" relied on faith in an Ozark-inflected evangelical culture as much as on fidelity to an abstract economic model. The Central American scholarship winners were themselves recruited largely from preexisting Protestant missionary ties. A transnational religious network of decidedly Sun Belt origins redefined the relevant community of moral accountability away from local networks to a global office culture knit together by individualistic evangelical probity. Conservative, neoliberal economics and its attendant politics of state-shrinking had transnational evangelical roots.[50]

Protestantism's political implications become more protean and complex when we expand the definition of politics away from economics, elections, and the state and toward related axes of social power like gender and race. Cecília Loreto Mariz, María das Dores Campos Machado, and Elizabeth Brusco all arrived at a surprising conclusion: in the Latin American context, evangelical Christianity may be a form of feminism. As Loreto Mariz and Campos Machado point out for the Brazilian case, in Pentecostalism God's grace frees individuals from the devil's grasp, liberating them from base natural passions and instincts.[51] As Colombia transformed into a postpeasant society in the late twentieth century, Brusco asserts, male and female realms diverged, and women became more economically dependent on their husbands, who inhabited a macho public sphere of street and work. Evangelical women successfully domesticated these men gone awry: shorn of Satan, male converts have the will to resist the public world's sensual temptations, especially alcohol, smoking, and gambling. Reformed men's domestic spending soared as demon rum gave way to kitchen tables and *electrodomésticos*; evangelical men, in short, embraced women's values of family and home. Where John Burdick found that Liberation Theology favored political and economic concerns of a structural sort and ignored domestic concerns, the evangelical and Pentecostal "reformation of machismo" provided a strong incentive for women to convert and to bring their husbands into the fold.[52]

Pentecostalism may also challenge racial hierarchies. CBCs mobilized small groups as they existed, Burdick argues, maintaining old identities and preserving light-skinned, better-off workers in positions of leadership. In Pentecostal communities, by contrast, social bonds depended not on old statuses but on the shared experiences of affliction. While neither Umbanda nor Pentecostalism offered blacks an unequivocal resolution to the affliction of racism, Burdick argued that they both offered effective "counterdiscourses" to racism. Those *umbandistas* who identified as blacks tended to upturn the dominant spiritual hierarchies, insisting on blacks' spiritual gifts and the primacy of African slave spirits. Among Pentecostals, black Brazilians rise to positions of institutional authority, and the insistence on equal access to charismatic gifts erodes some light-skinned *crentes*' racism. Moreover, Burdick found among Pentecostals a widespread understanding that blacks surpassed light-skinned people in fervor and in proximity to God. Perhaps for these reasons, blacks, who remained a small minority in the CBCs, constituted between one-third and one-half of Pentecostals in São Jorge.[53]

Protestantism's relationship to modernity is as disputed as its repercussions for power and politics. Far from constituting an evangelical awakening or a regional manifestation of a "world-transforming" Protestantism along Weberian lines, Bastian argued that the Protestant explosion represented little more than rural folk Catholicism without priests. Pentecostalism in particular betrayed the modernizing promise of the more sober nineteenth-century Latin American Protestantism. True agents of reform, these early Protestants attempted changes that Bastian tagged as the preconditions of democratic modernity. Bastian's theory is now hotly contested: Emilio García Pantojas, Daniel R. Rodríguez, and Margaret E. Crahan found that Protestant missionaries in the Caribbean were apologists for U.S. imperialism. These missionaries argued that Cubans needed U.S. tutelage; thus, their "civilizing mission" was anything but modernizing or democratic.[54] Martin disagreed with Bastian's skepticism about the current religious juncture: for him, Pentecostalism constituted the latest manifestation of an originally English branch of transformative Protestantism that has been spreading its ethic throughout Latin America. In the Protestant circles that nurture this ethic, Martin detected latent forces for the democratization and capitalization of society.[55]

Modernization theory, with its evolutionary stages of economic and political growth that all nations will pass through, lurks barely under the surface in both Martin's and Bastian's work. In both cases, as with Willems and Lalive d'Espinay, the stage theory of modernization goes unquestioned; the historical uniqueness of industrialization under postmodernity rather than modernity goes unnoticed, and late twentieth-century Protestantisms are tested by nineteenth-century criteria. Why should we be looking for *maquilas* to produce the sober Puritan investors of the first industrial revolution? If industrialization blazes new forms of "flexible" exploitation rather than building Detroit on the Amazon, shouldn't the real question be, as it is for the Comaroffs, how do elements of a particularly Latin American post-Fordism interact with recent conversions? Should we really be lamenting Pentecostalism's failure to modernize Latin America with Bastian or pinning our hopes on the Protestant ethic that Martin feels transformed England? Modernity was as modern on a Cuban sugar plantation as in a Birmingham steel mill: both were simultaneous articulations of a single process.[56] Just as world systems theories illuminated these coeval connections, transnational tools of analysis remind us of the mutual influences that modernization theory renders invisible.

Transnational history has much to offer one branch of the debate on Latin American Protestantism. The conversation around the region's recent conversions includes within it an impassioned argument about the extent to which Protestantism represents an alien import from the North. One wing of analysis has emphasized the inputs from foreign, and especially North American, missionary endeavors, with the most spectacular evidence coming from Reagan-era efforts in Central America.[57] Concerned as they are with political developments internal to the United States, the North American scholars writing in this vein imply unidirectional influence between bounded nation-states. Their model slights a generation of research on transnationalism and cultural reception, as well as world systems theory's challenge to the persistent myth of Western nations' autogenesis and autonomy.[58] The Christian fundamentalism spreading the globe, they assert, "is clearly stamped 'Made in the U.S.A.'"[59] Their own metaphor should have signaled the anachronism: if by the mid-nineties an "American-made" Boeing aircraft contained 30% foreign content, what are the odds that a complex, socially embedded belief system could be wholly constructed in one sovereign territory and shipped to another?[60]

Luis Martínez-Fernández has made the most systematic case against the characterization of Protestantism as an import. In *Protestantism and Political Conflict in the Nineteenth-Century Hispanic Caribbean*, he proposed that Protestantism was and remains a hybrid phenomenon that drew simultaneously from the cultural foundation of Mediterranean Catholicism and from a West African repertoire. His best evidence came from 1880s and 1890s Havana and Matanzas, where Episcopal and American Baptist proselytizers found favor with poor workers, many of them black and mulatto. The leaders and many members of these congregations were nationalist tobacco workers who converted to Protestantism while in exile during the Ten Year's War (1868–78). Samuel Silva Gotay, Anthony M. Stevens-Arroyo, and Nélida Agosto Cintrón all share Martínez-Fernández's distrust of the foreign-import model: all three found decidedly folk Catholic vestiges in Puerto Rican Pentecostalism, and Elizabeth Carrillo and Minerva Rodríguez noted similar tendencies in Cuba.[61]

Jason Yaremko's 2002 *U.S. Protestant Missions in Cuba* reconciles accounts that emphasize indigenization with those that insist on Protestantism's abiding foreignness. Yaremko argues that, despite Cuban efforts, congregations in eastern Cuba established during the first decades of the twentieth century did not constitute a Cuban church. The churches of the 1940s "remained North American, Anglo-Saxon, and middle-class institutions superimposed over an essentially impoverished, working-class, and structurally dependent society."[62] But things were not always that way. It was only after 1898 that missionaries saturated the formerly Cuban church. By Yaremko's reckoning, Cuban Protestantism was naturalized before it underwent a thorough and long-lasting denaturalization. U.S.-born missionaries blocked Cubans' attempts to take charge just as the neocolonial authorities prevented the full exercise of Cuban sovereignty. These developments help to explain why Cubans seeking better positions in the republican economy sought out Protestant education but did not join Protestant congregations in large numbers.

Conclusion

The study of Latin American popular religion remains divided along regional, period, and disciplinary lines; it is anything but a unified field of scholarship. In spite of shared interests in the dynamics of colonialism, ethnogenesis, and identity, the literature on creolization in the Hispanic Caribbean remains largely isolated from the scholarship on syncretism in Mesoamerica and the Andean region. Furthermore, while many Cuban and Brazilian officials speak of popular practices as a subset of broader national cultures, most scholars of African-derived practices typically employ different qualifiers, often replacing "popular" with Afro-, creole, or diasporic. The very rubric "popular religion" has been applied more readily to rural Catholicism than to urban Pentecostalism, despite a generation of accounts that document a genealogical connection between the two. It is not surprising, then, that at least since the 1980s, a growing number of Latin Americanists and Caribbeanists have questioned the usefulness of drawing categorical distinctions between popular and official religions, or between traditional and modern practices.[63]

Although Latin American religious studies remain a scattered field, there are areas of nascent consensus. Taken collectively, recent works suggest a tendency to view religion as a sphere possessed of autonomy. The effect of this shift can safely be called immense; while modernization and Marxian paradigms were dominant, religion was more commonly treated as a theater in which political and economic contests found symbolic staging. Modernization theory in particular tended to organize nations on an evolutionary ladder from religious and traditional to secular and modern—a teleology that transnational religious revivals in both the global north and south render obsolete. Although the relationships between religion, the modern order, and the nation-state remain central, religious practices are now commonly regarded as factors of consequence in their own right.

Although notions regarding periodization vary dramatically and the terms remain imprecise, the last generation of scholarship on Latin American religions shows a keen interest in the complex relationship between religious practices and the making of the modern order. Scholars such as Bastian, Ireland, and Martin, to mention only a few whose works are discussed above, remain preoccupied with Weberian questions regarding causal links between values, economic systems, and political orientations. But perhaps because the transitions to neoliberalism and democracy are no longer news, other questions regarding religion and modernity have gained prominence. Besides asking when and how modernity began in various locales—queries to which scholars as diverse as Voekel and Palmié have offered surprising answers—one finds a concern with the impact of modernity and postmodernity, whether early or late, on religious life. The theme is central in the accounts of millennial upheavals by Pereira de Queiroz, Pessar, and Vanderwood, as well as in the literature on secularization and the rise of religious pluralism. But this concern is also found in studies that ponder the extent and manner of the Christianization of indigenous peoples and in those that examine creolization, the signature cultural process of an earlier order of trans-Atlantic exploitation. Recent studies, however, also seek to reverse the formula: besides detailing the impact of modernity on religion, scholars are seeking to characterize how faith and practice function in a variety of modern venues. It is no longer possible to regard religion as a premodern vestige destined to wane as secular modernity waxes. Afro-Cuban religions are as modern as nuclear physics, as Palmié insists. Much of the emphasis in this respect has fallen on religion's capacity to define corporate and individual identities and reconstitute embattled communities.

The convergence of all of these interests has revitalized the study of witchcraft, Satanism, and "superstitious" healing practices. Gonzalo Aguirre Beltrán's 1963 opus now inhabits a crowded field—a field that boomed after the publication of Michael Taussig's book on commodity fetishism in 1980.[64] Studies featuring the devil and his acquaintances, sorcery, and healing now span the entire field from colonial Mexico, Peru, and Guatemala, to colonial Brazil, to the Hispanic Caribbean. Such topics are of course well suited for exploring the conflict-ridden interaction between religion and modernity and the production of discourses that gave birth to ethnic, racial, and national identities. For those reasons, the devil seems to voice the latest word when it comes to Latin American religions.

ACKNOWLEDGMENTS

In writing this essay, we accrued numerous intellectual and personal debts. We are grateful to Bethany Moreton, the Reverend Doctor Jennifer Hughes, Estela Roselló Soberón, Anne Rubenstein, Juan Pedro Viqueira, and Elliott Young for comments, corrections, and invaluable bibliographical suggestions. We also wish to thank our colleagues at the 2005 meeting of the Tepoztlán Institute for Transnational History of the Americas, University of Georgia graduate students Blake Scott and Hannah Waits, and our heroic research assistant Courtney Stallworth.

NOTES

1. For a synthesis of the debate in its formative years, see Walter Jackson, "Melville Herskovits and the Search for Afro-American Culture," in *Malinowski, Rivers, Benedict, and Others*, ed. George W. Stocking Jr. (Madison: University of Wisconsin Press, 1986). For an account of the development of the broader field, see O. Nigel Bolland, "Creolization and Creole Societies: A Cultural Nationalist View of Caribbean Social History," *Caribbean Quarterly* 44:1/2 (1998): 1–32, and Kevin A. Yelvington, "The Anthropology of Afro-Latin America and the Caribbean: Diasporic Dimensions," *Annual Review of Anthropology* 30 (2001): 227–60.

2. Fernando Ortiz, *Cuban Counterpoint*, translated by Harriet de Onís (Durham, N.C.: Duke University Press, 1995).

3. Roger Bastide, *The African Religions of Brazil: Towards a Sociology of the Interpenetration of Civilizations*, trans. Helen Sebba (Baltimore: Johns Hopkins University Press, 1978 [1960]).

4. Sidney W. Mintz and Richard Price, *The Birth of African-American Culture: An Anthropological Perspective* (Boston: Beacon Press, 1992).

5. Since the 1970s, Caribbeanists have associated creolization with Kamau Brathwaite, *The Development of Creole Society in Jamaica, 1770–1820* (Oxford: Clarendon Press, 1971). But the term has a history dating back to the sixteenth century, long before José Juan Arrom's scholarly usage in the 1950s. For a critique of the resurgence of the term in the globalization literature, see Sidney W. Mintz, "Enduring Substances, Trying Theories: The Caribbean Region as Oikoumene," *The Journal of the Royal Anthropological Institute* 2:2 (1996): 301–02. See also Verene A. Shepherd and Glen L. Richards, eds., *Questioning Creole: Creolisation Discourses in Caribbean Culture* (Kingston, Jamaica: Ian Randle; Oxford: James Currey, 2002).

6. Philip D. Curtin, *The Atlantic Slave Trade: A Census* (Madison: University of Wisconsin Press, 1969). John Thornton, *Africa and Africans in the Making of the Atlantic World, 1400–1800*, 2nd ed. (Cambridge, U.K.: Cambridge University Press, 1998). Michael A. Gomez, *Exchanging our Country Marks: The Transformation of African Identities in the Colonial and Antebellum South* (Chapel Hill, N.C.: University of North Carolina Press, 1998). Colin A. Palmer, "From Africa to the Americas: Ethnicity in the Early Black Communities of the Americas," *Journal of World History* 6 (1995): 223–36. Paul E. Lovejoy, "The African Diaspora: Revisionist Interpretations of Ethnicity, Culture and Religion under Slavery," *Studies in the World History of Slavery, Abolition, and Emancipation* 2 (1997): 1–23.

7. James H. Sweet, *Recreating Africa: Culture, Kinship and Religion in the African-Portuguese World, 1441–1770* (Chapel Hill and London: The University of North Carolina Press, 2003), 210.

8. Leslie G. Desmangles, *The Faces of the Gods: Vodou and Catholicism in Haiti* (Chapel Hill: University of North Carolina Press, 1992), 8.

9. Here Farriss parts company with Pedro Carrasco, although their positions may be based on regional differences. Carrasco found central Mexico to be characterized by public Christian rituals and private indigenous devotions; see his "La transformación de la cultura indígena durante la colonia," *Historia Mexicana* 25 (1975): 175–203.

10. Nancy M. Farriss, *Maya Society under Colonial Rule: The Collective Enterprise of Survival* (Princeton, N.J.: Princeton University Press, 1984).

11. Inga Clendinnen, "Ways to the Sacred: Reconstructing 'Religion' in Sixteenth-Century Mexico," *History and Anthropology* 5 (1990): 105–41. Clifford Geertz, *The Interpretation of Cultures: Selected Essays* (New York: Basic Books, 1973). Serge Gruzinski, *Man-Gods in the Mexican Highlands: Indian Power and Colonial Society, 1520–1800*, trans. Eileen Corrigan (Stanford, Calif.: Stanford University Press, 1989). Robert Ricard, *The Spiritual Conquest of Mexico: An Essay on the Apostolate and the Evangelizing Methods of the Mendicant Orders in New Spain, 1523–1572* (Berkeley: University of California Press, 1966), first published in French in 1933. A master storyteller with a knack for the felicitous phrase, Clendinnen has more than proven the utility of her approach: in her best-known work, *Ambivalent Conquests*, the key to Maya resistance to Spanish proselytizing is the endurance of their path to truth, their circular notion of time: Inga Clendinnen, *Ambivalent Conquests: Maya and Spaniard in Yucatan, 1517–1571* (Cambridge, U.K.: Cambridge University Press, 1987). Another interesting intervention on the continuity side of the debate is that of Louise M. Burkhart, who argues that a linguistic barrier prevented Spanish cultural concepts from passing into native culture; see her *The Slippery Earth: Nahua-Christian Moral Dialogue in Sixteenth-Century Mexico* (Stanford, Calif.: Stanford University Press, 1989).

12. Guillermo Bonfil Batalla, *México profundo: Una civilización negada* (Mexico City: CIESAS, 1987). The book was translated as *Mexico Profundo: Reclaiming a Civilization* (Austin: University of Texas Press, 1996).

13. Alberto Flores Galindo, *Buscando un Inca: Identidad y utopía en los Andes* (Havana: Casa de las Américas, 1986), 72. In a similar vein, Néstor García Canclini writes of cultural hybridity to underscore the impossibility of pristine, autonomous cultures. See his *Hybrid Cultures: Strategies for Entering and Leaving Modernity* (Minneapolis: University of Minnesota Press, 1995).

14. James Lockhart, *The Nahuas after the Conquest: A Social and Cultural History of the Indians of Central Mexico, Sixteenth through Eighteenth Centuries* (Stanford, Calif.: Stanford University Press, 1994).

15. On man-gods, see Gruzinski, *Man-Gods*. The concept was initially developed in Alfredo López Austin, *Hombre-Dios: Religión y política en el mundo náhuatl* (Mexico City: Universidad Autónoma de México, 1989). Juan Pedro Viqueira, *María de la Candelaria, india natural de Cancuc* (Mexico City: Fondo de Cultura Económica, 1993).

16. Laura Lewis, *Hall of Mirrors: Power, Witchcraft and Caste in Colonial Mexico* (Durham, N.C.: Duke University Press, 2003). Estela Roselló Soberón's careful reading of Fray Andres de Olmos's 1553 treatise on Satan revealed that the devil not only entered the polity through Indians but often appeared dressed as an Indian cacique. See Estela Roselló Soberón, "El Diablo en el *Tratado de sortilegios y hechicerías* de fray Andrés de Olmos: La caracterización de un marginal," paper presented at the Tepoztlán Institute for the Transnational History of the Americas, Tepoztlán, Morelos, Mexico, July 22–29, 2004.

17. Irene Silverblatt, *Moon, Sun, and Witches: Gender Ideologies and Class in Inca and Colonial Peru* (Princeton, N.J.: Princeton University Press, 1987). Sabine MacCormack, *Religion in the Andes: Visions and Images in Early Colonial Peru* (Princeton, N.J.: Princeton University Press, 1991). Other fine works include Kenneth Mills, *Idolatry and Its Enemies:*

Colonial Andean Religion and Extirpation, 1640–1750 (Princeton, N.J.: Princeton University Press, 1997), and Luiz R. B. Mott, *Escravidão, homosexualidade e demonologia* (São Paulo: Icone, 1988).

18. An informative discussion of the new scholarly concern with the magic of modernity can be found in Michael Saler, "Modernity and Enchantment: A Historiographical Review," *American Historical Review* 111:3 (2006): 692–717. Stephan Palmié, *Wizards and Scientists: Explorations in Afro-Cuban Modernity and Tradition* (Durham, N.C.: Duke University Press, 2002), 248. Brazilian messianic leader Antonio the Counselor's skull was similarly presented to Raimundo Nina Rodrigues for study at the Bahian Medical Faculty. Nina Rodrigues found a clear link between mental illness and messianic contagion in a piece entitled "Epidemic of Insanity at Canudos"; see Robert M. Levine, *Vale of Tears: Revisiting the Canudos Massacre in Northeastern Brazil, 1893–1897* (Berkeley: University of California Press, 1992), 207. The following works deal with witchcraft in Cuba but are not discussed here because their focus is not on religion: Ernesto Chávez Alvarez, *El crimen de la niña Cecilia: La brujería como fenómeno social, 1902–1925* (Havana: Editorial de Ciencias Sociales, 1991); Aline Helg, *Our Rightful Share: The Afro-Cuban Struggle for Equality, 1886–1912* (Chapel Hill: University of North Carolina Press, 1995); and Alejandra M. Bronfman, *Measures of Equality: Social Science, Citizenship, and Race in Cuba, 1902–1940* (Chapel Hill: University of North Carolina Press, 2004).

19. Stephen Palmié, *Wizards and Scientists*, 76.

20. Michael T. Taussig, *The Devil and Commodity Fetishism in South America* (Chapel Hill: University of North Carolina Press, 1980). James C. Scott, *Domination and the Arts of Resistance: Hidden Transcripts* (New Haven: Yale University Press, 1990). Paul Vanderwood, *The Power of God against the Guns of Government: Religious Upheaval in Mexico at the Turn of the Nineteenth Century* (Stanford, Calif.: Stanford University Press, 1998). Vanderwood's tale of a millenarian movement in northern Mexico is both well researched and engagingly written, a perfect book for graduate students and undergraduates alike.

21. Noemí Quezada, *Enfermedad y maleficio: El curandero en el México colonial* (Mexico City: Universidad Nacional Autónoma de México, 1989). Gonzalo Aguirre Beltrán, *Medicina y magia: El proceso de aculturación en la estructura colonial* (Mexico City: Instituto Nacional Indígena, 1963).

22. Laura de Mello e Souza, *O diablo e a Terra de Santa Cruz: Feitiçaria e religiosidade popular no Brasil colonial* (São Paulo: Companhia das Letras, 1986). The book was beautifully translated into English by Diane Grosklaus Whitty as *The Devil and the Land of the Holy Cross: Witchcraft, Slavery, and Popular Religion in Colonial Brazil* (Austin: University of Texas Press, 2004). Fernando Cervantes, *The Devil in the New World: The Impact of Diabolism in New Spain* (New Haven: Yale University Press, 1994).

23. Keith Thomas, *Religion and the Decline of Magic: Studies in Popular Belief in Sixteenth and Seventeenth Century England* (London: Weidenfeld and Nicolson, 1971), 643. In the modern Latin American context, Cristián Parker explains, capitalism and modernity do not lead inexorably to secularization, because the social and cultural uncertainty of life of the urban poor keeps them dependent on the supernatural. Secularization is the property of the few winners in a dependent capitalist context. See his *Popular Religion and Modernization in Latin America: A Different Logic* (Maryknoll, N.Y.: Maryknoll Press, 1996), 73–83.

24. Patricia Seed, *To Love, Honor, and Obey: Conflicts over Marriage Choice in Colonial Mexico, 1574–1821* (Stanford, Calif.: Stanford University Press, 1989). Ramón Gutiérrez, *When Jesus Came, the Corn Mothers Went Away: Marriage, Sexuality and Power in New Mexico, 1500–1846* (Stanford, Calif.: Stanford University Press, 1991). María Cristina

Sacristán, *Locura y disidencia en el México ilustrado, 1760–1810* (Zamora: El Colegio de Michoacán; Mexico City: Instituto Mora, 1994). Also see Brian Larkin, "Liturgy, Devotion, and Religious Reform in Eighteenth-Century Mexico City," *The Americas* 60:4 (April 2004): 493–518. Enrique Florescano provides a lucid summary of the forces of secularization and modernity at work in late-eighteenth-century Mexico in his *Memoria mexicana: Ensayo sobre la reconstrucción del pasado: Epoca prehispánica—1821* (Mexico City: Joaquín Mortiz, 1987), 265–80. Florescano is quick to point out that this process of secularization had less effect on the countryside than on the cities and less effect on the poor than on New Spain's elite Creoles and Spaniards; see pp. 280–300. María Elena Martínez's tour de force on religion, gender, and *limpieza de sangre* in Spain and Mexico also underscores the rise of secularism in the late eighteenth century; see her *Genealogical Fictions: Limpieza de Sangre, Religion and Gender in Colonial Mexico* (Stanford, Calif.: Stanford University Press, 2008).

25. From Joan Didion, "Mr. Bush & the Divine," *New York Review of Books*, Nov. 6, 2003, 81.

26. See Jeff Sharlet, "Soldiers of Christ I: Inside America's Most Powerful Megachurch," *Harper's*, May 2005, 41–54.

27. Rev. Peter J. Gomes, cited in Neil Swidey, "God on the Quad: New England's Liberal College Campuses Have Become Fertile Ground for the Evangelical Movement, Which Is Attracting Students in Record Numbers. But after They Graduate, Will They Keep the Faith?" *The Boston Globe*, Nov. 30, 2003, Sunday Magazine.

28. Eric Van Young, *The Other Rebellion: Popular Violence, Ideology, and the Mexican Struggle for Independence, 1810–1821* (Stanford, Calif.: Stanford University Press, 2001). Pamela Voekel, *Alone Before God*. Patricia Londoño Vega, *Religion, Culture, and Society in Colombia: Medellín and Antioquia, 1850–1930* (Oxford: Clarendon Press, 2002). Other historians share Londoño Vega's critique of the two-tiered model of elite and popular religiosity. Stephen Palmié, for example, provides a succinct discussion of the interpretive problems that can arise when scholars assume that literate and oral cultures or elite and popular religiosity constitute autonomous realms. He fears that "scholars have uncritically accepted the boundaries drawn by socially empowered orthodoxies intent on subjugating rival forms of knowledge and distinctive practices." Folk tradition is often in reality a congeries of diverse ideas and practices that are lumped together more by elite discursive agency than by any "features inherent in these phenomena themselves." See Palmié, *Wizards and Scientists*, p. 115. Paul Vanderwood fears that the two-tiered model of popular and elite religiosity tends to "create stereotypes, to make the Church monolithic, ordinary people passive, and their relationship static, all of which are very far from the reality of religiosity among humans": Paul Vanderwood, "Religion: Official, Popular, and Otherwise," *Mexican Studies/Estudios Mexicanos* 16:2 (Summer 2000), 413. As the previous discussion of works on the colonial period demonstrates, the two-tiered model of elite and popular religiosity has few champions. Michael P. Carroll, *The Penitente Brotherhood: Patriarchy and Hispano-Catholicism in New Mexico* (Baltimore, Md.: Johns Hopkins University Press, 2001). For an interesting discussion of trends in the historiography of popular religion in nineteenth- and twentieth-century Mexico, see Martin Austin Nesvig, "Introduction," in *Religious Culture in Modern Mexico*, ed. Martin Austin Nesvig (New York: Rowman & Littlefield, 2007), 1–13. Also indispensable is Alan Knight, "Superstition in Mexico: From Colonial Church to Secular State," *Past and Present* 199, Suppl. 3 (2008), 229–70. Also see Terry Rugeley, *Of Wonders and Wise Men: Religion and Popular Cultures in Southeast Mexico* (Austin: University of Texas Press, 2001). Alvaro Matute, Evelia Trejo, and Brian Connaughton, eds., *Estado, iglesia y sociedad en México, siglo XIX* (Mexico City: Facultad de Filosofía y Letras, UNAM/Grupo Editorial M.A. Porrúa, 1995). Luis Enrique Murillo, "The

Politics of the Miraculous: Popular Religious Practice in Porfirian Michoacán, 1876–1910" (PhD diss., University of California San Diego, 2002).

29. Sol Serrano, *Vírgenes viajeras: Diarios de religiosas francesas en su ruta a Chile 1838–1874* (Santiago: Ediciones Universidad Católica, 2000) and her work in progress "Catolicismo y secularización en Chile en el siglo XIX." Silvia Arrom, "Mexican Laywomen Spearhead a Catholic Revival: The Ladies of Charity, 1863–1910," in *Religious Culture in Modern Mexico*, ed. Martin Austin Nesvig (New York: Rowman & Littlefield, 2007): 50–78. Margaret Chowning, "Liberals, Women, and the Church in Mexico: Politics and the Feminization of Piety, 1700–1930," unpublished paper delivered to the Harvard Latin American Studies Seminar, 2002. Laura O'Dogherty Madrazo, "Restaurarlo todo en Cristo: Unión de Damas Católicas Mejicanas, 1920–1926," *Estudios de Historia Moderna y Contemporánea de México* 14 (1991): 129–58, and her "De urnas y sotanas: El Partido Católico Nacional en Jalisco" (PhD diss., Colegio de México, 1999). Patience Schell, *Church and State Education in Revolutionary Mexico City* (Tucson: University of Arizona Press, 2003).

30. And if there is increased attention to popular religion, there is also a call to give it the analytical weight it deserves. Adrian Bantjes's provocative 2004 review of the historiography of Mexico's Revolutionary-era *Kulturkampf* laments the tendency to reduce popular religion to a mere reflection of deeper political, economic, and social processes; he challenges historians to take religion seriously as a prime mover of the era's upheaval, especially at the local level: Adrian A. Bantjes, "Iglesia, estado, y religión en el México revolucionario: Una visión historiográfica del conjunto," *Prohistoria* 6:6 (2002): 203–24. A fine example of new work that places religion at the center of Mexico's revolutionary period is Jason Dormaday's, "A New Jerusalem for a New Mexico: Margarito Valencia Bautista and Religious Community in Post-Revolutionary Mexico, 1901–1954," unpublished paper, Santa Barbara, Calif., 2004.

31. The publication of *Rituals of Rule, Rituals of Resistance* signaled the generalization of these concerns. See William H. Beezley, Cheryl English Martin, and William E. French, eds., *Rituals of Rule, Rituals of Resistance: Public Celebrations and Popular Culture in Mexico* (Wilmington, Del.: SR Books, 1994). Jennifer Hughes, *Biography of a Mexican Crucifix: Lived Religion and Local Faith from the Conquest to the Present* (Oxford: Oxford University Press, 2009). Much of the turn towards local manifestations of piety has been influenced by several works on Spain by William A. Christian Jr.; see his *Apparitions in Late Medieval and Renaissance Spain* (Princeton, N.J.: Princeton University Press, 1981) and *Local Religion in Sixteenth Century Spain* (Princeton, N.J.: Princeton University Press, 1981). Important works include Martin Austin Nesvig, ed., *Local Religion in Colonial Mexico* (Albuquerque: University of New Mexico, 2006). Matthew Butler, "Trouble Afoot? Pilgrimage in Cristero Mexico City," in *Faith and Impiety in Revolutionary Mexico City*, ed. Matthew Butler (New York: Palgrave Macmillan, 2007): 149–57. Edward Wright-Rios, *Revolutions in Mexican Catholicism: Reform and Revelation in Oaxaca, 1887–1934* (Durham, N.C.: Duke University Press, 2009). Luiz R. B. Mott, *Rosa Egipcíaca: Uma santa africana no Brasil* (Rio de Janeiro: Bertrand Brasit, 1993). Linda Curcio-Nagy, *The Great Festivals of Colonial Mexico City: Performing Power and Identity* (Albuquerque: University of New Mexico Press, 2004). Carolyn Dean, *Inka Bodies and the Body of Christ: Corpus Christi in Colonial Cuzco, Peru* (Durham, N.C.: Duke University Press, 1999). Paul J. Vanderwood, *Juan Soldado: Rapist, Murderer, Martyr, Saint* (Durham, N.C.: Duke University Press, 2004). Clara García Ayluardo and Manuel Ramos Medina, eds., *Manifestaciones religiosas en el mundo colonial americano* (Mexico City: INAH/Condumex/UIA, 1992). María Elena Díaz, *The Virgin, the King, and the Royal Slaves of El Cobre: Negotiating Freedom in Colonial Cuba, 1670–1780*

(Stanford, Calif.: Stanford University Press, 2000). Mathew David O'Hara, "A Flock Divided: Religion and Community in Mexico City, 1749–1800" (PhD diss., University of California San Diego, 2003). Peter Herman Sigal, *From Moon Goddess to Virgins: The Colonization of Maya Sexual Desire* (Austin: University of Texas Press, 2000). The *obra maestra* of the literature on rituals and space remains Ramón Gutiérrez's *When Jesus Came*.

32. For a fascinating demonstration of the merits of attending to the underlying cultural assumptions of document producers, see James Krippner-Martínez, *Rereading the Conquest: Power, Politics, and the History of Early Colonial Michoacán, Mexico, 1521–1565* (University Park: Penn State University Press, 2001).

33. William B. Taylor, *Magistrates of the Sacred: Priests and Parishioners in Eighteenth-Century Mexico* (Stanford, Calif.: Stanford University Press, 1999). João José Reis, *Death Is a Festival: Funeral Rites and Rebellion in Nineteenth-Century Brazil*, trans. H. Sabrina Gledhill (Chapel Hill, N.C. and London: The University of North Carolina Press, 2003). Originally published as *A morte é uma festa: Ritos fúnebres e revolta popular no Brasil do século XIX* (Brazil: Companhias das Letras, 1991). Rachel A. Chico, "From the Pulpit to the Post: Anti-clericalism and Communication in Orizaba, 1857–1867," unpublished paper, Columbia S.C., 2008. Heather McCrea, "Medical Knowledge, Public Health, and Modernity in Early-Twentieth-Century Yucatán, Mexico," paper given at the Southwest Conference on Latin American Studies, Waco, Tex., January 2005; Adam Warren, "Piety and Danger: Popular Ritual, Epidemics, and Medical Reforms in Lima, Peru, 1750–1860" (PhD diss., University of California San Diego, 2004); Martina Will de Chaparro, *Death and Dying in New Mexico* (Albuquerque: University of New Mexico Press, 2007); Douglass Sullivan-González, *Piety, Power, and Politics: Religion and Nation Formation in Guatemala, 1821–1871* (Pittsburg, Pa.: University of Pittsburgh Press, 1998); Greg Grandin, *The Blood of Guatemala: A History of Race and Nation* (Durham, N.C.: Duke University Press, 2000). Pamela Voekel, *Alone Before God*.

34. Euclides da Cunha, *Rebellion in the Backlands*, trans. Samuel Putnam (Chicago and London: University of Chicago Press, 1944 [1906]).

35. Maria Isaura Pereira de Queiroz, *O messianismo no Brasil e no mundo* (São Paulo, 1965). Influenced by Pereira de Queiroz, Alida C. Metcalf stresses anomie as a causal factor in millenarian revolts in her discussion of a 1580s movement in the hinterlands of Salvador da Bahia. By her reckoning "the Santidade de Jaguaripe" is an example of slave millenarianism. She breaks with authors like Ronaldo Vainfas, who read the movement as an extension of precontact Indian religiosity blended with Catholicism. See Alida C. Metcalf, "Millenarian Slaves? The Santidade de Jaguaripe and Slave Resistance in the Americas," *The American Historical Review* 104:4 (October 1999): 1531–59. Ronaldo Vainfas, *A heresia dos índios: Catolicismo e rebeldia no Brasil colonial* (São Paulo: Companhia das Letras, 1995).

36. Todd A. Diacon, *Millenarian Vision, Capitalist Reality: Brazil's Contestado Rebellion, 1912–1916* (Durham, N.C.: Duke University Press, 1991). Scott, *Domination and the Arts of Resistance*. Writing about millenarian rebels in turn of the century Mexico, Paul Vanderwood employs a similar moral economy model, depicting the clash of modernity with traditional religious values; see his *The Power of God*. The moral economy model is also employed to good effect in Steve Stern's account of the Taqi Onqoy revolt, see his *Peru's Indian Peoples and the Challenge of Spanish Conquest: Huamanga to 1640* (Madison: University of Wisconsin Press, 1993). For an interesting work that takes religion seriously as a motivating factor in rural millenarianism, see Daniel Levine, *Vale of Tears*.

37. The insistent separation of the religious and the secular, Talal Asad explains, marches tellingly cheek by jowl with the overt claim that the latter produces the former.

The premodern world created superstitious and oppressive religion; the modern secular and scientific world spawned tolerant, rational religion. By Asad's reckoning, then, "the secular" is an empty category. For him, the real question is not whether it is marching forward, but how, when, and by whom are the categories of religion and the secular defined. See his *Formations of the Secular: Christianity, Islam, Modernity* (Stanford, Calif.: Stanford University Press, 2003). Peter Berger, the éminence grise of U.S. religious studies, has recanted his 1960s predictions of secularization and instead now urges considerations of "European exceptionalism." Berger's point is more forcefully made by isolating Western Europe and within it the native-born; further, if the United States and Canada are disaggregated into regions, the exception may prove to be the industrial, educated, nonimmigrant, and perhaps even the white North Atlantic. Peter Berger, "Epistemological Modesty: An Interview with Peter Berger," *Christian Century* 114 (1997): 974. Michael Hardt and Antonio Negri, *Empire* (Cambridge, Mass.: Harvard University Press, 2001). Michael Hardt and Antonio Negri, *Multitude: War and Democracy in the Age of Empire* (New York: Penguin, 2004). The most famous bard of consumer capitalism as history's telos is Francis Fukuyama; see his *The End of History and the Last Man* (New York: Penguin, 1992). Patricia Pessar, *From Fanatics to Folk: Brazilian Millenarianism and Popular Culture* (Durham, N.C.: Duke University Press, 2004). For an insightful review of the literature on Brazilian millenarianism, see Pessar's "Unmasking the Politics of Religion: The Case of Brazilian Millenarianism," *Journal of Latin American Lore* 7:2 (Winter 1981): 255–79, and her "Three Moments in Brazilian Millenarianism: The Interrelationship between Politics and Religion," *Luso-Brazilian Review* 28 (1991): 94–116. Scholars arguing for "alternative modernities" in the Latin American context have been influenced by subaltern studies. See, for example, Dipesh Chakrabarty, *Provincializing Europe* (Princeton: Princeton University Press, 2000) and Dilip Parameshwar Gaonkar, ed., *Alternative Modernities* (Durham, N.C.: Duke University Press, 2001). Influenced by the alternative modernities literature, Lia Schraeder argues that scholars have misread Mexico's Porfiriato as a time of increasing secularization; see her "The Spirits of Modern Mexico: Spiritism and Politics in Liberal and Revolutionary Eras" (PhD diss., University of California Davis, 2008). But see also Mark Overmyer-Velázquez, *Visions of the Emerald City: Modernity, Tradition, and the Formation of Porfirian Oaxaca, Mexico* (Durham, N.C.: Duke University Press, 2006). Gabriela Sánchez Hernández's work on Catholic magic in present-day Mexico City also comes out of this tradition; see her "De prácticas mágico religiosas en familias católicas del Distrito Federal (México)," presented at the Tepoztlán Institute for Transnational History of the Americas, Tepoztlán, Mexico, July 27–Aug. 3, 2005. Two recent interventions in the alternative modernities literature are Estela Roselló Soberón's *Así en la tierra como en el cielo: Manifestaciones cotidianas de la culpa y el perdón en la Nueva España* (Mexico City: Colegio de México, 2006) and Reinaldo L. Román's *Governing Spirits: Religion, Miracles, and Spectacles in Cuba and Puerto Rico, 1898–1956* (Chapel Hill: University of North Carolina Press, 2007).

38. Jean and John Comaroff, eds., *Millennial Capitalism and the Culture of Neoliberalism* (Durham, N.C. and London: Duke University Press, 2001), 1–56.

39. Robin Derby, "Vampires of Empire, or, Why the Chupacabras Stalks the Americas," and Reinaldo L. Román, "Of Dread and Laughter: Chupacabras and Vampires as Parodies," presented at the Association of Caribbean Historians, San Juan, Puerto Rico, May 1, 2003. A version of Derby's paper was later published as "Vampiros del imperio, o por qué el Chupacabras acecha las Américas," in *Culturas Imperiales: Experiencia y representación en América, Africa y Asia*, Ricardo Salvatorre ed. (Buenos Aires: Beatriz Viterbo, 2005) 317–44.

40. Robin Derby, "Vampires of Empire," 6.

41. Robin Derby, "Imperial Secrets: Vampires and Nationhood in Puerto Rico," *Past and Present* 199, Suppl. 3 (2008), 294, 308.

42. Román, *Governing Spirits*, 199.

43. Virginia Garrard-Burnett and David Stoll, eds., *Rethinking Protestantism in Latin America* (Philadelphia: Temple University Press, 1993), 2. In the 1990s, scholars anticipated uninterrupted Protestant growth. Figures gathered between 2003 and 2005 suggest that growth has slowed in many Latin American nations. See Religion in Latin America, "Statistics—Percentage of Protestants, Census or Estimated Percentages 2003, 2005," Latin American Network Information Center (LANIC) at the University of Texas, Austin, available at http://lanic.utexas.edu/project/rla/tables/protestants.html.

44. David Martin quotes Mintz's study extensively in *Tongues of Fire: The Explosion of Protestantism in Latin America* (Cambridge, Mass., and Oxford: Basil Blackwell, 1990), 192–97. But *Worker in the Cane: A Puerto Rican Life History* (New Haven: Yale University Press, 1960) is seldom mentioned in surveys of the literature.

45. R. Andrew Chesnut's recent claim that Pentecostalism grew in Belém—"the cradle of Brazilian Pentecostalism"—precisely because of its capacity to heal "the pathogens of poverty" can be read as a narrower, functionalist gloss on Mintz's argument. R. Andrew Chesnut, *Born Again in Brazil: The Pentecostal Boom and the Pathogens of Poverty* (New Brunswick, N.J.: Rutgers University Press, 1997), especially chap. 3.

46. Christian Lalive d'Epinay, *The Haven of the Masses* (London: Lutterworth Press, 1969), 38. Emilio Willems, *Followers of the New Faith* (Nashville, Tenn.: Vanderbilt University Press, 1967).

47. David Martin, *Tongues of Fire: The Explosion of Protestantism in Latin America* (Oxford and Cambridge, Mass.: Blackwell, 1990). David Stoll, *Is Latin America Turning Protestant?* (Berkeley: University of California Press, 1990). R. Andrew Chesnut, *Born Again in Brazil* and his *Competitive Spirits: Latin America's New Religious Economy* (New York: Oxford University Press, 2003). Anthony Gill, *Rendering Unto Caesar: The Catholic Church and the State in Latin America* (Chicago: University of Chicago Press, 1998). It is worth noting that neither the debate nor Gill and Chestnut's market model are new. Almost forty years ago, Willems and Lalive d'Epinay discussed the market model of religious change: Emilio Willems, *Followers*, 60; and Christian Lalive d'Epinay, *The Haven*, 30.

48. See among others Daniel H. Levine, *Popular Voices in Latin American Catholicism* (Princeton: Princeton University Press, 1992) and his "Popular Groups, Popular Culture, and Popular Religion," *Comparative Studies in Society and History* 32(4): 718–64.

49. Rowan Ireland, *Kingdoms Come: Religion and Politics in Brazil* (Pittsburgh: University of Pittsburgh Press, 1991). David Stoll, *Is Latin America Turning Protestant?* R. Andrew Chesnut, *Born Again in Brazil*. Jean-Pierre Bastian, "The Metamorphosis of Latin American Protestant Groups: A Socio-Historical Perspective," *Latin American Research Review* 28:2 (1993): 33–61.

50. Bethany Moreton, *To Serve God and Wal-Mart: The Making of Christian Free Enterprise* (Cambridge, Mass.: Harvard University Press, 2009). Important works on progressive Catholicism have shown equal sensitivity to the murkiness of religion and politics. The bloodletting in Central America in the 1980s went on under the sign of evangelical dictator Ríos Montt and the martyred Archbishop Oscar Romero. The literature from the region tends to be equally polarized on the religion and politics question. Roger Lancaster, for example, argued that Sandinista socialism was born not from Soviet machinations or even dependency theory's 1960s intellectual vogue, but from the womb of Managua's folk Catholicism, with its ethical imperatives against wealth accumulation and commodification; see his *Thanks to God and the Revolution: Popular*

Religion and Class Consciousness in the New Nicaragua (New York: Columbia University Press, 1988). For more on the link between radical Catholicism and revolutionary politics, see Deborah Levenson Estrada, *Trade Unionists against Terror: Guatemala City, 1954–1985* (Chapel Hill: University of North Carolina Press, 1994); and Ricardo Falla, *Quiché Rebelde: Religious Conversion, Politics, and Ethnic Identity in Guatemala*, trans. Philip Berryman (Austin: University of Texas Press, 2001). The deep history of liberation theology in Latin America is detailed in Gustavo Gutiérrez, *Dios o el oro en las Indias: Siglo XVI* (Lima: Instituto Bartolomé de las Casas, 1989) and in Susan Fitzpatrick Behrens, "Transforming Mission: Maryknoll Catholic Missionaries, Indian Catequists, and Liberation Theology in Peru and Guatemala, 1943–2000," unpublished manuscript, 2005. Historical treatments of liberation theology's influence on more recent social movements include Jean Meyer, Federico Anaya Gallardo, and Julio Ríos, *Samuel Ruíz en San Cristóbal, 1960–2000* (Mexico City: Tusquets, 2000); John Womack Jr., *Rebellion in Chiapas* (New York: New Press, 1999); Xóchitl Leyva Solano, "Catequistas, misioneros y tradiciones en Las Cañadas," in Mario Humberto Ruz and Juan Pedro Viquiera, eds., *Chiapas: Los rumbos de otra historia*, 3rd ed. (Mexico City: Universidad Nacional Autónoma de México, 2002): 375–407.

51. Cecília Loreto Mariz and María das Dores Campos Machado, "Pentecostalism and Women in Brazil," in Edward L. Cleary and Hannah W. Stewart-Gambino, eds, *Power, Politics, and Pentecostals in Latin America* (Boulder, Colo.: Westview Press, 1997), 41–55. Also see Maria das Dores Campos Machado, *Carismaticos e pentecostais: Adesão religiosa na esfera familiar* (Campinas: Autores Associados; São Paulo: ANPOCS, 1996). Cecilia Mariz, *Coping with Poverty: Pentecostals and Christian Base Communities in Brazil* (Philadelphia: Temple University Press, 1994); and Timothy J. Steigenga and David A. Smilde, "Wrapped in the Holy Shawl: The Strange Case of Conservative Christians and Gender Equality in Latin America," in *Latin American Religion in Motion*, ed. Christian Smith and Joshua Prokopy (New York: Routledge, 1999), 173–86.

52. Elizabeth Brusco, *The Reformation of Machismo: Evangelical Conversion and Gender in Colombia* (Austin: University of Texas Press, 1995). John Burdick, *Looking for God in Brazil*, 224. Ana L. Peterson disagrees with Burdick's assessment of liberation theology's neglect of gender issues; see her provocative "'The Only Way I can Walk': Women, Christianity, and Everyday Life in El Salvador," in Anna L. Peterson, Manuel A. Vásquez, and Philip J. Williams, *Christianity, Social Change, and Globalization in the Americas* (New Brunswick, N.J.: Rutgers University Press, 2001): 25–45. For a good example of how progressive Catholicism led directly to heightened feminist involvement, see Rose Marie Muraro with Philip Evanson, *Memórias de uma mulher brasileira* (Rio de Janeiro: Rosa dos Tempos, 1999). A leading Brazilian feminist, Muraro got her start in the 1960s in a progressive Catholic community under the leadership of Dom Hélder Câmara.

53. John Burdick, *Looking for God in Brazil* (Berkeley: University of California Press, 1993). Burdick challenged Diana Brown's conclusion that Umbanda promoted the status quo and its "whitening" discourse. He pointed out that his own conversations with black *umbandistas* led him to conclude that there were multiple discourses at work within the religion and that Brown had drawn her conclusions based on what light-skinned mediums asserted. See Diana D. G. Brown, *Umbanda: Religion and Politics in Urban Brazil* (New York: Columbia University Press, 1994).

54. Jean-Pierre Bastian, "The Metamorphosis," 35, 38. Much of the literature from Cuba and Puerto Rico questions Bastian's contentions regarding early Protestantism's radical liberalism. An often explicitly anticolonial scholarship has suggested since the 1970s that Protestants in the Hispanic Caribbean renounced what democratizing agendas they may have countenanced before the expansionist boom. Although Emilio García Pantojas,

Daniel R. Rodríguez, Margaret E. Crahan, and like-minded scholars recognize that Protestants figured prominently among the reformists and anticlerical revolutionaries agitating for change in Spain's last colonies, they argue that by the turn of the twentieth century, Protestants tended to legitimate the neocolonial designs of the United States. After 1898, missionaries from North America replaced the Cuban-born pastors who had established early Protestant communities in Havana and Matanzas. In Puerto Rico, new personnel took over flagging Anglican congregations of contract laborers from the British Caribbean and foreign-born plantation owners. The leaders in both islands aligned evangelization with a quest for "civilization" that proved decidedly undemocratic in practice. Emilio García Pantojas, *La iglesia protestante y la americanización de Puerto Rico* (Bayamón, P.R.: Prisa, 1976); Daniel R. Rodríguez, *La primera evangelización norteamericana en Puerto Rico* (Mexico City: Ediciones Borinquen, 1986); Margaret E. Crahan, "Religious Penetration and Nationalism in Cuba: U.S. Methodist Activities, 1898–1958," *Revista/Review Interamericana* 8:2 (Summer 1978): 204–24; and Margaret E. Crahan, "Protestantism in Cuba," Proceedings of the Pacific Coast Council on Latin American Studies, University of California, Los Angeles, 1982: 59–70.

55. Not all scholars who have shared in Martin's optimism have seen the Protestant boom as a force for ethical transformations. Ivan Vallier, for instance, saw competition itself as a decisive modernizing factor. In Chile, where communists and Pentecostals challenged the religious monopoly, the church was reportedly forced to specialize in religious activities, limiting its engagement with politics to Christian parties established outside the church. The episcopate also had to make concessions for lay participation and leadership. Vallier regarded these trends for "structural differentiation" as prerequisites for the establishment of a democratic order. Ivan Vallier, *Catholicism, Social Control, and Modernization in Latin America* (Englewood Cliffs, N.J.: Prentice-Hall, 1970).

56. Furthermore, as Sidney Mintz argues, the sugar factories in Caribbean fields existed in the seventeenth century, when factories were not even a gleam in the eye of Birmingham industrialists: Mintz, "Enduring Substances, Trying Theories." For a good summary of world systems theory and the myth of Western autogenesis, see Enrique Dussel, "Beyond Eurocentrism: The World-System and the Limits of Modernity," in *The Cultures of Globalization*, ed. Frederick Jameson and Masao Miyoshi (Durham, N.C.: Duke University Press, 2003).

57. Writing in the late 1980s from the context of the New Christian Right's political mobilization in the United States, Sara Diamond meticulously detailed the connections between the covert contra war against Nicaragua and a private aid network that funneled resources and personnel from such bedfellows as Pat Robertson's Christian Broadcasting Network, the Unification Church (often known as the Moonies), and the Catholic Knights of Malta, alongside national neoconservative lobbyists and paramilitary soldiers of fortune: Sara Diamond, *Spiritual Warfare: The Politics of the Christian Right* (Boston: South End Press, 1989), 161–81. Robertson had already cut his teeth on the brief but bloody Guatemalan presidency of Efraín Ríos Montt, a convert of the Gospel Outreach mission in California and leader in its affiliated El Verbo church of Guatemala City. Christian aid projects ranged from CBN's $3 million donation to the Nicaraguan Patriotic Association to "shoeboxes for liberty," small packages of candy, toiletries, and encouraging messages sent from U.S. churchgoers to contras encamped on the Honduran border: Diamond, *Spiritual Warfare*, 171, 173.

58. Steve Brouwer, Paul Gifford, and Susan D. Rose, *Exporting the American Gospel: Global Christian Fundamentalism* (New York: Routledge, 1996), 11. To see the loss to their analysis, it is instructive to place Brouwer et al.'s account of the role of U.S.-based religious

broadcasting alongside that of Vásquez and Marquardt in Manuel A. Vásquez and Marie Friedmann Marquardt, *Globalizing the Sacred: Religion Across the Americas* (New Brunswick, N.J., and London: Rutgers University Press, 2003), 197–222. Vásquez and Marquardt coined the term "glocalization" to underscore the importance of local understandings and uses of even the most global processes and products.

59. Brouwer, Gifford, and Rose, *Exporting the American Gospel*, 11.

60. The Boeing example, from 1994, appears in William Greider, *One World, Ready or Not: The Manic Logic of Global Capitalism* (New York: Simon & Schuster, 1997), 125. We are not suggesting that recent globalization alone has spawned transnational analysis of religion and culture. The transnational turn has deep intellectual and political precedents, particularly in the Caribbean. See, for example, Mintz, "Enduring Substances, Trying Theories." Mintz makes a persuasive argument that accelerated globalization has meant that the rest of the world may now be catching up to processes of modernity—especially immigration and hybridity—that have long held sway in the Caribbean. Micol Seigel provides a particularly lucid summary of the transnational turn's debt to anticolonial intellectuals like Franz Fanon and world systems theorists like Eric Williams, as well as a concise explanation of the differences between transnational and comparative history; see her "Beyond Compare: Comparative Method after the Transnational Turn," *Radical History Review* (December 2004): 62–89. For an introduction to transnational religious studies focused on the contemporary period, see Susanne Hoeber Rudolph and James Piscatori, eds., *Transnational Religion and Fading States* (Boulder, Colo.: Westview Press, 1997). Pamela Voekel, Bethany Moreton, and Michael Jo discuss transnational history and religion in their "Vaya con Diós: Religion and the Transnational History of the Americas," *History Compass* 5:5 (2007): 1604–39. A good example of the transnational as a unit of analysis in religious history is Derek Williams, "Networks of Catholic Journalism in Nineteenth-Century Latin America," paper presented at the Tepoztlán Institute for the Transnational History of the Americas, Tepoztlán, Mexico, July–August 2006.

61. See Anthony M. Stevens-Arroyo and Ana María Díaz-Stevens, *An Enduring Flame: Studies on Latino Popular Religiosity* (New York: Bindner Center for Western Hemisphere Studies, 1994); Nélida Agosto Cintrón, *Religión y cambio social en Puerto Rico (1898–1940)* (Río Piedras, P.R.: Ediciones Huracán, 1996); and Elizabeth Carrillo and Minerva Rodríguez, *Pentecostalismo y espiritismo* (Havana: Editorial Academia, 1997).

62. Jason M. Yaremko, *U.S. Protestant Missions in Cuba: From Independence to Castro* (Gainesville: University of Florida Press, 2000), 132. The doyen of Cuban studies, Louis A. Pérez Jr., has an interesting take on the debate on Protestantism's foreign origins. He has argued that Protestantism attracted the middle classes because they perceived the faith as compatible with modernity and associated it with the prestige of the United States. Pérez has shown that activities, material culture, and values derived from the United States were constitutive of Cuban nationalism. Among other factors, things American came to signify the rejection of Spanish colonialism. See Louis A. Pérez Jr., "North American Protestant Missionaries in Cuba and the Culture of Hegemony, 1898–1920," in his *Essays on Cuban History* (Gainesville: University of Florida Press, 1995), pp. 53–72; and his *On Becoming Cuban* (Chapel Hill: University of North Carolina Press, 2000).

63. Among other factors, Paul Vanderwood cites the influence of Natalie Zemon Davis and Jacques LeGoff on Latin Americanists, particularly on those specializing in Mexico. Paul Vanderwood, "Religion: Official, Popular, and Otherwise," 417.

64. Michael T. Taussig, *The Devil*.

Selected Bibliography

Abel, Christopher. *Health, Hygiene, and Sanitation in Latin America, 1870–1950*. London: Institute of Latin American Studies, University of London, 1996.

Abercrombie, Thomas. *Pathways of Memory and Power: Ethnography and History among an Andean People*. Madison: University of Wisconsin Press, 1998.

Adelman, Jeremy. *Frontier Development: Land, Labour, and Capital on the Wheatlands of Argentina and Canada, 1890–1914*. Oxford: The Clarendon Press, 1994.

———. *Sovereignty and Revolution in the Iberian Atlantic*. Princeton: Princeton University Press, 2006.

———, ed. *Colonial Legacies: The Problem of Persistence in Latin American History*. New York: Routledge, 1999.

Agostoni, Claudia. *Monuments of Progress: Modernization and Public Health in Mexico City, 1876–1910*. Calgary: University of Calgary Press, 2003.

Aguirre, Carlos. *Breve historia de la esclavitud en el Perú: Una herida que no deja de sangrar*. Lima: Fondo Editorial del Congreso del Perú, 2005.

Alchon, Suzanne Austin. *A Pest in the Land: New World Epidemics in a Global Perspective*. Albuquerque: University of New Mexico Press, 2003.

Alden, Dauril. *The Making of an Enterprise: The Society of Jesus in Portugal, Its Empire, and Beyond, 1540–1750*. Stanford, Calif.: Stanford University Press, 1996.

Alencastro, Luiz Felipe de. *O trato dos viventes. Formação do Brasil no Atlântico sul: Séculos XVI e XVII*. São Paulo: Companhia das Letras, 2000.

Alonso, Ana María. *Thread of Blood: Colonialism, Revolution and Gender on Mexico's Northern Frontier*. Tucson: University of Arizona Press, 1995.

Amaral, Samuel. *The Rise of Capitalism on the Pampas: The Estancias of Buenos Aires, 1785–1870*. New York: Cambridge University Press, 1998.

Amith, Jonathan D. *The Möbius Strip: A Spatial History of Colonial Society in Guerrero, Mexico*. Stanford, Calif.: Stanford University Press, 2005.

Andrews, George Reid. *Afro-Latin America, 1800–2000*. New York: Oxford University Press, 2004.

———. *Blacks and Whites in São Paulo, Brazil, 1888–1988*. Madison: University of Wisconsin Press, 1991.

Andrien, Kenneth J. "Economic Crisis, Taxes and the Quito Insurrection of 1765," *Past and Present* 129 (1990): 104–31.

Anna, Timothy. *Spain and the Loss of America*. Lincoln: University of Nebraska Press, 1983.

Annino, Antonio, ed. *Historia de las elecciones en Iberoamérica, siglo XIX*. Mexico City: Fondo de Cultura Económica, 1995.

Archer, Christon I., ed. *The Wars of Independence in Spanish America*. Wilmington, Del.: Scholarly Resources, 2000.

Archetti, Eduardo. *Masculinities: Football, Polo and the Tango in Argentina*. New York: Berg, 1999.

Armus, Diego, ed. *Disease in the History of Modern Latin America: From Malaria to AIDS*. Durham, N.C.: Duke University Press, 2003.

———. *La ciudad impura: Salud, tuberculosis y cultura en Buenos Aires, 1870–1950*. Buenos Aires: Edhasa, 2007 (forthcoming English version with Duke University Press).

Arrom, Silvia Marina. *The Women of Mexico City, 1790–1857*. Stanford, Calif.: Stanford University Press, 1985.

Baily, Samuel L. *Immigrants in the Lands of Promise: Italians in Buenos Aires and New York City, 1870–1914*. Ithaca: Cornell University Press, 1999.

Balderston, Daniel and Donna J. Guy, eds. *Sex and Sexuality in Latin America*. New York: New York University Press, 1997.

Balmori, Diana A., Stuart F. Voss, and Miles Wortman. *Notable Family Networks in Latin America*. Chicago: University of Chicago Press, 1984.

Barham, Bradford L., and Oliver T. Coomes. *Prosperity's Promise: The Amazon Rubber Boom and Distorted Economic Development*. Boulder, Colo.: Westview Press, 1996.

Barickman, B. J. *A Bahian Counterpoint: Sugar, Tobacco, Cassava, and Slavery in the Recôncavo, 1780–1860*. Stanford, Calif.: Stanford University Press, 1998.

Barman, Roderick J. *Brazil: The Forging of a Nation, 1798–1852*. Stanford, Calif.: Stanford University Press, 1988.

Barrán, José Pedro. *Medicina y sociedad en el Uruguay del novecientos*. Montevideo: Ediciones de la Banda Oriental, 1994.

Barsky, Osvaldo, ed. *Historia del capitalismo agrario pampeano*, Vol. 1: *La expansión ganadera hasta 1895*, by Osvando Barsky and Julio Djenderedjian; Vol. 2: *La vanguardia ganadera bonaerense, 1856–1900*, by Carmen Sesto. Buenos Aires: Universidad de Belgrano/Siglo Veintiuno, 2003–05.

Baskes, Jeremy. *Indians, Merchants, and Markets: A Reinterpretation of the* Repartimiento *and Spanish–Indian Economic Relations in Colonial Oaxaca, 1750–1821*. Stanford, Calif.: Stanford University Press, 2000.

Bastide, Roger. *The African Religions of Brazil*. Translated by Helen Sebba. Baltimore, Md.: Johns Hopkins University Press, 1978.

Bauer, Arnold J. *Goods, Power, History: Latin America's Material Culture*. Cambridge: Cambridge University Press, 2001.

Beattie, Peter M. *The Tribute of Blood: Army, Honor, Race, and Nation in Brazil, 1864–1945*. Durham, N.C.: Duke University Press, 2001.

Belmartino, Susana. *La atención médica argentina en el siglo XX: Instituciones y procesos*. Buenos Aires: Siglo XXI, 2005.

Benchimol, Jaime. *Do micróbios aos mosquitos: Febre amarela e a revoluçao pasteuriana no Brasil*. Rio de Janeiro: Fiocruz/UFJR, 1999.

Berco, Cristián. "Silencing the Unmentionable: Non-Reproductive Sex and the Creation of a Civilized Argentina." *The Americas* 53:3 (2002): 419–41.

Bergad, Laird W. *Cuban Rural Society in the Nineteenth Century: The Social and Economic History of Monoculture in Matanzas*. Princeton: Princeton University Press, 1990.

———. *Slavery and the Demographic and Economic History of Minas Gerais, Brazil, 1720–1888*. Cambridge: Cambridge University Press, 1999.

Bergad, Laird W., Fe Iglesias García, and María del Carmen Barcia. *The Cuban Slave Market, 1790–1880*. Cambridge, U.K.: Cambridge University Press, 1995.

Bergquist, Charles. *Labor in Latin America: Comparative Essays on Chile, Argentina, Venezuela, and Colombia*. Stanford, Calif.: Stanford University Press, 1986.

Besse, Susan K. *Restructuring Patriarchy: The Modernization of Gender Inequality in Brazil, 1914–1940*. Chapel Hill: University of North Carolina Press, 1996.

Bicalho, Maria Fernanda. *A cidade e o império: O Rio de Janeiro no século XVIII*. Rio de Janeiro: Civilização Brasileira, 2003.

Birn, Anne-Emanuelle. *Marriage of Convenience: Rockefeller International Health and Revolutionary Mexico*. Rochester, N.Y.: University of Rochester Press, 2006.

Blanchard, Peter. *Slavery and Abolition in Early Republican Peru*. Wilmington, Del.: Scholarly Resources, 1992.

Bliss, Katherine Elaine. *Compromised Positions: Prostitution, Public Health, and Gender Politics in Revolutionary Mexico City*. University Park: Penn State University Press, 2002.

Blum, Ann S. *Domestic Economies: Family, Work, and Welfare in Mexico City, 1884–1943*. Lincoln: University of Nebraska Press, 2010.

Bonfil Batalla, Guillermo. *México profundo: Una civilización negada*. Mexico City: Secretaría de Educación Pública/CIESAS, 1987.

Borges, Dain. *The Family in Bahia, Brazil, 1870–1945*. Stanford, Calif.: Stanford University Press, 1994.

Bortz, Jeffrey. *Industrial Wages in Mexico City, 1939–1975*. New York: Garland, 1987.

Bourgois, Philippe I. *Ethnicity at Work: Divided Labor on a Central American Banana Plantation*. Baltimore: Johns Hopkins University Press, 1989.

Boyer, Richard. *Lives of the Bigamists: Marriage, Family, and Community in Colonial Mexico*. Albuquerque: University of New Mexico Press, 1995.

Brading, David. *The First America: The Spanish Monarchy, Creole Patriots, and the Liberal State, 1492–1867*. Cambridge: Cambridge University Press, 1991.

Bragoni, Beatriz, ed. *Microanálisis: Ensayos de historiografía argentina*. Buenos Aires: Prometeo, 2004.

Brennan, James. P. *The Labor Wars in Córdoba, 1955–1976: Ideology, Work, and Labor Politics in an Argentine Industrial City*. Cambridge, Mass.: Harvard University Press, 1994.

Brennan, James P., and Mónica B. Gordillo. *Córdoba rebelde: El Cordobazo, el clasismo y la movilización social, 1969–1976*. Buenos Aires: Editorial de la Campana, 2008.

Brockington, Lolita Gutiérrez. *The Leverage of Labor: Managing the Cortés Haciendas in Tehuantepec, 1588–1688*. Durham, N.C.: Duke University Press, 1989.

Bulmer-Thomas, Victor, John H. Coatsworth, and Roberto Cortés Conde. *The Cambridge Economic History of Latin America*. 2 vols. Cambridge, U.K.: Cambridge University Press, 2006.

Burkhart, L. *The Slippery Earth: Nahua-Christian Moral Dialogue in Sixteenth-Century Mexico*. Tucson, University of Arizona Press, 1989.

Butler, Kim D. *Freedoms Given, Freedoms Won: Afro-Brazilians in Post-Abolition São Paulo and Salvador*. New Brunswick: Rutgers University Press, 1998.

Cabral de Mello, Evaldo. *A fronda dos mazombos*. São Paulo: Companhia das Letras, 1995.

———. *O Negócio do Brasil: Portugal, os Países Baixos e o Nordeste, 1641–1669*. Rio de Janeiro: Topbooks, 1998.

Cadena, Marisol de la. *Indigenous Mestizos: The Politics of Race and Culture in Cuzco, 1919–1991*. Durham, N.C.: Duke University Press, 2000.

Calero, Luis Fernando. *Chiefdoms under Siege: Spain's Rule and Native Adaptation in the Southern Colombian Andes, 1535–1700*. Albuquerque: University of New Mexico Press, 1997.

Cañizares-Esguerra, Jorge. *How to Write the History of the New World: Histories, Epistemologies, and Identities in the Eighteenth-Century Atlantic World*. Stanford, Calif.: Stanford University Press, 2001.

———. *Puritan Conquistadors: Iberianizing the Atlantic, 1550–1700*. Stanford, Calif.: Stanford University Press, 2006.

Cardoso, Ciro F. S., and Héctor Pérez Brignoli. *Historia económica de América Latina*, 2 vols. Barcelona: Crítica, 1984.

Carneiro da Cunha, Manuela, ed. *História dos índios do Brasil*. São Paulo: Companhia das Letras, 1992.

Carrara, Sergio. "Estrategias anticoloniales: Sífilis, raza e identidad nacional en el Brasil de Entreguerras." In *Avatares de la Medicalización en América Latina, 1870–1970*, ed. Diego Armus, 171–195. Buenos Aires: Lugar, 2005.

Carroll, Patrick J. *Blacks in Colonial Vera Cruz: Race, Ethnicity, and Regional Development*. Austin: University of Texas Press, 1991.

Carvalho Soares, Mariza de. *Devotos de cor: Identidade étnica, religiosidade e escravidão no Rio de Janeiro, século XVIII*. Rio de Janeiro: Civilização Brasileira, 2000.

Carvalho, José Murilo de. *Teatro de sombras: A política imperial*. São Paulo: Vértice, 1988.

Carvalho, Marcus J. M. *Liberdade: Rotinas e rupturas do escravismo, Recife, 1822–1850*. Recife: UFPE, 2002.

Castañeda, Carmen. *Violación, estupro y sexualidad: Nueva Galicia 1790–1821*. Guadalajara: Hexágono, 1989.

Castelnau-L'Estoile, Charlotte. *Les ouvriers d'une vigne stérile: Les jésuites et la conversion des Indien au Brasil*. Lisbon/Paris: Centre Culturel Calouste Gulbenkian, 2000.

Castro Gomes, Angela M. de. *A invenção do trabalhismo*. Rio de Janeiro: IUPERL/Vértice, 1988.

Castro Santos, Luiz Antonio de. "Poder, ideologias e saúde no Brasil da Primeira República: Ensaio de sociología histórica." In *Cuidar, controlar, curar: Ensaios históricos sobre saúde e doença na América Latina e Caribe*, ed. Gilberto Hochman and Diego Armus, 249–293. Rio de Janeiro: Fiocruz, 2004.

Caulfield, Sueann. *In Defense of Honor: Sexual Morality, Modernity, and Nation in Early Twentieth-Century Brazil*. Durham, N.C.: Duke University Press, 2000.

Cecelia F. Klein, ed. *Gender in Pre-Hispanic America*. Washington, D.C.: Dumbarton Oaks Research Library and Collection, 2001.

Cevallos-Candau, Francisco Javier, Jeffrey A. Cole, Nina M. Scott, and Nicomedes Suárez-Araúz. *Coded Encounters. Writing, Gender, and Ethnicity in Colonial Latin America*. Amherst: University of Massachusetts Press, 1994.

Chalhoub, Sidney. *Cidade febril: Cortiços e epidemias na Corte Imperial*. São Paulo: Companhia das Letras, 1996.

———. *Visões da liberdade: Uma história das últimas décadas da escravidão na Corte*. São Paulo: Companhia das Letras, 1990.

Chambers, Sarah C. *From Subjects to Citizens: Honor, Gender, and Politics in Arequipa, Peru, 1780–1854*. University Park: Penn State University Press, 1999.

Chance, John. *Race and Class in Colonial Oaxaca*. Stanford, Calif.: Stanford University Press, 1978.

Chasteen, John C. *Americanos: Latin America's Struggle for Independence*. Oxford: Oxford University Press, 2008.

———. *Heroes on Horseback: The Life and Times of the Last Gaucho Caudillos*. Albuquerque: University of New Mexico Press, 1995.

Chevalier, François. *La formación de los latifundios en México: Haciendas y sociedad en los siglos XVI, XVII y XVIII*. 3rd ed. Mexico City: Fondo de Cultura Económica, 1999.

Chiaramonte, José Carlos. *Ciudades, provincias, estados: Orígenes de la nación argentina (1800–1846)*. Buenos Aires: Ariel, 1997.

Chuchiak, John. "Secrets Behind the Screen: *Solicitantes* in the Colonial Diocese of Yucatan and the Yucatec Maya, 1570–1785." In *Religion in New Spain*, ed. Susan Schroeder and Stafford Poole, 83–109. Albuquerque: University of New Mexico Press, 2007.

———. "The Sins of the Fathers: Franciscan Friars, Parish Priests, and the Sexual Conquest of the Yucatec Maya, 1545–1808." *Ethnohistory* 54:1 (2007): 71–129.

Clarence-Smith, William Gervase, and Steven C. Topik, eds. *The Global Coffee Economy in Africa, Asia and Latin America, 1500–1989*. Cambridge: Cambridge University Press, 2003.

Coatsworth, John H. "Inequality, Institutions, and Economic Growth in Latin America." *Journal of Latin American Studies* 40 (2008): 545–69.

———. "Structures, Endowments, and Institutions in the Economic History of Latin America." *Latin American Research Review* 40:3 (2005): 126–44.

Coatsworth, John H., and Alan M. Taylor. *Latin America and the World Economy since 1800*. Cambridge, Mass.: Harvard University/David Rockefeller Center for Latin American Studies, 1998.

Coatsworth, John H., and Jeffrey G. Williamson. "Always Protectionist? Latin American Tariffs from Independence to Great Depression." *Journal of Latin American Studies* 36:2 (2004): 205–32.

Cook, Noble David. *Demographic Collapse: Indian Peru, 1520–1620*. New York: Cambridge University Press, 1981.

Cook, Noble David, and W. George Lovell, eds. *Secret Judgments of God: Old World Disease in Colonial Spanish America*. Norman: University of Oklahoma Press, 1991.

Cope, Douglas. *The Limits of Racial Domination*. Madison: University of Wisconsin Press, 1994.

Cortés Conde, Roberto, and Marcela Harriague. *Estimaciones del Producto Bruto Interno de Argentina, 1875–1935*. Buenos Aires: Universidad de San Andrés, 1994.

Cortés Conde, Roberto, and Shane J. Hunt. *The Latin American Economies: Growth and the Export Sector, 1880–1930*. New York: Holmes & Meier, 1985.

Cueto, Marcos. *Cold War, Deadly Fevers: Malaria Eradication in Mexico, 1955–1975*. Baltimore: Johns Hopkins University Press, 2007.

———. *El regreso de las epidemias. Salud y sociedad en el Perú del siglo XX*. Lima: Instituto de Estudios Peruanos, 1997.

Davis, Darién J., ed. *Beyond Slavery: The Multilayered Legacy of Africans in Latin America and the Caribbean*. Lanham, Md.: Rowman & Littlefield, 2007.

Dean, Carolyn. *Inka Bodies and the Body of Christ: Corpus Christi in Colonial Cuzco, Peru*. Durham, N.C.: Duke University Press, 1999.

Dean, Warren. *With Broadax and Firebrand: The Destruction of the Brazilian Atlantic Forest*. Berkeley: University of California Press, 1995.

Deans-Smith, Susan. *Bureaucrats, Planters, and Workers: The Making of the Tobacco Monopoly in Bourbon Mexico*. Austin: University of Texas Press, 1992.

Deeds, Susan. *Defiance and Deference in Mexico's Colonial North: Indians under Spanish Rule in Nueva Vizcaya*. Austin: University of Texas Press, 2003.

Deere, Carmen Diana, and Magdalena León de Leal. *Empowering Women: Land and Property Rights in Latin America*. Pittsburgh: Pittsburgh University Press, 2001.

Della Paolera, Gerardo, and Alan M. Taylor, eds. *A New Economic History of Argentina*. Cambridge, U.K.: Cambridge University Press, 2003.

DeShazo, Peter. *Urban Workers and Labor Unions in Chile, 1902–1927*. Madison: University of Wisconsin Press, 1983.

Deutsch, Sandra McGee. *Las Derechas: The Extreme Right in Argentina, Brazil, and Chile, 1890–1939*. Stanford, Calif.: Stanford University Press, 1999.

Di Stefano, Roberto. *El púlpito y la plaza: Clero, sociedad y política de la Monarquía Católica a la República Rosista*. Buenos Aires: Siglo Veintiuno, 2004.

Díaz, Arlene J. *Female Citizens, Patriarchy and the Law in Venezuela, 1786–1904*. Lincoln: University of Nebraska Press, 2004.

Díaz, María Elena. *The Virgin, the King, and the Royal Slaves of El Cobre: Negotiating Freedom in Colonial Cuba, 1670–1780*. Stanford, Calif.: Stanford University Press, 2000.

Dore, Elizabeth. *Myths of Modernity: Peonage and Patriarchy in Nicaragua*. Durham, N.C.: Duke University Press, 2006.

Dueñas Vargas, Guiomar. *Los hijos del pecado: Ilegitimidad y vida familiar en la Santafé de Bogotá colonial*. Bogotá: Editorial Universidad Nacional, 1997.

Duncan, Kenneth, and Ian Rutledge, eds. *Land and Labour in Latin America: Essays on the Development of Agrarian Capitalism in the Nineteenth and Twentieth Centuries*. Cambridge: Cambridge University Press, 1977.

Edelman, Marc. *The Logic of the Latifundio: The Large Estates of Northwestern Costa Rica Since the Late Nineteenth Century*. Stanford, Calif.: Stanford University Press, 1992.

Ehrick, Christine. *The Shield of the Weak: Feminism and the State in Uruguay, 1903–1933*. Albuquerque: University of New Mexico Press, 2005.

Escobar O., Antonio, ed. *Indio, Nación y Comunidad en el México del Siglo XIX*. Mexico City: Centro de Estudios Mexicanos y Centroamericanos/Centro de Investigaciones y Estudios Superiores en Antropología Social, 1993.

Escosura, Leandro Prados de la. "Economic Performance in Post-Independence Latin America." *Journal of Latin American Studies* 41 (2009): 279–307.

Estrada Urroz, Rosalina. *Del telar a la cadena de montaje: La condición obrera en Puebla, 1940–1976*. Puebla, Mexico: Universidad Autónoma de Puebla, 1997.

Farnsworth-Alvear, Ann. *Dulcinea in the Factory: Myths, Morals, Men, and Women in Colombia's Industrial Experiment*. Durham, N.C.: Duke University Press, 2000.

Farriss, Nancy. *Maya Society under Colonial Rule: The Collective Enterprise of Survival*. Princeton: Princeton University Press, 1984.

Fausto, Boris. *Trablho urbano e conflito social*. São Paulo: DIFEL, 1986.

Ferrer, Ada. *Insurgent Cuba: Race, Nation, and Revolution, 1868–1898*. Chapel Hill: University of North Carolina Press, 1999.

Ferry, Robert J. *The Colonial Elite of Early Caracas: Formation and Crisis, 1567–1767*. Berkeley: University of California Press, 1989.

Fico, Carlos. *Reinventando o otimismo: Ditadura, propaganda e imaginário social no Brasil*. Rio de Janeiro: FGV, 1997.

Fields, Sherry. *Pestilence and Headcolds: Encountering Illness in Colonial Mexico*. New York: Columbia University Press, 2009.

Findlay, Eileen A. Suárez. *Imposing Decency: The Politics of Sexuality and Race in Puerto Rico, 1870–1920*. Durham, N.C.: Duke University Press, 1999.

Fischer, Brodwyn. *A Poverty of Rights: Citizenship and Inequality in Twentieth-Century Rio de Janeiro*. Stanford, Calif.: Stanford University Press, 2008.

Florentino, Manolo, and José Roberto Góes. *A paz das senzalas: Famílias escravas e tráfico atlântico, Rio de Janeiro, c. 1790–c. 1850*. Rio de Janeiro: Civilização Brasileira, 1997.

Florescano, Enrique. *Memoria mexicana: Ensayo sobre la reconstrucción del pasado, época prehispánica–1821*. Mexico City: J. Mortiz, 1987.

———. *Precios del maíz y crisis agrícolas en México (1708–1810)*. Mexico City: El Colegio de México, 1969.

Fonseca, Cláudia Damasceno. *Des terres aux villes de l'or*. Paris: Centre Cultural Calouste Gulbenkian, 2003.

Font, Mauricio A., and Alfonso W. Quiroz, eds. *Cuban Counterpoints: The Legacy of Fernando Ortiz*. Lanham, Md.: Lexington Books, 2005.

Forment, Carlos A. *Democracy in Latin America, 1760–1900: Civic Selfhood and Public Life in Mexico and Peru*. Chicago: University of Chicago Press, 2003.

Fortes, Alexander et al. *Na luta por direitos: Estudos recentes em história social do trabalho*, Campinas, Brazil: Unicamp, 1999.

Fradkin, Raúl, ed. *La historia agraria del Río de la Plata colonial*. 2 vols. Buenos Aires: Centro Editor de América Latina, 1993.

Fradkin, Raúl, and Juan Carlos Garavaglia, eds. *En busca de un tiempo perdido: La economía de Buenos Aires en el pais de la abundancia 1750–1865*. Buenos Aires: Prometeo, 2004.

Fragoso, João. *Homens da grossa aventura: Acumulação e hierarquia na praça mercantile do Rio de Janeiro, 1790–1830*. 2nd ed. Rio de Janeiro: Civilização Brasileira, 1998.

Fragoso, João, Maria Fernanda Bicalho, and Maria de Fátima Gouvêa, eds. *O antigo regime nos trópicos: A dinâmica imperial portuguesa (séculos XVI–XVIII)*. Rio de Janeiro: Civilização Brasileira, 2001.

French, John D. *Drowning in Laws: Labor Law and Brazilian Political Culture*. Chapel Hill: University of North Carolina Press, 2004.

———. *The Brazilian Workers' ABC: Class Conflict and Alliances in Modern São Paulo*. Chapel Hill: University of North Carolina Press, 1992.

French, William E. *A Peaceful and Working People: Manners, Morals and Class Formation in Northern Mexico*. Albuquerque: University of New Mexico Press, 1996.

French, William E., and Katherine Elaine Bliss. *Gender, Sexuality and Power in Latin America Since Independence*. Lanham, Md.: Rowen & Littlefield, 2007.

Freyre, Gilberto. *The Masters and the Slaves: A Study in the Development of Brazilian Civilization*, translated by Samuel Putnam. New York: A.A. Knopf, [1933] 1944.

Fuente, Alejandro de la. *A Nation for All: Race, Inequality, and Politics in Twentieth-Century Cuba*. Chapel Hill: University of North Carolina Press, 2001.

Furtado, Júnia F. *Chica da Silva e o contratador de diamantes: O outro lado do mito*. São Paulo: Companhia das Letras, 2003. There is an English edition by Cambridge University Press.

Ganson, Barbara. *The Guaraní under Spanish Rule in the Rio de la Plata*. Stanford, Calif.: Stanford University Press, 2003.

Garavaglia, Juan Carlos. *Pastores y labradores de Buenos Aires: Una historia agraria de la campaña bonaerense 1700–1830*. Buenos Aires: Ediciones de la Flor, 1999.

Garavaglia, Juan Carlos, and Jorge D. Gelman. "Rural History of the Río de la Plata, 1600–1850: Results of a Historiographical Renaissance." *Latin American Research Review* 30:3 (1995): 75–105.

García Ugarte, Marta Eugenia. *Hacendados y rancheros queretanos (1780–1920)*. Mexico City: Consejo Nacional para la Cultura y las Artes, 1992.

Garner, Richard L. and Spiro E. Stefanou. *Economic Growth and Change in Bourbon Mexico*. Gainesville: University Press of Florida, 1993.

Geggus, David P., ed. *The Impact of the Haitian Revolution in the Atlantic World*. Charleston: University of South Carolina Press, 2001.

Gelman, Jorge D. *Campesinos y estancieros: Una región del Río de la Plata a fines de la época colonial*. Buenos Aires: Libros del Riel, 1998.

Gibson, Charles. *The Aztecs under Spanish Rule: A History of the Indians of the Valley of Mexico, 1519–1810*. Stanford, Calif.: Stanford University Press, 1964.

Golte, Jürgen. *Repartos y rebeliones: Túpac Amaru y las contradicciones de la economía colonial*. Lima: Instituto de Estudios Peruanos, 1980.

Gonzalbo Aizpuru, Pilar, and Cecilia Rabell Romero. *Familia y vida privada en la historia de Iberoamérica*. Mexico City: El Colegio de México/UNAM, 1996.

Gonzales, Michael J. *Plantation Agricultura and Social Control in Northern Peru, 1875–1933.* Austin: University of Texas Press, 1985.

González Marmolejo, Jorge René. *Sexo y confesión: La iglesia y la penitencia en los siglos XVIII y XIX en la Nueva España.* Mexico City: Conaculta/INAH/Plaza y Valdés, 2002.

Gootenberg, Paul. "Between a Rock and a Softer Place: Reflections on Some Recent Economic History of Latin America." *Latin American Research Review* 39:2 (2004): 239–57.

Gordillo, Mónica. *Córdoba en los '60: La experiencia del sindicalismo combativo.* Córdoba, Argentina: Universidad Nacional de Córdoba, 1996.

Gordon, Edmund T. *Disparate Diasporas: Identity and Politics in an African Nicaraguan Community.* Austin: University of Texas Press, 1998.

Graham, Richard. *Independence in Latin America: A Comparative Approach.* New York: McGraw-Hill, 1972.

———. *Patronage and Politics in Nineteenth-Century Brazil.* Stanford, Calif.: Stanford University Press, 1990.

———, ed. *The Idea of Race in Latin America, 1870–1940.* Austin: University of Texas Press, 1990.

Graubart, Karen B. *With our Labor and Sweat: Indigenous Women and the Formation of Colonial Society in Peru, 1550–1700.* Stanford, Calif.: Stanford University Press, 2007.

Green, James N. *Beyond Carnival: Male Homosexuality in Twentieth-Century Brazil.* Chicago: University of Chicago Press, 1999.

Gruzinski, Serge. *The Conquest of Mexico: The Incorporation of Indian Societies into the Western World, 16th–18th Centuries.* Cambridge: Polity Press, 1993.

Guardino, Peter F. *Peasants, Politics, and the Formation of Mexico's National State: Guerrero, 1800–1857.* Stanford, Calif.: Stanford University Press, 1996.

Gudmundson, Lowell. *Costa Rica before Coffee: Society and Economy on the Eve of the Export Boom.* Baton Rouge: Louisiana State University Press, 1986.

Guerra, François-Xavier. *Modernidad e independencias: Ensayos sobre las revoluciones hispánicas.* Mexico City: Fondo de Cultura Económica, 1993.

Guerrero, Andrés. *De la economía a las mentalidades.* Quito: El Conejo, 1991.

Gutiérrez, Ramón A. *When Jesus Came, the Corn Mothers Went Away: Marriage, Sexuality and Power in New Mexico, 1500–1846.* Stanford, Calif.: Stanford University Press, 1991.

Gutmann, Matthew. *The Meanings of Macho: Being a Man in Mexico City.* Berkeley: University of California Press, 1996.

Guy, Donna J. *Sex and Danger in Buenos Aires: Prostitution, Family and Nation in Argentina.* Lincoln: University of Nebraska Press, 1991.

———. *Women Build the Welfare State: Performing Charity, Creating Rights in Argentina, 1880–1955.* Durham, N.C.: Duke University Press, 2009.

Haber, Stephen H. "Industrial Concentration and the Capital Markets: A Comparative Study of Brazil, Mexico, and the United States, 1830–1930." *The Journal of Economic History* 51:3 (1991): 559–80.

———, ed. *How Latin America Fell Behind: Essays on the Economic Histories of Brazil and Mexico, 1800–1914.* Stanford, Calif.: Stanford University Press, 1997.

Haber, Stephen H., Noel Maurer, and Armando Razo. *The Politics of Property Rights: Political Instability, Credible Commitments, and Economic Growth in Mexico, 1876–1929.* Cambridge, U.K.: Cambridge University Press, 2003.

Hale, Charles R. *Resistance and Contradiction: Miskitu Indians and the Nicaraguan State, 1894–1987.* Stanford, Calif.: Stanford University Press, 1994.

Halperín Donghi, Tulio. *Reforma y disolución de los imperios ibéricos, 1750–1850.* Madrid: Alianza, 1985.

Hamnett, Brian. *Revolución y contrarrevolución en México y el Perú*. Mexico City: Fondo de Cultura Económica, 1978.

Hanley, Anne G. *Native Capital: Financial Institutions and Economic Development in São Paulo, Brazil, 1850–1920*. Stanford, Calif.: Stanford University Press, 2005.

Hart, Paul. *Bitter Harvest: The Social Transformation of Morelos, Mexico, and the Origins of the Zapatista Revolution, 1840–1910*. Albuquerque: University of New Mexico Press, 2005.

Hassig, Ross. *Trade, Tribute, and Transportation: The Sixteenth-Century Political Economy of the Valley of Mexico*. Norman: University of Oklahoma Press, 1985.

Helg, Aline. *Liberty and Equality in Caribbean Colombia, 1770–1835*. Chapel Hill: University of North Carolina Press, 2004.

——. *Our Rightful Share. The Afro-Cuban Struggle for Equality, 1886–1912*. Chapel Hill: University of North Carolina Press, 1995.

Herrera, Robinson. *Natives, Europeans, and Africans in Sixteenth-Century Santiago de Guatemala*. Austin: University of Texas Press, 2003.

Himmerich y Valencia, Robert. *The Encomenderos of New Spain, 1521–1555*. Austin: University of Texas Press, 1991.

Hoberman, Louisa Schell, and Susan Migden Socolow, eds. *The Countryside in Colonial Latin America*. Albuquerque: University of New Mexico Press, 1996.

Hochman, Gilberto, Nísia Trindade Lima, and Marcos Chor Maio. "The Paths of Eugenics in Brazil: Dilemmas of Miscegenation." In *The Oxford Handbook of the History of Eugenics*, ed. Allison Bashford and Philippa Levine. New York: Oxford University Press, 2010.

Hora, Roy. *The Landowners of the Argentine Pampas: A Social and Political History, 1860–1945*. New York: Oxford University Press, 2001.

Horowitz, Joel. *Argentine Unions, the State and the Rise of Perón, 1930–1945*, Berkeley: Institute of International Studies, 1990.

Horswell, Michael J. *Decolonizing the Sodomite: Queer Tropes of Sexuality in Colonial Andean Culture*. Austin: University of Texas Press, 2005.

Hughes, Jennifer. *Biography of a Mexican Crucifix: Lived Religion and Local Faith from the Conquest to the Present*. Oxford and New York: Oxford University Press, 2010.

Hunefeldt, Christine. *Liberalism in the Bedroom: Quarreling Spouses in Nineteenth-Century Lima*. University Park: Penn State University Press, 2000.

——. *Paying the Price of Freedom: Family and Labor among Lima's Slaves, 1800–1854*. Berkeley: University of California Press, 1994.

Hutchison, Elizabeth Quay. *Labors Appropriate to their Sex: Gender, Labor, and Politics in Urban Chile, 1900–1930*. Durham, N.C.: Duke University Press, 2001.

Instituto Nacional de Antropología e Historia. *Familia y sexualidad en Nueva España*. Mexico City: SEP/Fondo de Cultura Económica, 1982.

Jackson, Robert H. *Regional Markets and Agrarian Transformation in Bolivia: Cochabamba, 1539–1960*. Albuquerque: University of New Mexico Press, 1994.

Jacobsen, Nils. *Mirages of Transition: The Peruvian Altiplano, 1780–1930*. Berkeley: University of California Press, 1993.

James, Daniel. *Doña María's Story: Life History, Memory, and Political Identity*, Durham, N.C.: Duke University Press, 2000.

——. *Resistance and Integration: Peronism and the Argentine Working Class, 1946–1976*, Cambridge: Cambridge University Press, 1988.

Jancsó, István, and Kantor, Iris. *Festa: Cultura e sociabilidade na América portuguesa*. São Paulo: Hucitec, 2001.

Jiménez Pelayo, Agueda. *Haciendas y comunidades indígenas en el sur de Zacatecas*. Mexico City: Instituto Nacional de Antropología e Historia, 1989.

Johnson, Lyman L., and Enrique Tandeter, eds. *Essays on the Price History of Eighteenth-Century Latin America*. Albuquerque: University of New Mexico Press, 1990.

Johnson, Lyman L., and Zephyr Frank. "Cities and Wealth in the South Atlantic: Buenos Aires and Rio de Janeiro before 1860." *Comparative Studies in Society and History* 48:3 (2006): 634–68.

Kampwirth, Karen. *Radical Women in Latin America: Left and Right*. University Park: Penn State University Press, 2001.

Kantor, Iris. *Esquecidos e renascidos: Historiografia acadêmica luso-americana 1724–1759*. São Paulo: Hucitec/Centro de Estudos Bahianos, 2004.

Karasch, Mary C. *Slave Life in Rio de Janeiro, 1808–1850*. Princeton: Princeton University Press, 1987.

Katz, Friedrich, ed. *La servidumbre agraria en México en la época porfiriana*. Mexico City: Ediciones Era, 1984.

Kinsbruner, Jay. *Independence in Spanish America: Civil Wars, Revolutions, and Underdevelopment*. Albuquerque: University of New Mexico Press, 1994.

Klein, Herbert S. *African Slavery in Latin America and the Caribbean*. New York: Oxford University Press, 1986.

———. *Haciendas and 'Ayllus': Rural Society in the Bolivian Andes in the Eighteenth and Nineteenth Centuries*. Stanford, Calif.: Stanford University Press, 1993.

Klubock, Thomas M. *Contested Communities: Class, Gender, and Politics in Chile's El Teniente Copper Mine*. Durham, N.C.: Duke University Press, 1998.

Knight, Alan. *Mexico: The Colonial Era*. Cambridge: Cambridge University Press, 2002.

Kourí, Emilio. *A Pueblo Divided: Business, Property, and Community in Papantla, Mexico*. Stanford, Calif.: Stanford University Press, 2003.

Kramer, Wendy. *Encomienda Politics in Early Colonial Guatemala, 1524–1544: Dividing the Spoils*. Boulder, Colo.: Westview Press, 1994.

Kuznesof, Elizabeth Anne. *Household Economy and Urban Development, São Paulo, 1765–1836*. Boulder, Colo.: Westview Press, 1986.

Langfur, Hal. *The Forbidden Lands: Colonial Identity, Frontier Violence, and the Persistence of Brazil's Eastern Indians, 1750–1830*. Stanford, Calif.: Stanford University Press, 2006.

Langue, Frédérique. *Mines, terres et société a Zacatecas (Mexique) de la fin du XVIIe siècle a l'independence*. Paris: Publications de la Sorbonne, 1992.

Lara, Silvia H. *Campos da violencia: Esclavos e senhores na Capitania do Rio de Janeiro, 1750–1808*. Rio de Janeiro: Paz e Terra, 1988.

Larson, Brooke. "Andean Highland Peasants and the Trials of Nation Making During the Nineteenth Century." In *The Cambridge History of Native Peoples*, ed. Frank Salomon and Stuart Schwartz, Vol. III: Part 2, 558–703. Cambridge: Cambridge University Press, 1999.

———. *Cochabamba, 1550–1900: Colonialism and Agrarian Transformation in Bolivia*. Durham, N.C.: Duke University Press, [1988] 1998.

Lauderdale Graham, Sandra. *Caetana Says No: Women's Stories from a Brazilian Slave Society*. Cambridge: Cambridge University Press, 2002.

———. *House and Street: The Domestic World of Servants and Masters in Nineteenth-Century Rio de Janeiro*. Austin: University of Texas Press, 1992.

Lavallé, Bernard. *Amor y opresión en los Andes coloniales*. Lima: Instituto Francés de Estudios Andinos, 1999.

Lavrin, Asunción. *Brides of Christ: Conventual Life in Colonial Mexico*. Stanford, Calif.: Stanford University Press, 2008.

———. "Intimidades." In *Des Indes occidentales a l'Amérique latine*, ed. Alain Musset and Thomas Calvo, Vol. 1, 195–218. Paris: CEMCA/IHEAL, 1997.

———. *Women, Feminism, and Social Change in Argentina, Chile, and Uruguay, 1890–1940*. Lincoln: University of Nebraska Press, 1995.

———, ed. *Sexuality and Marriage in Colonial Latin America*. Lincoln: University of Nebraska Press, 1989.

Leal, Juan Felipe, and Mario Huacuja Rountree. *Economía y sistema de haciendas en México: La hacienda pulquera en el cambio, siglos XVIII, XIX y XX*. Mexico City: Ediciones Era, 1982.

Lear, John. *Workers, Neighbors, and Citizens: The Revolution in Mexico City*, Lincoln: University of Nebraska Press, 2001.

LeGrand, Catherine. *Frontier Expansion and Peasant Protest in Colombia, 1850–1936*. Albuquerque: University of New Mexico Press, 1986.

Lesser, Jeffrey. *Negotiating National Identity: Immigrants, Minorities, and the Struggle for Ethnicity in Brazil*. Durham, N.C.: Duke University Press, 1999.

Levine, Robert M. *Vale of Tears: Revisiting the Canudos Massacre in Northeastern Brazil, 1893–1897*. Berkeley: University of California Press, 1992.

Lewin, Linda. *Politics and Parentela in Paraíba: A Case Study of Family-Based Oligarchy in Brazil*. Princeton: Princeton University Press, 1987.

———. *Surprise Heirs: Illegitimacy, Patrimonial Rights, and Legal Nationalism in Luso-Brazilian Inheritance, 1750–1821*. Stanford, Calif.: Stanford University Press, 2003.

Lipsett-Rivera, Sonya. *To Defend Our Water with the Blood of Our Veins: The Struggle for Resources in Colonial Puebla*. Albuquerque: University of New Mexico Press, 1999.

Lobato, Marta Z. *La vida en las fábricas: Trabajo, protesta y política en una comunidad obrera, Berisso (1940–1970)*. Buenos Aires: Prometeo, 2001.

Lockhart, James. *The Nahuas after the Conquest: A Social and Cultural History of the Indians of Central Mexico, Sixteenth through Eighteenth Centuries*. Stanford, Calif.: Stanford University Press, 1992.

Londoño Vega, Patricia. *Religion, Culture, and Society in Colombia: Medellín and Antioquia, 1850–1930*. Oxford: Clarendon Press, 2002.

López Alonso, Moramay. "Growth with Inequality: Living Standards in Mexico, 1850–1950." *Journal of Latin American Studies* 39:1 (2007): 81–105.

López Austin, Alfredo. *Hombre-Dios: Religión y política en el mundo nahuatl*. Mexico City: UNAM, 1989.

López de Albornoz, Cristina. *Los dueños de la tierra: Economía, sociedad y poder, Tucumán, 1770–1820*. Tucumán: Universidad Nacional de Tucumán, 2003.

Luna, Francisco Vidal, and Herbert S. Klein. *Slavery and the Economy of São Paulo, 1750–1850*. Stanford, Calif.: Stanford University Press, 2003.

Lynch, John. *The Spanish American Revolutions, 1808–1826*. New York: W.W. Norton, 1973, 2nd ed. 1986.

MacCormack, Sabine. *Religion in the Andes: Visions and Images in Early Colonial Peru*. Princeton, N.J.: Princeton University Press, 1991.

Machado, Maria Helena P. T. *O plano e o pânico: Os movimentos sociais na década da abolição*. São Paulo: EDUSP/Rio de Janeiro: EDUFRJ, 1994.

Mallon, Florencia E. *Courage Tastes of Blood: The Mapuche Community of Nicolás Ailío and the Chilean State, 1906–2001*. Durham, N.C.: Duke University Press, 2005.

———. *Peasant and Nation: The Making of Postcolonial Mexico and Peru.* Berkeley: University of California Press, 1995.
Mandrini, Raúl, and Andrea Reguera. *Huellas en la tierra: Indios, agricultores y hacendados en la pampa bonaerense.* Tandil: Instituto de Estudios Histórico-Sociales, 1993.
Mannarelli, María Emma. *Hechiceras, beatas y expósitas: Mujeres y poder inquisitorial en Lima.* Lima: Ediciones del Congreso del Perú, 1999.
———. *Private Passions and Public Sins: Men and Women in Seventeenth-Century Lima.* Albuquerque: University of New Mexico Press, 2007.
Manrique, Nelson. *Campesinado y nación: Las guerrillas indígenas en la guerra con Chile.* Lima: Ital-Perú-C.I.C., 1981.
Marrero, Leví. *Cuba, economía y sociedad,* 15 vols. Rio Piedras, P.R.: Editorial San Juan, 1972.
Martin, Cheryl E. *Governance and Society in Colonial Mexico: Chihuahua in the Eighteenth Century.* Stanford, Calif.: Stanford University Press, 1996.
Martínez, Aída, and Pablo Rodríguez, eds. *Placer, dinero y pecado: Historia de la prostitución en Colombia.* Bogotá: Aguilar, 2002.
Martínez-Alier, Verena. *Marriage, Class and Colour in Nineteenth-Century Cuba: A Study of Racial Attitudes and Sexual Values in a Slave Society.* Ann Arbor: University of Michigan Press, 1974.
Mattos de Castro, Hebe M. *Das cores do silêncio: Os significados da liberdade no sudeste escravista,* 2d ed. Rio de Janeiro: Nova Fronteira, 1998.
Maurer, Noel. *The Power and the Money: The Mexican Financial System, 1876–1932.* Stanford, Calif.: Stanford University Press, 2002.
Maxwell, Kenneth R. *Conflicts and Conspiracies: Brazil and Portugal, 1750–1808.* Cambridge: Cambridge University Press, 1973.
Mayo, Carlos. *Estancia y sociedad en la pampa (1740–1820).* Buenos Aires: Biblos, 1995.
McCaa, Robert. *Marriage and Fertility in Chile: Demographic Turning Points in the Petorca Valley, 1840–1976.* Boulder, Colo.: Westview Press, 1983.
McCann, Bryan. *Hello, Hello Brazil: Popular Music in the Making of Modern Brazil.* Durham, N.C.: Duke University Press, 2004.
McCreery, David. *Rural Guatemala, 1760–1940.* Stanford, Calif.: Stanford University Press, 1994.
Meisel, Adolfo, and Margarita Vega. "The Biological Standard of Living (and Its Convergence) in Colombia, 1870–2003: A Tropical Success Story." *Economics and Human Biology* 5:1 (2007): 100–22.
Mello e Souza, Laura de. *O sol e a sombra: Política e administração na América portuguesa do século XVIII.* São Paulo: Compañía das Letras, 2006.
———. *The Devil in the Land of the Holy Cross.* Austin: University of Texas Press, 2003 (originally published as *O diablo e a terra da Santa Cruz,* São Paulo: Compañía das Letras, 1986).
Mello e Souza, Laura de, and Vera Lúcia Amaral Ferlini. *Modos de governar.* São Paulo: Alameda, 2005.
Melville, Elinor G. K. *A Plague of Sheep: Environmental Consequences of the Conquest of Mexico.* Cambridge: Cambridge University Press, 1994.
Mesquita Samara, Eni de. *A família brasileira.* São Paulo: Brasiliense, 1983.
Metcalf, Alida C. *Family and Frontier in Colonial Brazil: Santana de Parnaíba, 1580–1822.* Berkeley: University of California Press, 1992.
———. *Go-Betweens and the Colonization of Brazil, 1500–1600.* Austin: University of Texas Press, 2005.

Meyer, Jean. *Problemas campesinos y revueltas agrarias (1821–1910)*. Mexico City: Secretaría de Educación Pública, 1973.
Milanich, Nara. *Children of Fate: Childhood, Class, and the State in Chile, 1850–1930*. Durham, N.C.: Duke University Press, 2009.
Miller, Shawn. *Fruitless Trees: Portuguese Conservation and Brazil's Colonial Timber*. Stanford, Calif.: Stanford University Press, 2000.
Miller, Simon. *Landlords and Haciendas in Modernizing Mexico: Essays in Radical Reappraisal*. Amsterdam: CEDLA, 1995.
Mills, Kenneth. *Idolatry and its Enemies: Colonial Andean Religion and Extirpation, 1640–1750*. Princeton, N.J.: Princeton University Press, 1997.
Miño Grijalva, Manuel. *El mundo novohispano: Población, ciudades y economía, siglos XVII y XVIII*. Mexico City: El Colegio de México, 2001.
Mintz, Sidney. 1986. *Sweetness and Power: The Place of Sugar in Modern History*. New York: Penguin, 1986.
Molyneaux, Maxine, and Elizabeth Dore, eds. *The Hidden Histories of Gender and the State in Latin America*. Durham, N.C.: Duke University Press, 2000.
Monteiro, John. *Negros da terra: Índios e bandeirantes nas origens de São Paulo*. São Paulo: Companhia das Letras, 1994.
Moore, Robin Dale. *Nationalizing Blackness: Afrocubanismo and Artistic Revolution in Havana, 1920–1940*. Pittsburgh: University of Pittsburgh Press, 1997.
Moreira, Paulo Roberto S. *Os cativos e os homens de bem: Experiências negras no espaço urbano*. Porto Alegre, Brazil: EST, 2003.
Moritz Schwarcz, Lilia. *The Emperor's Beard: Dom Pedro II and the Tropical Monarchy of Brazil*. New York: Hill and Wang, 2004.
Mott, Luiz R. B. *Escravidão, homosexualidade e demonologia*. São Paulo: Icone, 1988.
Mott, Luiz. *Rosa Egipcíaca: Uma santa africana no Brasil*. Rio de Janeiro: Bertrand, 1993.
Motta, José Flávio. *Corpos escravos, vontades livres: Posse de cativos e família escrava em Bananal (1801–1829)*. São Paulo: FAPESP/Annablume, 1999.
Moya, José C. *Cousins and Strangers: Spanish Immigrants in Buenos Aires, 1850–1930*. Berkeley: University of California Press, 1998.
Muniz de Albuquerque Jr., Durval. *A invenção do Nordeste e outras artes*. Recife: Massangana, 2001.
Myers, Kathleen Ann. *Neither Saints nor Sinners: Writing the Lives of Women in Spanish America*. New York: Oxford University Press, 2003.
Naro, Nancy P. *A Slave's Place, a Master's World: Fashioning Dependency in Rural Brazil*. London: Continuum, 2000.
Naveda Chávez-Hita, Adriana. *Esclavos negros en las haciendas azucareras de Córdoba, Veracruz, 1690–1830*. Xalapa, Mexico: Universidad Veracruzana, Centro de Investigaciones Históricas, 1987.
Nazzari, Muriel. *Disappearance of the Dowry: Women, Families, and Social Change in São Paulo, Brazil, 1600–1900*. Stanford, Calif.: Stanford University Press, 1991.
Needell, Jeffrey D. *The Party of Order: The Conservatives, the State, and Slavery in the Brazilian Monarchy, 1831–1871*. Stanford, Calif.: Stanford University Press, 2006.
Newson, Linda A. *Life and Death in Early Colonial Ecuador*. Norman: University of Oklahoma Press, 1995.
Nickel, Herbert J. 1997. *El peonaje en las haciendas mexicanas: Interpretaciones, fuentes, hallazgos*. Mexico City: Universidad Iberoamericana, 1997.
Novais, Fernando A. *História da vida privada*, 4 vols. São Paulo: Companhia das Letras, 1997.

Nugent, Daniel. *Rural Revolt in Mexico: U.S. Intervention and the Domain of Subaltern Politics*. 2d ed., Durham, N.C.: Duke University Press, 1998.

Obregón Torres, Diana. *Batallas contra la lepra: Estado, medicina y ciencia en Colombia*. Medellín: EAFIT, 2002.

Ocampo, José Antonio. *Colombia y la economía mundial, 1830–1910*. Mexico City: Siglo Veintiuno, 1984.

O'Phelan Godoy, Scarlett. *Rebellions and Revolts in Eighteenth Century Peru and Upper Peru*. Vienna: Bohlau, 1985.

——, ed. *La independencia del Perú: De los Borbones a Bolívar*. Lima: Instituto Riva-Agüero, 2001.

Ortiz de la Tabla Ducasse, Javier. *Los encomenderos de Quito, 1534–1660: Origen y evolución de una elite colonial*. Seville: Escuela de Estudios Hispano-Americanos, 1993.

Ortiz de Montellano, Bernard. *Aztec Medicine, Health, and Nutrition*. New Brunswick, N.J.: Rutgers University Press, 1990.

Ouweneel, Arij. *Shadows over Anahuac: An Ecological Interpretation of Crisis and Development in Central Mexico, 1730–1800*. Albuquerque: University of New Mexico Press, 1996.

Palacios, Guillermo. *Cultivadores libres: Estado y crisis de la esclavitud en Brasil en la época de la Revolución industrial*. Mexico City: Colegio de México/Fondo de Cultura Económica, 1998.

Palacios, Marco. *El café en Colombia, 1850–1970: Una historia económica, social y política*, 3rd ed., rev. Bogotá: Planeta, 2002.

Palmer, Steven. *From Popular Medicine: Doctors, Healers, and Public Power in Costa Rica, 1800–1940*. Durham, N.C.: Duke University Press, 2003.

Palmié, Stephan. *Wizards and Scientists: Explorations in Afro-Cuban Modernity and Tradition*. Durham, N.C.: Duke University Press, 2002.

Pantelides, Edith A., Sarah Bott, et al. *Reproducción, salud y sexualidad en América Latina*. Buenos Aires: Biblos, 2000.

Parker, Richard. *Beneath the Equator: Cultures of Desire, Male Homosexuality, and Emerging Gay Communities in Brazil*. New York: Routledge, 1999.

Parodi, Jorge. *To Be a Worker: Identity and Politics in Peru*. Chapel Hill: University of North Carolina Press, 2000.

Patch, Robert W. *Maya and Spaniard in Yucatan, 1648–1812*. Stanford, Calif.: Stanford University Press, 1993.

Pease, Franklin. *Los ultimos Incas del Cuzco*. Lima: Alianza, 1991.

Perez, Louis A. Jr. *Cuba in the American Imagination: Metaphor and the Imperial Ethos*. Chapel Hill: University of North Carolina Press, 2008.

Pérez Brignoli, Héctor, and Mario Samper Kutschbach, eds. *Tierra, café y sociedad: Ensayos sobre la historia agraria centroamericana*. San José: Programa Costa Rica, FLACSO, 1994.

Pérez Herrero, Pedro, ed. *Región e historia en México (1750–1850): Métodos de análisis regional*. Mexico City: Instituto Doctor José María Luis Mora/Universidad Autónoma Metropolitana, 1992.

Perrone, Charles A., and Christopher Dunn, eds. *Brazilian Popular Music and Globalization*. Gainesville: University Press of Florida, 2001.

Pessar, Patricia. *From Fanatics to Folk: Brazilian Millenarianism and Popular Culture*. Durham, N.C.: Duke University Press, 2004.

Petraglia Kropf, Simone, Nara Azevedo, and Luiz Octavio Ferreira. "Biomedical Research and Public Health in Brazil: The Case of Chagas Disease." *Social History of Medicine* 16:1 (2003): 11–129.

Piccato, Pablo. *City of Suspects: Crime in Mexico City, 1900–1931.* Durham, N.C.: Duke University Press, 2001.
Pineda, Yovanna. *Industrial Development in a Frontier Economy: The Industrialization of Argentina, 1890–1930.* Stanford, Calif.: Stanford University Press, 2009.
Pinto Rodríguez, Jorge. *De la inclusión a la exclusión: La formación del estado, la nación y el pueblo mapuche.* Santiago: Instituto de Estudios Avanzados/Universidad de Santiago de Chile, 2000.
Pinto Vallejos, Julio. *Trabajos y rebeldías en la pampa salitre: El ciclo del salitre y la reconfiguración de las identidades populares (1850–1900).* Santiago: Universidad de Santiago, 1998.
Piqueras, José A., ed. *Azúcar y esclavitud en el final del trabajo forzado: Homenaje a M. Moreno Fraginals.* Madrid: Fondo de Cultura Económica, 2002.
Poole, Stafford. *Our Lady of Guadalupe: The Origin and Sources of a Mexican National Symbol, 1531–1797.* Tucson: University of Arizona Press, 1995.
Porter, Susie S. *Working Women in Mexico City; Public Discourses and Material Conditions, 1879–1931.* Tucson: University of Arizona Press, 2003.
Prados de la Escosura, Leandro, and Samuel Amaral, eds. *La Independencia americana: Consecuencias económicas.* Madrid: Alianza, 1993.
Premo, Bianca. *Children of the Father King: Youth, Authority and Legal Minority in Colonial Lima.* Chapel Hill: University of North Carolina Press, 2005.
Presta, Ana María. *Encomienda, familia y negocios en Charcas Colonial: Los encomenderos de La Plata 1550–1600.* Lima: IEP, 2000.
Przeworski, Adam. *Democracy and the Market: Political and Economic Reforms in Eastern Europe and Latin America, Studies in Rationality and Social Change.* Cambridge, U.K.: Cambridge University Press, 1991.
Puente Brunke, José de la. *Encomienda y encomenderos en el Perú: Estudio social y político de una institución colonial.* Seville: Excma. Diputación de Sevilla, 1992.
Putnam, Lara. *The Company They Kept: Migrants and the Politics of Gender in Caribbean Costa Rica, 1870–1960.* Chapel Hill: University of North Carolina Press, 2001.
Queirós Mattoso, Kátia M. de. *To Be a Slave in Brazil, 1550–1888.* New Brunswick, N.J.: Rutgers University Press, [1979] 1986.
Quezada, Noemí. *Sexualidad, amor y erotismo: México prehispánico y México colonial.* Mexico City: UNAM/Plaza y Valdés, 1996.
Ramírez Bacca, Renzo. *Formación y transformación de la cultura laboral cafetera en el siglo XX.* Medellín, Colombia: Carreta, 2004.
Ramírez, Maria Teresa. "Los ferrocarriles y su impacto sobre la economía colombiana." *Revista de Historia Económica* 19:1 (2001): 81–119.
Ramírez, Susan E. *To Feed and Be Fed: The Cosmological Bases of Authority and Identity in the Andes.* Stanford, Calif.: Stanford University Press, 2005.
Rappaport, Joanne. *The Politics of Memory: Native Historical Interpretation in the Colombian Andes.* New York: Cambridge University Press, 1990.
Reina, Leticia, ed. *La reindianización de América, siglo XIX.* Mexico City: Siglo XXI, 1997.
Reis, João José. *Death Is a Festival: Funeral Rites and Rebellion in Nineteenth-Century Brazil.* Translated by H. Sabrina Gledhill. Chapel Hill: University of North Carolina Press, 2003.
———. *Slave Rebellion in Brazil: The Muslim Uprising of 1835 in Bahia.* Baltimore: Johns Hopkins University Press, 1993.
Reis, João José, and Eduardo Silva. *Negociação e conflito: A resistencia negra no Brasil esclavista.* São Paulo: Companhia das Letras, 1989.

Restall, Matthew. *The Maya World: Yucatec Culture and Society, 1550–1850.* Stanford, Calif.: Stanford University Press, 1997.
Reuque Paillalef, Rosa Isolde. *When a Flower Is Reborn: The Life and Times of a Mapuche Feminist.* Translated, edited, and with an introduction by Florencia E. Mallon. Durham, N.C.: Duke University Press, 2002.
Rivera Garza, Cristina. "La vida en reclusión: Cotidianidad y estado en el manicomio general La Castañeda (México, 1910–1930)" in *Entre médicos y curanderos: Cultura, historia y enfermedad en la América Latina moderna,* ed. Diego Armus, 179–219. Buenos Aires: Norma, 2002.
Rocchi, Fernando. *Chimneys in the Desert: Industrialization in Argentina during the Export Boom Years, 1870–1930.* Stanford, Calif.: Stanford University Press, 2006.
Rodríguez O, Jaime E. *The Independence of Spanish America.* Cambridge: Cambridge University Press, 1998.
Rodríguez, José Angel. *Babilonia de pecados: Norma y transgresión en Venezuela, siglo XVIII.* Caracas: Alfadil, 1998.
Rodríguez, Julia. *Civilizing Argentina: Science, Medicine, and the Modern State.* Chapel Hill: University of North Carolina Press, 2006.
Rodríguez, Pablo. *Seducción, amancebamiento y abandono en la colonia.* Bogotá: Fundación Simón y Lola Guberek, 1991.
———, ed. *La familia en Iberoamérica, 1550–1980.* Bogotá: University Externada de Colombia, 2004.
Román, Reinaldo L. *Governing Spirits: Religion, Miracles, and Spectacles in Cuba and Puerto Rico, 1898–1956.* Chapel Hill: University of North Carolina Press, 2007.
Romano, Ruggiero. *Coyunturas opuestas: La crisis del siglo XVII en Europa e Hispanoamérica.* Mexico City: El Colegio de México, 1993.
Romero Frizzi, María de los Ángeles. *Economía y vida de los españoles en la Mixteca Alta: 1519–1720.* Mexico City: Instituto Nacional de Antropología e Historia, 1990.
Romero, Luis Alberto, and Hilda Sabato. *Los trabajadores de Buenos Aires: La experiencia del mercado, 1850–1880.* Buenos Aires: Sudamericana, 1992.
Roseberry, William, Lowell Gudmundson, and Mario Samper Kutschbach. *Coffee, Society, and Power in Latin America.* Baltimore: Johns Hopkins University Press, 1995.
Roselló Soberón, Estela. *Así en la tierra como en el cielo: Manifestaciones cotidianas de la culpa y el perdón en la Nueva España.* Mexico City: El Colegio de México, 2006.
Ruggiero, Kristin. *Modernity in the Flesh: Medicine, Law, and Society in Turn-of-the-Century Argentina.* Stanford, Calif.: Stanford University Press, 2003.
Sabato, Hilda. *Agrarian Capitalism and the World Market: Buenos Aires in the Pastoral Age, 1840–1890.* Albuquerque: University of New Mexico Press, 1990.
Sagás, Ernesto. *Race and Politics in the Dominican Republic.* Gainesville: University Press of Florida, 2000.
Sala de Touron, Lucía, Nelson de la Torre, and Julio C. Rodríguez. *Artigas y su revolución agraria, 1811–1820.* Mexico City: Siglo XXI, 1978.
Salazar, Gabriel. *Labradores, peones y proletarios: Formación y crisis de la sociedad popular chilena del siglo XIX.* Santiago: LOM Ediciones, 2000.
Salvatore, Ricardo D. *Wandering Paysanos: State Order and Subaltern Experience in Buenos Aires during the Rosas Era.* Durham, N.C.: Duke University Press, 2003.
Sánchez Santiró, Ernest. *Azúcar y poder: Estructura socioeconómica de las alcaldías mayores de Cuernavaca y Cuautla de Amilpas, 1730–1821.* Mexico City: Praxis, 2001.

Sánchez Silva, Carlos. *Indios, comerciantes y burocracia en la Oaxaca poscolonial, 1786–1860.* Oaxaca: Instituto Oaxaqueño de las Culturas/Fondo Estatal para la Cultura y las Artes/Universidad Autónoma Benito Juárez de Oaxaca, 1998.
Sanders, James E. *Contentious Republicans: Popular Politics, Race, and Class in Nineteenth-Century Colombia.* Durham, N.C.: Duke University Press, 2004.
Santos Gomes, Flávio dos. *A hydra e os pântanos: Mocambos, quilombos e comunidades de fugitives no Brasil (séculos XVII–XIX).* São Paulo: UNESP, 2005.
———. *História de quilombolas: Mocambos e comunidades de senzalas no Rio de Janeiro, século XIX.* São Paulo: Companhia das Letras, 2006.
Scarano, Francisco A. *Sugar and Slavery in Puerto Rico: The Plantation Economy of Ponce, 1800–1850.* Madison: University of Wisconsin Press, 1984.
Schell, William, Jr. *Medieval Iberian Tradition and the Development of the Mexican Hacienda.* Syracuse, N.Y.: Maxwell School of Citizenship and Public Affairs, Syracuse University, 1986.
Schettini Pereira, Cristiana. *Que tenhas teu corpo: Uma história social da prostituição no Rio de Janeiro das primeiras décadas republicanas.* Rio de Janeiro: Arquivo Nacional, 2006.
Schmit, Roberto. *Ruina y resurrección en tiempos de guerra: Sociedad, economía y poder en el Oriente entrerriano posrevolucionario, 1810–1852.* Buenos Aires: Prometeo, 2004.
Schwartz, Stuart B. *Slaves, Peasants, and Rebels: Reconsidering Brazilian Slavery.* Urbana and Chicago: University of Illinois Press, 1992.
———. *Sugar Plantations in the Formation of Brazilian Society: Bahia, 1550–1835.* Cambridge: Cambridge University Press, 1985.
Scott, Rebecca J. *Degrees of Freedom: Louisiana and Cuba after Slavery.* Cambridge, Mass.: Harvard University Press, 2005.
Seed, Patricia. *To Love, Honor and Obey in Colonial Mexico.* Stanford, Calif.: Stanford University Press, 1988.
Seigel, Micol. *Uneven Encounters: Making Black and White in Brazil and the United States, 1918–1933.* Durham, N.C.: Duke University Press, 2009.
Seminario de Historia de las Mentalidades. *Familia y sexualidad en Nueva España, México.* Mexico City: Fondo de Cultura Económica, 1982.
———. *Amor y desamor: Vivencia de parejas en la sociedad novohispana.* Mexico City: Instituto Nacional de Antropología e Historia, 1999.
Semo, Enrique. *The History of Capitalism in Mexico: Its Origins, 1521–1763.* Translated by Lidia Lozano. Austin: University of Texas Press, 1993.
Serulnikov, Sergio. *Subverting Colonial Authority: Challenges to Spanish Rule in Eighteenth-Century Southern Andes.* Durham, N.C.: Duke University Press, 2003.
Sevcenko, Nicolau. *Literatura como missão: Tensões sociais e criação cultural na Primeira República.* São Paulo: Brasiliense, 1983.
Shumway, Jeffrey. *The Case of the Ugly Suitor and Other Histories of Love, Gender, and Nation in Buenos Aires, 1776–1870.* Lincoln: University of Nebraska Press, 2005.
Sigal, Pete, ed. *Infamous Desire: Male Homosexuality in Colonial Latin America.* Chicago: University of Chicago Press, 2003.
Silva Gotay, Samuel. *Protestantismo y política en Puerto Rico, 1898–1930: Hacia una historia del protestantismo evangélico en Puerto Rico.* Río Piedras: Editorial de la Universidad de Puerto Rico, 1997.
Slenes, Robert. *Na senzala uma flor: Esperanças e recordações na formação da família escrava, Brasil sudeste, século XIX.* Rio de Janeiro: Nova Fronteira, 1999.
Smith, Raymond T. *Kinship Ideology and Practice in Latin America.* Chapel Hill: University of North Carolina, 1984.

Soares, Luiz Carlos. *O "povo de cam" na capital do Brasil: A escravidão urbana no Rio de Janeiro do século XIX*. Rio de Janeiro: Faperj/7Letras, 2007.

Soares, Mariza. *Devotos da cor: Identidade étnica, religiosidade e escravidão no Rio de Janeiro, século XVIII*. Rio de Janeiro: Civilização Brasileira, 2000.

Solberg, Carl E. *The Prairies and the Pampas: Agrarian Policy in Canada and Argentina, 1880–1930*. Stanford, Calif.: Stanford University Press, 1987.

Sowell, David. *The Early Colombian Labor Movement, 1832–1919: Artisans and Politics in Bogotá, 1832–1919*. Philadelphia: Temple University Press, 1992.

Spalding, Hobart. *Organized Labor in Latin America: Historical Case Studies of Workers in Dependent Societies*. New York: Harper and Row, 1977.

Stein, Stanley J. *Vassouras, a Brazilian Coffee County, 1850–1890: The Roles of Planter and Slave in a Changing Plantation Society*. New York: Atheneum, [1957] 1974.

Stepan, Nancy. *The Hour of Eugenics: Race, Gender, and Nation in Latin America*. Ithaca, N.Y.: Cornell University Press, 1991.

Stephen, Lynn, and George Collier, ed. *Reconfiguring Ethnicity, Identity and Citizenship in the Wake of the Zapatista Rebellion*, special issue of *Journal of Latin American Anthropology* 3:1 (1997).

Stern, Steve J., ed. *Resistance, Rebellion and Consciousness in the Andean Peasant World, 17th to 20th Centuries*. Madison: University of Wisconsin Press, 1987.

Stoll, David. *Is Latin America Turning Protestant?* Berkeley: University of California Press, 1990.

Storey, Rebecca. *Life and Death in the Ancient City of Teotihuacan: A Modern Paleodemographic Synthesis*. Tuscaloosa: University of Alabama Press, 1992.

Street, John. *Artigas and the Emancipation of Uruguay*. Cambridge: Cambridge University Press, 1959.

Summerhill, William Roderick. *Order against Progress: Government, Foreign Investment, and Railroads in Brazil, 1854–1913*. Stanford, Calif.: Stanford University Press, 2003.

Suriano, Juan. *Anarquistas: Cultura y política libertaria en Buenos Aires, 1890–1910*. Buenos Aires: Manantial, 2001.

Sweet, James H. *Recreating Africa: Culture, Kinship and Religion in the African-Portuguese World, 1441–1770*. Chapel Hill: University of North Carolina Press, 2003.

Tandeter, Enrique. *Coercion and Market: Silver Mining in Colonial Potosí, 1692–1826*. Albuquerque: University of New Mexico Press, 1993.

Taylor, William. *Magistrates of the Sacred: Priests and Parishioners in Eighteenth-Century Mexico*. Stanford, Calif.: Stanford University Press, 1996.

Terraciano, Kevin. *The Mixtecs of Colonial Oaxaca: Ñudzahui History, Sixteenth through Eighteenth Centuries*. Stanford, Calif.: Stanford University Press, 2001.

Thomas, Hugh. *The Slave Trade: The Story of the Atlantic Slave Trade, 1440–1870*. New York: Simon and Schuster, 1997.

Thomson, Sinclair. *We Alone Will Rule: Native Andean Politics in the Age of Insurgency*. Madison: University of Wisconsin Press, 2002.

Thurner, Mark. *From Two Republics to One Divided: Contradictions of Postcolonial Nationmaking in Andean Peru*. Durham, N.C.: Duke University Press, 1997.

Topik, Steven C., and Allen Wells, eds. *The Second Conquest of Latin America: Coffee, Henequen, and Oil During the Export Boom, 1850–1930*. Austin: University of Texas Press, 1998.

Triner, Gail D. *Banking and Economic Development: Brazil, 1889–1930*. New York: Palgrave, 2000.

Trujillo Bolio, Mario. *Operários fabriles en el valle de México, 1864–1884*. Mexico City: El Colegio de México, 1997.
Twinam, Ann. *Public Lives, Private Secrets: Gender, Honor, Sexuality, and Illegitimacy in Colonial Spanish America*. Stanford, Calif.: Stanford University Press, 1999.
Vainfas, Ronaldo. *A heresia dos índios: Catolicismo e rebeldia no Brasil colonial*. São Paulo: Companhia das Letras, 1995.
Vallecilla Gordillo, Jaime. *Café y crecimiento económico regional: El Antiguo Caldas, 1870–1970*. Manizales, Colombia: Universidad de Caldas, 2001.
Van Young, Eric. "Two Decades of Anglophone Historical Writing on Colonial Mexico: Continuity and Change since 1980." *Mexican Studies/Estudios Mexicanos* 20 (2004): 275–326.
———. *Hacienda and Market in Eighteenth-Century Mexico: The Rural Economy of the Guadalajara Region, 1675–1820*, 2nd ed., rev. Lanham, Md.: Rowman & Littlefield, 2006.
———. *The Other Rebellion: Popular Violence, Ideology, and the Mexican Struggle for Independence, 1810–1821*. Stanford, Calif.: Stanford University Press, 2001.
Vanderwood, Paul J. *The Power of God against the Guns of Government: Religious Upheaval in Mexico at the Turn of the Nineteenth Century*. Stanford, Calif.: Stanford University Press, 1998.
Verano, John W., and Douglas H. Ubelaker, eds. *Disease and Demography in the Americas*. Washington, D.C.: Smithsonian Institution Press, 1992.
Vidal Luna, Francisco, and Herbert S. Klein. *Slavery and the Economy of São Paulo, 1750–1850*. Stanford, Calif.: Stanford University Press, 2003; Portuguese edition, São Paulo, 2006.
Vidal Luna, Francisco, Iraci Nero da Costa, and Herbert S. Klein. *Escravismo em São Paulo e Minas Gerais*. São Paulo: EDUSP/Imprensa Oficial del Estado de São Paulo, 2009.
Vinson, Ben III. *Bearing Arms for His Majesty: The Free-Colored Militia in Colonial Mexico*. Stanford, Calif.: Stanford University Press, 2001.
Viquiera, Juan Pedro. *María de la Candelaria, india natural de Cancuc*. Mexico City: Fondo de Cultura Económica, 1993.
Voekel, Pamela. *Alone Before God: The Religious Origins of Modernity in Mexico*. Durham, N.C.: Duke University Press, 2002.
Wade, Peter. *Blackness and Race Mixture: The Dynamics of Racial Identity in Colombia*. Baltimore: Johns Hopkins University Press, 1993.
Walker, Charles F. *Smoldering Ashes: Cuzco and the Creation of Republican Peru, 1780–1840*. Durham, N.C.: Duke University Press, 1999.
Weaver, Karol K. *Medical Revolutionaries: The Enslaved Healers of Eighteenth-Century Saint Domingue*. Urbana and Chicago: University of Illinois Press, 2006.
Weinstein, Barbara. *For Social Peace in Brazil: Industrialists and the Remaking of the Working Class in São Paulo, 1920–1964*. Chapel Hill: University of North Carolina Press, 1996.
———. *The Amazon Rubber Boom, 1850–1920*. Stanford, Calif.: Stanford University Press, 1983.
Wells, Allen. *Yucatán's Gilded Age: Haciendas, Henequen, and International Harvester, 1860–1915*. Albuquerque: University of New Mexico Press, 1985.
Williams, Daryle. *Culture Wars in Brazil: The First Vargas Regime, 1930–1945*. Durham, N.C.: Duke University Press, 2001.
Williamson, Jeffrey G. "Real Wages, Inequality, and Globalization in Latin America before 1940." *Revista de Historia Económica* 17 (1999): 101–42.

Winn, Peter. *Weavers of Revolution: The Yarur Workers and Chile's Road to Socialism.* New York: Oxford University Press, 1986.

Wolfe, Joel. *Working Women, Working Men: São Paulo and the Rise of Brazil's Industrial Working Class, 1900–1955.* Durham, N.C.: Duke University Press, 1993.

Wolfe, Justin. *The Everyday Nation-State: Community and Ethnicity in Nineteenth-Century Nicaragua.* Lincoln: Nebraska University Press, 2007.

Womack, John Jr. *Posición estratégica obrera: Hacia una nueva historia de los movimientos obreros.* Mexico City: Fondo de Cultura Económica, 2008.

Woodard, James. *A Place in Politics: São Paulo, Brazil, from Seigneurial Republicanism to Regionalist Revolt.* Durham, N.C.: Duke University Press, 2009.

Wright, Winthrop R. *Café con Leche: Race, Class, and National Image in Venezuela.* Austin: University of Texas Press, 1990.

Wright-Rios, Edward. *Revolutions in Mexican Catholicism: Reform and Revelation in Oaxaca, 1887–1934.* Durham, N.C.: Duke University Press, 2009.

Zavala, Silvio A. *La encomienda indiana*, 3rd ed., rev. Mexico City: Porrúa, [1935] 1992.

Index

Aarão Reis, Daniel, 245
Abercrombie, Thomas, 67
Abreu Esteves, Martha de, 222
Abreu, Martha, 226
Acemoglu, Daron, 416, 417, 418
Adams, David, 32
Adams, Eleanor, 38
Adelman, Jeremy, xi, xvii, 320
Adorno, Rolena, 66, 68
Adorno, Sérgio, 213
Africa, 2, 22, 193–94, 262, 431. *See also* Africans; slavery
    Arab colonialism in, 6, 7, 18
    compared to Latin America, 6–8, 11–13, 17–18, 407
    connections to Latin America, 106–7, 117, 204, 271, 457
    slavery in, 188
Africans and Afro-descendants, 2–3, 4
    African ethnic origins, 2, 107, 111, 186, 193–94
    associations, 34, 107, 193, 263, 265
    black movements, 196, 218, 235, 245, 265–70
    Brazil, 105–7, 181–96, 217–19, 224–26
    Central America, 260, 266–67, 269
    Colombia, 173, 264–65
    colonial Mexico, 33–34
    colonial Spanish South America, 78, 79
    Cuba, 263, 265–68, 455, 462–63, 476
    Dominican Republic, 259, 264, 267, 318
    and European immigrants, 215, 218–19, 228
    family, 106, 392–93
    Haitian immigrants, 264, 277, 318
    health and disease, 431, 432
    independence movements, 164, 173–75, 259–61
    and indigenous people, 52, 104, 141, 182, 266, 270
    Islam, 186, 193
    Peru, 260, 265, 269
    post-abolition, 224–26, 257–71
    Puerto Rico, 2, 260, 263, 268, 327
    religion, 107, 242, 455–58, 463, 464, 473, 485
    return to Africa, 194
    sexuality, 136, 137, 141, 185
    slave-owners as, 110, 186, 213–14
    slavery, 33–34, 78, 105–7, 173, 181–96, 217–19
    Venezuela, 260, 264
    West Indian immigrants, 6, 266–67, 269, 392, 394
    women, 34, 36, 82, 136, 185, 191, 194, 196, 263, 269
Agosto Cintrón, Nélida, 474
agriculture, 6, 284, 287, 310–29, 345, 414–15, 470
    Argentina, 309, 319–22
    Brazil, 109–10, 190, 309, 324–26
    Chile, 314, 316, 330
    coffee, 218, 222, 312, 323–26
    colonial, 32, 44, 75–78
    Mexico, 32, 44, 309, 312–14
    Peru, 314, 318, 323–24
    plantations, 2, 3, 190, 265–66, 287, 324–28, 386, 416, 431
    smallholders, 109, 190, 218, 228, 321, 323–24, 392, 416
    sugar, 9, 33, 109, 311–12, 318, 324–28
    tobacco, 109, 311, 323, 327
Águeda Méndez, María, 137
Aguirre Beltrán, Gonzalo, 33, 327, 463, 476
Alberro, Solange, 35, 36, 38, 39
Alchon, Suzanne Austin, 81
Alden, Dauril, 104, 111
Alencastro, Luiz Felipe, 106
Alexandre, Valentim, 115
Algranti, Leila, 105, 110
Almeida, Celestino, 104
Almeida, Rita Heloísa de, 104

Alsina Franch, José, 30
Altman, Ida, 34
Alvarez de Toledo, Cayetana, 35
Amaral, Samuel, 320
anarchism, 11, 156, 228, 346–48, 350, 354
Anders, Ferdinand, 27
Anderson, Arthur J. O., 31
Andrade Arruda, José Jobson de, 115
Andrews, Reid, 217, 218–19, 225, 228, 235, 261, 265, 270
Andrien, Kenneth, 66, 76
Angola, 7, 33, 106, 117, 193, 207
Anguiano, Arturo, 351
Anna, Timothy, 156, 160, 161, 179
Annino, Antonio, 166, 286
Appelbaum, Nancy, 265
Aranda de los Rios, Ramón, 265
Araucanians. *See* Mapuches
Arazola Corvera, María Jesús, 77
Archer, Christon, 168
Archetti, Eduardo, 373
architecture, 7, 39, 42, 43, 236, 241
Arcondo, Anibal, 81
Argentina, 80, 157, 222, 269
   Afro-descendants, 4, 258, 265–66
   agriculture, 78, 309, 319–22
   economy, 3, 11, 15, 20, 77, 292, 411–15, 417
   education, 13, 22
   Europeans in, 1, 3, 68, 259, 292, 345, 346
   family, 370, 373, 374, 390
   gender, 13, 370–74
   health and disease, 81, 440, 441, 442
   independence, 74, 155, 161–62
   indigenous population, 20, 283, 291–93
   industrialization, 13, 343
   labor movement, 343–44, 346–48, 351–53, 356, 362
   politics, 12, 213, 234, 372
   religion, 72, 74
Ariès, Philippe, 79, 382
Armus, Diego, xiii, xvii, 442
Arrom, José Juan, 477
Arrom, Silvia, 35, 36, 42, 386, 400, 403, 465
art and literature, 16, 223, 362. *See also* architecture; music and dance
   Afro-descendants and, 268–70
   colonial, 43–44, 113–14
   Iberian influence, 7
   modernist, 230–31, 237
   religious, 38
Ashby, Joel, 351
Asia, 21
   compared to Latin America, 6–8, 11–13, 17–18, 19
   immigration from, 4, 225, 228, 260, 270
Atahualpa, 66
Atondo Rodríguez, Ana María, 36
Aymaras, 70, 288, 298
Azevedo, Elciene, 185
Azevedo Fernandes, João, 104
Azevedo Salomao, Eugenia María, 42
Aztecs. *See* Nahuas

Bacigalupo, Ana Mariella, 144
Badaró Mattos, Marcelo, 218
Bahia, 104–9, 185, 224, 242, 261
   economy, 414–15
   medicine, 225, 479
   millenarianism, 220, 466–68, 482
   religion, 456, 466
   slave revolts, 107, 193, 194, 215
   slavery, 184, 186, 188, 190
Bajío, 9, 32, 44–45, 284, 285
Bandeira, Moniz, 109
Bantus, 2, 6, 34, 193
Barbados, 2, 266, 267
Barham, Bradford, 323
Barickman, B. J., 109, 325
Barman, Roderick, 161, 216
Barnet, Miguel, 269
Barrett, Ward, 328
Barros de Castro, Antonio, 187
Barsky, Osvaldo, 320
Baskes, Jeremy, 317
Bastian, Jean-Pierre, 472, 473, 474, 476
Bastide, Roger, 193, 455, 456, 457
Baudot, Georges, 39
Bayer, Osvaldo, 348
Beattie, Peter, 226–27, 261
Behar, Ruth, 37, 141
Bender, Thomas, 154
Bennett, Herman, 33
Benson, Nettie Lee, 165–66
Berbel, Márcia Regina, 167
Berdan, Frances, 31
Bergad, Laird, 106, 195, 196, 327

Berger, Peter, 483
Bergquist, Charles, 343, 348, 360
Bernand, Carmen, 38, 266
Besse, Susan, 226, 232, 374
Besselaar, José van den, 113
Bethencourt, Francisco, 111, 112
Bicalho, Fernanda, 109, 116
Bieber, Judy, 220
Blackburn, Robin, 260
blacks. *See* Africans and Afro-descendants
Blanchard, Peter, 173
Bliss, Katherine, 368
Bolívar, Simón, 153, 155, 259
Bolivia, 7, 8, 260, 390, 441
   colonial, 67, 70
   economy, 11, 76, 317
   education, 22, 23
   indigenous population, 259, 283, 284, 288, 293, 298
   politics, 12, 297, 308
Bonfil Batalla, Guillermo, 460
Bonilla, Heraclio, 161, 163, 168
Borah, Woodrow, 28, 40
Bortz, Jeffrey, 357, 413
Boschi, Caio, 110
Bosi, Alfredo, 113, 215
Bourbon Reforms, 32, 45, 71, 74, 77, 83, 160, 284
Bourdieu, Pierre, 213, 236, 245, 361
Bourgois, Philippe, 267
Boxer, Charles, 106, 109, 114
Boyer, Richard, 36, 37, 139
Boylan, Kristin, 466
Brading, David, 39, 43, 314
Brazil, xii, 2, 33, 78
   1920s and 1930s, 231–33
   Afro-descendants, 105–7, 215, 218–19, 221, 224–28, 261–63
   agriculture, 109–10, 190, 218, 222, 309, 324–26
   Catholic Church, 111–14, 220, 238, 244, 466, 468
   colonial administration, 114–18
   economy, 3, 13, 108–9, 218, 227–30, 343, 411–15, 417
   education, xiv, 13, 22, 212, 225, 226, 244
   family, 101, 104, 106, 110, 188, 190, 194–95, 386–87, 389–90, 395
   gender, 110, 143, 226–27, 372, 485
   health and disease, 225, 429, 431, 441
   immigration, 218–19, 225, 227–28, 259, 260, 266, 346
   independence, 10, 117–18, 155, 158, 161–62, 166–73, 214–15
   indigenous population, 4, 20, 102–5, 182, 217, 235, 297
   Japanese in, viii–ix, 228, 270
   labor movement, 218, 221, 227–28, 232–34, 238–39, 348–49, 351–56
   millenarianism, 220, 466, 467, 468, 482
   national formation, 214–17
   politics, 11, 12, 213, 220–21, 233–37, 372
   Portuguese in, 6, 7, 16, 18, 21, 109, 214–16
   post-1945, 238–45
   Protestantism, 193, 469, 470, 471, 473
   race relations, 224–26, 261–63
   slavery, 105–7, 181–96, 217–19, 260, 324–26, 414
   urban history, 222–23, 240–42
Breña, Roberto, 168
Brennan, James, xiii, xvii, 12, 356, 365
Bricker, Victoria, 41
Broda, Johanna, 27
Brown, Jonathan, 320
Brown, Kendall, 81
Brusco, Elizabeth, 472
Buarque de Holanda, Sérgio, 158, 237
Buenos Aires, 11, 74, 77, 344, 346, 348, 441
Bulmer-Thomas, Victor, 409
Burdick, John, 471, 473, 485
Burke, Peter, 110
Burkett, Elinor, 79, 83
Burkhart, Louise, 31, 39, 136, 478
Bushnell, David, 156
Butler, Judith, 374
Butler, Kim, xii, xvii, 4, 218, 235, 261, 266

Cabral de Mello, Evaldo, 108
Caires Silva, Ricardo, 185
Calainho, Daniela, 107
Campbell, Leon, 70
Campos Machado, María, 472
Canada, viii, 3, 5, 11, 14, 20
Candido, Antonio, 237
candomblé, 186, 193, 456
   and ethnic identity, 194, 218, 242, 279
Cañeque, Alejandro, 35

Cañizares-Esguerra, Jorge, 19, 23, 43
Cano, Gabriela, 369
Capelato, Maria Helena, 234
Caplan, Karen, 167
Cardoso, Fernando Henrique, 182
Carmagnani, Marcelo, 38, 314
Carneiro da Cunha, Manuela, 102
Carnero, Tucci, 112
Carr, Barry, 267, 351
Carrasco, David, 27
Carrasco, Pedro, 27
Carrera Damas, Germán, 168
Carrier, Joseph, 373
Carrillo, Elizabeth, 474
Carroll, Michael, 465
Carroll, Patrick, 33, 327
Carvalho, Marcus, 187, 193
Carvalho Soares, Mariza de, 107, 118
Carvalho Souza, Lara Lis, 214
Caso, Alfonso, 42
Castañeda, Paulino, 141
Castelnau-L'Estoile, Charlotte de, 104, 111
Castillo Palma, Norma Angélica, 32
Castro, Fidel, 267, 468
Castro Gomes, Angela de, 232, 234, 237
Castro Gutiérrez, Felipe, 41
Catão, Luis, 413
Catholic Church, 6, 14, 238, 326, 386, 389, 425, 465, 472
  and African beliefs, 34, 107, 193, 455–56, 458
  in colonial Brazil, 111–14
  in colonial Mexico, 29, 31, 34, 35, 37–40, 458–62
  in colonial Spanish South America, 71–74
  convents, 36, 43–44, 73, 87, 151
  Counter-Reformation, 113, 132, 137, 142
  folk Catholicism, 470, 473, 474, 484
  and indigenous beliefs, 31, 68, 73, 136, 458–62
  left-wing Catholicism, 484, 485
  and liberalism, 9, 285–86, 310, 465
  liberation theology, 471, 473, 485
  in post-colonial Brazil, 220, 222, 244, 466, 468
  sexual morality, 132, 133, 136, 141, 142, 144, 369
  and women, 36, 71, 73, 110, 370–71, 466

Caulfield, Sueann, 223, 226, 233
Cavalcanti, Nireu, 109
Cervantes, Fernando, 464
Chalhoub, Sidney, 185, 187, 218, 221
Challu, Amílcar, 417
Chambers, Sarah, 172
Chamosa, Oscar, 265
Chance, John, 42
Chartier, Roger, 110, 213
Chasteen, John, 156, 221
Chauí, Marilena, 235
Chaunu, Pierre, 77
Chestnut, Andrew, 471, 472, 484
Chiaramonte, José Carlos, 167
Chihuahua, 32, 287
Chile, 3, 11, 260, 287
  agriculture, 314, 316, 330
  Communist Party, 11, 347, 486
  economy, 3, 15, 20, 411, 412
  education, 13, 22
  family, 383, 387, 389–90, 393, 396
  gender, 79, 374, 375
  health, 15, 441
  independence, 10, 158, 160, 260
  indigenous movements, 295–98
  indigenous population, 71, 283–84, 287–93
  industrialization, 13, 343, 414
  labor movement, 343–45, 347, 348, 349, 357, 374
  mining, 10, 319, 345
  politics, viii, 12, 288
  Protestantism, 469–71, 486
Chomsky, Aviva, 267
Chowning, Margaret, 465
Christian, William, 39
Christianity. *See* Catholic Church; Protestantism
Chuchiak, John, 38
cities. *See* urban society
citizenship, 5, 166–67, 170, 172–73
  and Afro-descendants, 224, 259, 260
  Brazil, 214, 215, 233, 254
  and gender, 226–27
  and indigenous people, 281–98
Clark, Marjorie, 351
Clastres, Hélène, 103
Clendinnen, Inga, 38, 459–61, 478
Cline, Sarah, 31, 39

Coates, Timothy, 113
Coatsworth, John, xiii, xviii, 409, 416
Cohen, Thomas, 113
Cold War, vii, 237, 242, 268, 351, 355, 358, 397
Collier, Simon, 160
Colombia, 2, 6, 8, 23, 349, 441
   Afro-descendants, 173, 264–65
   agriculture, 316, 318, 323
   economy, 20, 323, 411, 415, 417
   family, 385–86, 388–90
   independence, 153, 155
   indigenous population, 71, 295, 297
   labor movement, 343, 344
   politics, 213, 295, 319
   religion, 465, 472
colonial administration
   Brazil, 114–18
   Spanish South America, 74–75
Comaroff, Jean, 468, 474
Comaroff, John, 468, 474
Communist Party, 11, 295. *See* also Marxism
   Brazil, 237, 238
   Chile, 295, 347, 486
   and labor movement, 347–52, 354
Conniff, Michael, 267, 270
conquistadors, 43, 132, 163, 317, 458
Cook, Noble David, 67, 81
Cook, Sherbourne, 28
Coomes, Oliver, 323
Cooper, Frederic, 270
Cope, Douglas, 32, 42
Cornejo Bouroncle, Jorge, 174
Cortés Conde, Roberto, 408, 409, 413
Cortés Jacome, María Elena, 36
Costa Rica, 8, 13, 15, 260, 297
   agriculture, 323–24
   education, 13, 23
   family, 392, 394
   health, 15, 441
   West Indians in, 266–67, 269, 394
Costeloe, Michael, 161
Couturier, Edith, 35
Crahan, Margaret, 473
Cruz Santos, Beatriz, 112
Cuba, 10, 269, 311
   Afro-descendants, 263, 265–68, 462–63
   economy, 5, 9, 11, 13, 15, 20, 327, 411, 414, 474
   education, ix, 13, 22, 23, 263
   Europeans in, 8, 11
   gender, 13, 369, 374
   health, 9, 15
   labor movement, 12, 267, 357
   politics, 12, 213, 354
   race relations, 263, 265–68, 455
   religion, 473–75, 486
   slavery, 260, 263, 327, 414
   urbanization, 11, 21
Cuban Revolution, vii, 159, 242, 319, 355, 369
Cuche, Dennis, 265
Cunha, Euclides da, 220, 223
Curtin, Philip, 457
Cushner, Nicholas, 72, 314–15
Cuzco, 66, 70, 72, 78, 174

Daher, Andrea, 103
Damasceno Fonseca, Claudia, 109
Davies, Keith, 314
Dávila, Jerry, 226
Davis, Darién, 262
Davis, Thomas, 270
De Shazo, Peter, 347
Dean, Warren, 105, 217, 229, 323
Decca, Edgar de, 229, 232
Decoster, Jean-Jacques, 73
Deeds, Susan, 32
Deere, Carmen, 387
del Campo, Hugo, 352
demography, 12, 360
   colonial, 20–21, 42, 80–81, 137
   family, 384, 386, 388
   medical, 428, 430
   slavery, 195, 325
Derby, Robin, 264, 468–69
Derrida, Jacques, 361, 463
Desmangles, Leslie, 458
Deusen, Nancy van, 73
Di Stefano, Roberto, 74
Diacon, Todd, 467
Díaz, Arlene, 371
Díaz Polanco, Héctor, 41
Dibble, Charles, 31, 39
Domingues, Angela, 104

Domínguez, Jorge, 160
Dominican Republic, vii, 259
  education, 13, 23
  gender, 20, 392, 393
  race relations, 264, 267, 318
Dore, Elizabeth, 387
Ducey, Michael, 41
Dueñas Vargas, Guiomar, 83, 388
Duncan, Quince, 271
Dunn, Christopher, 240, 269
Durruty, Celia, 352
Dutch, 2, 7, 21
  in Brazil, 103, 104, 108, 109, 192
Dutra, Eliana, 235
Duverger, Christian, 37

Earle, Rebecca, 293
Ebert, Christopher, 108
Echeverri-Gent, Elisavinda, 267
economy, 100, 407–19
  colonial, 44–45, 75–78, 108, 115, 412
  finance, 45, 72, 77, 318, 415
  industrial, 9, 12, 13, 227–29, 238–39, 413–14
  inequality, 325, 416–17
  mining, 9, 45, 76, 77, 195, 313, 317, 321, 345, 412
  prices, 44, 75, 76, 196, 318, 322, 412–13
  rural, 2, 115, 218, 310–29, 412, 414–15
  slavery, 106, 187, 194, 324–26, 414
  transportation, 9, 266, 315, 415
Ecuador, 12, 13, 297, 411
  Afro-descendants, 2, 265
  education, 13, 23
  rural society, 76, 81, 314
Edgerton, Samuel, 39
education, 294, 348, 373, 418, 419, 438, 439
  colonial period, 44, 160
  gender, 13, 369
  literacy, 13, 22, 288
  public, 287, 358, 371
  religious, 74, 465, 475
  school enrollment, 13, 22–23, 348
  social policy, and, 226, 368, 369, 387
  university, vii, ix, xiv, 13, 212, 244, 269, 270
Ehrick, Christine, 372
Eisenberg, José, 111
Eisenberg, Peter, 325

El Salvador, 23, 297, 308
  colonial, 41
Enciso Rojas, Dolores, 37
Engerman, Stanley, 416, 417, 418
English language, 6–7, 15
environmental history, xvii, 42, 105, 329, 337, 364
Estenssoro, Juan Carlos, 68
Estrada Urroz, Rosalina, 357
Europeans and Euro-descendants, 3–8
  and Afro-descendants, 103–4, 190, 215, 218–19, 228, 264–65, 458
  Argentina, 3, 68, 292, 321, 345, 346, 353
  Brazil, 3, 103–4, 117, 213, 218–19, 227–28, 238
  Chile, 3, 292, 346
  colonial Mexico, 28–29, 32, 34–35, 39–40
  colonial Spanish South America, 67–75
  cultural syncretism, 103–4, 455
  farmers, 2, 228, 265
  and indigenous people, 28–29, 32, 39–40, 70, 76–77, 103–4, 283, 284
  Italian immigrants, 8, 228
  Jewish immigrants, 73, 112, 235, 379
  labor movement in, 218–19, 227–28, 346–50
  male sexuality, 135, 137, 138, 140, 185, 461–62
  Portuguese immigrants, 8, 16, 109, 215
  religion, 73, 107, 111, 112, 480
  sexuality, 136–45
  Spanish immigrants, 8, 52–53
  women, 73, 349, 379, 462
  working-class, 238, 259, 346–50, 438

family, 45, 78, 92, 101, 110, 382–97
  adultery, 41, 68, 134, 138, 139, 371, 387
  children, 45, 73, 137, 188, 371–74, 387, 393, 394
  divorce, 2, 139, 370, 371, 392
  dowry, 110, 387, 400
  elite, 67, 385, 396, 397
  female headship, 3, 92, 369, 386, 387, 392, 394
  illegitimacy, 79, 137, 373, 385, 387, 389, 392–93, 395
  marriage, 33, 36, 68, 139, 195, 371, 385–87, 389, 393

pre-Columbian, 68, 104
slavery, 33, 100, 106, 136, 188, 195
violence, 36, 135, 139, 149, 378
Fanon, Franz, 18, 487
Farage, Nadia, 104
Farberman, Judith, 80
Faria de Castro, Paulo, 106
Faria de Castro, Sheila, 106
Farnsworth-Alvear, Ann, 349
Farriss, Nancy, 30, 38, 57, 458–62
Fausto, Boris, 227, 348
Feitler, Bruno, 112
feminism, 226, 245, 369–74, 391, 472, 485
Ferlini, Vera, 109
Fernandes, Florestan, 182, 218, 219, 261
Ferreira, Jorge, 232, 235
Ferrer, Ada, 263
Ferrer, Aldo, 320
Ferry, Robert, 322
Few, Martha, 36, 37, 463
Fico, Carlos, 244
Fields, Barbara, 187
Figuereido, Luciano, 110, 191
Fischer, Brodwyn, 241
Fisher, John, 160, 168
Florentino, Manolo, 105, 106
Flores Galindo, Alberto, 173, 174, 460
Florescano, Enrique, 43, 412, 480
Font, Mauricio, 228
Fontes, Paulo, 238
Fortes, Alexandre, 238
Foucault, Michel, 36, 143, 213, 226, 361, 428, 462
Fradkin, Raúl, 322, 336
Fragoso, João, 115, 116
França Paiva, Eduardo, 191
France, 13, 15, 74, 103, 154
    Annales school, 29, 158, 384
    education, 13, 22
    empire, 2, 18, 260, 327
    French as colonial language, 6–7, 15
    French Revolution, 9, 161, 171
    medicine, 9, 425
    and Mexico, occupation of, 5, 286, 287, 290
Frank, Zephyr, 191
Fredrickson, George, 262
Freire, Paulo, 368, 369
Freire Costa, Leonor, 108

Freitas Monteiro, Nuno, 116
French, John, 229, 232, 234, 237, 353–55, 358–60
French, William, 348, 368
Freyre, Gilberto, 101, 158, 182, 223, 311, 383, 386
Fuente, Alejandro de la, 263
Fuller, Linda, 357
Furtado, Júnia, 107, 108

Galindo, Marcos, 103
Gama, Lúcia Helena, 237
Ganson, Barbara, 72
Garavaglia, Juan Carlos, 77, 321, 322
García Garagarza, León, 46, 55
García Pantojas, Emilio, 473, 486
García-Barrio, Constance, 266
Garfield, Seth, 232, 235
Garibay, Ángel María, 29, 31
Garrido, Margarita, 172
Garza Carvajal, Federico, 36, 143
Gaspar, Jeffrey Casey, 267
Gauderman, Kimberly, 80
Gebara, Ademir, 189
Geertz, Clifford, 112, 191, 459, 461
Gelman, Jorge, 322
gender. *See also* masculinity; sexuality; women
    Brazil, 110, 226–27
    colonial Mexico, xx, 35–37, 54, 135–45
    colonial Spanish America, 71–74, 79, 136–45
    family, 36, 73, 79, 82, 92, 370, 371, 382–97
    feminism, 226, 245, 369–74, 391, 472, 485
    and honor, 36, 79, 139–40, 150, 226, 233, 380
    migration, 20, 392
    patriarchalism, 14, 36, 226, 369–75, 384, 387, 392
    post-colonial Latin America, 13–14, 367–75
    pre-Columbian, 133–35
    and religion, 74, 454–55, 466, 472, 473, 485
    and slavery, 136, 185, 191
Gerhard, Peter, 28
Germany, viii, 11, 13, 15, 26, 234
Gibson, Charles, 27, 28, 37, 318, 412

Gill, Anthony, 471
Ginzburg, Carlo, 110, 113
Góes, José Roberto, 106
Gomes, Flavio, 188
Gomes da Cunha, Olívia, 225, 261
Gomez, Michael, 271, 457
Gómez-Galvarriato, Aurora, 413
Gonzalbo Aizpuru, Pilar, 37
Gonzales, Michael, 318
González Marmolejo, Jorge, 37, 141
Gootenberg, Paul, 419
Gordillo, Mónica, 356
Gordon, Edmund, 266
Gorender, Jacob, 187, 325
Gorenstein Ferreira da Silva, Lina, 112
Gosner, Kevin, 41
Goulart, Silvana, 235
Goulart Reis, Nestor, 109
Gouvêa, Maria da Fátima, 109
Graham, Richard, 159, 216, 219
Graham, Sandra Lauderdale, 389, 395
Grahn, Lance, 77
Grajales, Agustín, 35
Grandin, Greg, 466
Great Britain, viii, 21, 185, 260, 388
    economy, 9, 10, 45, 159, 292, 407, 414
    education, 9, 13, 22
    empire, 2, 18, 163, 260, 425
Green, James, 227
Green, Richard, 38
Grieco, Viviana, 77
Grinberg, Keila, 185, 215, 218, 224
Gruzinski, Serge, 29, 36, 37, 142, 459, 461
Guadalajara, 25, 39, 44, 45, 285, 315, 327
Guarani, 72, 103
Guardino, Peter, 162, 174
Guatemala, 1, 7, 8, 297, 342
    agriculture, 316, 323–24
        colonial, 25, 41, 42
        education, 22, 23
        family, 389, 393
        indigenous population, 288–89, 293, 298, 417
        religion, 463, 469, 471, 486
Gudmundson, Lowell, 323
Guedea, Virginia, 167
Guerra, François-Xavier, 170, 171
Guimarães Sá, Isabel dos, 109
Gutiérrez, Ramón, 36, 464

Guttman, Matthew, 374
Guy, Donna, xiii, xviii

Hahner, June, 226
Haiti, 5, 6, 7, 17, 264, 267, 319, 327, 458
Haitian Revolution, 2, 173, 193, 258, 259, 458
Halperín Donghi, Tulio, 162
Hamill, Hugh, 163, 164
Hamilton, Earl, 412
Hamnett, Brian, 160, 161, 174, 179
Hanchard, Michael, 262
Hansen, João Adolfo, 105, 113
Hardt, Michael, 468
Hart, Paul, 328
Hartman, Mary, 393
Hasenbalg, Carlos, 262
Haskett, Robert, 31, 36
Haslip-Viera, Gabriel, 41
Hassig, Ross, 315
health and disease, 424–42
    Brazil, 221, 222, 225, 479
    colonial period, 20–21, 37, 42, 53, 80–81, 317
    life expectancy, 12, 15
    popular medicine, 37, 80, 142, 221, 463
    and sexuality, 133, 227, 438, 440
    state interventions, 221, 371, 388, 417, 427–28, 434, 438
Helg, Aline, xii, xviii, 4, 173, 263, 264, 266
Hemming, John, 102
Hernández, Alicia, 351
Herschmann, Micael, 269
Hespanha, António Manuel, 115
Hidalgo, Miguel, 163, 164, 175, 285
Higgins, Kathleen, 105
Higgs, David, 113
Himmerich y Valencia, Robert, 35
historiography, ix, x, 83, 133, 213, 382.
    See also specific countries and topics
    Latin American, ix, 1, 4, 7, 10, 16, 21, 82, 212–13, 309
Hoberman, Louisa, 35
Hobsbawm, Eric, 67
Hoffman, Kelly, 396
Holloway, Thomas, 228
Holt, Thomas, 270
Holy Office. *See* Inquisition

homosexuality, 245, 370, 373, 440
  Brazil, 110, 143, 226–27
  and Catholic Church, 74, 141
  colonial Spanish America, 36, 138, 141–44
  among indigenous people, 133, 142
  lesbianism, 110, 227, 373, 375
  medicalization of, 227, 438
Honduras, 12, 81, 266, 393
  education, 13, 22, 23
honor
  in public life, 171, 172, 214
  and sexuality, 140, 150, 226, 380
Horowitz, Joel, 352
Howard, Philip, 263
Huerta, María Teresa, 41
Hughes, Jennifer, 476
Hunefeldt, Christine, 173, 260, 387
Hunt, Shane, 408
Hutchison, Elizabeth, 349

Ianni, Octavio, 182, 242, 261
Iberian colonialism, 5–8, 17, 18, 389, 433
Illades, Lilián, 35
immigration. *See* migration
Incas, 66, 72
independence movements, 5, 9–10, 82, 153–76
  Afro-descendants in, 33, 173–75, 259–61
  Argentina, 74, 155, 161–62
  Brazil, 108, 115, 117–18, 158, 172, 214–15
  Chile, 158, 160
  and indigenous people, 163, 283–85
  Mexico, 32, 39–41, 160–61, 167, 168, 174, 284–85
  Peru, 161–62, 168, 174
  structuralist interpretations of, 157–59
  Venezuela, 168, 173
indigenism, 157, 293–94, 304–5
indigenous people. *See also specific groups and places*
  and Afro-descendants, 52, 104, 141, 182, 266, 270
  in Americas, geographic distribution of, 2, 20, 181, 259
  Argentina, 20, 283, 291–93
  Bolivia, 259, 283, 284, 288, 293, 298
  Brazil, 4, 20, 102–5, 182, 217, 235, 297

  and Catholicism, 31, 34, 37–40, 68, 71–74, 136, 458–62
  Chile, 71, 283–84, 287–93
  colonial Mexico, 25–32, 37–44, 80, 134–36, 140–44, 458–64
  colonial Spanish South America, 66–74, 76, 80–81
  demography, 20–21, 28, 81, 293, 297, 318, 428, 430
  family, 68, 70, 104, 386, 387, 388, 389, 393
  gender, 27, 35–37, 136–45
  Guatemala, 1, 288–89, 293, 297, 298, 417
  health and disease, 29, 37, 42, 428, 432, 439
  and independence movements, 82, 163, 174, 283–85
  indigenous movements, 245, 281, 295–98
  Mexico, 283–89, 293–94, 297
  during nineteenth century, 285–93
  nobility, 28, 62, 66, 68, 72, 136
  Peru, 259, 283–85, 287–89, 293–94, 297
  pre-Columbian, 2, 17, 27, 68, 104, 133–35, 140, 144
  rebellions, 40–41, 67–71, 163, 284–85
  romantization of, 217, 293
  slavery, 211, 287, 316
  during twentieth century, 293–98
  women, 36, 79–80, 132, 134–35, 140, 143, 387, 462
Inquisition, 73, 388, 457, 463
  Brazil, 112–13, 193, 464
  Mexico, 35, 38, 40, 44, 55, 141, 466
  and sexuality, 133, 136–37, 139, 141
Ireland, Rowan, 472, 476
Islam, 186, 193, 316, 372
Italy, 9, 13, 15, 22, 112, 228, 234

Jacobsen, Nils, 323
Jaguaribe, Hélio, 237
Jamaica, 266–67
James, Daniel, 352–55, 358–60
Jancsó, István, 112, 117
Jansen, Maaten, 27
Japan, viii, 11, 12, 19, 228, 270
Jesuits, 32, 72, 75, 82
  Brazil, 111, 113
  land ownership, 310, 314, 315
  Portuguese empire, 103, 104

Jiménez Pelayo, Agueda, 32
Johnson, John J., 163
Johnson, Lyman, xi, xviii, 4, 21, 41, 412–13
Johnson, Simon, 416, 417
Jones, Grant, 41
Juiz de Fora, Teresina, 190

Kantor, Iris, 112, 114, 117
Karasch, Mary, 103, 105
Karttunen, Frances, 135
Keith, Robert, 314
Kicza, John, 35
Kiddy, Elizabeth, 107
Kinsbruner, Jay, 159
Klarén, Peter, 318
Klein, Cecilia, 62
Klein, Herbert, xii, xviii, 77, 106, 122, 208, 246, 326, 339, 412
Klubock, Thomas, 349, 374
Knaster, Meri, 367
Knight, Franklin, 327
Konder, Leandro, 237
Konrad, Herman, 314–15
Kourí, Emilio, 19
Kraay, Hendrik, 188, 215, 261
Kraut, Andrew, 41
Kubler, George, 39
Kuznesof, Elizabeth, 106, 385, 386

labor history, 232–34, 238–39, 342–62
labor movement
    1880–1930, 11, 346–50
    1930–1960, 350–55
    1960–2000, 355–58
    Afro-descendants in, 218–19, 266–67
    Argentina, 343–44, 346–48, 351–53, 356, 362
    Brazil, 221, 227–28, 232–34, 238–39, 242, 348–49
    European immigrants in, 218–19, 227–28, 346–50
    Mexico, 345–46, 347, 348, 351
Ladd, Doris, 35, 160
Lalive d'Epinay, Christian, 469, 470–71, 473–74, 484
Lancaster, Roger, 373, 484
Landázuri Benítez, Gisela, 327

Lane, Kris, 78
Langfur, Hal, 118
Lara, Jaime, 39
Lara, Silvia, 105, 107, 184
Larkin Nascimento, Elisa, 261
Lasso, Marixa, 173, 265
Latin America. *See also specific places and topics*
    distinguishing traits, 4–19, 257, 309
    ethno-racial geography, 2–3, 181
    historiography, ix, 1, 4, 7, 10, 16, 21, 82, 212–13, 309
    limitations of term, 1–3
    and the West, discursive exclusion from, 14–19
    and the West, similarities to, 9, 11, 12
    and Western Hemisphere, 4–5
Latin American studies, ix, vii–x, 1, 26, 408
Latinos, viii, 396
    racialization in the U.S., 15–16
Lavrin, Asunción, xi, xix, 35–36, 374
Lear, John, 347
legal history, 108–9, 115, 117, 226, 359
Leite da Silva Dias, Maria Odilia, 226
Lempérière, Annick, 171
León, Magdalena, 387
León-Portilla, Miguel, 29, 31, 37
Lesser, Jeffrey, 225, 228, 235, 270
Lestringant, Frank, 103
Levine, Daniel, 471
Levine, Robert, 219, 220
Lewis, Lancelot, 267
Lewis, Laura, 37, 142, 461–63
Libby, Douglas, 105
liberalism, 9, 157, 260, 282, 311, 387
    Brazil, 158, 214–16, 229–31, 348
    and Catholic Church, 9, 285–86, 310, 465
    and the family, 370, 386, 387
    and indigenous people, 285–93, 294
    Mexico, 157, 168, 175, 213, 285, 345, 387
    popular, 175, 213, 215, 286, 345
Lima, 71, 72, 73, 80, 160, 168, 173, 287, 387, 412
Lindo Fuentes, Hector, 412
Linebaugh, Peter, 106
Lipsett-Rivera, Sonya, 41, 42, 140
Little, Walter, 352
Lobato, Mirta, 353

Lockhart, James, 30, 39, 66, 76, 460–61
Lombardi, Peter, 260
Lomnitz, Claudio, 19
Lomnitz, Larissa, 385, 395
Londoño Vega, Patricia, 465
López, Celia, 72
López, Mario Luis, 266
López Austin, Alfredo, 31, 36, 37, 461
López Beltrán, Clara, 390
López Caballero, Paula, 31
López Denis, Adrián, xiii, xix
López Luján, Leonardo, 27
Lorandi, Ana María, 68
Loreto Mariz, Cecilia, 472
Love, Joseph, 219, 227
Lovejoy, Paul, 457
Lovell, George, 81
Lozano Armendares, Teresa, 41
Luca, Tania de, 230
Lynch, John, 156

Macaulay, Neill, 156
MacCormack, Sabine, 464
Machado, Maria Helena, 182, 218, 228
Maia, José, 188
Mallon, Florencia, xii, xix, 92
Mangan, Jane, 80
Mannarelli, Emma, 80
Mapuches, 71, 283–84, 289–96
Marcilio, Maria Luiza, 110
Mariátegui, José Carlos, 157, 158
Marquardt, Marie Friedmann, 487
Marquese, Rafael, 106
Martin, Cheryl, 327
Martin, David, 471, 473, 474, 476
Martínez, María Elena, 35, 42, 480
Martínez Peláez, Severo, 41
Martínez-Fernández, Luis, 474
Martínez-Vergne, Teresita, 263
Martins, Amílcar, 218
Martins, Roberto, 218
Martins Rodrigues, Leônicio, 353
Marx, Anthony, 262
Marxism, 8, 17, 231, 282. *See also* Communist Party
  in economic history, 114, 313, 410, 475
  on independence movements, 157–59, 162–63
  and labor movement, 239, 345, 349
  on slavery, 100, 182, 187, 316, 325
masculinity, xiii, 143, 369–76
  and fatherhood, 140, 374, 396
  and homosexuality, 36, 74, 143, 226–27, 373
  and labor movement, 349
  and legislation, 370–71
  and the military, 226–27
  pre-Columbian, 133, 142, 144
Matos Moctezuma, Eduardo, 27
Matos Rodríguez, Félix, 263
Mattos, Hebe, 185, 215, 218, 224
Maurer, Noel, 415
Mauss, Marcel, 115
Maxwell, Kenneth, 114, 117, 161
Maya, 27, 29, 41, 52, 289, 298
  language, 30, 38
  religion, 38, 458–62
  sexuality, 134, 143
Mayo, Carlos, 72, 322
Mazzeo, Cristina Ana, 77
McAndrew, Richard, 39
McCaa, Robert, 388
McCann, Bryan, 223, 240
McCrea, Heather, 466
McCreery, David, 323, 324
McFarlane, Anthony, 77
Meade, Teresa, 221
medicine. *See* health and disease
Mello e Souza, Laura de, 98, 109–11, 117, 193, 463–64
Mello e Souza, Marina de, 107
Melo Sampaio, Patricia, 104
Melville, Eleanor, 42
Mendonça, Joseli de, 218
Mendoza, Antonio de, 35
Merkerk, Nederveen, 109
mestizaje, 32, 132, 294, 297
  as national ideology, 33, 264, 281, 293, 298
  as a sexual issue, 137–38
Metcalf, Alida, 103–4, 110, 325, 482
Mexica. *See* Nahuas
Mexican Revolution, 293, 311, 315, 347, 374
Mexico, vii, ix, 5, 11, 46, 469
  Afro-descendants, 2, 4, 33–34, 52, 258, 270
  agriculture, 32, 44, 309, 312–14

Mexico (*continued*)
  Catholic Church, 29, 31, 34, 35, 37–40, 72, 458–62
  colonial, 25–46, 135–45
  economy, 9, 11, 20, 44–45, 408, 411–15, 417
  education, 13, 22, 23
  family, 385–88, 392, 393, 395
  gender, 35–37, 135–45, 369, 370, 374, 376
  health and disease, 37, 42, 53, 428, 432, 440, 441
  independence, 39–41, 160–61, 167, 168, 174, 284–85
  indigenous population, 25–32, 37–44, 134–36, 140–44, 283–89, 293–94, 458–64
  Inquisition, 35, 38, 40, 44, 55, 141, 466
  labor movement, 345–46, 347, 348, 351
  liberalism, 9, 157, 168, 175, 213, 285–86, 345, 387
  mining, 9, 10, 45, 63, 285, 319, 412
  politics, 12, 157, 167, 168, 285–87, 351
  rebellions, 40–41, 174–75, 327
  slavery, 260, 327, 328
  Spaniards in, 8, 28–29, 32, 34–35, 39–40, 135
  women, 34, 35–37, 42, 80, 135–45
Mexico City, 41–42, 174
  economy, 44–45, 412
  gender, 36, 371, 374, 393
  labor, 347, 357, 361
  population, 9, 32
Miceli, Sérgio, 236
Michoacan, 29, 42, 327
middle class, 359, 360, 428
  attitudes, 241, 487
  Brazil, 228, 230, 237, 244, 256
  and politics, 229, 230, 232
  and Protestantism, 475, 487
  and race, 228, 241, 264
Mignolo, Walter, 17
migration and migrants, ix, 18, 260
  to Argentina, 259, 292, 321, 345
  from Asia, 4, 225, 228, 260, 270
  to Brazil, 218–19, 227–28, 259, 266, 270
  to Costa Rica, 266–67, 277, 394
  to Cuba, 8, 266–67, 277
  from Europe, 4, 8, 218, 227–28, 259, 309, 346–50
  and gender, 13, 20, 392
  from Haiti, 264, 277, 318
  and health, 434, 438, 441
  indigenous, 81, 97
  policy, 260, 467
  from Portugal, 8, 16, 21, 109, 193
  from Spain, 7–8, 52, 53
  from West Indies, 6, 266–67, 277, 394
Mijares, María Marta, 264
Milanich, Nara, xiii, xix, 19, 405
military, 12, 165, 181, 242–45
  Afro-descendants in, 33, 69, 173–75, 191, 259–61
  colonial, 33, 67, 70, 74, 75, 78, 116
  during independence, 156, 163, 174
  and indigenous people, 70, 285–93, 295
  and masculinity, 226–27
  and religion, 467, 471, 472, 486
Millar, René, 141
Miller, Joseph, 106
Miller, Shawn, 105
Miller, Simon, 315
Mills, Kenneth, 73
Minas Gerais, 103, 105–13, 117, 220, 238, 415
  slavery, 184, 186, 195, 218
Mintz, Sidney, 315, 324, 456, 457, 469, 470, 486
Mixtecs, 27, 29, 30, 38, 40, 41
modernization theory, 14, 158, 418, 475
Molina, Lucía Dominga, 266
Monteiro, John, 102
Montoya, Gustavo, 173
Moore, Robin, 268
Moreira Leite, Miriam, 226
Morelos, 31, 285, 286, 328
Moreno, José Luis, 80
Moreno Fraginals, Manuel, 327
Moreton, Bethany, 472, 476
Moritz Schwarcz, Lilia, 114, 217, 225
Mota, Carlos Guilherme, 160, 161, 164
Mota, José Flávio, 106
Mott, Luiz, 107, 110–13, 143, 184, 191, 193, 227
Moutoukias, Zacarias, 77
Moya, José, xix, 350
Mundy, Barbara, 44
Muniz de Albuquerque, Durval, 220
Murilo de Carvalho, José, 172, 216, 217, 219, 221

Murmis, Miguel, 352
Murray, Stephen, 373
Musacchio, Aldo, 413, 415
music and dance, 23, 223, 240, 242, 269
   and Afro-descendants, 190, 262, 264, 269
   erotic, 137, 145
   and indigenous people, 29, 30, 459
   samba, 223, 240, 241
   tango, 268, 346, 353
Muslims. *See* Islam

Nahuas, 26–31, 39, 43, 134
   language, 29, 388
   religion, 37, 38, 136, 460–61
   sexuality, 140–42, 143
Nardi, Jean-Baptiste, 109
Naro, Nancy, 326
Navarro de Toledo, Caio, 239
Nazzari, Muriel, 110, 387
Needell, Jeffrey, 217, 221, 222
Negri, Antonio, 468
Negritude, 266, 267
Nero da Costa, Iraci del, 110, 195
Nesvig, Martin, 36, 40, 44
New Granada, 71, 73, 77, 78, 160, 260
Newson, Linda, 81
Newton, Velma, 267
Ngou-Mvé, Nicolas, 34
Nicaragua, 23, 266, 297, 319, 397, 486
   gender, 376, 380, 387, 392
Niemeyer, Oscar, 236, 241
Nina Rodrigues, Raimundo, 455
Nizza da Silva, Maria Beatriz, 110, 116, 117
Noguez, Xavier, 39
Novais, Fernando, 101, 114, 161, 162
Novinsky, Anita, 112

Oaxaca, 32, 41, 42, 45, 167, 317, 388
   indigenous people, 30, 38, 40, 286, 370
   pre-Columbian, 27, 29
O'Dogherty Madrazo, Laura, 466
O'Donnell, Guillermo, 242
O'Gorman, Edmundo, 39, 41
Olcott, Jocelyn, 369
Olival, Fernanda, 116
O'Phelan Godoy, Scarlett, 69, 72, 81, 168
orientalism, 14, 23

Ortega, Sergio, 36
Ortiz, Fernando, xiv, 311, 330, 455
Ortner, Sherry, 368, 369
Oudijk, Michel, 30
Owensby, Brian, 40, 59, 237, 238

Padden, Robert R., 135
Pádua, José Augusto, 105
Pagden, Anthony, 43
Paiva, Clotilde, 106, 195
Paiva, José Pedro, 111
Paiva França, Eduardo, 105
Palacios, Patricia, 41
Palafox, Juan de, 35
Palmer, Colin, 33, 327, 457
Palmié, Stephan, 456, 463, 464, 476
Panama, 2, 18, 71
   education, 13, 23
   West Indians in, 266–67
Paraguay, 7, 11, 12, 260, 411
   colonial, 70, 72
   education, ix, 13, 23
   Paraguayan War, 191, 192, 292
   rural society, 316, 322, 323
Pardo, Osvaldo, 39
Parker, Cristián, 479
Patch, Robert, 41
Paz, Octavio, 163, 169, 172
Peard, Julyan, 225
Pease, Frank, 66
Pécora, Alcir, 113–14
Pedreira, Jorge, 115
Peire, Jaime, 74
Penyak, Lee, 36, 41
Peralta, Víctor, 168
Pereira de Queiroz, Maria Isaura, 467, 476
Pérez-Lizaur, Marisol, 385, 395
Perlman, Janice, 241
Pernambuco, 103, 108, 113, 164
   slavery, 187, 192, 195
Peronism, 234, 352–53, 359, 370, 372
Perrone Moisés, Leyla, 103
Peru, ix, 7, 15, 288, 294, 313, 441
   Afro-descendants, 2, 260, 265, 269
   agriculture, 314, 318, 319, 323, 324
   colonial, 66–81
   economy, 11, 20, 23, 309, 319
   gender, 133, 141, 387

Peru (*continued*)
  independence, 77, 155, 157, 161–62, 163, 168, 174
  indigenous population, 259, 283–85, 287–89, 293–94, 297
  religion, 72–74
Pessar, Patricia, 467–68, 476
Petersen, Jeannette, 43
Peterson, Ana L., 485
Petiz, Silmei, 188
Petras, Elizabeth, 267
Phelan, John Leddy, 69
Piel, Jean, 314
Pieroni, Gerardo, 113
Pijning, Ernst, 115
Pino, Julio, 241
Pinto Furtado, J., 117
Pinto Vallejos, Julio, 348
Pollak-Eltz, Angelina, 264
Pompa, Christina, 104
Pompa, Claudia, 105
Poole, Stafford, 35, 39, 40
populism, 234, 238, 242, 350–55
Portantiero, Juan Carlos, 352
Portes, Alejandro, 396
Portugal, 14, 99, 115, 171, 326
  Braganza ruling house, 161, 164, 172
  and Brazilian identity, 18, 192, 214, 215, 216
  colonial administration, 108–9, 114–18, 167, 214
  education, 13, 22, 425
  empire, 104, 106, 108, 109, 111, 162, 166, 192
  immigration from, 8, 16, 21, 109
  Portuguese as colonial language, 6–7
  religion, 103, 110–13
postcolonial theory, x, 18, 213
Potosí, 8, 70, 412
  mining, 76, 77, 317, 321
Powers, Karen, 66
Prado, Maria Lígia, 229
Prado Júnior, Caio, 158
Prados de la Escosura, Leandro, 419
Premo, Bianca, 83, 387, 396
Presta, Ana María, 67
Price, Richard, 456, 457
Priore, Mary del, 110–11, 112
Prosperi, Adriano, 110

Protestantism, 14, 193, 425, 469–75
  colonial Spanish America, 73, 141
  Pentecostalism, 454, 469–75, 484
Puebla, 35, 37, 42, 44–45, 52, 141, 357
Puerto Rico, 10, 13
  demography, 12, 15
  gender, 263–64, 371
  race relations, 263–64
  racial geography, 2, 8
  religion, 468–69, 474, 485–86
  slavery, 260, 263, 327
Puntoni, Pedro, 103
Purcell, Trevor, 267
Putnam, Lara, 394

Quechua, xi, 297
Queirós de Mattoso, Katia, 105, 184, 326
Quezada, Noemí, 37, 141, 463
Quito, 69, 78, 80, 314

Rabell, Cecilia, 388
race relations
  Afro-Latin America, 257–71
  Brazil, 224–26, 261–63
  Indo-America, 281–98
  Spanish Caribbean, 263–65
Racine, Karen, 156
Radding, Cynthia, 32
Rago, Margareth, 226
Ramada Curto, Diogo, 113
Raminelli, Ronald, 117
Ramirez, Susan, 66
Ramos, Donald, 106
rebellions, 168, 174–75, 192
  colonial Mexico, 40–41
  colonial Spanish South America, 67–71
  indigenous, 163, 284–85, 295, 297
  religion and, 220, 248, 467, 466–68, 482
  slave, 187, 192–93, 215
Rediker, Marcus, 106
Reis, Isabel, 188
Reis, João, xii, xx, 107, 122, 173, 197, 215, 218, 224, 339, 466
religion, 454–76. *See also specific faiths*
  colonial Brazil, 103–5, 107, 111–14
  colonial Mexico, 37–40

colonial Spanish South America, 71–74
and gender, 136–45
idolatry, 38, 56, 57, 136, 142
messianism, 103, 111, 192
millenarianism, 103, 113, 220, 466–68, 479, 482
witchcraft, 37, 74, 80, 111, 136–38, 141–42, 458, 464, 476
Restall, Matthew, xx, 30, 34, 52
Reyes García, Luis, 27, 30, 31
Ribeiro, Gladys, 215
Ridenti, Marcelo, 244
Rio de Janeiro, 104, 112, 221, 226, 227, 346
governance, 114–18, 160, 164, 166, 167, 169
slavery, 105–7, 184–94
Rio Grande do Sul, 186, 188, 194, 221
Robinson, James, 416, 417, 418
Rodrigues, Jaime, 106
Rodríguez, Daniel R., 473
Rodríguez, Minerva, 474
Rodríguez, Pablo, 140, 385, 389, 390
Rodríguez, Romero, 265
Rodríguez O, Jaime, 169
Rohloff de Mattos, Ilmar, 216
Rojas, Rafael, 171
Rojas Rabiela, Teresa, 29
Roldán, Mary, 265
Román, Reinaldo, xiv, xx, 468, 469
Roman Catholic Church. *See* Catholic Church
Romano, Ruggiero, 412
Romeiro, Adriana, 113
Romero, Luis Alberto, 344–45
Romero Magalhães, Joaquim, 116
Roselló Soberón, Estela, 476
Rosemblatt, Karin, 375
Rout, Leslie, 270
Roys, Ralph, 30
Rubenstein, Anne, 476
Rubiera Castillo, Daisy, 269
Rudé, George, 67
Ruiz Medrano, Ethelia, 35
rural society, 104–9, 310–29. *See also* agriculture
Rushing, Fannie, 263
Russell-Wood, A. J. R., 109, 114
Rutledge, Ian, 320
Ruz, Mario Humberto, 29

Sabato, Hilda, 320–21, 344–45
Sacristán, María Cristina, 464
Saeger, James, 72
Sagás, Ernesto, 264
Salazar, Gabriel, 345
Salinas Mesa, René, 79
Salvatore, Ricardo, 322, 417
Salvucci, Richard, 44–45
San Luis Potosí, 25, 51
Sánchez, Ana, 142
Sánchez de Tagle, Esteban, 42
Sánchez Santiró, Ernest, 327
Sandinista Revolution, viii, 297, 397
Sandoval, Salvador, 239
Sandroni, Carlos, 223
Sansone, Livio, 262
Santamaría, Daniel, 74
São Paulo, 3, 109, 223, 227–31, 235, 237, 415
Afro-descendants, 218–19, 225, 261, 262
European immigrants, 218–19, 225
gender, 110, 226, 349, 386
labor, 218–19, 238, 346, 356
slavery, 106, 183, 184, 325
Scarano, Franciso, 327
Scharrer Tamm, Beatriz, 327
Schell, Patience, 466
Schmidt-Nowara, Christopher, 263
Scholes, France, 30, 38
Schroeder, Susan, 31, 36, 40, 41, 46
Schultz, Kirsten, 169, 214
Schwaller, Frederick, 72
Schwartz, Stuart, xi, xx, 4, 21, 103, 114, 184, 325, 326
Schwarz, Roberto, 214
Scott, James, 68, 191, 467
Scott, Joan, 369
Scott, Rebecca, 263, 270
Seed, Patricia, 464, 468
Seigel, Micol, 262
Sell, Barry, 31
Sempat Assadourian, Carlos, 321
Serbin, Kenneth, 244
Serrano, Sol, 465
Serulnikov, Sergio, 70
Sevcenko, Nicolau, 221, 222–23
sexuality. *See also* gender; homosexuality; masculinity
African, 136–37, 141, 185
colonial period, 35–37, 68, 74, 79, 136–45

sexuality (*continued*)
  and honor, 139–40, 150, 226, 380
  Iberian, 132–38, 140, 185
  indigenous, 133–35, 140–44
  and mestizaje, 137–38
  prostitution, 68, 80, 140, 142, 223, 226, 371–72, 438
  rape, 135, 138, 139–40, 371
Shumway, Jeffrey, 370
Sigal, Pete, 143
Silva, Diniz, 117
Silva, Eduardo, 189, 191, 218
Silva, Renán, 160
Silva Gotay, Samuel, 474
Silverblatt, Irene, 37, 462
Skidmore, Thomas, 225, 243
slavery
  abolition, 22, 185, 187, 191, 192, 217–19, 260, 324
  African ethnic origins, 2, 186, 193–94
  Brazil, 105–7, 181–96, 324–26
  children, 185, 188, 189
  Cuba, 260, 263, 327, 414
  demography, 194, 195
  economy, 100, 106, 116, 187, 194, 218, 324–26, 327, 414
  family, 33, 106, 136, 188, 195, 387
  and free persons of color, 109, 110, 113, 175, 193
  Independence Wars, and, 173, 180
  Indian, 211, 287, 316
  manumission, 100, 105, 106, 173, 184, 185–86, 196, 198
  Mexico, 33–34, 136
  Puerto Rico, 260, 263, 327
  resistance to, 100, 173, 184, 187, 189, 191–92, 218, 455
  women, 82, 136, 185, 191
Slenes, Robert, 105, 106, 193
Sloane, Katherinie, 370
Soares da Cunha, Mafalda, 116
socialism, 345–49, 354, 484
Socolow, Susan, xi, xx, 4, 21, 79, 388
Sokoloff, Kenneth, 416, 417, 418
Sommer, Barbara, 104
Sousa, Lisa, xi, xx, 4, 21, 30
Sowell, David, 344
Spain, 14, 21, 108, 171, 412
  anarchism in, 348
  colonial administration, 77, 117, 161, 165, 166, 316, 327
  education, 13, 22, 425
  empire, 2, 6, 192, 311
  immigration from, 7–8, 52, 53
  Latin Americans in, viii
  religion, 112, 141, 480
  sexuality, 140, 143, 461–62
  Spanish as colonial language, 6–7
  Spanish culture in Latin America, 5–8
Spalding, Hobart, 343
Spalding, Karen, 161, 163, 168
Spaniards, 2, 18, 169
  in colonial South America, 67–75
  and indigenous people, 28–29, 39–40, 70, 76–77, 461–62
  masculinity, 135, 137, 138, 140, 185, 461–62
  in Mexico, 8, 28–29, 32, 34–35, 39–40
  sexuality, 136–45
Stabili, María Rosaria, 396
Stavig, Ward, 68, 70
Stein, Stanley, 182, 325, 408
Stepan, Nancy, 225
Stern, Steve, 36, 68
Stevens-Arroyo, Anthony, 474
Stoll, David, 471
Stolze Lima, Ivana, 215
Stone, Lawrence, 23, 382
Stoner, Lynn, 367, 374
Street, John, 164
Stresser-Péan, Guy, 37
Studnicki-Gizbert, Daviken, 108
Suárez Findlay, Eileen, 263
Sullivan-González, Douglass, 466
Summerhill, William, xiii, xxi
Suriano, Juan, 348
Swann, Michael, 32
Sweet, James, 107, 193, 457, 458

Tandeter, Enrique, 76, 412
Taussig, Michael, 323, 463, 476
Tavárez, David, 30, 46
Taylor, William, 39, 40, 41, 71, 466
Teixeira da Silva, Fernando, 232
Telles, Edward, 262
Tena, Rafael, 31
Tenorio Trillo, Mauricio, 19

TePaske, John, 412
Terraciano, Kevin, xi, xxi, 4, 21, 30, 38, 41, 54, 57
Therborn, Göran, 389, 392
Thomas, Keith, 464
Thompson, E. P., 67, 185, 221, 228, 346, 353
Thomson, Sinclair, 70
Thornton, John, 106, 111, 457
Tilly, Louise, 391
Tinsman, Heidi, 394
Torre, Juan Carlos, 352
Torre Revello, José, 79
Tortorici, Zeb, 36, 46, 55
Townsend, Camilla, 135, 173
Trelles, Efraín, 317
Trevisan, Maria José, 239
Trexler, Richard, 143
Trujillo Bolio, Mario, 345
Tupac Amaru, 68, 70, 71, 163, 174, 284
Turits, Richard, 264
Tutino, John, 41
Twinam, Ann, 36, 37, 79, 83, 140

Umbanda, 471, 473
United States, 9, 22, 154, 234, 258, 260, 338
  America, appropriation of term by, 5
  economy, 3, 17, 19, 20, 407, 414, 416, 419
  gender, 13, 14, 367, 372, 392
  imperialism, 264, 266, 267, 468, 473, 474, 475
  indigenous population, 20, 32
  influence, 266, 358, 436, 469, 486, 487
  labor, 344, 346, 363
  Latinamericanists, vii–viii, ix, 1, 14, 16, 21, 34, 75, 76, 212–13, 361, 474
  and Puerto Rico, 263–64
  race, 2, 3, 262, 267, 270
  religion, 465, 470, 472, 475, 483, 486, 487
  slavery, 190, 195–96, 270, 316, 326, 414
  views of Latin America, 5, 14–16, 23
urban history, 31–32, 34, 45, 78, 109, 137, 222–23, 240–42
urban society, 7, 8–9
  Afro-descendants in, 33–34, 69, 78, 190, 227–28, 456
  arts and literature, 230–31
  colonial Mexico, 35, 41–42, 44–45
  economy, 109, 229, 238–39
  European immigrants in, 218–19, 238, 344–45, 346–50
  family in, 80, 383, 384–88, 395–96
  gender, 80, 140–41, 223, 226–27, 371–72, 374
  indigenous people in, 31–32, 69, 80, 297
  labor, 221, 227–28, 234, 238–39, 343–58
  political culture, 71, 109, 164, 169, 174, 221, 240
  popular culture, 137, 222, 223, 240–42, 262, 346–47
  public health, 429, 433, 434–35, 439
  religion, 112, 222, 471, 479
  riots, 41, 69, 222, 466
  rural economy, and, 314–15
  slavery in, 78, 105–7, 184–94, 218
  urban planning, 6, 109, 221, 240–41
urbanization, xii, 3, 8–9, 11, 13, 15, 21, 112, 309, 384
Uribe, Victor, 172
Urquiola, José, 45
Urrutia, Miguel, 419
Uruguay, 11, 20, 78, 441
  Afro-descendants, 265, 269
  economy, 3, 11, 13, 15, 20, 309, 322
  education, 13, 22
  gender, 13, 372, 390
  politics, 12, 164, 221, 265
  welfare state in, 11, 372

Vainfas, Ronaldo, 104, 110, 111
Valle Silva, Nelso do, 262
Vallier, Ivan, 486
van Doesburg, Sebastian, 30, 49
Van Young, Eric, xii, xxi, 26, 41, 44, 175, 301, 314, 331, 333, 465
Vanderwood, Paul, 476
Vargas, Getúlio, 231, 234–37, 239, 350, 351, 354, 372
Varón Gabai, Rafael, 67
Vaughn, Mary Kay, 369
Vázquez Mantecón, Verónica, 327
Velasco e Cruz, Maria Cecilia, 218
Velasco Murillo, Dana, 46
Velázquez, María Elisa, 34
Venezuela, 12, 23, 343, 371, 411
  agriculture, 322, 323
  economy, 15, 20, 412

Venezuela (*continued*)
   independence, 168, 173
   race relations, 260, 264
Verger, Pierre, 106
Viana Lyra, María de Lourdes, 168
Vidal Luna, Francisco, 106, 195, 326
Vilas, Carlos, 397
Vilela Santos, Maria Januária, 192
Villa, Marco Antonio, 220
Villella, Peter, 46
Vinson, Ben, 33, 270
Viotti da Costa, Emilia, 182, 215, 227
Viqueira, Carmen, 45
Viqueira Albán, Juan Pedro, 41, 461, 476
Virgin of Guadalupe, 38, 39
Viveiros de Castro, Eduardo, 103
Voekel, Pamela, xiv, xxi, 44, 465, 466, 476, 487
Voelz, Peter, 259
von Germeten, Nicole, 34

Walker, Charles, 70, 83, 162, 174
War of the Pacific (1879–83), 265, 287, 288
Warren, Adam, 466
Watkins-Owens, Irma, 267
Weber, Max, 158
Weffort, Francisco, 242, 353
Weinstein, Barbara, xii, xiv, xxi, 4, 323, 366
Weismantel, Mary, 134
Welch, Cliff, 232, 238
Wells, Allen, 323
West Indians, 6, 266–67, 269, 392, 394
whites. *See* Europeans and Euro-descendants
Will de Chaparro, Martina, 466
Willems, Emilio, 469, 470–71, 473–74, 484
Williams, Daryle, 236
Williams, Eric, 326, 487
Williams, Raymond, 353
Williamson, Jeffrey, 413, 416
Winn, Peter, 357
Wirth, John, 219

Wobeser, Gisela Von, 327
Wolf, Eric, 315
Wolfe, Joel, 349
women. *See also* gender; sexuality
   Afro-descendants, 34, 36, 82, 136, 185, 191, 194, 196, 263, 269
   and Catholic Church, 36, 71, 73, 110, 370–71, 466
   colonial Mexico, 35–37, 42, 45, 54, 134–35
   colonial Spanish South America, 66–68, 71, 73, 78, 79–80
   domestic service, 13, 395
   Euro-descendants, 36, 73, 349, 462
   family, 73, 382–97
   indigenous, 36, 54, 79–80, 104, 132, 134–35, 140, 143, 387, 462
   political empowerment, 13–14
   Protestantism, 470, 472–73
   slavery, 82, 185, 191
   suffrage, 13, 226, 231, 370, 372
   and witchcraft, 74, 80, 141
women's history, 36, 79–80, 110, 226, 372
   and family history, 78, 382, 386, 391
   versus gender studies, xiii, 349, 368
Wood, Stephanie, 31, 36
Woodard, James, 229
Wright, Robert, 102
Wright, Winthrop, 264

Yannakakis, Yanna, 40
Yaremko, Jason, 475
Yorubas, 107, 186, 191, 193, 242
Young, Elliot, 476
Yucatan, 25, 29, 30, 38, 56, 319

Zacatecas, 32, 42
Zapata, Emiliano, 327
Zapotecs, 27, 29, 30, 38
Zavala, Silvio, 33, 316
Zulawski, Ann, 76
Zuluaga, Francisco, 264